# Mission Handbook

## U.S. and Canadian Protestant Ministries Overseas
## 2007-2009
## (20th Edition)

Edited by Linda J. Weber
and Dotsey Welliver

www.missionhandbook.com

D1291862

## emis

Evangelism and Missions Information Service
P.O. Box 794, Wheaton, IL 60189

BILLY GRAHAM CENTER
WHEATON COLLEGE

## Mission Handbook
U.S. and Canadian Protestant Ministries Overseas (2007-2009)
20th Edition

Edited by Linda J. Weber and Dotsey Welliver
Executive editor, Kenneth D. Gill
Cover design and layout, Dona Diehl
Cover photos courtesy: Don Picker, Arab World Ministries, IMB

Copyright 2007 by Evangelism and Missions Information Service (EMIS) at the Billy Graham Center at Wheaton College. All rights reserved. No part of this publication may be reproduced, stored in a retrieval system or transmitted in any form by any means (electronic, photocopy, recording), without the prior written permission of the publisher. The only exception is brief quotations in printed reviews.

Published by EMIS, a division of the Billy Graham Center at Wheaton College, 500 College Ave., Wheaton, IL 60187

Printed in the United States of America.

For information about other resources or publications of EMIS or the Billy Graham Center:
Phone: 630.752.7158
Email: emis@wheaton.edu
Online: www.billygrahamcenter.org/emis

ISBN 978-1-879089-40-2

**To be included** in the next edition of the *Mission Handbook*, to update your agency's information or to check on current updates for mission agencies, go to: **www.missionhandbook.com**.

# Endorsements

"*To be good stewards of our opportunities, we need sound data. The* Handbook *provides it. Here we find strategies, many potential partners,* **a wealth of complementary approaches and a cornucopia of statistics** *to help us make wise decisions.*"

—**Miriam Adeney**, associate professor of global
and urban ministries, Seattle Pacific University

"*The* Mission Handbook *serves two significant purposes in my life and ministry. First, it is* **my up-to-date reference guide** *telling me the 'who, what, where and how many' details of North American missions. Second, it is an essential resource we in North America need in order to understand more fully where we fit in God's global purposes.*"

—**Paul Borthwick**, senior consultant, Development Associates International

"*Information is most helpful when it is carefully gathered, clearly reported and traced over time. The* Mission Handbook *does all three. That is what makes it* **the premier source of information** *about the status of North American missions and the best way to monitor trends.*"

—**George Hunsberger**, dean of Journey, a center for the
Church's learning, Western Theological Seminary

"*Global mission efforts are increasingly multifaceted initiatives. The* Mission Handbook *is* **the single source that I can go to** *for quick and thorough access to information for the networking and planning so necessary for mission effectiveness.*"

—**Byron Klaus**, president, Assemblies of God Theological Seminary

"*I receive a broad variety of mission questions, many which can be answered directly from the* Mission Handbook. *How much money do North American churches give to missions? Is the number of missionaries increasing or decreasing? With the* Mission Handbook, *church and mission leaders have* **a whole mission encyclopedia at their fingertips**."

—**David Mays**, nationally known missions consultant
and workshop leader, formerly with ACMC

"*As a mission executive,* **I wouldn't be without the most current edition of the** Mission Handbook. *The comprehensive listing of agencies with all the key information on each and the charts on mission activity and resources give me a pulse on global mission activity today.*"

—**Susan Perlman**, associate executive director, Jews for Jesus

"*There is not a week, and often not a day, that I do not refer to the* Mission Handbook. *It is* **an indispensable networking tool**. *The contact information, purpose statements, basic orientation, distribution and numbers of workers and financial resources for the hundreds of agencies listed give a quick grasp of the particulars. The summative opening chapter gives an excellent understanding of the big picture of North American sending agencies. This is the world of missions from North America at your fingertips.*"

—**Mike Pocock**, senior professor of world missions
and intercultural studies, Dallas Theological Seminary

117166

# Contents

# Abbreviations and Acronyms

| | | | |
|---|---|---|---|
| Admin. | Administrative, administrator | Natl. | National |
| Am. | America, American | NE | Northeast |
| Apt. | Apartment | NIV | New International Version |
| Assoc. | Associate, Association | NR | Not Reported |
| Ave. | Avenue | NW | Northwest |
| Bd. | Board | Org. | Organization |
| Blvd. | Boulevard | Pres. | President |
| Cen. | Central | P.O. | Post Office |
| CEO | Chief Executive Officer | Rd. | Road |
| Ch(s). | Church (es) | Rev. | Reverend |
| Co. | Company | Rm. | Room |
| Comm. | Commission | Rep. | Republic |
| Conf. | Conference | S. | South |
| Cong. | Congregational | SE | Southeast |
| Conv. | Convention | Soc. | Society |
| COO | Chief Operating Officer | St. | Saint, Street |
| Coord. | Coordinator, Coordination | Sta. | Station |
| Ctr. | Center | Supt. | Superintendent |
| Dept. | Department | Ste. | Suite |
| Dev. | Development | SVC(s) | Services |
| Dir. | Director | SW | Southwest |
| Div. | Division | TEE | Theological Education by Extension |
| Dr. | Doctor, Drive | Theol. | Theology, Theological |
| E. | East | U., Univ. | University |
| Ed. | Education | VP | Vice President |
| Exec. | Executive | W. | West |
| Frgn. | Foreign | Wld. | World |
| Gen. | General | | |
| Govt. | Government | **Canada** | |
| Hdq. | Headquarters | AB | Alberta |
| Hts. | Heights | BC | British Columbia |
| Hwy. | Highway | MB | Manitoba |
| Inc. | Incorporated | NB | New Brunswick |
| Inst. | Institute | NF | Newfoundland |
| Intl. | International | NS | Nova Scotia |
| Is (Is). | Islands | NT | Northwest Territories |
| Lit. | Literature | ON | Ontario |
| Mgr. | Manager | PE | Prince Edward Island |
| Min(s) | Ministry (ies) | PQ | Québec |
| Msn. | Mission | SK | Saskatchewan |
| Mtg. | Meeting | YT | Yukon Territory |
| N. | North | | |
| NA | Not Applicable | | |
| NASB | New American Standard Bible | | |

**United States**

| | | | |
|---|---|---|---|
| | | MT | Montana |
| AK | Alaska | NC | North Carolina |
| AL | Alabama | ND | North Dakota |
| AR | Arkansas | NE | Nebraska |
| AZ | Arizona | NH | New Hampshire |
| CA | California | NJ | New Jersey |
| CO | Colorado | NM | New Mexico |
| CT | Connecticut | NV | Nevada |
| DE | Delaware | NY | New York |
| DC | District of Columbia | OH | Ohio |
| FL | Florida | OK | Oklahoma |
| GA | Georgia | OR | Oregon |
| HI | Hawaii | PA | Pennsylvania |
| IA | Iowa | PR | Puerto Rico |
| ID | Idaho | RI | Rhode Island |
| IL | Illinois | SC | South Carolina |
| IN | Indiana | SD | South Dakota |
| KS | Kansas | TN | Tennessee |
| KY | Kentucky | TX | Texas |
| LA | Louisiana | UT | Utah |
| MA | Massachusetts | VA | Virginia |
| MD | Maryland | VT | Vermont |
| ME | Maine | WA | Washington |
| MI | Michigan | WI | Wisconsin |
| MN | Minnesota | WV | West Virginia |
| MO | Missouri | WY | Wyoming |
| MS | Mississippi | | |

**Mission Associations**

| | |
|---|---|
| AERDO | Association of Evangelical Relief and Development Organizations |
| AFMA | Alliance for Mission Advancement |
| AIMS | Accelerating International Mission Strategies |
| ANAM | Association of North American Missions |
| CCRDA | Canadian Christian Relief and Development Association |
| CWS | Church World Service |
| EFMA | Evangelical Fellowship of Mission Agencies |
| FOM | Fellowship of Missions |
| IFMA | Interdenominational Foreign Mission Association of North America |
| OCMC | Orthodox Christian Mission Center |
| USCMA | US Catholic Mission Association |

# Introduction

For more than fifty years the *Mission Handbook*, under different names, different publishers and in different formats, has been providing thousands of readers with comprehensive information on U.S. and Canadian-based Protestant mission agencies[1] engaged in overseas missions. With this edition of the *Handbook* you will find complete information on more than eight hundred U.S. and Canadian-based ministries that are changing the world for Jesus Christ. This invaluable resource includes information such as agency name and contact information, purpose statement, areas of ministry, countries of ministry, number of personnel and more.

It must be noted that although many of the agencies are involved in ministries in the U.S. and Canada, due to space concerns, this information is not included. The Handbook is concerned with what these agencies are doing overseas.

As God continues to grow his Church, so too do mission organizations around the world continue to engage in both evangelistic and social ministry. The *Handbook* includes only North American-based organizations. Mission activity for agencies based in other parts of the world can be found in other publications. See the bibliography for a list of these resources.

## This Edition of the *Mission Handbook*

The research for the 2007-2009 *Mission Handbook* took over a year. Research was gathered via mail, email, fax or phone. Each agency received the same questionnaire (see appendix). As times and mission agencies have changed, so too has certain aspects of the questionnaire. Key questions, however, have stayed the same. For example, questions relating to financial data have used the same definitions since the late 1970s. The countries of service and field personnel questions have remained the same since the early 1990s when the "more than four years" definition for long-term personnel was instituted. These definitions were determined in consultation with editors of other mission directories and leaders in national mission associations.

Dr. Scott Moreau, a former missionary to Africa who is currently serving as editor of *Evangelical Missions Quarterly* and as head of the Intercultural Studies department at Wheaton College Graduate School (Wheaton, Illinois), did an overview of the survey database. The result was a comprehensive analysis of trends in U.S. and Canadian-based ministries serving overseas (see chapter 1).

## History of the *Mission Handbook*

The *Mission Handbook* first appeared in 1953 with the title *Foreign Missionary*

*Agencies in the United States: A Check List.* It was compiled and mimeographed by the Missionary Research Library (MRL) in New York. The MRL was founded in 1914 at the initiative of John R. Mott who chaired the World Missionary Conference in Edinburgh, Scotland in 1910 and headed its continuation committee.

In 1968 the publication became a cooperative effort of MRL and the Missions Advanced Research and Communication (MARC) Center, a division of World Vision International near Los Angeles, California. The title was changed to *North American Protestant Ministries Overseas Directory.* In 1973 the title included "Mission Handbook" as the publication began to include related articles and expanded analyses of the survey data. In 1976 MARC became the sole publisher. The *Mission Handbooks* of the 1990s contained chapters by MARC director Bryant L. Myers which provided a global perspective of evangelism and missions using maps, charts, graphs and pictures. Also in the 1990s, chapters from the Catholic (www.uscatholicmission.org) and Orthodox (www.ocmc.org) mission communities were added and "Protestant" in the title was changed to "Christian." Presently, readers are referred to the websites of these two groups for their mission data.

For nearly two decades, John A. Siewert of MARC served as editor of the *Handbook.* In 2000 the Evangelism and Missions Information Service (EMIS) of the Billy Graham Center at Wheaton College near Chicago, Illinois became the publisher of the *Mission Handbook.* Under the transitional leadership of Siewert and the guidance of EMIS executive editor Kenneth Gill, the 18th edition (copyright 2000) was the first volume to be produced by EMIS. This edition is the third volume published by EMIS.

## A Word of Caution

Statistics relating to overseas missionary endeavors suffer from the same (and often more) problems as statistics in general. Although the questions have been worded to be as specific as possible, different interpretations will inevitably occur. Even within the same agency, some reporting practices may be inconsistent due to personnel changes or changes in the agency's policies or structure. Mission agencies may decide at different times and for various reasons not to report their activities in certain countries.

The reader should exercise caution when comparing statistics either between agencies or within the same agency from different years. They must also be cautious in combining statistics from different agencies. Wrong conclusions about a particular agency or group of agencies or missions within a particular country may result without being aware of, or securing, additional information not in the scope of this survey.

## Thanks and Acknowledgments

Our deep heartfelt thanks goes out to the individuals in each agency who completed the questionnaire. In larger agencies this may have been a collaborative effort involving executives, accountants, researchers, personnel department staff and others. The 2007-2009 edition of the *Mission Handbook* is possible because of the dedicated efforts of many individuals and organizations. We also owe a tremendous debt of gratitude to Dr. Moreau for using his detailed research skills to create the analysis chapter and to John Hayward for offering his technical database assistance. We also could not have completed this edition without the following members of the EMIS team: executive editor Ken Gill, editor Linda J. Weber, proof reader Dotsey Welliver, designer Dona Diehl, advertising manager Karen Rummel, editorial coordinator Laurie Fortunak, data entry specialist Deborah Ferguson and office assistant Wendy Walker.

## Update Information

Because the *Mission Handbook* only comes out every three years (with the next one not coming out until 2010!), we would appreciate being updated on any changes to the mission agencies included in this volume. To update any of the information in this directory or to suggest a new listing, please contact us in one of the following ways:

Website: www.missionhandbook.com
Email: missionhandbook@wheaton.edu
Phone : (630) 752-7159
Fax : (630) 752-7155
Address: EMIS, P.O. Box 794, Wheaton, IL 60189

### Endnote

1. The term "agency" is used in the broad sense referring to all denominational and nondenominational boards and societies, and other specialized organizations involved in overseas mission.

## Preparing missionaries and international Christian leaders for more effective service

### The Billy Graham Center Scholarship Program for Graduate Study

For more than thirty years the Billy Graham Center (BGC) Scholarship Program has been helping internationals, furloughing missionaries, pre-field missionaries and urban ministry leaders receive advanced degree training at the Wheaton College Graduate School. With world-renowned faculty, these students are developing solid skills and training to impact the world for Christ and to strengthen his Church.

The world is looking for answers to the hard questions in life. The Church worldwide needs individuals who can answer those questions effectively and lovingly. We help those individuals get the training they need to change the world for Jesus Christ.

**To date, more than 800 students have been in equipped in:**

- Biblical and Theological Studies
- Christian Formation and Ministry
- Clinical Psychology
- Counseling Ministries
- Evangelism and Leadership
- Intercultural Studies/TESOL

Billy Graham Center Scholarship Program at Wheaton College, Wheaton, IL 60187-5593
phone: 630.752.5903 • fax: 630.752.5916 • email: bgcscholar@wheaton.edu

# www.billygrahamcenter.org/scholarship

# Chapter 1

# Putting the Survey in Perspective

*A. Scott Moreau*

In this chapter we present selected findings on the survey that was used to collect data for the 822 North American Protestant mission agencies listed in this edition of the *Handbook*. Of these, 700 are in the United States and 122 in Canada. There are 6 more North American agencies in this *Handbook* than in the previous edition; 74 agencies from the previous edition are no longer listed (63 U.S.; 11 Canadian), while 80 agencies were added (69 U.S.; 11 Canadian). In the discussion that follows we offer statistical comparisons of the results of this survey with the results of previous surveys. Our hope is to paint the picture they portray of missions and missionaries being mobilized by North American agencies.

It must be noted that the tables and graphs we present are only as valid as the numbers received from each agency. Several factors contribute a certain softness to these numbers. First, the actual numbers fluctuate during the year. Second, agencies use different methods for counting their personnel. For example, some carefully tabulate and report painstakingly exact numbers for the month the survey is completed. Others, however, provide either highs or averages for the year. Still others provide estimates, especially for categories such as volunteers and short-term workers. Third, and finally, agencies do not always interpret the survey questions consistently with other agencies or even with their own answers in previous surveys. To help the reader keep this in mind, throughout this analysis we will typically use the term "reported" to refer to the numbers.

Table 1 summarizes the reported totals of the missionary force (for which we will use the terms missionary, worker and personnel interchangeably) employed by North American Protestant mission agencies from 2001 to 2005. The full-time[1] on-location North American missionary force deployed by those agencies[2] for 2005 was 132,399 people serving in 213 different countries and territories around the world. The 132,399 includes 43,899 North Americans, 6,156 non-North Americans[3] serving in countries other than their own, and 82,344 non-North Americans serving in their own countries. This is an increase in the total reported missionary force mobilized by North American Protestant agencies of 17.7% over the previous *Handbook*.

As seen in Table 1, this 17.7% increase happened even though the total reported number of U.S. and Canadian citizens in full-time on-location service under North American agencies declined from 2001. In fact, in the decade between 1996 and 2005, the total missionary force mobilized by North American

**Table 1: North American Mobilization from 2001 to 2005**

| | United States | | | Canada | | | North American Totals | | |
|---|---|---|---|---|---|---|---|---|---|
| | 2001 | 2005 | Change | 2001 | 2005 | Change | 2001 | 2005 | Change |
| U.S. or Canadian citizens in full-time service | 42,787 | 41,329 | -3.4% | 2,830 | 2,570 | -9.2% | 45,617 | 43,899 | -3.8% |
| Non-U.S. or Canadian citizens serving in another country | 5,029 | 5,428 | 7.9% | 873 | 728 | -16.6% | 5,902 | 6,156 | 4.3% |
| Non-U.S. or Canadian citizens serving in their own country | 59,843 | 80,834 | 35.1% | 1,128 | 1,510 | 33.9% | 60,971 | 82,344 | 35.1% |
| Total full-time on-location missionary force | 107,659 | 127,591 | 18.5% | 4,831 | 4,808 | -0.5% | 112,490 | 132,399 | 17.7% |

agencies increased by a strong 78.6%. However, virtually all of this increase has been the result of more non-U.S. and non-Canadian citizens serving as missionaries under U.S. and Canadian agencies.

As of 2005, for each U.S. or Canadian citizen serving an agency from his or her own country, there are roughly two non-U.S. or non-Canadian citizens also serving. The ratio in 2001 was about 1 to 1.3. The growth of this ratio is a strong reminder not only of the fact of the global presence of Christianity, but of the vibrancy of the faith of people from countries around the world who want to faithfully serve Christ in cross-cultural Christian service under the supervision of North American agencies. It also may imply a weakening of the mobilization of North Americans in missions, which we will discuss further below.

It should be clear that this is not the total picture of missionaries mobilized by North American Protestant agencies. Though it is representative, is likely well below the actual number of missionaries deployed out of North America. For example, numerous Christian organizations send Christian professionals to serve around the world and do not want to be labeled as "mission" agencies and so are not listed here. Additionally, uncounted individuals are sent as partial or fully supported cross-cultural workers by churches, and many other Christians simply go to serve Christ as business people not reporting to either a church or an agency. None of these types of cross-cultural workers is represented in this survey.

## United States Agencies

There are ten more U.S. agencies on which data are compiled for this edition than in the 2001 *Handbook* (700 versus 690).[4] The on-location, full-time United States missionary force was comprised of 127,591 people serving in 211 countries and territories.[5] As seen in Tables 1 and 2, 41,329 were U.S. citizens working in another country; 5,428 were non-U.S. citizens serving in countries other than

## Table 2: Summary of Changes in Reported
## U.S. Missions Statistics, 1992-2005

| Personnel from U.S. | 1992 | 1996 | 1998 | 2001 | 2005 | Change (2001-2005) | Change (1992-2001) |
|---|---|---|---|---|---|---|---|
| **Fully Supported U.S. Personnel Serving Overseas** | | | | | | | |
| Long-Term (Overseas more than 4 years) | 32,634 | 33,074 | 32,957 | 34,757 | 33,714 | -3.0% | 3.3% |
| Middle-Term[6] (Overseas from 1 to 4 years) | 5,115 | 6,562 | 6,930 | 8,030 | 7,615 | -5.2% | 48.9% |
| Nonresidential fully supported | 626 | 507 | 1,815 | 1,599 | 3,055 | 91.1% | 388.0% |
| Total fully supported U.S. personnel serving overseas | 38,375 | 40,143 | 41,702 | 44,386 | 44,384 | 0.0% | 15.7% |
| **Other U.S. Personnel Serving Overseas** | | | | | | | |
| Short-term of 2 weeks up to 1 year (1996 and 1999) | NA | 63,995 | 97,272 | 346,270 | 144,318 | -58.3% | NA |
| Bivocational associates sponsored or supervised | 1,040 | 1,336 | 3,220 | 1,748 | 1,934 | 10.6% | 86.0% |
| Nonresidential partially supported | 80 | 215 | 310 | 506 | 697 | 37.7% | 771.3% |
| **Non-U.S. Personnel Directly Supported** | | | | | | | |
| Those serving in their home country | NA | 28,535 | 71,150 | 59,843 | 80,834 | 35.1% | NA |
| Those serving in a country other than their home country | 1,898 | 1,791 | 3,179 | 5,029 | 5,428 | 7.9% | 186.0% |
| **U.S. Ministry and Home Office Staff** | | | | | | | |
| Full-time paid staff | 14,694 | 19,399 | 21,758 | 22,462 | 34,899 | 55.4% | 137.5% |
| Part-time staff/associates | 1,742 | 2,850 | 2,946 | 2,962 | 4,547 | 53.5% | 161.0% |
| Volunteer (ongoing) helpers[7] | 37,452 | 59,332 | 196,528 | 638,907 | 46,047 | -92.8% | 22.9% |

| Financial Support Raised in the U.S.— Income for Overseas Ministries (Adjusted for Inflation) | | | | | | |
|---|---|---|---|---|---|---|
| 1992 | 1996 | 1998 | 2001 | 2005 | Change 2001-2005 | Change 1992-2001 |
| $2,839,680,000 | $2,884,214,342 | $3,514,056,955 | 4,138,043,070 | $5,241,632,384 | 26.7% | 84.6% |

their own, and 80,834 were non-U.S. citizens serving in their own countries (occasionally referred to in this chapter as nationals).

As we observe the continuing development of the U.S. Protestant agencies through the surveys conducted as part of this *Handbook* and summarized in Table 2, several important changes may be noted from the data collected covering 1992 through 2005. We will identify a change as a trend if it has been consistent over the past decade or more. If the change has not been consistent over that time, we will identify what has happened as a shift. In our analysis of the data, we have isolated seven trends and five shifts seen in U.S. Protestant agencies that merit discussion.

**Trend 1: An Increase in the Reported Number of U.S. Citizens Working for U.S. Agencies.** Altogether, when we add the number of full-time U.S. citizens serving as residential missionaries, non-residential missionaries, tentmakers, and administrative or home-based staff, 86,461 U.S. citizens are reported to be fully engaged in the missionary task through U.S. agencies, a 20% increase over the number reported for these categories in the previous edition of the *Handbook* (Figure 1). While career and middle-term[6] missionary numbers were down, the number of U.S. citizens working as tentmakers or non-residential missionaries and the number of those working in the United States (whether as administrative staff or on home assignments) has risen enough to result in a net increase.

**Figure 1: U.S. Citizens Working for U.S. Agencies**

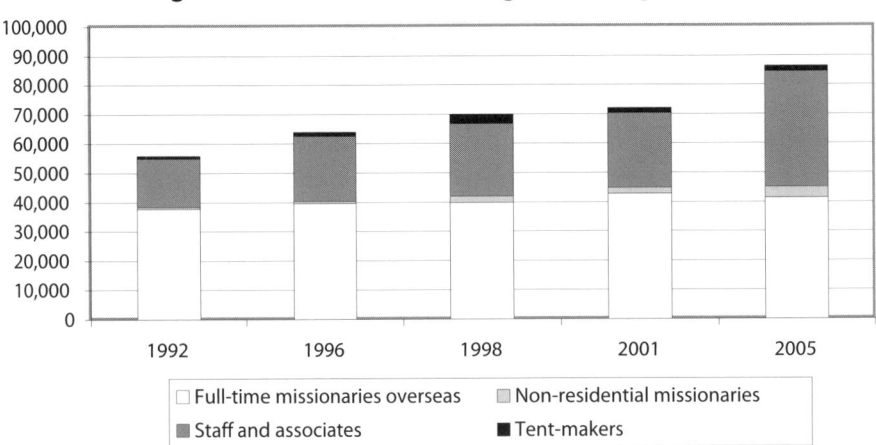

**Trend 2: An Increase in the Reported Number of Non-U.S. Citizens Working for U.S. Agencies.** There was also an increase in the total number of people (U.S. and non-U.S. citizens) serving full-time overseas under U.S. Protestant agencies of 18.5% (Figure 2), entirely due to the increase of non-U.S. citizens serving under U.S. agencies (Figure 3). Roughly speaking, for every four U.S. citizens there are eight non-U.S. citizens working under the employ of U.S. agencies. This is a significant increase from the last survey in which there were just over six nationals for every four Americans.

Figure 2 depicts this trend by showing the adjusted totals[7] of missionaries in both categories from 1992 to 2005. Figure 3 depicts the trend from 1996 to 2005 by showing the relative total share of U.S. citizens versus non-U.S. citizens employed by U.S. agencies. The share of non-U.S. citizens working for U.S. agencies rose from 42.4% of the total in 1996 to 67.6% of the total in 2005.

The non-U.S. citizens who are employed by U.S. Protestant agencies are primarily deployed in their own countries (93.3%; Figure 4). Non-U.S. citizens

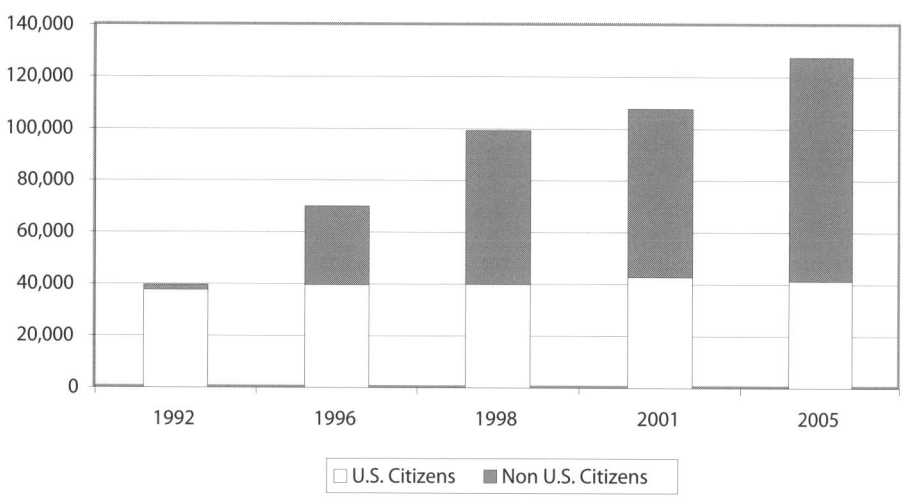

**Figure 2: Adjusted Total Full-time Missionary Force of U.S. Agencies**

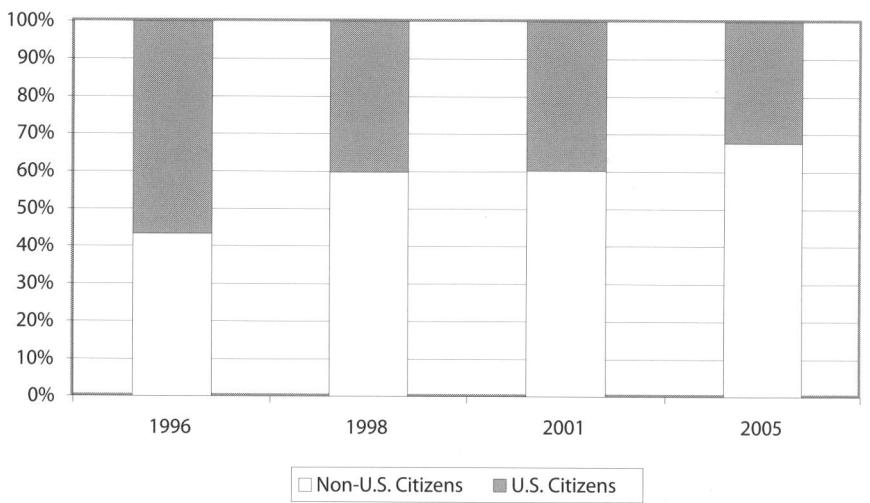

**Figure 3: Adjusted Share of U.S. and Non-U.S. Citizens Working for U.S. Agencies**

serving U.S. agencies in their home countries grew by 20,991 (35.1%) since 2001, continuing the trend seen since 1996 (Figure 4[8]). The gain was broadly-based across the agencies. Table 3 lists the 26 agencies reporting 500 or more non-U.S. citizens working for them; the corresponding table in the 2001 survey listed only 18 agencies.

The number of non-U.S. citizens reported as serving under U.S. agencies in a country other than their own increased by 399 people (7.9%) from 2001 to

### Figure 4: Adjusted Total Non-U.S. Citizens Deployed by U.S. Agencies

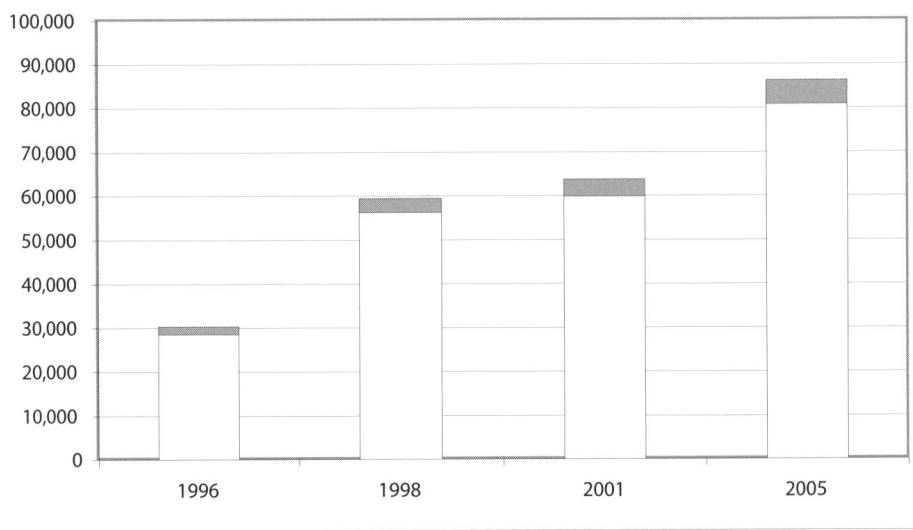

☐ Those serving in their home country    ■ Those serving in a country other than their home country

### Table 3: Agencies with 500 or More Non-U.S. Citizen Workers

| Rank | Agency | Nationals |
|------|--------|-----------|
| 1 | Gospel for Asia, Inc. | 16,377 |
| 2 | Campus Crusade for Christ, Intl. | 11,404 |
| 3 | AMG International | 8,284 |
| 4 | Partners International | 4,305 |
| 5 | Christian Aid Mission | 3,093 |
| 6 | Samaritan's Purse | 2,123 |
| 7 | India Gospel Outreach | 2,000 |
| 8 | World Missions Far Corners, Inc. | 1,661 |
| 9 | World Relief | 1,179 |
| 10 | Final Frontiers Foundation, Inc. | 1010 |
| 11 | Dayspring International | 1,000 |
| 12 | Global Fellowship Inc. | 923 |
| 13 | Lott Carey Baptist Foreign Mission Convention | 890 |
| 14 | World Concern | 850 |
| 15 | Christian Broadcasting Network Inc., the | 847 |
| 16 | Reaching Indians Ministries International | 810 |
| 17 | I. N. Network USA | 804 |
| 18 | Word of Life Fellowship, Inc.—International Ministries | 785 |
| 19 | Compassion International, Inc. | 778 |
| 20 | Gospelink, Inc. | 731 |

| 21 | Greater Grace World Outreach | 705 |
|----|------------------------------|-----|
| 22 | HBI Global Partners | 605 |
| 23 | Hosanna | 549 |
| 24 | Far East Broadcasting Company, Inc. | 515 |
| 25 | Churches of God, General Conference | 505 |
| 26 | Bible League, The | 500 |

2005, capping a run from 1992 in which the total gain was 186% (Figure 5).

There is no clear indicator to determine what accounts for the size of the increase between the 2001 and 2005 surveys. It may be primarily due to reporting variations,[9] as only seven of the 2005 top twenty agencies were also in the 2001 top twenty list, and there is no consistent indication from the data that explains why some agencies are now on the list and others have dropped off. Table 4 shows those agencies reporting 50 or more non-U.S. citizens working in a country other than their own. There are 21 such agencies in this edition versus 20 in the previous one.

While there should be no question of the potential effectiveness of the work of non-U.S. citizens, and across the majority world there are definite financial efficiencies gained through employing them rather than U.S. citizens, the extent to which these workers are actually serving as cross-cultural missionaries rather than same-culture evangelists is unknown. Even though Table 4 lists non-U.S. citizens working in a country other than their own, the survey does not ask if they are ministering cross-culturally in their country of service or if they are min-

**Figure 5: Adjusted Non-U.S. Citizens Working in a Country Other than Their Own and Deployed by U.S. Agencies**

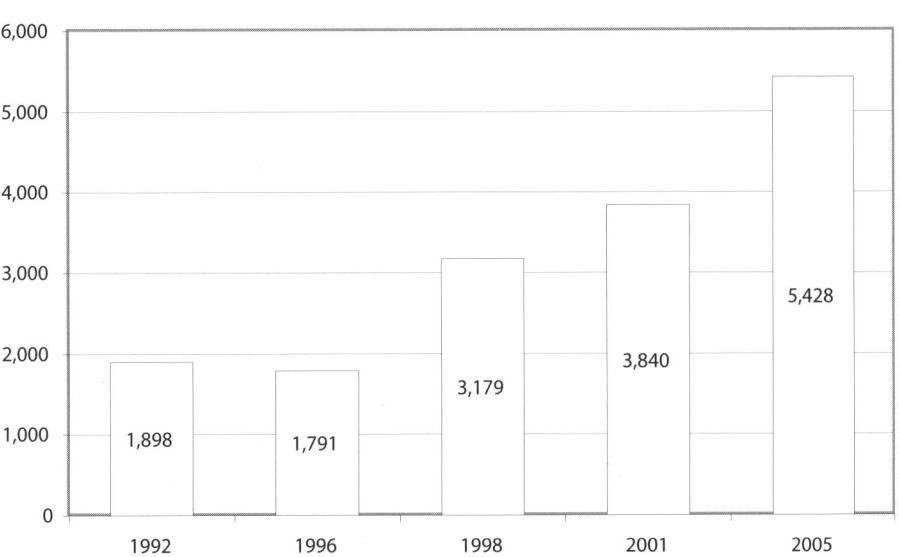

### Table 4: U.S. Agencies with 50 or More Non-U.S. Citizens Serving in Another Country

| Rank | Agency | No. |
|------|--------|-----|
| 1 | Campus Crusade for Christ, Intl. | 824 |
| 2 | OMF International | 575 |
| 3 | Seventh-day Adventists General Conference | 461 |
| 4 | International Teams, U.S.A. | 434 |
| 5 | Africa Inland Mission International | 257 |
| 6 | United Pentecostal Church Intl., Foreign Missions Division | 235 |
| 7 | Biblical Ministries Worldwide | 156 |
| 8 | Latin America Mission | 139 |
| 9 | Habitat for Humanity International | 110 |
| 10 | Church of the Nazarene, World Mission Department | 105 |
| 11 | SEND International USA | 79 |
| 12 | OMS International, Inc. | 73 |
| 13 | Greater Grace World Outreach | 70 |
| 14 | Cadence International | 69 |
| 15 | Operation Mobilization | 67 |
| 16 | Word of Life Fellowship, Inc. - International Ministries | 65 |
| 17 | Evangelism Explosion International | 64 |
| 18 | HCJB Global | 60 |
| 19 | Church of God (Cleveland, TN) World Missions | 55 |
| 20 | Trans World Radio, International | 54 |
| 21 | Middle East Christian Outreach (MECO) | 50 |

istering among same-culture pockets of people who have migrated there. For example, we do not know if a Korean missionary working under a U.S. agency in Germany is serving among the indigenous German nationals or among the Korean immigrant community in Germany.

We may further ask whether it is ultimately good or bad to have more non-U.S. citizens working for U.S. agencies. To what extent does this indicate we are headed toward a globalized mission world that parallels the multi-national corporate world? Is this simply a balancing between western and majority world missionaries? Is there greater status in working for a U.S. agency than for a majority world one? There is little doubt that U.S. agencies command a greater share of access to finances than majority world agencies, and we need to ask what role this reality plays among non-U.S. citizens choosing to work for U.S. agencies.

**Trend 3: An Increase in the Reported Number of Non-Residential Fully Supported Missionaries.** The number of non-residential fully-supported workers increased by 91.1% from 2001 to 2005 in a broad-based gain, while those partially supported rose 37.7% during the same period (see Figure 6[10]). Both are large enough to ask whether this is an evolving strategy—perhaps as a means of enabling people to serve in creative access countries while residing in countries where visas are easier to obtain—or more simply the realities of an aging missionary force returning to home to live there while still serving non-residentially for their prior country of service. In any event, the gain is broadly-based, with 47 agencies reporting at least 10 full-time non-residential workers and 219 agencies reporting at least 1 full-time non-residential worker (in contrast to 33 and 177 respectively in the 2001 survey).

**Figure 6: Adjusted Non-Residential Missionaries from U.S. Agencies**

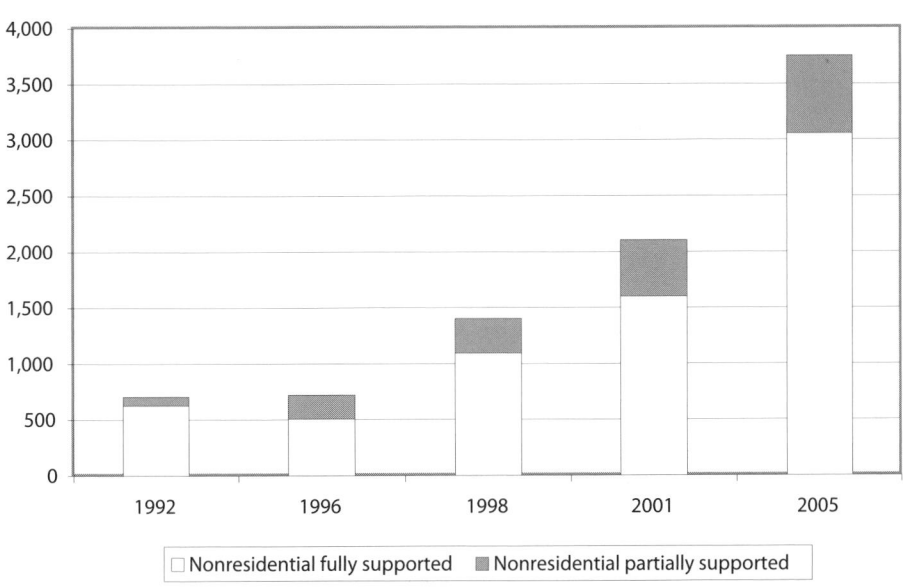

☐ Nonresidential fully supported    ■ Nonresidential partially supported

**Trend 4: An Increase in the Reported Number of Tentmakers.** Figure 7 illustrates the adjusted[11] gain in the number of reported tentmakers ("bivocational associates sponsored or supervised," in Table 2) of 186 (10.6%) from the previous survey. This gain was seen across the board by the agencies. As with short-term missions, this number can only be understood as representing a small fraction of the actual number of U.S. tentmakers. Many who consider themselves tentmakers find secular jobs working for multinational corporations or non-governmental organizations. Others are sent out by local churches without connecting with mission agencies, and still others establish their own international businesses without connection to a supporting church or mission agency.

**Trend 5: An Increase in the Reported Number of U.S. Agency Home Staff.** Figure 8 depicts both those who work behind the scenes to ensure the de-

**Figure 7: Adjusted Total U.S. Agency-Based Tentmakers**

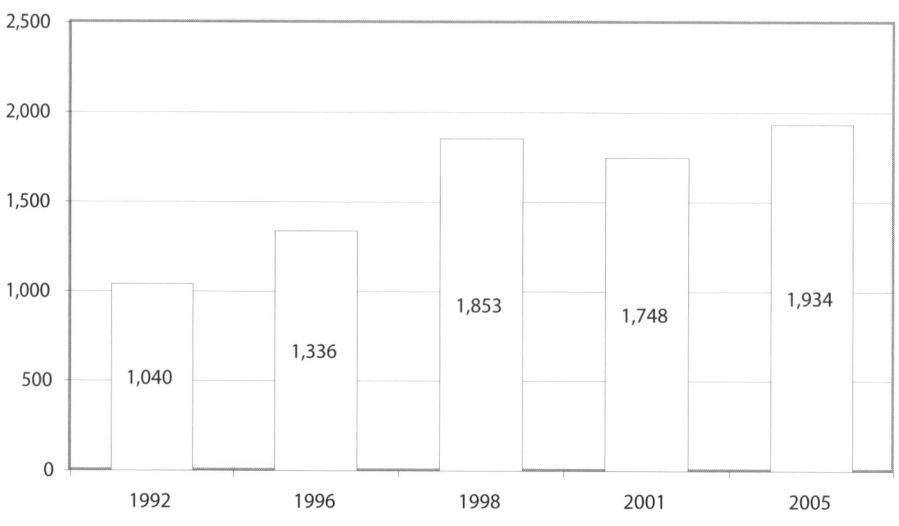

**Figure 8: U.S. Agency Home Staff (1992 to 2005)**

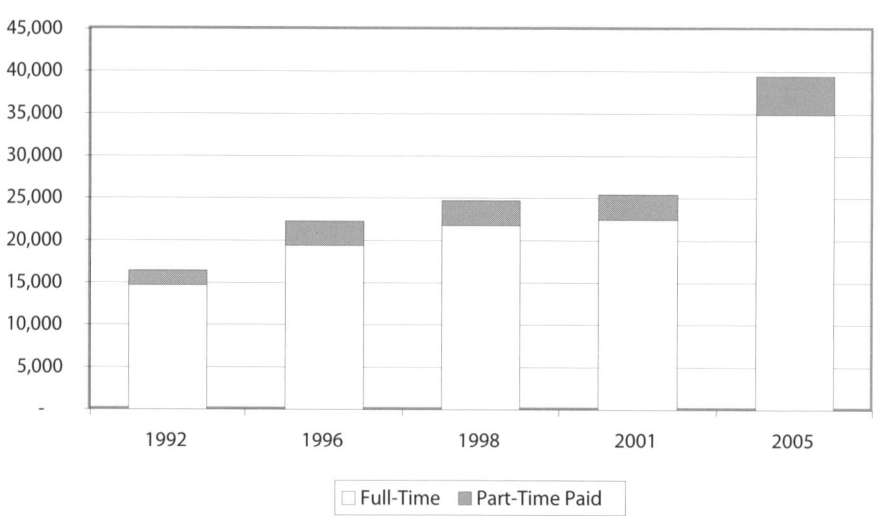

ployed field missionaries are able to accomplish their work and those who are working out of their home offices in ministry positions (e.g., among ethnic or migrant populations). As indicated in the chart, the number of reported home staff grew dramatically from 2001 to 2005. In fact, this number is now only slightly less than the number of full-time missionaries serving overseas through the agencies. This should not be read as a bloating of administrative staff. In this case, two organizations reported 60.3% of the total full-time home staff report-ed because of the way they defined their own workers. The other 698 agencies reported a total of 13,861 office staff, or just under 20 per agency. In the case of part-time office staff, the top two organizations reported 45.7% of the total. It helps to see that if the top 10 agencies are factored out, the average drops to 15 full-time office staff per agency and 2.5 part-time office staff, both of which are far more realistic numbers of the "behind-the-scenes" administrative people.

### Trend 6: An Increase in the Income Reported for Overseas Ministries

The total reported income for overseas missions for the U.S. Protestant agencies in 2005 was $5,241,632,384. In the previous edition we raised the question of what might happen to giving after the events of September 11, 2001 and in light of the drop in the U.S. stock market in 2000. However, as seen in Table 2 and Figure 9, the total giving in 2005 was up 26.7% after adjusting for inflation. This is a 6.7% annual growth rate, the strongest growth rate between surveys since 1992. Was this remarkable gain broadly-based or more narrowly-confined? Several indicators point towards it being a more narrowly-confined growth.

**Figure 9: Inflation-Adjusted Budget for Overseas Ministries**

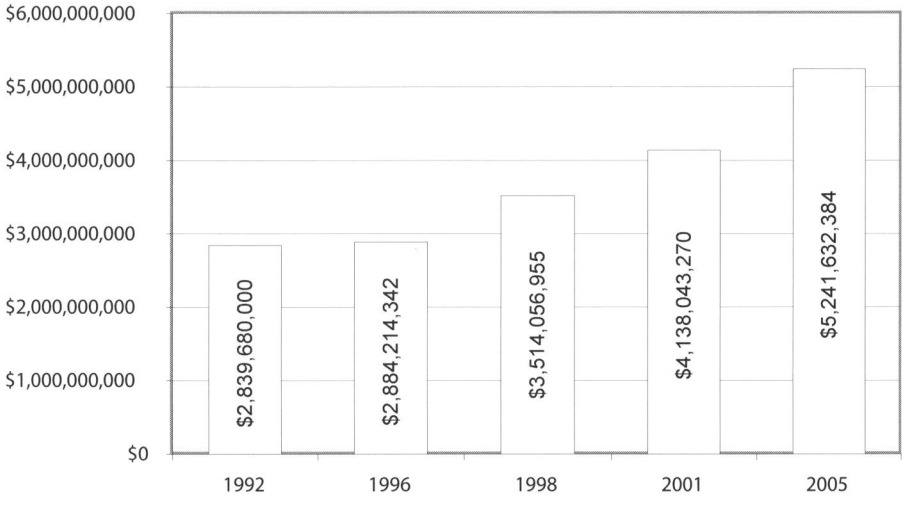

First, six agencies reported an overseas budget gain of over $40,000,000 between the surveys. Those six alone accounted for 76% of the inflation-adjusted gain reported, and five of them identify relief and development as their primary activities. This is further emphasized in that agencies that reported their primary activities as ones focused in the areas of evangelism and discipleship experienced a 2.7% inflation-adjusted budget growth during the four years between surveys, while agencies that reported their primary activities as ones focused in the areas of relief and development experienced a 74.3% inflation-adjusted budget growth (see Figure 24 and further discussion below).

Thus, while the overall reported numbers appear to indicate healthy growth for all of U.S. missions, the fact is that the bulk of the growth was among agencies whose primary activities were related to relief and development. This is not surprising in light of the influx of donations and government-based aid directed through these agencies as a result of the December 2004 Indian Ocean tsunami, the October 2005 earthquake in Pakistan, and other recent international emergency aid situations around the world.

A second indicator that this was narrowly-confined growth is that the number of U.S. agencies whose reported overseas income was $10,000,000 or more rose from 68 in 2001 to 72 in 2005 (after adjusting for inflation). In 2001 we reported that ten additional agencies had made the list in the span from 1998 to 2001. Thus, in this edition of the *Handbook*, only four agencies joined the ranks of those whose income exceeded $10,000,000 compared to ten agencies in the previous survey. Thus the gain was concentrated among the agencies with the largest incomes (in Table 5 we list the forty Protestant agencies which reported $25,000,000 or more in income for overseas ministries in 2005).

### Table 5: US Agencies with $25,000,000 or More Income for Overseas Ministries

| Rank | Agency | Overseas Income |
|---|---|---|
| 1 | World Vision Inc. | $752,348,000.00 |
| 2 | MAP International | $319,511,995.00 |
| 3 | Southern Baptist Convention International Mission Board | $242,140,000.00 |
| 4 | Northwest Medical Teams International, Inc. | $225,202,506.00 |
| 5 | Christian Aid Ministries | $190,608,201.00 |
| 6 | Assemblies of God World Missions | $181,178,453.00 |
| 7 | Compassion International, Inc. | $136,234,672.00 |
| 8 | Samaritan's Purse | $121,842,371.00 |
| 9 | Christian Broadcasting Network Inc., the | $115,104,000.00 |
| 10 | Opportunity International | $112,064,000.00 |
| 11 | Wycliffe Bible Translators, Inc. | $103,425,000.00 |
| 12 | Campus Crusade for Christ, Intl. | $98,321,000.00 |
| 13 | Habitat for Humanity International | $95,475,655.00 |
| 14 | Food for the Hungry, Inc. | $93,826,618.00 |
| 15 | United Methodist Church, General Bd. of Global Ministries | $91,200,000.00 |
| 16 | Church World Service | $63,665,788.00 |
| 17 | Blessings International | $61,002,351.00 |
| 18 | Heifer International | $56,625,000.00 |
| 19 | Church of the Nazarene, World Mission Department | $56,606,056.00 |
| 20 | Seventh-day Adventists General Conference | $55,803,094.00 |
| 21 | Christian Churches / Churches of Christ | $52,000,000.00 |
| 22 | Gideons International, The | $50,000,000.00 |
| 23 | Gospel for Asia, Inc. | $47,700,000.00 |
| 24 | Mission to the World (PCA), Inc. | $42,393,999.00 |

| 25 | Salvation Army, U.S.A. | $41,606,749.00 |
|----|------------------------|----------------|
| 26 | ABWE (Association of Baptists for World Evangelism) | $41,000,000.00 |
| 27 | Mennonite Central Committee (MCC) | $40,614,000.00 |
| 28 | Presbyterian Church (USA), Worldwide Ministries | $40,000,000.00 |
| 29 | Mercy Ships | $38,682,881.00 |
| 30 | Baptist Bible Fellowship International | $38,500,000.00 |
| 31 | International Aid | $36,611,986.00 |
| 32 | Evangelical Lutheran Ch. in Am., Div. for Global Mission | $34,434,240.00 |
| 33 | Church of God (Cleveland, TN) World Missions | $33,147,856.00 |
| 34 | New Tribes Mission | $32,400,000.00 |
| 35 | World Concern | $30,348,937.00 |
| 36 | SIM USA | $28,495,000.00 |
| 37 | Baptist International Missions, Inc. (BIMI) | $28,179,154.00 |
| 38 | TEAM (The Evangelical Alliance Mission) | $26,212,000.00 |
| 39 | Voice of the Martyrs, The | $25,305,375.00 |
| 40 | Cooperative Baptist Fellowship | $25,000,000.00 |

Finally, the agency ranked 100th in the 2005 survey reported an income for overseas missions of $6,500,000, which is an inflation-adjusted 3.7% increase over the agency listed as 100th in the 2001 survey. The gain of the 100th agency from 1998 to 2001 was 8.8%, so the net gain in the 2005 survey was less than half that in the 2001 survey even though the 2005 survey covered a longer period of time (one year longer).

The net result is that the growth, while large, was confined to the agencies with the largest incomes whose primary activities were related to relief and development.

In summary, we have identified six trends seen among U.S. Protestant mission agencies over the past decade, all indicating growth:

1. An increase in the reported number of U.S. citizens working for U.S. agencies;

2. An increase in the reported number of non-U.S. citizens working for U.S. agencies;

3. An increase in the reported number of non-residential fully-supported missionaries;

4. An increase in the reported number of tentmakers;

5. An increase in the reported number of U.S. agency home staff; and

6. An increase in the income reported for overseas ministries that was concentrated in the largest agencies whose primary activities focus on relief and development.

In addition to these trends, we have identified five changes that have not yet appeared over the course of a decade. In our discussion, we refer to these as shifts rather than trends.

**Shift 1: A Decrease in the Reported Number of Long Term U.S. Missionaries.** While in the previous *Handbook* we reported a 5.5% increase in long-term missionaries (four years or more) in the three-year span covered, Table 2 shows that over the four-year span between that survey and this one agencies reported a 3.0% decrease. The reported number of U.S. citizens deployed full-time in overseas service for one year or longer by U.S. agencies declined by 3.4%, the largest decline since the 1992 switch to our current use of terms (Figure 10).

**Figure 10: U.S. Citizens Serving
as Missionary through U.S. Agencies**

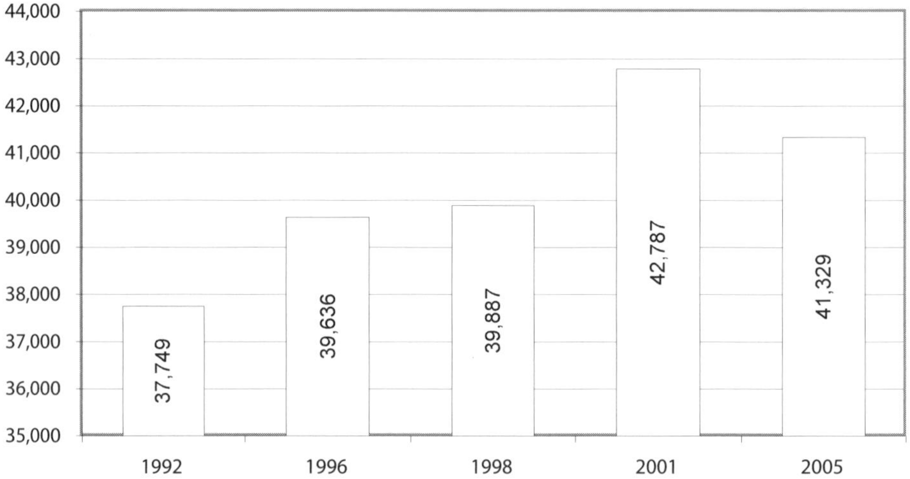

The 69 agencies that are listed for the first time in this *Handbook* account for 965 of the 1,043 fewer long-term workers (92.5% of the decrease) than the agencies that have been dropped for the first time from this edition. Thus, the long-term missionary drop reported here might not be as severe as it first appears because the bulk of the agencies that are no longer listed were dropped because new information was not made available, not because they ceased to deploy full-time missionaries. At the same time, however, 353 U.S. agencies reported at least one worker in this category compared to 316 in the 2001 survey, though the increase in the number of agencies reporting at least one long-term worker did not offset the total losses reported. Table 6 lists the 13 U.S. agencies that reported 500 or more U.S. citizens working as long-term missionaries.

**Table 6: U.S. Agencies with 500 or More Long-Term U.S. Workers**

| Rank | Organization | Workers |
|------|--------------|---------|
| 1 | Southern Baptist Convention International Mission Board | 4009 |
| 2 | Wycliffe Bible Translators, Inc. | 3496 |
| 3 | Assemblies of God World Missions | 1809 |
| 4 | New Tribes Mission | 1402 |
| 5 | Christian Churches / Churches of Christ | 915 |
| 6 | Campus Crusade for Christ, Intl. | 807 |

| 7 | Christian and Missionary Alliance | 761 |
|---|---|---|
| 8 | Baptist International Missions, Inc. (BIMI) | 708 |
| 9 | Churches of Christ | 695 |
| 10 | Baptist Bible Fellowship International | 682 |
| 11 | Mennonite Central Committee (MCC) | 606 |
| 12 | ABWE (Association of Baptists for World Evangelism) | 599 |
| 13 | TEAM (The Evangelical Alliance Mission) | 514 |

**Shift 2: A Decrease in the Reported Number of Middle-Term U.S. Missionaries.** As Figure 11 shows, there was also a reported 5.2% decrease of U.S. citizens serving overseas for 1 to 4 years, called here middle-term missionaries. This is the first decrease in this category since these demarcations were put into use in 1992. The reported decrease is actually more severe than indicated, as the agencies that are newly listed in this edition accounted for 158 more of these middle-term mission workers than the agencies that were dropped in this edition. In other words, without the newly listed agencies the drop would be even greater. To add to this, 199 agencies reported at least one worker in this category in 2005, compared to 188 in the 2001 survey, so even though 11 more agencies reported middle-missions workers than in 2001, the total still dropped. Table 7 lists the 19 U.S. agencies with more than 100 middle-term workers.

**Figure 11: Fully Supported Middle-Term
(1 to 4 years) U.S. Missionaries**

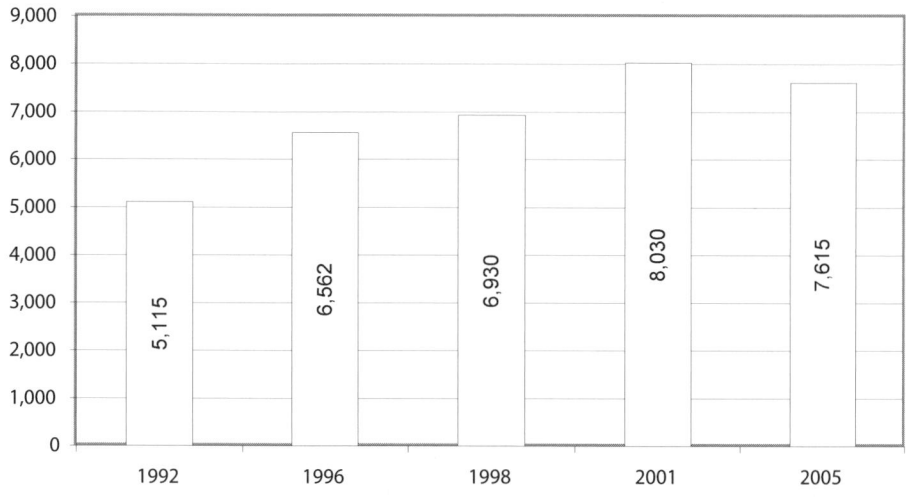

**Shift 3: A Decrease in the Reported Number of Short-Term Missionaries.** The largest decrease between the two editions is the enormous short-term (two weeks to 1 year) loss (from 346,270 to 144,318). This is a 58.3% drop in the four-year span. However, the magnitude of the drop is due to changes in reporting rather than actual decline. In this case, two agencies alone accounted for

## Table 7: U.S. Agencies with 100 or More Middle-Term U.S. Workers

| Rank | Organization | Workers |
|------|--------------|---------|
| 1 | Southern Baptist Convention International Mission Board | 1156 |
| 2 | Assemblies of God World Missions | 524 |
| 3 | Campus Crusade for Christ, Intl. | 480 |
| 4 | Mission to the World (PCA), Inc. | 403 |
| 5 | Presbyterian Church (USA), Worldwide Ministries | 385 |
| 6 | United Pentecostal Church Intl., Foreign Missions Division | 340 |
| 7 | Network of International Christian Schools | 236 |
| 8 | Church World Service | 204 |
| 9 | ABWE (Association of Baptists for World Evangelism) | 186 |
| 10 | Habitat for Humanity International | 184 |
| 11 | Educational Services International (ESI) | 165 |
| 12 | Operation Mobilization | 158 |
| 13 | Churches of Christ | 147 |
| 14 | Heifer International | 126 |
| 15 | United Church of Christ—Wider Church Ministries | 126 |
| 16 | Samaritan's Purse | 120 |
| 17 | CMF International | 119 |
| 18 | Global Partners / Wesleyan World Missions | 115 |
| 19 | Africa Inland Mission International | 109 |

97.5% of the total short-term losses reported in this survey. If the numbers from these two agencies are factored out for the 2001 and 2005 editions, the decline was 3.8% (see Figure 12). With recent research indicating that some 1.6 million people went on short-term missions trips from churches in 2005,[12] it is clear that our reported numbers are only the a fraction of this trend. For example, many more go through churches, schools, or other U.S. organizations not listed here in the *Handbook*.

While the agencies represented here do not tell the entire story of U.S. short-term missions, they still demonstrate the trend of tremendous expansion over the past decade. One question to ask is whether the leveling off seen in this survey is indicative of a wider trend. Two possible explanations may be noted:

1. Most simply, this might indicate that fewer people are choosing to take short-term missions trips through the agencies listed in this *Handbook*. There are many more means of going on a short-term trip than just through the agencies listed in this *Handbook*. Perhaps more people are utilizing these other means (especially their own churches).

2. It seems more likely, however that those going on two-week or longer trips through the agencies listed in the *Handbook* have hit a plateau. That this is more likely is seen in two factors:

   • In our survey agencies only report people who go on trips that are two weeks to one year, which is most likely a minority of the total number. For ex-

**Figure 12: Adjusted Long-Term
and Short-Term Missionaries 1996 to 2005**

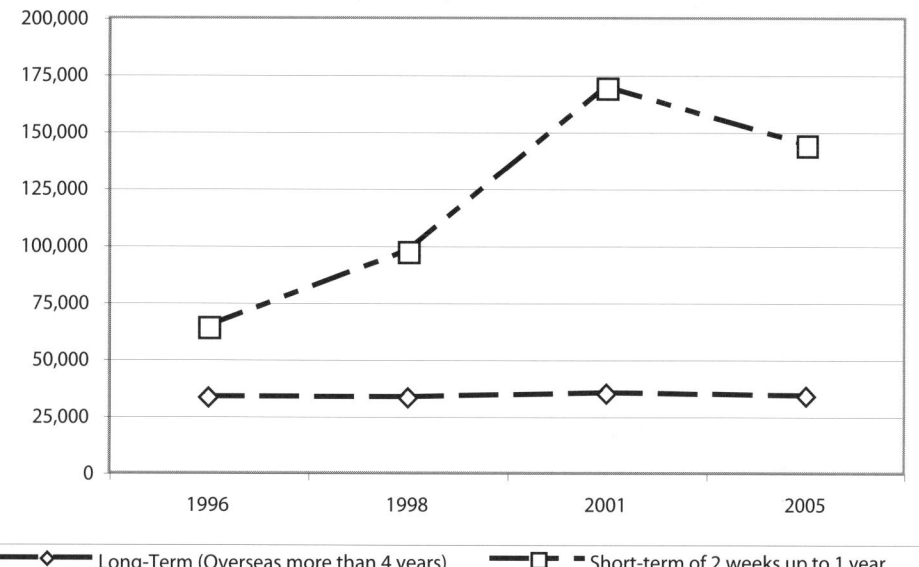

ample, in a recent survey of college students, seminary students and members of adult Sunday school classes it was discovered that more than two-thirds (67.6%) of the short-term trips they had taken were two weeks or less duration.[13]

• It may very well be that agencies are still experiencing short-term missions growth, but the growth is concentrated in trips of shorter duration. We do know that the agencies responding to this survey send out people on trips of less than two weeks. This can be seen, for example, in that 51 of them reported at least one staff member giving part-time or greater focus on short-term missions but with 0 short-term missionaries reported. This is not because these agencies did not send anyone, but most likely because the trips they sent people on lasted less than the minimum two-week time required to report in the *Handbook* survey.

Despite the flattening out of the reported short-term missions trips between 2001 and 2005, the number of people going on two-week to one-year short-term missions trips through the Protestant mission agencies listed in this *Handbook* still have risen by over 125% since 1996. During the same period, however, the number of long-term (four years or longer) missionaries has risen by just 1.9% (Figure 12). Thus, the explosion of short-term missions has yet to have any type of proportional impact on long-term missions. There are several possible types of explanations for this, each of which requires research beyond the scope of the survey conducted for the *Handbook*:

• Perhaps short-term missions experiences simply do not result in enough long-term interest for people to pursue missions as a career;

• It may be that the shift in generations from one focused on career to one focused on shorter term life objectives is impacting the number of career missionaries;

• Another possibility is that the budget of churches has shifted towards short-term missions to such an extent that new missionaries who want to go long term are finding it more difficult to raise their support.[14]

Table 8 shows the 20 agencies with 1,000 or more short-term missionaries reported (in the previous edition 22 agencies were listed). The organizations that are listed in the *Handbook* for the first time in this edition accounted for 1,764 more short-term workers than those that were removed from this edition. This gain was not enough to offset the overall loss, though it moderated the severity of it.

### Table 8: Agencies with 1,000 or More Short-Term Workers Sent

| Rank | Agency | No. Sent |
|------|--------|----------|
| 1 | Southern Baptist Convention International Mission Board | 30,000 |
| 2 | Youth With A Mission (YWAM) | 20,000 |
| 3 | Assemblies of God World Missions | 16,867 |
| 4 | Mission to the World (PCA), Inc. | 7,824 |
| 5 | Churches of Christ | 7,790 |
| 6 | Church of the Nazarene, World Mission Department | 6,600 |
| 7 | Habitat for Humanity International | 4,600 |
| 8 | Mennonite Mission Network | 3,000 |
| 9 | Church of God (Cleveland, TN) World Missions | 2,000 |
| 10 | Christian Churches / Churches of Christ | 2,000 |
| 11 | Missionary Ventures International | 1,800 |
| 12 | Evangelical Covenant Church - Covenant World Mission | 1,500 |
| 13 | Youth for Christ/USA - World Outreach | 1,400 |
| 14 | Christian and Missionary Alliance | 1,352 |
| 15 | Mercy Ships | 1,300 |
| 16 | Free Methodist World Missions | 1,200 |
| 17 | LeaderTreks | 1,100 |
| 18 | Global Outreach International | 1,007 |
| 19 | World Gospel Mission | 1,000 |
| 20 | On The Go Ministries / Keith Cook Evangelistic Association | 1,000 |

Figure 13 indicates a continuing increase in regular personnel (whether in the U.S. or overseas) who devote at least 10% of their work to supporting short-term missions. The number doing that has more than tripled since 1996, a strong indication that short-term missions growth continues and that agencies are putting considerable resources into ensuring that short-term efforts are adequately supported. The number of regular personnel (whether in the U.S. or overseas) whose full-time responsibilities were on short-term missions support grew by 147% from 2001 to 2005, a dramatic increase. While this may have been the agencies catching up to the demand or gearing up for anticipated future demand, the survey question does not enable us to confirm either possibility.

**Figure 13: U.S. Short-Term Support Personnel (1996 to 2005)**

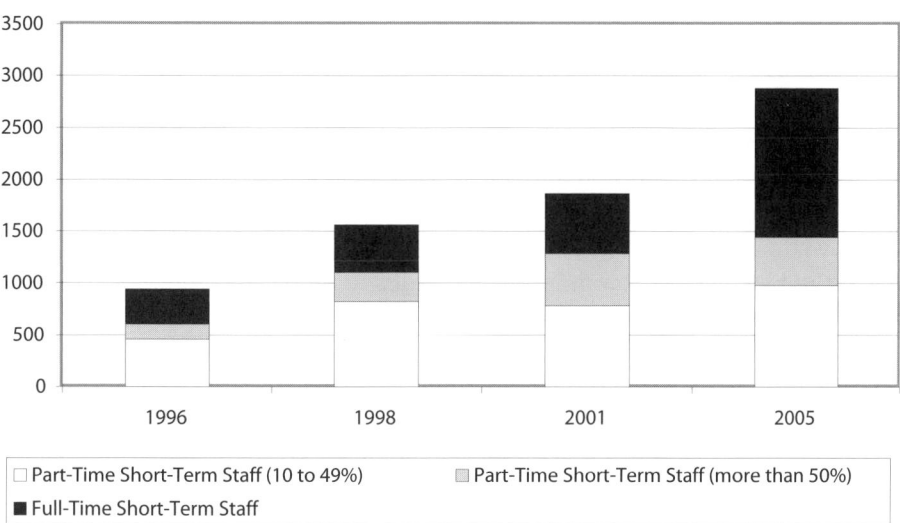

□ Part-Time Short-Term Staff (10 to 49%)          ▨ Part-Time Short-Term Staff (more than 50%)
■ Full-Time Short-Term Staff

Figure 14 shows how the agencies contact people for short-term missions. Nearly half the U.S. agencies now report that they contact potential short-term missionaries through churches—the largest number of agencies ever. An increasing number of agencies are also using conferences to recruit for short-term trips. However, the most dramatic increase was in the number of agencies recruiting through schools. This number grew from 41 to 131, a gain of almost 220% (the category "school" was added in the 1999 survey, and thus no number is avail-

**Figure 14: Contact Methods Used by U.S. Agencies
for Short-Term Missions Recruitment**

□ Church   ▨ Conference   ▨ Individual   ■ School

able for 1996). Clearly agencies are more actively recruiting for short-term trips than ever before and using a broader variety of contact methods in their mobilization efforts. Sixty-seven agencies indicated either internet or website. This will be added as a category in the next survey. Agencies are obviously taking advantage of the easy connectivity provided by the internet for short-term mobilization.

Agencies are pouring significant resources in short-term missions, seen in the vast numbers of people going on short-term trips, the rise in agency personnel resources devoted to short-term support, and the increasing mobilization efforts. Perhaps no single assumption drives this marshalling of resources more than the idea that short-term missions results in more long-term missionaries. The fact that this assumption has not yet been adequately demonstrated indicates the tremendous need for rigorous research into the costs and benefits of short-term missions work.[15]

**Shifts 4 and 5: Missionary Deployments: An Increase in the Reported Numbers of U.S. Agencies and Missionaries Deployed to Asia; An Increase in the Reported Numbers of U.S. Citizens Serving as Full-Time Missionaries in Europe.** Figures 15 through 20 depict the deployment of U.S. agencies and their personnel by region of the world. To ensure consistency with previous editions of the *Handbook*, Asia includes the Middle East. Three observations may be made.

First, more agencies are reporting activity on every continent of the world (Figure 15). With a decrease in the number of full-time U.S. missionaries, this may indicate a stretching of U.S. personnel.

Second, by a wide margin, the most significant increase is in the number of agencies reporting deployment in Asian countries (up 52.3% over 2001). Africa also saw a significant increase in the number of agencies reporting deployment (up 26.4%) (Figure 16).

Third, in 2005 U.S. agencies reported more full-time U.S. missionaries deployed to Europe (16.9%), Asia (5.4%), and South America (4.2) than in 2001, while they reported fewer being deployed in Oceania (down 17.1%), Central America and the Caribbean (down 4.3%) and Africa (down 3.0%) (Figures 17 and 18).

Why the increase to Europe? It would be hoped that the realities of an increasingly secularized Europe, possibly blended with a burgeoning immigrant population which is typically more open to exploring new faith options, have resulted in the significantly stronger full-time U.S. missionary presence there. At the same time, however, the shift might be more pragmatic in nature—perhaps people perceive Europe's more comfortable living conditions to be more desirable than those typically found in majority world countries or feel that the cultural adjustment needed is not as significant in Europe as it would be elsewhere in the world.

Fourth, and finally, U.S. agencies report a significant shift in deployment of all full-time residential missionaries (especially non-U.S. citizens) to Asia (Figures 19 and 20). On average, for each of the 26 Asian countries in which agencies reported they were active, there were 3 more active agencies, 29 fewer U.S.

## Figure 15: Number of U.S. Agencies Per Region

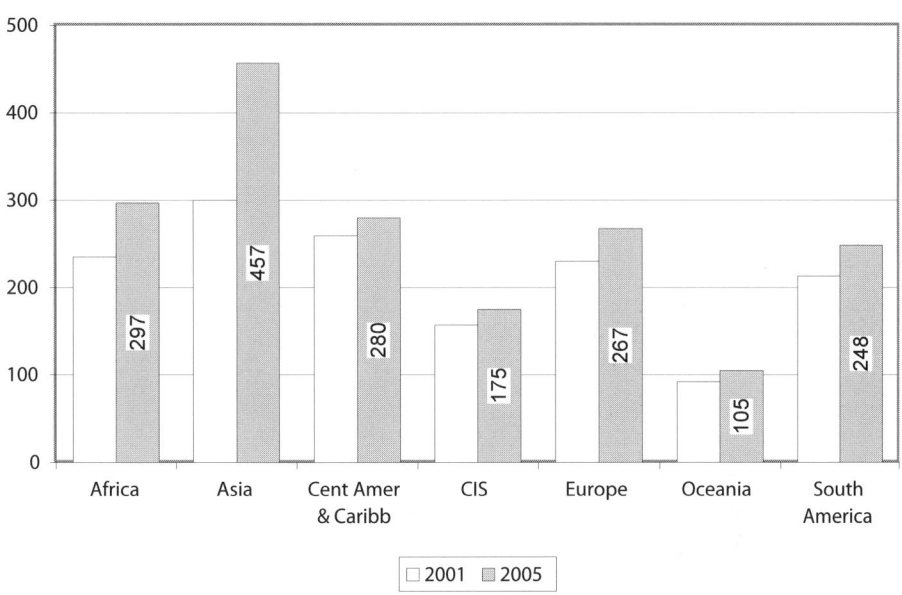

## Figure 16: Percent Increase in Number of Agencies in Region 2001 to 2005

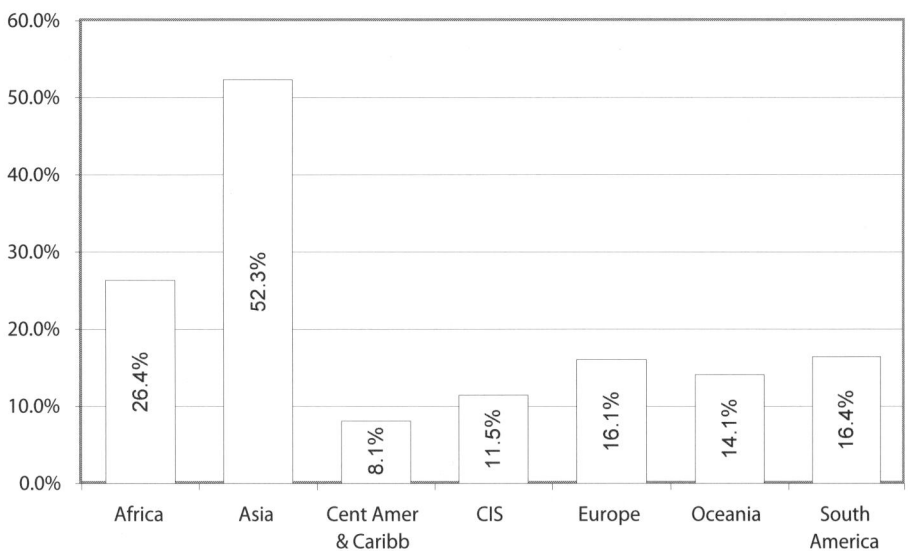

## Figure 17: Deployment of Full-Time
## U.S. Citizens as Missionaries  2001 and 2005

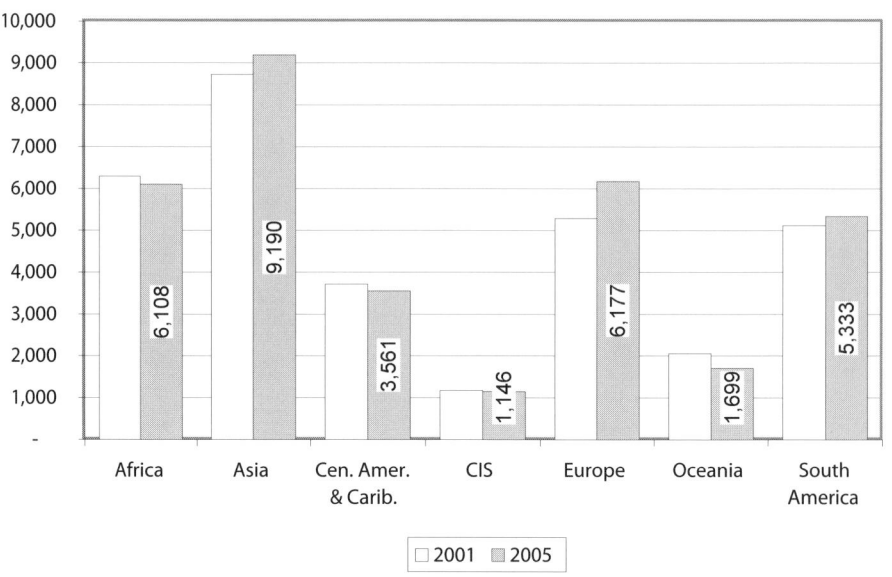

## Figure 18: Percent Gain/Loss Deployment of All Full-Time
## Missionaries through the U.S. Agencies 2001 to 2005

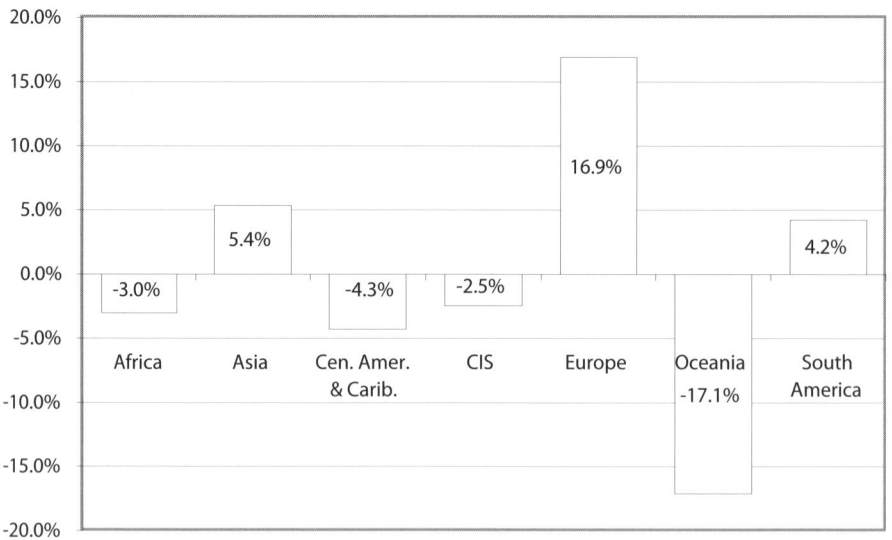

**Figure 19: 2001 vs 2005 Deployment of All
Full-Time Missionaries through U.S. Agencies**

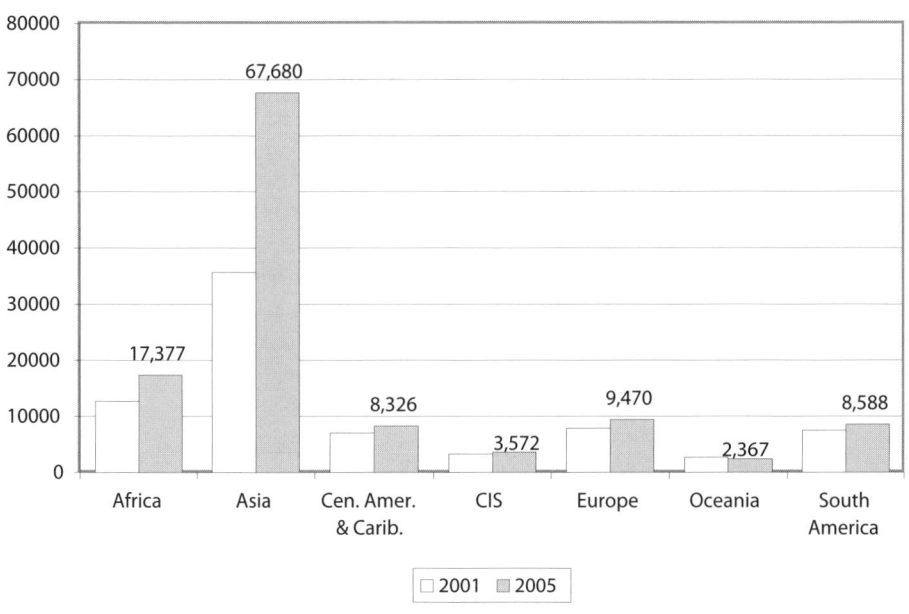

**Figure 20: Percent Gain/Loss in Full-Time
Missionaries per Region 2001 to 2005**

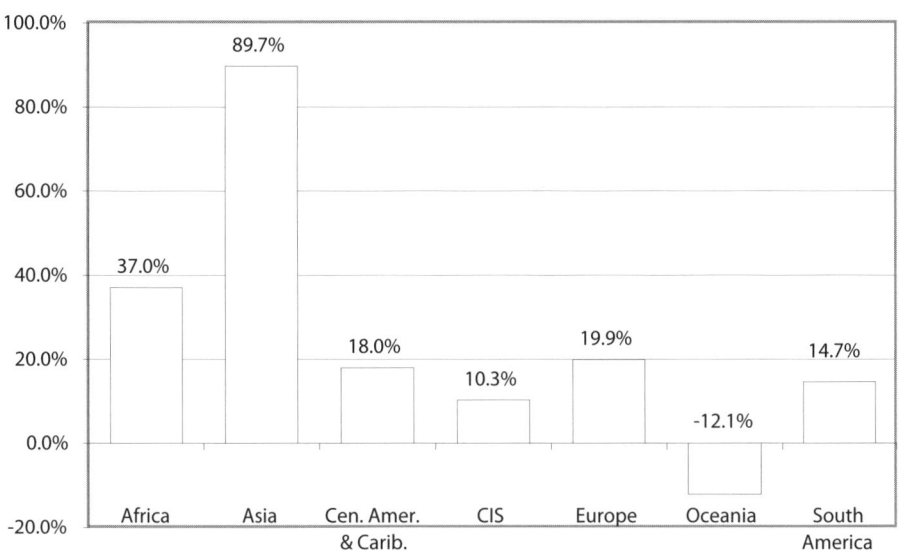

missionaries, and 1,225 more non-U.S. citizens working for U.S. agencies. On average, for each of the Middle Eastern countries in which agencies reported they were active, there were 2 more active agencies, 10 more U.S. missionaries, and 14 more non-U.S. citizens working for U.S. agencies. This is due in part to more agencies reporting the actual locations of their deployment in 2005 than in 2001 (there were only 10,197 "unspecified" deployments in 2005, compared to 30,919 in 2001). However, this is not just a redistribution due to more accurate reporting, seen through two facts. First, while we gained deployment information for some 20,700 more people than in 2001, the number of people reported as deployed to Asia increased by over 32,000. Second, reported deployments to each of the other specified regions were an average of 10.2%, but those in Asia were up 89.7% (Figure 20). Thus it appears that U.S. agencies are in the process of a large-scale shift of focus and deployment of non-U.S. personnel towards Asia (including the Middle East).

Table 9 indicates the 38 countries with 50 or more U.S. agencies present. The number of agencies for each country represent a minimum number, since several agencies did not choose to identify specific countries of deployment.[16] For the first time India has displaced Mexico as the country with the largest number of U.S. agencies reportedly active. The 38 countries that are on the 2005 list are 6 more than the 2001 list. Even though there are fewer total U.S. missionaries, there are more countries with more than 50 U.S. agencies active than ever before. This may indicate a focusing of attention on these countries as well as a possible

**Table 9: Countries with more than 50 US Agencies Reported**

| Rank | | Agencies |
|------|----|------|
| 1 | India | 173 |
| 2 | Mexico | 166 |
| 3 | Philippines | 129 |
| 4 | Brazil | 125 |
| 5 | Kenya | 120 |
| 6 | Russia | 101 |
| 7 | United Kingdom | 95 |
| 8 | Ukraine | 91 |
| 9 | South Africa | 90 |
| 10 | Japan | 87 |
| 11 | Thailand | 84 |
| 12 | Haiti | 82 |
| 13 | Honduras | 81 |
| 14 | Indonesia | 80 |
| 15 | Peru | 80 |
| 17 | Uganda | 79 |
| 16 | Spain | 79 |
| 18 | Romania | 77 |
| 19 | France | 76 |
| 20 | Guatemala | 74 |
| 21 | Ghana | 73 |
| 22 | Germany | 72 |
| 23 | Nigeria | 71 |
| 24 | China | 68 |
| 25 | Ecuador | 68 |
| 26 | Bolivia | 67 |
| 27 | Argentina | 66 |
| 28 | Australia | 65 |
| 29 | Colombia | 61 |
| 30 | Tanzania | 59 |
| 31 | Costa Rica | 58 |
| 32 | Hungary | 56 |
| 33 | Cambodia | 56 |
| 34 | Italy | 54 |
| 35 | Taiwan | 53 |
| 36 | Nicaragua | 53 |
| 37 | Dominican Republic | 52 |
| 38 | Chile | 51 |

dilution of the number of U.S. missionaries deployed in the rest of the world. On the other hand, since more agencies specified countries of service in the 2005 survey than the 2001 survey, this may simply be a more accurate picture than the 2001 survey gave rather than a genuine shift in deployment.

In contrast to the previous edition when 28.7% of all U.S. agency deployment was unspecified, in this edition only 8% were unspecified. In our last survey we indicated that due to security concerns we anticipated that it would be increasingly difficult to obtain hard data on deployment at the regional level. However, that was not proven to be true for this survey.

Finally, it should be noted that we do not collect data on the locations of deployment for short-term missionaries with less than one year of service commitment. Therefore the graphs do not include these short-term workers.

### Shift 6: Changes in the Reported Number of Primary Activities and Resources for Those Activities, including

- Increasing activities reported in the category of mission agency support;
- Decreasing activities reported in the category of evangelism and discipleship;
- Increasing number of agencies reporting primary activities in leadership development, community development, and theological education;
- Decreasing number of agencies reporting primary activities in personal and small group evangelism;
- Increasing number of agencies reporting activities in the areas of discipleship, community development, short-term missions coordination, personal and small group evangelism, partnership, childcare/orphanage and member care;
- Decreasing number of agencies reporting activities in the areas of mass evangelism and national church nurture/support; and

### Shift 7: Changes in the Reported Number of Resources for Agency Activities, including:

- Increasing financial and human resources shifted away from agencies reporting primary activities in the evangelism/discipleship category and towards agencies reporting primary activities in the relief and development category

In the 2005 survey agencies were given a list of 61 activities (including an "other" category with a blank to indicate what the "other" activities were) and asked to indicate a maximum of six of these as the primary activities of their organization. They were then asked to indicate which one of the activities was most commonly associated with their organization. In our discussion, that activity will be referred to as the "primary activity;" the others will be referred to simply as "activities" or "all activities."

Further, in our analysis we assume that the self-identified primary activity receives a larger share of an agency's resources and energy than any other activity indicated. It must be kept in mind that by indicating an activity as the one most commonly associated with the organization, an agency is not saying that this activity is all they do or even received the majority of their resources. Rather, they are simply indicating this activity is the one they are associated with. Thus, if an agency selects "church establishing/planting" as their primary activity, we assume that this will receive more personnel and financial resources than any of the other five activities reported by that agency. It is on the basis of this assumption that our analyses on the reported primary activities are made below, and it is important to keep this in mind in the discussion of Tables 10 through 14 and Figures 21 through 26.

Table 10 shows the ten activities most commonly chosen as the primary activity by U.S. agencies and the shifts in the number of agencies choosing those activities as primary from 2001 to 2005. As with the 1998 and 2001 surveys, church planting/establishing was by far the most frequently chosen primary activity (139, 19.9%),

### Table 10: Primary Activities: Comparing 2001 and 2005 Top Ten Survey Results

| 2005 Rank | Activity | 2005 No. | 2001 No. | Change 2001 to 2005 | % Change 2001 to 2005 |
|---|---|---|---|---|---|
| 1 | Church establishing/planting | 139 | 138 | 1 | 0.7% |
| 2 | Leadership development | 42 | 35 | 7 | 20.0% |
| 3 | Evangelism, personal and small group | 37 | 55 | -18 | -32.7% |
| 4 | Evangelism, mass | 30 | 29 | 1 | 3.4% |
| 5 | National church nurture/support | 28 | 34 | -6 | -17.6% |
| 6 | Education, theological | 26 | 21 | 5 | 23.8% |
| 7 | Support of national workers | 23 | 24 | -1 | -4.2% |
| 8 | Development, community and/or other | 23 | 17 | 6 | 35.3% |
| 9 | Short-term programs coordination | 20 | 19 | 1 | 5.3% |
| 10 | Medicine, incl. dental and public health | 18 | 20 | -2 | -10.0% |

The primary activities that have shown the largest increase of agencies indicating them since 2001 are "leadership development "(7 more agencies), "development, community or other" (6 more agencies) and "theological education" (5 more agencies). Those that show the biggest drop since 2001 are "evangelism, personal and small group" (18 fewer agencies), "national church nurture/support" (6 fewer agencies).

Table 11 shows all of the primary activities grouped into five major categories for 2001 and 2005: 1) activities related to evangelism and discipleship, 2) activi-

### Table 11: Primary Activities by Major Categories

| | 2005 | | 2001 | |
|---|---|---|---|---|
| | No. | % | No. | % |
| **Evangelism/Discipleship Activities** | **414** | **60.0%** | **425** | **61.7%** |
| Church establishing/planting | 139 | 20.1% | 138 | 20.0% |
| Leadership development | 42 | 6.1% | 35 | 5.1% |
| Evangelism, personal and small group | 38 | 5.5% | 55 | 8.0% |
| Evangelism, mass | 31 | 4.5% | 29 | 4.2% |
| National church nurture/support | 28 | 4.1% | 34 | 4.9% |
| Support of national workers | 23 | 3.3% | 24 | 3.5% |
| Broadcasting, radio and/or TV | 18 | 2.6% | 19 | 2.8% |
| Bible distribution | 12 | 1.7% | 14 | 2.0% |
| Literature distribution | 9 | 1.3% | 16 | 2.3% |
| Children's programs | 9 | 1.3% | 10 | 1.5% |
| Discipleship | 9 | 1.3% | 1 | 0.1% |
| Evangelism, student | 8 | 1.2% | 11 | 1.6% |
| Translation, Bible | 7 | 1.0% | 6 | 0.9% |
| Video/Film production/dist | 7 | 1.0% | 6 | 0.9% |
| Youth programs | 7 | 1.0% | 4 | 0.6% |
| Literature production | 6 | 0.9% | 6 | 0.9% |
| Audio recording/dist | 6 | 0.9% | 4 | 0.6% |
| Tentmaking & Related | 6 | 0.9% | 2 | 0.3% |
| Church construction | 2 | 0.3% | 4 | 0.6% |
| Translation, other | 2 | 0.3% | 3 | 0.4% |
| Literacy | 2 | 0.3% | 2 | 0.3% |
| Camping programs | 2 | 0.3% | 1 | 0.1% |
| Apologetics | 1 | 0.1% | 1 | 0.1% |
| **Education/Training Activities** | **65** | **9.4%** | **57** | **8.3%** |
| Education, theological | 26 | 3.8% | 21 | 3.0% |
| Training, Other | 15 | 2.2% | 19 | 2.8% |
| Education, ch/schl gen Christian | 14 | 2.0% | 8 | 1.2% |
| Correspondence courses | 6 | 0.9% | 3 | 0.4% |
| Education, extension (other) | 2 | 0.3% | 1 | 0.1% |
| Education (TEE) | 1 | 0.1% | 4 | 0.6% |
| Education, missy (cert/deg) | 1 | 0.1% | 1 | 0.1% |
| **Mission Agency Support Activities** | **116** | **6.8%** | **03** | **4.9%** |
| Short-term programs coordination | 20 | 2.9% | 19 | 2.8% |
| Training/Orientation, missionary | 17 | 2.5% | 20 | 2.9% |
| Recruiting/Mobilizing | 17 | 2.5% | 15 | 2.2% |
| Services for other agencies | 11 | 1.6% | 5 | 0.7% |
| Partnership development | 9 | 1.3% | 7 | 1.0% |
| Aviation services | 7 | 1.0% | 6 | 0.9% |
| Information services | 6 | 0.9% | 7 | 1.0% |
| Member Care | 6 | 0.9% | 4 | 0.6% |
| Association of Missions | 6 | 0.9% | 3 | 0.4% |

| | | | | |
|---|---|---|---|---|
| Technical assistance | 5 | 0.7% | 6 | 0.9% |
| Furloughed missionary support | 4 | 0.6% | 4 | 0.6% |
| Management consulting/training | 4 | 0.6% | 3 | 0.4% |
| Psychological counseling | 3 | 0.4% | 2 | 0.3% |
| Purchasing services | 1 | 0.1% | 2 | 0.3% |
| **Relief and Development Activities** | **83** | **12.0%** | **81** | **11.8%** |
| Development, community | 23 | 3.3% | 17 | 2.5% |
| Medicine, incl. dental and pub health | 18 | 2.6% | 20 | 2.9% |
| Childcare/orphanage | 17 | 2.5% | 16 | 2.3% |
| Relief and/or rehabilitation | 8 | 1.2% | 13 | 1.9% |
| Agricultural programs | 5 | 0.7% | 2 | 0.3% |
| Medical supplies | 4 | 0.6% | 3 | 0.4% |
| Supplying equipment | 3 | 0.4% | 4 | 0.6% |
| Disability assistance programs | 2 | 0.3% | 3 | 0.4% |
| Justice & Related | 2 | 0.3% | 2 | 0.3% |
| Adoption | 1 | 0.1% | 1 | 0.1% |
| **Other Activities** | **20** | **2.9%** | **24** | **3.5%** |
| Funds transmission | 10 | 1.4% | 11 | 1.6% |
| Other | 4 | 0.6% | 7 | 1.0% |
| Research | 4 | 0.6% | 5 | 0.7% |
| TESOL | 2 | 0.3% | 1 | 0.1% |

ties related to education and training, 3) activities related to agency support, 4) activities related to relief and development, and 5) other activities. In some cases the choice to list a particular activity in one category rather than another one was a matter of judgment on which not all will agree. For example, the activity of "Training/Orientation, missionary" could have fit under the "Education/Training" category or the "Mission Agency Support" category. It was deemed that training and orientation of missionaries, while educational, was primarily a support of missionaries and agencies rather than educating those of another culture, so it was placed in the "Mission Agency Support" category. Thus, there will be some fuzziness in the major categories used in the following analysis and care must be taken not to read too much into relatively minor changes in them.

Figures 21 and 22 show the trends from 1998 of these major groupings. Over the course of those years the percentage of agencies reporting some type of evangelism/discipleship related activity as their primary focus has gradually declined by 3.1%, while the number of agencies that reported activities related to mission agency support rose by 3.6%. The bulk of the latter increase was due to six more agencies designating their primary activity as "Services for other agencies" than in 2001.

It must be kept in mind that these category switches do not necessarily reflect a shift in organizational priorities. For example, Christian Aid mission changed their reported primary activity from "support of national workers"—which is in the category of evangelism/discipleship—to "funds transmission"—which is in the category "other." Likewise Global Mapping changed its primary activity from "information services"—which is in the category "mission agency services"—to

**Figure 21: Reported Primary Activities of U.S. Agencies**

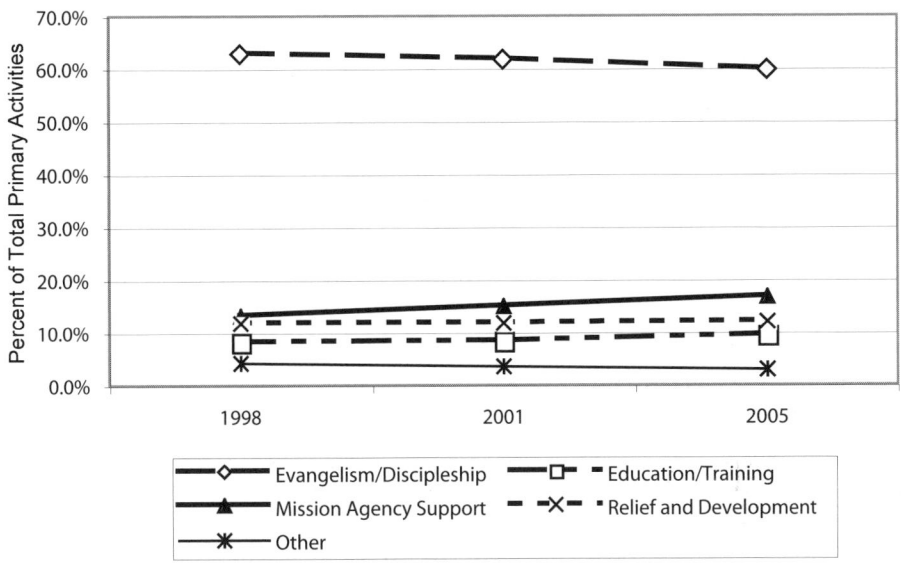

**Figure 22: Gain/Loss in Share of Percentage
of Reported  Primary Activities 1998 to 2005**

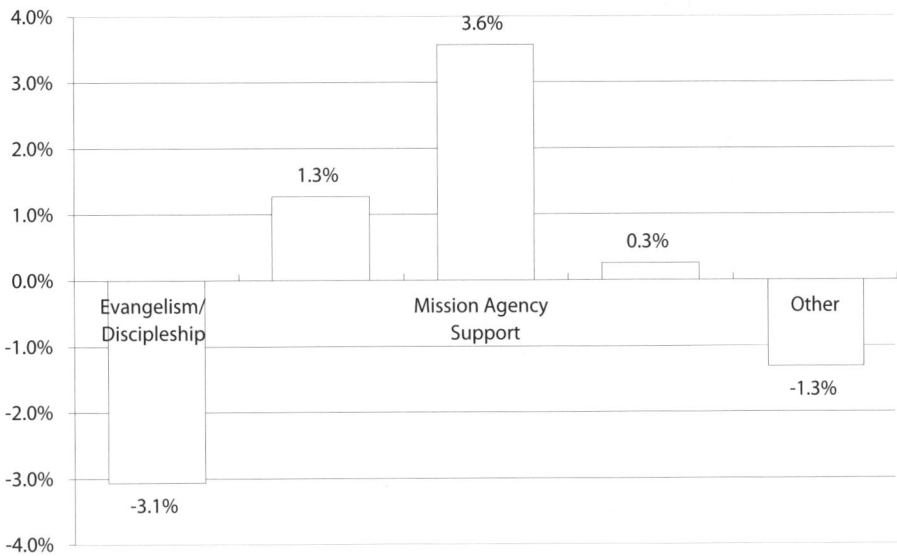

"research,"—which is in the "other" category. Neither of these changes reflect an actual shift in emphasis on the part of the reporting agency. Rather, both are simply changes in reporting and illustrate that the reported activities themselves—as well as the major categories into which they are sorted—are somewhat fuzzy.

Earlier we noted that each agency could select up to 6 activities they engage in. It is helpful to compile all of the indicated activities for every agency. We have done that in Tables 12 and 13 and Figure 23.

Table 12 shows the gain or loss for the top ten of all listed activities for the organizations. As in 1998 and 2001, "church establishing/planting," was the most commonly indicated activity, with 285 of the 700 U.S. Protestant agencies (40.8%) indicating that as one of their main activities. This is a gain of 18 agencies from the 2001 survey. Among the top ten activities, the activity seeing the largest number gain in agencies indicating it was "discipleship," (from 7 to 110). The reason this gain is so dramatic was that this category was indicated by 7 agencies in the "other" category in 2001, and so was added as a separate listing for the first time in 2005. The number of agencies reporting "Community development" as an activity grew by 21 (20.8%), and the number indicating "short-term programs coordination" grew by 13 (12%), as did "evangelism, personal and small group" (offsetting the decline in this being listed as a primary activity).

**Table 12: All Activities:**
**Comparing 2001 to 2005 Top Ten Survey Results**

|  | Activity | 2005 No. | 2001 No. | Change 2001 to 2005 | Change 2001 to 2005 |
|---|---|---|---|---|---|
| 1 | Church establishing/planting | 285 | 267 | 18 | 6.7% |
| 2 | Evangelism, personal and small group | 230 | 217 | 13 | 6.0% |
| 3 | Leadership development | 228 | 218 | 10 | 4.6% |
| 4 | Education, theological | 136 | 145 | -9 | -6.2% |
| 5 | National church nurture/support | 126 | 142 | -16 | -11.3% |
| 6 | Development, community and/or other | 122 | 101 | 21 | 20.8% |
| 6 | Short-term programs coordination | 121 | 108 | 13 | 12.0% |
| 8 | Evangelism, mass | 115 | 136 | -21 | -15.4% |
| 9 | Support of national workers | 114 | 123 | -9 | -7.3% |
| 10 | Discipleship | 110 | 7 | 103 | 1471.4% |

Among the top ten activities, those activities dropping the most in this survey are "mass evangelism" (from 138 to 115, a 16.7% loss) and "national church nurture/support" (from 143 to 126, an 11.9 % loss). One possible explanation for these drops is that agencies that formerly chose those activities now switched to "discipleship" instead.

Table 13 shows the 2001 and 2005 numbers for every activity arranged in the major categories. Outside of the top ten activities, the biggest gain was in the number of agencies reporting "partnership development" (from 20 to 70 agencies, a 250% gain). With the recent increase and focus of books, articles and seminars dealing with partnership issues, and the increasing number of non-U.S. citizens employed by U.S. agencies, this is not a surprising development, though the scale of the shift is quite large.

Another activity with a large percentage gain was "member care" (from 8 to

## Table 13: All Activities: Comparing 2001 and 2005 Survey Results

| | 2005 | | 2001 | |
|---|---|---|---|---|
| | No. | % | No. | % |
| **Evangelism/Discipleship Activities** | **1909** | **54.1%** | **822** | **54.3** |
| Church establishing/planting | 285 | 40.7% | 267 | 38.7% |
| Evangelism, personal and small group | 230 | 32.9% | 219 | 31.7% |
| Leadership development | 228 | 32.6% | 218 | 31.6% |
| National church nurture/support | 126 | 18.0% | 143 | 20.7% |
| Evangelism, mass | 115 | 16.4% | 138 | 20.0% |
| Support of national workers | 114 | 16.3% | 124 | 18.0% |
| Discipleship | 110 | 15.7% | 7 | 1.0% |
| Literature distribution | 99 | 14.1% | 122 | 17.7% |
| Bible distribution | 81 | 11.6% | 93 | 13.5% |
| Broadcasting, radio and/or TV | 62 | 8.9% | 68 | 9.9% |
| Children's programs | 62 | 8.9% | 50 | 7.2% |
| Literature production | 61 | 8.7% | 72 | 10.4% |
| Youth programs | 53 | 7.6% | 46 | 6.7% |
| Evangelism, student | 48 | 6.9% | 40 | 5.8% |
| Church construction | 40 | 5.7% | 44 | 6.4% |
| Translation, Bible | 38 | 5.4% | 32 | 4.6% |
| Camping programs | 33 | 4.7% | 28 | 4.1% |
| Audio recording/distribution | 28 | 4.0% | 28 | 4.1% |
| Video/Film prod./distrib. | 27 | 3.9% | 29 | 4.2% |
| Literacy | 24 | 3.4% | 20 | 2.9% |
| Translation, other | 14 | 2.0% | 14 | 2.0% |
| Tentmaking & related | 14 | 2.0% | 2 | 0.3% |
| Linguistics | 9 | 1.3% | 9 | 1.3% |
| Bible memorization | 5 | 0.7% | 3 | 0.4% |
| Apologetics | 2 | 0.3% | 2 | 0.3% |
| Urban ministry | 1 | 0.1% | 4 | 0.6% |
| **Education/Training Activities** | **451** | **12.8%** | **460** | **3.7%** |
| Education, theological | 136 | 19.4% | 145 | 21.0% |
| Training, Other | 100 | 14.3% | 107 | 15.5% |
| Education, ch/sch gen. Christ. | 91 | 13.0% | 83 | 12.0% |
| Education (TEE) | 39 | 5.6% | 45 | 6.5% |
| Correspondence courses | 33 | 4.7% | 30 | 4.3% |
| Education, extension (other) | 27 | 3.9% | 28 | 4.1% |
| Education, missy (cert./deg) | 25 | 3.6% | 22 | 3.2% |
| **Mission Agency Support Activities** | **551** | **15.6** | **52** | **15.6%** |
| Short-term programs coordination | 121 | 17.3% | 108 | 15.7% |
| Training/Orientation, missionary | 85 | 12.1% | 93 | 13.5% |
| Recruiting/Mobilizing | 72 | 10.3% | 77 | 11.2% |
| Partnership development | 70 | 10.0% | 20 | 2.9% |
| Services for other agencies | 42 | 6.0% | 57 | 8.3% |

| | | | | |
|---|---|---|---|---|
| Information services | 36 | 5.1% | 40 | 5.8% |
| Technical assistance | 26 | 3.7% | 40 | 5.8% |
| Management consulting/training | 26 | 3.7% | 34 | 4.9% |
| Member Care | 22 | 3.1% | 8 | 1.2% |
| Association of Missions | 15 | 2.1% | 8 | 1.2% |
| Furloughed missionary support | 14 | 2.0% | 17 | 2.5% |
| Aviation services | 11 | 1.6% | 14 | 2.0% |
| Psychological counseling | 7 | 1.0% | 3 | 0.4% |
| Purchasing services | 4 | 0.6% | 5 | 0.7% |
| **Relief and Development Activities** | **509** | **14.4%** | **452** | **13.5%** |
| Development, comm or other | 122 | 17.4% | 102 | 14.8% |
| Medicine, incl. dental and public health | 102 | 14.6% | 96 | 13.9% |
| Childcare/orphanage | 91 | 13.0% | 74 | 10.7% |
| Relief and/or rehabilitation | 88 | 12.6% | 76 | 11.0% |
| Medical supplies | 35 | 5.0% | 34 | 4.9% |
| Agricultural programs | 25 | 3.6% | 30 | 4.3% |
| Supplying equipment | 24 | 3.4% | 25 | 3.6% |
| Disability assistance programs | 10 | 1.4% | 10 | 1.4% |
| Justice & Related | 10 | 1.4% | 4 | 0.6% |
| Adoption | 2 | 0.3% | 1 | 0.1% |
| **Other Activities** | **97** | **2.8%** | **96** | **2.9%** |
| Funds transmission | 45 | 6.4% | 35 | 5.1% |
| Research | 34 | 4.9% | 33 | 4.8% |
| TESOL | 12 | 1.7% | 1 | 0.1% |
| Other | 6 | 0.9% | 27 | 3.9% |

22, an increase of 175%). Given the importance and wide distribution of the REMAP studies on missionary attrition, that agencies are paying more attention to member care is a good sign, though a total of 22 agencies indicated it as one of their significant activities, only 3.1% of all U.S. agencies.

The largest percentage drop was in "technical assistance" (from 40 to 26, a 35% loss), perhaps because agencies were choosing a more specific focus for how they assisted rather than indicating the more general category.

Another activity that agencies indicated significantly more often as one of the main activities was "childcare/orphanage" (from 74 to 91, a 23% gain). That over 13% of all mission agencies now list this as one of their main activities is solid evidence of the increasing attention given to children by mission agencies (especially when it is noted that the number of agencies reporting "children's programs" as one of their activities went from 50 to 62, a 24% gain).

Figure 23 illustrates the gain or loss for each major category. Overall, 3.4% fewer agencies reported activities in the category of evangelism/discipleship, while 2.0% more agencies reported activities in the category of mission agency support.

Tables 14 and 15 and Figures 24 to 26 offer comparisons related to the primary activities when sorted by the master categories shown in Table 11. While

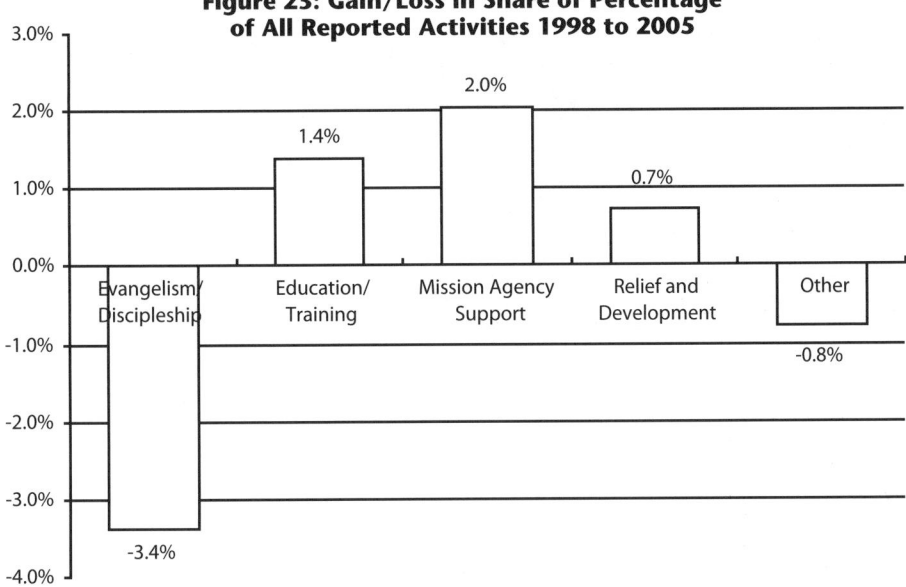

Figure 23: Gain/Loss in Share of Percentage of All Reported Activities 1998 to 2005

the numbers offered in these tables are exact, they represent the count of the number of U.S. agencies which report their primary activities in each area. For example, while Cities for Christ Worldwide reported "literature distribution" (which is in the category of evangelism/discipleship) as their primary activity for 2005, they also listed "services for other agencies" (which is in the category of mission agency support) as an activity. Thus, their activities were not confined to the "evangelism/discipleship" category. This means that the numbers seen in Tables 14 and 15 should be taken to indicate the focus of agencies rather than the exact budgets and personnel. For that reason, rather than reporting the calculated numbers, we have chosen to report the percentage shares as an indication of focus.

In our last survey agencies that reported relief and development activities as their primary ones deployed 2.9% of the workers (U.S. and non-U.S.) but had 35.1% the income for overseas. In this survey, that has changed to 14.4% of the workers and 46.1% of the income for overseas. Rather than an actual shift, this may simply be a more accurate picture than given last time, which included short-term missionaries, the numbers of which skewed the total picture (see discussion above on short-term missions).

While Table 14 shows the actual reported income for overseas (and the percentage of the total) for each major category, Figure 24 shows the inflation-adjusted increase seen between the surveys. The real increase of income of agencies whose primary activity was related to evangelism and discipleship was 2.7% over four years, while those whose primary activity was related to relief and development increased by 73.4%. As noted above, certainly a large fraction of this rise is attributable to the bump in giving that came after the December 2004 Indian Ocean

**Table 14: Resources Used by Primary Activity**

| Category of Primary Activity | No. of Agencies | | Income for Overseas | | Full Time US Workers | | Full Time Non US Workers | |
|---|---|---|---|---|---|---|---|---|
| Evangelism/ Discipleship | 414 | 59.3% | $2,490,417,384 | 47.5% | 36,155 | 87.5% | 59,056 | 68.4% |
| Education/ Training | 65 | 9.3% | $67,111,854 | 1.3% | 807 | 2.0% | 1,718 | 2.0% |
| Mission Agency Support | 116 | 16.6% | $236,358,525 | 4.5% | 2,181 | 5.3% | 5,522 | 6.4% |
| Relief and Development | 83 | 11.9% | $2,418,512,836 | 46.1% | 1,987 | 4.8% | 16,432 | 19.0% |
| Other Activities | 20 | 2.9% | $29,231,785 | 0.6% | 199 | 0.5% | 3,564 | 4.1% |

**Table 15: 2001 People Resources Used by Primary Activity**

| Category of Primary Activity | US Short Term | | Tentmakers | | US Long Term | | All US Workers | | Non-US | |
|---|---|---|---|---|---|---|---|---|---|---|
| Evangelism/ Discipleship | 328123 | 94.8% | 1446 | 82.7% | 31915 | 91.8% | 37800 | 88.4% | 58701 | 90.5% |
| Education/ Training | 1049 | 0.3% | 36 | 2.1% | 476 | 1.4% | 811 | 1.9% | 1678 | 2.6% |
| Mission Agency Support | 9984 | 2.9% | 169 | 9.7% | 975 | 2.8% | 1296 | 3.0% | 743 | 1.1% |
| Relief and Development | 6980 | 2.0% | 89 | 5.1% | 1341 | 3.9% | 2829 | 6.6% | 3433 | 5.3% |
| Other | 134 | 0.0% | 8 | 0.5% | 50 | 0.1% | 51 | 0.1% | 317 | 0.5% |

tsunami and the October 2005 earthquake in Pakistan. It also would include an increase in giving due to the introduction of faith-based initiative grants now being offered by the United States government. This last development merits further research to see how much it has affected the income shift being reported.

From Tables 14 and 15, we can see that agencies reporting primary activities related to evangelism/discipleship commanded the bulk of the human resources (74.6%) and just under half of the financial resources (47.5%), which is not a surprise. What is perhaps more interesting are the shifts in the relative share of the total pool of resources seen in each major category between 2001 and 2005 as charted in Figure 25.

It is tempting to say that the gains in every other category happened at the expense of the evangelism/discipleship category, but this graph indicates relative share of the totals rather than the total level of actual activities reported. For example, income for overseas budgets increased in every major category, but was

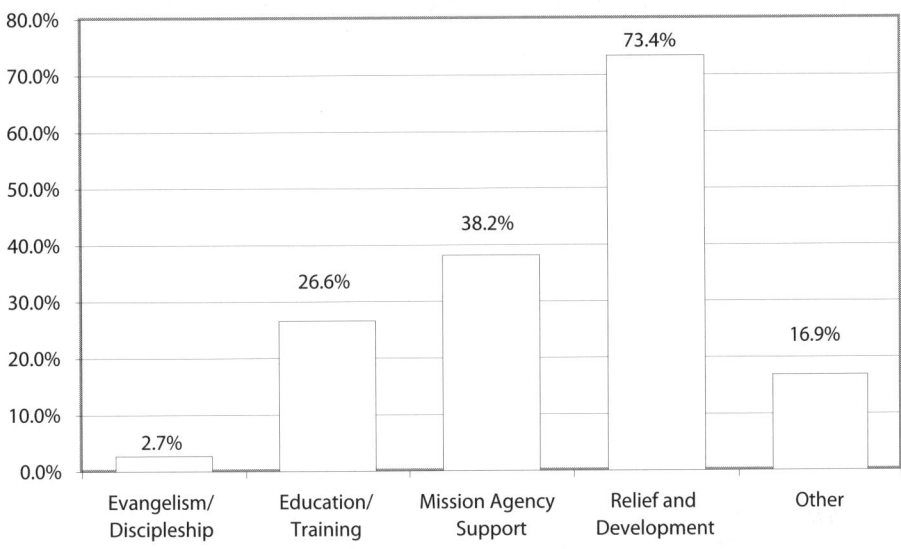

Figure 24: Inflation-adjusted Increase in Overseas Income by Major Category 2001-2005

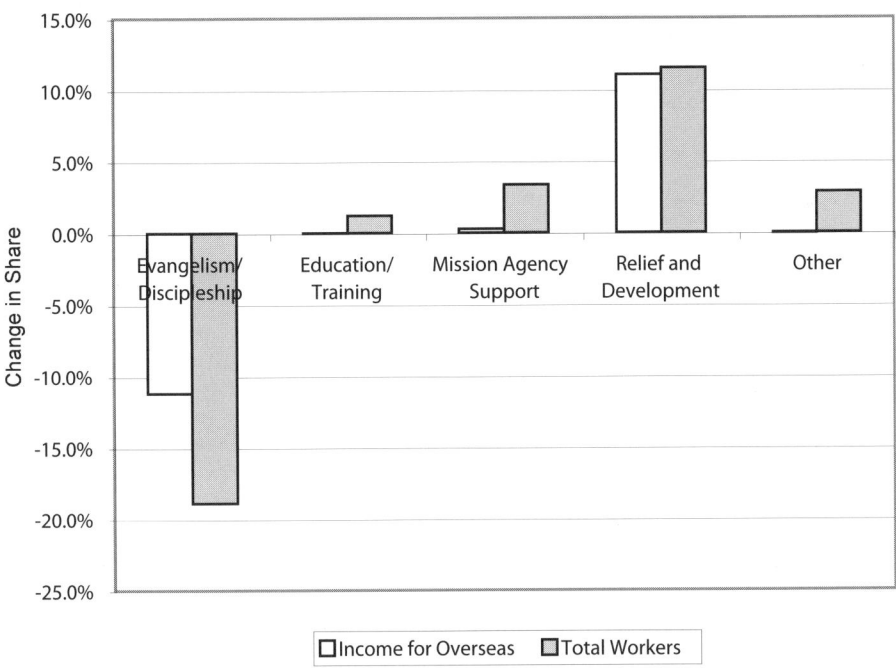

Figure 25: 2001 to 2005 Share Change in Resources by Activity

slowest for the category of evangelism/discipleship, and so that area lost ground relative to the other categories even though the budgets themselves increased (Figure 24). This means that agencies reporting as their primary activities those related to evangelism and discipleship oversaw less of the total pool of resources rather than fewer people or money in an absolute sense (as noted above, the budget for these agencies gained, but not as quickly as other agencies). The biggest gainers were agencies that reported their primary activities as those related to relief and development, which commanded 11.5% (up from 2.9% in 2001) of the total human resources and 46.1% (up from 35.1%) of the total financial resources.

Figure 26 indicates the relative pool of resources indicated in Tables 14 and 15 in graphic format. It makes it easy to see the relative number of agencies, overseas budget, U.S. full-time missionaries, and so on, for each major category of primary activity reported by the agencies. It is clear that agencies whose primary activity is in the major category of evangelism and discipleship continue to command the largest share of the total resources marshaled by U.S. Protestant mission agencies.

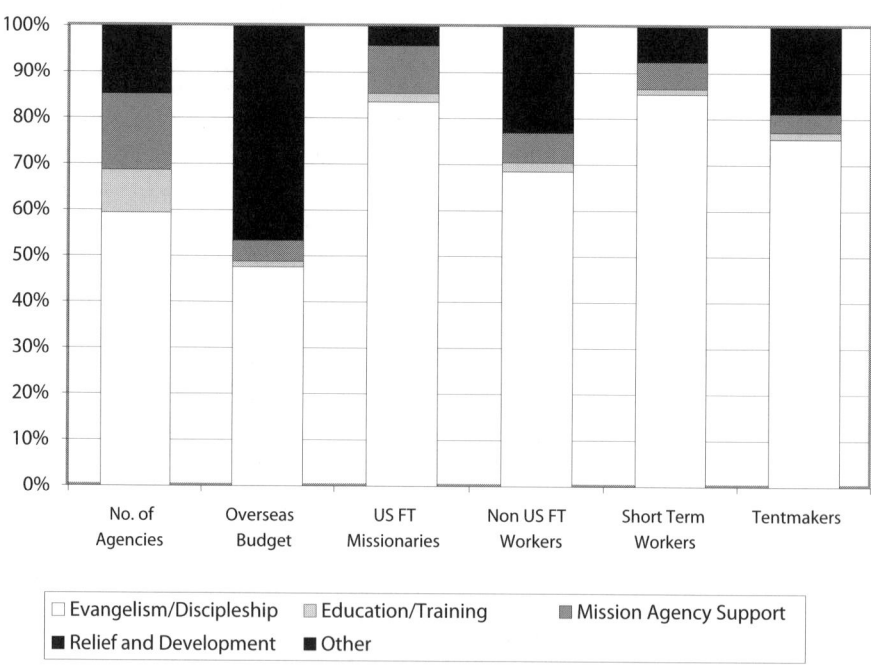

**Figure 26: Comparison of Support for Primary Activities of US Agencies**

In review, we have noted six shifts seen among U.S. Protestant mission agencies during the past decade:

1. A decrease in the reported number of long-term U.S. missionaries (and no apparent correlation with the increase seen in short-term missions over the past decade);

2. A decrease in the reported number of middle-term U.S. missionaries;

3. A decrease in the reported number of short-term missionaries;

4. An increase in the reported numbers of U.S. agencies and missionaries deployed in Asia;

5. An increase in the reported number of U.S. citizens serving as full-time missionaries in Europe; and

6. Shifts in the reported activities of agencies:

a. Increasing activities reported in the category of mission agency support;

b. Decreasing activities reported in the category of evangelism and discipleship;

c. Increasing number of agencies reporting primary activities in leadership development, community development, and theological education;

d. Decreasing number of agencies reporting primary activities in personal and small group evangelism;

e. Increasing number of agencies reporting activities in the areas of discipleship, community development, short-term missions coordination, personal and small group evangelism, partnership, childcare/orphanage and member care;

f. Decreasing number of agencies reporting activities in the areas of mass evangelism and national church nurture/support; and

7. Shifts in the reported number of resources for primary activities in the direction of relief and development, including

a. Increasing financial and human resources shifted away from agencies reporting primary activities in the evangelism/discipleship category and towards agencies reporting primary activities in the relief and development category.

With the trends and shifts we have identified, it appears that U.S. Protestant missions agencies have responded to some challenges that have been presented in the past decade even as new challenges have arisen.

The first such challenge is the need to mobilize more U.S. citizens to serve as full-time residential missionaries (whether middle- or long-term). A second challenge will be the appropriate care and support of the burgeoning non-U.S. citizens serving under U.S. agencies. A third challenge is deeper reflection and attention on the huge phenomena associated with short-term missions and its long-term impact on U.S. agencies. A fourth challenge will be to ensure that the increasing ranks of tentmakers are appropriately supported. Finally, a fifth challenge will be to ensure that agencies whose primary activities are in evangelism and discipleship are adequately staffed and financed so that this remains a central focus of the total pool of U.S. Protestant agencies.

**A Concluding Note on Denominationalism and U.S. Protestant Mission Agencies.** Finally, as noted in previous editions, agencies were asked to choose their orientation towards denominationalism from among six categories: 1) denominational, 2) interdenominational, 3) non-denominational, 4) transdenominational, 5) prefer that no orientation be used, and 6) other. Some agencies are very intentional in distinguishing nondenominational from interdenominational, while others change from edition to edition of the *Handbook*. In this survey there was a shift away from self-designation as "transdenominational" (down 20.3%) and towards "nondenominational" (up 13.4%).

Whatever the nomenclature, however, the most significant issue is whether an agency considers itself to be a denominational one or not. To distinguish the latter from the category "'nondenominational," in Figure 27 we use the term "not-denominational" to refer to the five categories that exclude the idea of being denominational. The response of the past three surveys has been fairly steady in that 16% to 18% of the agencies refer to themselves as denominational in orientation. Because this figure has not changed significantly, we will not offer additional analysis of the various categories that we did in previous versions of the *Handbook*.

**Figure 27: US Agency Orientations towards Denominationalism**

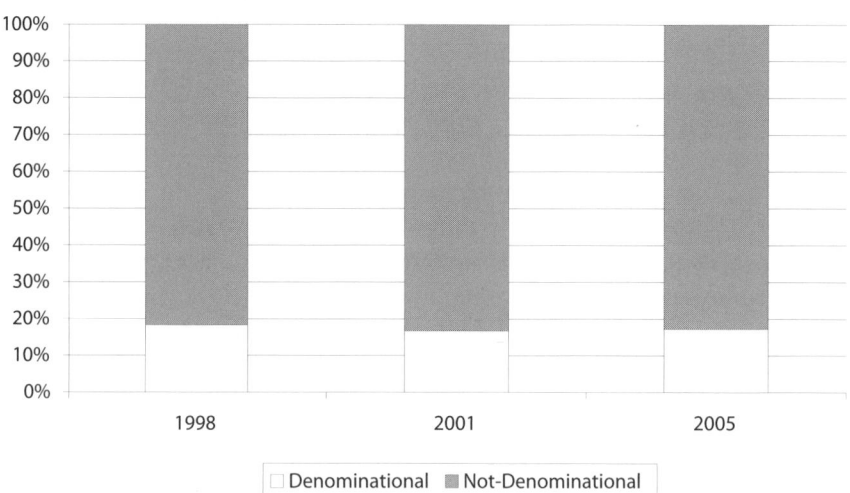

## Canadian Agencies

In Table 16 we provide a summary of the personnel and financial changes taking place in the Canadian missions movement. The 122 listed Canadian agencies mobilize a total full-time on location missionary force of 4,808 people working in 122 countries. This force is comprised of 2,750 Canadians, 728 non-Canadians working in a country other than their own and 1,510 non-Canadians working in their own countries.

To help put the following discussion in perspective,[17] throughout the analysis we refer to "reported" totals, since the totals we present are only as valid as the numbers received from each agency. Several factors contribute a certain softness to these numbers. First, the actual numbers fluctuate during the year. Second, agencies use different methods for counting their personnel. For example, some carefully tabulate and report painstakingly exact numbers for the month the survey is completed. Others, however, provide either highs or averages for the year. Still others provide estimates, especially for categories such as volunteers and short-term workers. Third, and finally, agencies do not always interpret the survey questions consistently with either other agencies or even with their own answers in previous surveys. To help the reader keep this in mind, throughout this analysis we will typically use the term "reported" to refer to the numbers.

As we observe the continuing development of the Canadian Protestant agencies through the surveys conducted as part of this *Handbook* and summarized in Table 16, several important changes may be noted from the data collected covering 1992 through 2005. We will identify a change as a trend if it has been consistent over the past decade or more. If the change has not been consistent over that time, we will identify what has happened as a shift. In our analysis of the Canadian data, we have isolated five trends and six shifts that merit discussion.

### Table 16: Summary of Changes in Reported Canadian Missions Statistics, 1992-2001

| Personnel from Canada | 1992 | 1996 | 1998 | 2001 | 2005 | Change 2001-2005 | Change 1992-2001 |
|---|---|---|---|---|---|---|---|
| **Fully Supported Canadian Personnel Serving Overseas** | | | | | | | |
| Long-Term (Overseas more than 4 years) | 3,075 | 2,961 | 2,613 | 2,493 | 2,059 | -17.4% | -33.0% |
| Middle-Term (Overseas from 1 to 4 years) | 304 | 416 | 421 | 337 | 511 | 51.6% | 68.1% |
| Nonresidential fully supported | 72 | 120 | 294 | 385 | 156 | -59.5% | 116.7% |
| Total fully supported Canadian personnel serving overseas | 3,451 | 3,497 | 3,328 | 3,215 | 2,726 | -15.2% | -21.0% |

| Other Canadian Personnel Serving Overseas | | | | | | |
|---|---|---|---|---|---|---|
| Short-term of 2 weeks up to 1 year | NA | 2,470 | 3,186 | 3,395 | 3,534 | 4.1% | 43.1% |
| Bivocational associates sponsored or supervised | 84 | 140 | 144 | 154 | 186 | 20.8% | 121.4% |
| Nonresidential partially supported | 13 | 17 | 38 | 27 | 38 | 40.7% | 192.3% |
| **Non-Canadian Personnel Directly Supported** | | | | | | |
| Those serving in their home country | NA | 707 | 1,725 | 1,128 | 1,510 | 33.9% | 113.6% |
| Those serving in a country other than their home country | 36 | 77 | 244 | 873 | 728 | -16.6% | 1922.2% |
| **Canadian Ministry and Home Office Staff** | | | | | | |
| Full-time paid staff | 1,412 | 1,622 | 1,838 | 2,515 | 2,145 | -14.7% | 51.9% |
| Part-time staff/associates | 249 | 389 | 496 | 431 | 570 | 32.3% | 128.9% |
| Volunteer (ongoing) helpers | 2,124 | 3,154 | 2,374 | 2,893 | 7,331 | 153.4% | 245.2% |

| Financial Support Raised in Canada—Income for Overseas Ministries (Adjusted for Inflation) | | | | | | |
|---|---|---|---|---|---|---|
| 1992 | 1996 | 1998 | 2001 | 2005 | Change 2001-2005 | Change 1992-2001 |
| $286,024,800 | $286,994,155 | $400,070,660 | $469,116,463 | $638,142,812 | 36.0% | 123.1% |

**Trend 1: A Decrease in the Reported Number of Fully-Supported Canadians Serving Overseas.** Canadian agencies mobilized a fully-supported missionary force 15.2% smaller than they did in 2001 (Figure 28). This continues a trend from 1992, in which the fully-supported missionary force mobilized by Canadian agencies has dropped 21%.

**Trend 2: A Decease in the Reported Number of Canadian Citizens Serving as Full-Time, Long-Term Missionaries.** The most significant decrease for Canadian agencies has been in the number of long-term Canadian missionaries, which dropped by 14.7% from 2001 to 2005. This extended the decline in Canadians serving long-term overseas observed since 1992, which is now 33% since then (Figure 29). This grim decline, and especially the acceleration seen from 2001 to 2005, is sobering. In the data collected there is no indication of whether this has happened through normal attrition (such as retirement) or downsizing. This is certainly one of the greatest challenges facing Canadian Protestant mission agencies in the 21st century.

Table 17 shows the nine Canadian agencies reporting fifty or more long-term

## Figure 28: Fully-supported Canadian Personnel Serving Overseas

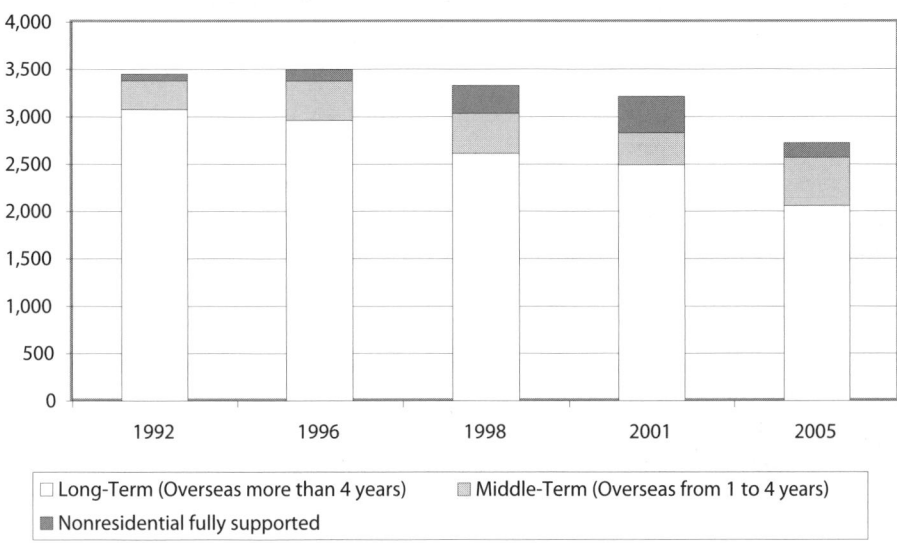

☐ Long-Term (Overseas more than 4 years)    ▨ Middle-Term (Overseas from 1 to 4 years)
■ Nonresidential fully supported

## Figure 29: Canadian Long-term Personnel Serving Overseas

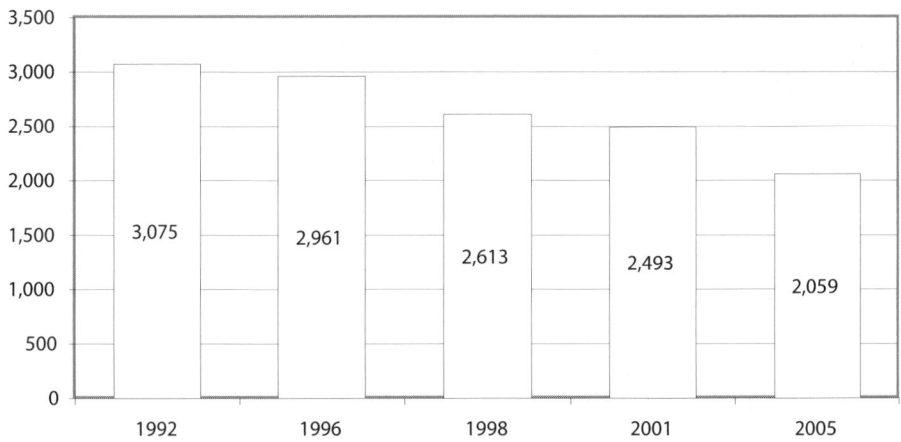

### Table 17: Canadian Agencies with 50 or More Long-Term Workers

| Rank | Agency | Workers |
|------|--------|---------|
| 1 | New Tribes Mission of Canada | 300 |
| 2 | Brethren Assemblies (Canada) | 236 |
| 3 | Wycliffe Bible Translators of Canada, Inc. | 170 |
| 4 | Christian and Missionary Alliance in Canada, The | 159 |
| 5 | SIM Canada | 111 |
| 6 | Pentecostal Assemblies of Canada | 85 |
| 7 | OMF International – Canada | 63 |

| 8 | Janz Team Ministries Inc. | 61 |
| 9 | Evangelical Free Church of Canada Mission | 55 |

workers. A comparable table in 2001 would have listed thirteen such agencies. Thus it was agencies at the top of the list that experienced significant decreases, confirmed in that the top ten agencies in 2001 reported an average of 153.7 long-term missionaries, while in 2005 the top ten agencies reported an average of 128.5 long-term missionaries, a drop of 16.4%.

**Trend 3: An Increase in Reported Number of Non-Canadian Citizens Working for Canadian Agencies.** The decrease in the on-location full-time workforce reported by Canadian agencies in this edition would be even greater if not for the 11.8% increase between 2001 and 2005 in the number of non-Canadian citizens working for Canadian agencies.

Roughly speaking, for every five Canadians working with Canadian agencies there are four non-Canadians working with Canadian agencies (see Figures 30 and 31). This continues the trend of more non-Canadians to Canadians ratio seen in the previous editions.[18] The sharpest increase was seen in the number of non-Canadians working in their own country (up 33.9%; the dark portion of the bar in Figure 31). If the current trend continues, Canadian agencies will have more non-Canadians than Canadians within their ranks by 2007.

In the last *Handbook*, we noted a sharp decline in the number of non-Canadians serving in their home countries. This number rebounded by 2005, so that almost as many were reported as in the 1998 survey. Non-Canadians serving in a country other than their home country dipped between 2001 and 2005 after a large increase from 1998 to 2001. This shift could indicate an increase in non-Canadian support personnel in the administrative offices of their home coun-

**Figure 30: Share of Missionaries Mobilized by Canadian Agency Missionaries (1992 to 2005)**

**Figure 31: Non-Canadian Personnel Working for Canadian Agencies**

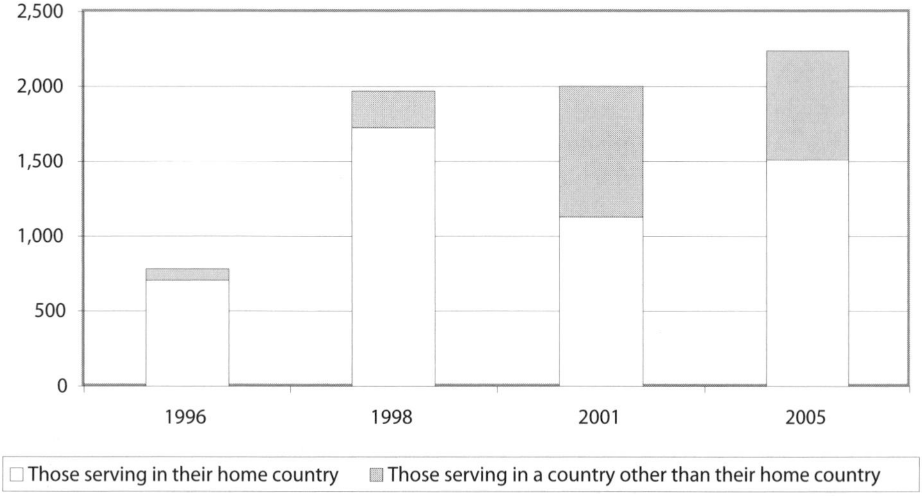
2,500
2,000
1,500
1,000
500
0
1996
1998
2001
2005
Those serving in their home country
Those serving in a country other than their home country

tries rather than an increase of field missionaries. However, the survey question did not ask for specific job responsibilities for the non-Canadians, so it would take further follow-up to determine the reasons for the shift.

Table 18 shows the eight Canadian agencies reporting fifty or more non-Canadian citizen workers. A comparable table in 2001 would have listed five such agencies. In this case the gain was broadly based. The top ten agencies in 2001 reported an average of 199.2 non-Canadian citizens, while in 2005 the top ten agencies reported an average of 208.4 non-Canadian citizens, a gain of 4.6% in comparison with a net gain for all agencies of 11.8%. Thus, the net gain was not confined to the top but spread across the 38 agencies that reported at least one non-Canadian in 2005.

**Table 18: Canadian Agencies with 50 or More Non-Canadian Citizens Workers**

| Rank | Agency | Non-Canadian Workers |
|---|---|---|
| 1 | I. N. (International Needs) Network Canada | 804 |
| 2 | Mennonite Central Committee Canada | 606 |
| 3 | World Team Canada | 159 |
| 4 | Mennonite Economic Development Associates (MEDA) | 156 |
| 5 | International Christian Aid Canada | 95 |
| 6 | Evangelical Free Church of Canada Mission | 80 |
| 7 | SEND International of Canada | 73 |
| 8 | OMF International - Canada | 66 |

**Trend 4: An Increase in the Reported Income for Overseas Missions.**
The total reported income for all Canadian agencies was $638,142,812 (Table 16; Figure 32). After adjusting for inflation, this is an increase of 36.9% over the last *Handbook*. Sixty organizations reported an income of $1,000,000 or more, up from fifty-one agencies in 2001. The following picture emerges from the data as reported in this survey:

• After adjusting for inflation, the increase in income reported by the top three agencies, all focused on relief and development, was almost 95% of the total income gains reported. In other words, the tremendous gain in Canadian agencies income for overseas missions reported in this edition is almost exclusively due to the gains in the top three agencies, all of which are focused on relief and development.

### Table 19: Canadian Agencies with $3,000,000 or More in Reported Income for Overseas Missions

| Rank | Agency | Income |
|:---:|---|---|
| 1 | World Vision Canada | $277,755,000.00 |
| 2 | Canadian Food for the Hungry International | $40,874,000.00 |
| 3 | Mennonite Central Committee Canada | $32,529,651.00 |
| 4 | Samaritan's Purse—Canada | $31,000,000.00 |
| 5 | HOPE International Development Agency | $18,000,000.00 |
| 6 | Pentecostal Assemblies of Canada | $14,732,000.00 |
| 7 | United Church of Canada, Justice, Global & Ecumenical Relations | $13,700,000.00 |
| 8 | Wycliffe Bible Translators of Canada, Inc. | $13,000,000.00 |
| 9 | SIM Canada | $11,511,259.00 |
| 10 | Mennonite Economic Development Associates (MEDA) | $10,179,658.00 |
| 11 | Salvation Army—Canada and Bermuda Territory, the | $10,000,000.00 |
| 12 | Canadian Baptist Ministries | $9,166,600.00 |
| 13 | Christian Blind Mission International - Canada | $8,540,527.00 |
| 14 | Youth with a Mission Canada, Inc. | $8,500,000.00 |
| 15 | Christian Reformed World Relief Committee of Canada | $8,275,036.00 |
| 16 | Christian and Missionary Alliance in Canada, The | $7,840,000.00 |
| 17 | Campus Crusade for Christ of Canada, Inc. | $6,884,009.00 |
| 18 | Compassion Canada | $6,640,000.00 |
| 19 | World Relief Canada | $5,492,053.00 |
| 20 | MSC Canada | $4,715,606.00 |
| 21 | Bible League of Canada, The | $4,500,000.00 |
| 22 | WorldServe Ministries Canada | $3,960,000.00 |
| 23 | New Tribes Mission of Canada | $3,943,909.00 |
| 24 | Evangelical Free Church of Canada Mission | $3,500,000.00 |
| 25 | Leprosy Mission Canada, The | $3,416,028.00 |
| 26 | Mission Aviation Fellowship of Canada (MAFC) | $3,210,703.00 |
| 27 | FEBInternational | $3,187,236.00 |
| 28 | MBMS International | $3,069,321.00 |

**Figure 32: Financial Support Raised in Canada**

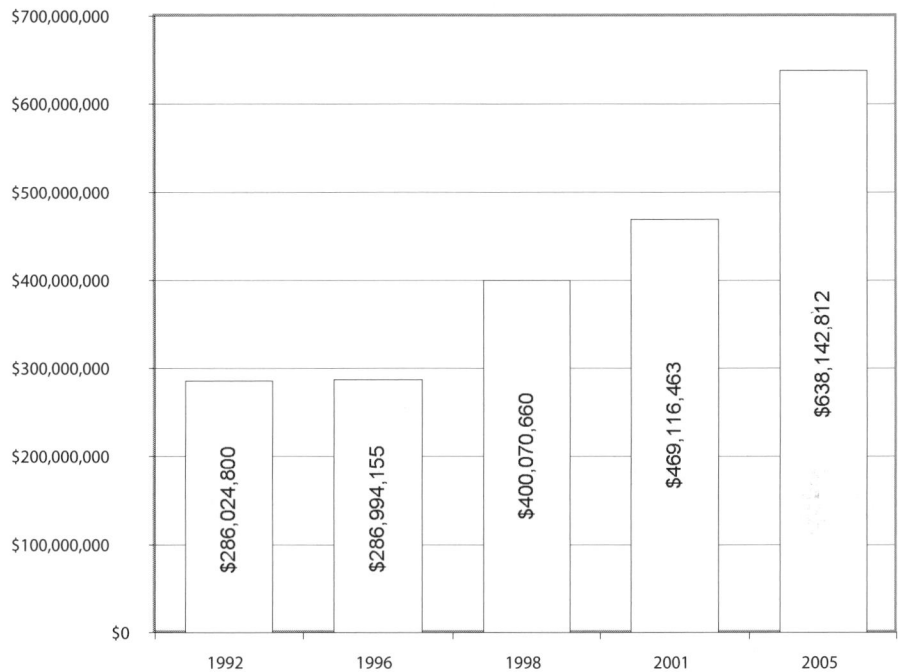

• The top 10 agencies received 72.6.5% of the total income, up from 66.7% in our last survey. The top 20 agencies received 84.5% of the total income, up from 82.5% in 2001. In other words, more of the total income for overseas work is being concentrated in fewer agencies.

• Organizations which reported a primary activity focused on relief and development received 73.6% ($469,491,505) of the total income. They received 93% of the inflation-adjusted gain, another reminder that while income was up, it was focused on relief and development activities (see Figure 40).

In 2005 101 of the 122 agencies reported some income for overseas missions, compared to 105 agencies in 2001. Table 19 gives the reported income for overseas mission work for the twenty-eight Canadian agencies with $3,000,000 or more. After adjusting for inflation, the same list in our 2001 survey would have included twenty-three agencies. This fits well with the fact that the growth in income was largely confined to the top agencies.

**Trend 5: An Increase in the Reported Number of Short-Term Missionaries.** While the 33% decline in long-term missionaries is sobering (Figure 29), it may be also important to point out that the number of middle-termers serving from 1 to 4 years rose by 68.1% since the last edition, which offers some hope for the recovery of Canadian long-term personnel.

Figure 33 offers a comparative look at the two trends of decreasing long-term and increasing short-term Canadian missionaries. It seems that after a decade of growth in short-term missionaries, there appears to have been no impact on long-term recruitment. It could be argued that the curve for long-term drop would be even steeper if not for short-term impact, but there is no evidence from our survey to justify such a claim.

### Figure 33: Canadian Long-term vs Short-term Workers 1996 to 2005

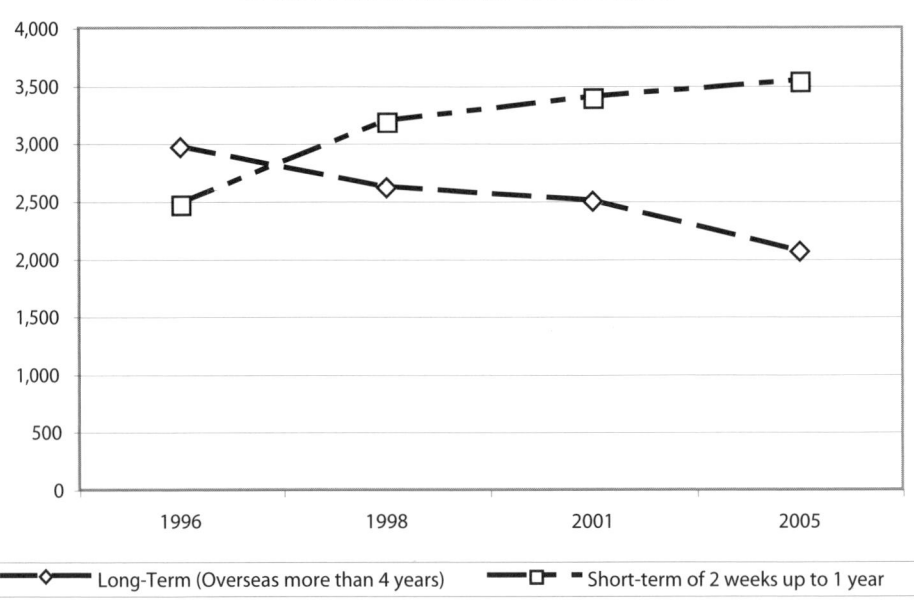

Long-Term (Overseas more than 4 years)    Short-term of 2 weeks up to 1 year

Since 1996, the year the terminology for this question in the survey was stabilized, short-term missionaries going through Canadian agencies has increased by 43.1% (Figure 34). Canadian mission agencies reported a total of 3,534 short-term workers (two weeks to one year), a modest increase of 4.1% over 2001 edition of the *Handbook*. As noted in the discussion of U.S. short-term efforts, this number at best represents only a small fraction of the actual number of Canadians going on short-term missions trips in 2005, as it does not reflect the people who are sent out directly from their churches or schools or Canadians going through U.S. organizations. Additionally, it does not reflect some who go for periods of time less than 2 weeks (as noted above, one U.S. survey indicated that 67.6% of the short-term trips last 2 weeks or less).

In summary, we have identified five trends seen among Canadian Protestant mission agencies over the past decade:

1. A decrease in the reported number of fully-supported Canadians serving overseas;

2. A decease in the reported number of Canadian citizens serving as full-time, long-term missionaries;

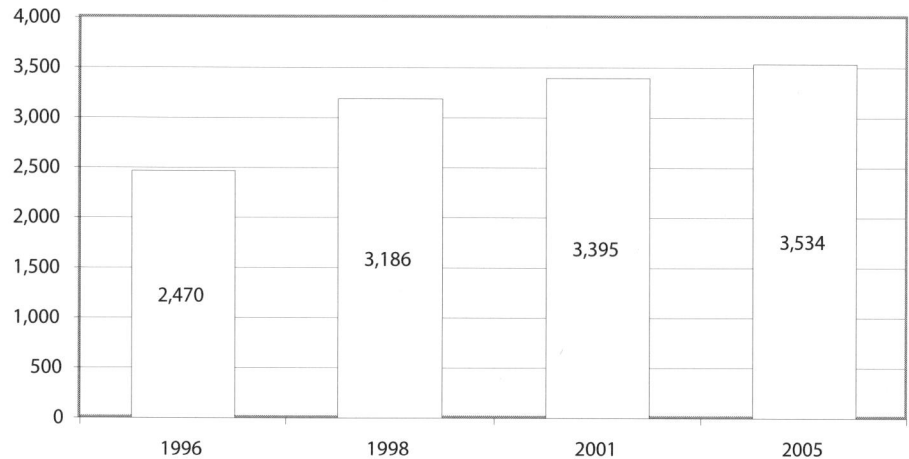

**Figure 34: Canadian Short-term Missionaries
(2 weeks up to 1 year)**

3. An increase in the reported number of non-Canadian citizens working for Canadian agencies;

4. An increase in the reported income for overseas missions; and

5. An increase in the reported number of short-term missionaries.

In addition to these trends, we have identified six changes that have appeared within the past decade. In our discussion, we refer to these as shifts rather than trends.

**Shift 1: A Decrease in the Reported Total Workforce of Canadian Agencies.** Canadian agencies engaged 0.5% fewer full-time on-location missionaries in 2005 than they did in 2001, though this is still 40.8% greater than the same totals reported in 1992. As Figure 35 clearly illustrates, and as discussed as Trend 3 above, the net increase is entirely due to the increasing number of non-Canadians being deployed by Canadian agencies.

**Shift 2: A Decrease in the Reported Number of Canadian Citizens Working for Canadian Agencies.** When we add the number of Canadian citizens working as full-time residential missionaries, non-residential missionaries, tentmakers, and home staff and associates, 5,471 of them are reported to be fully engaged in the missionary task through Canadian agencies, an 8.1% decrease over the number reported for these categories in 2001 (Figure 36). This is the first such reported decline since we began tracking these categories in 1992. While the number of career missionary, non-residential missionary and staff/associates were all down, the number of Canadians in middle missions[6] assignments and those working as tentmakers rose.

**Shift 3: A Decrease in the Number of Reported Short-Term Support**

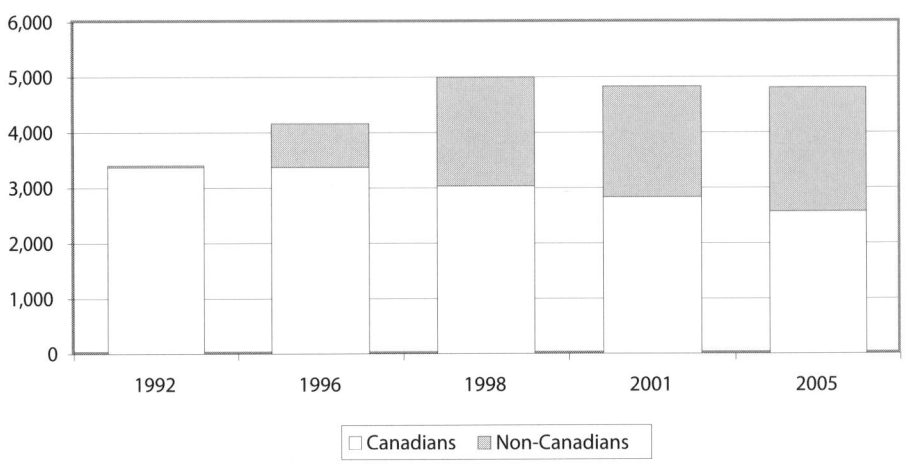

**Figure 35: Total On-location Canadian Agency Mission Force, 1992 to 2005**

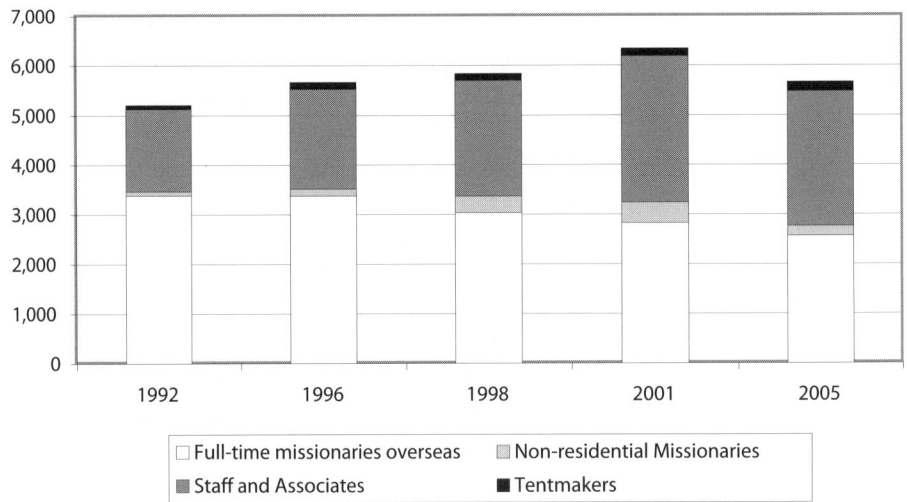

**Figure 36: Canadian Citizens Working for Canadian Agencies**

**Personnel.** While there was only a modest increase in the number of short-term workers, there was a 71.5% drop of the reported number of regular staff in Canada or overseas who have full-time responsibilities related to short-term missions programs (from 158 to 45; Figure 37) and a more moderate drop in the number of part-time (10 to 49%) short-term support staff (from 130 to 86, or 33.8%).

However, these drops can be accounted for from the variation in reports of two agencies (one organization reported 125 full-time short-term support

**Figure 37: Number of Short-term Support Personnel**

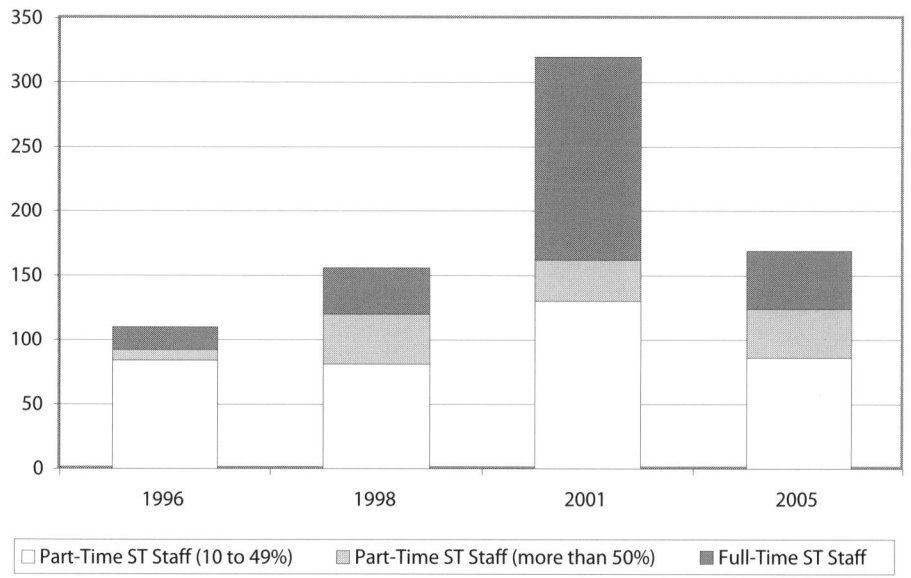

personnel in 2001, but 0 in 2005; another reported 30 part-time (10 to 49%) short-term support personnel in 2001 and only 4 in 2005). When these two are factored out, the loss from the 2001 report was far less dramatic. Thus, it appears as though the Canadian staff devoted to short-term care are proportionate to the modest increases reported in short-term activity between the 2001 and 2005 surveys.

How did the agencies find their people for their short-term mission projects? Figure 38 depicts the primary methods of initial contact as well as the changes from 1996 to 2005. Churches and individual contacts are the primary source of these contacts. The 22% increase in contacts through churches seems to reflect the growing desire of many agencies to connect more closely with the local church. However, the recent spike in developing contacts through schools from 2001 to 2005 may indicate a shift in focusing more in that direction for the future. Seventeen agencies indicated either internet or website. This will be added as a category in the next survey. Agencies are obviously taking advantage of the easy connectivity provided by the internet for short-term mobilization.

**Shift 4: Changes in Primary Activities and Resources Towards Relief and Development.** In the 2005 survey agencies were given a list of 61 activities (including an "other" category with a blank to indicate what the "other" activities were) and asked to indicate a maximum of six of these as the primary activities of their organization. They were then asked to indicate which one of the activities was most commonly associated with their organization. In our discussion, that activity will be referred to as the "primary activity;" the others will

**Figure 38: Contact Methods Used by Canadian
Agencies for Short-term Mission Recruitment**

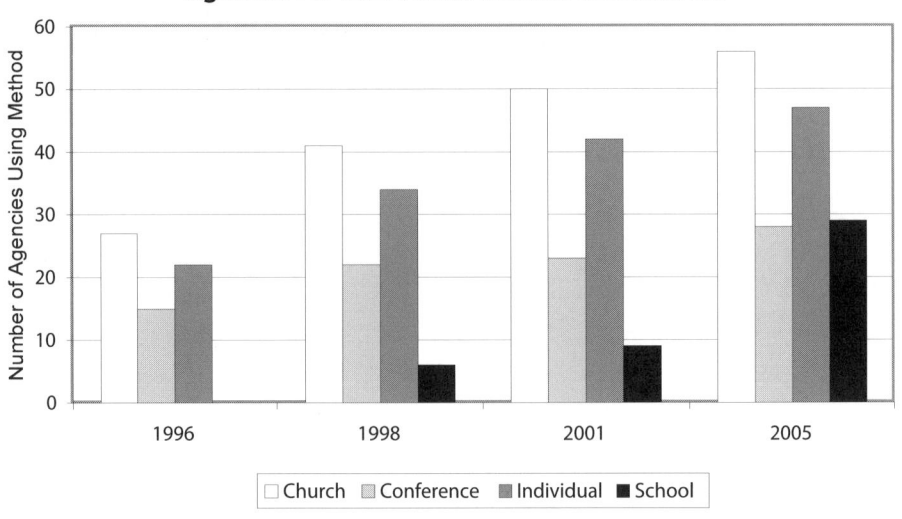

be referred to simply as "activities" or "all activities."

As noted in the discussion on U.S. agencies, in our analysis we assume that the self-identified primary activity receives a larger share of an agency's resources and energy than any other activity indicated. It must be kept in mind that by indicating an activity as the one most commonly associated with the organization, an agency is not saying that this activity is all they do or even received the majority of their resources. Rather, they are simply indicating this activity is the one they are associated with. Thus, if an agency selects "church establishing/ planting" as their primary activity, we assume that this will receive more personnel and financial resources than any of the other five activities reported by that agency. It is on the basis of this assumption that our analyses on the reported primary activities are made below, and it is important to keep this in mind in the discussion.

Table 20 depicts the top ten ranking of primary activities of Canadian agencies. The activity with the greatest reported gain was "church establishing/planting," with four more agencies reporting it as their primary activity in 2005 than in 2001. Three activities had three fewer agencies reporting them as their primary activities in 2005 than in 2001 were "evangelism, personal and small group", "relief and/or rehabilitation" and "support of national workers."

Table 21 lists the number of agencies indicating all the primary activities that had at least one agency indicate it as primary in either 2001 or 2005. They are grouped into the same five major categories used in the U.S. section: 1) activities related to evangelism and discipleship, 2) activities related to education and training, 3) activities related to agency support, 4) activities related to relief and development, and 5) other activities. As noted in the discussion of the U.S. agencies, in some cases the choice to list one activity in one particular category

## Table 20: Primary Activities: Comparing
## 1998 and 2005 Top Ten Survey Results

| 2005 Rank | Primary Activity | 2005 | 2001 | No. Change | % Change |
|---|---|---|---|---|---|
| 1 | Church establishing/planting | 38 | 34 | 4 | 11.8% |
| 2 | Development, community and/or other | 7 | 7 | 0 | 0.0% |
| 2 | Broadcasting, radio and/or TV | 7 | 5 | 2 | 40.0% |
| 4 | Evangelism, personal and small group | 6 | 9 | -3 | -33.3% |
| 5 | Relief and/or rehabilitation | 5 | 8 | -3 | -37.5% |
| 5 | Evangelism, mass | 5 | 4 | 1 | 25.0% |
| 7 | Support of national workers | 4 | 7 | -3 | -42.9% |
| 7 | National church nurture/support | 4 | 4 | 0 | 0.0% |
| 7 | Literature distribution | 4 | 5 | -1 | -20.0% |
| 7 | Bible distribution | 4 | 4 | 0 | 0.0% |

## Table 21: 2001 and 2005 Primary Activities by Major Category

| | 2005 | | 2001 | |
|---|---|---|---|---|
| | No. | % | No. | % |
| **Evangelism/Discipleship Activities** | **88** | **72.1%** | **82** | **68.3%** |
| Church establishing/planting | 39 | 32.0% | 34 | 28.3% |
| Broadcasting, radio and/or TV | 7 | 5.7% | 5 | 4.2% |
| Evangelism, personal and small group | 6 | 4.9% | 9 | 7.5% |
| Evangelism, mass | 5 | 4.1% | 4 | 3.3% |
| Bible distribution | 4 | 3.3% | 4 | 3.3% |
| Literature distribution | 4 | 3.3% | 5 | 4.2% |
| National church nurture/support | 4 | 3.3% | 3 | 2.5% |
| Support of national workers | 4 | 3.3% | 7 | 5.8% |
| Discipleship | 3 | 2.5% | 0 | 0.0% |
| Evangelism, student | 2 | 1.6% | 2 | 1.7% |
| Leadership development | 2 | 1.6% | 2 | 1.7% |
| Literature production | 2 | 1.6% | 1 | 0.8% |
| Youth programs | 2 | 1.6% | 1 | 0.8% |
| Audio recording/distribution | 1 | 0.8% | 1 | 0.8% |
| Childrens programs | 1 | 0.8% | 1 | 0.8% |
| Translation, Bible | 1 | 0.8% | 2 | 1.7% |
| Tentmaking and related | 1 | 0.8% | 1 | 0.8% |
| Church construction | 0 | 0.0% | 0 | 0.0% |
| **Education/Training Activities** | **8** | **6.6%** | **7** | **5.8%** |
| Education, church/sch. Gen. Christian | 3 | 2.5% | 2 | 1.7% |

| | | | | |
|---|---|---|---|---|
| Training, other | 2 | 1.6% | 0 | 0.0% |
| Correspondence courses | 1 | 0.8% | 1 | 0.8% |
| Education, extension (other) | 1 | 0.8% | 0 | 0.0% |
| Education, theological | 1 | 0.8% | 4 | 3.3% |
| **Mission Agency Support Activities** | **8** | **6.6%** | **8** | **6.7%** |
| Recruiting/Mobilizing | 3 | 2.5% | 2 | 1.7% |
| Short-term programs coordination | 2 | 1.6% | 2 | 1.7% |
| Training/Orientation, missionary | 2 | 1.6% | 3 | 2.5% |
| Aviation services | 1 | 0.8% | 1 | 0.8% |
| Association of Missions | 0 | 0.0% | 0 | 0.0% |
| Information Services | 0 | 0.0% | 0 | 0.0% |
| Services for other agencies | 0 | 0.0% | 0 | 0.0% |
| Technical assistance | 0 | 0.0% | 0 | 0.0% |
| **Relief and Development Activities** | **17** | **13.9%** | **17** | **14.2%** |
| Development, community and/or other | 7 | 5.7% | 7 | 5.8% |
| Relief and/or rehabilitation | 5 | 4.1% | 5 | 4.2% |
| Childcare/orphanage | 2 | 1.6% | 2 | 1.7% |
| Medicine, incl. dental and public health | 2 | 1.6% | 2 | 1.7% |
| Justice and related | 1 | 0.8% | 1 | 0.8% |
| Disability assistance programs | 0 | 0.0% | 0 | 0.0% |
| **Other Activities** | **1** | **0.8%** | **3** | **0.0%** |
| Funds transmission | 1 | 0.8% | 2 | 1.7% |
| Other | 0 | 0.0% | 1 | 0.8% |

rather than another was a matter of judgment on which not all will agree. For example, the activity of "training/orientation, missionary" could have fit under the "Education/Training" category or the "Mission Agency Support" category. It was deemed that training and orientation of missionaries, while educational, was primarily a support of missionaries and agencies rather than educating those of another culture, so it was placed in the "Mission Agency Support" category. Thus, there will be some fuzziness in the major categories used in the following analysis and care must be taken not to read too much into relatively minor shifts in them.

The most frequently indicated primary activity of Canadian agencies continues to be "church establishing/planting," which also saw the biggest increase in the number of agencies switching to it between the 2001 and 2005 surveys (an increase from 34 to 39). The second largest gain was the number of agencies indicating "discipleship" as their primary activity (from 0 to 3). The activity with the greatest loss in agencies selecting it as a primary activity was "Support of national workers," which went from 7 agencies in 2001 to 4 in 2005.

A somewhat clearer picture of the activity shifts appears when you examine

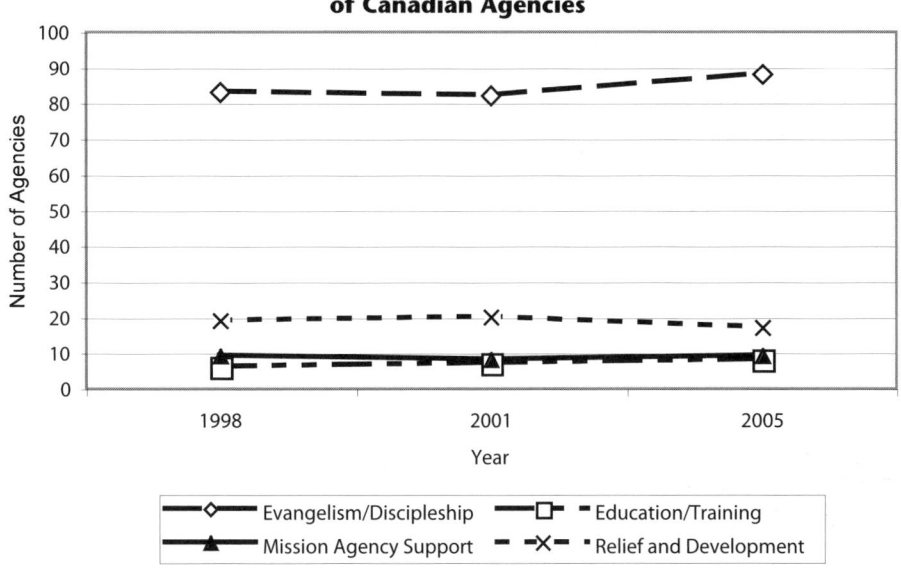

**Figure 39: Major Categories of Primary Activiies of Canadian Agencies**

the major categories of the primary activities of all Canadian agencies (Tables 22 through 24; Figure 39). As seen in Figure 39, the relative shifting of Canadian agencies has been towards reporting primary activities in the evangelism and discipleship category and away from reporting primary activities in the relief and development category.

The reported numbers for this shift are seen in Table 22, which also reflects the financial and people resources marshaled by each category. Figure 40 shows the inflation-adjusted gain or loss of income for overseas missions for each major category from 2001 to 2005, while Figure 41 shows that gain or loss for each major category in that category's share of the total percentage of workers mobilized by Canadian agencies from 2001 to 2005.

For 2005, 88 agencies (72.1%) indicated primary activities in the evangelism/ discipleship category, up by 6 (3.8%) from the 2001 survey. While these agencies reported an inflation-adjusted income gain of 9.5%, their share of the total

**Table 22: Canadian Resources Used by Primary Activity**

| Category of Primary Activity | # Agencies | | Income for Overseas | | All Workers | |
|---|---|---|---|---|---|---|
| Evangelism/Discipleship | 88 | 72.1% | $159,105,572 | 24.9% | 6,688 | 76.7% |
| Relief and Development | 17 | 13.9% | $469,491,505 | 73.6% | 1,667 | 19.1% |
| Education/Training | 8 | 6.6% | $4,864,568 | 0.8% | 270 | 3.1% |
| Mission Agency Support | 8 | 6.6% | $4,681,167 | 0.7% | 97 | 1.1% |
| Other | 1 | 0.8% | $0 | 0.0% | 0 | 0.0% |

**Figure 40: Inflation Adjusted Percent of Gain/Loss (2001 to 2005) of Income for Overseas Ministry by Major Category**

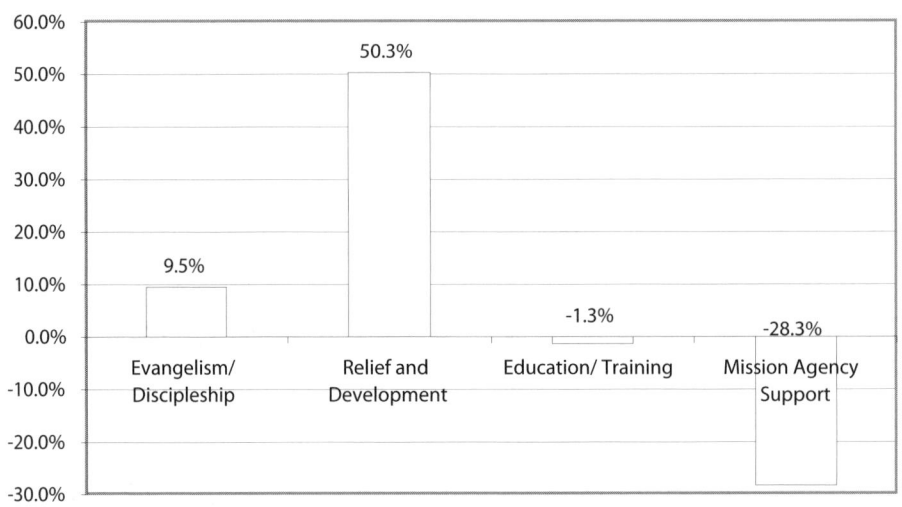

**Figure 41: Share Gain/Loss (2001 to 2005) of Total Percentage of All Workers**

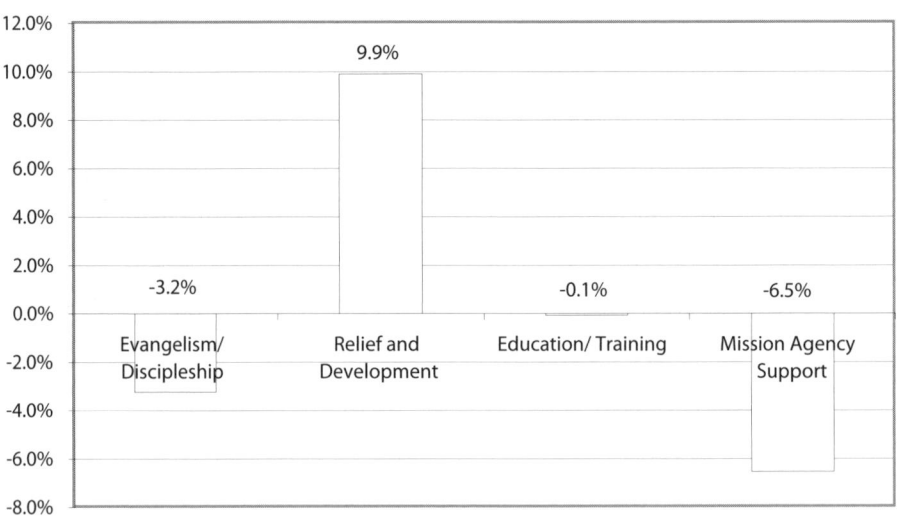

income for overseas missions actually dropped from 31% in 2001 to 24.9% in 2005. Over the same period they reported a loss of 444 total workers, so that their share of total workers dropped from 79.9% to 76.7%.

Seventeen agencies indicated primary activities in the relief and development category, down by 3 from 2001 (2.7%). They reported an inflation-adjusted gain of 50.3%, the largest of any category, and their share of the total income for overseas missions rose from 66.6% in 2001 to 73.6% in 2005. Additionally, they reported the total worker gain of 845, and their share in the total pool of workers increased from 9.2% in 2001 to 19.2% in 2005, the largest gain among the major categories.

Eight agencies indicated primary activities in the mission agency support category, the same number of agencies as 2001, but their income for overseas missions dropped by an inflation-adjusted 28.3%. Their share of the total income for overseas missions dropped from 1.4% in 2001 to 0.7% in 2005. They also reported a loss of 589 total workers, and their share of the total worker pool dropped from 9.6% in 2001 to 3.1% in 2005.

Table 23 shows the breakdown of reported personnel mobilized by Canadian agencies into the various categories. The most significant reported gains from 2001 to 2005 were seen among tentmakers (50.0%) working for agencies whose primary activity was in the evangelism discipleship category, and among and non-Canadians (335%), non-residential (272%) and short-term missionaries

### Table 23: Canadian People Resources Used by Primary Activity

| Category of Primary Activity | Short Term | | Tentmakers | | Non-Residential | |
|---|---|---|---|---|---|---|
| Evangelism/Discipleship | 2,773 | 78.5% | 180 | 96.8% | 121 | 62.4% |
| Relief and Development | 505 | 14.3% | 2 | 1.1% | 67 | 34.5% |
| Mission Agency Support | 217 | 6.1% | 0 | 0.0% | 0 | 0.0% |
| Education/Training | 39 | 1.1% | 4 | 2.2% | 6 | 3.1% |
| Other | 0 | 0.0% | 0 | 0.0% | 0 | 0.0% |

| Category of Primary Activity | Full-Time 1 to 4+ Years | | Non-Canadian Citizens | | All Workers | |
|---|---|---|---|---|---|---|
| Evangelism/Discipleship | 2,311 | 89.9% | 1,303 | 58.2% | 6,688 | 76.7% |
| Relief and Development | 180 | 7.0% | 913 | 40.8% | 1,667 | 19.1% |
| Mission Agency Support | 48 | 1.9% | 5 | 0.2% | 270 | 3.1% |
| Education/Training | 31 | 1.2% | 17 | 0.8% | 97 | 1.1% |
| Other | 0 | 0.0% | 0 | 0.0% | 0 | 0.0% |

(42.3%) working for agencies whose primary activity was in the relief and development category.

On the other hand, the most significant reported losses for 2001 to 2005 were for full-time missionaries (74.5%) and short-term missionaries (64.6%) working for agencies whose primary activity was in the mission agency support category and for non-residential missionaries (67.2%) and non-Canadian citizens (30.2%) working for agencies whose primary activity was in the evangelism and discipleship category.

Figure 42 indicates the relative pool of some of the resources listed in Tables 22 and 23, making it easier to see the relative number of agencies, overseas

**Figure 42: Comparison of Percent of Resources Support
for Primary Activities of Canadian Agencies**

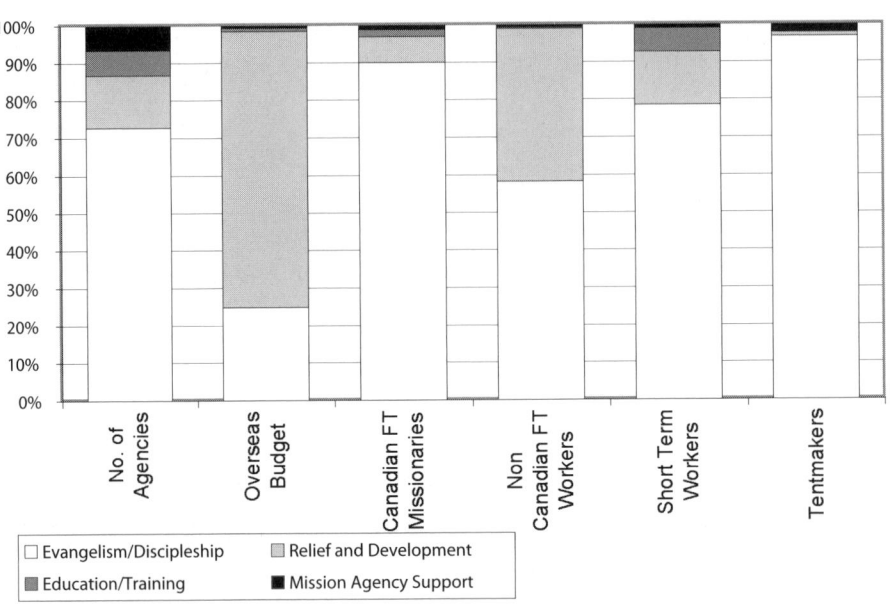

budget, Canadian full-time missionaries, and so on, for each major category of primary activity reported by the agencies. It is obvious that agencies whose primary activity is in the category of evangelism and discipleship continue to command the largest share of the total missionary resources with the exception of the income for overseas missions. Agencies that report their primary activities in the relief and development category report the largest share of the income for overseas mission as well as an increasing share in the number of non-Canadians working for them.

Tables 24 and 25 and Figures 43 and 44 offer information on all activities indicated by every Canadian agency. They enable comparisons among the activities and the categories of activities each represents. Because this section deals with all activities reported by every agency, and many agencies report activities across multiple categories, it is not possible to give a breakdown by major categories in any areas other than the number of agencies indicating each activity.

Among the top ten most commonly indicated activities, the most impressive gains were made by the number of agencies reporting "discipleship" (not added as a choice until this survey; up by 34), church "establishing/planting" (up by 10 or 23.3%), "mass evangelism" (up by 5 or 29.4%) and "support of national workers" (up by 5 or 29.4%). The largest decline was seen in " evangelism, personal and small group" (down by 16 or 27.6%) and "national church nurture/support" (down by 7 or 20.6%). The fuzziness of the activity listings may be a major factor in these shifts (e.g., agencies may have switched from listing "national church nurture/support" to listing "discipleship,") without actually

**Table 24: All Activities: Comparing 2001and 2005**
**Top Ten Survey Results**

| 2005 Rank | Activity | 2005 No. | 2001 No. | Change | % Change |
|---|---|---|---|---|---|
| 1 | Church establishing/planting | 53 | 50 | 3 | 6.0% |
| 2 | Evangelism, personal and small group | 42 | 49 | -7 | -14.3% |
| 3 | Leadership development | 36 | 31 | 5 | 16.1% |
| 4 | Discipleship | 34 | 0 | 34 | N/A |
| 5 | Development, community and/or other | 32 | 36 | -4 | -11.1% |
| 6 | National church nurture/support | 27 | 27 | 0 | 0.0% |
| 7 | Relief and/or rehabilitation | 23 | 24 | -1 | -4.2% |
| 8 | Evangelism, mass | 22 | 19 | 3 | 15.8% |
| 8 | Medicine, incl. dental and public health | 22 | 20 | 2 | 10.0% |
| 8 | Support of national workers | 22 | 20 | 2 | 10.0% |

**Table 25: Comparison of Total Canadian Activities**
**Reported for 1998, 2001 and 2005**

| Activity | 2005 | | 2001 | | 1998 | | 1998 to 2005 Change | |
|---|---|---|---|---|---|---|---|---|
| | | | | | | | No. | % |
| Evangelism/ Discipleship Activities | 360 | 56.2% | 311 | 53.1% | 307 | 57.1% | 53 | 17.3% |
| Education/Training Activities | 61 | 9.5% | 64 | 10.9% | 64 | 11.9% | -3 | -4.7% |
| Mission Agency Support Activities | 91 | 14.2% | 70 | 11.9% | 54 | 10.0% | 37 | 68.5% |
| Relief and Development Activities | 109 | 17.0% | 119 | 20.3% | 95 | 17.7% | 14 | 14.7% |
| Other Activities | 20 | 3.1% | 22 | 3.8% | 18 | 3.3% | 2 | 11.1% |

changing their emphasis.

As seen in Table 25, significant increases in the number of Canadian agencies reporting related activities are seen in two of the major categories. Fifty-three more agencies now indicate they are engaged in activities in the evangelism and discipleship category than in 1998, a 17.3% gain. Thirty-seven more agencies now indicate they are engaged in activities in the mission agency support category than in 1998, a 68.5% gain. However, these must be seen in the context of Canadian agencies reporting 103 more activities than in 1998, a 19.1% gain. In terms of the relative share of the total of all activities, then, mission agency support gained 4.2% while evangelism and discipleship lost 0.9% (see Figure 44). Thus, as impressive as the evangelism and discipleship gains were, they did not keep up with the total growth of activities reported by Canadian agencies. Both of these changes are clearly seen in Figure 43.

What do all these activities trends mean for the Canadian mission move-

**Figure 43: 1998 to 2005 Percent Gain/Loss in Percent of Total Share of All Reported Activities by Major Category**

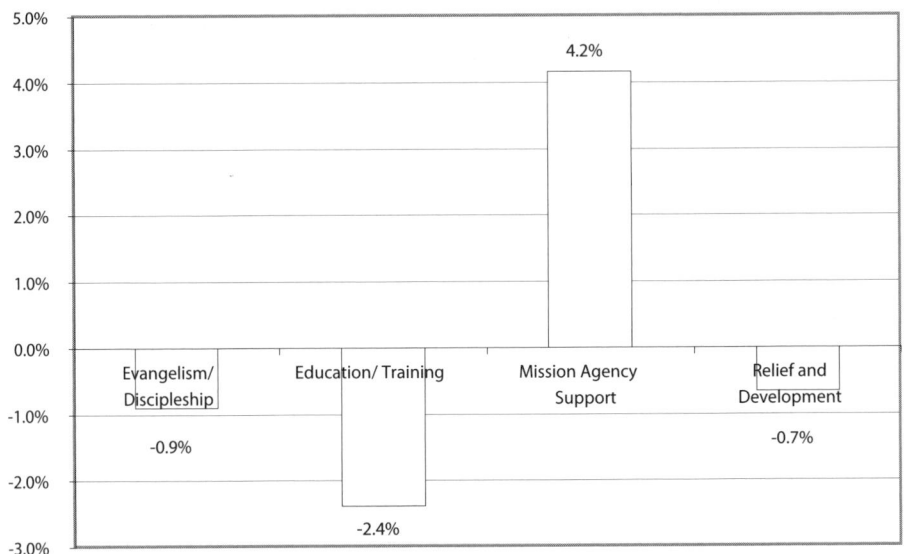

**Figure 44: Percent of Total Activites by Category for All Reported Activities of Canadian Agencies**

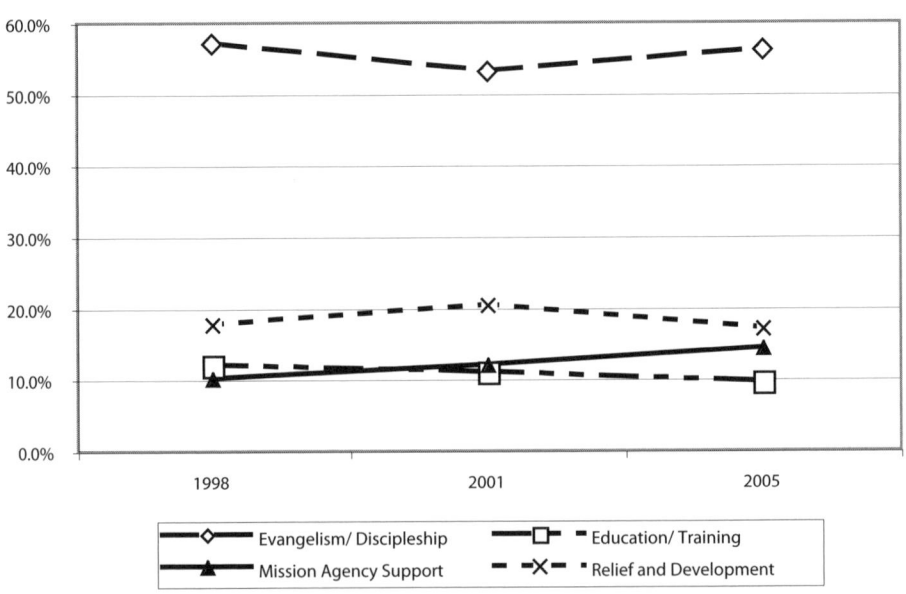

ment? While these major changes do beg for further research and study they also raise some profound questions, also asked in our previous survey:
- Are Canadian agencies developing a more holistic view of mission?
- Are Canadian agencies simply responding to the funding realities of the

Canadian Christian community which seems more inclined to give to relief and development activities?

• Are Canadian agencies making these changes because they reflect the changing role of the Canadian church in globalized community of faith?

### Shift 5: Changes in the Reported Deployment of Canadian Agencies and Missionaries:

• More Canadian agencies reported in every region of the world;

• More Canadians and non-Canadian citizens deployed in Africa and Central America/Caribbean; and

• Fewer Canadians deployed in Europe

Figure 45 maps the distribution of where Canadian agencies are sending their missionaries around the world for 2001 and 2005. Almost every continental region in this survey has more Canadian agencies reporting deployed missionaries. In light of the fact that there are fewer missionaries mobilized by Canadian agencies, this is an indicator that the resources are being stretched thinner than in the previous survey. As an illustration, note that the number of Canadian

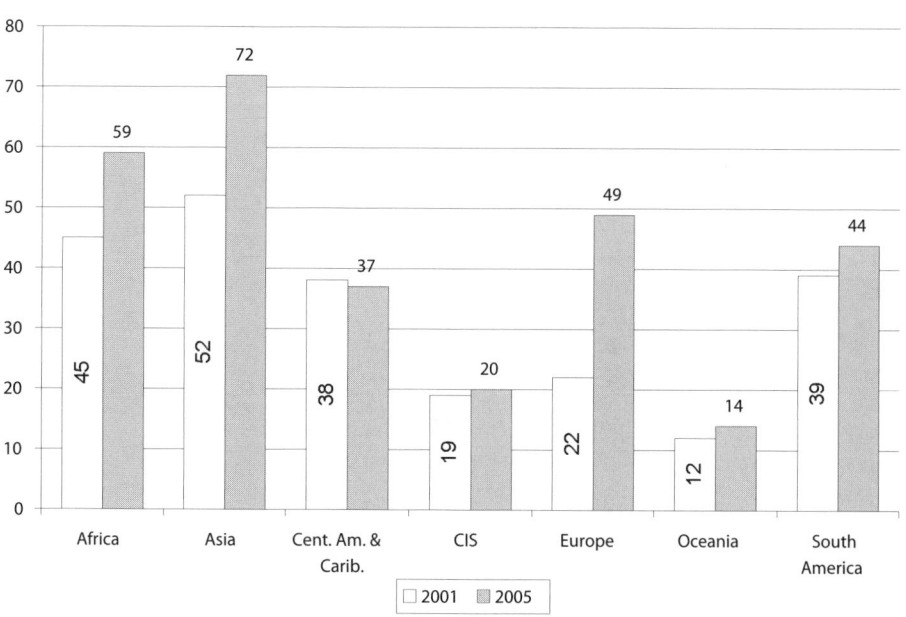

**Figure 45: Number of Canadian Agencies per Region for 2001 and 2005**

agencies now active in Europe more than doubled between the surveys. However, as seen in Figures 46 and 47, the actual number of Canadian missionaries reported working there increased by only 2.1% and the total number of missionaries deployed there dropped by 17.1%. The net result is a thinning of Canadian missionary presence in Europe.

**Figure 46: Number of Full-Time Canadian Missionaries by Region**

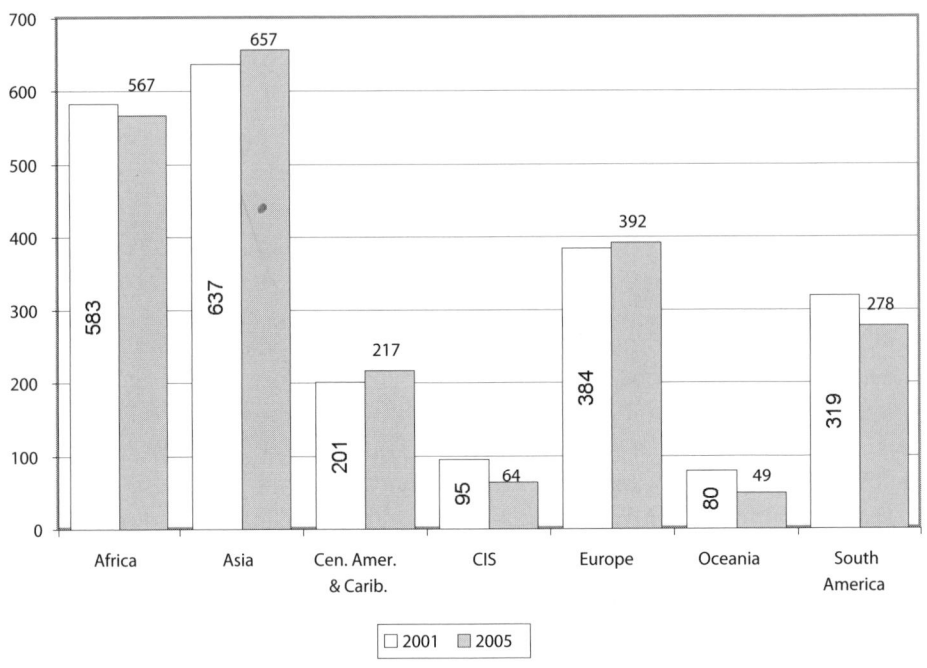

**Figure 47: Total Missionaries Deployed
through Canadian Agencies by Region**

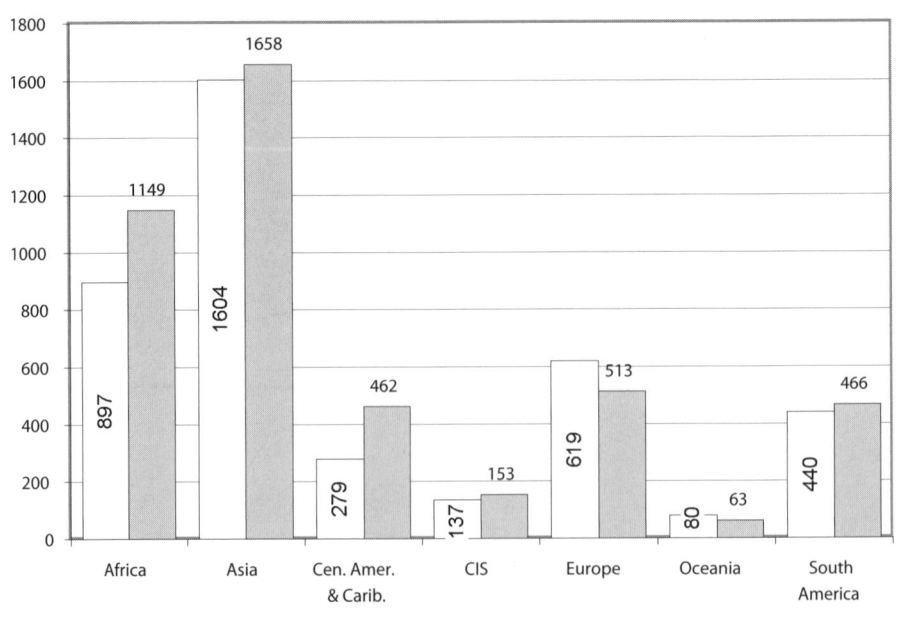

Figure 47 shows that the largest number of full-time Canadian-supported missionaries (both Canadian citizens and non-Canadians) is in Asia. However, the regions with the largest gains in missionaries deployed through Canadian agencies are Africa (28.1%) and Central America/Caribbean (65.6%). We must be careful not to read too much into this, as it may merely be a change in reporting by those agencies which did not specify the regions of deployment in 2001 but did so in 2005 (there was a 54.3% drop in unspecified, which were distributed among the other regions).

Figure 48 displays the deployment of non-Canadian workers for 2001 and 2005. The greatest gain was non-Canadians being reported as deployed in Africa

**Figure 48: Non-Canadians Deployed by Canadian Agencies 2001 and 2005**

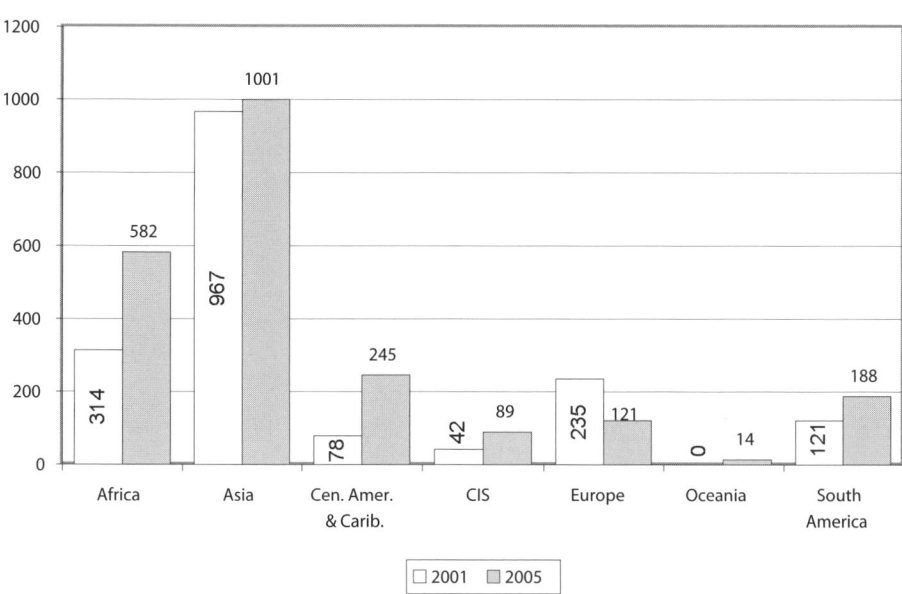

(85.4%) and Central America/Caribbean (214%), while the greatest drop was for non-Canadians reported as deployed in Europe (48.5%).

**Shift 6: A Decrease in the Number of Reported Canadian Home Staff.** Figure 49 indicates the number of employed people who make it possible for the Canadian missionaries and international programs to work. The full-time home staff decreased by 14.7%. The part-time staff increased by 32.3%, while the volunteers increased by a strong 153.4%.

In review, we have noted six shifts seen among Canadian Protestant mission agencies during the past decade:

1. A decrease in the reported total workforce of Canadian agencies;

2. A decrease in the reported number of Canadian citizens working for Canadian agencies;

3. A decrease in the number of reported short-term support personnel;

**Figure 49: Canadian Agency Home Staff**

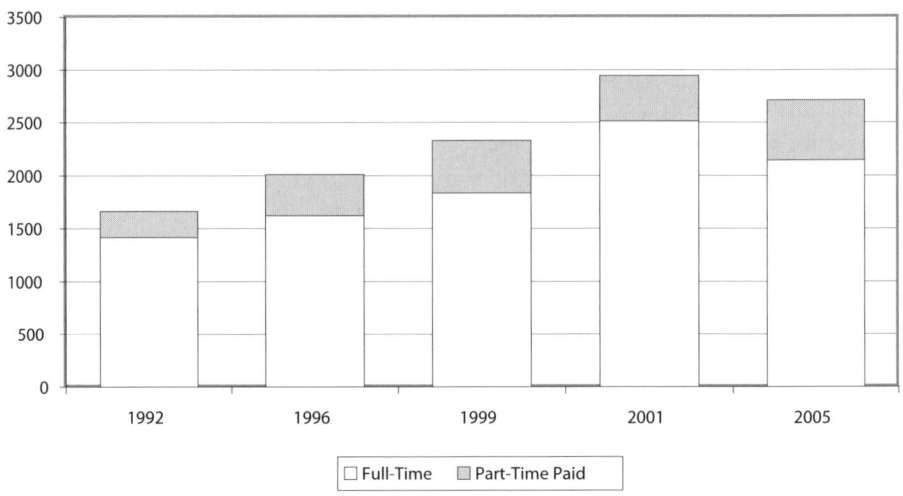

4. Changes in primary activities and resources towards relief and development;

5. Changes in the reported deployment of Canadian agencies and missionaries, namely:

a. More Canadian agencies reported in every region of the world;

b. More Canadians and non-Canadian citizens deployed in Africa and Central America/Caribbean; and

c. Fewer Canadians deployed in Europe; and

6. A decrease in the number of reported Canadian home staff.

## Conclusion

As the Canadian mission movement undergoes some profound changes there seem to be several overarching issues that are being faced by mission sending agencies. These include:

• An acceleration of the declining long-term missionary force

• An aging donor base

• Leadership transition challenges to the younger leaders

• The need to find appropriate ways to motivate the emerging postmodern generation.

Since 1985, Canada has seen relatively few new mission agencies (11 in this survey), and at this time there is scant evidence that the younger generation is stepping up to launch new structures for mission. As Canada continues to see more retirement of an aging missionary force, it does not appear that they are effectively being replaced. The next decade will continue to be critical not as much for Canadian agencies as it is for Canadians themselves to step out in missions within agency structures or to develop new structures that deploy Canadians in missionary efforts.

As noted in the 2001 edition of the *Handbook*, at the early part of the 21st century the Canadian mission enterprise finds itself at a crossroads. Some voices both within and outside the churches predict the Canadian missionary movement will be marginalized. Others argue mission organizations will adapt to a changing world. As evangelicals committed to taking God's Good News to the world, the Canadian mission community must find new ways of overcoming these challenges and working together. Mission organizations, denominations, churches and individuals with a passion for mission must be united in envisioning and equipping the Canadian church to utilize its strength, vitality and commitment to serve the least-reached people at home and beyond Canada's borders.

### Endnotes

1. By full-time we mean those who are in service for one year or longer.

2. There is important anecdotal evidence that this number, while representative, is likely significantly below the actual number of missionaries deployed out of North America. In addition to agencies that send primarily Christian professionals and do not want to be labeled "mission" agencies, uncounted individuals are sent as partial or fully supported cross-cultural workers by churches and other organizations that are not included in the totals given here.

3. That these are all "non-North Americans" is not completely accurate. The surveys ask for agencies to report non-U.S. or non-Canadian citizens, but does not distinguish U.S. citizens working for Canadian agencies (or vice-versa) from non-Canadian citizens of other countries. Thus, this number inevitably includes Americans working for Canadian agencies as well as Canadians working for American agencies.

4. While we only reported on 690 agencies in the last edition, we actually listed 694. The difference was caused by some agencies getting the information to us too late for the data analysis.

5. The numbers reported on country totals will always be the minimum confirmable number. There are two factors involved. First, this does not include countries of non-residential personnel, short-term workers, tentmakers, or where agencies have ongoing programs they support financially but without personnel. Second, several agencies report a general region but not specific countries for their missionary personnel. As agencies continue to evaluate security concerns, it seems likely that country statistics will become increasingly hard to report reliably.

6. Previously we called these "short-term" but as the same terminology is used for the 2 week to 1 year people, it was decided to adopt Sean Marston's suggestion of calling the 1 to 4 year people middle-term missionaries; Sean Marston, "Middle Mission," *Evangelical Missions Quarterly* 42:1 (2006), 90-45.

7. The reported number of volunteers dropped by almost 592,860 from the last edition (92%). It has become obvious that these numbers vary so widely from survey to survey that they are untrustworthy as indicators of the true extent of volunteerism within U.S. mission agencies, so no analysis will be done on them.

8. Adjusted for the reporting errors noted in endnotes 9 and 10.

9. For example, due to a category reporting error corrected in this survey, the top agency in the 2001 survey reported 1,189 people in this category, but 0 in 2005. However, that makes the increase seen in this survey even more impressive.

10. The sharp decline between 1998 and 2001 was, as noted in the previous edition of the *Handbook*, the result of the massive drop reported by a single organization.

11. As noted in the previous version, there was an anomalous spike in 1998 largely

due to one agency reporting a significant increase for 1998 followed by a corresponding decrease in 2001. We have adjusted Figure 10 to take that into account and provide a more accurate representation of the ongoing growth.

12. Robert J. Priest, Terry Dischinger, Steve Rasmussen and Steve Brown, "Researching the Short-Term Mission Movement." *Missiology: An International Review* 34:4 (October 2006), p. 432. This number includes international trips of any duration, while our survey asks about trips from 2 weeks to one year.

13. Ibid., p. 433.

14. Ibid., pp 435-41.

15. This was the motivation behind the October 2006 issue of *Missiology: An International Review of Mission*, which was entirely devoted to presenting research on short-term missions, and is an invaluable resource for anyone exploring this phenomenon.

16. Due to security reasons, the Southern Baptist Convention International Missions Board and Wycliffe Bible Translators report their missionaries by region only. As two of the largest sending agencies, they would be active in most—if not all—of the countries in this list.

17. For those who have read the U.S. section prior to reading the Canadian section, we ask that you excuse our redundancy in using some of the same explanations already found in the U.S. section. We do so under the assumption that some readers will only be interested in the Canadian section, and we wanted those readers to be able to understand our approach and terms without being forced to read the U.S. section.

18. In the 2001 edition, the ratio was eight Canadians for every four nationals working for Canadian agencies; in the 2004 edition it was six Canadians for every four nationals.

## Table 26: Agencies No Longer Listed

| Name of Agency | Reason No Longer Listed |
|---|---|
| ACMC, Inc. | Disbanded |
| AD2000 & Beyond Movement | Disbanded |
| American Baptist Association Missionary Council | Overseas data not available |
| American Tract Society | Overseas data not available |
| American Waldensian Society | Overseas data not available |
| Anglican Church of Canada, Partners in Mission | Overseas data not available |
| Associated Gospel Churches | No overseas ministries at present |
| Baptist Faith Missions | Overseas data not available |
| Baptist Missionary Association of America | Overseas data not available |
| Barnabas Ministries, Inc. | Overseas data not available |
| Berean Mission, Inc. | Merger |
| Bethany Missionary Association | Overseas data not available |
| Big World Ventures Inc. | Overseas data not available |
| Blossoming Rose | Overseas data not available |
| Caleb Project | Disbanded |
| Children of Promise International | Overseas data not available |
| Christian Indigenous Development Overseas | Choose not to be listed |
| Croisade du Livre Chretien / Christian Literature Crusade | Overseas relationship unknown |

| Door of Hope International (Canada) | Now considered non-mission |
|---|---|
| Episcopal World Mission | Overseas data not available |
| European Christian Mission | No office in Canada at present |
| European Missions Outreach | Overseas data not available |
| Eurovangelism | Overseas data not available |
| Evangelize China Fellowship, Inc. | Overseas data not available |
| Fellowship Travel Information, Inc. | Overseas data not available |
| Friendship Ministries | Overseas data not available |
| General Conf. Mennonite Church, Commission on Overseas Mission | Merger |
| Glad Tidings Missionary Society | Overseas relationship unknown |
| Harvest International Christian Outreach / Target Teams | Overseas data not available |
| Harvesting In Spanish | No office in USA at present |
| Institute of Chinese Studies | Merger |
| Institute of Hindu Studies | Inactive at present |
| International Bible Society | Choose not to be listed |
| International Children's Haven (Canada) | Overseas data not available |
| International Discipleship Mission | Overseas data not available |
| International Gospel League | Overseas data not available |
| Island Missionary Society | Overseas data not available |
| ISOH/Impact | Overseas data not available |
| Issachar Frontier Missions Strategies | Disbanded |
| Japan—North American Commission on Cooperative Mission | Overseas data not available |
| Liberia Christian Mission | Overseas data not available |
| Lion and Lamb Outreach | Inactive at present |
| Lutheran Bible Translators of Canada, Inc. | Choose not to be listed |
| Mennonite Board of Missions | Merger |
| Message of Life, Inc. | Overseas data not available |
| Mexican Border Missions | Disbanded |
| Mexican Christian Mission | Overseas data not available |
| Ministry of Jesus, Inc. | Overseas data not available |
| Moody Institute of Science Division of Moody Bible Institute | Overseas data not available |
| Pacific Northwest Mennonite Conference—Missions | Now considered non-mission |
| Reformed Presbyterian Church, Board of Foreign Missions | Overseas data not available |
| Romanian Mission of Chicago | No Financial Information |
| Scripture Union, USA | Overseas data not available |
| Society for Europe's Evangelization | Overseas data not available |
| Witnessing Ministries of Christ | Overseas data not available |
| World Gospel Mission—Canada | No office in Canada at present |
| World In Need—USA | Overseas data not available |

**Evangelical Missions Quarterly**

# A valuable resource for individuals and organizations involved in missions...

Since 1964 *Evangelical Missions Quarterly* (*EMQ*) has been providing practical information concerning missions. Today, *EMQ* has become the premier evangelical missions journal, read by thousands in North America and throughout the world.

## Available both in print and online, *EMQ* includes:

- articles by veteran missionaries and experts in fields pertinent to missions
- book reviews by experts in the missions field
- editorials on topics relevant to world missions today
- feedback from readers on past articles

## IN PRINT

The print edition allows you to build a valuable library with high-quality articles and editorials for future reference.

## ONLINE

The online edition allows you to access *EMQ* and *EMQ* archives from any computer, anytime. It includes additional valuable content such as:

- more than forty years of archived *EMQ* articles
- current news and events not found elsewhere
- updated feedback from readers on posted articles

### Check it out at:
### www.emqonline.com

### New Subscriber Rates

One year (four issues) of *EMQ*

**$18.95**

One year of EMQonline

**$13.95**

One year of both *EMQ* and EMQonline

**$28.95**

To order, call 630.752.7158 or go online to emisdirect.com

*EMQ* is published quarterly by the Evangelism and Missions Information Service (EMIS) at the Billy Graham Center at Wheaton College, 500 College Ave., Wheaton, IL 60189

# Special **EMQonline** Bulk Subscription Rates Available!

Evangelical Missions Quarterly (*EMQ*) is the premier evangelical missions journal, providing practical information for individuals and organizations committed to missions. *EMQ* is **ONLINE** at **www.emqonline.com**.

**EMQonline offers all the content found in the print edition, including:**

- articles written by veteran missionaries and experts in fields pertinent to missions

- book reviews by experts in the mission field

- editorials on topics relevant to world missions today

- feedback from readers concerning topics addressed in past EMQ editions

**PLUS**...current missions news and events not found on other websites **and** more than **forty years** of archived *EMQ* articles!

### SPECIAL BULK SUBSCRIPTIONS
26-50 subscriptions, only $12.95 per year
51-99 subscriptions, only $11.95 per year
100-499 subscriptions, only $10.95 per year
500-999 subscriptions, only $9.95 per year

To order: Call 630.752.7158 or go to: **www.emisdirect.com**

## Visit us at
# www.emqonline.com

Individual EMQonline subscriptions,
$13.95 per year (4 issues)

# Chapter 2
# U.S. Protestant Agencies

This chapter contains the basic information for U.S. Protestant agencies engaged in Christian mission ministries outside the U.S. and Canada. The comprehensive coverage includes agencies that directly support the work of such ministries or the work of overseas national churches/workers. The agencies supplied the information. The survey questionnaire used to gather the information is reproduced in the appendix.

The *Handbook* covers an agency's overseas ministry and support activities; it does not cover its mission work in the U.S. Agencies with both overseas and U.S. mission ministries, however, were asked to include U.S.-based ministry personnel in the total that appears in the "home ministry and office staff" line of the "Other Personnel" section.

Each agency will have at least seven of the basic categories of information listed below, with others included as applicable.

## Agency Name

Agencies are listed alphabetically. If the article "the" is in an agency's name, it will appear at the end of the name so the agency is in the most commonly referenced alphabetical order. Rare exceptions occur where the Christian public commonly uses the article "the" as the first word in the agency's name.

Agencies that have changed their name since the previous Handbook have their prior name listed also, with a cross-reference to the current or new name. A subdivision of a larger organization may be listed separately if it is organized to also serve the larger mission community rather than just its parent organization.

## Telephone and Fax Numbers

Area codes are in parentheses. Since area codes change rapidly, some may have changed since the time of publication.

## Email Address

The Internet format and standards for capitalization are used. In some cases, agencies have a general email address (i.e.,info@xxxx.org). Others have supplied an individual's address within the organization. In cases where only a web address is given, it generally means a web page provides access to several email addresses so an inquiry can be immediately directed to the relevant department or person.

## Web Address

The Internet format and standards for capitalization are used. Most agencies have a web address; however, a few have chosen not to list it for security reasons.

## Postal Mailing Address

A post office box number usually appears whenever the agency has one. Exceptions occur when the agency prefers the street address.

## Chief Executive Officer

In a few cases where there are multiple primary contacts, or due to agency preference, two officers may be listed.

## Short Descriptive Paragraph

A brief description appears based on the denominational orientation and primary activities information supplied by the agency. Additional specific information, such as name changes, mergers or other unique aspects may also be included.

## Purpose Statement

Purpose statements are included when available. Some of the statements are concise and shown in their entirety, straight from the agency or its promotional material. For most, however, common or similar phrases such as "exists for the purpose of" are replaced by ellipses to present a more concise statement.

## Year Founded in USA

This date is the year the agency or overseas mission component of a larger organization was founded or incorporated in the U.S. In some cases, the denomination or organization may have existed earlier in another country. For some organizations, the founding date of the missionary-sending component may be later than the founding of the larger organization. For organizations that have experienced mergers, the founding date is generally that of the oldest component involved in the merger.

## Income for Overseas Ministries

This is the part of an agency's overall income used or budgeted for ministry activities outside the U.S. and Canada or in activities that directly facilitate overseas ministries. "NA" indicates that income in this sense is not applicable, and usually applies to specialized service agencies or agencies whose income is reported under a sister or parent organization. "NR" indicates that the agency did not report income for overseas ministries, but may make this information available upon request.

## Gifts-in-Kind

If applicable, this is the portion of the income received in the form of donated gifts-in-kind commodities and/or services used for overseas ministries. Please note that some agencies do not include gifts-in-kind as part of their financial audit process, so the value of such gifts may not be included in their income for overseas ministries. Gifts-in-kind amounts that were an insignificant percentage (usually less than one percent) are not shown as a separate item.

## Fully Supported U.S. Personnel Overseas

Since not all agencies have overseas personnel in the following categories, the above heading will not always appear. If applicable, the following lines will appear with the appropriate numbers:

• "Expecting to serve more than four years" for persons from the U.S. who are fully supported by the agency

• "Expecting to serve one up to four years" for persons from the U.S. who are fully supported by the agency

• "Nonresidential mission personnel" for fully supported U.S. mission personnel not residing in the country or countries of their ministry, but assigned to work and travel overseas at least twelve weeks per year on operational aspects of the overseas ministry

## Other Personnel

If applicable for the agency, the following lines will appear:

• "Non-USA serving in own/other country" for persons with either citizenship in their country of service or another non-U.S. country, who are fully or partially supported from the U.S. Such individuals are not included in the specific numbers for individual countries listed under the "Countries" heading at the bottom of many entries.

• "Bivocational/Tentmaker from USA" for persons sponsored or supervised by the agency, but who support themselves partially or fully through non-church/non-mission vocations and live overseas for the purpose of Christian witness and/or encouraging believers

• "Short-Term less than one year from USA" for persons who went on overseas projects or mission trips that lasted at least two weeks but less than one year through the agency, either fully or partially supported, or raising their own support

• "Home Ministry and office staff in USA" for persons assigned to ministry and/or office duties in the U.S. either as full-time or part-time paid staff/associates

## Countries

These are the countries where the agency sends U.S. personnel or regularly supports national or other non-U.S. personnel. Following the name of the country is the number of U.S. personnel with terms of service of four years or more.

In some cases, a continent or other general region is shown instead of a country. This may be due to several reasons, such as mission personnel whose ministry covers several countries.

Where an agency's work is maintained by nationals of countries other than the U.S. or Canada, or by personnel serving less than four years, the country of activity may be listed without a number. Refer to the chapter entitled "Countries of Activity for U.S. Protestant Agencies" for more detailed country personnel totals.

"Unspecified Country" may also be listed for security reasons.

**Note:** Since the time we gathered the information, "Serbia/Montenegro" has been divided into two separate countries: Montenegro and the Republic of Serbia. Our statistical information uses the combined status.

# Abundant Life Association, Inc.

PO Box 883
Mount Prospect, IL 60056 USA

**Phone:** (630) 539-5481
**Fax:** (630) 539-5482
**E-mail:** eldon@abundantlifeassociation.com
**Web Site:** www.abundantlifeassociation.com
**Associations:** AFMA

*Mr. Eldon L. Tracy, President*

A nondenominational sending agency of Charismatic and Pentecostal tradition engaged in rescuing children, adults and communities, discipleship, association of missions, childrens programs, church planting, development, Christian education, missionary education, leadership development, literacy work and missionary training.

**Purpose:** "…to take the whole Gospel to the whole world so that men and women, boys and girls might become disciples of Christ Jesus."

**Year founded in US:** 1997

**Income for Overseas Min:** $60,000

**Gifts in Kind:** $2,000

**Fully Supported US Personnel Overseas:**
Expecting to serve 1 to 4 years: 2
Non-residential mission personnel: 2

**Other Personnel:**
Bi-vocational/tentmakers: 2
Non-US serving in own/other country: 213
Home ministry & office staff in US: 2

**Countries:** Angola; Brazil; Guinea-Bissau; Luxembourg; Mozambique; Portugal; Sao Tome and Principe

# ABWE (Association of Baptists for World Evangelism)
(See ad on page 83)
PO Box 8585
Harrisburg, PA 17105-8585 USA

**Phone:** (717) 774-7000
**Fax:** (717) 774-1919
**E-mail:** abwe@abwe.org
**Web Site:** www.abwe.org

*Dr. Michael G. Loftis, President*

An independent Baptist sending agency engaged in evangelism, discipleship, church planting, theological education,medical work and tentmaking.

**Income for Overseas Min:** $41,000,000

**Fully Supported US Personnel Overseas:**
Expecting to serve more than 4 years: 599
Expecting to serve 1 to 4 years: 186
Non-residential mission personnel: 50

**Other Personnel:**
Short-term less than 1 year: 200
Bi-vocational/tentmakers: 60
Home ministry & office staff in US: 80

**Countries:** Africa—General 79; Asia—General 141; Brazil 60; Caribbean—General 20; Europe—General 160; South America—General 70; Unspecified Country 69

# ACM International

619 Washington St.
Terre Haute, IN 47802 USA

**Phone:** (812) 238-2883
**Fax:** (812) 235-6646
**E-mail:** acmedbuell@aol.com
**Web Site:** www.acmint.org

*Mr. Ed D. Buell, Dir. Spiritual Formation & Recruitment*

A nondenominational sending agency of Christian (Restoration Movement) tradition engaged in leadership development, aviation services, broadcasting, church planting, discipleship and TEE.

**Purpose:** "…to establish and edify churches of Christ in strategic populations of the world."

**Year founded in US:** 1947

**Income for Overseas Min:** $995,000

**Fully Supported US Personnel Overseas:**
Expecting to serve more than 4 years: 17
Expecting to serve 1 to 4 years: 2
Non-residential mission personnel: 2

**Other Personnel:**
Short-term less than 1 year: 6
Home ministry & office staff in US: 3

**Countries:** Asia—General; Kenya 5; Nigeria 2; Philippines 2; South Africa 2; Tanzania 4; United Kingdom 2

# Action Intl. Ministries

PO Box 398
Mountlake Terrace, WA 98043-0398 USA

**Phone:** (425) 775-4800
**Fax:** (425) 775-0634
**E-mail:** info@actionusa.org
**Web Site:** www.actionintl.org

*Mr. Rex Lee Carlaw, USA Dir.*

P.O. Box 8585 • Harrisburg, PA 17105
**717-774-7000** • **www.abwe.org**

# TO THE ENDS
## of the EARTH

## *Looking for multipliers.*

### *Those who will reproduce themselves in the spirit of II Timothy 2*

*Evangelizing, discipling, planting churches, training national leaders, and mobilizing missions movements since 1927.*

# MISSION INSURANCE.
## NOTHING ELSE.

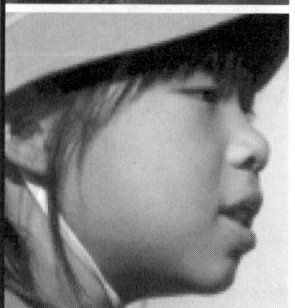

There's something to be said for insuring with a company that only offers mission-specific policies. For starters, our professionals are really specialists. They know the ins-and-outs of international insurance and travel hazards—and have helped thousands with unforeseen obstacles. That's why you place your trust in an insurance company in the first place, isn't it?

- Property Insurance Programs

- Mission Property & Casualty Program

- Volunteer Missionary Insurance Package

- Accident & Special Risk Insurance

- Group Medical Insurance

- Individual Medical Insurance

- Life Insurance & Related Products

- Automobile Insurance

## Adams & Associates®
### I N T E R N A T I O N A L

803.758.1400 • 800.922.8438 • Fax 803.252.1988

**www.aaintl.com**

A nondenominational sending agency of Evangelical tradition engaged in childrens programs, camping programs, development, literature distribution, medical work and relief and/or rehabilitation.

**Purpose:** "...to reach the masses for Christ, help individual Christians mature, and minister to the whole man, especially the poor..."

**Year founded in US:** 1974

**Income for Overseas Min:** $4,254,663

**Fully Supported US Personnel Overseas:**
Expecting to serve more than 4 years: 72
Expecting to serve 1 to 4 years: 7

**Other Personnel:**
Short-term less than 1 year: 26
Non-US serving in own/other country: 48
Home ministry & office staff in US: 14

**Countries:** Austria 1; Brazil 7; Cambodia 5; Colombia 3; Ecuador 3; Honduras 2; India 1; Malawi 2; Mexico 1; Philippines 29; Spain 3; Sri Lanka; Uganda 4; Ukraine 2; Zambia 9

## Advancing Indigenous Missions

PO Box 690042
San Antonio, TX 78269 USA
**Phone:** (830) 367-3513
**E-mail:** aim@omniglobal.net
*Mr. James W. Colley, Exec. Director, Exec. Dir.*

A transdenominational support agency of Charismatic and Evangelical tradition engaged in support of national churches, funds transmission and support of national workers.

**Purpose:** "...to plant churches...send missionaries to unreached peoples...evangelize the lost...train Christian workers...distribute Gospel literature and help people in need."

**Year founded in US:** 1990

**Personnel:**
Home ministry & office staff in US: 2

## Advancing Native Missions

PO Box 5303
Charlottesville, VA 22905 USA
**Phone:** (540) 456-7111
**Fax:** (540) 456-7222
**E-mail:** anm@adnamis.org
**Web Site:** www.adnamis.org
*Mr. Carl A. Gordon/Bo Barredo, Co-Pres./CEO*

An interdenominational support agency of

Evangelical tradition engaged in support of national workers, childcare/orphanage programs, funds transmission, support of national churches, relief and/or rehabilitation and mission-related research.

**Purpose:** "...to help take the Gospel of Jesus Christ to the world's remaining unreached peoples, standing behind 3,500 indigenous missionaries reaching their own people in more than 60 countries."

**Year founded in US:** 1992

**Income for Overseas Min:** $5,615,664

**Gifts in Kind:** $1,443,524

**Personnel:**
Short-term less than 1 year: 15
Home ministry & office staff in US: 28

## Advancing Renewal Ministries, Inc.

11616 Sir Francis Drake Dr.
Charlotte, NC 28277 USA
**Phone:** (704) 846-9355
**Fax:** (704) 846-9356
**E-mail:** arminc.@carolina.rr.com
**Web Site:** www.advancingrenewalministries.org
*Dr. Arthur M. Vincent, President*

A nondenominational sending agency of Lutheran and Charismatic tradition engaged in leadership development, Bible distribution, church planting, theological education, evangelism and support of national workers.

**Year founded in US:** 1983

**Income for Overseas Min:** $146,925

**Fully Supported US Personnel Overseas:**
Expecting to serve more than 4 years: 34

**Other Personnel:**
Non-US serving in own/other country: 34
Home ministry & office staff in US: 1

**Countries:** Africa —General 2; China 5; India 15; Japan 2; Kazakhstan 4; Laos 2; Nepal 2; Unspecified Country 2

## Advent Christian General Conf., Dept. of World Missions

PO Box 23152
Charlotte, NC 28227 USA
**Phone:** (704) 545-6161 x211
**Fax:** (704) 573-0712

**E-mail:** worldoutreach@acgc.us
**Web Site:** www.adventchristian.org
**Associations:** EFMA
*Rev. Ronald P. Thomas, Exec. Dir.*

A denominational sending agency of Adventist tradition engaged in ch. planting, TEE, theological education, evangelism, leadership dev. and support of national workers.

**Purpose:** "......to encourage, equip and empower Advent Christians worldwide to be obedient to His Great Commandment and Great Commission."

**Year founded in US:** 1865

**Income for Overseas Min:** $424,985

**Fully Supported US Personnel Overseas:**
Expecting to serve more than 4 years: 6
Non-residential mission personnel: 1

**Other Personnel:**
Short-term less than 1 year: 150
Non-US serving in own/other country: 159
Home ministry & office staff in US: 2

**Countries:** Croatia; Ghana; Honduras 1; India 2; Liberia; Malaysia; Mexico 1; Namibia; New Zealand; Nigeria; Philippines 2; South Africa

## Adventist World Aviation

PO Box 251
Berrien Springs, MI 49103-0251 USA
**Phone:** (269) 473-0135
**Fax:** (269) 471-4049
**E-mail:** info@flyawa.org
**Web Site:** www.flyawa.org
*Mr. Donald B. Starlin, President*

A denominational service agency of Adventist tradition engaged in missionary air service.

**Purpose:** "...to provide aviation and communications support to those serving the physical, mental and spiritual needs of the forgotten peoples of the earth."

**Year founded in US:** 1995

**Income for Overseas Min:** $717,276

**Gifts in Kind:** $60,850

**Fully Supported US Personnel Overseas:**
Expecting to serve more than 4 years: 5

**Other Personnel:**
Short-term less than 1 year: 3
Non-US serving in own/other country: 1
Home ministry & office staff in US: 1

**Countries:** Guyana 2; Philippines 3

## Adventures in Missions

6000 Wellspring Trail
Gainesville GA 30506 USA
**Phone:** (770) 983-5000
**Fax:** (770) 983-1061
**E-mail:** info@adventures.org
**Web Site:** www.adventures.org
*Mr. Seth Barnes, CEO*

An interdenominational sending agency engaged in missionary training, childcare/orphanage programs, evangelism, mobilization for mission, short-term programs and youth programs.

**Year founded in US:** 1989

**Income for Overseas Min:** $4,000,000

**Gifts in Kind:** $200,000

**Fully Supported US Personnel Overseas:**
Expecting to serve more than 4 years: 25
Expecting to serve 1 to 4 years: 5
Non-residential mission personnel: 30

**Other Personnel:**
Short-term less than 1 year: 500
Home ministry & office staff in US: 80

**Countries:** Dominican Republic 2; Kenya 3; Mexico 10; New Zealand 2; Swaziland 6; United Kingdom 2

## AFMA (Alliance for Missions Advancement)

PO Box 64534
Virginia Beach, VA 23467-4534 USA
**Phone:** (757) 226-5850
**Fax:** (757) 226-5851
**E-mail:** afma@aims.org
**Web Site:** www.theafma.org
*Dr. Howard Foltz, Founder/CEO*

A transdenominational association of missions for organizations and churches of Pentecostal and Charismatic tradition.

**Purpose:** "...to provide strategic and structured opportunities for its members to hear from God, network together, and share cutting-edge missions information."

## Africa Inland Mission Intl.

PO Box 178
Pearl River, NY 10965 USA
**Phone:** (845) 735-4014
**Fax:** (845) 735-1814
**E-mail:** go@aimint.net

**Web Site:** www.aim-us.org
**Associations:** IFMA
*Dr. W. Ted Barnett, U.S. Director*

A nondenominational sending agency of Evangelical and Independent tradition engaged in leadership development, church planting, development, Christian education, medical work and short-term programs.

**Purpose:** "...to reach Africa's unreached peoples with the Good News of Jesus Christ, working to develop leaders for a fast-growing church...and helping to meet the many physical and emotional needs facing Africa's peoples..."

**Year founded in US:** 1895
**Income for Overseas Min:** $16,266,000
**Fully Supported US Personnel Overseas:**
  Expecting to serve more than 4 years: 298
  Expecting to serve 1 to 4 years: 109
  Non-residential mission personnel: 10

**Other Personnel:**
  Short-term less than 1 year: 130
  Bi-vocational/tentmakers: 20
  Non-US serving in own/other country: 291
  Home ministry & office staff in US: 53

**Countries:** Africa—General 8; Angola 2; Australia; Central African Republic 1; Chad 4; Congo, Democratic Republic of 2; Kenya 185; Lesotho 1; Madagascar; Mozambique 21; Namibia 5; Rwanda; South Africa 5; Sudan; Tanzania 29; Uganda 16; United Kingdom 19

## Africa Inter-Mennonite Mission

PO Box 744
Goshen, IN 46527-0744 USA
**Phone:** (574) 535-0077
**Fax:** (574) 533-5275
**E-mail:** aimm@aimmintl.org
**Web Site:** www.aimmintl.org
*Rod Hollinger-Janzen, Executive Coordinator*

A denominational sending agency of Mennonite tradition engaged in church planting, evangelism, leadership development, linguistics, support of national churches and Bible translation. Statistical information from 2002.

**Purpose:** "...to make known the love of God in Jesus Christ to the people of Africa in ministries of word and deed, witness and service that God's people be brought to full stature in Christ."

**Year founded in US:** 1912
**Income for Overseas Min:** $696,591
**Fully Supported US Personnel Overseas:**
  Expecting to serve more than 4 years: 7
  Expecting to serve 1 to 4 years: 9

**Other Personnel:**
  Short-term less than 1 year: 16
  Non-US serving in own/other country: 12
  Home ministry & office staff in US: 2

**Countries:** Botswana 3; Burkina Faso 4; Senegal; South Africa

## African Bible Colleges, Inc.

PO Box 103
Clinton, MS 39060 USA
**Phone:** (601) 923-1679
**Fax:** (601) 924-6353
**E-mail:** ABCUSA@africanbiblecollege.com
**Web Site:** www.africanbiblecollege.com
*Rev. William L. Mosal, U.S. Director*

An interdenominational sending agency of Evangelical tradition engaged in leadership development, Bible distribution, broadcasting, correspondence courses, Christian education and evangelism. Data from 2001.

**Purpose:** "...to further evangelical Christian education through establishment and funding of Bible colleges in Africa and the acquisition of Christian teachers for African schools and colleges."

**Year founded in US:** 1977
**Income for Overseas Min:** $1,007,862
**Fully Supported US Personnel Overseas:**
  Expecting to serve more than 4 years: 14
  Expecting to serve 1 to 4 years: 12

**Other Personnel:**
  Non-US serving in own/other country: 25
  Home ministry & office staff in US: 2

**Countries:** Malawi 14; Uganda

## African Enterprise

PO Box 727
Monrovia, CA 91017 USA
**Phone:** (626) 357-8811
**Fax:** (626) 359-2069
**E-mail:** info@aeusa.org
**Web Site:** www.africanenterprise.org
**Associations:** EFMA
*Mr. Malcolm Graham, Exec. Director*

An interdenominational support agency of Evangelical tradition engaged in evangelism, development, leadership development, relief and/or rehabilitation and missionary training.

**Purpose:** "To evangelize the cities of Africa through Word & Deed in partnership with the Church."

**Year founded in US:** 1962

**Income for Overseas Min:** $429,660

**Personnel:**
  Short-term less than 1 year: 10
  Bi-vocational/tentmakers: 5
  Non-US serving in own/other country: 73
  Home ministry & office staff in US: 10

**Countries:** Congo, Republic of; Ethiopia; Ghana; Kenya; Malawi; Rwanda; South Africa; Tanzania; Uganda; Zimbabwe

## African Leadership, Inc.

PO Box 682444
Franklin, TN 37068-2444 USA

**Phone:** (615) 595-8238
**Fax:** (615) 595-7906
**E-mail:** info@africanleadership.org
**Web Site:** www.africanleadership.org

*Mr. Larry C. Warren, President/Founder*

A nondenominational support agency of Evangelical tradition engaged in pastor training, childcare/orphanage programs, development, Christian education, theological education and relief and/or rehabilitation.

**Purpose:** "...a Christian education, relief and development organization that offers Biblical training for church leaders across Africa, endeavoring to meet the physical needs of the poor in the communities where we provide instruction."

**Year founded in US:** 2000

**Income for Overseas Min:** $1,344,903

**Gifts in Kind:** $256,350

**Fully Supported US Personnel Overseas:**
  Non-residential mission personnel: 3

**Other Personnel:**
  Short-term less than 1 year: 4
  Non-US serving in own/other country: 23
  Home ministry & office staff in US: 10

**Countries:** Angola; Congo, Republic of; Ethiopia; Ghana; Kenya; Liberia; Malawi; Mozambique; Nigeria; Rwanda; Sierra Leone; South Africa; Sudan; Tanzania; Uganda; Zimbabwe

## African Methodist Episcopal Church, Dept. Global Witness

PO Box 20852
Charleston, SC 29413-0852 USA

**Phone:** (843) 852-2645
**Fax:** (843) 852-2648
**E-mail:** gwm@bellsouth.net
**Web Site:** www.globalmissions.com
**Associations:** CWS

*Rev. George F. Flowers, Exec. Director*

A denominational support agency of African Methodist Episcopal tradition engaged in partnership development, Bible distribution, evangelism, providing medical supplies, missionary training and technical assistance.

**Purpose:** "...ministry, witness and gospel proclamation so that people of God may be liberated spiritually and materially and reconciled to each other through the Holy Spirit."

**Year founded in US:** 1787

**Income for Overseas Min:** $104,956

**Gifts in Kind:** $62,000

**Personnel:**
  Home ministry & office staff in US: 2

## African Mission Evangelism, Inc.

2313 Bell Dr.
Knoxville, TN 37998 USA

**Phone:** (865) 579-1467
**Fax:** (865) 251-2258
**E-mail:** cbridges@jbc.edu
**Web Site:** www.ameghana.org

*Dr. Carl B. Bridges, President*

A nondenominational sending agency of Christian (Restoration Movement) tradition engaged in theological education and church planting.

**Year founded in US:** 1968

**Income for Overseas Min:** $585,761

**Fully Supported US Personnel Overseas:**
  Expecting to serve more than 4 years: 9

**Other Personnel:**
  Short-term less than 1 year: 15
  Non-US serving in own/other country: 15

**Countries:** Ghana 9

## Agape Gospel Mission

PO Box 1458

Manassas, VA 20108-1458 USA
**Phone:** (703) 361-3331
**Fax:** (703) 310-7551
**E-mail:** admin@agapegospelmission.org
**Web Site:** www.agapegospelmission.org
**Associations:** AFMA
*Rev. Richard C. Whitcomb, President*

A nondenominational sending agency engaged in evangelism, broadcasting, childcare/orphanage programs, church planting, theological education and leadership development.
**Year founded in US:** 1982
**Fully Supported US Personnel Overseas:**
  Expecting to serve more than 4 years: 2
**Other Personnel:**
  Short-term less than 1 year: 10
  Non-US serving in own/other country: 83
  Home ministry & office staff in US: 3
**Countries:** Benin; Ghana 2; Liberia; Nigeria

# AIMS (Accelerating International Mission Strategies)

PO Box 64534
Virginia Beach, VA 23467-4534 USA
**Phone:** (757) 226-5850
**Fax:** (757) 226-5851
**E-mail:** aims@aims.org
**Web Site:** www.aims.org
**Associations:** AFMA
*Dr. Howard Foltz, CEO/Founder*

A transdenominational support agency engaged in mobilization for mission, missionary training, association of missions, church planting and evangelism.
**Purpose:** "…Empowering the Church to take the Gospel where it has never been proclaimed…"
**Year founded in US:** 1985
**Income for Overseas Min:** $448,004
**Gifts in Kind:** $24,786
**Fully Supported US Personnel Overseas:**
  Expecting to serve more than 4 years: 1
**Other Personnel:**
  Short-term less than 1 year: 18
  Bi-vocational/tentmakers: 1
  Home ministry & office staff in US: 6
**Countries:** Asia—General 1

# Alberto Mottesi Evangelistic Association

PO Box 6290
Santa Ana, CA 92706 USA
**Phone:** (714) 265-0400
**Fax:** (714) 265-0444
**E-mail:** info@albertomottesi.org
**Web Site:** www.albertomottesi.org
*Dr. Alberto H. Mottesi, President*

An interdenominational service agency of Evangelical tradition engaged in evangelism, broadcasting, leadership development and family restoration in crusades, etc., in Latin America, the USA and Europe. Data from 2001.
**Year founded in US:** 1977
**Personnel:**
  Home ministry & office staff in US: 7

# All God's Children Int'l.

3308 NE Peerless Place
Portland, OR 97232 USA
**Phone:** (503) 282-7652
**Fax:** (503) 282-2582
**E-mail:** info@allgodschildren.org
**Web Site:** www.allgodschildren.org
*Mr. Ron Beazely, President*

A nondenominational service agency of Baptist tradition engaged in adoption, childrens programs and relief and/or rehabilitation.
**Year founded in US:** 1991
**Income for Overseas Min:** $3,500,000
**Fully Supported US Personnel Overseas:**
  Expecting to serve 1 to 4 years: 3
**Other Personnel:**
  Non-US serving in own/other country: 181
  Home ministry & office staff in US: 28
**Countries:** China; Guatemala; Kazakhstan; Nepal; Vietnam

# Allegheny Wesleyan Methodist Connection— Missions Department

PO Box 357
Salem, OH 44460 USA
**Phone:** (330) 337-9376
**Fax:** (330) 337-9700
**E-mail:** awmc@juno.com
**Web Site:** www.awmchurch.org

*Rev. William M. Cope, President*

A denominational sending agency of Wesleyan tradition engaged in Christian education, church construction, church planting, theological education, funds transmission and support of national workers.

**Purpose:** "...to recruit and send missionaries, collect and disburse funds, receive and invest annuities, dispatch information and acquire property, real or personal, as may be convenient."

**Year founded in US:** 1843

**Income for Overseas Min:** $399,514

**Fully Supported US Personnel Overseas:**
  Expecting to serve more than 4 years: 18
  Expecting to serve 1 to 4 years: 1

**Other Personnel:**
  Home ministry & office staff in US: 5

**Countries:** Ghana 3; Haiti 11; Peru 4

## ALM International
## See: American Leprosy Missions, Inc.

## Alongside Ministries Intl.

PO Box 504
Walnut Creek, CA 94597-0504 USA
**Phone:** (925) 280-6055
**Fax:** (925) 280-5577
**E-mail:** alongside@alongside.org
**Web Site:** www.alongside.org

*Margie Gilchrist, Exec. Director*

An interdenominational sending agency of Evangelical tradition engaged in support of national churches, discipleship, evangelism, leadership development, partnership development and short-term programs.

**Purpose:** "...to encourage and empower Christian leaders and churches through an international network of prayer, partnership and practical help."

**Year founded in US:** 1983

**Income for Overseas Min:** $602,372

**Fully Supported US Personnel Overseas:**
  Expecting to serve more than 4 years: 7
  Expecting to serve 1 to 4 years: 10

**Other Personnel:**
  Short-term less than 1 year: 17
  Non-US serving in own/other country: 3
  Home ministry & office staff in US: 4

**Countries:** Albania 3; Estonia 2; France 2; United Kingdom

## Alongside, Inc.

PO Box 587
Richland, MI 49083-0587 USA
**Phone:** (269) 671-4809
**Fax:** (269) 671-4977
**E-mail:** info@alongsidecares.net
**Web Site:** www.alongsidecares.net

*Jeanne L. Jensma, Exec. Director*

A nondenominational specialized agency of Evangelical tradition engaged in psychological counseling and member care.

**Purpose:** "...to restore hope, purpose, passion and relationships among Christian leaders who are making an impact around the world."

**Year founded in US:** 1984

**Personnel:**
  Home ministry & office staff in US: 2

## Amazon Focus

PO Box 5008
Florence, SC 29502 USA
**Phone:** (843) 676-0659
**Fax:** (843) 661-7458
**E-mail:** info@amazonfocus.com
**Web Site:** www.amazonfocus.com

*Greg Stuckey, CEO*

A nondenominational sending agency of Evangelical tradition engaged in development, leadership development, medical work, support of national churches, support of national workers and short-term programs. Statistical data from 2002.

**Purpose:** "...to empower and equip the indigenous tribes in the Amazon basin to assume responsibility for their long-term spiritual, economic and survival needs."

**Year founded in US:** 1995

**Income for Overseas Min:** $170,015

**Fully Supported US Personnel Overseas:**
  Expecting to serve more than 4 years: 4
  Non-residential mission personnel: 2

**Other Personnel:**
  Short-term less than 1 year: 30
  Non-US serving in own/other country: 29
  Home ministry & office staff in US: 7

**Countries:** Belize; Bolivia; Peru 4

## Ambassadors for Christ Intl.

PO Box 470
Tucker, GA 30085 USA
**Phone:** (678) 406-9669
**Fax:** (770) 621-9588
**E-mail:** info@afciworld.org
**Web Site:** www.afcinternational.org
*Rev. Paul Hanak, Intl. Director*

A nondenominational support agency of Evangelical tradition engaged in training, support of national workers and evangelism.

**Purpose:** "...to support spiritually gifted preachers and Bible teachers to reach their homelands for Jesus Christ."

**Year founded in US:** 1972

**Income for Overseas Min:** $1,000,000

**Personnel:**
  Home ministry & office staff in US: 9

## Ambassadors for Christ, Inc.

21 Ambassador Dr.
Paradise, PA 17562 USA
**Phone:** (717) 687-8564
**E-mail:** AFC@afcinc.org
**Web Site:** www.afcinc.org
*Mr. David Chow, Exec. Director*

A nondenominational support agency of Evangelical tradition engaged in translation and distribution of English language books into Chinese, Bible distribution, literature production and partnership development.

**Purpose:** "...to evangelize and disciple Chinese students and professionals in the United States, and other parts of the world, to motivate and equip them to impact the culture for the Lord."

**Year founded in US:** 1964

**Income for Overseas Min:** $135,000

**Personnel:**
  Short-term less than 1 year: 2
  Home ministry & office staff in US: 13

## American Association of Lutheran Churches— Commission for World Missions

801 W. 106th St., #203
Minneapolis, MN 55420-5603 USA
**Phone:** (952) 884-7784
**Fax:** (952) 884-7894
**E-mail:** theaalc@taalc.org
**Web Site:** www.taalc.org
*Rev. Orlando Hash, Chairman*

A denominational support agency of Lutheran tradition engaged in funds transmission, church planting, member care, relief and/or rehabilitation and Bible translation.

**Year founded in US:** 1987

**Income for Overseas Min:** $45,000

**Personnel:**
  Home ministry & office staff in US: 4

## American Baptist Churches of the U.S.A., Intl. Ministries

PO Box 851
Valley Forge, PA 19482-0851 USA
**Phone:** (800) 222-3872
**Fax:** (610) 768-2115
**E-mail:** Patricia.Williams@abc-usa.org
**Web Site:** www.internationalministries.org
**Associations:** CWS
*Mr. Reid S. Trulson, Exec. Director*

A denominational sending agency of Baptist tradition engaged in partnership development, community development, theological education, evangelism, leadership development and medical work.

**Purpose:** "...to glorify God in all the earth by crossing cultural boundaries to make disciples of Jesus Christ."

**Year founded in US:** 1814

**Income for Overseas Min:** $18,837,737

**Fully Supported US Personnel Overseas:**
  Expecting to serve more than 4 years: 59
  Non-residential mission personnel: 2

**Other Personnel:**
  Short-term less than 1 year: 68
  Non-US serving in own/other country: 15
  Home ministry & office staff in US: 40

**Countries:** Bahamas, The 1; Belgium 2; Bolivia 2; Brazil 4; Bulgaria 3; Chile 2; China 1; Congo, Democratic Republic of 13; Costa Rica 3; Cuba 1; Czech Republic; Dominican Republic 1; El Salvador; Haiti 2; India 4; Mexico 6; Nepal 2; Philippines 2; South Africa 2; United Kingdom; Unspecified Country 6; Zambia 2

## American Bible Society
**(See ad on page 93)**
1865 Broadway
New York, NY 10023 USA
**Phone:** (212) 408-1200
**E-mail:** info@americanbible.org
**Web Site:** www.americanbible.org
*Paul G. Irwin, President*

An interdenominational specialized service agency engaged in Scripture translation, publication and distribution in fellowship with 135 members of the United Bible Societies and other Bible Society offices operating in approximately 200 countries and territories.

**Purpose:** "...to make the Bible available to every person in a language and format each can understand and afford, so all people may experience its life-changing message."

**Year founded in US:** 1816
**Personnel:**
   Home ministry & office staff in US: 280

## American Council of the Ramabai Mukti Mission, Inc.
PO Box 4912
Clinton, NJ 08809-0912 USA
**Phone:** (908) 735-8770
**Fax:** (908) 638-3113
**E-mail:** mukti1@eclipse.net
**Web Site:** www.ramabaimuktimission.com
**Associations:** IFMA
*Rev. David L. Scott, Exec. Director*

A nondenominational support agency of Evangelical tradition engaged in childcare/orphanage programs, church planting, development, disability assistance programs, Christian education, support of national workers and short-term programs.

**Year founded in US:** 1889
**Income for Overseas Min:** $380,819
**Personnel:**
   Short-term less than 1 year: 3
   Non-US serving in own/other country: 2
   Home ministry & office staff in US: 3
**Countries:** India

## American Leprosy Missions, Inc.
1 ALM Way
Greenville, SC 29601 USA
**Phone:** (800) 537-7679
**Fax:** (864) 271-7062
**E-mail:** amlep@leprosy.org
**Web Site:** www.leprosy.org
*Mr. Christopher J. Doyle, President/CEO*

A nondenominational specialized agency of Evangelical tradition engaged in public health and medical work, development, disability assistance programs, providing medical supplies, relief and/or rehabilitation and technical assistance.

**Purpose:** "...to serve as a channel of Christ's love to persons affected by leprosy and related conditions, helping them to be healed in body and spirit and restored to lives of dignity and hope."

**Year founded in US:** 1906
**Income for Overseas Min:** $5,038,555
**Fully Supported US Personnel Overseas:**
   Expecting to serve more than 4 years: 1
   Non-residential mission personnel: 3
**Other Personnel:**
   Non-US serving in own/other country: 7
   Home ministry & office staff in US: 20
**Countries:** Angola; Brazil 1; Congo, Democratic Republic of; India; Myanmar/Burma; Philippines

## American Missionary Fellowship
672 Conestoga Rd.
Villanova, PA 19085 USA
**Phone:** (610) 527-4439
**Fax:** (610) 527-4720
**E-mail:** info@americanmissionary.org
**Web Site:** www.americanmissionary.org
**Associations:** IFMA
*Dr. Lee K. Iseley, Gen. Director*

A nondenominational support agency of Evangelical and Independent tradition engaged in camping programs, church establishing, discipleship, evangelism, support of national churches and youth programs in the USA leading to overseas missions.

**Purpose:** "...to evangelize, disciple and congregate the yet-unreached peoples of the United States for Jesus Christ."

**Year founded in US:** 1817
**Personnel:**
   Home ministry & office staff in US: 18

*Reach them with the Word of God in Their Language*

**Bibles.org** is your source for Scripture Resources
in the most languages and translations
for your U.S. and overseas work.

# BIBLES.ORG

*An American Bible Society Ministry*

**CALL: 1-800-32-BIBLE FOR A FREE CATALOG OR VISIT US ONLINE AT WWW.BIBLES.ORG**

The First Peoples of the Americas shouldn't be the last to hear!

# AMERITRIBES

- closely partnering with sending churches
- team approach to ministry
- focus on tribal peoples of western U.S. and Mexico
- servant evangelism through community development leading to the establishment of indigenous churches

Informative Brochure and Video Available
AmeriTribes, P.O. Box 27346, Tucson, AZ 85726-7346
Phone: (520) 670-9400  Fax: (520) 670-9444
E-mail: info@ameritribes.org

## American Scripture Gift Mission Inc. (SGM USA)

7862 W. Irlo Bronson Hwy., PMB 240
Melbourne, FL 34747 USA
**Phone:** (321) 255-7774
**Fax:** (321) 255-8986
**E-mail:** asgm@asgm.com
**Web Site:** www.asgm.com
*Mr. James R. Powell, Chairman*

A nondenominational support agency of Evangelical tradition distributing all-Scripture booklets and tracts in more than 400 languages, primarily for evangelism. The USA branch of SGM International, London, England. Data from 2001.

**Year founded in US:** 1937
**Income for Overseas Min:** $1,000
**Personnel:**
   Home ministry & office staff in US: 1

## AmeriTribes

**(See ad on page 94)**
PO Box 27346
Tucson, AZ 85726 USA
**Phone:** (520) 670-9400
**Fax:** (520) 670-9444
**E-mail:** info@ameritribes.org
**Web Site:** www.ameritribes.org
**Associations:** IFMA
*Mr. Timothy C. Brown, Exec. Director*

A nondenominational sending agency of Evangelical tradition engaged in church planting, camping programs, development, discipleship, literacy work and medical work.

**Purpose:** "...facilitating the development of reproducing, indigenous churches among tribal peoples of the Americas."

**Year founded in US:** 1944
**Income for Overseas Min:** $323,042

**Fully Supported US Personnel Overseas:**
   Expecting to serve more than 4 years: 8
   Non-residential mission personnel: 1

**Other Personnel:**
   Short-term less than 1 year: 3
   Home ministry & office staff in US: 16

**Countries:** Mexico 8

## AMF International

PO Box 5470
Lansing, IL 60438 USA
**Phone:** (708) 418-0020
**Fax:** (708) 418-0132
**E-mail:** office@amfi.org
**Web Site:** www.amfi.org
**Associations:** IFMA
*Mr. Wesley N. Taber, Exec. Director*

A sending agency of Evangelical tradition engaged in evangelism, Bible distribution, discipleship, literature distribution, short-term programs, training and missionary training.

**Purpose:** "Building bridges of understanding between Jewish and Christian communities for over 100 years."

**Year founded in US:** 1887
**Income for Overseas Min:** $147,183
**Gifts in Kind:** $330

**Fully Supported US Personnel Overseas:**
   Expecting to serve more than 4 years: 3
   Non-residential mission personnel: 1

**Other Personnel:**
   Short-term less than 1 year: 8
   Bi-vocational/tentmakers: 4
   Non-US serving in own/other country: 5
   Home ministry & office staff in US: 20

**Countries:** France; Israel 2; Netherlands 1

## AMG International

6815 Shallowford Rd.
Chattanooga, TN 37421 USA
**Phone:** (423) 894-6060
**Fax:** (423) 894-6863
**E-mail:** missions@amginternational.org
**Web Site:** www.amginternational.org
*Mr. Paul E. Jenks, President*

An interdenominational sending agency of Baptist and Evangelical tradition engaged in childcare/orphanage programs, broadcasting, church planting, theological education, evangelism and support of national workers.

**Purpose:** "...to give every person on earth at least one chance to hear and respond to a clear presentation of the Gospel...to express the compassion of Christ as the Lord gives us opportunity and means to do so...to serve the pastor and his local church, and to inform, challenge and encourage God's people in their worldwide responsibility."

**Year founded in US:** 1942
**Income for Overseas Min:** $5,015,203

**Fully Supported US Personnel Overseas:**
Expecting to serve more than 4 years: 14
Expecting to serve 1 to 4 years: 7

**Other Personnel:**
Short-term less than 1 year: 7
Non-US serving in own/other country: 8,307
Home ministry & office staff in US: 47

**Countries:** Albania; Argentina; Australia; Bangladesh; Brazil; Bulgaria; Cuba; Cyprus; Ghana; Greece 6; Guatemala; Haiti; India; Indonesia; Italy 2; Kosovo 2; Lebanon; Mexico 3; Mozambique; Myanmar/Burma; Peru; Philippines; Romania; Spain 1; Thailand; Turkey; Uganda

## AMOR Ministries

1664 Precision Park Ln.
San Diego, CA 92713 USA
**Phone:** (619) 662-1200
**Fax:** (619) 662-1295
**E-mail:** missionservices@amor.org
**Web Site:** www.amor.org
**Associations:** AERDO
*Mr. Scott Congdon, Founder/CEO*

A nondenominational sending agency of Evangelical tradition engaged in development, support of national churches, partnership development, relief and/or rehabilitation and short-term programs.
**Year founded in US:** 1980
**Income for Overseas Min:** $4,250,000
**Fully Supported US Personnel Overseas:**
Expecting to serve 1 to 4 years: 37

**Other Personnel:**
Non-US serving in own/other country: 10
Home ministry & office staff in US: 24
**Countries:** Mexico

## Anglican Frontier Missions

PO Box 18038
Richmond, VA 23226-8038 USA
**Phone:** (804) 355-8468
**Fax:** (804) 355-8260
**E-mail:** info@afm-us.org
**Web Site:** www.afm-us.org
*Rev. E. A. de Bordenave, Director*

A denominational sending agency of Anglican and Evangelical tradition engaged in strategic coordination leading to church planting, evangelism, partnership develop-

ment, mobilization for mission and mission-related research.
**Purpose:** "...to plant indigenous churches among the least evangelized people groups of the world."
**Year founded in US:** 1993
**Income for Overseas Min:** $497,121
**Fully Supported US Personnel Overseas:**
Expecting to serve more than 4 years: 9
Expecting to serve 1 to 4 years: 2

**Other Personnel:**
Short-term less than 1 year: 2
Bi-vocational/tentmakers: 4
Non-US serving in own/other country: 6
Home ministry & office staff in US: 4
**Countries:** Asia—General 5; Middle East 4; Uganda

## Anis Shorrosh Evangelistic Association

PO Box 949
Fairhope, AL 36533 USA
**Phone:** (251) 680-7770
**Fax:** (251) 626-1124
**E-mail:** asea777@truth-in-crisis.com
**Web Site:** www.islam-exposed.org
*Dr. Anis Shorrosh, Evangelist*

An interdenominational support agency of Baptist tradition engaged in evangelism, apologetics, audio recording/distribution, broadcasting and literature production.
**Year founded in US:** 1971
**Fully Supported US Personnel Overseas:**
Expecting to serve more than 4 years: 155

**Other Personnel:**
Short-term less than 1 year: 5
Home ministry & office staff in US: 4
**Countries:** India 35; Israel 40; Jordan 40; Palestine 40

## Apostolic Christian Church Foundation, Inc.— Missionary Committee

1135 Sholey Rd.
Richmond, VA 23231 USA
**Phone:** (804) 222-1943
**Fax:** (804) 236-0642
**E-mail:** info@accm.org
**Web Site:** www.accm.org
*Mr. Jim Hodges, Exec. Dir.*

# The bottom line of study at Alliance Graduate School of Mission: who I am becoming matters as much as what I am doing in the task of mission.

I left for Mali, West Africa as a missionary with great intercultural communication theory. But theory was like an unsharpened machete: I found I needed the experience of interacting with people from cultures and social structures different than my own. Mali became my laboratory, and I began to imagine a preparation process that encompassed both theory *and* practice.

Intercultural Studies at AGSM provides excellent academic preparation while living in the intercultural capital of the world—New York City! Students move beyond *talking* about poor people. Students begin *engaging* people whose lives are daily on the edge, or by eating naan and lentils with the local Mosque's Sufi Imam, or by ministering among recently arrived immigrant populations.

Through coaching by experienced professors and peer mentoring, we ask the challenging developmental questions that will prepare the student as person before servant. The bottom line of study at AGSM: *who I am becoming matters as much as what I am doing* in the task of mission.

I can think of no better environment in which to become what you are learning to do.

**Chuck Davis**
*Professor of Intercultural Studies*

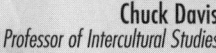

## NYACK

*Alliance Graduate School of Mission*
www.alliance.edu • 1-800-541-6891

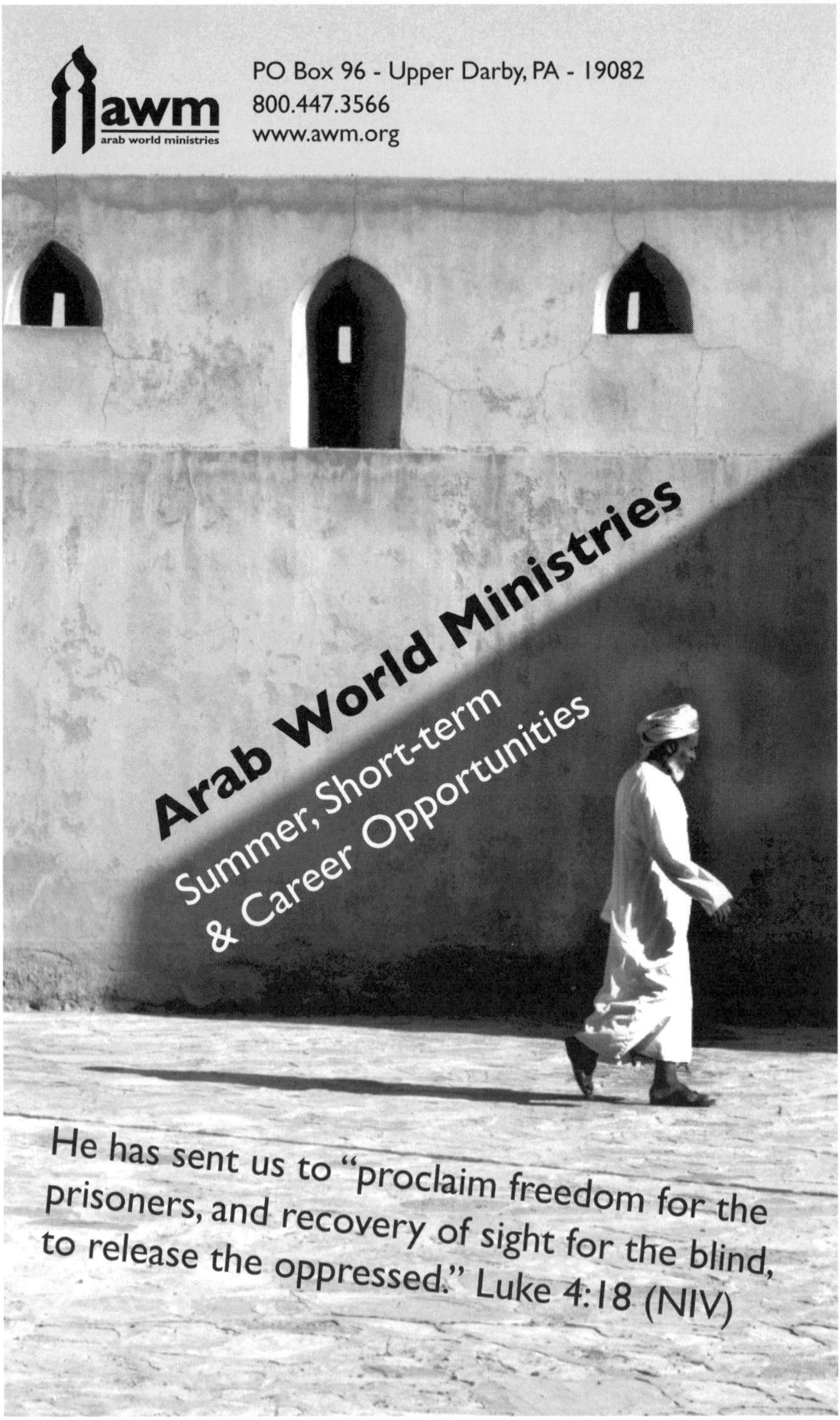

**awm**
arab world ministries

PO Box 96 - Upper Darby, PA - 19082
800.447.3566
www.awm.org

# Arab World Ministries

## Summer, Short-term & Career Opportunities

He has sent us to "proclaim freedom for the prisoners, and recovery of sight for the blind, to release the oppressed." Luke 4:18 (NIV)

A denominational sending agency of Anabaptist tradition engaged in funds transmission, church construction, relief aid, support of national workers and evangelism. Personnel data from 1998. Financial data from 2001.

**Purpose:** "...exists to help fulfill Christ's Commission by sending out members of the AC Church who are called by God to become foreign missionaries."

**Year founded in US:** 1953

**Income for Overseas Min:** $763,358

**Fully Supported US Personnel Overseas:**
Expecting to serve more than 4 years: 31

**Other Personnel:**
Non-US serving in own/other country: 24
Home ministry & office staff in US: 2

**Countries:** Argentina 1; Australia 2; Brazil 17; Czech Republic 1; Indonesia 2; Japan 2; Mexico 1; Papua New Guinea 2; Paraguay 1; Puerto Rico 2

## Apostolic Team Ministries, Intl.
529 North Walnut Street
Celina, OH 45822 USA
**Phone:** (419) 586-1095
**E-mail:** info@atmintl.org
**Web Site:** www.atmintl.org
*Rev. Bill Lewis, Admin. Dir.*

A nondenominational support agency of Charismatic tradition engaged in church planting and missionary training. Missionary personnel and financial information from 1998.

**Year founded in US:** 1980

**Income for Overseas Min:** $200,000

**Fully Supported US Personnel Overseas:**
Expecting to serve more than 4 years: 15

**Other Personnel:**
Non-US serving in own/other country: 8
Home ministry & office staff in US: 3

**Countries:** Albania 5; Bolivia 2; Brazil 2; France 4; United Kingdom 2

## Arab World Ministries
(See ad page 98)
PO Box 96
Upper Darby, PA 19083 USA
**Phone:** (800) 447-3566
**Fax:** (610) 352-2652
**E-mail:** awmusa@awm.org

**Web Site:** www.awm.org
**Associations:** IFMA
*Mr. Robert W. Sayer, U.S. Director*

An interdenominational sending agency of Evangelical tradition engaged in church planting, broadcasting, correspondence courses, TEE, tentmaking and video/film production/distribution.

**Purpose:** "...to exalt Jesus Christ through word and deed, making disciples and establishing mature, multiplying churches among Muslims of the Arab world wherever they reside."

**Year founded in US:** 1952

**Income for Overseas Min:** $5,287,763

**Fully Supported US Personnel Overseas:**
Expecting to serve more than 4 years: 110
Expecting to serve 1 to 4 years: 19

**Other Personnel:**
Short-term less than 1 year: 66
Bi-vocational/tentmakers: 10
Non-US serving in own/other country: 12
Home ministry & office staff in US: 30

**Countries:** Asia—General: 110

## ARISE International Mission
(See ad page 101)
PO Box 1014
College Park, MD 20741 USA
**Phone:** (301) 395-2385
**E-mail:** aim21century@yahoo.com
**Web Site:** www.arise-mission.org
*Rev. C. Daniel Kim, Director*

A support agency of Evangelical tradition engaged in leadership development, literature distribution, support of national workers and short-term programs.

**Purpose:** "...to evangelize the world with the Gospel of the Kingdom...reach the regions where the Gospel is most needed and equip and train Christian leaders/workers in overseas ministry."

**Year founded in US:** 1990

**Income for Overseas Min:** $72,000

**Gifts in Kind:** $12,000

**Personnel:**
Short-term less than 1 year: 3
Non-US serving in own/other country: 3
Home ministry & office staff in US: 4

## Armenian Missionary Association of America, Inc.

31 West Century Rd.
Paramus, NJ 07652 USA
**Phone:** (201) 265-2607
**Fax:** (201) 265-6015
**E-mail:** amaa@amaa.org
**Web Site:** www.amaa.org
*Mr. Andrew Torigian, Exec. Dir.*

A nondenominational service agency of Evangelical and Congregational tradition engaged in childrens programs, Bible distribution, camping programs, church planting, theological education and evangelism. Data from 2001.

**Year founded in US:** 1918
**Income for Overseas Min:** $3,285,018
**Gifts in Kind:** $247,023
**Fully Supported US Personnel Overseas:**
  Expecting to serve more than 4 years: 4
  Expecting to serve 1 to 4 years: 1
  Non-residential mission Personnel: 4
**Other Personnel:**
  Short-term less than 1 year: 30
  Non-US serving in own/other country: 4
  Home ministry & office staff in US: 12
**Countries:** Armenia 2; Lebanon 2

## Artists In Christian Testimony

PO Box 1649
Brentwood, TN 37024-1649 USA
**Phone:** (615) 376-7861
**Fax:** (615) 376-7863
**E-mail:** info@actinternational.org
**Web Site:** www.actinternational.org
*Rev. Byron L. Spradlin, President*

An interdenominational sending agency of Evangelical and Independent tradition engaged in arts in ministry and missions.
**Purpose:** "...to develop and deploy culture-sensitive arts missionaries and ministries throughout the world to grow and glorify Christ's Kingdom."
**Year founded in US:** 1973
**Income for Overseas Min:** $200,150
**Fully Supported US Personnel Overseas:**
  Expecting to serve more than 4 years: 14
  Expecting to serve 1 to 4 years: 2
**Other Personnel:**
  Short-term less than 1 year: 6

  Bi-vocational/tentmakers: 47
  Non-US serving in own/other country: 4
  Home ministry & office staff in US: 4
**Countries:** Brazil 4; Germany 1; Ghana; Hungary 1; India 1; Israel 2; Kenya 2; Russia 1; United Kingdom 2

## Asian Access

**(See ad page 102)**
PO Box 200
San Dimas, CA 91773 USA
**Phone:** (626) 914-8990
**Fax:** (626) 914-9572
**E-mail:** info@asianaccess.org
**Web Site:** www.asianaccess.org
**Associations:** EFMA
*Rev. S. Douglas Birdsall, President*

An interdenominational sending agency of Evangelical tradition engaged in leadership development, evangelism and church plantings.
**Purpose:** "...to strengthen and start Japanese churches in partnership with visionary pastors and congregations through innovation in evangelism and leadership training."
**Year founded in US:** 1967
**Income for Overseas Min:** $3,547,230
**Fully Supported US Personnel Overseas:**
  Expecting to serve more than 4 years: 21
  Expecting to serve 1 to 4 years: 8
**Other Personnel:**
  Short-term less than 1 year: 27
  Non-US serving in own/other country: 7
  Home ministry & office staff in US: 15
**Countries:** Cambodia; India; Japan 17; Mongolia; Myanmar/Burma; Nepal; Sri Lanka; Unspecified Country 4

## Asian Outreach U.S.A.

305 NE 192nd Ave.
Vancouver, WA 98684 USA
**Phone:** (360) 883-2421
**Fax:** (360) 893-8914
**E-mail:** mscheelsaousa@earthlink.net
**Web Site:** www.asianoutreach.org
*Mrs. Meghan Scheels, Exec. Director*

A nondenominational support agency of Evangelical and Charismatic tradition engaged in church planting, Bible distribution, correspondence courses, theological education, evangelism, leadership develop-

# *Arise*

## INTERNATIONAL MISSION

# Awake
# Renew
# Intercede
# Send
# Equip

### VISION
*To reach the least evangelized world.*
*To equip and train Christian leaders overseas.*
*To encourage and support national ministries involved in pioneering work.*

### MINISTRIES
**Emmanuel Training Institute:** Spiritual formation/training
**Century Intercession Ministry:** Prayer ministry for nations
**Dayspring Tech:** Technical Assistance

 *Arise*
## INTERNATIONAL MISSION

P.O. BOX 1014 • COLLEGE PARK, MD 20741

**(301) 395-2385**

**WWW.ARISE-MISSION.ORG**

# Developing shepherds to lead a movement

ASIAN ACCESS: CELEBRATING **40** YEARS IN ASIA

Developing Leaders. Multiplying Churches.

P.O. Box 200, San Dimas, CA 91773 USA
web: www.asianaccess.org • email: info@asianaccess.org • telephone: 1-800-543-3678

ment, literature distribution, literature production, short-term programs and training. Data from 2001.

**Purpose:** "…winning Asians to Christ."

**Year founded in US:** 1965

**Income for Overseas Min:** $790,000

**Personnel:**
Short-term less than 1 year: 40
Home ministry & office staff in US: 1

## Assemblies of God World Missions

1445 Boonville Ave.
Springfield, MO 65802 USA

**Phone:** (417) 862-2781 x3050
**Fax:** (417) 862-5274
**Web Site:** www.ag.org/worldmissions
**Associations:** EFMA

*Rev. L. John Bueno, Exec. Director*

A denominational sending agency of Pentecostal tradition engaged in church planting, Bible distribution, childrens programs, extension education, theological education, evangelism, leadership development, literature production/distribution, missionary training, relief and medical work.

**Purpose:** "…proclaiming the message of Jesus Christ to the spiritually lost…establishing churches, following the New Testament pattern…training leaders to proclaim the message of Jesus Christ to their own people and to other nations…touching poor and suffering people with the compassion of Jesus Christ…"

**Year founded in US:** 1914

**Income for Overseas Min:** $181,178,453

**Fully Supported US Personnel Overseas:**
Expecting to serve more than 4 years: 1809
Expecting to serve 1 to 4 years: 524
Non-residential mission Personnel: 219

**Other Personnel:**
Short-term less than 1 year: 16,867
Home ministry & office staff in US: 198

**Countries:** Africa—General 34; Albania 6; Algeria 2; American Samoa 1; Angola 6; Argentina 26; Armenia 5; Asia—General 122; Austria 13; Azerbaijan 6; Bahamas, The 2; Bangladesh 8; Belarus 4; Belgium 20; Belize 10; Benin 4; Bolivia 12; Bosnia and Herzegovina 2; Botswana 8; Brazil 13; Bulgaria 4; Burkina Faso 7; Burundi 4; Cambodia 18; Cameroon 8; Caribbean—General 2; Central Asia—General 42; Chad 2; Chile 16; Colombia 22; Congo, Democratic Republic of 6; Congo, Republic of the 2; Costa Rica 21; Croatia 6; Czech Republic 2; Denmark; Dominica 2; Dominican Republic 14; Ecuador 27; Egypt 7; El Salvador 14; Equatorial Guinea 7; Estonia 2; Ethiopia 5; Europe—General 77; Fiji 7; Finland 2; France 13; French Polynesia 2; Gambia, The 2; Georgia 4; Germany 40; Ghana 8; Greece 4; Guam 2; Guatemala 12; Haiti 2; Honduras 11; Hungary 6; Iceland 2; India 53; Indonesia 26; Ireland 14; Israel 11; Italy 10; Jamaica 10; Japan 37; Jordan 9; Kazakhstan 2; Kenya 32; Kiribati 1; Korea, South 4; Kosovo 4; Kyrgyzstan 10; Laos 4; Latin America—General 81; Latvia 3; Lebanon 8; Lesotho 2; Lithuania 8; Luxembourg 2; Macedonia 2; Madagascar 8; Malawi 7; Mali 6; Malta; Mauritius 2; Mexico 76; Middle East 21; Moldova 5; Mongolia 10; Mozambique 2; Myanmar/Burma 2; Namibia 11; Netherlands 15; Netherlands Antilles 2; Nicaragua 24; Niger 4; Nigeria 4; Oceania - General 9; Palau 2; Panama 8; Paraguay 14; Peru 12; Philippines 53; Poland 8; Portugal 9; Romania 10; Russia 41; Rwanda 8; Saint Lucia 2; Senegal 7; Serbia and Montenegro 4; Sierra Leone 4; Singapore 10; Slovakia 3; Slovenia 2; Solomon Islands 4; South Africa 44; Spain 46; Sri Lanka 6; Suriname 2; Swaziland 10; Taiwan 8; Tajikistan 7; Tanzania 10; Thailand 19; Togo 11; Tonga 6; Trinidad and Tobago 2; Ukraine 23; United Kingdom 15; Unspecified Country 68; Uruguay 10; Uzbekistan 4; Vanuatu 4; Venezuela 14; Vietnam 4; Yemen 2; Zambia 8; Zimbabwe 6

## ASSIST Ministries & ASSIST News Service

PO Box 609
Lake Forest, CA 92609-0609 USA

**Phone:** (949) 472-0974
**E-mail:** danjuma1@aol.com
**Web Site:** www.assistnews.net

*Mr. Dan Wooding, President*

A nondenominational support agency of Independent tradition engaged in missions information service. Also runs ASSIST News Service.

**Purpose:** "…encourages and supports

believers who, for religious, political or economic reasons, are unable to worship and witness freely for their faith."

**Year founded in US:** 1989

## Association of Christian Schools International (ACSI)

PO Box 65130
Colorado Springs, CO 80962-5130 USA

**Phone:** (719) 528-6906
**Fax:** (719) 531-0631
**E-mail:** info@acsi.org
**Web Site:** www.acsi.org

*Mr. Ken Smitherman, President*

A service agency of Evangelical tradition engaged in Christian education- K-12 and colleges, extension education, leadership development, management consulting/ training and short-term programs.

**Purpose:** "...to enable Christian Educators and schools worldwide by offering effective Christian School Education."

**Year founded in US:** 1978

**Income for Overseas Min:** $908,909

**Gifts in Kind:** $347,000

**Fully Supported US Personnel Overseas:**
Expecting to serve more than 4 years: 3
Non-residential mission personnel: 3

**Other Personnel:**
Short-term less than 1 year: 1
Home ministry & office staff in US: 175

**Countries:** Philippines 1; Ukraine 2

## Association of Free Lutheran Congregations— World Missions

3110 E. Medicine Lake Blvd.
Minneapolis, MN 55441 USA

**Phone:** (763) 545-5631
**Fax:** (763) 545-0079
**E-mail:** worldmis@aflc.org
**Web Site:** www.aflc.org

*Pastor Del Palmer, Director*

A denominational sending agency of Evangelical and Lutheran tradition engaged in evangelism, church planting, support of national workers, support of national churches, partnership development and missionary training.

**Year founded in US:** 1969

**Fully Supported US Personnel Overseas:**
Expecting to serve more than 4 years: 11
Expecting to serve 1 to 4 years: 4
Non-residential mission Personnel: 6

**Other Personnel:**
Short-term less than 1 year: 5
Non-US serving in own/other country: 47
Home ministry & office staff in US: 2

**Countries:** Africa—General; Brazil 5; India; Mexico 4; Poland 2; Ukraine

## Audio Scriptures International
## See: Talking Bibles Int'l.

## Audio Scripture Ministries

760 Waverly Rd.
Holland, MI 49423 USA

**Phone:** (616) 396-5291
**Fax:** (616) 396-5294
**E-mail:** asm@audioscriptureministries.org
**Web Site:** www.asmtoday.org

*Rev. Tom Dudenhofer, Exec. Director*

A nondenominational specialized agency of Evangelical tradition engaged in audio recording/distribution in more than 200 languages and services for other agencies.

**Year founded in US:** 1967

**Income for Overseas Min:** $221,000

**Fully Supported US Personnel Overseas:**
Expecting to serve more than 4 years: 4
Non-residential mission personnel: 2

**Other Personnel:**
Short-term less than 1 year: 2
Home ministry & office staff in US: 4

**Countries:** India 2; Kenya 1; Mexico 1

## Aurora Mission, Inc.

PO Box 1549
Bradenton, FL 34206 USA

**Phone:** (941) 748-4100
**Fax:** (941) 748-2625
**E-mail:** mission@auroramission.org
**Web Site:** www.auroramission.org

*Mr. David J. Standridge, Msn. Program Admin.*

A nondenominational support agency of Independent tradition engaged in theological education, Bible distribution, church planting, evangelism, literature distribution and short-term programs.

**Purpose:** "...to communicate the Gospel with the goal of evangelizing, discipling, establishing churches and providing training for pastors and church leaders."

**Year founded in US:** 1978

**Income for Overseas Min:** $522,114

**Fully Supported US Personnel Overseas:**
Expecting to serve more than 4 years: 6
Expecting to serve 1 to 4 years: 3
Non-residential mission personnel: 3

**Other Personnel:**
Short-term less than 1 year: 3
Non-US serving in own/other country: 13
Home ministry & office staff in US: 2

**Countries:** Italy 6

## Avant Ministries

10000 N. Oak Trafficway
Kansas City, MO 64155 USA
**Phone:** (816) 734-8500
**Fax:** (816) 734-4601
**E-mail:** info@avmi.org
**Web Site:** www.avantministries.org
**Associations:** IFMA

*Dr. J. Paul Nyquist, President/CEO*

An interdenominational sending agency of Evangelical tradition engaged in church planting, discipleship, evangelism and leadership development.

**Purpose:** "...a focus on church planting, with the goal of taking the gospel to unevangelized areas of the world."

**Year founded in US:** 1892

**Income for Overseas Min:** $8,847,885

**Gifts in Kind:** $303,087

**Fully Supported US Personnel Overseas:**
Expecting to serve more than 4 years: 144
Expecting to serve 1 to 4 years: 16

**Other Personnel:**
Short-term less than 1 year: 34
Non-US serving in own/other country: 52
Home ministry & office staff in US: 28

**Countries:** Argentina 14; Austria 1; Bahamas, The 3; Belgium 3; Belize; Bolivia 21; Brazil 17; Ecuador 19; France 5; Germany; Hungary 2; Italy 8; Jordan 2; Kyrgyzstan 2; Mali 6; Mexico 4; Panama 3; Poland 8; Russia 2; Spain 21; United Kingdom 3

## Awana Clubs International

1 East Bode Rd.
Streamwood, IL 60107 USA
**Phone:** (630) 213-2000
**Fax:** (630) 213-9704
**E-mail:** CustomerServiceHelp@awana.org
**Web Site:** www.awana.org

*Rev. Jack D. Eggar, CEO/President*

A specialized agency of Evangelical tradition providing Bible-based, Christ-centered weekly club programs and leadership training for local churches around the world. Awana manages more than 63,000 clubs in 72 countries.

**Purpose:** "...partnering with churches and mission organizations to reach children and teens with the gospel of Jesus Christ and to train them for Christian service."

**Year founded in US:** 1950

**Income for Overseas Min:** $2,000,000

**Gifts in Kind:** $2,500

**Fully Supported US Personnel Overseas:**
Expecting to serve more than 4 years: 23
Non-residential mission personnel: 2

**Other Personnel:**
Short-term less than 1 year: 131
Bi-vocational/tentmakers: 56
Non-US serving in own/other country: 254
Home ministry & office staff in US: 227

**Countries:** Argentina; Australia; Bahamas, the; Bangladesh 1; Belarus; Benin; Bolivia; Brazil; Cameroon; Columbia; Costa Rica 1; Czech Republic; Dominica; Dominican Republic 1; Ecuador 2; El Salvador 2; Fiji; Ghana; Guatemala; Haiti 1; Honduras; Hong Kong; Hungary; India; Indonesia 2; Jamaica; Japan; Kazakhstan; Kenya; Korea, South; Latvia; Liberia; Mexico 2; Middle East 3; Moldova; Mozambique; Nepal; Nicaragua 2; Papua New Guinea 2; Peru; Philippines; Romania; Russia; Singapore; Slovakia; South Africa; Sri Lanka; Taiwan 2; Togo; Uganda; Ukraine; Venezuela; Western Europe—General 2; Zambia; Zimbabwe

## Back to the Bible Intl.

PO Box 82808
Lincoln, NE 68501 USA
**Phone:** (402) 464-7200
**Fax:** (402) 464-7474
**E-mail:** info@backtothebible.org
**Web Site:** www.backtothebible.org

**Associations:** IFMA

*Dr. Woodrow Kroll, President*

A nondenominational service agency of Evangelical tradition engaged in broadcasting, support of national workers, literature production and literature distribution.

**Purpose:** "To lead believers into spiritual maturity and active service for Christ in the local church and the world, and to reach unbelievers with the Gospel of Christ by teaching the Bible through media."

**Year founded in US:** 1939

**Income for Overseas Min:** $1,586,109

**Personnel:**
Non-US serving in own/other country: 164
Home ministry & office staff in US: 85

**Countries:** Australia; Brazil; China; Ecuador; Egypt; India; Indonesia; Italy; Jamaica; Japan; Philippines; Poland; Russia; Sri Lanka; Turkmenistan

# Bakke Graduate University of Ministry

1013 8th Ave., Ste. 401
Seattle, WA 98104 USA

**Phone:** (206) 264-9100

**Fax:** (206) 264-8828

**E-mail:** bgu@bgu.edu

**Web Site:** www.bgu.edu

*Mr. Brad Smith, President*

A nondenominational information and service agency of Evangelical tradition engaged in leadership development through church consultations and theological education and training.

**Purpose:** "...to empower God's people in the largest cities of the world by means of leadership consultations that generate vision, partnerships, motivations and resources, so that the 'whole church can take the whole gospel to the whole city'."

**Year founded in US:** 1989

**Income for Overseas Min:** $450,000

**Personnel:**
Non-US serving in own/other country: 4
Home ministry & office staff in US: 3

# Baptist Bible Fellowship Intl.

PO Box 191
Springfield, MO 65801-0191 USA

**Phone:** (417) 862-5001

**Fax:** (417) 865-0794

**E-mail:** info@bbfimissions.com

**Web Site:** www.connectionpoint.net

*Dr. Jon Konnerup, Mission Director*

A sending agency of Baptist tradition engaged in church planting.

**Year founded in US:** 1950

**Income for Overseas Min:** $38,500,000

**Fully Supported US Personnel Overseas:**
Expecting to serve more than 4 years: 682
Expecting to serve 1 to 4 years: 17

**Other Personnel:**
Short-term less than 1 year: 28
Home ministry & office staff in US: 20

**Countries:** Argentina 21; Australia 28; Austria 8; Azores 2; Bahamas, The 2; Belgium 8; Belize 4; Bolivia 9; Botswana 2; Brazil 38; Bulgaria 2; Burkina Faso 8; Cambodia 6; Chile 11; Colombia 2; Congo, Democratic Republic of 4; Costa Rica 12; Cote d'Ivoire 2; Croatia 2; Denmark 2; Dominican Republic 6; Ecuador 13; El Salvador 2; Ethiopia 12; France 10; Germany 18; Greece 2; Guatemala 4; Haiti 3; Honduras 1; Hong Kong 6; Hungary 4; Iceland 2; India 2; Indonesia 4; Ireland 5; Italy 2; Jamaica 6; Japan 24; Kenya 34; Korea, South 11; Lithuania 2; Mexico 8; Mongolia 2; Nepal 2; Netherlands 2; New Zealand 16; Nicaragua 15; Nigeria 2; Pakistan 4; Panama 8; Papua New Guinea 10; Paraguay 2; Peru 17; Philippines 46; Poland 2; Portugal 10; Puerto Rico 5; Romania 9; Russia 22; Singapore 4; Slovakia 2; Slovenia 2; South Africa 14; Spain 12; Sweden 4; Taiwan 13; Tanzania 13; Thailand 5; Uganda 2; Ukraine 4; United Kingdom 55; Uruguay 2; Vanuatu 2; Venezuela 4; Zambia 16

# Baptist Bible Translators Institute

PO Box 1450
Bowie, TX 76230 USA

**Phone:** (940) 872-5751

**E-mail:** bbti@cleaninter.net

**Web Site:** www.baptisttranslators,com

*Mr. Rex L. Cobb, Director*

A denominational service agency of Baptist and Fundamental tradition engaged in missionary training, missionary education, linguistics and TESOL.

# MAKE YOUR MASTER'S PROGRAM WORK FOR YOU

*Earn a master's degree or certificate in TESOL and prepare to teach anywhere in the world.*

**APU's Master of Arts in Teaching English to Speakers of Other Languages (TESOL) and Certificate in TESOL allow you to:**

- Gain a superior education in a Christian environment.
- Blend course work with practical experiences to respond to a wide range of language needs and sociocultural differences.
- Study under qualified, experienced, and compassionate faculty.
- Open a host of career opportunities in international and domestic education.
- Choose between an on-campus or field-based program.

**Apply online at www.apu.edu!**

| | |
|---|---|
| call | (626) 815-4570 |
| click | www.apu.edu/tesol |
| email | graduatecenter@apu.edu |
| visit | Our Azusa Campus<br>901 E. Alosta Ave.<br>Azusa, CA 91702-7000<br>(26 miles northeast of L.A.). |

**AZUSA PACIFIC**
UNIVERSITY

# Global Perspectives *for* World Christian Missions

## Introducing World Missions
A BIBLICAL, HISTORICAL, AND PRACTICAL SURVEY
*A. Scott Moreau, Gary R. Corwin, and Gary B. McGee*
0801026482 • 352 pp. • $29.99c

"A remarkable text book containing the history of missions (biblical and modern era); a thorough guide to candidacy and choosing an organization; a discussion of personal and family life for missionaries; and a philosophical discussion of the current trends in (and future of) missions. . . . [An] educational and practical resource for missions pastors and would-be missionaries."—*Outreach*

## Globalizing Theology
BELIEF AND PRACTICE IN AN ERA OF WORLD CHRISTIANITY
*Craig Ott and Harold A. Netland, editors*
0801031125 • 384 pp. • $27.99p

"Some of the sharpest minds in the church have been gathered to discuss some of the most sensitive issues facing the church today. The result is an extremely helpful guide. A fitting tribute indeed to Paul G. Hiebert, the great Christian statesman this book honors."—**Ajith Fernando,** national director, Youth for Christ, Sri Lanka

## The Changing Face of World Missions
ENGAGING CONTEMPORARY ISSUES AND TRENDS
*Michael Pocock, Gailyn Van Rheenen, and Douglas McConnell*
080102661X • 400 pp. • $24.99p

"In a rapidly changing world, we can no longer carry out missions as usual. We need a renewed vision and new ways to reach a world in such desperate need. This excellent book can help all of us in the church grasp the nature and the importance of the mission God has given us in our day."—**Paul G. Hiebert,** Trinity Evangelical Divinity School

*Christianity Today* 2006 Book Award Winner
*Outreach Magazine* Year's Best Award Winner, 2005

## Bible and Mission
CHRISTIAN WITNESS IN A POSTMODERN WORLD
*Richard Bauckham*
0801027713 • 128 pp. • $15.00p

"A refreshing attempt to read the Bible with mission as the key hermeneutic. Richard Bauckham zeroes in on how the Scriptures interpret the relationship between the particular and the universal. The author's reading yields fresh insights on biblical stories and images that have been worn out by other interpretive viewpoints."—**Francis M. Macatangay,** *Mission Studies*

## ℟ Baker Academic
*Extending the Conversation*

**Available at your local bookstore, www.bakeracademic.com, or by calling 1-800-877-2665**
**Subscribe to Baker Academic's electronic newsletter (E-Notes) at www.bakeracademic.com**

**Purpose:** "...missionaries training missionaries to plant New Testament Baptist churches in every bibleless nation and translate the Scriptures into every bibleless language."

**Year founded in US:** 1973

## Baptist General Conference—International Ministries

2002 S. Arlington Hts. Rd
Arlington Heights, IL 60005 USA

**Phone:** (800) 323-4215
**Fax:** (847) 228-5376
**E-mail:** ncassell@baptistgeneral.org
**Web Site:** www.bgcworld.org
**Associations:** EFMA

*Rev. Stephen Doggett, Exec. Director*

A denominational sending agency of Baptist tradition engaged in church planting, discipleship, theological education, leadership development, medical work and short-term programs.

**Purpose:** "...helping member churches fulfill Christ's mission for His church in all communities God calls them to serve."

**Year founded in US:** 1944

**Income for Overseas Min:** $8,845,000

**Fully Supported US Personnel Overseas:**
Expecting to serve more than 4 years: 139
Expecting to serve 1 to 4 years: 12

**Other Personnel:**
Short-term less than 1 year: 15
Non-US serving in own/other country: 5
Home ministry & office staff in US: 10

**Countries:** Africa—General 12; Argentina 6; Belize 2; Brazil 13; Cambodia 2; Cameroon 12; Central Asia—General 2; Cote d'Ivoire 5; Estonia 2; Ethiopia 8; France 6; India 1; Japan 12; Mexico 15; Philippines 23; Senegal 6; Singapore 2; Thailand 8; Uruguay 2

## Baptist International Evangelistic Ministries

121 Commerce Drive Ste. #50
Danville, IN 46122 USA

**Phone:** (317) 718-1633
**E-mail:** missions@baptistinternational.org
**Web Site:** www.baptistinternational.org

*Dr. Sam Slobodian, President*

A denominational sending agency of Baptist and Fundamental tradition engaged in

church planting, Bible distribution, church construction, theological education, literature distribution and support of national workers. Data from 2001.

**Purpose:** "...fulfilling the missionary mandate in Russia and Eastern Europe through the support, training and equipping of dedicated and prepared nationals."

**Year founded in US:** 1981

**Income for Overseas Min:** $880,035

**Gifts in Kind:** $27,740

**Fully Supported US Personnel Overseas:**
Expecting to serve more than 4 years: 3
Non-residential mission personnel: 2

**Other Personnel:**
Short-term less than 1 year: 102
Non-US serving in own/other country: 93
Home ministry & office staff in US: 3

**Countries:** Moldova; Romania; Russia 3; Ukraine

## Baptist International Missions, Inc. (BIMI)

POBox 9215
Chattanooga, TN 37412 USA

**Phone:** (423) 344-5050
**Fax:** (423) 344-4774
**E-mail:** info@bimi.org
**Web Site:** www.bimi.org

*Dr. James R. Ray, Gen. Director*

A sending agency of Independent Baptist tradition engaged in church planting, Bible distribution, discipleship, evangelism and leadership development.

**Purpose:** "...to assist fundamental Baptist churches in fulfilling our Lord's command to evangelize the world with the Gospel of Jesus Christ."

**Year founded in US:** 1960

**Income for Overseas Min:** $28,179,154

**Gifts in Kind:** $485,615

**Fully Supported US Personnel Overseas:**
Expecting to serve more than 4 years: 708

**Other Personnel:**
Home ministry & office staff in US: 22

**Countries:** Africa—General 2; American Samoa 2; Anguilla 2; Antigua 6; Argentina 4; Australia 31; Austria 2; Bahamas, The 5; Barbados 2; Bolivia 10; Brazil 48; Cambodia 8; Cayman Islands 6; Chile 2; Costa Rica

10; Cote d'Ivoire 10; Cuba 2; Czech Republic 2; Dominican Republic 24; Ecuador 4; El Salvador 4; Estonia 2; Fiji 4; France 8; French Polynesia 2; Germany 30; Ghana 8; Guadeloupe 2; Guatemala 2; Haiti 6; Honduras 14; Hong Kong 2; Hungary 2; India 7; Indonesia 2; Ireland 14; Italy 4; Jamaica 4; Japan 45; Kenya 4; Latvia 4; Malawi 1; Mexico 55; N. Mariana Isls 4; Nepal 2; New Caledonia 2; New Zealand 6; Niger 2; Nigeria 6; Norway 2; Panama 2; Papua New Guinea 4; Paraguay 2; Peru 13; Philippines 35; Poland 2; Puerto Rico 13; Romania 12; Russia 16; Saint Kitts and Nevis 2; Senegal 4; Singapore 3; Slovakia 4; South Africa 19; Spain 7; Switzerland 2; Tanzania 6; Thailand 2; Togo 8; Trinidad and Tobago 9; Turks and Caicos Islands 1; Uganda 36; Ukraine 13; United Kingdom 39; Venezuela 18; Virgin Islands 2; Zambia 2

## Baptist Intl. Outreach

PO Box 639
Maynardville, TN 37807 USA
**Phone:** (865) 992-0999
**Fax:** (865) 992-4999
**E-mail:** execdir@biomissions.org
**Web Site:** www.biomissions.org
*Dr. Garvin Dykes, Exec. Director*

A sending agency of independent Baptist and Fundamental tradition engaged in church planting, disability assistance programs, theological education, evangelism and providing medical supplies. Personnel and financial data from 1998.

**Purpose:** "...to further the spread of the gospel of the Lord Jesus Christ with the ultimate goal of establishing New Testament Churches."

**Year founded in US:** 1985

**Income for Overseas Min:** $1,800,000

**Fully Supported US Personnel Overseas:**
    Expecting to serve more than 4 years: 39

**Other Personnel:**
    Non-US serving in own/other country: 25
    Home ministry & office staff in US: 6

**Countries:** Belarus 2; Belize 2; Botswana 4; Brazil 7; Cambodia; Costa Rica; Cuba; Ethiopia 1; India; Indonesia; Kenya 2; Mexico 4; Nigeria; Peru 4; Philippines 2; Russia; South Africa 4; Vietnam 2; Zambia 5

## Baptist Medical & Dental Mission International, Inc.

11 Plaza Dr.
Hattiesburg, MS 39402 USA
**Phone:** (601) 544-3586
**Fax:** (601) 544-6508
**E-mail:** info@bmdmi.org
**Web Site:** www.bmdmi.org
*Mr. Dwight G. Carr, President*

A specialized agency of Baptist tradition engaged in medical work, childcare/orphanage programs, church construction, church planting, theological education and evangelism. Data from 2001.

**Purpose:** "...to carry the message of salvation through the free grace of Jesus Christ."

**Year founded in US:** 1974

**Income for Overseas Min:** $9,944,707

**Gifts in Kind:** $7,729,094

**Fully Supported US Personnel Overseas:**
    Expecting to serve more than 4 years: 18

**Other Personnel:**
    Non-US serving in own/other country: 71
    Home ministry & office staff in US: 7

**Countries:** Honduras 10; Latin America—General 4; Nicaragua 4

## Baptist Mid-Missions

PO Box 308011
Cleveland, OH 44130 USA
**Phone:** (440) 826-3930
**Fax:** (440) 826-4457
**E-mail:** info@bmm.org
**Web Site:** www.bmm.org
*Dr. Gary L. Anderson, President*

A sending agency of Baptist and Fundamental tradition engaged in church planting, broadcasting, theological education, medical work, relief and/or rehabilitation and Bible translation.

**Purpose:** "...to strategically advance the building of Christ's church, with His passion and for His glory, in vital partnership with Baptist churches worldwide."

**Year founded in US:** 1920

**Income for Overseas Min:** $18,600,000

**Fully Supported US Personnel Overseas:**
    Expecting to serve more than 4 years: 466

**Other Personnel:**

Short-term less than 1 year: 381
Bi-vocational/tentmakers: 4
Non-US serving in own/other country: 20
Home ministry & office staff in US: 48

**Countries:** Argentina 5; Asia—General 7; Australia 17; Bangladesh; Botswana 2; Brazil 139; Cambodia 4; Cameroon 4; Central African Republic 5; Chad 7; Chile 4; Cote d'Ivoire 7; Dominican Republic 1; Ecuador 3; Ethiopia 2; Finland 2; France 29; Germany 17; Ghana 12; Guyana 2; Haiti 4; Honduras 10; India 8; Ireland 2; Italy 6; Jamaica 1; Japan 8; Kenya 2; Liberia 2; Luxembourg 2; Malta 2; Mexico 11; Micronesia, Federated States of 5; Middle East 2; Mozambique 2; Netherlands 10; New Zealand 6; Papua New Guinea 2; Peru 33; Puerto Rico 2; Romania 13; Russia 4; Saint Vincent and the Grenadines 6; Slovakia 2; Spain 8; Taiwan 2; Thailand 9; United Kingdom 11; Venezuela 7; Zambia 15

## Baptist Missions to Forgotten Peoples

PO Box 37043
Jacksonville, FL 32236-7043 USA
**Phone:** (904) 783-4007
**Fax:** (904) 778-8999
**E-mail:** bmfp@bmfp.org
**Web Site:** www.bmfp.org
*Dr. Gene Burge, Pres./Exec. Dir.*

A nondenominational sending agency of Baptist tradition engaged in church planting and evangelism. Data from 2001.

**Purpose:** "...to serve the local church by providing a faith-missions ministry committed to strategic church planting...among the unevangelized people groups of the world."

**Personnel:**
  Expecting to serve more than 4 years: 125
**Countries:** Unspecified Country 125

## Baptist World Mission

PO Box 2149
Decatur, AL 35602 USA
**Phone:** (256) 353-2221
**Fax:** (256) 353-2266
**E-mail:** office@baptistworldmission.org
**Web Site:** www.baptistworldmission.org
*Dr. Fred Moritz, Exec. Director*

A sending agency of independent Baptist and Fundamental tradition engaged in church planting.

**Purpose:** "...to furnish a channel for Bible-believing Baptist churches to carry out the Great Commission of our Lord through evangelism and the establishment of indigenous Baptist churches."

**Year founded in US:** 1961
**Fully Supported US Personnel Overseas:**
  Expecting to serve more than 4 years: 361
**Other Personnel:**
  Home ministry & office staff in US: 15
**Countries:** Unspecified Country 361

## Barnabas International

PO Box 11211
Rockford, IL 61108 USA
**Phone:** (815) 395-1335
**Fax:** (815) 395-1385
**E-mail:** Barnabas@barnabas.org
**Web Site:** www.barnabas.org
**Associations:** EFMA
*Rev. Lee Hotchkiss, Exec. Director*

An interdenominational support agency of Evangelical tradition engaged in member care, leadership development, support of national churches and psychological counseling.

**Purpose:** "...to edify, enrich, encourage, and strengthen missionaries, pastors, national church leaders and their families...through personal, small group and conference ministries."

**Year founded in US:** 1986
**Income for Overseas Min:** $964,095
**Personnel:**
  Home ministry & office staff in US: 2

## BCM International

PO Box 249
Akron, PA 17501-0249 USA
**Phone:** (717) 859-6404
**Fax:** (717) 859-6914
**E-mail:** info@bcmintl.org
**Web Site:** www.bcmintl.org
**Associations:** ANAM, IFMA
*Rev. Martin D. Windle, President*

A nondenominational sending agency of biblical tradition engaged in childrens programs, camping programs, discipleship, training and youth programs. Income figure from 1998.

**Purpose:** "...dedicated to making disciples

of all age groups for the Lord Jesus Christ through evangelism and diverse Bible Centered Ministries so that churches are established and the Church strengthened."

**Year founded in US:** 1936

**Income for Overseas Min:** $4,900,000

**Fully Supported US Personnel Overseas:**
Expecting to serve more than 4 years: 28

**Other Personnel:**
Short-term less than 1 year: 25
Non-US serving in own/other country: 457
Home ministry & office staff in US: 30

**Countries:** Antigua; Austria 1; Belize; Brazil; Cambodia; Cuba 1; Dominican Republic; Egypt; Finland; France 3; Germany 3; Greece; Guyana; Hungary; India; Indonesia; Ireland 2; Italy 2; Jamaica; Mexico; Mozambique; Myanmar/Burma; Nepal; Netherlands 1; Paraguay; Peru; Philippines; Poland 1; Portugal; Russia 1; St. Vincent and the Grenadines; South Africa; Spain; Sri Lanka; Suriname; Swaziland; Ukraine 2; United Kingdom 10; Zimbabwe 1

## Bethany Fellowship Missions
## See: Bethany Int'l. Ministries

## Bethany Intl. Ministries
6820 Auto Club Rd., Ste. D
Bloomington, MN 55438 USA
**Phone:** (952) 829-2492
**Fax:** (952) 829-2767
**E-mail:** ministries@bethanyinternational.org
**Web Site:** www.bethanyinternational.org
**Associations:** EFMA

*Mr. Dan Brokke, CEO*

A nondenominational sending agency of Charismatic and Evangelical tradition engaged in missionary training, missionary education, theological education, evangelism, literature distribution, church planting and partnership development.

**Purpose:** "...to witness, to train and send missionaries, to plant churches, to publish Christian literature, and to establish creative resource ventures for the expansion of Christ's Kingdom."

**Year founded in US:** 1963

**Income for Overseas Min:** $2,653,989

**Fully Supported US Personnel Overseas:**
Expecting to serve more than 4 years: 92

Expecting to serve 1 to 4 years: 11

**Other Personnel:**
Short-term less than 1 year: 95
Bi-vocational/tentmakers: 1
Non-US serving in own/other country: 97
Home ministry & office staff in US: 12

**Countries:** Bolivia 6; Brazil 15; Cambodia 2; Croatia 1; Dominican Republic 2; France 8; Ghana 2; Honduras 2; Hungary 2; Japan 2; Kenya 2; Kosovo 1; Mexico 10; Netherlands 1; Paraguay; Philippines 6; Slovenia 2; Spain 2; Thailand 1; Unspecified Country 25

## Bible League, The
PO Box 28000
Chicago, IL 60628 USA
**Phone:** (866) 825-4636
**Fax:** (708) 367-8600
**E-mail:** info@bibleleague.org
**Web Site:** www.bibleleague.org

*Mr. Robert Cole, President*

A nondenominational specialized agency of Evangelical tradition engaged in Bible distribution, church planting, evangelism, literacy work, support of national workers, Bible translation and training in more than 55 countries.

**Purpose:** "...to provide Scriptures and training worldwide to bring people into fellowship with Christ and His Church."

**Year founded in US:** 1938

**Income for Overseas Min:** $22,179,947

**Personnel:**
Non-US serving in own/other country: 500
Home ministry & office staff in US: 150

## Bible Training Centre for Pastors
2030 Tucker Industrial Rd., Ste. 126
Tucker, GA 30084 USA
**Phone:** (770) 938-6160
**Fax:** (770) 938-5884
**E-mail:** btcp@btcp.com
**Web Site:** www.bibletraining.com

*Mr. Dennis Mock, President*

A transdenominational sending agency of Evangelical tradition engaged in theological education.

**Purpose:** "...to extend non-formal theological training to the world's untrained pastors."

**Year founded in US:** 1988

**Income for Overseas Min:** $1,330,000

**Personnel:**
  Non-US serving in own/other country: 1
  Home ministry & office staff in US: 6

**Countries:** India

## Biblical Literature Fellowship
## See: Bibles & Literature
## in French

## Bibles & Literature in French
PO Box 629
Wheaton, IL 60189-0629 USA

**Phone:** (630) 221-1980
**Fax:** (630) 221-1982
**E-mail:** BLF@blfusa.org
**Web Site:** www.blfusa.org
**Associations:** IFMA

*Mr. Harry R. Enns, Exec. Director*

A nondenominational specialized agency of Evangelical and Independent tradition engaged in literature production, Bible distribution, Christian education, literature distribution and short-term programs.

**Purpose:** "...to glorify God through providing Christian materials to meet the needs of evangelism and discipleship in the French-speaking world."

**Year founded in US:** 1954

**Income for Overseas Min:** $357,094

**Fully Supported US Personnel Overseas:**
  Expecting to serve more than 4 years: 4
  Non-residential mission personnel: 10

**Other Personnel:**
  Short-term less than 1 year: 6
  Non-US serving in own/other country: 2
  Home ministry & office staff in US: 5

**Countries:** Belgium 2; France 2

## Bibles For The World, Inc.
PO Box 49759
Colorado Springs, CO 80949-9759 USA

**Phone:** (888) 382-4253
**Fax:** (719) 630-1449
**E-mail:** info@bftw.org
**Web Site:** www.biblesfortheworld.org

*Dr. Rochunga Pudaite, President*

A nondenominational support agency of Evangelical tradition engaged in Bible distribution, Christian education, theological education, support of national churches, support of national workers and childcare/orphanage programs. Data from 2001.

**Year founded in US:** 1972

**Income for Overseas Min:** $690,457

**Gifts in Kind:** $564,295

**Personnel:**
  Short-term less than 1 year: 30
  Non-US serving in own/other country: 400
  Home ministry & office staff in US: 15

**Countries:** India

## Biblical Ministries Worldwide
1595 Herrington Rd.
Lawrenceville, GA 30043 USA

**Phone:** (770) 339-3500
**Fax:** (770) 513-1254
**E-mail:** bmwhq@biblicalministries.org
**Web Site:** www.biblicalministries.org

*Rev. Paul G. Seger, Gen. Director*

A nondenominational sending agency of Independent tradition engaged in church planting, training and evangelism.

**Purpose:** "...to evangelize and develop leaders who will reproduce themselves and the churches we serve."

**Year founded in US:** 1948

**Income for Overseas Min:** $7,500,000

**Gifts in Kind:** $100,000

**Fully Supported US Personnel Overseas:**
  Expecting to serve more than 4 years: 183

**Other Personnel:**
  Bi-vocational/tentmakers: 16
  Non-US serving in own/other country: 185
  Home ministry & office staff in US: 9

**Countries:** Antigua 2; Argentina 12; Australia 6; Austria 2; Croatia 2; Ecuador 10; Fiji 8; France 8; Germany 10; Honduras 7; Hong Kong 5; Ireland 11; Italy 9; Japan 2; Luxembourg 2; Mexico 8; Netherlands 2; New Zealand 9; Palau 2; Puerto Rico 2; South Africa 12; Spain 6; Sweden 4; United Kingdom 7; Unspecified Country 11; Uruguay 24

## BILD International
2400 Oakwood Rd.
Ames, IA 50014-8417 USA

**Phone:** (515) 292-7012
**Fax:** (515) 292-1933

**E-mail:** info@bild.org
**Web Site:** www.bild.org
*Mr. Jeff Reed, President/CEO*

A transdenominational support agency of Evangelical tradition engaged in leadership development, church planting, discipleship, Christian education, missionary education and theological education.

**Purpose:** "...to train high impact networks of leaders, superbly trained in the "way of Christ and His Apostles," strategically rooted in each of the nine civilizations/240+ countries and to build several prototypical church planting movements, both large and small."

**Year founded in US:** 1974

**Income for Overseas Min:** $958,231

**Fully Supported US Personnel Overseas:**
Non-residential mission personnel: 3

**Other Personnel:**
Non-US serving in own/other country: 24
Home ministry & office staff in US: 11

**Countries:** Albania; Australia; Cambodia; Chad; France; Guatemala; India; Indonesia; Japan; Myanmar/Burma; Nigeria; Pakistan; Peru; Portugal

# Billy Graham Center, The
500 College Ave.
Wheaton, IL 60187 USA
**Phone:** (630) 752-5157
**Fax:** (630) 752-5916
**E-mail:** bgcadm@wheaton.edu
**Web Site:** www.billygrahamcenter.org
*Dr. Lon Allison, Director*

Stimulating global evangelism, a transdenominational service agency of Evangelical tradition engaged in training, evangelism, missions information service, leadership development and mission-related research.

**Purpose:** "...to develop strategies and skills for evangelism...through leadership training, research, networking, strategic planning and communicating the gospel."

**Year founded in US:** 1975

**Personnel:**
Home ministry & office staff in US: 25

# Blessings International
5881 S. Garnett St.
Tulsa, OK 74107 USA

**Phone:** (918) 250-8101
**Fax:** (918) 250-1281
**E-mail:** info@blessing.org
**Web Site:** www.blessing.org
**Associations:** AERDO
*Dr. Harold C. Harder, Exec. Director/President*

A nondenominational support agency of Evangelical and Charismatic tradition engaged in providing medical supplies, medical work and relief and/or rehabilitation. Conducts regular ongoing medical programs in 86 countries.

**Purpose:** "...to alleviate suffering and provide medicines world-wide by facilitating relationships that promote health."

**Year founded in US:** 1981

**Income for Overseas Min:** $61,002,351

**Gifts in Kind:** $61,085,667

**Fully Supported US Personnel Overseas:**
Non-residential mission personnel: 1

**Other Personnel:**
Short-term less than 1 year: 1
Home ministry & office staff in US: 7

# Brazil Gospel Fellowship Mission
125 W. Ash St.
Springfield, IL 62704 USA
**Phone:** (217) 523-7176
**Fax:** (217) 523-7186
**E-mail:** bgfm@bgfmission.org
**Web Site:** www.bgfmission.org
*Rev. Larry Lipka, Exec. Director*

A nondenominational sending agency of Independent tradition engaged in church planting, camping programs, discipleship, Christian education, theological education and evangelism.

**Year founded in US:** 1945

**Income for Overseas Min:** $893,000

**Fully Supported US Personnel Overseas:**
Expecting to serve more than 4 years: 45
Expecting to serve 1 to 4 years: 5

**Other Personnel:**
Short-term less than 1 year: 10
Home ministry & office staff in US: 4

**Countries:** Brazil 45

# Bread for the World
50 F St. NW, Ste. 500

# school of
# intercultural
# studies

BIOLA UNIVERSITY

*We are God's instruments.*
*We have a story to tell.*
*And the world is listening.*

With God's grace, we'll take
His Story and tell it on the
mountain, overseas, here at
home, and across the world.
Since 1908, Biola has been
training students to take God's
story to the ends of the earth.

We offer M.A. programs in
intercultural studies, TESOL,
and applied linguistics, a
doctorate in missiology, and a
Ph.D. in intercultural
education.

**Contact Biola's School of
Intercultural Studies today.**

BIOLA
UNIVERSITY
*School of Intercultural Studies*

*www.biola.edu*
*1.800.652.4652*

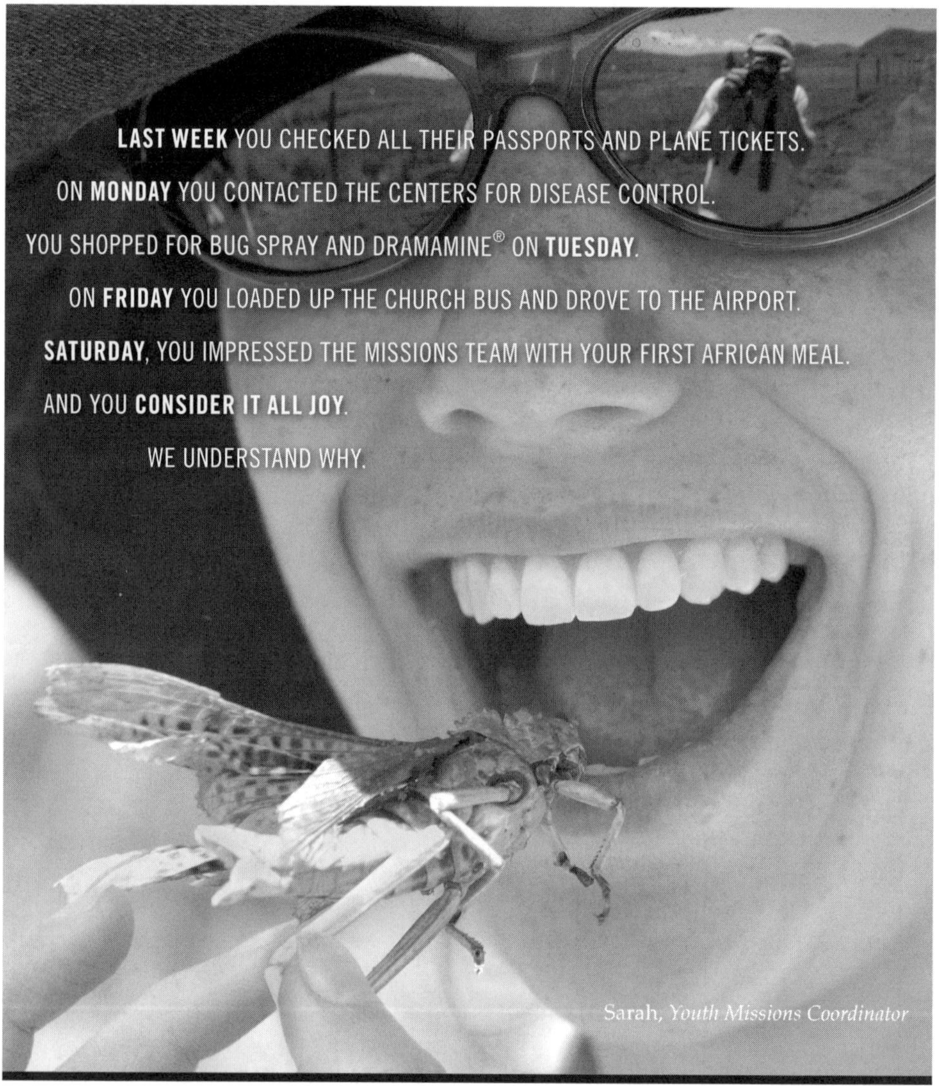

LAST **WEEK** YOU CHECKED ALL THEIR PASSPORTS AND PLANE TICKETS.

ON **MONDAY** YOU CONTACTED THE CENTERS FOR DISEASE CONTROL.

YOU SHOPPED FOR BUG SPRAY AND DRAMAMINE® ON **TUESDAY**.

ON **FRIDAY** YOU LOADED UP THE CHURCH BUS AND DROVE TO THE AIRPORT.

**SATURDAY**, YOU IMPRESSED THE MISSIONS TEAM WITH YOUR FIRST AFRICAN MEAL.

AND YOU **CONSIDER IT ALL JOY**.

WE UNDERSTAND WHY.

Sarah, *Youth Missions Coordinator*

Getting people out to help the world is important to you and your church. You care about spreading the Good News. You also care about the safety and health of the people you send. **So do we.**

That's why we created **Passport to Ministry**®, a unique package of liability insurance coverages designed to meet the specific needs of mission teams. To find out more, contact your agent, visit our comprehensive website at **www.brotherhoodmutual.com**, or call us at **800.876.4994**.

**Brotherhood Mutual**
Insurance Company

*We understand why.*®

www.brotherhoodmutual.com

Insuring America's churches and related ministries.® | Property/Liability Programs | Foreign Liability & Travel Assistance

Copyright © 2005 Brotherhood Mutual Insurance Company. All rights reserved.   Brotherhood Mutual is licensed in most states; for coverage availability, check our Web site, www.brotherhoodmutual.com or call 800.876.4994.

Washington, DC 20001 USA
**Phone:** (202) 639-9400
**Fax:** (202) 639-9401
**E-mail:** bread@bread.org
**Web Site:** www.bread.org
*Rev. David Beckmann, President*

An interdenominational Christian citizens movement of many traditions helping citizens be active in public-policy issues important to the reduction of hunger.

**Purpose:** "...seeking justice for the world's hungry people by lobbying our nation's decision makers."

**Year founded in US:** 1974
**Personnel:**
Home ministry & office staff in US: 80

## Brethren Assemblies

USA  (No central office)

The Brethren Assemblies are also known as "Christian Brethren" or "Plymouth Brethren." Missionaries are sent from each local assembly (church)  and not through a central agency. Personnel totals are from the Christian Mission in Many Lands service agency.

**Fully Supported US Personnel Overseas:**
Expecting to serve more than 4 years: 424
Non-residential mission personnel: 7
**Other Personnel:**
Bi-vocational/tentmakers: 2

**Countries:** Albania 7; Argentina 6; Austria 7; Bahamas, The 10; Belgium 2; Belize 1; Bolivia 19; Brazil 9; Burundi 2; Chad 1; Chile 4; Colombia 13; Dominican Republic 5; Ecuador 7; El Salvador 6; France 15; Germany 4; Greece 4; Guatemala 2; Honduras 9; Hong Kong 4; Hungary 2; India 14; Indonesia 3; Ireland 14; Italy 8; Jamaica 2; Japan 11; Kenya 1; Korea, South 2; Mexico 44; Mozambique 2; Netherlands 2; Nicaragua 6; Nigeria 4; Papua New Guinea 8; Paraguay 14; Peru 22; Philippines 14; Poland 6; Portugal 3; Puerto Rico 2; Romania 4; Senegal 5; Serbia and Montenegro 2; Sierra Leone 2; South Africa 7; Spain 11; Tanzania 2; Uganda 3; Unspecified Country 41; Venezuela 1; Zambia 25

## Brethren in Christ World Missions

PO Box 390
Grantham, PA 17027-0390 USA

**Phone:** (717) 697-2634
**Fax:** (717) 691-6053
**E-mail:** bicwm@messiah.edu
**Web Site:** www.bic-church.org/wm
**Associations:** EFMA
*Rev. John A. Brubaker, Exec. Director*

A denominational sending agency of Brethren and Wesleyan tradition engaged in leadership development, church planting, TEE, evangelism, support of national churches, support of national workers, mobilization for mission, mission-related research and missionary training.

**Purpose:** "A church for every people...the Gospel to every person...Jesus worshipped in the nations."

**Year founded in US:** 1895

**Income for Overseas Min:** $1,807,897

**Fully Supported US Personnel Overseas:**
Expecting to serve more than 4 years: 32
Expecting to serve 1 to 4 years: 2
**Other Personnel:**
Short-term less than 1 year: 51
Bi-vocational/tentmakers: 10
Non-US serving in own/other country: 101
Home ministry & office staff in US: 14

**Countries:** Colombia 2; Honduras 4; India 2; Malawi 4; Mexico 2; Nepal; Nicaragua 2; Spain 2; United Kingdom 2; Unspecified Country 3; Venezuela 2; Zambia 3; Zimbabwe 4

## Bridge Builders International

PO Box 625
Philomath, OR 97370 USA

**Phone:** (541) 929-5627
**Fax:** (541) 929-5628
**E-mail:** info@bridgebuildersint.com
**Web Site:** www.bridgebuildersint.com
*Mr. Charles D. Kelley, President*

A nondenominational mobilization agency of Baptist tradition specializing in facilitating international partnerships for ministry & mission training.

**Purpose:** "...builds partnerships for effective ministry, mission, development and assistance [and] cultivates relationships that lead to strategic partnerships..."

**Year founded in US:** 1994

**Income for Overseas Min:** $460,907

**Fully Supported US Personnel Overseas:**

Expecting to serve more than 4 years: 1
Expecting to serve 1 to 4 years: 2
Non-residential mission Personnel: 2
**Other Personnel:**
Short-term less than 1 year: 12
Bi-vocational/tentmakers: 2
Home ministry & office staff in US: 6
**Countries:** Latvia 1

## Bright Hope International
2060 Stonington Ave.
Hoffman Estates, IL 60195 USA
**Phone:** (847) 519-0012
**Fax:** (847) 519-0024
**E-mail:** info@brighthope.org
**Web Site:** www.brighthope.org
**Associations:** AERDO
*Mr. Craig H. Dyer, President*

A nondenominational service agency of Independent tradition engaged in relief and/or rehabilitation, development and evangelism.
**Year founded in US:** 1968
**Income for Overseas Min:** $1,773,000
**Gifts in Kind:** $939,980
**Fully Supported US Personnel Overseas:**
Non-residential mission personnel: 1
**Other Personnel:**
Short-term less than 1 year: 3
Bi-vocational/tentmakers: 5
Non-US serving in own/other country: 348
Home ministry & office staff in US: 5
**Countries:** Costa Rica; Côte d'Ivoire; Cuba; Ethiopia; Ghana; Haiti; India; Indonesia; Kenya; Malawi; Mozambique; Papua New Guinea; Philippines; Thailand; Uganda

## Cadence International
PO Box 1268
Englewood, CO 80150 USA
**Phone:** (303) 762-1400
**Fax:** (303) 788-0661
**E-mail:** maryetta@cadence.org
**Web Site:** www.cadence.org
**Associations:** IFMA
*Mr. David Schroeder, Gen. Director*

A nondenominational service agency of Evangelical tradition engaged in hospitality ministry to the military around the world, evangelism, childrens programs, disciple-

ship and partnership development. Financial data from 2003.
**Year founded in US:** 1954
**Income for Overseas Min:** $2,627,634
**Gifts in Kind:** $4,245
**Fully Supported US Personnel Overseas:**
Expecting to serve 1 to 4 years: 91
**Other Personnel:**
Non-US serving in own/other country: 91
Home ministry & office staff in US: 7
**Countries:** Germany; Italy; Japan; Korea, South; Philippines; Russia; Spain; United Kingdom

## Calvary Commission, Inc.
PO Box 100
Lindale, TX 75771 USA
**Phone:** (903) 882-5501
**Fax:** (903) 882-7282
**E-mail:** missions@calvarycommission.org
**Web Site:** www.calvarycommission.org
*Rev. Joe L. Fauss, Intl. Director*

A transdenominational sending agency of Charismatic and Evangelical tradition engaged in missionary training, childcare/orphanage programs, missionary education, evangelism, support of national workers and short-term programs. Data from 2001.
**Year founded in US:** 1977
**Income for Overseas Min:** $150,000
**Gifts in Kind:** $125,000
**Fully Supported US Personnel Overseas:**
Expecting to serve more than 4 years: 18
Expecting to serve 1 to 4 years: 7
**Other Personnel:**
Short-term less than 1 year: 25
Bi-vocational/tentmakers: 3
Home ministry & office staff in US: 45
**Countries:** Belize 6; Mexico 10; Romania 2

## Calvary Evangelistic Mission, Inc.
PO Box 367000
San Juan, PR 00936-7000 USA
**Phone:** (787) 724-2727
**Fax:** (787) 723-9633
**E-mail:** cem@therockradio.org
**Web Site:** www.therockradio.org
*Janet Luttrell, President/CEO*

An interdenominational specialized agency of Baptist tradition engaged in broadcasting and extension education.

**Purpose:** "...to glorify God by assisting the church in fulfilling the Great Commission of Jesus Christ, primarily in the Caribbean."

**Year founded in US:** 1953

**Income for Overseas Min:** $660,067

**Gifts in Kind:** $73,428

**Fully Supported US Personnel Overseas:**
   Expecting to serve more than 4 years: 7
   Expecting to serve 1 to 4 years: 8
   Non-residential mission personnel: 2

**Other Personnel:**
   Home ministry & office staff in US: 11

**Countries:** Caribbean—General 7

# Calvary International
PO Box 10305
Jacksonville, FL 32247-0305 USA
**Phone:** (904) 398-6559
**Fax:** (904) 398-6840
**E-mail:** calvary@gotonations.com
**Web Site:** www.gotonations.com
**Associations:** AFMA

*Mr. Jerry L. Williamson, President*

An interdenominational sending agency of Charismatic tradition engaged in missionary training, church planting, evangelism, leadership development, mobilization for mission and short-term programs.

**Purpose:** "...a servant ministry helping the Body of Christ reap a global harvest."

**Year founded in US:** 1981

**Income for Overseas Min:** $1,664,409

**Gifts in Kind:** $17,040

**Fully Supported US Personnel Overseas:**
   Expecting to serve more than 4 years: 65
   Expecting to serve 1 to 4 years: 9
   Non-residential mission personnel: 16

**Other Personnel:**
   Short-term less than 1 year: 34
   Bi-vocational/tentmakers: 32
   Non-US serving in own/other country: 14
   Home ministry & office staff in US: 20

**Countries:** Brazil; Burkina Faso 8; China 1; Costa Rica 4; Guatemala 13; Honduras 2; Latvia 1; Mexico 6; Niger 1; Peru 2; Philippines 13; Russia 2; South Africa 2; Tanzania; Thailand 4; Ukraine 2; Vietnam 4

# CAM International
8625 La Prada Dr.
Dallas, TX 75228 USA
**Phone:** (214) 327-8206
**Fax:** (214) 327-8201
**E-mail:** info@caminternational.org
**Web Site:** www.caminternational.org
**Associations:** IFMA

*Mr. Daniel Wicher, President*

An evangelical sending agency engaged in evangelism, discipleship, church planting, leadership development, theological education, global mission mobilization and various other ministry initiatives.

**Purpose:** "...to produce and empower committed followers of Jesus Christ in Spanish speaking areas to reach the world."

**Year founded in US:** 1890

**Income for Overseas Min:** $5,780,354

**Fully Supported US Personnel Overseas:**
   Expecting to serve more than 4 years: 187

**Other Personnel:**
   Short-term less than 1 year: 30
   Non-US serving in own/other country: 42
   Home ministry & office staff in US: 18

**Countries:** Albania 4; El Salvador 3; Guatemala 48; Honduras 26; Mexico 80; Nicaragua 4; Panama 6; Spain 16

# Campus Crusade for Christ, International
100 Lake Hart Dr.
Orlando, FL 32832-0100 USA
**Phone:** (407) 826-2000
**Fax:** (407) 826-2851
**E-mail:** postmaster@ccci.org
**Web Site:** www.ccci.org
**Associations:** EFMA

*Dr. Steven B. Douglass, President*

An interdenominational sending agency of Evangelical tradition engaged in evangelism, support of national workers, training and discipleship.

**Purpose:** "...to boldly proclaim Jesus Christ and His life-changing love and truth to every person, and urgently mobilize co-laborers for the global harvest."

**Year founded in US:** 1951

**Income for Overseas Min:** $98,321,000

**Gifts in Kind:** $1,861,000

**Fully Supported US Personnel Overseas:**
Expecting to serve more than 4 years: 807
Expecting to serve 1 to 4 years: 480

**Other Personnel:**
Short-term less than 1 year: 776
Non-US serving in own/other country: 12,228
Home ministry & office staff in US: 6,415

**Countries:** Africa—General 2; Albania 7; Angola; Argentina 6; Armenia; Asia—General 163; Australia 10; Austria; Bangladesh; Barbados; Belarus 9; Belgium; Bolivia 4; Bosnia and Herzegovina; Botswana; Brazil 9; Bulgaria 4; Burkina Faso 2; Burundi; Cambodia 2; Cameroon; Central African Republic; Central Asia—General 60; Chad; Chile 2; Costa Rica; Croatia 16; Czech Republic 7; Dominican Republic; East Timor; Ecuador; Egypt 3; El Salvador 2; Estonia 2; Ethiopia; Europe—General 11; Fiji; France 57; Gabon; Germany 29; Ghana 1; Greece 3; Guatemala; Guinea; Haiti; Honduras; Hong Kong; Hungary 69; India; Indonesia 2; Italy 13; Jamaica; Japan 18; Kenya 6; Korea, South; Latvia 8; Lebanon; Lesotho; Liberia; Lithuania 5; Macau; Macedonia 4; Madagascar; Malawi; Malaysia; Mali; Mexico 9; Moldova; Mozambique; Myanmar/Burma; Namibia; Nepal; Netherlands 2; New Zealand 17; Nicaragua 2; Niger; Nigeria 4; Pakistan; Panama 2; Papua New Guinea; Paraguay; Peru; Philippines 21; Poland; Portugal; Romania 8; Russia 65; Rwanda; Serbia and Montenegro; Senegal 1; Sierra Leone; Singapore 41; Slovakia 9; Slovenia 3; Solomon Islands; South Africa 6; Spain 30; Sri Lanka; Suriname; Swaziland; Sweden; Switzerland; Taiwan; Tanzania; Thailand 8; Togo; Tonga; Trinidad and Tobago; Uganda 2; Ukraine 13; United Kingdom 17; Uruguay; Venezuela 3; Zambia; Zimbabwe 8

## Caring Partners Intl., Inc.

PO Box 44707
Middletown, OH 45044-0707 USA

**Phone:** (513) 727-1400
**Fax:** (513) 727-1401
**E-mail:** r.cline@caringpartners.org
**Web Site:** www.caringpartners.org

*Mr. Roy W. Cline, President & CEO*

A transdenominational specialized agency of Evangelical tradition engaged in short-term programs, evangelism, providing medical supplies, medical work, support of national churches.

**Purpose:** "...to open the minds & hearts of people around the world to the Gospel of Jesus Christ while serving their health needs with treatment, training and materials."

**Year founded in US:** 1975

**Income for Overseas Min:** $248,000

**Gifts in Kind:** $360,000

**Personnel:**
Short-term less than 1 year: 35
Home ministry & office staff in US: 6

## Carver Intl. Missions, Inc.

PO Box 92543
Atlanta, GA 30314 USA

**Phone:** (770) 484-0610
**Fax:** (770) 484-0615
**E-mail:** carverfm@aol.com

*Rev. Glenn T. Mason, Exec. Director*

A nondenominational missionary agency of Evangelical tradition specializing in training and deploying national disciples to biblically analyze, attack and resolve issues in their homes, communities, churches and workplaces.

**Year founded in US:** 1955

**Income for Overseas Min:** $300,000

**Fully Supported US Personnel Overseas:**
Expecting to serve more than 4 years: 5
Expecting to serve 1 to 4 years: 1

**Other Personnel:**
Short-term less than 1 year: 2
Non-US serving in own/other country: 3
Home ministry & office staff in US: 1

**Countries:** Liberia 5

## Catalyst Services

PO Box 152
Newtown, PA 18940 USA

**Phone:** (215) 579-4346
**Fax:** (215) 579-4826
**E-mail:** info@catalystservices.org
**Web Site:** www.catalystservices.org

*Ellen Livingood, President*

A service agency of Evangelical tradition engaged in services for other agencies and partnership development.

**Purpose:** "...to assist mission agencies and

denominations to collaborate more effectively with local churches to accelerate their global impact."

**Year founded in US:** 2006

**Personnel:**
  Home ministry & office staff in US: 2

## CBI International
## See: World Venture

## Cedar Lane Missionary Homes, Inc.
103 Cedar Lane
Laurel Springs, NJ 08021 USA
**Phone:** (856) 783-6525
**Fax:** (856) 783-6525
**E-mail:** cedarlane@furloughhomes.org
**Web Site:** www.furloughhomes.org
*Rev. James Callahan, Director*

An interdenominational support agency of Evangelical tradition engaged in furloughed missionary support and housing for missionaries.

**Purpose:** "...providing restful homes and otherwise assisting missionaries on furlough."

**Year founded in US:** 1949

**Personnel:**
  Short-term less than 1 year: 2
  Home ministry & office staff in US: 2

## Celebrant Singers
420 N. Dudley St.
Visalia, CA 93291 USA
**Phone:** (559) 740-4000
**Fax:** (559) 740-4040
**E-mail:** celebrants@celebrants.org
**Web Site:** www.celebrants.org
*Mr. Jon F. Stemkoski, Founder/President*

An interdenominational service agency of Charismatic and Evangelical tradition engaged in music ministry evangelism, audio recording/distribution and broadcasting. Data from 2001.

**Purpose:** "Teaching young adults by proclaiming His greatness and sharing His love with a hurting world through music, testimony, the preaching of the Word and our lives."

**Year founded in US:** 1977

**Income for Overseas Min:** $1,200,000

**Fully Supported US Personnel Overseas:**
  Non-residential mission personnel: 44

**Other Personnel:**
  Short-term less than 1 year: 125
  Home ministry & office staff in US: 22

## Centers for Apologetics Research (CFAR), The
PO Box 1196
San Juan Capistrano, CA 92693 USA
**Phone:** (949) 496-2000
**Fax:** (949) 496-2244
**E-mail:** TheCenters@aol.com
**Web Site:** www.thecenters.org
*Mr. Paul Carden, Exec. Director*

A nondenominational service agency of Evangelical tradition engaged in apologetics, broadcasting, evangelism, literature production and mission-related research.

**Purpose:** "...to equip God's people across borders and cultures for discernment, the defense of the faith and cult evangelism."

**Year founded in US:** 1995

**Fully Supported US Personnel Overseas:**
  Expecting to serve 1 to 4 years: 2

**Other Personnel:**
  Short-term less than 1 year: 1
  Non-US serving in own/other country: 10
  Home ministry & office staff in US: 3

**Countries:** Belize; Hungary; Russia; Ukraine

## Central Missionary Fellowship
## See: Seed International

## Central Yearly Meeting of Friends Missions
PO Box 542
Westfield, IN 46074 USA
**Phone:** (317) 896-5082
*Rev. Joseph A. Enyart, President*

A denominational sending agency of Friends tradition engaged in church planting, Bible distribution and evangelism.

**Year founded in US:** 1925

## Child Evangelism Fellowship, Inc.
PO Box 348
Warrenton, MO 63383 USA

**Phone:** (636) 456-4321
**Fax:** (636) 456-5000
**E-mail:** webmaster@cefonline.com
**Web Site:** www.cefonline.com
*Mr. Reese R. Kauffman, President*

A sending agency of Independent tradition engaged in evangelism, childrens programs, literature distribution, literature production, partnership development and training. Field personnel from 2002.

**Purpose:** "...to evangelize boys and girls... and establish them in the Word of God and the local church..."

**Year founded in US:** 1937

**Income for Overseas Min:** $4,663,827

**Fully Supported US Personnel Overseas:**
  Expecting to serve more than 4 years: 69
  Expecting to serve 1 to 4 years: 3

**Other Personnel:**
  Short-term less than 1 year: 31
  Non-US serving in own/other country: 196
  Home ministry & office staff in US: 132

**Countries:** Albania 1; Angola; Argentina 1; Armenia 2; Australia 2; Austria 1; Belgium 2; Belize 2; Benin; Bolivia; Botswana 1; Brazil; Burkina Faso; Burundi; Cameroon; Chad; Chile; Colombia; Congo, Democratic Republic of; Côte d'Ivoire; Croatia 2; Cuba; Cyprus 7; Denmark 2; Ecuador; Estonia; Fiji 3; France 2; Gambia, The 2; Germany 4; Ghana; Greece 2; Guatemala; Guinea; Haiti 2; Hong Kong 1; Hungary 1; Israel 2; Japan; Jordan; Kenya 5; Liberia; Macau; Madagascar; Malawi; Mali; Mexico 1; Micronesia, Federated States of 2; Moldova 1; Mozambique; Namibia 3; Nepal; Netherlands Antilles 2; Niger; Nigeria; Pakistan; Peru; Philippines; Poland; Russia; Serbia and Montenegro 2; Singapore; Slovakia; Slovenia; South Africa 3; Suriname; Switzerland 6; Taiwan 2; Thailand; Togo; Uganda; Ukraine; Zambia; Zimbabwe

## Childcare International
## See: Childcare Worldwide

## Childcare Worldwide
PO Box W
Bellingham, WA 98227-1582 USA
**Phone:** (800) 553-2328
**Fax:** (360) 647-2392

**E-mail:** info@childcareworldwide.org
**Web Site:** www.childcareworldwide.org
*Dr. G. Max Lange, President*

A nondenominational service agency of Evangelical tradition engaged in extension education, childcare/orphanage programs, development, medical work and relief and/or rehabilitation.

**Year founded in US:** 1981

**Income for Overseas Min:** $14,415,698

**Gifts in Kind:** $12,198,526

**Personnel:**
  Non-US serving in own/other country: 109
  Home ministry & office staff in US: 14

**Countries:** Belarus; China; Haiti; India; Kenya; Liberia; Mexico; Peru; Philippines; Sri Lanka; Thailand; Uganda

## Children's Haven Intl.
400 E. Minnesota Rd.
Pharr, TX 78577 USA
**Phone:** (956) 787-7378
**Fax:** (956) 783-4637
**E-mail:** chii@prodigy.net
**Web Site:** www.childrenshaven.org
*Alfredo Tamayo, US Director*

A nondenominational service agency of Mennonite tradition engaged in childcare/orphanage programs, services for other agencies and short-term programs. Data from 2001.

**Year founded in US:** 1972

**Fully Supported US Personnel Overseas:**
  Expecting to serve more than 4 years: 2
  Non-residential mission personnel: 12

**Other Personnel:**
  Short-term less than 1 year: 4

**Countries:** Mexico 2

## Children's HopeChest
PO Box 69
Palmer Lake, CO 80133 USA
**Phone:** (719) 487-7800
**Fax:** (719) 487-7799
**E-mail:** lmercer@hopechest.org
**Web Site:** www.hopechest.org
*Mr. George Steiner, CEO/Founder*

An interdenominational support agency of Evangelical tradition engaged in childcare/orphanage programs, Bible distribution, childrens programs, discipleship and youth programs.

**Purpose:** "...to respond to God's desire to create a world where every orphan knows Him, experiences the blessing of family, and acquires the skills necessary for independent life."

**Year founded in US:** 1994

**Income for Overseas Min:** $1,964,877

**Gifts in Kind:** $240,143

**Fully Supported US Personnel Overseas:**
  Expecting to serve more than 4 years: 1

**Other Personnel:**
  Short-term less than 1 year: 480
  Non-US serving in own/other country: 92
  Home ministry & office staff in US: 12

**Countries:** Russia 1; Swaziland; Ukraine

## Childspring International

1328 Peachtree St. NE
Atlanta, GA 30309 USA

**Phone:** (404) 228-7733
**Fax:** (404) 228-7759
**E-mail:** REB@childspringintl.org
**Web Site:** www.childspringintl.org
**Associations:** EFMA Candidate

*Mrs. Rose Emily Bermudez, Exec. Director*

An interdenominational support agency of Christian (Restoration Movement) tradition engaged in medical work, relief and/or rehabilitation.

**Purpose:** "...brings children to the United States for medical care not available in their own countries and returns them home with opportunities for a better life."

**Income for Overseas Min:** $3,204,805

**Gifts in Kind:** $2,946,461

**Personnel:**
  Bi-vocational/tentmakers: 1
  Home ministry & office staff in US: 4

## China Connection

458 S. Pasadena Ave.
Pasadena, CA 91105 USA

**Phone:** (626) 793-3737
**Fax:** (626) 793-3362
**E-mail:** kathycall@juno.com
**Web Site:** www.chinaconnection.org

*Ms. Kathy Call, Executive Director*

A nondenominational support agency of Evangelical tradition engaged in missions information service, agricultural programs, Bible distribution, church construction, childcare/orphanage programs and medical work. Data from 2003.

**Year founded in US:** 1989

**Income for Overseas Min:** $340,871

**Gifts in Kind:** $65,834

**Personnel:**
  Home ministry & office staff in US: 1

## China Ministries Intl.

PO Box 40489
Pasadena, CA 91114 USA

**Phone:** (626) 398-2343
**Fax:** (626) 398-2361
**E-mail:** cmius@compuserve.com
**Web Site:** www.cmius.org

*Dr. Samuel Chao, US Director*

A nondenominational support agency of Evangelical tradition engaged in theological education, extension education, Bible distribution, TEE, evangelism, mission-related research and missionary training.

**Purpose:** "...for the evangelization of China, the strengthening of the Chinese Church...by engaging in ministries of research, training of workers and sending them to the harvest field..."

**Year founded in US:** 1987

**Income for Overseas Min:** $362,515

**Personnel:**
  Bi-vocational/tentmakers: 5
  Home ministry & office staff in US: 5

## China Outreach Ministries, Inc.

PO Box 35
Mechanicsburg, PA 17055 USA

**Phone:** (717) 591-3500
**Fax:** (717) 591-0412
**E-mail:** chinaout@aol.com
**Web Site:** www.chinaoutreach.org

*Rev. Glendon W. Osborn, President*

A nondenominational support agency of Evangelical tradition engaged in evangelism and discipleship, primarily among Chinese intellectuals on U.S. university campuses.

**Purpose:** "...focuses on giving Christ to China's future leaders by...showing them the love of Christ...leading them to faith in Christ...discipling, training and mentoring them and equipping them to minister creatively to other Chinese people."

**Year founded in US:** 1959

**Income for Overseas Min:** $103,297

**Personnel:**
Bi-vocational/tentmakers: 1
Home ministry & office staff in US: 4

## ChinaSource

PO Box 4343
Fullerton, CA 92834-4343 USA
**Phone:** (714) 449-0611
**Fax:** (714) 449-0624
**E-mail:** info@chsource.org
**Web Site:** www.chsource.org

*Dr. Brent Fulton, President*

A specialized agency engaged in mission-related research, partnership development, and consulting/training. Founded as a cooperative effort of the EFMA, IFMA, WEF, Chinese Coordination Centre for World Evangelization, and the Billy Graham Center at Wheaton College.

**Purpose:** "Strategically connecting knowledge and leaders to advance the kingdom of God in China."

**Year founded in US:** 1995

**Personnel:**
Non-US serving in own/other country: 3
Home ministry & office staff in US: 6

**Countries:** Hong Kong

## Chosen Inc.
## See: Chosen Mission Project

## Chosen Mission Project

3638 W. 26th St.
Erie, PA 16506 USA
**Phone:** (814) 833-3023
**Fax:** (814) 833-4091
**E-mail:** rick@chosenmissionproject.org
**Web Site:** www.chosenmissionproject.org

*Mr. Rick King, Exec. Director*

A nondenominational specialized agency of Evangelical tradition engaged in supplying equipment, providing medical supplies and technical assistance.

**Purpose:** "...to promote health care programs in conjunction with missionaries and national Christian health care workers in a tangible effort to bring the love of Christ to those least able to help themselves."

**Year founded in US:** 1969

**Gifts in Kind:** $787,622

**Personnel:**
Home ministry & office staff in US: 4

## Chosen People Ministries

241 E. 51st St.
New York, NY 10022 USA
**Phone:** (212) 223-2252
**Fax:** (212) 223-2576
**E-mail:** cpm@chosenpeople.com
**Web Site:** www.chosenpeople.com
**Associations:** IFMA

*Dr. Mitch Glaser, Pres./CEO*

A nondenominational service agency of Independent and Evangelical tradition engaged in evangelism, church planting, literature distribution and missionary training. Financial information from 1998.

**Year founded in US:** 1894

**Income for Overseas Min:** $297,112

**Personnel:**
Home ministry & office staff in US: 39

**Countries:** Argentina; Australia; France; Germany; Israel; Mexico; Ukraine; United Kingdom

## Christ Community Church

2500 Dowie Memorial Dr.
Zion, IL 60099 USA
**Phone:** (847) 746-1411
**Fax:** (847) 746-1452
**E-mail:** mmcdowell@ccczion.org
**Web Site:** www.ccczion.org

*Dr. Mike McDowell, Missions Pastor*

A denominational sending agency of Evangelical tradition engaged in support of national workers, camping programs, church planting, TEE, leadership development, short-term programs and TESOL.

**Year founded in US:** 1896

**Income for Overseas Min:** $300,000

**Personnel:**

do you?

# Know. Go.

## need Seminary training now.

In a world crunched for time, Columbia Biblical Seminary & School of Missions offers realistic options for furthering your education.

**Distance Education**
Audio, video, and online courses enable you to complete a Biblical Ministry Certificate or work toward a M.A. or M. Div. degree completely from your home.

**Winter and Summer Modular Courses**
Each January and summer, Columbia Biblical Seminary offers one- and two-week intensive courses on missions, ministry, and Bible, taught by expert professors.

**Advancement In Ministry (AIM)**
You'll take courses from home most of the year, and come to campus for a week or two twice a year. Earn your seminary degree without ever relocating to Columbia, South Carolina.

## Columbia Biblical Seminary
### & School of Missions

**Equipping Great
Commission Christians**

Admissions 800.777.2227

www.**ciu**.edu/seminary

Columbia.South Carolina

# "Someone is counting on you."

**Christ to the Nations Missions** supports both national and American missionaries, and is engaged in church planting, missionary training, and Bible distribution.

- Church planting
- Bible and literature distribution
- Children's programs
- Supporting national churches
- Supporting national workers
- Missionary training

**Bless the Children Program**, a ministry of Christ to the Nations Missions, is helping to meet the needs of children in Eastern Europe, Africa, and Asia.

# Christ to the Nations World Missions and Bless the Children Program

Christ to the Nations first began ministering to nations suffering under communist rule. Since 1989, we've grown to include other countries. We have sent God's word to thousands in Ukraine, India, Poland, Cuba, Lithuania, Russia, Kazakstan, and the Philippines. We continue to focus on establishing local New Testament Churches and reaching and teaching national peoples.

**Founder and Director:**
David Ralston and family
P.O. Box 1824, Cocoa, FL 32923
Phone/Fax: 321-504-0778
E-mail: DLRCTTN@aol.com
Website: www.CTTN.org

Triple your church's mission giving!
Ask us how!

David and Georgia Ralson

Short-term less than 1 year: 27
Non-US serving in own/other country: 120
Home ministry & office staff in US: 13

**Countries:** Guyana; Indonesia; Japan; Palestine; Philippines; South Africa

## Christ for India, Inc.
PO Box 271086
Dallas, TX 75227 USA
**Phone:** (972) 771-7221
**Fax:** (972) 771-4021
**E-mail:** jtitus@christforindia.org
**Web Site:** www.christforindia.org
**Associations:** AFMA

*Mr. Jameson Titus, Pres./Chief Devel. Officer*

A nondenominational service agency of Charismatic and Evangelical tradition engaged in theological education, childcare/orphanage programs, church construction, church planting, medical work and training. Data from 2001.

**Purpose:** "...to make ready a people, prepared for the coming of the Lord'."
**Year founded in US:** 1981
**Income for Overseas Min:** $253,156
**Gifts in Kind:** $1,147
**Fully Supported US Personnel Overseas:**
  Expecting to serve more than 4 years: 1
**Other Personnel:**
  Short-term less than 1 year: 30
  Non-US serving in own/other country: 1
  Home ministry & office staff in US: 2
**Countries:** India 1

## Christ for the City Intl.
PO Box 241827
Omaha, NE 68124 USA
**Phone:** (402) 592-8332
**Fax:** (402) 592-8312
**E-mail:** info@cfci.org
**Web Site:** www.cfci.org
**Associations:** EFMA

*Dr. Duane "Chip" Anderson, President*

An interdenominational support agency of Evangelical tradition engaged in childcare/orphanage programs, leadership development, support of national churches, evangelism and short-term programs.

**Purpose:** "To multiply churches...which in turn...send multinational teams into the

least evangelized cities of the world."
**Year founded in US:** 1995
**Income for Overseas Min:** $1,417,220
**Gifts in Kind:** $13,496
**Fully Supported US Personnel Overseas:**
  Expecting to serve more than 4 years: 14
  Expecting to serve 1 to 4 years: 10
  Non-residential mission personnel: 1
**Other Personnel:**
  Short-term less than 1 year: 35
  Non-US serving in own/other country: 63
  Home ministry & office staff in US: 12

**Countries:** Bolivia; Colombia 2; Costa Rica 7; Mali; Mexico; Nicaragua; Peru 1; Spain 2

## Christ for the Nations, Inc.
3404 Conway St.
Dallas, TX 75224 USA
**Phone:** (214) 376-1711
**Fax:** (214) 302-6301
**E-mail:** info@cfni.org
**Web Site:** www.cfni.org

*Dr. Dennis Lindsay, President/CEO*

An interdenominational support agency of Pentecostal tradition engaged in missionary education, church construction, theological education, evangelism, literature distribution and literature production.

**Purpose:** "...to provide resources for the completion of church buildings, caring for orphans, supporting the nation of Israel, humanitarian relief efforts, establishing and strengthening international Bible schools and the distribution of Christian literature."
**Year founded in US:** 1948
**Income for Overseas Min:** $1,500,000
**Personnel:**
  Short-term less than 1 year: 400
  Home ministry & office staff in US: 110

## Christ to the Nations
**(See ad page 126)**
PO Box 1824
Cocoa, FL 32923 USA
**Phone:** (321) 504-0778
**Fax:** (321) 504-0778
**E-mail:** inhisfields@aol.com
**Web Site:** www.cttn.org

*Dr. David L. Ralston, Founder/Director*

A sending agency engaged in church planting, Bible distribution, childcare/orphanage programs, extension education, evangelism and support of national churches.

**Purpose:** "...to help local churches and God's people reach the unreached millions with the Gospel of Jesus Christ and the Word of God."

**Year founded in US:** 1989

**Income for Overseas Min:** $185,000

**Fully Supported US Personnel Overseas:**
Expecting to serve more than 4 years: 6
Expecting to serve 1 to 4 years: 2

**Other Personnel:**
Short-term less than 1 year: 2
Non-US serving in own/other country: 56
Home ministry & office staff in US: 1

**Countries:** Bahamas, The 2; Ghana; India; Kenya; Lithuania; Pakistan; Philippines; Romania; Russia; Uganda; Ukraine 2; Unspecified Country 2

## Christar

PO Box 14866
Reading, PA 19612-4866 USA

**Phone:** (610) 375-0300
**Fax:** (610) 375-6862
**E-mail:** info@christar.org
**Web Site:** www.christar.org
**Associations:** IFMA

*Rev. R. Stephen Coffey, President*

A nondenominational sending agency of evangelical tradition engaged in church planting, correspondence courses, development, theological education, evangelism and mobilization for mission.

**Purpose:** "...to establish churches, primarily within least-reached Buddhist, Hindu, Muslim and Asian communities worldwide."

**Year founded in US:** 1930

**Income for Overseas Min:** $10,108,599

**Fully Supported US Personnel Overseas:**
Expecting to serve more than 4 years: 254
Expecting to serve 1 to 4 years: 1
Non-residential mission personnel: 300

**Other Personnel:**
Short-term less than 1 year: 90
Bi-vocational/tentmakers: 10
Non-US serving in own/other country: 16
Home ministry & office staff in US: 40

**Countries:** Africa—General 8; Albania 10; Asia—General 24; Central Asia—General

3; China 37; France 15; Germany 5; Hong Kong 8; Indonesia 2; Japan 12; Jordan 18; Kazakhstan 12; Middle East 8; Mongolia 5; Netherlands 5; Pakistan 10; Philippines 17; Russia 1; Tajikistan 7; Turkey 35; United Kingdom 12; Yemen

## Christian Aid Ministries

PO Box 360
Berlin, OH 44610 USA

**Phone:** (330) 893-2428
**Fax:** (330) 893-2305

*Mr. David N. Troyer, Gen. Director*

An interdenominational service agency of Mennonite tradition engaged in relief and/or rehabilitation, childcare/orphanage programs and literature distribution. Field personnel data from 2002.

**Purpose:** "...to provide a channel for Amish and conservative Mennonite churches to minister to physical and spiritual needs around the world."

**Year founded in US:** 1981

**Income for Overseas Min:** $190,608,201

**Gifts in Kind:** $169,231,381

**Fully Supported US Personnel Overseas:**
Expecting to serve 1 to 4 years: 75

**Other Personnel:**
Short-term less than 1 year: 200
Non-US serving in own/other country: 163
Home ministry & office staff in US: 64

**Countries:** Haiti; Liberia; Moldova; Nicaragua; Romania; Ukraine

## Christian Aid Mission

PO Box 9037
Charlottesville, VA 22906 USA

**Phone:** (434) 977-5650
**Fax:** (434) 295-6814
**E-mail:** info@christianaid.org
**Web Site:** www.christianaid.org
*Mr. Axel Lanausse, President/CEO*

A transdenominational service agency of Evangelical and Fundamental tradition providing financial assistance for indigenous missions, Bible distribution, childcare, church planting, missionary education and evangelism. Assists over 700 ministries with a missionary force of more than 80,000.

**Purpose:** "...providing financial support

for indigenous missionary ministries in poorer countries overseas."

**Year founded in US:** 1953

**Income for Overseas Min:** $10,117,197

**Fully Supported US Personnel Overseas:**
Non-residential mission personnel: 4

**Other Personnel:**
Non-US serving in own/other country: 3,093
Home ministry & office staff in US: 66

**Countries:** Albania; Argentina; Bangladesh; Belarus; Benin; Bolivia; Bulgaria; Cambodia; Chile; China; Colombia; Cuba; Czech Republic; Ecuador; Ghana; Honduras; India; Indonesia; Kazakhstan; Kenya; Kyrgyzstan; Laos; Liberia; Mexico; Middle East; Myanmar/Burma; Nepal; Nigeria; Pakistan; Papua New Guinea; Paraguay; Peru; Philippines; Romania; Russia; Senegal; Sierra Leone; Sri Lanka; Tanzania; Thailand; Ukraine; Uruguay; Uzbekistan; Vietnam

## Christian and Missionary Alliance

PO Box 35000
Colorado Springs, CO 80935-3500 USA

**Phone:** (719) 599-5999
**Fax:** (719) 262-5393
**E-mail:** info@cmalliance.org
**Web Site:** www.cmalliance.org

**Associations:** IFMA

*Dr. Gary M. Benedict, President*

A denominational sending agency of Evangelical tradition engaged in church planting, correspondence courses, discipleship, theological education, evangelism and leadership development. Short-term data from 2002.

**Purpose:** "...to develop missionary church-multiplication movements among unreached and responsive peoples worldwide, as an extension of the local church."

**Year founded in US:** 1887

**Income for Overseas Min:** $20,545,803

**Fully Supported US Personnel Overseas:**
Expecting to serve more than 4 years: 761

**Other Personnel:**
Short-term less than 1 year: 1,352
Bi-vocational/tentmakers: 89
Home ministry & office staff in US: 15

**Countries:** Africa—General 148; Asia—General 201; Central Asia—General 5; Europe—General 159; Latin America—General 171; Unspecified Country 77

## Christian Associates Intl.

1534 N. Moorpark Rd. #356
Thousand Oaks, CA 91360 USA

**Phone:** (818) 865-1816
**Fax:** (818) 865-0317
**E-mail:** usoffice@christianassociates.org
**Web Site:** www.christianassociates.org

*Dr. Linus J. Morris, President*

A transdenominational sending agency of Evangelical tradition engaged in church planting and support of national churches, with 150 missionaries. Financial data from 2001.

**Purpose:** "...to reach the unchurched through the multiplication of high-impact leaders and high-impact churches."

**Year founded in US:** 1968

**Income for Overseas Min:** $2,330,050

**Personnel:**
Short-term less than 1 year: 100
Home ministry & office staff in US: 17

**Countries:** Belgium; Czech Republic; France; Germany; Ireland; Italy; Latvia; Netherlands; Poland; Portugal; Romania; Russia; Spain; Sweden; Switzerland; United Kingdom

## Christian Aviation and Radio Mission

PO Box 514
Ankeny, IA 50021-0514 USA

**Phone:** (515) 480-9099
**Fax:** (515) 967-7128
**E-mail:** carmstan@aol.com
**Web Site:** www.carm-intl.org

*Mr. Stanley Smelser, Admin./Mission Rep.*

A nondenominational specialized agency of Christian (Restoration Movement) tradition engaged in audio recording/distribution, aviation services, broadcasting, leadership development, supplying equipment and technical assistance.

**Purpose:** "...to strive to take on the responsibility of meeting the logistical and technical needs...in order to allow the Ministers, Evangelists and Missionaries to give their attention to prayer and the ministry of the Word."

**Year founded in US:** 1989

Income for Overseas Min: $27,476

Personnel:
  Short-term less than 1 year: 1
  Non-US serving in own/other country: 4

Countries: Philippines

## Christian Blind Mission Intl.

450 E. Park Ave.
Greenville, SC 29601 USA
**Phone:** (864) 239-0065
**Fax:** (864) 239-0069
**E-mail:** jwood@cbmiusa.org
**Web Site:** www.cbmiusa.org
*Mr. Alan Harkey, Natl. Director*

A transdenominational service agency engaged in medical work, providing medical supplies, support of national workers and relief and/or rehabilitation. Personnel data from 1998.

**Purpose:** "…Worldwide Christian service in eye care and projects for people with disabilities."

Year founded in US: 1976

Income for Overseas Min: $22,575,172

Gifts in Kind: $21,057,740

Fully Supported US Personnel Overseas:
  Expecting to serve more than 4 years: 1
  Expecting to serve 1 to 4 years: 18
  Non-residential mission personnel: 1

Other Personnel:
  Home ministry & office staff in US: 8

Countries: Cameroon; Congo, Republic of the; Dominican Republic; Ecuador; Jordan; Kenya; Madagascar; Nigeria; Pakistan; Papua New Guinea; Philippines; Tanzania 1; Thailand; Togo; Uganda

## Christian Broadcasting Network Inc., The

977 Centerville Turnpike
Virginia Beach, VA 23463 USA
**Phone:** (757) 226-7000
**Fax:** (757) 226-2017
**E-mail:** cbnonline@cbn.com
**Web Site:** www.cbn.com
**Associations:** AERDO
*Mr. Pat Robertson, Chairman & CEO*

The Christian Broadcasting Network (CBN) is one of the largest Christian television ministries in the world. A multifaceted nonprofit organization, CBN provides programming by cable, broadcast and satellite to 180 countries produced in 71 languages. CBN's humanitarian arm, Operation Blessing International, includes The Hunger Strike Force and event-driven outreaches designed to provide relief and ministry to those in need.

Year founded in US: 1960

Income for Overseas Min: $115,104,000

Gifts in Kind: $96,600,000

Fully Supported US Personnel Overseas:
  Expecting to serve more than 4 years: 6
  Expecting to serve 1 to 4 years: 9
  Non-residential mission personnel: 15

Other Personnel:
  Short-term less than 1 year: 35
  Non-US serving in own/other country: 853
  Home ministry & office staff in US: 50

Countries: Brazil; Cambodia; China 1; Costa Rica; Ghana; Hong Kong; India; Indonesia 1; Kazakhstan; Mexico; Nigeria; Philippines; Russia; Senegal 2; Singapore; South Africa; Thailand 1; Ukraine 1; United Kingdom

## Christian Business Men's Committee
## See: Connecting Business Men to Christ

## Christian Church (Disciples of Christ)—Global Ministries

PO Box 1986
Indianapolis, IN 46206 USA
**Phone:** (317) 635-3100
**Fax:** (317) 635-4323
**E-mail:** dom@disciples.org
**Web Site:** www.globalministries.org
*Julia Brown Karimu, Mission Exec.*

A denominational sending agency of Christian (Restoration Movement) tradition engaged in support of missionaries and national churches through a combined Global Ministries partnership with the Wider Church Ministries of the United Church of Christ. Statistics are from 2003.

Year founded in US: 1849

Personnel:
  Home ministry & office staff in US: 21

## Christian Church of North America—Missions

1294 Rutledge Rd.
Transfer, PA 16154 USA
**Phone:** (724) 962-3501
**Fax:** (724) 962-1766
**E-mail:** ccnamissions@yahoo.com
**Web Site:** www.ccna.org
*Rev. Mark Charles, Missions Director*

A denominational sending agency of Pentecostal and Charismatic tradition engaged in evangelism, childcare/orphanage programs, church construction, church planting, support of national workers and relief and/or rehabilitation. Personnel figures from 1998. Financial data from 2001.

**Year founded in US:** 1907

**Income for Overseas Min:** $408,000

**Fully Supported US Personnel Overseas:**
Expecting to serve more than 4 years: 12
Expecting to serve 1 to 4 years: 2

**Other Personnel:**
Short-term less than 1 year: 50
Home ministry & office staff in US: 3

**Countries:** Colombia 1; Europe—General 2; India 4; Italy 1; Kenya; South Africa 4

## Christian Churches/ Churches of Christ

USA  (No central office)
A body of autonomous congregations and agencies of Christian (Restoration Movement) tradition (using instrumental music in worship) which sends and supports missionaries directly from local congregations. Data provided by Mission Services Association (all information based upon best estimates for an independent brotherhood of churches). Data from 2001.

**Income for Overseas Min:** $52,000,000

**Fully Supported US Personnel Overseas:**
Expecting to serve more than 4 years: 915
Expecting to serve 1 to 4 years: 100
Non-residential mission personnel: 50

**Other Personnel:**
Short-term less than 1 year: 2,000
Non-US serving in own/other country: 422

**Countries:** Africa—General 4; Argentina 4; Asia—General 6; Australia 20; Austria 6; Bahamas, The 2; Bangladesh; Barbados 6; Belgium 1; Bosnia and Herzegovina 2; Brazil 28; Cayman Islands 2; Chile 32; Cote d'Ivoire 6; Czech Republic 2; Dominica 5; Dominican Republic 12; Ecuador 4; Equatorial Guinea 2; Ethiopia 8; France 5; Germany 8; Ghana 13; Grenada 2; Guatemala 2; Guinea 15; Guyana; Haiti 4; Honduras 19; Hong Kong 10; India 17; Indonesia 15; Ireland 6; Israel 2; Italy 14; Jamaica 12; Japan 30; Kenya 35; Korea, South 4; Kosovo 2; Liberia 2; Mali 2; Mexico 50; Mozambique 6; Myanmar/Burma; New Zealand 8; Nigeria 2; Pakistan; Panama 2; Papua New Guinea 30; Philippines 40; Poland 2; Portugal 4; Puerto Rico 5; Russia 16; Singapore 4; South Africa 32; Spain 1; Taiwan 21; Tanzania 21; Thailand 41; Ukraine 30; United Kingdom 20; Unspecified Country 160; Venezuela 15; Zimbabwe 34

## Christian Cultural Development Foundation

417 NE Third Ave.
Fort Lauderdale, FL 33301 USA
**Phone:** (954) 828-1505
**E-mail:** robin@christiancultural.com
**Web Site:** www.christiancultural.com
*Robin Haines Merrill, Founder/Director*

An interdenominational service agency of Ecumenical and Evangelical tradition engaged in development, evangelism, prostitution ministry, justice, leadership development and support of national workers.

**Purpose:** "...to provide creative alternatives to prostitutes and street children in the Philippines who want to change their lifestyles and follow Jesus Christ."

**Year founded in US:** 1990

**Income for Overseas Min:** $14,408

**Gifts in Kind:** $2,000

**Fully Supported US Personnel Overseas:**
Expecting to serve more than 4 years: 2
Non-residential mission personnel: 1

**Other Personnel:**
Bi-vocational/tentmakers: 2
Non-US serving in own/other country: 6
Home ministry & office staff in US: 1

**Countries:** Philippines 2

## Christian Dental Society

PO Box 296
Sumner, IA 50674 USA

**Phone:** (563) 578-8887
**Fax:** (563) 578-8887
**E-mail:** cdssent@iowatelecom.net
**Web Site:** www.christiandental.org

*Dr. Robert F. Liebler, Exec. Director*

An nondenominational specialized agency of Ecumenical tradition engaged in dental work, training local dentists in new techniques in 22 countries.

**Purpose:** "...to carry out the Great Commission given by Christ in Matthew 28:19 & 20 through dentists and dentistry."

**Year founded in US:** 1963

**Personnel:**
  Home ministry & office staff in US: 1

## Christian Discipleship Ministries, Inc.

PO Box 1084
Eagle Point, OR 97524 USA

**Phone:** (541) 830-8161
**Fax:** (541) 830-1565
**E-mail:** rcook@ccountry.com

*Mr. Richard E. Cook, Director*

A nondenominational sending agency of Baptist tradition engaged in church planting, discipleship, literature distribution, management consulting/training and training. Personnel data from 2002.

**Purpose:** "...to support and strengthen mission work in India."

**Year founded in US:** 1994

**Gifts in Kind:** $129,245

**Fully Supported US Personnel Overseas:**
  Expecting to serve more than 4 years: 1
  Non-residential mission personnel: 2

**Other Personnel:**
  Non-US serving in own/other country: 7

**Countries:** India 1

## Christian Fellowship Union, Inc.

PO Box 909
McAllen, TX 78505-0909 USA

**Phone:** (956) 686-5886
**Fax:** (956) 686-3049
**E-mail:** cfunion@sbcglobal.net

*Rev. Steven P. Johnson, Gen. Director*

An interdenominational support agency of Charismatic tradition engaged in support of national churches, church planting, discipleship, TEE, evangelism and leadership development.

**Purpose:** "...to proclaim Jesus Christ, make disciples, establish churches and equip believers in Mexico and south Texas for worldwide ministry."

**Year founded in US:** 1945

**Income for Overseas Min:** $9,581

**Fully Supported US Personnel Overseas:**
  Expecting to serve more than 4 years: 4
  Non-residential mission personnel: 2

**Other Personnel:**
  Bi-vocational/tentmakers: 2
  Home ministry & office staff in US: 3

**Countries:** Mexico 2; Spain 2

## Christian Laymen's Missionary Evangelism Association

826 Ford St.
Prosser, WA 99350 USA

**Phone:** (509) 241-0530
**E-mail:** clmealaymen@earthlink.net
**Web Site:** www.clmea.com

*Mr. Larry Taylor, President*

A support agency of Charismatic tradition engaged in evangelism, broadcasting, short-term programs and support of national workers.

**Purpose:** "To raise up laymen for world evangelism."

**Year founded in US:** 1977

**Income for Overseas Min:** $2,982

**Gifts in Kind:** $300

**Personnel:**
  Short-term less than 1 year: 5
  Home ministry & office staff in US: 1

## Christian Literacy Associates

541 Perry Highway
Pittsburgh, PA 15229-1851 USA

**Phone:** (412) 364-3777
**E-mail:** drliteracy@aol.com
**Web Site:** www.christianliteracy.com

*Dr. William E. Kofmehl Jr., President*

An interdenominational specialized agency of Ecumenical tradition engaged in literacy work. The "Christian Literacy Series" has been used in 54 countries.

**Purpose:** "...committed to reaching functionally illiterate adults and children throughout the world by helping them develop reading skills."

**Year founded in US:** 1975

**Personnel:**
  Home ministry & office staff in US: 4

## Christian Literature Crusade
## See: CLC Ministries Int'l.

## Christian Literature Intl.
PO Box 777
Canby, OR 97013 USA

**Phone:** (503) 266-9734
**Fax:** (503) 266-1143
**E-mail:** newlife1@canby.com
**Web Site:** www.newlifebible.org

*Joyce E. Moore, President*

A nondenominational support agency of Evangelical tradition engaged in Bible distribution, literacy work, TESOL and Bible translation.

**Purpose:** "...to provide the Word of God in a form that can be understood by new readers and the well-educated at an affordable price."

**Year founded in US:** 1967

**Income for Overseas Min:** $102,000

**Personnel:**
  Home ministry & office staff in US: 2

**Countries:** Australia; Cameroon; Ghana; India; Liberia; Malaysia; Mexico; Myanmar/Burma; Nigeria; Philippines; Tanzania; Uganda; United Kingdom; Zambia

## Christian Medical & Dental Associations—Global Health Outreach
PO Box 7500
Bristol, TN 37621 USA

**Phone:** (423) 844-1000
**Fax:** (423) 764-1417
**E-mail:** gho@cmda.org
**Web Site:** www.cmda.org/go/gho

*Mr. David L. Stevens, CEO/CMDA*

A service agency engaged in medical work, management consulting/training, mobilization for mission, short-term programs and

missionary training. Conducts over 70 ministries to and by CMDA members.

**Purpose:** "...to motivate, educate and equip Christian physicians and dentists to glorify God."

**Year founded in US:** 1935

**Income for Overseas Min:** $5,602,827

**Gifts in Kind:** $3,932,595

**Fully Supported US Personnel Overseas:**
  Expecting to serve more than 4 years: 1
  Non-residential mission personnel: 3

**Other Personnel:**
  Short-term less than 1 year: 287
  Non-US serving in own/other country: 1
  Home ministry & office staff in US: 70

**Countries:** Honduras 1

## Christian Ministries Intl. (CMI)
1665 SW Brisbane St.
Port St. Lucie, FL 34984 USA

**Phone:** (772) 201-2077
**Fax:** (772) 398-9236
**E-mail:** cmihood@yahoo.com
**Web Site:** www.glowmi.org/cmi

*Dr. L. Lynn Hood, President*

A transdenominational sending agency of Charismatic and Independent tradition engaged in leadership development, church planting, discipleship, TEE, evangelism and management consulting/training.

**Purpose:** "...preparing national indigenous leaders of the local church to be empowered by New Testament principles of leadership to assist them in world evangelization and church planting in their generation."

**Year founded in US:** 1985

**Income for Overseas Min:** $450,000

**Fully Supported US Personnel Overseas:**
  Expecting to serve more than 4 years: 7
  Non-residential mission personnel: 2

**Other Personnel:**
  Short-term less than 1 year: 35
  Bi-vocational/tentmakers: 2
  Non-US serving in own/other country: 28
  Home ministry & office staff in US: 4

**Countries:** Brazil 2; China 2; Colombia 2; Russia; Thailand 1; Ukraine

## Christian Mission for the Deaf
PO Box 28005

Detroit, MI 48228-0005 USA
**Phone:** (313) 933-1424
**Fax:** (313) 933-1424
**E-mail:** cmd@cmdeaf.org
**Web Site:** www.cmdeaf.org
*Mrs. Berta Foster, Administrator*

A denominational support agency of Brethren tradition engaged in Christian education, camping programs and funds transmission.

**Purpose:** "...to organize, operate, maintain, promote and encourage Gospel and education work among the deaf of Africa."

**Year founded in US:** 1956

**Income for Overseas Min:** $114,047

**Fully Supported US Personnel Overseas:**
  Expecting to serve more than 4 years: 2

**Other Personnel:**
  Short-term less than 1 year: 1
  Home ministry & office staff in US: 2

**Countries:** Congo, Democratic Republic of 2

## Christian Missions in Many Lands, Inc.

PO Box 13
Spring Lake, NJ 07762-0013 USA
**Phone:** (732) 449-8880
**Fax:** (732) 974-0888
**E-mail:** cmml@cmmlusa.org
**Web Site:** www.cmmlusa.org
*Mr. Thomas J. Turner, President*

A nondenominational service agency of Christian/Plymouth Brethren tradition assisting missionaries through funds transmission and missions information service. Overseas personnel included under Brethren Assemblies.

**Purpose:** "...to provide necessary services which are difficult or impossible for the individual missionary or assembly to provide."

**Year founded in US:** 1921

**Income for Overseas Min:** $12,600,000
**Personnel:**
  Home ministry & office staff in US: 7

## Christian Missions Unlimited

PO Box 58
Hope Hull, AL 36043 USA
**Phone:** (334) 284-0878
**Fax:** (334) 284-1039

**E-mail:** cmu@mindspring.com
**Web Site:** www.christianmissions.org
*Mr. Charles Conner, Jr., Exec. Dir.*

A specialized agency of Baptist tradition engaged in church construction, Bible distribution, evangelism, support of national workers, mobilization for mission and short-term programs. Data from 2001.

**Purpose:** "Church construction is the main focus."

**Year founded in US:** 1973

**Fully Supported US Personnel Overseas:**
  Non-residential mission personnel: 3

**Other Personnel:**
  Short-term less than 1 year: 300
  Home ministry & office staff in US: 4

## Christian Outreach Intl.

PO Box 2823
Vero Beach, FL 32961-2823 USA
**Phone:** (772) 778-0575
**Fax:** (772) 778-6781
**E-mail:** missions@coiusa.com
**Web Site:** www.coiusa.com
*Mr. Jack Isleib, Founder/Exec. Dir.*

A nondenominational service agency of Evangelical tradition engaged in evangelism, leadership development, mobilization for mission, short-term programs, missionary training and TESOL. Data from 2001.

**Purpose:** "...reaching the lost, and the development and training of believers."

**Year founded in US:** 1984

**Income for Overseas Min:** $2,190,659

**Fully Supported US Personnel Overseas:**
  Expecting to serve more than 4 years: 13

**Other Personnel:**
  Short-term less than 1 year: 115
  Non-US serving in own/other country: 17
  Home ministry & office staff in US: 14

**Countries:** Czech Republic 7; France 1; Mexico 3; Romania; Ukraine 1; United Kingdom; Venezuela 1

## Christian Pilots Association

4100 Newport Place, Suite 620
Newport Beach, CA 92660 USA
**Phone:** (562) 208-2912
**E-mail:** info@christianpilots.org
**Web Site:** www.christianpilots.org

*Mr. Andy Pike, Chairman*

An interdenominational specialized agency of Evangelical tradition engaged in aviation services and providing medical supplies. Data from 2001.

**Year founded in US:** 1972

**Income for Overseas Min:** $17,000

**Gifts in Kind:** $10,000

## Christian Reformed World Missions

2850 Kalamazoo Ave., SE
Grand Rapids, MI 49508 USA

**Phone:** (616) 224-0700
**Fax:** (616) 224-0707
**E-mail:** crwm@crcna.org
**Web Site:** www.crwm.org
**Associations:** EFMA

*Dr. Gary J. Bekker, Exec. Director*

A denominational sending agency of Reformed and Evangelical tradition engaged in church planting, Christian education, theological education, leadership development, support of national churches and mobilization for mission.

**Purpose:** "…to bring salvation to the ends of the earth…to proclaim the Gospel and develop churches around the world."

**Year founded in US:** 1888

**Income for Overseas Min:** $8,081,894

**Fully Supported US Personnel Overseas:**
  Expecting to serve more than 4 years: 109
  Expecting to serve 1 to 4 years: 25

**Other Personnel:**
  Short-term less than 1 year: 60
  Home ministry & office staff in US: 20

**Countries:** Bangladesh; China 2; Costa Rica 3; Dominican Republic 8; El Salvador 1; France 2; Guinea 13; Haiti 4; Honduras 2; Hungary 5; Japan 12; Mali 6; Mexico 16; Nicaragua 2; Nigeria 22; Philippines 10; Russia 1

## Christian Reformed World Relief Committee

2850 Kalamazoo Ave. SE
Grand Rapids, MI 49560 USA

**Phone:** (800) 552-7972
**Fax:** (616) 224-0806
**E-mail:** crwrc@crcna.org

**Web Site:** www.crwrc.org
**Associations:** AERDO

*Mr. Andy Ryskamp, U.S. Director*

A denominational service agency of Reformed tradition engaged in development, justice, leadership development, partnership development and relief and/or rehabilitation.

**Purpose:** "…a Christian relief, development & justice organization working for love, life, justice and mercy around the world."

**Year founded in US:** 1962

**Income for Overseas Min:** $7,740,630

**Fully Supported US Personnel Overseas:**
  Expecting to serve more than 4 years: 15
  Expecting to serve 1 to 4 years: 4
  Non-residential mission personnel: 1

**Other Personnel:**
  Short-term less than 1 year: 404
  Non-US serving in own/other country: 34
  Home ministry & office staff in US: 26

**Countries:** Bangladesh 1; Cambodia; Cuba; Dominican Republic 1; Ecuador; El Salvador; Guatemala; Haiti 1; Honduras; India; Indonesia 1; Kenya 1; Laos; Malawi 3; Mali 1; Mexico; Mozambique; Nicaragua; Niger; Nigeria; Philippines; Romania; Senegal 1; Sierra Leone; South Africa 1; Tanzania 1; Uganda 2; Zambia 1

## Christian Resources Intl.

PO Box 356
Fowlerville, MI 48836-0356 USA

**Phone:** (517) 223-3193
**Fax:** (517) 223-7668
**E-mail:** admin@cribooks.org
**Web Site:** www.cribooks.org

*Mr. Fred Palmerton, Exec. Dir.*

An interdenominational specialized agency of Evangelical tradition engaged in literature distribution worldwide by sending overseas surplus and reusable Christian literature and Bibles. Personnel data from 2001.

**Year founded in US:** 1956

**Income for Overseas Min:** $216,037

**Personnel:**
  Home ministry & office staff in US: 6

## Christian Service International
## See: CSI Ministries, Inc.

## Christian Union Churches of North America—Missions

PO Box 454
Liberty Corner, OH 43532 USA

**Phone:** (419) 237-2015
**E-mail:** JoeRoseRedmond@juno.com
**Web Site:** www.christianunion.com

*Rev. Phil Harris, President*

A sending agency of Evangelical tradition engaged in evangelism, broadcasting, camping programs, church construction, church planting and literature distribution.

**Year founded in US:** 1864

**Fully Supported US Personnel Overseas:**
  Non-residential mission personnel: 1

**Other Personnel:**
  Short-term less than 1 year: 50
  Home ministry & office staff in US: 2

## Christians In Action Missions International

PO Box 728
Woodlake, CA 93286-0728 USA

**Phone:** (559) 564-3762
**Fax:** (559) 564-1231
**E-mail:** cinamissions@christiansinaction.org
**Web Site:** www.christiansinaction.org

*Mr. David W. Konold, Jr., President/CEO*

A transdenominational sending agency of Evangelical tradition engaged in evangelism, childcare/orphanage programs, church planting, medical work, support of national churches and missionary training.

**Year founded in US:** 1957

**Income for Overseas Min:** $766,189

**Fully Supported US Personnel Overseas:**
  Expecting to serve more than 4 years: 21
  Non-residential mission personnel: 1

**Other Personnel:**
  Short-term less than 1 year: 45
  Non-US serving in own/other country: 78
  Home ministry & office staff in US: 9

**Countries:** Brazil 2; Colombia 3; Ecuador 2; El Salvador; Germany 3; Ghana 1; Guatemala 2; Guinea-Bissau; Honduras 1; India; Japan 2; Korea, South; Macau 1; Madagascar; Mexico; Peru; Philippines; Sierra Leone; United Kingdom 4

## Christ's Mandate for Missions

(See ad page 137)
PO Box 7705
Charlotte, NC 28241 USA

**Phone:** (704) 225-3927
**Fax:** (888) 816-0725
**E-mail:** info@cmmissions.net
**Web Site:** www.cmmissions.net

*Rev. Jorge Parrott, President*

A service agency of Charismatic tradition engaged in mobilization for mission, discipleship, Christian education, literature distribution, medical work, short-term programs and tentmaking.

**Purpose:** "…to network with existing, proven and new missionaries and leaders globally…to join with anointed men and women of God and unifying ministries, developing national pastors and workers in many nations, who are leaders, equipping current and emerging leaders, in their own culture, all for God's glory."

**Year founded in US:** 1978

**Income for Overseas Min:** $250,000

**Gifts in Kind:** $150,000

**Fully Supported US Personnel Overseas:**
  Expecting to serve more than 4 years: 17
  Non-residential mission personnel: 9

**Other Personnel:**
  Short-term less than 1 year: 500
  Bi-vocational/tentmakers: 3
  Non-US serving in own/other country: 287
  Home ministry & office staff in US: 2

**Countries:** Bolivia; Dominican Republic; Ghana 5; Guatemala 5; Hong Kong 2; India; Mexico 5; Nigeria; Philippines; Spain; Thailand

## Church Leadership Development International

8000 Research Forest Dr.
Suite 115, #280
The Woodlands, TX 77382-1506 USA

**Phone:** (281) 363-2534
**E-mail:** info@cldi.org
**Web Site:** www.cldi.org

*Mr. Craig Ludrick, President*

A nondenominational support agency of Evangelical tradition engaged in training pastors, church planting, leadership development and literature distribution.

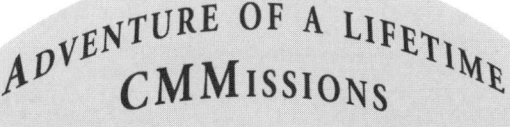

ADVENTURE OF A LIFETIME
CMMISSIONS

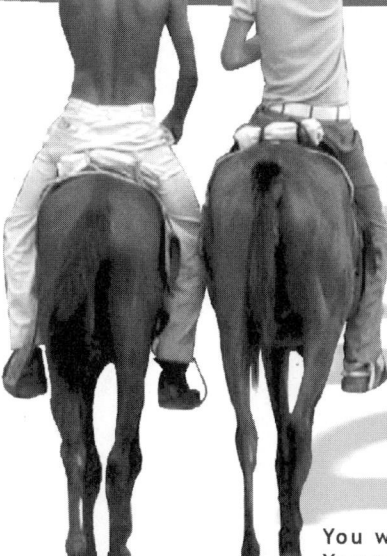

**CMM CONNECTING DESTINIES**
We have invitations to Bible
schools, churches, crusades,
mission festivals, Christian
Schools & hospitals.

You will work
You will get dirty
You may even get broken

What must you do to go on a CMM missions trip? First contact our
office at 704-225-3927. We will give you all the details and put you
in contact with trip leaders. We provide training, support, encouragement and even sample support letters! Team leader training available.

CMM     P O 7705     CHARLOTTE, NC   28241     704-225-3927

WWW.**CMM**ISSIONS.NET

Those who had been scattered preached
the word wherever they went.

ACTS 8:4

LIVE

Pastors Training Pastors to Transform the World

1.800.264.8064   www.covenantseminary.edu
Saint Louis, Missouri

**Purpose:** "...to equip pastors in Eurasia and India with training, encouragement and resources to strengthen and multiply their churches."

**Year founded in US:** 1996

**Personnel:**
Non-US serving in own/other country: 7
Home ministry & office staff in US: 1

**Countries:** Central Asia; Georgia; India; Ukraine

## Church Ministries Intl.

1919 S. Shiloh Rd., Ste. 600, LB # 33
Garland, TX 75042-8292 USA
**Phone:** (972) 926-5200
**Fax:** (972) 926-5211
**E-mail:** cmioffice@churchministries.org
**Web Site:** www.churchministries.org

*Mr. James R. Murray, Exec. Director*

An interdenominational support agency of Evangelical tradition engaged in support of national churches, church construction, church planting, discipleship, evangelism and partnership development. Financial data from 2002.

**Purpose:** "...to reach the world for Christ by serving as a catalyst to established mission teams and churches for strategic planning and implementation of programs that specifically address the goal of evangelizing and discipling an entire nation."

**Year founded in US:** 1988

**Income for Overseas Min:** $285,731

**Fully Supported US Personnel Overseas:**
Non-residential mission personnel: 2

**Other Personnel:**
Non-US serving in own/other country: 2
Home ministry & office staff in US: 3

## Church Missions Link

PO Box 14175
Spokane, WA 99214 USA
**Phone:** (509) 891-5595
**Fax:** (509) 891-5595
**E-mail:** cmlink@worldnet.att.net

*Rev. Ken Parker, Director*

An interdenominational support agency of Brethren and Independent tradition engaged in leadership development, Christian education, management consulting/training, support of national workers, short-term programs and missionary training.

**Year founded in US:** 1998

**Income for Overseas Min:** $10,000

**Personnel:**
Non-US serving in own/other country: 6
Home ministry & office staff in US: 1

**Countries:** Cameroon

## Church of God (Anderson, Indiana), Global Missions

1201 E. 5th St.
Anderson, IN 46012 USA
**Phone:** (765) 648-2140
**Fax:** (765) 642-4279
**E-mail:** bedwards@chog.org
**Web Site:** www.chogmissions.org

*Dr. Robert E. Edwards, Global Msns. Coordinator*

A sending agency of Holiness and Wesleyan tradition engaged in mobilization for mission, church planting, discipleship, leadership development and support of national workers.

**Year founded in US:** 1909

**Income for Overseas Min:** $5,300,000

**Fully Supported US Personnel Overseas:**
Expecting to serve more than 4 years: 56
Expecting to serve 1 to 4 years: 30

**Other Personnel:**
Non-US serving in own/other country: 13
Home ministry & office staff in US: 10

**Countries:** Angola; Australia 2; Belize; Bolivia 3; Brazil 5; Bulgaria 2; Costa Rica 2; Cote d'Ivoire 4; Ecuador 6; Guam; Haiti 4; Hong Kong 2; Hungary 2; Japan 2; Kenya 5; Lebanon 1; New Zealand 3; Paraguay; Russia 2; Tanzania 5; Uganda 1; Unspecified Country 2; Zambia 3

## Church of God (Cleveland, TN) World Missions

PO Box 8016
Cleveland, TN 37320 USA
**Phone:** (423) 478-7190
**Fax:** (423) 478-7155
**E-mail:** info@cogwm.org
**Web Site:** www.cogwm.org
**Associations:** AFMA, EFMA

*Dr. Roland E. Vaughn, Gen. Director*

A denominational sending agency of Pentecostal tradition engaged in church planting, childcare/orphanage programs, church construction, TEE, theological education, evangelism and support of national workers.

**Purpose:** "...to help unchurched or nominal Christians become committed disciples of Christ and non-Christian people become Christians..."

**Year founded in US:** 1910

**Income for Overseas Min:** $33,147,856

**Fully Supported US Personnel Overseas:**
  Expecting to serve more than 4 years: 159
  Expecting to serve 1 to 4 years: 31

**Other Personnel:**
  Short-term less than 1 year: 2,000
  Bi-vocational/tentmakers: 8
  Non-US serving in own/other country: 55
  Home ministry & office staff in US: 67

**Countries:** Albania; Aruba 2; Australia; Austria 2; Bahrain; Belgium 5; Brazil 4; Bulgaria 1; Caribbean—General 2; Chile 3; China 6; Colombia 3; Croatia 2; Czech Republic 2; Ecuador 8; Europe—General 2; Fiji 2; France 3; Germany 10; Ghana 4; Greece 2; Guatemala 2; Haiti 2; Honduras 5; Indonesia 2; Ireland 4; Italy 2; Kenya 9; Liberia; Malaysia 4; Mexico; Nicaragua; Nigeria; Pakistan; Panama 2; Paraguay 2; Peru 2; Philippines 16; Romania 2; Russia 6; Singapore 2; South Africa 1; South America—General 2; Spain 4; Ukraine 3; United Kingdom; Unspecified Country 18; Venezuela 3; Vietnam; Zambia 3

## Church of God (Holiness), World Mission Dept., Inc.

PO Box 4711
Overland Park, KS 66204 USA

**Phone:** (913) 432-0303
**Fax:** (913) 722-0351
**E-mail:** worldmissions@cogh.net
**Web Site:** www.coghworldmissions.org

*Silas McGehee, Exec. Secretary*

A denominational sending agency of Holiness and Wesleyan tradition engaged in church planting, Christian education, evangelism, literature production, partnership development and Bible translation.

**Purpose:** "...to promote God's Kingdom

through proclaiming the Gospel of Jesus Christ and providing opportunities to develop mission fields into self-propagating missionary forces."

**Year founded in US:** 1917

**Income for Overseas Min:** $89,743

**Fully Supported US Personnel Overseas:**
  Expecting to serve more than 4 years: 2
  Expecting to serve 1 to 4 years: 1

**Other Personnel:**
  Non-US serving in own/other country: 62
  Home ministry & office staff in US: 2

**Countries:** Bolivia; Cayman Islands; Haiti; India; Jamaica; Liberia; Middle East; Myanmar/Burma; Nigeria; Panama; Papua New Guinea; Ukraine 2

## Church of God (Seventh Day) Gen. Conference—Missions Abroad

PO Box 33677
Denver, CO 80233 USA

**Phone:** (303) 452-7973
**Fax:** (303) 452-0657
**E-mail:** missions@cog7.org
**Web Site:** www.cog7.org

*Mr. William C. Hicks, Missions Min. Dir.*

A denominational support agency of Evangelical tradition engaged in funds transmission, Bible and literature distribution, and support of national churches in 16 countries. Data from 2001.

**Year founded in US:** 1860

**Income for Overseas Min:** $109,950

**Gifts in Kind:** $30,000

**Personnel:**
  Home ministry & office staff in US: 14

## Church of God in Christ, Mennonite General Mission Board

PO Box 230
Moundridge, KS 67107 USA

**Phone:** (620) 345-2532
**Fax:** (620) 345-2582

*Dale Koehn, Information Contact*

A denominational sending agency of Mennonite tradition engaged in evangelism, Bible distribution, support of national churches and relief and/or rehabilitation in 21 countries. Includes U.S. and Canadian totals. Statistics from 2003.

**Year founded in US:** 1933

**Income for Overseas Min:** $1,461,920

**Personnel:**
Expecting to serve more than 4 years: 94

**Countries:** Unspecified Country 94

## Church of God of Prophecy— Global Outreach

PO Box 2910
Cleveland, TN 37320-2910 USA

**Phone:** (423) 559-5100
**Fax:** (423) 472-5037
**E-mail:** Global@cogop.org
**Web Site:** www.cogop.org

*Mr. Randy Howard, General Overseer*

A denominational sending agency of Pentecostal tradition engaged in church planting, evangelism, leadership development, support of national churches and support of national workers. Data from 2001.

**Year founded in US:** 1903

**Income for Overseas Min:** $2,000,000

**Fully Supported US Personnel Overseas:**
Expecting to serve more than 4 years: 15
Non-residential mission personnel: 8

**Other Personnel:**
Short-term less than 1 year: 50
Bi-vocational/tentmakers: 1
Non-US serving in own/other country: 352

**Countries:** Angola; Argentina; Australia 2; Azerbaijan; Barbados; Belarus; Belgium; Belize; Benin; Bermuda; Bolivia; Botswana; Brazil; Bulgaria; Burkina Faso; Cameroon; Caribbean—General; Central African Republic; Chad; Chile; China 2; Colombia; Congo, Democratic Republic of; Congo, Republic of the; Costa Rica; Côte d'Ivoire; Cuba; Cyprus; Ecuador; Egypt; El Salvador; Ethiopia; Fiji; Finland; France; French Guiana; Gabon; Gambia, The; Germany 4; Greece; Guyana; Haiti; Hungary; India; Indonesia; Israel; Japan 2; Kazakhstan; Kenya; Korea, South; Liberia; Malawi; Malta; Mozambique; Namibia; Netherlands Antilles; New Zealand; Pakistan; Panama; Paraguay; Peru; Philippines; Portugal; Romania; Russia; Rwanda; Samoa 2; Senegal; Sierra Leone; South Africa; Spain; Sri Lanka; Sudan; Suriname; Swaziland; Tanzania; Thailand; Togo; Trinidad and Tobago; Uganda; Ukraine 3; Uruguay; Venezuela; Virgin Islands; Zambia; Zimbabwe

## Church of the Brethren— Global Mission Partnerships

1451 Dundee Ave.
Elgin, IL 60120 USA

**Phone:** (847) 742-5100
**Fax:** (847) 742-6103
**E-mail:** mission_gb@brethren.org
**Web Site:** www.brethren.org

**Associations:** CWS

*Mervin Keeney, Dir. Global Misn. Partnerships*

A denominational sending agency of Brethren tradition engaged in support of national churches, development and relief and/or rehabilitation. Data from 2001.

**Year founded in US:** 1884

**Income for Overseas Min:** $2,260,000

**Personnel:**
Home ministry & office staff in US: 3

## Church of the Nazarene, World Mission Department

6401 The Paseo
Kansas City, MO 64131 USA

**Phone:** (816) 333-7000
**Fax:** (816) 363-3100
**Web Site:** www.nazareneworldmission.org

**Associations:** EFMA

*Dr. Louie E. Bustle, Director*

A denominational sending agency of Holiness and Wesleyan tradition engaged in church planting, TEE, evangelism, missionary education, providing medical supplies, medical work, relief and/or rehabilitation, missionary training, Christian education, theological education, evangelism, literature distribution, literature production, support of national workers, short-term programs and video/film production/distribution.

**Purpose:** "...fulfilling the Great Commission through a denominational structure and contextualized system of evangelism, discipleship and development of a multiplying, indigenous, holiness church."

**Year founded in US:** 1895

**Income for Overseas Min:** $56,606,056

**Fully Supported US Personnel Overseas:**
Expecting to serve more than 4 years: 363
**Other Personnel:**
Short-term less than 1 year: 6,600
Bi-vocational/tentmakers: 25
Non-US serving in own/other country: 105
Home ministry & office staff in US: 70

**Countries:** Albania 3; American Samoa; Angola 2; Antigua; Argentina 17; Armenia; Aruba; Australia 5; Azores; Bahamas, The; Bangladesh; Barbados; Belize; Benin 6; Bolivia 2; Botswana 1; Brazil 6; Bulgaria 2; Burkina Faso; Burundi; Cambodia 2; Cameroon; Cape Verde; Chile 2; Colombia; Congo, Democratic Republic of; Congo, Republic of the; Costa Rica 11; Cote d'Ivoire 10; Croatia 1; Cuba; Cyprus 2; Denmark; Dominica 3; Dominican Republic 10; East Timor 2; Ecuador 6; Egypt; El Salvador; Equatorial Guinea; Eritrea; Ethiopia 6; Fiji 2; France 4; French Guiana; Gabon; Germany; Ghana 2; Greece; Grenada; Guadeloupe; Guam 2; Guatemala 20; Guinea-Bissau; Guyana; Haiti 6; Honduras; Hong Kong; Hungary; India; Indonesia 4; Ireland; Israel 3; Italy 2; Jamaica; Japan 2; Jordan 3; Kazakhstan; Kenya 20; Korea, South 6; Kosovo; Lebanon 2; Lesotho 2; Liberia; Macedonia 1; Madagascar 4; Malawi 5; Martinique; Micronesia, Federated States; Mexico 3; Mozambique 9; Myanmar/Burma; N. Mariana Isls.; Namibia 2; Nepal; Netherlands; New Zealand; Nicaragua; Nigeria; Pakistan; Palau; Panama; Papua New Guinea 28; Paraguay; Peru 8; Philippines 22; Poland; Portugal 3; Puerto Rico 1; Reunion 1; Romania 1; Russia 7; Rwanda; Saint Kitts and Nevis; Saint Lucia; Saint Vincent and the Grenadines; Samoa; Sao Tome and Principe 2; Senegal 2; Sierra Leone 2; Slovenia 1; Solomon Islands 2; South Africa 30; Spain; Sri Lanka; Sudan; Suriname; Swaziland 1; Switzerland 19; Syria; Thailand 6; Taiwan; Tanzania; Togo; Tonga; Trinidad and Tobago; Uganda 2; Ukraine; United Kingdom; Unspecified Country 10; Uruguay; Vanuatu 2; Venezuela 6; Virgin Islands; Zambia 4; Zimbabwe

## Church Planting Intl.

PO Box 836
Gainesville, GA 30503 USA

**Phone:** (770) 535-7008
**Fax:** (770) 534-1025
**E-mail:** cpimission@juno.com

*Rev. George P. Hutchinson, Exec. Director*

A transdenominational support agency of Evangelical and Presbyterian tradition engaged in support of indigenous church planting movements in developing countries. Statistics are from 2003.

**Purpose:** "Assisting indigenous church planting ministries in developing countries."
**Year founded in US:** 1983
**Income for Overseas Min:** $100,000
**Personnel:**
Short-term less than 1 year: 9
Bi-vocational/tentmakers: 1
Non-US serving in own/other country: 1
Home ministry & office staff in US: 1

**Countries:** Myanmar/Burma; Portugal; Uganda

## Church Resource Ministries (CRM)

1240 N. Lakeview Ave., Ste.120
Anaheim, CA 92807 USA

**Phone:** (714) 779-0370
**Fax:** (714) 779-0189
**E-mail:** crm@crmleaders.org
**Web Site:** www.crmnet.org

*Dr. Samuel F. Metcalf, President*

A transdenominational sending agency of Evangelical tradition engaged in leadership development, church planting, development and support of national churches. Data from 2001.

**Purpose:** "...to develop leaders to strengthen and start churches worldwide."
**Year founded in US:** 1980
**Income for Overseas Min:** $4,029,112
**Gifts in Kind:** $48,503
**Fully Supported US Personnel Overseas:**
Expecting to serve more than 4 years: 74
Expecting to serve 1 to 4 years: 3
Non-residential mission personnel: 3
**Other Personnel:**
Short-term less than 1 year: 51
Non-US serving in own/other country: 1
Home ministry & office staff in US: 19

**Countries:** Asia—General 2; Cambodia 9; France 4; Hungary 9; Indonesia 2; Japan 8; Poland 2; Romania 6; Russia 12; Singapore 4; South Africa 2; Venezuela 14

# Church World Service

PO Box 968
Elkhart, IN 46515 USA
**Phone:** (800) 297-1516
**Fax:** (574) 262-1966
**E-mail:** info@churchworldservice.org
**Web Site:** www.churchworldservice.org
*John L. McCullough, Exec. Dir./CEO*

An ecumenical service agency of Anglican and Orthodox tradition engaged in agricultural programs, development, leadership development, literacy work, relief and/or rehabilitation and technical assistance. Countries of service and personnel from 1998.

**Purpose:** "...meets basic needs of people in peril, works for justice and dignity with the poor and vulnerable, promotes peace and understanding among people of different faiths, races, and nations and affirms and preserves the diversity and integrity of God's creation."

**Year founded in US:** 1946
**Income for Overseas Min:** $63,665,788
**Gifts in Kind:** $12,462,165
**Fully Supported US Personnel Overseas:**
  Expecting to serve more than 4 years: 8
  Expecting to serve 1 to 4 years: 204
  Non-residential mission personnel: 10
**Other Personnel:**
  Non-US serving in own/other country: 92
  Home ministry & office staff in US: 35
**Countries:** Africa—General 5; Asia—General; Cambodia 1; Europe—General 1; Indonesia; Laos 1; Latin America—General; Pakistan; Thailand; Vietnam

# Churches of Christ

USA  (No Central Office)

A body of autonomous congregations and agencies of the Christian "Restoration Movement" (not using instrumental music in worship) which sends and supports missionaries directly from local congregations. Data furnished by Missions Resource Network.

**Fully Supported US Personnel Overseas:**
  Expecting to serve more than 4 years: 695
  Expecting to serve 1 to 4 years: 147
**Other Personnel:**
  Short-term less than 1 year: 7,790
  Bi-vocational/tentmakers: 14

Non-US serving in own/other country: 453
Home ministry & office staff in US: 51

**Countries:** Albania 12; American Samoa 2; Antigua 2; Argentina 7; Australia; Austria 9; Bahamas, The 4; Bangladesh 2; Barbados 1; Belarus 3; Belgium 6; Belize 4; Benin 6; Bosnia and Herzegovina 2; Botswana 2; Brazil 103; Bulgaria 3; Burkina Faso 6; Cameroon; Central African Republic; Chile 17; China 6; Colombia; Costa Rica 4; Cote d'Ivoire 3; Croatia 2; Czech Republic 4; Denmark; Dominican Republic 5; Ecuador 12; Egypt 2; El Salvador; Estonia 8; Ethiopia; Fiji 1; Finland 1; France 14; Germany 28; Ghana 6; Greece 2; Guatemala 4; Guyana 6; Haiti 2; Honduras 8; Hungary 7; India 8; Indonesia 5; Israel; Italy 18; Jamaica 1; Japan 10; Kazakhstan 2; Kenya 22; Korea, South 1; Latvia 1; Lithuania 4; Malawi 5; Malaysia 2; Mexico 38; Mozambique 2; Nepal 2; Netherlands 4; New Zealand 3; Nicaragua 3; Nigeria 12; Norway; Panama 1; Papua New Guinea 5; Paraguay 8; Peru 4; Philippines 20; Poland 4; Portugal 2; Romania 12; Russia 12; Serbia and Montenegro 2; South Africa 14; Spain 2; Swaziland 3; Switzerland 4; Taiwan 2; Tanzania 5; Thailand 16; Togo 18; Trinidad and Tobago 2; Uganda 24; Ukraine 18; United Kingdom 52; Uruguay; Venezuela 2; Zambia 2; Zimbabwe 2

# Churches of God, General Conference

PO Box 926
Findlay, OH 45839 USA
**Phone:** (419) 424-1961
**Fax:** (419) 424-3433
**E-mail:** missions@cggc.org
**Web Site:** www.cggc.org
**Associations:** EFMA
*Rev. Wayne W. Boyer, Exec. Director*

A denominational support agency engaged in support of national churches, church planting, Christian education, leadership development, medical work and support of national workers.

**Purpose:** "...to evangelize, disciple and equip a community of Christians for effective witness and meaningful service within their own culture."

**Year founded in US:** 1825
**Income for Overseas Min:** $939,458

**Fully Supported US Personnel Overseas:**
Expecting to serve more than 4 years: 8

**Other Personnel:**
Short-term less than 1 year: 1
Non-US serving in own/other country: 505
Home ministry & office staff in US: 6

**Countries:** Bangladesh; Brazil 4; Haiti 2; India; Sweden 2

## Cities for Christ Worldwide
2474 Boise Ave.
Loveland, CO 80538 USA
**Phone:** (970) 663-0477
**Fax:** (970) 663-0477
**E-mail:** Monsmatd@comcast.net

*Dr. Timothy Monsma, Director*

An interdenominational sending agency of Presbyterian and Reformed tradition engaged in literature distribution and services for other agencies.

**Year founded in US:** 1985

**Income for Overseas Min:** $12,000

**Fully Supported US Personnel Overseas:**
Expecting to serve more than 4 years: 6
Non-residential mission personnel: 1

**Other Personnel:**
Short-term less than 1 year: 2
Bi-vocational/tentmakers: 2
Home ministry & office staff in US: 3

**Countries:** Africa—General 2; Asia—General 2; Latin America—General 2

## CityTeam Ministries
2304 Zanker Rd.
San Jose, CA 95131 USA
**Phone:** (408) 232-5600
**Fax:** (408) 436-0702
**E-mail:** kjurgens@cityteam.org
**Web Site:** www.cityteam.org

*Patrick J. Robertson, President*

A nondenominational support agency engaged in church planting, discipleship, partnership development, relief and/or rehabilitation and training.

**Purpose:** "...serving people in need, proclaiming the gospel, and establishing disciples among disadvantaged people of cities."

**Year founded in US:** 1957

**Fully Supported US Personnel Overseas:**
Expecting to serve more than 4 years: 1

Non-residential mission personnel: 3
**Other Personnel:**
Non-US serving in own/other country: 11
**Countries:** Côte d'Ivoire; Ethiopia 1; Indonesia; Sierra Leone; South Africa

## CLC Ministries International
PO Box 1449
Ft. Washington, PA 19034 USA
**Phone:** (215) 542-1242
**Fax:** (215) 542-7580
**E-mail:** debalmack@clcusa.org
**Web Site:** clcusa.org
**Associations:** EFMA

*Mr. David W. Almack, President*

An interdenominational support agency of Evangelical tradition engaged in literature distribution, literature production, funds transmission, mobilization for mission and Bible translation.

**Year founded in US:** 1957

**Income for Overseas Min:** $265,029

**Fully Supported US Personnel Overseas:**
Expecting to serve more than 4 years: 12
Expecting to serve 1 to 4 years: 1

**Other Personnel:**
Home ministry & office staff in US: 33

**Countries:** Central Asia—General 2; Colombia 2; Hong Kong 2; Italy 1; Portugal 2; Russia 2; United Kingdom 1

## CMF International
5525 E. 82nd St.
Indianapolis, IN 46250 USA
**Phone:** (317) 578-2700
**Fax:** (317) 578-2827
**E-mail:** missions@cmfi.org
**Web Site:** www.cmfi.org

*Dr. Doug Priest, Exec. Director*

A nondenominational sending agency of Christian (Restoration Movement) tradition engaged in church planting, development, evangelism, leadership development and tentmaking.

**Purpose:** "...to mobilize Christians to draw people from all nations into relationship with Christ and His church."

**Year founded in US:** 1949

**Income for Overseas Min:** $8,379,179

And how will anyone

# go

...without being sent?

*Romans 10:15*

In the challenging task of raising support, *Creative Plus* offers a suite of team building tools that will maximize the impact of your support-raising efforts.

*Prayer cards* – Whether you favor a traditional prayer card or response card, *Creative Plus* can create a design that communicates to your support team the exciting story of your ministry.

*Magnets* – Our Photo Magnets are becoming more popular every day because they make your job so easy; no peeling and sticking each piece, just mail it with your prayer letter.

*Bookmarks* – Send your support team a bookmark. What better way to stay on their hearts and minds? When it finds its way into their Bible, they will be reminded of your ministry every time they open the Word.

*Displays* – When sharing your story with groups or at missions conferences, our table-top displays make a handy backdrop. Designed with the missionary in mind, our displays are professional, durable, portable and affordable.

 **Creative Plus**   1-800-347-2848   www.creativeplus.com

Team building tools for missionaries   *Prayer Cards • Magnets • Bookmarks • Response Cards • Displays*

Most mission agencies invite you to join them to accomplish their God-given mission.

*What if* God has called you to do something unique that does not fit the mold?

CTEN **serves** by providing pastoral care, service and oversight to help missionaries fulfill their unique call.

# Commission

## TO EVERY NATION

# International

Serving along side faith-based missionaries and their churches in the U.S. and Canada.

## www.CTEN.org

ECFA MEMBER

In the U.S. 800.872.5404 or usa@cten.org

In Canada 519.735.8620 or canada@cten.org

Helping Ordinary People Partner With God To Accomplish The Extraordinary

Gifts in Kind: $29,285

Fully Supported US Personnel Overseas:
Expecting to serve 1 to 4 years: 119

Other Personnel:
Short-term less than 1 year: 40
Bi-vocational/tentmakers: 10
Home ministry & office staff in US: 25

Countries: Brazil; Chile; Cote d'Ivoire; Ethiopia; Indonesia; Kenya; Mexico; Spain; Tanzania; Thailand; Ukraine; United Kingdom

## CMTS Ministries, Inc.
321 Focht Rd.
Bernville, PA 19506 USA
Phone: (610) 488-6975
Fax: (610) 488-6111
E-mail: CMTSmin@aol.com
Web Site: www.cmtsministries.org
*Mr. Andrew Merrick, Sr., Exec. Dir.*

An interdenominational service agency of Evangelical tradition engaged in technical assistance, furloughed missionary support, short-term programs, supplying equipment, training and video/film production/distribution. Data from 2001.

Purpose: "…providing technical assistance, materials and equipment for use by Bible-believing missionaries and Christian organizations."

Year founded in US: 1982

Income for Overseas Min: $43,731

Personnel:
Home ministry & office staff in US: 11

## ComCare International
3027 Split Rock Circle
Bulverde, TX 78163 USA
Phone: (210) 317-9998
E-mail: cci@comcareinternational.org
Web Site: www.comcareinternational.org
*Scotta Williams, Exec. Dir.*

An interdenominational specialized agency of Evangelical tradition engaged in medical work, technical assistance, and training, including solar powered hearing aids for unreached people. Statistical data from 2001.

Year founded in US: 1989

Income for Overseas Min: $24,000

Fully Supported US Personnel Overseas:
Expecting to serve more than 4 years: 2

Other Personnel:
Short-term less than 1 year: 1
Non-US serving in own/other country: 2

Countries: Mexico 2

## COMHINA—Cooperacion Misionera De Hispanos De North America
PO Box 593754
Orlando, FL 32859-3754 USA
Phone: (407) 858-9363
Fax: (407) 858-9364
E-mail: comhinanacional@comhina.org
Web Site: www.comhina.org
Associations: EFMA
*Rev. Diana E. Barrera, Exec. Director*

An interdenominational sending agency of Evangelical tradition engaged in Christian education, extension education, funds transmission, leadership development, partnership development and youth programs.

Income for Overseas Min: $12,391.39

Gifts in Kind: $10,814

## Commission to Every Nation
(See ad page 146)
PO Box 291307
Kerrville, TX 78029-1307 USA
Phone: (830) 896-8326
Fax: (830) 896-5262
E-mail: usa@cten.org
Web Site: www.cten.org
*Mr. Richard Malm, Exec. Director*

A transdenominational sending agency of Baptist and Charismatic tradition engaged in member care, funds transmission and missions information service.

Purpose: "…partnering with churches to help Christians become personally involved in fulfilling the Great Commission to every nation."

Year founded in US: 1994

Income for Overseas Min: $2,044,500

Gifts in Kind: $4,815

Fully Supported US Personnel Overseas:
Expecting to serve more than 4 years: 28
Expecting to serve 1 to 4 years: 38
Non-residential mission personnel: 66

**Other Personnel:**
  Short-term less than 1 year: 19
  Non-US serving in own/other country: 5
  Home ministry & office staff in US: 8

**Countries:** Albania; Asia—General; Cameroon 4; Costa Rica 1; Cyprus; El Salvador; Guatemala 9; Honduras; Indonesia; Mexico 5; Mongolia 1; Nicaragua 2; Peru; Philippines 2; Poland 2; Romania 2

## Compassion Intl., Inc.

12290 Voyager Pkwy.
Colorado Springs, CO 80921 USA
**Phone:** (719) 487-7000
**Fax:** (719) 481-5805
**E-mail:** ciinfo@us.ci.org
**Web Site:** www.compassion.com
**Associations:** EFMA

*Dr. Wesley K. Stafford, President/CEO*

A nondenominational support agency engaged in youth programs, development, Christian education, evangelism, leadership development, childrens programs and medical work.

**Purpose:** "...an advocate for children to release them from their spiritual, economic, social and physical poverty and enable them to become responsible and fulfilled Christian adults."

**Year founded in US:** 1952

**Income for Overseas Min:** $136,234,672

**Gifts in Kind:** $206,722

**Fully Supported US Personnel Overseas:**
  Expecting to serve more than 4 years: 3

**Other Personnel:**
  Non-US serving in own/other country: 782
  Home ministry & office staff in US: 464

**Countries:** Bangladesh; Bolivia; Brazil; Burkina Faso; Colombia; Dominican Republic; Ecuador; El Salvador; Ethiopia; Guatemala; Haiti; Honduras; Hong Kong 2; India; Indonesia; Kenya 1; Mexico; Nicaragua; Peru; Philippines; Rwanda; Tanzania; Thailand; Uganda

## Concordia Gospel Outreach

PO Box 201
St. Louis, MO 63166-0201 USA
**Phone:** (314) 268-1363
**Fax:** (314) 268-1202
**E-mail:** outreach@cph.org

**Web Site:** www.cgo-online.org

*Annette Frank, Manager*

A specialized agency of Lutheran tradition engaged in literature distribution. Data from 2001.

**Purpose:** "...distributes Gospel materials and supports the expansion of the Gospel worldwide."

**Year founded in US:** 1992

**Personnel:**
  Home ministry & office staff in US: 1

## Congregational Holiness Church—World Missions

3888 Fayetteville Hwy.
Griffin, GA 30223 USA
**Phone:** (770) 228-4833
**Fax:** (770) 228-1177
**E-mail:** headquarters@cchurch.com
**Web Site:** www.chchurch.com

*Rev. Billy Anderson, World Missions Director*

A denominational support agency of Holiness and Pentecostal tradition engaged in support of national workers, church construction, Christian education and providing medical supplies in 17 countries. Data from 2001.

**Year founded in US:** 1921

**Personnel:**
  Home ministry & office staff in US: 4

## Congregational Methodist Church, Division of Mission Ministries

PO Box 9
Florence, MS 39073 USA
**Phone:** (601) 845-8787
**Fax:** (601) 845-8788
**E-mail:** dmmissions@aol.com
**Web Site:** www.congregationalmethodist.net

*Rev. Jerry M. Jones, Director*

A denominational sending agency of Wesleyan tradition engaged in church planting, discipleship, evangelism, leadership development, support of national workers and support of national churches.

**Purpose:** "...to promote evangelism of non-Christans, equipping of believers, empowering of leaders and the planting of churches..."

**Year founded in US:** 1945

**Income for Overseas Min:** $600,000

**Fully Supported US Personnel Overseas:**
Expecting to serve more than 4 years: 8
Non-residential mission **Personnel:** 1

**Other Personnel:**
Short-term less than 1 year: 4
Non-US serving in own/other country: 2
Home ministry & office staff in US: 1

**Countries:** Belize 2; Bolivia 1; Mexico 5

## Connecting Businessmen to Christ

PO Box 8009
Chattanooga, TN 37414-0009 USA

**Phone:** (423) 698-4444
**Fax:** (423) 629-4434
**E-mail:** poneal@cbmc.com
**Web Site**: www.cbmc.com

*Mr. Patrick O'Neal, Exec. Director*

An interdenominational support agency of Evangelical tradition engaged in evangelism.

**Purpose:** "...saturating the business and professional community with the Gospel... by establishing, equipping and mobilizing teams where we work and live that yield spiritual reproducers."

**Year founded in US:** 1950

## Conservative Baptist Foreign Mission Society (CBFMS) See: World Venture

## Conservative Congregational Christian Conference— Missions Committee

7582 Currell Blvd. #108
St. Paul, MN 55125 USA

**Phone:** (651) 739-1474
**Fax:** (651) 739-0750
**E-mail:** clonguevan@cs.com
**Web Site:** www.ccccusa.org

*Rev. Clair Longuevan, Msns. Committee Chair.*

A denominational support agency of Congregational and Evangelical tradition engaged in support of national churches and short-term programs.

**Year founded in US:** 1948

**Income for Overseas Min:** $6,375,000

**Fully Supported US Personnel Overseas:**

Expecting to serve more than 4 years: 4

**Other Personnel:**
Short-term less than 1 year: 90
Home ministry & office staff in US: 3

**Countries:** Micronesia, Federated States of 4

## Cook Communications Ministries International

4050 Lee Vance View
Colorado Springs, CO 80920 USA

**Phone:** (719) 536-0100
**Fax:** (719) 536-3266
**E-mail:** gatesr@ccmi.org
**Web Site:** www.ccmi.org
**Associations:** EFMA

*Mr. David Mehlis, President*

An interdenominational ministry of evangelical tradition engaged in making Christian literature available from translations of their English language product and through training Christian publishers to provide Christian literature in their own language and country.

**Purpose:** "To encourage the acceptance of Jesus Christ as personal Savior and to aid, promote and contribute to the teaching and putting into practice of His two great commands..."

**Year founded in US:** 1944

**Income for Overseas Min:** $1,900,000

Countries: Brazil; China; Europe—General; India; Latin America—General; Myanmar/Burma; Vietnam

## Cooperative Baptist Fellowship

PO Box 450329
Atlanta, GA 31145-0329 USA

**Phone:** (770) 220-1600
**Fax:** (770) 220-1685
**E-mail:** contact@thefellowship.info
**Web Site:** www.thefellowship.info

*Dr. Daniel Vestal, Exec. Coordinator*

A sending agency of Baptist Renewal Movement tradition engaged in discipleship, development and leadership development.

**Purpose:** "...to serve Christians and churches as they discover and fulfill their God-given mission."

**Year founded in US:** 1991

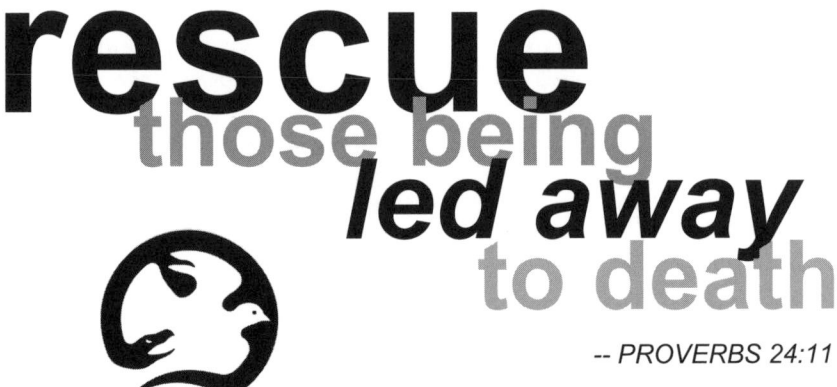

# rescue
those being
*led away*
to death

*-- PROVERBS 24:11*

# Crisis Consulting
# International

## *Serving the Missionary & NGO Communities*

- **Personal Security & Crisis Prevention Training**
- **Risk Assessment & Contingency Planning**
- **Emergency Assistance**
- **Crisis Management**
- **Hostage Negotiations**
- **Security Services**

# www.CriCon.org

**Crisis Consulting International**
9452 Telephone Rd., #223, Ventura, CA  93004  USA
PH: 805-642-2549     FAX: 805-642-1748
EMAIL: info@cricon.org

Income for Overseas Min: $25,000,000

Fully Supported US Personnel Overseas:
Expecting to serve more than 4 years: 83

Other Personnel:
Bi-vocational/tentmakers: 28
Home ministry & office staff in US: 50

Countries: Africa—General 21; Asia—General 24; Europe—General 38

## Cornerstone International
PO Box 192
Wilmore, KY 40390 USA
Phone: (859) 858-4578
Fax: (859) 858-0981
E-mail: duane@cornerstoneinternational.org
Web Site: www.cornerstoneinternational.org
Mr. E. Duane Jones, Director

A nondenominational sending agency of Wesleyan and Charismatic tradition engaged in church planting, mobilization for mission, childrens programs, TEE, evangelism and short-term programs. Data from 2001.

Purpose: "...to evangelize and disciple... [in] partnership with local churches in the launching of short-term and career missionaries."

Year founded in US: 1972

Income for Overseas Min: $565,226

Personnel:
Home ministry & office staff in US: 4

## Correll Missionary Ministries
See: Christ's Mandate for Missions

## Crisis Consulting Intl.
(See ad on page 150)
9452 Telephone Rd., #223
Ventura, CA 93004 USA
Phone: (805) 642-2549
Fax: (805) 642-1748
E-mail: info@cricon.org
Web Site: www.cricon.org
Mr. Robert Klamser, Exec. Director

A nondenominational service agency of Evangelical tradition engaged in management consulting/training, training and services for other agencies.

Purpose: "...to assist the Global Christian Community in fulfilling the Great Commission by providing security and crisis management services."

Year founded in US: 1985

Personnel:
Home ministry & office staff in US: 1

## CrossLink International
427 North Maple Ave.
Falls Church, VA 22046 USA
Phone: (703) 534-5465
Fax: (703) 536-8349
E-mail: info@crosslinkinternational.net
Web Site: www.crosslinkinternational.net
Associations: AERDO
Linda L. Cook, Exec. Director

An interdenominational specialized agency of Baptist tradition engaged in providing medical supplies, relief and/or rehabilitation and supplying medical equipment.

Purpose: "...to change the world one life at a time through Christ-like missions, by equipping mission volunteers, medical mission teams and missionaries as they witness the love of Jesus Christ."

Year founded in US: 1993

Income for Overseas Min: $3,577,818

Gifts in Kind: $3,004,912

Personnel:
Home ministry & office staff in US: 9

## Crossover Communications International
PO Box 211755
Columbia, SC 29221-1755 USA
Phone: (803) 691-0688
Fax: (803) 691-9355
E-mail: info@crossoverusa.org
Web Site: www.crossoverusa.org
Associations: IFMA
Dr. William H. Jones, President

An interdenominational service agency of Baptist and Independent tradition engaged in church planting, evangelism, short-term programs and training.

Purpose: "In the power of the Spirit...to communicate the message of Christ...to the peoples of the world."

Year founded in US: 1987

Income for Overseas Min: $202,735

Fully Supported US Personnel Overseas:

Expecting to serve more than 4 years: 10
Non-residential mission personnel: 2

**Other Personnel:**
Short-term less than 1 year: 11
Non-US serving in own/other country: 1
Home ministry & office staff in US: 9

**Countries:** Brazil 4; Central Asia—General 4; Moldova 2

## CrossWorld
PO Box 306
Bala-Cynwyd, PA 19004 USA
**Phone:** (610) 667-7660
**Fax:** (610) 660-9068
**E-mail:** info@crossworld.org
**Web Site:** www.crossworld.org
**Associations:** IFMA

*Rev. D. James O'Neill, President*

A transdenominational sending agency of Independent tradition engaged in church planting, childrens programs, Christian education, theological education, evangelism and leadership development.

**Purpose:** "...serves the church by mobilizing teams to make disciples and train leaders which will result in movements of reproducing churches among the unreached."

**Year founded in US:** 1931
**Income for Overseas Min:** $15,000,000
**Fully Supported US Personnel Overseas:**
Expecting to serve more than 4 years: 257
Expecting to serve 1 to 4 years: 5
Non-residential mission personnel: 8

**Other Personnel:**
Short-term less than 1 year: 157
Home ministry & office staff in US: 49

**Countries:** Afghanistan 3; Bosnia and Herzegovina 6; Brazil 58; Congo, Democratic Republic of 6; Dominican Republic 10; Ecuador 12; France 23; Germany 23; Guyana 8; Haiti 20; Indonesia 25; Ireland 11; Italy 19; Mexico 8; Philippines 5; Romania 4; Serbia and Montenegro 5; Slovakia 4; South Africa 3; Spain 4

## CSI Ministries, Inc.
**(See ads on page 154 & 155)**
1714 W. Royale Dr.
Muncie, IN 47304 USA
**Phone:** (765) 286-0711

**Fax:** (765) 286-5773
**E-mail:** csi@csiministries.org
**Web Site:** www.csiministries.org

*Mr. Lenville Gross, President*

An interdenominational service agency of Evangelical tradition engaged in short-term programs, mobilization for mission, relief and/or rehabilitation and services for other agencies. Financial and personnel data from 2003.

**Purpose:** "...promotes world missions by taking people to see firsthand what God is doing to get His Word to a lost world."

**Year founded in US:** 1963
**Income for Overseas Min:** $1,607,855
**Fully Supported US Personnel Overseas:**
Expecting to serve more than 4 years: 10

**Other Personnel:**
Short-term less than 1 year: 975
Non-US serving in own/other country: 22
Home ministry & office staff in US: 10

**Countries:** Haiti 5; Jamaica 5

## CTI Music Ministries (Carpenter's Tools Intl.)
PO Box 100
Willmar, MN 56201-0100 USA
**Phone:** (800) 543-6205
**Fax:** (320) 235-0185
**E-mail:** info@ctimusic.org
**Web Site:** www.ctimusic.org

*Mr. David Lanning, President*

An interdenominational support agency of Evangelical tradition engaged in evangelism, short-term programs, music performance and youth programs. An associate ministry of Youth for Christ International.

**Purpose:** "...to recruit, train and send music teams to work with established Christian ministries worldwide to reach young people with the Gospel."

**Year founded in US:** 1975
**Income for Overseas Min:** $230,000
**Personnel:**
Short-term less than 1 year: 45
Home ministry & office staff in US: 7

## Cumberland Presbyterian Church Board of Missions
1978 Union Ave.

Unlike any other college experience.

# Uncompromising Education

Uncommon Personal Mentoring • Unparalleled Community • Unchanging Christian Worldview • Unmatched Value

Some students choose a college; Crown College students are called. They are called to lives of excellence and relevance in a full range of professions. The call includes living out their faith in the classroom, through extracurriculars, on short-term mission trips, and while living in community with each other.

Crown's faculty and staff are also called and provide the foundation of a life changing faith that integrates what students learn in the classroom and what they experience around the world.

**MEMBER**
Council for Christian
Colleges & Universities

**Number of Students:** 1300

**Faculty/Student Ratio:** 14:1

**Percentage of Students Receiving Aid:** 90+

**Athletics:** 11 sports in NCAA Division III

**Location:** 215-acre campus located in the lake-dotted west metro region of the Twin Cities near St. Bonifacius, Minnesota.

## 1-800-68-CROWN
www.crown.edu
email: info@crown.edu

CROWN COLLEGE

# Christian Service International

## CSI Facts

Christian Service International (CSI Ministries, Inc.) is an evangelical, interdenominational, non-profit organization, that promotes missions and mission
projects worldwide. It is approved by the IRS as a tax-exempt 501 (c)(3) organization. Gifts to CSI are tax-deductible in accordance with federal and state
laws.

Founded in 1963, the international headquarters is in Muncie, Indiana.
Missionaries with CSI are currently ministering in Haiti, Jamaica, Guatemala,
Mozambique, Ireland and North America. Missionary opportunities are also
available in additional countries.

We have speakers available for church meetings, mission conferences, college
groups, and other interested organizations.

Visit our website:
**www.csiministries.org**

ECFA
MEMBER

# Helping You Serve

Are you ready to say, "Send me", but are uncertain how to take the next step? This is where our 40 plus years of experience will help you explore all the many possibilities of serving the needy, advancing God's Kingdom, and bringing all the glory to Him.

# The CSI Ministry

Ministering to the soul, mind and body of people, is at the heart of our mission ministry. We need you to help us achieve our goals by touching souls through personal evangelism, VBS, music, and Bible study; touching minds by assisting in schools, Sunday school classes, and building and repairing schools; and reaching out to the body by building houses and churches, serving on medical teams, and painting and making repairs at children's homes.

# CSI Services

CSI assists in all aspects of planning your team's mission trip. We will help you choose the country and the project. We can organize your travel plans and arrange for housing and transportation within the host country. We will supply the equipment needed for your project and make arrangements for all necessary supplies. Teams pay for materials for building projects.

We have many years of experience ministering with teams to many countries including Haiti, Jamaica, Guatemala, Belize, Dominican Republic, Brazil, Kenya, Mozambique, and Ireland. Tell us where you want to serve and we will work to see your ministry goals accomplished.

If you would prefer to stay within our borders, our North American Ministry can assist you in serving in the Appalachians, inner city, with Native Americans or in the Gulf Coast area.

# Serving on a Team

We welcome all who have a heart for the needs of others and wish to serve the Lord on the mission field for short periods of time. We'll give assistance in helping you form a team from your church, college, or other organization. We will help you in selecting a country to serve in and the projects needed there. We all have been blessed with various talents and gifts that can be utilized on the mission field.

If physical problems keep you from traveling to the mission field, we still need you to give prayer support to CSI as well as the many teams. We firmly believe that all short-term mission efforts must be covered by prayer.

**Christian Service International**
1714 W. Royale Drive • Muncie, IN 47304-2240
Phone: (765) 286-0711• Fax: (765) 286-5773
Email: csi@csiministries.org

# EASTERN UNIVERSITY

## SCHOOL OF LEADERSHIP AND DEVELOPMENT

**Offering degree programs to a global audience for over 20 years**

### Degree Programs:

- MA in Organizational Leadership
- MA in International Development
- MBA in Economic Development

### 3 Certificate Programs:

- NGO Leadership
- Development Studies
- Small Enterprise Development
  (beginning 2008)

### Convenient Delivery Options:

- Full-time at US campus
- Hybrid residency model
  (online and short residencies)

*As the first Christian university in the United States to offer holistic, community-based development programs, Eastern has been helping change the world, one community at a time, for over 22 years. The proof of this long-term commitment is an experienced team of faculty and a dynamic curriculum, which combines classroom learning with extensive hands-on experience. To find out more, call us or visit our website today.*

1-800-597-9324 (US Only)      + 610-341-1398      sld@eastern.edu

EASTERN†UNIVERSITY
*Light Your Future.*

# www.eastern.edu/sld

Memphis, TN 38104 USA
**Phone:** (901) 276-9988
**Fax:** (901) 276-4578
**E-mail:** missions@cumberland.org
**Web Site:** www.cumberland.org/bom
**Associations:** CWS

*Rev. Michael Sharpe, Exec. Director*

A denominational sending agency of Presbyterian tradition engaged in church planting, missions information service, leadership development, partnership development, relief and/or rehabilitation and short-term programs.

**Year founded in US:** 1845

**Income for Overseas Min:** $437,720

**Personnel:**
Short-term less than 1 year: 30
Bi-vocational/tentmakers: 4
Home ministry & office staff in US: 11

## D & D Missionary Homes, Inc.
4020 58th Ave. North
St. Petersburg, FL 33714 USA
**Phone:** (727) 522-0522
**Fax:** (727) 522-0524
**E-mail:** ddmissionaryhomes@juno.com
**Web Site:** www.ddmissionaryhomes.org

*Mr. Philip R. Fogle, President*

A service agency of Independent and Evangelical tradition engaged in furloughed missionary support, missions information service and member care.

**Purpose:** "...to provide quality hospitality and support services to active evangelical missionaries and pastors of all nationalities during their transitional periods."

**Year founded in US:** 1949

**Personnel:**
Home ministry & office staff in US: 7

## David Livingstone KURE Foundation
PO Box 232
Tulsa, OK 74102 USA
**Phone:** (918) 742-9902
**Fax:** (918) 496-2873
**E-mail:** DLMFKURE@aol.com
**Web Site:** www.dlmfkure.org

*Mr. H. Dwain Griffin, Chairman/CEO*

A nondenominational service agency of Independent tradition engaged in support of

national workers. Statistical data from 1998.

**Year founded in US:** 1969

**Income for Overseas Min:** $1,500,000

**Personnel:**
Non-US serving in own/other country: 113
Home ministry & office staff in US: 9

**Countries:** Korea, South; Mexico; Philippines; Thailand; Ukraine

## Dawn Ministries, Inc.
PO Box 690787
Orlando, FL 32869-0787 USA
**Phone:** (407) 370-9312
**Fax:** (407) 226-9713
**E-mail:** inquiries@dawnministries.org
**Web Site:** www.dawnministries.org

*Ngwiza Mnkandla, President*

A nondenominational service agency of Charismatic and Evangelical tradition engaged in church planting, discipleship, justice, leadership development, literature distribution, mission-related research and training.

**Purpose:** "...to see saturation church planting become the generally accepted and fervently practiced strategy for completing the task of making disciples of all peoples in our generation."

**Year founded in US:** 1985

**Income for Overseas Min:** $3,900,000

**Personnel:**
Non-US serving in own/other country: 8
Home ministry & office staff in US: 10

## Dayspring International
PO Box 3309
Virginia Beach, VA 23454 USA
**Phone:** (757) 428-1092
**Fax:** (757) 428-0257
**E-mail:** webmaster@dayspringinternational.org
**Web Site:** www.dayspringinternational.org
**Associations:** EFMA

*Rev. John E. Gilman, President*

A nondenominational support agency of Evangelical tradition engaged in evangelism, church planting, funds transmission, support of national workers and supplying equipment.

**Purpose:** "...to be an enabling servant to the national church through culturally relevant multi-media tools and humanitarian programs to assist in evangelization and discipling of unreached and under-reached people groups."

**Year founded in US:** 1979
**Income for Overseas Min:** $11,947,641
**Gifts in Kind:** $9,544,533
**Personnel:**
  Non-US serving in own/other country: 1,000
**Countries:** India

## Daystar U.S.
5701 Normandale Rd., Ste. 325
Edina, MN 55424 USA
**Phone:** (952) 928-2550
**Fax:** (952) 928-2551
**E-mail:** info@daystarus.org
**Web Site:** www.daystarus.org
*Mr. Todd Rasmuson, Exec. Director*

A nondenominational sending agency of Evangelical tradition engaged in providing support for Daystar Univ. in Nairobi, in theological education, leadership, management consulting/training, missionary training, postsecondary education and mission-related research.

**Purpose:** "...to expand God's Kingdom in Africa by equipping Christian servant leaders through B.A./M.A. programs, short courses and research services."

**Year founded in US:** 1963
**Income for Overseas Min:** $1,044,537
**Gifts in Kind:** $17,046
**Fully Supported US Personnel Overseas:**
  Expecting to serve more than 4 years: 6
**Other Personnel:**
  Short-term less than 1 year: 20
  Home ministry & office staff in US: 5
**Countries:** Kenya 4; Sri Lanka 2

## Deaf Missions International
PO Box 8514
Clearwater, FL 33758 USA
**Phone:** (727) 530-3020
**E-mail:** deafmissions@netzero.net
*M. Eldeny Hale, Director*

A transdenominational specialized agency of Evangelical tradition engaged in ministry to those with hearing disabilities through mission projects including missionary orientation and training.

**Year founded in US:** 1967
**Personnel:**
  Home ministry & office staff in US: 1

## DeNike Ministries
PO Box 1231
McAlester, OK 74502 USA
**Phone:** (918) 423-2431
**E-mail:** denikeministries@emptychair.net
**Web Site:** www.denikeministries.org
*Mr. Frank DeNike, President*

A nondenominational support agency of Charismatic and Independent tradition engaged in short-term programs, training the nationals in Mexico and Kenya, church construction, church planting, theological education, partnership development and supplying equipment.

**Purpose:** "...to encourage others to come alongside of them to provide the necessary resources, both spiritual and physical, for the training and strengthening of God's people in Mexico, so they can more effectively fulfill their burden to reach the lost for Jesus as stated in Matt. 28:18-20."

**Year founded in US:** 1995
**Fully Supported US Personnel Overseas:**
  Expecting to serve more than 4 years: 1
**Other Personnel:**
  Short-term less than 1 year: 120
  Home ministry & office staff in US: 1
**Countries:** Mexico 1

## Derek Prince Ministries, Intl.
PO Box 19501
Charlotte, NC 28219 USA
**Phone:** (704) 357-3556
**Fax:** (704) 357-1413
**E-mail:** ContactUs@derekprince.org
**Web Site:** www.derekprince.org
*Mr. Dick Leggatt, President*

A nondenominational support agency engaged in audio/video recording, production and distribution, broadcasting in 13 languages, and literature translation, production and distribution in up to 50 languages.

**Purpose:** "...seeking to reach the unreached, teach the untaught and touch the untouched with the pure truths of God's

Word in all nations through the distribution of teaching material by Derek Prince..."

**Year founded in US:** 1963

**Income for Overseas Min:** $227,999

**Personnel:**
Short-term less than 1 year: 1
Home ministry & office staff in US: 21

## Development Associates International (DAI)
PO Box 49278
Colorado Springs, CO 80949 USA

**Phone:** (719) 598-7970
**Fax:** (425) 988-8126
**E-mail:** info@daintl.org
**Web Site:** www.daintl.org
**Associations:** EFMA

*Mrs. Jane Overstreet, President/CEO*

A transdenominational support agency of Evangelical and Ecumenical tradition engaged in leadership development, extension education and management consulting/training.

**Purpose:** "Development Associates International is committed to develop the integrity and effectiveness of Christian leaders worldwide so that the church can fulfill its role in extending the Kingdom of God."

**Year founded in US:** 1996

**Income for Overseas Min:** $1,654,398

**Fully Supported US Personnel Overseas:**
Expecting to serve more than 4 years: 1
Non-residential mission personnel: 6

**Other Personnel:**
Non-US serving in own/other country: 22
Home ministry & office staff in US: 7

**Countries:** Australia; Belgium; Côte d'Ivoire; Egypt; Ghana 1; Haiti; India; Nigeria; Russia; South Africa; Uganda

## Disciples International
PO Box 466
Wallingford, PA 19013 USA

**Phone:** (610) 872-8742
**Fax:** (610) 872-8762
**E-mail:** disciples.international@verizon.net
**Web Site:** www.disciplesinternational.org

*Mr. David Komarnicki, President/CEO*

A specialized agency of Evangelical and Independent tradition engaged in literature

production, bible memorization, discipleship, Christian education, leadership development and literature distribution.

**Purpose:** "...to share the Good News of salvation and eternal life with every man, woman and child on God's earth."

**Year founded in US:** 2001

**Income for Overseas Min:** $5,000

## Donetsk Christian University
PO Box 521144
Tulsa, OK 74152-1144 USA

**Phone:** (918) 249-2011
**E-mail:** JWhite@dcu.donetsk.ua
**Web Site:** www.dcu.donbass.com

*Mr. David Anderson, U.S. Director*

An interdenominational specialized agency of Evangelical and Baptist tradition engaged in theological education, church planting, missionary education, TESOL, missionary training and Christian education.

**Purpose:** "...to work on behalf of the evangelical community of the former Soviet Union to engage in theological as well as other academic research and reflection, and to prepare people to fulfill the mission of the Church in both the spiritual and social spheres."

**Year founded in US:** 2001

**Income for Overseas Min:** $194,201

**Gifts in Kind:** $8,000

**Fully Supported US Personnel Overseas:**
Expecting to serve more than 4 years: 5
Expecting to serve 1 to 4 years: 2

**Other Personnel:**
Short-term less than 1 year: 25
Non-US serving in own/other country: 50
Home ministry & office staff in US: 1

**Countries:** Ukraine 5

## Door of Hope International
PO Box 303
Glendale, CA 91209 USA

**Phone:** (888) 541-9942
**Fax:** (818) 279-8334
**E-mail:** info@dohi.org
**Web Site:** www.dohi.org

*Paul H. Popov, Intl. President*

An interdenominational support agency engaged in Bible distribution, childcare/orphanage programs, missions information service, relief and/or rehabilitation, Bible translation and youth programs.

**Purpose:** "...to provide help and bring spiritual, practical and humanitarian assistance to Eastern Europe through the development and support of leadership in the indigenous church and the education of believers in the West."

**Year founded in US:** 1972

**Income for Overseas Min:** $158,985

**Gifts in Kind:** $48,937

**Personnel:**
  Home ministry & office staff in US: 4

## DualReach
PO Box 427
Dana Point, CA 92629 USA
**Phone:** (949) 248-1236
**E-mail:** info@dualreach.org
**Web Site:** www.dualreach.org
*Dr. Bruce Camp, President/CEO*

A transdenominational service agency of Evangelical tradition engaged in missions mobilization of churches and assistance to the church-mobilization ministry of mission agencies via consulting, training and production of resources to increase their global impact.

**Purpose:** "...to provide resources, training and consulting to churches and mission agencies to help them mobilize local congregations' potential to reach the world globally and locally."

**Year founded in US:** 2001

**Personnel:**
  Home ministry & office staff in US: 1

## East Gates Ministries Intl.
PO Box 2010
Sumner, WA 98390-0440 USA
**Phone:** (253) 770-2625
**Fax:** (253) 770-2817
**E-mail:** egmi@eastgates.org
**Web Site:** www.eastgates.org
*Rev. Nelson Graham, President*

A specialized agency of Evangelical and Ecumenical tradition engaged in Bible distribution, audio recording/distribution, church construction, literature distribution, literature production and support of na-

tional workers. Data from 2001.

**Purpose:** "...to have a positive impact on the Church history of China through diplomatic activity that helps Chinese leaders, at all levels, better understand and appreciate their Christian population."

**Year founded in US:** 1990

**Income for Overseas Min:** $846,986

**Personnel:**
  Short-term less than 1 year: 4
  Non-US serving in own/other country: 4
  Home ministry & office staff in US: 8

**Countries:** China; Hong Kong

## East West Ministries
## See: East West Interknit

## East West Interknit
P.O. Box 270333
St. Paul, MN 55127
**Phone:** (651) 765-2550
**Fax:** (651) 765-2523
**E-mail:** info@ew-interknit.org
**Web Site:** www.ew-interknit.org
*Annette L. Jones, Executive Director*

A nondenominational support agency of Baptist tradition engaged in support of national workers, childcare/orphanage programs, funds transmission, leadership development, literature distribution and supplying equipment.

**Purpose:** "...to provide for training, tools and resources that enhance the outreach efforts of developing world Christians serving to meet the spiritual and physical needs of people in their sphere of influence."

**Year founded in US:** 1991

**Income for Overseas Min:** $266,000

**Gifts in Kind:** $200,000

**Personnel:**
  Home ministry & office staff in US: 20

**Countries:** Cuba; Haiti; India; Indonesia

## Eastern European Outreach, Inc.
PO Box 685
Murrieta, CA 92564 USA
**Phone:** (951) 696-5244
**Fax:** (951) 696-5247
**E-mail:** info@eeo.org

**Web Site:** www.eeo.org

**Associations:** AERDO

*Mr. Jeff L. Thompson, President*

A nondenominational service agency of Evangelical tradition engaged in child sponsorship, camping programs, evangelism, literature distribution, support of national workers and short-term programs.

**Purpose:** "...to make disciples (followers of Christ) of all peoples (Matt. 28:18-19) ...the emphasis is on the needy children and young people of Eastern Europe."

**Year founded in US:** 1980

**Income for Overseas Min:** $1,250,000

**Gifts in Kind:** $10,000

**Fully Supported US Personnel Overseas:**
    Non-residential mission personnel: 1

**Other Personnel:**
    Short-term less than 1 year: 125
    Non-US serving in own/other country: 40
    Home ministry & office staff in US: 7

## Eastern Mennonite Missions

53 Brandt Blvd.
Salunga, PA 17538 USA

**Phone:** (717) 898-2251
**Fax:** (717) 898-8092
**E-mail:** info@emm.org
**Web Site:** www.emm.org

**Associations:** EFMA Candidate

*Dr. Richard Showalter, President*

A denominational sending agency of Mennonite tradition engaged in church planting, development, theological education, leadership development, relief and/or rehabilitation and youth programs.

**Purpose:** "To envision many people worldwide experiencing salvation in Jesus Christ, a new generation of leaders raised up and new Christ-centered congregations established from which more workers are sent."

**Year founded in US:** 1914

**Income for Overseas Min:** $4,658,715

**Fully Supported US Personnel Overseas:**
    Expecting to serve more than 4 years: 34
    Expecting to serve 1 to 4 years: 47

**Other Personnel:**
    Short-term less than 1 year: 108
    Non-US serving in own/other country: 6
    Home ministry & office staff in US: 9

**Countries:** Albania 2; Cambodia 2; Ethiopia; Germany 2; Guatemala 2; Hong Kong 2; Kenya 2; Lithuania 3; Peru; Tanzania 2; Thailand 2; United Kingdom 4; Unspecified Country 11

## East-West Ministries Intl.

4450 Sojourn Dr.
Addison, TX 75001 USA

**Phone:** (214) 265-8300
**Fax:** (214) 265-8503
**E-mail:** llittle@eastwest.org
**Web Site:** www.eastwest.org

*Mr. John Maisel, President*

A sending agency of Evangelical tradition engaged in church planting, theological education, evangelism and literature distribution.

**Purpose:** "...to provide church planting training and coordination of evangelistic resources to help plant churches that are doctrinally sound, spiritually alive, grace oriented and multiplying..."

**Year founded in US:** 1993

**Income for Overseas Min:** $9,000,000

**Fully Supported US Personnel Overseas:**
    Expecting to serve more than 4 years: 27
    Non-residential mission personnel: 40

**Other Personnel:**
    Short-term less than 1 year: 10
    Bi-vocational/tentmakers: 2
    Non-US serving in own/other country: 128
    Home ministry & office staff in US: 25

**Countries:** Albania 1; China 4; India; Kazakhstan 6; Kenya 2; Russia 10; Spain 4

## ECHO (Educational Concerns for Hunger Organization)

17391 Durance Rd.
N. Ft. Myers, FL 33917 USA

**Phone:** (239) 543-3246
**Fax:** (239) 543-5317
**E-mail:** echo@echonet.org
**Web Site:** www.echonet.org

**Associations:** AERDO

*Mr. Stan Doerr, CEO*

An interdenominational service agency of Evangelical tradition engaged in agricultural programs, development, missions information service, mission-related research, services for other agencies and technical assistance.

**Purpose:** "...to strengthen the ministries of

missionaries and national churches as they assist small-scale farmers or urban gardeners in the Third World."

**Year founded in US:** 1973

**Personnel:**
Short-term less than 1 year: 6
Home ministry & office staff in US: 15

## Educational Services Intl. (ESI)

444 E. Huntington Dr., Ste. 200
Arcadia, CA 91006 USA

**Phone:** (626) 294-9400
**Fax:** (626) 821-2022
**Web Site:** www.teachoverseas.org

*Mr. Ron Nicholas, President*

An interdenominational specialized agency of Evangelical tradition engaged in TESOL and tentmaking.

**Purpose:** "...to share Christ's love in creative-access nations through teaching."

**Year founded in US:** 1989

**Income for Overseas Min:** $1,400,000

**Fully Supported US Personnel Overseas:**
Expecting to serve 1 to 4 years: 165

**Other Personnel:**
Short-term less than 1 year: 105
Home ministry & office staff in US: 20

**Countries:** China; CIS - General; Europe—General; Morocco; Vietnam

## Edwin L. Hodges Ministries

PO Box 1921
Decatur, AL 35602 USA

**Phone:** (256) 355-3004
**Fax:** (256) 350-3502
**E-mail:** ehodges169@aol.com
**Web Site:** www.elhm.org

**Associations:** EFMA Candidate

*Rev. Edwin L. Hodges, President/Founder*

A support agency engaged in literature production/distribution, Bible distribution, discipleship, leadership development and support of national workers in 11 countries.

**Year founded in US:** 1994

**Income for Overseas Min:** $158,000

**Gifts in Kind:** $2,727,248

**Personnel:**
Home ministry & office staff in US: 6

## EFCA International Mission

901 E. 78th St.
Minneapolis, MN 55420-1300 USA

**Phone:** (952) 854-1300
**Fax:** (952) 853-8474
**E-mail:** efcaim@efca.org
**Web Site:** www.efca.org/international

**Associations:** EFMA

*Rev. Timothy J. Addington, Exec. Director*

A denominational sending agency of Evangelical tradition engaged in church planting, theological education, evangelism, leadership development, mobilization for mission and short-term programs.

**Purpose:** "...making disciples of Jesus Christ and incorporating them into reproducing congregations with the goal of launching church planting movements internationally."

**Year founded in US:** 1887

**Income for Overseas Min:** $20,692,657

**Gifts in Kind:** $300,000

**Fully Supported US Personnel Overseas:**
Expecting to serve more than 4 years: 300
Expecting to serve 1 to 4 years: 76
Non-residential mission personnel: 36

**Other Personnel:**
Short-term less than 1 year: 274
Non-US serving in own/other country: 71
Home ministry & office staff in US: 29

**Countries:** Austria 3; Belgium 12; Bosnia and Herzegovina 6; Brazil 5; Central African Republic 12; China; Colombia; Congo, Democratic Republic of; Costa Rica 7; Czech Republic 11; France 12; Germany 10; Honduras 2; Hong Kong 9; Hungary 10; India; Japan 19; Kenya 8; Macau; Malaysia; Mexico 10; Mongolia; Netherlands 4; Peru 11; Philippines 14; Poland 4; Portugal 4; Romania 16; Russia 16; Rwanda; Singapore; Slovakia 4; Spain 8; Sudan; Taiwan 1; Tanzania 9; Thailand 10; Turkey; Ukraine 8; United Kingdom 2; Unspecified Country 44; Uzbekistan; Venezuela 9

## EFMA (Evangelical Fellowship of Mission Agencies)

(See ad page 163)
4201 N. Peachtree Rd. #300
Atlanta, GA 30341 USA

**Phone:** (770) 457-6677
**Fax:** (770) 457-0037

# We'd like to help you **Increase Effectiveness** by **Adding Value** and **Stimulating Partnership.**

→ Our mission is to facilitate relational and developmental initiatives that increase the effectiveness of mission organizations by adding value to their leaders and stimulating partnership in the missions community.

## EVANGELICAL FELLOWSHIP OF MISSION AGENCIES

4201 North Peachtree Road, Suite 300
Atlanta, GA 30341
770-457-6677
www.efmamissions.org
efma@efmamissions.org

**ECIM**

**kingdom BUILDING**

**ECCU**

Banking, financing, and investment

**kingdom BUILDING**

**FINANCING**

1. *Strategize.*
2. *Find the right tools.*
3. *Build.*

## BANKING, FINANCING, AND INVESTING. TOOLS FOR KINGDOM BUILDING.

Whether you're constructing a new worship facility or seeking to wisely steward your ministry's cash flow, the financial choices you make can have an eternal impact. At Evangelical Christian Credit Union (ECCU), we believe that our biblically-based financial tools make all the difference.

For more information on how ECCU can help build your ministry through banking, financing, and investing, contact us today.

**ECCU**

**800.634.3228   WWW.ECCU.ORG**

© 2006 ECCU

**E-mail:** efma@efmamissions.org
**Web Site:** www.efmamissions.org
*Rev. Steve Moore, President/CEO*

A confederation of mission agencies which serves for the exchange of ideas and building of supportive relationships.

**Purpose:** "...to aid agencies and boards to work more efficiently, tapping into the rich resource of all our members so that the gifts God gives can be used most effectively in the task of world evangelization."

**Year founded in US:** 1945

**Personnel:**
   Home ministry & office staff in US: 3

## Elim Fellowship—Intl. Dept.
PO Box 57A
Lima, NY 14485-0857 USA
**Phone:** (585) 582-2790
**Fax:** (585) 624-1229
**E-mail:** international@elimfellowship.org
**Web Site:** www.elimfellowship.org
*Rev./Dr. Ronald Burgio, President*

A nondenominational sending agency of Charismatic and Pentecostal tradition engaged in evangelism, church planting, discipleship, theological education, leadership development and medical work. See Teen World Outreach for short-term program.

**Purpose:** "...to glorify God and His Son Jesus Christ and to obey Christ's mandate to preach the Gospel and make disciples of all nations. To this end we are committed to serving and equipping our worldwide constituency in carrying out their respective missions."

**Year founded in US:** 1933

**Income for Overseas Min:** $2,681,233

**Gifts in Kind:** $15,000

**Fully Supported US Personnel Overseas:**
   Expecting to serve more than 4 years: 68
   Expecting to serve 1 to 4 years: 4
   Non-residential mission personnel: 29

**Other Personnel:**
   Short-term less than 1 year: 3
   Non-US serving in own/other country: 36
   Home ministry & office staff in US: 4

**Countries:** Argentina 3; Asia—General 13; Australia 1; Austria 2; Bosnia and Herzegovina 1; Brazil 2; Ghana 1; Guam 1; Haiti 2; Jamaica 2; Kenya 5; Mexico 10; Middle East 2; New Zealand 2; Niger 4; Nigeria; Peru 1; Philippines 1; Poland 1; Singapore; Sweden 2; Tanzania 10; United Kingdom 2

## Emmanuel Intl. Mission
3878 Concord Rd.
York, SC 29745 USA
**Phone:** (803) 831-1356
**Fax:** (803) 831-1369
**E-mail:** agraham@e-i.org
**Web Site:** www.eim-us.org
*Mr. Alan C. Graham, Chairman*

An interdenominational service agency of Evangelical tradition engaged in support of national churches, development, TEE, evangelism, leadership development and relief and/or rehabilitation.

**Purpose:** "...assists local churches worldwide to meet physical and spiritual needs of the poor."

**Year founded in US:** 1978

**Income for Overseas Min:** $133,115

**Fully Supported US Personnel Overseas:**
   Expecting to serve more than 4 years: 2
   Expecting to serve 1 to 4 years: 1

**Other Personnel:**
   Short-term less than 1 year: 12
   Non-US serving in own/other country: 23

**Countries:** Brazil; Ethiopia; Haiti; Indonesia; Malawi 1; Philippines 1; South Africa; Sudan; Tanzania; Uganda

## Emmaus Road International
7150 Tanner Ct.
San Diego, CA 92111 USA
**Phone:** (858) 292-7020
**Fax:** (858) 292-7020
**E-mail:** Emmaus_Road@eri.org
**Web Site:** www.eri.org
*Mr. Neal Pirolo, Director*

A transdenominational service agency engaged in church level member care, furloughed missionary support, leadership development and missionary training.

**Purpose:** "...to mobilize, train and network cross-cultural workers in effective cross-cultural outreach ministry."

**Year founded in US:** 1983

**Income for Overseas Min:** $60,000

**Fully Supported US Personnel Overseas:**
Expecting to serve more than 4 years: 2
**Other Personnel:**
Short-term less than 1 year: 17
Home ministry & office staff in US: 1
**Countries:** Unspecified Country 2

## Empowering Lives Intl.
PO Box 67
Upland, CA 91785 USA
**Phone:** (909) 476-6822
**Fax:** (909) 476-6618
**E-mail:** info@empoweringlives.org
**Web Site:** www.empoweringlives.org
*Mr. Donald P. Rogers, Founder/Director*

A nondenominational service agency of Evangelical tradition engaged in development, agricultural programs, childcare/orphanage programs, Christian education, evangelism, medical work, support of national churches and short-term programs.
**Purpose:** "…to provide training, resources and encouragement to break the cycle of poverty and help people recognize their importance in the eyes of God."
**Year founded in US:** 1994
**Income for Overseas Min:** $600,464
**Fully Supported US Personnel Overseas:**
Expecting to serve more than 4 years: 2
Expecting to serve 1 to 4 years: 3
Non-residential mission personnel: 3
**Other Personnel:**
Short-term less than 1 year: 65
Non-US serving in own/other country: 122
Home ministry & office staff in US: 4
**Countries:** Congo, Democratic Republic of; Kenya 2; Sudan; Tanzania

## Engineering Ministries Intl.
103 E. Kiowa, Ste. 200
Colorado Springs, CO 80903 USA
**Phone:** (719) 633-2078
**Fax:** (719) 633-2970
**E-mail:** info@emiusa.org
**Web Site:** www.emiusa.org
*Mr. Glen Woodruff, CEO*

A nondenominational specialized agency of Evangelical tradition engaged in offering design services to ministries serving the poor and preaching the Gospel in developing nations.

**Purpose:** "…to mobilize Christian design professionals to serve the poor in developing countries…by empowering people to transform their world through the design and development of hospitals, schools, orphanages, bridges, water supplies, wastewater facilities and more."
**Year founded in US:** 1981
**Income for Overseas Min:** $4,687,664
**Gifts in Kind:** $2,859,095
**Fully Supported US Personnel Overseas:**
Expecting to serve more than 4 years: 18
Non-residential mission personnel: 15
**Other Personnel:**
Short-term less than 1 year: 183
Non-US serving in own/other country: 4
Home ministry & office staff in US: 4
**Countries:** Guatemala 6; India 7; Uganda 5

## Enterprise Development Intl.
10395-B Democracy Lane
Fairfax, VA 22030 USA
**Phone:** (703) 277-3360
**Fax:** (703) 277-3348
**E-mail:** enterprise@endpoverty.org
**Web Site:** www.endpoverty.org
*Mr. Kenneth W. Wesche, Exec. Dir.*

A transdenominational service agency engaged in management consulting, training and technical assistance for partner implementing agencies.
**Purpose:** "…enabling the poor to become productive, self supporting citizens."
**Year founded in US:** 1985
**Gifts in Kind:** $20,000
**Personnel:**
Home ministry & office staff in US: 6

## Entrust
**(See ad on page 167)**
PO Box 25520
Colorado Springs, CO 80936-5520 USA
**Phone:** (719) 622-1980
**Fax:** (719) 622-1992
**E-mail:** info@entrust4.org
**Web Site:** www.entrust4.org
*Dr. David P. Bohn, President*

A nondenominational sending agency of Evangelical tradition engaged in theological education, Christian education, missionary

## enTRUST⁴

*Multiplying Leaders for Multiplying Churches*

Entrust assists the church in responding to the global cry for servant-leaders through accessible, transformational, biblical training.

**The need for trained leaders is paramount** as we move into an era of unprecedented growth of Christian believers. Approximately 4,000 new churches start each week, while over 2 million pastors are serving without any biblical education.

**Now is the time** to take seriously the need to exponentially expand servant-leader training for the church. We hear God's call to see the number of leaders being trained grow to 250,000. Please join with us in this new chapter of training church leaders throughout the world.

Entrust • P.O. Box 25520 • Colorado Springs • CO • 80936-5520
719.622.1980 • info@entrust4.org • www.entrust4.org

# Your Heart's Calling.

**Incoming call:**
**Beijing, China**

Answer    Silence

# How Will You Answer?

By doing something significant? Something much bigger than yourself? Something that will last forever?

Thousands have answered that call by teaching English in Asia with ELIC. We have rewarding and fulfilling teaching positions available now in China, Mongolia, Vietnam, Laos, and Cambodia. If you have a bachelor's degree and feel your heart's calling to serve, contact us and we will get you on your way.

**Answer that call . . . and *Go* with us.**

*GO* With Us.        **www.elic.org**
**800.366.3542**

education, TEE, extension education, leadership development and missionary training.

**Purpose:** "...to assist the church in responding to the global cry for servant-leaders through accessible, transformational, biblical training."

**Year founded in US:** 1979

**Income for Overseas Min:** $2,602,236

**Gifts in Kind:** $377,304

**Fully Supported US Personnel Overseas:**
  Expecting to serve more than 4 years: 60
  Non-residential mission personnel: 7

**Other Personnel:**
  Short-term less than 1 year: 12
  Bi-vocational/tentmakers: 2
  Non-US serving in own/other country: 24
  Home ministry & office staff in US: 13

**Countries:** Africa—General; Austria 2; Bulgaria; Central Asia—General 4; Czech Republic 4; Georgia; Greece 4; Hungary 9; Middle East 6; Moldova 6; Romania 9; Russia 13; Slovakia 3

## Envoy International

2051 Warrington
Rochester Hills, MI 48307 USA

**Phone:** (248) 650-8974
**E-mail:** dandersen@envoyinternational.org
*Rev. David L. Andersen, President*

A nondenominational service agency of Baptist and Independent tradition engaged in leadership development, support of national churches, mission-related research, services for other agencies and training.

**Purpose:** "...to help the local church develop and implement a personalized involvement in world evangelization and discipleship."

**Year founded in US:** 1995

**Income for Overseas Min:** $164,000

**Fully Supported US Personnel Overseas:**
  Non-residential mission personnel: 6

**Other Personnel:**
  Short-term less than 1 year: 20
  Non-US serving in own/other country: 4

## Episcopal Church Missionary Community
## See: New Wineskins Missionary Network

## Episcopal Church USA— Domestic & Foreign Missionary Society

815 Second Ave.
New York, NY 10017 USA

**Phone:** (212) 922-5461
**Fax:** (212) 983-6377
**E-mail:** dcopley@episcopalchurch.org
**Web Site:** www.episcopalchurch.org
*Katharine Jefferts Schori, Presiding Bishop-Elect*

A denominational sending agency of Anglican tradition engaged in support of national churches, discipleship, evangelism, furloughed missionary support, partnership development and youth programs. Financial data from 2002.

**Purpose:** "...to ensure, in the most comprehensive and coordinated manner possible, the full participation of Episcopalians in the worldwide mission of the church..."

**Year founded in US:** 1785

**Income for Overseas Min:** $11,915,649

**Fully Supported US Personnel Overseas:**
  Expecting to serve more than 4 years: 59

**Other Personnel:**
  Home ministry & office staff in US: 4

**Countries:** China 3; Cyprus 2; Dominican Republic 6; Ecuador 1; Egypt 2; El Salvador 1; France 1; Germany 1; Ghana 1; Haiti 1; Honduras 1; India 1; Japan 2; Kenya 5; Liberia 2; Lithuania 2; Malawi 1; Mozambique 1; Myanmar/Burma 1; Pakistan 3; Panama 4; Romania 1; Rwanda 2; South Africa 7; Sudan 1; Syria 1; Tanzania 4; United Kingdom 1

## EQUIP Foundation

12000 Findley Rd., Ste. 150
Duluth, GA 30097 USA

**Phone:** (678) 225-3300
**Fax:** (678) 225-3349
**E-mail:** equipinfo@iequip.org
**Web Site:** www.iequip.org
**Associations:** EFMA
*Dr. John D. Hull, President*

An interdenominational support agency engaged in leadership development and training.

**Purpose:** "To see effective Christian leaders fulfill the Great Commission in every nation."

**Year founded in US:** 1996

**Income for Overseas Min:** $2,448,925

**Gifts in Kind:** $5,000

**Personnel:**
  Home ministry & office staff in US: 22

**Countries:** Africa—General; Asia—General

## Equip, Inc.

PO Box 1126
Marion, NC 28752-1126 USA

**Phone:** (828) 738-3891
**Fax:** (828) 738-3846
**Web Site:** www.equipinternational.com

*Rev. Barrie G. Flitcroft, Gen. Director*

An interdenominational sending agency of Baptist and Reformed tradition engaged in missionary training, agricultural programs, childcare/orphanage programs, development, disability assistance programs and medical work.

**Purpose:** "...to assist the church around the world to be responsive to the poor, sensitive to the Holy Spirit, focused on personal evangelism and practically engaged in strengthening the Body of Christ."

**Year founded in US:** 1983

**Income for Overseas Min:** $1,182,505

**Fully Supported US Personnel Overseas:**
  Expecting to serve more than 4 years: 24
  Expecting to serve 1 to 4 years: 3

**Other Personnel:**
  Short-term less than 1 year: 6
  Non-US serving in own/other country: 16
  Home ministry & office staff in US: 10

**Countries:** Belize 2; Brazil 5; Ethiopia 4; Ghana; Japan 1; Kenya; Liberia; Mexico 6; Nicaragua 2; Nigeria; Spain 2; Tanzania 2

## Equipping the Saints

1254 Keezletown Road
Weyers Cave, VA 24486 USA

**Phone:** (540) 234-6222
**Fax:** (540) 234-6262
**E-mail:** ets@rica.net
**Web Site:** www.etsusa.org

*Rev. Keith A. Jones, Exec. Director*

A nondenominational service agency of Evangelical tradition engaged in supplying equipment, missions information service, literature distribution, providing medical supplies, purchasing services and services for other agencies.

**Purpose:** "...to serve evangelical Christian ministries worldwide by providing all types of information, materials and equipment."

**Year founded in US:** 1991

**Income for Overseas Min:** $240,454

**Gifts in Kind:** $72,789

**Personnel:**
  Home ministry & office staff in US: 6

## European Christian Mission International—USA

161 Strasburg Pike
Lancaster, PA 17602-1323 USA

**Phone:** (717) 397-0390
**Fax:** (717) 397-5455
**E-mail:** ecm.usa@ecmi.org
**Web Site:** www.ecmi.org

**Associations:** IFMA

*Mr. Curtis Edwards, U.S. Director*

An interdenominational sending agency of Evangelical tradition engaged in church planting, discipleship, evangelism, support of national churches, support of national workers and short-term programs.

**Purpose:** "...to glorify by God by obeying His leading to develop a nationwide network of people passionate in prayer and support for promoting the planting and developing of churches which evangelize and disciple the peoples of Europe."

**Year founded in US:** 1960

**Income for Overseas Min:** $463,805

**Fully Supported US Personnel Overseas:**
  Expecting to serve more than 4 years: 136

**Other Personnel:**
  Short-term less than 1 year: 50
  Non-US serving in own/other country: 10
  Home ministry & office staff in US: 1

**Countries:** Albania 6; Austria 13; Bosnia and Herzegovina 4; Croatia 7; France 13; Germany 4; Ireland 15; Italy 11; Kosovo 4; Poland 4; Portugal 15; Romania 5; Serbia and Montenegro 2; Spain 29; Sweden 2; Ukraine 2

## European Evangelistic Society

PO Drawer 90150
East Point, GA 30364 USA
**Phone:** (404) 460-2443
**Fax:** (404) 460-2446
**E-mail:** wyehuxford@earthlink.net
**Web Site:** www.eesatlanta.org
*Mr. Samuel W. Huxford, Exec. Dir.*

A nondenominational specialized agency of Christian (Restoration Movement) tradition engaged in theological education, church planting, evangelism and mission-related research. Statistical data from 2001.

**Purpose:** "...to study, disseminate, and demonstrate the gospel, primarily, but not exclusively in Europe ... through scholarly research in Christian origins, the publication of research, and the establishment and development of congregations reflecting the understanding of the early church..."

**Year founded in US:** 1932
**Income for Overseas Min:** $205,817
**Personnel:**
Home ministry & office staff in US: 2

## Evangel Bible Translators

PO Box 669
Rockwall, TX 75087-0669 USA
**Phone:** (972) 771-8886
**Fax:** (972) 722-1721
**E-mail:** info@evangelbible.org
**Web Site:** www.evangelbible.org
*Rev. H. Syvelle Phillips, Founder/President*

A nondenominational sending agency of Pentecostal tradition engaged in Bible translation, Bible distribution, church planting, literacy work and translation work.

**Year founded in US:** 1976
**Income for Overseas Min:** $701,405
**Fully Supported US Personnel Overseas:**
Expecting to serve more than 4 years: 17
**Other Personnel:**
Short-term less than 1 year: 8
Non-US serving in own/other country: 37
Home ministry & office staff in US: 10
**Countries:** Azerbaijan 1; Benin; France 2; Ghana 2; Guatemala 2; India 6; Israel 1; Kenya; Liberia 1; Myanmar/Burma; Nepal; Papua New Guinea 2

## Evangelical Baptist Missions

PO Box 781438
Indianapolis, IN 46278 USA
**Phone:** (317) 872-4488
**Fax:** (317) 872-4489
**E-mail:** ebm@ebm.org
**Web Site:** www.ebm.org
*Dr. W. Paul Jackson, President*

A sending agency of Independent and Baptist tradition engaged in church planting, childcare/orphanage programs, discipleship, extension education, partnership development and Bible translation.

**Purpose:** "...help churches reach the world."
**Year founded in US:** 1928
**Income for Overseas Min:** $4,599,000
**Gifts in Kind:** $29,000
**Fully Supported US Personnel Overseas:**
Expecting to serve more than 4 years: 109
Expecting to serve 1 to 4 years: 6
Non-residential mission personnel: 15
**Other Personnel:**
Bi-vocational/tentmakers: 2
Non-US serving in own/other country: 12
Home ministry & office staff in US: 13
**Countries:** Argentina 8; Belgium 2; Benin 4; Brazil 5; France 12; Germany 8; Haiti: Italy 3; Japan 4; Mali 10; Mexico 6; Niger 8; Nigeria; Romania 3; Russia 1; South Africa 20; Sweden 1; United Arab Emirates; Unspecified Country 14

## Evangelical Bible Mission

5200 SE 145thStreet
Summerfield, FL 34491 USA
**Phone:** (352) 245-2560
**Fax:** (352) 245-9783
**E-mail:** info@ebminternational.com
**Web Site:** www.ebminternational.com
*Rev. Gerald Bustin, President*

An interdenominational sending agency of Holiness tradition engaged in church planting, Bible distribution, evangelism, literature distribution and supplying equipment. Data from 2001.

**Year founded in US:** 1939
**Personnel:**
Home ministry & office staff in US: 5

## Evangelical Congregational Church—Global Ministries Commission

100 W Park Ave.
Myerstown, PA 17067-1235 USA
**Phone:** (800) 866-7584
**Fax:** (717) 866-7383
**E-mail:** ecglobalministries@eccenter.com
**Web Site:** www.eccenter.com
*Mr. James Ehrman, Director Global Mins.*

A denominational service agency of Wesley-an tradition engaged in support of national churches, childcare/orphanage programs, church planting, theological education and Bible translation. Additional missionaries sent under other mission agencies. Statistical data from 2002.

**Year founded in US:** 1922
**Income for Overseas Min:** $826,955
**Gifts in Kind:** $10,000
**Fully Supported US Personnel Overseas:**
  Expecting to serve more than 4 years: 2
  Non-residential mission personnel: 2
**Other Personnel:**
  Bi-vocational/tentmakers: 1
  Non-US serving in own/other country: 2
  Home ministry & office staff in US: 3
**Countries:** Japan; Malaysia 1; Mexico 1

## Evangelical Covenant Church —Covenant World Mission

5101 N. Francisco Ave.
Chicago, IL 60625 USA
**Phone:** (773) 784-3000
**Fax:** (773) 784-4366
**E-mail:** world.mission@covchurch.org
**Web Site:** www.covchurch.org
*Mr. Glenn Palmberg, President*

A denominational sending agency of Evangelical tradition engaged in church planting, development, leadership development, support of national churches and partnership development.

**Year founded in US:** 1885
**Income for Overseas Min:** $7,255,518
**Fully Supported US Personnel Overseas:**
  Expecting to serve more than 4 years: 73
  Expecting to serve 1 to 4 years: 36
  Non-residential mission personnel: 2

**Other Personnel:**
  Short-term less than 1 year: 1,500
  Home ministry & office staff in US: 10
**Countries:** Africa—General 8; Argentina 2; Asia—General 4; Chile; Colombia 3; Czech Republic 2; Ecuador 5; France 3; Japan 10; Kenya; Laos 2; Mexico 14; Russia 2; Spain 6; Sudan; Taiwan 2; Thailand 10

## Evangelical Free Church Mission
## See: EFCA Int'l. Mission

## Evangelical Friends Church Southwest

PO Box 1607
Whittier CA 90609-1607 USA
**Phone:** (562) 947-2883
**Fax:** (562) 947-9385
**E-mail:** office@efcsw.org
**Web Site:** www.efcsw.org
*Mr. Stan Leach, Superintendent*

A denominational sending agency of Evangelical and Friends tradition engaged in church planting, furloughed missionary support, mobilization for mission and short-term programs.

**Year founded in US:** 1895
**Income for Overseas Min:** $500,000
**Fully Supported US Personnel Overseas:**
  Expecting to serve more than 4 years: 5
  Expecting to serve 1 to 4 years: 2
**Other Personnel:**
  Home ministry & office staff in US: 3
**Countries:** Cambodia; El Salvador 5

## Evangelical Friends Mission

PO Box 525
Arvada, CO 80001 USA
**Phone:** (303) 421-8100
**Fax:** (303) 431-6455
**E-mail:** efm@friendsmission.com
**Web Site:** www.friendsmission.com
**Associations:** EFMA
*Dr. Chuck Mylander, Exec. Director*

A denominational sending agency of Friends tradition engaged in church planting, evangelism, leadership development, development, Christian education and TEE.

**Purpose:** "...to fuel a worldwide multiplication movement of worshipping, God-glorifying Evangelical Friends Churches through evangelism, leadership development and missionary-sending."

**Year founded in US:** 1978

**Income for Overseas Min:** $1,050,814

**Gifts in Kind:** $500

**Fully Supported US Personnel Overseas:**
  Expecting to serve more than 4 years: 12

**Other Personnel:**
  Short-term less than 1 year: 30
  Non-US serving in own/other country: 22
  Home ministry & office staff in US: 6

**Countries:** Bangladesh; India; Ireland 3; Mexico 6; Nepal 1; Philippines; Rwanda 2; Unspecified Country

## Evangelical Lutheran Church in America, Div. for Global Mission

8765 W. Higgins Rd.
Chicago, IL 60631 USA

**Phone:** (800) 638-3522
**Fax:** (773) 380-3406
**E-mail:** info@elca.org
**Web Site:** www.elca.org
**Associations:** CWS

*Rev. Rafael Malpica-Padilla, Exec. Director*

A denominational sending agency of Lutheran tradition engaged in partnership development, development, evangelism, leadership development and relief and/or rehabilitation.

**Purpose:** "Marked with the cross of Christ forever, we are claimed, gathered and sent for the sake of the world."

**Year founded in US:** 1987

**Income for Overseas Min:** $34,434,240

**Fully Supported US Personnel Overseas:**
  Expecting to serve more than 4 years: 101
  Expecting to serve 1 to 4 years: 62

**Other Personnel:**
  Short-term less than 1 year: 83
  Non-US serving in own/other country: 15
  Home ministry & office staff in US: 44

**Countries:** Argentina 1; Brazil 2; Cameroon 6; Central African Republic 1; China 4; Costa Rica 1; Denmark 2; Egypt 2; El Salvador; Ethiopia 2; Germany 6; Guam 2; Guyana 2; Honduras; Hong Kong 6; India 1; Indo-nesia 1; Jamaica 2; Japan 13; Kenya 4; Korea, South; Lebanon; Liberia 1; Madagascar 5; Mexico 2; Namibia 1; Nigeria 1; Palestine; Papua New Guinea 2; Russia 1; Senegal 7; Singapore 1; Slovakia 2; South Africa 1; Tanzania 19; Thailand

## Evangelical Mennonite Church Int'l. Ministries See: Fellowship of Evangelical Churches—International Ministries

## Evangelical Methodist Church, Inc.—Board of Missions

PO Box 17070
Indianapolis, IN 46217 USA

**Phone:** (317) 780-8017
**Fax:** (317) 780-8078
**E-mail:** headquarters@emchurch.org
**Web Site:** www.emchurch.org

*Dr. Edward W. Williamson, General Supt.*

A denominational sending agency of Wesleyan tradition engaged in evangelism, childrens programs, church planting, discipleship and theological education.

**Year founded in US:** 1946

**Income for Overseas Min:** $344,145

**Fully Supported US Personnel Overseas:**
  Expecting to serve more than 4 years: 5

**Other Personnel:**
  Non-US serving in own/other country: 1
  Home ministry & office staff in US: 3

**Countries:** Mexico 5; Spain

## Evangelical Presbyterian Church—World Outreach

17197 N. Laurel Park Dr., Ste. 567
Livonia, MI 48152 USA

**Phone:** (734) 742-2020
**Fax:** (734) 742-2033
**E-mail:** jeff.chadwick@epc.org
**Web Site:** www.epcwo.org
**Associations:** EFMA

*Rev. Jeffrey Chadwick, Director*

A denominational sending agency of Presbyterian and Evangelical tradition engaged in church planting, theological education, evangelism, support of national churches and support of national workers.

**Purpose:** "...to establish the church of Jesus Christ in those cultures and people groups where opportunity and our ability to respond intersect."

**Year founded in US:** 1981

**Income for Overseas Min:** $1,981,264

**Fully Supported US Personnel Overseas:**
Expecting to serve more than 4 years: 74
Non-residential mission personnel: 1

**Other Personnel:**
Bi-vocational/tentmakers: 1
Non-US serving in own/other country: 10
Home ministry & office staff in US: 4

**Countries:** Argentina 6; Ethiopia 4; France 2; Germany 2; Hungary 2; Kazakhstan; Nigeria 2; Singapore 2; Thailand 4; Uganda 2; United Kingdom 3; Unspecified Country 45

## Evangelism and Missions Information Service (EMIS)
**(See ad on page 176)**
PO Box 794
Wheaton, IL 60189 USA
**Phone:** (630) 752-7158
**Fax:** (630) 752-7155
**E-mail:** EMIS@wheaton.edu
**Web Site:** www.billygrahamcenter.org/emis
*Dr. Kenneth D. Gill, Director*

The publishing department of the Billy Graham Center, providing evangelism and missions information through publications such as "Evangelical Missions Quarterly", "Lausanne World Pulse", " Mission Handbook", and books about evangelism and missions.

**Year founded in US:** 1964

**Personnel:**
Home ministry & office staff in US: 9

## Evangelism Explosion Intl.
PO Box 23820
Ft. Lauderdale, FL 33307 USA
**Phone:** (954) 491-6100
**Fax:** (954) 771-2256
**E-mail:** info@eeinternational.org
**Web Site:** www.eeinternational.org
**Associations:** EFMA
*Dr. D. James Kennedy, President*

An interdenominational support agency of

Evangelical tradition engaged in evangelism, leadership development, support of national workers, mobilization for mission and missionary training. Support mission with contacts, volunteers and representatives in more than 200 nations. Income data from 2002.

**Purpose:** "To glorify God...equipping believers to multiply in and through local churches worldwide."

**Year founded in US:** 1970

**Income for Overseas Min:** $1,000,000

**Fully Supported US Personnel Overseas:**
Expecting to serve more than 4 years: 2
Non-residential mission personnel: 2

**Other Personnel:**
Short-term less than 1 year: 130
Non-US serving in own/other country: 64
Home ministry & office staff in US: 40

**Countries:** Argentina; Armenia; Belgium; Ghana; Guatemala; India 2; Indonesia; Kazakhstan; Mexico; Moldava; Papua New Guinea; Russia; Turkmenistan; Ukraine; Uzbekistan

## Evangelism Resources
**(See ad on page 175)**
425 Epworth Ave.
Wilmore, KY 40390 USA
**Phone:** (859) 858-0777
**Fax:** (859) 858-2907
**E-mail:** eroffice@qx.net
**Web Site:** www.erinfo.org
*Mr. Stephen Liversedge, President*

An interdenominational sending agency of Evangelical tradition engaged in evangelism, church planting, discipleship, extension education, leadership development and training.

**Purpose:** "...equipping overseas churches for accelerated evangelism and church growth."

**Year founded in US:** 1976

**Income for Overseas Min:** $356,243

**Gifts in Kind:** $4,471

**Personnel:**
Non-US serving in own/other country: 4
Home ministry & office staff in US: 6

**Countries:** India; Nigeria

## Evangelistic Faith Missions
PO Box 609
Bedford, IN 47421 USA

Equipping overseas churches to complete the Great Commission...

*in their own lands!*

# EVANGELISM
## *Resources*

- Equipping evangelists
- Training lay pastors
- Providing literature
- Building bridges between denominations

425 Epworth Avenue • Wilmore, KY 40390 • (859)858-0777

## www.erinfo.org

# www.emisdirect.com

## Missions and Evangelism Resources for Ministry

**For more than four decades Evangelism and Mission Information**
Service (EMIS) has been publishing practical materials to equip
those involved in ministry both at home and overseas. Whether
you are just getting involved in missions or whether you have
been serving for decades, EMIS Direct is the place to visit.

   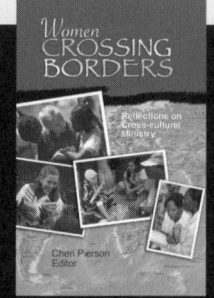

**Equip**
you as you
serve the Lord.

**Educate**
you on the
global Church
and world
missions and
evangelism.

**Strengthen**
your devotional
and prayer life.

**Encourage**
you with stories
of others who have
given their lives
to missions.

## Serving the Lord requires preparation—physically, emotionally and spiritually.

## We can prepare you.

**Help**
you make the
transitions
necessary to the
missionary life.

For a complete list of EMIS publications
or to make a purchase, visit
**www.emisdirect.com**

**Phone:** (812) 275-7531
**Fax:** (812) 275-7532
**E-mail:** efmjsm@juno.com
**Web Site:** www.efm-missions.org
**Associations:** EFMA

*Rev. J. Stevan Manley, President*

An interdenominational sending agency of Holiness and Wesleyan tradition engaged in church planting, support of national workers, theological education, medical work and support of national churches.

**Year founded in US:** 1905

**Income for Overseas Min:** $925,534

**Fully Supported US Personnel Overseas:**
Expecting to serve 1 to 4 years: 14
Non-residential mission personnel: 6

**Other Personnel:**
Short-term less than 1 year: 20
Non-US serving in own/other country: 4
Home ministry & office staff in US: 4

**Countries:** Bolivia; Costa Rica; Dominican Republic; El Salvador; Egypt; Eritrea; Ethiopia; Guatemala; Honduras; Korea, South; Unspecified Country

## Every Child Ministries, Inc.
PO Box 810
Hebron, IN 46341-0810 USA
**Phone:** (219) 996-4201
**Fax:** (219) 996-4203
**E-mail:** ecmafrica@ecmafrica.org
**Web Site:** www.ecmafrica.org

*John Rouster, Intl. Director*

A service agency of Evangelical tradition engaged in childrens programs, justice, childcare/orphanage programs, evangelism, leadership development and relief and/or rehabilitation for the forgotten children of Africa.

**Purpose:** "...encouraging and empowering African churches to reach the youth of their continent."

**Year founded in US:** 1985

**Income for Overseas Min:** $348,566

**Gifts in Kind:** $30,135

**Fully Supported US Personnel Overseas:**
Non-residential mission personnel: 2

**Other Personnel:**
Short-term less than 1 year: 16
Non-US serving in own/other country: 48
Home ministry & office staff in US: 1

**Countries:** Congo, Democratic Republic of; Ghana

## Every Home for Christ
640 Chapel Hills Dr.
Colorado Springs, CO 80920 USA
**Phone:** (719) 260-8888
**Fax:** (719) 260-7505
**E-mail:** info@ehc.org
**Web Site:** www.ehc.org
**Associations:** EFMA, IFMA

*Dr. Dick Eastman, Intl. President*

An interdenominational service agency of Evangelical tradition engaged in evangelism, church planting, correspondence courses, literature distribution, Bible distribution and training.

**Purpose:** "...equipping and mobilizing believers everywhere to pray for and actively participate in the personal presentation of a printed or repeatable message of the Gospel of Jesus Christ, systematically,to every home in the whole world..."

**Year founded in US:** 1946

**Income for Overseas Min:** $13,648,253

**Personnel:**
Home ministry & office staff in US: 32

## Family Aid International
## See: Ukranian Children's Fund

## Far East Broadcasting Company, Inc.
PO Box 1
La Mirada, CA 90638 USA
**Phone:** (562) 947-4651
**Fax:** (562) 947-0391
**Web Site:** www.febc.org
**Associations:** EFMA

*Mr. Gregg J. Harris, President*

A nondenominational sending agency of Evangelical tradition engaged in broadcasting, audio recording/distribution, evangelism and support of national workers.

**Purpose:** "...to develop radio programming and deliver it to listeners in Asia in such a way that they move toward Jesus Christ and into His Kingdom..."

**Year founded in US:** 1945

**Income for Overseas Min:** $5,484,932
**Gifts in Kind:** $8,134,728
**Fully Supported US Personnel Overseas:**
  Expecting to serve more than 4 years: 14
  Non-residential mission personnel: 4
**Other Personnel:**
  Non-US serving in own/other country: 516
  Home ministry & office staff in US: 59
**Countries:** Cambodia; Finland 1; Indonesia; Korea, South 1; Mongolia; N. Mariana Isls 4; Philippines 7; Russia; United Kingdom 1

## FARMS International
PO Box 270
Knife River, MN 55609 USA
**Phone:** (218) 834-2676
**Fax:** (218) 834-2676
**E-mail:** info@farmsinternational.com
**Web Site:** www.farmsinternational.com
**Associations:** AERDO
*Mr. Joseph E. Richter, Exec. Director*
A nondenominational specialized agency of Evangelical tradition engaged in development, agricultural programs, discipleship, funds transmission, management consulting/training and technical assistance.
**Purpose:** "...serving the church by equipping Christian families in poverty with the means for self-support...[to help]...families find a biblical path out of poverty."
**Year founded in US:** 1967
**Income for Overseas Min:** $117,580
**Personnel:**
  Home ministry & office staff in US: 4

## Fellowship Intl. Mission
555 S. 24th St.
Allentown, PA 18104 USA
**Phone:** (610) 435-9099
**Fax:** (610) 435-2641
**E-mail:** info@fimworldwide.org
**Web Site:** www.fimworldwide.org
**Associations:** IFMA
*Dr. Stephen Wilt, Gen. Director*
A nondenominational sending agency of Independent tradition engaged in church planting, camping programs, childcare/orphanage programs, childrens programs, theological education and youth programs.

**Purpose:** "...to assist local churches to fulfill their missionary vision and missionaries to fulfill their call."
**Year founded in US:** 1950
**Income for Overseas Min:** $2,586,202
**Fully Supported US Personnel Overseas:**
  Expecting to serve more than 4 years: 66
**Other Personnel:**
  Non-US serving in own/other country: 38
  Home ministry & office staff in US: 8
**Countries:** Australia 1; Belgium; Bolivia 2; Brazil 13; China 1; Fiji; France; Germany; Ghana; Greece; Guatemala 1; Japan 3; Kenya 2; Mexico 13; Morocco 13; Nepal 2; New Zealand; Niger 1; Nigeria 4; Poland 1; Senegal 2; Sweden 3; Uganda; Ukraine 2; United Kingdom 2

## Fellowship of Associates of Medical Evangelism
PO Box 33548
Indianapolis, IN 46203 USA
**Phone:** (317) 358-2480
**Fax:** (317) 358-2483
**E-mail:** medicalmissions@fameworld.org
**Web Site:** www.fameworld.org
*Rick Wolford, Executive Director*
A nondenominational support agency of Christian (Restoration Movement) tradition engaged in church planting, providing medical supplies, medical work, support of national workers, mobilization for mission and short-term programs. Data from 2001.
**Year founded in US:** 1970
**Income for Overseas Min:** $1,132,576
**Personnel:**
  Bi-vocational/tentmakers: 1
  Non-US serving in own/other country: 41
  Home ministry & office staff in US: 8
**Countries:** Ghana; Honduras; Panama; Zimbabwe

## Fellowship of Evangelical Churches—Intl. Ministries
1420 Kerrway Ct.
Fort Wayne, IN 46805 USA
**Phone:** (260) 423-3649
**Fax:** (260) 420-1905
**E-mail:** FECmissions@aol.com
**Web Site:** www.fecministries.org

*Rev. Earl I. Cecil, Director*

A denominational sending agency of Evangelical and Anabaptist tradition engaged in church planting, discipleship, Christian education, evangelism, leadership development and short-term programs.

**Purpose:** "...exists to facilitate local churches to spread the Gospel in worldwide cross-cultural ministry situations among unreached and unevangelized peoples with the goal of generating a reproducing church planting movement."

**Year founded in US:** 1865

**Income for Overseas Min:** $785,676

**Fully Supported US Personnel Overseas:**
  Expecting to serve more than 4 years: 19

**Other Personnel:**
  Short-term less than 1 year: 66
  Non-US serving in own/other country: 19
  Home ministry & office staff in US: 3

**Countries:** Albania 4; Asia—General 3; Ecuador 2; Hungary 2; Ukraine 2; United Kingdom 3; Venezuela 3

## Final Frontiers Foundation, Inc.

1200 Peachtree St.
Louisville, GA 30434 USA
**Phone:** (706) 955-4916
**E-mail:** webmaster@finalfrontiers.org
**Web Site:** www.finalfrontiers.org

*Rev. Jon Nelms, President*

A nondenominational support agency of Baptist tradition engaged in support of national workers, Bible distribution, childcare/orphanage programs, church planting, funds transmission and support of national churches, serving in 73 countries and more than 25,000 churches.

**Year founded in US:** 1986

**Income for Overseas Min:** $806,561

**Personnel:**
  Short-term less than 1 year: 4
  Non-US serving in own/other country: 1,010
  Home ministry & office staff in US: 6

## FLET University/ Universidad FLET

14540 SW 136 St., Ste. 108
Miami, FL 33186 USA

**Phone:** (305) 378-8700
**Fax:** (305) 232-5832
**E-mail:** informacion@flet.edu
**Web Site:** www.flet.edu

*Dr. Larry McCullough, President*

An interdenominational service agency of Evangelical tradition engaged in theological education, correspondence courses, Christian education, TEE, extension education and leadership development, with students located in 29 countries.

**Purpose:** "...to provide biblical and theological training to pastors, teacher and church leaders by means of distance education throughout the Spanish-speaking world."

**Year founded in US:** 1968

**Personnel:**
  Home ministry & office staff in US: 5

## Floresta USA, Inc.

4903 Morena Blvd., Ste.1215
San Diego, CA 92117-7352 USA
**Phone:** (858) 274-3718
**Fax:** (858) 274-3728
**E-mail:** floresta@xc.org
**Web Site:** www.floresta.org
**Associations:** AERDO

*Mr. Scott C. Sabin, Exec. Director*

A nondenominational support agency of Evangelical tradition engaged in agricultural programs, development and discipleship.

**Purpose:** "...reversing deforestation and poverty by transforming the lives of the rural poor."

**Year founded in US:** 1984

**Income for Overseas Min:** $814,837

**Personnel:**
  Non-US serving in own/other country: 47
  Home ministry & office staff in US: 7

**Countries:** Dominican Republic; Haiti; Mexico; Tanzania

## Flying Doctors of America (Medical Mercy Missions, Inc.)

15 Medical Dr.
Cartersville, GA 30121 USA
**Phone:** (770) 386-5221
**Fax:** (404) 254-3097
**E-mail:** fdoamissions@aol.com
**Web Site:** www.fdoamerica.org

*Mr. Ed Atwell, Exec. Director*

An interdenominational service agency engaged in providing medical and dental work, providing medical supplies and rehabilitation through short-term medical missions in 14 countries. A division of Medical Mercy Missions, Inc.

**Purpose:** "...helping people help people... [by]...creating a network of God's love that reaches into the farthest corners of the world and the human heart."

**Year founded in US:** 1990

**Income for Overseas Min:** $70,984

**Personnel:**
    Short-term less than 1 year: 60

**Countries:** Guatemala; Honduras; Mexico; Peru

## FOCAS (Foundation of Compassionate American Samaritans)

PO Box 428760
Cincinnati, OH 45242 USA

**Phone:** (513) 621-5300
**Fax:** (513) 621-5307
**E-mail:** rptaylor@focas-us.org
**Web Site:** www.focas-us.org
**Associations:** AERDO

*Mr. Richard P. Taylor, Exec. Director*

An interdenominational service agency of Charismatic tradition engaged in medical work, childrens programs, Christian education, evangelism and short-term programs.

**Purpose:** "...to seek the transformation of lives by proclaiming the gospel of Jesus Christ and, through discipleship and practical expressions of God's love, to open hearts to the work of the Holy Spirit."

**Year founded in US:** 1986

**Income for Overseas Min:** $400,000

**Gifts in Kind:** $80,000

**Personnel:**
    Non-US serving in own/other country: 8
    Home ministry & office staff in US: 3

**Countries:** Haiti

## FOM (Fellowship of Missions)

35 Maranatha Blvd.
Sebring, FL 33870 USA

**Phone:** (863) 214-4859
**E-mail:** mbcwebb@earthlink.net
**Web Site:** www.fellowshipofmissions.org

*Dr. Gerald K. Webber, President*

An inter-mission service agency of fundamental tradition engaged in research and information service, acting as an accrediting agency for its constituents and encouraging the formation of missionary and church fellowships.

**Year founded in US:** 1969

## Food for the Hungry, Inc.

1224 E. Washington St.
Phoenix, AZ 85034 USA

**Phone:** (480) 998-3100
**Fax:** (480) 998-9448
**E-mail:** hunger@fh.org
**Web Site:** www.fh.org
**Associations:** EFMA

*Mr. Benjamin Homan, CEO/President*

A parachurch service agency engaged in relief and/or rehabilitation, agricultural programs, development and leadership development.

**Purpose:** "...an organization of Christian motivation committed to helping the poor and needy throughout the world, by generating cash and in-kind gifts and fostering world hunger advocacy in the United States."

**Year founded in US:** 1971

**Income for Overseas Min:** $93,826,618

**Gifts in Kind:** $68,694,675

**Fully Supported US Personnel Overseas:**
    Expecting to serve more than 4 years: 19
    Expecting to serve 1 to 4 years: 63

**Other Personnel:**
    Short-term less than 1 year: 374
    Bi-vocational/tentmakers: 1
    Non-US serving in own/other country: 6
    Home ministry & office staff in US: 83

**Countries:** Bangladesh; Bolivia 4; Brazil; Cambodia; China 2; Congo, Democratic Republic of; Costa Rica; Dominican Republic; Ethiopia; Guatemala 3; India; Kenya 1; Laos; Malaysia 2; Mongolia; Mozambique; Nicaragua; Nigeria; Peru; Philippines 1; Romania 4; Rwanda; Tajikistan; Thailand 2; Uzbekistan

## For Haiti with Love Inc.

4767 Simcoe St.

Palm Harbor, FL 34683 USA
**Phone:** (727) 938-3245
**Fax:** (727) 942-6945
**E-mail:** forhaiti@aol.com
**Web Site:** www.forhaitiwithlove.org
*Mrs. Eva DeHart, President*
A service agency engaged in medical work, a food program, and home and marketplace construction.
**Year founded in US:** 1982
**Income for Overseas Min:** $410,350
**Gifts in Kind:** $95,000
**Personnel:**
   Expecting to serve more than 4 years: 1
   Non-residential mission personnel: 1
**Countries:** Haiti 1

## Forward Edge International
15121 NE 72nd Ave.
Vancouver, WA 98686 USA
**Phone:** (360) 574-3343
**Fax:** (360) 574-2118
**E-mail:** fei@forwardedge.org
**Web Site:** www.forwardedge.org
**Associations:** AFMA
*Rev. Joseph Anfuso, Founder/Director*
A transdenominational service agency of Evangelical tradition engaged in short-term programs, childcare/orphanage programs, development, medical work and relief and/or rehabilitation.
**Purpose:** "...mobilizing ordinary Christians to spread the gospel and serve the poor... on U.S. Indian reservations and overseas."
**Year founded in US:** 1983
**Income for Overseas Min:** $165,000
**Fully Supported US Personnel Overseas:**
   Expecting to serve 1 to 4 years: 1
**Other Personnel:**
   Short-term less than 1 year: 950
   Non-US serving in own/other country: 1
   Home ministry & office staff in US: 13
**Countries:** Nicaragua

## Foundation For His Ministry
PO Box 74000
San Clemente, CA 92673-0134 USA
**Phone:** (949) 492-2200
**Fax:** (949) 492-0900

**E-mail:** info@ffhm.org
**Web Site:** www.ffhm.org
*Charla Pereau, Exec. Dir.*
A transdenominational service agency of Charismatic and Evangelical tradition engaged in childcare/orphanage programs, church planting, Christian education, evangelism, literacy work, medical work, relief and/or rehabilitation and support of national workers. Personnel data from 2001.
**Purpose:** "...to glorify God by making disciples of Jesus Christ...by sharing and demonstrating God's love through the power of the Holy Spirit by meeting basic spiritual, physical and educational needs of those in Mexico and beyond."
**Year founded in US:** 1967
**Income for Overseas Min:** $2,971,813
**Gifts in Kind:** $900,000
**Personnel:**
   Non-US serving in own/other country: 124
**Countries:** Mexico

## Foursquare Missions Intl.
1910 W. Sunset Blvd., #200
Los Angeles, CA 90026 USA
**Phone:** (213) 989-4320
**Fax:** (213) 989-4559
**E-mail:** fmi@foursquare.org
**Web Site:** www.foursquare.org
**Associations:** EFMA
*Dr. Jack Hayford, President*
A denominational sending agency of Evangelical and Pentecostal tradition engaged in church planting, Christian education, TEE, evangelism, leadership development and support of national churches.
**Purpose:** "...to glorify God and advance His kingdom in obedience to Jesus Christ's mandate to preach the gospel and make disciples of all nations/peoples."
**Year founded in US:** 1923
**Income for Overseas Min:** $7,483,082
**Fully Supported US Personnel Overseas:**
   Expecting to serve more than 4 years: 61
   Expecting to serve 1 to 4 years: 13
   Non-residential mission personnel: 4
**Other Personnel:**
   Short-term less than 1 year: 40
   Home ministry & office staff in US: 19

**Countries:** Albania 2; Australia 2; Brazil 2; Cambodia 2; Costa Rica 2; Croatia; Dominican Republic 2; Grenada 1; India 2; Israel 4; Italy 2; Japan 4; Malaysia; Mexico 4; Nepal 2; Nigeria 2; Panama 2; Papua New Guinea 2; Paraguay 2; Puerto Rico 2; Rwanda 2; Singapore 2; South Africa 4; Spain 2; Taiwan 2; Tajikistan 2; Thailand 2; Uganda 4; Unspecified Country

## Free Gospel Church, Inc.— Missions Department

PO Box 477
Export, PA 15632 USA

**Phone:** (412) 373-0307
**Fax:** (412) 373-0307
**E-mail:** fgmd@juno.com
**Web Site:** www.fgbi.org

*Rev. Chester H. Heath, Gen. Superintendent*

A denominational support agency of Pentecostal and Holiness tradition engaged in evangelism, Bible distribution, church planting, Christian education, support of national churches and support of national workers.

**Year founded in US:** 1905

**Income for Overseas Min:** $175,000

**Fully Supported US Personnel Overseas:**
   Expecting to serve 1 to 4 years: 2

**Other Personnel:**
   Short-term less than 1 year: 22
   Non-US serving in own/other country: 57

**Countries:** India; Philippines; Sierra Leone

## Free Methodist World Missions

PO Box 535002
Indianapolis, IN 46253-5002 USA

**Phone:** (317) 244-3660
**Fax:** (317) 241-1248
**E-mail:** missions@fmcna.org
**Web Site:** www.freemethodistchurch.org
**Associations:** EFMA

*Dr. Arthur Brown, Exec. Director*

A denominational sending agency of Wesleyan tradition engaged in church planting, childcare/orphanage programs, leadership development, support of national churches, mobilization for mission and missionary training.

**Purpose:** "To help Free Methodists establish a mature church among the peoples of the world."

**Year founded in US:** 1885

**Income for Overseas Min:** $6,369,338

**Fully Supported US Personnel Overseas:**
   Expecting to serve more than 4 years: 100
   Non-residential mission personnel: 2

**Other Personnel:**
   Short-term less than 1 year: 1,200
   Non-US serving in own/other country: 4
   Home ministry & office staff in US: 22

**Countries:** Africa—General 2; Asia—General 5; Belgium 2; Bolivia; Brazil 2; Burundi; Cambodia 2; Chile 2; Colombia; Congo, Democratic Republic of 1; Costa Rica 2; Ecuador 2; Ethiopia; Europe—General 2; France 2; Greece 2; Haiti 6; Hong Kong 4; Hungary 5; Kenya 2; Latin America—General 3; Malawi 2; Mexico 10; Nigeria 2; Peru 4; Philippines 6; Romania 2; Rwanda 1; Slovakia 2; Spain 2; Taiwan 6; Tanzania 2; Thailand 2; Ukraine 5; Unspecified Country 8; Venezuela

## Free Will Baptist, Inc. Board of International Missions

PO Box 5002
Antioch, TN 37013 USA

**Phone:** (615) 760-6120
**Fax:** (615) 731-5345
**E-mail:** kiley@fwbgo.com
**Web Site:** www.fwbgo.com
**Associations:** EFMA

*Rev. James Forlines, Gen. Director*

A denominational sending agency of Baptist tradition engaged in church planting, development, theological education, evangelism, leadership development and mobilization for mission.

**Year founded in US:** 1935

**Income for Overseas Min:** $5,499,000

**Fully Supported US Personnel Overseas:**
   Expecting to serve more than 4 years: 84
   Expecting to serve 1 to 4 years: 10

**Other Personnel:**
   Home ministry & office staff in US: 17

**Countries:** Brazil 16; Cote d'Ivoire 15; France 18; India 1; Japan 10; Panama 8; Russia 2; Spain 9; Uruguay 5

## FRIENDS in Action, Intl.

PO Box 168

Mansfield, MO 65704 USA
**Phone:** (417) 924-3220
**Fax:** (417) 924-3228
**E-mail:** FIA@fiaintl.org
**Web Site:** www.fiaintl.org
*Mr. Timothy Johnston, Exec. Director*

A nondenominational service agency of Evangelical and Fundamental tradition engaged in technical assistance, development, providing medical supplies, purchasing services and supplying equipment.

**Purpose:** "...to accelerate the work of proclaiming the Gospel to remote peoples around the world that have not had the opportunity to hear the Good News of Jesus Christ."

**Year founded in US:** 1992

**Income for Overseas Min:** $656,028

**Fully Supported US Personnel Overseas:**
Expecting to serve more than 4 years: 2
Expecting to serve 1 to 4 years: 10
Non-residential mission personnel: 3

**Other Personnel:**
Short-term less than 1 year: 48
Bi-vocational/tentmakers: 1
Home ministry & office staff in US: 20

**Countries:** Africa—General; Nicaragua; Papua New Guinea 2; Vanuatu

## Friends of Israel Gospel Ministry, Inc.
PO Box 908
Bellmawr, NJ 08099 USA
**Phone:** (800) 257-7843
**Fax:** (856) 853-9565
**E-mail:** foi@foi.org
**Web Site:** www.foi.org
*Mr. William E. Sutter, Exec. Director*

A nondenominational support agency of Evangelical tradition engaged in evangelism, audio recording/distribution, broadcasting, development, theological education, literature distribution and literature production.

**Purpose:** "...to communicate Biblical truth about Israel and the Messiah, while fostering solidarity with the Jewish people."

**Year founded in US:** 1938

**Income for Overseas Min:** $842,234

**Fully Supported US Personnel Overseas:**

Non-residential mission personnel: 1
**Other Personnel:**
Non-US serving in own/other country: 32
Home ministry & office staff in US: 37
**Countries:** Argentina; Australia; France; India; Israel; Poland; Russia; United Kingdom

## Friends United Meeting— Global Ministries
101 Quaker Hill Dr.
Richmond, IN 47374 USA
**Phone:** (765) 962-7573
**Fax:** (765) 966-1293
**E-mail:** info@fum.org
**Web Site:** www.fum.org
*Sylvia Graves, Gen. Secretary*

A denominational sending agency of Friends tradition engaged in foreign missions, TEE, leadership development, literature distribution, literature production, medical work and support of national churches.

**Purpose:** "...to energize and equip Friends through the power of the Holy Spirit to gather people into fellowships where Jesus Christ is known..."

**Year founded in US:** 1902

**Income for Overseas Min:** $3,181,134

**Fully Supported US Personnel Overseas:**
Expecting to serve more than 4 years: 7
Expecting to serve 1 to 4 years: 1

**Other Personnel:**
Short-term less than 1 year: 9
Non-US serving in own/other country: 1
Home ministry & office staff in US: 12

**Countries:** Belize 2; Cuba; Jamaica; Kenya 4; Palestine 1

## Friendship Intl. Ministries, Inc.
PO Box 50884
Colorado Springs, CO 80949-0884 USA
**Phone:** (719) 386-8808
**Fax:** (719) 594-4992
**E-mail:** FRINT@aol.com
**Web Site:** www.friendshipintl.org
*Rev. Del Huff, Exec. Director*

An interdenominational service agency of Evangelical tradition engaged in evangelism, camping programs, discipleship, short-term programs and youth programs.

**Year founded in US:** 1990

Income for Overseas Min: $200,000

Gifts in Kind: $50,000

Fully Supported US Personnel Overseas:
Expecting to serve more than 4 years: 7
Expecting to serve 1 to 4 years: 7
Non-residential mission personnel: 3

Other Personnel:
Short-term less than 1 year: 25
Bi-vocational/tentmakers: 5
Non-US serving in own/other country: 14
Home ministry & office staff in US: 4

Countries: Chile 1; Hungary 4; Romania 2

## Frontier Mission Fellowship
See: U.S. Center for World Mission

## Frontiers
P.O. Box 31690
Mesa, AZ 85275 USA

Phone: (480) 834-1500
Fax: (480) 834-1974
E-mail: info@frontiers.org
Web Site: www.frontiers.org
Associations: EFMA

*Rev. Robert A. Blincoe, US Director*

A nondenominational sending agency of Evangelical tradition engaged in church planting, evangelism, mobilization for mission, development and leadership development.

Purpose: "...planting reproducing churches among unreached Muslim peoples."

Year founded in US: 1982

Income for Overseas Min: $12,100,000

Fully Supported US Personnel Overseas:
Expecting to serve more than 4 years: 303

Other Personnel:
Short-term less than 1 year: 121
Bi-vocational/tentmakers: 10
Non-US serving in own/other country: 8
Home ministry & office staff in US: 86

Countries: Unspecified Country 303

## Full Gospel Evangelistic Association
1400 E. Skelley Dr.
Tulsa, OK 74105-4742 USA

Phone: (918) 749-3432

Fax: (918) 749-1171
E-mail: fgeatulsa@juno.com
Web Site: www.fgeaonline.org

*Mr. Curt Bezingve, President*

An association of missions of Pentecostal and Full Gospel tradition helping to support full-time missionaries and national churches engaged in church construction, church planting, member care and services for other agencies.

Year founded in US: 1951

Fully Supported US Personnel Overseas:
Expecting to serve more than 4 years: 12
Expecting to serve 1 to 4 years: 6

Other Personnel:
Short-term less than 1 year: 25
Non-US serving in own/other country: 2
Home ministry & office staff in US: 2

Countries: El Salvador 2; Honduras 2; Kenya 1; Mexico 5; Nicaragua 2; Pakistan; Russia

## Full Gospel Grace Fellowship
PO Box 4564
Tulsa, OK 74159 USA

Phone: (918) 224-3540
E-mail: fggf@juno.com
Web Site: www.fggf.org

*Rev. Harley Hunt, Chairman*

A nondenominational sending agency of Pentecostal and Independent tradition engaged in funds transmission and literature distribution.

Year founded in US: 1945

Income for Overseas Min: $70,000

Personnel:
Short-term less than 1 year: 2
Non-US serving in own/other country: 8

Countries: Argentina; Belarus; Belize; Paraguay

## Fundamental Baptist Mission of Trinidad & Tobago
3050 Magazine Drive
Winston-Salem, NC 27106 USA

Phone: (336) 768-2739
E-mail: fbmtt@earthlink.net

*Rev. Ken Best, Exec. Dir.*

A sending agency of Baptist and Fundamental tradition engaged in church planting, evangelism and support of national workers. Statistical data from 1998.

# Quality Personal Service
# PRINTING
# for Christian Ministries
# Since 1921

- Paperback and cloth-bound books
- Brilliant color prayer cards

PHONE US TOLL-FREE, 800-253-9315
FAX: 574-773-5934
E-MAIL: sales@evangelpress.com
OUR WEBSITE: evangelpress.com

EVANGEL PRESS
2000 EVANGEL WAY, P.O. Box 189
NAPPANEE, IN 46550-0189

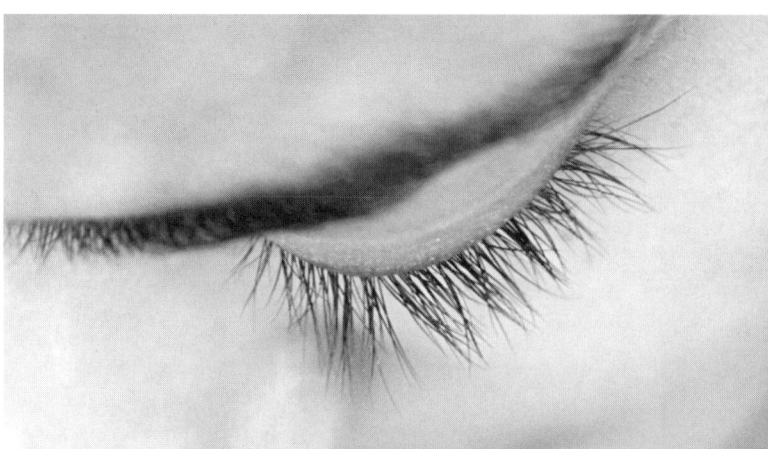

billions of people have not seen

or heard the gospel of hope.

are you prepared to communicate

it with them?

*The need for committed and well-prepared workers is growing. In Fuller's School of Intercultural Studies, you will acquire greater knowledge, learn new skills, and form strategic relationships that will enable you to share your hope effectively. If you feel called to service for Jesus Christ, we encourage you to consider joining us at Fuller.*

1-800-2FULLER

www.fuller.edu

FULLER
THEOLOGICAL SEMINARY

**Year founded in US:** 1921
**Income for Overseas Min:** $139,000
**Fully Supported US Personnel Overseas:**
  Expecting to serve more than 4 years: 5
**Other Personnel:**
  Non-US serving in own/other country: 6
**Countries:** Trinidad and Tobago 5

## Galcom Intl. USA, Inc.
PO Box 270956
Tampa, FL 33618-0956 USA
**Phone:** (813) 933-8111
**Fax:** (813) 933-8886
**E-mail:** GalcomUSA@galcom.org
**Web Site:** www.galcomusa.org
**Associations:** IFMA
*Mr. Gary Nelson, President*

A nondenominational support agency of Independent and Evangelical tradition engaged in radio distribution for Christian broadcasting, Bible distribution, church planting and evangelism in 124 countries. Income data from 2002.
**Purpose:** "To provide durable technical equipment for communicating the Gospel worldwide."
**Year founded in US:** 1991
**Income for Overseas Min:** $300,000
**Personnel:**
  Home ministry & office staff in US: 2

## General Association of Regular Baptist Churches
1300 N. Meacham Rd.
Schaumburg, IL 60173 USA
**Phone:** (847) 843-1600
**Fax:** (847) 843-3757
**E-mail:** dgreening@garbc.org
**Web Site:** www.garbc.org
*Mr. John Greening, Natl. Representative*

An association of Baptist tradition providing information for its associated local churches relative to cooperating mission agencies.
**Year founded in US:** 1932

## General Baptists Intl.
100 Stinson Dr.
Poplar Bluff, MO 63901 USA
**Phone:** (573) 785-7746

**Fax:** (573) 785-0564
**E-mail:** imdir@generalbaptist.com
**Web Site:** www.generalbaptist.com
**Associations:** EFMA
*Rev. Jack Eberhardt, Director*

A denominational sending agency of Baptist tradition engaged in church planting, childcare/orphanage programs, medical work, Christian education, leadership development, short-term programs and training.
**Purpose:** "...to assist [local associations and churches of General Baptists] in the task of winning people to Christ at home and abroad..."
**Year founded in US:** 1903
**Income for Overseas Min:** $994,781
**Fully Supported US Personnel Overseas:**
  Expecting to serve more than 4 years: 20
  Expecting to serve 1 to 4 years: 7
**Other Personnel:**
  Short-term less than 1 year: 8
  Bi-vocational/tentmakers: 7
  Non-US serving in own/other country: 1
  Home ministry & office staff in US: 3
**Countries:** Honduras 8; Mexico 4; N. Mariana Isls 2; Philippines 6; Unspecified Country

## Gideons International, The
PO Box 140800
Nashville, TN 37214-0800 USA
**Phone:** (615) 564-5000
**Fax:** (615) 564-6000
**E-mail:** tgi@gideons.org
**Web Site:** www.gideons.org
*Mr. Jerry Burden, Exec. Director*

An international Christian professional men's association engaged in Bible distribution and evangelism. Active in 172 countries with 58,500 overseas members. Statistical data from 1998.
**Year founded in US:** 1899
**Income for Overseas Min:** $50,000,000
**Personnel:**
  Home ministry & office staff in US: 63

## Global Action
7680 Goddard Street, Ste. 200
Colorado Springs, CO 80920 USA
**Phone:** (719) 528-8728

**Fax:** (719) 528-8718
**E-mail:** globalaction@global-act.org
**Web Site:** www.globalaction.nu
*Dr. Lars B. Dunberg, President*

A nondenominational sending agency engaged in evangelism, childrens programs, church planting, short-term programs, training and youth programs. Data from 2001.

**Purpose:** "To proclaim the Kingdom of God in word and deed around the world and to serve the Church by empowering, training, motivating and mobilizing people to become fully devoted followers of Christ."

**Year founded in US:** 1998

**Income for Overseas Min:** $966,077

**Gifts in Kind:** $222,333

**Fully Supported US Personnel Overseas:**
   Expecting to serve more than 4 years: 3
   Non-residential mission personnel: 2

**Other Personnel:**
   Short-term less than 1 year: 108
   Non-US serving in own/other country: 21
   Home ministry & office staff in US: 10

**Countries:** India; Latin America—General 2; Serbia and Montenegro; Ukraine 1

## Global Advance

PO Box 742077
Dallas, TX 75374-2077 USA
**Phone:** (972) 771-9042
**Fax:** (972) 771-3315
**E-mail:** info@globaladvance.org
**Web Site:** www.globaladvance.org
*Dr. David Shibley, Founder/President*

An interdenominational service agency of Evangelical tradition engaged in leadership development, discipleship, theological education, evangelism, support of national churches and training. Staff does short-term trips to more than 72 nations.

**Purpose:** "...to help fulfill the Great Commission...by empowering national leaders to evangelize and disciple their own and surrounding nations..."

**Year founded in US:** 1990

**Income for Overseas Min:** $1,068,645

**Fully Supported US Personnel Overseas:**
   Expecting to serve more than 4 years: 8

**Other Personnel:**
   Short-term less than 1 year: 3

Home ministry & office staff in US: 9
**Countries:** Unspecified Country 8

## Global Fellowship Inc.

PO Box 1
Meadow Vista, CA 95722 USA
**Phone:** (530) 888-9208
**Fax:** (530) 888-8680
**E-mail:** globaldon@hotmail.com
**Web Site:** www.globalfellowship.org
*Mr. Don Oates, President*

A nondenominational sending agency of Evangelical tradition engaged in church planting, childcare/orphanage programs, evangelism, support of national workers and mission-related research.

**Year founded in US:** 1989

**Income for Overseas Min:** $335,000

**Personnel:**
   Non-US serving in own/other country: 923
   Home ministry & office staff in US: 2

**Countries:** Bangladesh; Chile; India; Kenya; Laos; Mexico; Myanmar/Burma; Romania; Sierra Leone; Slovenia; Sri Lanka; Thailand

## Global Focus

PO Box 1058
Acworth, GA 30101 USA
**Phone:** (770) 529-8610
**Fax:** (770) 529-8611
**E-mail:** contact.info@globalfocus.info
**Web Site:** www.globalfocus.info
**Associations:** EFMA Candidate
*Dr. Larry D. Reesor, President*

A nondenominational service agency of Baptist and Evangelical tradition engaged in church mobilization, church mission development, missions information service and Acts 1:8 strategies.

**Purpose:** "...to glorify God by helping pastors or church leaders to be more effective in mobilizing the church to reach the world for Christ."

**Year founded in US:** 1995

**Personnel:**
   Home ministry & office staff in US: 8

## Global Harvest Ministries

PO Box 63060
Colorado Springs, CO 80962-3060 USA

**Phone:** (719) 262-9922
**Fax:** (719) 262-9920
**E-mail:** info@globalharvest.org
**Web Site:** www.globalharvestministries.org
*Dr. C. Peter Wagner, President*

A transdenominational support agency of Evangelical and Charismatic tradition engaged in leadership development and training.

**Purpose:** "...to strengthen global forces for evangelism; engage in apostolic ministries to train, encourage, network, and resource leaders; mobilize prayer for world evangelization; train leaders in prayer, spiritual warfare, practical ministry and deliverance."

**Year founded in US:** 1991

**Personnel:**
Short-term less than 1 year: 8
Home ministry & office staff in US: 19

## Global Health Ministries
7831 Hickory St. NE
Minneapolis, MN 55432 USA
**Phone:** (763) 586-9590
**Fax:** (763) 586-9591
**E-mail:** ghmoffice@cs.com
**Web Site:** www.ghm.org
*Rev. Timon C. Iverson, Exec. Director*

A denominational support agency of Lutheran tradition engaged in providing medical supplies, development, missions information service, medical work, relief and/or rehabilitation and supplying equipment. Ongoing programs in 19 countries.

**Purpose:** "...providing financial support, shipping of urgently needed medical supplies, assisting in recruiting of medical personnel, funding for training of national health care givers."

**Year founded in US:** 1987

**Income for Overseas Min:** $2,407,878

**Gifts in Kind:** $1,057,436

**Personnel:**
Short-term less than 1 year: 6
Home ministry & office staff in US: 5

## Global Mapping Intl.
15435 Gleneagle Dr., Ste. 100
Colorado Springs, CO 80921 USA
**Phone:** (719) 531-3599

**Fax:** (719) 548-7459
**E-mail:** info@gmi.org
**Web Site:** www.gmi.org
**Associations:** EFMA
*Mr. Michael O'Rear, President*

An interdenominational support agency of Evangelical tradition engaged in missions information service, leadership development, mission-related research, services for other agencies, technical assistance and missionary training.

**Purpose:** "...to produce and present world-class research that fuels emerging mission movements and leaders."

**Year founded in US:** 1983

**Income for Overseas Min:** $556,807

**Personnel:**
Home ministry & office staff in US: 9

## Global Ministries, Church of the United Brethren in Christ
302 Lake St.
Huntington, IN 46750 USA
**Phone:** (260) 356-2312
**Fax:** (260) 356-4730
**E-mail:** gary@ub.org
**Web Site:** www.ub.org
**Associations:** EFMA
*Rev. Gary Dilley, Director*

A denominational support agency of Evangelical tradition engaged in church planting, evangelism, missions information service, partnership development and support of national churches.

**Purpose:** "...to grow and multiply churches through worship, evangelism, discipleship and social concern by actively seeking and winning the lost..."

**Year founded in US:** 1853

**Income for Overseas Min:** $301,646

**Fully Supported US Personnel Overseas:**
Expecting to serve more than 4 years: 6
Expecting to serve 1 to 4 years: 1
Non-residential mission personnel: 7

**Other Personnel:**
Short-term less than 1 year: 170
Home ministry & office staff in US: 3

**Countries:** India 2; Jamaica; Macau 4

## Global Opportunities

1600 Elizabeth St.
Pasadena, CA 91104 USA
**Phone:** (626) 376-4086
**E-mail:** info@globalopps.org
**Web Site:** www.globalopps.org

*Mr. David E. English, Exec. Director*

A nondenominational support agency of Evangelical tradition engaged in tentmaking, church planting, mobilization for mission and training.

**Purpose:** "...mobilize and equip missions-committed lay Christians to serve abroad as effective tentmakers, especially in countries of greatest spiritual need."

**Year founded in US:** 1984

**Personnel:**
  Bi-vocational/tentmakers: 100
  Home ministry & office staff in US: 3

## Global Outreach, Ltd.
## See: Global Outreach Int'l.

## Global Outreach Intl.

PO Box 1
Tupelo, MS 38802 USA
**Phone:** (662) 842-4615
**Fax:** (662) 842-4620
**E-mail:** mnunnelee@globaloutreach.org
**Web Site:** www.globaloutreach.org

*Mr. Wes White, Exec. Director*

A nondenominational sending agency of Evangelical tradition engaged in missionary training, childcare/orphanage programs, church construction, evangelism, leadership development and medical work.

**Year founded in US:** 1970

**Income for Overseas Min:** $4,789,009

**Fully Supported US Personnel Overseas:**
  Expecting to serve more than 4 years: 165

**Other Personnel:**
  Short-term less than 1 year: 1,007
  Non-US serving in own/other country: 9
  Home ministry & office staff in US: 9

**Countries:** Argentina 5; Barbados 2; Belize 11; Brazil 3; Cambodia 2; Cameroon 2; Chile 1; China 13; Costa Rica 2; Ecuador 13; Guatemala 1; Guyana 5; Haiti 8; Honduras 11; India 4; Kenya 7; Mexico 9; Moldova 2; Mozambique 2; Myanmar/Burma 2; Nicaragua 2; Peru 2; Philippines 2; Poland 2; Romania 14; Rwanda 2; Slovakia 1; Sudan 1; Uganda 22; Ukraine 5; United Kingdom 5; Vietnam 2

## Global Outreach Mission, Inc.

PO Box 2010
Buffalo, NY 14231-2010 USA
**Phone:** (716) 688-5048
**Fax:** (716) 688-5049
**E-mail:** gomhq1670@missiongo.org
**Web Site:** www.missiongo.org
**Associations:** IFMA

*Dr. Brian M. Albrecht, President*

An interdenominational sending agency of Baptist and Independent tradition engaged in church planting, broadcasting, evangelism, medical work, support of national workers and mobilization for mission.

**Purpose:** "...sharing the Gospel of Jesus Christ around the world, planting and encouraging His church, helping the hurting physically and serving in every area of Christian development."

**Year founded in US:** 1944

**Income for Overseas Min:** $2,454,000

**Fully Supported US Personnel Overseas:**
  Expecting to serve more than 4 years: 135

**Other Personnel:**
  Short-term less than 1 year: 34
  Non-US serving in own/other country: 142
  Home ministry & office staff in US: 38

**Countries:** Australia 2; Austria 1; Bangladesh; Belize 4; Bolivia 3; Brazil 6; Congo, Republic of the 8; France 35; Gabon 1; Germany 6; Greece 2; Guatemala 11; Guyana; Haiti; Honduras 4; Hong Kong; India 2; Ireland 10; Israel; Jamaica; Jordan; Korea, South; Mexico 17; Myanmar/Burma; Netherlands; Netherlands Antilles 2; Paraguay 4; Peru; Romania; Russia 3; South Africa 1; Spain; Sweden; Switzerland 1; Ukraine; United Kingdom 9; Unspecified Country 3

## Global Partners/Wesleyan World Missions

PO Box 50434
Indianapolis, IN 46250 USA
**Phone:** (317) 774-7950
**Fax:** (317) 774-7958
**E-mail:** globalpartners@wesleyan.org

**Web Site:** www.praygivego.com
**Associations:** EFMA

*Dr. Donald L. Bray, Gen. Director*

A denominational sending agency of Wesleyan tradition engaged in church planting, theological education, TEE, evangelism, leadership development and support of national churches.

**Purpose:** "...to exalt Jesus Christ by calling and mobilizing believers to global ministries of evangelism, church planting, leadership development and ministries of compassion."
**Year founded in US:** 1889
**Income for Overseas Min:** $8,814,196
**Fully Supported US Personnel Overseas:**
  Expecting to serve 1 to 4 years: 115
  Non-residential mission personnel: 13
**Other Personnel:**
  Short-term less than 1 year: 90
  Non-US serving in own/other country: 13
  Home ministry & office staff in US: 21
**Countries:** Africa—General; Albania; Australia; Austria; Brazil; Cambodia; Croatia; Czech Republic; Dominican Republic; Ecuador; Guatemala; Guyana; Haiti; Kenya; Mexico; Mozambique; Nepal; Papua New Guinea; Peru; Philippines; Puerto Rico; Russia; South Africa; Suriname; Thailand; United Kingdom; Unspecified Country; Zambia

## Global Recordings Network
41823 Enterprise Cir. N.
Temecula, CA 92590 USA
**Phone:** (951) 719-1650
**Fax:** (951) 719-1651
**E-mail:** info@globalrecordings.net
**Web Site:** www/globalrecordings.net
**Associations:** IFMA

*Mr. Colin Stott, Exec. Director*

A nondenominational specialized agency of Evangelical tradition engaged in audio recording/distribution, support of national workers, mobilization for mission, mission-related research, services for other agencies and short-term programs.

**Purpose:** "...to help spread the Gospel by recording and distributing evangelistic messages in the thousands of languages and dialects."
**Year founded in US:** 1939

**Income for Overseas Min:** $377,881
**Fully Supported US Personnel Overseas:**
  Expecting to serve more than 4 years: 7
  Non-residential mission personnel: 2
**Other Personnel:**
  Non-US serving in own/other country: 6
  Home ministry & office staff in US: 20
**Countries:** Brazil 1; Mexico 2; Thailand 4

## Global University
1211 S. Glenstone Ave.
Springfield, MO 65804 USA
**Phone:** (417) 862-9533
**Fax:** (417) 865-7167
**E-mail:** info@globaluniversity.edu
**Web Site:** www.globaluniversity.edu

*Dr. Ronald A. Iwasko, President*

A denominational service agency of Pentecostal tradition engaged in correspondence courses, missionary education, TEE, extension education, theological education and evangelism. Financial data from 2003.

**Purpose:** "...to integrate education and service through a worldwide network for student support."
**Year founded in US:** 1999
**Income for Overseas Min:** $2,137,000
**Gifts in Kind:** $1,957,000
**Personnel:**
  Home ministry & office staff in US: 83

## Global Youth Ministry Network
283 Cline Ave., Ste. A
Mansfield, OH 44907 USA
**Phone:** (419) 756-4433
**Fax:** (419) 756-3041
**E-mail:** office@global-youth.com
**Web Site:** www.global-youth.com

*Mr. Chris Davis, Exec. Director*

A transdenominational specialized agency of Evangelical and Reformed tradition engaged in leadership development, evangelism, support of national workers, support of national churches, training and youth programs.

**Year founded in US:** 1997
**Income for Overseas Min:** $75,000
**Gifts in Kind:** $1,000
**Fully Supported US Personnel Overseas:**

Expecting to serve more than 4 years: 1
**Other Personnel:**
  Non-US serving in own/other country: 6
  Home ministry & office staff in US: 2
**Countries:** Unspecified Country 1

## Globe Missionary Evangelism
PO Box 3040
Pensacola, FL 32516-3040 USA
**Phone:** (850) 453-3453
**Fax:** (850) 456-6001
**E-mail:** info@gme.org
**Web Site:** www.gme.org
**Associations:** AFMA
*Mr. Doug Gehman, President/Director*
An interdenominational sending agency of
Independent tradition engaged in church
planting, childrens programs, discipleship,
evangelism and leadership development.
**Purpose:** "...to carry the Gospel across
cultural boundaries to unreached people,
encouraging them to accept Christ as Lord
and Savior...to draw disciples together into
clusters of churches...to help the churches,
under the Holy Spirit's leadership, to multi-
ply, serve their communities and send out
their own cross-cultural missionaries."
**Year founded in US:** 1973
**Income for Overseas Min:** $3,690,668
**Fully Supported US Personnel Overseas:**
  Expecting to serve more than 4 years: 97
  Expecting to serve 1 to 4 years: 4
**Other Personnel:**
  Short-term less than 1 year: 8
  Home ministry & office staff in US: 10
**Countries:** Africa—General 2; Albania 6;
Argentina 2; China 2; Costa Rica; Ecuador
2; Germany 2; Guatemala 6; Haiti 2; Hon-
duras 2; India 7; Indonesia 2; Israel 6; Italy
2; Kenya 2; Laos 2; Malaysia 2; Mexico 11;
Mozambique 2; Nepal 2; Nicaragua 3; Phil-
ippines 2; Russia 2; South Africa 2; Sri Lan-
ka 2; Taiwan 2; Thailand 6; Ukraine 2; Unit-
ed Kingdom 10; Vietnam 2

## GO InterNational
PO Box 123
Wilmore, KY 40390 USA
**Phone:** (859) 858-3171
**Fax:** (859) 858-4324

**E-mail:** gointernational@gointernational.org
**Web Site:** www.gointernational.org
*Rev. Larry G. Cochran, President*
An interdenominational support agency
of Wesleyan tradition providing assistance
through ministry teams of believers from
other countries engaged in development,
childrens programs, church planting, evan-
gelism, leadership development and short-
term programs. Statistical data from 1998.
**Purpose:** "...[to] collaborate with indig-
enous ministries [and] give Christians in the
USA the opportunity to become directly in-
volved in the life and ministry of the church
in the Two-Thirds World..."
**Year founded in US:** 1968
**Income for Overseas Min:** $615,194
**Fully Supported US Personnel Overseas:**
  Non-residential mission personnel: 3
**Other Personnel:**
  Short-term less than 1 year: 250
  Home ministry & office staff in US: 13

## Go Ye Fellowship
PO Box 40039
Pasadena, CA 91114-7039 USA
**Phone:** (626) 398-2305
**Fax:** (626) 797-5576
**E-mail:** gyfint@cs.com
**Web Site:** www.goyefellowship.org
*Rev. Gordon Rohn, President*
A nondenominational sending agency of
Evangelical tradition sending missionaries
wherever God has called them, to do what-
ever He has called them to do.
**Purpose:** "...enabling missionaries to pur-
sue their God-given call and vision by serv-
ing as the link between missionaries and
those who send them."
**Year founded in US:** 1932
**Income for Overseas Min:** $1,376,009
**Fully Supported US Personnel Overseas:**
  Expecting to serve more than 4 years: 28
  Expecting to serve 1 to 4 years: 9
  Non-residential mission personnel: 5
**Other Personnel:**
  Short-term less than 1 year: 2
  Bi-vocational/tentmakers: 9
  Non-US serving in own/other country: 14
  Home ministry & office staff in US: 6

**Countries:** Africa—General 3; Argentina 1; Asia—General 7; Austria 1; Brazil 5; Central Asia—General 2; Costa Rica; Equatorial Guinea 1; Germany 1; Korea, South 1; Mexico 4; Middle East; Romania; Slovakia 1; Tanzania 1; United Kingdom

## Good News for India
PO Box 7576
LaVerne, CA 91750-7576 USA
**Phone:** (909) 593-7753
**Fax:** (909) 593-1155
**E-mail:** gnfi@aol.com
**Web Site:** www.goodnewsforindia.org
*Mr. George Kuruvila Chavanikamannil, Pres.*

An interdenominational support agency of Charismatic and Pentecostal tradition engaged in theological education, church planting, discipleship, evangelism, funds transmission and Bible translation.

**Purpose:** "To train, send out and support 'national missionaries' to plant churches in the unreached areas of India and neighboring countries."

**Year founded in US:** 1986
**Income for Overseas Min:** $1,150,000
**Personnel:**
   Short-term less than 1 year: 15
   Non-US serving in own/other country: 300
   Home ministry & office staff in US: 2

## Good News Productions Intl.
PO Box 222
Joplin, MO 64802-0222 USA
**Phone:** (417) 782-0060
**Fax:** (417) 782-3999
**E-mail:** gnpi@gnpi.org
**Web Site:** www.gnpi.org
*Mr. Rich Sheeley, Exec. Director*

A nondenominational specialized agency of Christian (Restoration Movement) tradition engaged in video/film production/distribution, broadcasting, evangelism, partnership development and mission-related research. Data from 2001.

**Purpose:** "...works in partnership with Christians around the world to develop culturally-relevant strategies and resources which are used to effectively proclaim the gospel of Christ to the peoples of the world."

**Year founded in US:** 1976

**Income for Overseas Min:** $800,000
**Fully Supported US Personnel Overseas:**
   Expecting to serve more than 4 years: 15
   Expecting to serve 1 to 4 years: 2
   Non-residential mission personnel: 2
**Other Personnel:**
   Short-term less than 1 year: 5
   Non-US serving in own/other country: 34
   Home ministry & office staff in US: 18
**Countries:** Africa—General 2; India 2; Mexico 2; Philippines 1; Singapore 2; Thailand 4; Ukraine 2

## Good Shepherd Ministries Intl.
PO Box 11909
San Bernardino, CA 92423 USA
**Phone:** (909) 478-3330
**Fax:** (909) 478-3331
**E-mail:** info@isom.org
**Web Site:** www.isom.org
**Associations:** AFMA
*Dr. Berin Gilfillan, President/Founder*

A nondenominational sending agency of Charismatic tradition engaged in leadership development, church planting, correspondence courses, discipleship, video/film production/distribution and youth programs.

**Year founded in US:** 1991
**Income for Overseas Min:** $184,787
**Fully Supported US Personnel Overseas:**
   Expecting to serve 1 to 4 years: 4
**Other Personnel:**
   Short-term less than 1 year: 7
   Home ministry & office staff in US: 35
**Countries:** Germany; Uganda

## Good Shepherd Ministries, Inc.
PO Box 360963
Melbourne, FL 32936-0963 USA
**Phone:** (321) 752-0072
**Fax:** (321) 752-7209
**E-mail:** goodshepmin@juno.com
**Web Site:** www.gsmi-haiti.org
*Mr. Jeffrey Mitchell, President*

An interdenominational support agency of Baptist and Evangelical tradition engaged in theological education, extension education, evangelism, literature distribution, providing medical supplies, medical work and supplying equipment.

**Year founded in US:** 1975

**Income for Overseas Min:** $203,343

**Fully Supported US Personnel Overseas:**
  Expecting to serve more than 4 years: 2
  Non-residential mission personnel: 1

**Other Personnel:**
  Short-term less than 1 year: 6
  Non-US serving in own/other country: 48
  Home ministry & office staff in US: 1

**Countries:** Haiti 2

## Gospel Communications International, Inc.

PO Box 455
Muskegon, MI 49443-0455 USA

**Phone:** (231) 773-3361
**Fax:** (231) 777-1847
**E-mail:** info@gospelcom.net
**Web Site:** www.gospelcommunications.org

*Rev. J. R. Whitby, President/CEO*

A nondenominational specialized agency of Ecumenical tradition engaged in video/film production/distribution, broadcasting, evangelism, partnership development and training.

**Purpose:** "...to proclaim the Gospel of Jesus Christ and empower the Body of Christ for ministry, worldwide, through the effective use of media resources and communication technologies."

**Year founded in US:** 1950

**Income for Overseas Min:** $750,000

**Gifts in Kind:** $10,000

**Fully Supported US Personnel Overseas:**
  Non-residential mission personnel: 5

**Other Personnel:**
  Bi-vocational/tentmakers: 40
  Non-US serving in own/other country: 26
  Home ministry & office staff in US: 5

**Countries:** Ghana; Nigeria; Philippines; Romania; Tanzania; Uganda

## Gospel Fellowship Association

1809 Wade Hampton Blvd., #110
Greenville, SC 29609 USA

**Phone:** (864) 609-5500
**Fax:** (864) 609-5501
**E-mail:** GFA@gfamissions.org
**Web Site:** www.gfamissions.org

*Dr. Mark Batory, Exec. Director*

A nondenominational sending agency of Fundamental tradition engaged in church planting, camping programs, correspondence courses, theological education, evangelism and medical work.

**Year founded in US:** 1961

**Fully Supported US Personnel Overseas:**
  Expecting to serve more than 4 years: 168
  Expecting to serve 1 to 4 years: 19
  Non-residential mission personnel: 3

**Other Personnel:**
  Short-term less than 1 year: 9
  Home ministry & office staff in US: 10

**Countries:** Albania 2; Argentina 2; Asia—General 2; Australia 4; Austria 7; Botswana 2; Brazil 4; Cambodia 4; Cameroon 18; Chile 2; Costa Rica 4; Dominica 2; Ecuador 2; Equatorial Guinea 2; Germany 20; Italy 2; Japan 1; Korea, South 4; Marshall Islands 4; Mexico 10; New Zealand 2; Panama 2; Papua New Guinea 11; Philippines 14; Puerto Rico 4; South Africa 4; Spain 6; United Kingdom 19; Zambia 8

## Gospel for Asia, Inc.

1800 Golden Trail Ct.
Carrollton, TX 75010 USA

**Phone:** (972) 300-7777
**Fax:** (972) 300-7778
**E-mail:** info@gfa.org
**Web Site:** www.gfa.org

*Rev. K. P. Yohannan, President/Founder*

A nondenominational service agency of Evangelical tradition engaged in church planting, broadcasting, childrens programs, discipleship, leadership development and literature distribution.

**Purpose:** "...to be devout followers of Christ and fulfill the Great Commission among the unreached in Asia through training, sending and assisting qualified laborers who will win the lost and plant local churches in partnership with the Body of Christ."

**Year founded in US:** 1979

**Income for Overseas Min:** $47,700,000

**Personnel:**
  Non-US serving in own/other country: 16,377
  Home ministry & office staff in US: 82

**Countries:** Bangladesh; Bhutan; China; India; Nepal; Sri Lanka

## Gospel Furthering Fellowship, The

221 Hamilton Ave.
Myerstown, PA 17067 USA
**Phone:** (717) 866-1964
**Fax:** (717) 866-8527
**E-mail:** gff@comcast.net
**Web Site:** www.gffministries.com
*Rev. Bruce P. Busch, Gen. Director*

A sending agency of Independent Baptist tradition engaged in church planting, discipleship, theological education, evangelism and Bible translation.

**Purpose:** "…to serve fundamentalist-oriented churches in their missions outreach to start homogeneous churches…to go to any unreached people group in any country if there are no other fundamental ministries to reach them, and if there is a team of people who feel that God is leading them to partner with GFF to get the job done."

**Year founded in US:** 1935
**Income for Overseas Min:** $240,000
**Fully Supported US Personnel Overseas:**
  Expecting to serve more than 4 years: 8
  Expecting to serve 1 to 4 years: 2
**Other Personnel:**
  Short-term less than 1 year: 6
  Non-US serving in own/other country: 4
  Home ministry & office staff in US: 2
**Countries:** Asia—General 2; France 2; Kenya; South Africa 2; Spain; Tanzania 2

## Gospel Literature Intl., Inc.

PO Box 4060
Ontario, CA 91761-1003 USA
**Phone:** (909) 481-5222
**Fax:** (909) 481-5216
**E-mail:** glintint@aol.com
**Web Site:** www.glint.org
*Georgalyn B. Wilkinson, President*

An interdenominational service agency of Evangelical and Independent tradition providing copyrighted English Christian education curriculum and literature for adaptation, translation and publication in more than 70 non-English languages. Data from 2001.

**Purpose:** "…to provide resources for Christian publishers worldwide in producing effective Bible teaching curriculum, discipleship materials and other Christian literature

in national languages, with the goal of making disciples, developing godly christian leaders and building up God's church."

**Year founded in US:** 1961
**Personnel:**
  Home ministry & office staff in US: 5

## Gospel Mission of South America

1401 SW 21st Ave.
Fort Lauderdale, FL 33312 USA
**Phone:** (954) 587-2975
**Fax:** (954) 587-2058
**E-mail:** gmsausa@gmsa.org
**Web Site:** www.gmsa.org
*Mr. David L. Rozelle, U.S. Director*

A nondenominational sending agency of Baptist and Fundamental tradition engaged in church planting, theological education and leadership development.

**Purpose:** "…to evangelize the people of Latin America by means of itinerant and localized work, with the object of establishing and developing indigenous churches."

**Year founded in US:** 1923
**Income for Overseas Min:** $930,930
**Fully Supported US Personnel Overseas:**
  Expecting to serve more than 4 years: 24
**Other Personnel:**
  Short-term less than 1 year: 5
  Home ministry & office staff in US: 4
**Countries:** Argentina 8; Chile 10; Uruguay 6

## Gospel Missionary Union
## See: Avant Ministries

## Gospel Outreach Ministries International

PO Box 380
Hillsboro, MO 63050-0380 USA
**Phone:** (636) 948-9836
**Fax:** (636) 948-9835
**E-mail:** gomint@aol.com
*Dr. Sam Paul Gokanakonda, Pres./CEO*

A nondenominational support agency of Evangelical tradition engaged in evangelism, church planting, support of national workers, mission-related research, literacy work, development, childcare/orphanage programs, leadership development, short-term programs and relief and/or rehabilitation. Primary focus is the most unreached people groups in India.

**Purpose:** "...to fulfill the responsibility of the Great Commission to disciple the lost through a relationship with God and forming a community of local believers."

**Year founded in US:** 1988

**Income for Overseas Min:** $144,000

**Personnel:**
    Short-term less than 1 year: 7
    Non-US serving in own/other country: 250
    Home ministry & office staff in US: 2

**Countries:** India

## Gospel Recordings, Inc.
## See: Global Recordings
## Network

## Gospel Revival Ministries
PO Box 705
DeSoto, TX 75115 USA
**Phone:** (972) 230-4660
**Fax:** (972) 274-1318
**E-mail:** staff@gogoodnews.com
**Web Site:** www.gogoodnews.com
*Mr. John Musser, President*

A nondenominational support agency of Pentecostal tradition engaged in support of national workers, Bible distribution, church construction, development, evangelism, funds transmission, literature distribution, mobilization for mission, mission-related research, short-term programs and supplying equipment.

**Purpose:** "...to equip native workers to reach their nations for Christ, especially the unreached people groups - small rural villages that are usually inaccessible to western missionaries..."

**Year founded in US:** 1980

**Income for Overseas Min:** $159,000

**Gifts in Kind:** $40,000

**Personnel:**
    Short-term less than 1 year: 5
    Non-US serving in own/other country: 59
    Home ministry & office staff in US: 8

**Countries:** Cameroon; Chad; Ghana; India; Malaysia; Niger; Nigeria; Pakistan; Philippines; Sri Lanka; Sudan

## Gospelink, Inc.
220 Royal Palm Beach Blvd.
Royal Palm Beach, FL 33411 USA
**Phone:** (561) 204-1919
**Fax:** (561) 204-1920
**E-mail:** lnelms@gospelink.org
**Web Site:** www.gospelink.org
*Mr. Lewis Nelms, President/CEO*

A nondenominational support agency of Evangelical and Independent tradition engaged in support of national churches, church planting, discipleship, evangelism, funds transmission and support of national workers.

**Purpose:** "...to advance the gospel of Jesus Christ by linking the strength of Christianity in America with national preachers throughout the world."

**Year founded in US:** 1998

**Income for Overseas Min:** $1,525,000

**Personnel:**
    Short-term less than 1 year: 104
    Non-US serving in own/other country: 731
    Home ministry & office staff in US: 11

**Countries:** Congo, Democratic Republic of; India; Malawi; Mozambique; Russia; Tanzania; Ukraine; Zambia; Zimbabwe

## Grace and Truth, Inc.
210 Chestnut St.
Danville, IL 61832 USA
**Phone:** (217) 442-1120
**Fax:** (217) 442-1163
**E-mail:** gtpress@gtpress.org
**Web Site:** www.gtpress.org
*Mr. Sam O. Hadley, President*

A nondenominational support agency of Christian/Plymouth Brethren tradition engaged in lliterature production and correspondence courses.

**Year founded in US:** 1931

**Income for Overseas Min:** $300,000

**Personnel:**
    Home ministry & office staff in US: 9

## Grace Baptist Missions Intl.
PO Box 9
Mehoopany, PA 18629-4192 USA
**Phone:** (570) 833-5403
**Fax:** (570) 833-5403

**E-mail:** GBMI99@aol.com
**Web Site:** www.gracebaptistmissions.org
*Dr. David A. Denny, Exec. Director*
A denominational specialized agency of Baptist tradition engaged in missions information service, association of missions, church planting, extension education, support of national churches and mission-related research.
**Purpose:** "...to provide education and research services to local Baptist churches sending missionaries directly to the field."
**Year founded in US:** 1989

## Grace Brethren Intl. Missions
PO Box 588
Winona Lake, IN 46590 USA
**Phone:** (574) 268-1888
**Fax:** (574) 267-5210
**E-mail:** info@gbim.org
**Web Site:** www.gbim.org
**Associations:** EFMA
*Rev. David Guiles, Exec. Director*
A denominational sending agency of Brethren tradition engaged in church planting, development, theological education, evangelism, leadership development and mobilization for mission.
**Purpose:** "...to mobilize men and women to evangelize and disciple the nations through church multiplication movements."
**Year founded in US:** 1900
**Income for Overseas Min:** $6,093,017
**Fully Supported US Personnel Overseas:**
  Expecting to serve more than 4 years: 83
  Expecting to serve 1 to 4 years: 12
**Other Personnel:**
  Short-term less than 1 year: 208
  Bi-vocational/tentmakers: 7
  Non-US serving in own/other country: 40
  Home ministry & office staff in US: 23
**Countries:** Argentina 9; Brazil 6; Cambodia 2; Cameroon 3; Central African Republic 1; Chad 2; Chile; Czech Republic 2; France 17; Germany 4; Ireland 6; Japan 2; Kyrgyzstan 2; Mexico 2; Paraguay; Philippines 6; Portugal 5; Russia; Spain 4; United Kingdom 8; Unspecified Country 2

## Grace Ministries Intl.
PO Box 9405

Grand Rapids, MI 49509 USA
**Phone:** (616) 241-5666
**Fax:** (616) 538-0599
**E-mail:** gmi@gracem.org
**Web Site:** www.gracem.org
**Associations:** EFMA
*Dr. Samuel R. Vinton, Jr., Exec. Director*
A nondenominational sending agency of Evangelical tradition engaged in church planting, Christian education, theological education, leadership development, medical work and literature production.
**Year founded in US:** 1939
**Income for Overseas Min:** $2,229,198
**Gifts in Kind:** $9,000
**Fully Supported US Personnel Overseas:**
  Expecting to serve 1 to 4 years: 41
**Other Personnel:**
  Short-term less than 1 year: 40
  Non-US serving in own/other country: 20
  Home ministry & office staff in US: 5
**Countries:** Australia; Bolivia; Congo, Democratic Republic of; Costa Rica; Puerto Rico; Tanzania; Zambia

## Grand Old Gospel Fellowship
160 E. Main St.
Lansdale, PA 19446-2519 USA
**Phone:** (215) 361-8111
**Fax:** (215) 643-2288
**E-mail:** tonyhart@gogf.org
**Web Site:** www.gogf.org
*Mr. Tony Hart, President*
A nondenominational support agency of Evangelical tradition engaged in broadcasting, audio recording/distribution, church planting and evangelism. Data from 2001.
**Year founded in US:** 1962
**Income for Overseas Min:** $50,000
**Gifts in Kind:** $10,000
**Personnel:**
  Non-US serving in own/other country: 2
**Countries:** Bahamas; Jamaica

## Great Commission Center International
848 Stewart Dr. #200
Sunnyvale, CA 94085 USA
**Phone:** (408) 636-0030

**Fax:** (408) 636-0033
**E-mail:** info@gcciusa.org
**Web Site:** www.gcciusa.org
*Dr. Thomas Wang, President*
An interdenominational support agency of Evangelical tradition engaged in mobilization for mission, literature distribution, literature production, short-term programs and training. Data from 2001.
**Year founded in US:** 1989
**Income for Overseas Min:** $207,550
**Personnel:**
    Non-US serving in own/other country: 1
    Home ministry & office staff in US: 6

## Great Commission Ministries, Inc.
PO Box 7101
Winter Park, FL 32793 USA
**Phone:** (407) 671-9700
**Fax:** (407) 671-9776
**E-mail:** gcm@gcmweb.org
**Web Site:** www.gcmweb.org
**Associations:** EFMA, IFMA
*Mr. David Meldrum, Dir. Finance & Admin.*
A nondenominational sending agency of Evangelical tradition engaged in leadership development, church planting, evangelism, recruiting/mobilizing and short-term programs.
**Year founded in US:** 1990
**Income for Overseas Min:** $3,140,788
**Fully Supported US Personnel Overseas:**
    Expecting to serve more than 4 years: 32
    Expecting to serve 1 to 4 years: 18
    Non-residential mission personnel: 2
**Other Personnel:**
    Short-term less than 1 year: 15
    Bi-vocational/tentmakers: 12
    Non-US serving in own/other country: 5
    Home ministry & office staff in US: 277
**Countries:** Germany 4; Italy 7; Netherlands 9; Poland 2; Taiwan; Ukraine 10

## Greater Europe Mission
18950 Base Camp Rd.
Monument, CO 80132-8009 USA
**Phone:** (719) 488-8008
**Fax:** (719) 488-8018
**E-mail:** info@gemission.com

**Web Site:** www.gemission.org
**Associations:** IFMA
*Mr. Jay Butler, U.S. Director*
A nondenominational sending agency of Evangelical tradition engaged in church planting, camping programs, theological education, evangelism, leadership development and TESOL.
**Year founded in US:** 1949
**Income for Overseas Min:** $2,661,364
**Gifts in Kind:** $78,865
**Fully Supported US Personnel Overseas:**
    Expecting to serve more than 4 years: 255
    Expecting to serve 1 to 4 years: 24
    Non-residential mission personnel: 1
**Other Personnel:**
    Short-term less than 1 year: 296
    Home ministry & office staff in US: 39
**Countries:** Albania; Austria 15; Belgium 6; Croatia 6; Czech Republic 8; France 28; Germany 66; Greece 12; Hungary 6; Iceland 2; Ireland 17; Italy 7; Kosovo 3; Latvia 4; Luxembourg; Netherlands 12; Poland 4; Portugal 13; Romania 12; Russia 1; Serbia and Montenegro 2; Slovakia 4; Spain 19; Sweden 4; Ukraine 2; United Kingdom 2

## Greater Grace World Outreach
6025 Moravia Park Dr.
Baltimore, MD 21206 USA
**Phone:** (410) 483-3700
**Fax:** (410) 483-3708
**E-mail:** missions@ggwo.org
**Web Site:** www.ggwo.org/missions
*Mr. Thomas Schaller, Pastor*
A nondenominational support agency of Evangelical tradition engaged in church planting, broadcasting, childcare/orphanage programs, discipleship, theological education and evangelism.
**Year founded in US:** 1987
**Income for Overseas Min:** $1,745,000
**Gifts in Kind:** $200,000
**Fully Supported US Personnel Overseas:**
    Expecting to serve more than 4 years: 56
    Expecting to serve 1 to 4 years: 8
    Non-residential mission personnel: 1
**Other Personnel:**
    Short-term less than 1 year: 90

Bi-vocational/tentmakers: 9
Non-US serving in own/other country: 775
Home ministry & office staff in US: 5

**Countries:** Albania; Argentina; Asia—General 2; Austria 2; Azerbaijan; Brazil; Burkina Faso; Bulgaria; Burundi; Chile; Congo, Democratic Republic of; Croatia 2; Ecuador 3; Finland; France; Germany 2; Ghana 2; Hungary 11; India 2; Ireland 1; Kazakhstan; Kenya; Korea, South 3; Kyrgyzstan 2; Liberia; Lithuania; Mexico 3; Middle East 3; Moldova; Mozambique; Nepal; Peru 2; Philippines 1; Portugal 1; Romania 1; Russia 1; Rwanda; South Africa 2; Sudan; Sweden; Switzerland 2; Tajikistan; Tanzania; Thailand 2; Turkey 2; Turkmenistan; Uganda; United Kingdom 1; Uzbekistan; Zambia 3

## Habitat for Humanity Intl.

121 Habitat St.
Americus, GA 31709 USA
**Phone:** (229) 924-6935
**Fax:** (229) 928-4157
**E-mail:** publicinfo@habitat.org
**Web Site:** www.habitat.org
*Mr. Jonathan T.M. Reckford, CEO*

An interdenominational specialized service agency of Ecumenical tradition engaged in building low-income housing in partnership with/for people in need. Since 1976, Habitat has built more than 200,000 houses in nearly 100 countries.

**Purpose:** "...works in partnership with God and people everywhere to develop communities with God's people in need by building and renovating houses...in which people can live and grow into all that God intended."

**Year founded in US:** 1976

**Income for Overseas Min:** $95,475,655

**Gifts in Kind:** $2,348,081

**Fully Supported US Personnel Overseas:**
Expecting to serve more than 4 years: 22
Expecting to serve 1 to 4 years: 184
Non-residential mission personnel: 50

**Other Personnel:**
Short-term less than 1 year: 4,600
Non-US serving in own/other country: 206
Home ministry & office staff in US: 20

**Countries:** Afghanistan; Australia; Bangladesh; Botswana; Brazil; China; Congo, Democratic Republic of; Costa Rica 6; Dominican Republic; Ecuador; Fiji; Ghana; Hong Kong; Hungary 4; India; Indonesia; Jordan; Kenya; Lesotho; Malawi; Mongolia; Mozambique; Nepal; Nicaragua; Philippines; Senegal; Singapore 3; South Africa 4; Sri Lanka; Tanzania; Thailand 5; Uganda; United Kingdom; Vietnam

## Haiti Lutheran Mission Society

PO Box 22544
Lincoln, NE 68542-2544 USA
**Phone:** (402) 474-2063
**Fax:** (402) 474-2596
**E-mail:** rnnbuethe@alltel.net
**Web Site:** www.haitilutheran.org
*Dick Buethe, Executive Director*

A denominational support agency of Lutheran tradition engaged in church planting, Christian education, theological education, medical work and relief and/or rehabilitation.

**Purpose:** "...to minister to the spiritual and physical needs of the Haitian people so that they might be won by the Holy Spirit to be disciples of Jesus Christ."

**Year founded in US:** 1979

**Income for Overseas Min:** $250,000

**Gifts in Kind:** $40,000

**Personnel:**
Short-term less than 1 year: 300
Non-US serving in own/other country: 75

## Haitian Christian Outreach

PO Box 1052
Mahomet, IL 61853 USA
**Phone:** (217) 778-6023
**E-mail:** mac@haitianchristian.org
**Web Site:** www.haitianchristian.org
*Mr. Mac Burberry, Exec. Director*

A support agency of Christian (Restoration Movement) tradition engaged in church planting, discipleship, Christian education, evangelism, leadership development and medical work.

**Year founded in US:** 1985

**Income for Overseas Min:** $240,000

**Personnel:**
Short-term less than 1 year: 30
Non-US serving in own/other country: 70
Home ministry & office staff in US: 2

# Handclasp International, Inc.

PO Box 233
Crest Park, CA 92326 USA
**Phone:** (909) 337-1894
**Fax:** (909) 336-1674

*Mr. Daniel J. Henrich, President*

A transdenominational service agency of Baptist tradition engaged in video/film production/distribution, extension education, mission-related research and services for other agencies. Data from 2002.

**Year founded in US:** 1970
**Personnel:**
  Home ministry & office staff in US: 1

# Harvest

PO Box 2670
Phoenix, AZ 85002-2670 USA
**Phone:** (602) 258-1083
**Fax:** (602) 258-1318
**E-mail:** info@harvestfoundation.org
**Web Site:** www.harvestfoundation.org
**Associations:** AERDO

*Mr. Robert C. Moffitt, President*

A nondenominational service agency of Evangelical tradition engaged in wholistic ministry training for local church leaders, curriculum development, and training services and conferences.

**Purpose:** "...to equip local churches worldwide to demonstrate God's intentions in every area of life."

**Year founded in US:** 1981
**Income for Overseas Min:** $583,000
**Fully Supported US Personnel Overseas:**
  Expecting to serve 1 to 4 years: 2
  Non-residential mission personnel: 1
**Other Personnel:**
  Short-term less than 1 year: 4
  Non-US serving in own/other country: 26
  Home ministry & office staff in US: 3
**Countries:** Brazil; Congo, Democratic Republic of; Dominican Republic; Ethiopia; Ghana; Haiti; Honduras; India; Kenya; Peru; Philippines; Rwanda; Thailand; Venezuela

# Harvest Evangelism, Inc.

PO Box 20310
San Jose, CA 95160 USA
**Phone:** (408) 927-9052
**Fax:** (408) 927-9830
**E-mail:** info@harvestevan.org
**Web Site:** www.harvestevan.org

*Rev. Ed Silvoso, President*

An interdenominational specialized agency of Evangelical tradition engaged in missionary training, evangelism, support of national churches, mobilization for mission and short-term programs. Statistical data from 1998.

**Purpose:** "...to help the Church of the city, comprised of its various congregations, implement a comprehensive strategy to effectively saturate the city with the Good News of the gospel..."

**Year founded in US:** 1980
**Income for Overseas Min:** $200,000
**Fully Supported US Personnel Overseas:**
  Non-residential mission personnel: 4
**Other Personnel:**
  Short-term less than 1 year: 20
  Bi-vocational/tentmakers: 5
  Home ministry & office staff in US: 20

# Harvest International, Inc.

PO Box 6690
Ocala, FL 34478-6690 USA
**Phone:** (352) 622-1818
**Fax:** (352) 622-2569
**E-mail:** danny@harvestinternational.org
**Web Site:** www.harvestinternational.org

*Mr. Danny Thomas, Director*

A nondenominational sending agency of Evangelical tradition engaged in team/missionary member care, childcare/orphanage programs, childrens programs, evangelism, providing medical supplies, medical work and short-term programs.

**Year founded in US:** 1987
**Income for Overseas Min:** $1,461,000
**Fully Supported US Personnel Overseas:**
  Expecting to serve 1 to 4 years: 11
  Non-residential mission personnel: 2
**Other Personnel:**
  Short-term less than 1 year: 100
  Non-US serving in own/other country: 14
  Home ministry & office staff in US: 3
**Countries:** Haiti; Kenya; Romania; Uganda; Ukraine

# International Health Insurance for Missionaries

With more than 30 years of overseas missionary service and options offered by 8 major international and 5 major domestic health insurance carriers, Good Neighbor Insurance can meet your health insurance needs.

> Career & Short-Term Health Plans for Individuals & Families
> Large & Small Group Coverage

Good Neighbor Insurance

480.813.9100
www.gninsurance.com
info@gninsurance.com

Call today for a FREE quote
**866-636-9100**
(toll free)

In addition, we provide plans for internationals visiting, studying and working in the U.S., and for non-Americans serving in and outside of their home country.

## HBI GLOBAL PARTNERS
HINDUSTAN BIBLE INSTITUTE · SERVING CHRIST IN INDIA SINCE 1952

"HBIGP exists to glorify God through the local churches in the U.S. by mobilizing its resources in people, finances, skills and abilities to fulfill the great commission in India and beyond."

Since 1990, HBI Global Partners has been working in partnership with the North American Church and the ministries of Hindustan Bible Institute & college, located in Chennai, India. Each year, a growing number of churches have furthered both the vision of their churches and the ministries and HBI through the paradigm of short-term mission.

## Opportunities for service

- Churches to send short term teams
- Individuals to come to teach English as second language
- Theological faculty on sabbatical looking for an opportunity to equip theologians
- Librarians interested in developing skills for nationals to build effective library
- Nurses interested in preparing Indian nurses to send as Cross cultural missionaries globally.
- Children workers to stay and parent children in orphanages
- Veteran Cross cultural missionaries interested in mentoring national teams to reach Unreached People groups.
- Media and computer Personnel
- People with writing skills to produce reports, articles and train people to produce quality reports.

Dr. Paul R. Gupta *President* • P.O. Box 584, Forest, VA 24551 *Phone:* (434) 525-5847
*e-mail:* bgpt214@cs.com • *website:* globalpartners.org

## Have Christ Will Travel Ministries

528 E. Church Ln.
Philadelphia, PA 19144 USA
**Phone:** (215) 438-6308
*Dr. Joseph C. Jeter, President/Director*

An interdenominational support agency of Baptist tradition engaged in Christian education, camping programs, childrens programs, short-term programs and missionary training.

**Year founded in US:** 1965

**Income for Overseas Min:** $203,003

**Gifts in Kind:** $7,450

**Personnel:**
Non-US serving in own/other country: 50
Home ministry & office staff in US: 2

**Countries:** Haiti; India; Kenya; Liberia

## HBI Global Partners

**(See ad on page 202)**
PO Box 584
Forest, VA 24551 USA
**Phone:** (336) 595-3891
**E-mail:** bgpt214@cs.com
**Web Site:** www.globalpartners.org
*Dr. Paul R. Gupta, President/Director*

A sending agency of Baptist tradition engaged in leadership development, church planting, discipleship, support of national workers, relief and/or rehabilitation and short-term programs.

**Purpose:** "...enabling the North American Church to develop partnerships with national movements to reach the unreached in India and beyond."

**Year founded in US:** 1950

**Income for Overseas Min:** $1,069,020

**Personnel:**
Short-term less than 1 year: 40
Non-US serving in own/other country: 605
Home ministry & office staff in US: 2

**Countries:** India; Nepal

## HCJB Global

**(See ad on page 205)**
1065 Garden of the Gods Rd.
Colorado Springs, CO 80907-3405 USA
**Phone:** (719) 590-9800
**Fax:** (719) 590-9801

**E-mail:** info@hcjb.org
**Web Site:** www.hcjb.org
**Associations:** IFMA
*Mr. David Johnson, President*

An interdenominational service agency of Evangelical tradition engaged in broadcasting, discipleship, Christian education, medical work, partnership development and video/film production/distribution.

**Purpose:** "...to communicate the gospel of Jesus Christ to all nations so that people are transformed and become active, vital parts of the Body of Christ."

**Year founded in US:** 1931

**Income for Overseas Min:** $13,300,016

**Gifts in Kind:** $1,231,700

**Fully Supported US Personnel Overseas:**
Expecting to serve more than 4 years: 24
Expecting to serve 1 to 4 years: 18
Non-residential mission personnel: 274

**Other Personnel:**
Short-term less than 1 year: 40
Non-US serving in own/other country: 188
Home ministry & office staff in US: 72

**Countries:** Argentina; Australia 7; Bolivia 1; Czech Republic 2; Ecuador; Ghana 2; Russia 2; Singapore 6; South Africa 2; Spain; Switzerland; Ukraine 2

## HCJB World Radio
## See: HCJB Global

## Health Emergent International Services

PO Box 1225
Issaquah, WA 98027 USA
**Phone:** (425) 837-0991
**Fax:** (425) 837-0992
**E-mail:** info@heis.org
**Web Site:** www.heis.org
*Mr. Marvin G. Taylor, Medical Director*

A service agency of Evangelical and Pentecostal tradition engaged in medical work, development, management consulting/ training, providing medical supplies, relief and/or rehabilitation and Christian education. Data from 2001.

**Purpose:** "...strives to show love and compassion to international communities, continually delivering health care services, medical education and supporting indigenous medical communities."

**Year founded in US:** 1999

**Income for Overseas Min:** $2,700,000

**Gifts in Kind:** $1,200,000

**Fully Supported US Personnel Overseas:**
Expecting to serve more than 4 years: 4
Expecting to serve 1 to 4 years: 12
Non-residential mission personnel: 2

**Other Personnel:**
Short-term less than 1 year: 53
Non-US serving in own/other country: 1

**Countries:** Afghanistan 2; Tajikistan 2

## Health Teams Intl., Inc.

10056 Applegate Ln.
Brighton, MI 48114 USA

**Phone:** (810) 229-9247

**Fax:** (810) 229-4336

**E-mail:** ddchar@ismi.net

**Web Site:** www.healthteamsintl.org

*Dr. Richard E. Charlick, President/CEO*

An interdenominational specialized agency of Baptist tradition engaged in medical work and evangelism in more than 60 countries.

**Purpose:** "...to assist in the evangelization of the unreached people groups of the world through the ministrations of short-term Christian health care teams."

**Year founded in US:** 1986

**Income for Overseas Min:** $100,000

**Gifts in Kind:** $1,500,000

**Personnel:**
Short-term less than 1 year: 80

## Heart of God Ministries

3720 S. Hiwassee Rd.
Choctaw, OK 73020 USA

**Phone:** (405) 737-9446

**Fax:** (405) 737-9448

**E-mail:** jim@heartofgod.com

**Web Site:** www.heartofgod.com

*Rev. Dr. James Lee West, Exec. Director*

A transdenominational specialized agency of Evangelical and Holiness tradition engaged in missionary training, church planting, missionary education and literature production.

**Year founded in US:** 1996

**Income for Overseas Min:** $700,000

**Gifts in Kind:** $15,000

**Fully Supported US Personnel Overseas:**
Expecting to serve more than 4 years: 37
Expecting to serve 1 to 4 years: 23

**Other Personnel:**
Short-term less than 1 year: 15
Home ministry & office staff in US: 30

**Countries:** Africa—General 9; China; India 12; Indonesia 6; Middle East 3; Taiwan 7

## Heart to Heart International Ministries

PO Box 1832
Ramona, CA 92065 USA

**Phone:** (760) 789-8798

**Fax:** (760) 789-8798

**E-mail:** info@h2hint.org

**Web Site:** www.h2hint.org

*Mr. James Sorrels, President*

A nondenominational support agency of Evangelical tradition engaged in childcare/orphanage ministry, camping programs, childrens programs, discipleship, medical work and youth programs. Financial data from 2003.

**Purpose:** "...helping the orphans and poor in Romania, sharing God's love."

**Year founded in US:** 1994

**Income for Overseas Min:** $420,363

**Fully Supported US Personnel Overseas:**
Expecting to serve 1 to 4 years: 14
Non-residential mission personnel: 4

**Other Personnel:**
Short-term less than 1 year: 200
Non-US serving in own/other country: 10
Home ministry & office staff in US: 4

**Countries:** Romania

## Heifer International

1 World Ave.
Little Rock, AR 72202 USA

**Phone:** (501) 907-2600

**Fax:** (501) 907-2602

**E-mail:** info@heifer.org

**Web Site:** www.heifer.org

*Jo Luck, President/CEO*

A support agency engaged in environmental and sustainable agricultural development, extension education, and training.

HCJB World Radio is now

# hcjb global

www.hcjbglobal.org

HCJB
WORLD RADIO

*is now*

hcjb global

OUR MISSION:
Empowering dynamic media and healthcare ministries
that declare and demonstrate Jesus Christ.

# PREPARE FOR CROSS-CULTURAL MISSIONS

Pre-field training in
how to learn another language

Teaching English to
speakers of other languages (TESOL)

Intercultural communication

Children's programs

**Credit or non-credit courses
Three weeks each June**

## Institute for Cross-Cultural Training

Billy Graham Center, Wheaton College
Wheaton, IL 60187-5593
Phone: 630/752-7950    Fax: 630/752-7125
E-mail: Lonna.J.Dickerson@wheaton.edu
Website: www.wheaton.edu/bgc/icct

Wheaton College

*For Christ and His Kingdom*

Eleven denominations have "covenant agency representatives" on the board. Personnel data from 2002.

**Purpose:** "...to work with communities to end hunger and poverty and care for the earth."

**Year founded in US:** 1944

**Income for Overseas Min:** $56,625,000

**Fully Supported US Personnel Overseas:**
 Expecting to serve more than 4 years: 53
 Expecting to serve 1 to 4 years: 126

**Other Personnel:**
 Short-term less than 1 year: 50
 Non-US serving in own/other country: 217

**Countries:** Asia—General 35; Europe—General 4; Latin America—General 14

## Hellenic Ministries

PO Box 726
Wheaton, IL 60189 USA
**Phone:** (630) 462-7088
**Fax:** (630) 462-3740
**E-mail:** info@hmnet.org
**Web Site:** www.hmnet.org

*Mr. Trevor Eby, Director*

A nondenominational sending agency of Evangelical tradition engaged in evangelism, church planting, discipleship, relief and/or rehabilitation and youth programs.

**Purpose:** "Christ for Greece and the nations."

**Year founded in US:** 1986

**Income for Overseas Min:** $219,936

**Fully Supported US Personnel Overseas:**
 Expecting to serve more than 4 years: 4
 Expecting to serve 1 to 4 years: 1

**Other Personnel:**
 Short-term less than 1 year: 2
 Non-US serving in own/other country: 9
 Home ministry & office staff in US: 2

**Countries:** Greece 4

## Help for Christian Nationals, Inc.

PO Box 381006
Duncanville, TX 75138 USA
**Phone:** (972) 780-5909
**Fax:** (972) 780-5909
**E-mail:** hcninc@swbell.net

*Dr. John S. Jauchen, President*

An interdenominational sending agency of Evangelical tradition engaged in leadership development, theological education and evangelism.

**Purpose:** "...serving Christian national workers through economic and educational assistance, equipping them to be more effective in reaching their own people for Jesus Christ."

**Year founded in US:** 1982

**Income for Overseas Min:** $674,000

**Fully Supported US Personnel Overseas:**
 Expecting to serve more than 4 years: 7
 Non-residential mission personnel: 1

**Other Personnel:**
 Non-US serving in own/other country: 7
 Home ministry & office staff in US: 2

**Countries:** Guatemala 2; India 1; Latin America—General 2; Philippines; Russia; Spain 2

## Helps Intl. Ministries

573 Fairview Rd.
Asheville, NC 28803 USA
**Phone:** (828) 277-3812
**Fax:** (828) 274-7770
**E-mail:** him@helpsintl.com
**Web Site:** www.helpsintl.com

*Rev. David A. Summey, CEO*

A nondenominational specialized agency of Evangelical and Fundamental tradition engaged in services for other agencies and technical assistance. Statistical data from 1998.

**Purpose:** "...strengthening and equipping ministries serving God's kingdom by providing various 'helps'..."

**Year founded in US:** 1976

**Income for Overseas Min:** $121,661

**Fully Supported US Personnel Overseas:**
 Expecting to serve more than 4 years: 4
 Non-residential mission personnel: 4

**Other Personnel:**
 Short-term less than 1 year: 12
 Home ministry & office staff in US: 19

**Countries:** United Kingdom 2; West Bank 2

## Hermano Pablo Ministries

POBox 100
Costa Mesa, CA 92628 USA
**Phone:** (949) 645-0676

**Fax:** (949) 645-0374
**E-mail:** hpm@box100.org
**Web Site:** www.box100.org
*Dr. Charles R. Stewart, President*

An interdenominational agency of Evangelical tradition whose four-minute "Message to the Conscience" is broadcast more than 3,200 times per day in more than 30 countries throughout the Spanish-speaking world.

**Purpose:** "...to be God's voice to the conscience of every Hispanic in the world."

**Year founded in US:** 1964

**Personnel:**
Home ministry & office staff in US: 5

## High Adventure Ministries/ Voice of Hope Broadcasting Network

PO Box 197569
Louisville, KY 40259 USA

**Phone:** (502) 254-9960
**Fax:** (502) 254-9962
**E-mail:** mail@highadventure.net
**Web Site:** www.highadventure.org
*Jacqueline G.Yockey, President/CEO*

An interdenominational service agency of Evangelical tradition engaged in broadcasting, evangelism and relief and/or rehabilitation.

**Year founded in US:** 1972

**Personnel:**
Non-US serving in own/other country: 3
Home ministry & office staff in US: 6

**Countries:** Israel

## Hisportic Christian Mission

93 Crown Ave.
Riverside, RI 02915 USA

**Phone:** (401) 438-9197
**Fax:** (401) 438-9190
**E-mail:** wlong@hcm.org
**Web Site:** www.hcm.org
*Mr. Wayne A. Long, Exec. Director*

A denominational support agency of Christian (Restoration Movement) tradition engaged in church planting.

**Purpose:** "...enables mission-minded Christians to evangelize and plant churches among Portuguese speaking people."

**Year founded in US:** 1984

**Income for Overseas Min:** $1,200
**Personnel:**
Bi-vocational/tentmakers: 18
Non-US serving in own/other country: 1
Home ministry & office staff in US: 5

**Countries:** Guinea-Bissau

## Hope for the Hungry

PO Box 786
Belton, TX 76513 USA

**Phone:** (254) 939-0124
**Fax:** (254) 939-0882
**E-mail:** hope@hopeforthehungry.org
**Web Site:** www.hopeforthehungry.org
*Dan Kirkley, President*

An interdenominational sending agency of Evangelical tradition engaged in childcare/ orphanage programs, childrens programs, evangelism, support of national workers, short-term programs and missionary training. Data from 2001.

**Purpose:** "To share Jesus Christ with those in the world who do not know Him and will suffer eternal death without Him."

**Year founded in US:** 1982

**Income for Overseas Min:** $515,416

**Fully Supported US Personnel Overseas:**
Expecting to serve more than 4 years: 20
Expecting to serve 1 to 4 years: 3

**Other Personnel:**
Non-US serving in own/other country: 21
Home ministry & office staff in US: 15

**Countries:** Africa—General 2; Belize 1; China 1; Colombia 1; Costa Rica 1; France 1; Guatemala 2; Haiti 3; India 1; Indonesia 1; Israel 1; Japan 1; Mexico 1; South Africa 1; Sri Lanka 2; Sudan; Uganda

## HOPE International

214A Willow Valley Lakes Dr.
Willow Street, PA 17584 USA

**Phone:** (717) 464-3220
**Fax:** (717) 464-9046
**E-mail:** info@hopeinternational.org
**Web Site:** www.hopeinternational.org
*Mr. Peter Greer, President*

A nondenominational support agency of Evangelical tradition engaged in development, childrens programs, evangelism and training.

**Purpose:** "...to enable sustainable economic development that results in significant and lasting change, temporal and eternal, in the lives of many people living in proverty."

**Year founded in US:** 1997

**Income for Overseas Min:** $1,950,169

**Fully Supported US Personnel Overseas:**
Expecting to serve more than 4 years: 2
Expecting to serve 1 to 4 years: 6
Non-residential mission personnel: 2

**Other Personnel:**
Short-term less than 1 year: 138
Home ministry & office staff in US: 9

**Countries:** China; Congo, Democratic Republic of; Uganda; Ukraine 2

## Hosanna

2421 Aztec Rd. NE
Albuquerque, NM 87107 USA
**Phone:** (505) 881-3321
**Fax:** (505) 884-5381
**E-mail:** info@fcbhmail.org
**Web Site:** www.fcbh.org
*Gerald A. Jackson, President*

An interdenominational service agency engaged in discipleship, Bible distribution, evangelism, literacy work and partnership development.

**Purpose:** "...to make recordings of the Bible available in every language, and to encourage the use of audio Scriptures in every church/community throughout the world."

**Year founded in US:** 1973

**Income for Overseas Min:** $6,910,000

**Personnel:**
Non-US serving in own/other country: 549
Home ministry & office staff in US: 29

**Countries:** Bolivia; Colombia; Ghana; Guatemala; Hong Kong; India; Kenya; Mexico; Mozambique; Nigeria; Pakistan; Papua New Guinea; Peru; Suriname; Uganda; Ukraine; Unspecified Country

## Hosanna/Faith Comes by Hearing
See: Hosanna

## Hundredfold Ministries Intl.

PO Box 625
Blue Jay, CA 92317 USA

**Phone:** (909) 336-9701
**E-mail:** jomurphy1936@cs.com
**Web Site:** www.hundredfold.org
*Mr. James O. Murphy, President*

An interdenominational service agency of Charismatic and Ecumenical tradition engaged in leadership development, audio recording/distribution, theological education, literature distribution and literature production.

**Purpose:** "...to provide sound, balanced, easy to understand Bible training for church leaders of the Developing Nations of the world regardless of their denominational affiliation."

**Year founded in US:** 1988

**Income for Overseas Min:** $49,000

**Fully Supported US Personnel Overseas:**
Non-residential mission personnel: 1

**Other Personnel:**
Short-term less than 1 year: 1
Home ministry & office staff in US: 2

## I. N. Network USA

10432 Chicago Dr., Ste. 2
Zeeland, MI 49464 USA
**Phone:** (616) 748-9620
**Fax:** (616) 748-9641
**E-mail:** info@innetworkusa.org
**Web Site:** www.innetworkusa.org
*Mr. LaDoyt "Rody" Rodeheaver, Pres./CEO*

A nondenominational service agency of Evangelical and Reformed tradition engaged in support of national workers, church planting, development, Christian education, evangelism and child sponsorship program. Field personnel data from 2002.

**Year founded in US:** 1975

**Income for Overseas Min:** $1,369,236

**Personnel:**
Bi-vocational/tentmakers: 2
Non-US serving in own/other country: 804
Home ministry & office staff in US: 7

**Countries:** Bangladesh; Colombia; Czech Republic; Egypt; Eritrea; Ethiopia; Ghana; India; Morocco; Nepal; Philippines; Romania; Slovakia; Sri Lanka; Tanzania; Uganda; Vietnam; Zambia

## IFMA (Interdenominational Foreign Mission Association)
**(See ad page 211)**
PO Box 398
Wheaton, IL 60189-0398 USA

**Phone:** (630) 682-9270
**Fax:** (630) 682-9278
**E-mail:** ifma@aol.com
**Web Site:** www.ifmamissions.org

*Dr. Marvin J. Newell, Exec. Director*

An association of mission agencies without denominational affiliation organized for the purpose of strengthening the effectiveness and outreach of interdenominational missions.

**Year founded in US:** 1917

**Personnel:**
　Home ministry & office staff in US: 3

## Impact International
PO Box 160
Boca Raton, FL 33429 USA

**Phone:** (561) 338-7000
**E-mail:** bdm4@msn.com
**Web Site:** www.impacto-radio.org

*Rev. Bruce Woodman, Exec. Director*

A nondenominational sending agency of Baptist tradition engaged in evangelism, broadcasting and church planting.

**Year founded in US:** 1959

**Income for Overseas Min:** $545,500

**Gifts in Kind:** $6,500

**Fully Supported US Personnel Overseas:**
　Expecting to serve more than 4 years: 42
　Non-residential mission personnel: 35

**Other Personnel:**
　Non-US serving in own/other country: 8
　Home ministry & office staff in US: 1

**Countries:** Argentina 2; Guatemala 2; Honduras 4; Mexico 2; Unspecified Country 32

## In Touch Mission Intl.
PO Box 7575
Tempe, AZ 85281 USA

**Phone:** (480) 968-4100
**Fax:** (480) 968-5462
**E-mail:** info@intouchmission.org
**Web Site:** www.intouchmission.org

*Mr. Steve Evers, Director*

A nondenominational service agency of Baptist and Reformed tradition engaged in support of national workers, Bible distribution, childcare/orphanage programs, literature distribution, support of national churches and partnership development.

**Purpose:** "...to find and partner with Christians who are already living and doing ministry in their home country for the purpose of connecting them with resources that will empower them to fulfill their calling by exposing their ministries to others in the Body of Christ."

**Year founded in US:** 1981

**Income for Overseas Min:** $1,055,116

**Gifts in Kind:** $21,311

**Fully Supported US Personnel Overseas:**
　Expecting to serve more than 4 years: 14
　Non-residential mission personnel: 1

**Other Personnel:**
　Short-term less than 1 year: 6
　Non-US serving in own/other country: 49
　Home ministry & office staff in US: 6

**Countries:** Poland 7; South Africa 6; Uganda 1

## Independent Faith Mission, Inc.
PO Box 7791
Greensboro, NC 27417 USA

**Phone:** (336) 292-1255
**Fax:** (336) 292-9348
**E-mail:** kurtz.robert@ifmnews.com
**Web Site:** www.ifmnews.com

*Rev. Robert F. Kurtz, Exec. Director*

A nondenominational service agency of Baptist and Fundamental tradition providing various services to local churches sending missionaries engaged in church planting, evangelism and training.

**Year founded in US:** 1950

**Income for Overseas Min:** $2,850,000

**Fully Supported US Personnel Overseas:**
　Expecting to serve more than 4 years: 53
　Expecting to serve 1 to 4 years: 13

**Other Personnel:**
　Short-term less than 1 year: 8
　Home ministry & office staff in US: 5

**Countries:** Australia 2; Caribbean—General 2; Congo, Democratic Republic of 5; Israel; Kenya 6; Korea, South 2; Mexico 2; Mi-

# The symbol makes all the difference.

With the IFMA symbol you can trust its member missions' stewardship of the Gospel, Finances, Relationships, and Morals.

The Interdenominational Foreign Mission Association of North America plays a vital role in the missions community providing encouragement and essential resources.

But most importantly, since 1917 the IFMA has helped ensure the integrity of its member organizations. When Christians and churches see the IFMA symbol they know their mission agency deploys its people and resources under the accountability of highly stringent membership standards.

Because the IFMA has never deviated from these standards, its members can be trusted to be true to the Lord Jesus Christ and therefore, true to the gospel, and true to the high moral and ethical demands of Scripture through annual affirmations.

Look for the IFMA symbol of integrity.

www.ifmamissions.org

# MULTI-LANGUAGE
# COUNTER-CULT RESOURCES
## Accurate. Biblical. Compassionate.

*"The Institute for Religious Research is leading the way in providing outstanding resources that respond effectively to these seductive heresies, yet reflect genuine compassion for the lost."* Ruth A. Tucker, Ph.D., Missiologist, Author

**Resources Available in:**
- Albanian • Amharic
- Armenian • Bulgarian
- Chinese • Dutch • English
- Estonian • Finnish
- French • German • Greek
- Hungarian • Italian

- Korean • Latvian
- Malagasy • Polish
- Portuguese
- Quechua • Romanian
- Russian • Spanish
- Swahili • Tagalog
- Ukrainian

View and order materials online at:
## www.irr.org/resources
Free samples available on request.

**IRR**
**INSTITUTE FOR RELIGIOUS RESEARCH**
1340 Monroe Ave. NW • Grand Rapids, MI 49505
616-451-4562 • 877-888-4477 (toll-free)
e-mail: info@irr.org • web: www.irr.org

cronesia, Federated States of 2; Philippines 2; South Africa 6; Suriname 13; Zambia 9; Zimbabwe 2

## Independent Gospel Missions: A Baptist Mission Agency

990 Calkins Rd.
Rochester, NY 14623 USA
**Phone:** (585) 334-9048
**Fax:** (585) 334-9418
**E-mail:** igm@igmonline.org
**Web Site:** www.igmonline.org
*Rev. Gary E. Newhart, Exec. Director*

An agency of Baptist and Independent tradition engaged in church planting, childcare/orphanage programs, leadership development, national worker support, short-term programs and training. IGM is a total faith missionary agency, operating solely on the support of individuals and churches. Financial figure from 1998.

**Purpose:** "...serving the church, missionary, and national pastor to produce a concerted effort in the areas of accountability, responsibility, need, and the harvest of souls for the glory and kingdom of God."

**Year founded in US:** 1968
**Income for Overseas Min:** $900,000
**Personnel:**
    Home ministry & office staff in US: 1

## India Evangelical Mission

PO Box 1633
Lakewood, CA 90716-0633 USA
**Phone:** (562) 484-0881
**E-mail:** iemusa@jps.net
**Web Site:** www.indiaevangelical.org
*Dr. G. V. Mathai, President*

A nondenominational service agency of Evangelical tradition engaged in evangelism, Bible distribution, childcare/orphanage programs and training.

**Purpose:** "...winning the lost, building and equipping the saints and then sending them forth to fulfill the Great Commission of our Lord."

**Year founded in US:** 1966
**Personnel:**
    Short-term less than 1 year: 10
    Home ministry & office staff in US: 1

## India Gospel League, NA

1521 Georgetown Rd. Ste. 305
Hudson, OH 44236 USA
**Phone:** (330) 650-5900
**Fax:** (330) 650-5911
**E-mail:** igl@iglworld.org
**Web Site:** www.iglworld.org
*Rev. James Colledge, Exec. Director*

A support agency of Evangelical tradition engaged in church planting, childcare/orphanage programs, development, leadership development, support of national churches and relief and/or rehabilitation.

**Purpose:** "..to bring the gospel and the love of Jesus Christ to unreached peoples and through effective discipleship extend God's reign over the nations."

**Year founded in US:** 1994
**Income for Overseas Min:** $3,400,000
**Personnel:**
    Short-term less than 1 year: 75
    Home ministry & office staff in US: 4

## India Gospel Outreach

PO Box 550
Rancho Cucamonga, CA 91729-0550 USA
**Phone:** (909) 948-2404
**Fax:** (909) 948-2406
**E-mail:** IGO@indiago.org
**Web Site:** www.indiago.org
*Rev. T. Valson Abraham, Founder/President*

A service agency of Charismatic and Evangelical tradition engaged in church planting, evangelism, leadership development, support of national workers, mobilization for mission and training.

**Purpose:** "...planting dynamic churches in all 3,000 castes and tribes...and establishing Bible training centers in all states of India."

**Year founded in US:** 1984
**Income for Overseas Min:** $1,082,311
**Gifts in Kind:** $12,000
**Fully Supported US Personnel Overseas:**
    Expecting to serve more than 4 years: 1
    Non-residential mission personnel: 1
**Other Personnel:**
    Short-term less than 1 year: 11
    Non-US serving in own/other country: 2,000
    Home ministry & office staff in US: 6
**Countries:** India 1

## India National Inland Mission

PO Box 13422
Roanoke, VA 24033-3422 USA

**Phone:** (540) 400-8684
**E-mail:** ajaybpillai@hotmail.com

*Dr. Ajay Pillai, Director*

A nondenominational support agency of Evangelical tradition engaged in church planting, Bible distribution, childcare/orphanage programs, discipleship, theological education and evangelism.

**Year founded in US:** 1963

**Income for Overseas Min:** $1,632,000

**Personnel:**
   Non-US serving in own/other country: 350
   Home ministry & office staff in US: 1

## India Partners

PO Box 5470
Eugene, OR 97405 USA

**Phone:** (888) 870-9085
**Fax:** (541) 683-2773
**E-mail:** info@indiapartners.org
**Web Site:** www.indiapartners.org

*Mr. Brent Hample, Exec. Director*

A nondenominational service agency of Ecumenical tradition engaged in partnership development, childcare/orphanage programs, development, disability assistance programs, evangelism and relief and/or rehabilitation.

**Purpose:** "...to partner with the people of India in ministry by cultivating relationships, sharing resources and encouraging self-sufficiency through the compassion and wisdom of Jesus Christ."

**Year founded in US:** 1984

**Income for Overseas Min:** $313,321

**Gifts in Kind:** $4,020

**Personnel:**
   Short-term less than 1 year: 5
   Non-US serving in own/other country: 1
   Home ministry & office staff in US: 4

## India Rural Evangelical Fellowship

PO Box 65
White Lake, WI 54491-0065 USA

**Phone:** (847) 604-3776
**Fax:** (847) 680-4270
**E-mail:** Info@irefusa.org

**Web Site:** www.irefusa.org

*Mr. Emmanuel Rebba, President*

An interdenominational service agency of Evangelical tradition engaged in evangelism, Bible distribution, childcare/orphanage programs, church planting, Christian education and theological education. Statistical data from 1998.

**Purpose:** "...to promote the gospel within the state of Andhra Pradesh; to print and publish Christian literature...to establish and maintain individual churches...Christian schools...homes for orphans and destitute children; to provide financial assistance in supporting medical services for the rural poor; and to encourage human development..."

**Year founded in US:** 1985

**Income for Overseas Min:** $476,258

**Personnel:**
   Short-term less than 1 year: 48
   Non-US serving in own/other country: 127
   Home ministry & office staff in US: 1

## Institute for International Christian Communication WorldView Center

6012 SE Yamhill St.
Portland, OR 97215 USA

**Phone:** (503) 235-3818
**Fax:** (503) 234-1639
**E-mail:** office@worldviewcenter.org
**Web Site:** www.worldviewcenter.org

*Dr. David Stockamp, Exec. Director*

A transdenominational service agency of Evangelical tradition supporting the leadership of Third World churches by forging meaningful collaborations that result in sharing resources of research, education, personnel, and materials. Sponsors of WorldView Center, a residential and training center for international students and missionary candidates.

**Year founded in US:** 1967

**Personnel:**
   Home ministry & office staff in US: 11

## Institute of Strategic Languages and Cultures

PO Box 212667

Columbia, SC 29221 USA
**Phone:** (803) 333-9119
**Fax:** (803) 333-9117
**E-mail:** rlmoffice@russianlanguage.org
**Web Site:** www.russianlanguage.org
*Mr. Marc T. Canner, Director*

A nondenominational support agency of Evangelical and Independent tradition engaged in missionary training, missionary education, linguistics, mission-related research and services for other agencies.

**Year founded in US:** 1992

**Income for Overseas Min:** $1,358

**Personnel:**
Short-term less than 1 year: 3
Home ministry & office staff in US: 7

## Institute of Theological Studies—Division of Outreach Inc.

3140 Three Mile Rd. NE
Grand Rapids, MI 49525 USA
**Phone:** (616) 363-7864
**Fax:** (616) 363-7880
**E-mail:** info@itscourses.org
**Web Site:** www.itscourses.org
*Mr. Darrell Yoder, Chief Operations Officer*

A nondenominational theological education agency of Evangelical tradition engaged in independent study course development and training resources for students, pastors and laity worldwide.

**Purpose:** "...to make the proven resources of ITS more available and more affordable to more people worldwide, through global partnerships, new delivery systems, translated and contextualized versions and creative financial options."

**Year founded in US:** 1973

**Income for Overseas Min:** $6,344

**Personnel:**
Home ministry & office staff in US: 4

## INTENT

5840 W. Midway Park
Chicago, IL 60644-1803 USA
**Phone:** (773) 921-0457
**Fax:** (773) 921-9738
**E-mail:** info@intent.org
**Web Site:** www.intent.org

*Mr. Gary D. Ginter, Chairman*

A nondenominational service agency of Baptist tradition engaged in tentmaking-related services.

**Year founded in US:** 1987

## InterAct Ministries

31000 SE Kelso Rd.
Boring, OR 97009 USA
**Phone:** (503) 668-5571
**Fax:** (503) 668-6814
**E-mail:** info@interactministries.org
**Web Site:** www.interactministries.org
**Associations:** IFMA
*Rev. Gary Brumbelow, Gen. Director*

A nondenominational sending agency of Evangelical tradition engaged in church planting, discipleship, extension education, evangelism and support of national churches.

**Purpose:** "...to see culturally relevant churches in every community in the North Pacific Crescent."

**Year founded in US:** 1951

**Income for Overseas Min:** $243,399

**Fully Supported US Personnel Overseas:**
Expecting to serve more than 4 years: 9

**Other Personnel:**
Short-term less than 1 year: 4
Bi-vocational/tentmakers: 10
Home ministry & office staff in US: 50

**Countries:** Russia 9

## Interaction International

PO Box 863
Wheaton, IL 60189 USA
**Phone:** (630) 653-8780
**Fax:** (815) 846-1778
**E-mail:** office@interactionintl.org
**Web Site:** www.interactionintl.org
*Janet Blomberg, Exec. Director*

An interdenominational service agency of Evangelical tradition engaged in training and orientation of missionaries/third-culture kids, Christian education, furloughed missionary support, member care and services for other agencies.

**Purpose:** "...to be a catalyst and resource working cooperatively in the development of programs, services and publications to provide and contribute to a flow of care that meets the needs of third-culture kids (TCKS) and internationally mobile personnel."

**Year founded in US:** 1968

**Personnel:**
　Home ministry & office staff in US: 7

## Interchurch Medical Assistance, Inc.

500 Main St., Old Main Bldg.
New Windsor, MD 21157 USA

**Phone:** (410) 635-8720
**Fax:** (410) 635-8726
**E-mail:** imainfo@interchurch.org
**Web Site:** www.interchurch.org
**Associations:** CWS

*Mr. Paul Derstine, President*

An interdenominational support agency of Christian ("Restoration Movement") and Ecumenical tradition distributing medical supplies to healthcare facilities in more than 50 countries affiliated with member and associate organizations.

**Purpose:** "...to provide essential products and services for emergency, health and development programs of interest to members, which serve people in need with preference given to the poorest of the poor..."

**Year founded in US:** 1960

**Income for Overseas Min:** $20,511,465

**Gifts in Kind:** $75,654,708

**Personnel:**
　Home ministry & office staff in US: 23

## INTERCOMM

PO Box 618
Winona Lake, IN 46590 USA

**Phone:** (574) 267-6175
**Fax:** (574) 267-5876
**E-mail:** lanejill@intercommedia.org
**Web Site:** www.intercommedia.org

*Mr. Lane Anderson, Director*

A nondenominational support agency of Evangelical tradition engaged in video/film production/distribution, audio recording/distribution and evangelism, equipping national workers in more than 100 countries in evangelism outreach. A ministry of Ken Anderson Films.

**Purpose:** "...to equip national Christian

leaders with appropriate Christian media to help them evangelize their country."

**Year founded in US:** 1991

**Income for Overseas Min:** $400,000

**Personnel:**
　Short-term less than 1 year: 2
　Home ministry & office staff in US: 3

## Intercristo, a CRISTA Ministry

19303 Fremont Ave. N., MS #20
Seattle, WA 98133 USA

**Phone:** (206) 546-7330
**Fax:** (206) 289-7150
**E-mail:** employeehelp@intercristo.com
**Web Site:** www.intercristo.com

*Mr. Ron Rutherford, Exec. Director*

An interdenominational service agency of Evangelical tradition providing assistance and information to mission agencies in locating qualified personnel for positions at home and abroad, serving more than 500 organizations worldwide. An affiliate of CRISTA Ministries.

**Purpose:** "...to provide a Christ-centered pathway, helping organizations holding Christian values make the best hire to fulfill their Kingdom purpose."

**Year founded in US:** 1967

**Personnel:**
　Home ministry & office staff in US: 3

## INTERDEV
## See: Interdev Partnership Associates

## Interdev Partnership Associates

PO Box 1331
Edmonds, WA 98020 USA

**Phone:** (206) 972-1662
**Fax:** (425) 778-3456
**E-mail:** aaraujo@ipassociates.org
**Web Site:** www.ipassociates.org

*Mr. Alex Araujo, President*

A nondenominational service agency of Evangelical tradition engaged in partnership development, leadership development, management consulting/training, services for other agencies and training. An association of 25 individuals affiliated with other agencies, serving in various regions of the world.

**Purpose:** "...to serve the Church in its mission to the least-reached peoples by equipping, encouraging and catalyzing the partnering movement."

**Year founded in US:** 2004

## International Aid

17011 W. Hickory St.
Spring Lake, MI 49456 USA
**Phone:** (616) 846-7490
**Fax:** (616) 846-3842
**E-mail:** ia@internationalaid.org
**Web Site:** www.internationalaid.org
**Associations:** AERDO

*Rev. Myles D. Fish, President/CEO*

A nondenominational specialized agency of Evangelical tradition engaged in services for other agencies, development, providing medical supplies, relief and/or rehabilitation, supplying equipment and training.

**Purpose:** "...responding to Biblical mandates by providing and supporting solutions in healthcare."

**Year founded in US:** 1980

**Income for Overseas Min:** $36,611,986

**Gifts in Kind:** $31,792,434

**Personnel:**
  Home ministry & office staff in US: 66

## International Board of Jewish Missions, Inc.

PO Box 1386
Hixson, TN 37343 USA
**Phone:** (423) 876-8150
**Fax:** (423) 876-8156
**E-mail:** amolam@ibjm.org
**Web Site:** www.ibjm.org

*Dr. Orman L. Norwood, President*

A sending agency of Baptist and Independent tradition engaged in missionary training, Bible distribution, broadcasting, evangelism, leadership development and literature distribution.

**Year founded in US:** 1949

**Income for Overseas Min:** $2,240,000

**Fully Supported US Personnel Overseas:**
  Expecting to serve more than 4 years: 14
  Expecting to serve 1 to 4 years: 6

**Other Personnel:**
  Short-term less than 1 year: 4
  Home ministry & office staff in US: 17

**Countries:** Argentina 2; Australia 2; Israel 2; South Africa 2; United Kingdom 2; Uruguay 2; Venezuela 2

## International Child Care, USA, Inc.

3620 N. High St., Ste. 110
Columbus, OH 43214 USA
**Phone:** (614) 447-9952
**Fax:** (614) 447-1123
**E-mail:** iccusa@intlchildcare.org
**Web Site:** www.intlchildcare.org

*Mr. Keith Mumma, Natl. Director*

A nondenominational service agency of Methodist tradition engaged in fundraising, childrens programs, development, disability assistance programs, Christian education and medical work.

**Purpose:** "...to respond to a loving God by promoting health and well-being for the children and families of Haiti and the Dominican Republic through caring service and the education of others."

**Year founded in US:** 1965

**Income for Overseas Min:** $516,192

**Gifts in Kind:** $8,393

## International Christian Leprosy Mission, Inc. (USA)

PO Box 596
Forest Grove, OR 97116 USA
**Phone:** (503) 357-7830
**Fax:** (503) 285-6535
**E-mail:** HealingHands8414@aol.com
**Web Site:** www.christian-relief.org

*Dr. Daniel G. Pulliam, President*

An interdenominational support agency of Evangelical tradition engaged in childcare/orphanage programs, church planting, medical work, partnership development and relief and/or rehabilitation. Financial data from 2002.

**Year founded in US:** 1948

**Income for Overseas Min:** $70,000

**Personnel:**
  Non-US serving in own/other country: 14
  Home ministry & office staff in US: 3

## International Christian Ministries

PO Box 9071
Bakersfield, CA 93389 USA
**Phone:** (661) 832-9740
**Fax:** (661) 832-9741
**E-mail:** info@icm-intl.org
**Web Site:** www.icmusa.org
**Associations:** EFMA Candidate
*Dr. Phillip R. Walker, President*

An interdenominational sending agency of Ecumenical tradition engaged in leadership development, theological education and support of national churches.

**Year founded in US:** 1990
**Income for Overseas Min:** $1,900,000
**Fully Supported US Personnel Overseas:**
Expecting to serve more than 4 years: 4
Expecting to serve 1 to 4 years: 2
Non-residential mission personnel: 3
**Other Personnel:**
Short-term less than 1 year: 30
Non-US serving in own/other country: 39
Home ministry & office staff in US: 11
**Countries:** Congo, Democratic Republic of; Egypt; Ethiopia; Kenya 4; Nigeria; Sierra Leone; South Africa; Tanzania; Uganda

## International Cooperating Ministries (A Ministry of the Rosser Foundation)

606 Aberdeen Rd.
Hampton, VA 23661 USA
**Phone:** (757) 827-6704
**Fax:** (757) 838-6486
**E-mail:** icm@icm.org
**Web Site:** www.icm.org
*Mr. Thomas C. Pratt, President/CEO*

International Cooperating Ministries (ICM) is a ministry committed to transforming nations through Jesus Christ by building churches and broadcasting God's Word. Through God's grace and the partnership of donors and indigenous church organizations, ICM has 1,175 churches either built or under construction in 18 countries.

**Purpose:** "...to nurture believers and assist Church growth worldwide."
**Year founded in US:** 1988
**Income for Overseas Min:** $5,969,022

**Fully Supported US Personnel Overseas:**
Non-residential mission personnel: 2
**Other Personnel:**
Short-term less than 1 year: 4
Home ministry & office staff in US: 25

## International Family Missions

PO Box 309
Lafayette, CO 80026 USA
**Phone:** (303) 665-7635
**Fax:** (303) 287-7617
**E-mail:** ifm@ifmus.org
**Web Site:** www.ifmus.org
*Rev. Joseph Hart, Pres., Minister/Director*

A transdenominational support agency of Evangelical tradition engaged in short-term programs, Bible distribution, discipleship, evangelism, partnership development, mobilization for mission and missionary training.

**Year founded in US:** 1987
**Income for Overseas Min:** $175,000
**Gifts in Kind:** $40,000
**Fully Supported US Personnel Overseas:**
Expecting to serve more than 4 years: 8
**Other Personnel:**
Short-term less than 1 year: 420
Home ministry & office staff in US: 33
**Countries:** Mexico 8

## International Foundation for EWHA Woman's University

475 Riverside Dr. Rm. 1359
New York, NY 10115 USA
**Phone:** (212) 864-5759
**Fax:** (212) 864-2552
**E-mail:** admin@ewhafoundation.org
**Web Site:** www.ewhafoundation.org
*Mrs. Ji-yei Park, Exec. Director*

An interdenominational support agency of Ecumenical tradition providing financial and other support to EWHA University in South Korea.

**Year founded in US:** 1969

## International Gospel Outreach

PO Drawer 1008
Semmes, AL 36575 USA

**Phone:** (251) 645-2117
**Fax:** (251) 645-2118
**E-mail:** info@igoministries.org
**Web Site:** www.igoministries.org
*Dr. James G. Graham, President*

An interdenominational sending agency of Charismatic and Wesleyan tradition engaged in missionary training, association of missions, church planting, correspondence courses, theological education and leadership development.

**Year founded in US:** 1973

**Income for Overseas Min:** $700,000

**Fully Supported US Personnel Overseas:**
Expecting to serve more than 4 years: 46
Expecting to serve 1 to 4 years: 3
Non-residential mission personnel: 4

**Other Personnel:**
Non-US serving in own/other country: 56
Home ministry & office staff in US: 11

**Countries:** Brazil 2; Bulgaria 1; Chile; Cuba; Egypt 1; Ethiopia 2; Gambia, The 1; Georgia 1; Ghana 1; Greece 2; Guatemala 2; Guinea 1; Guinea-Bissau 1; Honduras 2; India; Indonesia 2; Israel; Italy 6; Kenya 4; Korea, South; Liberia; Mexico 2; Morocco 1; Philippines 2; Romania 2; Russia 4; Rwanda 1; Senegal 1; Sierra Leone 1; Sudan; Taiwan 2; Tanzania 1

# International Health Services
PO Box 265
Southeastern, PA 19399-0265 USA

**Phone:** (610) 935-6030
**Fax:** (610) 240-9518
**E-mail:** info@internationalhealthservices.org
**Web Site:** www.internationalhealthservices.org
*Dr. Robert Snyder, President*

An interdenominational service agency of Evangelical tradition engaged in leadership development, evangelism and medical work. Financial data from 2001.

**Year founded in US:** 1995

**Income for Overseas Min:** $490,122

**Gifts in Kind:** $5,600

**Personnel:**
Home ministry & office staff in US: 2

# International Institute for Christian Studies
PO Box 12147
Overland Park, KS 66282 USA

**Phone:** (913) 962-4422
**Fax:** (913) 962-1912
**E-mail:** iics@iics.com
**Web Site:** www.iics.com
**Associations:** EFMA
*Dr. Daryl McCarthy, President*

A nondenominational sending agency of Evangelical tradition engaged in theological education and recruiting/mobilizing.

**Purpose:** "To develop leaders who think and live Christianly, by establishing Departments of Christian Studies in secular universities and by providing evangelical academicians, business leaders and professional teaching with a Christian worldview overseas."

**Year founded in US:** 1986

**Income for Overseas Min:** $1,763,160

**Gifts in Kind:** $489,650

**Fully Supported US Personnel Overseas:**
Expecting to serve more than 4 years: 15
Expecting to serve 1 to 4 years: 7

**Other Personnel:**
Short-term less than 1 year: 10
Bi-vocational/tentmakers: 18
Non-US serving in own/other country: 13
Home ministry & office staff in US: 8

**Countries:** Brazil 3; Czech Republic 6; Hungary; Lithuania; Nigeria 3; Romania 1; Unspecified Country 2

# International Justice Mission
PO Box 58147
Washington, DC 20037-8147 USA

**Phone:** (703) 465-5495
**Fax:** (703) 465-5499
**E-mail:** contact@ijm.org
**Web Site:** www.ijm.org
**Associations:** AERDO, EFMA
*Mr. Gary A. Haugen, President/CEO*

A service agency of Protestant tradition engaged primarily in international justice ministry.

**Year founded in US:** 1994

**Income for Overseas Min:** $5,452,090

**Fully Supported US Personnel Overseas:**
Expecting to serve more than 4 years: 1
Expecting to serve 1 to 4 years: 12

Non-residential mission personnel: 6

**Other Personnel:**
Short-term less than 1 year: 30
Non-US serving in own/other country: 130
Home ministry & office staff in US: 62

**Countries:** Cambodia; India; Kenya; Philippines; Thailand 1; Uganda; Zambia

# International Lutheran Laymen's League/Lutheran Hour Ministries
# See: Lutheran Hour Mins.

# International Messengers
PO Box R
Clearlake, IA 50428 USA
**Phone:** (641) 357-6700
**Fax:** (641) 357-6791
**E-mail:** office@internationalmessengers.org
**Web Site:** www.internationalmessengers.org
*Darwin Anderson, President*

A nondenominational sending agency of Evangelical tradition engaged in evangelism, camping programs, childcare/orphanage programs, childrens programs, church construction, short-term programs and missionary training. Statistics from 2003.

**Purpose:** "...partnering with local churches to renew, train and mobilize believers for active involvement in reaching the world for Christ."

**Year founded in US:** 1984

**Fully Supported US Personnel Overseas:**
Expecting to serve more than 4 years: 24
Expecting to serve 1 to 4 years: 4

**Other Personnel:**
Short-term less than 1 year: 300
Bi-vocational/tentmakers: 14
Non-US serving in own/other country: 47
Home ministry & office staff in US: 33

**Countries:** Czech Republic; Germany; Hungary 2; Poland 12; Romania 7; Slovakia 3; Ukraine

# International Needs
# See: I.N. Network USA

# International Partnership Ministries, Inc.
PO Box 337

Hanover, PA 17331-0337 USA
**Phone:** (717) 637-7388
**Fax:** (717) 637-1618
**E-mail:** ipm@ipmworld.org
**Web Site:** www.ipmworld.org
*Dr. Timothy B. Shorb, President*

A sending agency of Baptist and Independent tradition engaged in partnership development, church planting, theological education, leadership development, support of national workers and support of national churches.

**Purpose:** "...to glorify God through the reaching of men and women with the gospel, the training of Christian leaders and the planting of fundamental churches through partnerships with national missionaries and indigenous national ministries."

**Year founded in US:** 1982

**Income for Overseas Min:** $2,174,520

**Fully Supported US Personnel Overseas:**
Expecting to serve 1 to 4 years: 5
Non-residential mission personnel: 4

**Other Personnel:**
Non-US serving in own/other country: 335
Home ministry & office staff in US: 10

**Countries:** Bangladesh; Bhutan; Bolivia; Chad; Chile; Côte d'Ivoire; Cuba; Dominican Republic; Ghana; Guatemala; Haiti; India; Iraq; Jordan; Lebanon; Liberia; Mexico; Myanmar/Burma; Nepal; Paraguay; Peru; Philippines; Puerto Rico; Spain; Taiwan; Togo; Uruguay; Zambia

# International Pentecostal Church of Christ—Global Missions Dept.
PO Box 439
London, OH 43140-0439 USA
**Phone:** (740) 852-4722
**Fax:** (740) 852-0348
**E-mail:** hqipcc@aol.com
**Web Site:** www.ipcc.cc
*Bishop Clyde M. Hughes, General Overseer*

A denominational sending agency of Pentecostal tradition engaged in church planting, discipleship, leadership development, support of national churches and training.

**Year founded in US:** 1917

**Income for Overseas Min:** $162,699

**Gifts in Kind:** $162,699

**Fully Supported US Personnel Overseas:**
Expecting to serve more than 4 years: 21

**Other Personnel:**
Non-US serving in own/other country: 21
Home ministry & office staff in US: 7

**Countries:** Brazil 5; French Guiana 1; India 2; Kenya 8; Mexico 1; Philippines 1; Uruguay 3

## International Pentecostal Holiness Church World Missions Ministries

PO Box 12609
Oklahoma City, OK 73157 USA

**Phone:** (405) 787-7110
**Fax:** (405) 787-7729
**E-mail:** info@wmmiphc.org
**Web Site:** www.iphc.org
**Associations:** AFMA, EFMA

*Dr. Doug Beacham, Exec. Director*

A denominational sending agency of Pentecostal and Holiness tradition engaged in church planting, theological education, evangelism, partnership development and relief and/or rehabilitation.

**Year founded in US:** 1904

**Income for Overseas Min:** $3,679,000

**Fully Supported US Personnel Overseas:**
Expecting to serve more than 4 years: 128
Expecting to serve 1 to 4 years: 7
Non-residential mission personnel: 14

**Other Personnel:**
Short-term less than 1 year: 8
Bi-vocational/tentmakers: 2
Non-US serving in own/other country: 35
Home ministry & office staff in US: 17

**Countries:** Albania; Australia; Azerbaijan; Belgium 6; Belize 2; Costa Rica 4; Cote d'Ivoire 2; Dominican Republic 2; Ecuador 2; Estonia 2; France 1; Germany 2; Ghana 2; Guatemala 2; Guyana 2; Haiti; Honduras 2; Hong Kong; Hungary 4; India 2; Japan 4; Kenya 6; Malawi 4; Mexico 6; Netherlands 2; Nicaragua 1; Norway 2; Panama 2; Paraguay; Peru 2; Philippines 6; Portugal 2; Romania 2; Singapore 6; South Africa 19; Spain 4; Tanzania 4; Thailand 4; Turkey; Uganda 2; Ukraine; United Kingdom 8; Unspecified Country 5; Uruguay; Zambia

## International Street Kids Outreach Ministries (ISKOM)

PO Box 8551
Clearwater, FL 33758-8551 USA

**Phone:** (800) 265-1970
**E-mail:** jschmidt/iskom@tampabay.rr.com
**Web Site:** www.internationalstreetkids.com

*Rev. John M. Schmidt, President*

A nondenominational support agency of Evangelical tradition engaged in childcare/orphanage programs, church planting, discipleship, support of national workers, support of national churches and partnership development.

**Purpose:** "...to reach, rescue and disciple abandoned and orphaned children for Christ, one at a time."

**Year founded in US:** 1995

**Income for Overseas Min:** $367,000

**Fully Supported US Personnel Overseas:**
Expecting to serve more than 4 years: 2
Expecting to serve 1 to 4 years: 2
Non-residential mission personnel: 3

**Other Personnel:**
Short-term less than 1 year: 1
Non-US serving in own/other country: 232
Home ministry & office staff in US: 2

**Countries:** Asia—General; Brazil 2; Eastern Europe—General

## International Students, Inc (ISI)

PO Box C
Colorado Springs, CO 80901-2901 USA

**Phone:** (719) 576-2700
**Fax:** (719) 576-5363
**E-mail:** team@isiwebnet.net
**Web Site:** www.isionline.org

*Dr. Douglas Shaw, President*

A transdenominational support agency of Evangelical and Ecumenical tradition engaged in international student friendship, evangelism and discipleship in the USA with students from other countries. Statistical data from 1998.

**Year founded in US:** 1953

**Fully Supported US Personnel Overseas:**
Expecting to serve more than 4 years: 3

**Other Personnel:**
Bi-vocational/tentmakers: 1

Home ministry & office staff in US: 180
Countries: Israel 1; Singapore 1; Taiwan 1

## International Teams, U.S.A.

411 W. River Rd.
Elgin, IL 60123 USA
**Phone:** (847) 429-0900
**Fax:** (847) 429-0800
**E-mail:** mark.foshager@iteams.org
**Web Site:** www.iteams.org
**Associations:** EFMA

*Dr. David E. Schroeder, President*

An interdenominational sending agency of Evangelical tradition engaged in evangelism, childcare/orphanage programs, church planting, development, leadership development, support of national workers and youth programs.

**Year founded in US:** 1960
**Income for Overseas Min:** $7,020,000
**Gifts in Kind:** $255,000
**Fully Supported US Personnel Overseas:**
   Expecting to serve more than 4 years: 211
   Expecting to serve 1 to 4 years: 38
   Non-residential mission personnel: 7
**Other Personnel:**
   Short-term less than 1 year: 460
   Bi-vocational/tentmakers: 21
   Non-US serving in own/other country: 487
   Home ministry & office staff in US: 85
**Countries:** Albania 4; Australia 3; Austria 28; Belarus; Belgium; Bhutan; Bolivia 3; Bosnia and Herzegovina 3; Brazil; Bulgaria 3; Cambodia 6; Colombia 2; Costa Rica 15; Cuba; Czech Republic 3; Ecuador 18; Fiji; France 16; Greece 9; Honduras 2; Indonesia 3; Ireland 4; Israel 2; Italy; Japan; Kenya 2; Kosovo 2; Mexico 13; Nepal 2; Netherlands; New Zealand 2; Nicaragua; Norway; Philippines 2; Romania 6; Russia 4; Rwanda; Spain 6; Thailand; Turkey 3; Ukraine 9; Uganda; United Kingdom 13; Unspecified Country 23; Zambia

## International Urban Assocs. See: Bakke Graduate University

## InterServe USA (International Service Fellowship)

**(See ad on page 223)**
PO Box 418
Upper Darby, PA 19082-0418 USA
**Phone:** (610) 352-0581
**Fax:** (610) 352-4394
**E-mail:** ea@ludlow.net
**Web Site:** www.interserveusa.org
**Associations:** IFMA

*Doug Van Bronkhurst, Exec. Director*

An interdenominational sending agency of Evangelical, Ecumenical and Independent tradition engaged in tentmaking, development, discipleship, evangelism, medical work, relief and/or rehabilitation and TESOL.

**Year founded in US:** 1964
**Income for Overseas Min:** $4,670,270
**Fully Supported US Personnel Overseas:**
   Expecting to serve more than 4 years: 104
**Other Personnel:**
   Short-term less than 1 year: 30
   Bi-vocational/tentmakers: 14
   Home ministry & office staff in US: 9
**Countries:** Asia—General 47; Bangladesh 8; China 10; Cyprus 2; India 5; Middle East 11; Nepal 4; Thailand 2; Turkey 15

## InterVarsity Christian Fellowship/USA— Missions Department

PO Box 7895
Madison, WI 53707-7895 USA
**Phone:** (608) 274-3702
**Fax:** (608) 274-7882
**E-mail:** jtebbe@intervarsity.org
**Web Site:** www.intervarsity.org
**Associations:** EFMA

*Mr. Jim Tebbe, VP Missions/Urbana Director*

A nondenominational sending agency of Evangelical tradition engaged in student ministry, leadership development and discipleship. As a member movement of the International Fellowship of Evangelical Students, IVCF/USA supports work with student ministries in 141 countries.

**Income for Overseas Min:** $1,200,000
**Fully Supported US Personnel Overseas:**
   Expecting to serve more than 4 years: 36
   Expecting to serve 1 to 4 years: 20

# IT TAKES ALL KINDS OF
# PEOPLE
## TO REACH

## ALL KINDS
## OF
## PEOPLE

For over 150 years Interserve's partners have used their God-given talents, interests and abilities to carry the Good News to the ends of the earth.

## Now it's your turn.

www.interserveusa.org
1-800-809-4440
email: InterserveUSA@xc.org

# In service to missions
# by providing
# continuous protection...

Sponsored by the National Association of
Evangelicals (since 1991) providing worldwide
health insurance for long term and short term
mission trips.

## KUFFEL, COLLIMORE & CO.
### WORLDWIDE INSURANCE
1761 S. Naperville Road, Suite 105 – Wheaton, IL 60187
## (800) 488-4302
(630) 221-6000  FAX (630) 221-1453
www.missionaryinsurance.com
email: keccompany@iwic.net

**Other Personnel:**
Short-term less than 1 year: 800
Home ministry & office staff in US: 9

**Countries:** Asia—General 4; Central Asia—General 3; France; Gabon 2; Italy; Kenya 2; Latin America—General 1; Moldova 2; Romania 3; Russia 6; South Africa; Ukraine 1; United Kingdom 5; Unspecified Country 6; Uzbekistan 1; Zimbabwe

## Iranian Christians Intl.
PO Box 25607
Colorado Springs, CO 80936 USA
**Phone:** (719) 596-0010
**Fax:** (719) 574-1141
**E-mail:** info@iranchristians.org
**Web Site:** www.iranchristians.org
*Mr. Ebrahim (Abe) Ghaffari, Exec. Director*

A transdenominational support agency of Evangelical tradition engaged in support of national churches, Bible distribution, church planting, evangelism, literature distribution and translation work, focused on Persian speaking peoples. Statistical data from 2001.

**Purpose:** An interdenominational agency of evangelical tradition engaged in support of national and diaspora churches, evangelism, literature production/distribution and training focused on Persian speaking peoples.
**Year founded in US:** 1981
**Income for Overseas Min:** $50,000
**Personnel:**
Home ministry & office staff in US: 3

## Ireland Outreach Intl. Inc.
PO Box 1772
Waterloo, IA 50704-1772 USA
**Phone:** (319) 296-2216
**E-mail:** charleville@eircom.net
**Web Site:** www.irelandoutreach.org
*Mr. James W. Gillett, President*

A nondenominational sending agency of Christian/Plymouth Brethren tradition engaged in evangelism, Bible distribution, church planting, correspondence courses, theological education, literature distribution, literature production, literacy work, medical work, short-term programs. Gospel literature and correspondence courses are sent from Ireland to 40 countries around the world.

**Year founded in US:** 1981
**Fully Supported US Personnel Overseas:**
Expecting to serve more than 4 years: 10
Expecting to serve 1 to 4 years: 3
**Other Personnel:**
Short-term less than 1 year: 50
Non-US serving in own/other country: 19
**Countries:** Ghana; Ireland 10; Nigeria; Zambia

## Italy for Christ
1301 Shiloh Rd., #1720
Kennesaw, GA 30144-7170 USA
**Phone:** (770) 274-2800
**Fax:** (770) 274-2833
**E-mail:** info@italyforchrist.com
**Web Site:** www.italyforchrist.it
*Gaetano Sottile, President*

A nondenominational sending agency of Baptist and Pentecostal tradition engaged in evangelism, Bible distribution, leadership development and youth programs.

**Purpose:** "...to present the Gospel of Christ to every Italian in this generation, in cooperation with the local churches."
**Year founded in US:** 1983
**Income for Overseas Min:** $13,000
**Fully Supported US Personnel Overseas:**
Expecting to serve more than 4 years: 6
**Other Personnel:**
Non-US serving in own/other country: 6
Home ministry & office staff in US: 1
**Countries:** Italy 6

## JAARS Inc.
PO Box 248
Waxhaw, NC 28173 USA
**Phone:** (704) 843-6000
**Fax:** (704) 843-6200
**E-mail:** info@jaars.org
**Web Site:** www.jaars.org
*Mr. James S. Akovenko, President*

An interdenominational service agency of Evangelical tradition serving Wycliffe Bible Translators with various technical support services including aviation and radio. Personnel serves more than 70 countries.

**Purpose:** "...provides quality technical support services and resources to speed Bible translation for all people, serving

Wycliffe Bible Translators."
**Year founded in US:** 1948
**Income for Overseas Min:** $4,460,743
**Gifts in Kind:** $394,727
**Personnel:**
Short-term less than 1 year: 25
Home ministry & office staff in US: 10

## Janz Team Ministries USA

PO Box 2010
Buffalo, NY 14231 USA
**Phone:** (716) 688-0276
**Fax:** (716) 688-5049
**E-mail:** jtm@janzteam.org
**Web Site:** www.janzteam.org
**Associations:** IFMA

*Mr. Jack Stenekes, Director*

An interdenominational sending agency of Evangelical tradition engaged in evangelism, camping programs, Christian education and TESOL, and music outreach.

**Purpose:** "...to be obedient to the Great Commission of Jesus Christ through evangelism and Christian education, contributing to the establishment and growth of vibrant churches."
**Year founded in US:** 1980
**Income for Overseas Min:** $1,345,299
**Fully Supported US Personnel Overseas:**
Expecting to serve more than 4 years: 36
Expecting to serve 1 to 4 years: 8
**Other Personnel:**
Short-term less than 1 year: 9
Non-US serving in own/other country: 2
**Countries:** Brazil; Germany 36; Hungary

## Japanese Evangelical Missionary Society (JEMS)

948 E. 2nd St.
Los Angeles, CA 90012-4317 USA
**Phone:** (213) 613-0022
**Fax:** (213) 613-0211
**E-mail:** info@jems.org
**Web Site:** www.jems.org
*Rev. Sam Tonomura, Exec. Director*

An interdenominational service agency of Evangelical tradition engaged in camping programs, evangelism, support of national workers, support of national churches,

sports outreach, music ministry and short-term programs.
**Year founded in US:** 1950
**Income for Overseas Min:** $100,000
**Fully Supported US Personnel Overseas:**
Expecting to serve more than 4 years: 3
Expecting to serve 1 to 4 years: 5
**Other Personnel:**
Short-term less than 1 year: 20
Non-US serving in own/other country: 10
Home ministry & office staff in US: 9
**Countries:** Japan 3

## Japanese Evangelization Center (Institute of Japanese Studies)

1605 Elizabeth St.
Pasadena, CA 91104 USA
**Phone:** (626) 398-2235
**Fax:** (562) 402-2903
*Dr. John Mizuki, Exec. Director*

A nondenominational specialized agency of Evangelical tradition engaged in research and information on Japanese evangelization and church planting.

**Purpose:** "...to provide information to churches, mission agencies, pastors, missionaries, missionary candidates, students and to serve as consultants to those interested in Japanese culture and evangelization."
**Year founded in US:** 1981

## JARON Ministries Intl.

5150 North 6th St., Ste. 132
Fresno, CA 93710 USA
**Phone:** (559) 227-7997
**Fax:** (559) 227-9603
**E-mail:** info@jaron.org
**Web Site:** www.jaron.org
*Rev. Eugene E. Beck, Executive Director*

An interdenominational support agency of Baptist tradition engaged in leadership development, theological education, literature production and short-term programs. Statistical data from 2001.

**Purpose:** "...to teach, disciple, counsel, and encourage Christian leaders...serve as a ministry of instruction and motivation...produce and provide biblically sound and currently

WWW.MVTI.COM
MISSIONS@MVTI.US

# WHOLESALE TRAVEL
**AFRICA | ASIA | EUROPE | MIDDLE EAST | SOUTH AMERICA**

# MISSIONARY
# INDIVIDUAL
# GROUP

# 877-565-7468
**112 COOPERATIVE WAY | KALISPELL MT 59901**

# JEWS F✡R JESUS

**We exist to make the messiahship of Jesus
an unavoidable issue to our Jewish people worldwide.**

If you'd like to partner with us in any of the 22 cities we're working in,
we'd love to hear from you!

## US BRANCH LOCATIONS

Boston, Chicago, Fort Lauderdale, Los Angeles, New York,
Phoenix,San Francisco, Washington D.C.
(contact jfj@jewsforjesus.org)

## INTERNATIONAL LOCATIONS

Sydney, Australia
australia@jewsforjesus.org
www.jewsforjesus.com.au

Rio De Janeiro, Brazil
judeusporjesus@aol.com

Toronto/Montreal
montreal@jewsforjesus.ca
www.jewsforjesus.ca

London, England
uk@jewsforjesus.org.uk
www.jewsforjesus.uk

Paris, France
france@jewsforjesus.org/france
www.jewsforjesus.org/France

Essen, Germany
judenfuerjesus@aol.com

Tel Aviv, Israel
jfjisreal@jewsforjesus.co.il
www.jewsforjesus.co.il

Moscow, Russia
moscow@jewsforjesus.org
www.jewsforjesus.org/CIS

Johannesburg, South Africa
southafrica@jewsforjesus.org
www.jewsforjesus.org/sa

Ukraine
dnepr@jewsforjesus.org
kharkov@jewsforjesus.org
kiev@jewsforjesus.org
odessa@jewsforjesus.org

**International Headquarters**
60 Haight Street, San Francisco, CA 94102 USA
Phone: (415) 864-2600  Fax: (415) 552-8325
jfj@jewsforjesus.org • www.jewsforjesus.org

relevant written, audio, and video training materials and organize and lead short-term ministry teams to other parts of the world."

**Year founded in US:** 1992
**Income for Overseas Min:** $96,328
**Fully Supported US Personnel Overseas:**
Non-residential mission personnel: 5
**Other Personnel:**
Short-term less than 1 year: 68
Home ministry & office staff in US: 6

## Jewish Awareness Ministries
PO Box 706
Ramseur, NC 27316 USA
**Phone:** (336) 824-1477
**Fax:** (336) 824-1577
**E-mail:** jewishawareness@cs.com
**Web Site:** www.jewishawareness.org
*Mr. Mark Robinson, Exec. Director*

A nondenominational sending agency of Baptist and Fundamental tradition engaged in evangelism, broadcasting, literature distribution, literature production and missionary training.

**Year founded in US:** 1946
**Income for Overseas Min:** $40,000
**Fully Supported US Personnel Overseas:**
Expecting to serve more than 4 years: 2
**Other Personnel:**
Home ministry & office staff in US: 1
**Countries:** Israel 2

## Jews for Jesus
(See ad on page 228)
60 Haight St.
San Francisco, CA 94102 USA
**Phone:** (415) 864-2600
**Fax:** (415) 552-8325
**E-mail:** jfj@jewsforjesus.org
**Web Site:** www.jewsforjesus.org
**Associations:** EFMA, IFMA
*Mr. David Brickner, Exec. Director*

A nondenominational sending agency of Evangelical tradition engaged in Jewish evangelism, childrens programs, Christian education,literature distribution, literature production, short-term programs and missionary training.

**Purpose:** "...to make the Messiahship of Jesus an unavoidable issue to our Jewish

people worldwide."

**Year founded in US:** 1973
**Income for Overseas Min:** $1,180,349
**Gifts in Kind:** $867,253
**Fully Supported US Personnel Overseas:**
Expecting to serve more than 4 years: 11
**Other Personnel:**
Non-US serving in own/other country: 57
Home ministry & office staff in US: 203
**Countries:** Australia 3; Brazil; France 1; Germany 2; Israel 3; Russia; South Africa; Ukraine; United Kingdom 2

## Joni and Friends
PO Box 3333
Agoura Hills, CA 91376 USA
**Phone:** (818) 707-5664
**Fax:** (818) 707-2391
**E-mail:** dmarkham@joniandfriends.org
**Web Site:** www.joniandfriends.org
*Mrs. Joni Eareckson Tada, Founder/CEO*

An interdenominational service agency of Evangelical tradition engaged in disability assistance programs, broadcasting, Christian education, evangelism, short-term programs and missionary training.

**Purpose:** "...to communicate the Gospel and equip Christ-honoring churches worldwide to evangelize and disciple people affected by disabilities."

**Year founded in US:** 1979
**Income for Overseas Min:** $6,218,959
**Gifts in Kind:** $4,796,959
**Personnel:**
Short-term less than 1 year: 194
Home ministry & office staff in US: 99

## Josue Yrion World Evangelism and Missions, Inc.
PO Box 876018
Los Angeles, CA 90087-1118 USA
**Phone:** (562) 928-8892
**Fax:** (562) 947-2268
**E-mail:** josueyrion@josueyrion.org
**Web Site:** www.josueyrion.org
*Rev. Josue Yrion, President/CEO*

An interdenominational sending agency of Evangelical and Pentecostal tradition engaged in evangelism, audio recording/distribution,

Bible distribution, theological education, leadership development, missionary training and video/film production/distribution.

**Purpose:** "...to serve the Body of Christ, to edify, teach and prepare an effective evangelistic ministry that can change lives by the power of God's Word."

**Year founded in US:** 1986

**Income for Overseas Min:** $28,389

**Personnel:**
   Non-US serving in own/other country: 21
   Home ministry & office staff in US: 1

**Countries:** Africa—General; Argentina; Australia; Brazil; India; Mexico; Peru; Spain; United Kingdom

## Key Communications
PO Box 13620
Portland, OR 97213 USA
**Phone:** (503) 233-7680
**Fax:** (503) 236-0733
**E-mail:** lee@keycom.org
*Mr. Bryan L. Turner, Director*

A specialized agency of Christian (Restoration Movement)  and Independent tradition engaged in broadcasting, audio recording/distribution, evangelism, literature distribution and Bible translation.

**Purpose:** "...to bring the gospel of grace and peace to Muslims throughout the world."

**Year founded in US:** 1977

**Income for Overseas Min:** $85,876

**Personnel:**
   Short-term less than 1 year: 1
   Non-US serving in own/other country: 2
   Home ministry & office staff in US: 5

**Countries:** Pakistan

## Kids Alive International
2507 Cumberland Dr.
Valparaiso, IN 46383 USA
**Phone:** (219) 464-9035
**Fax:** (219) 462-5611
**E-mail:** kidsalive@kidsalive.org
**Web Site:** www.kidsalive.org
**Associations:** IFMA
*Mr. Alfred Lackey, President*

An interdenominational sending agency of Evangelical tradition engaged in childcare/orphanage programs, Christian education, medical work, relief and/or rehabilitation, short-term programs and missionary training.

**Purpose:** "...to reflect the love of Christ by rescuing suffering children in crisis, nurturing them with quality holistic care and introducing them to the transforming power of Jesus Christ so they are enabled to instill hope in others."

**Year founded in US:** 1916

**Income for Overseas Min:** $2,957,992

**Gifts in Kind:** $28,168

**Fully Supported US Personnel Overseas:**
   Expecting to serve more than 4 years: 23
   Expecting to serve 1 to 4 years: 21
   Non-residential mission personnel: 3

**Other Personnel:**
   Short-term less than 1 year: 229
   Non-US serving in own/other country: 423
   Home ministry & office staff in US: 11

**Countries:** Dominican Republic 10; Guatemala 3; Haiti 2; Kenya 2; Lebanon 1; Papua New Guinea 1; Peru 2; Taiwan 2

## Kids Around the World, Inc.
2424 Charles St.
Rockford, IL 61108 USA
**Phone:** (815) 229-8731
**Fax:** (815) 229-8931
**Web Site:** www.kidsaroundtheworld.com
*Mr. Jim Rosene, President*

A nondenominational service agency of Evangelical tradition engaged in building playgrounds, childrens programs, support of national workers and training.

**Purpose:** "...to reach children around the world with the gospel of Jesus Christ and to help those who work with children through evangelizing and building playgrounds."

**Year founded in US:** 1994

**Income for Overseas Min:** $531,926

**Gifts in Kind:** $16,961

**Fully Supported US Personnel Overseas:**
   Non-residential mission personnel: 3

**Other Personnel:**
   Non-US serving in own/other country: 2
   Home ministry & office staff in US: 5

## Latin America Assistance, Inc.
PO Box 123
Solvang, CA 93464-0123 USA

# TRANSPORTATION
## to the world
by *air,* *land* or *sea*

BIG or small. A whole shipload of containers or just a few cartons.

## **We know** relief and missionary cargoes!

**Tell us about your shipment:**

—what is it?

—how big is it?

—how heavy is it?

—where is it coming from?

—where is it going to?

**Using state of the art systems, we manage your shipment with:**

- a Project Plan Proposal which shows you the best value of budget options

- a Routing Plan which keeps the shipment flow in control

# Missionary Expediters, Inc.
Federal Maritime Commission license no. 268

Fax: 504-891-6365

Email: query@solvenet.com

Website: www.solvenet.com

## *Serving those who serve Him*
for over 50 years

call us at
# 1-800-299-6363

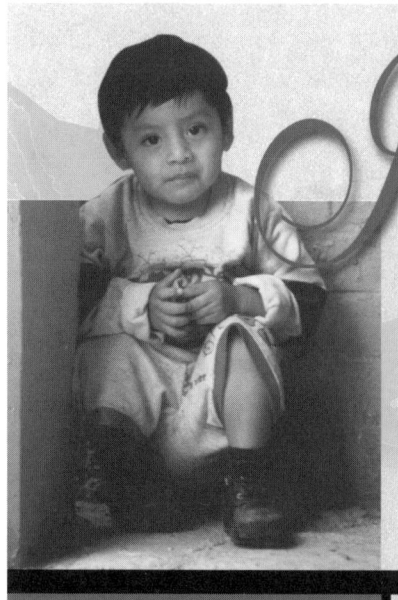

*J*S God calling
you to serve in
Latin America?

*LAM can help you
explore that calling.*

*Latin America
Mission offers
opportunities for
meaningful pro-
fessional service
with grass-roots
Latin ministries.
If the Lord is
calling you, count
the cost. Then call
Latin America
Mission.*

• *Summer*   • *Limited-term*
• *YearOut*   • *Career*

*Contact us today to
find out more!*

 **Latin America
Mission**

PO Box 52-7900 • Miami, FL 33152-7900
1-800-275-8410
mobilization@lam.org
**www.lam.org**

**Phone:** (805) 693-9222
**Fax:** (805) 693-9222
**E-mail:** info@lam.org
**Web Site:** www.lamontana.org

*Mr. Joseph B. Pent, President*

An interdenominational service agency of Evangelical and Independent tradition engaged in camping programs, evangelism, leadership development and partnership development.

**Purpose:** "...to equip youth leaders for aggressive evangelism and radical discipleship."

**Year founded in US:** 1976

**Income for Overseas Min:** $400,000

**Fully Supported US Personnel Overseas:**
  Expecting to serve more than 4 years: 8
  Non-residential mission personnel: 1

**Other Personnel:**
  Short-term less than 1 year: 12
  Non-US serving in own/other country: 18
  Home ministry & office staff in US: 19

**Countries:** Costa Rica 8

## Latin America Mission
**(See ad on page 232)**
PO Box 52-7900
Miami, FL 33152-7900 USA
**Phone:** (305) 884-8400
**Fax:** (305) 885-8649
**E-mail:** info@lamcanada.ca
**Web Site:** www.lam.org
**Associations:** IFMA

*Dr. David R. Befus, President*

An interdenominational sending agency of Evangelical tradition engaged in Christian education, camping programs, childrens programs, theological education, short-term programs and development.

**Purpose:** "...to encourage, assist and participate with the Latin church in the task of building the church of Jesus Christ in the Latin world and beyond."

**Year founded in US:** 1921

**Income for Overseas Min:** $781,356

**Fully Supported US Personnel Overseas:**
  Expecting to serve more than 4 years: 122
  Expecting to serve 1 to 4 years: 35

**Other Personnel:**
  Short-term less than 1 year: 40
  Non-US serving in own/other country: 157

Home ministry & office staff in US: 19

**Countries:** Argentina 2; Brazil 6; Chile; Colombia 12; Costa Rica 52; Ecuador 4; El Salvador 1; Honduras 5; Mexico 27; Panama; Paraguay 2; Peru 6; Spain 4; Venezuela 1

## Latin American Indian Ministries
PO Box 2050
Orange, CA 92859 USA
**Phone:** (626) 398-2105
**E-mail:** Dale.Kietzman@laim.org
**Web Site:** www.laim.org

*Mr. Dale W. Kietzman, President*

A nondenominational service agency of Evangelical and Independent tradition engaged in support of national churches and support of national workers.

**Purpose:** "...to encourage, strengthen and support the indigenous communities of Latin America in their efforts to evangelize and disciple their own people, as well as to help them improve living standards for their families..."

**Year founded in US:** 1976

**Income for Overseas Min:** $68,000

**Personnel:**
  Short-term less than 1 year: 4
  Home ministry & office staff in US: 1

**Countries:** Brazil; Mexico; Peru

## Latin American Lutheran Mission
3519 Salinas Ave.
Laredo, TX 78041 USA
**Phone:** (956) 722-4047
**Fax:** (956) 722-0997
**E-mail:** lalmelcm@sbcglobal.net
**Web Site:** www.lalm-elcm.org

*Mr. Richard G. Erickson, Director*

A denominational support agency of Lutheran tradition engaged in short-term programs, Bible distribution, church construction, church planting, discipleship, TEE, evangelism, literature distribution and support of national churches.

**Purpose:** "...to encourage Bible study and discipleship, and to train and equip the Mexican people to fulfill Christ's 'Great Commission.'"

**Year founded in US:** 1936

**Income for Overseas Min:** $87,045

**Fully Supported US Personnel Overseas:**
Expecting to serve more than 4 years: 3
Non-residential mission personnel: 3

**Other Personnel:**
Short-term less than 1 year: 650
Non-US serving in own/other country: 1
Home ministry & office staff in US: 4

**Countries:** Mexico 3

## Leadership Ministries Worldwide

PO Box 21310
Chattanooga, TN 37424 USA

**Phone:** (423) 855-2181
**Fax:** (423) 855-8616
**E-mail:** info@outlinebible.org
**Web Site:** www.outlinebible.org

*Mr. John W. Burkett, Gen. Director*

A service agency of Evangelical tradition publishing and distributing the Preacher's OUTLINE and Sermon Bible and related OUTLINE Bible series.

**Purpose:** "...equipping God's servants worldwide in their understanding, preaching and teaching of God's Word by publishing and distributing OUTLINE Bible materials, to reach and disciple people for Jesus Christ."

**Year founded in US:** 1992

**Income for Overseas Min:** $431,960

**Personnel:**
Short-term less than 1 year: 1
Home ministry & office staff in US: 9

## Leadership Training Intl.

PO Box 9882
Chesapeake, VA 23321 USA

**Phone:** (757) 673-6581
**Fax:** (757) 673-6584
**E-mail:** info@lti-va.org
**Web Site:** www.ltiworld.com
**Associations:** AFMA

*Mr. Kevin Hinman, Founder/President*

An interdenominational service agency of Charismatic and Evangelical tradition engaged in leadership development.

**Purpose:** "...to provide training and resources to multiply ministry leaders to fulfill

the Great Commission."

**Year founded in US:** 1992

**Income for Overseas Min:** $23,000

**Gifts in Kind:** $10,000

**Personnel:**
Home ministry & office staff in US: 6

## LeaderTreks

25W560 Geneva Rd., #30
Carol Stream, IL 60188 USA

**Phone:** (630) 668-0936
**Fax:** (630) 668-0980
**E-mail:** info@leadertreks.com
**Web Site:** www.leadertreks.com

*Mr. Doug Franklin, President*

An interdenominational service agency engaged in leadership development.

**Purpose:** "...developing leaders to fulfill the Great Commission."

**Year founded in US:** 1994

**Fully Supported US Personnel Overseas:**
Expecting to serve 1 to 4 years: 18

**Other Personnel:**
Short-term less than 1 year: 1,100
Home ministry & office staff in US: 17

**Countries:** Bolivia; Costa Rica; South Africa

## Liberty Corner Mission

PO Box 204
Liberty Corner, NJ 07938 USA

**Phone:** (908) 647-1777
**Fax:** (908) 647-4117
**E-mail:** lcmissions@fellowshipdeaconry.org
**Web Site:** www.fellowshipdeaconry.org

*Rev. E. E. Achenbach, President*

An interdenominational sending agency of Evangelical tradition engaged in evangelism, church planting, childcare and support of national churches, working together with Marburg Mission of Germany.

**Year founded in US:** 1933

**Fully Supported US Personnel Overseas:**
Expecting to serve more than 4 years: 3

**Other Personnel:**
Home ministry & office staff in US: 1
**Countries:** Japan 1; Taiwan 2

## Liebenzell USA

PO Box 66

# 24/7 Missionary Airfares

## From the U.S. Leader in Missions Travel

- On-Line Booking
- Short-Term Mission Experts
- Special Airfares for Family, Friends & Partners
- Fund Raising Assistance

Offices in 4 time zones to serve you.

Since 1955
**MTS ▸ TRAVEL**
mtstravel.com

**Call or email at:**
(877) 908-8899
service@mtstravel.com
CST 2013363-40

Schooleys Mtn., NJ 07870-0066 USA

**Phone:** (908) 852-3044
**Fax:** (908) 852-4531
**E-mail:** missions@liebenzellusa.org
**Web Site:** www.liebenzellusa.org

**Associations:** IFMA

An interdenominational sending agency of Evangelical tradition engaged in evangelism, church planting, development, Christian education, TEE and theological education.

**Purpose:** "...to bring glory to God by preaching the Gospel and making disciples of the nations."

**Year founded in US:** 1941

**Income for Overseas Min:** $950,000

**Fully Supported US Personnel Overseas:**
Expecting to serve more than 4 years: 25
Expecting to serve 1 to 4 years: 4

**Other Personnel:**
Bi-vocational/tentmakers: 3
Non-US serving in own/other country: 14
Home ministry & office staff in US: 5

**Countries:** Central Asia—General 6; Ecuador 4; Germany 1; Guam 6; Micronesia, Federated States of 3; Nigeria 1; Palau 1; Papua New Guinea; Spain 2; Taiwan; Zambia 1

## LIFE Ministries
## See: Asian Access

## Lifewater International
PO Box 3131
San Luis Obispo, CA 93403 USA

**Phone:** (805) 541-6634
**Fax:** (805) 541-6649
**E-mail:** info@lifewater.org
**Web Site:** www.lifewater.org

*Mr. Dan Stevens, Exec. Director*

An interdenominational specialized agency of Reformed tradition engaged in development and training.

**Purpose:** "...trains the rural poor to develop clean water supplies...works with mission agencies, local agencies and missionaries to train in shallow well drilling, pump repair, spring development, hygiene education and cottage industries."

**Year founded in US:** 1979

**Income for Overseas Min:** $1,306,318

**Gifts in Kind:** $534,000

**Personnel:**
Short-term less than 1 year: 105
Home ministry & office staff in US: 22

## LIGHT International, Inc.
PO Box 714
Etna, CA 96027 USA

**Phone:** (530) 467-5373
**E-mail:** bwaymire@sisqtel.net

*Mr. Robert H. Waymire, President*

A nondenominational specialized agency of Evangelical tradition engaged in church mobilization and mission-related research and training in 65 countries. Statistical information from 2003.

**Year founded in US:** 1991

**Income for Overseas Min:** $30,000

**Gifts in Kind:** $30,000

**Personnel:**
Home ministry & office staff in US: 2

## Link Care Foundation
**(See ad on page 237)**
1734 W. Shaw Ave.
Fresno, CA 93711 USA

**Phone:** (559) 439-5920
**Fax:** (559) 439-2214
**E-mail:** info@linkcare.org
**Web Site:** www.linkcare.org

**Associations:** EFMA

*Dr. Brent Lindquist, President/CEO*

A nondenominational specialized agency of Evangelical tradition engaged in psychological counseling.

**Year founded in US:** 1965

**Personnel:**
Home ministry & office staff in US: 26

## Literacy & Evangelism Intl.
1800 S. Jackson Ave.
Tulsa, OK 74107-1897 USA

**Phone:** (918) 585-3826
**Fax:** (918) 585-3224
**E-mail:** general@literacyevangelism.org
**Web Site:** www.literacyevangelism.org

*Rev. Sid Rice, Exec. Director*

An interdenominational sending agency of Evangelical tradition engaged in literacy work, literature production, services for

# Link Care Center

**ENHANCING EFFECTIVENESS IN LIVING, WITNESSING, AND WORKING WITH MISSIONARIES AND PASTORS AROUND THE WORLD.**

**SINCE 1965**, Link Care Center has been providing comprehensive counseling, pastoral care, and training resources across the wide human resources spectrum for mission agencies, denominations, and local churches.

**IN FRESNO**, our Restoration/Personal Growth Program combines intensive counseling and pastoral care in community for up to 25 individual and family units at a time. Each year, at least 60% to 70% of the people that come to us for help return to their arena of ministry, saving the entire Great Commission community substantial funds and heartache. Our licensed psychologists, marriage and family therapists and social workers qualify for many insurance plans, also reducing the out of pocket expenses.

**AROUND THE WORLD** we provide many services, including candidate assessment, training, consulting, crisis debriefing, intensive counseling and pastoral care.

**IN PRINT** and electronic media we provide books, newsletters, and other resources.

**VISIT OUR WEBSITE** for further details.

**LINK CARE CENTER**
1734 W. Shaw Ave.
Fresno, CA 93711
Phone 559-439-5920
Fax 559-439-2214
Website linkcare.org
E-mail info@linkcare.org

other agencies, TESOL and missionary and other training.

**Purpose:** "To encourage, equip and enable the Church worldwide to empower the functionally illiterate with God's Word, through literacy ministries."

**Year founded in US:** 1967

**Income for Overseas Min:** $200,000

**Fully Supported US Personnel Overseas:**
Expecting to serve more than 4 years: 4

**Other Personnel:**
Short-term less than 1 year: 4
Non-US serving in own/other country: 14
Home ministry & office staff in US: 6

**Countries:** Asia—General; Benin; Bolivia; Brazil; Burundi; China; Dominican Republic; Ghana; India; Malawi; Pakistan; Peru 2; Philippines 2; Poland; Switzerland; Togo

## Living Hope Ministries Int'l.

PO Box 2765
Acworth, GA 30102 USA

**Phone:** (770) 917-1307
**Fax:** (770) 917-1307
**E-mail:** bob2c@mindspring.com
**Web Site:** www.lhmi.org

*Robert A. Carter, President*

A nondenominational service agency of Baptist tradition engaged in childcare/orphanage programs, church planting, evangelism, medical work, training and youth programs.

**Year founded in US:** 2001

**Income for Overseas Min:** $57,909

**Fully Supported US Personnel Overseas:**
Expecting to serve more than 4 years: 1

**Other Personnel:**
Short-term less than 1 year: 12
**Countries:** Kenya 1

## Living Water Teaching

PO Box 1190
Caddo Mills, TX 75135 USA

**Phone:** (903) 527-4160
**Fax:** (903) 527-2134
**E-mail:** lwt@lwtusa.org
**Web Site:** www.livingwaterteaching.org

*Keith & Debbie Spanberger, Exec. Directors*

A nondenominational sending agency of Pentecostal tradition engaged in theological education, association of missions, childrens programs, evangelism, missionary

training and youth programs.

**Year founded in US:** 1979

**Income for Overseas Min:** $913,415

**Fully Supported US Personnel Overseas:**
Expecting to serve more than 4 years: 12
Expecting to serve 1 to 4 years: 2

**Other Personnel:**
Short-term less than 1 year: 250
Non-US serving in own/other country: 10
Home ministry & office staff in US: 7

**Countries:** Costa Rica; El Salvador 3; Guatemala 5; Honduras 2; Nicaragua; Panama; Paraguay 2

## LOGOI, Inc./FLET
## See: FLET University/
## Universidad FLET

## LOGOI, Inc./FLET
## See: LOGOI Ministries

## LOGOI Ministries

14540 SW 136th St., Ste. 200
Miami, FL 33186 USA

**Phone:** (305) 232-5880
**Fax:** (305) 232-3592
**E-mail:** logoi@logoi.org
**Web Site:** www.logoi.org

*Rev. Leslie J. Thompson, Founder/President*

A nondenominational service agency of Reformed tradition engaged in training national Spanish pastors, discipleship, TEE, theological education, leadership development, literature distribution and literature production.

**Purpose:** "...to help equip national Spanish pastors to become effective ministers of the Gospel."

**Year founded in US:** 1962

**Income for Overseas Min:** $715,000

**Personnel:**
Short-term less than 1 year: 2
Non-US serving in own/other country: 19
Home ministry & office staff in US: 8

**Countries:** Argentina; Bolivia; Chile; Colombia; Cuba; Ecuador; Mexico; Peru; Uruguay; Venezuela

## Lott Carey Baptist Foreign Mission Convention

220 I Street NE, Ste. 220
Washington, DC 20002 USA
**Phone:** (202) 543-3200
**Fax:** (202) 543-6300
**E-mail:** lottcarey@lottcarey.org
**Web Site:** www.lottcarey.org
*Dr. David E. Goatley, Exec. Sec.-Treas.*

A transdenominational sending agency of Baptist tradition engaged in support of national churches, Christian education, medical work, support of national workers, relief and/or rehabilitation and short-term programs.

**Year founded in US:** 1897

**Income for Overseas Min:** $2,800,000

**Fully Supported US Personnel Overseas:**
   Non-residential mission **Personnel:** 5
**Other Personnel:**
   Short-term less than 1 year: 50
   Non-US serving in own/other country: 890
   Home ministry & office staff in US: 3
**Countries:** Australia; Guyana; Haiti; India; Italy; Jamaica; Kenya; Liberia; Nigeria; South Africa; Zimbabwe

## Ludhiana Christian Medical College Board, USA, Inc.

7121 Vasalias Heights
Colorado Springs, CO 80918 USA
**Phone:** (719) 272-0200
**Fax:** (719) 272-0201
**E-mail:** Ludhianamc@aol.com
**Web Site:** www.ludhianaus.org
*Rev. Roberta K. Jones, Exec. Director*

An interdenominational service agency of Methodist tradition engaged in medical work, extension education, leadership development, providing medical supplies, relief and/or rehabilitation and missionary training.

**Year founded in US:** 1910

**Income for Overseas Min:** $200,000

**Gifts in Kind:** $150,000

**Personnel:**
   Short-term less than 1 year: 25
   Home ministry & office staff in US: 1

## Luis Palau Evangelistic Assoc.

PO Box 50
Portland, OR 97207 USA
**Phone:** (503) 614-1500
**Fax:** (503) 614-1599
**E-mail:** info@palau.org
**Web Site:** www.palau.org
**Associations:** EFMA
*Dr. Luis Palau, President*

A nondenominational service agency of Evangelical tradition engaged in evangelism, broadcasting, partnership development and video/film production/distribution.

**Purpose:** "…to proclaim the Good News, mobilize the church and equip the next generation."

**Year founded in US:** 1978

**Income for Overseas Min:** $6,250,000

**Fully Supported US Personnel Overseas:**
   Non-residential mission personnel: 14
**Other Personnel:**
   Non-US serving in own/other country: 8
**Countries:** Argentina; United Kingdom

## Luke Society, Inc., The

3409 Gateway Blvd., Ste. 1000
Sioux Falls, SD 57106 USA
**Phone:** (605) 373-9686
**Fax:** (605) 373-9711
**E-mail:** office@lukesociety.org
**Web Site:** www.lukesociety.org
*Dr. Wrede Vogel, Exec. Director*

An interdenominational service agency of Evangelical tradition engaged in support of national workers, development, discipleship, evangelism and medical work.

**Year founded in US:** 1964

**Income for Overseas Min:** $1,941,529

**Personnel:**
   Home ministry & office staff in US: 7
**Countries:** Bolivia; Colombia; Ecuador; Guatemala; Honduras; Mexico; Nicaragua; Paraguay; Peru

## Lutheran Bible Translators, Inc.

PO Box 2050
Aurora, IL 60507 USA

**Phone:** (630) 897-0660
**Fax:** (630) 897-3567
**E-mail:** info@lbt.org
**Web Site:** www.lbt.org
**Associations:** EFMA Candidate
*Dr. Marshall R. Gillam, Exec. Director*
A denominational sending agency of Lutheran tradition engaged in Bible translation, leadership development, linguistics, literacy work and translation work.
**Purpose:** "...to help bring people to faith in Jesus Christ by making the Word of God available to those who do not yet have it in the language of their hearts."
**Year founded in US:** 1964
**Income for Overseas Min:** $1,082,932
**Fully Supported US Personnel Overseas:**
  Expecting to serve more than 4 years: 25
  Expecting to serve 1 to 4 years: 5
  Non-residential mission Personnel: 2
**Other Personnel:**
  Short-term less than 1 year: 4
  Non-US serving in own/other country: 94
  Home ministry & office staff in US: 19
**Countries:** Botswana 6; Cameroon; Ecuador; Ghana 5; Guatemala 10; Liberia; Namibia; Nigeria 2; Papua New Guinea 2; Sierra Leone; Togo

## Lutheran Brethren World Missions

PO Box 655
Fergus Falls, MN 56538 USA
**Phone:** (218) 739-3336
**Fax:** (775) 522-1552
**E-mail:** lbwm@lbwm.org
**Web Site:** www.lbwm.org
**Associations:** EFMA
*Rev. Matthew Rogness, Exec. Director*
A denominational sending agency of Evangelical tradition engaged in church planting, development, leadership development, literature production, support of national churches and Bible translation.
**Purpose:** "...serving the congregations of the Church of the Lutheran Brethren to facilitate their task of fulfilling the Great Commission..."
**Year founded in US:** 1900
**Income for Overseas Min:** $90,000

**Fully Supported US Personnel Overseas:**
  Expecting to serve more than 4 years: 16
**Other Personnel:**
  Short-term less than 1 year: 6
  Bi-vocational/tentmakers: 2
  Home ministry & office staff in US: 7
**Countries:** Chad 8; Japan 4; Taiwan 4

## Lutheran Church-Missouri Synod, Board for Mission Services

1333 S. Kirkwood Rd.
St. Louis, MO 63122 USA
**Phone:** (314) 996-1349
**Fax:** (314) 965-0959
**E-mail:** namissions@aol.com
**Web Site:** www.lcms.org
*Rev./Dr. Robert Scudieri, Assoc. Exec. Dir.*
A denominational sending agency of Lutheran tradition engaged in church planting, evangelism, leadership development, partnership development, missionary training and training.
**Purpose:** "Praying to the Lord of the harvest, LCMS World Mission in collaboration with its North American and worldwide partners will share the good news of Jesus with 100 million unreached people or uncommitted people by the 500th anniversary of the Reformation in 2017."
**Year founded in US:** 1839
**Income for Overseas Min:** $15,000,000
**Gifts in Kind:** $5,000,000
**Fully Supported US Personnel Overseas:**
  Expecting to serve more than 4 years: 59
  Expecting to serve 1 to 4 years: 9
**Other Personnel:**
  Home ministry & office staff in US: 34
**Countries:** Argentina 1; Asia—General 2; Central Asia—General 2; Guatemala 1; Jamaica 2; Japan 7; Kenya 2; Macau 3; Nigeria 2; Panama 6; Papua New Guinea 1; Poland 3; Puerto Rico 8; Russia 5; Taiwan 9; Togo 2; Venezuela 3

## Lutheran Hour Ministries

660 Mason Ridge Center Dr.
St. Louis, MO 63141 USA
**Phone:** (314) 317-4100
**Fax:** (314) 317-4297

**E-mail:** lh_min@lhm.org.
**Web Site:** www.lhm.org

*Mr. Greg Lewis, Exec. Director*

A denominational specialized agency of Lutheran tradition engaged in evangelism through broadcasting in 41 countries through 290 national staff.

**Purpose:** "...to bring Christ to the Nations and the Nations to the church through Christian radio and TV programming, the Internet, print communications, dramas, music and congregational outreach training."

**Year founded in US:** 1917

**Income for Overseas Min:** $650,000

**Fully Supported US Personnel Overseas:**
Expecting to serve more than 4 years: 1
Non-residential mission personnel: 4

**Other Personnel:**
Short-term less than 1 year: 72
Non-US serving in own/other country: 290
Home ministry & office staff in US: 142

**Countries:** Unspecified Country 1

## Lutheran World Relief

700 Light St.
Baltimore, MD 21230 USA
**Phone:** (410) 230-2800
**Fax:** (410) 230-2882
**E-mail:** lwr@lwr.org
**Web Site:** www.lwr.org

*Mr. Jeff Whisenant, Acting President*

A denominational service agency of Lutheran tradition engaged in relief and/or rehabilitation, development, leadership development and agricultural programs. Financial information from 1998.

**Purpose:** "...to alleviate suffering caused by natural disaster, conflict or poverty; through development efforts to enable marginalized people to realize more fully their God-given potential; and through education and advocacy efforts to promote a peaceful, just and sustainable global community."

**Year founded in US:** 1945

**Income for Overseas Min:** $22,598,621

**Gifts in Kind:** $11,763,386

**Personnel:**
Home ministry & office staff in US: 45

## Lutheran Youth Encounter
## See: Youth Encounter

## M/E International, Inc. (Missionary Electronics)

655 Shadow Lake Dr.
Brea, CA 92821 USA
**Phone:** (714) 624-3547
**Fax:** (909) 336-1674
**E-mail:** jford767@aol.com
**Web Site:** www.me-intl.org

*Mr. James R. Ford, President*

An interdenominational support agency of Baptist and Evangelical tradition engaged in providing equipment and technical support for the Cassette Discipleship Program used by 6,500 village evangelists in 186 countries.

**Purpose:** "To enable nationals in developing countries to reach their own with the Gospel of the Lord Jesus Christ...using cassette discipleship programs...structured dialog messages with village evangelists."

**Year founded in US:** 1948

**Income for Overseas Min:** $84,000

## Macedonia World Baptist Missions, Inc.

PO Box 519
Braselton, GA 30517 USA
**Phone:** (706) 654-2818
**Fax:** (706) 654-2816
**E-mail:** mwbm@mwbm.org
**Web Site:** www.mwbm.org

*Dr. Don Richards, Gen. Director*

A denominational sending agency of Baptist and Independent tradition engaged in church planting, childcare/orphanage programs, correspondence courses, theological education and short-term programs.

**Year founded in US:** 1967

**Income for Overseas Min:** $5,000,000

**Fully Supported US Personnel Overseas:**
Expecting to serve more than 4 years: 152
Non-residential mission personnel: 7

**Other Personnel:**
Short-term less than 1 year: 30
Bi-vocational/tentmakers: 3
Non-US serving in own/other country: 13
Home ministry & office staff in US: 14

**Countries:** Argentina 2; Armenia 2; Asia—General 4; Australia 2; Bahamas, The 2; Bolivia 2; Brazil 16; Bulgaria 2; Burkina Faso 2; Chile 10; Colombia 2; Costa Rica 2; Cyprus 2; Dominica 4; Germany 4; Guam 2; Guatemala 2; Guyana; Haiti 2; Indonesia 4; Ireland 6; Jamaica 4; Japan 2; Kenya; Korea, South 2; Mali 2; Mexico 17; Middle East 4; Peru 15; Puerto Rico 6; Romania 2; Russia 1; Saint Lucia 6; South Africa 4; Spain 2; Taiwan 2; United Kingdom 5; Venezuela 4

## Macedonian Missionary Service

PO Box 68
Polk City, FL 33868-0068 USA
**Phone:** (863) 984-4060
**Fax:** (863) 984-4505
**E-mail:** secretary@macedonianms.org
**Web Site:** www.macedonianms.org

*Mr. Leon Jasper, President*

A denominational support agency of Baptist tradition engaged in short-term programs, Bible distribution, broadcasting, church construction, church planting, missionary education, missions information service, literature distribution, literature production, providing medical supplies, medical work, supplying equipment and missionary training.

**Year founded in US:** 1973
**Income for Overseas Min:** $500,000
**Fully Supported US Personnel Overseas:**
  Non-residential mission personnel: 7
**Other Personnel:**
  Short-term less than 1 year: 100
  Home ministry & office staff in US: 11

## Mahesh Chavda Ministries Intl.

PO Box 411008
Charlotte, NC 28241-1008 USA
**Phone:** (704) 543-7272
**Fax:** (704) 541-5300
**E-mail:** Info@maheshchavda.com
**Web Site:** www.maheshchavda.com
**Associations:** AFMA

*Rev. Mahesh Chavda, Founder/President*

A nondenominational support agency of Charismatic tradition engaged in evangelism, leadership development, literature production and support of national church-es. Financial data from 1998.

**Year founded in US:** 1985
**Income for Overseas Min:** $20,000
**Personnel:**
  Home ministry & office staff in US: 9

## Mailbox Club Intl. Inc., The
(See ad on page 243)

404 Eager Rd.
Valdosta, GA 31602 USA
**Phone:** (229) 244-6812
**Fax:** (229) 245-8977
**E-mail:** email@mailboxclub.org
**Web Site:** www.mailboxclub.org
**Associations:** ANAM

*Mr. John Mark Eager, Director/CEO*

A nondenominational support agency of Christian/Plymouth Brethren and Fundamental tradition engaged in correspondence courses, discipleship, evangelism, literature distribution, partnership development and services for other agencies.

**Purpose:** "...to win the children and young people of the world to Christ, help nurture them into spiritual maturity through Bible correspondence courses and into local churches...accomplished through direct ministry and by multiplying our efforts through key partnerships and the Body of Christ around the world."

**Year founded in US:** 1965
**Income for Overseas Min:** $1,800,000
**Fully Supported US Personnel Overseas:**
  Expecting to serve more than 4 years: 4
  Non-residential mission personnel: 4
**Other Personnel:**
  Non-US serving in own/other country: 5
  Home ministry & office staff in US: 16
**Countries:** Africa—General 1; Asia—General 1; Eastern Europe—General 1; Latin America—General 1

## MAP International

PO Box 215000
Brunswick, GA 31521-5000 USA
**Phone:** (912) 265-6010
**Fax:** (912) 265-6170
**E-mail:** map@map.org
**Web Site:** www.map.org
**Associations:** AERDO

# the Mailbox Club®
## INTERNATIONAL

Bible Lessons for the Childern of the World

Since 1965 The Mailbox Club has presented the Gospel to children through the use of Bible correspondence lessons.

These easy to use Bible lessons have proven to be a very effective tool to evangelize and disciple children around the word.

Through active participation with other ministries, millions of Mailbox Club lessons are being distributed annually worldwide.

*"Our partnership with The Mailbox Club enables local churches to continue their relationship with the children, even their families, by providing solid Biblical teaching through the study lessons. We praise God for the way He has brought us together to further His Kingdom!"*
**–Franklin Graham, President and CEO, Samaritan's Purse**

## Highlights of Ministry:

- Lessons for ages 4 years-adults
- Fun and exciting
- Over 40 years of experience in discipleship
- Christ-centered materials
- International Training
- Strategic partners
- Relevant to every culture

## Testimonies:

*"I received Jesus as my Savior after reading this lesson which I learned that I need forgiveness for my sins."***Florin–Romania**

*"I'm very happy that I've got to know Jesus as my Savior from all the sins I've done…"* **Siwaporn–Thailand**

*"Thank you for giving me the opportunity to learn more about God."* **Alyssa–Georgia, USA**

## the Mailbox Club®
404 Eager Road, Valdosta, GA 31602
229-244-6812
Fax 229-245-8977
www.mailboxclub.org

NO TURN ON RED

www.multnomah.edu

Ellisha, Dr. Metzger, and Matt from New Wine, New Wineskins

# next»

# culture

**Study at Multnomah and experience the "living lab" of Portland, Oregon. Discover how to take your accredited education into real-life ministry. Explore the Institute for the Theology of Culture:** *New Wine, New Wineskins* **with Dr. Paul Metzger and engage biblically the tough questions common in today's culture. Prepare for your own intercultural ministry... wherever it takes you!**

» **Interested in teaching English as a 2nd language? Ask about our TESOL program!**

MULTNOMAH BIBLE COLLEGE   MULTNOMAH BIBLICAL SEMINARY

ACCREDITED BY ATS, ABHE, & NWCCU

800.275.4672   admiss@multnomah.edu
**www.multnomah.edu**

*Mr. Michael Nyenhuis, President/CEO*

A nondenominational specialized agency engaged in providing medical supplies, childrens programs, development, theological education, partnership development and relief and/or rehabilitation.

**Purpose:** "...to promote the total health of people living in the world's poorest communities by partnering in the provision of essential medicines, prevention and eradication of disease and the promotion of community health development."

**Year founded in US:** 1954

**Income for Overseas Min:** $319,511,995

**Gifts in Kind:** $338,971,358

**Personnel:**
Non-US serving in own/other country: 111
Home ministry & office staff in US: 58

**Countries:** Bolivia; Côte d'Ivoire; Ecuador; Honduras; Indonesia; Kenya; Tanzania; Uganda

# Marriage Ministries Intl.
# See: University of the Family

# MATS International, Inc.
4444 National Rd. E.
Richmond, IN 47374 USA
**Phone:** (765) 965-7777
**Fax:** (765) 962-9966
**E-mail:** car@mats.org
**Web Site:** www.mats.org
*Mr. Josh Nottingham, President*

A nondenominational support agency engaged in purchasing services, furloughed missionary support, support of national workers, supplying equipment and technical assistance.

**Year founded in US:** 1977

**Personnel:**
Home ministry & office staff in US: 2

# MBMS International
4867 E. Townsend Ave.
Fresno, CA 93727 USA
**Phone:** (559) 456-4600
**Fax:** (559) 251-1432
**E-mail:** mbmsi@mbmsi.org
**Web Site:** www.mbmsinternational.org
**Associations:** EFMA

*Mr. Randy Friesen, Regional Mobilizer, US West*

A denominational sending agency of Mennonite tradition engaged in church planting, development, evangelism, recruiting/mobilizing, training and youth programs. MBMS is a bi-national organization and statistics cannot be separated into U.S. and Canadian. For statistical information see the Canadian listing.

**Purpose:** "...to participate in making disciples of all people groups, sharing the gospel of Jesus Christ cross-culturally and globally, in Spirit-empowered obedience to Christ's Commission and in partnership with local Mennonite Brethren churches."

**Year founded in US:** 1878

# Media Associates Intl.
351 S. Main Place, Ste. 230
Carol Stream, IL 60188 USA
**Phone:** (630) 260-9063
**Fax:** (630) 260-9265
**E-mail:** mailittworld@sbcglobal.net
**Web Site:** www.littworld.org
*Mr. John D. Maust, President*

A nondenominational specialized agency of Evangelical tradition engaged in training of Christian publishers, editors and authors in countries where Christian publishing and witness are limited and difficult, leadership development, literature production, management consulting/training and technical assistance.

**Purpose:** "...to train, particularly in countries and cultures with limited Christian publishing or witness, MAI stimulates the creation of books, periodicals and other written materials that nurture the church and attract general readers to Christ."

**Year founded in US:** 1985

**Income for Overseas Min:** $260,000

**Gifts in Kind:** $21,080

**Personnel:**
Non-US serving in own/other country: 2
Home ministry & office staff in US: 4

**Countries:** Costa Rica; Ghana

# Medical Ambassadors Intl. Inc.
PO Box 576645
Modesto, CA 95357-6645 USA

**Phone:** (209) 524-0600
**Fax:** (209) 571-3538
**E-mail:** info@med-amb.org
**Web Site:** www.medicalambassadors.org
**Associations:** EFMA

*Dr. Paul Calhoun, Exec. Director*

An interdenominational support agency of Evangelical tradition engaged in development, agricultural programs, evangelism, management consulting/training, medical work and support of national workers.

**Purpose:** "...recruits, trains and supports national leaders among developing peoples...to reach their own people physically and spiritually..."

**Year founded in US:** 1974

**Income for Overseas Min:** $2,144,624

**Fully Supported US Personnel Overseas:**
  Expecting to serve more than 4 years: 13
  Non-residential mission personnel: 17

**Other Personnel:**
  Short-term less than 1 year: 15
  Non-US serving in own/other country: 354
  Home ministry & office staff in US: 44

**Countries:** Albania 2; Argentina; Bangladesh; Belize; Bosnia and Herzegovina; Brazil; Cambodia; Congo, Democratic Republic of; Costa Rica; Cuba; Dominican Republic; East Timor; El Salvador; Ethiopia; Gabon; Guatemala; Haiti; Honduras; India; Indonesia; Kenya 6; Kiribati; Kosovo; Laos; Malaysia; Mexico 1; Mozambique; Myanmar/Burma; Nepal; Nicaragua; Niger; Nigeria; Panama; Papua New Guinea; Paraguay; Peru; Philippines; Romania; Russia; Sierra Leone; Solomon Islands; South Africa; Sudan; Tanzania; Thailand; Uganda 2; Ukraine; Unspecified Country 2; Venezuela; Vietnam; Zambia

## Medical Missions Philippines, Inc.
PO Box 3656
Modesto, CA 95352 USA
**Phone:** (209) 531-3031
**Fax:** (209) 848-2346

*Mr. Richard G. Hagerty, President*

A support agency of Evangelical tradition engaged in funds transmission to their Manila-based charitable corporation for community health ministry.

**Year founded in US:** 1987
**Income for Overseas Min:** $46,771
**Countries:** Philippines

## Men for Missions Intl.
941 Fry Road
Greenwood, IN 46142 USA
**Phone:** (317) 881-6752
**Fax:** (317) 865-1076
**E-mail:** whardig@omsinternational.org
**Web Site:** www.mfmi.org

*Mr. Warren Hardig, Intl. Exec. Director*

An interdenominational support agency of Evangelical tradition engaged in overseas missionary housing construction, literature production and providing other technical assistance as a short-term arm of OMS International for laymen.

**Purpose:** "Reaching the nations for Christ in this generation by doing whatever God asks us to do, going wherever God asks us to go and giving whatever God asks us to give."

**Year founded in US:** 1954

**Personnel:**
  Short-term less than 1 year: 700
  Home ministry & office staff in US: 12

## Mennonite Central Committee (MCC)
PO Box 500
Akron, PA 17501-0500 USA
**Phone:** (717) 859-1151
**Fax:** (717) 859-2171
**E-mail:** mailbox@mcc.org
**Web Site:** www.mcc.org

*Mr. Robb Davis, Exec. Director*

A denominational service agency of Mennonite and Brethren tradition engaged in development, agricultural programs, extension education, justice, medical work, relief and/or rehabilitation, technical assistance and training. Overseas personnel includes 287 locally appointed citizens within more than 70 countries where MCC works.

**Purpose:** "...to demonstrate God's love by working among people suffering from poverty, conflict, oppression and natural disaster."

**Year founded in US:** 1920

**Income for Overseas Min:** $40,614,000

Gifts in Kind: $6,345,000

Fully Supported US Personnel Overseas:
Expecting to serve more than 4 years: 606

Other Personnel:
Home ministry & office staff in US: 217

Countries: Africa—General 153; Asia—General 212; Europe—General 26; Latin America—General 181; Middle East 34

# Mennonite Economic Development Associates —US (MEDA)

1821 Oregon Pike, Ste. 201
Lancaster, PA 17601 USA

Phone: (717) 560-6546
Fax: (717) 560-6549

A service agency. Details for MEDA—US listed under their Canadian corporate office.

# Mennonite Mission Network

PO Box 370
Elkhart, IN 46515-0370 USA

Phone: (574) 294-7523
Fax: (574) 294-8669
E-mail: info@mennonitemission.net
Web Site: www.mennonitemission.net

Mr. Stanley W. Green, Exec. Director/CEO

A denominational mobilizing, partnering and resource/equipping agency of Mennonite/Anabaptist tradition engaged in leadership development, church planting, partnership development, short-term programs and video/film production/distribution. Country and personnel data from 2003.

Purpose: "With a vision for every congregation and all parts of the church to be fully engaged in God's mission, Mennonite Mission Network exists to lead, mobilize and equip the church for holistic witness to Jesus Christ in a broken world."

Year founded in US: 1899

Income for Overseas Min: $3,910,000

Fully Supported US Personnel Overseas:
Expecting to serve more than 4 years: 72
Non-residential mission personnel: 2

Other Personnel:
Short-term less than 1 year: 3,000
Bi-vocational/tentmakers: 1
Non-US serving in own/other country: 37
Home ministry & office staff in US: 98

Countries: Afghanistan 4; Argentina 4; Asia—General 2; Australia; Belgium; Benin 3; Bolivia 1; Botswana 2; Brazil; Burkina Faso; Chile; China 4; Colombia 2; Congo, Democratic Republic of; Cote d'Ivoire 2; Dominican Republic; Ecuador 2; Egypt 2; Finland; France 3; Germany; Ghana; Hong Kong 2; Hungary; India; Iran; Ireland 2; Israel 6; Japan 7; Korea, South; Lesotho; Liberia; Lithuania; Macau; Malaysia; Mexico 4; Mongolia 5; Nepal 2; Netherlands; Nigeria; Paraguay; Philippines; Russia 2; Senegal 7; South Africa; Spain 2; Sweden; Taiwan; Thailand; Togo; Ukraine; United Kingdom 2; Uruguay

# Mercy Ships

PO Box 2020
Garden Valley, TX 75771-2020 USA

Phone: (903) 939-7000
Fax: (903) 882-0336
E-mail: info@mercyships.org
Web Site: www.mercyships.org

Mr. Donald K. Stephens, President/Founder

An interdenominational service agency of Evangelical tradition engaged in medical work, development, evangelism, literacy work, support of national churches and relief and/or rehabilitation.

Purpose: "Mercy Ships, a global charity with land offices in 17 countries, is staffed by 1200+ staff coming from many Christian denominations and traditions with staff coming from over 40 nations. It runs the world's largest fleet of non-governmental hospital ships. Seeking to follow the example of Jesus, Mercy Ships brings hope and healing to the poor, mobilizing people and resources worldwide."

Year founded in US: 1978

Income for Overseas Min: $38,682,881

Gifts in Kind: $14,039,508

Personnel:
Short-term less than 1 year: 1,300
Bi-vocational/tentmakers: 350
Home ministry & office staff in US: 22

# Mexican Gospel Mission See: Mission Gospel Ministries International

## Mexican Medical Ministries

251 Landis Ave.
Chula Vista, CA 91910 USA
**Phone:** (619) 420-9750
**Fax:** (619) 420-9570
**E-mail:** info@mexicanmedical.com
**Web Site:** www.mexicanmedical.com

*Mr. Stephen M. Crews, President*

A nondenominational service agency of Evangelical tradition engaged in short-term programs, childcare/orphanage programs, development, evangelism, medical work, support of national churches and Bible translation.

**Purpose:** "...to bring the Gospel of Jesus Christ to the various age groups of Mexican people through a variety of ministries."

**Year founded in US:** 1966

**Income for Overseas Min:** $880,610

**Fully Supported US Personnel Overseas:**
  Expecting to serve more than 4 years: 22
  Expecting to serve 1 to 4 years: 9
  Non-residential mission personnel: 6

**Other Personnel:**
  Short-term less than 1 year: 12
  Non-US serving in own/other country: 6
  Home ministry & office staff in US: 2

**Countries:** Mexico 22

## Middle East Christian Outreach (MECO)

PO Box 531151
Indianapolis, IN 46253-1151 USA
**Phone:** (317) 271-4026
**Fax:** (317) 271-4026
**E-mail:** info@mecousa.org
**Web Site:** www.aboutmeco.org
**Associations:** EFMA

*Rev. James R. Smith, U.S. Representative*

An interdenominational support agency of Evangelical tradition engaged in support of national churches, Christian education, theological education, literature distribution, mobilization for mission and video/film production/distribution.

**Year founded in US:** 1978

**Income for Overseas Min:** $103,066

**Fully Supported US Personnel Overseas:**
  Expecting to serve more than 4 years: 4
  Expecting to serve 1 to 4 years: 2

**Other Personnel:**
  Short-term less than 1 year: 2
  Bi-vocational/tentmakers: 5
  Non-US serving in own/other country: 50
  Home ministry & office staff in US: 2

**Countries:** Australia; Cyprus; Middle East; Unspecified Country 4

## Middle East Media—USA

PO Box 4949
Wheaton, IL 60189-4949 USA
**Phone:** (425) 488-9429
**Fax:** (425) 672-9222
**E-mail:** info@mem-usa.org
**Web Site:** www.mem.org
**Associations:** EFMA

*Wayne Larson, Exec. Director*

A nondenominational support agency engaged in video/film production/distribution, broadcasting, evangelism, support of national churches, missionary training, literature production and translation work.

**Year founded in US:** 1976

**Income for Overseas Min:** $286,870

**Fully Supported US Personnel Overseas:**
  Expecting to serve more than 4 years: 2

**Other Personnel:**
  Non-US serving in own/other country: 89
  Home ministry & office staff in US: 4

**Countries:** Africa—General; Iran; Middle East; Turkey; Unspecified Country 2

## Middle Eastern Outreach

PO Box 405
Duarte, CA 91009-0405 USA
**Phone:** (818) 482-5242
**E-mail:** meo.e@usa.net
**Web Site:** www.middleeasternoutreach.com

*Dr./Rev. Elie Elbayadi, Founder/President*

A support agency engaged in evangelism, missions information service, missionary training, literature distribution, support of national churches, and Muslim and jail ministry. Statistics are from 2003.

**Year founded in US:** 1995

**Income for Overseas Min:** $22,000

**Personnel:**
  Home ministry & office staff in US: 3

## Ministries In Action

PO Box 571357
Miami, FL 33257-1357 USA
**Phone:** (305) 234-7855
**Fax:** (305) 234-7825
**E-mail:** info@mia.org
**Web Site:** www.mia.org

*Rev./Dr. E. Walford Thompson, President*

An interdenominational sending agency of Evangelical tradition engaged in support of national churches, development, discipleship, TEE, evangelism, relief and/or rehabilitation and short-term programs.

**Purpose:** "...to help the Church internationally to grow holistically and in accordance with the Great Commission."

**Year founded in US:** 1961

**Income for Overseas Min:** $345,035

**Fully Supported US Personnel Overseas:**
Expecting to serve more than 4 years: 5
Non-residential mission personnel: 6

**Other Personnel:**
Short-term less than 1 year: 302
Non-US serving in own/other country: 10
Home ministry & office staff in US: 11

**Countries:** Bolivia; Brazil; Dominican Republic; Grenada; Guadeloupe; Haiti 1; Jamaica 2; Mexico; Peru; Puerto Rico 2; Saint Lucia; Saint Martin; Saint Vincent and the Grenadines

## Ministry to Eastern Europe

2520 Professional Rd., Suite C
Richmond, VA 23235 USA
**Phone:** (804) 320-6456
**Fax:** (804) 320-6456
**E-mail:** mtee@verizon.net
**Web Site:** www.mtee.org

*Mr. Ernest R. Campe, President*

A nondenominational sending agency of Charismatic and Evangelical tradition engaged in theological education, childrens programs, Christian education, leadership development and Bible translation. Statistical data from 2002.

**Year founded in US:** 1983

**Income for Overseas Min:** $258,500

**Personnel:**
Short-term less than 1 year: 10
Home ministry & office staff in US: 2

## Ministry to Educate and Equip International (MTEE)

2520 Professional Rd., Ste. C
Richmond, VA 23235 USA
**Phone:** (804) 320-6456
**Fax:** (804) 320-6456
**E-mail:** mtee@verizon.net
**Web Site:** www.mtee.org
**Associations:** AFMA

*Ernest R. Campe, President*

A nondenominational sending agency of Evangelical tradition engaged in theological education, childrens programs, leadership development, literature production, support of national workers and translation work.

**Year founded in US:** 1991

**Income for Overseas Min:** $280,817

**Fully Supported US Personnel Overseas:**
Expecting to serve 1 to 4 years: 8
Non-residential mission personnel: 3

**Other Personnel:**
Non-US serving in own/other country: 18
Home ministry & office staff in US: 3

**Countries:** Belarus; Bulgaria; Hungary; Moldova; Romania; Ukraine

## Mission Aviation Fellowship

PO Box 47
Nampa, ID 83653 USA
**Phone:** (208) 498-0800
**Fax:** (208) 498-0801
**E-mail:** maf-us@maf.org
**Web Site:** www.maf.org
**Associations:** EFMA

*Mr. Kevin Swanson, President/CEO*

An interdenominational specialized agency of Evangelical tradition engaged in aviation services and missions information service.

**Purpose:** "...to multiply the effectiveness of the Church using aviation and other strategic technologies that overcome barriers in reaching the world for Christ."

**Year founded in US:** 1945

**Income for Overseas Min:** $8,555,670

**Gifts in Kind:** $154,883

**Fully Supported US Personnel Overseas:**
Expecting to serve more than 4 years: 76
Expecting to serve 1 to 4 years: 68

**Other Personnel:**

Short-term less than 1 year: 5
Home ministry & office staff in US: 147
**Countries:** Africa—General 2; Asia—General 6; Brazil 3; Congo, Democratic Republic of 7; Ecuador 5; Germany 1; Guatemala; Haiti 3; Indonesia 24; Latin America—General 1; Lesotho 4; Mali 5; Mexico; Mozambique 1; Russia 1; Uganda 2; Unspecified Country 7; Venezuela 3; Zimbabwe 1

## Mission Catalyst Intl.

PO Box 73047
Houston, TX 77273-3047 USA
**Phone:** (281) 705-7877
**Fax:** (936) 273-1232
**E-mail:** jre@mci3.org
**Web Site:** www.mci3.org
**Associations:** AFMA
*Mr. James R. Eby, President/Founder*
An interdenominational support agency of Charismatic and Evangelical tradition engaged in training nationals for church planting among unreached people groups.
**Purpose:** "...to help equip and mobilize church-planting missionaries from the Two-Thirds World to more effectively evangelize the least reached people of the earth with the Gospel of Jesus Christ."
**Year founded in US:** 2002
**Income for Overseas Min:** $215,279
**Fully Supported US Personnel Overseas:**
Expecting to serve more than 4 years: 4
**Other Personnel:**
Short-term less than 1 year: 15
Non-US serving in own/other country: 2
Home ministry & office staff in US: 2
**Countries:** India 4

## Mission India

PO Box 141312
Grand Rapids, MI 49514 USA
**Phone:** (616) 453-8855
**Fax:** (616) 791-9926
**E-mail:** info@missionindia.org
**Web Site:** www.missionindia.org
*Rev. Dave Stravers, President/CEO*
A support agency of Evangelical tradition engaged in church planting, childrens programs, evangelism, literacy work, partnership development and training.The entire staff in India are Indian nationals.
**Purpose:** "...assists national Indian Christians in the planting of 'Reproducing Churches' in a systematic and measurable pattern throughout India."
**Year founded in US:** 1980
**Income for Overseas Min:** $9,116,918
**Gifts in Kind:** $3,626,370
**Personnel:**
Non-US serving in own/other country: 196
Home ministry & office staff in US: 24
**Countries:** India

## Mission Ministries, Inc.

PO Box 10044
Costa Mesa, CA 92627 USA
**Phone:** (714) 957-8787
**Fax:** (714) 444-3347
**E-mail:** missionmin@aol.com
**Web Site:** www.missionministries.org
*Mr. John Mark Lindvall, President*
A transdenominational sending agency of Baptist and Pentecostal tradition engaged in support of national workers, childcare/orphanage programs, church planting, evangelism, leadership development and tentmaking.
**Purpose:** "...to serve wherever there are needs."
**Year founded in US:** 1980
**Income for Overseas Min:** $331,340
**Gifts in Kind:** $2,000
**Fully Supported US Personnel Overseas:**
Expecting to serve more than 4 years: 11
Non-residential mission personnel: 7
**Other Personnel:**
Bi-vocational/tentmakers: 2
Non-US serving in own/other country: 53
Home ministry & office staff in US: 4
**Countries:** Asia—General 2; Congo, Democratic Republic of; India; Kenya 1; Mexico 1; Middle East 2; Nigeria; Philippines 1; Romania 1; Uganda 3

## Mission Nannys

PO Box 61805
Santa Barbara, CA 93160-1805 USA
**Phone:** (805) 683-7476
**E-mail:** bettysullins@juno.com
**Web Site:** www.missionnannys.org

*Betty Sullins, Director*

A nondenominational service agency of Baptist tradition engaged in childcare/orphanage programs, Christian education, short-term programs and providing domestic help for missionary families.

**Purpose:** "...to seek to glorify God among missionary families through the domestic and teaching services of mature humble women who volunteer to travel and meet particular needs."

**Year founded in US:** 1990

**Personnel:**
Short-term less than 1 year: 10

## Mission of Mercy

PO Box 62600
Colorado Springs, CO 80962 USA
**Phone:** (800) 864-0200
**Fax:** (719) 481-4649
**E-mail:** mominfo@mofm.org
**Web Site:** www.missionofmercy.org
**Associations:** AERDO

*Mr. David Perkin, Chairman/CEO*

A nondenominational support agency of Evangelical tradition engaged in childrens programs, childcare/orphanage programs, development, discipleship, Christian education and youth programs in more than 23 countries.

**Purpose:** "...to rescue forgotten children, with Jesus' Love."

**Year founded in US:** 1954

**Income for Overseas Min:** $13,736,718

**Fully Supported US Personnel Overseas:**
Expecting to serve more than 4 years: 1

**Other Personnel:**
Non-US serving in own/other country: 1
Home ministry & office staff in US: 18

**Countries:** Algeria; China; Ethiopia; India 1; Iraq; Jordan; Kenya; Laos; Lebanon; Nepal; Pakistan; Sudan; Tanzania; Uganda; Vietnam

## Mission ONE, Inc.

PO Box 5960
Scottsdale, AZ 85261 USA
**Phone:** (480) 951-0900
**Fax:** (480) 951-1016
**E-mail:** info@mission1.org
**Web Site:** www.mission1.org

*Mr. Robert Schindler, President*

An interdenominational support agency of Baptist and Evangelical tradition engaged in support of national workers, church planting, Christian education, evangelism and support of national churches.

**Purpose:** "...to mobilize the Church for partnership with national missionaries, focusing on unreached people groups, and serving the poor and oppressed."

**Year founded in US:** 1991

**Income for Overseas Min:** $385,323

**Personnel:**
Short-term less than 1 year: 12
Non-US serving in own/other country: 214
Home ministry & office staff in US: 15

**Countries:** Algeria; China; Ethiopia; India; Iraq; Jordan; Kenya; Laos; Lebanon; Nepal; Pakistan; Sudan; Tanzania; Uganda; Vietnam

## Mission Possible Foundation, Inc.

404 E. Gregory St., Ste. 8
Mount Prospect, IL 60056 USA
**Phone:** (847) 259-1270
**Fax:** (847) 259-1270
**E-mail:** mpusa@mp.org
**Web Site:** www.mp.org

*Nasko Lazarov, USA Director*

An interdenominational support agency of Evangelical and Pentecostal tradition engaged in church planting, childrens programs, leadership development, literature distribution and literature production.

**Purpose:** "...to serve local national churches and enable them to evangelize unbelievers and disciple new believers..."

**Year founded in US:** 1974

**Income for Overseas Min:** $139,526

**Personnel:**
Non-US serving in own/other country: 52
Home ministry & office staff in US: 1

**Countries:** Albania; Bulgaria; Finland; Russia; Sweden; Ukraine

## Mission Possible, Inc.

PO Box 1026
Findlay, OH 45839-1026 USA
**Phone:** (419) 422-3364
**Fax:** (419) 422-3342

**E-mail:** office@ourmissionispossible.org
**Web Site:** www.ourmissionispossible.org
*Mr. Kurt Bishop, President*

An interdenominational support agency of Evangelical tradition engaged in Christian education, childcare/orphanage programs, development, discipleship, leadership development and short-term programs.

**Purpose:** "...to equip a new generation of Christ-centered leaders for the harvest."

**Year founded in US:** 1974

**Income for Overseas Min:** $697,129

**Gifts in Kind:** $100,542

**Personnel:**
Non-US serving in own/other country: 141
Home ministry & office staff in US: 5

**Countries:** Dominican Republic; Haiti

## Mission Safety International

328 E. Elk Ave. #1
Elizabethton, TN 37643-3351 USA
**Phone:** (423) 542-8892
**Fax:** (423) 542-5464
**E-mail:** info@msisafety.org
**Web Site:** www.msisafety.org
*Mr. Jonathan A. Egeler, President/CEO*

A nondenominational specialized agency engaged in aviation safety services for other agencies in 10 countries.

**Purpose:** "...to provide educational and consulting services to mission and mission aviation training organizations and related agencies in the areas of operational safety and organizational security."

**Year founded in US:** 1983

**Income for Overseas Min:** $10,258

**Gifts in Kind:** $211,045

**Personnel:**
Home ministry & office staff in US: 3

## Mission Services Association, Inc.

PO Box 13111
Knoxville, TN 37920-0111 USA
**Phone:** (865) 577-9740
**Web Site:** www.missionservices.org
*Mr. W. Reggie Hundley, Exec. Director*

A nondenominational support agency of Christian (Restoration Movement) tradition engaged in communication, print publishing, web development and missions information service.

**Year founded in US:** 1960

**Income for Overseas Min:** $400,000

**Personnel:**
Short-term less than 1 year: 2
Home ministry & office staff in US: 8

## Mission Society for United Methodists
## See: The Mission Society

## Mission to the Americas

2530 Washington St.
Denver, CO 80205-3142 USA
**Phone:** (303) 308-1818
**Fax:** (303) 295-9090
**E-mail:** mta@mtta.org
**Web Site:** www.mtta.org
*Rev. Richard A. Miller, President*

A sending agency of Baptist tradition engaged in church planting, urban ministry, campus ministry, evangelism, leadership development and support of national churches in North and Central America (including Canada, USA, Mexico and the Caribbean).

**Purpose:** "...to assist local churches of like faith and practice in their efforts to evangelize, disciple and plant churches among the unreached of the Americas and beyond."

**Year founded in US:** 1950

**Income for Overseas Min:** $2,260,000

**Fully Supported US Personnel Overseas:**
Expecting to serve more than 4 years: 32
Expecting to serve 1 to 4 years: 1
Non-residential mission personnel: 4

**Other Personnel:**
Short-term less than 1 year: 2
Non-US serving in own/other country: 50
Home ministry & office staff in US: 15

**Countries:** Belize 2; Cambodia 8; Costa Rica 2; Dominican Republic; El Salvador; Guatemala 4; Haiti; Honduras 9; Kenya 1; Mexico 6; Nicaragua; Panama

## Mission to the World (PCA), Inc.

1700 North Brown Rd.
Lawrenceville, GA 30043 USA

**Phone:** (678) 823-0004
**Fax:** (678) 823-0027
**E-mail:** info@mtw.org
**Web Site:** www.pcanet.org
**Associations:** EFMA

*Dr. Paul D. Kooistra, Coordinator*

A denominational sending agency of Presbyterian tradition engaged in church planting, TEE, leadership development, support of national churches and youth programs.

**Purpose:** "To reach the world's unreached responsive peoples with God's Good News through the testimony of church-planting teams and strategic technical and support personnel..."

**Year founded in US:** 1973

**Income for Overseas Min:** $42,393,999

**Fully Supported US Personnel Overseas:**
Expecting to serve 1 to 4 years: 403
Non-residential mission personnel: 1

**Other Personnel:**
Short-term less than 1 year: 7,824
Bi-vocational/tentmakers: 25
Home ministry & office staff in US: 130

**Countries:** Australia; Austria; Belgium; Belize; Brazil; Bulgaria; Chile; Cote d'Ivoire; Czech Republic; Dominican Republic; Ecuador; Egypt; El Salvador; Ethiopia; France; Germany; Haiti; Honduras; India; Italy; Jamaica; Japan; Kazakhstan; Kenya; Korea, South; Mexico; New Zealand; Nicaragua; Panama; Peru; Philippines; Romania; Senegal; Slovakia; South Africa; Spain; Sweden; Taiwan; Tanzania; Thailand; Uganda; Ukraine; United Kingdom; Unspecified Country; Zambia

## Mission To Unreached Peoples

PO Box 30947
Seattle, WA 98113 USA
**Phone:** (206) 781-3151
**Fax:** (206) 781-3182
**E-mail:** mupinfo@gatiwa.com
**Web Site:** www.mup.org
**Associations:** AFMA, EFMA

*Mr. David M. Hupp, U.S. Director*

A nondenominational sending agency of Evangelical tradition engaged in church planting, childcare/orphanage programs, development, medical work, member care and youth programs.

**Purpose:** " ...to obey the Great Commission of Jesus Christ by investing our lives, gifts, resources and vocational skills in God's work throughout Asia and Europe... to model Christ so that the peoples of the world will come to worship and glorify His name."

**Year founded in US:** 1982

**Income for Overseas Min:** $3,343,992

**Gifts in Kind:** $25,297

**Fully Supported US Personnel Overseas:**
Expecting to serve more than 4 years: 130
Non-residential mission personnel: 11

**Other Personnel:**
Short-term less than 1 year: 11
Bi-vocational/tentmakers: 49
Non-US serving in own/other country: 10
Home ministry & office staff in US: 25

**Countries:** Albania 2; Cambodia 16; China 30; Hungary 3; India 12; Indonesia 4; Japan 5; Kazakhstan; Korea, South; Macedonia 2; Malaysia; Mongolia 2; Nepal 3; Philippines 4; Poland 4; Russia 2; Taiwan 2; Thailand 27; Turkey 8; Ukraine 2; Vietnam 2

## Mission Training and Resource Center

PO Box 41155
Pasadena, CA 91114 USA
**Phone:** (626) 797-7903
**Fax:** (626) 797-7906
**E-mail:** Phil@MEF-LA.org

*Mr. Phillip Elkins, President*

A nondenominational specialized agency of Evangelical tradition engaged in community experience-based cross-cultural training preparing people to work in 42 countries.

**Year founded in US:** 1979

**Personnel:**
Home ministry & office staff in US: 10

## Mission Training Intl.

PO Box 1220
Palmer Lake, CO 80133 USA
**Phone:** (719) 487-0111
**Fax:** (719) 487-9350
**E-mail:** info@mti.org
**Web Site:** www.mti.org
**Associations:** EFMA

*Dr. Stephen Sweatman, President*

An interdenominational support agency of Evangelical tradition engaged in missionary training, linguistics, member care and services for other agencies.

**Purpose:** "...to serve mission boards, churches and other organizations by equipping their missionaries with vital skills and cross-cultural tools for the furtherance of Christ's Kingdom."

**Year founded in US:** 1954

**Personnel:**
   Home ministry & office staff in US: 13

## Mission: Moving Mountains, Inc.

6001 Egan Dr, Suite. 190
Savage, MN 55378-4913 USA
**Phone:** (952) 440-9100
**Fax:** (952) 440-9104
**E-mail:** mmm@movingmountains.org
**Web Site:** www.movingmountains.org
**Associations:** EFMA
*Dr. Gary T. Hipp, CEO*

An interdenominational sending agency of Evangelical tradition engaged in development, agricultural programs, church planting, evangelism, leadership development and medical work.

**Purpose:** "...to facilitate the physical and spiritual well-being of impoverished people in developing countries."

**Year founded in US:** 1978

**Income for Overseas Min:** $602,980

**Fully Supported US Personnel Overseas:**
   Expecting to serve more than 4 years: 26
   Non-residential mission personnel: 5

**Other Personnel:**
   Short-term less than 1 year: 17
   Non-US serving in own/other country: 27
   Home ministry & office staff in US: 13

**Countries:** Ghana; Kenya 16; Nigeria; Senegal 10; Uganda

## Missionaire International

PO Box 474
Kimball, NE 69145-0474 USA
**Phone:** (308) 235-4147
**E-mail:** serve@missionaire.org
**Web Site:** www.missionaire.org
*Mr. Jon O. Foote, Director Operations*

An interdenominational service agency of Evangelical tradition engaged in aviation maintenance and flight training, education, services for other agencies and youth programs.

**Purpose:** "...to supply other mission organizations with suitable aircraft for use in their ministry of spreading the gospel and to train people for a career in missionary aviation."

**Year founded in US:** 1988

**Fully Supported US Personnel Overseas:**
   Non-residential mission personnel: 6

**Other Personnel:**
   Home ministry & office staff in US: 2

## Missionary Athletes Intl.

PO Box 2938
Indian Trail, NC 28079 USA
**Phone:** (704) 841-8644
**Fax:** (704) 841-8652
**E-mail:** info@maisoccer.com
**Web Site:** www.maisoccer.com
*Mr. Patrick Stewart, CEO*

A nondenominational specialized agency of Evangelical tradition engaged in evangelism and youth programs.

**Year founded in US:** 1983

**Income for Overseas Min:** $651,581

**Personnel:**
   Short-term less than 1 year: 151
   Home ministry & office staff in US: 32

## Missionary Flights Intl.

3170 Airmans Dr.
Ft. Pierce, FL 34951 USA
**Phone:** (772) 462-2395
**Fax:** (772) 462-2397
**E-mail:** MFI@missionaryflights.org
**Web Site:** www.missionaryflights.org
*Mr. Richard Snook, President*

A nondenominational support agency of Evangelical tradition engaged in missionary air transportation of personnel and cargo, Bible distribution and relief and/or rehabilitation.

**Year founded in US:** 1964

**Income for Overseas Min:** $2,600,000

**Gifts in Kind:** $2,600,000

**Personnel:**
   Home ministry & office staff in US: 16

## Missionary Gospel Fellowship

PO Box 1535
Turlock, CA 95381 USA
**Phone:** (209) 634-8575
**Fax:** (209) 634-8472
**E-mail:** mgfhq@mgfhq.org
**Web Site:** www.mgfhq.org

*Mr. A. J. Hyatt III, CEO*

An interdenominational sending agency of Evangelical tradition engaged in multi-ethnic ministries of evangelism, church planting, correspondence courses, discipleship, theological education and member care in the USA, Canada and Mexico.

**Purpose:** "...to share the Gospel and to disciple various ethnic or unreached groups of people in or near the USA."

**Year founded in US:** 1939

**Income for Overseas Min:** $50,000

**Fully Supported US Personnel Overseas:**
Expecting to serve more than 4 years: 19
Non-residential mission personnel: 1

**Other Personnel:**
Bi-vocational/tentmakers: 5
Home ministry & office staff in US: 3

**Countries:** Mexico 19

## Missionary Outreach Support Services (MOSS)

1000 Regent University Dr., CRB 163
Virginia Beach, VA 23464 USA
**Phone:** (757) 226-4341
**E-mail:** support@missionaryoutreach.net
**Web Site:** www.missionaryoutreach.net
**Associations:** AFMA

*Mr. Glen L. Moriarty, Director*

A nondenominational specialized agency of Evangelical tradition engaged in member care, furloughed missionary support, missions information service, leadership development, psychological counseling and relief and/or rehabilitation.

**Year founded in US:** 2005

## Missionary Retreat Fellowship Inc.

R.R. #4, Box 4590
Lake Ariel, PA 18436 USA
**Phone:** (570) 689-2984

**Fax:** (570) 689-2984
**E-mail:** MRF65@juno.com
**Web Site:** www.missionaryretreat.org

*Mr. Donald E. Schuit, Director*

A nondenominational support agency of Evangelical tradition engaged in furloughed missionary support.

**Purpose:** "...to provide the furloughing missionary with fully furnished housing...at subsidized rates."

**Year founded in US:** 1965

## Missionary Revival Crusade

PO Box 764979
Dallas TX 75376-4979 USA
**Phone:** (972) 283-8900
**Fax:** (972) 283-8908
**E-mail:** mrcsupport@sbcglobal.net

*Rev. Roger J. West, President*

A nondenominational support agency engaged in association of missions, church planting, correspondence courses, evangelism, Bible translation and video/film production/distribution.

**Year founded in US:** 1958

**Income for Overseas Min:** $960,939

**Fully Supported US Personnel Overseas:**
Expecting to serve more than 4 years: 43
Expecting to serve 1 to 4 years: 8

**Other Personnel:**
Non-US serving in own/other country: 13
Home ministry & office staff in US: 2

**Countries:** Argentina 2; Brazil 1; Bulgaria; Colombia 1; France 4; Greece; Italy; Mexico 19; Nicaragua 3; Portugal; Russia; Spain 11; United Kingdom; Unspecified Country 2; Venezuela

## Missionary TECH Team

25 FRJ Dr.
Longview, TX 75602 USA
**Phone:** (903) 757-4530
**Fax:** (903) 758-2799
**E-mail:** bwiley@techteam.org
**Web Site:** www.techteam.org
**Associations:** ANAM, IFMA

*Mr. Birne D. Wiley, President*

A nondenominational service agency of Independent tradition engaged in services for other agencies, literature production, management consulting/training, short-term programs, technical assistance and training. Worked in 65 countries on more than 770 projects.

**Purpose:** "...providing technical assistance, 'know-how' and support services to mission organizations around the world."

**Year founded in US:** 1969

**Income for Overseas Min:** $225,000

**Gifts in Kind:** $18,393

**Fully Supported US Personnel Overseas:**
Non-residential mission personnel: 3

**Other Personnel:**
Short-term less than 1 year: 10
Home ministry & office staff in US: 23

## Missionary Ventures Intl.

PO Box 593550
Orlando, FL 32859-3550 USA
**Phone:** (407) 859-7322
**Fax:** (407) 856-7934
**E-mail:** info@mvi.org
**Web Site:** www.mvi.org
*Mr. Steven G. Beam, President/Founder*

An interdenominational specialized agency of Evangelical tradition engaged in support of national churches, childrens programs, church planting, support of national workers and short-term programs.

**Purpose:** "...to encourage and support indigenous missions through personal involvement, financial sponsorship and ministry development."

**Year founded in US:** 1984

**Income for Overseas Min:** $6,031,772

**Fully Supported US Personnel Overseas:**
Expecting to serve more than 4 years: 64
Non-residential mission personnel: 15

**Other Personnel:**
Short-term less than 1 year: 1,800
Non-US serving in own/other country: 30
Home ministry & office staff in US: 14

**Countries:** Belize 2; Bolivia 4; Colombia 2; Costa Rica 1; Dominican Republic 5; Ecuador 4; Egypt; Gabon; Guatemala 8; Haiti 1; Honduras 4; Indonesia 2; Israel; Malaysia; Marshall Islands 2; Mexico 4; Nicaragua 6; Nigeria; Paraguay 2; Peru 8; Philippines 2; Russia; Singapore 1; South Africa; Thailand 2; Uganda; United Kingdom 2; Zambia 2

## Missions Resource Network

4001 Airport FWY, Ste. 550
Bedford, TX 76021 USA
**Phone:** (817) 267-2727
**Fax:** (817) 267-2626
**E-mail:** missions@MRNet.org
**Web Site:** www.MRNet.org
*Mr. Robert T. Waldron, Exec. Director*

A nondenominational service agency of Christian (Restoration Movement) tradition engaged in mobilization for mission, church planting, missions information service, member care, mission-related research and missionary training.

**Purpose:** "...to help churches plant churches worldwide."

**Year founded in US:** 1998

**Income for Overseas Min:** $350,000

**Personnel:**
Home ministry & office staff in US: 10

## Missions To Japan, Inc.

PO Box 1203
Campbell, CA 95009-1203 USA
**Phone:** (408) 998-1768
*Rev. Joe Weigand, President*

An interdenominational support agency of Charismatic and Evangelical tradition engaged in discipleship, Bible distribution, bible memorization, broadcasting, evangelism and funds transmission.

**Purpose:** "...to promote fellowship, cooperation, protection, recognition and the propagation of the Christian Gospel at home and abroad..."

**Year founded in US:** 1959

**Income for Overseas Min:** $17,801

**Personnel:**
Home ministry & office staff in US: 2

## Missions to Military, Inc.

PO Box 6
Norfolk, VA 23501 USA
**Phone:** (757) 479-2288
**Fax:** (757) 479-3705
**E-mail:** hq@mtmi.org
**Web Site:** www.mtmi.org
*Dr. Keith H. Davey, President*

A sending agency of Independent Baptist

tradition engaged in operating military Christian centers for active military personnel. Data from 2001.

**Year founded in US:** 1958

**Income for Overseas Min:** $190,000

**Fully Supported US Personnel Overseas:**
Expecting to serve more than 4 years: 7
Non-residential mission personnel: 7

**Other Personnel:**
Short-term less than 1 year: 2
Home ministry & office staff in US: 6

**Countries:** France 5; Ukraine 2

## MMS Aviation

24387 Airport Rd.
Coshocton, OH 43812 USA

**Phone:** (740) 622-6848
**Fax:** (740) 622-8277
**E-mail:** admin@mmsaviation.org
**Web Site:** www.mmsaviation.org

*Mr. Dwight Jarboe, President/ CEO*

A nondenominational support agency of Evangelical tradition providing technical assistance and training in mission aviation for others.

**Purpose:** "Preparing people and planes for worldwide mission service."

**Year founded in US:** 1975

**Personnel:**
Home ministry & office staff in US: 24

## Moravian Church in North America, Board of World Mission

PO Box 1245
Bethlehem, PA 18016-1245 USA

**Phone:** (610) 868-1732
**Fax:** (610) 868-1732
**E-mail:** will@mcnp.org
**Web Site:** www.moravianmission.org
**Associations:** CWS

*Mr. William C. Sibert, Jr., Exec. Director*

A denominational sending agency of Ecumenical and Moravian tradition engaged in short-term programs, Christian education, leadership development, missionary training and youth programs.

**Year founded in US:** 1742

**Income for Overseas Min:** $1,200,000

**Personnel:**
Short-term less than 1 year: 12
Non-US serving in own/other country: 4
Home ministry & office staff in US: 5

**Countries:** Honduras; Kenya; Tanzania

## Morelli Ministries Intl.

PO Box 700026
Tulsa, OK 74170 USA

**Phone:** (918) 664-2552
**E-mail:** michael@morelliministries.org
**Web Site:** www.morelliministries.org

*Rev. Michael Morelli, Founder-President*

An interdenominational support agency of Evangelical tradition engaged in support of national churches, church planting, evangelism, leadership development, literature distribution and supplying equipment in 7 countries. Statistical data from 1998.

**Year founded in US:** 1995

**Income for Overseas Min:** $32,000

**Fully Supported US Personnel Overseas:**
Non-residential mission personnel: 1

**Other Personnel:**
Short-term less than 1 year: 2
Home ministry & office staff in US: 3

## Mustard Seed, Inc. The See: Mustard Seed Int'l.

## Mustard Seed International

PO Box 20188
Charleston, SC 29413-0188 USA

**Phone:** (843) 388-9314
**Fax:** (843) 388-9315
**E-mail:** info@mustardseed.org
**Web Site:** www.mustardseed.org

*Mr. William N. Deans, President/CEO*

An interdenominational sending agency of Evangelical tradition engaged in Christian education, agricultural programs, childcare/orphanage programs, church planting, TEE and medical work.

**Purpose:** "...to present Christ to all we meet, to heal disease and all manner of suffering and to love sincerely and deeply those people whose lives we are privileged to touch."

**Year founded in US:** 1948

**Income for Overseas Min:** $837,916

**Fully Supported US Personnel Overseas:**
Expecting to serve more than 4 years: 7
**Other Personnel:**
Short-term less than 1 year: 100
**Countries:** India; Indonesia 7; Papua New Guinea; Sudan; Taiwan

## Mutual Faith Ministries Intl.
PO Box 951060
Mission Hills, CA 91395-1060 USA
**Phone:** (818) 837-3400
**Fax:** (818) 837-4686
**E-mail:** ckrouzian@mutualfaith.org
**Web Site:** www.mutualfaith.org
*Keith Hershey, President/Founder*
A nondenominational support agency of Independent tradition engaged in short-term programs for evangelism teams in Central America, Africa, Asia, India and other nations. Financial data from 1998.
**Year founded in US:** 1984
**Income for Overseas Min:** $250,000
**Gifts in Kind:** $100,000
**Fully Supported US Personnel Overseas:**
Expecting to serve more than 4 years: 3
**Other Personnel:**
Short-term less than 1 year: 100
Home ministry & office staff in US: 5
**Countries:** Costa Rica 1; Ghana; Guatemala 2; Lebanon; Nigeria; Philippines

## Narramore Christian Foundation
250 W. Colorado Blvd., Ste. 200
Arcadia, CA 91007 USA
**Phone:** (626) 821-8400
**Fax:** (626) 821-8409
**E-mail:** bruce@ncfliving.org
**Web Site:** www.ncfliving.org
*Dr. Bruce Narramore, President*
A nondenominational specialized agency of Evangelical tradition providing missionary kids reentry training and literature and also helps develop and support overseas missionary counseling and training programs. NCF's ministries include a Christian mental health website, literature on psychological problems and issues, reentry programs for missionary children and overseas seminars for missionaries.

**Purpose:** "…to serve individuals and families through biblically-based psychological counseling, consulting, publications, education, research and training…targeting toward missionaries and pastors and their families, laypersons and counseling/psychology students."
**Year founded in US:** 1958
**Income for Overseas Min:** $48,000
**Personnel:**
Home ministry & office staff in US: 8

## National Baptist Convention of America—Foreign Mission Board
PO Box 223665
Dallas, TX 75222 USA
**Phone:** (214) 507-7567
**E-mail:** glover-c@sbcglobal.net
**Web Site:** www.nbcamerica.net
*Rev. Q.E. Hammonds, Chairman*
A denominational support agency of Baptist tradition engaged in evangelism, church construction, Christian education, funds transmission and support of national workers. Statistical data from 1998.
**Purpose:** "…operates as 'partner in ministry' with indigenous Christians and church bodies."
**Year founded in US:** 1915
**Income for Overseas Min:** $222,071
**Personnel:**
Short-term less than 1 year: 26
Non-US serving in own/other country: 87
Home ministry & office staff in US: 4
**Countries:** Ghana; Haiti; Jamaica; Panama; Virgin Islands

## National Baptist Convention USA, Inc.—Foreign Mission Board
701 South 19th Street
Philadelphia, PA 19146 USA
**Phone:** (215) 735-7868
**Fax:** (215) 735-1721
**E-mail:** FMB@nationalbaptist.com
**Web Site:** www.fmbusainc.org
**Associations:** CWS
*Dr. William J. Shaw, President*

A denominational sending agency of Baptist tradition engaged in evangelism, church construction, church planting, Christian education, furloughed missionary support and providing medical supplies. Data from 2002.

**Purpose:** "...to accomplish the Great Commission by training ministers and mission workers and providing health services and occupational training and services at each mission station with the goal of self-sufficiency."

**Year founded in US:** 1880

**Income for Overseas Min:** $793,787

**Fully Supported US Personnel Overseas:**
Expecting to serve more than 4 years: 1
Expecting to serve 1 to 4 years: 2

**Other Personnel:**
Non-US serving in own/other country: 7
Home ministry & office staff in US: 6

**Countries:** Bahamas, The; Barbados; Guinea 1; Lesotho; Malawi; Nicaragua; Sierra Leone; South Africa; Swaziland; Zambia

## National Religious Broadcasters

9510 Technology Dr.
Manassas, VA 20110 USA

**Phone:** (703) 330-7000
**Fax:** (703) 330-7100
**E-mail:** info@nrb.org
**Web Site:** www.nrb.com

*Dr. Frank Wright, President/CEO*

An interdenominational service agency of Evangelical tradition engaged in broadcasting and leadership development, including a Caribbean chapter and International Committee involving overseas associate members.

**Year founded in US:** 1944

**Personnel:**
Home ministry & office staff in US: 19

## Navigators, U.S. International Missions Group

PO Box 6000
Colorado Springs, CO 80934 USA

**Phone:** (719) 598-1212
**Fax:** (719) 260-0479
**E-mail:** info@usimg.org
**Web Site:** www.usimg.org
**Associations:** EFMA

*Mr. Alan Andrews, U.S. Director*

An interdenominational sending agency of Evangelical tradition engaged in discipleship, evangelism and leadership development. U.S. staff and tentmaker data from 2002.

**Purpose:** "To reach, disciple and equip people to know Christ and to make Him known through successive generations."

**Year founded in US:** 1933

**Income for Overseas Min:** $16,873,357

**Fully Supported US Personnel Overseas:**
Expecting to serve more than 4 years: 301
Expecting to serve 1 to 4 years: 33
Non-residential mission personnel: 21

**Other Personnel:**
Short-term less than 1 year: 272
Bi-vocational/tentmakers: 78
Home ministry & office staff in US: 85

**Countries:** Argentina 6; Australia 6; Brazil 10; Bulgaria 6; Cameroon 4; Chile 4; Costa Rica 1; France 2; Germany; Ghana 1; Guatemala 1; Hungary 3; Iceland 2; Italy 4; Japan 24; Kenya 2; Mexico 8; New Zealand 4; Nigeria 2; Norway 2; Philippines 10; South Africa 4; Spain 8; Taiwan 4; United Kingdom 2; Unspecified Country 179; Zambia 2

## Network of International Christian Schools

PO Box 1260
Southaven, MS 38671 USA

**Phone:** (662) 796-1830
**Fax:** (662) 796-1840
**E-mail:** info@nics.org
**Web Site:** www.nics.org
**Associations:** IFMA

*Dr. Joe Hale, President*

A nondenominational service agency of Evangelical tradition engaged in international Christian education.

**Purpose:** "...to establish a worldwide network of international Christian schools staffed by qualified Christian educators, instilling in each student a Biblical worldview in an environment of academic excellence and respect for people of all cultures and religions."

**Year founded in US:** 1991

**Income for Overseas Min:** $3,120,850

**Fully Supported US Personnel Overseas:**
Expecting to serve more than 4 years: 87

Expecting to serve 1 to 4 years: 236
**Other Personnel:**
Non-US serving in own/other country: 18
Home ministry & office staff in US: 14
**Countries:** Asia—General 5; Bolivia 2; Brazil 6; Central Asia—General 5; Germany 1; Indonesia 6; Japan 2; Kenya 2; Korea, South 48; Peru 2; Singapore 6; Suriname 2

## New Directions Int'l., Inc.

PO Box 2347
Burlington, NC 27216 USA
**Phone:** (336) 227-1273
**Fax:** (336) 570-1392
**E-mail:** ndi@newdirections.org
**Web Site:** www.newdirections.org
**Associations:** EFMA Candidate
*Dr. J. L. Williams, Founder & Director*
A nondenominational support agency of Evangelical tradition engaged in leadership development, childcare/orphanage programs, childrens programs, church construction, church planting, support of national churches and support of national workers.
**Purpose:** "...encouraging, equipping and empowering indigenous national leaders to evangelize the unreached and edify the church in their respective countries."
**Year founded in US:** 1968
**Income for Overseas Min:** $1,339,917
**Gifts in Kind:** $309,102
**Fully Supported US Personnel Overseas:**
Non-residential mission personnel: 4
**Other Personnel:**
Short-term less than 1 year: 4
Non-US serving in own/other country: 81
Home ministry & office staff in US: 15
**Countries:** Bhutan; Haiti; India; Kenya; Nepal

## New Hope International

PO Box 25490
Colorado Springs, CO 80936-5490 USA
**Phone:** (719) 577-4450
**Fax:** (719) 577-4453
**E-mail:** cindy.mefford@newhopeinternational.org
**Web Site:** www.newhopeinternational.org
*Mr. Hank Paulson, President*
A nondenominational support agency of Evangelical tradition engaged in support of national workers, childcare/orphanage programs, leadership development, literature production, support of national churches, partnership development, short-term programs and youth programs.
**Year founded in US:** 1971
**Income for Overseas Min:** $350,000
**Gifts in Kind:** $1,000
**Fully Supported US Personnel Overseas:**
Expecting to serve more than 4 years: 3
Expecting to serve 1 to 4 years: 3
Non-residential mission personnel: 1
**Other Personnel:**
Short-term less than 1 year: 20
Non-US serving in own/other country: 34
Home ministry & office staff in US: 9
**Countries:** Czech Republic; Eastern Europe—General 3; Hungary; Moldova; Romania; Slovakia; Ukraine

## New Life Advance Intl.

PO 35857
Houston, TX 77235 USA
**Phone:** (832) 242-7750
**Fax:** (832) 242-7751
**E-mail:** Info@nlai.org
**Web Site:** www.nlai.org
*Mr. David Depew, President*
A nondenominational sending agency of Charismatic and Evangelical tradition engaged in Bible distribution, childcare/orphanage programs, church planting, development, evangelism, mobilization for mission and relief and/or rehabilitation. Data from 2001.
**Purpose:** "...in partnership with local churches, to make disciples among the nations, to plant churches, to work for the relief of human suffering and to print the Word of God and distribute it to the nations of the world."
**Year founded in US:** 1954
**Income for Overseas Min:** $728,595
**Gifts in Kind:** $8,000
**Fully Supported US Personnel Overseas:**
Expecting to serve more than 4 years: 14
Expecting to serve 1 to 4 years: 1
Non-residential mission personnel: 4
**Other Personnel:**
Short-term less than 1 year: 60

Non-US serving in own/other country: 12
Home ministry & office staff in US: 1

**Countries:** Brazil 1; Bhutan; China; Cuba; Guatemala 6; Haiti 2; India; Israel; Japan; Mexico 1; Nepal; Papua New Guinea; Philippines; Thailand 2; Turkey 2; Ukraine

## New Life League Int'l: See: New Life Advance Int'l.

## New Mission Systems Intl.

PO Box 547
Fort Myers, FL 33902 USA

**Phone:** (239) 337-4336
**Fax:** (239) 461-0686
**E-mail:** info@nms-intl.com
**Web Site:** www.nms-intl.org

*Mr. Phil Hudson, CEO*

A transdenominational sending agency of Christian (Restoration Movement) and Reformed tradition engaged in discipleship, church planting, development, partnership development and short-term programs.

**Purpose:** "...fosters the emergence of Christian communities globally."

**Year founded in US:** 1989

**Income for Overseas Min:** $1,206,601

**Fully Supported US Personnel Overseas:**
  Expecting to serve more than 4 years: 33
  Expecting to serve 1 to 4 years: 2
  Non-residential mission personnel: 2

**Other Personnel:**
  Non-US serving in own/other country: 28
  Home ministry & office staff in US: 50

**Countries:** Asia—General 3; Brazil; Bulgaria 1; Central African Republic; Chile 2; Czech Republic 1; Estonia 1; Germany 1; Haiti; Honduras 2; India 4; Kenya 9; Malawi 3; Middle East 2; Myanmar/Burma; Russia 2; Serbia and Montenegro 2; Zimbabwe

## New Tribes Mission

1000 E. First St.
Sanford, FL 32771 USA

**Phone:** (407) 323-3430
**Fax:** (407) 330-0376
**E-mail:** NTM@ntm.org
**Web Site:** www.ntm.org
**Associations:** IFMA

*Mr. Oli Jacobsen, Chairman*

A nondenominational sending agency of Baptist and Brethren tradition engaged in church planting, linguistics, literacy work and Bible translation.

**Purpose:** "...to assist the ministry of the local church through mobilizing, equipping, and coordinating of missionaries to evangelize unreached people groups, translate the Scriptures, and see indigenous New Testament churches established..."

**Year founded in US:** 1942

**Income for Overseas Min:** $32,400,000

**Gifts in Kind:** $500,000

**Fully Supported US Personnel Overseas:**
  Expecting to serve more than 4 years: 1,402
  Expecting to serve 1 to 4 years: 62
  Non-residential mission personnel: 10

**Other Personnel:**
  Non-US serving in own/other country: 408
  Home ministry & office staff in US: 240

**Countries:** Asia—General 23; Australia 6; Bolivia 97; Brazil 160; Cambodia 2; Colombia 55; Cote d'Ivoire 61; Denmark 2; Germany 2; Greenland 2; Guinea 25; Indonesia 80; Korea, South 2; Malaysia 2; Mexico 80; Mongolia 7; Mozambique 4; Netherlands; Norway; Panama 50; Papua New Guinea 400; Paraguay 60; Philippines 100; Senegal 60; Singapore 2; South Africa 2; Thailand 60; United Kingdom 8; Venezuela 50

## New Way Missions

1501 Loretta Ct.
Brandon, FL 33511 USA

**Phone:** (813) 684-1289
**Fax:** (813) 684-1289
**E-mail:** linda.h.parker@att.net
**Web Site:** www.newwaymissions.org

*Linda H. Parker, Co-Founder/President*

An interdenominational specialized agency of Charismatic and Pentecostal tradition engaged in short-term mission projects/ministry trips, Bible distribution, discipleship, evangelism, medical work and support of national churches.

**Year founded in US:** 2000

**Income for Overseas Min:** $13,470

**Personnel:**
  Short-term less than 1 year: 18

**Countries:** Dominican Republic; Mexico; Peru

## New Wineskins Missionary Network

PO Box 278
Ambridge, PA 15003-0278 USA
**Phone:** (724) 266-2810
**Fax:** (724) 266-6773
**E-mail:** info@newwineskins.org
**Web Site:** www.newwineskins.org
*Sharon Stockdale Steinmiller, Director*

A denominational support agency of Anglican tradition engaged in mobilization for mission, missions information service and missionary training.

**Purpose:** "...a voluntary society, raising mission vision in parishes and dioceses, promoting and providing training for missionaries and mission committees, equipping Anglicans to reach unreached people groups around the world and raising prayer support for Anglican missionaries."

**Year founded in US:** 1974

**Income for Overseas Min:** $5,020

**Personnel:**
   Home ministry & office staff in US: 3

## No Greater Love Ministries, Inc.

PO Box 263
DuQuoin, IL 62832 USA
**Phone:** (618) 542-4503
**Fax:** (618) 542-4503
**E-mail:** NGL1FRED@onecliq.net
**Web Site:** www.nogreaterlove.org
*Rev. Fred L. Bishop, President*

An interdenominational support agency of Evangelical tradition engaged in leadership development, evangelism, literature distribution and short-term programs. Financial data from 1998.

**Purpose:** "...to develop and equip men to become Christian leaders."

**Year founded in US:** 1975

**Income for Overseas Min:** $10,000

**Personnel:**
   Short-term less than 1 year: 40
   Bi-vocational/tentmakers: 2
   Home ministry & office staff in US: 25

## North American Baptist Conference—Worldwide Outreach

1 S. 210 Summit Ave.
Oakbrook Terrace, IL 60181 USA
**Phone:** (630) 495-2000
**Fax:** (630) 495-3301
**E-mail:** jblack@nabconf.org
**Web Site:** www.nabconference.org
**Associations:** EFMA

*Rev. Jim Black, Sr. Leader/Worldwide Outreach*

A denominational sending agency of Baptist tradition engaged in church planting, childcare/orphanage programs, theological education, medical work, mobilization for mission and relief and/or rehabilitation.

**Purpose:** "...to glorify God by making disciplemakers of Jesus Christ internationally on behalf of and with the churches of the North American Baptist Conference."

**Year founded in US:** 1891

**Income for Overseas Min:** $2,865,639

**Fully Supported US Personnel Overseas:**
   Expecting to serve more than 4 years: 25
   Expecting to serve 1 to 4 years: 4
**Other Personnel:**
   Short-term less than 1 year: 56
   Non-US serving in own/other country: 26
   Home ministry & office staff in US: 9

**Countries:** Brazil 1; Cameroon 11; Japan 9; Mexico 2; Nigeria 2

## Northwest Medical Teams International, Inc.

PO Box 10
Portland, OR 97207-0010 USA
**Phone:** (800) 959-4325
**Fax:** (503) 624-1001
**E-mail:** info@nwmti.org
**Web Site:** www.nwmedicalteams.org
**Associations:** AERDO

*Mr. Bas Vanderzalm, President*

An interdenominational specialized agency engaged in medical work and volunteers, development, providing medical supplies, psychological counseling and relief and/or rehabilitation.

**Purpose:** "...to demonstrate the love of Christ to people affected by disaster, conflict and poverty."

# *Be Prepared for Today's Missions Opportunities*

The Great Commission challenges believers to be on mission with Jesus, equipped with both the knowledge and personal experience of the gospel. As you respond to God's call to cross-cultural ministry, consider enhancing your effectiveness through the Avery T. Willis Center for Global Outreach at Oklahoma Baptist University.

**Resources include:**
- Orality Studies
- Missiological Research
- Global Outreach Trips
- Academic Preparation

## Learn more at www.obu-go.org

**Avery T. Willis Center**

*for* **Global Outreach**

## Oklahoma Baptist University
OBU Box 61143 | 500 W. University | Shawnee, OK 74804

**405.878.2372 • 800.654.3285 • go@okbu.edu**

# Hope for East Asia

## SIX WAYS YOU CAN GIVE EAST ASIA HOPE:

❖ GO SHORT-TERM OR LONG-TERM

❖ PRAY FOR EAST ASIA'S PEOPLES

❖ SEND WORKERS

❖ MOBILIZE WORKERS, PRAYER AND SUPPORT

❖ WELCOME EAST ASIANS WHO LIVE HERE

❖ LEARN ABOUT EAST ASIA AND ITS NEEDS

WWW.US.OMF.ORG
INFO@OMF.ORG
800-422-5330

SINCE 1865
CHINA INLAND MISSION

OMF
INTERNATIONAL

Year founded in US: 1979
Income for Overseas Min: $225,202,506
Gifts in Kind: $216,233,732
Fully Supported US Personnel Overseas:
Expecting to serve 1 to 4 years: 6
Other Personnel:
Short-term less than 1 year: 937
Non-US serving in own/other country: 204
Home ministry & office staff in US: 25
Countries: Cambodia; Indonesia; Liberia; Mexico; Moldova; Sri Lanka; Sudan; Tajikistan; Uganda; Uzbekistan; Vietnam

## OC International, Inc.
PO Box 36900
Colorado Springs, CO 80936-6900 USA
Phone: (719) 592-9292
Fax: (719) 592-0693
E-mail: info@oci.org
Web Site: www.onechallenge.org
Associations: EFMA
*Dr. Greg Gripentrog, President*
A nondenominational sending agency of Evangelical tradition engaged in leadership development, church planting, theological education, support of national churches, partnership development, mission-related research and missionary training.
Purpose: "Using research, motivation and training, we mobilize church leaders to reach their nations and beyond."
Year founded in US: 1950
Income for Overseas Min: $8,253,133
Fully Supported US Personnel Overseas:
Expecting to serve more than 4 years: 200
Non-residential mission personnel: 6
Other Personnel:
Short-term less than 1 year: 819
Bi-vocational/tentmakers: 3
Non-US serving in own/other country: 17
Home ministry & office staff in US: 20
Countries: Argentina; Brazil 13; Bulgaria 4; Colombia 2; Germany 13; Guatemala 13; India; Japan 2; Kenya 6; Mexico 4; Mozambique 2; Philippines 18; Romania 11; Singapore 6; South Africa 14; Spain 13; Taiwan 5; United Kingdom 4; Unspecified Country 70

## OMF International
(See ad on page 264)
10 W. Dry Creek Cir.
Littleton, CO 80120 USA
Phone: (800) 422-5330
Fax: (303) 730-4165
E-mail: omfus@omf.org
Web Site: www.us.omf.org
Associations: IFMA
*Dr. Neil O.Thompson, US Natl. Director*
An interdenominational sending agency of Evangelical tradition engaged in church planting, development, evangelism, leadership development and mobilization for mission.
Purpose: "...to see an indigenous biblical church movement in each people group of East Asia, evangelizing their own people and reaching out in mission to other peoples."
Year founded in US: 1888
Income for Overseas Min: $9,800,000
Fully Supported US Personnel Overseas:
Expecting to serve more than 4 years: 251
Expecting to serve 1 to 4 years: 42
Non-residential mission personnel: 6
Other Personnel:
Short-term less than 1 year: 200
Bi-vocational/tentmakers: 150
Non-US serving in own/other country: 629
Home ministry & office staff in US: 15
Countries: Asia—General 133; Cambodia 23; Japan 25; Philippines 15; Singapore 3; Taiwan 8; Thailand 44

## OMS International, Inc.
PO Box A
941 Fry Rd.
Greenwood, IN 46142 USA
Phone: (317) 881-6751
Fax: (317) 888-5275
E-mail: info@omsinternational.org
Web Site: www.omsinternational.org
Associations: EFMA
*Rev. David Long, President*
An interdenominational sending agency of Evangelical and Wesleyan tradition engaged in evangelism, church planting, broadcasting, TEE, theological education, mobilization for mission and missionary training.
Purpose: "...to reach around the world with the good news of Jesus Christ...in co-

operation with national churches..."

**Year founded in US:** 1901

**Income for Overseas Min:** $16,000,000

**Gifts in Kind:** $694,073

**Fully Supported US Personnel Overseas:**
Expecting to serve more than 4 years: 125
Expecting to serve 1 to 4 years: 2

**Other Personnel:**
Short-term less than 1 year: 522
Bi-vocational/tentmakers: 5
Non-US serving in own/other country: 73
Home ministry & office staff in US: 105

**Countries:** Australia; Brazil 6; China 3; Colombia 6; Ecuador 7; Haiti 10; Hong Kong 5; Hungary 8; India 1; Indonesia 9; Ireland 1; Japan 12; Kazakhstan 1; Korea, South 2; Mexico 9; Mozambique 8; Philippines 6; Russia 5; South Africa; Spain 11; Taiwan 5; Ukraine 4; United Kingdom; Unspecified Country; Uruguay 6

## On The Go Ministries/Keith Cook Evangelistic Association

PO Box 963
Springfield, TN 37172 USA

**Phone:** (615) 299-0222
**Fax:** (615) 299-0232
**E-mail:** keithcook@onthego.org
**Web Site:** www.onthego.org

*Rev. Keith Cook, President*

A transdenominational support agency of Evangelical tradition engaged in evangelism, leadership development, short-term programs, training and youth programs in 9 countries. Data from 2001.

**Year founded in US:** 1980

**Income for Overseas Min:** $200,000

**Gifts in Kind:** $100,000

**Fully Supported US Personnel Overseas:**
Non-residential mission personnel: 12

**Other Personnel:**
Short-term less than 1 year: 1,000
Bi-vocational/tentmakers: 4
Home ministry & office staff in US: 12

## Open Air Campaigners— Overseas Ministries

PO Box 602
Woodstock, GA 30188 USA

**Phone:** (770) 924-9055

**E-mail:** david.wilson@oaci.org
**Web Site:** www.oacom.org

*Rev. David Wilson, Director*

An interdenominational ministry of evangelism of Evangelical tradition engaged in evangelism and training. Each national branch is autonomous, with national evangelists.

**Purpose:** "committed to preaching the gospel to the unreached through open air and other outreaches in partnership with the church."

**Year founded in US:** 1989

**Income for Overseas Min:** $467,631

**Fully Supported US Personnel Overseas:**
Expecting to serve more than 4 years: 32
Expecting to serve 1 to 4 years: 18
Non-residential mission personnel: 1

**Other Personnel:**
Non-US serving in own/other country: 50
Home ministry & office staff in US: 1

**Countries:** Brazil 2; Ecuador 2; India 22; Jamaica 2; Mexico; Paraguay 4; Russia; Ukraine

## Open Bible Churches, International Ministries

2020 Bell Ave.
Des Moines, IA 50315 USA

**Phone:** (515) 288-6761
**Fax:** (515) 288-2510
**E-mail:** missions@openbible.org
**Web Site:** www.openbible.org/intl

**Associations:** EFMA

*Rev. Paul V. Canfield, Exec. Director*

A denominational sending agency of Pentecostal and Charismatic tradition engaged in church planting, church construction, TEE, evangelism, leadership development and support of national churches.

**Purpose:** "...exists to serve, equip and resource churches, missionaries and leaders committed to global evangelism, discipleship and church planting."

**Year founded in US:** 1935

**Income for Overseas Min:** $1,953,301

**Fully Supported US Personnel Overseas:**
Expecting to serve more than 4 years: 21

**Other Personnel:**
Home ministry & office staff in US: 4

**Countries:** Africa—General 2; Australia 2; Central Asia—General 1; Eastern Europe—

General 2; El Salvador 2; Guinea 2; Mexico 6; Nicaragua 2; Papua New Guinea 2

## Open Bible Standard Churches, Int'l. Ministries
See: Open Bible Churches, International Ministries

## Open Door Baptist Missions
1115 Pelham Rd.
Greenville, SC 29615 USA
**Phone:** (864) 297-7890
**Fax:** (864) 297-5222
**E-mail:** info@odbm.org
**Web Site:** www.odbm.org
*Dr. John Burnette, Director*

A sending agency of Independent Baptist and Fundamental tradition engaged in church planting, Bible distribution, evangelism, leadership development, literature distribution and support of national churches. Statistics from 1998.

**Purpose:** "...to promote the work of Christ in regions that have been closed to the gospel or that presently have little or no fundamental gospel witness."

**Year founded in US:** 1990

**Income for Overseas Min:** $265,500

**Fully Supported US Personnel Overseas:**
Expecting to serve more than 4 years: 17

**Other Personnel:**
Short-term less than 1 year: 1
Non-US serving in own/other country: 2
Home ministry & office staff in US: 15

**Countries:** Haiti 4; India; Israel 2; Lithuania 4; Puerto Rico 2; Senegal 2; Spain 2; Taiwan 1

## Open Doors with Brother Andrew USA
PO Box 27001
Santa Ana, CA 92799 USA
**Phone:** (949) 752-6600
**Fax:** (949) 752-6442
**E-mail:** usa@opendoors.org
**Web Site:** www.opendoorsusa.org
*Mr. Carl A. Moeller, President/CEO*

A nondenominational support agency of Evangelical tradition engaged in Bible distribution to persecuted Christians, leadership development, literacy work, literature distribution, support of national churches and relief and/or rehabilitation.

**Purpose:** "To strengthen and equip the Body of Christ living under or facing restriction and persecution because of their faith in Jesus Christ, and to encourage their involvement in world evangelism."

**Year founded in US:** 1973

**Income for Overseas Min:** $6,016,038

**Gifts in Kind:** $98,592

**Personnel:**
Home ministry & office staff in US: 39

## Operation Blessing International Relief and Development Corporation
977 Centerville Turnpike
Virginia Beach, VA 23463 USA
**Phone:** (757) 226-3401
**Fax:** (757) 226-6228
**E-mail:** operation.blessing@ob.org
**Web Site:** www.ob.org
**Associations:** AERDO
*Mr. William Horan, President/COO*

A nondenominational relief agency that has helped more than 184.9 million people in 96 countries, distributing more than $1.1 billion in goods. Engaged in hunger relief, medical aid, disaster relief, childrens programs and community development that will make a significant, long-term impact. Operating methodology focuses on capacity building and collaboration between indigenously-staffed field offices and local indigenous partners (including other NGOs, government agencies, community-based social service agencies, and grassroots relief groups) .

**Purpose:** "...to demonstrate God's love by alleviating human need and suffering in the United States and around the world."

**Year founded in US:** 1978

**Personnel:**
Home ministry & office staff in US: 85

## Operation Mobilization
PO Box 444
Tyrone, GA 30290 USA
**Phone:** (770) 631-0432
**Fax:** (770) 631-0439
**E-mail:** info@usa.om.org

**Web Site:** www.usa.om.org
**Associations:** EFMA
*Dr. Rick Hicks, President*
An interdenominational sending agency of Evangelical tradition engaged in evangelism, church planting, development, literature distribution, mobilization for mission and missionary training.
**Purpose:** "...to motivate, develop and equip people for world evangelization, and to strengthen and help plant churches, especially among the unreached in the Middle East, South and Central Asia and Europe."
**Year founded in US:** 1957
**Income for Overseas Min:** $9,800,000
**Gifts in Kind:** $305,000
**Fully Supported US Personnel Overseas:**
  Expecting to serve more than 4 years: 173
  Expecting to serve 1 to 4 years: 158
**Other Personnel:**
  Short-term less than 1 year: 458
  Bi-vocational/tentmakers: 11
  Non-US serving in own/other country: 67
  Home ministry & office staff in US: 128
**Countries:** Africa—General 13; Albania 2; Asia—General 2; Australia; Belgium 5; Caucasus; Central Asia—General 17; Chile; Czech Republic 1; Egypt 7; Europe—General 14; France 2; Hungary 3; India 7; Ireland 2; Israel; Italy 4; Latin America—General 6; Mexico 2; Middle East 23; Nepal 2; Netherlands; Romania; Russia; South Africa 6; Spain 3; Sweden 1; Turkey 8; Ukraine; United Kingdom 21; Unspecified Country 21; Uzbekistan 1

## Opportunity International
2122 York Rd., Ste. 340
Oak Brook, IL 60523 USA
**Phone:** (630) 242-4100
**Fax:** (630) 645-1458
**E-mail:** getinfo@opportunity.org
**Web Site:** www.opportunity.org
*Mr. Christopher A. Crane, President/CEO*
An interdenominational service agency of Ecumenical tradition engaged in microfinancing, leadership development, funds transmission and training, working in 26 countries.
**Purpose:** "...to provide opportunities for people in chronic poverty to transform their lives."

**Year founded in US:** 1971
**Income for Overseas Min:** $112,064,000
**Personnel:**
  Home ministry & office staff in US: 65

## Orthodox Presbyterian Church—Committee on Foreign Missions
PO Box P
Willow Grove, PA 19090-0920 USA
**Phone:** (215) 830-0900
**Fax:** (215) 830-0350
**E-mail:** OPForeignMissions@opc.org
**Web Site:** www.opc.org
*Mr. Mark T. Bube, Gen. Secretary*
A denominational sending agency committed to the establishment of indigenous churches in the Presbyterian and Reformed tradition, primarily through the ministry of the Word. Actively engaged in church planting, theological education, evangelism and literature distribution, medicine and national church support. Medical ministries of mercy supplement the gospel proclamation.
**Year founded in US:** 1937
**Income for Overseas Min:** $2,200,000
**Fully Supported US Personnel Overseas:**
  Expecting to serve more than 4 years: 30
  Expecting to serve 1 to 4 years: 14
  Non-residential mission personnel: 2
**Other Personnel:**
  Short-term less than 1 year: 35
  Bi-vocational/tentmakers: 14
  Home ministry & office staff in US: 4
**Countries:** China 4; Eritrea 4; Haiti 2; Japan 8; Korea, South 2; Suriname 2; Uganda 8

## Outreach To Asia Nationals
PO Box 2440
Winchester, VA 22604 USA
**Phone:** (540) 665-6418
**Fax:** (540) 665-0793
**E-mail:** outreachtoasianationals@mailbox20.com
**Associations:** IFMA
*Mr. Otis S. Goodwin, President/CEO*
A denominational support agency of Baptist and Independent tradition engaged in support of national workers, Bible distribution, childcare/orphanage programs, church

**Buy a variety of
International Insurance
Products online at**

**www.globalNsure.com**

- tripNsure
- usaNsure
- healthNsure
- bizNsure
- studentNsure
- termNsure
- warRisk

**Review Products**

**Apply and Pay Online
Via Secure Server**

# Choose a *FREE* gift
# when you subscribe
### or renew your subscription

**International Bulletin**

Vol. 30, No. 2
April 2006

**Beyond Babel: Pentecost and Mission**

**On Page**

**of Missionary Research**

**Every issue offers thought-provoking research and reflection. You will receive:**

- Reports on mission trends and major conferences
- Annual statistical updates on global Christianity
- Profiles of current and past missionary leaders
- Book reviews and notices

**Subscription options and current issues online. Visit www.omsc.org/onlinehelp.html for details.**

Visit www.OMSC.org/ibmr.html to purchase a subscription using a credit card, call (203) 624-6672, ext. 309, or mail a check payable in U.S. funds to: *IBMR*, P.O. Box 3000, Denville, NJ 07834

Published quarterly by the
**OVERSEAS MINISTRIES
STUDY CENTER**

3A10

---

# Invest your
# SUMMER
# in research and writing

Mission scholars and their families are welcome to apply for short-term summer residency.

Send your summer reservation request to:
Judy C. Stebbins, Director of Finance and Housing,
**Overseas Ministries Study Center**
490 Prospect Street
New Haven, CT 06511 USA
stebbins@OMSC.org

Current weekly rates are online. Discount of $25 per week for members of American Society of Missiology (ASM), Association of Professors of Mission (APM), International Association for Mission Studies (IAMS), Evangelical Missiological Society (EMS), and International Association of Catholic Missiologists (IACM).

**www.OMSC.org/summer.pdf**

planting, theological education, evangelism and translation work.

**Purpose:** "...to serve, train, equip and empower national church workers in Asia to plant evangelistic, disciple-making and reproducing churches among the different people groups."

**Year founded in US:** 1986

**Income for Overseas Min:** $1,300,000

**Fully Supported US Personnel Overseas:**
  Expecting to serve more than 4 years: 7
  Expecting to serve 1 to 4 years: 11

**Other Personnel:**
  Short-term less than 1 year: 188
  Non-US serving in own/other country: 188
  Home ministry & office staff in US: 45

**Countries:** Asia—General 7; Central Asia—General

## Overseas Council Intl.

PO Box 17368
Indianapolis, IN 46217 USA

**Phone:** (317) 788-7250
**Fax:** (317) 788-7257
**E-mail:** Info@overseas.org
**Web Site:** www.overseas.org
**Associations:** EFMA Candidate

*Dr. David A. Baer, President/CEO*

An interdenominational support agency of Evangelical tradition engaged in establishing partnerships between Western Christians and non-Western students and evangelical theological schools. Affiliated organizations in Australia, Canada, Europe, New Zealand, and UK.

**Purpose:** "...to equip biblical leaders to be effective pastors, teachers, evangelists, missionaries and Christian leaders in their own countries."

**Year founded in US:** 1974

**Income for Overseas Min:** $3,370,383

**Personnel:**
  Home ministry & office staff in US: 28

## Overseas Ministries Study Center

**(See ad on page 270)**

490 Prospect St.
New Haven, CT 06511 USA

**Phone:** (203) 624-6672

**Fax:** (203) 865-2857
**Web Site:** www.omsc.org

*Dr. Jonathan J. Bonk, Exec. Director*

A nondenominational study center of Ecumenical tradition providing education and related activities. Publishes the "International Bulletin of Missionary Research" and the "Dictionary of African Christian Biography" (web only at www.dacb.org) .

**Purpose:** "...to strengthen the Christian world mission by providing residential programs for the renewal of missionaries and international church leaders, continuing education in cross-cultural Christian ministries and advancement of mission scholarship through research and publication."

**Year founded in US:** 1922

**Personnel:**
  Home ministry & office staff in US: 17

## Overseas Radio & Television, Inc. (ORTV)

130 S. First St.
Arcadia, CA 91006 USA

**Phone:** (626) 462-0880
**Fax:** (626) 462-0008
**E-mail:** susan@ortv.com
**Web Site:** www.ortv.com

*Susan Cheng, Director N. America*

An interdenominational support agency engaged in TESOL, audio recording/distribution, extension education, evangelism, short-term programs and video/film production/distribution.

**Year founded in US:** 1952

**Fully Supported US Personnel Overseas:**
  Non-residential mission personnel: 20

**Other Personnel:**
  Bi-vocational/tentmakers: 5
  Non-US serving in own/other country: 225
  Home ministry & office staff in US: 12

**Countries:** Taiwan

## Palm Missionary Ministries

**(See ad on page 273)**

1702 Parks Lake Rd.
Lake Wales, FL 33898-8430 USA

**Phone:** (863) 696-7131
**Fax:** (863) 696-7122
**E-mail:** info@palmministries.com

**Web Site:** www.palmministries.com

*Mr. Arthur B. Patray, President/CEO*

An interdenominational sending agency of Evangelical tradition engaged in support of national workers, church planting, Christian education, support of national churches and national prison ministry.

**Purpose:** "...to enable and facilitate the development of national missionaries and workers to go into all nations."

**Year founded in US:** 1987

**Income for Overseas Min:** $292,091

**Fully Supported US Personnel Overseas:**
Expecting to serve more than 4 years: 1
Expecting to serve 1 to 4 years: 1

**Other Personnel:**
Short-term less than 1 year: 90
Non-US serving in own/other country: 40
Home ministry & office staff in US: 2

**Countries:** Bolivia; Colombia; Ecuador 1; Mexico; Spain

## Pan American Missions

PO Box 710097
Santee, CA 92072-0097 USA

**Phone:** (619) 469-0970
**Fax:** (619) 469-0970
**E-mail:** dllasher@cox.net

*Mr. Fred Jappe, President*

An interdenominational support agency of Baptist and Wesleyan tradition engaged in Bible distribution, childcare/orphanage programs and church planting.

**Purpose:** "...ministers in Mexico and other Spanish-speaking countries of Latin America for the establishing and building up of indigenous churches."

**Year founded in US:** 1960

**Income for Overseas Min:** $33,000

**Fully Supported US Personnel Overseas:**
Expecting to serve more than 4 years: 2

**Other Personnel:**
Home ministry & office staff in US: 2

**Countries:** Mexico 2

## Paraclete, Inc.

PO Box 6507
Mesa, AZ 85216 USA

**Phone:** (480) 854-4444
**Fax:** (480) 854-4741

**E-mail:** info@paraclete.net
**Web Site:** www.paraclete.net
**Associations:** EFMA Candidate

*Rev. Donald Parrott, President/CEO*

A nondenominational sending agency of Evangelical tradition engaged in services for other agencies, church planting, leadership development, management consulting/training, member care and missionary training.

**Purpose:** "...to come alongside mission agencies and churches to help them strengthen their efforts to share God's love with those who have least access to the gospel."

**Year founded in US:** 1988

**Income for Overseas Min:** $180,625

**Fully Supported US Personnel Overseas:**
Expecting to serve 1 to 4 years: 4
Non-residential mission personnel: 17

**Other Personnel:**
Short-term less than 1 year: 11
Home ministry & office staff in US: 10

**Countries:** Bangladesh; China; India; Kosovo; Pakistan; Turkey

## Partners in Asian Missions

PO Box 531011
Birmingham, AL 35253 USA

**Phone:** (205) 854-8418
**E-mail:** js1@quickbox.com
**Web Site:** www.pam-ee.org

*Rev. Jerry F. Sharpe, Intl. Director*

A nondenominational support agency of Reformed tradition engaged in support of national workers, childcare/orphanage programs, church construction, church planting, evangelism and leadership development.

**Purpose:** "...to mobilize and equip top leaders in every Asian country for developing and implementing an effective national church-planting project...to enlist groups that will take responsibility for evangelization of a particular geographic territory or ethnolinguistic group..."

**Year founded in US:** 1972

**Income for Overseas Min:** $150,000

**Fully Supported US Personnel Overseas:**
Non-residential mission personnel: 1

**Other Personnel:**
Non-US serving in own/other country: 159

**PALM MISSIONARY MINISTRIES, INC**

# NATIONAL PASTORS'/MINISTRIES' EMPOWERMENT

By recruiting, training, placing and supporting National pastors and workers in their own countries, while instilling accountability measures in their practices. Also through various kinds of ministerial assistance including financial help, prayer base, community projects, and work teams (construction, healthcare, medical and dental) for existing national churches and para church ministries (prison, educational, camping, homeless, etc.).

*"Missions-inclined Christians really desire closer contact with their missionaries and their outreach in the field. They also want to know that their financial gifts are being used for the purposes intended. PMM provides an organized administrative structure for national pastors, missionaries and independent ministries that assures accountability is always maintained in the areas of doctrine, work ethic/integrity and finances. PMM national affiliates also teach Biblical Stewardship to their flocks, a vital step in becoming a spiritually balanced people. Such measures build trust as well as good and personal relationships with their supporting partners. "*
Art Patray, Palm Missionary Ministries, Inc.

### Presently Working in:
Bolivia, Ecuador, Mexico, Spain and the U.S.A.

Areas of ministry include church planting, evangelism, schools/education, healthcare, camping, prisons, community development, delinquents, leadership training, projects, short-term missionaries, radio and television production, video productions, and, seconding trained Latin nationals to other missions working in other countries.

**ECFA**

**CONTACT US:**
www.palmministries.com
**HEADQUARTERS:**
1702 Parks Lake Road. Lake Wales. FL.33898-8430 Phone:(863)696-7131 Fax:(863)696-7122
**GIFTS/BOOKKEPING:**
1315 Campo Sano Avenue. Coral Gables, FL 33146-1165 Phone:(305)665-0903 Fax:(305)665-0859

# PARTNERS
*International*

• LIVES •

• CHURCHES •

• LEADERS •

• COMMUNITIES •

www.partnersintl.org

Home ministry & office staff in US: 1
Countries: Asia—General

## Partners in Christ Intl.

PO Box 237
Tempe, AZ 85280 USA
**Phone:** (480) 731-9170
**Fax:** (480) 731-9166
**E-mail:** partnersinchrist@qwest.net
**Web Site:** www.partnersinchrist-intl.org
*Mr. Nicholas J. Beezhold, Exec. Director*

A nondenominational sending agency of Evangelical tradition engaged in short-term programs, Bible distribution, broadcasting, TEE, theological education and medical work.

**Purpose:** "Bringing people together across geographical and cultural boundaries for ministry together as we impact the world for Christ."

**Year founded in US:** 1986
**Income for Overseas Min:** $300,000
**Fully Supported US Personnel Overseas:**
  Expecting to serve more than 4 years: 1
  Non-residential mission personnel: 1
**Other Personnel:**
  Short-term less than 1 year: 1
  Non-US serving in own/other country: 4
  Home ministry & office staff in US: 1
**Countries:** Mexico 1

## Partners International
**(See ad page 274)**
1117 E. Westview Ct.
Spokane, WA 99218 USA
**Phone:** (509) 343-4000
**Fax:** (509) 343-4015
**E-mail:** info@partnersintl.org
**Web Site:** www.partnersintl.org
**Associations:** EFMA, IFMA
*Mr. Jon Lewis, President/CEO*

A nondenominational sending agency of Evangelical tradition engaged in partnership development, development, funds transmission, leadership development, support of national churches and support of national workers.

**Purpose:** "...to multiply the effectiveness of indigenous Christian ministries who are taking Christ to neglected peoples around the world."

**Year founded in US:** 1943
**Income for Overseas Min:** $10,636,414
**Gifts in Kind:** $2,678,000
**Fully Supported US Personnel Overseas:**
  Expecting to serve more than 4 years: 9
  Non-residential mission personnel: 5
**Other Personnel:**
  Short-term less than 1 year: 50
  Bi-vocational/tentmakers: 1
  Non-US serving in own/other country: 4325
  Home ministry & office staff in US: 49
**Countries:** Africa—General; Asia—General 6; Bangladesh; Cambodia; China 1; Egypt; Ghana; Hong Kong; India; Indonesia; Iran; Iraq; Jordan; Liberia; Malaysia; Mali; Middle East 2; Myanmar/Burma; Philippines; Senegal; Sudan; Taiwan; Thailand; Turkey

## Pass the Torch Ministries
PO Box 7392
Bismarck, ND 58507 USA
**Phone:** (701) 667-6325
**E-mail:** ptm@btinet.net
*Mr. Greg S. Runyon, President*

A nondenominational support agency of Christian (Restoration Movement) and Charismatic tradition engaged in training, church planting, discipleship and leadership development.

**Purpose:** "...to train national Christian leaders."

**Year founded in US:** 1988
**Income for Overseas Min:** $11,060
**Fully Supported US Personnel Overseas:**
  Expecting to serve more than 4 years: 2
**Other Personnel:**
  Short-term less than 1 year: 3
  Non-US serving in own/other country: 4
  Home ministry & office staff in US: 2
**Countries:** Philippines 1; Thailand 1

## Pentecostal Church of God— World Missions Department
PO Box 2248
Joplin, MO 64803 USA
**Phone:** (417) 624-7050
**Fax:** (417) 624-7102
**E-mail:** wm@pcg.org
**Web Site:** www.pcg.org
*Loyd L. Naten, Director of World Missions*

A denominational sending agency of Pentecostal tradition engaged in church planting, support of national churches, support of national workers, church construction, evangelism, and literature/Bible distribution. Statistical information from 1998.

**Year founded in US:** 1919

**Income for Overseas Min:** $1,367,284

**Fully Supported US Personnel Overseas:**
  Expecting to serve more than 4 years: 32

**Other Personnel:**
  Home ministry & office staff in US: 4

**Countries:** Africa—General 4; Belize 2; Bolivia 2; Haiti 2; Honduras 2; India 2; Mexico 6; Nicaragua 2; Philippines 6; Russia 2; Trinidad and Tobago 2

## Pentecostal Free Will Baptist Church, Inc.— World Witness Dept.

PO Box 1568
Dunn, NC 28335 USA
**Phone:** (910) 892-4161
**Fax:** (910) 892-6876
**E-mail:** dockhpfwbc@intrstar.net
**Web Site:** www.pfwb.org

*Dr. Preston Heath, Gen. Superintendent*

A denominational sending agency of Holiness, Pentecostal and Wesleyan tradition engaged in church planting, Church revitalization, missions, extension education, theological education, funds transmission, furloughed missionary support, member care and youth programs.

**Year founded in US:** 1600

**Fully Supported US Personnel Overseas:**
  Expecting to serve more than 4 years: 2

**Other Personnel:**
  Short-term less than 1 year: 50
  Non-US serving in own/other country: 10
  Home ministry & office staff in US: 2

**Countries:** Costa Rica; Dominican Republic; Guatemala; Honduras; Mexico; Nicaragua; Nigeria; Peru; Philippines 2; Puerto Rico; Venezuela

## Pentecostal Holiness Church See: Intl. Pentecostal Holiness Church World Missions Ministries

## People International USA

PO Box 3005
Vancouver, WA 98668-3005 USA
**Phone:** (360) 567-3757
**Fax:** (360) 567-3757
**E-mail:** peoplemail@msn.com
**Web Site:** www.gopeople.org

*Mr. Tom Houser, Exec. Director*

An interdenominational sending agency of Evangelical tradition engaged in church planting, childcare/orphanage programs, development, medical work, tentmaking and Bible translation.

**Purpose:** "...to see churches established that proclaim the Good News among the Muslim peoples of Central Asia and model true Christian living on the example of Jesus Christ."

**Year founded in US:** 1987

**Income for Overseas Min:** $910,000

**Gifts in Kind:** $10,000

**Fully Supported US Personnel Overseas:**
  Expecting to serve more than 4 years: 27
  Expecting to serve 1 to 4 years: 11
  Non-residential mission personnel: 4

**Other Personnel:**
  Short-term less than 1 year: 25
  Bi-vocational/tentmakers: 4
  Non-US serving in own/other country: 11
  Home ministry & office staff in US: 5

**Countries:** Afghanistan 5; Caucasus 1; Kazakhstan 5; Kyrgyzstan 2; Pakistan; Tajikistan; Turkey 4; Turkmenistan; United Kingdom; Uzbekistan 10

## Perimeter Church, Global Outreach

9500 Medlock Bridge Pkwy.
Duluth, GA 30097 USA
**Phone:** (678) 405-2270
**Fax:** (678) 405-2008
**E-mail:** allisonb@perimeter.org
**Web Site:** www.perimeter.org/globaloutreach
**Associations:** EFMA Candidate

*Mr. Tom Mullis, Dir. Global Outreach*

A denominational support agency of Presbyterian tradition engaged in support of national churches, childcare/orphanage programs, church planting, development, disability assistance programs, Christian education, theological education, evangelism, leadership development, management consulting/training, medical work, member care, support of national workers, partnership development, mobilization for mission, relief and/or rehabilitation, mission-related research, short-term programs and missionary training.

**Purpose:** "To faciliate movements of discipleship-based, saturation church planting in the United States and abroad by providing strategic, human and financial resources to Perimeter Ministries International and to nationals of other countries who share our vision for planting churches..."

**Year founded in US:** 1996

**Income for Overseas Min:** $1,100,000

**Fully Supported US Personnel Overseas:**
   Non-residential mission personnel: 3

**Other Personnel:**
   Short-term less than 1 year: 309
   Home ministry & office staff in US: 7

**Countries:** China; India; Russia; Tanzania; Thailand

## Persecuted Church Fellowship See: Ukrainian Children's Fund

## Peter Deyneka Russian Ministries

PO Box 496
Wheaton, IL 60189 USA

**Phone:** (630) 462-1739
**Fax:** (630) 690-2976
**E-mail:** info@russian-ministries.org
**Web Site:** www.russian-ministries.org
**Associations:** EFMA

*Mrs. Anita Deyneka, President*

An interdenominational support agency of Evangelical tradition engaged in literature distribution, camping programs, church planting, extension education, evangelism, support of national workers and youth programs.

**Purpose:** "To promote indigenous evangelism, church planting and church growth in the former Soviet Union by developing creative and strategic ministries and facilitating partnerships between nationals and Western Christians."

**Year founded in US:** 1991

**Income for Overseas Min:** $7,121,303
**Gifts in Kind:** $4,880,417
**Personnel:**
   Short-term less than 1 year: 2
   Home ministry & office staff in US: 9
**Countries:** Belarus; Latvia; Russia; Ukraine

## Pillar of Fire Missions Intl.

1302 Sherman St.
Denver, CO 80203 USA

**Phone:** (303) 839-1500
**Fax:** (303) 832-8560
**E-mail:** pillaroffiredenver@msn.com

*Rev. Bernard Dawson, Director*

A sending agency of Holiness tradition engaged in Christian education, church construction, theological education and support of national workers.

**Year founded in US:** 1960

**Income for Overseas Min:** $113,204
**Personnel:**
   Home ministry & office staff in US: 2

## Pioneer Bible Translators

7500 W. Camp Wisdom Rd.
Dallas, TX 75137 USA

**Phone:** (972) 708-7460
**Fax:** (972) 708-7463
**E-mail:** secretary@pbtusa.org
**Web Site:** www.pbtusa.org

*Dr. Rondal B. Smith, President*

A nondenominational sending agency of Christian (Restoration Movement) tradition engaged in Bible translation, development, evangelism, literacy work, support of national churches and mobilization for mission. Statistical data from 2003.

**Purpose:** "...discipling of the nations by: Providing Scripture in the language of the people.Developing mother-tongue literacy programs.Establishing and strengthening congregations.Training leadership among nationals for partnership in reaching our goals."

**Year founded in US:** 1976

**Income for Overseas Min:** $2,245,982
**Gifts in Kind:** $29,954

**Fully Supported US Personnel Overseas:**
   Expecting to serve more than 4 years: 70
   Non-residential mission personnel: 70

**Other Personnel:**
 Short-term less than 1 year: 10
 Non-US serving in own/other country: 3
 Home ministry & office staff in US: 27

**Countries:** Guinea 27; Papua New Guinea 33; Tanzania 6; Ukraine 4

## Pioneer Clubs

PO Box 788
Wheaton, IL 60189-0788 USA

**Phone:** (630) 293-1600
**Fax:** (630) 293-3053
**E-mail:** info@pioneerclubs.org
**Web Site:** www.pioneerclubs.org

*Judy Bryson, President*

A nondenominational service agency of Evangelical and Fundamental tradition engaged in childrens programs, bible memorization, camping programs, discipleship, evangelism and youth programs.

**Purpose:** "...to serve God by providing the most effective and educationally sound programs to help children follow Christ in every aspect of life."

**Year founded in US:** 1939

**Personnel:**
 Home ministry & office staff in US: 37

## Pioneers USA

10123 William Carey Dr.
Orlando, FL 32832 USA

**Phone:** (407) 382-6000
**Fax:** (407) 382-1008
**E-mail:** info@pioneers.org
**Web Site:** www.pioneers.org
**Associations:** IFMA

*Mr. Stephen L. Richardson, President*

An interdenominational sending agency of Evangelical tradition engaged in church planting, development, evangelism, leadership development, short-term programs and tentmaking.

**Purpose:** "...partners with churches to mobilize, prepare and support missionaries for effective church planting ministry among unreached peoples."

**Year founded in US:** 1979

**Income for Overseas Min:** $15,600,000

**Fully Supported US Personnel Overseas:**
 Expecting to serve more than 4 years: 441

 Expecting to serve 1 to 4 years: 48

**Other Personnel:**
 Short-term less than 1 year: 89
 Non-US serving in own/other country: 22
 Home ministry & office staff in US: 91

**Countries:** Asia—General 158; Belize 2; Bolivia 13; Bosnia and Herzegovina 23; Brazil 2; Cambodia 6; Central Asia—General 80; CIS - General 11; Croatia 7; Eastern Europe—General 15; Fiji 1; Hungary 10; India 24; Japan 3; Kenya 2; Middle East 12; N. Mariana Isls 2; Papua New Guinea 14; Peru 17; Poland 4; Senegal 5; Slovenia 1; Thailand 29

## Prakash Association, USA

2130 Stoney Point Farms Rd.
Cumming, GA 30041 USA

**Phone:** (770) 844-1651
**Fax:** (770) 844-1651
**E-mail:** loren@prakash4india.org
**Web Site:** www.prakash4india.org

*Mr. Loren D. Eckhardt, Exec. Director*

An interdenominational support agency of Baptist tradition engaged in vocational and skill training, agricultural programs, development, leadership development and youth programs.

**Purpose:** "...to empower marginalized young Indian nationals by teaching marketable trades and life skills so they can build self-supporting, spiritually vibrant, transformed lives."

**Year founded in US:** 1968

**Income for Overseas Min:** $193,000

**Fully Supported US Personnel Overseas:**
 Non-residential mission personnel: 1

**Other Personnel:**
 Non-US serving in own/other country: 40
 Home ministry & office staff in US: 1

**Countries:** India

## Precept Ministries Intl.

PO Box 182218
Chattanooga, TN 37422 USA

**Phone:** (423) 892-6814
**Fax:** (423) 894-2449
**E-mail:** info@precept.org
**Web Site:** www.precept.org

*Mr. Jack Arthur, President/CEO*

A transdenominational sending agency

of Evangelical and Independent tradition engaged in extension education, broadcasting, leadership development, literature distribution, literature production and training. Data from 2001.

**Year founded in US:** 1970

**Income for Overseas Min:** $1,503,140

**Gifts in Kind:** $63,000

**Fully Supported US Personnel Overseas:**
    Expecting to serve more than 4 years: 2

**Other Personnel:**
    Non-US serving in own/other country: 90

**Countries:** Australia; Austria 1; Bahamas, The; Bolivia; Brazil; Bulgaria; Colombia; Costa Rica; El Salvador; Estonia; Germany; Guatemala; India; Korea, South; Mexico; Moldova; Nigeria; Peru; Philippines; Russia; Serbia and Montenegro; Slovakia; South Africa; Spain 1; Taiwan

## Precious Seed Ministries

1115 S. Maryland St.
Alton, TX 78573 USA

**Phone:** (956) 585-9966
**Fax:** (956) 583-7838
**E-mail:** wymanpylant@yahoo.com

*Mr. Wyman Pylant, President*

A nondenominational support agency of Charismatic tradition engaged in childcare/orphanage programs, church construction, church planting, theological education, leadership development and relief and/or rehabilitation.

**Year founded in US:** 1985

**Income for Overseas Min:** $57,000

**Fully Supported US Personnel Overseas:**
    Expecting to serve more than 4 years: 1
    Non-residential mission personnel: 2

**Other Personnel:**
    Non-US serving in own/other country: 10
    Home ministry & office staff in US: 2

**Countries:** Mexico 1; Nicaragua

## Presbyterian Church in America
## See: Mission to the World (PCA), Inc.

## Presbyterian Church (USA), Worldwide Ministries

100 Witherspoon St.
Louisville, KY 40202 USA

**Phone:** (502) 569-5000
**Fax:** (502) 569-8039
**Web Site:** www.pcusa.org/pcusa/wmd

**Associations:** CWS

*Linda Valentine, Exec. Director*

A denominational sending agency of Presbyterian and Reformed tradition engaged in mobilization for mission, development, leadership development, medical work, partnership development and relief and/or rehabilitation.

**Purpose:** "...to share the transforming power of the Gospel of Jesus Christ and to carry out this mission by being committed to the whole church, the whole Gospel and the whole inhabited earth...assist the church in the quest for Christian unity and ecumenical commitment...nourish and strengthen the global perspective and mission effort of the General Assembly Council, the Divisions and the church-at-large."

**Year founded in US:** 1837

**Income for Overseas Min:** $40,000,000

**Fully Supported US Personnel Overseas:**
    Expecting to serve more than 4 years: 350
    Expecting to serve 1 to 4 years: 385
    Non-residential mission personnel: 275

**Countries:** Africa—General 80; Asia—General 65; Australia 2; Europe—General 37; Latin America—General 88; Unspecified Country 78

## Presbyterian Evangelistic Fellowship

425 State St. Ste. 312
Bristol, VA 24201 USA

**Phone:** (276) 591-5336
**Fax:** (276) 591-5349
**E-mail:** admin@pefministry.org
**Web Site:** www.pefministry.org

*Rev. Rick Light, Exec. Director*

An interdenominational sending agency of Presbyterian and Reformed tradition engaged in evangelism, camping programs, literature distribution, support of national workers and youth programs. Overseas personnel data from 1998.

**Purpose:** "...to practice, train and equip God's people to do Biblical evangelism, anywhere, anytime, with anyone."

**Year founded in US:** 1958

**Income for Overseas Min:** $1,000,000

**Fully Supported US Personnel Overseas:**
  Expecting to serve more than 4 years: 47

**Other Personnel:**
  Bi-vocational/tentmakers: 49
  Non-US serving in own/other country: 24
  Home ministry & office staff in US: 8

**Countries:** Bulgaria 2; Chile 1; Costa Rica 1; Europe—General 9; France 5; Greece 1; India; Japan 2; Kazakhstan 1; Kenya 2; Latin America—General 2; Liberia; Mexico 8; Nigeria 1; Peru 4; Russia 2; Uganda 2; United Kingdom 4

## Presbyterian Mission International (PMI)

12330 Conway Rd.
St. Louis, MO 63141 USA

**Phone:** (314) 434-4044
**Fax:** (314) 434-4819
**E-mail:** pmi@covenantseminary.edu
**Web Site:** www.pmiweb.org

*Dr. J. Nelson Jennings, President*

An interdenominational sending agency of Presbyterian and Reformed tradition engaged in support of national workers, church planting, development, theological education, evangelism and partnership development.

**Purpose:** "...to enhance worldwide reformed and presbyterian gospel ministry through relationships with nationals who labor in evangelism, church planting, leadership training, holistic ministries and connecting churches internationally."

**Year founded in US:** 1988

**Income for Overseas Min:** $1,794,247

**Personnel:**
  Non-US serving in own/other country: 13
  Home ministry & office staff in US: 2

**Countries:** Brazil; France; Hungary; India; Italy; Japan; Netherlands; New Zealand; Philippines; Thailand; Ukraine

## Presbyterian Missionary Union

1650 Love Rd
Grand Island, NY 14072-2399 USA

**Phone:** (716) 775-0442
**Fax:** (716) 775-0442
**E-mail:** office@presbyterianmissions.org
**Web Site:** www.presbyterianmissions.org

*Dr. Len Pine, Field Rep.*

A denominational sending agency of Presbyterian tradition engaged in church planting, Bible distribution, evangelism, funds transmission, literature distribution and support of national churches.

**Purpose:** "...to establish and strengthen indigenous Bible believing churches, related institutions and works agreeable to the (Westminster) doctrinal standards and principles of (Presbyterian) church government."

**Year founded in US:** 1985

**Fully Supported US Personnel Overseas:**
  Expecting to serve more than 4 years: 3

**Other Personnel:**
  Short-term less than 1 year: 8
  Bi-vocational/tentmakers: 1
  Non-US serving in own/other country: 2
  Home ministry & office staff in US: 2

**Countries:** Australia 2; Cambodia 1; Myanmar/Burma

## Presbyterian Order for World Evangelization

542 E. Ingram
Mesa, AZ 95203 USA

**Phone:** (480) 834-1500
**Fax:** (480) 834-6643
**E-mail:** robertblincoe@cox.net

*Rev. Robert Blincoe, Gen. Director*

A denominational support agency of Presbyterian tradition engaged in evangelism, mobilization for mission, mission-related research and training.

**Purpose:** "...attracting, coordinating, sponsoring, managing and establishing whatever project, activities, program or organizations that contribute strategically toward the fulfilment of the Great Commission."

**Year founded in US:** 1974

**Income for Overseas Min:** $50,000

**Personnel:**
  Home ministry & office staff in US: 3

## Primitive Methodist Church in the USA—Intl. Mission Bd.

33 W. Barrows St.
Cumberland, RI 02864-7404 USA
**Phone:** (215) 675-2639
**Fax:** (215) 675-1576
**E-mail:** fjeffrey@juno.com
**Web Site:** www.primitivemethodistchurch.org

*Rev. Fred Jeffrey, Dir. Intl. Mission Board*

A denominational sending agency of Wesleyan and Methodist tradition engaged in support of national churches, church planting, correspondence courses, theological education, TEE and medical work. Financial figure from 1998.

**Year founded in US:** 1922
**Income for Overseas Min:** $455,000
**Fully Supported US Personnel Overseas:**
  Expecting to serve more than 4 years: 7
**Other Personnel:**
  Short-term less than 1 year: 25
**Countries:** Dominican Republic 2; Guatemala 5

## Prison Mission Association

PO Box 2300
Port Orchard, WA 98366 USA
**Phone:** (360) 876-0918
**E-mail:** pma@pmabcf.org
**Web Site:** www.pmabcf.org

*Dr. Donald Sommer, Exec. Director*

A nondenominational specialized agency engaged in prison ministry, correspondence courses to 33 nations worldwide, Bible distribution, discipleship, evangelism, literature distribution.

**Year founded in US:** 1955
**Personnel:**
  Home ministry & office staff in US: 2

## Progressive National Baptist Convention, Inc.—Missions

601 50th St., NE
Washington, DC 20019 USA
**Phone:** (202) 396-0558
**Fax:** (202) 398-4998
**E-mail:** info@pnbc.org
**Web Site:** www.pnbc.org

*Dr. Major L. Jemison, President*

A denominational support agency of Baptist tradition engaged in supplying equipment, Bible distribution, church construction and childrens programs. Data from 2001.

**Year founded in US:** 1962

## Progressive Vision

PO Box 670
Coeur d' Alene, ID 83816 USA
**Phone:** (208) 665-9998
**E-mail:** info@progressivevision.org
**Web Site:** www.progressivevision.org

*Mr. Marcus Vegh, President*

A nondenominational service agency of Evangelical tradition engaged in services for other agencies, discipleship and leadership development.

**Purpose:** "...to radically influence the way oral cultures are evangelized and discipled."

**Year founded in US:** 1995
**Income for Overseas Min:** $376,000
**Personnel:**
  Home ministry & office staff in US: 8

## Project AmaZon

PO Box 913
Morton, IL 61550 USA
**Phone:** (309) 263-2299
**E-mail:** dove@dpc.net
**Web Site:** www.projectamazon.org

*Jeffrey P. Hrubik, President*

An interdenominational sending agency of Evangelical tradition engaged in church planting, Christian education, evangelism, leadership development and medical work.

**Purpose:** "...fulfilling the great commission by planting nationally-led churches, focusing on the Amazon Basin."

**Year founded in US:** 1987
**Income for Overseas Min:** $1,804,546
**Fully Supported US Personnel Overseas:**
  Expecting to serve more than 4 years: 32
**Other Personnel:**
  Short-term less than 1 year: 4
  Non-US serving in own/other country: 4
  Home ministry & office staff in US: 2
**Countries:** Brazil 29; Japan 3

## Project Christ International

124-08 Linden Blvd.
Jamaica, NY 11420 USA
**Phone:** (718) 845-6992
**E-mail:** pcintl@aol.com
**Web Site:** www.projectchristinternational.org

*Mr. John Stephen, President*

A nondenominational support agency of Baptist and Brethren tradition engaged in Christian education, childcare/orphanage programs, childrens programs, church construction, church planting and missionary education.

**Year founded in US:** 1984
**Income for Overseas Min:** $25,000
**Gifts in Kind:** $25,000
**Personnel:**
  Short-term less than 1 year: 2
  Bi-vocational/tentmakers: 2
  Non-US serving in own/other country: 80
**Countries:** India; Nepal

## Project Mercy, Inc.

7011 Ardmore Ave.
Fort Wayne, IN 46809 USA
**Phone:** (260) 747-2559
**Fax:** (260) 478-1361
**E-mail:** pminfo@projectmercy.org
**Web Site:** www.projectmercy.org

*Marta Gabre-Tsadick, Exec. Director*

A nondenominational support agency of Evangelical tradition engaged in community development, agricultural programs, KG-11 skills training and medical work.

**Purpose:** "...providing aid, comfort and support to those in need anywhere in Africa...also participates to alleviate human suffering anywhere in the world in the name of Jesus Christ."

**Year founded in US:** 1977
**Income for Overseas Min:** $1,178,079
**Fully Supported US Personnel Overseas:**
  Expecting to serve more than 4 years: 2
  Non-residential mission personnel: 2
**Other Personnel:**
  Short-term less than 1 year: 119
  Home ministry & office staff in US: 7
**Countries:** Ethiopia 2

## Providence Mission Homes, Inc.

PO Box 40727
Pasadena, CA 91114-7727 USA
**Phone:** (626) 398-2487
**Fax:** (626) 398-2488
**E-mail:** providencehomes1@yahoo.com

*Dr. Marvin Eyler, Director*

An interdenominational support agency of Congregational and Evangelical tradition engaged in housing for missionaries.

**Year founded in US:** 1973
**Personnel:**
  Home ministry & office staff in US: 3

## Ramesh Richard Evangelism and Church Health

5500 W. Plano Pkwy. #100
Plano, TX 75093 USA
**Phone:** (972) 733-3402
**Fax:** (972) 733-3495
**E-mail:** info@rreach.org
**Web Site:** www.rreach.org

*Dr. Ramesh P. Richard, President*

A nondenominational support agency engaged in training, broadcasting, evangelism and Christian education.

**Purpose:** "A global proclamation ministry, RREACH International implements God's calling on Ramesh Richard to proclaim the message of the Lord Jesus Christ worldwide, with a strategic burden for strengthening pastoral leaders and evangelizing opinion leaders of weaker economies."

**Year founded in US:** 1987
**Income for Overseas Min:** $317,000
**Personnel:**
  Home ministry & office staff in US: 8

## Raul Zaldivar Ministries

PO Box 8601
Northfield, IL 60093 USA
**Phone:** (847) 441-6861
**E-mail:** ministerio@raulzaldivar.com
**Web Site:** www.raulzaldivar.com

*Dr. Raul Zaldivar, President*

An interdenominational service agency engaged in evangelism, broadcasting, Christian education, TEE and funds transmission.

Financial data from 2002.

**Year founded in US:** 1997

**Income for Overseas Min:** $40,000

**Personnel:**
Home ministry & office staff in US: 8

## Ravi Zacharias International Ministries

4725 Peachtree Corners Circle, #250
Norcross, GA 30092 USA

**Phone:** (770) 449-6766
**Fax:** (770) 729-1729
**E-mail:** rzim@rzim.com
**Web Site:** www.rzim.org

*Rev. Ravi Zacharias, President*

An interdenominational specialized agency of Evangelical tradition involved in apologetics training with professionals, theological education, evangelism and leadership development. Statistics from 1998.

**Purpose:** "...to support, expand and enhance the preaching and teaching ministry of Ravi Zacharias, distinctive in its strong evangelistic and apologetic foundation, intended to touch both the heart and the intellect of the thinkers and opinion-makers of society..."

**Year founded in US:** 1984

**Income for Overseas Min:** $1,000,000

**Gifts in Kind:** $500,000

**Fully Supported US Personnel Overseas:**
Expecting to serve more than 4 years: 4
Non-residential mission personnel: 2

**Other Personnel:**
Short-term less than 1 year: 4
Home ministry & office staff in US: 26

**Countries:** India 2; United Kingdom 2

## Reach Ministries Intl.

PO Box 2060
Orange, CA 92859 USA

**Phone:** (562) 690-4252
**Fax:** (562) 690-5612
**E-mail:** reachmin@cosmoslink.net

*Loring E. Tabor, CEO/President*

A nondenominational sending agency of Evangelical tradition engaged in discipleship, bible memorization, development, evangelism, leadership development and Bible translation.

**Purpose:** "...to propagate the gospel of the Lord Jesus Christ and to promote aid and develop contextualized, holistic disciplemaking ministries in the Philippines and India with expansion to other countries and cultures as the Lord leads."

**Year founded in US:** 1985

**Income for Overseas Min:** $126,236

**Fully Supported US Personnel Overseas:**
Expecting to serve more than 4 years: 7

**Other Personnel:**
Non-US serving in own/other country: 2
Home ministry & office staff in US: 3

**Countries:** Hong Kong 1; India; Philippines 6

## Reaching Indians Ministries International

PO Box 688
Round Lake Beach, IL 60073 USA

**Phone:** (847) 265-0630
**Fax:** (847) 265-0642
**E-mail:** Slukos@rimi.org
**Web Site:** www.rimi.org

*Saji Lukos, President*

An interdenominational support agency of Independent tradition engaged in evangelism, church planting, discipleship, missionary education, leadership development and support of national workers.

**Purpose:** "...to serve the people of India and others with the message of Jesus Christ."

**Year founded in US:** 1993

**Income for Overseas Min:** $1,612,427

**Fully Supported US Personnel Overseas:**
Non-residential mission personnel: 1

**Other Personnel:**
Short-term less than 1 year: 30
Non-US serving in own/other country: 810
Home ministry & office staff in US: 3

**Countries:** India

## Reciprocal Ministries Intl.

5471 Lee St., Ste. 301
Lehigh Acres, FL 33971 USA

**Phone:** (239) 368-8390
**Fax:** (941) 876-6633
**E-mail:** rmioffice.florida@rminet.org
**Web Site:** www.rminet.org

*Mr. Dan Shoemaker, President*

An interdenominational sending agency of Baptist and Evangelical tradition engaged in partnership development, development and short-term programs.

**Purpose:** "...to see Christian laypersons ministering, through the vehicle of the Sister Church Program, to Christians in a church of a different culture, and together with them, minister to each other's community."

**Year founded in US:** 1986

**Income for Overseas Min:** $700,000

**Fully Supported US Personnel Overseas:**
    Expecting to serve more than 4 years: 12

**Other Personnel:**
    Short-term less than 1 year: 2
    Home ministry & office staff in US: 2

**Countries:** Guatemala 4; Haiti 8

## Red Sea Team International

PO Box 2047
Lexington, SC 29071-2047 USA
**Phone:** (803) 358-2330
**Fax:** (803) 358-2330
**E-mail:** rsti@sc.rr.com
**Web Site:** www.rsti.com
**Associations:** IFMA

*Rev. Herb Brasher, US Director*

An interdenominational support agency of Evangelical tradition engaged in medical work, church planting, evangelism and TESOL.

**Purpose:** "...to glorify God through our lives and testimony in order to proclaim the Gospel of Christ's redeeming love to Muslims."

**Year founded in US:** 1953

**Income for Overseas Min:** $1,460,000

**Fully Supported US Personnel Overseas:**
    Expecting to serve more than 4 years: 2
    Expecting to serve 1 to 4 years: 1

**Other Personnel:**
    Short-term less than 1 year: 4
    Non-US serving in own/other country: 30
    Home ministry & office staff in US: 4

**Countries:** Africa—General; Central Asia—General; Middle East 2; Pakistan; United Kingdom

## Reformation Translation Fellowship (RTF)

302 E. First St.
Bloomington, IN 47401 USA
**Phone:** (812) 339-1922
**E-mail:** Bill4RTF@aol.com
**Web Site:** www.members.aol.com/Bill4RTF/rtf/

*Rev. William L. Roberts, American Rep.*

A nondenominational service agency of Reformed tradition engaged in translation work, literature production and literature distribution. Statistical data from 2001.

**Year founded in US:** 1950

**Income for Overseas Min:** $60,000

## Reformed Baptist Mission Services

PO Box 289
Carlisle, PA 17013 USA
**Phone:** (717) 249-7473
**Fax:** (717) 258-0614
**E-mail:** arbca@reformedbaptist.com
**Web Site:** www.reformedbaptist.com

*Rev. Robert B. Selph, Coordinator*

A mission service coordinating member churches to assist one another to send missionaries and plant churches worldwide.

**Purpose:** "...to advance Christ's kingdom by providing an association in which churches of common confession may find mutual encouragement, assistance, edification and counsel, and to participate in cooperative efforts in church planting, foreign missions, ministerial training, publications and other endeavors deemed appropriate by the Association."

**Year founded in US:** 1985

**Income for Overseas Min:** $674,213

**Fully Supported US Personnel Overseas:**
    Expecting to serve more than 4 years: 3

**Other Personnel:**
    Non-US serving in own/other country: 22
    Home ministry & office staff in US: 3

**Countries:** Argentina; Asia—General; Chile; Colombia; France; Ireland; Israel; Jamaica; Kenya; Switzerland; United Kingdom; Unspecified Country 3

## Reformed Church in America, Gen. Synod Council, Mission Services

4500 - 60th St.
Grand Rapids, MI 49512 USA

**Phone:** (616) 698-7071
**Fax:** (616) 698-6606
**E-mail:** bmenning@rca.org
**Web Site:** www.rca.org

*Rev. Bruce Menning, Director Global Msn.*

A denominational sending agency of Reformed tradition engaged in development, agricultural programs, church planting, theological education, evangelism and medical work.

**Year founded in US:** 1857

**Income for Overseas Min:** $6,480,000

**Fully Supported US Personnel Overseas:**
   Expecting to serve more than 4 years: 62
   Non-residential mission personnel: 2

**Other Personnel:**
   Short-term less than 1 year: 195
   Non-US serving in own/other country: 34
   Home ministry & office staff in US: 18

**Countries:** Albania 2; Bahrain 5; Bangladesh 1; China; Croatia 2; Cyprus 2; Egypt 2; Estonia 2; Ethiopia 5; Guatemala; Honduras; Hungary 2; India 2; Indonesia 2; Israel 2; Italy 2; Japan 6; Kenya 6; Malawi 2; Mexico 4; Mozambique 2; Myanmar/Burma; Nicaragua; Niger 2; Oman 4; Senegal; South Africa; Sudan 2; Taiwan 3; Ukraine; Venezuela

## Reformed Episcopal Board of Foreign Missions

4142 Dayflower Dr.
Katy, TX 77449 USA

**Phone:** (800) 732-3433
**Fax:** (281) 463-9575
**E-mail:** RoyalREC1@aol.com
**Web Site:** www.recus.org

*Bishop Royal U. Grote, President*

A denominational sending agency of Anglican tradition engaged in church planting, medical work and Bible translation.

**Year founded in US:** 1892

**Income for Overseas Min:** $220,000

**Fully Supported US Personnel Overseas:**
   Expecting to serve more than 4 years: 3

**Other Personnel:**
   Short-term less than 1 year: 50
   Non-US serving in own/other country: 15

**Countries:** Brazil 1; France 1; Germany 1; Liberia

## Rehoboth Ministries, Inc

333 Hilliard Dr.
Fayetteville, NC 28311-8751 USA

**Phone:** (910) 630-3730
**E-mail:** pgiba@aol.com

*Rev. Pritchard Adams, III, President*

A transdenominational sending agency of Pentecostal tradition engaged in evangelism, Christian education, theological education, leadership development and broadcasting.

**Year founded in US:** 1985

**Income for Overseas Min:** $76,939

**Personnel:**
   Expecting to serve more than 4 years: 2

**Countries:** Haiti 2

## Remnant Ministries, Inc.

PO Box 24398
Cleveland, OH 44124-0398 USA

**Phone:** (440) 684-0220
**Fax:** (440) 684-0219
**E-mail:** rmi1@ix.netcom.com
**Web Site:** www.remininc.org

*Rev. Joel S. Kettenring, Exec. Director*

A nondenominational sending agency of Fundamental and Independent tradition engaged in Jewish evangelism, Bible distribution, discipleship and literature production.

**Purpose:** "...to evangelize Jews in this present age...to reach the 'remnant according to the election of grace' Romans 11:5."

**Year founded in US:** 1904

**Income for Overseas Min:** $100,000

**Fully Supported US Personnel Overseas:**
   Expecting to serve more than 4 years: 3

**Other Personnel:**
   Home ministry & office staff in US: 2

**Countries:** Brazil 1; Israel 2

## Rio Grande Bible Institute

4300 S. Business Hwy. #281
Edinburg, TX 78539 USA

**Phone:** (956) 380-8100

**Fax:** (956) 380-8256
**E-mail:** rgbimail@riogrande.edu
**Web Site:** www.riogrande.edu
**Associations:** IFMA

*Mr. Lawrence B. Windle, President*

A nondenominational service agency of Independent tradition engaged in theological education, broadcasting, correspondence courses, missionary education, leadership development and literature production.

**Purpose:** "…exists to glorify God by serving the Hispanic church through equipping leaders, edifying believers and evangelizing the lost."

**Year founded in US:** 1946

**Personnel:**
   Home ministry & office staff in US: 37

## Ripe for Harvest, Inc.

2824 N.Power Rd. #113282
Mesa, AZ 85215-1674 USA

**Phone:** (480) 373-9387
**E-mail:** TimSmith@ripeforharvest.org
**Web Site:** www.ripeforharvest.org

*Dr. Tim Smith, Exec. Director*

A nondenominational sending agency of Evangelical tradition engaged in evangelism, Bible distribution, church planting, funds transmission and literature distribution. Data from 2001.

**Year founded in US:** 1979

**Income for Overseas Min:** $570,673

**Fully Supported US Personnel Overseas:**
   Expecting to serve more than 4 years: 61
   Expecting to serve 1 to 4 years: 15

**Other Personnel:**
   Bi-vocational/tentmakers: 40
   Non-US serving in own/other country: 1
   Home ministry & office staff in US: 6

**Countries:** Bolivia 2; Brazil 1; China 2; Colombia 1; Costa Rica 1; Cyprus 3; Denmark 1; Finland 2; France 7; Germany 2; Greece 2; Guatemala 5; Honduras 2; Hungary 2; India 2; Japan 2; Malaysia 2; Malta 1; Mexico; Middle East 2; Nigeria 1; Peru 1; Philippines 1; Poland 1; Puerto Rico 1; Romania 1; Russia 3; Taiwan 1; Thailand 3; Turkey 2; United Kingdom 4

## Rock the World Youth Mission Alliance

PO Box 43
Ambridge, PA 15003 USA

**Phone:** (724) 266-8876
**Fax:** (724) 266-5916
**E-mail:** info@rocktheworld.org
**Web Site:** www.rocktheworld.org

*Mr. Whis Hays, Exec. Dir.*

A nondenominational support agency of Episcopal and Evangelical tradition engaged in youth programs, theological education, evangelism, leadership development, mobilization for mission and short-term programs. Data from 2002.

**Purpose:** "Mobilize young people to make an impact for God."

**Year founded in US:** 1989

**Income for Overseas Min:** $38,000

**Fully Supported US Personnel Overseas:**
   Non-residential mission personnel: 1

**Other Personnel:**
   Short-term less than 1 year: 13
   Home ministry & office staff in US: 7

**Countries:** Belize; Honduras; Nepal; Peru

## Rogma International, Inc.

PO Box 2008
Easley, SC 29641 USA

**Phone:** (864) 855-2887
**Fax:** (864) 859-0100
**E-mail:** info@rogma.org
**Web Site:** www.rogma.org

*Dr. John Vanden Akker, President*

A service agency of Baptist and Fundamental tradition engaged in correspondence courses, discipleship and evangelism with 160 directors in 88 countries.

**Purpose:** "…to share the Word with the world."

**Year founded in US:** 1985

**Income for Overseas Min:** $42,500

**Personnel:**
   Home ministry & office staff in US: 1

## Romanian Missionary Society

PO Box 527
Wheaton, IL 60189-0527 USA

**Phone:** (630) 665-6503

**Fax:** (630) 665-6538
**E-mail:** rms@rmsonline.org
**Web Site:** www.rmsonline.org
*Rev. Stuart Erdenberg, Exec. Director*

An interdenominational sending agency of Baptist and Presbyterian tradition engaged in evangelism, broadcasting, childrens programs, theological education, literature production and support of national workers.

**Purpose:** "...to support Christian projects and ministries in Romania."

**Year founded in US:** 1968

**Income for Overseas Min:** $425,000

**Fully Supported US Personnel Overseas:**
Non-residential mission personnel: 1

**Other Personnel:**
Short-term less than 1 year: 1
Non-US serving in own/other country: 70
Home ministry & office staff in US: 3

## Rosedale Mennonite Missions

9920 Rosedale Milford Ctr. Rd.
Irwin, OH 43029-9537 USA
**Phone:** (740) 857-1366
**Fax:** (740) 857-1605
**E-mail:** info@rmmoffice.org
**Web Site:** www.rosedalemennonitemissions.org
*Mr. Joseph Showalter, President*

A denominational sending agency of Mennonite tradition engaged in church planting, childcare/orphanage programs, discipleship, leadership development, support of national churches and short-term programs.

**Purpose:** "...to establish locally rooted and led, rapidly reproducing churches, prioritizing people groups and locations that are least reached with the Good News."

**Year founded in US:** 1919

**Income for Overseas Min:** $1,207,119

**Fully Supported US Personnel Overseas:**
Expecting to serve more than 4 years: 28
Expecting to serve 1 to 4 years: 8

**Other Personnel:**
Short-term less than 1 year: 58
Bi-vocational/tentmakers: 9
Non-US serving in own/other country: 36
Home ministry & office staff in US: 15

**Countries:** Albania 2; Belarus 2; China; Costa Rica 2; Ecuador 7; India 2; Mexico 2; Nicaragua 2; Thailand 1; Turkey 6; Uzbekistan 2

## RUN Ministries

PO Box 6543
Virginia Beach, VA 23546 USA
**Phone:** (757) 213-2060
**Fax:** (757) 420-4670
**E-mail:** eric.watt@earthlink.net
**Web Site:** www.runministries.org
**Associations:** EFMA
*Mr. Eric Watt, President*

An interdenominational sending agency of Charismatic and Evangelical tradition engaged in leadership development, church planting, missions information service, literature distribution, training and Bible translation.

**Income for Overseas Min:** $209,909

**Personnel:**
Bi-vocational/tentmakers: 4
Home ministry & office staff in US: 5

**Countries:** Kazakhstan; Malaysia

## Russian Bible Society, Inc.

PO Box 6068
Asheville, NC 28816 USA
**Phone:** (828) 681-0370
**Fax:** (828) 681-0371
**E-mail:** russianbibles@bellsouth.net
*Dr. Robert Doom, Director*

An interdenominational specialized agency of Baptist and Fundamental tradition engaged in Bible distribution, literature distribution, literature production, Bible translation and translation work. Data from 2001.

**Purpose:** "...to continue providing the 'Synodal Translation' of the Russian Bible... and its translation into many of the minority languages [of Russia]."

**Year founded in US:** 1944

**Income for Overseas Min:** $105,437

**Personnel:**
Short-term less than 1 year: 10
Home ministry & office staff in US: 1

## Russian Christian Radio

PO Box 1667
Estes Park, CO 80517 USA
**Phone:** (970) 586-8638
**E-mail:** radiorcr@earthlink.net
*Mr. Sergei Matveyuk, Director*

A specialized agency of Evangelical tradition engaged in broadcasting, audio recording/distribution, literature distribution and literature production. Data from 2002.

**Year founded in US:** 1982

**Income for Overseas Min:** $428,478

**Personnel:**
  Home ministry & office staff in US: 5

## Russian Language Ministries See: Institute of Strategic Languages and Cultures

## Salvation Army, U.S.A.
PO Box 269
Alexandria, VA 22313 USA
**Phone:** (703) 684-5500
**Fax:** (703) 684-3478
**E-mail:** usn_Chief_Secretary@usn.salvationarmy.org
**Web Site:** www.salvationarmy.org
**Associations:** AERDO

*Commissioner Israel L. Gaither, Natl. Commander*

A denominational sending agency of Evangelical and Holiness tradition engaged in evangelism expressed through worship services and social services including relief and/or rehabilitation, disaster, camping programs, children's programs, evangelism and youth programs in 108 countries.

**Purpose:** "...to preach the Gospel of Jesus Christ and to meet human needs in His name without discrimination."

**Year founded in US:** 1880

**Income for Overseas Min:** $41,606,749

**Fully Supported US Personnel Overseas:**
  Expecting to serve more than 4 years: 61
  Non-residential mission personnel: 63

**Other Personnel:**
  Short-term less than 1 year: 4
  Home ministry & office staff in US: 17

**Countries:** Argentina 2; Australia 4; Belize 1; Chile 1; Costa Rica 1; El Salvador 1; Estonia 3; Georgia 1; Germany 2; Haiti 3; Italy 1; Jamaica 3; Kenya 5; Latvia 1; Liberia 1; Malaysia 1; Mexico 5; Moldova 1; New Zealand 1; Nigeria 1; Paraguay 1; Portugal 1; Romania 1; Russia 2; Singapore 1; Spain 5; Sri Lanka 2; Uganda 1; United Kingdom 7; Zambia 1

## Samaritan's Purse
PO Box 3000
Boone, NC 28607 USA
**Phone:** (828) 262-1980
**Fax:** (828) 266-1056
**E-mail:** info@samaritan.org
**Web Site:** www.samaritanspurse.org

*Mr. Franklin Graham, President*

A nondenominational specialized agency of Evangelical tradition engaged in relief and/or rehabilitation, agricultural programs, development, evangelism, providing medical supplies and partnership development.

**Purpose:** "...providing spiritual and physical aid to hurting people around the world... meeting needs of people who are victims of war, poverty, natural disaster, disease and famine with the purpose of sharing God's love through his Son, Jesus Christ."

**Year founded in US:** 1970

**Income for Overseas Min:** $121,842,371

**Gifts in Kind:** $150,658,844

**Fully Supported US Personnel Overseas:**
  Expecting to serve more than 4 years: 1
  Expecting to serve 1 to 4 years: 120
  Non-residential mission personnel: 5

**Other Personnel:**
  Short-term less than 1 year: 45
  Non-US serving in own/other country: 2,163
  Home ministry & office staff in US: 1,180

**Countries:** Afghanistan 1; Angola; Cambodia; El Salvador; Eritrea; Ethiopia; Honduras; Indonesia; Jordan; Kenya; Kosovo; Liberia; Mozambique; Niger; Pakistan; Sri Lanka; Sudan; Uganda; Vietnam

## SAND International
693 Naoma Dr.
Crete, IL 60417 USA
**Phone:** (708) 367-1605
**Fax:** (708) 367-1605
**E-mail:** sand32@juno.com
**Web Site:** www.sandinternational.org

*Mr. Donald Sobkoviak, President*

An interdenominational support agency of Charismatic and Independent tradition engaged in agricultural programs, development, Christian education and evangelism.

**Purpose:** "...to help needy people everywhere to know and receive the Two-Hand-

## scholarship with a
# shepherd's heart

**Dr. Wayne Grudem**
*Research Professor,
Bible and Theology,
Phoenix Seminary*

PHOENIX
SEMINARY.

"I don't know of any other seminary in the U.S.
that does such an excellent job of combining a
strong mentoring program, care for students'
spiritual growth and solid academic training."

Training spiritual leaders is our vision. At Phoenix Seminary,
we are committed to combining a challenging and diverse
theological education with personal mentoring and practical
ministry training.

**Our Programs:** Doctor of Ministry, Master of Divinity,
Master of Arts in Biblical Leadership and Graduate Diploma

ACCREDITED

For more information, contact us at:
888.443.1020 or phoenixseminary.edu

# HOW WILL THEY HEAR,

www.send.org

**SEND**
INTERNATIONAL

## unless...

**S**tarting churches
**E**vangelizing the unreched
**N**urturing disciples
**D**eveloping leaders

Romans 10:14,15

ed Gospel."

**Year founded in US:** 1982

**Income for Overseas Min:** $7,645

**Personnel:**
  Short-term less than 1 year: 2

## SAT-7 North America
PO Box 2770
Easton, MD 21601 USA

**Phone:** (410) 770-9804
**Fax:** (410) 770-9807
**E-mail:** usa@sat7.org
**Web Site:** www.sat7.org
**Associations:** EFMA

*Miss Debra A. Brink, Exec. Director*

An interdenominational specialized agency of Evangelical tradition engaged in broadcasting, childrens programs, evangelism and funds transmission.

**Purpose:** "...to provide the churches and Christians of the Middle East and North Africa with an opportunity to witness to Jesus Christ through inspirational, informative and educational television services."

**Year founded in US:** 1997

**Income for Overseas Min:** $3,500,000

**Personnel:**
  Home ministry & office staff in US: 9

## Seed International
PO Box 69
Merrifield, VA 22116 USA

**Phone:** (703) 996-0717
**Fax:** (703) 996-0740
**E-mail:** email@seedusa.org
**Web Site:** www.seedusa.org
**Associations:** EFMA

*Rev. John Park, Exec. Director*

An interdenominational sending agency of Presbyterian and Independent tradition engaged in church planting, theological education, leadership development, support of national churches, mobilization for mission and short-term programs.

**Year founded in US:** 1990

**Income for Overseas Min:** $1,474,632

**Fully Supported US Personnel Overseas:**
  Expecting to serve more than 4 years: 26
  Expecting to serve 1 to 4 years: 4

**Other Personnel:**
  Short-term less than 1 year: 1
  Bi-vocational/tentmakers: 1
  Home ministry & office staff in US: 3

**Countries:** Brazil 2; Cambodia 1; Croatia 1; Czech Republic 1; Honduras 1; India 1; Japan 2; Kenya 1; Mexico 3; Philippines 1; Russia 1; Tanzania 1; Thailand 1; Uganda 1; Unspecified Country 9

## Self-Help International
805 W. Bremer Ave.
Waverly, IA 50677 USA

**Phone:** (319) 352-4040
**Fax:** (319) 352-4040
**E-mail:** selfhelp@dybb.com
**Web Site:** www.selfhelpinternational.org

*Merry Fredrick, Exec. Director*

An interdenominational service agency of Ecumenical tradition engaged in agricultural programs, childrens programs, development, leadership development, management consulting/training and training.

**Purpose:** "To train small-scale farmers... improve and maintain their farming and transport methods; train people in developing countries...increase crop yields and improve nutrition...; cooperate with others in the introduction of appropriate farming practices...and help the people of the United States understand the problems of life in developing countries."

**Year founded in US:** 1959

**Income for Overseas Min:** $265,000

**Gifts in Kind:** $50,000

**Fully Supported US Personnel Overseas:**
  Non-residential mission personnel: 5

**Other Personnel:**
  Short-term less than 1 year: 3
  Non-US serving in own/other country: 8
  Home ministry & office staff in US: 2

**Countries:** Ghana; Nicaragua

## SEND International USA
**(See ad page 290)**
PO Box 513
Farmington, MI 48332 USA

**Phone:** (248) 477-4210
**Fax:** (248) 477-4232
**E-mail:** info@send.org
**Web Site:** www.send.org

**Associations:** IFMA

*Rev. Warren Janzen, Gen. Director*

An interdenominational sending agency of Evangelical tradition engaged in church planting, discipleship, theological education, evangelism, leadership development and support of national churches.

**Purpose:** "...to glorify God through establishing the Church of Jesus Christ where it does not exist and serving it through aggressive evangelism, intensive discipling and international leadership development."

**Year founded in US:** 1947

**Income for Overseas Min:** $13,069,261

**Fully Supported US Personnel Overseas:**
Expecting to serve more than 4 years: 257
Expecting to serve 1 to 4 years: 3
Non-residential mission personnel: 18

**Other Personnel:**
Short-term less than 1 year: 355
Non-US serving in own/other country: 89
Home ministry & office staff in US: 63

**Countries:** Asia—General 8; Bulgaria 19; Croatia 2; Czech Republic 5; Hungary 6; Japan 44; Kazakhstan 5; Macedonia 11; Philippines 29; Poland 10; Russia 30; Spain 18; Taiwan 19; Ukraine 48; Unspecified Country 3

## Sending Experienced Retired Volunteers Everywhere

3007 Bimini Bay
Boynton Beach, FL 33436 USA
**Phone:** (802) 676-9908
**Fax:** (800) 606-8260
**E-mail:** admin@serveintl.com
**Web Site:** www.serve-intl.org

*Mr. Terry Kennedy, Director*

An interdenominational specialized agency of Reformed tradition engaged in sending volunteer short and long-term teams overseas to twelve countries.

**Purpose:** "...to enhance the missions vision of retirees primarily and assist the church in building kingdom communities for worship and the glory of God worldwide."

**Year founded in US:** 1993

**Income for Overseas Min:** $150,000

**Gifts in Kind:** $100,000

**Personnel:**
Short-term less than 1 year: 49

## Sentinel Group, The

PO Box 6334
Lynnwood, WA 98036 USA
**Phone:** (425) 672-2989
**Fax:** (425) 672-3028
**E-mail:** info@sentinelgroup.org
**Web Site:** www.sentinelgroup.org

*Mr. George K. Otis, Jr., President*

A nondenominational support agency of Lausanne Covenant tradition engaged in video/film production/distribution, mission-related research, networking and training.

**Purpose:** "...to help the church pray knowledgably for end-time global evangelization and to enable communities to discover the pathway to genuine revival and societal transformation."

**Year founded in US:** 1990

**Income for Overseas Min:** $98,921

**Personnel:**
Home ministry & office staff in US: 10

## Servants in Faith & Technology (SIFAT)

2944 County Rd. 113
Lineville, AL 36266 USA
**Phone:** (256) 396-2015
**Fax:** (256) 396-2501
**E-mail:** corsont@aol.com
**Web Site:** www.sifat.org

*Mr. Thomas Corson, Exec. Director*

A service agency of Baptist and Methodist tradition engaged in youth programs, camping programs, Christian education, missions information service, leadership development, short-term programs and missionary training.

**Purpose:** "...to share God's love through service, education and personal involvement...providing training and technical assistance in meeting basic human needs..."

**Year founded in US:** 1979

**Income for Overseas Min:** $885,240

**Fully Supported US Personnel Overseas:**
Expecting to serve more than 4 years: 2
Expecting to serve 1 to 4 years: 1
Non-residential mission personnel: 2

**Other Personnel:**
Short-term less than 1 year: 345
Bi-vocational/tentmakers: 2

Non-US serving in own/other country: 28
Home ministry & office staff in US: 14
**Countries:** Bolivia 1; Ecuador 1; Uganda

## ServLife International

PO Box 79675
Houston, TX 77279 USA
**Phone:** (713) 464-8400
**E-mail:** info@servlife.org
**Web Site:** www.servlife.org
*Mr. Joel Vestal, President*

An interdenominational support agency of Evangelical tradition engaged in support of national workers, church planting, development, funds transmission and support of national churches. Data from 2001.
**Year founded in US:** 1996

## Seventh Day Baptist Missionary Society

119 Main St.
Westerly, RI 02891 USA
**Phone:** (401) 596-4326
**Fax:** (401) 348-9494
**E-mail:** sdbmissoc@verizon.net
**Web Site:** www.sdbmissions.org
*Mr. G. Kirk Looper, Exec. Director*

An associational agency of Baptist tradition engaged in church planting, evangelism, funds transmission, leadership development, short-term programs and missionary training.
**Purpose:** "...to coordinate and carry out... the message of salvation through faith in Christ to all who will hear, so they may accept Him as Savior."
**Year founded in US:** 1828
**Income for Overseas Min:** $58,000
**Personnel:**
Home ministry & office staff in US: 3

## Seventh-day Adventists General Conference

12501 Old Columbia Pike
Silver Spring, MD 20904 USA
**Phone:** (301) 680-6000
**Fax:** (301) 680-6090
**E-mail:** information@global-mission.org
**Web Site:** www.adventist.org
*Dr. Jan Paulsen, President*

A denominational sending agency of Adventist tradition engaged in evangelism, childrens programs, church planting, development, Christian education, TEE, theological education, literature distribution, literature production, medical work, support of national churches, relief and/or rehabilitation and training.
**Purpose:** "...to proclaim to all peoples the everlasting gospel in the context of the three angels' messages of Revelation 14:6-12, leading them to accept Jesus as personal Savior and to unite with His church."
**Year founded in US:** 1863
**Income for Overseas Min:** $55,803,094
**Fully Supported US Personnel Overseas:**
Expecting to serve more than 4 years: 329
Non-residential mission personnel: 7
**Other Personnel:**
Short-term less than 1 year: 412
Bi-vocational/tentmakers: 124
Non-US serving in own/other country: 461
Home ministry & office staff in US: 30
**Countries:** Albania 2; Algeria; Angola; Antigua 2; Argentina; Armenia; Australia 4; Bangladesh; Bolivia; Botswana 2; Brazil; Burkina Faso; Cambodia 8; Cameroon 2; Chad 2; Chile 6; Colombia 2; Congo, Democratic Republic of 2; Costa Rica 2; Côte d'Ivoire; Cyprus 4; Djibouti; Dominican Republic 2; Egypt 4; Equatorial Guinea 2; Ethiopia; France; French Guiana; French Polynesia; Gambia, The; Georgia 2; Germany; Ghana; Greece; Guam 58; Guyana 4; Haiti 2; Honduras 2; Hong Kong 10; India 10; Indonesia 4; Israel; Jamaica 14; Japan 4; Kazakhstan; Kenya 17; Korea, North; Korea, South 8; Kuwait; Laos; Lebanon; Lesotho 2; Liberia; Macau 2; Madagascar 2; Malawi 2; Mali; Marshall Islands 2; Mauritania; Mexico 10; Mongolia 2; Myanmar/Burma; Nepal 4; Netherlands Antilles 2; New Caledonia; Nicaragua; Niger; Nigeria 4; Pakistan; Papua New Guinea; Paraguay; Philippines 26; Puerto Rico 8; Russia 5; Rwanda 4; Sao Tome and Principe; Saint Vincent and the Grenadines 2; Senegal; Sierra Leone; Singapore 2; Solomon Islands; South Africa 2; Sudan 2; Swaziland; Switzerland; Taiwan 9; Tanzania 4; Thailand 22; Togo 2; Trinidad and Tobago 4; Tunisia; Uganda 6; United Arab Emirates; United Kingdom 6; Venezuela 2; Vietnam 2; Yemen 2; Zambia 2; Zimbabwe 4

## Shalom Outreach Ministries
## See: Jewish Awareness Mins.

## Share International
207 N. Service Rd. East, PMB210
Ruston, LA 71270 USA
**Phone:** (318) 513-2535
**Fax:** (318) 513-2535
**E-mail:** share123@bellsouth.net
**Web Site:** www.shareinternationalinc.com
*Sammy Murimi, President*

An interdenominational support agency of Evangelical tradition engaged in support of national workers, mobilization for mission and training. Data from 2001.

**Purpose:** "...challenging, training, sending, and supporting missionaries in partnership with the Church, with an initial emphasis on African nationals."

**Year founded in US:** 1989

**Income for Overseas Min:** $154,419

**Personnel:**
Short-term less than 1 year: 5
Non-US serving in own/other country: 9
Home ministry & office staff in US: 1

## Shelter for Life International, Inc.
502 E. New York Ave.
Oshkosh, WI 54901 USA
**Phone:** (920) 426-1207
**Fax:** (920) 426-4321
**E-mail:** info@shelter.org
**Web Site:** www.shelter.org
**Associations:** AERDO
*Mr. Randall Olson, President/CEO*

A Christian relief and development agency committed to serving refugees and the poor all over the world, regardless of race, religion or country of origin.

**Purpose:** "...to demonstrate God's love by enabling people affected by conflict and disaster to rebuild their communities and restore their lives."

**Year founded in US:** 1989

**Income for Overseas Min:** $13,600,000

**Gifts in Kind:** $103,000

**Fully Supported US Personnel Overseas:**
Expecting to serve more than 4 years: 1
Expecting to serve 1 to 4 years: 7

**Other Personnel:**
Short-term less than 1 year: 1
Non-US serving in own/other country: 290
Home ministry & office staff in US: 8

**Countries:** Central Asia—General 1; Middle East

## Shield of Faith Ministries
PO Box 327
Texas City, TX 77590 USA
**Phone:** (888) 241-9185
**Fax:** (713) 440-4139
**E-mail:** sofministries@hotmail.com
**Web Site:** www.sofministries.com
*Mr. Kyle Dickson, Exec. Director*

A nondenominational support agency of Charismatic and Evangelical tradition engaged in evangelism, church planting, Christian education, leadership development, community development and partnership development. Financial data from 2004.

**Year founded in US:** 1990

**Income for Overseas Min:** $145,839

**Personnel:**
Short-term less than 1 year: 25

## Shield of Faith Mission Intl.
PO Box 144
Bend, OR 97709 USA
**Phone:** (541) 382-7081
**Fax:** (541) 382-4471
**E-mail:** sfmi@sfmiusa.org
**Web Site:** www.sfmiusa.org
*Mr. Jim Lucas, President*

A sending agency of Evangelical tradition engaged in evangelism whose goal is to reach the unreached/unevangelized people groups, church planting, discipleship, missionary training and regional conferences for encouraging believers.

**Year founded in US:** 1953

**Fully Supported US Personnel Overseas:**
Expecting to serve more than 4 years: 10
Expecting to serve 1 to 4 years: 6
Non-residential mission personnel: 2

**Other Personnel:**
Short-term less than 1 year: 2
Home ministry & office staff in US: 2

**Countries:** Africa—General 4; Asia—General; Australia; Belize; Korea, South; Mexico 6

## SIM USA

PO Box 7900
Charlotte, NC 28241-7900 USA
**Phone:** (704) 588-4300
**Fax:** (704) 587-1518
**E-mail:** info@sim.org
**Web Site:** www.sim.org
**Associations:** EFMA, IFMA

*Dr. Steve Strauss, U.S. Director*

An interdenominational sending agency of Evangelical tradition engaged in church planting, development, theological education, medical work, Bible translation and mobilization for mission.

**Purpose:** "...to glorify God by planting, strengthening and partnering with churches around the world as we evangelize the unreached, minister to human need, disciple believers into churches and equip churches to fulfill Christ's Commission."

**Year founded in US:** 1893

**Income for Overseas Min:** $28,495,000

**Fully Supported US Personnel Overseas:**
Expecting to serve more than 4 years: 469
Expecting to serve 1 to 4 years: 50

**Other Personnel:**
Short-term less than 1 year: 95
Bi-vocational/tentmakers: 6
Home ministry & office staff in US: 233

**Countries:** Angola 7; Bangladesh 9; Benin 11; Bolivia 47; Botswana 5; Burkina Faso 9; Central African Republic 1; Chile 5; China; Cote d'Ivoire 2; Ecuador 5; Ethiopia 58; Ghana 12; Guatemala 2; Guinea 11; India 16; Italy 2; Kenya 21; Korea, South 2; Liberia 3; Malawi 15; Mozambique 8; Namibia 2; Niger 61; Nigeria 56; Paraguay 16; Peru 12; Senegal 13; South Africa 8; Switzerland 2; Tanzania 2; Thailand 5; Togo 2; Unspecified Country 12; Uruguay 6; Zambia 18; Zimbabwe 3

## Slavic Gospel Association

6151 Commonwealth Dr.
Loves Park, IL 61111 USA
**Phone:** (815) 282-8900
**Fax:** (815) 282-8901
**E-mail:** sga@sga.org
**Web Site:** www.sga.org
**Associations:** IFMA

*Dr. Robert W. Provost, President*

A support agency of Evangelical and Independent tradition engaged in theological education, Bible distribution, literature distribution, support of national workers and Bible translation.

**Purpose:** "...to serve evangelical churches, helping make disciples of the people in the lands of Russia."

**Year founded in US:** 1934

**Income for Overseas Min:** $8,100,000

**Gifts in Kind:** $750,000

**Fully Supported US Personnel Overseas:**
Expecting to serve more than 4 years: 5
Non-residential mission personnel: 2

**Other Personnel:**
Short-term less than 1 year: 25
Home ministry & office staff in US: 30

**Countries:** CIS—General 5

## Slavic Missionary Service, Inc.

PO Box 307
South River, NJ 08882 USA
**Phone:** (732) 873-8981
**Fax:** (732) 873-1625
**E-mail:** smsusa@smsusa.org
**Web Site:** www.smsusa.org

*Rev. Alex Leonovich, Exec. Director*

An interdenominational support agency of Baptist and Evangelical tradition engaged in support of national workers, broadcasting, church construction, church planting, funds transmission and support of national churches.

**Year founded in US:** 1933

**Fully Supported US Personnel Overseas:**
Non-residential mission personnel: 2

**Other Personnel:**
Home ministry & office staff in US: 3

## Society of St. Margaret

17 Highland Park St.
Boston, MA 02119-1436 USA
**Phone:** (617) 445-8961
**Fax:** (617) 445-7120
**E-mail:** ssmconvent@ssmbos.com
**Web Site:** www.ssmbos.com

*Sister Carolyn Darr, Reverend Mother*

A religious order of Episcopal tradition engaged in Christian education, childrens programs, development, leadership development, literacy work and support of national churches. Data from 2002.

**Purpose:** "...seeking to find Jesus present in the common life, and in ministries which concentrate on responding to the needs of the time."

**Year founded in US:** 1873

**Fully Supported US Personnel Overseas:**
Expecting to serve more than 4 years: 2

**Other Personnel:**
Non-US serving in own/other country: 2

**Countries:** Haiti 2

## Son Shine Ministries Intl.

PO Box 456
Azle, TX 76098-0456 USA

**Phone:** (817) 444-3777
**Fax:** (817) 270-0199
**Web Site:** www.sonshineonline.org
*Mr. David A. Shaffer, Director*

An interdenominational sending agency of Baptist and Methodist tradition engaged in evangelism, missionary training, correspondence courses and training. Data is from 2003.

**Year founded in US:** 1977

**Personnel:**
Home ministry & office staff in US: 6

## Source of Light Ministries International, Inc.

1011 Mission Rd.
Madison, GA 30650 USA

**Phone:** (706) 342-0397
**Fax:** (706) 342-9072
**E-mail:** solm@sourcelight.org
**Web Site:** www.sourcelight.org
**Associations:** IFMA
*Dr. William Shade, General Director*

An interdenominational sending agency of Baptist tradition engaged in correspondence courses, church planting, TEE, literature distribution, literature production and support of national workers, evangelizing in more than 80 countries.

**Purpose:** "...to bring people of every nation, language and ethnicity into a mature relationship with Jesus Christ and into fellowship with a local church family through disseminating Gospel literature, portions of Scripture and Bible correspondence courses into the hands of the multitudes in as many lands and languages as possible (Matt. 28:19-20) .

**Year founded in US:** 1952

**Income for Overseas Min:** $1,403,238

**Fully Supported US Personnel Overseas:**
Expecting to serve more than 4 years: 4

**Other Personnel:**
Short-term less than 1 year: 18
Non-US serving in own/other country: 39
Home ministry & office staff in US: 48

**Countries:** Argentina; Bolivia; Chile; Congo, Democratic Republic of 2; Côte d'Ivoire; Ghana; Guyana; Haiti 2; India; Jamaica; Japan; Korea, South; Mexico; Nigeria; Peru; Philippines; Romania; Singapore; South Africa; Togo; Uganda

## South America Mission, Inc.

5217 S. Military Trail
Lake Worth, FL 33463 USA

**Phone:** (561) 965-1833
**Fax:** (561) 439-8950
**E-mail:** samusa@southamericamission.org
**Web Site:** www.southamericamission.org
**Associations:** IFMA
*Rev. William K. Ogden, Exec. Director*

An interdenominational sending agency of Evangelical tradition engaged in theological education, aviation services, Christian education, leadership development and mobilization for mission.

**Purpose:** "...to intentionally and strategically build leaders to build churches across South America - churches that will transform communities to the glory of God."

**Year founded in US:** 1910

**Income for Overseas Min:** $3,432,229

**Gifts in Kind:** $27,563

**Fully Supported US Personnel Overseas:**
Expecting to serve more than 4 years: 81
Expecting to serve 1 to 4 years: 8
Non-residential mission personnel: 1

**Other Personnel:**
Short-term less than 1 year: 250
Non-US serving in own/other country: 14
Home ministry & office staff in US: 9

**Countries:** Bolivia 29; Brazil 19; Colombia; Paraguay 5; Peru 28

## South American Missionary Society (USA)

PO Box 399
Ambridge, PA 15003 USA
**Phone:** (724) 266-0669
**Fax:** (724) 266-5681
**E-mail:** info@sams-usa.org
**Web Site:** www.sams-usa.org
**Associations:** EFMA

*Mr. Stewart Wicker, President & Mission Dir.*

A denominational sending agency of Anglican and Evangelical tradition engaged in church planting, development, Christian education, evangelism, leadership development and support of national churches.

**Purpose:** "...to be witnesses and make disciples for Jesus Christ in fellowship with the Episcopal/Anglican Church in Latin America and Spain."

**Year founded in US:** 1976
**Income for Overseas Min:** $1,348,004
**Fully Supported US Personnel Overseas:**
  Expecting to serve more than 4 years: 19
  Expecting to serve 1 to 4 years: 12
**Other Personnel:**
  Short-term less than 1 year: 4
  Non-US serving in own/other country: 6
  Home ministry & office staff in US: 8
**Countries:** Bolivia 4; Chile; Dominican Republic 2; Ecuador 1; Honduras; Panama; Paraguay 1; Peru 6; Spain 3; Uganda 2

## Southern Baptist Convention International Mission Board

PO Box 6767
Richmond, VA 23230 USA
**Phone:** (804) 219-1209
**Fax:** (804) 254-8987
**E-mail:** dsteverson@imb.org
**Web Site:** www.imb.org
**Associations:** EFMA

*Dr. Jerry Rankin, President*

A denominational sending agency of Baptist tradition engaged in church planting, theological education, leadership development, evangelism, mission-related research and missionary training.

**Purpose:** "...to lead Southern Baptists in international missions efforts to evangelize the lost, disciple believers, develop church-

es and minister to people in need..."

**Year founded in US:** 1845
**Income for Overseas Min:** $242,140,000
**Fully Supported US Personnel Overseas:**
  Expecting to serve more than 4 years:
  4,009
  Expecting to serve 1 to 4 years: 1,156
**Other Personnel:**
  Short-term less than 1 year: 30,000
  Home ministry & office staff in US: 457
**Countries:** Unspecified Country 4,009

## Sowers International, The

26347 Governor Ave.
Harbor City, CA 90719 USA
**Phone:** (310) 325-0950
**Fax:** (310) 325-0503
**E-mail:** gwynn@sower.org
**Web Site:** www.sower.org

*Mr. Gwynn Lewis, Exec. Director*

A transdenominational support agency of Evangelical tradition engaged in support of national workers, Bible distribution, evangelism, short-term programs and missionary training. Statistical data and countries of service from 2002.

**Purpose:** "...to sow the word by raising up, equipping and sending out workers into the harvest."

**Year founded in US:** 1993
**Income for Overseas Min:** $479,971
**Fully Supported US Personnel Overseas:**
  Expecting to serve more than 4 years: 1
  Non-residential mission personnel: 3
**Other Personnel:**
  Short-term less than 1 year: 125
  Non-US serving in own/other country: 30
  Home ministry & office staff in US: 5
**Countries:** Brazil 1; China; Colombia; Philippines; Taiwan; Thailand

## Spanish American Evangelistic Ministries

650 Linwood Dr.
El Paso, TX 79928 USA
**Phone:** (915) 852-2525
**Fax:** (915) 852-4747
**E-mail:** staff@spanam.org
**Web Site:** www.spanam.org

*Mr. Eric Hupp, Director*

A nondenominational service agency engaged in printing ministry and benevolence, Bible distribution, correspondence courses, missionary education, literature distribution and translation work including evangelizing and teaching tracts.

**Purpose:** "...to provide New Testaments, Bibles, books and tracts to Spanish-speaking people all over the world."

**Year founded in US:** 1964

**Income for Overseas Min:** $29,022

**Fully Supported US Personnel Overseas:**
Non-residential mission personnel: 1

**Other Personnel:**
Home ministry & office staff in US: 1

## Spanish World Ministries

PO Box 542
Winona Lake, IN 46590 USA

**Phone:** (574) 267-8821
**Fax:** (574) 267-3524
**E-mail:** info@spanishworld.org
**Web Site:** www.spanishworld.org

*Mr. Cornelius Rivera, Exec. Director*

A nondenominational support agency of Independent and Fundamental tradition engaged in broadcasting, audio recording/distribution, correspondence courses, literature distribution, providing medical supplies and support of national workers.

**Purpose:** "...to assist local churches in the Spanish speaking world to carry out the ministry of communicating the Gospel of the Lord Jesus Christ and making disciples."

**Year founded in US:** 1959

**Income for Overseas Min:** $275,000

**Fully Supported US Personnel Overseas:**
Expecting to serve more than 4 years: 22
Non-residential mission personnel: 1

**Other Personnel:**
Short-term less than 1 year: 10
Non-US serving in own/other country: 22
Home ministry & office staff in US: 6

**Countries:** Argentina 3; Bolivia 1; Chile 2; Colombia 1; Guatemala 1; Honduras 2; Mexico 5; Paraguay 1; Peru 2; Spain 2; Uruguay 1; Venezuela 1

## Spiritual Growth Resources, Inc.

PO Box 2081
Gilroy, CA 95021-2081 USA

**Phone:** (408) 848-5608
**Fax:** (408) 848-4198
**E-mail:** SGR@sgrresources.org

*Rev. Royal L. Peck, President*

An interdenominational support agency of Baptist and Christian/Plymouth Brethren tradition engaged in support of national churches, discipleship, evangelism and support of national workers.

**Year founded in US:** 1984

**Income for Overseas Min:** $80,000

**Fully Supported US Personnel Overseas:**
Non-residential mission personnel: 2

**Other Personnel:**
Non-US serving in own/other country: 8
Home ministry & office staff in US: 1

**Countries:** Albania; Italy

## Spiritual Overseers Service International

PO Box 5985
La Quinta, CA 92248 USA

**Phone:** (760) 345-0906
**E-mail:** sosinternational@gmail.com
**Web Site:** www.sosinternational.us
**Associations:** EFMA

*Dr. Richard J. Frazer, President*

An interdenominational support agency of Evangelical tradition engaged in leadership development, childrens programs, support of national churches and training.

**Income for Overseas Min:** $100,000

**Fully Supported US Personnel Overseas:**
Non-residential mission personnel: 2

**Other Personnel:**
Short-term less than 1 year: 3
Non-US serving in own/other country: 1
Home ministry & office staff in US: 3

**Countries:** India

## Sports & Rec Plus

4121 Plank Rd., #433
Fredericksburg, VA 22407 USA

**Phone:** (540) 854-0210
**Fax:** (540) 854-0210

*Raptim International Travel:*

# $aving Church/Mission Workers Around the Globe since 1947

Africa • Asia • Central America • Europe • The Orient • Russia • South America • ANYWHERE World-Wide

*European Offices:*
- Germany
- Holland
- Italy
- Spain
- Switzerland

*USA Offices:*
- Chicago
- Colorado Springs
- Dallas
- Lewiston, NY

*Canadian Office:*
- Abbotsford, BC

## ALL YOU NEED TO KNOW...

## Raptim International Travel

**1-800-777-9232**
Toll-Free Fax: 1-800-766-2881
E-Mail: raptim@raptimusa.com
Lewiston, New York, 14092

**1-800-777-9232 ➤ www.raptimusa.com**

STRAIGHTWAY INC
TRANSPORTATION WITH A MISSION

**28666 Hildebrandt Road**
**P. O. Box 74068**
**Romulus, MI 48174**
**Web Site: www.straightway.com**

**Phone: (800)Say Amen**
*(729-2636)*
**Fax:     (734) 946-1419**

### MISSIONARY AND RELIEF AGENCY SERVICES

**Straightway** provides domestic & international transportation assistance to missionaries moving to all corners of the world.  Many *Mission Boards* rely on our services to either transport our missionary friends to their new overseas homes or assist with their return to the U.S after the completion of their service.

**Straightway** can handle shipments of all sizes to facilitate your overseas ministry & help guide you through the process from start to finish.

Many relief good agencies & humanitarian aid organizations rely on the transportation services provided by **Straightway** to deliver their precious cargo to remote destinations worldwide.  We can handle most all necessary arrangements for all modes of transport from origin to des-tination, no matter what size shipment your organization is forwarding.

**Straightway, Inc**. Was founded in 1968 with one objective in mind:
To provide a full range of quality air, marine and domestic transportation services to importers, exporters & domestic shippers around the country and world through an integrated network of expert companies.
We offer a ***"one call that's all"*** total transportation service throughout the entire world.

Call us today at 1-800-SAY AMEN for more information.

**E-mail:** 104063.2435@compuserve.com
**Web Site:** www.sportsrecplus.org

An interdenominational specialized agency of Baptist and Evangelical tradition engaged in evangelism, camping programs, church planting, evangelism and short-term programs.

**Purpose:** "...helping churches and mission organizations use sports and all forms of recreation--camping, drama, trips, arts & crafts and social activities--for outreach, evangelism, church planting and church growth."

**Year founded in US:** 1995

**Income for Overseas Min:** $15,000

**Gifts in Kind:** $10,000

**Personnel:**
Short-term less than 1 year: 15
Bi-vocational/tentmakers: 2
Home ministry & office staff in US: 1

## STEER, Inc.

PO Box 1236
Bismarck, ND 58502 USA
**Phone:** (701) 258-4911
**Fax:** (701) 258-7684
**E-mail:** steerinc@steerinc.com
**Web Site:** www.steerinc.com

*Mr. Keith Kost, Exec. Director*

A nondenominational support agency of Evangelical tradition engaged in a three-way partnership program to help raise funds, agricultural programs and services for other agencies.

**Purpose:** "...raising money to help existing missionary societies get the Gospel to the ends of the earth in the shortest possible time..."

**Year founded in US:** 1957

**Personnel:**
Home ministry & office staff in US: 6

## STEM (Short-Term Evangelical Missions) International

PO Box 386001
Minneapolis, MN 55438 USA
**Phone:** (952) 996-1385
**Fax:** (952) 996-1384
**E-mail:** info@stemintl.org
**Web Site:** www.stemintl.org
**Associations:** EFMA

*Rev. Roger P. Peterson, CEO*

An interdenominational sending agency

of Evangelical tradition engaged in evangelism, childrens programs, literature distribution, support of national workers, mobilization for mission, short-term programs and Christian education.

**Purpose:** "...to extend God's glory through strategic partnerships in short-term mission outreaches, training and publications."

**Year founded in US:** 1984

**Income for Overseas Min:** $620,313

**Fully Supported US Personnel Overseas:**
Expecting to serve more than 4 years: 4

**Other Personnel:**
Short-term less than 1 year: 185
Home ministry & office staff in US: 11

**Countries:** Belize; Dominican Republic; Haiti 4; Honduras; Jamaica; Mexico; Paraguay; Trinidad and Tobago; Venezuela

## Straightway Inc.

**(See ad page 300)**
PO Box 74068
Romulus, MI 48174-0068 USA
**Phone:** (800) 729-2636
**Fax:** (734) 946-1419
**E-mail:** fshrum@straightway.com
**Web Site:** www.straightway.com
**Associations:** AFMA

*Mr. Daniel T. Gregg, Owner*

An interdenominational service agency engaged in services for other agencies and technical assistance.

**Purpose:** "...to provide a full range of quality air, marine and transportation services."

**Year founded in US:** 1968

**Personnel:**
Home ministry & office staff in US: 7

## Supreme Task Intl., Inc.

PO Box 490245
Lawrenceville, GA 30044 USA
**Phone:** (678) 377-0179
**Fax:** (678) 377-0179
**E-mail:** supremetask@aol.com
**Web Site:** www.supremetask.org
**Associations:** AFMA

*Mr. Larry E. Derstine, President*

An interdenominational support agency of Charismatic tradition engaged in discipleship, leadership development, literacy work, literature distribution, relief and/or rehabilitation and training.

**Purpose:** "...to train and aid national leaders to reach the unreached."

**Year founded in US:** 1989

**Income for Overseas Min:** $92,418

**Fully Supported US Personnel Overseas:**
  Expecting to serve 1 to 4 years: 1

**Other Personnel:**
  Short-term less than 1 year: 12
  Non-US serving in own/other country: 4
  Home ministry & office staff in US: 2

**Countries:** India

## Surfing the Nations

PO Box 29393
Honolulu, HI 96819 USA

**Phone:** (808) 843-2342
**Fax:** (808) 853-1174
**E-mail:** info@surfingthenations.com
**Web Site:** www.surfingthenations.com

*Mr. Tom Bauer, Director*

An interdenominational specialized agency of Charismatic tradition engaged in short-term programs, discipleship, evangelism, leadership development, relief and/or rehabilitation and youth programs.

**Purpose:** "...to use the sport of surfing as a tool to communicate the Gospel locally and internationally."

**Year founded in US:** 1998

**Income for Overseas Min:** $246,380

**Fully Supported US Personnel Overseas:**
  Non-residential mission personnel: 8

**Other Personnel:**
  Short-term less than 1 year: 102
  Non-US serving in own/other country: 2
  Home ministry & office staff in US: 11

## Talking Bibles International

419 E. Grand Ave.
Escondido, CA 92025 USA

**Phone:** (760) 745-8105
**Fax:** (760) 745-8150
**E-mail:** info@talkingbibles.org
**Web Site:** www.talkingbibles.org

*Mr. Mark S. Hoekstra, President*

A specialized agency of Reformed tradition engaged in Bible distribution, audio recording/distribution, church planting, discipleship, services for other agencies and Bible translation.

**Purpose:** "A Talking Bible in every language and village...A Talking Bible on Sunday in every church."

**Year founded in US:** 1989

**Income for Overseas Min:** $453,146

**Fully Supported US Personnel Overseas:**
  Expecting to serve more than 4 years: 2
  Non-residential mission personnel: 1

**Other Personnel:**
  Short-term less than 1 year: 3
  Non-US serving in own/other country: 5
  Home ministry & office staff in US: 1

**Countries:** Africa—General; India; Unspecified Country 2

## TCM International
## See: TCM International Institute

## TCM International Institute

PO Box 24560
Indianapolis, IN 46224 USA

**Phone:** (317) 299-0333
**Fax:** (317) 290-8607
**E-mail:** tcm@tcmi.org
**Web Site:** www.tcmi.org

*Dr. Tony Twist, President*

A service agency of Christian (Restoration Movement) tradition engaged in theological education, benevolence and support of national churches in Eastern Europe.

**Purpose:** "...to assist, disciple, encourage and equip Eastern and Central European Christians to reach their own people for Christ."

**Year founded in US:** 1957

**Income for Overseas Min:** $2,274,432

**Fully Supported US Personnel Overseas:**
  Expecting to serve more than 4 years: 4
  Expecting to serve 1 to 4 years: 8
  Non-residential mission personnel: 12

**Other Personnel:**
  Short-term less than 1 year: 200
  Non-US serving in own/other country: 10
  Home ministry & office staff in US: 6

**Countries:** Austria 4; Belarus; Bulgaria; Czech Republic; Estonia; Hungary; Moldova; Poland; Romania; Russia; Ukraine

## TEAM (The Evangelical Alliance Mission)

PO Box 969
Wheaton, IL 60189-0969 USA

**Phone:** (630) 653-5300
**Fax:** (630) 653-1826
**E-mail:** info@teamworld.org
**Web Site:** www.teamworld.org
**Associations:** IFMA

*Dr. Charles Davis, Exec. Director*

An interdenominational sending agency of Evangelical tradition engaged in establishing churches through evangelism, discipleship, leadership development, theological education, and medical work.

**Purpose:** "...to help churches send missionaries to establish reproducing churches among the nations..."

**Year founded in US:** 1890

**Income for Overseas Min:** $26,212,000

**Fully Supported US Personnel Overseas:**
Expecting to serve more than 4 years: 514
Expecting to serve 1 to 4 years: 11

**Other Personnel:**
Short-term less than 1 year: 130
Non-US serving in own/other country: 2
Home ministry & office staff in US: 74

**Countries:** Asia—General 72; Australia 2; Austria 11; Brazil 6; Central Asia—General 6; Chad 18; Colombia 9; Croatia 2; Czech Republic 9; France 35; Germany 18; Honduras 6; India 2; Indonesia 15; Ireland 5; Italy 20; Japan 76; Mexico 15; Middle East 22; Mozambique 2; Nicaragua 2; Peru 6; Philippines 12; Portugal 8; Russia 10; South Africa 21; Spain 42; Sri Lanka 2; Swaziland 2; Sweden 2; Taiwan 16; Turkey 2; Ukraine 7; Venezuela 16; Zimbabwe 15

## Team Expansion, Inc.

3700 Hopewell Rd.
Louisville, KY 40299 USA

**Phone:** (502) 719-0007
**Fax:** (502) 719-0008
**E-mail:** info@teamexpansion.org
**Web Site:** www.teamexpansion.org

*Mr. Doug K. Lucas, President*

A nondenominational sending agency of Christian (Restoration Movement) tradition engaged in church planting, discipleship, evangelism, leadership development, partnership development and mobilization for mission.

**Purpose:** "...partnering with local churches to plant new churches worldwide, focusing on global ministries of prayer, mobilization, outreach and operations."

**Year founded in US:** 1978

**Income for Overseas Min:** $5,977,317

**Gifts in Kind:** $10,000

**Fully Supported US Personnel Overseas:**
Expecting to serve more than 4 years: 161
Expecting to serve 1 to 4 years: 24

**Other Personnel:**
Short-term less than 1 year: 75
Bi-vocational/tentmakers: 30
Non-US serving in own/other country: 5
Home ministry & office staff in US: 25

**Countries:** Africa—General 14; Asia—General 31; Cambodia 2; Central Asia—General 3; Colombia 5; Ecuador 6; Europe—General 16; Ireland 6; Italy 8; Japan 10; Mongolia 2; Mozambique; Peru; Philippines 4; Poland; Taiwan 21; Tanzania 2; Thailand 5; Ukraine 4; Venezuela 22

## Team World Outreach

PO Box 57A
Lima, NY 14485 USA

**Phone:** (585) 582-2792
**Fax:** (585) 624-1229
**E-mail:** international@elimfellowship.org
**Web Site:** www.elimfellowship.org

*Rev. Gary Ham, Intl. Min. Dir.*

A transdenominational service agency of Pentecostal tradition engaged in short-term programs, evangelism, medical work, support of national churches and youth programs. An affiliate of ELIM Fellowship. Statistics from 1998.

**Year founded in US:** 1981

**Income for Overseas Min:** $670,000

**Personnel:**
Short-term less than 1 year: 240
Home ministry & office staff in US: 3

## TEAMS for Medical Missions

PO Box 215
Macungie, PA 18062 USA

**Phone:** (610) 398-0070
**Fax:** (610) 710-5884
**E-mail:** t4mm@juno.com
**Web Site:** www.t4mm.org
*Mr. Raymond Shive, Director*

A nondenominational sending agency of Evangelical tradition engaged in medical work, church planting, evangelism, support of national churches and short-term programs.

**Purpose:** "...to build strong Jamaican churches with the commitment, ability and resources to make disciples of Jesus Christ locally and worldwide...linking them with the church in America in ministries of teaching, evangelism and medical services."

**Year founded in US:** 1992

**Income for Overseas Min:** $425,282

**Gifts in Kind:** $147,046

**Fully Supported US Personnel Overseas:**
   Expecting to serve more than 4 years: 2

**Other Personnel:**
   Short-term less than 1 year: 60
   Home ministry & office staff in US: 1

**Countries:** Jamaica 2

## Tech Serve International, Inc.
PO Box 598
Greenbrier, AR 72058 USA
**Phone:** (501) 679-2120
**Fax:** (501) 679-2017
**E-mail:** info@tech-serve.org
**Web Site:** www.techserve.org
*Mr. Wes Syverson, President*

A specialized agency engaged in utilities systems and construction, services for other agencies and supplying equipment.

**Purpose:** "...to assist missionary organizations by meeting their needs for facilities and equipment...to provide an opportunity for the service of Christian laymen skilled in the various technical areas."

**Year founded in US:** 1989

**Income for Overseas Min:** $500,000

**Gifts in Kind:** $250,000

**Fully Supported US Personnel Overseas:**
   Non-residential mission personnel: 12

**Other Personnel:**
   Short-term less than 1 year: 60
   Home ministry & office staff in US: 5

## Teen Missions Intl., Inc.
885 E. Hall Rd.
Merrit Island, FL 32953 USA
**Phone:** (321) 453-0350
**Fax:** (321) 452-7988
**E-mail:** info@teenmissions.org
**Web Site:** www.teenmissions.org
*Rev. Robert M. Bland, Founder/Director*

An interdenominational sending agency of Evangelical tradition engaged in short-term programs, childcare/orphanage programs, discipleship, missionary education, evangelism and youth programs.

**Purpose:** "...to challenge, train, and disciple young people, exposing them to worldwide missions."

**Year founded in US:** 1970

**Income for Overseas Min:** $960,000

**Gifts in Kind:** $500

**Fully Supported US Personnel Overseas:**
   Expecting to serve more than 4 years: 18
   Non-residential mission personnel: 4

**Other Personnel:**
   Short-term less than 1 year: 800
   Non-US serving in own/other country: 156
   Home ministry & office staff in US: 43

**Countries:** Australia 2; Belize 2; Brazil; Cambodia 1; Cameroon 2; Ecuador; Honduras 3; India; Indonesia 2; Madagascar; New Zealand; Philippines; South Africa 3; Uganda 1; Zambia 2

## Teen World Outreach
## See: Team World Outreach

## Tentmakers International
PO Box 30947
Seattle, WA 98113 USA
**Phone:** (206) 781-3151 x243
**Fax:** (206) 781-3182
**E-mail:** ti@gatiwa.com
**Web Site:** www.tentmakersinternational.org
*Mr. Kenneth Smith, TI Intl. Coordinator*

A nondenominational specialized agency of Evangelical tradition engaged in tentmaking, church planting, evangelism, missions information service, member care and missionary training.

**Purpose:** "...to promote tentmaking worldwide and to provide training and resources for tentmakers and tentmaking organizations including the exchange of ideas, information and opportunities."

**Year founded in US:** 1994

**Countries:** Africa—General; Asia—General; Australia; Brazil; China; Europe—General; Finland; India; Korea, South; Netherlands; Norway; Philippines; Thailand

## The Brethren Church, Inc.

524 College Ave.
Ashland, OH 44805 USA

**Phone:** (419) 289-1708
**Fax:** (419) 281-0450
**E-mail:** brethren@brethrenchurch.org
**Web Site:** www.brethrenchurch.org

*Rev. Kenneth D. Hunn, Exec. Director*

A denominational sending agency of Brethren tradition engaged in church planting, TEE, theological education, evangelism, support of national workers and youth programs.

**Year founded in US:** 1892

**Income for Overseas Min:** $800,000

**Fully Supported US Personnel Overseas:**
    Expecting to serve more than 4 years: 3

**Other Personnel:**
    Non-US serving in own/other country: 114
    Home ministry & office staff in US: 5

**Countries:** Argentina; Colombia; India; Ireland 1; Malaysia; Mexico 2; Paraguay; Peru; Philippines

## The Church of God of the Apostolic Faith, Inc.

PO Box 691745
Tulsa, OK 74169-1745 USA

**Phone:** (918) 437-7652
**Fax:** (918) 438-5633
**E-mail:** cogaf@tulsacoxmail.com
**Web Site:** www.cogaf.org

*Rev. Joseph L. Edmonson, Gen. Supt.*

A denominational sending agency of Pentecostal tradition engaged in theological education, Bible distribution, church construction, church planting, evangelism, literature distribution, providing medical supplies, training, video/film production/distribution and youth programs. Data from 2001.

**Purpose:** "Knowing Him...making Him known...that others may believe."

**Year founded in US:** 1914

**Fully Supported US Personnel Overseas:**
    Expecting to serve more than 4 years: 5
    Non-residential mission personnel: 2

**Other Personnel:**
    Short-term less than 1 year: 3
    Home ministry & office staff in US: 5

**Countries:** Honduras 1; Mexico 4

## The God's Story Project

PO Box 187
Hemet, CA 92546 USA

**Phone:** (951) 658-1619
**Fax:** (951) 658-9189
**E-mail:** info@gods-story.org
**Web Site:** www.gods-story.org

*Dorothy A. Miller, Exec. Director*

A transdenominational sending agency of Evangelical tradition engaged in video/film production/distribution, audio recording/distribution, church planting, evangelism and partnership development.

**Year founded in US:** 1998

**Income for Overseas Min:** $325,000

**Personnel:**
    Short-term less than 1 year: 2
    Non-US serving in own/other country: 10

**Countries:** Ethiopia; India; Kenya; Mozambique; Myanmar/Burma; Nepal; Nigeria; Zambia

## The Master's Mission, Inc.

PO Box 547
Robbinsville, NC 28771 USA

**Phone:** (828) 479-6873
**Fax:** (828) 479-2471
**E-mail:** info@mastersmission.org
**Web Site:** www.mastersmission.org

*Rev. Paul Teasdale, Exec. Director*

An interdenominational sending agency of Baptist tradition engaged in missionary training, childcare/orphanage programs, church planting, development, missionary education and services for other agencies.

**Year founded in US:** 1979

**Income for Overseas Min:** $1,803,690

**Gifts in Kind:** $16,615

**Fully Supported US Personnel Overseas:**
    Expecting to serve more than 4 years: 26

**Other Personnel:**
  Short-term less than 1 year: 130
  Non-US serving in own/other country: 19
  Home ministry & office staff in US: 15
**Countries:** Congo, Democratic Republic of; Ecuador 2; India; Israel; Kazakhstan 2; Kenya 20; Nigeria; Romania 2; Uganda

## The Mission Society

PO Box 9222637
Norcross, GA 30010 USA
**Phone:** (770) 446-1381
**Fax:** (770) 446-3044
**E-mail:** info@msum.org
**Web Site:** www.msum.org
**Associations:** EFMA

*Dr. Philip R. Granger, President & CFO*

A sending agency of Methodist and Wesleyan tradition engaged in evangelism, childcare/orphanage programs, church planting, Christian education, medical work and support of national churches.

**Purpose:** "...reaching the unreached with the Gospel, and helping national churches finish the task of winning their own people for Christ."

**Year founded in US:** 1984
**Income for Overseas Min:** $4,980,305
**Gifts in Kind:** $7,379
**Fully Supported US Personnel Overseas:**
  Expecting to serve more than 4 years: 46
  Expecting to serve 1 to 4 years: 30
  Non-residential mission personnel: 1
**Other Personnel:**
  Short-term less than 1 year: 6
  Bi-vocational/tentmakers: 3
  Home ministry & office staff in US: 29
**Countries:** China 3; Colombia; Costa Rica 2; France 6; Ghana 6; Hungary; India 2; Japan 2; Kazakhstan 6; Mexico 2; Paraguay 6; Peru 4; Philippines 2; Russia 4; Tanzania 1

## The Waray-Waray Project

414 Highland Dr.
Bartlesville, OK 74003 USA
**Phone:** (918) 336-0750
**Fax:** (918) 336-3977
**E-mail:** snider_dan@yahoo.org
**Web Site:** www.waray.org

*Mr. Gordon Clymer, Director/Chairman*

A nondenominational service agency of Christian (Restoration Movement) tradition engaged in church planting, broadcasting, church construction, funds transmission, support of national workers and support of national churches.

**Purpose:** "...to assist Filipino natives in evangelizing the Waray-Waray tribal group."
**Year founded in US:** 1992
**Income for Overseas Min:** $11,201
**Personnel:**
  Non-US serving in own/other country: 12
**Countries:** Philippines

## The Word for the World

PO Box 26363
Colorado Springs, CO 80920 USA
**Phone:** (719) 594-2052
**Fax:** (719) 594-4046
**E-mail:** info@twftw.org
**Web Site:** www.twftw.org

*Veroni Kruger, President*

A nondenominational sending agency of Evangelical tradition engaged in Bible translation, Bible distribution, linguistics, literacy work, support of national workers and training.

**Purpose:** "...to recruit, train and assist pioneer Bible translators (i.e. Bible translators working in languages into which the Bible has never before been translated) ."
**Year founded in US:** 1997
**Income for Overseas Min:** $660,000
**Gifts in Kind:** $80,000
**Fully Supported US Personnel Overseas:**
  Expecting to serve more than 4 years: 4
  Expecting to serve 1 to 4 years: 3
  Non-residential mission personnel: 2
**Other Personnel:**
  Non-US serving in own/other country: 21
  Home ministry & office staff in US: 4
**Countries:** Congo, Democratic Republic of; Ethiopia; Malawi; Slovakia 2; South Africa; Tanzania; Zambia 2; Zimbabwe

## Things To Come Mission, Inc.

2200 English Ave.
Indianapolis, IN 46201 USA
**Phone:** (317) 262-8806
**Fax:** (317) 262-8852

**E-mail:** tcm@tcmusa.org
**Web Site:** www.tcmusa.org
*Mr. Ben N. Anderson, Exec. Director*

A nondenominational sending agency engaged in church planting, childrens programs, church construction, theological education, evangelism and leadership development.

**Purpose:** "...preaching of the gospel of salvation through faith in the shed blood of Jesus Christ, training believers for ministry and leadership and establishing indigenous, local churches..."

**Year founded in US:** 1955

**Income for Overseas Min:** $1,000,000

**Fully Supported US Personnel Overseas:**
Expecting to serve more than 4 years: 2
Expecting to serve 1 to 4 years: 2
Non-residential mission personnel: 2

**Other Personnel:**
Short-term less than 1 year: 27
Bi-vocational/tentmakers: 1
Non-US serving in own/other country: 371
Home ministry & office staff in US: 4

**Countries:** Brazil 2; China; Indonesia; Kenya; Philippines; South Africa; Turkey; Uganda; United Kingdom

## TITUS International

1515 McBrien Rd.
Chattanooga, TN 37412 USA
**Phone:** (423) 867-7079
**Fax:** (423) 867-7263
**E-mail:** info@titusinternational.org
**Web Site:** www.titusinternational.org
*Mr. Lowell David Marcum, President*

A nondenominational service agency of Baptist tradition engaged in support of national workers, camping programs, church planting, discipleship and evangelism.

**Purpose:** "...to teach nationals to reach their world for Christ."

**Year founded in US:** 1984

**Income for Overseas Min:** $800,000

**Fully Supported US Personnel Overseas:**
Expecting to serve more than 4 years: 16
Non-residential mission personnel: 14

**Other Personnel:**
Short-term less than 1 year: 20
Non-US serving in own/other country: 80

Home ministry & office staff in US: 3
**Countries:** Austria 2; Czech Republic 2; Moldova 1; Romania 5; Ukraine 6

## TMA Ministries

PO Box 49060
St. Petersburg, FL 33743 USA
**Phone:** (901) 301-1550
**Fax:** (727) 321-2924
**E-mail:** TMAjl3@msn.com
*Dr. John L. Langston III, President*

A nondenominational service agency of Baptist and Evangelical tradition engaged in theological education, evangelism and architectual support services for global missionary enterprise.

**Purpose:** "...to focus on architectural support services for the global missionary enterprise, worldwide evangelism among the architectural professional community and preaching/teaching for theological education."

**Year founded in US:** 1982

**Income for Overseas Min:** $17,000

**Fully Supported US Personnel Overseas:**
Expecting to serve 1 to 4 years: 8
Non-residential mission personnel: 2

**Other Personnel:**
Short-term less than 1 year: 10
Bi-vocational/tentmakers: 2
Home ministry & office staff in US: 1

**Countries:** Belize; Europe—General; Guyana; India; Indonesia; Mexico; Serbia and Montenegro; Trinidad and Tobago; United Kingdom; Western Europe—General

## Touch the World Ministries
## See: Touch the World Youth Ministries

## Touch the World Youth Ministries

1 Maple St.
Allendale, NJ 07401 USA
**Phone:** (201) 760-9925
**Fax:** (201) 760-9926
**E-mail:** info@touchtheworld.org
**Web Site:** www.touchtheworld.org
*Rev. Jeff Boucher, President*

A nondenominational sending agency of

Charismatic and Evangelical tradition engaged in short-term programs, evangelism and youth programs. Financial data from 2002.

**Purpose:** "...to introduce teenagers to Jesus Christ as their Savior and Lord, and to disciple Christian students to share Christ."

**Year founded in US:** 1990

**Income for Overseas Min:** $350,825

**Fully Supported US Personnel Overseas:**
Expecting to serve more than 4 years: 3

**Other Personnel:**
Non-US serving in own/other country: 12
Home ministry & office staff in US: 3

**Countries:** Cuba; Japan; Uganda 3

## Training Evangelistic Leadership (T.E.L.) , Inc.
PO Box E
Denton, TX 76202-1650 USA
**Phone:** (940) 382-8365
**E-mail:** roy.rob@verizon.net
**Web Site:** www.tel-intl.org
*Dr. Sean Collins, American Director*

An interdenominational sending agency of Evangelical tradition engaged in evangelism, follow-up discipleship training, evangelism and support of national workers.

**Purpose:** "...to serve alongside existing national churches called to develop multi-national gospel teams which major in evangelism, follow-up and discipleship."

**Year founded in US:** 1976

**Income for Overseas Min:** $741,728

**Fully Supported US Personnel Overseas:**
Expecting to serve more than 4 years: 39
Expecting to serve 1 to 4 years: 7

**Other Personnel:**
Short-term less than 1 year: 12
Bi-vocational/tentmakers: 18
Non-US serving in own/other country: 55
Home ministry & office staff in US: 5

**Countries:** China 15; Hong Kong 7; India 4; Indonesia 4; Philippines 7; Singapore; Vietnam 2

## Trans World Missions
PO Box 10
Glendale, CA 91209-0010 USA
**Phone:** (818) 830-3437
**Fax:** (818) 830-3437

**E-mail:** LuisM@aol.com
*Rev. Luis R. Mejia, President*

A nondenominational support agency of Charismatic and Evangelical tradition engaged in church planting, camping programs, child-care/orphanage programs, discipleship, evangelism and leadership development.

**Purpose:** "...ministering to the whole man spiritually, physically, emotionally and mentally..."

**Year founded in US:** 1949

**Income for Overseas Min:** $138,728

**Personnel:**
Non-US serving in own/other country: 21
Home ministry & office staff in US: 3

**Countries:** Colombia; Costa Rica; El Salvador; Guatemala; Honduras; Nicaragua; Panama; Venezuela

## Trans World Radio, Intl.
PO Box 8700
Cary, NC 27512-8700 USA
**Phone:** (800) 456-7897
**Fax:** (919) 460-3702
**E-mail:** info@twr.org
**Web Site:** www.twr.org
**Associations:** IFMA
*Dr. David G. Tucker, President/CEO*

An interdenominational specialized agency of Evangelical tradition engaged in broadcasting, audio recording/distribution, church planting, correspondence courses, evangelism and technical assistance.

**Purpose:** "...to assist the Church to fulfill the command of Jesus Christ to make disciples of all peoples and to do so by using and making available mass media..."

**Year founded in US:** 1952

**Income for Overseas Min:** $24,258,000

**Fully Supported US Personnel Overseas:**
Expecting to serve more than 4 years: 82
Expecting to serve 1 to 4 years: 17

**Other Personnel:**
Short-term less than 1 year: 6
Non-US serving in own/other country: 148
Home ministry & office staff in US: 51

**Countries:** Aruba 8; Austria 9; Cambodia 4; Germany 2; Guam 9; Monaco 2; Netherlands 8; Singapore 11; Slovakia 6; South Africa 17; Swaziland 4; Unspecified Country 2

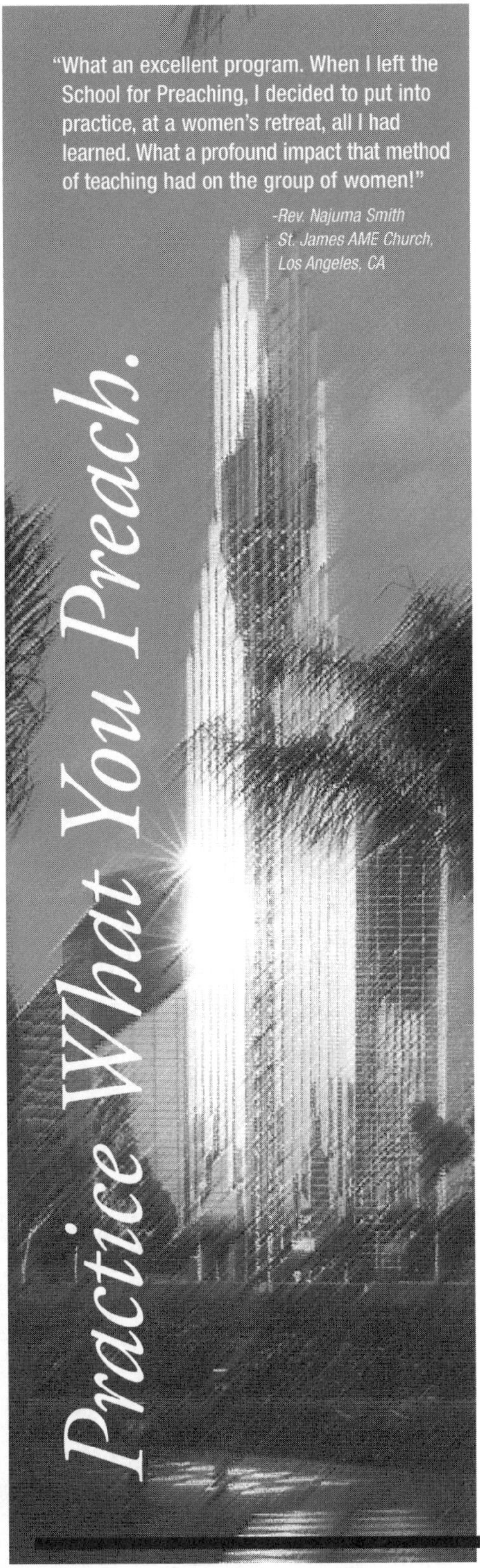

*Practice What You Preach.*

> "What an excellent program. When I left the School for Preaching, I decided to put into practice, at a women's retreat, all I had learned. What a profound impact that method of teaching had on the group of women!"
>
> *-Rev. Najuma Smith*
> *St. James AME Church,*
> *Los Angeles, CA*

## DATES FOR BASIC INTENSIVES

September 18-22, 2006
February 5-9, 2007
September 17-21, 2007

## DATES FOR ADVANCED INTENSIVES

October 2-6, 2006  *(The Method)*
October 23-27, 2006  *(The Messenger)*
March 5-9, 2007  *(The Message)*
April 23-27, 2007  *(The Milieu)*
October 1-5, 2007  *(The Method)*
October 22-26, 2007  *(The Messenger)*

## FACULTY

Dr. Robert H. Schuller
Dr. Robert A. Schuller
Dr. Lawrence Wilkes
Dr. Paul D. Borden
Capt. Donald E. den Dulk
Dr. Sandra Herron
Dr. Juan Carlos Ortiz

## CONTACT INFORMATION

Robert Schuller School for Preaching
13280 Chapman Avenue
Garden Grove, CA  92840

**Phone:** 714-971-4238
**Fax:** 714-971-4204
**Email:** Preaching@crystalcathedral.org
**Website:** www.crystalcathedral.org then
scroll to School for Preaching

## Robert Schuller School for Preaching

# Travel King Tours

## ROYAL VALUES SINCE 1980

- DISCOUNTED FARES FOR ALL CHURCH & MISSION GROUPS

- OVER 25 YEARS EXPERIENCE IN PROVIDING WORLD TRAVEL

- EXCEPTIONAL SERVICES TO MEET EVERY TRAVEL NEED

- $100 WELOME BONUS GIVEN FIRST TIME BOOKING (WITH GROUP OF FOUR OR MORE)

Call Us Toll Free
**1-866-773-8355**

**www.travelkingtours.com**
info@travelkingtours.com

# Tribes and Nations Outreach

PO Box 1454
Baldwin Park, CA 91706 USA
**Phone:** (626) 373-4963
**E-mail:** tnousa@aol.com
*Arlene del Campo, Develop. Dir.*

A nondenominational support agency of Charismatic and Pentecostal tradition engaged in missionary training, agricultural programs, Bible distribution, church planting, medical work and short-term programs. Data from 2002.

**Purpose:** "...to build the body of Christ in Asia through training of nationals and provision of Bibles and other encouragement like sending medical missions. It seeks to mobilize, equip and involve the body of Christ worldwide for missions in Asia."

**Year founded in US:** 1986

**Income for Overseas Min:** $21,300

# Turkish World Outreach

508 Fruitvale Ct.
Grand Junction, CO 81504 USA
**Phone:** (970) 434-1942
**Fax:** (970) 434-1461
**E-mail:** TWO@onlinecol.com
**Web Site:** www.two-fot.org
*Rev. Steven E. Hagerman, U.S. Director*

A nondenominational support agency of Evangelical tradition engaged in evangelism, Bible distribution, church planting, literature distribution, mobilization for mission, services for other agencies and prayer mobilization.

**Purpose:** "...to evangelize Turks by any means possible."

**Year founded in US:** 1969

**Income for Overseas Min:** $964,618

**Fully Supported US Personnel Overseas:**
Expecting to serve more than 4 years: 24

**Other Personnel:**
Short-term less than 1 year: 2
Bi-vocational/tentmakers: 36
Non-US serving in own/other country: 6
Home ministry & office staff in US: 11

**Countries:** Germany 2; Turkey 22

# UFM International
# See: CrossWorld

# U.S. Center for World Mission

1605 E. Elizabeth St.
Pasadena, CA 91104 USA
**Phone:** (626) 797-1111
**Fax:** (626) 398-2263
**E-mail:** personnel@uscwm.org
**Web Site:** www.uscwm.org
**Associations:** EFMA, IFMA
*Rev. Greg Parsons, Gen. Director*

An interdenominational support agency of Evangelical tradition engaged in mobilization for mission, theological education and missions information service. Home staff data from 2002.

**Purpose:** "To stimulate and encourage the growth of a movement for frontier missions throughout the United States and the world..."

**Year founded in US:** 1976

**Fully Supported US Personnel Overseas:**
Expecting to serve more than 4 years: 10
Expecting to serve 1 to 4 years: 6

**Other Personnel:**
Non-US serving in own/other country: 5
Home ministry & office staff in US: 95

**Countries:** China; India 4; Korea, South 1; Mexico; Philippines 3; United Kingdom 2

# Ukrainian Childrens Fund

1629 Pine Dr.
Grove, OK 74344 USA
**Phone:** (918) 786-7278
**E-mail:** david.tinney@gmail.com
**Web Site:** www.ukrainianchildrensfund.org
*Mr. David L. Tinney, Founder/President*

A support agency of Evangelical tradition engaged in childcare/orphanage programs, childrens programs, providing medical supplies and relief and/or rehabilitation.

**Year founded in US:** 2001

**Income for Overseas Min:** $10,000

**Personnel:**
Short-term less than 1 year: 20
Non-US serving in own/other country: 2

**Countries:** Ukraine

# United Board for Christian Higher Education in Asia

475 Riverside Dr. Rm. 1221
New York, NY 10115 USA

**Phone:** (212) 870-2600
**Fax:** (212) 870-2322
**Web Site:** www.unitedboard.org
*Patricia S. Stranahan, President*

An interdenominational service agency of Ecumenical tradition engaged in leadership development, technical assistance and training. Statistical data from 2002.

**Purpose:** "...to contribute to higher education and to the exchange of resources in and with Asia for the pursuit of truth and knowledge...and full human development understood from the perspective of Christian faith."

**Year founded in US:** 1932

**Income for Overseas Min:** $5,425,196

**Personnel:**
  Home ministry & office staff in US: 11

# United Church Board for World Ministries
## See: United Church of Christ —Wider Church Ministries

# United Church of Christ— Wider Church Ministries
700 Prospect Ave. E.
Cleveland, OH 44115 USA

**Phone:** (216) 736-3200
**Fax:** (216) 736-3203
**E-mail:** rogersc@ucc.org
**Web Site:** www.ucc.org
*Rev. Cally Rogers-Witte, Executive Minister*

A denominational sending agency of Reformed, Ecumenical and Congregational tradition engaged in development, Christian education, theological education, leadership development and medical work. Statistical data from 1998.

**Year founded in US:** 1812

**Income for Overseas Min:** $13,379,044

**Fully Supported US Personnel Overseas:**
  Expecting to serve 1 to 4 years: 126

**Other Personnel:**
  Home ministry & office staff in US: 48

**Countries:** Argentina; Asia—General; Australia; Botswana; Brazil; Chile; China; Dominican Republic; Ecuador; El Salvador; Fiji; Germany; Guatemala; Haiti; Honduras; Hong Kong; Hungary; India; Indonesia; Israel; Jamaica; Japan; Kenya; Korea, South; Lebanon; Lesotho; Marshall Islands; Mexico; Namibia; Nepal; Nicaragua; Paraguay; Philippines; South Africa; Sri Lanka; Swaziland; Taiwan; Thailand; Turkey; Vietnam; Zimbabwe

# United Evangelical Churches
PO Box 1000
San Juan Bautista, CA 95045-1000 USA

**Phone:** (800) 595-4832
**Fax:** (831) 635-0909
**E-mail:** admin@uecol.org
**Web Site:** www.uecol.org
*Mr. Robert B. Fort, Chairman/CEO*

A transdenominational service agency of Charismatic and Evangelical tradition engaged in services for other agencies, association of missions, church planting, leadership development, member care and support of national churches. Has outreaches and/or personnel in more than 70 nations.

**Year founded in US:** 1958

# United Methodist Church, General Board of Global Ministries
475 Riverside Dr., Rm. 350
New York, NY 10115 USA

**Phone:** (800) 862-4246
**Fax:** (212) 870-3748
**E-mail:** info@gbgm-umc.org
**Web Site:** www.gbgm-umc.org
**Associations:** CWS
*Rev. Randy Day, Gen. Secretary*

A denominational sending agency of Methodist tradition responding to program and personnel needs through relationships to partner churches and ecumenical organizations all over the world, including support of national churches, education, information service, relief and/or rehabilitation, short-term programs and missionary training.

**Year founded in US:** 1820

**Income for Overseas Min:** $91,200,000

**Fully Supported US Personnel Overseas:**
  Expecting to serve more than 4 years: 486

**Other Personnel:**
  Short-term less than 1 year: 93
  Non-US serving in own/other country: 308
**Countries:** Unspecified Country 486

## United Pentecostal Church Intl., Foreign Missions Div.

8855 Dunn Rd.
Hazelwood, MO 63042 USA
**Phone:** (314) 837-7300
**Fax:** (314) 837-2387
**E-mail:** fmwebmaster@upci.org
**Web Site:** www.upci.org
*Rev. Bruce Allen Howell, Gen. Director*

A denominational sending agency of Pentecostal and Apostolic tradition engaged in evangelism, church planting, discipleship, theological education, evangelism and leadership development. Financial data from 2002.

**Year founded in US:** 1945

**Income for Overseas Min:** $19,352,247

**Fully Supported US Personnel Overseas:**
Expecting to serve 1 to 4 years: 340
Non-residential mission personnel: 317

**Other Personnel:**
Short-term less than 1 year: 300
Non-US serving in own/other country: 236
Home ministry & office staff in US: 35

**Countries:** Albania; American Samoa; Argentina; Armenia; Aruba; Australia; Austria; Azerbaijan; Bahamas, The; Bangladesh; Belarus; Belgium; Belize; Benin; Bhutan; Bolivia; Bosnia and Herzegovina; Botswana; Brazil; Bulgaria; Burkina Faso; Burundi; Cambodia; Cameroon; Caribbean—General; Cayman Islands; Central African Republic; Chile; Colombia; Congo, Democratic Republic of; Costa Rica; Cote d'Ivoire; Croatia; Cuba; Cyprus; Czech Republic; Dominican Republic; Ecuador; Egypt; El Salvador; Equatorial Guinea; Europe—General; Fiji; Finland; France; French Guiana; Gabon; Gambia, The; Georgia; Germany; Ghana; Greece; Guam; Guatemala; Guyana; Haiti; Honduras; Hong Kong; Hungary; India; Indonesia; Israel; Italy; Jamaica; Japan; Jordan; Kazakhstan; Kenya; Korea, South; Laos; Latvia; Lebanon; Lesotho; Liberia; Lithuania; Macedonia; Madagascar; Malawi; Malaysia; Malta; Mauritius; Mexico; Micronesia, Federated States of; Middle East; Morocco; Mozambique; Myanmar/Burma; Namibia; Nepal; Netherlands; New Caledonia; New Zealand; Nicaragua; Niger; Nigeria; Norway; Oceania—General; Pakistan; Palestine; Panama; Papua New Guinea; Paraguay; Peru; Philippines; Poland; Portugal; Puerto Rico; Reunion; Romania; Russia; Rwanda; Samoa; Serbia and Montenegro; Seychelles; Sierra Leone; Singapore; Slovakia; Solomon Islands; South Africa; Spain; Sri Lanka; Sudan; Suriname; Swaziland; Sweden; Switzerland; Taiwan; Tanzania; Thailand; Togo; Tonga; Trinidad and Tobago; Turkey; Uganda; Ukraine; United Kingdom; Uruguay; Vanuatu; Venezuela; Vietnam; Zambia; Zimbabwe

## United World Mission

9401-B Southern Pines Blvd.
Charlotte, NC 28270 USA
**Phone:** (704) 357-3355
**Fax:** (704) 357-6389
**E-mail:** info@uwm.org
**Web Site:** www.unitedworldmission.org
**Associations:** EFMA, IFMA
*Dr. John Bernard, Exec. Director*

A nondenominational sending agency engaged in church planting, development, leadership development, support of national churches and missionary training.

**Purpose:** "...to advance church planting movements throughout the world."

**Year founded in US:** 1946

**Income for Overseas Min:** $6,500,000

**Fully Supported US Personnel Overseas:**
Expecting to serve more than 4 years: 95
Expecting to serve 1 to 4 years: 21
Non-residential mission personnel: 125

**Other Personnel:**
Short-term less than 1 year: 45
Bi-vocational/tentmakers: 1
Home ministry & office staff in US: 3

**Countries:** Africa—General 18; Central Asia—General 39; Eastern Europe—General 9; Europe—General 2; Latin America—General 15; Western Europe—General 12

## University of the Family

12211 W. Alameda Pkwy. #200
Lakewood, CO 80228 USA
**Phone:** (303) 933-3331
**Fax:** (303) 933-2153
**E-mail:** inquire@marriage.org
**Web Site:** www.marriage.org
**Associations:** AFMA

*Mike & Marilyn Phillipps, Co-Presidents*
A specialized agency providing training materials in 90 countries and 30 languages for strengthening married couples for evangelism and other ministries. More than 20,000 leaders lead marriage classes in their homes around the world. Statistical data for 1998.

**Purpose:** "To help couples establish their homes as powerful lighthouses in their neighborhoods, reaching out to those around in the storms of life."

**Year founded in US:** 1983

**Income for Overseas Min:** $70,000

**Personnel:**
  Short-term less than 1 year: 6
  Bi-vocational/tentmakers: 10
  Non-US serving in own/other country: 10
  Home ministry & office staff in US: 20

## UWEZO International

PO Box 434
Hudson, WI 54016 USA
**Phone:** (715) 760-1882
**E-mail:** uwezo413@hotmail.com

*Andrea Kela, Exec. Director*
A nondenominational specialized agency of Evangelical tradition engaged in discipleship, evangelism, management consulting/training and partnership development. Their primary activity is recovery/aftercare/family support.

**Purpose:** "...to share the Good News of salvation to inmates, addicts, and their families through outreach ministries, so that they can live free in Christ..."

**Year founded in US:** 2000

**Income for Overseas Min:** $1,510

**Fully Supported US Personnel Overseas:**
  Expecting to serve more than 4 years: 1

**Other Personnel:**
  Short-term less than 1 year: 6
  Non-US serving in own/other country: 1
  Home ministry & office staff in US: 1

**Countries:** Kenya 1

## VELA Ministries International

PO Box 28850
San Jose, CA 95159-8840 USA
**Phone:** (408) 995-5090
**Fax:** (408) 995-5092

**E-mail:** galo@velaministries.org
**Web Site:** www.velaministries.org
*Galo Vasquez, Founder/CEO*
An interdenominational support agency of Evangelical tradition engaged in leadership development, church planting, evangelism, mission-related research and training. Statistical data from 2002.

**Year founded in US:** 1990

**Income for Overseas Min:** $102,235

**Fully Supported US Personnel Overseas:**
  Expecting to serve 1 to 4 years: 1

**Other Personnel:**
  Non-US serving in own/other country: 1
  Home ministry & office staff in US: 2

**Countries:** Latin America—General; Russia

## Vellore Christian Medical College Board (USA) , Inc.

475 Riverside Dr. Ste. 243
New York, NY 10115 USA
**Phone:** (212) 870-2640
**Fax:** (212) 870-2173
**E-mail:** usaboard@vellorecmc.org
**Web Site:** www.vellorecmc.org

*Rev. Louis L. Knowles, President*
An interdenominational specialized agency of Ecumenical tradition engaged in medical work, development, funds transmission, volunteer recruitment, providing medical supplies, supplying equipment and training. Statistical data from 2001.

**Purpose:** "...to provide a focus for excellence and integrity through the support of the wide range of programs of Vellore Christian Medical College and Hospital, Vellore, India."

**Year founded in US:** 1948

**Income for Overseas Min:** $1,041,423

**Gifts in Kind:** $118,000

**Personnel:**
  Home ministry & office staff in US: 6

## Venture International

PO Box 7396
Tempe, AZ 85281 USA
**Phone:** (480) 730-2702
**Fax:** (480) 730-2720
**E-mail:** info@ventureint.org
**Web Site:** www.ventureint.org

*Mr. Leonard Rodgers, President/CEO*

An interdenominational service agency of Evangelical tradition engaged in development, disability assistance programs, support of national churches, partnership development, relief and/or rehabilitation.

**Purpose:** "...serves as a bridge between those in need and those who want to help God's people in the Middle East; empowering and enhancing their work through strategic partnerships, emergency relief, small business creation and people development."

**Year founded in US:** 1986

**Personnel:**
    Non-US serving in own/other country: 51
    Home ministry & office staff in US: 6

**Countries:** Egypt; Iraq; Israel; Jordan; Kyrgyzstan; Lebanon

## Village Ministries Intl.

5350 S. Western, Ste. 200
Oklahoma, City OK 73109 USA

**Phone:** (405) 634-4373
**Fax:** (405) 634-4465
**E-mail:** bobt@villageministries.org
**Web Site:** www.villageministries.org

*Mr. Bob Thompson, CEO*

A nondenominational service agency of Fundamental tradition engaged in training pastors to be pastors in their own country and evangelism.

**Purpose:** "...to fulfill the Great Commission of making disciples through going into all the world to train and develop nationals for ministry, evangelizing the lost by developing the opportunities for Christians to experience missionary activity through short-term mission trips and by teaching through Biblical study materials on the printed page and via Internet technology."

**Year founded in US:** 1991

**Income for Overseas Min:** $412,000

**Personnel:**
    Short-term less than 1 year: 126
    Non-US serving in own/other country: 63
    Home ministry & office staff in US: 4

**Countries:** Belarus; Ghana; India; Myanmar/Burma; Nicaragua; Nigeria; Sri Lanka

## Vineyard Church USA— Missions

112 Harvard Ave., #265
Claremont, CA 91711 USA

**Phone:** (909) 626-0773
**E-mail:** missions@vineyardusa.org
**Web Site:** www.vineyardusa.org

*Rev. Mark Fields, Missions Coordinator*

A consortium of 8 different associations of Charismatic and Evangelical tradition engaged in church planting, evangelism, leadership development and support of national churches. There are approximately 380 Vineyard Churches outside the USA in 52 countries. The eight associations oversee the work being done in different areas of the world.

**Purpose:** "...to equip the saints for the advancement of the Kingdom of God through evangelizing and church planting."

**Year founded in US:** 1982

## Virginia Mennonite Board of Missions

901 Parkwood Dr.
Harrisonburg, VA 22802 USA

**Phone:** (540) 434-9727
**Fax:** (540) 434-7627
**E-mail:** info@vmbm.org
**Web Site:** www.vmbm.org

*Mr. Loren E. Horst, President*

An interdenominational sending agency of Mennonite tradition engaged in church planting, TEE, missions information service, leadership development, management consulting/training and short-term programs.

**Purpose:** "...to build and connect worldwide communities of faith."

**Year founded in US:** 1919

**Income for Overseas Min:** $1,047,567

**Gifts in Kind:** $2,500

**Fully Supported US Personnel Overseas:**
    Expecting to serve more than 4 years: 6
    Expecting to serve 1 to 4 years: 8

**Other Personnel:**
    Short-term less than 1 year: 120
    Non-US serving in own/other country: 2
    Home ministry & office staff in US: 11

**Countries:** Albania 1; Italy 2; Jamaica 2; Trinidad and Tobago 1

## Voice of the Martyrs, The

PO Box 443
Bartlesville, OK 74005-0443 USA
**Phone:** (877) 337-0302
**Fax:** (918) 338-0189
**E-mail:** thevoice@vom-usa.org
**Web Site:** www.persecution.com
*Mr. Tom White, Exec. Director*

A nondenominational support agency of Evangelical tradition engaged in Bible distribution, audio recording/distribution, broadcasting, literature distribution, providing medical supplies and support of national workers, working in 71 countries.

**Purpose:** "...to serve the persecuted church through practical and spiritual assistance while leading Christians in the free world into fellowship with them."

**Year founded in US:** 1967
**Income for Overseas Min:** $25,305,375
**Gifts in Kind:** $14,183,885
**Personnel:**
   Home ministry & office staff in US: 111

## Walk Thru the Bible Ministries, Inc.

4201 N. Peachtree Rd.
Atlanta, GA 30341 USA
**Phone:** (770) 458-9300
**Fax:** (770) 454-9313
**E-mail:** tsparks@walkthru.org
**Web Site:** www.walkthru.org
**Associations:** EFMA

*Mr. Chip Ingram, President*

A nondenominational support agency of Evangelical tradition engaged in training, broadcasting, literature production, support of national churches and support of national workers.

**Purpose:** "...to contribute to the spiritual growth of Christians worldwide through Bible teaching, tools, and training."

**Year founded in US:** 1976
**Income for Overseas Min:** $1,951,167
**Gifts in Kind:** $382,136
**Fully Supported US Personnel Overseas:**
   Non-residential mission personnel: 3
**Other Personnel:**
   Non-US serving in own/other country: 275

Home ministry & office staff in US: 47

**Countries:** Armenia; Bangladesh; Belarus; Bhutan; Botswana; Brazil; China; Congo, Democratic Republic of; Cuba; Egypt; Honduras; India; Indonesia; Japan; Kenya; Korea, South; Latvia; Lesotho; Liberia; Mexico; Moldova; Morocco; Mozambique; Myanmar/Burma; Namibia; Nepal; Nigeria; Philippines; Romania; Russia; Singapore; South Africa; Sri Lanka; Sudan; Swaziland; Tanzania; Uganda; Ukraine; United Kingdom; Zambia; Zimbabwe

## Waymakers International

PO Box 203131
Austin, TX 78720-3131 USA
**Phone:** (800) 264-5214
**Fax:** (512) 323-9066
**E-mail:** info@waymakers.org
**Web Site:** www.waymakers.org
*Mr. Steve Hawthorne, Director*

An interdenominational service agency of Evangelical tradition engaged in prayer mobilization.

**Purpose:** "...to impart vision and training for leaders of local movements of united prayer that will prepare communities for evangelization and spiritual awakening."

**Year founded in US:** 1994
**Income for Overseas Min:** $15,000
**Gifts in Kind:** $9,000
**Personnel:**
   Short-term less than 1 year: 2
   Home ministry & office staff in US: 7

## Waymarks International Radio Ministries

PO Box 2324
Macon, GA 31203 USA
**Phone:** (478) 750-1422
**E-mail:** loren@waymarks.org
**Web Site:** www.waymarks.org
*Rev. Loren H. Wilson, Radio Pastor*

A nondenominational specialized agency of Baptist and Charismatic tradition engaged in broadcasting, audio recording/distribution, correspondence courses and theological education. Volunteers in 7 countries.

**Year founded in US:** 1987
**Income for Overseas Min:** $22,514
**Personnel:**

Bi-vocational/tentmakers: 1
Home ministry & office staff in US: 1

## WEC International

PO Box 1707
Fort Washington, PA 19034 USA
**Phone:** (215) 646-2322
**Fax:** (215) 646-6202
**E-mail:** info@wec-usa.org
**Web Site:** www.wec-int.org
**Associations:** EFMA

*Dr. Louis V. Sutton, Director*

An interdenominational sending agency of Evangelical tradition engaged in church planting, childrens programs, furloughed missionary support, mobilization for mission, short-term programs and missionary training.

**Purpose:** "To bring the gospel . . . to the remaining unevangelized peoples with the utmost urgency, to demonstrate the compassion of Christ to a needy world, to plant churches and lead them to spiritual maturity and to inspire, mobilize and train for cross-cultural mission."

**Year founded in US:** 1939

**Income for Overseas Min:** $3,960,800

**Fully Supported US Personnel Overseas:**
Expecting to serve more than 4 years: 166
Non-residential mission personnel: 2

**Other Personnel:**
Short-term less than 1 year: 16
Home ministry & office staff in US: 59

**Countries:** Brazil 4; Cambodia 2; Chad 5; Cote d'Ivoire 7; El Salvador 2; Equatorial Guinea 2; France 2; Ghana 3; Guinea 2; Guinea-Bissau 2; Italy 6; Macedonia 1; Mexico 18; Mongolia 1; New Zealand 2; Russia 3; Senegal 1; South Africa 3; Spain 13; Thailand 6; United Kingdom 9; Unspecified Country 71; Venezuela 1

## Weiner Ministries Intl.

PO Box 1799
Gainesville, GA 32602 USA
**Phone:** (352) 375-4455
**Fax:** (352) 335-0080
**E-mail:** YouthNow@aol.com
**Web Site:** www.weinerministries.com

*Mr. Robert Weiner, President*

A nondenominational support agency of

Charismatic tradition engaged in youth programs and training, discipleship, evangelism and mobilization for mission.

**Year founded in US:** 1991

**Income for Overseas Min:** $433,938

**Fully Supported US Personnel Overseas:**
Expecting to serve more than 4 years: 1

**Other Personnel:**
Home ministry & office staff in US: 4

**Countries:** Unspecified Country 1

## Wesleyan World Missions
## See: Global Partners/
## Wesleyan World Missions

## Westminster Biblical Missions

PO Box 602
Carbondale, PA 18407 USA
**Phone:** (530) 273-6280
**Web Site:** www.wbminc.org

*Rev. Dennis E. Roe, Gen. Secretary*

A transdenominational sending agency of Presbyterian tradition engaged in theological education, literature production and support of national churches. Financial figure from 1998. Countries of service data from 2001.

**Purpose:** "...planting and multiplying Reformed churches on the foreign field."

**Year founded in US:** 1974

**Income for Overseas Min:** $375,000

**Fully Supported US Personnel Overseas:**
Expecting to serve more than 4 years: 3

**Other Personnel:**
Non-US serving in own/other country: 51
Home ministry & office staff in US: 3

**Countries:** Hungary 1; Korea, South 1; Mexico; Pakistan 1

## White Fields Inc.

PO Box 226
Stillwater, MN 55082 USA
**Phone:** (651) 430-0090
**Fax:** (651) 430-0090
**E-mail:** usa@whitefields.org
**Web Site:** www.whitefields.org
**Associations:** IFMA

*Mr. Stephen Lonetti, Gen. Director*

A nondenominational service agency of Evangelical tradition engaged in church planting and evangelism.

**Purpose:** "...to provide collaborative start-up support to pastors and churches among their own people in other parts of the world."

**Year founded in US:** 1953

**Income for Overseas Min:** $200,000

**Personnel:**
  Short-term less than 1 year: 12
  Non-US serving in own/other country: 92
  Home ministry & office staff in US: 1

**Countries:** Argentina; Brazil; China; Ghana; Indonesia; Japan; Myanmar/Burma; Paraguay; Peru; Philippines; Russia; South Africa; Zimbabwe

# Wisconsin Evangelical Lutheran Synod, Board for World Missions

2929 N. Mayfair Rd.
Milwaukee, WI 53222 USA

**Phone:** (414) 256-3233
**Fax:** (414) 256-6480
**E-mail:** worldmissionsgroup@sab.wels.net
**Web Site:** www.wels.net

*Rev. Daniel H. Koelpin, Administrator*

A denominational sending agency of Lutheran tradition engaged in church planting, broadcasting, correspondence courses, TEE, theological education, literature production, providing medical supplies, support of national churches and partnership development.

**Purpose:** "...to make disciples throughout the world...using the gospel to win the lost for Christ and to nurture believers for lives of Christian service..."

**Year founded in US:** 1955

**Income for Overseas Min:** $8,000,000

**Gifts in Kind:** $1,000,000

**Fully Supported US Personnel Overseas:**
  Expecting to serve more than 4 years: 38
  Expecting to serve 1 to 4 years: 3

**Other Personnel:**
  Home ministry & office staff in US: 8

**Countries:** Albania; Brazil 3; Bulgaria 1; Dominican Republic 1; Hong Kong 2; India 2; Indonesia 1; Japan 4; Malawi 7; Mexico 2; Russia 4; Sweden 1; Taiwan 1; Thailand 1; Zambia 8

# Women to the World

PMB Suite, 581
2341 College Station Road
Athens, GA 30605

**Phone:** (706) 548-0000
**Fax:** (706) 548-5368
**E-mail:** wttw@bellsouth.net
**Web Site:** www.womentotheworld.org

*Doris Aldrich, President*

An interdenominational specialized agency of Evangelical tradition engaged in tentmaking, extension education, leadership development, literacy work, psychological counseling and training.

**Purpose:** "...to improve the lives of poor women and children in developing countries...to connect women of resource with women of need."

**Year founded in US:** 1985

**Income for Overseas Min:** $630,831

**Gifts in Kind:** $523,003

**Personnel:**
  Short-term less than 1 year: 7
  Non-US serving in own/other country: 13
  Home ministry & office staff in US: 5

**Countries:** Afghanistan; Burkina Faso; Kenya; Peru; Tajikistan; Turkey; Ukraine; Zambia

# Word of Life Fellowship, Inc. —International Ministries

PO Box 600
Schroon Lake, NY 12870 USA

**Phone:** (518) 494-6000
**Fax:** (518) 494-6306
**E-mail:** info@wol.org
**Web Site:** www.wol.org

*Dr. Joe Jordan, Exec. Director*

A nondenominational sending agency of Baptist and Independent tradition engaged in youth programs, broadcasting, camping programs, theological education and short-term programs.

**Year founded in US:** 1940

**Income for Overseas Min:** $12,550,973

**Fully Supported US Personnel Overseas:**
  Expecting to serve more than 4 years: 98
  Non-residential mission personnel: 17

**Other Personnel:**
  Short-term less than 1 year: 777
  Non-US serving in own/other country: 850

Home ministry & office staff in US: 495

**Countries:** Argentina 11; Australia 6; Brazil 25; Bulgaria; Czech Republic 4; France 6; Germany 6; Guatemala; Honduras 1; Hungary 4; Italy; Japan; Kenya 2; Korea, South 4; Mexico; Netherlands Antilles; New Zealand; Nigeria 2; Panama 1; Papua New Guinea; Paraguay; Peru; Philippines 9; Poland 1; Portugal 3; Romania 1; South Africa 6; Spain 2; Uganda; Ukraine 2; United Kingdom 2; Uruguay; Venezuela

## Word To Russia

PO Box 1521
West Sacramento, CA 95691 USA

**Phone:** (916) 372-4610
**Fax:** (916) 375-6770
**E-mail:** wtrmlokteff@sbcglobal.net
**Web Site:** www.wordtorussia.org

*Sergey Lopuga, Exec. Director*

A nondenominational support agency of Baptist and Evangelical tradition engaged in broadcasting, audio recording/distribution, camping programs, childcare/orphanage support, childrens radio/music programs and literature distribution to Russian-speaking immigrants, with outreach in the former Soviet Union and Ukraine. Emphasis is on the children and youth.

**Year founded in US:** 1972

**Income for Overseas Min:** $95,000

**Fully Supported US Personnel Overseas:**
Expecting to serve more than 4 years: 5

**Other Personnel:**
Non-US serving in own/other country: 5
Home ministry & office staff in US: 2

**Countries:** Russia 5

## World Baptist Fellowship Mission Agency, Inc.

PO Box 13459
Arlington, TX 76094-0459 USA

**Phone:** (817) 274-7161
**Fax:** (817) 861-1992
**E-mail:** wbfraley@earthlink.net
**Web Site:** www.wbfi.net

*Rev. Thomas M. Raley, Missions Director*

A denominational sending agency of Baptist tradition engaged in church planting, Bible distribution and evangelism.

**Year founded in US:** 1939

**Income for Overseas Min:** $5,794,950

**Fully Supported US Personnel Overseas:**
Expecting to serve more than 4 years: 107
Expecting to serve 1 to 4 years: 16
Non-residential mission personnel: 4

**Other Personnel:**
Short-term less than 1 year: 21
Non-US serving in own/other country: 4
Home ministry & office staff in US: 7

**Countries:** Australia 2; Brazil 26; Cambodia 2; Chile 2; Colombia 2; Dominica 2; Dominican Republic; Ecuador 8; France 2; Guatemala 2; Honduras 4; Indonesia 5; Latvia 2; Mali; Mexico 23; N. Mariana Isls 2; New Zealand 8; Palau 2; Portugal 2; Spain 4; Thailand 1; Ukraine 2; United Kingdom 2; Virgin Islands 2

## World Bible Translation Center

PO Box 820648
Fort Worth, TX 76182 USA

**Phone:** (817) 595-1664
**Fax:** (817) 589-7013
**E-mail:** info@wbtc.com
**Web Site:** www.wbtc.com

*Mr. Dale Randolph, CEO*

A nondenominational specialized agency of Christian (Restoration Movement) tradition engaged in Bible translation and Bible distribution.

**Purpose:** "...to translate and distribute faithful, easy-to-understand translations of the Scriptures in the world's major languages to lead people to Jesus and help believers grow in faith."

**Year founded in US:** 1973

**Personnel:**
Non-US serving in own/other country: 48
Home ministry & office staff in US: 20

**Countries:** Bulgaria; China; Colombia; Croatia; Egypt; Hungary; India; Indonesia; Jordan; Myanmar/Burma; Romania; Russia; Serbia and Montenegro; Vietnam

## World Concern

19303 Fremont Ave. N.
Seattle, WA 98133 USA

**Phone:** (206) 546-7201
**Fax:** (206) 546-7269

**E-mail:** info@worldconcern.org
**Web Site:** www.worldconcern.org
**Associations:** EFMA

*Mr. Paul Kennel, President*

A nondenominational sending agency of Evangelical tradition engaged in development, agricultural programs, broadcasting, disability assistance programs, evangelism, leadership development, providing medical supplies and relief and/or rehabilitation.

**Purpose:** "To overcome human suffering through emergency relief, rehabilitation and long-term development programs so that families and individuals can be in right relationship with God, with one another and with creation."

**Year founded in US:** 1973

**Income for Overseas Min:** $30,348,937

**Gifts in Kind:** $29,709,058

**Fully Supported US Personnel Overseas:**
Expecting to serve more than 4 years: 13
Expecting to serve 1 to 4 years: 19
Non-residential mission personnel: 40

**Other Personnel:**
Short-term less than 1 year: 3
Non-US serving in own/other country: 858
Home ministry & office staff in US: 27

**Countries:** Afghanistan 2; Bolivia 1; Burkina Faso; Cambodia; Ethiopia 1; Haiti; Honduras 1; Kenya 3; Laos; Myanmar/Burma; Peru; Rwanda; Thailand 4; Uganda; Uzbekistan 1; Vietnam

# World Gospel Mission

PO Box 948
Marion, IN 46952 USA
**Phone:** (765) 664-7331
**Fax:** (765) 671-7230
**E-mail:** wgm@wgm.org
**Web Site:** www.wgm.org
**Associations:** EFMA

*Dr. Hubert P. Harriman, President*

An interdenominational sending agency of Wesleyan and Holiness tradition engaged in church planting, Christian education, theological education, evangelism, leadership development and medical work.

**Purpose:** "...to proclaim the good news of salvation through faith in Jesus Christ by calling believers to scriptural holiness as a

doctrine to be believed, an experience to be received, a message to be declared and a lifestyle to be demonstrated."

**Year founded in US:** 1910

**Income for Overseas Min:** $13,017,133

**Gifts in Kind:** $86,771

**Fully Supported US Personnel Overseas:**
Expecting to serve more than 4 years: 177
Expecting to serve 1 to 4 years: 6

**Other Personnel:**
Short-term less than 1 year: 1,000
Bi-vocational/tentmakers: 3
Non-US serving in own/other country: 3
Home ministry & office staff in US: 82

**Countries:** Argentina 8; Bolivia 37; Dominica 4; Honduras 29; Hungary 5; India 2; Japan 4; Kenya 46; Mexico 12; Papua New Guinea 5; Paraguay 4; Taiwan 2; Uganda 10; Ukraine 6; Unspecified Country 3

# World Harvest Mission

100 West Ave., Ste. W960
Jenkintown, PA 19046 USA
**Phone:** (215) 885-1811
**Fax:** (215) 885-4762
**E-mail:** info@whm.org
**Web Site:** www.whm.org
**Associations:** EFMA

*Mr. Bob Osborne, Acting Director*

A nondenominational sending agency of Evangelical and Reformed tradition engaged in discipleship, church planting, development, evangelism, leadership development and support of national churches.

**Purpose:** "...[to see] local churches revived, mobilized and...sending teams of trained men and women to plant churches overseas."

**Year founded in US:** 1983

**Income for Overseas Min:** $6,132,313

**Fully Supported US Personnel Overseas:**
Expecting to serve more than 4 years: 72
Expecting to serve 1 to 4 years: 12

**Other Personnel:**
Short-term less than 1 year: 137
Bi-vocational/tentmakers: 2
Home ministry & office staff in US: 22

**Countries:** Chile 2; Czech Republic 2; Germany 3; Hungary 2; India 2; Ireland 16; Italy 2; Kenya 6; Netherlands 2; Romania 2; Spain 6; Uganda 11; Ukraine 2; United Kingdom 14

"The faculty are all experts in their own right, and they contribute to the richness of the program not only by their theological insights but also by their years of significant intercultural experience. The diversity of the students, both in terms of their cultural background and their cross-cultural ministry experience, creates a unique community where theological and missiological thinking is forged in a highly stimulating context."

—Doctoral student How-Chuang Chua came to Trinity after four years of church planting work as a missionary in Japan.

Our full-time Mission and Evangelism faculty members include:

**Richard R. Cook,** PhD
*Mission History and Global Christianity*
**Paul G. Hiebert,** PhD
*Anthropology and Missiology*
**Harold A. Netland,** PhD
*Religion and Intercultural Studies*
**John W. Nyquist,** PhD
*Evangelism and Discipleship*
**Craig Ott,** PhD
*Church Planting and Contextualization*
**James F. Plueddemann,** PhD
*Leadership and Education*
**Robert J. Priest,** PhD
*Anthropology and Intercultural Studies*
**Tite Tiénou,** PhD
*Theology of Mission and Ethnicity*

# Trinity Evangelical Divinity School

*Expand your understanding*
*Explore different perspectives*
*Ask tough questions*
*Experience relevant ministry*

GO deeper

## Is God leading you toward intercultural ministry?

At Trinity we offer several degree options to help you deepen your theological understanding, cultural insights, and missionary skills for cross-cultural ministry and theological leadership both globally and locally. Trinity's faculty combine international experience with quality scholarship to help you reflect, explore, and grow to achieve your educational and ministry goals.

*Intercultural degree programs at Trinity:*

• **MDiv** (cross-cultural focus) • **MA** (Intercultural Studies or Evangelism) • **ThM** (Mission and Evangelism)
• **PhD** (Intercultural Studies, Educational Studies, or Theological Studies) • **DMin** (Missions and Evangelism)

## Contact our Admissions Office today: 877.270.0834

Trinity Evangelical Divinity School | 2065 Half Day Road, Deerfield, IL 60015 | 847.945.8800 | www.teds.edu

# Prepare for intercultural service

## With a Masters in Intercultural Studies from Wheaton College

*Scholarship Committed to Servanthood*

Is your ministry culturally relevant? Wheaton College can give you the foundational training and multifaceted skills needed in today's ever changing world. A Masters degree from Wheaton will prepare you for service in evangelism, church planting, leadership development, community health and development, or teaching English as a second language.

As a student you'll get all the benefits of a Wheaton College experience, plus close proximity to local ministries and mission agencies which will help you relate classroom experiences to real life.

Begin your Masters in Intercultural Studies at Wheaton College by contacting us today, toll-free at 800-888-0141.

**Master of Arts Degrees in:**

Evangelism

Missions

Teaching English to Speakers of Other Languages (TESOL)

Wheaton College
Graduate School
*For Christ and His Kingdom*

Graduate Admissions
Local: 630.752.5195
Toll Free: 800.888.0141
gradadm@wheaton.edu
www.wheatongrad.com

# World Harvest Now, Inc.

PO Box 911
Denton, TX 76202 USA
**Phone:** (940) 891-4400
**Fax:** (940) 484-6097
**E-mail:** whn@whn.org
**Web Site:** www.whn.org

*Mr. Lamont Brown, President/Founder*

A nondenominational sending agency of Evangelical tradition engaged in church planting, evangelism, leadership development, support of national churches and missionary training. Statistics from 1998.

**Purpose:** "...to facilitate the planting of cell group churches among the least evangelized people in or near the 10/40 Window."

**Year founded in US:** 1992

**Income for Overseas Min:** $687,400

**Gifts in Kind:** $430,000

**Fully Supported US Personnel Overseas:**
Expecting to serve more than 4 years: 2
Expecting to serve 1 to 4 years: 7
Non-residential mission personnel: 1

**Other Personnel:**
Short-term less than 1 year: 2
Bi-vocational/tentmakers: 3
Non-US serving in own/other country: 11
Home ministry & office staff in US: 8

**Countries:** Asia—General 2; Russia

# World Help

PO Box 501
Forest, VA 24551 USA
**Phone:** (434) 525-4657
**Fax:** (434) 525-4727
**E-mail:** info@worldhelp.net
**Web Site:** www.worldhelp.net

**Associations:** EFMA

*Dr. Vernon Brewer, President*

An interdenominational support agency of Evangelical tradition engaged in Bible distribution, childcare/orphanage programs, church construction, church planting, literature distribution and providing medical supplies.

**Purpose:** "...to fulfill the Great Commission and the Great Commandment through partnering, training, helping and serving, especially in the unreached areas of the world."

**Year founded in US:** 1992

**Income for Overseas Min:** $10,663,775

**Gifts in Kind:** $8,139,891

**Personnel:**
Short-term less than 1 year: 30
Home ministry & office staff in US: 60

# World Horizons

2102 E. Main St.
Richmond, VA 23223 USA
**Phone:** (804) 225-5517
**Fax:** (804) 225-5517
**E-mail:** usinfo@worldhorizons.org
**Web Site:** www.worldhorizons.org

*Mr. Andrew Fuller, Exec. Director*

An interdenominational support agency of Charismatic and Evangelical tradition engaged in mobilization for mission, church planting, evangelism, support of national churches and missionary training.

**Purpose:** "...to serve on behalf of souls as yet unsaved; churches as yet unplanted; missionaries as yet unsent...ministering through creative evangelism, church-planting and the establishment of a trained missionary presence..."

**Year founded in US:** 1985

**Income for Overseas Min:** $316,000

**Fully Supported US Personnel Overseas:**
Expecting to serve more than 4 years: 15

**Other Personnel:**
Bi-vocational/tentmakers: 8
Non-US serving in own/other country: 16
Home ministry & office staff in US: 2

**Countries:** Africa—General 1; Austria 2; Brazil 2; France 5; Middle East 2; Spain 1; Turkey 2

# World Indigenous Missions

2409 Lifehaus Industrial Dr.
New Braunfels, TX 78130 USA
**Phone:** (830) 629-0863
**Fax:** (830) 629-0357
**E-mail:** wim@worldim.com
**Web Site:** www.worldim.org

*Mr. Charles E. Hall, President*

A nondenominational sending agency of Charismatic and Independent tradition engaged in church planting, funds transmission, short-term programs and missionary training.

**Purpose:** "...to disciple the nations to

reach the world."

**Year founded in US:** 1981

**Income for Overseas Min:** $1,643,091

**Fully Supported US Personnel Overseas:**
 Expecting to serve more than 4 years: 56
 Non-residential mission personnel: 10

**Other Personnel:**
 Short-term less than 1 year: 2
 Bi-vocational/tentmakers: 2
 Non-US serving in own/other country: 7
 Home ministry & office staff in US: 5

**Countries:** Bolivia 5; China 6; Mexico 23; Philippines 4; Romania 2; Russia 2; Spain 5; Thailand 2; Venezuela 5; Vietnam 2

## World Link Ministries
PO Box 153026
Irving, TX 75015-3026 USA

**Phone:** (972) 253-6800
**Fax:** (972) 253-6803
**E-mail:** wlmsefovan@aol.com
**Web Site:** www.worldlinkministries.org

*Dr. Manny Fernandez, President/CEO*

A transdenominational sending agency of Evangelical tradition engaged in church planting, extension education, theological education, evangelism, leadership development and support of national workers.

**Year founded in US:** 1994

**Income for Overseas Min:** $933,000

**Fully Supported US Personnel Overseas:**
 Expecting to serve more than 4 years: 6
 Non-residential mission personnel: 1

**Other Personnel:**
 Short-term less than 1 year: 7
 Non-US serving in own/other country: 446
 Home ministry & office staff in US: 8

**Countries:** Africa—General 4; Cuba; Romania; Spain 2; Ukraine

## World Mission
1701 Porter St., Ste. 6
Wyoming, MI 49519 USA

**Phone:** (616) 534-5689
**Fax:** (616) 257-5248
**E-mail:** staff@worldmission.cc
**Web Site:** www.worldmission.cc
**Associations:** EFMA

*Mr. Greg Kelley, Exec. Director*

A nondenominational support agency of

Evangelical tradition engaged in audio recording/distribution, Bible distribution, discipleship, evangelism, partnership development and Bible translation.

**Year founded in US:** 1994

**Income for Overseas Min:** $840,439

**Personnel:**
 Short-term less than 1 year: 50

## World Mission Associates
600-C Eden Rd.
Lancaster, PA 17601 USA

**Phone:** (717) 299-1427
**Fax:** (717) 299-2943
**E-mail:** wmausa@wmausa.org
**Web Site:** www.wmausa.org

*Rev. Glenn J. Schwartz, Exec. Director*

A denominational service agency of Evangelical tradition engaged in mobilization of local resources for missions through seminars, training and video production/distribution.

**Year founded in US:** 1983

**Personnel:**
 Bi-vocational/tentmakers: 2
 Home ministry & office staff in US: 3

## World Mission Prayer League
232 Clifton Ave.
Minneapolis, MN 55403-3466 USA

**Phone:** (612) 871-6843
**Fax:** (612) 871-6844
**E-mail:** wmpl@wmpl.org
**Web Site:** www.wmpl.org
**Associations:** EFMA

*Rev. Charles R. Lindquist, Gen. Director*

A denominational sending agency of Lutheran tradition engaged in leadership development, church planting, theological education, evangelism, medical work and translation work.

**Purpose:** "...committed to know Christ, pray for the advance of His Kingdom, share the Gospel and ourselves with those who do not know him and encourage Christians everywhere in this global task."

**Year founded in US:** 1937

**Income for Overseas Min:** $1,421,800

**Fully Supported US Personnel Overseas:**
 Expecting to serve more than 4 years: 46

Expecting to serve 1 to 4 years: 2

**Other Personnel:**
Short-term less than 1 year: 4
Non-US serving in own/other country: 11
Home ministry & office staff in US: 25

**Countries:** Bangladesh 5; Bolivia 8; Ecuador 3; Eritrea 1; Kenya 8; Mexico 2; Nepal 5; Pakistan 2; Peru 2; Philippines 5; Romania 2; Unspecified Country 3

# World Missionary Assistance Plan
1419 N. San Fernando Blvd., Suite 200
Burbank, CA 91504-4194 USA
**Phone:** (818) 843-7233
**Fax:** (818) 845-5000
**E-mail:** wmap01@aol.com
**Web Site:** www.world-map.com
*Rev. Frank R. Parrish, President*

A transdenominational service agency of Charismatic and Evangelical tradition engaged in leadership development, theological education, literature distribution, literature production, training and translation work.

**Purpose:** "...to make disciples of all nations by equipping indigenous church leaders in Third-World nations through biblically-based, Spirit-filled teaching resources and by sharing their triumphs with believers in Western nations."

**Year founded in US:** 1964
**Income for Overseas Min:** $797,377
**Personnel:**
Short-term less than 1 year: 2
Home ministry & office staff in US: 8

# World Missionary Press, Inc.
PO Box 120
New Paris, IN 46553 USA
**Phone:** (574) 831-2111
**Fax:** (574) 831-2161
**E-mail:** Jay@wmpress.org
**Web Site:** www.wmpress.org
*Mr. Jay E. Benson, President*

A nondenominational evangelical literature ministry producing topical Scripture booklets in 313 languages and Bible study booklets and New Testaments in a variety of languages for free distribution in 209 countries.

**Year founded in US:** 1961
**Income for Overseas Min:** $2,018,196
**Personnel:**
Home ministry & office staff in US: 42

# World Missions & Evangelism, Inc.
PO Box 790
Benton, KY 42025 USA
**Phone:** (270) 527-8369 x131
**Fax:** (270) 527-6982
**E-mail:** rclendenen@christianfellowhip.org
**Web Site:** www.christianfellowship.org
**Associations:** EFMA Candidate
*Dr. David T. Parish, President*

A transdenominational sending agency of Evangelical tradition engaged in church planting, development, Christian education, funds transmission, leadership development and support of national workers.

**Income for Overseas Min:** $812,913

**Fully Supported US Personnel Overseas:**
Expecting to serve more than 4 years: 42
Expecting to serve 1 to 4 years: 6
Non-residential mission personnel: 43

**Other Personnel:**
Short-term less than 1 year: 3
Non-US serving in own/other country: 52
Home ministry & office staff in US: 4

**Countries:** Costa Rica; France 2; Guatemala; Honduras 4; Hungary 2; Jamaica 3; Kenya 10; Mexico 2; Niger 2; Romania 2; South Africa 2; Spain 2; Unspecified Country 10; Vietnam 1

# World Missions Far Corners, Inc.
PO Box 2611
Long Beach, CA 90801 USA
**Phone:** (562) 402-4400
**Fax:** (562) 402-9039
**Web Site:** www.worldmissionsfarcorners.com
*Patricia L. Murdock-Cook, Exec. Secty./Treas.*

A nondenominational sending agency of Evangelical tradition engaged in evangelism, church planting, literature distribution, medical work, support of national workers and relief and/or rehabilitation. Statistical data from 2003.

**Purpose:** "A unique outreach carried on by missionaries and an army of national workers including medical work and preaching the gospel on five continents."

**Year founded in US:** 1958

**Income for Overseas Min:** $1,025,000

**Fully Supported US Personnel Overseas:**
Expecting to serve more than 4 years: 36

**Other Personnel:**
Non-US serving in own/other country: 1665
Home ministry & office staff in US: 10

**Countries:** China 2; Cote d'Ivoire 2; Cuba 1; Ecuador 8; Ethiopia; India; Kenya; Korea, South 2; Mexico 7; Nepal; Peru 4; Philippines 2; South Africa 2; Thailand 2; United Kingdom 2; Vietnam 2

## World Orphans

1880 Office Club Pointe, Suite 2100
Colorado Springs, CO 80920 USA

**Phone:** (719) 487-1700
**Fax:** (719) 487-1800
**E-mail:** info@worldorphans.org
**Web Site:** www.worldorphans.org

*Mr. Paul Myhill, CEO/President*

A nondenominational specialized agency of Evangelical tradition engaged in childcare/orphanage programs and funds transmission by partnering with local indigenous churches who rescue the children and construct orphan homes as a part of their ongoing ministries.

**Purpose:** "...to rescue orphaned and abandoned children in underdeveloped countries by funding construction of the orphan homes required for local Christian churches to meet the spiritual, physical, nutritional, social, educational, economic and skills training needs of these children."

**Year founded in US:** 1993

**Fully Supported US Personnel Overseas:**
Non-residential mission personnel: 5

**Other Personnel:**
Non-US serving in own/other country: 2
Home ministry & office staff in US: 5

**Countries:** Kenya; Uganda

## World Outreach Intl.—US

615 E. 9800 South
Sandy, UT 84070 USA

**Phone:** (801) 572-0211
**Fax:** (801) 576-1092
**E-mail:** admin@wousa.org
**Web Site:** www.wointl.com

*Mr. Jack Rudd, US Director*

A nondenominational sending agency of Charismatic and Evangelical tradition engaged in church planting, childcare/orphanage programs, childrens programs, discipleship, evangelism and leadership development.

**Purpose:** "...to impact least reached people groups with the Gospel of Jesus through raising leaders, evangelism, assisting emerging missions, children's ministry and humanitarian aid."

**Year founded in US:** 1994

**Fully Supported US Personnel Overseas:**
Expecting to serve more than 4 years: 5
Expecting to serve 1 to 4 years: 2

**Other Personnel:**
Short-term less than 1 year: 50
Bi-vocational/tentmakers: 6
Home ministry & office staff in US: 10

**Countries:** Burkina Faso 1; Indonesia; Tanzania 2; Vanuatu 2

## World Outreach Ministries

PO Box B
Marietta, GA 30061 USA

**Phone:** (770) 424-1545
**Fax:** (770) 424-1545
**E-mail:** wom@worldoutreach.org
**Web Site:** www.worldoutreach.org

*Mr. Jason R. Peebles, Founder/President*

An interdenominational agency of Charismatic and Evangelical tradition performing a variety of home office duties for residential missionaries engaged in church planting, evangelism and missionary training in 40 nations.

**Year founded in US:** 1979

**Income for Overseas Min:** $1,700,000

**Personnel:**
Home ministry & office staff in US: 3

## World Partners USA

PO Box 9127
Fort Wayne, IN 46899 USA

**Phone:** (260) 747-2027
**Fax:** (260) 747-5331
**E-mail:** wpusa@Worldpartnersusa.com

**Web Site:** www.worldpartnersusa.com

**Associations:** EFMA

*Rev. David W. Mann, Director*

A denominational sending agency of Evangelical tradition engaged in church planting, development, theological education, leadership development and mobilization for mission.

**Purpose:** "...to assist Missionary Churches in responding to their cross-cultural calling to the Great Commission."

**Year founded in US:** 1969

**Income for Overseas Min:** $4,454,062

**Gifts in Kind:** $14,000

**Fully Supported US Personnel Overseas:**
Expecting to serve more than 4 years: 68
Expecting to serve 1 to 4 years: 1
Non-residential mission personnel: 13

**Other Personnel:**
Short-term less than 1 year: 258
Home ministry & office staff in US: 22

**Countries:** Brazil 2; Bulgaria 2; Cyprus 2; Ecuador 12; France 3; Guinea 6; Ireland 2; Portugal 2; Russia 8; Sierra Leone 1; South Africa 2; Spain 9; Thailand 2; Unspecified Country 15

## World Reach, Inc.

PO Box 26155
Birmingham, AL 35260-6155 USA

**Phone:** (205) 979-2400

**Fax:** (205) 979-6289

**E-mail:** info@world-reach.org

**Web Site:** www.world-reach.org

**Associations:** IFMA

*Rev. Timothy Q. Prewitt, Gen. Director*

A nondenominational sending agency of Evangelical tradition engaged in church planting, discipleship, evangelism, leadership development, relief and/or rehabilitation and short-term programs.

**Purpose:** "...to reach the world with the gospel of Christ through the local church."

**Year founded in US:** 1982

**Income for Overseas Min:** $1,243,927

**Fully Supported US Personnel Overseas:**
Expecting to serve more than 4 years: 13
Non-residential mission personnel: 1

**Other Personnel:**
Short-term less than 1 year: 15
Non-US serving in own/other country: 41

Home ministry & office staff in US: 5

**Countries:** Albania; Colombia; El Salvador 4; Germany; Honduras 5; Kenya; Peru 2; Romania; Ukraine 2

## World Relief

7 East Baltimore St.
Baltimore, MD 21202 USA

**Phone:** (443) 451-1900

**Fax:** (443) 410-1985

**E-mail:** worldrelief@worldrelief.com

**Web Site:** www.wr.org

**Associations:** EFMA

*Mr. Sammy Mah, President/CEO*

A nondenominational sending agency of Evangelical tradition engaged in development, agricultural programs and relief and/or rehabilitation.

**Purpose:** "...to work with the church in alleviating human suffering worldwide in the name of Christ."

**Year founded in US:** 1944

**Income for Overseas Min:** $16,461,539

**Gifts in Kind:** $466,283

**Fully Supported US Personnel Overseas:**
Expecting to serve more than 4 years: 10
Expecting to serve 1 to 4 years: 23
Non-residential mission personnel: 6

**Other Personnel:**
Short-term less than 1 year: 23
Non-US serving in own/other country: 1196
Home ministry & office staff in US: 515

**Countries:** Burkina Faso; Burundi 4; Cambodia 2; China 1; Congo, Republic of the; Grenada; Haiti; India; Indonesia; Kenya; Kosovo; Liberia; Malawi 1; Mongolia; Mozambique; Nicaragua 1; Rwanda 1; Sierra Leone; Sudan; Zimbabwe

## World Servants, Inc.

7130 Portland Ave. S.
Richfield, MN 55423 USA

**Phone:** (612) 866-0010

**Fax:** (612) 866-0078

**Web Site:** www.worldservants.org

*Rev. Timothy N. Gibson, President*

A specialized agency of Ecumenical tradition engaged in short-term programs, development, leadership development and training. Short-term teams serving in 22 countries.

**Purpose:** "...to assist in the transformation of people to be Christ-centered servants and leaders through training and short-term cross-cultural mission experiences."

**Year founded in US:** 1986

**Personnel:**
Short-term less than 1 year: 14
Home ministry & office staff in US: 15

## World Team

1431 Stuckert Rd.
Warrington, PA 18976 USA

**Phone:** (215) 491-4900
**Fax:** (215) 491-4910
**E-mail:** wt-usa@worldteam.org
**Web Site:** www.worldteam.org

**Associations:** IFMA

*Mr. Albert Ehmann, President*

A nondenominational sending agency of Evangelical tradition engaged in church planting, aviation services, evangelism, support of national churches, training and Bible translation.

**Purpose:** "Glorifying God by working together to plant reproducing churches among the unreached people groups of the world."

**Year founded in US:** 1928

**Income for Overseas Min:** $8,765,000

**Gifts in Kind:** $38,000

**Fully Supported US Personnel Overseas:**
Expecting to serve more than 4 years: 173
Expecting to serve 1 to 4 years: 2

**Other Personnel:**
Short-term less than 1 year: 2
Bi-vocational/tentmakers: 14
Non-US serving in own/other country: 38
Home ministry & office staff in US: 16

**Countries:** Australia 1; Brazil 6; Cambodia 30; Cameroon 17; Chile 6; Dominican Republic 8; Europe—General 14; France 15; Greece 2; Guadeloupe 2; Haiti 5; Indonesia 14; Italy 4; Mexico 2; Peru; Philippines 13; Saint Vincent and the Grenadines 2; Singapore; Spain 5; Suriname 2; Taiwan 6; Trinidad and Tobago; United Kingdom 2; Unspecified Country 17

## World Thrust Intl., Inc.

3545 Cruse Rd., Ste. 309-A

Lawrenceville, GA 30044-3162 USA

**Phone:** (770) 923-5215
**Fax:** (770) 923-3933
**E-mail:** info@worldthrust.com
**Web Site:** www.worldthrust.com

*Dr. Bill H. Boerop, Founder/President*

A nondenominational support agency of Evangelical tradition engaged in mobilization for mission, theological education, leadership development and training.

**Purpose:** "...to serve...as a catalyst to help mobilize the local church toward a more effective involvement in the evangelization of the world."

**Year founded in US:** 1984

**Income for Overseas Min:** $119,804

**Personnel:**
Non-US serving in own/other country: 4
Home ministry & office staff in US: 2

**Countries:** Africa—General; South Africa

## World Venture

1501 W. Mineral Ave.
Littleton, CO 80120-5612 USA

**Phone:** (720) 283-2000
**Fax:** (720) 283-9383
**E-mail:** info@worldventure.com
**Web Site:** www.worldventure.com

**Associations:** EFMA

*Dr. Hans Finzel, President*

A sending agency of Baptist tradition engaged in leadership development, church planting, development, evangelism, mobilization for mission and partnership development.

**Purpose:** "We see people of all nations transformed by Jesus Christ through partnership with his church."

**Year founded in US:** 1943

**Income for Overseas Min:** $22,407,400

**Fully Supported US Personnel Overseas:**
Expecting to serve more than 4 years: 373
Expecting to serve 1 to 4 years: 24

**Other Personnel:**
Short-term less than 1 year: 14
Non-US serving in own/other country: 21
Home ministry & office staff in US: 67

**Countries:** Albania 2; Argentina 11; Asia—General 4; Austria 21; Belgium 6; Bolivia 2; Brazil 20; Central Asia—General 2; China

3; Congo, Democratic Republic of 2; Cote d'Ivoire 11; Czech Republic 3; Ecuador 4; France 10; Germany; Ghana 2; Guinea 5; Hong Kong 6; Hungary 2; India 4; Indonesia 8; Ireland 4; Italy 11; Japan 13; Jordan 4; Kenya 7; Lebanon 2; Lithuania 3; Macau 11; Madagascar 2; Mali 8; Mongolia 1; Mozambique 4; Pakistan 4; Philippines 28; Poland 9; Portugal 4; Romania 6; Russia 12; Rwanda 6; Senegal 23; Sierra Leone 2; Singapore 6; Slovenia 2; South Africa 4; Spain 13; Taiwan 11; Thailand 2; Uganda 18; Ukraine 11; United Kingdom 6; Uruguay 4; Venezuela 4

## World Vision Inc.

PO Box 9716
Federal Way, WA 98063-9716 USA
**Phone:** (253) 815-1000
**Fax:** (253) 815-3343
**E-mail:** info@worldvision.org
**Web Site:** www.worldvision.org
**Associations:** EFMA

*Mr. Richard E. Stearns, President*

An interdenominational service agency of Evangelical tradition engaged in development, agricultural programs, childcare/orphanage programs, evangelism, funds transmission and relief and/or rehabilitation. Personnel and country information from 2002.

**Purpose:** "...to follow our Lord and Savior Jesus Christ in working with the poor and oppressed to promote human transformation, seek justice and bear witness to the good news of the Kingdom of God."

**Year founded in US:** 1950

**Income for Overseas Min:** $752,348,000

**Personnel:**
  Home ministry & office staff in US: 679

## World Vision International

800 W. Chestnut Ave.
Monrovia, CA 91016 USA
**Phone:** (626) 303-8811
**Fax:** (626) 301-7786
**Web Site:** www.wvi.org
**Associations:** EFMA

*Dr. Dean R. Hirsch, Intl . President*

The international coordination office for the regional and national offices and other entities of the World Vision Partnership engaged in development, children's programs, justice, relief/rehabilitation and technical assistance. North American personnel serving overseas, income for overseas ministries, and countries of activity included in World Vision (USA) and World Vision Canada.

**Purpose:** "...working with the poor and oppressed to promote human transformation, seek justice and bear witness to the good news of the Kingdom of God."

**Year founded in US:** 1978

**Personnel:**
  Home ministry & office staff in US: 185

## World Witness, The Board of Foreign Missions, Associate Reformed Presbyterian Church

One Cleveland St.
Greenville, SC 29601 USA
**Phone:** (864) 233-5226
**Fax:** (864) 233-5226
**E-mail:** worldwitness@worldwitness.org
**Web Site:** www.worldwitness.org
**Associations:** EFMA

*Mr. Frank Van Dalen, Exec. Director*

A denominational sending agency of Presbyterian and Reformed tradition engaged in church planting, theological education, evangelism, providing medical supplies, support of national churches and youth programs.

**Purpose:** "Proclaim Christ as the only Savior and Lord through the means of evangelism, church planting, theological education and works of compassion."

**Year founded in US:** 1876

**Income for Overseas Min:** $3,646,440

**Fully Supported US Personnel Overseas:**
  Expecting to serve more than 4 years: 41
  Expecting to serve 1 to 4 years: 2
  Non-residential mission personnel: 4

**Other Personnel:**
  Short-term less than 1 year: 4
  Non-US serving in own/other country: 411
  Home ministry & office staff in US: 8

**Countries:** Germany 8; Mexico 12; Pakistan; Russia 10; Turkey 6; United Kingdom 3; Unspecified Country 2

## WorldServe Ministries

5795 Genesis Ct.
Frisco, TX 75034
**Phone:** (469) 633-9600
**Fax:** (469) 633-9604
**E-mail:** info@worldserve.org
**Web Site:** www.worldserve.org

*Mr. David Hunt, LLD, President*

A nondenominational sending agency of Evangelical tradition engaged in church planting, Bible distribution, leadership development, literature production, support of national churches and training

**Purpose:** "...to equip indigenous believers in closed or restricted access countries with tools and resources to strategically fuel the fires of dynamic church growth."

**Year Founded in US:** 1992
**Income for Overseas Min:** $11,825,511
**Gifts in Kind:** $8,679,668
**Fully Supported US Personnel Overseas:**
  Expecting to serve more than 4 years: 2
  Non-residential mission personnel: 3
**Other Personnel:**
  Non-US serving in own/other country: 3
  Home ministry & office staff in US: 7
**Countries:** China; Cuba; Ethiopia; India; Vietnam

## WorldHarvest

301 E. Foothill Blvd. Ste. 201
Arcadia, CA 91006 USA
**Phone:** (626) 359-8500
**Fax:** (626) 359-8181
**E-mail:** contact@worldharvest.cc
**Web Site:** www.worldharvest.cc
**Associations:** AFMA

*Heintje Tjahja, USA Director*

An interdenominational support agency of Charismatic tradition engaged in development, adoption, childcare/orphanage programs, missionary education, leadership development, support of national churches, relief and/or rehabilitation and short-term programs.

**Purpose:** "...to impact the world through creative community, education and media services."

**Year founded in US:** 1989
**Income for Overseas Min:** $1,900,000

**Gifts in Kind:** $700,000
**Personnel:**
  Short-term less than 1 year: 50
  Non-US serving in own/other country: 175
  Home ministry & office staff in US: 4

## WorldTeach

4201 N. Peachtree Rd
Atlanta, GA 30341 USA
**Phone:** (770) 458-9300
**Fax:** (770) 454-9313
**E-mail:** info@walkthru.org
**Web Site:** www.walkthru.org
**Associations:** EFMA

*Chip Ingram, President/CEO*

An interdenominational support agency of Evangelical tradition engaged in broadcasting, discipleship, Christian education, literature distribution, literature production and training. See Walk Thru the Bible for statistical information.

**Year founded in US:** 1976
**Personnel:**
  Non-residential mission personnel: 3

## Worldwide Discipleship Assoc.

110 Carnegie Place, Ste.100
Fayetteville, GA 30214 USA
**Phone:** (770) 460-1337
**Fax:** (770) 460-1339
**E-mail:** info@disciplebuilding.org
**Web Site:** www.disciplebuilding.org

*Mr. Robert D. Dukes, President/Exec. Dir.*

An interdenominational support agency of Evangelical tradition engaged in training, evangelism and missions information service. Data from 2002.

**Year founded in US:** 1974
**Income for Overseas Min:** $98,416
**Personnel:**
  Home ministry & office staff in US: 13

## Worldwide Lab Improvement

3607 Gembrit Cir.
Kalamazoo, MI 49001 USA
**Phone:** (269) 323-8407
**Fax:** (269) 323-2030
**E-mail:** mail@wwlab.org
**Web Site:** www.wwlab.org

*Mr. Edwin J. Bos, President*

A non-profit agency of Evangelical tradition which assists any evangelical mission hospital or clinic or short-term medical missionary.

**Purpose:** "…to serve Jesus Christ by providing mission hospitals, clinics and short-term teams in developing countries with quality clinical laboratory equipment, supplies, consulting and on-site training at reasonable costs."

**Year founded in US:** 1995

**Income for Overseas Min:** $285,647

**Gifts in Kind:** $29,154

**Fully Supported US Personnel Overseas:**
 Non-residential mission personnel: 1

**Other Personnel:**
 Short-term less than 1 year: 4
 Home ministry & office staff in US: 2

## World-Wide Missions

PO Box 2300
Redlands, CA 92373 USA

**Phone:** (909) 793-2009
**Fax:** (909) 793-6880
**E-mail:** info@world-widemissions.org
**Web Site:** www.world-widemissions.org

*Rev. Fred M. Johnson, President*

A nondenominational support agency of Evangelical and Independent tradition engaged in support of national workers, childcare/orphanage programs, church planting, Christian education, medical work and relief and/or rehabilitation.

**Purpose:** "…to touch the suffering people of our world with the love of Jesus Christ, changing the lives of men, women and children forever."

**Year founded in US:** 1950

**Income for Overseas Min:** $13,027,064

**Gifts in Kind:** $11,967,647

**Fully Supported US Personnel Overseas:**
 Expecting to serve more than 4 years: 16
 Expecting to serve 1 to 4 years: 6

**Other Personnel:**
 Non-US serving in own/other country: 43
 Home ministry & office staff in US: 4

**Countries:** Bolivia; Brazil 7; Chile; China 2; Colombia; Congo, Democratic Republic of; Egypt; Guatemala; Honduras; India; Italy 2; Jordan; Kenya; Liberia; Macau 1; Malawi; Mexico 1; Nepal 1; Nigeria; Papua New Guinea; Paraguay; Peru 2; Philippines; Russia; Switzerland; Taiwan; Thailand; Turkey; Venezuela

## Worldwide Tentmakers, Inc.

423 Townes St.
Greenville, SC 29601 USA

**Phone:** (864) 370-0475
**Fax:** (864) 235-3369
**E-mail:** wtijobs@aol.com
**Web Site:** www.worldwidetentmakers.com

*Mr. Thomas J.Stultz, President*

A nondenominational service agency of Baptist and Fundamental tradition engaged in tentmaking and evangelism. Data from 2002.

**Purpose:** "…committed to assisting local fundamentalist churches in the promotion, preparation and placement of self-supporting witnesses worldwide."

**Year founded in US:** 1987

**Income for Overseas Min:** $225,000

**Fully Supported US Personnel Overseas:**
 Non-residential mission personnel: 2

**Other Personnel:**
 Short-term less than 1 year: 60
 Bi-vocational/tentmakers: 23
 Home ministry & office staff in US: 2

## Wycliffe Associates, Inc.

PO Box 2000
Orange, CA 92859 USA

**Phone:** (800) 843-9673
**E-mail:** info@wycliffeassociates.org
**Web Site:** www.wycliffeassociates.org

*Mr. Bruce Smith, President/CEO*

A nondenominational service agency of Evangelical tradition engaged in mobilization of volunteers for mission to accelerate Bible translation, construction of translation facilities, services for other agencies and short-term programs.

**Purpose:** "…supports Wycliffe Bible Translators through programs and services that enable God's people to become involved in Bible translation through their prayers and resources."

**Year founded in US:** 1967

**Income for Overseas Min:** $2,169,000

**Gifts in Kind:** $200,000

**Fully Supported US Personnel Overseas:**
Expecting to serve 1 to 4 years: 13

**Other Personnel:**
Short-term less than 1 year: 1
Home ministry & office staff in US: 62

**Countries:** Africa—General; Asia—General

## Wycliffe Bible Translators, Inc.

PO Box 628200
Orlando, FL 32862-8200 USA

**Phone:** (407) 852-3600
**Fax:** (407) 852-3601
**E-mail:** info.usa@wycliffe.org
**Web Site:** www.wycliffe.org
**Associations:** EFMA

*Mr. Bob Creson,, President*

An interdenominational sending agency engaged in translation work, missionary training, linguistics, literacy work, funds transmission and mobilization for mission.

**Purpose:** "...to assist the church in making disciples of all nations through Bible translation."

**Year founded in US:** 1934

**Income for Overseas Min:** $103,425,000

**Fully Supported US Personnel Overseas:**
Expecting to serve more than 4 years: 3,496

**Other Personnel:**
Short-term less than 1 year: 90
Home ministry & office staff in US: 390

**Countries:** Africa—General 918; Asia—General 1065; Europe—General 160; Latin America—General 678; Oceania - General 25; Papua New Guinea 430; Philippines 220

## Wycliffe International

7500 W. Camp Wisdom Rd.
Dallas, TX 75236 USA

**Phone:** (972) 708-7575
**E-mail:** info_WBTI@wycliffe.org
**Web Site:** www.wycliffe.net

*Dr. John Watters, Exec. Director*

An interdenominational support agency of Evangelical tradition that is the international coordination center for 31 Wycliffe national sending agencies and 14 affiliates around the world. Wycliffe is engaged in Bible translation, linguistics, literacy work and other activities needed to support these primary ministries. Income and overseas personnel totals from the USA and Canada shown under Wycliffe USA and Wycliffe Canada.

**Purpose:** "...to integrate Scripture translation, scholarship and service so that all people will have access to God's Word in their own language."

**Year founded in US:** 1934

## Young Life

PO Box 520
Colorado Springs, CO 80901 USA

**Phone:** (877) 438-9572
**Fax:** (719) 381-1750
**E-mail:** mat@sc.younglife.org
**Web Site:** www.younglife.org

*Mr. Denny Rydberg, President*

A nondenominational sending agency of Evangelical tradition engaged in youth programs, camping programs, discipleship and evangelism.

**Purpose:** "...to introduce adolescents to Jesus Christ and help them grow in their faith."

**Year founded in US:** 1940

**Income for Overseas Min:** $8,063,032

**Fully Supported US Personnel Overseas:**
Expecting to serve more than 4 years: 39
Expecting to serve 1 to 4 years: 47

**Other Personnel:**
Home ministry & office staff in US: 580

**Countries:** Africa—General 4; Asia—General 1; Caribbean—General 3; Europe—General 14; Latin America—General 10; Russia 1; United Kingdom 6

## Youth Encounter

3490 Lexington Ave. N.
St. Paul, MN 55126 USA

**Phone:** (651) 287-9688
**Fax:** (651) 287-9689
**Web Site:** www.youthencounter.org

*Rev. Dr. Larry Dean Johnson, President*

A specialized agency of Lutheran tradition engaged in youth programs, childrens programs, evangelism and leadership development.

**Purpose:** "...to strengthen the church through the Christian faith and ministry of its youth."

# Your Source for the Latest Frontier Mission Books

A Ministry of the U.S. Center for World Mission

**WILLIAM CAREY**
LIBRARY
Publishers and Distributors

Living Water
and Indian Bowl
Swami Dayanand Bharati

Paul Hattaway
PEOPLES OF THE
BUDDHIST
WORLD
A Christian Prayer Guide

Must read for students of India
## Living Water Indian Bowl

An insightful analysis of Christian work among Hindus and the error and inadequacy of Western Christianity in the Hindu world. Numerous telling anecdotes are the greatest strength of this important book. A must read for anyone interested in Hindu ministry. Call for discount pricing!

From the author of Operation China
## Peoples of the Buddhist World

Paul Hattaway has meticulously collected the available information on all the Buddhist people groups of the world. Readers will learn about the different forms of Buddhism, where and how these are practiced, and what special challenges they present for Christians who want to bring the good news of Jesus to Buddhists. Call for discount pricing!

**For these frontier mission books and more, visit the William Carey Library at www.missionbooks.org or by calling 1-800-Mission.**

# Women Crossing Borders:
## Reflections on Cross-cultural Ministry

edited by Cheri Pierson

W̲e̲ all have a call to go out and share the good news of Jesus Christ with others. For some this is done in their local community. For others, like the women featured in **Women Crossing Borders**, this means reaching out to people cross-culturally, both in their homelands and in other regions of the world. The women featured in this book reflect on lessons learned in seeking to share Christ around the world.

**Women Crossing Borders** can be used to:

- promote discussion in academic settings and missions classes
- encourage women either involved in or going into missions
- help women discern where God may be calling them
- serve as a devotional

**Only $9.99**

## To order call
630.752.7158
## or purchase it online at
# www.emisdirect.com

Published by Evangelism and Missions Information Service (EMIS) of the
Billy Graham Center at Wheaton College, Wheaton, Illinois

**Year founded in US:** 1963
**Income for Overseas Min:** $1,319,000
**Gifts in Kind:** $1,878,000
**Fully Supported US Personnel Overseas:**
Non-residential mission personnel: 30
**Other Personnel:**
Short-term less than 1 year: 36
Home ministry & office staff in US: 48

## Youth for Christ Intl.

PO Box 4555
Englewood, CO 80155-4555 USA
**Phone:** (303) 843-9000
**Fax:** (303) 843-6017
**E-mail:** info@yfci.org
**Web Site:** www.yfci.org
*Mr. David Wraight, President/CEO*

An interdenominational support agency of Evangelical tradition engaged in youth programs, discipleship, evangelism, leadership development and training.

**Purpose:** "...to see that every young person in every people group in every nation has the opportunity to make an informed decision to be a follower of Jesus Christ and become part of a local church...to participate in the body of Christ in responsible evangelism of youth, presenting them with the person, work and teachings of Christ and discipling them into a local church."

**Year founded in US:** 1968
**Income for Overseas Min:** $3,600,000
**Fully Supported US Personnel Overseas:**
Expecting to serve more than 4 years: 4
Non-residential mission personnel: 5
**Other Personnel:**
Home ministry & office staff in US: 17
**Countries:** Africa—General 2; Asia—General 2

## Youth for Christ/USA— World Outreach

PO Box 4478
Englewood, CO 80155 USA
**Phone:** (303) 843-9000
**Fax:** (303) 843-9002
**E-mail:** worldinfo@yfc.net
**Web Site:** www.yfc.org
*Mr. Dan Wolgemuth, CEO*

A nondenominational sending agency of Evangelical tradition engaged in youth evangelism and youth programs.

**Purpose:** "...facilitate USA citizens to serve the YFC International movement in reaching youth in nearly 100 countries in the world."

**Year founded in US:** 1945
**Income for Overseas Min:** $4,500,000
**Fully Supported US Personnel Overseas:**
Expecting to serve more than 4 years: 92
Non-residential mission personnel: 6
**Other Personnel:**
Short-term less than 1 year: 1,400
Home ministry & office staff in US: 16
**Countries:** Africa—General 2; Australia 2; Belgium 1; Bolivia 3; Brazil 2; Cayman Islands 1; Europe—General 8; France 2; Germany 9; Guinea-Bissau 6; Honduras 3; Ireland 1; Italy 4; Japan 1; Kenya 3; Middle East 6; New Zealand 3; Philippines 1; Portugal 2; Rwanda 4; Slovakia 1; South Africa 5; Spain 4; Switzerland 7; Thailand 2; Uganda 1; United Kingdom 8

## Youth With A Mission (YWAM)

75-5851 Kwakini Hwy.
Kailua Kona, HI 96740 USA
**Phone:** (808) 326-7228
**Fax:** (808) 329-2387
**E-mail:** info@ywam.org
**Web Site:** www.ywam.org
*Mr. John Dawson, President*

An interdenominational sending agency of Charismatic and Evangelical tradition engaged in youth programs, discipleship, evangelism, evangelism, missionary training and relief and/or rehabilitation. Full-time staff serve in 149 countries.

**Year founded in US:** 1960
**Personnel:**
Short-term less than 1 year: 20,000
Home ministry & office staff in US: 15,700

## YUGO Ministries (Youth Unlimited Gospel Outreach, Inc.)

PO Box 25
San Dimas, CA 91773-0025 USA
**Phone:** (909) 592-6621
**Fax:** (909) 394-1210
**E-mail:** outreach@yugo.org

**Web Site:** www.yugo.org

*Mr. Leonard K. Janssen, Exec. Director*

A nondenominational sending agency of Evangelical tradition engaged in short-term evangelistic outreach trips for small groups, childcare/orphanage programs, church planting, evangelism, support of national workers and mobilization for mission.

**Year founded in US:** 1964

**Income for Overseas Min:** $2,000,000

**Personnel:**
  Expecting to serve more than 4 years: 26
  Expecting to serve 1 to 4 years: 5

**Countries:** Mexico 26

# Zion Evangelical Ministries of Africa

PO Box 727
Zion, IL 60099 USA

**Phone:** (847) 872-7363
**Fax:** (847) 872-7363
**E-mail:** zemausa@aol.com
**Web Site:** www.zema.org

**Associations:** IFMA

*Mr. Tom Lex, Board Chairman*

A nondenominational sending agency of Evangelical tradition engaged in TEE, Bible distribution, camping programs, Christian education, theological education and leadership development.

**Year founded in US:** 1900

**Income for Overseas Min:** $277,458

**Fully Supported US Personnel Overseas:**
  Expecting to serve more than 4 years: 5

**Other Personnel:**
  Short-term less than 1 year: 100
  Non-US serving in own/other country: 21
  Home ministry and office staff in US: 1

**Countries:** South Africa 5

# Addressing the Cares and Concerns of Missionaries

Spending time in an overseas mission field brings many challenges. Stress, depression, fear and uncertainty are common. You need wisdom and resources to know how to deal with each person and situation you encounter. We are here for you.

### Don't Pig Out on Junk Food:
### The MK's Guide to Survival in the U.S.
*Alma Daugherty Gordon*

Although the life of a Missionary Kid (MK) can provide opportunities for learning about various cultures and languages, there are also many challenges upon reentry into the "home" culture. This book is an open and honest discussion on issues MKs face during this time: preparing for reentry, stress and depression, transitioning to a new cultural setting and more.

**REDUCED PRICE: $6.95**. Regularly $13.95.

### Families on the Move:
### Growing Up Overseas and Loving It!
*Marion Knell*

In a highly mobile world, even missionaries are moving from one country to another in service to the Lord. For those crossing cultural boundaries, this book helps Third Culture Kids (TCKs) deal with issues such as: nourishing family relationships; coping with the grief of moving and overcoming cultural barriers.

**REDUCED PRICE: $6.95**. Regularly $14.95.

### Honourably Wounded:
### Stress among Christian Workers
*Marjory Foyle*

Stresses can occur to missionaries in any setting or area of service and this book helps individuals deal with those. Topics include: dealing with depression, interpersonal relationships and caring for other missionaries. For those serving overseas, special emphasis is also given to culture shock, burnout and reentry.

**REDUCED PRICE: $6.95**. Regularly $13.95.

## To order, call 630.752.7158
## or go online @ www.emisdirect.com

**Order 10 or more copies and pay only $4.95 per book!**

# Prepare to Lead in Evangelism

*Lon Allison*

## With a Masters in Evangelism & Leadership from Wheaton College

*Rick Richardson*

*Scholarship Committed to Servanthood*

Wheaton College has launched a new Master of Arts degree in Evangelism that is designed to equip leaders to think critically, and act creatively to communicate the gospel in our contemporary, multi-ethnic world.

### A master's degree in Evangelism will equip you to:

- Generate ministry strategies that are theologically sound and contextually relevant.
- Lead and train others in effective evangelism.
- Grow in your critical thinking skills about the gospel and contemporary culture.
- Understand and communicate the gospel as the good news of the kingdom of God.
- Learn crucial cross cultural communication skills.

As a student you will not only benefit from Wheaton's outstanding faculty, but also from the opportunity to intern at cutting edge churches and para church ministries, and have contact with national leaders in effective evangelism.

> "My goal is to preach the Good News about Jesus Christ and train leadership and laity in the church on how to share the Gospel."
>
> *—Yreille Belizaire, from Nassau, Bahamas*

### Who should apply?

- Pastors and emerging leaders in the local church
- Para-church Evangelism leaders and potential leaders
- Evangelists and missionaries
- Aspiring scholars in areas of gospel and culture
- Lay people wanting greater evangelistic impact

## Wheaton College Graduate School
*For Christ and His Kingdom*

Graduate Admissions
Local: 630.752.5195
Toll Free: 800.888.0141
gradadm@wheaton.edu
www.wheatongrad.com

# Chapter 3
# Indices to U.S. Protestant Agencies

M any *Handbook* users find it valuable to locate agencies by particular categories of church tradition or ministry activity. This chapter provides the user with those indices. Agency responses on the Mission Handbook survey questionnaire helped define the listed categories. The organizations in each category appear in alphabetical order by organization name.

## Index by Church Tradition

If an agency needed more than one generic or denominational category to describe its traditional doctrinal and/or ecclesiastical stance, the agency may appear under as many as two of the given categories. We have arranged the list alphabetically by category and within each category by agency name. See question #8 of the survey questionnaire (in appendix) for the actual wording of the question and the check-off list of choices.

## Index by Ministry Activity

Almost all agencies are involved in several types of ministry activities. Each agency may be listed under as many as six primary categories of activity. We asked those with more than six primary activities to indicate the six activities toward which they had committed the largest amount of resources.

We have divided the broad activities of education and evangelism into subcategories. For example, the evangelism category appears as "evangelism, mass" and "evangelism, student" and so on. See question #9 of the survey questionnaire (in appendix) for the actual wording of the question and the check-off list of activities.

Agencies sometimes have written in new categories under the "other" choice in previous surveys. Some of these, if used often enough, may be included in the check-off list for the next edition's survey questionnaire. Categories are occasionally dropped for lack of use. The most used categories have remained the same.

# Church Tradition

## Adventist
Advent Christian General Conf.
Adventist World Aviation
Seventh-day Adventists General Conf.

## Anglican
Anglican Frontier Missions
Church World Service
Episcopal Ch. USA—Domestic & Foreign
New Wineskins Missionary Network
Reformed Episcopal Bd. of Foreign Msns.
South American Missionary Society (USA)

## Baptist
ABWE
All God's Children International
Am. Baptist Chs. of the U.S.A., Intl. Mns
AMG International
Anis Shorrosh Evangelistic Association
Baptist Bible Fellowship International
Baptist Bible Translators Institute
Baptist General Conf.—Intl. Ministries
Baptist International Evangelistic Ministries
Baptist International Missions, Inc. (BIMI)
Baptist International Outreach
Baptist Medical & Dental Mission Intl., Inc.
Baptist Mid-Missions
Baptist Missions to Forgotten Peoples
Baptist World Mission
Bridge Builders International
Calvary Evangelistic Mission, Inc.
CAM International
Children's Medical Ministries
Christ to the Nations
Christian Discipleship Ministries, Inc.
Christian Missions Unlimited
Commission to Every Nation
Cooperative Baptist Fellowship
CrossLink International
Crossover Communications International
East West Ministries International
Envoy International
Equip, Inc.
Final Frontiers Foundation, Inc.
Free Will Baptist, Inc. Bd. of Int'l. Missions
Fundamental Baptist Msn. Trinidad/Tobago
General Assoc. of Regular Baptist Chs.
General Baptists International
Global Focus
Global Outreach Mission, Inc.
Good Shepherd Ministries, Inc.
Gospel Mission of South America
Grace Baptist Missions International
Handclasp International, Inc.

Have Christ Will Travel Ministries
HBI Global Partners
Health Teams International, Inc.
Impact International
In Touch Mission International
Independent Faith Mission, Inc.
Independent Gospel Missions
Institute for Intl. Christian Communication
    WorldView Center
INTENT
International Board of Jewish Missions, Inc.
International Partnership Ministries, Inc.
Italy for Christ
JARON Ministries International
Jewish Awareness Ministries
Living Hope Ministries International
Lott Carey Baptist Foreign Msn. Conv.
M/E Intl., Inc. (Missionary Electronics)
Macedonia World Baptist Missions, Inc.
Macedonian Missionary Service
Mission Ministries, Inc.
Mission Nannys
Mission ONE, Inc.
Mission to the Americas
Natl. Baptist Conv. of Am.
National Baptist Convention USA, Inc.
New Tribes Mission
North American Baptist Conference
Open Door Baptist Missions
Outreach To Asia Nationals
Pan American Missions
Prakash Association, USA
Priority One International
Progressive Natl. Baptist Convention, Inc.
Project Christ International
Reciprocal Ministries International
Reformed Baptist Mission Services
Rogma International, Inc.
Romanian Missionary Society
Russian Bible Society, Inc.
Servants in Faith & Technology (SIFAT)
Seventh Day Baptist Missionary Society
Slavic Missionary Service, Inc.
Son Shine Ministries International
Source of Light Ministries Intl., Inc.
Southern Baptist Conv. Intl. Mission Bd.
Spiritual Growth Resources, Inc.
Sports & Rec Plus
The Master's Harvest
The Master's Mission, Inc.
TITUS International
TMA Ministries
Waymarks International Radio Ministries
Word of Life Fellowship, Inc.—Intl. Mins.
Word To Russia
World Baptist Fellowship Msn. Agency, Inc.

World Venture
Worldwide Tentmakers, Inc.

## Brethren

Brethren in Christ World Missions
Christian Mission for the Deaf
Church Missions Link
Church of the Brethren
Grace Brethren International Missions
The Brethren Church, Inc.

## Charismatic

Abundant Life Association, Inc.
Advancing Indigenous Missions
Apostolic Team Ministries, Intl.
Bethany International Ministries
Calvary Commission, Inc.
Calvary International
Celebrant Singers
Christ for India, Inc.
Christian Fellowship Union, Inc.
Christian Laymen's Missionary
Evangelism Association
Christian Ministries International (CMI)
Christ's Mandate for Missions
Covenant Celebration Ch. Global Outreach
Dawn Ministries, Inc.
DeNike Ministries
Elim Fellowship
FOCAS
Foundation For His Ministry
Full Gospel Evangelistic Association
Good News for India
Good Shepherd Ministries International
Hundredfold Ministries International
India Gospel Outreach
International Gospel Outreach
International Leadership Seminars
International Outreach Ministries (IOM)
Leadership Training International
Mahesh Chavda Ministries Intl.
Ministry to Eastern Europe
Mission Catalyst International
Missions To Japan, Inc.
New Life Advance International
New Way Missions
Precious Seed Ministries
RUN Ministries
SAND International
Shield of Faith Ministries
Supreme Task International, Inc.
Surfing the Nations
Touch the World Youth Ministries
Trans World Missions
Tribes and Nations Outreach
United Evangelical Churches

University of the Family
Vineyard Church USA—Missions
Weiner Ministries International
World Horizons
World Indigenous Missions
World Missionary Assistance Plan
World Outreach International—US
World Outreach Ministries
WorldHarvest
Youth With A Mission (YWAM)

## Christian (Restoration Movement)

ACM International
African Mission Evangelism, Inc.
Childspring International
Christian Aviation and Radio Mission
Christian Church (Disciples of Christ)
Christian Churches / Churches of Christ
Churches of Christ
CMF International
European Evangelistic Society
Fellowship of Assocs. of Medical Evangelism
Good News Productions International
Haitian Christian Outreach
Hisportic Christian Mission
Interchurch Medical Assistance, Inc.
Key Communications
Mission Services Association, Inc.
Missions Resource Center
Missions Resource Network
New Mission Systems International
Pass the Torch Ministries
Pioneer Bible Translators
TCM International Institute
Team Expansion, Inc.
The Waray-Waray Project
World Bible Translation Center

## Christian/Plymouth Brethren

Brethren Assemblies
Christian Missions in Many Lands, Inc.
Grace and Truth, Inc.
Ireland Outreach International Inc.
Mailbox Club International Inc., The

## Congregational

Conservative Cong. Christian Conf.
Missions Committee
Providence Mission Homes, Inc.

## Ecumenical

Bread for the World
Christian Cultural Development Foundation
Christian Dental Society
Christian Literacy Associates
Gospel Communications International, Inc.

Habitat for Humanity International
India Partners
International Christian Ministries
Intl. Found. for EWHA Woman's University
Moravian Church in North America
Opportunity International
Overseas Ministries Study Center
Self-Help International
United Bd. for Christian Higher Ed. in Asia
United Ch. of Christ—Wider Ch. Mns.
Vellore Christian Med. College Bd. (USA), Inc.
World Servants, Inc.

## Episcopal

International Justice Mission
Rock the World Youth Mission Alliance
Society of St. Margaret

## Evangelical

ACMC, Inc.
Action International Ministries
ACTS International Ministries
Advancing Native Missions
Adventures in Missions
Africa Inland Mission International
African Bible Colleges, Inc.
African Enterprise
African Leadership, Inc.
Alberto Mottesi Evangelistic Association
Alongside Ministries International
Alongside, Inc.
Amazon Focus
Ambassadors for Christ Intl.
Ambassadors for Christ, Inc.
Am. Council of the Ramabai Mukti Msn., Inc.
American Leprosy Missions, Inc.
American Missionary Fellowship
Am. Scripture Gift Mission Inc. (SGM USA)
AmeriTribes
AMF International
AMOR Ministries
Arab World Ministries
ARISE International Mission
Armenian Missionary Assoc. of America, Inc.
Artists In Christian Testimony
Asian Access
Asian Outreach U.S.A.
Association of Christian Schools Intl. (ACSI)
Association of Free Lutheran Congregations
Audio Scripture Ministries
Avant Ministries
Awana Clubs International
Back to the Bible International
Bakke Graduate University of Ministry
Barnabas International
BCM International

Bible League, The
Bible Literature International
Bible Training Centre for Pastors
Bibles & Literature in French
Bibles For The World, Inc.
BILD International
Billy Graham Center, The
Blessings International
Cadence International
Caleb Project
Campus Crusade for Christ, Intl.
Caring Partners International, Inc.
Carver International Missions, Inc.
Catalyst Services
Cedar Lane Missionary Homes, Inc.
Centers for Apologetics Research (CFAR)
Childcare Worldwide
Children's HopeChest
China Connection
China Ministries International
China Outreach Ministries, Inc.
ChinaSource
Chosen Mission Project
Christ Community Church
Christ for the City International
Christar
Christian Aid Mission
Christian and Missionary Alliance
Christian Associates International
Christian Broadcasting Network Inc., the
Christian Info. Service, Inc. Missions Div.
Christian Literature International
Christian Outreach International
Christian Pilots Association
Christian Resources International
Christian Union Churches of N. Am.
Christian World Publishers
Christians In Action Missions International
Church Leadership Dev. Intl.
Church Ministries International
Church of God (Seventh Day) Gen. Con
Church Planting International
Church Resource Ministries (CRM)
CLC Ministries International
CMTS Ministries, Inc.
ComCare International
COMHINA
Connecting Businessmen to Christ
Cook Communications Ministries Intl.
Crisis Consulting International
CSI Ministries, Inc.
CTI Music Ministries
Dayspring International
Daystar U.S.
Deaf Missions International
Development Associates International (DAI)

Latin America Assistance, Inc.
Latin America Mission
Latin American Indian Ministries
Leadership Ministries Worldwide
Liberty Corner Mission
Liebenzell USA
LIGHT International, Inc.
Link Care Foundation
Literacy & Evangelism International
Luis Palau Evangelistic Assoc.
Luke Society, Inc., The
Lutheran Brethren World Missions
Media Associates International
Medical Ambassadors International, Inc.
Medical Missions Philippines, Inc.
Men for Missions International
Mercy Ships
Mexican Medical Ministries
Ministries In Action
Ministry to Educate and Equip Intl. (MTEE)
Mission Aviation Fellowship
Mission India
Mission of Mercy
Mission Possible Foundation, Inc.
Mission Possible, Inc.
Mission To Unreached Peoples
Mission Training and Resource Center
Mission Training International
Mission: Moving Mountains, Inc.
Missionaire International
Missionary Athletes International
Missionary Flights International
Missionary Gospel Fellowship
Missionary Outreach Support Svcs. (MOSS)
Missionary Retreat Fellowship Inc.
Missionary Ventures International
MMS Aviation
Morelli Ministries International
Mustard Seed International
Narramore Christian Foundation
National Religious Broadcasters
Navigators, U.S. Intl. Missions Group
Network of International Christian Schools
New Directions International, Inc.
New Hope International
No Greater Love Ministries, Inc.
OC International, Inc.
OMF International
OMS International, Inc.
On The Go Ministries/Keith Cook
    Evangelistic Association
Open Air Campaigners—Overseas Ministries
Open Doors with Brother Andrew USA
Operation Blessing International Relief
    and Development Corporation
Operation Mobilization

Overseas Council International
Palm Missionary Ministries
Paraclete, Inc.
Partners in Christ International
Partners International
People International USA
Peter Deyneka Russian Ministries
Pioneer Clubs
Pioneers USA
Precept Ministries International
Prison Mission Association
Progressive Vision
Project AmaZon
Project Mercy, Inc.
Ravi Zacharias International Ministries
Reach Ministries International
Red Sea Team International
Ripe for Harvest, Inc.
Russian Christian Radio
Salvation Army, U.S.A.
Samaritan's Purse
SAT-7 North America
SEND International USA
ServLife International
Share International
Shelter for Life International, Inc.
Shield of Faith Mission International
SIM USA
Slavic Gospel Association
South America Mission, Inc.
Sowers International, The
Spiritual Overseers Service International
STEER, Inc.
STEM
TEAM (The Evangelical Alliance Mission)
TEAMS for Medical Missions
Teen Missions International, Inc.
Tentmakers International
The God's Story Project
The Word for the World
Training Evangelistic Leadership (T.E.L.), Inc.
Trans World Radio, International
Turkish World Outreach
U.S. Center for World Mission
Ukrainian Childrens Fund
UWEZO International
VELA Ministries International
Venture International
Voice of the Martyrs, The
Walk Thru the Bible Ministries, Inc.
Waymakers International
WEC International
White Fields Inc.
Women to the World
World Concern
World Harvest Mission

World Harvest Now, Inc.
World Help
World Link Ministries
World Mission
World Mission Associates
World Missionary Press, Inc.
World Missions & Evangelism, Inc.
World Missions Far Corners, Inc.
World Opportunities International
World Orphans
World Partners USA
World Reach, Inc.
World Relief
World Team
World Thrust International, Inc.
World Vision Inc.
WorldTeach
Worldwide Discipleship Assoc.
Worldwide Lab Improvement
World-Wide Missions
Wycliffe Associates, Inc.
Wycliffe International
Young Life
Youth for Christ International
Youth for Christ/USA—World Outreach
Youth with a Mission (YWAM), N. Am. Office
YUGO Ministries
Zion Evangelical Ministries of Africa

## Friends

Central Yearly Meeting of Friends Missions
Evangelical Friends Mission
Friends United Meeting—Global Ministries

## Fundamental

FOM (Fellowship of Missions)
Gideons International, The
Gospel Fellowship Association
Remnant Ministries, Inc.
Village Ministries International

## Holiness

Ch. of God (Anderson, Ind.), Global Msns.
Ch. of God (Holiness), Wld. Msn. Dept., Inc.
Ch. of the Nazarene, Wld. Msn. Dept.
Congregational Holiness Ch.—Wld. Msns.
Evangelical Bible Mission
Evangelistic Faith Missions
Pentecostal Free Will Baptist Church, Inc.
Pillar of Fire Missions Intl.

## Independent

ASSIST Ministries & ASSIST News Service
Aurora Mission, Inc.
Biblical Ministries Worldwide
Brazil Gospel Fellowship Mission

Bright Hope International
Child Evangelism Fellowship, Inc.
Chosen People Ministries
CrossWorld
D & D Missionary Homes, Inc.
David Livingstone KURE Foundation
Evangelical Baptist Missions
Fellowship International Mission
Galcom International USA, Inc.
Globe Missionary Evangelism
Gospel Furthering Fellowship, The
INTERCOMM
Missionary TECH Team
Missions to Military, Inc.
Mutual Faith Ministries Intl.
Reaching Indians Ministries International
Rio Grande Bible Institute
Spanish World Ministries
Strategic Ventures Network

## Lutheran

Advancing Renewal Ministries, Inc.
Am. Assoc. of Lutheran Churches
Concordia Gospel Outreach
Evangelical Lutheran Church in America
Global Health Ministries
Haiti Lutheran Mission Society
Latin American Lutheran Mission
Lutheran Bible Translators, Inc.
Lutheran Church-Missouri Synod
Lutheran Hour Ministries
Lutheran World Relief
Wisconsin Evangelical Lutheran Synod
World Mission Prayer League
Youth Encounter

## Mennonite

Africa Inter-Mennonite Mission
Children's Haven International
Christian Aid Ministries
Church of God in Christ, Mennonite
Eastern Mennonite Missions
MBMS International
Mennonite Central Committee (MCC)
Mennonite Mission Network
Pacific Northwest Mennonite Conf.—Msns.
Rosedale Mennonite Missions
Virginia Mennonite Board of Missions

## Methodist

African Methodist Episcopal Church
International Child Care, USA, Inc.
Ludhiana Christian Medical College
     Board, USA, Inc.
The Mission Society
United Methodist Church

## None Preferred

Derek Prince Ministries, International
Emmaus Road International
Enterprise Development Intl.

## Other Tradition

Apostolic Christian Church Foundation, Inc.
Christian Medical & Dental Associations
   Global Health Outreach
Food for the Hungry, Inc.
Global Action
Middle East Media—USA

## Pentecostal

AFMA
AIMS
Assemblies of God World Missions
Christ for the Nations, Inc.
Christian Church of North America Missions
Ch. of God (Cleveland, Tenn.) World Msns.
Church of God of Prophecy
Evangel Bible Translators
Free Gospel Church, Inc.—Missions Dept.
Full Gospel Grace Fellowship
Global University
Gospel Revival Ministries
International Pentecostal Church of Christ
Intl. Pentecostal Holiness Church
Living Water Teaching
Open Bible Churches, Intl. Ministries
Pentecostal Ch. of God—World Msns. Dept.
Rehoboth Ministries, Inc
Team World Outreach
The Ch. of God of the Apostolic Faith, Inc.
United Pentecostal Church Intl.

## Presbyterian

Arabic Communication Center
Cities for Christ Worldwide
Cumberland Presbyterian Ch. Bd. of Msns.
Evangelical Presbyterian Church
Mission to the World (PCA), Inc.
Orthodox Presbyterian Church
Perimeter Church, Global Outreach
Presbyterian Center for Mission Studies
Presbyterian Ch. (USA), Worldwide Mns.
Presbyterian Evangelistic Fellowship
Presbyterian Mission International (PMI)
Presbyterian Missionary Union
Presbyterian Order for World Evangelization
Seed International
Westminster Biblical Missions
World Witness, Assoc. Reformed Presb.Ch.

## Reformed

Christian Reformed World Missions

Christian Reformed World Relief Committee
Lifewater International
LOGOI Ministries
Partners in Asian Missions
Reformation Translation Fellowship (RTF)
Reformed Ch. in Am., Gen. Synod Council
Sending Experienced Retired Volunteers
   Everywhere
Talking Bibles International

## Wesleyan

Allegheny Wesleyan Methodist Connection
Congregational Methodist Church
Cornerstone International
Evangelical Congregational Ch. Commission
Evangelical Methodist Church, Inc.
Free Methodist World Missions
Global Partners/Wesleyan World Missions
GO InterNational
Primitive Methodist Church in the USA
World Gospel Mission

# Ministry Activity

## Adoption

All God's Children International
WorldHarvest

## Agricultural programs

China Connection Church World Service
ECHO
Empowering Lives International
Equip, Inc.
FARMS International
Floresta USA, Inc.
Food for the Hungry, Inc.
Heifer International
Lutheran World Relief
Medical Ambassadors International, Inc
Mennonite Central Committee (MCC)
Mission: Moving Mountains, Inc.
Mustard Seed International
Prakash Association, USA
Project Mercy, Inc.
Reformed Ch. in Am., Gen. Synod Council
Samaritan's Purse
SAND International
Self-Help International
STEER, Inc.
Tribes and Nations Outreach
World Concern
World Relief
World Vision Inc.

## Apologetics

Anis Shorrosh Evangelistic Association

Centers for Apologetics Research (CFAR),
Abundant Life Association, Inc.
ACMC, Inc.
AFMA (Alliance for Missions Advancement)
AIMS (Accelerating Intl. Mission Strategies)
EFMA
FOM (Fellowship of Missions)
Full Gospel Evangelistic Association
Grace Baptist Missions International
IFMA
International Gospel Outreach
Living Water Teaching
Missionary Revival Crusade
Reformed Baptist Mission Services
United Evangelical Churches
World Outreach Ministries

## Audio recording/distribution

Anis Shorrosh Evangelistic Association
Assemblies of God World Missions
Audio Scripture Ministries
Celebrant Singers
Christian Aviation and Radio Mission
Christian Resources International
Derek Prince Ministries, International
East Gates Ministries Intl.
Far East Broadcasting Company, Inc.
Friends of Israel Gospel Ministry, Inc.
Global Recordings Network
Grand Old Gospel Fellowship
Hundredfold Ministries International
Institute of Theological Studies—Division
   of Outreach Inc.
JAARS Inc.
Josue Yrion Wld. Evangelism and Msns., Inc.
Key Communications
M/E International, Inc.
Overseas Radio & Television, Inc. (ORTV)
Russian Christian Radio
Spanish World Ministries
Talking Bibles International
The God's Story Project
Trans World Radio, International
Voice of the Martyrs, The
Waymarks International Radio Ministries
Word To Russia
World Mission

## Aviation services

ACM International
Christian Aviation and Radio Mission
Christian Pilots Association
JAARS Inc.
Mission Aviation Fellowship
Mission Safety International
Missionaire International

Missionary Flights International
MMS Aviation
South America Mission, Inc.
World Team

## Bible distribution

Advancing Renewal Ministries, Inc.
African Bible Colleges, Inc.
African Methodist Episcopal Church
Ambassadors for Christ, Inc.
American Bible Society
AMF International
Armenian Missionary Assoc. of America, Inc.
Asian Outreach U.S.A.
Assemblies of God World Missions
Aurora Mission, Inc.
Baptist International Evangelistic Ministries
Baptist International Missions, Inc. (BIMI)
Bible League, The
Bibles & Literature in French
Bibles For The World, Inc.
Central Yearly Meeting of Friends Missions
Children's HopeChest
China Connection
China Ministries International
Christ to the Nations
Christian Aid Mission
Christian Literature International
Christian Missions Unlimited
Christian Resources International
Church of God (Seventh Day) Gen. Conf.
Church of God in Christ, Mennonite
Cook Communications Ministries Intl.
Door of Hope International
East Gates Ministries Intl.
Edwin L. Hodges Ministries
Evangel Bible Translators
Evangelical Bible Mission
Every Home for Christ
Final Frontiers Foundation, Inc.
Free Gospel Church, Inc.
Galcom International USA, Inc.
Gideons International, The
Gospel Revival Ministries
Hosanna
In Touch Mission International
India Evangelical Mission
India National Inland Mission
India Rural Evangelical Fellowship
International Board of Jewish Missions, Inc.
International Family Missions
Iranian Christians International
Ireland Outreach International Inc.
Italy for Christ
Josue Yrion Wld. Evangelism and Msns., Inc.
Latin American Lutheran Mission

Macedonian Missionary Service
Missionary Flights International
Missions To Japan, Inc.
New Life Advance International
New Way Missions
Open Door Baptist Missions
Open Doors with Brother Andrew USA
Outreach To Asia Nationals
Pan American Missions
Partners in Christ International
Pentecostal Ch. of God—World Msns. Dept.
Presbyterian Missionary Union
Prison Mission Association
Progressive Natl. Baptist Convention, Inc.
Remnant Ministries, Inc.
Ripe for Harvest, Inc.
Russian Bible Society, Inc.
Slavic Gospel Association
Sowers International, The
Spanish American Evangelistic Ministries
Talking Bibles International
The Ch. of God of the Apostolic Faith, Inc.
The Word for the World
Tribes and Nations Outreach
Turkish World Outreach
Voice of the Martyrs, The
World Baptist Fellowship Msn. Agency, Inc.
World Bible Translation Center
World Help
World Mission
Zion Evangelical Ministries of Africa

## Bible memorization

Awana Clubs International
Disciples International
Missions To Japan, Inc.
Pioneer Clubs
Reach Ministries International

## Broadcasting, radio and/or TV

ACM International
African Bible Colleges, Inc.
Agape Gospel Mission
Alberto Mottesi Evangelistic Association
AMG International
Anis Shorrosh Evangelistic Association
Arab World Ministries
Assemblies of God World Missions
Back to the Bible International
Baptist Mid-Missions
Calvary Evangelistic Mission, Inc.
Celebrant Singers
Centers for Apologetics Research (CFAR)
Christian Aviation and Radio Mission
Christian Broadcasting Network Inc., the
Christian Laymen's Missionary Evangelism

Association
Christian Union Churches of N. America
Derek Prince Ministries, International
Far East Broadcasting Company, Inc.
Friends of Israel Gospel Ministry, Inc.
Global Outreach Mission, Inc.
Good News Productions International
Gospel Communications International, Inc.
Gospel for Asia, Inc.
Grand Old Gospel Fellowship
Greater Grace World Outreach
HCJB Global
Hermano Pablo Ministries
High Adventure Ministries/Voice of Hope
   Broadcasting Network
Impact International
INTERCOMM
International Board of Jewish Missions, Inc
Jewish Awareness Ministries
Joni and Friends
Key Communications
Luis Palau Evangelistic Assoc.
Lutheran Hour Ministries
Macedonian Missionary Service
Middle East Media—USA
Missions To Japan, Inc.
National Religious Broadcasters
OMS International, Inc.
Partners in Christ International
Precept Ministries International
Ramesh Richard Evangelism and Ch. Health
Raul Zaldivar Ministries
Rehoboth Ministries, Inc
Rio Grande Bible Institute
Romanian Missionary Society
Russian Christian Radio
SAT-7 North America
Slavic Missionary Service, Inc.
Spanish World Ministries
The Waray-Waray Project
Trans World Radio, International
Voice of the Martyrs, The
Walk Thru the Bible Ministries, Inc.
Waymarks International Radio Ministries
Wisconsin Evangelical Lutheran Synod
Word of Life Fellowship, Inc.—Intl. Mns
Word To Russia
WorldTeach

## Camping programs

Action International Ministries
American Missionary Fellowship
AmeriTribes
Armenian Missionary Assoc. of America, Inc.
BCM International
Brazil Gospel Fellowship Mission

Christ Community Church
Christian Mission for the Deaf
Christian Union Churches of North America
Eastern European Outreach, Inc.
Fellowship International Mission
Friendship International Ministries, Inc.
Gospel Fellowship Association
Greater Europe Mission
Have Christ Will Travel Ministries
Heart to Heart Intl. Ministries
International Messengers
Janz Team Ministries USA
Japanese Evangelical Missionary Society
Latin America Assistance, Inc.
Latin America Mission
Peter Deyneka Russian Ministries
Pioneer Clubs
Presbyterian Evangelistic Fellowship
Salvation Army, U.S.A.
Servants in Faith & Technology (SIFAT)
Sports & Rec Plus
TITUS International
Trans World Missions
Word of Life Fellowship, Inc.—Intl. Mins.
Word To Russia
Young Life
Zion Evangelical Ministries of Africa

## Childcare/orphanage

Advancing Native Missions
Adventures in Missions
African Leadership, Inc.
Agape Gospel Mission
Am. Council of the Ramabai Mukti Msn., Inc.
AMG International
Assemblies of God World Missions
Baptist Medical & Dental Mission Intl., Inc.
Bibles For The World, Inc.
Calvary Commission, Inc.
Childcare Worldwide
Children's Haven International
Children's HopeChest
China Connection
Christ for India, Inc.
Christ for the City International
Christ to the Nations
Christian Aid Ministries
Christian Aid Mission
Christian Broadcasting Network Inc.
Christian Church of North America
Christians In Action Missions International
Church of God (Cleveland, TN)
Door of Hope International
East West Ministries International
Eastern European Outreach, Inc.
Empowering Lives International

Equip, Inc.
Evangelical Baptist Missions
Evangelical Congregational Church
   Commission
Every Child Ministries, Inc.
Fellowship International Mission
Final Frontiers Foundation, Inc.
Forward Edge International
Foundation For His Ministry
Free Methodist World Missions
General Baptists International
Global Fellowship Inc.
Global Outreach International
Gospel Outreach Ministries Intl.
Greater Grace World Outreach
Harvest International, Inc.
Heart to Heart Intl. Ministries
Hope for the Hungry
In Touch Mission International
Independent Gospel Missions: A Baptist
   Mission Agency
India Evangelical Mission
India Gospel League, NA
India National Inland Mission
India Partners
India Rural Evangelical Fellowship
Intl. Christian Leprosy Mission, Inc. (USA)
International Messengers
International Street Kids Outreach Mins.
International Teams, U.S.A.
Kids Alive International
Liberty Corner Mission
Living Hope Ministries International
Macedonia World Baptist Missions, Inc.
Mexican Medical Ministries
Mission Ministries, Inc.
Mission Nannys
Mission of Mercy
Mission Possible, Inc.
Mission To Unreached Peoples
Mustard Seed International
New Directions International, Inc.
New Hope International
New Life Advance International
North American Baptist Conference
Outreach To Asia Nationals
Pan American Missions
Partners in Asian Missions
People International USA
Perimeter Church, Global Outreach
Precious Seed Ministries
Project Christ International
Rosedale Mennonite Missions
Teen Missions International, Inc.
The Master's Mission, Inc.
The Mission Society

Trans World Missions
Ukrainian Childrens Fund
Word To Russia
World Help
World Orphans
World Outreach International—US
World Vision Inc.
WorldHarvest
World-Wide Missions
YUGO Ministries

## Childrens programs

Abundant Life Association, Inc.
Action International Ministries
All God's Children International
American Scripture Gift Mission Inc.
Armenian Missionary Assoc. of America, Inc.
Assemblies of God World Missions
Awana Clubs International
BCM International
Cadence International
Carver International Missions, Inc.
Child Evangelism Fellowship, Inc.
Children's HopeChest
Compassion International, Inc.
Cornerstone International
CrossWorld
Evangelical Methodist Church, Inc.
Every Child Ministries, Inc.
Fellowship International Mission
FOCAS
Global Action
Globe Missionary Evangelism
GO InterNational
Gospel for Asia, Inc.
Harvest International, Inc.
Have Christ Will Travel Ministries
Heart to Heart Intl. Ministries
Hope for the Hungry
HOPE International
International Child Care, USA, Inc.
International Messengers
Jews for Jesus
Kids Around the World, Inc.
Latin America Mission
Living Water Teaching
MAP International
Ministry to Eastern Europe
Ministry to Educate and Equip International
Mission India
Mission of Mercy
Mission Possible Foundation, Inc.
Missionary Ventures International
New Directions International, Inc.
Operation Blessing International Relief and
    Development Corporation

Pioneer Clubs
Progressive Natl. Baptist Convention, Inc.
Project Christ International
Romanian Missionary Society
Salvation Army, U.S.A.
SAT-7 North America
Self-Help International
Sending Experienced Retired Volunteers
    Everywhere
Seventh-day Adventists General Conference
Society of St. Margaret
Spiritual Overseers Service International
STEM International
Things To Come Mission, Inc.
Ukrainian Childrens Fund
WEC International
Word To Russia
World Outreach International—US
World Vision International
Youth Encounter

## Church construction

Allegheny Wesleyan Methodist Connection
Apostolic Christian Church Foundation, Inc.
Assemblies of God World Missions
Baptist International Evangelistic Ministries
Baptist Medical & Dental Mission Intl., Inc.
China Connection
Christ for India, Inc.
Christ for the Nations, Inc.
Christian Church of North America
Christian Missions Unlimited
Christian Union Churches of North America
Church Ministries International
Church of God (Cleveland, TN)
Church Planting International
Congregational Holiness Church
DeNike Ministries
East Gates Ministries Intl.
Full Gospel Evangelistic Association
Global Outreach International
Gospel Revival Ministries
International Cooperating Ministries
International Messengers
Latin American Lutheran Mission
Macedonian Missionary Service
Men for Missions International
Natl. Baptist Conv. of Am.—Foreign Msn. Bd.
National Baptist Convention USA, Inc.
New Directions International, Inc.
Open Bible Churches, Intl. Ministries
Partners in Asian Missions
Pentecostal Ch. of God—World Msns. Dept.
Pillar of Fire Missions Intl.
Precious Seed Ministries
Progressive Natl. Baptist Convention, Inc.

Project Christ International
Slavic Missionary Service, Inc.
The Ch. of God of the Apostolic Faith, Inc.
The Waray-Waray Project
Things To Come Mission, Inc.
World Help

## Church establishing/planting

Abundant Life Association, Inc.
ABWE
ACM International
Advancing Renewal Ministries, Inc.
Advent Christian General Conf.
Africa Inland Mission International
Africa Inter-Mennonite Mission
African Mission Evangelism, Inc.
Agape Gospel Mission
AIMS
Allegheny Wesleyan Methodist Connection
American Association of Lutheran Churches
Am. Council of the Ramabai Mukti Msn., Inc.
AmeriTribes
AMG International
Anglican Frontier Missions
Apostolic Team Ministries, Intl.
Arab World Ministries
Armenian Missionary Assoc. of America, Inc.
Artists In Christian Testimony
Asian Access
Asian Outreach U.S.A.
Assemblies of God World Missions
Association of Free Lutheran Congregations
Aurora Mission, Inc.
Avant Ministries
Baptist Bible Fellowship International
Baptist General Conference—Intl. Mns.
Baptist International Evangelistic Ministries
Baptist International Missions, Inc. (BIMI)
Baptist International Outreach
Baptist Medical & Dental Mission Intl., Inc.
Baptist Mid-Missions
Baptist Missions to Forgotten Peoples
Baptist World Mission
Bethany International Ministries
Bible League, The
Biblical Ministries Worldwide
BILD International
Brazil Gospel Fellowship Mission
Brethren Assemblies
Brethren in Christ World Missions
Calvary International
CAM International
Central Yearly Meeting of Friends Missions
Chosen People Ministries
Christ Community Church
Christ for India, Inc.

Christ to the Nations
Christar
Christian Aid Mission
Christian and Missionary Alliance
Christian Associates International
Christian Church of North America
Christian Churches / Churches of Christ
Christian Discipleship Ministries, Inc.
Christian Fellowship Union, Inc.
Christian Ministries International (CMI)
Christian Reformed World Missions
Christian Union Churches of N. America
Christians In Action Missions International
Church Leadership Development Intl.
Church Ministries International
Ch. of God (Anderson, Ind.), Global Missions
Ch. of God (Cleveland, Tenn.) World Msns.
Ch. of God (Holiness), Wld. Msn. Dept., Inc
Church of God of Prophecy
Church of the Nazarene, World Msn. Dept.
Church Planting International
Church Resource Ministries (CRM)
Churches of Christ
Churches of God, General Conference
CityTeam Ministries
CMF International
Congregational Methodist Church
Cornerstone International
Crossover Communications International
CrossWorld
Cumberland Presbyterian Ch. Bd. of Msns.
Dawn Ministries, Inc.
Dayspring International
DeNike Ministries
Donetsk Christian University
Eastern Mennonite Missions
East-West Ministries International
EFCA International Mission
Elim Fellowship—International Department
European Christian Mission Intl.—USA
European Evangelistic Society
Evangel Bible Translators
Evangelical Baptist Missions
Evangelical Bible Mission
Evangelical Congregational Church
Evangelical Covenant Church
Evangelical Friends Church Southwest
Evangelical Friends Mission
Evangelical Methodist Church, Inc.
Evangelical Presbyterian Church
Evangelism Resources
Evangelistic Faith Missions
Every Home for Christ
Fellowship International Mission
Fellowship of Assocs. of Medical Evangelism
Fellowship of Evangelical Churches

Final Frontiers Foundation, Inc.
Foundation For His Ministry
Foursquare Missions International
Free Gospel Church, Inc.—Missions Dept.
Free Methodist World Missions
Free Will Baptist, Inc. Board of Intl. Missions
Frontiers
Full Gospel Evangelistic Association
Fundamental Baptist Msn. Trinidad/ Tobago
Galcom International USA, Inc.
General Baptists International
Global Action
Global Fellowship Inc.
Global Ministries, Church of the United
    Brethren in Christ
Global Opportunities
Global Outreach Mission, Inc.
Global Partners / Wesleyan World Missions
Globe Missionary Evangelism
GO InterNational
Good News for India
Good Shepherd Ministries International
Gospel Fellowship Association
Gospel for Asia, Inc.
Gospel Furthering Fellowship, The
Gospel Mission of South America
Gospel Outreach Ministries Intl.
Gospelink, Inc.
Grace Baptist Missions International
Grace Brethren International Missions
Grace Ministries International
Grand Old Gospel Fellowship
Great Commission Ministries, Inc.
Greater Europe Mission
Greater Grace World Outreach
Haiti Lutheran Mission Society
Haitian Christian Outreach
HBI Global Partners
Heart of God Ministries
Hellenic Ministries
Hisportic Christian Mission
I. N. Network USA
Impact International
Independent Faith Mission, Inc.
Independent Gospel Missions: A Baptist
    Mission Agency
India Gospel League, NA
India Gospel Outreach
India National Inland Mission
India Rural Evangelical Fellowship
InterAct Ministries
Intl. Christian Leprosy Mission, Inc. (USA)
International Gospel Outreach
International Partnership Ministries, Inc.
International Pentecostal Church of Christ
Intl. Pentecostal Holiness Ch. Wld. Msns. Mns.

International Street Kids Outreach Ministries
International Teams, U.S.A.
Iranian Christians International
Ireland Outreach International Inc.
Japanese Evangelization Center
Latin American Lutheran Mission
Liberty Corner Mission
Liebenzell USA
Living Hope Ministries International
Lutheran Brethren World Missions
Lutheran Church-Missouri Synod
M/E International, Inc.
Macedonia World Baptist Missions, Inc.
Macedonian Missionary Service
MBMS International
Mennonite Mission Network Mission India
Mission Ministries, Inc.
Mission ONE, Inc.
Mission Possible Foundation, Inc.
Mission to the Americas
Mission to the World (PCA), Inc.
Mission To Unreached Peoples
Mission: Moving Mountains, Inc.
Missionary Gospel Fellowship
Missionary Revival Crusade
Missionary Ventures International
Missions Resource Network
Missions to Military, Inc.
Morelli Ministries International
Mustard Seed International
National Baptist Convention USA, Inc.
New Directions International, Inc.
New Life Advance International
New Mission Systems International
New Tribes Mission
N. Am. Baptist Conf.—Worldwide Outreach
OC International, Inc.
OMF International
OMS International, Inc.
Open Bible Churches, Intl. Ministries
Open Door Baptist Missions
Operation Mobilization
Orthodox Presbyterian Church
Outreach To Asia Nationals
Palm Missionary Ministries
Pan American Missions
Paraclete, Inc.
Partners in Asian Missions
Pass the Torch Ministries
Pentecostal Ch. of God—World Msns. Dept.
Pentecostal Free Will Baptist Church, Inc.
People International USA
Perimeter Church, Global Outreach
Peter Deyneka Russian Ministries
Pioneers USA
Precious Seed Ministries

## Correspondence courses

## Development, community

African Leadership, Inc.
Amazon Focus
American Baptist Churches of the U.S.A.
Am. Council of the Ramabai Mukti Msn., Inc.
American Leprosy Missions, Inc.
AmeriTribes
AMOR Ministries
Assemblies of God World Missions
Bright Hope International
Childcare Worldwide
Christar
Christian Broadcasting Network Inc.
Christian Church (Disciples of Christ)
Christian Cultural Development Foundation
Christian Reformed World Relief Committee
Church of the Brethren
Church Resource Ministries (CRM)
Church World Service
CMF International
Compassion International, Inc.
Cooperative Baptist Fellowship
Eastern Mennonite Missions
ECHO
Emmanuel International Mission
Empowering Lives International
Engineering Ministries International
Equip, Inc.
Evangelical Covenant Church
Evangelical Friends Mission
Evangelical Lutheran Church in America
FARMS International
Floresta USA, Inc.
Food for the Hungry, Inc.
Forward Edge International
Free Will Baptist, Inc. Board of Intl. Missions
FRIENDS in Action, International
Friends of Israel Gospel Ministry, Inc.
Frontiers
Global Health Ministries
GO InterNational
Gospel Outreach Ministries Intl.
Gospel Revival Ministries
Grace Brethren International Missions
Habitat for Humanity International
Health Emergent International Services
Heifer International
HOPE International
I. N. Network USA
India Gospel League, NA
India Partners
Interchurch Medical Assistance, Inc.
International Aid
International Child Care, USA, Inc.
International Teams, U.S.A.
InterServe USA (Intl. Service Fellowship)
Latin America Mission

Liebenzell USA
Lifewater International
Luke Society, Inc., The
Lutheran Brethren World Missions
Lutheran World Relief
MAP International MBMS International
Medical Ambassadors International, Inc
Medical Missions Philippines, Inc.
Mennonite Central Committee (MCC)
Mercy Ships
Mexican Medical Ministries
Ministries In Action
Mission of Mercy
Mission Possible, Inc.
Mission To Unreached Peoples
Mission: Moving Mountains, Inc.
New Life Advance International
New Mission Systems International
Northwest Medical Teams International, Inc.
OMF International
Operation Blessing International Relief
    and Development Corporation
Operation Mobilization
Opportunity International
Partners International
People International USA
Perimeter Church, Global Outreach
Pioneer Bible Translators
Pioneers USA
Prakash Association, USA
Presbyterian Ch. (USA), Worldwide Mins.
Presbyterian Mission International (PMI)
Project Mercy, Inc.
Reach Ministries International
Reciprocal Ministries International
Reformed Ch. in Am., Gen. Synod Council
Samaritan's Purse
SAND International
Self-Help International
Sending Experienced Retired Volunteers
    Everywhere
ServLife International
Seventh-day Adventists General Conference
Shelter for Life International, Inc.
Shield of Faith Ministries
SIM USA
Society of St. Margaret
South American Missionary Society (USA)
The Master's Mission, Inc.
United Church of Christ—Wider Ch. Mns.
United World Mission
Vellore Christian Med. College Bd. (USA), Inc.
Venture International
World Concern
World Harvest Mission
World Missions & Evangelism, Inc.

World Partners USA
World Relief
World Servants, Inc.
World Venture
World Vision Inc.
World Vision International
WorldHarvest

## Disability assistance programs

Am. Council of the Ramabai Mukti Msn., Inc.
American Leprosy Missions, Inc.
Baptist International Outreach
Deaf Missions International
Equip, Inc.
India Partners
International Child Care, USA, Inc.
Joni and Friends
Perimeter Church, Global Outreach
Venture International

## Discipleship

Abundant Life Association, Inc.
ABWE
ACM International
Alongside Ministries International
American Missionary Fellowship
AmeriTribes
AMF International
Artists In Christian Testimony
Avant Ministries
Awana Clubs International
Baptist General Conference—Intl. Ministries
Baptist International Missions, Inc. (BIMI)
BCM International
BILD International
Brazil Gospel Fellowship Mission
Cadence International
Campus Crusade for Christ, Intl.
Children's HopeChest
China Outreach Ministries, Inc.
Christian and Missionary Alliance
Christian Discipleship Ministries, Inc.
Christian Fellowship Union, Inc.
Christian Ministries International (CMI)
Christ's Mandate for Missions
Church Ministries International
Church of God (Anderson, Indiana)
CityTeam Ministries
Congregational Methodist Church
Cooperative Baptist Fellowship
Dawn Ministries, Inc.
Disciples International
Edwin L. Hodges Ministries
Elim Fellowship—International Department
Episcopal Church USA—Domestic &
   Foreign Missionary Society

European Christian Mission Intl.—USA
Evangelical Baptist Missions
Evangelical Methodist Church, Inc.
Evangelism Resources
FARMS International
Fellowship of Evangelical Churches
Floresta USA, Inc.
Friendship International Ministries, Inc.
Global Advance
Globe Missionary Evangelism
Good News for India
Good Shepherd Ministries International
Gospel for Asia, Inc.
Gospel Furthering Fellowship, The
Gospelink, Inc.
Greater Grace World Outreach
Haitian Christian Outreach
Harvest
HBI Global Partners
HCJB Global
Heart to Heart Intl. Ministries
Hellenic Ministries
Hosanna
India National Inland Mission
InterAct Ministries
International Family Missions
International Pentecostal Church of Christ
International Street Kids Outreach Ministries
InterServe USA (Intl. Service Fellowship)
InterVarsity Christian Fellowship/USA
Latin American Lutheran Mission
LOGOI Ministries
Luke Society, Inc., The
M/E International, Inc.
Mailbox Club International Inc., The
Ministries In Action
Mission of Mercy
Mission Possible, Inc.
Missionary Gospel Fellowship
Missions To Japan, Inc.
Navigators, U.S. Intl. Missions Group
New Mission Systems International
New Way Missions
Pass the Torch Ministries
Pioneer Clubs
Prison Mission Association
Progressive Vision
Reach Ministries International
Reaching Indians Ministries International
Remnant Ministries, Inc.
Rogma International, Inc.
Rosedale Mennonite Missions
SEND International USA
Shield of Faith Mission International
Spiritual Growth Resources, Inc.
Supreme Task International, Inc.

Surfing the Nations
Talking Bibles International
TEAM (The Evangelical Alliance Mission)
Team Expansion, Inc.
Teen Missions International, Inc.
TITUS International
Training Evangelistic Leadership (T.E.L.), Inc.
Trans World Missions
United Pentecostal Church Intl.,
UWEZO International
Weiner Ministries International
World Harvest Mission
World Mission
World Missionary Press, Inc.
World Outreach International—US
World Reach, Inc.
WorldTeach
Young Life
Youth for Christ International
Youth With A Mission (YWAM)

## Education, church/sch. general

Abundant Life Association, Inc.
Africa Inland Mission International
African Bible Colleges, Inc.
African Leadership, Inc.
Allegheny Wesleyan Methodist Connection
Am. Council of the Ramabai Mukti Msn., Inc.
Assemblies of God World Missions
Association of Christian Schools Intl.
Bibles & Literature in French
Bibles For The World, Inc.
BILD International
Brazil Gospel Fellowship Mission
Caleb Project
CAM International
Carver International Missions, Inc.
Christian Mission for the Deaf
Christian Reformed World Missions
Christ's Mandate for Missions
Church Missions Link
Ch. of God (Holiness), World Mn. Dept., Inc.
Church of the Nazarene, World Msn. Dept.
Church Planting International
Churches of Christ
Churches of God, General Conference
COMHINA
Compassion International, Inc.
Congregational Holiness Church
CrossWorld
Disciples International
Donetsk Christian University
Empowering Lives International
Entrust
Evangelical Friends Mission
Fellowship of Evangelical Churches

FLET University/Universidad FLET
FOCAS
Foundation For His Ministry
Foursquare Missions International
Free Gospel Church, Inc.—Msns. Dept.
General Baptists International
Grace Ministries International
Haiti Lutheran Mission Society
Haitian Christian Outreach
Have Christ Will Travel Ministries
HCJB Global
I. N. Network USA
India Rural Evangelical Fellowship
Interaction International
International Child Care, USA, Inc.
International Justice Mission
Janz Team Ministries USA
Jews for Jesus
Joni and Friends
Kids Alive International
Latin America Mission
Liebenzell USA
Lott Carey Baptist Foreign Msn. Convention
Ministry to Eastern Europe
Mission Nannys
Mission of Mercy
Mission ONE, Inc.
Mission Possible, Inc.
Moravian Church in North America
Mustard Seed International
National Baptist Convention of America
National Baptist Convention USA, Inc.
Network of International Christian Schools
Palm Missionary Ministries
Perimeter Church, Global Outreach
Pillar of Fire Missions Intl.
Project AmaZon
Project Christ International
Project Mercy, Inc.
Ramesh Richard Evangelism and Ch. Health
Raul Zaldivar Ministries
Rehoboth Ministries, Inc
SAND International
Servants in Faith & Technology (SIFAT)
Seventh-day Adventists General Conference
Shield of Faith Ministries
Society of St. Margaret
South America Mission, Inc.
South American Missionary Society (USA)
The Mission Society
United Church of Chris—Wider Ch. Mns.
World Gospel Mission
World Missions & Evangelism, Inc.
WorldTeach
World-Wide Missions
Zion Evangelical Ministries of Africa

## Education, extension (other)

Alberto Mottesi Evangelistic Association
Association of Christian Schools Intl.
Calvary Evangelistic Mission, Inc.
Childcare Worldwide
China Ministries International
Christ to the Nations
COMHINA
Development Associates International (DAI)
Entrust
Evangelical Baptist Missions
Evangelism Resources
FLET University/Universidad FLET
Global University
Good Shepherd Ministries, Inc.
Grace Baptist Missions International
Handclasp International, Inc.
IFMA
Institute for Intl. Christian Communication
WorldView Center
InterAct Ministries
Ludhiana Christian Medical College
    Board, USA, Inc.
Mennonite Central Committee (MCC)
Overseas Radio & Television, Inc. (ORTV)
Pentecostal Free Will Baptist Church, Inc.
Peter Deyneka Russian Ministries
Precept Ministries International
Women to the World
World Link Ministries

## Education, missionary

Abundant Life Association, Inc.
Baptist Bible Translators Institute
Bethany International Ministries
BILD International
Calvary Commission, Inc.
Christ for the Nations, Inc.
Christian Aid Mission
Church of the Nazarene, World Msn. Dept.
Donetsk Christian University
Entrust
Global University
Heart of God Ministries
Institute for Intl. Christian Communication
WorldView Center
Institute of Strategic Languages and Cultures
Macedonian Missionary Service
Missionaire International
Overseas Ministries Study Center
Project Christ International
Reaching Indians Ministries International
Rio Grande Bible Institute
Spanish American Evangelistic Ministries
Teen Missions International, Inc.
The Master's Mission, Inc.

United Methodist Church
WorldHarvest

## Education, theological

ABWE
Advancing Renewal Ministries, Inc.
Advent Christian General Conf.
African Leadership, Inc.
African Mission Evangelism, Inc.
Agape Gospel Mission
Allegheny Wesleyan Methodist Connection
Am. Baptist Chs. of the U.S.A., Intl. Mins.
AMG International
Armenian Missionary Assoc. of America, Inc.
Asian Outreach U.S.A.
Assemblies of God World Missions
Aurora Mission, Inc.
Bakke Graduate University of Ministry
Baptist General Conference—Intl. Mins.
Baptist International Evangelistic Ministries
Baptist International Outreach
Baptist Medical & Dental Mission Intl., Inc.
Baptist Mid-Missions
Bethany International Ministries
Bible Training Centre for Pastors
Bibles For The World, Inc.
BILD International
Brazil Gospel Fellowship Mission
CAM International
Carver International Missions, Inc.
China Ministries International
Christ for India, Inc.
Christ for the Nations, Inc.
Christar
Christian and Missionary Alliance
Christian Reformed World Missions
Church of God (Cleveland, TN)
Church of the Nazarene, World Ms. Dept
CrossWorld
Daystar U.S.
DeNike Ministries
Donetsk Christian University
Eastern Mennonite Missions
East-West Ministries International
EFCA International Mission
Elim Fellowship—Intl. Department
Entrust
European Evangelistic Society
Evangelical Congregational Church
Evangelical Methodist Church, Inc.
Evangelical Presbyterian Church
Evangelistic Faith Missions
Fellowship International Mission
FLET University/Universidad FLET
Free Will Baptist, Inc. Bd. of Intl. Missions
Friends of Israel Gospel Ministry, Inc.

Global Advance
Global Partners / Wesleyan World Missions
Global University
Good News for India
Good Shepherd Ministries, Inc.
Gospel Fellowship Association
Gospel Furthering Fellowship, The
Gospel Mission of South America
Grace Brethren International Missions
Grace Ministries International
Greater Europe Mission
Greater Grace World Outreach
Haiti Lutheran Mission Society
Help for Christian Nationals, Inc.
Hundredfold Ministries International
India National Inland Mission
India Rural Evangelical Fellowship
Institute of Theological Studies—Division
   of Outreach Inc.
International Christian Ministries
International Gospel Outreach
International Institute for Christian Studies
International Partnership Ministries, Inc.
Intl. Pentecostal Holiness Ch. Wld. Msns. Mins.
Ireland Outreach International Inc.
JARON Ministries International
Josue Yrion Wld. Evangelism and Msns., Inc.
Latin America Mission
Liebenzell USA
Living Water Teaching
LOGOI Ministries
Macedonia World Baptist Missions, Inc.
MAP International
Middle East Christian Outreach (MECO)
Ministry to Eastern Europe
Ministry to Educate and Equip International
Missionary Gospel Fellowship
N. Am. Baptist Conf.—Worldwide Outreach
OC International, Inc.
OMS International, Inc.
Orthodox Presbyterian Church
Outreach To Asia Nationals
Overseas Council International
Partners in Christ International
Pentecostal Free Will Baptist Church, Inc.
Perimeter Church, Global Outreach
Pillar of Fire Missions Intl.
Precious Seed Ministries
Presbyterian Mission International (PMI)
Primitive Methodist Church in the USA
Ravi Zacharias International Ministries
Reformed Baptist Mission Services
Reformed Ch. in Am., Gen. Synod Counci
Rehoboth Ministries, Inc
Rio Grande Bible Institute
Rock the World Youth Mission Alliance

Romanian Missionary Society
Seed International
SEND International USA
Seventh-day Adventists General Conference
SIM USA
Slavic Gospel Association
South America Mission, Inc.
Southern Baptist Conv. Intl. Mission Board
TCM International Institute
TEAM (The Evangelical Alliance Mission)
The Brethren Church, Inc.
The Ch. of God of the Apostolic Faith, Inc.
Things To Come Mission, Inc.
TMA Ministries
U.S. Center for World Mission
United Ch. of Christ—Wider Ch. Mins.
United Pentecostal Church Intl.
Waymarks International Radio Ministries
Westminster Biblical Missions
Wisconsin Evangelical Lutheran Synod
Word of Life Fellowship, Inc.—Intl. Mins.
World Gospel Mission
World Link Ministries
World Mission Prayer League
World Missionary Assistance Plan
World Partners USA
World Thrust International, Inc.
World Witness, Assoc. Reformed Presb. Ch.
Zion Evangelical Ministries of Africa

## Education, theological by extension
ACM International
Advent Christian General Conf.
Arab World Ministries
Brethren in Christ World Missions
CAM International
China Ministries International
Christ Community Church
Christian Fellowship Union, Inc.
Christian Ministries International (CMI)
Church of God (Cleveland, TN)
Church of the Nazarene, World Msn. Dept.
Cornerstone International
Emmanuel International Mission
Entrust  Evangelical Friends Mission
FLET University/Universidad FLET
Foursquare Missions International
Friends United Meeting—Global Ministries
Global Partners/Wesleyan World Missions
Global University
Institute of Theological Studies—Division
   of Outreach Inc.
Latin American Lutheran Mission
Liebenzell USA
LOGOI Ministries
Ministries In Action

Mission to the Americas
Mission to the World (PCA), Inc.
Mustard Seed International
OMS International, Inc.
Open Bible Churches, Intl. Ministries
Partners in Christ International
Primitive Methodist Church in the USA
Raul Zaldivar Ministries
Seventh-day Adventists General Conference
Source of Light Ministries International, Inc.
The Brethren Church, Inc.
Virginia Mennonite Board of Missions
Wisconsin Evangelical Lutheran Synod
Zion Evangelical Ministries of Africa

## Evangelism, mass

Advent Christian General Conf.
African Bible Colleges, Inc.
African Enterprise
African Methodist Episcopal Church
Agape Gospel Mission
Alberto Mottesi Evangelistic Association
Alongside Ministries International
AMG International
Anis Shorrosh Evangelistic Association
Apostolic Christian Church Foundation, Inc.
Assemblies of God World Missions
Baptist International Missions, Inc. (BIMI)
Baptist Medical & Dental Mission Intl., Inc.
Billy Graham Center, The
Bright Hope International
Calvary International
Campus Crusade for Christ, Intl.
Celebrant Singers
Centers for Apologetics Research (CFAR)
Chosen People Ministries
Christ for the City International
Christ to the Nations
Christar
Christian Aid Mission
Christian Church of N. America—Missions
Christian Laymen's Missionary Evangelism
 Association
Church of God of Prophecy
Church of the Nazarene, World Msn. Dept.
Church Planting International
CTI Music Ministries
Dayspring International
East-West Ministries International
Emmanuel International Mission
Evangelical Lutheran Church in America
Evangelism Resources
FOCAS
Foursquare Missions International
Friends of Israel Gospel Ministry, Inc.
Fundamental Baptist Msn.Trinidad/Tobago

Galcom International USA, Inc.
Global Action
Global Advance
Globe Missionary Evangelism
GO InterNational
Good News Productions International
Gospel Communications International, Inc.
Gospel Furthering Fellowship, The
Gospel Outreach Ministries Intl.
Gospel Revival Ministries
Grand Old Gospel Fellowship
Harvest Evangelism, Inc.
Harvest International, Inc.
Hellenic Ministries Hermano Pablo Ministries
High Adventure Ministries/Voice of Hope
 Broadcasting Network
Impact International
India Gospel Outreach
India National Inland Mission
India Rural Evangelical Fellowship
International Board of Jewish Missions, Inc.
International Pentecostal Holiness Church
Iranian Christians International
Italy for Christ
Janz Team Ministries USA
Jews for Jesus
Joni and Friends
Josue Yrion Wld. Evangelism and Msns., Inc.
Key Communications
Latin America Assistance, Inc.
Luis Palau Evangelistic Assoc.
Lutheran Hour Ministries
M/E International, Inc.
Mahesh Chavda Ministries Intl.
Middle East Media—USA
Middle Eastern Outreach
Ministries In Action
Missionary Revival Crusade
Morelli Ministries International
Natl. Baptist Conv. of Am. —Foreign Msn. Bd.
Natl. Baptist Conv. USA, Inc.—Foreign Msn. Bd.
New Life Advance International
No Greater Love Ministries, Inc.
OMS International, Inc.
On The Go Ministries / Keith Cook
 Evangelistic Association
Open Air Campaigners—Overseas Ministries
Operation Mobilization
Outreach To Asia Nationals
Overseas Radio & Television, Inc. (ORTV)
Pentecostal Ch. of God—Wld. Msns. Dept.
Perimeter Church, Global Outreach
Pioneer Bible Translators
Presbyterian Evangelistic Fellowship
Presbyterian Order for World Evangelization
Project AmaZon

Raul Zaldivar Ministries
Ripe for Harvest, Inc.
Rogma International, Inc.
SAT-7 North America
Seventh-day Adventists General Conference
Son Shine Ministries International
Spiritual Growth Resources, Inc.
Sports & Rec Plus
The Ch. of God of the Apostolic Faith, Inc.
TITUS International
Training Evangelistic Leadership (T.E.L.), Inc.
Trans World Radio, International
United Pentecostal Ch. Intl., Foreign Msns. Div.
VELA Ministries International
Weiner Ministries International
World Link Ministries
World Missionary Press, Inc.
World Missions Far Corners, Inc.
World Reach, Inc.
Youth for Christ/USA—World Outreach
Youth With A Mission (YWAM)

**Evangelism, personal and small group**
ABWE
Advancing Renewal Ministries, Inc.
Africa Inter-Mennonite Mission
African Enterprise
AIMS
Alongside Ministries International
Ambassadors for Christ Intl.
Am. Baptist Chs. of the U.S.A., Intl. Mins.
American Missionary Fellowship
American Scripture Gift Mission Inc.
AMF International Anglican Frontier Missions
Anis Shorrosh Evangelistic Association
Armenian Missionary Assoc. of America, Inc.
Asian Access
Asian Outreach U.S.A.
Assemblies of God World Missions
Association of Free Lutheran Congregations
Aurora Mission, Inc.
Avant Ministries
Baptist International Missions, Inc. (BIMI)
Baptist International Outreach
Baptist Missions to Forgotten Peoples
Bethany International Ministries
Bible League, The
Biblical Ministries Worldwide
Brazil Gospel Fellowship Mission
Brethren in Christ World Missions
Bright Hope International
Cadence International
CAM International
Campus Crusade for Christ, Intl.
Caring Partners International, Inc.
Central Yearly Meeting of Friends Missions

China Ministries International
China Outreach Ministries, Inc.
Chosen People Ministries
Christ for the Nations, Inc.
Christ to the Nations
Christian and Missionary Alliance
Christian Ch. of North America—Missions
Christian Cultural Development Foundation
Christian Dental Society
Christian Fellowship Union, Inc.
Christian Laymen's Missionary Evangelism
   Association
Christian Ministries International (CMI)
Christian Missions Unlimited
Christian Outreach International
Christian Union Chs. of N. Am.—Missions
Christians In Action Missions International
Church Ministries International
Church of God (Cleveland, TN)
Church of God (Holiness)
Church of God in Christ, Mennonite
Ch. of God of Prophecy—Global Outreach
Church of the Nazarene, World Msn. Dept.
Churches of Christ
Congregational Methodist Church
Connecting Businessmen to Christ
Cornerstone International
Crossover Communications International
CrossWorld
Dayspring International
Eastern European Outreach, Inc.
East-West Ministries International
EFCA International Mission
Elim Fellowship—Intl. Department
Empowering Lives International
Episcopal Church USA—Domestic &
   Foreign Missionary Society
European Christian Mission Intl. —USA
European Evangelistic Society
Evangelical Bible Mission
Evangelical Friends Mission
Evangelical Methodist Ch., Inc.—Bd. of Msns.
Evangelical Presbyterian Ch.—Wld. Outreach
Evangelism Explosion International
Every Home for Christ
Far East Broadcasting Company, Inc.
Fellowship of Evangelical Chs.—Intl. Mins.
Foundation For His Ministry
Free Gospel Church, Inc.—MissionsDept.
Free Will Baptist, Inc. Board of Intl. Missions
Friendship International Ministries, Inc
Frontiers
Global Fellowship Inc.
Global Mins., Ch. of the United Brethren
   in Christ
Global Outreach Mission, Inc.
Global Partners / Wesleyan World Missions

TITUS International
TMA Ministries
Training Evangelistic Leadership (T.E.L.), Inc.
Trans World Missions
Turkish World Outreach
United Pentecostal Church Intl.
UWEZO International
VELA Ministries International
Village Ministries International
Vineyard Church USA—Missions
White Fields Inc.
World Baptist Fellowship Msn. Agency, Inc.
World Concern
World Gospel Mission
World Harvest Mission
World Harvest Now, Inc.
World Horizons
World Mission
World Mission Prayer League
World Outreach International—US
World Team
World Venture
World Vision Inc.
World Witness, Assoc. Reformed Presb. Ch.
Worldwide Tentmakers, Inc.  Young Life
Youth Encounter
Youth for Christ International
Youth for Christ/USA—World Outreach
Youth With A Mission (YWAM)
YUGO Ministries

## Evangelism, student

Adventures in Missions
AMF International
Assemblies of God World Missions
Awana Clubs International
Cadence International
Calvary Commission, Inc.
Campus Crusade for Christ, Intl.
Carver International Missions, Inc.
Child Evangelism Fellowship, Inc.
China Outreach Ministries, Inc.
Chosen People Ministries
Christian Dental Society
Christian Laymen's Missionary Evangelism
   Association
CMF International
Compassion International, Inc.
CTI Music Ministries
Evangelism Explosion International
Every Child Ministries, Inc.
Global Outreach International
Global Youth Ministry Network
Good Shepherd Ministries, Inc.
Gospel Communications International, Inc.
Great Commission Ministries, Inc.

International Messengers
International Students, Inc (ISI)
InterVarsity Christian Fellowship/USA—
   Missions Department
Italy for Christ
Japanese Evangelical Missionary Society
Latin America Assistance, Inc.
Living Hope Ministries International
Mailbox Club International Inc., The
Mission India
Mission to the Americas
Missionary Revival Crusade
Navigators, U.S. International Missions
Group
OMF International
On The Go Ministries/Keith Cook
   Evangelistic Association
Perimeter Church, Global Outreach
Ravi Zacharias International Ministries
Rock the World Youth Mission Alliance
Sowers International, The
Teen Missions International, Inc.
Touch the World Youth Ministries
World Team
Worldwide Discipleship Assoc.
Young Life
Youth for Christ International
Youth for Christ/USA—World Outreach

## Funds transmission

Advancing Indigenous Missions
Advancing Native Missions
Allegheny Wesleyan Methodist Connection
American Assoc. of Lutheran Churches
Apostolic Christian Church Foundation, Inc.
Christian Aid Mission
Christian Mission for the Deaf
Christian Missions in Many Lands, Inc.
Ch. of God (Seventh Day) Gen. Conf.
CLC Ministries International
COMHINA
Commission to Every Nation
Dayspring International
East West Ministries International
Far East Broadcasting Company, Inc.
FARMS International
Final Frontiers Foundation, Inc.
Full Gospel Grace Fellowship
Good News for India
Gospel Revival Ministries
Gospelink, Inc.
International Child Care, USA, Inc.
Intl. Found. for EWHA Woman's University
M/E International, Inc.
Medical Missions Philippines, Inc.
Missions To Japan, Inc.

Natl. Baptist Conv. of Am.—Foreign Msn. Bd.
Opportunity International
Partners International
Pentecostal Free Will Baptist Church, Inc.
Presbyterian Missionary Union
Raul Zaldivar Ministries
Ripe for Harvest, Inc.
SAT-7 North America
ServLife International
Seventh Day Baptist Missionary Society
Slavic Missionary Service, Inc.
The Waray-Waray Project
Vellore Christian Med. College Bd. (USA), Inc.
World Indigenous Missions
World Missions & Evangelism, Inc.
World Orphans
World Outreach Ministries
World Vision Inc.
Wycliffe Bible Translators, Inc.

## Furloughed missionary support

Cedar Lane Missionary Homes, Inc.
CMTS Ministries, Inc.
D & D Missionary Homes, Inc.
Emmaus Road International
Episcopal Church USA—Domestic &
    Foreign Missionary Society
Evangelical Friends Church Southwest
Interaction International
MATS International, Inc.
Missionary Outreach Support Services
Missionary Retreat Fellowship Inc.
Natl. Baptist Conv. USA, Inc.—Foreign Msn. Bd.
Pentecostal Free Will Baptist Church, Inc.
Providence Mission Homes, Inc.
WEC International

## Information services

ASSIST Ministries & ASSIST News Service
Billy Graham Center, The
China Connection
Christian Missions in Many Lands, Inc.
Commission to Every Nation
Cumberland Presbyterian Ch. Bd. of Msns.
D & D Missionary Homes, Inc.
Door of Hope International
ECHO
Equipping the Saints
Evangelism and Missions Information Service
FOM (Fellowship of Missions)
General Assoc. of Regular Baptist Churches
Global Focus
Global Health Ministries
Global Mapping International
Global Ministries, Church of the United
    Brethren in Christ

Grace Baptist Missions International
IFMA
Japanese Evangelization Center (Institute of
Japanese Studies) LIGHT International, Inc.
Macedonian Missionary Service
Middle Eastern Outreach
Mission Aviation Fellowship
Mission Safety International
Mission Services Association, Inc.
Missionary Outreach Support Services
Missions Resource Network
New Wineskins Missionary Network
RUN Ministries
Servants in Faith & Technology (SIFAT)
Tentmakers International
U.S. Center for World Mission
United Methodist Ch., Gen. Bd. of
    Global Ministries
Virginia Mennonite Board of Missions
Worldwide Discipleship Assoc.

## Justice & Related

Bread for the World
Christian Cultural Development Foundation
Christian Reformed World Relief Committee
Dawn Ministries, Inc.
Every Child Ministries, Inc.
Heifer International
International Justice Mission
Lutheran World Relief
Mennonite Central Committee (MCC)
World Vision International

## Leadership development

Abundant Life Association, Inc.
ACM International
Advancing Renewal Ministries, Inc.
Advent Christian General Conf.
Africa Inland Mission International
Africa Inter-Mennonite Mission
African Bible Colleges, Inc.
African Enterprise
Agape Gospel Mission
Alberto Mottesi Evangelistic Association
Alongside Ministries International
Amazon Focus
Am. Baptist Chs. of the USA, Intl. Mins.
ARISE International Mission
Artists In Christian Testimony
Asian Access
Asian Outreach U.S.A.
Assemblies of God World Missions
Association of Christian Schools Intl.
Avant Ministries
Bakke Graduate University of Ministry
Baptist General Conference—Intl. Mins.

Baptist International Missions, Inc. (BIMI)
Barnabas International
BILD International
Billy Graham Center, The
Bread for the World
Brethren in Christ World Missions
Bridge Builders International
Calvary International
CAM International
Carver International Missions, Inc.
Christ Community Church
Christ for the City International
Christian and Missionary Alliance
Christian Aviation and Radio Mission
Christian Church (Disciples of Christ)
Christian Cultural Development Foundation
Christian Fellowship Union, Inc.
Christian Ministries International (CMI)
Christian Outreach International
Christian Reformed World Missions
Christian Reformed World Relief Committee
Church Leadership Development Intl.
Church Missions Link
Ch. of God (Anderson, Ind.), Global Missions
Ch. of God of Prophecy—Global Outreach
Church Planting International
Church Resource Ministries (CRM)
Church World Service
Churches of Christ Churches of God
CMF International
COMHINA
Compassion International, Inc.
Congregational Methodist Church
Cook Communications Ministries Intl.
Cooperative Baptist Fellowship
CrossWorld
Cumberland Presbyterian Ch. Bd. of Msns.
Dawn Ministries, Inc.
Daystar U.S.
Development Associates International (DAI)
Disciples International
East West Ministries International
Eastern Mennonite Missions
Edwin L. Hodges Ministries
EFCA International Mission
Elim Fellowship—International Department
Emmanuel International Mission
Emmaus Road International
Entrust
Envoy International
EQUIP Foundation
Evangelical Covenant Church
Evangelical Friends Mission
Evangelical Lutheran Church in America
Evangelism Explosion International
Evangelism Resources

Every Child Ministries, Inc.
Fellowship of Evangelical Churches—
    International Ministries
FLET University/Universidad FLET
Food for the Hungry, Inc.
Foursquare Missions International
Free Methodist World Missions
Free Will Baptist, Inc. Board of Intl. Missions
Friends United Meeting—Global Ministries
Frontiers
General Baptists International
Global Advance
Global Harvest Ministries
Global Mapping International
Global Outreach International
Global Partners / Wesleyan World Missions
Global Youth Ministry Network
Globe Missionary Evangelism
GO InterNational
Good Shepherd Ministries International
Gospel for Asia, Inc.
Gospel Mission of South America
Gospel Outreach Ministries Intl.
Grace Brethren International Missions
Grace Ministries International
Great Commission Ministries, Inc.
Greater Europe Mission
Haitian Christian Outreach
Harvest
HBI Global Partners
Help for Christian Nationals, Inc.
Hundredfold Ministries International
IFMA
Independent Gospel Missions: A Baptist
    Mission Agency
India Gospel League, NA
India Gospel Outreach
Institute for International Christian
    Communication WorldView Center
Institute of Theological Studies—Division
    of Outreach Inc.
Interdev Partnership Associates
International Board of Jewish Missions, Inc.
International Christian Ministries
International Gospel Outreach
International Health Services
International Partnership Ministries, Inc.
Intl. Pentecostal Church of Christ
International Teams, U.S.A.
InterVarsity Christian Fellowship/USA
Italy for Christ
JARON Ministries International
Josue Yrion Wld. Evangelism and Missions, Inc.
Latin America Assistance, Inc.
Leadership Training International
LeaderTreks
LOGOI Ministries

## Linguistics

## Literacy

AmeriTribes
Bible League, The
Christian Literacy Associates
Christian Literature International
Church World Service
Evangel Bible Translators
Foundation For His Ministry
Gospel Outreach Ministries Intl.
Hosanna
Ireland Outreach International Inc.
Literacy & Evangelism International
Lutheran Bible Translators, Inc.
Mercy Ships
Mission India
New Tribes Mission
Open Doors with Brother Andrew USA
Pioneer Bible Translators
Society of St. Margaret
Supreme Task International, Inc.
The Word for the World
Women to the World
Wycliffe Bible Translators, Inc.
Wycliffe International

## Literature distribution

Action International Ministries
Ambassadors for Christ, Inc.
American Bible Society
American Scripture Gift Mission Inc.
AMF International
ARISE International Mission
Asian Outreach U.S.A.
Assemblies of God World Missions
Aurora Mission, Inc.
Back to the Bible International
Baptist International Evangelistic Ministries
Bethany International Ministries
Bibles & Literature in French
Child Evangelism Fellowship, Inc.
Chosen People Ministries
Christ for the Nations, Inc.
Christian Aid Ministries
Christian Discipleship Ministries, Inc.
Christian Resources International
Christian Union Chs. of N. America—Msns.
Christ's Mandate for Missions
Church Leadership Development Intol.
Church of God (Seventh Day) Gen. Conf
Church of the Nazarene, World Msn. Dept.
Cities for Christ Worldwide
CLC Ministries International
Concordia Gospel Outreach
Cook Communications Ministries Intl.
Dawn Ministries, Inc.
Derek Prince Ministries, International
Disciples International

East Gates Ministries Intl.
East West Ministries International
Eastern European Outreach, Inc.
East-West Ministries International
Edwin L. Hodges Ministries
Equipping the Saints
Evangelical Bible Mission
Evangelism and Missions Information Service
Every Home for Christ
Friends of Israel Gospel Ministry, Inc.
Friends United Meeting—Global Ministries
Full Gospel Grace Fellowship
Good Shepherd Ministries, Inc.
Gospel for Asia, Inc.
Gospel Revival Ministries
Great Commission Center International
Harvest
Hundredfold Ministries International
In Touch Mission International
International Board of Jewish Missions, Inc.
Iranian Christians International
Ireland Outreach International Inc.
Jewish Awareness Ministries
Jews for Jesus
Key Communications
Latin American Lutheran Mission
Leadership Ministries Worldwide
LOGOI Ministries  Lutheran Hour Ministries
Macedonian Missionary Service
Mailbox Club International Inc., The
Middle East Christian Outreach (MECO)
Middle Eastern Outreach
Mission Possible Foundation, Inc.
Morelli Ministries International
No Greater Love Ministries, Inc.
Open Door Baptist Missions
Open Doors with Brother Andrew USA
Operation Mobilization
Orthodox Presbyterian Church—
     Committee on Foreign Missions
Overseas Ministries Study Center
Pentecostal Ch. of God—World Msns. Dept.
Peter Deyneka Russian Ministries
Precept Ministries International
Presbyterian Evangelistic Fellowship
Presbyterian Missionary Union
Prison Mission Association
Reformation Translation Fellowship (RTF)
Ripe for Harvest, Inc.
RUN Ministries
Russian Bible Society, Inc.
Russian Christian Radio
Seventh-day Adventists General Conference
Slavic Gospel Association
Source of Light Ministries International, Inc.
Spanish American Evangelistic Ministries

Spanish World Ministries
STEM
Supreme Task International, Inc.
The Ch. of God of the Apostolic Faith, Inc.
Turkish World Outreach
Voice of the Martyrs, The
Word To Russia
World Help
World Missionary Assistance Plan
World Missionary Press, Inc.
World Missions Far Corners, Inc.
WorldTeach

## Literature production

Ambassadors for Christ, Inc.
American Bible Society
Anis Shorrosh Evangelistic Association
Asian Outreach U.S.A.
Assemblies of God World Missions
Back to the Bible International
Bibles & Literature in French
Centers for Apologetics Research (CFAR)
Child Evangelism Fellowship, Inc.
Christ for the Nations, Inc.
Ch. of God (Holiness), Wld. Msn. Dept., Inc.
Church of the Nazarene, World Msn. Dept.
CLC Ministries International
Cook Communications Ministries Intl.
Derek Prince Ministries, International
Disciples International
East Gates Ministries Intl.
Edwin L. Hodges Ministries
Evangelism and Missions Information Service
Friends of Israel Gospel Ministry, Inc.
Friends United Meeting—Global Ministries
Gospel Literature International, Inc.
Grace and Truth, Inc.
Grace Ministries International
Great Commission Center International
Harvest
Heart of God Ministries
Hundredfold Ministries International
Ireland Outreach International Inc.
JARON Ministries International
Jewish Awareness Ministries
Jews for Jesus
Leadership Ministries Worldwide
Literacy & Evangelism International
LOGOI Ministries
Lutheran Brethren World Missions
Lutheran Hour Ministries
Macedonian Missionary Service
Mahesh Chavda Ministries Intl.
Media Associates International
Middle East Media—USA
Ministry to Educate and Equip International

Mission Possible Foundation, Inc.
Missionary TECH Team
New Hope International
Precept Ministries International
Reformation Translation Fellowship (RTF)
Reformed Baptist Mission Services
Remnant Ministries, Inc.
Rio Grande Bible Institute
Romanian Missionary Society
Russian Bible Society, Inc.
Russian Christian Radio
Seventh-day Adventists General Conference
Source of Light Ministries International, Inc.
Walk Thru the Bible Ministries, Inc.
Westminster Biblical Missions
Wisconsin Evangelical Lutheran Synod
World Missionary Assistance Plan
World Missionary Press, Inc.
WorldTeach

## Management

Association of Christian Schools Intl. (ACSI)
ChinaSource
Christian Discipleship Ministries, Inc.
Christian Medical & Dental Associations
   —Global Health Outreach
Christian Ministries International (CMI)\
Church Missions Link
Crisis Consulting International
Daystar U.S.
Development Associates International (DAI)
Enterprise Development Intl.
FARMS International
Health Emergent International Services
Intercristo, a CRISTA Ministry
Interdev Partnership Associates
LIGHT International, Inc.
Media Associates International
Medical Ambassadors International, Inc.
Men for Missions International
Missionary TECH Team
Paraclete, Inc.
Perimeter Church, Global Outreach
Self-Help International
UWEZO International
Virginia Mennonite Board of Missions
World Mission Associates
World Outreach Ministries

## Medical supplies

African Methodist Episcopal Church
American Leprosy Missions, Inc.
Baptist International Outreach
Blessings International
Caring Partners International, Inc.
Chosen Mission Project

Christian Blind Mission International
Christian Pilots Association
Church of the Nazarene, World Msn. Dept.
Congregational Holiness Ch.—World Msns.
CrossLink International
Equipping the Saints
Fellowship of Assocs. of Medical Evangelism
FRIENDS in Action, International
Global Health Ministries
Good Shepherd Ministries, Inc.
Harvest International, Inc.
Health Emergent International Services
Interchurch Medical Assistance, Inc.
International Aid
Ludhiana Christian Medical College
    Board, USA, Inc.
Macedonian Missionary Service
MAP International
Natl. Baptist Conv. USA, Inc.—Foreign Msn. Bd.
Northwest Medical Teams International, Inc.
Samaritan's Purse
Spanish World Ministries
The Ch. of God of the Apostolic Faith, Inc.
Ukrainian Childrens Fund
Vellore Christian Medical College Board
    (USA), Inc.
Voice of the Martyrs, The
Wisconsin Evangelical Lutheran Synod
World Concern
World Help
World Witness, Assoc. Reformed Presb. Ch.

## Medicine, incl. dental and public health

ABWE
Action International Ministries
Africa Inland Mission International
Amazon Focus
Am. Baptist Chs. of the U.S.A., Intl. Mins.
American Leprosy Missions, Inc.
AmeriTribes
Assemblies of God World Missions
Baptist General Conf.—Intl. Ministries
Baptist Medical & Dental Mission Intl., Inc.
Baptist Mid-Missions
Blessings International
Caring Partners International, Inc.
Childcare Worldwide
Childspring International
China Connection
Christ for India, Inc.
Christian Blind Mission International
Christian Broadcasting Network Inc., the
Christian Dental Society
Christian Medical & Dental Associations
    —Global Health Outreach
Christians In Action Missions International

Christ's Mandate for Missions
Church of the Nazarene, World Msn. Dept.
Churches of God, General Conference
ComCare International
Compassion International, Inc.
Elim Fellowship—International Department
Empowering Lives International
Equip, Inc.
Evangelistic Faith Missions
Fellowship of Assocs. of Medical Evangelism
Flying Doctors of America (Medical
    Mercy Missions, Inc.)
FOCAS
For Haiti with Love Inc.
Forward Edge International
Foundation For His Ministry
Friends United Meeting—Global Ministries
General Baptists International
Global Health Ministries
Global Outreach International
Global Outreach Mission, Inc.
Good Shepherd Ministries, Inc.
Gospel Fellowship Association
Grace Ministries International
Haiti Lutheran Mission Society
Haitian Christian Outreach
Harvest International, Inc.
HCJB Global
Health Emergent International Services
Health Teams International, Inc.
Heart to Heart Intl. Ministries
Interchurch Medical Assistance, Inc.
International Child Care, USA, Inc.
Intl. Christian Leprosy Mission, Inc. (USA)
International Health Services InterServe USA
Ireland Outreach International Inc.
Kids Alive International
Living Hope Ministries International
Lott Carey Baptist Foreign Mission Conv.
Ludhiana Christian Medical College
    Board, USA, Inc.
Luke Society, Inc., The
M/E International, Inc.
Macedonian Missionary Service
Medical Ambassadors International, Inc.
Men for Missions International
Mennonite Central Committee (MCC)
Mercy Ships
Mexican Medical Ministries
Mission To Unreached Peoples
Mission: Moving Mountains, Inc.
Mustard Seed International
New Way Missions
North American Baptist Conference
Northwest Medical Teams International, Inc.
Operation Blessing Intl. Relief and
    Development Corporation

Orthodox Presbyterian Church—Committee on Foreign Missions
Partners in Christ International
People International USA
Perimeter Church, Global Outreach
Presbyterian Ch. (USA), Worldwide Mins.
Primitive Methodist Church in the USA
Project AmaZon
Project Mercy, Inc.
Red Sea Team International
Reformed Church in America
Reformed Episcopal Bd. of Foreign Missions
Seventh-day Adventists General Conference
SIM USA
TEAM (The Evangelical Alliance Mission)
Team World Outreach
TEAMS for Medical Missions
The Mission Society
Tribes and Nations Outreach
United Ch. of Christ—Wider Ch. Mins.
Vellore Christian Medical College Board (USA), Inc.
World Concern
World Gospel Mission
World Mission Prayer League
World Missions Far Corners, Inc.
World-Wide Missions

## Member Care

Alongside, Inc.
American Association of Lutheran Churches —Commission for World Missions
Barnabas International
Commission to Every Nation
D & D Missionary Homes, Inc.
Emmaus Road International
Full Gospel Evangelistic Association
Harvest International, Inc.
Interaction International
Mission To Unreached Peoples
Mission Training International
Missionary Gospel Fellowship
Missionary Outreach Support Services
Missions Resource Network
Narramore Christian Foundation
Paraclete, Inc.
Pentecostal Free Will Baptist Church, Inc.
Perimeter Church, Global Outreach
Reformed Baptist Mission Services
Tentmakers International
United Evangelical Churches
University of the Family

## National church nurture/support

Advancing Indigenous Missions
Advancing Native Missions

Africa Inter-Mennonite Mission
Alongside Ministries International
Amazon Focus
American Missionary Fellowship
AMOR Ministries
Association of Free Lutheran Congregations
Barnabas International
Bibles For The World, Inc.
Brethren in Christ World Missions
Caring Partners International, Inc.
Christ for the City International
Christ to the Nations
Christian Aid Mission
Christian Associates International
Christian Church (Disciples of Christ)— Global Ministries
Christian Fellowship Union, Inc.
Christian Reformed World Missions
Christians In Action Missions International
Church Ministries International
Ch. of God (Seventh Day) Gen. Conference
Church of God in Christ, Mennonite
Ch. of God of Prophecy—Global Outreach
Ch. of the Brethren—Global Msn. Partnerships
Church Planting International
Church Resource Ministries (CRM)
Churches of Christ
Churches of God, General Conference
Congregational Methodist Church, Division of Mission Ministries
Conservative Congregational Christian Conference—Missions Committee
Edwin L. Hodges Ministries
Emmanuel International Mission
Empowering Lives International
Envoy International
Episcopal Church USA—Domestic & Foreign Missionary Society
European Christian Mission Intl.—USA
Evangelical Congregational Church
Evangelical Covenant Church
Evangelical Presbyterian Church
Evangelistic Faith Missions
Final Frontiers Foundation, Inc.
Foursquare Missions International
Free Gospel Church, Inc.—Missions Dept.
Free Methodist World Missions
Friends United Meeting—Global Ministries
Full Gospel Evangelistic Association
Global Advance
Global Ministries, Church of the United Brethren in Christ
Global Partners / Wesleyan World Missions
Global Youth Ministry Network
Gospelink, Inc.
Grace Baptist Missions International
Harvest Evangelism, Inc.

In Touch Mission International
India Gospel League, NA
InterAct Ministries
International Christian Ministries
International Cooperating Ministries
International Partnership Ministries, Inc.
International Pentecostal Church of Christ
International Street Kids Outreach Ministries
Iranian Christians International
Ireland Outreach International Inc.
Japanese Evangelical Missionary Society
Latin American Indian Ministries
Latin American Lutheran Mission
Liberty Corner Mission
Lott Carey Baptist Foreign Mission Conv.
Lutheran Brethren World Missions
Mahesh Chavda Ministries Intl.
Mercy Ships
Mexican Medical Ministries
Middle East Media - USA
Middle Eastern Outreach
Ministries In Action
Mission ONE, Inc. Mission to the Americas
Mission to the World (PCA), Inc.
Missionary Ventures International
Morelli Ministries International
New Directions International, Inc.
New Hope International
New Way Missions
OC International, Inc.
Open Bible Churches, Intl. Ministries
Open Door Baptist Missions
Open Doors with Brother Andrew USA
Orthodox Presbyterian Church
Palm Missionary Ministries
Partners International
Pentecostal Church of God
Perimeter Church, Global Outreach
Pioneer Bible Translators
Presbyterian Missionary Union
Primitive Methodist Church in the USA
Rosedale Mennonite Missions
Seed International
SEND International USA
Sending Experienced Retired
  Volunteers Everywhere
ServLife International
Seventh-day Adventists General Conf.
Slavic Missionary Service, Inc.
Society of St. Margaret
South American Missionary Society (USA)
Spiritual Growth Resources, Inc.
Spiritual Overseers Service International
Team World Outreach
TEAMS for Medical Missions
The Mission Society
The Waray-Waray Project

United Evangelical Churches
United Methodist Church
United World Mission
Venture International
Vineyard Church USA—Missions
Walk Thru the Bible Ministries, Inc.
Westminster Biblical Missions
Wisconsin Evangelical Lutheran Synod,
  Board for World Missions
World Harvest Mission
World Harvest Now, Inc.
World Horizons
World Team
World Witness, Assoc. Reformed Presb. Ch.
WorldHarvest

## Partnership development

African Methodist Episcopal Church
Alongside Ministries International
Ambassadors for Christ, Inc.
Am. Baptist Chs. of the U.S.A., Intl. Mins.
American Bible Society
AMOR Ministries
Anglican Frontier Missions
Association of Free Lutheran Congregations
Bakke Graduate University of Ministry
Bethany International Ministries
Bridge Builders International
Cadence International
Catalyst Services
Child Evangelism Fellowship, Inc.
ChinaSource
Christian Reformed World Relief Committee
Church Ministries International
Church of God (Holiness), World Mission
CityTeam Ministries
COMHINA
Cumberland Presbyterian Ch. Bd. of Msns.
DeNike Ministries
Episcopal Church USA—Domestic & Foreign
  Missionary Society
Evangelical Baptist Missions
Evangelical Covenant Church
Evangelical Lutheran Church in America
Global Ministries, Church of the United
  Brethren in Christ
Good News Productions International
Gospel Communications International, Inc.
Habitat for Humanity International
HCJB Global
Hosanna
In Touch Mission International
India Partners
Institute for International Christian
  Communication WorldView Center
Interchurch Medical Assistance, Inc.

Interdev Partnership Associates
Intl. Christian Leprosy Mission, Inc. (USA)
International Cooperating Ministries
International Family Missions
International Partnership Ministries, Inc.
International Pentecostal Holiness Church
International Street Kids Outreach Ministries
Latin America Assistance, Inc.
Luis Palau Evangelistic Assoc.
Lutheran Church-Missouri Synod
Mailbox Club International Inc., The
MAP International
Mennonite Mission Network
Mission India
Mission Safety International
New Hope International
New Mission Systems International
OC International, Inc.
Partners International
Perimeter Church, Global Outreach
Presbyterian Ch. (USA), Worldwide Mins.
Presbyterian Mission International (PMI)
Reciprocal Ministries International
Samaritan's Purse
Shield of Faith Ministries
STEER, Inc.
Team Expansion, Inc.
The God's Story Project
UWEZO International
Venture International
Wisconsin Evangelical Lutheran Synod
World Mission
World Outreach Ministries
World Venture

## Psychological counseling
Alongside, Inc.
Barnabas International
Link Care Foundation
Missionary Outreach Support Services
Narramore Christian Foundation
Northwest Medical Teams International, Inc.
Women to the World

## Purchasing services
Equipping the Saints
FRIENDS in Action, International
JAARS Inc.
MATS International, Inc.

## Recruiting/Mobilizing
ACMC, Inc.
Adventures in Missions
AIMS
Anglican Frontier Missions
Brethren in Christ World Missions

Caleb Project
Calvary International
Christar
Christian Medical & Dental
  Associations—Global Health Outreach
Christian Missions Unlimited
Christian Outreach International
Christian Reformed World Missions
Christ's Mandate for Missions
Ch. of God (Anderson, Ind.), Global Msns.
CLC Ministries International
Cornerstone International
CSI Ministries, Inc.
DualReach
EFCA International Mission
Evangelical Friends Church Southwest
Evangelism Explosion International
Fellowship of Assocs. of Medical Evangelism
Free Methodist World Missions
Free Will Baptist, Inc. Board of Intl. Missions
Frontiers
Global Focus
Global Opportunities
Global Outreach Mission, Inc.
Global Recordings Network
Go Ye Fellowship
Gospel Revival Ministries
Grace Brethren International Missions
Great Commission Center International
Great Commission Ministries, Inc.
Habitat for Humanity International
Harvest Evangelism, Inc.
India Gospel Outreach
International Family Missions
International Institute for Christian Studies
International Students, Inc (ISI)
MBMS International
Middle East Christian Outreach (MECO)
Missions Resource Network
New Life Advance International
New Wineskins Missionary Network
N. Am. Baptist Conf.—Worldwide Outreach
OMF International
OMS International, Inc.
Operation Mobilization
Perimeter Church, Global Outreach
Pioneer Bible Translators
Presbyterian Ch. (USA), Worldwide Mins.
Presbyterian Order for World Evangelization
Rock the World Youth Mission Alliance
Seed International
Sending Experienced Retired Volunteers
  Everywhere
Share International
SIM USA
South America Mission, Inc.

STEM International
Team Expansion, Inc.
Turkish World Outreach
U.S. Center for World Mission
WEC International
Weiner Ministries International
World Horizons
World Partners USA
World Thrust International, Inc.
World Venture
Wycliffe Associates, Inc.
Wycliffe Bible Translators, Inc.
YUGO Ministries

## Relief and/or rehabilitation

Action International Ministries
Advancing Native Missions
African Enterprise
African Leadership, Inc.
All God's Children International
American Association of Lutheran Churches
American Leprosy Missions, Inc.
AMOR Ministries
Apostolic Christian Church Foundation, Inc.
Assemblies of God World Missions
Baptist Mid-Missions
Blessings International
Bright Hope International
Childcare Worldwide
Childspring International
Christian Aid Ministries
Christian Blind Mission International
Christian Broadcasting Network Inc., the
Christian Church of North America
Christian Reformed World Relief Committee
Church of God in Christ, Mennonite
Church of the Brethren—Global Mission
    Partnerships
Church of the Nazarene, World Msn. Dept.
Church World Service
CityTeam Ministries
CrossLink International
CSI Ministries, Inc.
Cumberland Presbyterian Ch. Bd. of Msns
Door of Hope International
Eastern Mennonite Missions
Emmanuel International Mission
Engineering Ministries International
Evangelical Lutheran Church in America
Every Child Ministries, Inc.
Food for the Hungry, Inc.
Forward Edge International
Foundation For His Ministry
Global Health Ministries
Gospel Outreach Ministries Intl.
Habitat for Humanity International

Haiti Lutheran Mission Society
HBI Global Partners
Health Emergent International Services
Hellenic Ministries
High Adventure Ministries/Voice of Hope
    Broadcasting Network
India Gospel League, NA
India Partners
International Aid
Intl. Christian Leprosy Mission, Inc. (USA)
International Justice Mission
International Pentecostal Holiness Church
    World Missions Ministries
InterServe USA (Intl. Service Fellowship)
Kids Alive International
Lott Carey Baptist Foreign Mission Conv.
Ludhiana Christian Medical College
    Board, USA, Inc.
Lutheran World Relief
MAP International
Mennonite Central Committee (MCC)
Mercy Ships
Ministries In Action
Missionary Flights International
Missionary Outreach Support Services
New Life Advance International
N. Am. Baptist Conf.—Worldwide Outreach
Northwest Medical Teams International, Inc.
Open Doors with Brother Andrew USA
Operation Blessing International Relief
    and Development Corporation
Perimeter Church, Global Outreach
Precious Seed Ministries
Presbyterian Ch. (USA), Worldwide Mins.
Salvation Army, U.S.A.
Samaritan's Purse
Seventh-day Adventists General Conference
Shelter for Life International, Inc.
Supreme Task International, Inc.
Surfing the Nations
Ukrainian Childrens Fund
United Methodist Church
Venture International
World Concern
World Missions Far Corners, Inc.
World Reach, Inc.
World Relief
World Vision Inc.
World Vision International
WorldHarvest
World-Wide Missions
Youth With A Mission (YWAM)

## Research

Advancing Native Missions
Anglican Frontier Missions

Billy Graham Center, The
Brethren in Christ World Missions
Caleb Project
Centers for Apologetics Research (CFAR)
China Ministries International
ChinaSource
Dawn Ministries, Inc.
Daystar U.S.
ECHO
Envoy International
European Evangelistic Society
Evangelism and Missions Information Service
FOM (Fellowship of Missions)
Global Fellowship Inc.
Global Mapping International
Global Recordings Network
Good News Productions International
Gospel Outreach Ministries Intl.
Gospel Revival Ministries
Grace Baptist Missions International
Handclasp International, Inc.
Institute of Strategic Languages and Cultures
Japanese Evangelization Center
LIGHT International, Inc.
Missions Resource Network
OC International, Inc.
Overseas Ministries Study Center
Perimeter Church, Global Outreach
Presbyterian Order for World Evangelization
Sentinel Group, The
So. Baptist Convention Intl. Mission Board
VELA Ministries International

## Services for other agencies

Adventist World Aviation
Audio Scripture Ministries
Catalyst Services
Children's Haven International
ChinaSource
Cities for Christ Worldwide
Crisis Consulting International
CSI Ministries, Inc.
ECHO
Engineering Ministries International
Envoy International
Equipping the Saints
Full Gospel Evangelistic Association
Global Mapping International
Global Recordings Network
Gospel Literature International, Inc.
Handclasp International, Inc.
Helps International Ministries
IFMA
Institute for International Christian
    Communication WorldView Center
Institute of Strategic Languages and Cultures

Interaction International
Interchurch Medical Assistance, Inc.
Intercristo, a CRISTA Ministry
Interdev Partnership Associates
International Aid
Literacy & Evangelism International
Mailbox Club International Inc., The
Mission Safety International
Mission Training International
Missionaire International
Missionary TECH Team
Paraclete, Inc.
Progressive Vision  Straightway Inc.
Talking Bibles International
Tech Serve International, Inc.
The Master's Mission, Inc.
Turkish World Outreach
United Evangelical Churches
World Missionary Press, Inc.
Wycliffe Associates, Inc.

## Short-term programs

Adventures in Missions
Africa Inland Mission International
Alongside Ministries International
Amazon Focus
Am. Council of the Ramabai Mukti Msn., Inc.
AMF International
AMOR Ministries
ARISE International Mission
Artists In Christian Testimony
Asian Outreach U.S.A.
Association of Christian Schools Intl. (ACSI)
Aurora Mission, Inc.
Baptist General Conf.—Intl. Ministries
Bibles & Literature in French
Caleb Project
Calvary Commission, Inc.
Calvary International
Caring Partners International, Inc.
Children's Haven International
Christ Community Church
Christ for the City International
Christian Laymen's Missionary Evangelism
    Association
Christian Medical & Dental Associations
    —Global Health Outreach
Christian Missions Unlimited
Christian Outreach International
Christ's Mandate for Missions
Church Missions Link
Church of the Nazarene, World Msn. Dept.
CMTS Ministries, Inc.
Conservative Congregational Christian
    Conference—Missions Committee
Cornerstone International

Crossover Communications International
CSI Ministries, Inc.
CTI Music Ministries (Carpenter's Tools Intl.)
Cumberland Presbyterian Ch. Bd. of Msns.
DeNike Ministries
Eastern European Outreach, Inc.
EFCA International Mission
Empowering Lives International
European Christian Mission Intl.—USA
Evangelical Friends Church Southwest
Fellowship of Assocs. of Medical Evangelism
Fellowship of Evangelical Churches
FOCAS
Forward Edge International
Friendship International Ministries, Inc.
General Baptists International
Global Action
Global Ministries, Church of the
    United Brethren in Christ
Global Recordings Network
GO InterNational
Gospel Outreach Ministries Intl.
Gospel Revival Ministries
Great Commission Center International
Great Commission Ministries, Inc.
Habitat for Humanity International
Harvest Evangelism, Inc.
Harvest International, Inc.
Have Christ Will Travel Ministries
HBI Global Partners
Hope for the Hungry
Independent Gospel Missions: A Baptist
    Mission Agency
International Family Missions
International Messengers
Ireland Outreach International Inc.
Japanese Evangelical Missionary Society
JARON Ministries International
Jews for Jesus
Joni and Friends
Kids Alive International
Latin America Mission
Latin American Lutheran Mission
Lott Carey Baptist Foreign Mission Conv.
Macedonia World Baptist Missions, Inc.
Macedonian Missionary Service
Men for Missions International
Mennonite Mission Network
Mexican Medical Ministries
Ministries In Action
Mission Nannys
Mission Possible, Inc.
Mission to the Americas
Missionary TECH Team
Missionary Ventures International
Moravian Church in North America

Mutual Faith Ministries Intl.
New Hope International
New Mission Systems International
New Way Missions
No Greater Love Ministries, Inc.
On The Go Ministries / Keith Cook
    Evangelistic Association
Overseas Radio & Television, Inc. (ORTV)
Partners in Christ International
Perimeter Church, Global Outreach
Pioneers USA
Reciprocal Ministries International
Rock the World Youth Mission Alliance
Rosedale Mennonite Missions
Seed International
Sending Experienced Retired Volunteers
    Everywhere
Servants in Faith & Technology (SIFAT)
Seventh Day Baptist Missionary Society
Sowers International, The
Sports & Rec Plus
STEM International
Surfing the Nations
Team World Outreach
TEAMS for Medical Missions
Teen Missions International, Inc.
Touch the World Youth Ministries
Tribes and Nations Outreach
United Methodist Church
Virginia Mennonite Board of Missions
WEC International
Word of Life Fellowship, Inc.—Intl. Mins.
World Indigenous Missions
World Reach, Inc.
World Servants, Inc.
WorldHarvest
Wycliffe Associates, Inc.
YUGO Ministries

## Supplying equipment

Chosen Mission Project
Christian Aviation and Radio Mission
Christian Dental Society
CMTS Ministries, Inc.
ComCare International
CrossLink International
Dayspring International
DeNike Ministries
East West Ministries International
Equipping the Saints
Evangelical Bible Mission
FRIENDS in Action, International
Global Health Ministries
Good Shepherd Ministries, Inc.
Gospel Revival Ministries
INTERCOMM

International Aid
JAARS Inc.
Macedonian Missionary Service
MATS International, Inc.
Morelli Ministries International
Progressive National Baptist Conv., Inc.
Tech Serve International, Inc.
Vellore Christian Medical College Board
   (USA), Inc.

**Support of national workers**

Advancing Indigenous Missions
Advancing Native Missions
Advancing Renewal Ministries, Inc.
Advent Christian General Conf.
Allegheny Wesleyan Methodist Connection
Amazon Focus
Ambassadors for Christ Intl.
American Council of the Ramabai Mukti
   Mission, Inc.
AMG International
Apostolic Christian Church Foundation, Inc.
ARISE International Mission
Artists In Christian Testimony
Assemblies of God World Missions
Association of Free Lutheran Congregations
Awana Clubs International
Back to the Bible International
Baptist International Evangelistic Ministries
Bible League, The
Bibles For The World, Inc.
Brethren in Christ World Missions
Calvary Commission, Inc.
Campus Crusade for Christ, Intl.
Christ Community Church
Christian Blind Mission International
Christian Church of North America
Christian Cultural Development Foundation
Christian Laymen's Missionary Evangelism
   Association
Christian Missions Unlimited
Church Missions Link
Ch. of God (Anderson, Ind.), Global Missions
Ch. of God (Cleveland, TN) World Missions
Church of God of Prophecy
Church of the Nazarene, World Msn. Dept.
Churches of God, General Conference
Congregational Holiness Church
Congregational Methodist Church
David Livingstone KURE Foundation
Dayspring International
East Gates Ministries Intl.
East West Ministries International
Eastern European Outreach, Inc.
European Christian Mission Intl.—USA
Evangelical Presbyterian Church

Evangelism Explosion International
Far East Broadcasting Company, Inc.
Fellowship of Assocs. of Medical Evangelism
Final Frontiers Foundation, Inc.
Foundation For His Ministry
Free Gospel Church, Inc.
Fundamental Baptist Msn. Trinidad/Tobago
Global Fellowship Inc.
Global Outreach Mission, Inc.
Global Recordings Network
Global Youth Ministry Network
Gospel Outreach Ministries Intl.
Gospel Revival Ministries
Gospelink, Inc.
Habitat for Humanity International
HBI Global Partners
Hope for the Hungry
I. N. Network USA
In Touch Mission International
Independent Gospel Missions: A Baptist
   Mission Agency
India Gospel Outreach
International Partnership Ministries, Inc.
International Street Kids Outreach Ministries
International Teams, U.S.A.
Japanese Evangelical Missionary Society
Kids Around the World, Inc.
Latin American Indian Ministries
Lott Carey Baptist Foreign Mission Conv.
Luke Society, Inc., The
MATS International, Inc.
Medical Ambassadors International, Inc.
Ministry to Educate and Equip Intl.
Mission Ministries, Inc.
Mission ONE, Inc.
Missionary Ventures International
National Baptist Convention of America
   —Foreign Mission Board
New Directions International, Inc.
New Hope International
Outreach To Asia Nationals
Palm Missionary Ministries
Partners in Asian Missions
Partners International
Pentecostal Ch. of God—World Msns. Dept.
Perimeter Church, Global Outreach
Peter Deyneka Russian Ministries
Pillar of Fire Missions Intl.
Presbyterian Evangelistic Fellowship
Presbyterian Mission International (PMI)
Reaching Indians Ministries International
Romanian Missionary Society
ServLife International
Share International
Slavic Gospel Association
Slavic Missionary Service, Inc.

Source of Light Ministries International, Inc.
Sowers International, The
Spanish World Ministries
Spiritual Growth Resources, Inc.
STEM International
The Brethren Church, Inc.
The Waray-Waray Project
The Word for the World
TITUS International
Training Evangelistic Leadership (T.E.L.), Inc.
Voice of the Martyrs, The
Walk Thru the Bible Ministries, Inc.
World Link Ministries
World Missions & Evangelism, Inc.
World Missions Far Corners, Inc.
World-Wide Missions
YUGO Ministries

### Technical assistance
African Methodist Episcopal Church
American Leprosy Missions, Inc.
Chosen Mission Project
Christian Aviation and Radio Mission
Church World Service
CMTS Ministries, Inc.
ComCare International
ECHO
Enterprise Development Intl.
FARMS International
FRIENDS in Action, International
Global Mapping International
Helps International Ministries
Interchurch Medical Assistance, Inc.
JAARS Inc.
M/E International, Inc.
MATS International, Inc.
Media Associates International
Mennonite Central Committee (MCC)
Missionary TECH Team
Straightway Inc.
Tech Serve International, Inc.
Trans World Radio, International
United Board for Christian Higher
    Education in Asia
World Vision International
Worldwide Lab Improvement

### Tentmaking & Related
ABWE
Arab World MinistriesChrist's
Mandate for MissionsCMF International
Educational Services International (ESI)
Global Opportunities
INTENT
InterServe USA (Intl. Service Fellowship)
Mission Ministries, Inc.

People International USA
Pioneers USA
Tentmakers International
Women to the World
Worldwide Tentmakers, Inc.

### TESOL
Baptist Bible Translators Institute
Christ Community Church
Christian Literature International
Christian Outreach International
Donetsk Christian University
Educational Services International (ESI)
Greater Europe Mission
InterServe USA (Intl. Service Fellowship)
Janz Team Ministries USA
Literacy & Evangelism International
Overseas Radio & Television, Inc. (ORTV)
Red Sea Team International

### Training, other
African Leadership, Inc.
Ambassadors for Christ Intl.
AMF International
Asian Outreach U.S.A.
BCM International
Bible League, The
Biblical Ministries Worldwide
Billy Graham Center, The
Bridge Builders International
Campus Crusade for Christ, Intl.
Child Evangelism Fellowship, Inc.
Christ for India, Inc.
Christian Discipleship Ministries, Inc.
Church Leadership Development Intl.
CityTeam Ministries
CMTS Ministries, Inc.
ComCare International
Crisis Consulting International
Crossover Communications International
Dawn Ministries, Inc.
DeNike Ministries
Derek Prince Ministries, International
nterprise Development Intl.
Envoy International
EQUIP Foundation Evangelism Resources
Every Home for Christ
General Baptists International
Global Action
Global Advance
Global Harvest Ministries
Global Opportunities
Global Youth Ministry Network
Gospel Communications International, Inc.
Gospel Literature International, Inc.
Great Commission Center International

Harvest Heifer International
HOPE International
IFMA
Independent Faith Mission, Inc.
Independent Gospel Missions: A
     Baptist Mission Agency
India Evangelical Mission
India Gospel Outreach
Interdev Partnership Associates
International Aid
International Pentecostal Church of Christ
International Students, Inc (ISI)
Kids Around the World, Inc.
Leadership Ministries Worldwide
Lifewater International
Literacy & Evangelism International
Living Hope Ministries International
LOGOI Ministries
Lutheran Church-Missouri Synod
Media Associates International
Mennonite Central Committee (MCC)
Mission Catalyst International
Mission India
Missionary TECH Team
MMS Aviation
On The Go Ministries/Keith Cook
     Evangelistic Association
Open Air Campaigners—Overseas Mins.
Opportunity International
Pass the Torch Ministries
Prakash Association, USA
Precept Ministries International
Presbyterian Order for Wld. Evangelization
Project Mercy, Inc.
Ramesh Richard Evangelism and Ch. Health
Ravi Zacharias International Ministries
RUN Ministries
Self-Help International
Sentinel Group, The
Seventh-day Adventists General Conf.
Share International
Son Shine Ministries International
Spiritual Overseers Service International
Supreme Task International, Inc.
TCM International Institute
The Ch. of God of the Apostolic Faith, Inc.
The Word for the World
Training Evangelistic Leadership, Inc.
United Board for Christian Higher
     Education in Asia
University of the Family
VELA Ministries International
Vellore Christian Medical College Board
     (USA), Inc.
Village Ministries International
Walk Thru the Bible Ministries, Inc.
Weiner Ministries International

Women to the World
World Indigenous Missions
World Missionary Assistance Plan
World Servants, Inc.
World Team
World Thrust International, Inc.
WorldTeach
Worldwide Discipleship Assoc.
Wycliffe International
Youth for Christ International

## Training/Orientation

Abundant Life Association, Inc.
Adventures in Missions
African Enterprise
African Methodist Episcopal Church
AIMS
AMF International
Apostolic Team Ministries, Intl.
Assemblies of God World Missions
Association of Free Lutheran Congregations
Baptist Bible Translators Institute
Brethren in Christ World Missions
Caleb Project
Calvary Commission, Inc.
Calvary International
China Ministries International
Chosen People Ministries
Christian Churches / Churches of Christ
Christian Medical & Dental Associations
     —Global Health Outreach
Christian Outreach International
Christians In Action Missions International
Church Missions Link
Church of the Nazarene, World Msn. Dept.
Daystar U.S.
Deaf Missions International
Donetsk Christian University
Emmaus Road International
Entrust
Equip, Inc.
Evangelism Explosion International
Free Methodist World Missions
Global Mapping International
Global Outreach International
Harvest Evangelism, Inc.
Have Christ Will Travel Ministries
Heart of God Ministries
Hope for the Hungry
Institute for International Christian
     Communication WorldView Center
Inst. of Strategic Languages and Cultures
Interaction International
International Board of Jewish Missions, Inc.
International Family Missions
International Gospel Outreach

International Messengers
Jewish Awareness Ministries
Jews for Jesus
Joni and Friends
Josue Yrion Wld. Evangelism and Msns., Inc.
Kids Alive International
Literacy & Evangelism International
Living Water Teaching
Ludhiana Christian Medical College
    Board, USA, Inc.
Lutheran Church-Missouri Synod
Macedonian Missionary Service
MBMS International
Middle East Media - USA
Middle Eastern Outreach
Mission Training International
Missionaire International
Missions Resource Network
Moravian Church in North America
New Wineskins Missionary Network
OC International, Inc.
OMS International, Inc.
Operation Mobilization
Paraclete, Inc.
Perimeter Church, Global Outreach
Servants in Faith & Technology (SIFAT)
Seventh Day Baptist Missionary Society
Shield of Faith Mission International
Son Shine Ministries International
Southern Baptist Conv. Intl. Mission Bd.
Sowers International, The
Tentmakers International
The Master's Mission, Inc.
Tribes and Nations Outreach
United Methodist Church
United World Mission
WEC International
World Harvest Now, Inc.
World Horizons
World Indigenous Missions
World Mission Associates
World Outreach Ministries
Wycliffe Bible Translators, Inc.
Youth With A Mission (YWAM)

## Translation, Bible

Africa Inter-Mennonite Mission
American Association of Lutheran Churches
American Bible Society
Baptist Mid-Missions
Bible League, The
Christian Literature International
Ch. of God (Holiness), Wld. Msn. Dept., Inc.
CLC Ministries International
Door of Hope International
Evangel Bible Translators

Evangelical Baptist Missions
Evangelical Congregational Church—
    Global Ministries Commission
Good News for India
Gospel Furthering Fellowship, The
JAARS Inc.
Key Communications
Leadership Ministries Worldwide
Lutheran Bible Translators, Inc.
Lutheran Brethren World Missions
Mexican Medical Ministries
Ministry to Eastern Europe
Missionary Revival Crusade
New Tribes Mission
People International USA
Pioneer Bible Translators
Reach Ministries International
Reformed Episcopal Bd. of Foreign Msns.
RUN Ministries
Russian Bible Society, Inc.
SIM USA
Slavic Gospel Association
Talking Bibles International
The Word for the World
World Bible Translation Center
World Mission
World Team
Wycliffe Associates, Inc.
Wycliffe International

## Translation, other

Evangel Bible Translators
Gospel Literature International, Inc.
Iranian Christians International
Lutheran Bible Translators, Inc.
Middle East Media—USA
Ministry to Educate and Equip Intl.
Outreach To Asia Nationals
Reformation Translation Fellowship (RTF)
Russian Bible Society, Inc.
Spanish American Evangelistic Ministries
World Mission Prayer League
World Missionary Assistance Plan
World Missionary Press, Inc.
Wycliffe Bible Translators, Inc.

## Urban Ministry

LIGHT International, Inc.

## Video/Film

Arab World Ministries
Assemblies of God World Missions
Caleb Project
Christian Broadcasting Network Inc.
Christian Resources International
Ch. of the Nazarene, World Mission Dept.

CMTS Ministries, Inc.
Derek Prince Ministries, International
Good News Productions International
Good Shepherd Ministries International
Gospel Communications International, Inc.
Habitat for Humanity International
Handclasp International, Inc.
HCJB Global
INTERCOMM
Josue Yrion World Evangelism and
    Missions, Inc.
Luis Palau Evangelistic Assoc.
Lutheran Hour Ministries
Mennonite Mission Network
Middle East Christian Outreach (MECO)
Middle East Media—USA
Missionary Revival Crusade
Overseas Radio & Television, Inc. (ORTV)
Sentinel Group, The
The Ch. of God of the Apostolic Faith, Inc.
The God's Story Project
World Mission Associates

Pentecostal Free Will Baptist Church, Inc.
Peter Deyneka Russian Ministries
Pioneer Clubs
Prakash Association, USA
Presbyterian Evangelistic Fellowship
Rock the World Youth Mission Alliance
Salvation Army, U.S.A.
Servants in Faith & Technology (SIFAT)
Surfing the Nations
Team World Outreach
Teen Missions International, Inc.
The Brethren Church, Inc.
The Ch. of God of the Apostolic Faith, Inc.
Touch the World Youth Ministries
Weiner Ministries International
Word of Life Fellowship, Inc.
World Witness, Assoc. Reformed Presb. Ch.
Young Life
Youth Encounter
Youth for Christ International
Youth for Christ/USA—World Outreach
Youth With A Mission (YWAM)

## Youth programs

Adventures in Missions
American Missionary Fellowship
BCM International
Children's Hope Chest
COMHINA
Compassion International, Inc.
CTI Music Ministries
Door of Hope International
Eastern Mennonite Missions
Episcopal Church USA—Domestic &
    Foreign Missionary Society
Fellowship International Mission
Friendship International Ministries, Inc.
Global Action
Global Youth Ministry Network
Good Shepherd Ministries International
Habitat for Humanity International
Heart to Heart Intl. Ministries
Hellenic Ministries Intl. Teams, U.S.A.
Italy for Christ
Living Hope Ministries International
Living Water Teaching
MBMS International
Mission of Mercy
Mission to the World (PCA), Inc.
Mission To Unreached Peoples
Missionaire International
Missionary Athletes International
Moravian Church in North America
New Hope International
On The Go Ministries/Keith Cook
    Evangelistic Association

# Lausanne **w⊙rld pulse**.com

**Free monthly online publication** with
comprehensive news, analysis and information
on evangelism and world missions.

**Each issue includes:**

—Regional reports from key
  leaders and practitioners
  in evangelism and missions

—Updates on news and
  events around the world

—Trends and statistics
  on the global church

—Information on various
  unreached people groups

—Resources and tools for
  those involved in
  evangelism and missions

**LWP is committed to:**

—Communicating the call to
  global evangelism

—Connecting the global body
  of Christ through
  the sharing of information

—Serving as a catalytic force for
  collaborative evangelism
  efforts and initiatives

—Providing a theological
  foundation for working
  toward the fulfillment of the
  Great Commission

*LWP readers include: international Christian leaders, missions
professors, denominational leaders, missionaries, evangelists
and pastors, and others interested in missions and evangelism.*

## FREE!
## Visit Us Today!

## www.lausanneworldpulse.com
Email: info@lausanneworldpulse.com

Lausanne World Pulse is a collaborative effort of the Institute of Strategic Evangelism, Evangelism
and Missions Information Service and Intercultural Studies Department (Wheaton College,
Wheaton, IL USA) and the Lausanne Committee for World Evangelization.

A global event that will

# UNIFY, ENERGIZE AND FOCUS

God's church on advancing world evangelization!

# 2010 LAUSANNE

## INTERNATIONAL CONGRESS ON WORLD EVANGELIZATION

"The 1974 Lausanne Congress was critical to the evangelism efforts of that day. But the issues facing today's generation are radically different. That's why I strongly support the need for a new congress in 2010."

— Billy Graham
Founder, Lausanne Movement

"The church needs renewed momentum, passion and focus on the unique problems facing this generation. The 2010 Lausanne Congress on World Evangelization will be a historic opportunity for discussion, strategy and action."

— Rick Warren
Senior Pastor,
Saddleback Church

"I'm impressed with the current Lausanne leadership. This gifted team shares the spirit of Lausanne and I believe that God will use them to unite the church in world evangelization."

— John Stott
Chief architect of the Lausanne Covenant

"The 2010 Lausanne Congress will emphasize that true evangelism means reaching out in Jesus' name to every part of society — including those who are sick, hungry, poor and disabled."

— Joni Eareckson Tada
Founder, Joni and Friends International Disability Center

### For more information about how you might participate, sign up for the Lausanne *Connecting Point* enewsletter at www.lausanne.org.

*Details of the Congress will be announced soon. But you'll want to begin now preparing for and praying about this historic gathering.*

The Lausanne Committee for World Evangelization
Email: info@lausanne.org • Web: www.lausanne.org • www.lausanneworldpulse.com

# 3 self-study courses
## to equip you in evangelism and discipleship

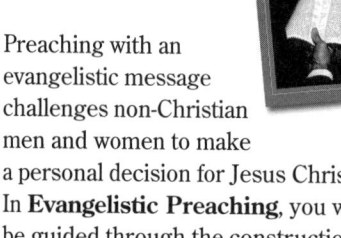

Preaching with an evangelistic message challenges non-Christian men and women to make a personal decision for Jesus Christ. In **Evangelistic Preaching**, you will be guided through the construction

**NOW ONLY $19.95 each.**
**Order online today!**

of your own sermon. You will hear and analyze sermons by Billy Graham, D. James Kennedy, Luis Palau, Leighton Ford, Charles Swindoll and others. Includes one manual and six cassette tapes.

Discipleship is critical to establishing new believers in their Christian life. In **Disciple Making**, you will learn how to equip new disciples. You will be instructed and inspired by Bill Bright, Tony Evans, Howard Hendricks, Dollee Meredith and others. Includes one manual and six cassette tapes.

Women have a unique part to play in sharing the gospel message with others. In **Women & Evangelism**, you will explore how women are fulfilling the Great Commission. You will hear from more than three dozen well-known evangelical women, including Jill Briscoe, Elisabeth Elliot and Anne Graham Lotz. Includes one manual and six cassette tapes.

Each course (which includes one manual and six cassette tapes) **NOW ONLY $19.95!** Originally $41.95.

Extra manuals **NOW ONLY $4.95!** Originally $10.95.

Now available on CD!

Visit us at: **www.billygrahamcenter.org/emis**

To order, call 630.752.7158 or go online to
## www.emisdirect.com

# Chapter 4
# Countries of Activity for U.S. Protestant Agencies

In this chapter you will find the countries where agencies reported field personnel in answer to question #14 of the survey questionnaire (see appendix). The few exceptions are agencies whose whole program supports (with funds raised in the U.S., but which may not be designated to specific personnel on a regular basis) churches or other initiatives in a country.

All countries are listed in alphabetical order according to the name most commonly recognized in North America. Countries that are part of the Commonwealth of Independent States (most of the former Soviet Union) have been listed separately. Examples of this include Armenia, Kyrgyzstan and Belarus. In a few cases we have listed a territory or other administrative district of a country because it is commonly viewed as a separate entity and mission agencies report it that way. The country of Serbia/Montenegro has separated into two separate countries as we go to print.

We have separated the personnel totals for all agencies into five categories. Under the "Personnel from U.S." heading, the term of expected service has been divided into three categories: 4+ years, 2-4 years and 1-2 years for fully supported personnel. For non-U.S. personnel in the "Other Countries" heading, the categories are those who are citizens of that ministry country and those who are not citizens, and are fully or partially supported by funds raised in the U.S. by the associated agency. For example, a Korean with specific mission/ministry duties serving in Korea would be included in an agency's "citizens" column of the Korea section. A Korean serving in Russia would be listed in the "not citizen" column of the Russia section.

At the end of each country section, totals of each category for that country are given. Please note that the totals for the "other countries" heading do not necessarily reflect all non-U.S. mission personnel who draw support from U.S. agencies. Some agencies give grants for ongoing institutions and other programs without specifying individual recipients. This may be in addition to U.S. mission personnel based in that country or the agency may not have U.S. personnel living in that country.

Please note also that the totals will be minimum numbers only because of the bigger number of large agencies in this edition that reported their personnel only by general regions and not by specific countries. Their numbers are not included in this "countries of activity" section.

| | First Year | Personnel from U.S. | | | Other Countries | |
|---|---|---|---|---|---|---|
| | | 1-2 yrs. | 2-4 yrs. | 4+ yrs. | Citizens | Non-Citizens |

## Afghanistan

| | First Year | 1-2 yrs. | 2-4 yrs. | 4+ yrs. | Citizens | Non-Citizens |
|---|---|---|---|---|---|---|
| CrossWorld | | - | - | 3 | - | - |
| Habitat for Humanity International | | - | 1 | - | - | 1 |
| Health Emergent International Services | 1999 | 2 | 10 | 2 | - | 1 |
| Mennonite Mission Network | 1966 | - | - | 4 | - | - |
| People International USA | 1996 | - | 2 | 5 | - | - |
| Samaritan's Purse | 2001 | 7 | 2 | 1 | 31 | 3 |
| Women to the World | 2001 | - | - | - | 13 | - |
| World Concern | 1982 | 2 | - | 2 | 16 | - |
| | Totals: | 11 | 15 | 17 | 60 | 5 |

## Africa—General

| | First Year | 1-2 yrs. | 2-4 yrs. | 4+ yrs. | Citizens | Non-Citizens |
|---|---|---|---|---|---|---|
| ABWE (Assoc. of Baptists for World Evang.) | 1966 | - | 19 | 79 | - | - |
| Advancing Renewal Ministries, Inc. | | - | - | 2 | - | 2 |
| Africa Inland Mission International | 2001 | - | 2 | 8 | - | - |
| ARISE International Mission | | - | - | - | 3 | - |
| Assemblies of God World Missions | | 9 | - | 34 | - | - |
| Assoc. of Free Lutheran Congregations | 2006 | - | 2 | - | - | - |
| Bakke Graduate University of Ministry | 2005 | - | - | - | - | 1 |
| Baptist General Conf.—Intl. Ministries | | - | - | 12 | - | - |
| Baptist International Missions, Inc. (BIMI) | 1960 | - | - | 2 | - | - |
| Campus Crusade for Christ, Intl. | | - | - | 2 | 2 | 2 |
| Christar | 1984 | - | - | 8 | - | - |
| Christian and Missionary Alliance | 1996 | - | - | 148 | - | - |
| Christian Churches / Churches of Christ | | - | - | 4 | - | - |
| Church World Service | 1946 | - | - | 5 | 35 | 10 |
| Cities for Christ Worldwide | 1963 | - | - | 2 | - | - |
| Cooperative Baptist Fellowship | 1991 | - | - | 21 | - | - |
| Dawn Ministries, Inc. | | - | - | - | - | 1 |
| Eastern Mennonite Missions | | - | - | - | - | |
| Entrust | 2004 | - | - | - | 8 | 2 |
| EQUIP Foundation | 2004 | - | - | - | - | - |
| Evangelical Covenant Ch.—Covenant Wld. Msn. | 1999 | 4 | - | 8 | - | - |
| Final Frontiers Foundation, Inc. | 1990 | - | - | - | 200 | - |
| Free Methodist World Missions | | - | - | 2 | - | - |
| FRIENDS in Action, International | 1998 | - | 4 | - | - | - |
| Global Partners / Wesleyan World Missions | | 2 | 5 | - | - | - |
| Global Youth Ministry Network | | - | - | - | 2 | - |
| Globe Missionary Evangelism | 1993 | - | - | 2 | - | - |
| Go Ye Fellowship | | 1 | - | 3 | 1 | 2 |
| Good News Productions International | 1995 | - | - | 2 | 8 | - |
| Heart of God Ministries | 2003 | - | - | 9 | - | - |
| Hope for the Hungry | | - | 1 | 2 | 1 | - |
| International Cooperating Ministries | | - | - | - | - | - |
| Josue Yrion World Evangelism and Missions, Inc. | 2001 | - | - | - | 1 | - |
| Mailbox Club International Inc., The | 2001 | - | - | 1 | 2 | 2 |
| Mennonite Central Committee (MCC) | | - | - | 153 | - | - |
| Middle East Media—USA | 1976 | - | - | - | - | - |
| Mission Aviation Fellowship | | - | - | 2 | - | - |

| | First Year | Personnel from U.S. | | | Other Countries | |
|---|---|---|---|---|---|---|
| | | 1-2 yrs. | 2-4 yrs. | 4+ yrs. | Citizens | Non-Citizens |
| Open Bible Churches, International Ministries | 2004 | - | - | 2 | - | - |
| Operation Mobilization | | 5 | 2 | 13 | - | 4 |
| Partners International | 1964 | - | - | - | - | 2 |
| Pentecostal Ch. of God—World Missions Dept. | | - | - | 4 | - | - |
| Presbyterian Ch. (USA), Worldwide Ministries | | - | 85 | 80 | - | - |
| Red Sea Team International | 1953 | - | - | - | 1 | 16 |
| Shield of Faith Mission International | 1980 | - | - | 4 | - | - |
| Source of Light Ministries International, Inc. | | - | - | - | - | - |
| Southern Baptist Convention Intl. Mission Bd. | | - | - | - | - | - |
| Talking Bibles International | 2002 | - | - | - | 1 | - |
| Team Expansion, Inc. | 2001 | - | - | 14 | - | 2 |
| Tentmakers International | | - | - | - | - | - |
| United World Mission | | - | 1 | 18 | - | - |
| World Concern | 1980 | - | - | - | 30 | - |
| World Horizons | 1981 | - | - | 1 | - | 2 |
| World Link Ministries | 1995 | - | - | 4 | 11 | 2 |
| World Thrust International, Inc. | 1999 | - | - | - | - | 2 |
| Wycliffe Associates, Inc. | | 3 | 3 | - | - | - |
| Wycliffe Bible Translators, Inc. | 1963 | - | - | 918 | - | - |
| Young Life | | 2 | - | 4 | - | - |
| Youth for Christ International | | - | - | 2 | - | - |
| Youth for Christ/USA—World Outreach | | - | - | 2 | - | - |
| Totals: | | 26 | 124 | 1577 | 306 | 52 |

## Albania

| | First Year | 1-2 yrs. | 2-4 yrs. | 4+ yrs. | Citizens | Non-Citizens |
|---|---|---|---|---|---|---|
| Alongside Ministries International | 1994 | 2 | - | 3 | 2 | - |
| AMG International | 1992 | - | - | - | 1 | - |
| Apostolic Team Ministries, Intl. | | - | - | 5 | 3 | - |
| Assemblies of God World Missions | 1991 | - | - | 6 | - | - |
| BILD International | | - | - | - | - | 1 |
| Brethren Assemblies | | - | - | 7 | - | - |
| CAM International | 2005 | - | - | 4 | - | - |
| Campus Crusade for Christ, Intl. | 1991 | - | - | 7 | 83 | 3 |
| Child Evangelism Fellowship, Inc. | 1992 | - | - | 1 | - | - |
| Christar | 1993 | - | - | 10 | - | - |
| Christian Aid Mission | | - | - | - | 3 | - |
| Church of God (Cleveland, TN) World Missions | 1993 | - | 2 | - | - | 2 |
| Church of the Nazarene, World Mission Dept. | 1993 | - | - | 3 | - | 1 |
| Churches of Christ | 1991 | - | - | 12 | 6 | - |
| Commission to Every Nation | 2003 | 1 | - | - | - | - |
| Eastern Mennonite Missions | | - | 1 | 2 | - | - |
| East-West Ministries International | 1999 | - | - | 1 | 10 | - |
| European Christian Mission Intl.—USA | | - | - | 6 | - | - |
| Fellowship of Evangelical Churches—Intl. Mns. | 1995 | - | - | 4 | - | 4 |
| Foursquare Missions International | 1996 | - | - | 2 | - | - |
| Global Partners / Wesleyan World Missions | 1993 | - | 2 | - | - | - |
| Globe Missionary Evangelism | 1995 | - | - | 6 | - | - |
| Gospel Fellowship Association | 1997 | - | - | 2 | - | - |
| Greater Europe Mission | 1992 | - | 2 | - | - | - |
| Greater Grace World Outreach | 1995 | - | - | - | - | 2 |

| | First Year | Personnel from U.S. | | | Other Countries | |
| --- | --- | --- | --- | --- | --- | --- |
| | | 1-2 yrs. | 2-4 yrs. | 4+ yrs. | Citizens | Non-Citizens |
| Intl. Pentecostal Holiness Ch. World Missions Mins. | 2001 | - | 2 | - | 2 | - |
| International Teams, U.S.A. | | 1 | - | 4 | - | 2 |
| Larry Jones Intl. Ministries (Feed the Children) | 1999 | - | - | - | 2 | 2 |
| Medical Ambassadors International, Inc. | 1995 | - | - | 2 | 3 | - |
| Mission Possible Foundation, Inc. | 1992 | - | - | - | 8 | - |
| Mission To Unreached Peoples | 2005 | - | - | 2 | - | - |
| Operation Mobilization | 1991 | - | - | 2 | - | 2 |
| Reformed Ch. in America, Gen. Synod Council | 2000 | - | - | 2 | - | - |
| Rosedale Mennonite Missions | 2005 | - | - | 2 | - | 2 |
| Seventh-day Adventists General Conference | 1992 | - | - | 2 | - | 2 |
| Spiritual Growth Resources, Inc. | 1998 | - | - | - | 5 | - |
| United Pentecostal Ch. Intl., Foreign Missions Div. | | - | 1 | - | - | - |
| Virginia Mennonite Board of Missions | 1991 | - | - | 1 | - | 1 |
| Wisc. Evangelical Luth. Synod, Bd. for Wld. Msns. | 1996 | - | 1 | - | - | - |
| World Reach, Inc. | 1999 | - | - | - | 1 | 3 |
| World Venture | 1993 | - | - | 2 | - | - |
| Totals: | | 4 | 11 | 100 | 129 | 27 |

## Algeria

| | | | | | | |
| --- | --- | --- | --- | --- | --- | --- |
| Assemblies of God World Missions | 2002 | - | - | 2 | - | - |
| Mission ONE, Inc. | 1990 | - | - | - | 3 | - |
| Partners International | 1992 | - | - | - | 12 | - |
| Seventh-day Adventists General Conference | | - | - | - | - | 2 |
| Totals: | | - | - | 2 | 15 | 2 |

## American Samoa

| | | | | | | |
| --- | --- | --- | --- | --- | --- | --- |
| Assemblies of God World Missions | 1926 | - | - | 1 | - | - |
| Baptist International Missions, Inc. (BIMI) | | - | - | 2 | - | - |
| Church of the Nazarene, World Mission Dept. | 1958 | - | - | - | - | - |
| Churches of Christ | | 2 | - | 2 | 1 | - |
| United Pentecostal Ch. Intl., Foreign Missions Div. | 1999 | - | 2 | - | - | 2 |
| Totals: | | 2 | 2 | 5 | 1 | 2 |

## Angola

| | | | | | | |
| --- | --- | --- | --- | --- | --- | --- |
| Abudant Life Association, Inc. | 1990 | - | 2 | - | 90 | 2 |
| Africa Inland Mission International | | 2 | - | 2 | - | 1 |
| African Leadership, Inc. | 1998 | - | - | - | 1 | - |
| American Leprosy Missions, Inc. | 1948 | - | - | - | - | 1 |
| Assemblies of God World Missions | 1985 | - | - | 6 | - | - |
| Campus Crusade for Christ, Intl. | 1997 | - | - | - | 10 | - |
| Child Evangelism Fellowship, Inc. | 1993 | - | - | - | 1 | - |
| Ch. of God (Anderson, Ind.), Global Missions | 1998 | - | - | - | - | 2 |
| Church of God of Prophecy—Global Outreach | | - | - | - | 2 | - |
| Church of the Nazarene, World Mission Dept. | 1992 | - | - | 2 | - | 2 |
| Larry Jones Intl. Ministries (Feed the Children) | 1995 | - | - | - | 7 | - |
| Samaritan's Purse | 2001 | 3 | - | - | 11 | 2 |
| Seventh-day Adventists General Conference | | - | - | - | - | 2 |
| SIM USA | 1914 | 2 | - | 7 | - | - |
| Walk Thru the Bible Ministries, Inc. | 2001 | - | - | - | - | - |
| Totals: | | 7 | 2 | 17 | 122 | 12 |

| | First Year | Personnel from U.S. 1-2 yrs. | 2-4 yrs. | 4+ yrs. | Other Countries Citizens | Non-Citizens |
|---|---|---|---|---|---|---|

**Anguilla**

| | First Year | 1-2 yrs. | 2-4 yrs. | 4+ yrs. | Citizens | Non-Citizens |
|---|---|---|---|---|---|---|
| Baptist International Missions, Inc. (BIMI) | | - | - | 2 | - | - |
| Totals: | | - | - | 2 | - | - |

**Antigua**

| | First Year | 1-2 yrs. | 2-4 yrs. | 4+ yrs. | Citizens | Non-Citizens |
|---|---|---|---|---|---|---|
| Assemblies of God World Missions | 1997 | - | - | - | - | - |
| Baptist International Missions, Inc. (BIMI) | | - | - | 6 | - | - |
| BCM International | | - | - | - | 1 | - |
| Biblical Ministries Worldwide | 2005 | - | - | 2 | - | 2 |
| Church of the Nazarene, World Mission Dept. | 1973 | - | - | - | - | - |
| Churches of Christ | 1971 | - | - | 2 | - | - |
| Seventh-day Adventists General Conference | 1944 | - | - | 2 | - | 2 |
| Totals: | | - | - | 12 | 1 | 4 |

**Argentina**

| | First Year | 1-2 yrs. | 2-4 yrs. | 4+ yrs. | Citizens | Non-Citizens |
|---|---|---|---|---|---|---|
| AMG International | | - | - | - | 2 | - |
| Apostolic Christian Church Foundation, Inc. | 1969 | - | - | 1 | 11 | - |
| Armenian Missionary Assoc. of America, Inc. | 1950 | - | - | - | - | - |
| Assemblies of God World Missions | 1910 | 6 | - | 26 | - | - |
| Avant Ministries | 1911 | - | - | 14 | - | 3 |
| Awana Clubs International | 1983 | - | - | - | 2 | - |
| Baptist Bible Fellowship International | 1959 | - | - | 21 | - | - |
| Baptist General Conference—Intl. Ministries | 1957 | - | - | 6 | - | - |
| Baptist International Missions, Inc. (BIMI) | | - | - | 4 | - | - |
| Baptist Mid-Missions | 1987 | - | - | 5 | - | |
| Biblical Ministries Worldwide | 1979 | - | - | 12 | 2 | 10 |
| Brethren Assemblies | | - | - | 6 | - | - |
| Campus Crusade for Christ, Intl. | 1963 | 14 | - | 6 | 41 | 1 |
| Child Evangelism Fellowship, Inc. | 1944 | - | - | 1 | - | - |
| Chosen People Ministries | 1942 | - | - | - | - | - |
| Christian Aid Mission | | - | - | - | 39 | - |
| Christian Churches / Churches of Christ | | - | - | 4 | 4 | - |
| Church of God of Prophecy—Global Outreach | | - | - | - | 3 | 2 |
| Church of the Nazarene, World Mission Dept. | 1909 | - | - | 17 | - | 5 |
| Churches of Christ | 1957 | - | - | 7 | 3 | - |
| Elim Fellowship—International Department | 1956 | - | - | 3 | - | - |
| Envoy International | | - | - | - | - | - |
| Evangelical Baptist Missions | | - | - | 8 | - | - |
| Evangelical Covenant Ch.—Covenant Wld. Msn. | 2003 | - | - | 2 | - | - |
| Evangelical Lutheran Ch. in Am., Div. for Global Msn. | 1948 | - | - | 1 | - | - |
| Evangelical Presbyterian Ch.—World Outreach | 1991 | - | - | 6 | 5 | - |
| Evangelism Explosion International | | - | - | - | - | 2 |
| Friends of Israel Gospel Ministry, Inc. | 1970 | - | - | - | 2 | - |
| Full Gospel Grace Fellowship | 1940 | - | - | - | 3 | - |
| Global Outreach International | 2001 | - | - | 5 | 3 | - |
| Globe Missionary Evangelism | 2001 | - | - | 2 | - | - |
| Go Ye Fellowship | | - | - | 1 | - | - |
| Gospel Fellowship Association | 2005 | - | - | 2 | - | - |
| Gospel Mission of South America | 1970 | - | - | 8 | - | - |
| Grace Brethren International Missions | 1909 | - | 2 | 9 | - | - |

| | First Year | Personnel from U.S. 1-2 yrs. | 2-4 yrs. | 4+ yrs. | Other Countries Citizens | Non-Citizens |
|---|---|---|---|---|---|---|
| Greater Grace World Outreach | 1994 | - | - | - | 2 | - |
| HCJB Global | | - | - | - | - | 2 |
| Impact International | 1959 | - | - | 2 | - | - |
| International Board of Jewish Missions, Inc. | 1989 | - | - | 2 | - | - |
| Intl. Pentecostal Holiness Ch. World Missions Mins. | | - | - | - | - | - |
| International Teams, U.S.A. | | - | - | - | - | 2 |
| Josue Yrion World Evangelism and Missions, Inc. | 2003 | - | - | - | 1 | - |
| Latin America Mission | 1976 | - | 1 | 2 | - | 3 |
| LOGOI Ministries | 1972 | - | - | - | 1 | - |
| Luis Palau Evangelistic Assoc. | 1963 | - | - | - | 5 | - |
| Lutheran Ch.—Missouri Synod, Bd. for Msn. Svcs. | 1902 | - | - | 1 | - | - |
| Macedonia World Baptist Missions, Inc. | 2002 | - | - | 2 | - | - |
| Medical Ambassadors International, Inc. | 1995 | - | - | - | 3 | - |
| Mennonite Mission Network | 1917 | - | - | 4 | - | - |
| Mission to the World (PCA), Inc. | 1983 | - | - | - | - | - |
| Missionary Revival Crusade | 1991 | - | 4 | 2 | 1 | - |
| Navigators, U.S. International Missions Group | | 1 | - | 6 | - | - |
| OC International, Inc. | 1956 | - | - | - | - | 1 |
| Reformed Baptist Mission Services | | - | - | - | - | 2 |
| Salvation Army, U.S.A. | | - | - | 2 | - | - |
| Seventh-day Adventists General Conference | 1890 | - | - | - | - | 6 |
| Source of Light Ministries International, Inc. | 1999 | - | - | - | 2 | - |
| Spanish World Ministries | | - | - | 3 | 3 | - |
| The Brethren Church, Inc. | 1941 | - | - | - | 3 | - |
| United Church of Christ—Wider Ch. Ministries | | - | 2 | - | - | - |
| United Pentecostal Ch. Intl., Foreign Missions Div. | 1967 | - | 2 | - | - | 4 |
| Walk Thru the Bible Ministries, Inc. | 2001 | - | - | - | - | - |
| White Fields Inc. | | - | - | - | 12 | - |
| Word of Life Fellowship, Inc.—Intl. Ministries | 1971 | - | - | 11 | 172 | - |
| World Gospel Mission | 1970 | - | - | 8 | - | - |
| World Venture | 1947 | - | - | 11 | - | - |
| | Totals: | 21 | 11 | 233 | 325 | 43 |

## Armenia

| | First Year | 1-2 yrs. | 2-4 yrs. | 4+ yrs. | Citizens | Non-Citizens |
|---|---|---|---|---|---|---|
| Armenian Missionary Assoc. of America, Inc. | 1988 | - | - | 2 | - | 4 |
| Assemblies of God World Missions | 1999 | - | - | 5 | - | - |
| Campus Crusade for Christ, Intl. | 1993 | - | - | - | 30 | - |
| Child Evangelism Fellowship, Inc. | 1992 | - | - | 2 | - | 1 |
| Church of the Nazarene, World Mission Dept. | 2002 | - | - | - | - | - |
| Evangelism Explosion International | | - | - | - | - | 3 |
| Macedonia World Baptist Missions, Inc. | 2000 | - | - | 2 | - | - |
| Seventh-day Adventists General Conference | | - | - | - | - | 2 |
| United Pentecostal Ch. Intl., Foreign Msns. Div. | | - | 1 | - | - | - |
| Walk Thru the Bible Ministries, Inc. | 2000 | - | - | - | 1 | - |
| | Totals: | - | 1 | 11 | 31 | 10 |

## Aruba

| | First Year | 1-2 yrs. | 2-4 yrs. | 4+ yrs. | Citizens | Non-Citizens |
|---|---|---|---|---|---|---|
| Church of God (Cleveland, TN) World Missions | 1968 | - | - | 2 | - | - |
| Church of the Nazarene, World Mission Dept. | 2000 | - | - | - | - | - |

| | First Year | 1-2 yrs. | 2-4 yrs. | 4+ yrs. | Citizens | Non-Citizens |
|---|---|---|---|---|---|---|
| | | **Personnel from U.S.** | | | **Other Countries** | |
| Trans World Radio, International | 1964 | - | 2 | 8 | - | - |
| United Pentecostal Ch. Intl., Foreign Msns. Div. | | - | 2 | - | - | 3 |
| Totals: | | - | 4 | 10 | - | 3 |

## Asia—General

| | First Year | 1-2 yrs. | 2-4 yrs. | 4+ yrs. | Citizens | Non-Citizens |
|---|---|---|---|---|---|---|
| ABWE (Assoc. of Baptists for World Evangelism) | 1970 | - | 45 | 141 | - | - |
| ACM International | 2004 | - | 2 | - | - | - |
| AIMS (Accelerating Intl. Mission Strategies) | 2002 | - | - | 1 | - | - |
| Anglican Frontier Missions | 1999 | - | - | 5 | - | - |
| ARISE International Mission | | - | - | - | 7 | - |
| Asian Access | 2000 | - | - | - | - | - |
| Assemblies of God World Missions | 1926 | 52 | - | 122 | - | - |
| Bakke Graduate University of Ministry | | - | - | - | 1 | - |
| Baptist Mid-Missions | 1988 | - | - | 7 | - | - |
| Campus Crusade for Christ, Intl. | | 141 | - | 163 | 2770 | 462 |
| Christar | 1930 | - | - | 24 | - | 8 |
| Christian and Missionary Alliance | | - | - | 201 | - | - |
| Christian Churches / Churches of Christ | | - | - | 6 | 2 | - |
| Church Resource Ministries (CRM) | 1998 | - | - | 2 | - | - |
| Church World Service | 1946 | 17 | 10 | - | - | - |
| Cities for Christ Worldwide | 1985 | - | - | 2 | - | - |
| Commission to Every Nation | 2002 | 1 | 1 | - | - | - |
| Cooperative Baptist Fellowship | 1991 | - | - | 24 | - | - |
| Dawn Ministries, Inc. | | - | - | - | 1 | - |
| Eastern Mennonite Missions | | - | - | - | - | - |
| Elim Fellowship—International Department | | 2 | - | 13 | 2 | 1 |
| EQUIP Foundation | 2003 | - | - | - | - | - |
| Evangelical Covenant Ch.—Covenant Wld. Msn. | 1999 | 8 | - | 4 | - | - |
| Fellowship of Evangelical Churches—Intl. Mins. | 1994 | - | - | 3 | - | 3 |
| Final Frontiers Foundation, Inc. | 1986 | - | - | - | 550 | - |
| Free Methodist World Missions | | - | - | 5 | - | - |
| Global Action | 1998 | - | - | - | 1 | - |
| Global Fellowship Inc. | 1990 | - | - | - | 15 | - |
| Global Youth Ministry Network | | - | - | - | 3 | - |
| Go Ye Fellowship | 1935 | - | 1 | 7 | 3 | - |
| Gospel Fellowship Association | 2005 | - | - | 2 | - | - |
| Gospel Furthering Fellowship, The | | 2 | - | 2 | - | - |
| Greater Grace World Outreach | 1987 | - | - | 2 | 8 | 3 |
| Heifer International | 1954 | 20 | 26 | 35 | 111 | 4 |
| India National Inland Mission | | - | - | - | - | - |
| Intl. Christian Leprosy Mission, Inc. (USA) | 1954 | - | - | - | 14 | - |
| International Cooperating Ministries | | - | - | - | - | - |
| International Institute for Christian Studies | 1995 | - | - | - | - | 3 |
| Intl. Street Kids Outreach Ministries (ISKOM) | 1998 | 1 | - | - | 164 | - |
| InterServe USA (Intl. Service Fellowship) | 1966 | - | - | 47 | - | - |
| InterVarsity Christian Fellowship/USA—Msns. Dept. | | 3 | 1 | 4 | - | - |
| Literacy & Evangelism International | 2004 | - | - | - | 2 | - |
| Lutheran Church-Missouri Synod | | - | - | 2 | - | - |
| Macedonia World Baptist Missions, Inc. | 1994 | - | - | 4 | - | - |
| Mailbox Club International Inc., The | 2003 | - | - | 1 | - | - |

| | First Year | Personnel from U.S. | | | Other Countries | |
| --- | --- | --- | --- | --- | --- | --- |
| | | 1-2 yrs. | 2-4 yrs. | 4+ yrs. | Citizens | Non-Citizens |
| Mennonite Central Committee (MCC) | | - | - | 212 | - | - |
| Mennonite Mission Network | | - | - | 2 | - | - |
| Mission Aviation Fellowship | | - | - | 6 | - | - |
| Mission Ministries, Inc. | 2000 | - | - | 2 | - | - |
| Network of International Christian Schools | 1994 | - | 17 | 5 | - | 2 |
| New Mission Systems International | | - | - | 3 | - | - |
| New Tribes Mission | 1988 | - | - | 23 | - | - |
| OMF International | 1865 | 36 | - | 133 | 17 | 237 |
| Operation Mobilization | 1995 | - | 2 | 2 | | - |
| Outreach To Asia Nationals | 1986 | 2 | 3 | 7 | 180 | 4 |
| Partners in Asian Missions | 1972 | - | - | - | 159 | - |
| Partners International | 1954 | - | - | 6 | - | 2 |
| Pioneers USA | | 17 | - | 158 | 2 | 4 |
| Presbyterian Ch. (USA), Worldwide Ministries | | - | 70 | 65 | - | - |
| Reformed Baptist Mission Services | | - | - | - | - | 2 |
| SEND International USA | 1988 | - | - | 8 | 8 | 9 |
| Shelter for Life International, Inc. | 1999 | - | - | - | 10 | 4 |
| Shield of Faith Mission International | 1990 | - | 2 | - | - | - |
| Southern Baptist Convention Intl. Mission Bd. | | - | - | - | - | - |
| TEAM (The Evangelical Alliance Mission) | | - | - | 72 | - | - |
| Team Expansion, Inc. | 1996 | - | - | 31 | - | - |
| Tentmakers International | | - | - | - | - | - |
| United Church of Christ—Wider Church Ministries | | - | 1 | - | - | - |
| World Concern | | - | - | - | 30 | - |
| World Harvest Now, Inc. | | - | 3 | 2 | 4 | 4 |
| World Venture | 1993 | - | - | 4 | - | - |
| Wycliffe Associates, Inc. | | 3 | 4 | - | - | - |
| Wycliffe Bible Translators, Inc. | 1953 | - | - | 1065 | - | - |
| Young Life | | 4 | 1 | 1 | - | - |
| Youth for Christ International | | - | - | 2 | - | - |
| Totals: | | 309 | 189 | 2638 | 4064 | 752 |

## Australia

| | First Year | 1-2 yrs. | 2-4 yrs. | 4+ yrs. | Citizens | Non-Citizens |
| --- | --- | --- | --- | --- | --- | --- |
| Africa Inland Mission International | | 2 | - | - | 9 | - |
| AMG International | | - | - | - | - | 2 |
| Apostolic Christian Church Foundation, Inc. | 1978 | - | - | 2 | - | - |
| Armenian Missionary Assoc. of America, Inc. | 1975 | - | - | - | - | - |
| Asian Outreach U.S.A. | | - | - | - | - | - |
| Awana Clubs International | 1972 | - | - | - | 5 | - |
| Back to the Bible International | 1957 | - | - | - | 4 | - |
| Baptist Bible Fellowship International | 1968 | - | - | 28 | - | - |
| Baptist International Missions, Inc. (BIMI) | | - | - | 31 | - | - |
| Baptist Mid-Missions | 1968 | - | - | 17 | - | - |
| Biblical Ministries Worldwide | 1981 | - | - | 6 | 2 | 4 |
| BILD International | | - | - | - | 3 | - |
| Campus Crusade for Christ, Intl. | 1967 | 10 | - | 10 | 126 | 3 |
| Child Evangelism Fellowship, Inc. | 1944 | - | - | 2 | - | - |
| Chosen People Ministries | | - | - | - | - | - |
| Christian Churches / Churches of Christ | | - | - | 20 | 4 | - |
| Christian Literature International | | - | - | - | - | - |

| | First Year | Personnel from U.S. | | | Other Countries | |
|---|---|---|---|---|---|---|
| | | 1-2 yrs. | 2-4 yrs. | 4+ yrs. | Citizens | Non-Citizens |
| Ch. of God (Anderson, Ind.), Global Missions | 1977 | - | - | 2 | - | - |
| Church of God (Cleveland, TN) World Missions | 1976 | 2 | 2 | - | - | 4 |
| Church of God of Prophecy—Global Outreach | | - | - | 2 | 1 | - |
| Church of the Nazarene, World Mission Dept. | 1946 | - | - | 5 | - | 4 |
| Churches of Christ | 1847 | - | 3 | - | 31 | - |
| Development Associates International (DAI) | 2003 | - | - | - | 1 | - |
| Elim Fellowship—International Department | | - | - | 1 | 1 | - |
| Fellowship International Mission | 1987 | - | - | 1 | 1 | 2 |
| Foursquare Missions International | 1954 | - | - | 2 | - | - |
| Friends of Israel Gospel Ministry, Inc. | 1991 | - | - | - | 4 | - |
| Global Outreach Mission, Inc. | 1994 | - | - | 2 | - | - |
| Global Partners / Wesleyan World Missions | 1945 | - | 5 | - | - | 2 |
| Gospel Fellowship Association | 1973 | - | - | 4 | - | - |
| Grace Ministries International | 1976 | - | 6 | - | - | - |
| Habitat for Humanity International | 1988 | - | 1 | - | 1 | - |
| HCJB Global | 1950 | - | - | 7 | - | 5 |
| Independent Faith Mission, Inc. | | - | - | 2 | - | - |
| International Board of Jewish Missions, Inc. | 2001 | - | - | 2 | - | - |
| Intl. Pentecostal Holiness Ch. World Missions Mins. | 1995 | - | - | - | - | - |
| International Teams, U.S.A. | | 2 | - | 3 | - | 17 |
| Jews for Jesus | 1998 | - | - | 3 | - | 1 |
| Josue Yrion World Evangelism and Missions, Inc. | 2003 | - | - | - | 1 | - |
| Lott Carey Baptist Foreign Mission Convention | 2005 | - | - | - | 4 | - |
| Macedonia World Baptist Missions, Inc. | 1982 | - | - | 2 | 1 | - |
| Mennonite Mission Network | 2000 | - | - | - | - | - |
| Middle East Christian Outreach (MECO) | 1976 | - | - | - | - | 2 |
| Mission to the World (PCA), Inc. | 1984 | - | 2 | - | - | - |
| Navigators, U.S. International Missions Group | | 1 | - | 6 | - | - |
| New Tribes Mission | 1958 | - | - | 6 | 30 | - |
| OMS International, Inc. | | - | - | - | - | 3 |
| Open Bible Churches, International Ministries | 2003 | - | - | 2 | - | - |
| Operation Mobilization | | - | 1 | - | - | - |
| Precept Ministries International | 1988 | - | - | - | 3 | - |
| Presbyterian Ch. (USA), Worldwide Ministries | | - | - | 2 | - | - |
| Presbyterian Missionary Union | 2004 | - | - | 2 | - | - |
| Salvation Army, U.S.A. | | - | - | 4 | - | - |
| Seventh-day Adventists General Conference | 1885 | - | - | 4 | - | 6 |
| Shield of Faith Mission International | 1992 | - | 2 | - | - | - |
| TEAM (The Evangelical Alliance Mission) | | - | - | 2 | - | - |
| Teen Missions International, Inc. | 1986 | - | - | 2 | 5 | - |
| Tentmakers International | | - | - | - | - | - |
| United Ch. of Christ—Wider Church Ministries | | - | 2 | - | - | - |
| United Pentecostal Ch. Intl., Foreign Msns. Div. | 1973 | - | 4 | - | - | 6 |
| Walk Thru the Bible Ministries, Inc. | 2002 | - | - | - | - | - |
| Word of Life Fellowship, Inc.—Intl. Ministries | 1970 | - | - | 6 | - | 6 |
| World Baptist Fellowship Mission Agency, Inc. | | - | - | 2 | - | - |
| World Team | 1942 | - | - | 1 | - | - |
| Youth for Christ/USA—World Outreach | | - | - | 2 | - | - |
| Totals: | | 17 | 28 | 195 | 237 | 67 |

| | Personnel from U.S. | | | | Other Countries | |
|---|---|---|---|---|---|---|
| | First Year | 1-2 yrs. | 2-4 yrs. | 4+ yrs. | Citizens | Non-Citizens |

## Austria

| | First Year | 1-2 yrs. | 2-4 yrs. | 4+ yrs. | Citizens | Non-Citizens |
|---|---|---|---|---|---|---|
| Action International Ministries | 1987 | - | - | 1 | - | 1 |
| Apostolic Team Ministries, Intl. | | - | - | - | 2 | - |
| Assemblies of God World Missions | 1967 | 10 | - | 13 | - | - |
| Avant Ministries | 1966 | - | - | 1 | - | 1 |
| Baptist Bible Fellowship International | 1984 | - | - | 8 | - | - |
| Baptist International Missions, Inc. (BIMI) | | - | - | 2 | - | - |
| BCM International | | - | - | 1 | - | - |
| Biblical Ministries Worldwide | 1964 | - | - | 2 | - | 2 |
| Brethren Assemblies | | - | - | 7 | - | - |
| Campus Crusade for Christ, Intl. | 1974 | - | - | - | - | 2 |
| Child Evangelism Fellowship, Inc. | 1955 | - | - | 1 | - | - |
| Christian Churches / Churches of Christ | | - | 2 | 6 | 9 | - |
| Church of God (Cleveland, TN) World Missions | 1980 | - | - | 2 | - | - |
| Churches of Christ | 1953 | - | - | 9 | - | - |
| EFCA International Mission | 1971 | - | - | 3 | - | - |
| Elim Fellowship— International Department | 1991 | - | - | 2 | - | - |
| Entrust | 2001 | - | - | 2 | - | - |
| European Christian Mission International—USA | | - | - | 13 | - | - |
| Global Outreach Mission, Inc. | | - | - | 1 | - | - |
| Global Partners / Wesleyan World Missions | | - | 4 | - | - | - |
| Go Ye Fellowship | | - | - | 1 | - | 1 |
| Gospel Fellowship Association | 1997 | 1 | - | 7 | - | - |
| Greater Europe Mission | 1964 | - | 3 | 15 | - | - |
| Greater Grace World Outreach | 1984 | - | - | 2 | 2 | 1 |
| International Teams, U.S.A. | 1978 | - | - | 28 | 4 | 4 |
| Mission to the World (PCA), Inc. | 1991 | - | 2 | - | - | - |
| Precept Ministries International | 1992 | - | - | 1 | 1 | - |
| TCM International Institute | 1957 | 6 | 2 | 4 | - | - |
| TEAM (The Evangelical Alliance Mission) | | - | - | 11 | - | - |
| TITUS International | 2005 | - | - | 2 | - | - |
| Trans World Radio, International | | - | - | 9 | 5 | 15 |
| United Pentecostal Ch. Intl., Foreign Missions Div. | 1971 | - | 2 | - | - | 1 |
| Walk Thru the Bible Ministries, Inc. | 2002 | - | - | - | - | - |
| Word of Life Fellowship, Inc.—Intl. Ministries | 1997 | - | - | - | - | 4 |
| World Horizons | 2005 | - | - | 2 | - | - |
| World Venture | 1970 | - | - | 21 | 2 | - |
| Worldwide Tentmakers, Inc. | 2001 | - | - | - | - | - |
| **Totals:** | | 17 | 15 | 177 | 25 | 32 |

## Azerbaijan

| | First Year | 1-2 yrs. | 2-4 yrs. | 4+ yrs. | Citizens | Non-Citizens |
|---|---|---|---|---|---|---|
| Assemblies of God World Missions | 1993 | - | - | 6 | - | - |
| Church of God of Prophecy—Global Outreach | | - | - | - | 1 | - |
| Evangel Bible Translators | 1998 | - | - | 1 | - | - |
| Greater Grace World Outreach | 1991 | - | - | - | 8 | - |
| Intl. Pentecostal Holiness Ch. World Missions Mins. | 2003 | - | - | - | - | - |
| United Pentecostal Ch. Intl., Foreign Msns. Div. | 2004 | - | 1 | - | - | - |
| Walk Thru the Bible Ministries, Inc. | 2002 | - | - | - | - | - |
| **Totals:** | | - | 1 | 7 | 9 | - |

| | Personnel from U.S. | | | | Other Countries | |
|---|---|---|---|---|---|---|
| | First Year | 1-2 yrs. | 2-4 yrs. | 4+ yrs. | Citizens | Non-Citizens |

### Azores
| | | | | | | |
|---|---|---|---|---|---|---|
| Baptist Bible Fellowship International | 1993 | - | - | 2 | - | - |
| Church of the Nazarene, World Mission Dept. | 1984 | - | - | - | - | |
| | Totals: | - | - | 2 | - | - |

### Bahamas, The
| | | | | | | |
|---|---|---|---|---|---|---|
| Am. Baptist Chs. of the U.S.A., Intl. Ministries | 2000 | - | - | 1 | - | 1 |
| Assemblies of God World Missions | 1942 | - | - | 2 | - | - |
| Avant Ministries | 1956 | - | - | 3 | - | 1 |
| Awana Clubs International | 1974 | - | - | - | 2 | - |
| Baptist Bible Fellowship International | 1999 | - | - | 2 | - | - |
| Baptist International Missions, Inc. (BIMI) | | - | - | 5 | - | - |
| Brethren Assemblies | | - | - | 10 | - | - |
| Christ to the Nations | 2001 | - | - | 2 | 2 | - |
| Christian Churches / Churches of Christ | | - | - | 2 | - | - |
| Church of the Nazarene, World Mission Dept. | 1971 | - | - | - | - | - |
| Churches of Christ | 1959 | - | - | 4 | 3 | - |
| Grand Old Gospel Fellowship | | - | - | - | 1 | - |
| Macedonia World Baptist Missions, Inc. | 1985 | - | - | 2 | - | - |
| Natl. Baptist Conv. USA, Inc.—Foreign Msn. Bd. | 1946 | - | - | - | 1 | - |
| Precept Ministries International | 2001 | - | - | - | 2 | - |
| United Pentecostal Ch. Intl., Foreign Missions Div. | | - | - | - | - | 2 |
| Word of Life Fellowship, Inc.—Intl. Ministries | 2001 | - | - | - | - | |
| | Totals: | - | - | 33 | 11 | 4 |

### Bahrain
| | | | | | | |
|---|---|---|---|---|---|---|
| Arab World Ministries | | - | - | 2 | - | - |
| Church of God (Cleveland, TN) World Missions | 1984 | - | - | - | - | 2 |
| Reformed Church in Am., Gen. Synod Council | 1988 | - | - | 5 | - | 2 |
| University of the Family | 1993 | - | - | - | - | 2 |
| Walk Thru the Bible Ministries, Inc. | 2002 | - | - | - | - | - |
| | Totals: | - | - | 7 | - | 6 |

### Bangladesh
| | | | | | | |
|---|---|---|---|---|---|---|
| AMG International | | - | - | - | 16 | - |
| Assemblies of God World Missions | 1949 | 2 | - | 8 | - | - |
| Awana Clubs International | 1984 | - | - | 1 | 4 | 2 |
| Baptist Mid-Missions | 1979 | - | - | - | 2 | - |
| Campus Crusade for Christ, Intl. | 1975 | - | - | - | 398 | - |
| Christian Aid Mission | | - | - | - | 20 | - |
| Christian Churches / Churches of Christ | | - | - | - | 2 | - |
| Christian Reformed World Missions | 2001 | - | 2 | - | - | - |
| Christian Reformed World Relief Committee | 1972 | - | 1 | 1 | 1 | - |
| Church of the Nazarene, World Mission Dept. | 1992 | - | - | - | - | - |
| Churches of Christ | 1970 | - | - | 2 | 1 | - |
| Churches of God, General Conference | 1905 | - | - | - | 330 | - |
| Compassion International, Inc. | 2004 | - | - | - | 9 | - |
| Evangelical Friends Mission | 2005 | - | - | - | - | - |
| Food for the Hungry, Inc. | 1972 | - | - | - | - | - |
| Global Fellowship Inc. | 1998 | - | - | - | 35 | - |

| | | Personnel from U.S. | | | Other Countries | |
|---|---|---|---|---|---|---|
| | First Year | 1-2 yrs. | 2-4 yrs. | 4+ yrs. | Citizens | Non-Citizens |
| Global Outreach Mission, Inc. | | - | - | - | 6 | - |
| Gospel for Asia, Inc. | 1979 | - | - | - | 163 | - |
| Habitat for Humanity International | 1999 | - | 1 | - | - | 1 |
| I. N. Network USA | 1974 | - | - | - | 93 | - |
| International Partnership Ministries, Inc. | 2004 | - | - | - | - | 2 |
| InterServe USA (Intl. Service Fellowship) | 1865 | - | - | 8 | - | - |
| Medical Ambassadors International, Inc. | 1998 | - | - | - | 17 | - |
| Paraclete, Inc. | 2000 | - | - | - | - | - |
| Partners International | 1984 | - | - | - | 2 | - |
| Reformed Church in Am., Gen. Synod Council | 1999 | - | - | 1 | 1 | - |
| Seventh-day Adventists General Conference | 1906 | - | - | - | - | 8 |
| SIM USA | 1958 | 2 | - | 9 | - | - |
| Surfing the Nations | 2004 | - | - | - | 1 | - |
| United Pentecostal Ch. Intl., Foreign Missions Div. | 2004 | - | 2 | - | - | - |
| Walk Thru the Bible Ministries, Inc. | 2000 | - | - | - | 1 | - |
| World Concern | 1978 | - | - | - | 251 | - |
| World Mission Prayer League | 1972 | - | - | 5 | - | 2 |
| World Vision Inc. | 1970 | - | - | - | - | - |
| Totals: | | 4 | 6 | 35 | 1353 | 15 |

## Barbados

| | | | | | | |
|---|---|---|---|---|---|---|
| Baptist International Missions, Inc. (BIMI) | | - | - | 2 | - | - |
| Campus Crusade for Christ, Intl. | | 1 | - | - | - | - |
| Christian Churches / Churches of Christ | | - | - | 6 | - | - |
| Church of God of Prophecy—Global Outreach | | - | - | - | 4 | - |
| Church of the Nazarene, World Mission Dept. | 1926 | - | - | - | - | - |
| Churches of Christ | 1957 | - | - | 1 | - | - |
| Global Outreach International | 2005 | - | - | 2 | - | - |
| Intl. Pentecostal Holiness Ch. World Missions Mins. | | - | - | - | - | - |
| Mission to the World (PCA), Inc. | 2002 | - | - | - | - | - |
| Natl. Baptist Conv. USA, Inc.—Foreign Msn. Bd. | 1975 | - | - | - | 1 | - |
| Totals: | | 1 | - | 11 | 5 | - |

## Belarus

| | | | | | | |
|---|---|---|---|---|---|---|
| Assemblies of God World Missions | 1991 | - | - | 4 | - | - |
| Awana Clubs International | 1999 | - | - | - | 2 | - |
| Baptist International Outreach | 1994 | - | - | 2 | - | - |
| Campus Crusade for Christ, Intl. | 1992 | - | - | 9 | 23 | - |
| Childcare Worldwide | 1991 | - | - | - | - | - |
| Christian Aid Mission | | - | - | - | 17 | - |
| Church of God of Prophecy—Global Outreach | | - | - | - | 2 | 2 |
| Churches of Christ | 1991 | - | - | 3 | - | - |
| Full Gospel Grace Fellowship | 1990 | - | - | - | - | 1 |
| International Teams, U.S.A. | | - | - | - | - | 2 |
| Ministry to Educate and Equip Intl. (MTEE) | 1998 | - | - | - | 1 | - |
| Peter Deyneka Russian Ministries | | - | - | - | - | - |
| Rosedale Mennonite Missions | 2004 | 1 | - | 2 | - | 3 |
| TCM International Institute | | - | - | - | 1 | - |
| United Pentecostal Ch. Intl., Foreign Missions Div. | 1990 | - | 2 | - | - | - |
| Village Ministries International | 1993 | - | - | - | 4 | - |

| | Personnel from U.S. | | | Other Countries | |
| --- | --- | --- | --- | --- | --- |
| | First Year | 1-2 yrs. | 2-4 yrs. | 4+ yrs. | Citizens | Non-Citizens |
| Walk Thru the Bible Ministries, Inc. | 2000 | - | - | - | 4 | - |
| Totals: | | 1 | 2 | 20 | 54 | 8 |

## Belgium

| | | | | | | |
| --- | --- | --- | --- | --- | --- | --- |
| Am. Baptist Chs. of the U.S.A., Intl. Ministries | 1861 | - | - | 2 | - | - |
| Armenian Missionary Assoc. of America, Inc. | 1988 | - | - | - | - | - |
| Assemblies of God World Missions | 1969 | 10 | - | 20 | - | - |
| Avant Ministries | 1966 | - | - | 3 | 1 | - |
| Baptist Bible Fellowship International | 1962 | - | - | 8 | - | - |
| Bibles & Literature in French | 1958 | - | - | 2 | - | - |
| Brethren Assemblies | | - | - | 2 | - | - |
| Campus Crusade for Christ, Intl. | 2001 | - | - | - | - | 2 |
| Child Evangelism Fellowship, Inc. | 1955 | - | - | 2 | 3 | - |
| Christian Associates International | | - | - | - | - | - |
| Christian Churches / Churches of Christ | | - | - | 1 | - | - |
| Church of God (Cleveland, TN) World Missions | 1973 | - | - | 5 | - | - |
| Church of God of Prophecy—Global Outreach | | - | - | - | 1 | - |
| Churches of Christ | 1947 | - | - | 6 | - | - |
| Development Associates International (DAI) | 2001 | - | - | - | 2 | - |
| EFCA International Mission | 1977 | 2 | - | 12 | - | - |
| Evangelical Baptist Missions | | - | - | 2 | - | - |
| Evangelism Explosion International | | - | - | - | - | 2 |
| Fellowship International Mission | 1991 | - | - | - | - | 1 |
| Free Methodist World Missions | | - | - | 2 | - | - |
| Greater Europe Mission | 1972 | - | - | 6 | - | - |
| International Outreach Ministries (IOM) | 1986 | - | - | 6 | - | - |
| Intl. Pentecostal Holiness Ch. World Missions Mins. | 1999 | - | - | 6 | - | - |
| International Teams, U.S.A. | | - | - | - | - | 2 |
| Mennonite Mission Network | 1950 | - | - | - | - | - |
| Mission to the World (PCA), Inc. | 2001 | - | 6 | - | - | - |
| Operation Mobilization | 1961 | - | - | 5 | - | 3 |
| United Pentecostal Ch. Intl., Foreign Missions Div. | | - | 2 | - | - | - |
| World Venture | 1990 | - | - | 6 | - | - |
| Youth for Christ/USA—World Outreach | | - | - | 1 | - | - |
| Totals: | | 12 | 8 | 97 | 7 | 10 |

## Belize

| | | | | | | |
| --- | --- | --- | --- | --- | --- | --- |
| Amazon Focus | 1995 | - | - | - | 1 | - |
| Assemblies of God World Missions | 1950 | 8 | - | 10 | - | - |
| Avant Ministries | 1955 | 2 | - | - | 2 | 4 |
| Baptist Bible Fellowship International | 1979 | - | - | 4 | - | - |
| Baptist General Conference—Intl. Ministries | | 1 | - | 2 | - | - |
| Baptist International Outreach | | - | - | 2 | - | - |
| BCM International | | - | - | - | 1 | - |
| Brethren Assemblies | | - | - | 1 | - | - |
| Calvary Commission, Inc. | 1984 | - | - | 6 | - | - |
| Centers for Apologetics Research (CFAR), the | | - | 1 | - | - | - |
| Child Evangelism Fellowship, Inc. | 1997 | - | - | 2 | - | - |
| Ch. of God (Anderson, Ind.), Global Missions | 1998 | - | - | - | - | 2 |
| Church of God of Prophecy—Global Outreach | | - | - | - | 3 | 2 |

| | Personnel from U.S. | | | | Other Countries | |
|---|---|---|---|---|---|---|
| | First Year | 1-2 yrs. | 2-4 yrs. | 4+ yrs. | Citizens | Non-Citizens |
| Church of the Nazarene, World Mission Dept. | 1934 | - | - | - | - | - |
| Churches of Christ | | - | - | 4 | 2 | - |
| Cong. Methodist Ch., Div. of Msn. Mins. | 2002 | - | - | 2 | - | - |
| Equip, Inc. | 1999 | - | - | 2 | 2 | - |
| Friends United Meeting—Global Ministries | | - | - | 2 | - | - |
| Full Gospel Grace Fellowship | 1989 | - | - | - | - | 2 |
| Global Outreach International | 1991 | - | - | 11 | - | - |
| Global Outreach Mission, Inc. | | - | - | 4 | - | - |
| Hope for the Hungry | | - | - | 1 | - | 1 |
| Intl. Pentecostal Holiness Ch. World Missions Mins. | 2000 | - | - | 2 | - | - |
| Medical Ambassadors International, Inc. | 2003 | - | - | - | - | - |
| Mission to the Americas | 1960 | - | - | 2 | 2 | - |
| Mission to the World (PCA), Inc. | 1996 | 8 | 9 | - | - | - |
| Missionary Ventures International | | - | - | 2 | - | - |
| Pentecostal Ch. of God—World Missions Dept. | | - | - | 2 | - | - |
| Pioneers USA | 1986 | - | - | 2 | - | - |
| Rock the World Youth Mission Alliance | | - | - | - | - | - |
| Salvation Army, U.S.A. | | - | - | 1 | - | - |
| Shield of Faith Mission International | 1983 | - | 1 | - | - | - |
| STEM (Short-Term Evangelical Missions) Intl. | 1998 | - | - | - | - | - |
| Teen Missions International, Inc. | | - | - | 2 | - | - |
| TMA Ministries | 1995 | - | - | - | - | - |
| United Pentecostal Ch. Intl., Foreign Missions Div. | 1984 | - | 3 | - | - | 3 |
| **Totals:** | | 19 | 14 | 66 | 13 | 14 |
| **Benin** | | | | | | |
| Agape Gospel Mission | | - | - | - | 4 | - |
| Assemblies of God World Missions | 1937 | - | - | 4 | - | - |
| Awana Clubs International | 1995 | - | - | - | 2 | - |
| Campus Crusade for Christ, Intl. | 1988 | - | - | - | 19 | - |
| Child Evangelism Fellowship, Inc. | 1987 | - | - | - | 2 | - |
| Christian Aid Mission | | - | - | - | 41 | - |
| Church of God of Prophecy—Global Outreach | | - | - | - | 4 | - |
| Church of the Nazarene, World Mission Dept. | 1998 | - | - | 6 | - | - |
| Churches of Christ | 1988 | - | - | 6 | - | - |
| Evangel Bible Translators | 1989 | - | - | - | 1 | - |
| Evangelical Baptist Missions | | - | - | 4 | - | - |
| Greater Grace World Outreach | 2003 | - | - | - | 4 | - |
| Intl. Pentecostal Holiness Ch. World Missions Mins. | | - | - | - | - | - |
| Literacy & Evangelism International | 2005 | - | - | - | 2 | - |
| Mennonite Mission Network | 1986 | - | - | 3 | - | 1 |
| SIM USA | 1946 | - | - | 11 | - | - |
| United Pentecostal Ch. Intl., Foreign Missions Div. | 1988 | - | 2 | - | - | 4 |
| **Totals:** | | - | 2 | 34 | 79 | 5 |
| **Bermuda** | | | | | | |
| Church of God of Prophecy—Global Outreach | | - | - | - | 1 | - |
| Word of Life Fellowship, Inc.—Intl.I Ministries | 1986 | - | - | - | 7 | - |
| **Totals:** | | - | - | - | 8 | - |

| | First Year | Personnel from U.S. | | | Other Countries | |
|---|---|---|---|---|---|---|
| | | 1-2 yrs. | 2-4 yrs. | 4+ yrs. | Citizens | Non-Citizens |
| **Bhutan** | | | | - | | |
| Assemblies of God World Missions | 1995 | - | - | - | - | - |
| Gospel for Asia, Inc. | 1995 | - | - | - | - | - |
| International Partnership Ministries, Inc. | 2000 | - | - | - | - | 2 |
| International Teams, U.S.A. | | - | - | - | - | 2 |
| New Directions International, Inc. | 1998 | - | - | - | 9 | - |
| New Life Advance International | | - | - | - | 4 | - |
| United Pentecostal Ch. Intl., Foreign Missions Div. | 2004 | - | 1 | - | - | - |
| Walk Thru the Bible Ministries, Inc. | 2002 | - | - | - | 1 | - |
| Totals: | | - | 1 | - | 14 | 4 |
| **Bolivia** | | | | | | |
| Amazon Focus | 1995 | - | - | - | 3 | - |
| Am. Baptist Chs. of the U.S.A., Intl. Ministries | 1986 | - | - | 2 | - | - |
| Apostolic Team Ministries, Intl. | | - | - | 2 | - | - |
| Assemblies of God World Missions | 1946 | 4 | - | 12 | - | - |
| Avant Ministries | 1928 | - | - | 21 | - | 11 |
| Awana Clubs International | 1974 | - | - | - | 5 | - |
| Baptist Bible Fellowship International | 1978 | - | - | 9 | - | - |
| Baptist International Missions, Inc. (BIMI) | | - | - | 10 | - | - |
| BCM International | | - | - | - | 20 | - |
| Bethany International Ministries | 2001 | - | - | 6 | - | - |
| Brethren Assemblies | | - | - | 19 | - | - |
| Campus Crusade for Christ, Intl. | 1965 | - | - | 4 | 16 | - |
| Child Evangelism Fellowship, Inc. | 1943 | - | - | - | 1 | - |
| Christ for the City International | 2005 | - | - | - | - | 2 |
| Christian Aid Mission | | - | - | - | 15 | - |
| Christ's Mandate for Missions | 1985 | - | - | - | 6 | - |
| Ch. of God (Anderson, Ind.), Global Missions | 1974 | - | - | 3 | - | 1 |
| Ch. of God (Holiness), World Mission Dept., Inc. | 1945 | - | - | - | - | - |
| Church of God of Prophecy—Global Outreach | | - | - | - | 2 | - |
| Church of the Nazarene, World Mission Dept. | 1945 | - | - | 2 | - | - |
| Compassion International, Inc. | 1975 | - | - | - | 36 | - |
| Cong. Methodist Ch., Division of Msn. Mins. | 2001 | - | - | 1 | - | - |
| Envoy International | 1998 | - | - | - | 1 | - |
| Evangelistic Faith Missions | 1978 | - | - | - | - | 2 |
| Fellowship International Mission | 1998 | - | - | 2 | - | - |
| Food for the Hungry, Inc. | 1978 | - | 12 | 4 | - | - |
| Free Methodist World Missions | | - | - | - | - | - |
| Global Outreach Mission, Inc. | | - | - | 3 | 4 | - |
| Grace Ministries International | 1954 | - | 2 | - | - | - |
| HCJB Global | | - | - | 1 | - | - |
| Hosanna | 2000 | - | - | - | 2 | - |
| International Partnership Ministries, Inc. | 2001 | - | - | - | 1 | 1 |
| Intl. Pentecostal Holiness Ch. World Missions Mins. | | - | - | - | - | - |
| International Teams, U.S.A. | | 4 | 2 | 3 | - | 3 |
| LeaderTreks | 2003 | 15 | - | - | - | - |
| Literacy & Evangelism International | | - | - | - | - | - |
| LOGOI Ministries | 1972 | - | - | - | 1 | - |
| Luke Society, Inc., The | 2004 | - | - | - | - | - |

| | Personnel from U.S. | | | | Other Countries | |
|---|---|---|---|---|---|---|
| | First Year | 1-2 yrs. | 2-4 yrs. | 4+ yrs. | Citizens | Non-Citizens |
| Macedonia World Baptist Missions, Inc. | 2004 | - | - | 2 | - | - |
| MAP International | 1989 | - | - | - | 36 | 2 |
| Mennonite Mission Network | 1971 | - | - | 1 | - | - |
| Ministries In Action | 2004 | - | - | - | - | - |
| Missionary Ventures International | 2002 | - | - | 4 | - | - |
| Network of International Christian Schools | 2002 | - | 4 | 2 | - | - |
| New Tribes Mission | 1942 | 8 | - | 97 | - | - |
| Palm Missionary Ministries | 2004 | 1 | - | - | 1 | 2 |
| Pentecostal Ch. of God—World Missions Dept. | | - | - | 2 | - | - |
| Pioneers USA | 1984 | 2 | - | 13 | - | - |
| Precept Ministries International | 1993 | - | - | - | 1 | - |
| Ripe for Harvest, Inc. | 1990 | - | - | 2 | - | - |
| Servants in Faith & Technology (SIFAT) | 1982 | - | - | 1 | 23 | 1 |
| Seventh-day Adventists General Conference | 1907 | - | - | - | - | 4 |
| SIM USA | 1907 | 6 | - | 47 | - | - |
| Source of Light Ministries International, Inc. | 1993 | - | - | - | 2 | - |
| South America Mission, Inc. | 1922 | - | 6 | 29 | 4 | - |
| South American Missionary Society (USA) | 1996 | 2 | - | 4 | - | - |
| Spanish World Ministries | | - | - | 1 | 1 | - |
| United Pentecostal Ch. Intl., Foreign Missions Div. | 1974 | - | 4 | - | - | 4 |
| Walk Thru the Bible Ministries, Inc. | 2001 | - | - | - | - | - |
| Word of Life Fellowship, Inc.—Intl. Ministries | 1990 | - | - | - | 15 | 10 |
| World Concern | 1997 | 3 | 1 | 1 | 25 | 1 |
| World Gospel Mission | 1944 | - | 1 | 37 | - | - |
| World Indigenous Missions | 1993 | - | - | 5 | 2 | - |
| World Mission Prayer League | 1939 | - | - | 8 | - | - |
| World Venture | | - | - | 2 | - | - |
| World-Wide Missions | 1962 | - | - | - | 1 | - |
| Youth for Christ/USA—World Outreach | | - | - | 3 | - | - |
| Totals: | | 45 | 32 | 365 | 224 | 44 |

### Bosnia and Herzegovina

| | First Year | 1-2 yrs. | 2-4 yrs. | 4+ yrs. | Citizens | Non-Citizens |
|---|---|---|---|---|---|---|
| Assemblies of God World Missions | 1992 | 1 | - | 2 | - | - |
| Campus Crusade for Christ, Intl. | 1994 | 5 | - | - | 1 | 2 |
| Christian Churches / Churches of Christ | | | 1 | 2 | - | - |
| Churches of Christ | | - | - | 2 | - | - |
| CrossWorld | 1996 | 2 | - | 6 | - | - |
| EFCA International Mission | 1997 | - | - | 6 | - | - |
| Elim Fellowship—International Department | 1987 | - | - | 1 | - | - |
| European Christian Mission International—USA | | - | - | 4 | - | - |
| International Teams, U.S.A. | | - | - | 3 | - | 2 |
| Medical Ambassadors International, Inc. | 2004 | - | - | - | - | - |
| Pioneers USA | 1992 | 3 | - | 23 | - | - |
| United Pentecostal Ch. Intl., Foreign Missions Div. | | - | 1 | - | - | - |
| Totals: | | 11 | 2 | 49 | 1 | 4 |

### Botswana

| | First Year | 1-2 yrs. | 2-4 yrs. | 4+ yrs. | Citizens | Non-Citizens |
|---|---|---|---|---|---|---|
| Africa Inter-Mennonite Mission | 1975 | 2 | - | 3 | - | 4 |
| Assemblies of God World Missions | 1963 | - | - | 8 | - | - |
| Baptist Bible Fellowship International | 2001 | - | - | 2 | - | - |

| | First Year | Personnel from U.S. | | | Other Countries | |
| --- | --- | --- | --- | --- | --- | --- |
| | | 1-2 yrs. | 2-4 yrs. | 4+ yrs. | Citizens | Non-Citizens |
| Baptist International Outreach | 1996 | - | - | 4 | - | - |
| Baptist Mid-Missions | 1999 | - | - | 2 | - | - |
| Campus Crusade for Christ, Intl. | 1993 | - | - | - | 7 | 4 |
| Child Evangelism Fellowship, Inc. | 1996 | - | - | 1 | - | - |
| Church of God of Prophecy—Global Outreach | | - | - | - | 3 | 2 |
| Church of the Nazarene, World Mission Dept. | 1984 | - | - | 1 | - | - |
| Churches of Christ | 1974 | - | - | 2 | 1 | - |
| Gospel Fellowship Association | 2002 | | - | 2 | - | - |
| Habitat for Humanity International | 1992 | 1 | | - | | 1 |
| Intl. Pentecostal Holiness Ch. World Missions Mins. | | | - | - | - | - |
| Lutheran Bible Translators, Inc. | 1993 | | - | 6 | 7 | - |
| Mennonite Mission Network | 1975 | | - | 2 | - | 2 |
| Seventh-day Adventists General Conference | 1921 | - | - | 2 | - | 10 |
| SIM USA | 1973 | 2 | - | 5 | - | - |
| United Church of Christ—Wider Church Mins. | | - | 2 | - | - | - |
| United Pentecostal Ch. Intl., Foreign Missions Div. | 1980 | - | 2 | - | - | 2 |
| Walk Thru the Bible Ministries, Inc. | 1999 | - | - | - | 2 | - |
| | Totals: | 4 | 5 | 40 | 20 | 25 |

## Brazil

| | First Year | 1-2 yrs. | 2-4 yrs. | 4+ yrs. | Citizens | Non-Citizens |
| --- | --- | --- | --- | --- | --- | --- |
| Abundant Life Association, Inc. | 1995 | - | - | - | 4 | - |
| ABWE (Assoc. of Baptists for World Evangelism) | 1939 | - | 23 | 60 | - | - |
| ACMC, Inc. | 2001 | - | - | 1 | - | - |
| Action International Ministries | 1991 | 1 | - | 7 | 6 | 5 |
| Am. Baptist Chs. of the U.S.A., Intl. Ministries | 1999 | - | - | 4 | - | - |
| American Leprosy Missions, Inc. | 1935 | - | - | 1 | - | - |
| AMG International | | - | - | - | 1 | - |
| Apostolic Christian Church Foundation, Inc. | 1961 | - | - | 17 | 3 | 2 |
| Apostolic Team Ministries, Intl. | | - | - | 2 | - | - |
| Armenian Missionary Assoc. of America, Inc. | 1956 | - | - | - | - | - |
| Artists In Christian Testimony | 2001 | - | - | 4 | 1 | - |
| Assemblies of God World Missions | 1910 | 2 | - | 13 | - | - |
| Association of Free Lutheran Congregations | 1969 | - | - | 5 | 12 | - |
| Avant Ministries | 1911 | - | - | 17 | 2 | 2 |
| Awana Clubs International | 1975 | - | - | - | 10 | - |
| Back to the Bible International | 2000 | - | - | - | 3 | - |
| Baptist Bible Fellowship International | 1952 | - | - | 38 | - | - |
| Baptist General Conference—Intl. Ministries | 1955 | - | - | 13 | - | - |
| Baptist International Missions, Inc. (BIMI) | | - | - | 48 | - | - |
| Baptist International Outreach | 1993 | - | - | 7 | - | - |
| Baptist Mid-Missions | 1935 | - | - | 139 | 1 | - |
| BCM International | | - | - | - | 10 | - |
| Bethany International Ministries | 1963 | - | - | 15 | - | - |
| Brazil Gospel Fellowship Mission | 1939 | 2 | 3 | 45 | - | - |
| Brethren Assemblies | | - | - | 9 | - | - |
| Calvary International | | 2 | - | - | - | - |
| Campus Crusade for Christ, Intl. | 1968 | 15 | - | 9 | 120 | - |
| Centers for Apologetics Research (CFAR), the | 1997 | - | - | - | 1 | - |
| Child Evangelism Fellowship, Inc. | 1941 | - | - | - | - | 2 |
| Christian Broadcasting Network Inc., the | 2004 | - | - | - | 4 | - |

| | First Year | Personnel from U.S. | | | Other Countries | |
|---|---|---|---|---|---|---|
| | | 1-2 yrs. | 2-4 yrs. | 4+ yrs. | Citizens | Non-Citizens |
| Christian Churches / Churches of Christ | | 1 | 4 | 28 | 6 | - |
| Christian Ministries International (CMI) | 1985 | - | - | 2 | 10 | 2 |
| Christian Missions Unlimited | 1973 | - | - | - | - | - |
| Christians In Action Missions International | 1960 | - | - | 2 | - | - |
| Ch. of God (Anderson, Ind.), Global Missions | 1923 | - | - | 5 | - | - |
| Church of God (Cleveland, TN) World Missions | 1951 | - | - | 4 | - | - |
| Church of God of Prophecy—Global Outreach | | - | - | - | 5 | - |
| Church of the Nazarene, World Mission Dept. | 1958 | - | - | 6 | - | 4 |
| Churches of Christ | 1927 | - | - | 103 | 25 | - |
| Churches of God, General Conference | 1994 | - | - | 4 | 10 | - |
| CMF International | 1957 | - | 2 | - | - | - |
| Compassion International, Inc. | 1974 | - | - | - | 26 | - |
| Cook Communications Ministries International | 1995 | - | - | - | - | - |
| Crossover Communications International | 1996 | - | - | 4 | 1 | - |
| CrossWorld | 1931 | 1 | - | 58 | - | - |
| EFCA International Mission | 1986 | - | 1 | 5 | - | - |
| Elim Fellowship—International Department | | - | - | 2 | - | - |
| Emmanuel International Mission | 1980 | - | - | - | 2 | 2 |
| Equip, Inc. | 1995 | - | - | 5 | - | - |
| Evangelical Baptist Missions | | - | - | 5 | 1 | - |
| Evangelical Luth. Ch. in Am., Div. for Global Msn. | 1958 | - | - | 2 | - | - |
| Fellowship International Mission | 1983 | - | - | 13 | 2 | - |
| Food for the Hungry, Inc. | 1997 | - | 2 | - | - | - |
| Foursquare Missions International | 1946 | - | - | 2 | - | - |
| Free Methodist World Missions | 1928 | - | - | 2 | - | - |
| Free Will Baptist, Inc. Board of Intl. Missions | 1958 | - | 1 | 16 | - | - |
| Global Outreach International | 2000 | - | - | 3 | - | - |
| Global Outreach Mission, Inc. | 1973 | - | - | 6 | - | - |
| Global Partners / Wesleyan World Missions | 1958 | - | 2 | - | - | - |
| Global Recordings Network | 1970 | - | - | 1 | 2 | - |
| Go Ye Fellowship | 1962 | - | - | 5 | 1 | - |
| Gospel Fellowship Association | 1965 | - | - | 4 | - | - |
| Grace Brethren International Missions | 1949 | - | - | 6 | - | - |
| Greater Grace World Outreach | 2002 | - | - | - | 2 | - |
| Habitat for Humanity International | 1987 | - | 1 | - | - | 1 |
| Harvest | 2000 | - | - | - | 4 | - |
| International Gospel Outreach | 2001 | - | - | 2 | - | - |
| International Institute for Christian Studies | 2003 | - | - | 3 | - | - |
| Intl. Pentecostal Ch. of Christ—Global Msns. Dept. | 1938 | - | - | 5 | 5 | - |
| Intl. Pentecostal Holiness Ch. World Missions Mins. | | - | - | - | - | - |
| Intl. Street Kids Outreach Ministries (ISKOM) | 1992 | - | - | 2 | 47 | - |
| International Teams, U.S.A. | | - | - | - | - | 1 |
| Janz Team Ministries USA | 1970 | - | - | - | 2 | - |
| Jews for Jesus | 2002 | - | - | - | 2 | - |
| Josue Yrion World Evangelism and Missions, Inc. | 1993 | - | - | - | 2 | 1 |
| Latin America Mission | 1973 | - | - | 6 | 3 | 3 |
| Latin American Indian Ministries | 1995 | - | - | - | - | - |
| Literacy & Evangelism International | 2003 | - | - | - | 1 | - |
| Macedonia World Baptist Missions, Inc. | 1975 | - | - | 16 | - | - |
| Medical Ambassadors International, Inc. | 1999 | - | - | - | 3 | - |

| | First Year | Personnel from U.S. 1-2 yrs. | 2-4 yrs. | 4+ yrs. | Other Countries Citizens | Non-Citizens |
|---|---|---|---|---|---|---|
| Mennonite Mission Network | 1954 | - | - | - | - | - |
| Ministries In Action | 2002 | - | - | - | - | - |
| Mission Aviation Fellowship | 1957 | - | 1 | 3 | - | - |
| Mission to the World (PCA), Inc. | 1993 | - | 3 | - | - | - |
| Missionary Revival Crusade | | - | - | 1 | 1 | - |
| Navigators, U.S. International Missions Group | | - | - | 10 | - | - |
| Network of International Christian Schools | 1958 | 2 | 22 | 6 | - | 2 |
| New Life Advance International | 1984 | - | - | 1 | - | - |
| New Mission Systems International | | - | - | - | - | - |
| New Tribes Mission | 1946 | 5 | - | 160 | 300 | - |
| N. American Baptist Conf.—Worldwide Outreach | 1966 | - | - | 1 | 1 | 5 |
| OC International, Inc. | 1963 | - | - | 13 | - | - |
| OMS International, Inc. | 1950 | - | - | 6 | - | 1 |
| Open Air Campaigners—Overseas Ministries | 1991 | - | - | 2 | 2 | - |
| Pioneers USA | | - | - | 2 | 1 | - |
| Precept Ministries International | 2000 | - | - | - | 6 | - |
| Presbyterian Mission International (PMI) | 2002 | - | - | - | 1 | - |
| Project AmaZon | 1976 | - | - | 29 | 2 | - |
| Reformed Episcopal Board of Foreign Missions | | - | - | 1 | 2 | - |
| Remnant Ministries, Inc. | 1956 | - | - | 1 | - | - |
| Ripe for Harvest, Inc. | 1998 | - | - | 1 | - | - |
| Seed International | 1995 | - | - | 2 | - | - |
| Seventh-day Adventists General Conference | 1894 | - | - | - | - | 2 |
| Source of Light Ministries International, Inc. | 1982 | - | - | - | - | - |
| South America Mission, Inc. | 1913 | - | - | 19 | 3 | - |
| Sowers International, The | 2000 | - | - | 1 | 1 | - |
| TEAM (The Evangelical Alliance Mission) | | - | - | 6 | - | - |
| Teen Missions International, Inc. | 1985 | - | - | - | 8 | 1 |
| Tentmakers International | | - | - | - | - | - |
| Things To Come Mission, Inc. | 1956 | - | - | 2 | 25 | - |
| United Church of Christ—Wider Church Mins. | | - | 1 | - | - | - |
| United Pentecostal Ch. Intl., Foreign Missions Div. | 1956 | - | 12 | - | - | 1 |
| Walk Thru the Bible Ministries, Inc. | 2003 | - | - | - | 2 | - |
| WEC International | 1957 | - | - | 4 | - | - |
| White Fields Inc. | | - | - | - | 10 | - |
| Wisc. Evangelical Luth. Synod, Bd. for Wld. Msns. | 1985 | - | - | 3 | - | - |
| Word of Life Fellowship, Inc.—Intl. Ministries | 1958 | - | - | 25 | 145 | - |
| World Baptist Fellowship Mission Agency, Inc. | | - | - | 26 | 2 | - |
| World Horizons | 1991 | - | - | 2 | 1 | - |
| World Partners USA | 1955 | - | - | 2 | - | - |
| World Servants, Inc. | 2005 | - | - | - | - | - |
| World Team | 1957 | - | - | 6 | - | - |
| World Venture | 1946 | 2 | - | 20 | 2 | - |
| World-Wide Missions | 1965 | - | - | 7 | - | - |
| Youth for Christ/USA—World Outreach | 1950 | - | - | 2 | - | - |
| Totals: | | 33 | 78 | 1145 | 855 | 37 |

## British Virgin Islands

| | First Year | | | | | |
|---|---|---|---|---|---|---|
| Mission to the World (PCA), Inc. | 1991 | - | - | - | - | - |
| Totals: | | - | - | - | - | - |

| | First Year | Personnel from U.S. 1-2 yrs. | 2-4 yrs. | 4+ yrs. | Other Countries Citizens | Non-Citizens |
|---|---|---|---|---|---|---|

### Bulgaria

| | First Year | 1-2 yrs. | 2-4 yrs. | 4+ yrs. | Citizens | Non-Citizens |
|---|---|---|---|---|---|---|
| Am. Baptist Chs. of the U.S.A., Intl. Ministries | 2001 | - | - | 3 | - | - |
| AMG International | | - | - | - | 8 | - |
| Armenian Missionary Assoc. of America, Inc. | 1950 | - | - | - | - | - |
| Assemblies of God World Missions | 1926 | 2 | - | 4 | - | - |
| Baptist Bible Fellowship International | 1995 | - | - | 2 | - | - |
| Campus Crusade for Christ, Intl. | 1991 | - | - | 4 | 42 | - |
| Christian Aid Mission | | - | - | - | 17 | - |
| Ch. of God (Anderson, Ind.), Global Missions | 1940 | - | - | 2 | - | - |
| Church of God (Cleveland, TN) World Missions | 1982 | - | - | 1 | - | 1 |
| Church of God of Prophecy—Global Outreach | | - | - | - | 4 | - |
| Church of the Nazarene, World Mission Dept. | 1994 | - | - | 2 | - | - |
| Churches of Christ | 1990 | - | - | 3 | 2 | - |
| Entrust | 2003 | - | - | - | 2 | - |
| Envoy International | | - | - | - | - | - |
| Greater Grace World Outreach | 2004 | 1 | 2 | - | - | - |
| International Gospel Outreach | 1997 | - | - | 1 | - | - |
| International Teams, U.S.A. | | - | - | 3 | - | 5 |
| Macedonia World Baptist Missions, Inc. | 2001 | - | - | 2 | - | - |
| Ministry to Educate and Equip Intl. (MTEE) | 1995 | - | 1 | - | 4 | - |
| Mission Possible Foundation, Inc. | 1991 | - | - | - | 8 | - |
| Mission to the World (PCA), Inc. | 1994 | 5 | 10 | - | - | - |
| Missionary Revival Crusade | | - | - | - | - | - |
| Navigators, U.S. International Missions Group | | - | - | 6 | - | - |
| New Mission Systems International | 2002 | - | - | 1 | - | - |
| OC International, Inc. | | - | - | 4 | - | - |
| Precept Ministries International | 1991 | - | - | - | 1 | - |
| Presbyterian Evangelistic Fellowship | | - | - | 2 | 8 | - |
| SEND International USA | 1992 | - | - | 19 | - | 1 |
| TCM International Institute | | - | - | - | 1 | - |
| United Pentecostal Ch. Intl., Foreign Missions Div. | 1991 | - | 1 | - | - | - |
| Walk Thru the Bible Ministries, Inc. | 2003 | - | - | - | - | - |
| Wisc. Evangelical Luth. Synod, Bd. for Wld. Msns. | 1992 | - | - | 1 | - | - |
| Word of Life Fellowship, Inc.—Intl. Ministries | 2002 | - | - | - | - | 4 |
| World Bible Translation Center | | - | - | - | 2 | - |
| World Partners USA | 2003 | - | - | 2 | - | - |
| | Totals: | 8 | 14 | 62 | 99 | 11 |

### Burkina Faso

| | First Year | 1-2 yrs. | 2-4 yrs. | 4+ yrs. | Citizens | Non-Citizens |
|---|---|---|---|---|---|---|
| Africa Inter-Mennonite Mission | 1978 | - | - | 4 | - | 6 |
| Assemblies of God World Missions | 1919 | - | - | 7 | - | - |
| Baptist Bible Fellowship International | 1994 | - | - | 8 | - | - |
| Calvary International | | - | 2 | 8 | - | - |
| Campus Crusade for Christ, Intl. | 1991 | - | - | 2 | 17 | - |
| Child Evangelism Fellowship, Inc. | 1982 | - | - | - | 2 | - |
| Church of God of Prophecy—Global Outreach | | - | - | - | 2 | - |
| Church of the Nazarene, World Mission Dept. | 1997 | - | - | - | - | - |
| Churches of Christ | 1986 | - | - | 6 | - | - |
| Compassion International, Inc. | 2004 | - | - | - | 9 | 1 |
| Greater Grace World Outreach | 2001 | - | - | - | 28 | - |

| | First Year | Personnel from U.S. | | | Other Countries | |
|---|---|---|---|---|---|---|
| | | 1-2 yrs. | 2-4 yrs. | 4+ yrs. | Citizens | Non-Citizens |
| Macedonia World Baptist Missions, Inc. | 2005 | - | - | 2 | - | - |
| Mennonite Mission Network | 1977 | - | - | - | - | - |
| Seventh-day Adventists General Conference | 1972 | - | - | - | - | 4 |
| SIM USA | 1930 | 1 | - | 9 | - | - |
| United Pentecostal Ch. Intl., Foreign Missions Div. | 1994 | - | 2 | - | - | - |
| Women to the World | 2004 | - | - | - | - | - |
| World Concern | 2003 | 4 | - | - | - | - |
| World Outreach International—US | 2002 | - | - | 1 | - | - |
| World Relief | 1982 | 4 | | - | 6 | - |
| | Totals: | 9 | 4 | 47 | 64 | 11 |

## Burundi

| | First Year | 1-2 yrs. | 2-4 yrs. | 4+ yrs. | Citizens | Non-Citizens |
|---|---|---|---|---|---|---|
| Assemblies of God World Missions | 2002 | - | - | 4 | - | - |
| Brethren Assemblies | | - | - | 2 | - | - |
| Campus Crusade for Christ, Intl. | 1980 | - | - | - | 22 | - |
| Child Evangelism Fellowship, Inc. | 1952 | - | - | - | 1 | - |
| Church of the Nazarene, World Mission Dept. | 1999 | - | - | - | - | - |
| Free Methodist World Missions | 1935 | - | - | 0 | - | - |
| Greater Grace World Outreach | 2005 | - | - | - | 3 | - |
| Intl. Pentecostal Holiness Ch. Wld. Msns. Mins. | | - | - | - | - | - |
| Literacy & Evangelism International | 2006 | - | - | - | 2 | - |
| United Pentecostal Ch. Intl., Foreign Missions Div. | | - | 4 | - | - | - |
| World Gospel Mission | | - | - | - | - | - |
| World Relief | 1994 | - | - | 4 | 8 | - |
| | Totals: | - | 4 | 10 | 36 | - |

## Cambodia

| | First Year | 1-2 yrs. | 2-4 yrs. | 4+ yrs. | Citizens | Non-Citizens |
|---|---|---|---|---|---|---|
| Action International Ministries | 2003 | - | 1 | 5 | - | - |
| Am. Baptist Chs. of the U.S.A., Intl. Ministries | 1996 | - | - | - | - | - |
| Asian Access | 2003 | - | - | - | - | - |
| Asian Outreach U.S.A. | | - | - | - | - | - |
| Assemblies of God World Missions | 1990 | 12 | - | 18 | - | - |
| Baptist Bible Fellowship International | 1997 | - | - | 6 | - | - |
| Baptist General Conference—Intl. Ministries | | - | - | 2 | - | - |
| Baptist International Missions, Inc. (BIMI) | | - | - | 8 | - | - |
| Baptist International Outreach | | - | - | - | - | - |
| Baptist Mid-Missions | 1998 | - | - | 4 | - | - |
| BCM International | | - | - | - | 2 | - |
| Bethany International Ministries | 1999 | - | - | 2 | - | - |
| BILD International | | - | - | - | 3 | - |
| Campus Crusade for Christ, Intl. | 1989 | - | - | 2 | 33 | - |
| Christian Aid Mission | | - | - | - | 11 | - |
| Christian Broadcasting Network Inc., the | 2000 | - | - | - | 10 | - |
| Christian Reformed World Relief Committee | 1998 | - | - | - | 1 | 1 |
| Church of the Nazarene, World Mission Dept. | 1992 | - | - | 2 | - | 2 |
| Church Resource Ministries (CRM) | 1995 | 2 | - | 9 | - | 1 |
| Church World Service | | - | - | 1 | 10 | 4 |
| Eastern Mennonite Missions | | - | 2 | 2 | - | - |
| Evangelical Friends Church Southwest | 1995 | 2 | - | - | - | - |
| Far East Broadcasting Company, Inc. | 1993 | - | - | - | 26 | - |

| | First Year | Personnel from U.S. 1-2 yrs. | 2-4 yrs. | 4+ yrs. | Other Countries Citizens | Non-Citizens |
|---|---|---|---|---|---|---|
| Food for the Hungry, Inc. | 1991 | - | 2 | - | - | - |
| Foursquare Missions International | 1995 | - | - | 2 | - | - |
| Free Methodist World Missions | | - | - | 2 | - | - |
| Global Outreach International | 2006 | - | - | 2 | - | - |
| Global Partners / Wesleyan World Missions | 1995 | - | - | - | - | 4 |
| Gospel Fellowship Association | 2000 | 1 | - | 4 | - | - |
| Gospel for Asia, Inc. | | - | - | - | - | - |
| Grace Brethren International Missions | 1998 | - | 2 | 2 | - | 9 |
| International Justice Mission | | 1 | 1 | - | 12 | 1 |
| International Teams, U.S.A. | | - | - | 6 | - | 5 |
| Medical Ambassadors International, Inc. | 1998 | - | - | - | 3 | - |
| Mission to the Americas | 2001 | - | - | 8 | - | - |
| Mission To Unreached Peoples | 1989 | - | - | 16 | 2 | - |
| New Tribes Mission | 2001 | - | - | 2 | - | - |
| Northwest Medical Teams International, Inc. | 1979 | - | - | - | 1 | - |
| OMF International | 1970 | 1 | - | 23 | - | 53 |
| Partners International | 1993 | - | - | - | 112 | - |
| Pioneers USA | | - | - | 6 | - | - |
| Presbyterian Missionary Union | | - | - | 1 | - | - |
| Samaritan's Purse | 2003 | 4 | - | - | 2 | 1 |
| Seed International | 2005 | 1 | - | 1 | - | - |
| Seventh-day Adventists General Conference | 1991 | - | - | 8 | - | 2 |
| Team Expansion, Inc. | | - | - | 2 | - | - |
| Teen Missions International, Inc. | | - | - | 1 | 10 | - |
| Trans World Radio, International | | - | - | 4 | 13 | 2 |
| United Pentecostal Ch. Intl., Foreign Missions Div. | | - | - | - | - | - |
| Walk Thru the Bible Ministries, Inc. | 2002 | - | - | - | - | - |
| WEC International | 1992 | - | - | 2 | - | - |
| World Baptist Fellowship Mission Agency, Inc. | | - | - | 2 | - | - |
| World Concern | 1991 | - | - | - | - | 2 |
| World Horizons | 1993 | - | - | - | - | - |
| World Relief | 1989 | - | - | 2 | 318 | 3 |
| World Team | 1996 | - | - | 30 | - | - |
| | Totals: | 24 | 8 | 187 | 569 | 90 |

## Cameroon

| | First Year | 1-2 yrs. | 2-4 yrs. | 4+ yrs. | Citizens | Non-Citizens |
|---|---|---|---|---|---|---|
| Assemblies of God World Missions | 1976 | 1 | - | 8 | - | - |
| Awana Clubs International | 1992 | - | - | - | - | 2 |
| Baptist General Conference—Intl. Ministries | 1982 | 5 | - | 12 | 1 | - |
| Baptist Mid-Missions | 2006 | - | - | 4 | - | - |
| Campus Crusade for Christ, Intl. | 1992 | - | - | - | 66 | - |
| Child Evangelism Fellowship, Inc. | 1995 | - | - | - | 2 | - |
| Christian Blind Mission International | 1982 | - | 1 | - | - | - |
| Christian Literature International | | - | - | - | - | - |
| Church Missions Link | 2002 | - | - | - | 6 | - |
| Church of God of Prophecy—Global Outreach | | - | - | - | 5 | - |
| Church of the Nazarene, World Mission Dept. | 1999 | - | - | - | - | - |
| Churches of Christ | 1960 | - | 1 | - | 3 | - |
| Commission to Every Nation | 1999 | - | - | 4 | - | - |
| Evangelical Luth. Ch. in Am., Div. for Global Msn. | 1923 | 4 | - | 6 | - | - |

| | First Year | Personnel from U.S. | | | Other Countries | |
|---|---|---|---|---|---|---|
| | | 1-2 yrs. | 2-4 yrs. | 4+ yrs. | Citizens | Non-Citizens |
| Global Outreach International | 2002 | - | - | 2 | - | - |
| Gospel Fellowship Association | 1987 | 3 | - | 18 | - | - |
| Gospel Revival Ministries | 1998 | - | - | - | 1 | - |
| Grace Brethren International Missions | 2003 | 1 | - | 3 | - | - |
| Intl. Pentecostal Holiness Ch. World Missions Mins. | | - | - | - | - | - |
| Lutheran Bible Translators, Inc. | 1980 | - | 2 | - | 9 | - |
| Navigators, U.S. International Missions Group | | - | - | 4 | - | - |
| N. Am. Baptist Conf.—Worldwide Outreach | 1935 | - | - | 11 | - | 8 |
| Seventh-day Adventists General Conference | 1928 | - | - | 2 | - | 5 |
| Teen Missions International, Inc. | 2002 | - | - | 2 | 3 | - |
| United Pentecostal Ch. Intl., Foreign Missions Div. | 1971 | - | 2 | - | - | 2 |
| Walk Thru the Bible Ministries, Inc. | 2002 | - | - | - | - | - |
| Wisc. Evangelical Luth. Synod, Bd. for Wld. Msns. | 1969 | - | - | - | - | - |
| World Team | 1985 | - | 1 | 17 | - | - |
| Totals: | | 14 | 7 | 93 | 96 | 17 |

**Cape Verde**

| | First Year | 1-2 yrs. | 2-4 yrs. | 4+ yrs. | Citizens | Non-Citizens |
|---|---|---|---|---|---|---|
| Assemblies of God World Missions | 1989 | - | - | - | - | - |
| Church of the Nazarene, World Mission Dept. | 1901 | - | - | - | - | - |
| Totals: | | - | - | - | - | - |

**Caribbean—General**

| | First Year | 1-2 yrs. | 2-4 yrs. | 4+ yrs. | Citizens | Non-Citizens |
|---|---|---|---|---|---|---|
| ABWE (Assoc. of Baptists for World Evangelism) | 1990 | - | 17 | 20 | - | - |
| Assemblies of God World Missions | 1920 | - | - | 2 | - | - |
| Calvary Evangelistic Mission, Inc. | 1953 | 8 | - | 7 | - | - |
| Church of God (Cleveland, TN) World Missions | | - | - | 2 | - | - |
| Church of God of Prophecy—Global Outreach | | - | - | - | 7 | - |
| Final Frontiers Foundation, Inc. | 1989 | - | - | - | 3 | - |
| Global Partners / Wesleyan World Missions | 1904 | - | - | - | - | - |
| Independent Faith Mission, Inc. | | 2 | - | 2 | - | - |
| International Cooperating Ministries | | - | - | - | - | - |
| Southern Baptist Convention Intl. Mission Bd. | | - | - | - | - | - |
| United Pentecostal Ch. Intl., Foreign Missions Div. | 1974 | - | 8 | - | - | - |
| Young Life | | - | 2 | 3 | - | - |
| Totals: | | 10 | 27 | 36 | 10 | - |

**Caucasus**

| | First Year | 1-2 yrs. | 2-4 yrs. | 4+ yrs. | Citizens | Non-Citizens |
|---|---|---|---|---|---|---|
| Operation Mobilization | 1998 | - | 2 | - | - | - |
| People International USA | 2004 | - | - | 1 | - | - |
| Totals: | | - | 2 | 1 | - | - |

**Cayman Islands**

| | First Year | 1-2 yrs. | 2-4 yrs. | 4+ yrs. | Citizens | Non-Citizens |
|---|---|---|---|---|---|---|
| Assemblies of God World Missions | 1992 | - | - | - | - | - |
| Baptist International Missions, Inc. (BIMI) | | - | - | 6 | - | - |
| Christian Churches / Churches of Christ | | - | - | 2 | - | - |
| Ch. of God (Holiness), World Mission Dept., Inc. | 1954 | - | - | - | 2 | - |
| United Pentecostal Ch. Intl., Foreign Missions Div. | | - | - | - | - | - |
| Word of Life Fellowship, Inc.—Intl. Ministries | 2005 | - | - | - | - | - |
| Youth for Christ/USA—World Outreach | | - | - | 1 | - | - |
| Totals: | | - | - | 9 | 2 | - |

|  | First Year | Personnel from U.S. | | | Other Countries | |
|---|---|---|---|---|---|---|
|  |  | 1-2 yrs. | 2-4 yrs. | 4+ yrs. | Citizens | Non-Citizens |

### Central African Republic

| | | | | | | |
|---|---|---|---|---|---|---|
| Africa Inland Mission International | 1924 | - | - | 1 | - | - |
| Assemblies of God World Missions | 1997 | - | - | - | - | - |
| Baptist Mid-Missions | 1920 | - | - | 5 | - | - |
| Campus Crusade for Christ, Intl. | 1987 | - | - | - | 35 | - |
| Church of God of Prophecy—Global Outreach | | - | - | - | 1 | - |
| Churches of Christ | 1990 | - | - | - | 1 | - |
| EFCA International Mission | 1997 | 1 | - | 12 | - | - |
| Evangelical Luth. Ch. in Am., Div. for Global Msn. | 1974 | 1 | - | 1 | - | 1 |
| Grace Brethren International Missions | 1918 | 2 | - | 1 | - | - |
| New Mission Systems International | 2005 | - | 2 | - | - | 2 |
| SIM USA | 1990 | - | - | 1 | - | - |
| United Pentecostal Ch. Intl., Foreign Missions Div. | 2000 | - | 2 | - | - | - |
| Totals: | | 4 | 4 | 21 | 37 | 3 |

### Central Asia—General

| | | | | | | |
|---|---|---|---|---|---|---|
| Assemblies of God World Missions | | 1 | - | 42 | - | - |
| Baptist General Conference—Intl. Ministries | | - | - | 2 | - | - |
| Campus Crusade for Christ, Intl. | | 52 | - | 60 | 383 | 81 |
| Christar | 1992 | - | - | 3 | - | - |
| Christian and Missionary Alliance | | - | - | 5 | - | - |
| Church Leadership Development Intl. | 2005 | - | - | - | 1 | - |
| CLC Ministries International | 1956 | - | - | 2 | - | - |
| Crossover Communications International | 2003 | - | - | 4 | - | - |
| Dawn Ministries, Inc. | | - | - | - | - | 1 |
| Entrust | 1993 | - | - | 4 | - | - |
| Final Frontiers Foundation, Inc. | 2004 | - | - | - | 15 | - |
| Go Ye Fellowship | | - | - | 2 | - | - |
| InterVarsity Christian Fellowship/USA—Msns. Dept. | | - | 2 | 3 | - | - |
| Liebenzell USA | 1995 | - | - | 6 | - | - |
| Lutheran Church-Missouri Synod | | - | - | 2 | - | - |
| Network of International Christian Schools | 2003 | 10 | 15 | 5 | - | 2 |
| Open Bible Churches, International Ministries | | - | - | 1 | - | - |
| Operation Mobilization | 1995 | 7 | 6 | 17 | - | 6 |
| Outreach To Asia Nationals | 1987 | 2 | 4 | - | 4 | - |
| Pioneers USA | | 3 | - | 80 | - | 2 |
| Red Sea Team International | 2004 | 1 | - | - | - | - |
| Shelter for Life International, Inc. | 1994 | 5 | 1 | 1 | 70 | 5 |
| So. Baptist Convention Intl. Mission Board | | - | - | - | - | - |
| TEAM (The Evangelical Alliance Mission) | | - | - | 6 | - | - |
| Team Expansion, Inc. | | 6 | 2 | 3 | - | - |
| United World Mission | | 3 | - | 39 | - | - |
| World Venture | 1993 | - | - | 2 | - | - |
| Totals: | | 90 | 30 | 289 | 473 | 97 |

### Chad

| | | | | | | |
|---|---|---|---|---|---|---|
| Africa Inland Mission International | 1986 | - | - | 4 | - | 12 |
| Assemblies of God World Missions | 1996 | - | - | 2 | - | - |
| Baptist Mid-Missions | 1925 | - | - | 7 | - | - |
| BILD International | | - | - | - | 2 | - |

| | First Year | Personnel from U.S. | | | Other Countries | |
|---|---|---|---|---|---|---|
| | | 1-2 yrs. | 2-4 yrs. | 4+ yrs. | Citizens | Non-Citizens |
| Brethren Assemblies | | - | - | 1 | - | - |
| Campus Crusade for Christ, Intl. | 1996 | - | - | - | 14 | - |
| Child Evangelism Fellowship, Inc. | 1997 | - | - | - | 1 | 1 |
| Church of God of Prophecy—Global Outreach | | - | - | - | 1 | - |
| Gospel Revival Ministries | 1997 | - | - | - | 4 | - |
| Grace Brethren International Missions | 1960 | - | - | 2 | - | 5 |
| International Partnership Ministries, Inc. | 2004 | - | - | - | 2 | - |
| Lutheran Brethren World Missions | 1918 | - | - | 8 | - | - |
| Seventh-day Adventists General Conference | 1870 | - | - | 2 | - | - |
| TEAM (The Evangelical Alliance Mission) | | 2 | - | 18 | - | - |
| WEC International | 1962 | - | - | 5 | - | - |
| Totals: | | 2 | - | 49 | 24 | 18 |

## Chile

| | First Year | 1-2 yrs. | 2-4 yrs. | 4+ yrs. | Citizens | Non-Citizens |
|---|---|---|---|---|---|---|
| Am. Baptist Chs of the U.S.A., Intl. Ministries | 1993 | - | - | 2 | - | 2 |
| Assemblies of God World Missions | 1941 | - | - | 16 | - | - |
| Baptist Bible Fellowship International | 1954 | - | - | 11 | - | - |
| Baptist International Missions, Inc. (BIMI) | | - | - | 2 | - | - |
| Baptist Mid-Missions | 1992 | - | - | 4 | - | - |
| Brethren Assemblies | | - | - | 4 | - | - |
| Campus Crusade for Christ, Intl. | 1963 | - | - | 2 | 4 | 4 |
| Child Evangelism Fellowship, Inc. | 1942 | 1 | - | - | - | - |
| Christian Aid Mission | | - | - | - | 15 | - |
| Christian Churches / Churches of Christ | | - | - | 32 | 4 | - |
| Church of God (Cleveland, TN) World Missions | 1954 | - | - | 3 | - | - |
| Church of God of Prophecy—Global Outreach | | - | - | - | 1 | - |
| Church of the Nazarene, World Mission Dept. | 1962 | - | - | 2 | - | - |
| Churches of Christ | 1958 | - | - | 17 | 4 | - |
| CMF International | 1988 | - | 7 | - | - | - |
| Evangelical Covenant Ch.—Covenant Wld. Msn. | 1994 | - | - | - | - | - |
| Free Methodist World Missions | 1986 | - | - | 2 | - | - |
| Friendship International Ministries, Inc. | 2000 | 5 | - | 1 | 6 | - |
| Global Fellowship Inc. | 2003 | - | - | - | 12 | - |
| Global Outreach International | 2001 | - | - | 1 | - | - |
| Global Partners / Wesleyan World Missions | 1998 | - | - | - | - | - |
| Gospel Fellowship Association | 1963 | - | - | 2 | - | - |
| Gospel Mission of South America | 1923 | - | - | 10 | - | - |
| Grace Brethren International Missions | 2001 | - | - | - | - | 4 |
| Greater Grace World Outreach | 1985 | - | - | - | 2 | - |
| International Gospel Outreach | 1973 | - | - | - | 2 | - |
| International Partnership Ministries, Inc. | 1992 | - | - | - | 6 | - |
| Intl. Pentecostal Holiness Ch. World Missions Mins. | 1967 | - | - | - | - | - |
| Latin America Mission | | - | 2 | - | - | 2 |
| LOGOI Ministries | 1972 | - | - | - | 2 | - |
| Macedonia World Baptist Missions, Inc. | 1999 | - | - | 10 | - | 2 |
| Mennonite Mission Network | 1963 | - | - | - | 2 | - |
| Mission to the World (PCA), Inc. | 1977 | 3 | 14 | - | - | - |
| Navigators, U.S. International Missions Group | | - | - | 4 | - | - |
| New Mission Systems International | 1999 | - | - | 2 | - | - |
| Operation Mobilization | | 2 | - | - | - | - |

| | First Year | Personnel from U.S. | | | Other Countries | |
|---|---|---|---|---|---|---|
| | | 1-2 yrs. | 2-4 yrs. | 4+ yrs. | Citizens | Non-Citizens |
| Presbyterian Evangelistic Fellowship | | - | - | 1 | - | - |
| Reformed Baptist Mission Services | | - | - | - | 2 | - |
| Salvation Army, U.S.A. | 1909 | - | - | 1 | - | - |
| Seventh-day Adventists General Conference | 1895 | - | - | 6 | - | 2 |
| SIM USA | 1988 | - | - | 5 | - | - |
| Source of Light Ministries International, Inc. | 1979 | - | - | - | 2 | - |
| South American Missionary Society (USA) | 1979 | - | 1 | - | - | 2 |
| Spanish World Ministries | | - | - | 2 | 2 | - |
| United Ch. of Christ—Wider Church Ministries | | - | 1 | - | - | - |
| United Pentecostal Ch. Intl., Foreign Missions Div. | 1964 | - | 2 | - | - | - |
| Word of Life Fellowship, Inc.—Intl. Ministries | 1976 | - | - | - | 23 | 2 |
| World Baptist Fellowship Mission Agency, Inc. | | - | - | 2 | - | - |
| World Harvest Mission | 2000 | - | - | 2 | - | - |
| World Team | 1982 | - | - | 6 | - | - |
| World-Wide Missions | 1964 | - | - | - | 1 | - |
| Totals: | | 11 | 27 | 152 | 90 | 20 |

## China

| | First Year | 1-2 yrs. | 2-4 yrs. | 4+ yrs. | Citizens | Non-Citizens |
|---|---|---|---|---|---|---|
| Advancing Renewal Ministries, Inc. | | - | - | 5 | 4 | 1 |
| All God's Children International | 1995 | 2 | - | - | 25 | - |
| Ambassadors for Christ, Inc. | 1963 | - | - | - | - | - |
| Am. Baptist Chs. of the U.S.A., Intl. Ministries | 1843 | - | - | 1 | - | - |
| Artists In Christian Testimony | 2005 | - | - | - | - | - |
| Asian Outreach U.S.A. | | - | - | - | - | - |
| Back to the Bible International | 1994 | - | - | - | 6 | - |
| Calvary International | 1995 | - | - | 1 | 1 | - |
| Caring Partners International, Inc. | 1989 | - | - | - | - | - |
| Childcare Worldwide | 2004 | - | - | - | - | - |
| Christar | 1912 | - | - | 37 | - | - |
| Christian Aid Mission | | - | - | - | 400 | - |
| Christian Broadcasting Network Inc., the | 1997 | 1 | 3 | 1 | 44 | - |
| Christian Ministries International (CMI) | 1987 | - | - | 2 | 2 | 4 |
| Christian Reformed World Missions | 1986 | - | - | 2 | - | - |
| Church of God (Cleveland, TN) World Missions | 1937 | - | - | 6 | - | - |
| Church of God of Prophecy—Global Outreach | | - | - | 2 | - | - |
| Churches of Christ | 1930 | 20 | 6 | 6 | - | - |
| Cook Communications Ministries International | 1998 | - | - | - | - | - |
| East Gates Ministries Intl. | 1990 | - | - | - | 1 | - |
| East-West Ministries International | 1999 | - | - | 4 | - | - |
| Educational Services International (ESI) | 1981 | 60 | - | - | - | - |
| EFCA International Mission | 1887 | - | - | - | 5 | - |
| Episcopal Ch. USA—Domestic & Foreign | | - | - | 3 | - | - |
| Evangelical Luth. Ch. in Am., Div. for Global Msn. | 1986 | 7 | - | 4 | - | - |
| Fellowship International Mission | 2003 | - | - | 1 | - | - |
| Food for the Hungry, Inc. | 1992 | - | 3 | 2 | - | - |
| Global Outreach International | 1992 | - | - | 13 | - | - |
| Globe Missionary Evangelism | 2003 | - | - | 2 | - | - |
| Gospel for Asia | 1998 | - | - | - | - | - |
| Great Commission Center International | 2000 | - | - | - | - | 1 |
| Habitat for Humanity International | | - | 2 | - | - | 2 |

| | First Year | Personnel from U.S. | | | Other Countries | |
|---|---|---|---|---|---|---|
| | | 1-2 yrs. | 2-4 yrs. | 4+ yrs. | Citizens | Non-Citizens |
| Heart of God Ministries | 2004 | - | 20 | - | - | - |
| Hope for the Hungry | | - | - | 1 | - | 1 |
| HOPE International | 1999 | 1 | - | - | - | - |
| International Outreach Ministries (IOM) | 1996 | - | 5 | - | - | - |
| InterServe USA (International Service Fellowship) | 1870 | - | - | 10 | - | - |
| Literacy & Evangelism International | | - | - | - | - | - |
| Mennonite Mission Network | 1909 | - | - | 4 | - | 4 |
| Mission ONE, Inc. | 1990 | - | - | - | 6 | - |
| Mission To Unreached Peoples | 1986 | - | - | 30 | - | 2 |
| New Life Advance International | | - | - | - | - | - |
| OMS International, Inc. | 1999 | - | - | 3 | - | 2 |
| Orthodox Presbyterian Church | 1994 | 5 | 2 | 4 | - | - |
| Paraclete, Inc. | 1999 | - | - | - | - | - |
| Partners International | 1943 | - | - | 1 | 523 | 14 |
| Perimeter Church, Global Outreach | | - | - | - | - | - |
| Reformed Ch. in Am., Gen. Synod Council | 2000 | - | - | - | 2 | - |
| Ripe for Harvest, Inc. | 1999 | - | - | 2 | - | - |
| Rosedale Mennonite Missions | 2005 | 2 | - | - | - | 2 |
| SIM USA | 1997 | 3 | - | - | - | - |
| Sowers International, The | 1994 | - | - | - | 3 | - |
| Tentmakers International | | - | - | - | - | - |
| The Mission Society | 1994 | - | - | 3 | - | - |
| Things To Come Mission, Inc. | 2005 | - | - | - | - | 1 |
| Training Evangelistic Leadership (T.E.L.), Inc. | 1985 | - | 7 | 15 | 6 | 5 |
| U.S. Center for World Mission | | 2 | - | - | - | - |
| United Church of Christ—Wider Church Ministries | | - | 2 | - | - | - |
| United Pentecostal Ch. Intl., Foreign Missions Div. | | - | - | - | - | 1 |
| Walk Thru the Bible Ministries, Inc. | 2004 | - | - | - | 1 | - |
| White Fields Inc. | | - | - | - | 3 | - |
| World Bible Translation Center | | - | - | - | 2 | - |
| World Help | 1992 | - | - | - | - | - |
| World Indigenous Missions | 2002 | - | - | 6 | - | - |
| World Missions Far Corners, Inc. | 1988 | - | - | 2 | 2 | - |
| World Relief | | - | - | 1 | - | - |
| World Venture | 2005 | - | - | 3 | - | - |
| World-Wide Missions | | - | 2 | 2 | - | - |
| Worldwide Tentmakers, Inc. | 1993 | - | - | - | - | - |
| | Totals: | 103 | 52 | 179 | 1036 | 40 |

## CIS—General

| | First Year | 1-2 yrs. | 2-4 yrs. | 4+ yrs. | Citizens | Non-Citizens |
|---|---|---|---|---|---|---|
| Educational Services International (ESI) | 1991 | 20 | - | - | - | - |
| Pioneers USA | 1993 | - | - | 11 | 1 | - |
| Slavic Gospel Association | | - | - | 5 | - | - |
| | Totals: | 20 | - | 16 | 1 | - |

## Colombia

| | First Year | 1-2 yrs. | 2-4 yrs. | 4+ yrs. | Citizens | Non-Citizens |
|---|---|---|---|---|---|---|
| Action International Ministries | 1992 | - | - | 3 | 3 | 3 |
| Assemblies of God World Missions | 1951 | 7 | - | 22 | - | - |
| Awana Clubs International | 1987 | - | - | - | 4 | - |
| Baptist Bible Fellowship International | 1971 | 2 | - | 2 | - | - |

| | First Year | Personnel from U.S. | | | Other Countries | |
| --- | --- | --- | --- | --- | --- | --- |
| | | 1-2 yrs. | 2-4 yrs. | 4+ yrs. | Citizens | Non-Citizens |
| Brethren Assemblies | | - | - | 13 | - | - |
| Brethren in Christ World Missions | 1984 | - | - | 2 | - | - |
| Campus Crusade for Christ, Intl. | 1963 | - | - | - | 21 | - |
| Child Evangelism Fellowship, Inc. | 1943 | - | - | - | 1 | - |
| Christ for the City International | 1988 | - | 1 | 2 | 2 | 2 |
| Christian Aid Mission | | - | - | - | 40 | - |
| Christian Church of North America—Missions | 1965 | - | - | 1 | - | - |
| Christian Ministries International (CMI) | 1997 | - | - | 2 | 1 | 4 |
| Christians In Action Missions International | 1970 | - | - | 3 | 14 | - |
| Church of God (Cleveland, TN) World Missions | 1954 | - | - | 3 | - | - |
| Church of God of Prophecy—Global Outreach | | - | - | - | 3 | - |
| Church of the Nazarene, World Mission Dept. | 1975 | - | - | - | - | - |
| Churches of Christ | 1958 | 2 | - | - | - | - |
| CLC Ministries International | 1973 | - | - | 2 | - | - |
| Compassion International, Inc. | 1976 | - | - | - | 32 | - |
| EFCA International Mission | 2002 | - | - | - | - | - |
| Evangelical Covenant Ch.—Covenant Wld. Msn. | 1968 | - | - | 3 | - | - |
| Free Methodist World Missions | | - | - | - | - | - |
| Global Partners / Wesleyan World Missions | 1943 | - | - | - | - | - |
| Hope for the Hungry | | - | - | 1 | 1 | - |
| Hosanna | 2002 | - | - | - | 2 | - |
| I. N. Network USA | 1994 | - | - | - | 8 | - |
| International Outreach Ministries (IOM) | 1986 | - | - | 2 | - | - |
| Intl. Pentecostal Holiness Ch. World Missions Mins. | 1993 | - | - | - | - | - |
| International Teams, U.S.A. | | - | - | 2 | - | 2 |
| Latin America Mission | 1953 | - | 3 | 12 | 3 | 12 |
| LOGOI Ministries | 1972 | - | - | - | 3 | - |
| Luke Society, Inc., The | 1998 | - | - | - | - | - |
| Macedonia World Baptist Missions, Inc. | 2002 | - | - | 2 | - | - |
| Mennonite Mission Network | 1945 | - | - | 2 | - | 2 |
| Mission to the World (PCA), Inc. | 2002 | - | - | - | - | - |
| Missionary Revival Crusade | 1974 | - | - | 1 | 1 | - |
| Missionary Ventures International | 2001 | - | - | 2 | - | - |
| New Tribes Mission | 1944 | 2 | - | 55 | 15 | - |
| OC International, Inc. | | - | - | 2 | - | - |
| OMS International, Inc. | 1943 | - | - | 6 | - | 2 |
| Palm Missionary Ministries | 1995 | - | - | - | 2 | - |
| Precept Ministries International | 1995 | - | - | - | 2 | - |
| Reformed Baptist Mission Services | | - | - | - | - | 2 |
| Ripe for Harvest, Inc. | 2001 | - | - | 1 | - | - |
| Seventh-day Adventists General Conference | 1921 | - | - | 2 | - | 2 |
| South America Mission, Inc. | 1934 | - | 1 | - | 1 | - |
| Sowers International, The | 1985 | - | - | - | - | 4 |
| Spanish World Ministries | | - | - | 1 | 1 | - |
| TEAM (The Evangelical Alliance Mission) | | - | - | 9 | - | - |
| Team Expansion, Inc. | 1989 | - | - | 5 | - | - |
| The Brethren Church, Inc. | 1997 | - | - | - | - | 1 |
| The Mission Society | 1985 | - | - | - | - | - |
| Trans World Missions | | - | - | - | 4 | 2 |
| United Pentecostal Ch. Intl., Foreign Missions Div. | 1936 | - | 1 | - | - | - |

| | First Year | Personnel from U.S. | | | Other Countries | |
|---|---|---|---|---|---|---|
| | | 1-2 yrs. | 2-4 yrs. | 4+ yrs. | Citizens | Non-Citizens |
| Walk Thru the Bible Ministries, Inc. | 2000 | - | - | - | - | - |
| Wisc. Evangelical Luth. Synod, Bd. for Wld. Msns. | 1974 | - | - | - | - | - |
| Word of Life Fellowship, Inc.—Intl. Ministries | 1980 | - | - | - | 3 | 2 |
| World Baptist Fellowship Mission Agency, Inc. | | - | - | 2 | - | - |
| World Bible Translation Center | | - | - | - | 2 | - |
| World Reach, Inc. | 2005 | - | - | - | - | 2 |
| World Vision Inc. | 1960 | - | - | - | - | - |
| World-Wide Missions | 1966 | - | - | - | 1 | |
| | Totals: | 13 | 6 | 165 | 170 | 42 |

## Congo, Democratic Republic of

| | First Year | 1-2 yrs. | 2-4 yrs. | 4+ yrs. | Citizens | Non-Citizens |
|---|---|---|---|---|---|---|
| Africa Inland Mission International | 1912 | - | - | 2 | - | 5 |
| Africa Inter-Mennonite Mission | 1912 | - | - | - | - | - |
| Am. Baptist Chs. of the U.S.A., Intl. Ministries | 1884 | - | - | 13 | - | - |
| American Leprosy Missions, Inc. | 1906 | - | - | - | 1 | - |
| Assemblies of God World Missions | 1921 | - | - | 6 | - | - |
| Baptist Bible Fellowship International | 1957 | - | - | 4 | - | - |
| Campus Crusade for Christ, Intl. | 1979 | - | - | - | 166 | 12 |
| Child Evangelism Fellowship, Inc. | 1952 | - | - | - | 3 | - |
| Christian Mission for the Deaf | 1990 | - | - | 2 | - | - |
| Church of God of Prophecy—Global Outreach | | - | - | - | 20 | - |
| Church of the Nazarene, World Mission Dept. | 1990 | - | - | - | - | - |
| CrossWorld | 1931 | - | - | 6 | - | - |
| EFCA International Mission | 1922 | - | - | - | - | - |
| Empowering Lives International | 2001 | - | - | - | 36 | - |
| Every Child Ministries, Inc. | 1985 | - | - | - | 14 | - |
| Food for the Hungry, Inc. | 1994 | - | - | - | - | - |
| Free Methodist World Missions | | - | - | 1 | - | - |
| Global Partners / Wesleyan World Missions | 2003 | - | - | - | - | - |
| Gospelink, Inc. | | - | - | - | 60 | - |
| Grace Ministries International | 1928 | - | 4 | - | 12 | - |
| Greater Grace World Outreach | 2005 | - | - | - | 42 | - |
| Habitat for Humanity International | 1974 | - | 1 | - | - | 1 |
| Harvest | 2003 | - | - | - | 2 | - |
| HOPE International | 2204 | 2 | 2 | - | - | - |
| Independent Faith Mission, Inc. | | - | - | 5 | - | - |
| International Christian Ministries | 2002 | - | - | - | 4 | - |
| International Outreach Ministries (IOM) | 1986 | - | - | 6 | - | - |
| Intl. Pentecostal Holiness Ch. World Missions Mins. | 1992 | - | - | - | - | - |
| Medical Ambassadors International, Inc. | 1987 | - | - | - | 28 | - |
| Mennonite Mission Network | 1906 | - | - | - | - | - |
| Mission Aviation Fellowship | 1960 | 2 | 1 | 7 | - | - |
| Mission Ministries, Inc. | 2000 | - | - | - | 2 | - |
| Seventh-day Adventists General Conference | 1965 | - | - | 2 | - | 7 |
| Source of Light Ministries International, Inc. | | - | - | 2 | - | - |
| The Master's Mission, Inc. | 1986 | - | - | - | 2 | - |
| The Word for the World | 2004 | - | - | - | 6 | 2 |
| United Pentecostal Ch. Intl., Foreign Missions Div. | 1985 | - | 2 | - | - | - |
| Walk Thru the Bible Ministries, Inc. | 2002 | - | - | - | 2 | - |
| World Venture | 1946 | - | - | 2 | - | - |

| | First Year | Personnel from U.S. | | | Other Countries | |
|---|---|---|---|---|---|---|
| | | 1-2 yrs. | 2-4 yrs. | 4+ yrs. | Citizens | Non-Citizens |
| Totals: | | 4 | 10 | 58 | 400 | 27 |

### Congo, Republic of the

| | First Year | 1-2 yrs. | 2-4 yrs. | 4+ yrs. | Citizens | Non-Citizens |
|---|---|---|---|---|---|---|
| African Enterprise | 1994 | - | - | - | 5 | - |
| African Leadership, Inc. | 1998 | - | - | - | 1 | - |
| Assemblies of God World Missions | 1996 | 3 | - | 2 | - | - |
| Campus Crusade for Christ, Intl. | 1990 | - | - | - | 18 | - |
| Christian Blind Mission International | 1991 | - | 1 | - | - | - |
| Church of God of Prophecy—Global Outreach | | - | - | - | 2 | - |
| Ch. of the Nazarene, World Mission Dept. | 1997 | - | - | - | - | - |
| Global Outreach Mission, Inc. | 1974 | - | - | 8 | - | - |
| World Relief | 1994 | - | 1 | - | 26 | - |
| World-Wide Missions | 1961 | - | - | - | 2 | - |
| Totals: | | 3 | 2 | 10 | 54 | - |

### Cook Islands

| | First Year | 1-2 yrs. | 2-4 yrs. | 4+ yrs. | Citizens | Non-Citizens |
|---|---|---|---|---|---|---|
| Assemblies of God World Missions | 1992 | - | - | - | - | - |
| Totals: | | - | - | - | - | - |

### Costa Rica

| | First Year | 1-2 yrs. | 2-4 yrs. | 4+ yrs. | Citizens | Non-Citizens |
|---|---|---|---|---|---|---|
| Am. Baptist Chs. of the U.S.A., Intl. Ministries | 1980 | - | - | 3 | - | - |
| Assemblies of God World Missions | 1943 | 7 | - | 21 | - | - |
| Awana Clubs International | 1985 | - | - | 1 | 1 | - |
| Baptist Bible Fellowship International | 1970 | - | - | 12 | - | - |
| Baptist International Missions, Inc. (BIMI) | | - | - | 10 | - | - |
| Baptist International Outreach | 1990 | - | - | - | 2 | - |
| Bright Hope International | 2000 | - | - | - | 1 | - |
| Calvary International | 1982 | - | - | 4 | - | 0 |
| Campus Crusade for Christ, Intl. | 1976 | - | 2 | - | 6 | - |
| Christ for the City International | 1985 | 1 | 3 | 7 | 20 | 18 |
| Christian Broadcasting Network Inc., the | 1998 | - | - | - | 8 | 1 |
| Christian Reformed World Missions | 1981 | - | 2 | 3 | - | - |
| Ch. of God (Anderson, Ind.), Global Missions | 1939 | - | - | 2 | - | - |
| Church of God of Prophecy—Global Outreach | | - | - | - | 3 | 2 |
| Church of the Nazarene, World Mission Dept. | 1964 | - | - | 11 | - | 5 |
| Churches of Christ | 1967 | - | - | 4 | 2 | - |
| Commission to Every Nation | 1998 | 1 | - | 1 | - | - |
| EFCA International Mission | 2000 | 2 | 2 | 7 | 2 | - |
| Envoy International | 2001 | - | - | - | 3 | - |
| Evangelical Luth. Ch. in Am., Div. for Global Msn. | 1998 | 1 | - | 1 | - | 1 |
| Evangelistic Faith Missions | 1982 | - | - | - | - | 2 |
| Food for the Hungry, Inc. | 1992 | - | 3 | - | - | - |
| Foursquare Missions International | 1953 | - | - | 2 | - | - |
| Free Methodist World Missions | | - | - | 2 | - | - |
| Global Outreach International | 2002 | - | - | 2 | - | - |
| Global Partners / Wesleyan World Missions | 1995 | - | - | - | - | - |
| Globe Missionary Evangelism | 2006 | 1 | - | - | - | - |
| Go Ye Fellowship | 1998 | - | 2 | - | - | - |
| Gospel Fellowship Association | 1991 | - | - | 4 | - | - |
| Grace Ministries International | 1984 | - | 5 | - | - | - |

| | First Year | Personnel from U.S. | | | Other Countries | |
|---|---|---|---|---|---|---|
| | | 1-2 yrs. | 2-4 yrs. | 4+ yrs. | Citizens | Non-Citizens |
| Habitat for Humanity International | 1987 | - | 45 | 6 | 37 | 14 |
| Hope for the Hungry | | - | - | 1 | - | 1 |
| International Outreach Ministries (IOM) | 1994 | 1 | - | 6 | - | - |
| Intl. Pentecostal Holiness Ch. World Missions Mins. | 1951 | - | - | 4 | - | - |
| International Teams, U.S.A. | 1993 | 5 | - | 15 | 7 | 11 |
| Latin America Assistance, Inc. | 2000 | - | - | 8 | 18 | - |
| Latin America Mission | 1921 | 5 | 9 | 52 | 2 | 64 |
| LeaderTreks | 2002 | 1 | 1 | - | - | - |
| Living Water Teaching | 1983 | - | - | - | - | - |
| Macedonia World Baptist Missions, Inc. | 1996 | - | - | 2 | - | - |
| Media Associates International | | - | - | - | - | 1 |
| Medical Ambassadors International, Inc. | 1999 | - | - | - | 4 | - |
| Mission to the Americas | 1955 | - | - | 2 | - | - |
| Missionary Ventures International | 2001 | - | - | 1 | - | - |
| Mutual Faith Ministries Intl. | 1992 | - | - | 1 | - | - |
| Navigators, U.S. International Missions Group | | - | - | 1 | - | - |
| Pentecostal Free Will Baptist Church, Inc. | | - | - | - | 1 | - |
| Precept Ministries International | 1994 | - | - | - | - | 1 |
| Presbyterian Evangelistic Fellowship | | - | - | 1 | - | - |
| Ripe for Harvest, Inc. | 2000 | - | - | 1 | - | - |
| Rosedale Mennonite Missions | 1961 | 1 | 2 | 2 | - | 5 |
| Salvation Army, U.S.A. | 1907 | - | - | 1 | - | - |
| Seventh-day Adventists General Conference | 1903 | - | - | 2 | - | 2 |
| The Mission Society | 1986 | - | - | 2 | - | - |
| Trans World Missions | | - | - | - | - | - |
| United Pentecostal Ch. Intl., Foreign Missions Div. | 1975 | - | 2 | - | - | 2 |
| Walk Thru the Bible Ministries, Inc. | 2004 | - | - | - | - | - |
| Word of Life Fellowship, Inc.—Intl. Ministries | 1986 | - | - | - | 20 | 2 |
| World Missions & Evangelism, Inc. | | - | 3 | | - | - |
| Totals: | | 26 | 81 | 205 | 137 | 132 |

## Cote d'Ivoire

| | First Year | 1-2 yrs. | 2-4 yrs. | 4+ yrs. | Citizens | Non-Citizens |
|---|---|---|---|---|---|---|
| Assemblies of God World Missions | 1927 | - | - | - | - | - |
| Baptist Bible Fellowship International | 1988 | - | - | 2 | - | - |
| Baptist General Conference—Intl. Ministries | 1977 | - | - | 5 | - | 2 |
| Baptist International Missions, Inc. (BIMI) | | - | - | 10 | - | - |
| Baptist Mid-Missions | 1974 | - | - | 7 | - | - |
| Bright Hope International | 2004 | - | - | - | 1 | - |
| Campus Crusade for Christ, Intl. | 1975 | - | - | - | 34 | 2 |
| Child Evangelism Fellowship, Inc. | 1976 | - | - | - | 4 | - |
| Christian Churches / Churches of Christ | | - | - | 6 | - | - |
| Ch. of God (Anderson, Ind.), Global Missions | 1997 | - | - | 4 | - | - |
| Church of God of Prophecy—Global Outreach | | - | - | - | 7 | - |
| Church of the Nazarene, World Mission Dept. | 1987 | - | - | 10 | - | 6 |
| Churches of Christ | | - | 4 | 3 | - | - |
| CityTeam Ministries | | - | - | - | 2 | - |
| CMF International | 1999 | - | 11 | - | - | - |
| Development Associates International (DAI) | 2001 | - | - | - | 3 | - |
| Free Will Baptist, Inc. Board of Intl. Missions | 1958 | - | - | 15 | - | - |
| International Partnership Ministries, Inc. | 1998 | - | - | - | 13 | - |

| | | Personnel from U.S. | | | Other Countries | |
|---|---|---|---|---|---|---|
| | First Year | 1-2 yrs. | 2-4 yrs. | 4+ yrs. | Citizens | Non-Citizens |
| Intl. Pentecostal Holiness Ch. World Missions Mins. | 1993 | - | - | 2 | - | - |
| MAP International | 1993 | - | - | - | 23 | - |
| Mennonite Mission Network | 1978 | - | - | 2 | 1 | - |
| Mission to the World (PCA), Inc. | 1985 | - | 6 | - | - | - |
| New Tribes Mission | 1982 | 7 | - | 61 | - | - |
| Seventh-day Adventists General Conference | | - | - | - | - | 6 |
| SIM USA | 1967 | 2 | - | 2 | - | - |
| Source of Light Ministries International, Inc. | 2001 | - | - | - | 1 | - |
| United Pentecostal Ch. Intl., Foreign Missions Div. | 1975 | - | 2 | - | - | - |
| WEC International | | - | - | 7 | - | - |
| World Missions Far Corners, Inc. | 1992 | - | - | 2 | - | - |
| World Venture | 1947 | - | - | 11 | - | - |
| Totals: | | 9 | 23 | 151 | 87 | 16 |

## Croatia

| | | | | | | |
|---|---|---|---|---|---|---|
| Advent Christian Gen. Conf., Dept. of Wld. Msns. | 1996 | - | - | - | 1 | - |
| Assemblies of God World Missions | 1992 | - | - | 6 | - | - |
| Baptist Bible Fellowship International | 1992 | - | - | 2 | - | - |
| Bethany International Ministries | 1999 | - | - | 1 | - | 1 |
| Biblical Ministries Worldwide | | - | - | 2 | 2 | - |
| Campus Crusade for Christ, Intl. | 1993 | - | - | 16 | 16 | - |
| Child Evangelism Fellowship, Inc. | 1989 | - | - | 2 | 2 | - |
| Church of God (Cleveland, TN) World Missions | 1968 | - | - | 2 | - | - |
| Church of the Nazarene, World Mission Dept. | 1999 | - | - | 1 | - | - |
| Churches of Christ | 1969 | 4 | - | 2 | 8 | - |
| Envoy International | | - | - | - | - | - |
| European Christian Mission International—USA | | - | - | 7 | - | - |
| Foursquare Missions International | 1997 | - | 2 | - | - | - |
| Global Partners / Wesleyan World Missions | 1993 | - | 6 | - | - | - |
| Greater Europe Mission | 1974 | - | - | 6 | - | - |
| Greater Grace World Outreach | 2005 | - | - | 2 | - | 2 |
| Intl. Pentecostal Holiness Ch. World Missions Mins. | 2003 | - | - | - | - | - |
| Pioneers USA | 1992 | - | - | 7 | - | - |
| Reformed Church in Am., Gen. Synod Council | 2006 | - | - | 2 | - | - |
| Seed International | 2000 | - | - | 1 | - | - |
| SEND International USA | 1995 | - | - | 2 | - | - |
| TEAM (The Evangelical Alliance Mission) | | - | - | 2 | - | - |
| United Pentecostal Ch. Intl., Foreign Missions Div. | | - | 1 | - | - | - |
| World Bible Translation Center | | - | - | - | 2 | - |
| Totals: | | 4 | 9 | 63 | 31 | 3 |

## Cuba

| | | | | | | |
|---|---|---|---|---|---|---|
| Am. Baptist Chs. of the U.S.A., Intl. Ministries | 1898 | - | - | 1 | - | - |
| AMG International | | - | - | - | 8 | - |
| Assemblies of God World Missions | 1920 | - | - | - | - | - |
| Baptist International Missions, Inc. (BIMI) | | - | - | 2 | - | - |
| Baptist International Outreach | | - | - | - | - | - |
| BCM International | | - | - | 1 | - | - |
| Bright Hope International | 2001 | - | - | - | 310 | - |
| Caring Partners International, Inc. | 1996 | - | - | - | - | - |

| | First Year | Personnel from U.S. | | | Other Countries | |
|---|---|---|---|---|---|---|
| | | 1-2 yrs. | 2-4 yrs. | 4+ yrs. | Citizens | Non-Citizens |
| Child Evangelism Fellowship, Inc. | 1949 | - | - | - | 2 | - |
| Christian Aid Mission | | - | - | - | 64 | - |
| Christian Reformed World Relief Committee | 2002 | - | - | - | - | - |
| Church of God of Prophecy—Global Outreach | | - | - | - | 4 | - |
| Church of the Nazarene, World Mission Dept. | 1902 | - | - | - | - | - |
| East-West Ministries International | 1997 | - | - | - | 2 | - |
| Friends United Meeting—Global Ministries | | - | - | - | - | - |
| International Gospel Outreach | 1999 | - | - | - | 4 | 2 |
| International Partnership Ministries, Inc. | 1999 | - | - | - | 45 | - |
| Intl. Pentecostal Holiness Ch. World Missions Mins. | | - | - | - | - | - |
| International Teams, U.S.A. | | - | - | - | - | 4 |
| LOGOI Ministries | 1972 | - | - | - | 4 | - |
| Medical Ambassadors International, Inc. | 2001 | - | - | - | 1 | - |
| New Life Advance International | | - | - | - | - | - |
| Touch the World Youth Ministries | 2000 | - | - | - | 2 | - |
| United Pentecostal Ch. Intl., Foreign Missions Div. | | - | 2 | - | - | - |
| University of the Family | 1993 | - | - | - | 2 | - |
| Walk Thru the Bible Ministries, Inc. | | - | - | - | 1 | - |
| Wisc. Evangelical Luth. Synod, Bd. for Wld. Msns. | 1994 | - | - | - | - | - |
| Word of Life Fellowship, Inc.—Intl. Ministries | 2001 | - | - | - | 3 | - |
| World Help | 1997 | - | - | - | - | - |
| World Link Ministries | 2000 | - | - | - | 338 | - |
| World Missions Far Corners, Inc. | 1977 | - | - | 1 | - | - |
| | Totals: | - | 2 | 1 | 790 | 6 |

## Cyprus

| | First Year | 1-2 yrs. | 2-4 yrs. | 4+ yrs. | Citizens | Non-Citizens |
|---|---|---|---|---|---|---|
| AMG International | 1984 | - | - | - | 3 | 3 |
| Armenian Missionary Association of America, Inc. | 1950 | - | - | - | - | - |
| Assemblies of God World Missions | 1984 | - | - | - | - | - |
| Child Evangelism Fellowship, Inc. | 1952 | - | - | 7 | - | - |
| Church of God of Prophecy—Global Outreach | | - | - | - | 2 | 2 |
| Church of the Nazarene, World Mission Dept. | 1985 | - | - | 2 | - | - |
| Commission to Every Nation | 2000 | - | 2 | - | - | - |
| Episcopal Church USA—Domestic & Foreign | | - | - | 2 | - | - |
| InterServe USA (International Service Fellowship) | 1970 | - | - | 2 | - | - |
| Macedonia World Baptist Missions, Inc. | 1993 | - | - | 2 | - | - |
| Middle East Christian Outreach (MECO) | 1976 | - | - | - | - | 16 |
| Reformed Church in Am., Gen. Synod Council | 1966 | - | - | 2 | - | - |
| Ripe for Harvest, Inc. | 2001 | - | - | 3 | - | - |
| Seventh-day Adventists General Conference | 1932 | - | - | 4 | - | 8 |
| United Pentecostal Ch. Intl., Foreign Missions Div. | 1989 | - | 2 | - | - | - |
| World Partners USA | 1966 | - | - | 2 | - | - |
| | Totals: | - | 4 | 26 | 5 | 29 |

## Czech Republic

| | First Year | 1-2 yrs. | 2-4 yrs. | 4+ yrs. | Citizens | Non-Citizens |
|---|---|---|---|---|---|---|
| Am. Baptist Chs. of the U.S.A., Intl. Ministries | 1995 | - | - | - | - | 2 |
| Apostolic Christian Church Foundation, Inc. | 1998 | - | - | 1 | - | - |
| Assemblies of God World Missions | 1992 | - | - | 2 | - | - |
| Awana Clubs International | 1999 | - | - | - | 2 | - |
| Baptist International Missions, Inc. (BIMI) | | - | - | 2 | - | - |

| | First Year | Personnel from U.S. | | | Other Countries | |
|---|---|---|---|---|---|---|
| | | 1-2 yrs. | 2-4 yrs. | 4+ yrs. | Citizens | Non-Citizens |
| Campus Crusade for Christ, Intl. | 1981 | 3 | - | 7 | 13 | - |
| Christian Aid Mission | | - | - | - | 8 | - |
| Christian Associates International | | - | - | - | - | - |
| Christian Churches / Churches of Christ | | - | - | 2 | - | - |
| Christian Outreach International | 1992 | - | - | 7 | 1 | 3 |
| Church of God (Cleveland, TN) World Missions | 2001 | 1 | - | 2 | - | 2 |
| Churches of Christ | 1990 | - | 2 | 4 | - | - |
| EFCA International Mission | 1991 | 1 | 2 | 11 | - | - |
| Entrust | 1994 | - | - | 4 | - | - |
| Envoy International | | - | - | - | - | - |
| Evangelical Covenant Ch.—Covenant Wld. Msn. | 1999 | 1 | - | 2 | - | - |
| Global Partners / Wesleyan World Missions | 1994 | - | 4 | - | - | - |
| Grace Brethren International Missions | 1994 | - | - | 2 | - | 2 |
| Greater Europe Mission | 1991 | - | 2 | 8 | - | - |
| Greater Grace World Outreach | 1991 | - | - | - | 2 | - |
| HCJB Global | 1992 | - | - | 2 | 2 | - |
| I. N. Network USA | 1993 | - | - | - | 6 | - |
| International Institute for Christian Studies | 1994 | - | 2 | 6 | 1 | - |
| International Messengers | 1994 | - | - | - | 2 | - |
| International Teams, U.S.A. | | - | - | 3 | - | - |
| Mission to the World (PCA), Inc. | 1989 | 1 | 6 | - | - | - |
| New Hope International | 1971 | - | - | - | 2 | - |
| New Mission Systems International | 2003 | - | - | 1 | - | - |
| Operation Mobilization | 1991 | - | - | 1 | - | 1 |
| Seed International | 2004 | - | - | 1 | - | - |
| SEND International USA | 1992 | - | - | 5 | - | 6 |
| TCM International Institute | | - | - | - | 1 | - |
| TEAM (The Evangelical Alliance Mission) | | 1 | - | 9 | - | 2 |
| TITUS International | 2006 | - | - | 2 | - | - |
| United Pentecostal Ch. Intl., Foreign Missions Div. | 1995 | - | 2 | - | - | - |
| Word of Life Fellowship, Inc.—Intl. Ministries | 1997 | - | - | 4 | 5 | - |
| World Harvest Mission | 2004 | - | - | 2 | - | - |
| World Venture | 1993 | 1 | - | 3 | - | - |
| | Totals: | 9 | 20 | 93 | 45 | 18 |

**Denmark**

| | | | | | | |
|---|---|---|---|---|---|---|
| Assemblies of God World Missions | 2000 | 1 | - | - | - | - |
| Baptist Bible Fellowship International | 1980 | - | - | 2 | - | - |
| Child Evangelism Fellowship, Inc. | 1947 | - | - | 2 | - | - |
| Church of the Nazarene, World Mission Dept. | 1960 | - | - | - | - | - |
| Churches of Christ | 1950 | - | - | - | 1 | - |
| Evangelical Luth. Ch. in Am., Div. for Global Msn. | 1995 | 1 | - | 2 | - | - |
| New Tribes Mission | 2004 | - | - | 2 | 6 | - |
| Ripe for Harvest, Inc. | 2001 | - | - | 1 | - | - |
| | Totals: | 2 | - | 9 | 7 | - |

**Djibouti**

| | | | | | | |
|---|---|---|---|---|---|---|
| Seventh-day Adventists General Conference | 1980 | - | - | - | - | 4 |
| | Totals: | - | - | - | - | 4 |

| | First Year | Personnel from U.S. | | | Other Countries | |
|---|---|---|---|---|---|---|
| | | 1-2 yrs. | 2-4 yrs. | 4+ yrs. | Citizens | Non-Citizens |

## Dominica

| | First Year | 1-2 yrs. | 2-4 yrs. | 4+ yrs. | Citizens | Non-Citizens |
|---|---|---|---|---|---|---|
| Assemblies of God World Missions | 1996 | - | - | 2 | - | - |
| Awana Clubs International | 1989 | - | - | - | 2 | - |
| Christian Churches / Churches of Christ | | - | - | 5 | 15 | - |
| Church of the Nazarene, World Mission Dept. | 1974 | - | - | 3 | - | 1 |
| Gospel Fellowship Association | 1994 | 1 | - | 2 | - | - |
| Macedonia World Baptist Missions, Inc. | 1967 | - | - | 4 | - | - |
| World Baptist Fellowship Mission Agency, Inc. | | - | - | 2 | - | - |
| World Gospel Mission | 1996 | - | - | 4 | - | - |
| | Totals: | 1 | - | 22 | 17 | 1 |

## Dominican Republic

| | First Year | 1-2 yrs. | 2-4 yrs. | 4+ yrs. | Citizens | Non-Citizens |
|---|---|---|---|---|---|---|
| | | - | - | - | - | - |
| Adventures in Missions | 1990 | - | - | 2 | - | - |
| Am. Baptist Chs. of the U.S.A., Intl. Ministries | 1980 | - | - | 1 | - | 1 |
| Assemblies of God World Missions | 1933 | 1 | - | 14 | - | - |
| Awana Clubs International | 1989 | - | - | 1 | 1 | - |
| Baptist Bible Fellowship International | 1996 | - | - | 6 | - | - |
| Baptist International Missions, Inc. (BIMI) | | - | - | 24 | - | - |
| Baptist Mid-Missions | 1950 | - | - | 1 | - | - |
| BCM International | | - | - | - | 1 | - |
| Bethany International Ministries | 1978 | - | - | 2 | - | - |
| Brethren Assemblies | | - | - | 5 | - | - |
| Campus Crusade for Christ, Intl. | 1977 | - | - | - | 36 | - |
| Christian Blind Mission International | 1985 | 1 | - | - | - | - |
| Christian Churches / Churches of Christ | | - | - | 12 | - | - |
| Christian Reformed World Missions | 1979 | - | 1 | 8 | - | - |
| Christian Reformed World Relief Committee | 1983 | - | - | 1 | - | - |
| Christ's Mandate for Missions | 2003 | - | - | - | 2 | - |
| Church of the Nazarene, World Mission Dept. | 1974 | - | - | 10 | - | 3 |
| Churches of Christ | 1963 | - | - | 5 | 3 | - |
| Compassion International, Inc. | 1970 | - | - | - | 36 | - |
| CrossWorld | 1949 | - | - | 10 | - | - |
| Episcopal Church USA—Domestic & Foreign | | - | - | 6 | - | - |
| Evangelistic Faith Missions | 1981 | 2 | - | - | - | - |
| Floresta USA, Inc. | 1984 | - | - | - | 20 | - |
| Food for the Hungry, Inc. | 1979 | - | 3 | - | 1 | - |
| Foursquare Missions International | 1996 | 1 | 2 | 2 | - | - |
| Global Partners / Wesleyan World Missions | 2001 | - | 2 | - | - | - |
| Habitat for Humanity International | 1987 | - | 1 | - | - | 1 |
| Harvest | 1981 | - | - | - | 2 | - |
| International Partnership Ministries, Inc. | 2000 | - | - | - | 6 | - |
| Intl. Pentecostal Holiness Ch. World Missions Mins. | 1996 | - | - | 2 | - | - |
| Kids Alive International | 1989 | 6 | 6 | 10 | 99 | 2 |
| Literacy & Evangelism International | 2003 | - | - | - | 2 | - |
| Medical Ambassadors International, Inc. | 1988 | - | - | - | 4 | - |
| Mennonite Mission Network | 1906 | - | - | - | - | - |
| Ministries In Action | 1995 | - | - | - | 1 | - |
| Mission Possible, Inc. | 1992 | - | - | - | 16 | - |
| Mission to the Americas | 1981 | - | - | - | 7 | - |
| Missionary Ventures International | 1999 | - | - | 5 | - | - |

| | First Year | Personnel from U.S. | | | Other Countries | |
|---|---|---|---|---|---|---|
| | | 1-2 yrs. | 2-4 yrs. | 4+ yrs. | Citizens | Non-Citizens |
| New Way Missions | 2000 | - | - | - | - | - |
| Pentecostal Free Will Baptist Church, Inc. | | - | - | - | 1 | - |
| Primitive Methodist Church in the USA | | - | - | 2 | - | - |
| Seventh-day Adventists General Conference | 1908 | - | - | 2 | - | 4 |
| South American Missionary Society (USA) | 1987 | - | 1 | 2 | - | - |
| STEM (Short-Term Evangelical Missions) Intl. | 1994 | - | - | - | - | - |
| United Church of Christ—Wider Church Ministries | | - | 1 | - | - | - |
| United Pentecostal Ch. Intl., Foreign Msns. Div. | 1965 | - | 4 | - | - | 2 |
| Walk Thru the Bible Ministries, Inc. | 2001 | - | - | - | - | - |
| Wisc. Evangelical Luth. Synod, Bd. for Wld. Msns. | 1993 | - | - | 1 | - | - |
| Word of Life Fellowship, Inc.—Intl. Ministries | 1994 | - | - | - | 12 | - |
| World Baptist Fellowship Mission Agency, Inc. | | 1 | - | - | - | 1 |
| World Servants, Inc. | 1986 | - | - | - | - | - |
| World Team | 1939 | - | - | 8 | - | - |
| | Totals: | 12 | 21 | 142 | 250 | 14 |

## East Timor

| | | | | | | |
|---|---|---|---|---|---|---|
| Assemblies of God World Missions | 2001 | - | - | - | - | - |
| Campus Crusade for Christ, Intl. | 2002 | - | - | - | - | 4 |
| Church of the Nazarene, World Mission Dept. | 2001 | - | - | 2 | - | - |
| Medical Ambassadors International, Inc. | 2003 | - | - | - | - | - |
| | Totals: | - | - | 2 | - | 4 |

## Eastern Europe—General

| | | | | | | |
|---|---|---|---|---|---|---|
| Dawn Ministries, Inc. | | - | - | - | - | 1 |
| Final Frontiers Foundation, Inc. | 1992 | - | - | - | 25 | - |
| International Cooperating Ministries | | - | - | - | - | - |
| Intl. Street Kids Outreach Ministries (ISKOM) | 1998 | 1 | - | - | 21 | - |
| Mailbox Club International Inc., The | 1993 | - | - | 1 | 1 | - |
| New Hope International | 1971 | 3 | - | 3 | - | - |
| Open Bible Churches, International Ministries | 1996 | - | - | 2 | - | - |
| Pioneers USA | | 1 | - | 15 | - | 1 |
| Source of Light Ministries International, Inc. | | - | - | - | 2 | - |
| United World Mission | | 4 | 2 | 9 | - | - |
| | Totals: | 9 | 2 | 30 | 49 | 2 |

## Ecuador

| | | | | | | |
|---|---|---|---|---|---|---|
| Action International Ministries | 1993 | - | - | 3 | 3 | 1 |
| Assemblies of God World Missions | 1962 | 7 | - | 27 | - | - |
| Avant Ministries | 1896 | 5 | - | 19 | - | 5 |
| Awana Clubs International | 1988 | - | - | 2 | 4 | 2 |
| Back to the Bible International | 1970 | - | - | - | 10 | - |
| Baptist Bible Fellowship International | 1975 | 1 | - | 13 | - | - |
| Baptist International Missions, Inc. (BIMI) | | - | - | 4 | - | - |
| Baptist Mid-Missions | 1988 | - | - | 3 | 2 | - |
| Biblical Ministries Worldwide | | - | - | 10 | - | 10 |
| Brethren Assemblies | | - | - | 7 | - | - |
| Campus Crusade for Christ, Intl. | 1965 | - | - | - | 21 | - |
| Caring Partners International, Inc. | 1998 | - | - | - | - | - |
| Child Evangelism Fellowship, Inc. | 1941 | - | - | - | 2 | - |

| | First Year | Personnel from U.S. | | | Other Countries | |
|---|---|---|---|---|---|---|
| | | 1-2 yrs. | 2-4 yrs. | 4+ yrs. | Citizens | Non-Citizens |
| Christian Aid Mission | | - | - | - | 23 | - |
| Christian Blind Mission International | 1980 | - | 1 | - | - | - |
| Christian Churches / Churches of Christ | | - | 4 | 4 | - | - |
| Christian Reformed World Relief Committee | 1983 | - | - | - | 2 | - |
| Christians In Action Missions International | 1979 | - | - | 2 | - | - |
| Ch. of God (Anderson, Ind.), Global Missions | 1986 | 1 | - | 6 | - | - |
| Church of God (Cleveland, TN) World Missions | 1971 | 4 | - | 8 | - | 2 |
| Church of God of Prophecy—Global Outreach | | - | - | - | 2 | 2 |
| Church of the Nazarene, World Mission Dept. | 1972 | - | - | 6 | - | - |
| Churches of Christ | 1966 | 8 | - | 12 | 4 | - |
| Compassion International, Inc. | 1974 | - | - | - | 33 | - |
| CrossWorld | 2000 | - | - | 12 | - | - |
| Episcopal Church USA—Domestic & Foreign | | - | - | 1 | - | - |
| Evangelical Covenant Ch.—Covenant Wld. Msn. | 1947 | 5 | - | 5 | - | - |
| Fellowship of Evangelical Churches—Intl. Ministries | 2003 | - | - | 2 | - | 2 |
| Free Methodist World Missions | 1981 | - | - | 2 | - | - |
| Global Outreach International | 1976 | - | - | 13 | - | - |
| Global Partners / Wesleyan World Missions | 2001 | - | 2 | - | - | - |
| Globe Missionary Evangelism | 2006 | - | - | 2 | - | - |
| Gospel Fellowship Association | 2006 | 1 | - | 2 | - | - |
| Greater Grace World Outreach | 1985 | - | - | 3 | 2 | - |
| Habitat for Humanity International | 1998 | - | 1 | - | - | 1 |
| HCJB Global | 1931 | 16 | 2 | - | 114 | 39 |
| Intl. Pentecostal Holiness Ch. Wld. Msns. Mins. | 2002 | - | - | 2 | 2 | - |
| International Teams, U.S.A. | 1994 | 5 | 1 | 18 | 6 | 9 |
| Latin America Mission | 1974 | - | 1 | 4 | 1 | 4 |
| Liebenzell USA | 1989 | - | - | 4 | 4 | - |
| LOGOI Ministries | 1972 | - | - | - | - | - |
| Luke Society, Inc., The | 2002 | - | - | - | - | - |
| Lutheran Bible Translators, Inc. | 1984 | - | - | - | 2 | - |
| MAP International | 1988 | - | - | - | 17 | - |
| Mennonite Mission Network | 1969 | - | - | 2 | 2 | - |
| Mission Aviation Fellowship | 1948 | 5 | 4 | 5 | - | - |
| Mission to the World (PCA), Inc. | 1975 | 1 | 14 | - | - | - |
| Missionary Ventures International | | - | - | 4 | - | - |
| OMS International, Inc. | 1952 | - | - | 7 | - | 8 |
| Open Air Campaigners—Overseas Ministries | 2001 | - | - | 2 | 2 | - |
| Palm Missionary Ministries | 1989 | - | - | 1 | 26 | 5 |
| Rosedale Mennonite Missions | 1980 | 1 | - | 7 | - | 8 |
| Servants in Faith & Technology (SIFAT) | 1999 | - | - | 1 | 3 | - |
| SIM USA | 1989 | - | - | 5 | - | - |
| South American Missionary Society (USA) | 2001 | - | - | 1 | - | - |
| Team Expansion, Inc. | 1990 | - | - | 6 | - | - |
| Teen Missions International, Inc. | 1999 | - | - | - | 3 | - |
| The Master's Mission, Inc. | 2003 | - | - | 2 | - | - |
| United Church of Christ—Wider Church Ministries | | - | 2 | - | - | - |
| United Pentecostal Ch. Intl., Foreign Missions Div. | 1964 | - | 1 | - | - | - |
| Walk Thru the Bible Ministries, Inc. | 2001 | - | - | - | - | - |
| Word of Life Fellowship, Inc.—Intl. Ministries | 1970 | - | - | - | 13 | 2 |
| World Baptist Fellowship Mission Agency, Inc. | | - | - | 8 | - | - |

| | First Year | Personnel from U.S. | | | Other Countries | |
|---|---|---|---|---|---|---|
| | | 1-2 yrs. | 2-4 yrs. | 4+ yrs. | Citizens | Non-Citizens |
| World Mission Prayer League | 1951 | - | - | 3 | - | 1 |
| World Missions Far Corners, Inc. | 1984 | - | - | 8 | - | - |
| World Partners USA | 1945 | - | - | 12 | - | - |
| World Servants, Inc. | 1988 | - | - | - | - | - |
| World Venture | | - | - | 4 | - | - |
| Totals: | | 60 | 33 | 274 | 303 | 101 |

## Egypt

| | First Year | 1-2 yrs. | 2-4 yrs. | 4+ yrs. | Citizens | Non-Citizens |
|---|---|---|---|---|---|---|
| Arab World Ministries | | 1 | 3 | 8 | - | - |
| Armenian Missionary Association of America, Inc. | 1950 | - | - | - | - | - |
| Assemblies of God World Missions | 1910 | - | - | 7 | - | - |
| Back to the Bible International | 1998 | - | - | - | 8 | - |
| BCM International | | - | - | - | 10 | - |
| Campus Crusade for Christ, Intl. | 1972 | - | - | 3 | 140 | - |
| Church of God of Prophecy—Global Outreach | | - | - | - | 6 | - |
| Church of the Nazarene, World Mission Dept. | 1986 | - | - | - | - | - |
| Churches of Christ | 1960 | - | - | 2 | - | - |
| Development Associates International (DAI) | 2002 | - | - | - | 3 | - |
| Episcopal Church USA—Domestic & Foreign | | - | - | 2 | - | - |
| Evangelical Luth. Ch. in Am., Div. for Global Msn. | 1967 | - | 2 | 2 | - | - |
| Evangelistic Faith Missions | 1905 | 2 | - | - | - | - |
| Global Partners / Wesleyan World Missions | 2004 | - | - | - | - | - |
| I. N. Network USA | 1997 | - | - | - | 2 | - |
| International Christian Ministries | 2003 | - | - | - | 4 | - |
| International Gospel Outreach | 2005 | - | - | 1 | - | - |
| Intl. Pentecostal Holiness Ch. World Missions Mins. | | - | - | - | - | - |
| Mennonite Mission Network | 1985 | - | - | 2 | - | - |
| Mission to the World (PCA), Inc. | | - | 6 | - | - | - |
| Missionary Ventures International | 1997 | - | - | - | 2 | - |
| Operation Mobilization | | - | 2 | 7 | - | - |
| Partners International | 1989 | - | - | - | 111 | - |
| Reformed Church in Am., Gen. Synod Council | 2001 | - | - | 2 | - | - |
| Seventh-day Adventists General Conference | 1879 | - | - | 4 | - | 4 |
| United Pentecostal Ch. Intl., Foreign Missions Div. | 1950 | - | 2 | - | - | - |
| University of the Family | 1992 | - | - | - | 1 | 1 |
| Venture International | 1994 | - | - | - | 2 | - |
| Walk Thru the Bible Ministries, Inc. | 2001 | - | - | - | 4 | - |
| World Bible Translation Center | | - | - | - | 2 | - |
| World-Wide Missions | 1963 | - | - | - | 10 | - |
| Totals: | | 3 | 15 | 40 | 305 | 5 |

## El Salvador

| | First Year | 1-2 yrs. | 2-4 yrs. | 4+ yrs. | Citizens | Non-Citizens |
|---|---|---|---|---|---|---|
| Am. Baptist Chs. of the U.S.A., Intl. Ministries | 1911 | - | - | - | - | 2 |
| Assemblies of God World Missions | 1925 | 37 | - | 14 | - | - |
| Awana Clubs International | 1993 | - | - | 2 | - | - |
| Baptist Bible Fellowship International | 1976 | - | - | 2 | - | - |
| Baptist International Missions, Inc. (BIMI) | | - | - | 4 | - | - |
| Brethren Assemblies | | - | - | 6 | - | - |
| CAM International | 1890 | - | - | 3 | - | - |
| Campus Crusade for Christ, Intl. | 1966 | - | - | 2 | 13 | - |

| | Personnel from U.S. | | | Other Countries | |
|---|---|---|---|---|---|
| | First Year | 1-2 yrs. | 2-4 yrs. | 4+ yrs. | Citizens | Non-Citizens |
| Child Evangelism Fellowship, Inc. | 1942 | - | - | - | 1 | - |
| Christian Reformed World Missions | 1996 | - | - | 1 | - | - |
| Christian Reformed World Relief Committee | 1976 | - | - | - | - | - |
| Christians In Action Missions International | | - | - | - | - | - |
| Church of God of Prophecy—Global Outreach | | - | - | - | 4 | - |
| Church of the Nazarene, World Mission Dept. | 1964 | - | - | - | - | - |
| Churches of Christ | 1964 | - | - | - | 5 | - |
| Commission to Every Nation | 2004 | 1 | - | - | - | - |
| Compassion International, Inc. | 1977 | - | - | - | 27 | - |
| Envoy International | | - | - | - | - | - |
| Episcopal Church USA—Domestic & Foreign | | - | - | 1 | - | - |
| Evangelical Friends Church Southwest | | - | - | 5 | - | - |
| Evangelical Luth. Ch. in Am., Div. for Global Msn. | 1985 | 1 | 1 | - | - | - |
| Evangelistic Faith Missions | 1964 | - | - | - | - | - |
| Full Gospel Evangelistic Association | 2000 | - | 1 | 2 | - | - |
| Global Partners / Wesleyan World Missions | 2002 | - | - | - | - | - |
| Larry Jones Intl. Ministries (Feed the Children) | 1983 | - | - | - | 6 | - |
| Latin America Mission | 2001 | - | 2 | 1 | - | 3 |
| Living Water Teaching | 1985 | - | - | 3 | 1 | 1 |
| Medical Ambassadors International, Inc. | 1984 | - | - | - | 6 | - |
| Mission to the Americas | 1996 | - | - | - | 2 | - |
| Open Bible Churches, International Ministries | 1973 | - | - | 2 | - | - |
| Precept Ministries International | 1988 | - | - | - | 1 | - |
| Salvation Army, U.S.A. | | - | - | 1 | - | - |
| Samaritan's Purse | 2001 | - | 2 | - | 15 | - |
| Trans World Missions | | - | - | - | 2 | - |
| United Church of Christ—Wider Church Ministries | | - | 2 | - | - | - |
| United Pentecostal Ch. Intl., Foreign Missions Div. | 1975 | - | 1 | - | - | 9 |
| Walk Thru the Bible Ministries, Inc. | 2000 | - | - | - | - | - |
| WEC International | | - | - | 2 | - | - |
| Word of Life Fellowship, Inc.—Intl. Ministries | 1993 | - | - | - | 6 | 2 |
| World Reach, Inc. | 1996 | - | - | 4 | 3 | - |
| World Vision Inc. | 1975 | - | - | - | - | - |
| | Totals: | 39 | 9 | 55 | 92 | 17 |

**Equatorial Guinea**

| | | | | | | |
|---|---|---|---|---|---|---|
| Assemblies of God World Missions | 1987 | 4 | - | 7 | - | - |
| Christian Churches / Churches of Christ | | - | - | 2 | - | - |
| Church of the Nazarene, World Mission Dept. | 2002 | - | - | - | - | - |
| Go Ye Fellowship | | - | - | 1 | - | - |
| Gospel Fellowship Association | 1999 | - | - | 2 | - | - |
| Seventh-day Adventists General Conference | 1986 | - | - | 2 | - | - |
| United Pentecostal Ch. Intl., Foreign Msns. Div. | | - | 2 | - | - | - |
| WEC International | 1933 | - | - | 2 | - | - |
| | Totals: | 4 | 2 | 16 | - | - |

**Eritrea**

| | | | | | | |
|---|---|---|---|---|---|---|
| Assemblies of God World Missions | 1995 | - | - | - | - | - |
| Church of the Nazarene, World Mission Dept. | 1993 | - | - | - | - | - |
| Evangelistic Faith Missions | 1950 | - | - | - | - | - |

| | First Year | Personnel from U.S. | | | Other Countries | |
|---|---|---|---|---|---|---|
| | | 1-2 yrs. | 2-4 yrs. | 4+ yrs. | Citizens | Non-Citizens |
| I. N. Network USA | 1980 | - | - | - | - | - |
| Orthodox Presbyterian Church | 1944 | - | - | 4 | - | - |
| Samaritan's Purse | 2002 | 2 | 2 | - | 42 | 2 |
| World Mission Prayer League | 1996 | - | - | 1 | - | 1 |
| | Totals: | 2 | 2 | 5 | 42 | 3 |

## Estonia

| | First Year | 1-2 yrs. | 2-4 yrs. | 4+ yrs. | Citizens | Non-Citizens |
|---|---|---|---|---|---|---|
| Alongside Ministries International | 1998 | - | - | 2 | 1 | - |
| Assemblies of God World Missions | 2001 | - | - | 2 | - | - |
| Baptist General Conference—Intl. Ministries | | - | - | 2 | - | - |
| Baptist International Missions, Inc. (BIMI) | | - | - | 2 | - | - |
| Campus Crusade for Christ, Intl. | 1991 | - | - | 2 | 11 | - |
| Child Evangelism Fellowship, Inc. | 1989 | - | - | - | 1 | - |
| Churches of Christ | 1990 | - | - | 8 | 4 | - |
| Intl. Pentecostal Holiness Ch. World Missions Mins. | 2002 | - | - | 2 | - | - |
| New Mission Systems International | 2005 | - | - | 1 | - | 1 |
| Precept Ministries International | 1994 | - | - | - | 1 | - |
| Reformed Church in Am., Gen. Synod Council | 1994 | - | - | 2 | 3 | - |
| Salvation Army, U.S.A. | | - | - | 3 | - | - |
| TCM International Institute | | - | - | - | 1 | - |
| Walk Thru the Bible Ministries, Inc. | 2001 | - | - | - | - | - |
| | Totals: | - | - | 26 | 22 | 1 |

## Ethiopia

| | First Year | 1-2 yrs. | 2-4 yrs. | 4+ yrs. | Citizens | Non-Citizens |
|---|---|---|---|---|---|---|
| African Enterprise | 1995 | - | - | - | 3 | - |
| African Leadership, Inc. | 1998 | - | - | - | 1 | - |
| Assemblies of God World Missions | 1975 | 2 | - | 5 | - | - |
| Baptist Bible Fellowship International | 1960 | - | - | 12 | - | - |
| Baptist General Conf.—International Ministries | 1950 | 2 | - | 8 | - | - |
| Baptist International Outreach | 1985 | - | - | 1 | 7 | - |
| Baptist Mid-Missions | 1993 | - | - | 2 | 1 | - |
| Bright Hope International | 2004 | - | - | - | 7 | - |
| Campus Crusade for Christ, Intl. | 1980 | - | - | - | 160 | - |
| Christian Churches / Churches of Christ | | - | - | 8 | 2 | - |
| Church of God of Prophecy—Global Outreach | | - | - | - | 9 | - |
| Church of the Nazarene, World Mission Dept. | 1992 | - | - | 6 | - | 2 |
| Churches of Christ | 1961 | - | - | - | 4 | - |
| CityTeam Ministries | | - | - | 1 | - | 2 |
| CMF International | 1963 | - | 14 | - | - | - |
| Compassion International, Inc. | 1993 | - | - | - | 47 | - |
| Eastern Mennonite Missions | | - | 2 | - | - | - |
| Emmanuel International Mission | 1978 | - | - | - | - | - |
| Equip, Inc. | 1995 | - | - | 4 | - | - |
| Evangelical Luth. Ch. in Am., Div. for Global Msn. | 1957 | - | - | 2 | - | - |
| Evangelical Presbyterian Church—World Outreach | 2002 | - | - | 4 | - | - |
| Evangelistic Faith Missions | 1961 | - | - | - | - | - |
| Food for the Hungry, Inc. | 1984 | - | - | - | - | - |
| Free Methodist World Missions | | - | - | - | - | - |
| Harvest | 1999 | - | - | - | 2 | - |
| I. N. Network USA | 1996 | - | - | - | 50 | - |

| | First Year | Personnel from U.S. | | | Other Countries | |
|---|---|---|---|---|---|---|
| | | 1-2 yrs. | 2-4 yrs. | 4+ yrs. | Citizens | Non-Citizens |
| International Christian Ministries | 2001 | - | - | - | 2 | - |
| International Gospel Outreach | 2004 | - | - | 2 | 4 | - |
| Intl. Pentecostal Holiness Ch. World Missions Mins. | 1995 | - | - | - | - | - |
| Larry Jones Intl. Ministries (Feed the Children) | 1983 | - | - | - | 12 | - |
| Medical Ambassadors International, Inc. | 1993 | - | - | - | 4 | - |
| Mission ONE, Inc. | 1990 | - | - | - | 32 | - |
| Mission to the World (PCA), Inc. | 1990 | 1 | 2 | - | - | - |
| Project Mercy, Inc. | 1977 | - | - | 2 | - | - |
| Reformed Church in Am., Gen. Synod Council | 1981 | - | - | 5 | 1 | - |
| Samaritan's Purse | 2004 | 2 | - | - | 46 | - |
| Seventh-day Adventists General Conference | 1907 | - | - | - | - | 13 |
| SIM USA | 1927 | 10 | - | 58 | - | - |
| Source of Light Ministries International, Inc. | | - | - | - | - | - |
| The God's Story Project | 2004 | - | - | - | - | 1 |
| The Word for the World | 1995 | 3 | - | - | - | 2 |
| Walk Thru the Bible Ministries, Inc. | 2001 | - | - | - | - | - |
| World Concern | 1983 | - | - | 1 | 16 | 2 |
| World Missions Far Corners, Inc. | 1982 | - | - | - | 2 | - |
| World Vision Inc. | 1971 | - | - | - | - | - |
| | Totals: | 20 | 18 | 121 | 412 | 22 |

## Europe—General

| | First Year | Personnel from U.S. | | | Other Countries | |
|---|---|---|---|---|---|---|
| | | 1-2 yrs. | 2-4 yrs. | 4+ yrs. | Citizens | Non-Citizens |
| ABWE (Assoc. of Baptists for World Evangelism) | 1970 | - | 42 | 160 | - | - |
| Assemblies of God World Missions | 1925 | 9 | - | 77 | - | - |
| Bakke Graduate University of Ministry | | - | - | - | 2 | - |
| Campus Crusade for Christ, Intl. | | 4 | - | 11 | 9 | - |
| Christian and Missionary Alliance | | - | - | 159 | - | - |
| Christian Church of North America—Missions | 1945 | - | - | 2 | - | - |
| Church of God (Cleveland, TN) World Missions | | - | - | 2 | - | - |
| Church World Service | 1946 | - | - | 1 | 4 | 1 |
| Cook Communications Ministries International | 1991 | - | - | - | - | - |
| Cooperative Baptist Fellowship | 1991 | - | - | 38 | - | - |
| Eastern Mennonite Missions | | - | - | - | - | - |
| Educational Services International (ESI) | 1990 | 40 | - | - | - | - |
| Final Frontiers Foundation, Inc. | 1992 | - | - | - | 25 | - |
| Free Methodist World Missions | | - | - | 2 | - | - |
| Heifer International | 1992 | 10 | 14 | 4 | 31 | 1 |
| Mennonite Central Committee (MCC) | | - | - | 26 | - | - |
| Operation Mobilization | 1963 | - | 2 | 14 | - | 3 |
| Presbyterian Church (USA), Worldwide Ministries | | - | 40 | 37 | - | - |
| Presbyterian Evangelistic Fellowship | | - | - | 9 | - | - |
| Southern Baptist Convention Intl. Mission Board | | - | - | - | - | - |
| Team Expansion, Inc. | 1997 | 2 | - | 16 | - | - |
| Tentmakers International | | - | - | - | - | - |
| TMA Ministries | 1987 | 4 | - | - | - | - |
| United Pentecostal Ch. Intl., Foreign Missions Div. | | - | 6 | - | - | 23 |
| United World Mission | | 1 | 3 | 2 | - | - |
| World Team | 1993 | - | 1 | 14 | - | - |
| Wycliffe Bible Translators, Inc. | 1980 | - | - | 160 | - | - |
| Young Life | | 17 | 8 | 14 | - | - |

| | Personnel from U.S. | | | | Other Countries | |
| --- | --- | --- | --- | --- | --- | --- |
| | First Year | 1-2 yrs. | 2-4 yrs. | 4+ yrs. | Citizens | Non-Citizens |
| Youth for Christ/USA—World Outreach | - | - | 8 | | - | - |
| Totals: | 87 | 116 | 756 | | 71 | 28 |

## Fiji

| | | | | | | |
| --- | --- | --- | --- | --- | --- | --- |
| Assemblies of God World Missions | 1918 | 2 | - | 7 | - | - |
| Awana Clubs International | 1993 | - | - | - | 2 | - |
| Baptist International Missions, Inc. (BIMI) | | - | - | 4 | - | - |
| Biblical Ministries Worldwide | 1990 | - | - | 8 | - | 8 |
| Campus Crusade for Christ, Intl. | 1974 | - | - | - | 11 | 5 |
| Child Evangelism Fellowship, Inc. | 1953 | - | - | 3 | - | - |
| Church of God (Cleveland, TN) World Missions | 1990 | - | - | 2 | - | - |
| Church of God of Prophecy—Global Outreach | | - | - | - | 3 | - |
| Church of the Nazarene, World Mission Dept. | 1995 | - | - | 2 | - | - |
| Churches of Christ | 1961 | - | - | 1 | 2 | - |
| Fellowship International Mission | 1995 | - | - | - | 2 | - |
| Habitat for Humanity International | 1991 | - | 1 | - | - | 1 |
| International Teams, U.S.A. | | - | - | - | - | 2 |
| Pioneers USA | | - | - | 1 | - | 1 |
| United Church of Christ—Wider Church Ministries | | - | 2 | - | - | - |
| United Pentecostal Ch. Intl., Foreign Missions Div. | 1980 | - | 2 | - | - | 2 |
| Walk Thru the Bible Ministries, Inc. | 2002 | - | - | - | - | - |
| Word of Life Fellowship, Inc.—Intl. Ministries | 1986 | - | - | - | - | - |
| Totals: | 2 | 5 | 28 | | 20 | 19 |

## Finland

| | | | | | | |
| --- | --- | --- | --- | --- | --- | --- |
| Arab World Ministries | | - | - | 2 | - | - |
| Assemblies of God World Missions | 2000 | - | - | 2 | - | - |
| Baptist Mid-Missions | 1980 | - | - | 2 | - | - |
| BCM International | | - | - | - | 2 | - |
| Church of God of Prophecy—Global Outreach | | - | - | - | 1 | - |
| Churches of Christ | 1960 | 2 | 2 | 1 | - | - |
| Far East Broadcasting Company, Inc. | 1999 | - | - | 1 | - | - |
| Greater Grace World Outreach | 1975 | - | - | - | 16 | 2 |
| Mennonite Mission Network | 1995 | - | - | - | 1 | 1 |
| Mission Possible Foundation, Inc. | 1985 | - | - | - | - | - |
| Ripe for Harvest, Inc. | 2000 | - | - | 2 | - | - |
| Tentmakers International | | - | - | - | - | - |
| United Pentecostal Ch. Intl., Foreign Missions Div. | | - | - | - | - | 4 |
| Totals: | 2 | 2 | 10 | | 20 | 7 |

## France

| | | | | | | |
| --- | --- | --- | --- | --- | --- | --- |
| Alongside Ministries International | 1980 | 2 | 2 | 2 | - | - |
| AMF International | 1998 | - | - | - | 2 | - |
| Apostolic Team Ministries, Intl. | | - | - | 4 | 1 | - |
| Arab World Ministries | | - | 2 | 25 | - | - |
| Armenian Missionary Association of America, Inc. | 1950 | - | - | - | - | - |
| Assemblies of God World Missions | 1952 | 2 | - | 13 | - | - |
| Avant Ministries | 1960 | - | - | 5 | - | - |
| Baptist Bible Fellowship International | 1970 | - | - | 10 | - | - |
| Baptist General Conference—Intl. Ministries | 1989 | - | - | 6 | - | - |

| | First Year | Personnel from U.S. | | | Other Countries | |
|---|---|---|---|---|---|---|
| | | 1-2 yrs. | 2-4 yrs. | 4+ yrs. | Citizens | Non-Citizens |
| Baptist International Missions, Inc. (BIMI) | | - | - | 8 | - | - |
| Baptist Mid-Missions | 1948 | - | - | 29 | - | - |
| BCM International | | - | - | 3 | 1 | - |
| Bethany International Ministries | 1987 | - | - | 8 | - | 2 |
| Bibles & Literature in French | 2006 | - | - | 2 | 2 | - |
| Biblical Ministries Worldwide | 1996 | - | - | 8 | - | 8 |
| BILD International | | - | - | - | 2 | - |
| Brethren Assemblies | | - | - | 15 | - | - |
| Campus Crusade for Christ, Intl. | 1970 | 17 | - | 57 | - | 9 |
| Child Evangelism Fellowship, Inc. | 1949 | - | - | 2 | - | - |
| Chosen People Ministries | | - | - | - | - | - |
| Christar | 1988 | - | - | 15 | - | 1 |
| Christian Associates International | | - | - | - | - | - |
| Christian Churches / Churches of Christ | | - | 1 | 5 | - | - |
| Christian Outreach International | 1992 | - | - | 1 | 1 | - |
| Christian Reformed World Missions | 1989 | - | - | 2 | - | - |
| Church of God (Cleveland, TN) World Missions | 1960 | - | - | 3 | - | - |
| Church of God of Prophecy—Global Outreach | | - | - | - | 3 | - |
| Church of the Nazarene, World Mission Dept. | 1977 | - | - | 4 | - | - |
| Church Resource Ministries (CRM) | 1996 | - | - | 4 | - | - |
| Churches of Christ | 1949 | - | - | 14 | 4 | - |
| CrossWorld | 1962 | - | - | 23 | - | - |
| EFCA International Mission | 1988 | - | 2 | 12 | - | - |
| Episcopal Church USA—Domestic & Foreign | | - | - | 1 | - | - |
| European Christian Mission International—USA | | - | - | 13 | - | - |
| Evangel Bible Translators | 1978 | - | - | 2 | - | - |
| Evangelical Baptist Missions | | - | 1 | 12 | - | - |
| Evangelical Covenant Ch.—Covenant Wld. Msn. | 1996 | - | - | 3 | - | - |
| Evangelical Presbyterian Church—World Outreach | 1983 | - | - | 2 | - | - |
| Fellowship International Mission | 1986 | - | - | - | - | 1 |
| Free Methodist World Missions | | - | - | 2 | - | - |
| Free Will Baptist, Inc. Board of Intl. Missions | 1966 | - | 1 | 18 | - | - |
| Friends of Israel Gospel Ministry, Inc. | 1990 | - | - | - | 2 | - |
| Global Outreach Mission, Inc. | 1946 | - | - | 35 | 15 | - |
| Gospel Furthering Fellowship, The | | - | - | 2 | - | - |
| Grace Brethren International Missions | 1951 | 1 | - | 17 | - | 2 |
| Greater Europe Mission | 1949 | - | 7 | 28 | - | - |
| Greater Grace World Outreach | 1981 | - | - | - | 8 | - |
| Hope for the Hungry | | - | - | 1 | - | 1 |
| International Outreach Ministries (IOM) | 1996 | - | - | 4 | - | - |
| Intl. Pentecostal Holiness Ch. World Missions Mins. | 1981 | - | - | 1 | - | - |
| International Teams, U.S.A. | | - | - | 16 | - | 5 |
| InterVarsity Christian Fellowship/USA—Msns. Dept. | | - | 4 | - | - | - |
| Jews for Jesus | 1992 | - | - | 1 | 1 | 4 |
| Mennonite Mission Network | 1953 | - | - | 3 | - | - |
| Mission to the World (PCA), Inc. | 1978 | - | 15 | - | - | - |
| Missionary Revival Crusade | 1983 | - | 1 | 4 | 1 | - |
| Missions to Military, Inc. | 1972 | - | - | 5 | - | - |
| Navigators, U.S. International Missions Group | | - | - | 2 | - | - |
| Operation Mobilization | 1961 | - | 1 | 2 | - | 2 |

| | Personnel from U.S. | | | | Other Countries | |
| --- | --- | --- | --- | --- | --- | --- |
| | First Year | 1-2 yrs. | 2-4 yrs. | 4+ yrs. | Citizens | Non-Citizens |
| Presbyterian Evangelistic Fellowship | | - | - | 5 | - | - |
| Presbyterian Mission International (PMI) | 2003 | - | - | - | 1 | - |
| Reformed Baptist Mission Services | | - | - | - | - | 2 |
| Reformed Episcopal Board of Foreign Missions | | - | - | 1 | - | - |
| Ripe for Harvest, Inc. | 2001 | - | - | 7 | - | - |
| Seventh-day Adventists General Conference | 1876 | - | - | - | - | 2 |
| TEAM (The Evangelical Alliance Mission) | | - | - | 35 | - | - |
| The Mission Society | 1986 | - | 1 | 6 | - | - |
| United Pentecostal Ch. Intl., Foreign Missions Div. | 1930 | - | 8 | - | - | - |
| WEC International | 1950 | - | - | 2 | - | - |
| Word of Life Fellowship, Inc.—Intl. Ministries | 1999 | - | - | 6 | 2 | 2 |
| World Baptist Fellowship Mission Agency, Inc. | | - | - | 2 | - | - |
| World Horizons | 1982 | - | - | 5 | - | 2 |
| World Missions & Evangelism, Inc. | | - | - | 2 | - | - |
| World Partners USA | 1979 | - | - | 3 | - | - |
| World Team | 1980 | - | - | 15 | - | - |
| World Venture | 1962 | - | - | 10 | 2 | - |
| Youth for Christ/USA—World Outreach | 1949 | - | - | 2 | - | - |
| | Totals: | 22 | 46 | 555 | 48 | 43 |

### French Guiana

| | First Year | 1-2 yrs. | 2-4 yrs. | 4+ yrs. | Citizens | Non-Citizens |
| --- | --- | --- | --- | --- | --- | --- |
| Church of God of Prophecy—Global Outreach | | - | - | - | 1 | - |
| Church of the Nazarene, World Mission Dept. | 1988 | - | - | - | - | - |
| Intl. Pentecostal Ch. of Christ—Global Msns. Dept. | 1998 | - | - | 1 | 1 | - |
| Seventh-day Adventists General Conference | 1946 | - | - | - | - | 2 |
| United Pentecostal Ch. Intl., Foreign Missions Div. | 1991 | - | 2 | - | - | - |
| | Totals: | - | 2 | 1 | 2 | 2 |

### French Polynesia

| | First Year | 1-2 yrs. | 2-4 yrs. | 4+ yrs. | Citizens | Non-Citizens |
| --- | --- | --- | --- | --- | --- | --- |
| Assemblies of God World Missions | 1979 | - | - | 2 | - | - |
| Baptist International Missions, Inc. (BIMI) | | - | - | 2 | - | - |
| Seventh-day Adventists General Conference | 1891 | - | - | - | - | 2 |
| | Totals: | - | - | 4 | - | 2 |

### Gabon

| | First Year | 1-2 yrs. | 2-4 yrs. | 4+ yrs. | Citizens | Non-Citizens |
| --- | --- | --- | --- | --- | --- | --- |
| Assemblies of God World Missions | 2000 | - | - | - | - | - |
| Campus Crusade for Christ, Intl. | 1989 | - | - | - | 7 | - |
| Church of God of Prophecy—Global Outreach | | - | - | - | 2 | - |
| Church of the Nazarene, World Mission Dept. | 1999 | - | - | - | - | - |
| Global Outreach Mission, Inc. | | - | - | 1 | - | - |
| InterVarsity Christian Fellowship/USA—Msns. Dept. | | - | - | 2 | - | - |
| Medical Ambassadors International, Inc. | 1993 | - | - | - | - | - |
| Missionary Ventures International | | - | - | - | - | 2 |
| United Pentecostal Ch. Intl., Foreign Missions Div. | 2001 | - | 2 | - | - | - |
| | Totals: | - | 2 | 3 | 9 | 2 |

### Gambia, The

| | First Year | 1-2 yrs. | 2-4 yrs. | 4+ yrs. | Citizens | Non-Citizens |
| --- | --- | --- | --- | --- | --- | --- |
| Assemblies of God World Missions | 1996 | - | - | 2 | - | - |
| Child Evangelism Fellowship, Inc. | 1986 | - | - | 2 | - | - |
| Church of God of Prophecy—Global Outreach | | - | - | - | 1 | - |

| | First Year | Personnel from U.S. | | | Other Countries | |
|---|---|---|---|---|---|---|
| | | 1-2 yrs. | 2-4 yrs. | 4+ yrs. | Citizens | Non-Citizens |
| International Gospel Outreach | 1988 | - | - | 1 | 2 | - |
| Seventh-day Adventists General Conference | 1973 | - | - | - | - | 2 |
| United Pentecostal Ch. Intl., Foreign Missions Div. | 2003 | - | 2 | - | - | - |
| Totals: | | - | 2 | 5 | 3 | 2 |

## Georgia

| | First Year | 1-2 yrs. | 2-4 yrs. | 4+ yrs. | Citizens | Non-Citizens |
|---|---|---|---|---|---|---|
| Armenian Missionary Association of America, Inc. | 1988 | - | - | - | - | - |
| Assemblies of God World Missions | 1999 | 5 | - | 4 | - | - |
| Church Leadership Development International | 1996 | - | - | - | 1 | - |
| Entrust | 1991 | - | - | - | - | - |
| International Gospel Outreach | 2003 | - | - | 1 | 1 | - |
| Salvation Army, U.S.A. | 1993 | - | - | 1 | - | - |
| Seventh-day Adventists General Conference | 1886 | - | - | 2 | - | - |
| United Pentecostal Ch. Intl., Foreign Missions Div. | | - | - | - | - | 2 |
| Walk Thru the Bible Ministries, Inc. | 2001 | - | - | - | - | - |
| Totals: | | 5 | - | 8 | 2 | 2 |

## Germany

| | First Year | 1-2 yrs. | 2-4 yrs. | 4+ yrs. | Citizens | Non-Citizens |
|---|---|---|---|---|---|---|
| Apostolic Team Ministries, Intl. | | - | - | - | 2 | - |
| Artists In Christian Testimony | 2005 | - | - | 1 | - | - |
| Assemblies of God World Missions | 1948 | 9 | - | 40 | - | - |
| Avant Ministries | 1961 | 3 | - | - | - | - |
| Baptist Bible Fellowship International | 1970 | - | - | 18 | - | - |
| Baptist International Missions, Inc. (BIMI) | | - | - | 30 | - | - |
| Baptist Mid-Missions | 1952 | - | - | 17 | - | - |
| BCM International | | - | - | 3 | 6 | - |
| Biblical Ministries Worldwide | 1958 | - | - | 10 | - | 10 |
| Brethren Assemblies | | - | - | 4 | - | - |
| Cadence International | | - | 36 | - | - | 36 |
| Campus Crusade for Christ, Intl. | 1966 | 16 | - | 29 | - | 10 |
| Child Evangelism Fellowship, Inc. | 1949 | - | - | 4 | - | - |
| Chosen People Ministries | 1995 | - | - | - | - | - |
| Christar | 1989 | - | - | 5 | - | - |
| Christian Associates International | 1996 | - | - | - | - | - |
| Christian Churches / Churches of Christ | | - | 2 | 8 | - | - |
| Christians In Action Missions International | 1972 | - | - | 3 | 1 | - |
| Church of God (Cleveland, TN) World Missions | 1936 | 2 | 2 | 10 | - | 4 |
| Church of God of Prophecy—Global Outreach | | - | - | 4 | 1 | - |
| Church of the Nazarene, World Mission Dept. | 1958 | - | - | - | - | - |
| Churches of Christ | 1947 | - | - | 28 | 20 | - |
| CrossWorld | 1976 | - | - | 23 | - | - |
| Eastern Mennonite Missions | | 1 | 4 | 2 | - | - |
| EFCA International Mission | 1958 | 1 | - | 10 | - | - |
| Episcopal Church USA—Domestic & Foreign | | - | - | 1 | - | - |
| European Christian Mission International—USA | | - | - | 4 | - | - |
| Evangelical Baptist Missions | | - | - | 8 | 1 | 1 |
| Evangelical Lutheran Church in America | 1972 | 3 | - | 6 | - | - |
| Evangelical Presbyterian Church—World Outreach | 2003 | - | - | 2 | - | - |
| Fellowship International Mission | 1984 | - | - | - | - | 2 |
| Global Outreach Mission, Inc. | 1946 | - | - | 6 | 8 | - |

| | First Year | Personnel from U.S. | | | Other Countries | |
|---|---|---|---|---|---|---|
| | | 1-2 yrs. | 2-4 yrs. | 4+ yrs. | Citizens | Non-Citizens |
| Global Partners / Wesleyan World Missions | 1987 | - | - | - | - | - |
| Globe Missionary Evangelism | 1987 | - | - | 2 | - | - |
| Go Ye Fellowship | | - | - | 1 | - | 1 |
| Good Shepherd Ministries International | 2005 | 2 | - | - | - | - |
| Gospel Fellowship Association | 1963 | 1 | - | 20 | - | - |
| Grace Brethren International Missions | 1969 | - | - | 4 | - | 2 |
| Great Commission Ministries, Inc. | | 2 | - | 4 | - | - |
| Greater Europe Mission | 1954 | - | 2 | 66 | - | - |
| Greater Grace World Outreach | 1998 | - | - | 2 | - | 3 |
| International Messengers | 1996 | - | 1 | - | 2 | - |
| Intl. Pentecostal Holiness Ch. World Missions Mins. | 1987 | - | 2 | 2 | - | - |
| Janz Team Ministries USA | 1955 | 6 | - | 36 | - | - |
| Jews for Jesus | | - | - | 2 | - | 1 |
| Liebenzell USA | 1993 | - | - | 1 | - | - |
| Macedonia World Baptist Missions, Inc. | 1990 | - | - | 4 | - | - |
| Mennonite Mission Network | 1994 | - | - | - | - | 2 |
| Mission Aviation Fellowship | | - | - | 1 | - | - |
| Mission to the World (PCA), Inc. | 1991 | 1 | 8 | - | - | - |
| Navigators, U.S. International Missions Group | | - | 1 | - | - | - |
| Network of International Christian Schools | 2002 | - | 2 | 1 | - | 1 |
| New Mission Systems International | | - | - | 1 | 3 | - |
| New Tribes Mission | 1991 | - | - | 2 | 15 | - |
| OC International, Inc. | 1981 | - | - | 13 | - | - |
| Precept Ministries International | 1992 | - | - | - | 1 | - |
| Reformed Episcopal Board of Foreign Missions | | - | - | 1 | 5 | - |
| Ripe for Harvest, Inc. | 1996 | - | - | 2 | - | - |
| Salvation Army, U.S.A. | 1886 | - | - | 2 | - | - |
| Seventh-day Adventists General Conference | 1875 | - | - | - | - | 2 |
| Source of Light Ministries International, Inc. | | - | - | - | - | - |
| TEAM (The Evangelical Alliance Mission) | | - | 2 | 18 | - | - |
| Trans World Radio, International | | - | - | 2 | 5 | - |
| Turkish World Outreach | 1988 | - | - | 2 | 2 | - |
| United Church of Christ—Wider Church Ministries | | - | 2 | - | - | - |
| United Pentecostal Ch. Intl., Foreign Missions Div. | 1960 | - | 4 | - | - | - |
| Word of Life Fellowship, Inc.—Intl. Ministries | 1965 | - | - | 6 | 48 | - |
| World Harvest Mission | 1996 | - | - | 3 | - | - |
| World Reach, Inc. | 1998 | - | - | - | 2 | - |
| World Venture | 1981 | 1 | 2 | - | - | - |
| World Witness, Assoc. Reformed Presbyterian Ch. | 1991 | - | - | 8 | 1 | - |
| Youth for Christ/USA—World Outreach | | - | - | 9 | - | - |
| Totals: | | 48 | 70 | 491 | 123 | 75 |

## Ghana

| | First Year | 1-2 yrs. | 2-4 yrs. | 4+ yrs. | Citizens | Non-Citizens |
|---|---|---|---|---|---|---|
| Advent Christian Gen. Conf., Dept. of Wld. Msns. | 1995 | - | - | - | 10 | - |
| African Enterprise | 1995 | - | - | - | 4 | - |
| African Leadership, Inc. | 1998 | - | - | - | 1 | - |
| African Mission Evangelism, Inc. | 1966 | - | - | 9 | 15 | - |
| Agape Gospel Mission | | - | - | 2 | 60 | 1 |
| Allegheny Wesleyan Methodist Connection | 1997 | - | - | 3 | - | - |
| AMG International | | - | - | - | 2 | - |

| | First Year | Personnel from U.S. | | | Other Countries | |
|---|---|---|---|---|---|---|
| | | 1-2 yrs. | 2-4 yrs. | 4+ yrs. | Citizens | Non-Citizens |
| Anis Shorrosh Evangelistic Association | | - | - | - | - | - |
| Apostolic Christian Church Foundation, Inc. | 1975 | - | - | - | 2 | - |
| Artists In Christian Testimony | 1999 | - | 2 | - | - | - |
| Assemblies of God World Missions | 1930 | - | - | 8 | - | - |
| Awana Clubs International | 1984 | - | - | - | 4 | - |
| Baptist International Missions, Inc. (BIMI) | | - | - | 8 | - | - |
| Baptist Mid-Missions | 1946 | - | - | 12 | - | - |
| Bethany International Ministries | 1995 | - | - | 2 | - | 2 |
| Bright Hope International | 2004 | - | - | - | 1 | - |
| Campus Crusade for Christ, Intl. | 1969 | - | - | 1 | 86 | 6 |
| Child Evangelism Fellowship, Inc. | 1971 | - | - | - | 12 | - |
| Christ to the Nations | 2002 | - | - | - | 4 | - |
| Christian Aid Mission | | - | - | - | 1 | - |
| Christian Broadcasting Network Inc., the | 1999 | - | - | - | 2 | - |
| Christian Churches / Churches of Christ | | - | 1 | 13 | 2 | - |
| Christian Literature International | | - | - | - | - | - |
| Christians In Action Missions International | 1994 | - | - | 1 | - | - |
| Christ's Mandate for Missions | 2002 | - | - | 5 | - | - |
| Church of God (Cleveland, TN) World Missions | 1950 | 2 | - | 4 | - | - |
| Church of the Nazarene, World Mission Dept. | 1990 | - | - | 2 | - | - |
| Churches of Christ | 1961 | - | - | 6 | 15 | - |
| Development Associates International (DAI) | 1999 | - | - | 1 | - | - |
| Elim Fellowship—International Department | 2000 | - | - | 1 | - | 1 |
| Episcopal Church USA—Domestic & Foreign | | - | - | 1 | - | - |
| Equip, Inc. | 2001 | - | - | - | 2 | - |
| Evangel Bible Translators | 1992 | - | - | 2 | - | - |
| Evangelism Explosion International | | - | - | - | - | 2 |
| Every Child Ministries, Inc. | 1999 | - | - | - | 34 | - |
| Fellowship International Mission | 2002 | - | - | - | 2 | - |
| Fellowship of Associates of Medical Evangelism | 1987 | - | - | - | 16 | - |
| Global Partners / Wesleyan World Missions | 2004 | - | - | - | - | - |
| Gospel Communications International, Inc. | 1990 | - | - | - | 7 | - |
| Gospel Revival Ministries | 1996 | - | - | - | 2 | - |
| Greater Grace World Outreach | 1986 | - | - | 2 | 152 | - |
| Habitat for Humanity International | 1987 | - | 1 | - | 1 | - |
| Harvest | 2001 | - | - | - | 2 | - |
| HCJB Global | 2005 | - | - | 2 | - | - |
| Hosanna | 1989 | - | - | - | 12 | - |
| I. N. Network USA | 1986 | - | - | - | 91 | - |
| International Gospel Outreach | 1988 | - | - | 1 | 2 | - |
| International Partnership Ministries, Inc. | 1987 | 2 | - | - | 19 | - |
| Intl. Pentecostal Holiness Ch. World Missions Mins. | 1992 | - | - | 2 | - | - |
| Ireland Outreach International Inc. | 1997 | - | - | - | 6 | - |
| Kids Around the World, Inc. | 1998 | - | - | - | 2 | - |
| Literacy & Evangelism International | 2006 | - | - | - | 2 | - |
| Lutheran Bible Translators, Inc. | 2000 | - | - | 5 | 3 | - |
| Media Associates International | | - | - | - | 1 | - |
| Mennonite Mission Network | 1957 | - | - | - | - | - |
| Mission: Moving Mountains, Inc. | 2002 | - | - | - | - | - |
| Mutual Faith Ministries Intl. | | - | - | - | - | - |

| | | Personnel from U.S. | | | Other Countries | |
|---|---|---|---|---|---|---|
| | First Year | 1-2 yrs. | 2-4 yrs. | 4+ yrs. | Citizens | Non-Citizens |
| Natl. Baptist Conv. of Am.—Foreign Msn. Bd. | 1984 | - | - | - | 14 | - |
| Navigators, U.S. International Missions Group | | - | - | 1 | - | - |
| Partners International | 1973 | - | - | - | 333 | - |
| Self-Help International | 1990 | - | - | - | 5 | - |
| Seventh-day Adventists General Conference | 1894 | - | - | - | - | 6 |
| SIM USA | 1952 | 1 | - | 12 | - | - |
| Source of Light Ministries International, Inc. | 1995 | - | - | - | 2 | - |
| The Mission Society | 1985 | 2 | - | 6 | - | - |
| United Pentecostal Ch. Intl., Foreign Missions Div. | 1969 | - | 4 | - | - | 3 |
| Village Ministries International | 1997 | - | - | - | 6 | - |
| Walk Thru the Bible Ministries, Inc. | 2001 | - | - | - | - | - |
| WEC International | 1946 | - | - | 3 | - | - |
| White Fields Inc. | | - | - | - | 6 | - |
| Word of Life Fellowship, Inc.—Intl. Ministries | 2003 | - | - | - | 1 | 1 |
| World Venture | | - | - | 2 | - | - |
| World Vision Inc. | 1958 | - | - | - | - | - |
| Totals: | | 7 | 8 | 117 | 944 | 22 |

## Greece

| | | | | | | |
|---|---|---|---|---|---|---|
| AMG International | 1945 | - | - | 6 | 401 | - |
| Armenian Missionary Association of America, Inc. | 1950 | - | - | - | - | - |
| Assemblies of God World Missions | 1935 | 4 | - | 4 | - | - |
| Avant Ministries | 1959 | - | - | - | 1 | - |
| Baptist Bible Fellowship International | 1993 | - | - | 2 | - | - |
| BCM International | | - | - | - | 1 | - |
| Brethren Assemblies | | - | - | 4 | - | - |
| Campus Crusade for Christ, Intl. | 1978 | - | - | 3 | - | - |
| Child Evangelism Fellowship, Inc. | 1971 | - | - | 2 | 2 | - |
| Church of God (Cleveland, TN) World Missions | 1972 | - | - | 2 | - | - |
| Church of God of Prophecy—Global Outreach | | - | - | - | 1 | - |
| Church of the Nazarene, World Mission Dept. | 2002 | - | - | - | - | - |
| Churches of Christ | 1960 | - | - | 2 | 10 | - |
| Entrust | 1991 | - | - | 4 | - | - |
| Fellowship International Mission | 2002 | - | - | - | 2 | - |
| Free Methodist World Missions | 1998 | - | - | 2 | - | - |
| Global Outreach Mission, Inc. | 1994 | - | - | 2 | - | - |
| Greater Europe Mission | 1966 | - | - | 12 | - | - |
| Hellenic Ministries | 1980 | - | 1 | 4 | 9 | - |
| International Gospel Outreach | 2005 | - | - | 2 | - | - |
| International Teams, U.S.A. | 1984 | - | - | 9 | 4 | 11 |
| Missionary Revival Crusade | | - | - | - | - | - |
| Presbyterian Evangelistic Fellowship | | - | - | 1 | - | - |
| Ripe for Harvest, Inc. | 1999 | - | - | 2 | - | - |
| Seventh-day Adventists General Conference | 1907 | - | - | - | - | 1 |
| United Pentecostal Ch. Intl., Foreign Missions Div. | 1975 | - | 4 | - | - | 1 |
| World Team | | - | - | 2 | - | - |
| Totals: | | 4 | 5 | 65 | 431 | 13 |

## Greenland

| | | | | | | |
|---|---|---|---|---|---|---|
| Assemblies of God World Missions | 1989 | - | - | - | - | - |

| | Personnel from U.S. | | | | Other Countries | |
|---|---|---|---|---|---|---|
| | First Year | 1-2 yrs. | 2-4 yrs. | 4+ yrs. | Citizens | Non-Citizens |
| New Tribes Mission | 1986 | - | - | 2 | - | - |
| Totals: | | - | - | 2 | - | - |
| **Grenada** | | | | | | - |
| Christian Churches / Churches of Christ | | - | - | 2 | - | - |
| Church of the Nazarene, World Mission Dept. | 1977 | - | - | - | - | - |
| Foursquare Missions International | 1987 | - | - | 1 | - | - |
| Ministries In Action | 1974 | - | - | - | 2 | - |
| United Pentecostal Ch. Intl., Foreign Missions Div. | | - | - | - | - | 2 |
| World Relief | | 2 | - | - | - | - |
| Totals: | | 2 | - | 3 | 2 | 2 |
| **Guadeloupe** | | | | | | |
| Baptist International Missions, Inc. (BIMI) | | - | - | 2 | - | - |
| Church of the Nazarene, World Mission Dept. | 1986 | - | - | - | - | - |
| Ministries In Action | 2004 | - | - | - | - | - |
| World Team | 1947 | - | - | 2 | - | - |
| Totals: | | - | - | 4 | - | - |
| **Guam** | | | | | | |
| Assemblies of God World Missions | 1957 | - | - | 2 | - | - |
| Church of God (Anderson, Ind.), Global Missions | 1955 | - | 4 | - | - | - |
| Church of the Nazarene, World Mission Dept. | 1971 | - | - | 2 | - | - |
| Elim Fellowship—International Department | 1991 | - | - | 1 | - | 1 |
| Evangelical Luth. Ch. in Am., Div. for Global Msn. | 1961 | - | - | 2 | - | - |
| Liebenzell USA | 1972 | 3 | - | 6 | - | - |
| Macedonia World Baptist Missions, Inc. | 1988 | - | - | 2 | - | - |
| Mission to the World (PCA), Inc. | 1996 | - | - | - | - | - |
| Seventh-day Adventists General Conference | 1930 | - | - | 58 | - | 6 |
| Trans World Radio, International | 1977 | 7 | - | 9 | - | - |
| United Pentecostal Ch. Intl., Foreign Missions Div. | | - | - | - | - | 2 |
| Totals: | | 10 | 4 | 82 | - | 9 |
| **Guatemala** | | | | | | |
| All God's Children International | 2000 | 1 | - | - | 130 | 1 |
| AMG International | 1978 | 2 | 4 | - | 460 | - |
| Assemblies of God World Missions | 1935 | 5 | - | 12 | - | - |
| Awana Clubs International | 1987 | - | - | - | 2 | 3 |
| Baptist Bible Fellowship International | 1975 | - | - | 4 | - | - |
| Baptist International Missions, Inc. (BIMI) | | - | - | 2 | - | - |
| BILD International | | - | - | - | 1 | - |
| Brethren Assemblies | | - | - | 2 | - | - |
| Calvary International | 1987 | - | 1 | 13 | 1 | 1 |
| CAM International | 1890 | - | - | 48 | - | - |
| Campus Crusade for Christ, Intl. | 1963 | - | - | - | 40 | - |
| Caring Partners International, Inc. | 1993 | - | - | - | - | - |
| Child Evangelism Fellowship, Inc. | 1943 | - | - | - | 1 | - |
| Christian Churches / Churches of Christ | | - | - | 2 | 2 | - |
| Christian Reformed World Relief Committee | 1976 | - | 2 | - | 1 | - |
| Christians In Action Missions International | 1970 | - | - | 2 | 7 | - |

| | First Year | Personnel from U.S. | | | Other Countries | |
|---|---|---|---|---|---|---|
| | | 1-2 yrs. | 2-4 yrs. | 4+ yrs. | Citizens | Non-Citizens |
| Christ's Mandate for Missions | 1985 | - | - | 5 | 5 | - |
| Church of God (Cleveland, TN) World Missions | 1934 | - | - | 2 | - | - |
| Church of the Nazarene, World Mission Dept. | 1904 | - | - | 20 | - | 12 |
| Churches of Christ | 1960 | - | - | 4 | 8 | - |
| Commission to Every Nation | 1995 | 11 | 6 | 9 | 2 | - |
| Compassion International, Inc. | 1976 | - | - | - | 31 | - |
| Eastern Mennonite Missions | | - | 2 | 2 | - | - |
| Engineering Ministries International | 1999 | - | - | 6 | 1 | - |
| Envoy International | | - | - | - | - | - |
| Evangel Bible Translators | 1999 | - | - | 2 | - | - |
| Evangelism Explosion International | | - | - | - | - | 2 |
| Evangelistic Faith Missions | 1960 | 2 | - | - | - | - |
| Fellowship International Mission | 1997 | - | - | 1 | - | - |
| Flying Doctors of Am. (Medical Mercy Msns., Inc.) | 1990 | - | - | - | - | - |
| Food for the Hungry, Inc. | 1976 | - | 3 | 3 | 1 | - |
| Global Outreach International | 1998 | - | - | 1 | - | - |
| Global Outreach Mission, Inc. | | - | - | 11 | 11 | - |
| Global Partners / Wesleyan World Missions | 1997 | - | 2 | - | - | - |
| Globe Missionary Evangelism | 1980 | - | - | 6 | - | - |
| Help for Christian Nationals, Inc. | 1994 | - | - | 2 | - | 2 |
| Hope for the Hungry | | - | - | 2 | - | 2 |
| Hosanna | 1995 | - | - | - | 2 | - |
| Impact International | 1970 | - | - | 2 | 2 | - |
| International Gospel Outreach | 2003 | - | - | 2 | - | - |
| International Justice Mission | | - | - | - | 4 | - |
| International Partnership Ministries, Inc. | 1994 | - | - | - | 1 | 1 |
| Intl. Pentecostal Holiness Ch. World Missions Mins. | 1995 | - | - | 2 | - | - |
| Kids Alive International | 1993 | 2 | 4 | 3 | 15 | 1 |
| Larry Jones Intl. Ministries (Feed the Children) | 1984 | - | - | - | 11 | - |
| Living Water Teaching | 1979 | - | 2 | 5 | 4 | - |
| Luke Society, Inc., The | 1996 | - | - | - | - | - |
| Lutheran Bible Translators, Inc. | 1996 | - | - | 10 | 5 | - |
| Lutheran Church-Missouri Synod | 1947 | - | - | 1 | - | - |
| Macedonia World Baptist Missions, Inc. | 2005 | - | - | 2 | - | - |
| Medical Ambassadors International, Inc. | 1983 | - | - | - | 21 | - |
| Mission Aviation Fellowship | | 1 | - | - | - | - |
| Mission to the Americas | 1990 | - | - | 4 | 2 | - |
| Missionary Ventures International | 1985 | - | - | 8 | 4 | - |
| Mutual Faith Ministries Intl. | 1993 | - | - | 2 | - | - |
| Navigators, U.S. International Missions Group | | 1 | - | 1 | - | - |
| New Life Advance International | 1976 | - | - | 6 | - | - |
| OC International, Inc. | 1979 | - | - | 13 | - | 2 |
| Pentecostal Free Will Baptist Church, Inc. | | - | - | - | 1 | - |
| Precept Ministries International | 1983 | - | - | - | 1 | - |
| Primitive Methodist Church in the USA | | - | - | 5 | - | - |
| Reciprocal Ministries International | 1996 | - | - | 4 | - | - |
| Reformed Church in Am., Gen. Synod Council | 2001 | - | - | - | 1 | - |
| Ripe for Harvest, Inc. | 1995 | 4 | 2 | 5 | - | - |
| SIM USA | | - | - | 2 | - | - |
| Source of Light Ministries International, Inc. | | - | - | - | - | - |

| | Personnel from U.S. | | | | Other Countries | |
|---|---|---|---|---|---|---|
| | First Year | 1-2 yrs. | 2-4 yrs. | 4+ yrs. | Citizens | Non-Citizens |
| Spanish World Ministries | | - | - | 1 | 1 | - |
| Trans World Missions | | - | - | - | - | 2 |
| United Church of Christ—Wider Church Ministries | | - | 1 | - | - | - |
| United Pentecostal Ch. Intl., Foreign Missions Div. | 1977 | - | 3 | - | - | 4 |
| Walk Thru the Bible Ministries, Inc. | 2000 | - | - | - | - | - |
| Word of Life Fellowship, Inc.—Intl. Ministries | 1998 | - | - | - | 12 | 2 |
| World Baptist Fellowship Mission Agency, Inc. | | - | 2 | 2 | - | - |
| World Missions & Evangelism, Inc. | | - | 2 | - | - | - |
| World-Wide Missions | 1968 | - | - | - | 1 | - |
| Totals: | | 29 | 36 | 241 | 792 | 35 |

## Guinea

| | | | | | | |
|---|---|---|---|---|---|---|
| Campus Crusade for Christ, Intl. | 1977 | - | - | - | 29 | - |
| Child Evangelism Fellowship, Inc. | 1992 | - | - | - | 1 | - |
| Christian Churches / Churches of Christ | | - | 5 | 15 | - | - |
| Christian Reformed World Missions | 1984 | 2 | - | 13 | - | - |
| International Gospel Outreach | 1988 | - | - | 1 | 2 | - |
| Natl. Baptist Conv. USA, Inc.—Foreign Msn. Bd. | 1990 | - | - | 1 | - | - |
| New Tribes Mission | 1988 | - | - | 25 | - | - |
| Open Bible Churches, International Ministries | 1987 | - | - | 2 | - | - |
| Pioneer Bible Translators | 1988 | - | - | 27 | - | 1 |
| SIM USA | 1986 | - | - | 11 | - | - |
| WEC International | 1984 | - | - | 2 | - | - |
| World Partners USA | 1995 | - | - | 6 | - | - |
| World Venture | 2003 | - | - | 5 | - | - |
| Totals: | | 2 | 5 | 108 | 32 | 1 |

## Guinea-Bissau

| | | | | | | |
|---|---|---|---|---|---|---|
| | | - | - | - | - | - |
| Abundant Life Association, Inc. | 1990 | - | - | - | 2 | - |
| Assemblies of God World Missions | 1991 | - | - | - | - | - |
| Campus Crusade for Christ, Intl. | 1996 | - | - | - | 3 | 2 |
| Christians In Action Missions International | 2002 | - | - | - | - | 2 |
| Church of the Nazarene, World Mission Dept. | 2004 | - | - | - | - | - |
| Hisportic Christian Mission | | - | - | - | - | 1 |
| International Gospel Outreach | 1988 | - | - | 1 | 2 | - |
| WEC International | 1939 | - | - | 2 | - | - |
| Youth for Christ/USA—World Outreach | | - | - | 6 | - | - |
| Totals: | | - | - | 9 | 7 | 5 |

## Guyana

| | | | | | | |
|---|---|---|---|---|---|---|
| Adventist World Aviation | 2005 | - | - | 2 | - | - |
| Assemblies of God World Missions | 1953 | - | - | - | - | - |
| Baptist Mid-Missions | 1954 | - | - | 2 | - | - |
| BCM International | | - | - | - | 4 | - |
| Campus Crusade for Christ, Intl. | 1977 | - | - | - | 8 | - |
| Christ Community Church | 1948 | - | - | - | 4 | - |
| Christian Churches / Churches of Christ | | - | - | - | 2 | - |
| Church of God of Prophecy—Global Outreach | | - | - | - | 2 | - |
| Church of the Nazarene, World Mission Dept. | 1946 | - | - | - | - | - |
| Churches of Christ | 1982 | - | - | 6 | 4 | - |

| | First Year | Personnel from U.S. | | | Other Countries | |
|---|---|---|---|---|---|---|
| | | 1-2 yrs. | 2-4 yrs. | 4+ yrs. | Citizens | Non-Citizens |
| CrossWorld | 1949 | - | - | 8 | - | - |
| Evangelical Luth. Ch. in Am., Div. for Global Msn. | 1914 | - | - | 2 | - | - |
| Global Outreach International | 1994 | - | - | 5 | - | - |
| Global Outreach Mission, Inc. | | - | - | - | 2 | - |
| Global Partners / Wesleyan World Missions | 1913 | - | 3 | - | - | - |
| Intl. Pentecostal Holiness Ch. Wld. Missions Mins. | 1996 | - | - | 2 | - | - |
| Lott Carey Baptist Foreign Mission Convention | 1961 | - | - | - | 100 | - |
| Macedonia World Baptist Missions, Inc. | 1998 | - | - | - | - | 4 |
| Seventh-day Adventists General Conference | 1883 | - | - | 4 | - | 2 |
| Source of Light Ministries International, Inc. | 1960 | - | - | - | 1 | - |
| TMA Ministries | 1998 | - | - | - | - | - |
| United Pentecostal Ch. Intl., Foreign Missions Div. | 1976 | - | 2 | - | - | 2 |
| | Totals: | - | 5 | 31 | 127 | 8 |

## Haiti

| | First Year | 1-2 yrs. | 2-4 yrs. | 4+ yrs. | Citizens | Non-Citizens |
|---|---|---|---|---|---|---|
| Allegheny Wesleyan Methodist Connection | 1968 | 1 | - | 11 | - | - |
| Am. Baptist Chs. of the U.S.A., Intl. Ministries | 1923 | - | - | 2 | - | 2 |
| AMG International | | - | - | - | 20 | - |
| Assemblies of God World Missions | 1957 | 4 | - | 2 | - | - |
| Awana Clubs International | 2000 | - | - | 1 | 1 | - |
| Baptist Bible Fellowship International | 1982 | - | - | 3 | - | - |
| Baptist International Missions, Inc. (BIMI) | | - | - | 6 | - | - |
| Baptist Mid-Missions | 1934 | - | - | 4 | - | - |
| Bright Hope International | 1999 | - | - | - | 1 | - |
| Campus Crusade for Christ, Intl. | 1977 | - | - | - | 10 | - |
| Child Evangelism Fellowship, Inc. | 1946 | - | - | 2 | 1 | - |
| Childcare Worldwide | 1983 | - | - | - | 10 | - |
| Christian Aid Ministries | | - | 18 | - | 29 | - |
| Christian Churches / Churches of Christ | | - | 4 | 4 | 30 | - |
| Christian Reformed World Missions | 1985 | - | - | 4 | - | - |
| Christian Reformed World Relief Committee | 1975 | - | - | 1 | 1 | 1 |
| Ch. of God (Anderson, Ind.), Global Missions | 1968 | - | - | 4 | - | - |
| Church of God (Cleveland, TN) World Missions | 1933 | 1 | - | 2 | - | - |
| Ch. of God (Holiness), World Mission Dept., Inc. | 1966 | - | - | - | 4 | - |
| Church of God of Prophecy—Global Outreach | | - | - | - | 10 | - |
| Church of the Nazarene, World Mission Dept. | 1950 | - | - | 6 | - | - |
| Churches of Christ | 1989 | 3 | - | 2 | 4 | - |
| Churches of God, General Conference | 1967 | - | - | 2 | 150 | - |
| Compassion International, Inc. | 1968 | - | - | - | 43 | - |
| CrossWorld | 1943 | - | - | 20 | - | - |
| CSI Ministries, Inc. | 1963 | - | - | 5 | 17 | - |
| Development Associates International (DAI) | 2001 | - | - | - | 1 | - |
| East-West Ministries International | 2002 | - | - | - | 2 | - |
| Elim Fellowship—International Department | 1986 | 1 | - | 2 | - | - |
| Emmanuel International Mission | 1978 | - | - | - | 2 | 1 |
| Episcopal Church USA—Domestic & Foreign | | - | - | 1 | - | - |
| Evangelical Baptist Missions | | - | - | - | 2 | - |
| Floresta USA, Inc. | 1997 | - | - | - | 15 | - |
| FOCAS | 1986 | - | - | - | 8 | - |
| For Haiti with Love Inc. | 1969 | - | - | 1 | - | - |

| | Personnel from U.S. | | | Other Countries | |
| --- | First Year | 1-2 yrs. | 2-4 yrs. | 4+ yrs. | Citizens | Non-Citizens |
| --- | --- | --- | --- | --- | --- | --- |
| Free Methodist World Missions | 1964 | - | - | 6 | - | - |
| Global Outreach International | 1988 | - | - | 8 | - | - |
| Global Outreach Mission, Inc. | | - | - | - | 4 | - |
| Global Partners / Wesleyan World Missions | 1948 | - | 7 | - | - | 1 |
| Globe Missionary Evangelism | 2002 | - | - | 2 | - | - |
| Good Shepherd Ministries, Inc. | 1975 | - | - | 2 | 48 | - |
| Haiti Lutheran Mission Society | | - | - | - | 75 | - |
| Haitian Christian Outreach | 1985 | - | - | - | 70 | - |
| Harvest | 1986 | - | - | - | 2 | - |
| Harvest International, Inc. | 1987 | - | 2 | - | 6 | - |
| Have Christ Will Travel Ministries | 1970 | - | - | - | 15 | - |
| Hope for the Hungry | | - | - | 3 | 1 | 2 |
| International Partnership Ministries, Inc. | 1982 | - | - | - | 20 | - |
| Intl. Pentecostal Holiness Ch. World Missions Mins. | 1976 | - | - | - | - | - |
| Kids Alive International | 2003 | 1 | - | 2 | - | 2 |
| Larry Jones Intl. Ministries (Feed the Children) | 1979 | - | - | - | 7 | - |
| Lott Carey Baptist Foreign Mission Convention | 2001 | - | - | - | 116 | - |
| Macedonia World Baptist Missions, Inc. | 1967 | - | - | 2 | - | - |
| Medical Ambassadors International, Inc. | 1981 | - | - | - | 8 | 2 |
| Ministries In Action | 1974 | - | - | 1 | 2 | 1 |
| Mission Aviation Fellowship | 1981 | 4 | 1 | 3 | - | - |
| Mission Possible, Inc. | 1974 | - | - | - | 125 | - |
| Mission to the Americas | 1954 | - | - | - | 6 | - |
| Missionary Ventures International | 1999 | - | - | 1 | - | - |
| Natl. Baptist Conv. of Am.—Foreign Msn. Bd. | 1975 | - | - | - | 25 | - |
| New Directions International, Inc. | 1969 | - | - | - | 3 | - |
| New Life Advance International | 1975 | - | - | 2 | - | - |
| New Mission Systems International | | - | - | - | 6 | - |
| OMS International, Inc. | 1958 | - | 1 | 10 | - | 6 |
| Open Door Baptist Missions | 1995 | - | - | 4 | - | - |
| Orthodox Presbyterian Church | 2004 | - | - | 2 | - | - |
| Pentecostal Church of God—World Missions Dept. | | - | - | 2 | - | - |
| Reciprocal Ministries International | 1986 | - | - | 8 | - | - |
| Rehoboth Ministries, Inc | | - | - | 2 | - | - |
| Salvation Army, U.S.A. | | - | - | 3 | - | - |
| Seventh-day Adventists General Conference | 1905 | - | - | 2 | - | - |
| Society of St. Margaret | 1927 | - | - | 2 | 2 | - |
| Source of Light Ministries International, Inc. | 1999 | - | - | 2 | - | - |
| STEM (Short-Term Evangelical Missions) Intl. | 1985 | - | - | 4 | - | - |
| United Church of Christ—Wider Church Ministries | | - | 2 | - | - | - |
| United Pentecostal Ch. Intl., Foreign Msns. Div. | 1966 | - | 2 | - | - | - |
| Walk Thru the Bible Ministries, Inc. | 2005 | - | - | - | - | - |
| World Concern | 1995 | - | - | - | 120 | - |
| World Gospel Mission | 1962 | - | - | - | - | - |
| World Relief | 1987 | - | - | - | 18 | 1 |
| World Servants, Inc. | 2001 | - | - | - | - | - |
| World Team | 1936 | - | - | 5 | - | - |
| World Vision Inc. | 1959 | - | - | - | - | - |
| Totals: | | 15 | 37 | 163 | 1040 | 19 |

| | Personnel from U.S. | | | Other Countries | |
| First Year | 1-2 yrs. | 2-4 yrs. | 4+ yrs. | Citizens | Non-Citizens |
| --- | --- | --- | --- | --- | --- |

## Honduras

| | First Year | 1-2 yrs. | 2-4 yrs. | 4+ yrs. | Citizens | Non-Citizens |
| --- | --- | --- | --- | --- | --- |
| Action International Ministries | 2005 | - | - | 2 | - | 2 |
| Advent Christian Gen. Conf., Dept. of Wld. Msns. | 2002 | - | - | 1 | - | - |
| Assemblies of God World Missions | 1940 | 10 | - | 11 | - | - |
| Awana Clubs International | 1987 | - | - | - | 6 | - |
| Baptist Bible Fellowship International | 1974 | - | - | 1 | - | - |
| Baptist International Missions, Inc. (BIMI) | | - | - | 14 | - | - |
| Baptist Medical & Dental Mission Intl., Inc. | 1974 | - | - | 10 | 45 | - |
| Baptist Mid-Missions | 1959 | - | - | 10 | - | - |
| Bethany International Ministries | 2002 | - | - | 2 | - | - |
| Biblical Ministries Worldwide | 1949 | - | - | 7 | - | 7 |
| Brethren Assemblies | | - | - | 9 | - | - |
| Brethren in Christ World Missions | 1989 | - | - | 4 | - | - |
| Calvary International | | - | - | 2 | - | - |
| CAM International | 1890 | - | - | 26 | - | - |
| Campus Crusade for Christ, Intl. | 1966 | - | - | - | 20 | - |
| Christian Aid Mission | | - | - | - | 26 | - |
| Christian Churches / Churches of Christ | | 2 | - | 19 | 2 | - |
| Christian Medical & Dental Associations | 2000 | - | - | 1 | 1 | - |
| Christian Reformed World Missions | 1971 | - | 1 | 2 | - | - |
| Christian Reformed World Relief Committee | 1974 | - | - | - | 1 | - |
| Christians In Action Missions International | 2002 | - | - | 1 | - | - |
| Church of God (Cleveland, TN) World Missions | 1944 | 2 | - | 5 | - | - |
| Church of the Nazarene, World Mission Dept. | 1970 | - | - | - | - | - |
| Churches of Christ | 1978 | 2 | 1 | 8 | 8 | - |
| Commission to Every Nation | 2004 | 1 | - | - | - | - |
| Compassion International, Inc. | 1974 | - | - | - | 29 | - |
| EFCA International Mission | 2002 | - | 5 | 2 | - | - |
| Episcopal Church USA—Domestic & Foreign | | - | - | 1 | - | - |
| Evangelical Luth. Ch. in Am., Div. for Global Msn. | | 1 | - | - | - | - |
| Evangelistic Faith Missions | 1968 | 4 | - | - | - | - |
| Fellowship of Associates of Medical Evangelism | 1997 | - | - | - | - | 3 |
| Flying Doctors of Am. (Medical Mercy Msns., Inc.) | 1990 | - | - | - | - | - |
| Full Gospel Evangelistic Association | 1970 | - | - | 2 | - | - |
| General Baptists International | 1995 | - | - | 8 | - | - |
| Global Outreach International | 1990 | - | - | 11 | - | - |
| Global Outreach Mission, Inc. | | - | - | 4 | 1 | - |
| Global Partners / Wesleyan World Missions | 1957 | - | - | - | - | - |
| Globe Missionary Evangelism | 1986 | - | - | 2 | - | - |
| Harvest | 1987 | - | - | - | 2 | - |
| Impact International | 1970 | - | - | 4 | 2 | 2 |
| International Gospel Outreach | 1996 | - | 2 | 2 | 1 | - |
| Intl. Pentecostal Holiness Ch. World Missions Mins. | 1993 | - | - | 2 | 2 | - |
| International Teams, U.S.A. | | - | - | 2 | - | - |
| Larry Jones Intl. Ministries (Feed the Children) | 1983 | - | - | - | 7 | - |
| Latin America Mission | 1987 | - | 1 | 5 | - | 6 |
| Living Water Teaching | 1983 | - | - | 2 | - | - |
| Luke Society, Inc., The | 1983 | - | - | - | - | - |
| MAP International | 2006 | - | - | - | - | - |
| Medical Ambassadors International, Inc. | 1999 | - | - | - | 3 | - |

| | | Personnel from U.S. | | | Other Countries | |
| --- | --- | --- | --- | --- | --- | --- |
| | First Year | 1-2 yrs. | 2-4 yrs. | 4+ yrs. | Citizens | Non-Citizens |
| Mission to the Americas | 1951 | - | - | 9 | 10 | - |
| Mission to the World (PCA), Inc. | 2001 | 4 | - | - | - | - |
| Missionary Ventures International | 1992 | - | - | 4 | - | - |
| Moravian Ch. in N. Am., Bd. of Wld. Msn. | 1994 | - | - | - | 2 | - |
| New Mission Systems International | | - | - | 2 | - | - |
| Pentecostal Church of God—World Missions Dept. | | - | - | 2 | - | - |
| Pentecostal Free Will Baptist Church, Inc. | | - | - | - | 1 | - |
| Reformed Ch. in Am., Gen. Synod Council | 1995 | - | - | - | 5 | - |
| Ripe for Harvest, Inc. | 1994 | 1 | 1 | 2 | - | - |
| Rock the World Youth Mission Alliance | | - | - | - | - | - |
| Samaritan's Purse | 2000 | 4 | - | - | 40 | 1 |
| Seed International | 2001 | - | 1 | - | - | - |
| Seventh-day Adventists General Conference | 1891 | - | - | 2 | - | 2 |
| South American Missionary Society (USA) | 1981 | - | 6 | - | - | 2 |
| Spanish World Ministries | | - | - | 2 | 2 | - |
| STEM (Short-Term Evangelical Missions) Intl. | 1997 | - | - | - | - | - |
| TEAM (The Evangelical Alliance Mission) | | - | - | 6 | - | - |
| Teen Missions International, Inc. | 1990 | - | - | 3 | 2 | - |
| The Church of God of the Apostolic Faith, Inc. | 1989 | - | - | 1 | - | - |
| Trans World Missions | | - | - | - | - | 2 |
| United Church of Christ—Wider Church Ministries | | - | 2 | - | - | - |
| United Pentecostal Ch. Intl., Foreign Missions Div. | 1997 | - | 4 | - | - | - |
| Walk Thru the Bible Ministries, Inc. | 2002 | - | - | - | 4 | - |
| Word of Life Fellowship, Inc.—Intl. Ministries | 1998 | - | - | 1 | 5 | 1 |
| World Baptist Fellowship Mission Agency, Inc. | | - | - | 4 | - | - |
| World Concern | 1998 | - | - | 1 | - | 1 |
| World Gospel Mission | 1944 | - | - | 29 | - | - |
| World Help | 1994 | - | - | - | - | - |
| World Missions & Evangelism, Inc. | | - | - | 4 | - | - |
| World Reach, Inc. | 1982 | - | - | 5 | 9 | - |
| World Vision Inc. | 1974 | - | - | - | - | - |
| World-Wide Missions | 1963 | 2 | - | - | 1 | - |
| Youth for Christ/USA—World Outreach | | - | - | 3 | - | - |
| Totals: | | 33 | 24 | 262 | 237 | 29 |

## Hong Kong

| | | | | | | |
| --- | --- | --- | --- | --- | --- | --- |
| Asian Outreach U.S.A. | | - | - | - | - | - |
| Awana Clubs International | 1996 | - | - | - | 2 | - |
| Bakke Graduate University of Ministry | 2005 | - | - | - | - | - |
| Baptist Bible Fellowship International | 1969 | - | - | 6 | - | - |
| Baptist International Missions, Inc. (BIMI) | | - | - | 2 | - | - |
| Biblical Ministries Worldwide | 1988 | - | - | 5 | - | 5 |
| Brethren Assemblies | | - | - | 4 | - | - |
| Campus Crusade for Christ, Intl. | 1972 | - | - | - | 119 | - |
| Child Evangelism Fellowship, Inc. | 1948 | - | - | 1 | - | 2 |
| ChinaSource | | - | - | - | 3 | - |
| Christar | 1909 | - | - | 8 | - | - |
| Christian Broadcasting Network Inc., the | 2004 | - | 1 | - | 11 | - |
| Christian Churches / Churches of Christ | | - | - | 10 | 4 | - |
| Christ's Mandate for Missions | 2005 | - | - | 2 | - | - |

| | First Year | Personnel from U.S. | | | Other Countries | |
|---|---|---|---|---|---|---|
| | | 1-2 yrs. | 2-4 yrs. | 4+ yrs. | Citizens | Non-Citizens |
| Ch. of God (Anderson, Ind.), Global Missions | 1979 | - | - | 2 | - | - |
| Church of the Nazarene, World Mission Dept. | 1974 | - | - | - | - | - |
| CLC Ministries International | 1976 | - | - | 2 | - | - |
| Compassion International, Inc. | | - | - | 2 | 2 | 2 |
| East Gates Ministries Intl. | 1990 | - | - | - | 3 | - |
| Eastern Mennonite Missions | | - | - | 2 | - | 1 |
| EFCA International Mission | 1987 | - | - | 9 | - | - |
| Evangelical Luth. Ch. in Am., Div. for Global Msn. | 1890 | 1 | - | 6 | 2 | - |
| Free Methodist World Missions | | - | - | 4 | - | - |
| Global Outreach Mission, Inc. | | - | - | - | 4 | - |
| Habitat for Humanity International | | - | 2 | - | - | 2 |
| Hosanna | 2005 | - | - | - | 1 | - |
| Intl. Pentecostal Holiness Ch. World Missions Mins. | 1911 | - | - | - | - | - |
| Mennonite Mission Network | 1980 | - | - | 2 | - | 2 |
| Mission to the World (PCA), Inc. | 1982 | - | - | - | - | - |
| OMS International, Inc. | 1954 | - | - | 5 | - | 1 |
| Partners International | 1950 | - | - | - | 2 | - |
| Reach Ministries International | 1985 | - | - | 1 | - | - |
| Seventh-day Adventists General Conference | | - | - | 10 | - | 4 |
| Training Evangelistic Leadership (T.E.L.), Inc. | 1986 | - | - | 7 | 2 | - |
| United Church of Christ—Wider Church Ministries | | - | 1 | - | - | - |
| United Pentecostal Ch. Intl., Foreign Missions Div. | 1976 | - | 2 | - | - | - |
| Wisconsin Evangelical Lutheran Synod | 1964 | - | - | 2 | - | - |
| World Venture | 1963 | - | - | 6 | - | - |
| Worldwide Tentmakers, Inc. | 2001 | - | - | - | - | - |
| | Totals: | 1 | 6 | 98 | 155 | 19 |

## Hungary

| | First Year | 1-2 yrs. | 2-4 yrs. | 4+ yrs. | Citizens | Non-Citizens |
|---|---|---|---|---|---|---|
| Artists In Christian Testimony | 2003 | - | - | 1 | - | - |
| Assemblies of God World Missions | 1926 | - | - | 6 | - | - |
| Avant Ministries | | - | - | 2 | - | - |
| Awana Clubs International | 1993 | - | - | - | 7 | - |
| Baptist Bible Fellowship International | 1990 | - | - | 4 | - | - |
| Baptist International Missions, Inc. (BIMI) | | - | - | 2 | - | - |
| BCM International | | - | - | - | 2 | - |
| Bethany International Ministries | 1999 | - | - | 2 | - | - |
| Brethren Assemblies | | - | - | 2 | - | - |
| Campus Crusade for Christ, Intl. | 1978 | 18 | - | 69 | 31 | 6 |
| Centers for Apologetics Research (CFAR), the | 2000 | - | - | - | 2 | - |
| Child Evangelism Fellowship, Inc. | 1989 | - | - | 1 | 5 | 2 |
| Christian Reformed World Missions | 1990 | - | - | 5 | - | - |
| Ch. of God (Anderson, Ind.), Global Missions | 1907 | 2 | - | 2 | - | - |
| Church of God of Prophecy—Global Outreach | | - | - | - | 1 | - |
| Church of the Nazarene, World Mission Dept. | 1996 | - | - | - | - | - |
| Church Resource Ministries (CRM) | 1987 | - | - | 9 | - | - |
| Churches of Christ | 1971 | - | 3 | 7 | 1 | - |
| EFCA International Mission | 1997 | - | 2 | 10 | 3 | - |
| Entrust | 1990 | - | - | 9 | - | 3 |
| Evangelical Presbyterian Church—World Outreach | 2003 | - | - | 2 | - | - |
| Fellowship of Evangelical Churches—Intl. Mins. | 2000 | - | - | 2 | 1 | 1 |

| | First Year | Personnel from U.S. | | | Other Countries | |
|---|---|---|---|---|---|---|
| | | 1-2 yrs. | 2-4 yrs. | 4+ yrs. | Citizens | Non-Citizens |
| Free Methodist World Missions | 1998 | - | - | 5 | - | - |
| Friendship International Ministries, Inc. | 1990 | - | - | 4 | 3 | 1 |
| Greater Europe Mission | 1996 | - | 1 | 6 | - | - |
| Greater Grace World Outreach | 1990 | - | - | 11 | 57 | 7 |
| Habitat for Humanity International | 1994 | - | 25 | 4 | 15 | 14 |
| International Institute for Christian Studies | 1993 | - | 4 | - | - | 2 |
| International Messengers | 1992 | - | 1 | 2 | 9 | 1 |
| Intl. Pentecostal Holiness Ch. World Missions Mins. | 1989 | - | - | 4 | - | - |
| Janz Team Ministries USA | | 2 | - | - | - | - |
| Mennonite Mission Network | 1993 | - | - | - | - | - |
| Ministry to Educate and Equip Intl. (MTEE) | 1995 | - | 4 | - | - | - |
| Mission to the World (PCA), Inc. | 2000 | - | - | - | - | - |
| Mission To Unreached Peoples | 1996 | - | - | 3 | - | - |
| Navigators, U.S. International Missions Group | | 1 | 1 | 3 | - | - |
| New Hope International | 1971 | - | - | - | 2 | - |
| OMS International, Inc. | 1992 | - | - | 8 | - | 1 |
| Operation Mobilization | | - | 2 | 3 | - | 1 |
| Pioneers USA | 1992 | 1 | - | 10 | - | - |
| Presbyterian Mission International (PMI) | 2000 | - | - | - | 1 | - |
| Reformed Church in Am., Gen. Synod Council | 2002 | - | - | 2 | 1 | - |
| Ripe for Harvest, Inc. | 1996 | - | - | 2 | - | - |
| SEND International USA | 1992 | - | - | 6 | - | - |
| TCM International Institute | | - | - | - | 1 | - |
| The Mission Society | 2001 | 2 | - | - | - | - |
| United Church of Christ—Wider Church Ministries | | - | 2 | - | - | - |
| United Pentecostal Ch. Intl., Foreign Msns. Div. | | - | - | - | - | - |
| Walk Thru the Bible Ministries, Inc. | 2000 | - | - | - | - | - |
| Westminster Biblical Missions | 1990 | - | - | 1 | 10 | 3 |
| Word of Life Fellowship, Inc.—Intl. Ministries | 1987 | - | - | 4 | 26 | 2 |
| World Bible Translation Center | | - | - | - | 2 | - |
| World Gospel Mission | 1992 | - | - | 5 | - | - |
| World Harvest Mission | 1999 | - | - | 2 | - | - |
| World Missions & Evangelism, Inc. | | - | - | 2 | - | - |
| World Venture | 1990 | - | - | 2 | - | - |
| | Totals: | 26 | 45 | 224 | 180 | 44 |

## Iceland

| | First Year | Personnel from U.S. | | | Other Countries | |
|---|---|---|---|---|---|---|
| Assemblies of God World Missions | 1992 | 2 | - | 2 | - | - |
| Baptist Bible Fellowship International | 1984 | - | - | 2 | - | - |
| Greater Europe Mission | 1985 | - | - | 2 | - | - |
| Navigators, U.S. International Missions Group | | - | - | 2 | - | - |
| | Totals: | 2 | - | 8 | - | - |

## India

| | First Year | Personnel from U.S. | | | Other Countries | |
|---|---|---|---|---|---|---|
| Action International Ministries | 1994 | - | - | 1 | 8 | 2 |
| Advancing Renewal Ministries, Inc. | | - | - | 15 | 15 | - |
| Advent Christian Gen. Conf., Dept. of Wld. Msns. | 1882 | - | - | 2 | 65 | 1 |
| Am. Baptist Chs. of the U.S.A., Intl. Ministries | 1836 | - | - | 4 | - | - |
| Am. Council of the Ramabai Mukti Msn., Inc. | 1929 | - | - | - | 2 | - |
| American Leprosy Missions, Inc. | 1906 | - | - | - | 1 | - |

| | Personnel from U.S. | | | Other Countries | |
|---|---|---|---|---|---|
| | First Year | 1-2 yrs. | 2-4 yrs. | 4+ yrs. | Citizens | Non-Citizens |
| AMG International | 1970 | - | - | - | 6400 | - |
| Anis Shorrosh Evangelistic Association | | - | - | 35 | - | - |
| Armenian Missionary Association of America, Inc. | 1999 | - | - | - | - | - |
| Artists In Christian Testimony | 2005 | - | - | 1 | - | - |
| Asian Access | 2002 | - | - | - | - | - |
| Assemblies of God World Missions | 1914 | 10 | - | 53 | - | - |
| Association of Free Lutheran Congregations | | - | - | - | 30 | - |
| Audio Scripture Ministries | 2005 | - | - | 2 | - | - |
| Awana Clubs International | 1991 | - | - | - | 23 | 2 |
| Back to the Bible International | 1970 | - | - | - | 36 | - |
| Baptist Bible Fellowship International | 1952 | - | - | 2 | - | - |
| Baptist General Conference—Intl. Ministries | | - | - | 1 | 1 | - |
| Baptist International Missions, Inc. (BIMI) | | - | - | 7 | - | - |
| Baptist International Outreach | 1993 | - | - | - | 2 | - |
| Baptist Mid-Missions | 1935 | - | - | 8 | 6 | - |
| BCM International | | - | - | - | 275 | - |
| Bible Training Centre for Pastors | 1999 | - | - | - | 1 | - |
| Bibles For The World, Inc. | 1972 | - | - | - | 400 | - |
| BILD International | | - | - | - | 3 | - |
| Brethren Assemblies | | - | - | 14 | - | - |
| Brethren in Christ World Missions | 1904 | - | - | 2 | 74 | - |
| Bright Hope International | 1990 | - | - | - | 5 | - |
| Campus Crusade for Christ, Intl. | 1963 | - | - | 0 | 1721 | 2 |
| Caring Partners International, Inc. | 1991 | - | - | - | - | - |
| Childcare Worldwide | 1981 | - | - | - | 7 | - |
| Christ for India, Inc. | 1981 | - | - | 1 | 1 | - |
| Christ to the Nations | 1991 | 2 | - | - | 18 | - |
| Christian Aid Mission | | - | - | - | 872 | - |
| Christian Broadcasting Network Inc., the | 1997 | - | 1 | - | 151 | - |
| Christian Church of North America—Missions | 1965 | - | - | 4 | - | - |
| Christian Churches / Churches of Christ | | - | - | 17 | 35 | - |
| Christian Discipleship Ministries, Inc. | 1994 | - | - | 1 | 5 | 2 |
| Christian Literature International | | - | - | - | - | - |
| Christian Reformed World Relief Committee | 1965 | - | - | - | - | - |
| Christians In Action Missions International | 1972 | - | - | - | 8 | 1 |
| Christ's Mandate for Missions | 1978 | - | - | - | 190 | - |
| Church Leadership Development International | 1996 | - | - | - | 3 | - |
| Ch. of God (Holiness), World Mission Dept., Inc. | 2005 | - | - | - | 35 | - |
| Church of God of Prophecy—Global Outreach | | - | - | - | 25 | - |
| Church of the Nazarene, World Mission Dept. | 1898 | - | - | - | - | - |
| Churches of Christ | 1960 | - | - | 8 | 15 | - |
| Churches of God, General Conference | 1898 | - | - | - | 15 | - |
| Compassion International, Inc. | 1968 | - | - | - | 70 | - |
| Cook Communications Ministries International | 1999 | - | - | - | - | - |
| Dayspring International | 1979 | - | - | - | 1000 | - |
| Development Associates International (DAI) | 2000 | - | - | - | 5 | - |
| East-West Ministries International | 2001 | - | - | - | 2 | - |
| EFCA International Mission | 1995 | - | - | - | 33 | - |
| Engineering Ministries International | 1998 | - | - | 7 | 3 | - |
| Envoy International | | - | - | - | - | - |

| | Personnel from U.S. | | | Other Countries | |
|---|---|---|---|---|---|
| | First Year | 1-2 yrs. | 2-4 yrs. | 4+ yrs. | Citizens | Non-Citizens |
| Episcopal Church USA—Domestic & Foreign | | - | - | 1 | - | - |
| Evangel Bible Translators | 1978 | - | - | 6 | 28 | - |
| Evangelical Friends Mission | 1992 | - | - | - | 4 | - |
| Evangelical Luth. Ch. in Am., Div. for Global Msn. | 1842 | - | - | 1 | - | - |
| Evangelism Explosion International | | - | - | 2 | - | - |
| Evangelism Resources | 1999 | - | - | - | 2 | - |
| Food for the Hungry, Inc. | 1998 | - | 1 | - | - | - |
| Foursquare Missions International | | - | 2 | 2 | - | - |
| Free Gospel Church, Inc.—Missions Department | 1935 | - | - | - | 2 | - |
| Free Will Baptist, Inc. Board of Intl. Missions | 1935 | - | - | 1 | - | - |
| Friends of Israel Gospel Ministry, Inc. | 1969 | - | - | - | 2 | - |
| General Baptists International | 1982 | - | - | - | 1 | - |
| Global Action | 1998 | - | - | - | 10 | - |
| Global Fellowship Inc. | 1989 | - | - | - | 750 | - |
| Global Mins., Ch. of the United Brethren in Christ | 1978 | - | - | 2 | - | - |
| Global Outreach International | 1977 | - | - | 4 | - | - |
| Global Outreach Mission, Inc. | | - | - | 2 | 33 | - |
| Global Partners / Wesleyan World Missions | 1910 | - | - | - | - | - |
| Globe Missionary Evangelism | 1989 | - | - | 7 | - | - |
| Good News for India | 1986 | - | - | - | 300 | - |
| Good News Productions International | 1989 | - | - | 2 | 10 | - |
| Gospel for Asia, Inc. | 1980 | - | - | - | 14754 | - |
| Gospel Outreach Ministries Intl. | 1988 | - | - | - | 250 | - |
| Gospel Revival Ministries | 1995 | - | - | - | 35 | - |
| Gospelink, Inc. | | - | - | - | 9 | - |
| Grace Ministries International | 1969 | - | - | - | - | 2 |
| Greater Grace World Outreach | 1984 | - | - | 2 | 120 | 1 |
| Habitat for Humanity International | 1983 | - | 22 | - | 1 | 21 |
| Harvest | 1996 | - | - | - | 2 | - |
| Harvest International, Inc. | 2000 | - | - | - | 2 | - |
| Have Christ Will Travel Ministries | 1978 | - | - | - | 10 | - |
| HBI Global Partners | 1984 | - | - | - | 595 | - |
| Heart of God Ministries | 1997 | - | - | 12 | - | - |
| Help for Christian Nationals, Inc. | 1996 | - | - | 1 | 1 | - |
| Hope for the Hungry | | - | - | 1 | 1 | - |
| Hosanna | 2000 | - | - | - | 10 | - |
| I. N. Network USA | 1979 | - | - | - | 202 | - |
| India Gospel Outreach | 1984 | - | - | 1 | 2000 | - |
| India National Inland Mission | 1964 | - | - | - | 350 | - |
| India Partners | 2001 | - | - | - | 1 | - |
| India Rural Evangelical Fellowship | 1950 | - | - | - | 127 | - |
| International Gospel Outreach | 1989 | - | - | - | 4 | - |
| International Justice Mission | 2000 | 5 | 1 | - | 57 | - |
| International Partnership Ministries, Inc. | 1988 | - | - | - | 114 | - |
| Intl. Pentecostal Ch. of Christ— Global Msns. Dept. | 1947 | - | - | 2 | 1 | 1 |
| Intl. Pentecostal Holiness Ch. World Missions Mins. | 1911 | - | - | 2 | - | - |
| InterServe USA (International Service Fellowship) | 1852 | - | - | 5 | - | - |
| Josue Yrion World Evangelism and Missions, Inc. | 1997 | - | - | - | 11 | - |
| Literacy & Evangelism International | 2003 | - | - | - | 2 | - |
| Lott Carey Baptist Foreign Mission Convention | 1948 | - | - | - | 300 | - |

| | First Year | Personnel from U.S. | | | Other Countries | |
|---|---|---|---|---|---|---|
| | | 1-2 yrs. | 2-4 yrs. | 4+ yrs. | Citizens | Non-Citizens |
| Medical Ambassadors International, Inc. | 1982 | - | - | - | 38 | - |
| Mennonite Mission Network | 1899 | - | - | - | - | - |
| Mission Catalyst International | 2006 | - | - | 4 | 2 | - |
| Mission India | 1980 | - | - | - | 196 | - |
| Mission Ministries, Inc. | 2004 | - | - | - | 5 | - |
| Mission of Mercy | 1954 | - | - | 1 | 1 | - |
| Mission ONE, Inc. | 1990 | - | - | - | 70 | - |
| Mission to the World (PCA), Inc. | 1973 | 2 | 10 | - | - | - |
| Mission To Unreached Peoples | 1987 | - | - | 12 | 3 | 1 |
| Mustard Seed International | 1998 | - | - | - | - | - |
| New Directions International, Inc. | 1985 | - | - | - | 25 | - |
| New Life Advance International | 1970 | - | - | - | 2 | - |
| New Mission Systems International | | - | - | 4 | 2 | - |
| OC International, Inc. | 1984 | - | - | - | - | 1 |
| OMS International, Inc. | 1941 | - | - | 1 | - | 1 |
| Open Air Campaigners—Overseas Ministries | 1990 | 4 | 2 | 22 | 28 | - |
| Open Door Baptist Missions | 1995 | - | - | - | 2 | - |
| Operation Mobilization | 1964 | 2 | - | 7 | - | 2 |
| Paraclete, Inc. | 2000 | - | - | - | - | - |
| Partners International | 1969 | - | - | - | 881 | - |
| Pentecostal Ch. of God—World Missions Dept. | | - | - | 2 | - | - |
| Perimeter Church, Global Outreach | 1998 | - | - | - | - | - |
| Pioneers USA | | 11 | - | 24 | 2 | 4 |
| Prakash Association, USA | 1968 | - | - | - | 40 | - |
| Precept Ministries International | 2000 | - | - | - | 5 | - |
| Presbyterian Evangelistic Fellowship | | - | - | - | 5 | - |
| Presbyterian Mission International (PMI) | 1988 | - | - | - | 3 | - |
| Project Christ International | 1985 | - | - | - | 75 | - |
| Ravi Zacharias International Ministries | | - | - | 2 | - | - |
| Reach Ministries International | 1985 | - | - | - | 2 | - |
| Reaching Indians Ministries International | 1993 | - | - | - | 810 | - |
| Reformed Church in Am., Gen. Synod Council | 1990 | - | - | 2 | - | - |
| Ripe for Harvest, Inc. | 1997 | 1 | 1 | 2 | - | - |
| Rosedale Mennonite Missions | 2000 | - | - | 2 | - | 2 |
| Seed International | 2000 | - | - | 1 | - | - |
| Seventh-day Adventists General Conference | 1895 | - | - | 10 | - | 10 |
| SIM USA | 1894 | 2 | - | 16 | - | - |
| Source of Light Ministries International, Inc. | 1978 | - | - | - | 3 | - |
| Spiritual Overseers Service International | 1985 | - | - | - | 1 | - |
| Supreme Task International, Inc. | 2006 | 1 | - | - | 4 | - |
| Talking Bibles International | 1997 | - | - | - | 4 | - |
| TEAM (The Evangelical Alliance Mission) | | - | - | 2 | - | - |
| Teen Missions International, Inc. | 1983 | - | - | - | 11 | - |
| Tentmakers International | | - | - | - | - | - |
| The Brethren Church, Inc. | 1970 | - | - | - | 102 | - |
| The God's Story Project | 2000 | - | - | - | 2 | - |
| The Master's Mission, Inc. | 1993 | - | - | - | 2 | - |
| The Mission Society | 1995 | - | - | 2 | - | - |
| TMA Ministries | 1989 | - | - | - | - | - |
| Training Evangelistic Leadership (T.E.L.), Inc. | 1975 | - | - | 4 | 16 | - |

| | | Personnel from U.S. | | | Other Countries | |
|---|---|---|---|---|---|---|
| | First Year | 1-2 yrs. | 2-4 yrs. | 4+ yrs. | Citizens | Non-Citizens |
| U.S. Center for World Mission | | - | 2 | 4 | - | - |
| United Church of Christ—Wider Church Ministries | | - | 4 | - | - | - |
| United Pentecostal Ch. Intl., Foreign Missions Div. | 1909 | - | 1 | - | - | 3 |
| Village Ministries International | 2000 | - | - | - | 3 | - |
| Walk Thru the Bible Ministries, Inc. | 1998 | - | - | - | 21 | - |
| Wisc. Evangelical Luth. Synod, Bd. for Wld. Msns. | 1970 | - | - | 2 | - | - |
| World Bible Translation Center | | - | - | - | 20 | - |
| World Gospel Mission | 1937 | - | - | 2 | - | - |
| World Harvest Mission | 1998 | - | - | 2 | - | - |
| World Help | 1996 | - | - | - | - | - |
| World Horizons | 2001 | - | - | - | - | 2 |
| World Missions & Evangelism, Inc. | 1997 | - | - | - | 33 | 2 |
| World Missions Far Corners, Inc. | 1965 | - | - | - | 1500 | - |
| World Relief | 2000 | 1 | - | - | 2 | 1 |
| World Venture | 1945 | - | - | 4 | 2 | - |
| World Vision Inc. | 1953 | - | - | - | - | - |
| World-Wide Missions | 1965 | - | - | - | 4 | - |
| **Totals:** | | 41 | 47 | 345 | 35589 | 64 |
| **Indonesia** | | | | | | |
| AMG International | 1975 | - | - | - | 493 | 1 |
| Apostolic Christian Church Foundation, Inc. | 1986 | - | - | 2 | - | - |
| Asian Outreach U.S.A. | | - | - | - | - | - |
| Assemblies of God World Missions | 1920 | 13 | - | 26 | | - |
| Awana Clubs International | 1990 | - | - | 2 | 5 | - |
| Back to the Bible International | 2001 | - | - | - | 4 | - |
| Baptist Bible Fellowship International | 1972 | - | - | 4 | - | - |
| Baptist International Missions, Inc. (BIMI) | | - | - | 2 | - | - |
| Baptist International Outreach | | - | - | - | - | - |
| BCM International | | - | - | - | 6 | - |
| BILD International | | - | - | - | 1 | - |
| Brethren Assemblies | | - | - | 3 | - | - |
| Bright Hope International | 2000 | - | - | - | 1 | - |
| Campus Crusade for Christ, Intl. | 1968 | - | - | 2 | 445 | 4 |
| Christ Community Church | 2000 | - | - | - | - | 2 |
| Christar | 2000 | - | - | 2 | - | - |
| Christian Aid Mission | | - | - | - | 30 | - |
| Christian Broadcasting Network Inc., the | 1998 | - | - | 1 | 216 | 1 |
| Christian Churches / Churches of Christ | | - | - | 15 | - | - |
| Christian Reformed World Relief Committee | 1984 | - | - | 1 | - | - |
| Church of God (Cleveland, TN) World Missions | 1967 | - | - | 2 | - | - |
| Church of God of Prophecy—Global Outreach | | - | - | - | 2 | - |
| Church of the Nazarene, World Mission Dept. | 1973 | - | - | 4 | - | - |
| Church Resource Ministries (CRM) | 2001 | - | - | 2 | - | - |
| Church World Service | | - | 1 | - | 10 | - |
| Churches of Christ | 1967 | - | - | 5 | 4 | - |
| CityTeam Ministries | | - | - | - | - | 3 |
| CMF International | 1978 | - | 4 | - | - | - |
| Commission to Every Nation | 1992 | - | 2 | - | - | - |
| Compassion International, Inc. | 1968 | - | - | - | 47 | - |

| | First Year | Personnel from U.S. | | | Other Countries | |
|---|---|---|---|---|---|---|
| | | 1-2 yrs. | 2-4 yrs. | 4+ yrs. | Citizens | Non-Citizens |
| CrossWorld | 1957 | - | - | 25 | - | - |
| East-West Ministries International | 2006 | - | - | - | 2 | - |
| Emmanuel International Mission | 2003 | - | - | - | - | - |
| Evangelical Luth. Ch. in Am., Div. for Global Msn. | 1970 | - | - | 1 | - | - |
| Evangelism Explosion International | | - | - | - | - | 10 |
| Far East Broadcasting Company, Inc. | 1951 | - | - | - | 80 | - |
| Global Partners / Wesleyan World Missions | 1975 | - | - | - | - | - |
| Globe Missionary Evangelism | 1989 | - | - | 2 | - | - |
| Habitat for Humanity International | | - | 2 | - | - | 2 |
| Heart of God Ministries | 2002 | 2 | 1 | 6 | - | - |
| Hope for the Hungry | | - | - | 1 | - | 1 |
| International Gospel Outreach | 1995 | - | - | 2 | 2 | - |
| International Outreach Ministries (IOM) | 1996 | - | - | 1 | - | - |
| Intl. Pentecostal Holiness Ch. World Missions Mins. | 1986 | - | - | - | - | - |
| International Teams, U.S.A. | | - | - | 3 | - | 18 |
| Macedonia World Baptist Missions, Inc. | 1980 | - | - | 4 | - | - |
| MAP International | 2005 | - | - | - | 6 | 1 |
| Medical Ambassadors International, Inc. | 1998 | - | - | - | 20 | - |
| Mission Aviation Fellowship | 1952 | 6 | 7 | 24 | - | - |
| Mission to the World (PCA), Inc. | 1977 | - | - | - | - | - |
| Mission To Unreached Peoples | 2002 | - | - | 4 | - | - |
| Missionary Ventures International | 2002 | - | - | 2 | - | - |
| Mustard Seed International | 1972 | - | - | 7 | - | - |
| Network of International Christian Schools | 1956 | 1 | 24 | 6 | - | 1 |
| New Tribes Mission | 1970 | - | - | 80 | - | - |
| Northwest Medical Teams International, Inc. | 2005 | - | - | - | 50 | - |
| OMS International, Inc. | 1971 | - | - | 9 | - | 6 |
| Partners International | 1971 | - | - | - | 842 | - |
| Reformed Church in Am., Gen. Synod Council | 2000 | - | - | 2 | - | - |
| Samaritan's Purse | 2005 | 13 | - | - | 1050 | 5 |
| Seventh-day Adventists General Conference | 1900 | - | - | 4 | - | 2 |
| Surfing the Nations | 1998 | - | - | - | - | - |
| TEAM (The Evangelical Alliance Mission) | | - | - | 15 | - | - |
| Teen Missions International, Inc. | | - | - | 2 | 41 | - |
| Things To Come Mission, Inc. | 1973 | - | - | - | 20 | 1 |
| TMA Ministries | 1981 | - | - | - | - | - |
| Training Evangelistic Leadership (T.E.L.), Inc. | 1976 | - | - | 4 | 10 | - |
| United Church of Christ—Wider Church Ministries | | - | 2 | - | - | - |
| United Pentecostal Ch. Intl., Foreign Missions Div. | 1938 | - | 2 | - | - | - |
| Walk Thru the Bible Ministries, Inc. | 2001 | - | - | - | 6 | - |
| White Fields Inc. | | - | - | - | 2 | - |
| Wisc. Evangelical Luth. Synod, Bd. for Wld. Msns. | 1969 | - | - | 1 | - | - |
| World Baptist Fellowship Mission Agency, Inc. | | - | - | 5 | - | - |
| World Bible Translation Center | | - | - | - | 4 | - |
| World Indigenous Missions | 1994 | - | - | - | 1 | - |
| World Outreach International—US | 2004 | 2 | - | - | - | - |
| World Relief | 2004 | 2 | - | - | - | - |
| World Team | 1948 | - | - | 14 | - | 6 |
| World Venture | 1961 | - | - | 8 | - | - |
| World Vision Inc. | 1961 | - | - | - | - | - |

| | Personnel from U.S. | | | Other Countries | |
|---|---|---|---|---|---|
| First Year | 1-2 yrs. | 2-4 yrs. | 4+ yrs. | Citizens | Non-Citizens |
| WorldHarvest | 1989 | - | - | - | 175 | - |
| | Totals: | 39 | 45 | 305 | 3575 | 64 |

## Iran

| | | | | | | |
|---|---|---|---|---|---|---|
| Armenian Missionary Association of America, Inc. | 1950 | - | - | - | - | - |
| Mennonite Mission Network | 2001 | - | - | - | - | - |
| Middle East Media—USA | 1976 | - | - | - | - | - |
| Partners International | 2002 | - | - | - | 4 | - |
| | Totals: | - | - | - | 4 | - |

## Iraq

| | | | | | | |
|---|---|---|---|---|---|---|
| International Partnership Ministries, Inc. | 2004 | - | - | - | 1 | 1 |
| Mission ONE, Inc. | 1990 | - | - | - | 1 | - |
| Partners International | 1997 | - | - | - | 121 | - |
| Venture International | 2003 | - | - | - | 25 | - |
| Walk Thru the Bible Ministries, Inc. | 2001 | - | - | - | - | - |
| | Totals: | - | - | - | 148 | 1 |

## Ireland

| | | | | | | |
|---|---|---|---|---|---|---|
| Assemblies of God World Missions | 1978 | 10 | - | 14 | - | - |
| Baptist Bible Fellowship International | 1977 | - | - | 5 | - | - |
| Baptist International Missions, Inc. (BIMI) | | - | - | 14 | - | - |
| Baptist Mid-Missions | 1978 | - | - | 2 | - | - |
| BCM International | | - | - | 2 | 5 | - |
| Biblical Ministries Worldwide | 1975 | - | - | 11 | - | 11 |
| Brethren Assemblies | | - | - | 14 | - | - |
| Christian Associates International | | - | - | - | - | - |
| Christian Churches / Churches of Christ | | 1 | - | 6 | - | - |
| Church of God (Cleveland, TN) World Missions | 1995 | 2 | - | 4 | - | - |
| Church of the Nazarene, World Mission Dept. | 1987 | - | - | - | - | 2 |
| CrossWorld | 1980 | - | - | 11 | - | - |
| European Christian Mission International—USA | | - | - | 15 | - | - |
| Evangelical Friends Mission | 1998 | - | - | 3 | - | - |
| Global Outreach Mission, Inc. | 1965 | - | - | 10 | 4 | - |
| Grace Brethren International Missions | 2002 | - | - | 6 | - | - |
| Greater Europe Mission | 1974 | - | - | 17 | - | - |
| Greater Grace World Outreach | 1997 | - | - | 1 | - | 2 |
| International Teams, U.S.A. | | - | - | 4 | - | - |
| Ireland Outreach International Inc. | 1970 | - | 3 | 10 | - | 3 |
| Macedonia World Baptist Missions, Inc. | 2000 | - | - | 6 | - | - |
| Mennonite Mission Network | 1978 | - | - | 2 | - | - |
| Mission to the World (PCA), Inc. | 1995 | - | - | - | - | - |
| Missionary Ventures International | 1998 | - | - | - | 2 | - |
| OMS International, Inc. | 1996 | - | - | 1 | - | 1 |
| Operation Mobilization | | 1 | - | 2 | - | - |
| Reformed Baptist Mission Services | | - | - | - | 2 | - |
| TEAM (The Evangelical Alliance Mission) | | - | - | 5 | - | - |
| Team Expansion, Inc. | 1987 | - | - | 6 | - | - |
| The Brethren Church, Inc. | 2004 | - | - | 1 | - | - |
| Walk Thru the Bible Ministries, Inc. | 2000 | - | - | - | - | - |

| | | Personnel from U.S. | | | Other Countries | |
|---|---|---|---|---|---|---|
| | First Year | 1-2 yrs. | 2-4 yrs. | 4+ yrs. | Citizens | Non-Citizens |
| World Harvest Mission | 1986 | - | - | 16 | - | - |
| World Partners USA | 2003 | - | - | 2 | - | - |
| World Venture | 1993 | - | - | 4 | - | - |
| Youth for Christ/USA—World Outreach | | - | - | 1 | - | - |
| | Totals: | 14 | 3 | 195 | 13 | 19 |

## Israel

| | | | | | | |
|---|---|---|---|---|---|---|
| AMF International | 1940 | - | - | 2 | 2 | - |
| Anis Shorrosh Evangelistic Association | | - | - | 40 | - | - |
| Arab World Ministries | | - | - | 2 | - | - |
| Artists In Christian Testimony | 2005 | - | - | 2 | - | - |
| Assemblies of God World Missions | 1917 | 6 | - | 11 | - | - |
| Child Evangelism Fellowship, Inc. | 1951 | - | - | 2 | 2 | - |
| Chosen People Ministries | 1968 | - | - | - | - | - |
| Christian Churches / Churches of Christ | | - | - | 2 | 1 | - |
| Church of God of Prophecy—Global Outreach | | - | - | - | - | 2 |
| Church of the Nazarene, World Mission Dept. | 1921 | - | - | 3 | - | 2 |
| Churches of Christ | 1960 | - | - | - | 7 | - |
| Evangel Bible Translators | 1998 | - | - | 1 | - | - |
| Foursquare Missions International | 1998 | - | - | 4 | - | - |
| Friends of Israel Gospel Ministry, Inc. | 1958 | - | - | - | 8 | - |
| Global Outreach Mission, Inc. | | - | - | - | 2 | - |
| Globe Missionary Evangelism | 2001 | - | - | 6 | - | - |
| High Adventure Ministries/Voice of Hope | 1979 | - | - | - | 3 | - |
| Hope for the Hungry | | - | - | 1 | 1 | - |
| Independent Faith Mission, Inc. | | 2 | - | - | - | - |
| International Board of Jewish Missions, Inc. | 1991 | 2 | 4 | 2 | - | - |
| International Gospel Outreach | 2004 | - | 1 | - | - | - |
| International Students, Inc (ISI) | | - | - | 1 | - | - |
| International Teams, U.S.A. | | - | - | 2 | - | 2 |
| Jewish Awareness Ministries | 2002 | - | - | 2 | - | - |
| Jews for Jesus | 1994 | - | - | 3 | 6 | 1 |
| Mennonite Mission Network | 1953 | - | - | 6 | - | - |
| Missionary Ventures International | 1997 | - | - | - | 2 | - |
| New Life Advance International | | - | - | - | - | - |
| Open Door Baptist Missions | 1997 | - | - | 2 | - | - |
| Operation Mobilization | | 5 | 3 | - | - | 5 |
| Reformed Baptist Mission Services | | - | - | - | 2 | - |
| Reformed Church in Am., Gen. Synod Council | 2005 | - | - | 2 | - | - |
| Remnant Ministries, Inc. | 2000 | - | - | 2 | - | - |
| Seventh-day Adventists General Conference | 1898 | - | - | - | - | 4 |
| The Master's Mission, Inc. | 1990 | - | - | - | 2 | - |
| United Church of Christ—Wider Church Ministries | | - | 2 | - | - | - |
| United Pentecostal Ch. Intl., Foreign Missions Div. | | - | 2 | - | - | 4 |
| Venture International | 1989 | - | - | - | 3 | - |
| Walk Thru the Bible Ministries, Inc. | | - | - | - | - | - |
| | Totals: | 15 | 12 | 98 | 41 | 20 |

## Italy

| | | | | | | |
|---|---|---|---|---|---|---|
| AMG International | 2002 | - | - | 2 | - | - |

| | | Personnel from U.S. | | | Other Countries | |
|---|---|---|---|---|---|---|
| | First Year | 1-2 yrs. | 2-4 yrs. | 4+ yrs. | Citizens | Non-Citizens |
| Assemblies of God World Missions | 1908 | 1 | - | 10 | - | - |
| Aurora Mission, Inc. | 1998 | 3 | - | 6 | 9 | 4 |
| Avant Ministries | 1950 | 1 | - | 8 | 2 | - |
| Back to the Bible International | 1961 | - | - | - | 8 | - |
| Baptist Bible Fellowship International | 1978 | - | - | 2 | - | - |
| Baptist International Missions, Inc. (BIMI) | | - | - | 4 | - | - |
| Baptist Mid-Missions | 1951 | - | - | 6 | - | - |
| BCM International | | - | - | 2 | - | - |
| Biblical Ministries Worldwide | 1962 | - | - | 9 | - | 9 |
| Brethren Assemblies | | - | - | 8 | - | - |
| Cadence International | | - | 2 | - | - | 2 |
| Campus Crusade for Christ, Intl. | 1969 | 25 | - | 13 | - | - |
| Christian Associates International | | - | - | - | - | - |
| Christian Church of North America—Missions | 1927 | - | - | 1 | - | - |
| Christian Churches / Churches of Christ | | - | - | 14 | 6 | - |
| Church of God (Cleveland, TN) World Missions | 1959 | - | - | 2 | - | 2 |
| Church of the Nazarene, World Mission Dept. | 1948 | - | - | 2 | - | - |
| Churches of Christ | 1948 | 4 | - | 18 | 12 | - |
| CLC Ministries International | 1956 | 1 | - | 1 | - | - |
| CrossWorld | 1974 | 1 | - | 19 | - | - |
| European Christian Mission International—USA | | - | - | 11 | - | - |
| Evangelical Baptist Missions | | - | - | 3 | 1 | - |
| Foursquare Missions International | 1993 | - | - | 2 | - | - |
| Globe Missionary Evangelism | 2002 | - | - | 2 | - | - |
| Gospel Fellowship Association | 1983 | - | - | 2 | - | - |
| Great Commission Ministries, Inc. | | 1 | - | 7 | - | - |
| Greater Europe Mission | 1956 | - | - | 7 | - | - |
| International Gospel Outreach | 2006 | - | - | 6 | - | - |
| Intl. Pentecostal Holiness Ch. World Missions Mins. | 1987 | - | - | - | - | - |
| International Teams, U.S.A. | | 2 | - | - | - | - |
| InterVarsity Christian Fellowship/USA—Msns. Dept. | | - | 1 | - | - | - |
| Italy for Christ | 1983 | - | - | 6 | 2 | 4 |
| Lott Carey Baptist Foreign Mission Convention | 2005 | - | - | - | 1 | - |
| Mission to the World (PCA), Inc. | 1988 | - | 2 | - | - | - |
| Missionary Revival Crusade | | - | - | - | - | - |
| Navigators, U.S. International Missions Group | | - | - | 4 | - | - |
| Operation Mobilization | 1962 | 1 | 3 | 4 | - | - |
| Presbyterian Mission International (PMI) | 2003 | - | - | - | 1 | - |
| Reformed Church in Am., Gen. Synod Council | 2004 | - | - | 2 | - | - |
| Salvation Army, U.S.A. | 1887 | - | - | 1 | - | - |
| SIM USA | 1979 | - | - | 2 | - | - |
| Spiritual Growth Resources, Inc. | 1998 | - | - | - | 3 | - |
| TEAM (The Evangelical Alliance Mission) | | - | - | 20 | - | - |
| Team Expansion, Inc. | 2000 | - | - | 8 | - | - |
| United Pentecostal Ch. Intl., Foreign Missions Div. | 1959 | - | 1 | - | - | - |
| Virginia Mennonite Board of Missions | 1949 | - | 4 | 2 | - | - |
| WEC International | 1964 | - | - | 6 | - | - |
| Word of Life Fellowship, Inc.—Intl. Ministries | 1985 | - | - | - | 2 | 2 |
| World Harvest Mission | 2000 | - | - | 2 | - | - |
| World Team | 1997 | - | - | 4 | - | - |

| | | Personnel from U.S. | | | Other Countries | |
|---|---|---|---|---|---|---|
| | First Year | 1-2 yrs. | 2-4 yrs. | 4+ yrs. | Citizens | Non-Citizens |
| World Venture | 1947 | 1 | 1 | 11 | 3 | - |
| World-Wide Missions | 1999 | - | - | 2 | - | - |
| Youth for Christ/USA—World Outreach | | - | - | 4 | - | - |
| Totals: | | 41 | 14 | 245 | 50 | 23 |

## Jamaica

| | | | | | | |
|---|---|---|---|---|---|---|
| Assemblies of God World Missions | 1936 | 5 | - | 10 | - | - |
| Awana Clubs International | 1997 | - | - | - | 2 | - |
| Back to the Bible International | 1958 | - | - | - | 7 | - |
| Baptist Bible Fellowship International | 1972 | - | - | 6 | - | - |
| Baptist International Missions, Inc. (BIMI) | | - | - | 4 | - | - |
| Baptist Mid-Missions | 1939 | - | - | 1 | - | - |
| BCM International | | - | - | - | 2 | - |
| Brethren Assemblies | | - | - | 2 | - | - |
| Campus Crusade for Christ, Intl. | 1990 | 2 | - | - | 3 | - |
| Christian Churches / Churches of Christ | | - | - | 12 | 6 | - |
| Ch. of God (Holiness), World Mission Dept., Inc. | 1946 | - | - | - | - | - |
| Church of the Nazarene, World Mission Dept. | 1966 | - | - | - | - | - |
| Churches of Christ | 1930 | 2 | - | 1 | 4 | - |
| CSI Ministries, Inc. | 1979 | - | - | 5 | 5 | - |
| Elim Fellowship—International Department | 1998 | - | - | 2 | - | 2 |
| Evangelical Luth. Ch. in Am., Div. for Global Msn. | 1990 | - | - | 2 | - | - |
| Friends United Meeting—Global Ministries | | - | - | - | - | - |
| Global Mins., Ch. of the United Brethren in Christ | 2003 | 1 | - | - | - | - |
| Global Outreach Mission, Inc. | | - | - | - | 2 | - |
| Grand Old Gospel Fellowship | | - | - | - | 1 | - |
| Greater Grace World Outreach | 1995 | - | - | - | 2 | - |
| Intl. Pentecostal Holiness Ch. World Missions Mins. | | - | - | - | - | - |
| Lott Carey Baptist Foreign Mission Convention | 1997 | - | - | - | 12 | - |
| Lutheran Church-Missouri Synod | 1993 | - | - | 2 | - | - |
| Macedonia World Baptist Missions, Inc. | 1980 | - | - | 4 | - | - |
| Ministries In Action | 1974 | - | - | 2 | 2 | - |
| Mission to the World (PCA), Inc. | 1981 | - | 2 | - | - | - |
| Natl. Baptist Conv. of Am.—Foreign Msn. Bd. | 1945 | - | - | - | 38 | - |
| Open Air Campaigners—Overseas Ministries | 1984 | 1 | - | 2 | 3 | - |
| Reformed Baptist Mission Services | | - | - | - | 2 | - |
| Salvation Army, U.S.A. | 1887 | - | - | 3 | - | - |
| Seventh-day Adventists General Conference | 1893 | - | - | 14 | - | - |
| Source of Light Ministries International, Inc. | 1952 | - | - | - | 2 | - |
| STEM (Short-Term Evangelical Missions) Intl. | 1985 | - | - | - | - | - |
| TEAMS for Medical Missions | | - | - | 2 | - | - |
| United Church of Christ—Wider Church Ministries | | - | 2 | - | - | - |
| United Pentecostal Ch. Intl., Foreign Missions Div. | 1930 | - | - | - | - | - |
| Virginia Mennonite Board of Missions | 1955 | 2 | - | 2 | - | - |
| World Missions & Evangelism, Inc. | | - | - | 3 | - | - |
| World Servants, Inc. | 1987 | - | - | - | - | - |
| Totals: | | 13 | 4 | 79 | 93 | 2 |

## Japan

| | | | | | | |
|---|---|---|---|---|---|---|
| Advancing Renewal Ministries, Inc. | | - | - | 2 | 2 | - |

| | First Year | Personnel from U.S. | | | Other Countries | |
|---|---|---|---|---|---|---|
| | | 1-2 yrs. | 2-4 yrs. | 4+ yrs. | Citizens | Non-Citizens |
| Am. Baptist Chs. of the U.S.A., Intl. Ministries | 1872 | - | - | - | - | - |
| Apostolic Christian Church Foundation, Inc. | 1985 | - | - | 2 | - | - |
| Artists In Christian Testimony | 2003 | - | - | - | 1 | 2 |
| Asian Access | 1967 | - | 8 | 17 | 7 | - |
| Asian Outreach U.S.A. | | - | - | - | - | - |
| Assemblies of God World Missions | 1913 | 16 | - | 37 | - | - |
| Awana Clubs International | 1983 | - | - | - | 4 | - |
| Back to the Bible International | 2004 | - | - | - | 1 | - |
| Baptist Bible Fellowship International | 1948 | - | - | 24 | - | - |
| Baptist General Conference—Intl. Ministries | 1948 | 2 | - | 12 | - | - |
| Baptist International Missions, Inc. (BIMI) | | - | - | 45 | - | - |
| Baptist Mid-Missions | 1949 | - | - | 8 | 3 | - |
| Bethany International Ministries | 1985 | - | 1 | 2 | - | 6 |
| Biblical Ministries Worldwide | 1987 | - | - | 2 | - | 2 |
| BILD International | | - | - | - | - | - |
| Brethren Assemblies | | - | - | 11 | - | - |
| Cadence International | | - | 18 | - | - | 18 |
| Campus Crusade for Christ, Intl. | 1962 | 13 | - | 18 | 42 | 50 |
| Child Evangelism Fellowship, Inc. | 1948 | - | - | - | - | 2 |
| Christ Community Church | 1951 | - | - | - | 4 | - |
| Christar | 1950 | - | - | 12 | - | - |
| Christian Churches / Churches of Christ | | - | 4 | 30 | - | - |
| Christian Reformed World Missions | 1951 | - | 2 | 12 | - | - |
| Christians In Action Missions International | 1957 | - | - | 2 | - | - |
| Ch. of God (Anderson, Ind.), Global Missions | 1908 | 7 | - | 2 | 1 | - |
| Church of God of Prophecy—Global Outreach | | - | - | 2 | - | - |
| Church of the Nazarene, World Mission Dept. | 1905 | - | - | 2 | - | - |
| Church Resource Ministries (CRM) | 1998 | 1 | - | 8 | - | - |
| Churches of Christ | 1892 | 8 | - | 10 | 6 | - |
| EFCA International Mission | 1949 | - | - | 19 | - | - |
| Episcopal Church USA—Domestic & Foreign | | - | - | 2 | - | - |
| Equip, Inc. | 1997 | - | - | 1 | - | - |
| Evangelical Baptist Missions | | - | - | 4 | - | - |
| Evangelical Congregational Ch.—Global Mins. | | - | - | - | 2 | - |
| Evangelical Covenant Ch.—Covenant Wld. Msn. | 1949 | 1 | - | 10 | - | - |
| Evangelical Luth. Ch. in Am., Div. for Global Msn. | 1892 | - | 13 | 13 | 2 | - |
| Fellowship International Mission | 1984 | - | - | 3 | 4 | 3 |
| Foursquare Missions International | 1951 | - | - | 4 | - | - |
| Free Will Baptist, Inc. Board of Intl.Missions | 1954 | - | 4 | 10 | - | - |
| Global Partners / Wesleyan World Missions | 1949 | - | - | - | - | - |
| Gospel Fellowship Association | 1958 | - | - | 1 | - | - |
| Grace Brethren International Missions | 1984 | - | - | 2 | - | 2 |
| Hope for the Hungry | | - | - | 1 | - | 1 |
| International Institute for Christian Studies | 2004 | - | - | - | - | - |
| Intl. Pentecostal Holiness Ch. World Missions Mins. | 1989 | - | - | 4 | - | - |
| International Teams, U.S.A. | | - | - | - | - | 8 |
| Japanese Evangelical Missionary Society (JEMS) | 1953 | 4 | 1 | 3 | 10 | - |
| Liberty Corner Mission | | - | - | 1 | - | - |
| Lutheran Brethren World Missions | 1949 | - | - | 4 | - | - |
| Lutheran Church-Missouri Synod | 1948 | - | 9 | 7 | - | - |

| | First Year | Personnel from U.S. | | | Other Countries | |
|---|---|---|---|---|---|---|
| | | 1-2 yrs. | 2-4 yrs. | 4+ yrs. | Citizens | Non-Citizens |
| Macedonia World Baptist Missions, Inc. | 2003 | - | - | 2 | - | - |
| Mennonite Mission Network | 1949 | - | - | 7 | - | 1 |
| Mission to the World (PCA), Inc. | 1985 | 4 | 25 | - | - | - |
| Mission To Unreached Peoples | 1990 | - | - | 5 | - | - |
| Navigators, U.S. International Missions Group | | - | 12 | 24 | - | - |
| Network of International Christian Schools | 1998 | - | 9 | 2 | - | - |
| New Life Advance International | | - | - | - | - | - |
| N. Am. Baptist Conf.—Worldwide Outreach | 1951 | 2 | 2 | 9 | - | - |
| OC International, Inc. | 1985 | - | - | 2 | - | - |
| OMF International | 1950 | 2 | - | 25 | 10 | 68 |
| OMS International, Inc. | 1922 | - | - | 12 | - | 3 |
| Orthodox Presbyterian Church | 1938 | 1 | 1 | 8 | - | - |
| Pioneers USA | | 2 | - | 3 | 1 | - |
| Presbyterian Evangelistic Fellowship | | - | - | 2 | - | - |
| Presbyterian Mission International (PMI) | 1994 | - | - | - | 1 | - |
| Project AmaZon | 1989 | - | - | 3 | - | 2 |
| Reformed Church in Am., Gen. Synod Council | 1987 | - | - | 6 | - | - |
| Ripe for Harvest, Inc. | 1992 | - | - | 2 | - | - |
| Seed International | 2003 | - | - | 2 | - | - |
| SEND International USA | 1948 | - | 3 | 44 | 2 | 6 |
| Seventh-day Adventists General Conference | 1896 | - | - | 4 | - | - |
| Source of Light Ministries International, Inc. | 2000 | - | - | - | 2 | - |
| TEAM (The Evangelical Alliance Mission) | | 5 | - | 76 | - | - |
| Team Expansion, Inc. | | - | - | 10 | - | - |
| The Mission Society | 1997 | - | - | 2 | - | - |
| Touch the World Youth Ministries | | - | - | - | 10 | - |
| United Church of Christ—Wider Church Ministries | | - | 15 | - | - | - |
| United Pentecostal Ch. Intl., Foreign Missions Div. | 1900 | - | 8 | - | - | 4 |
| Walk Thru the Bible Ministries, Inc. | 2002 | - | - | - | 1 | - |
| White Fields Inc. | | - | - | - | 5 | - |
| Wisc. Evangelical Lutheran Synod, Bd. for Wld. Msns. | 1952 | - | - | 4 | - | - |
| Word of Life Fellowship, Inc.—Intl. Ministries | 1981 | - | - | - | 5 | - |
| World Gospel Mission | 1952 | - | - | 4 | - | - |
| World Venture | 1947 | - | 2 | 13 | - | - |
| WorldHarvest | | - | - | - | - | - |
| Youth for Christ/USA—World Outreach | | - | - | 1 | - | - |
| Totals: | | 68 | 137 | 621 | 126 | 178 |

## Jordan

| | First Year | 1-2 yrs. | 2-4 yrs. | 4+ yrs. | Citizens | Non-Citizens |
|---|---|---|---|---|---|---|
| Anis Shorrosh Evangelistic Association | | - | - | 40 | - | - |
| Arab World Ministries | | 5 | 4 | 17 | - | - |
| Assemblies of God World Missions | 1920 | 5 | - | 9 | - | - |
| Avant Ministries | | - | - | 2 | - | - |
| Child Evangelism Fellowship, Inc. | 1991 | - | - | - | 2 | - |
| Christar | 1983 | - | - | 18 | - | - |
| Christian Blind Mission International | 1990 | - | 1 | - | - | - |
| Church of the Nazarene, World Mission Dept. | 1950 | - | - | 3 | - | - |
| Global Outreach Mission, Inc. | | - | - | - | 2 | - |
| Habitat for Humanity International | 2002 | - | 1 | - | - | 1 |
| International Partnership Ministries, Inc. | 2004 | 2 | - | - | - | - |

| | First Year | Personnel from U.S. | | | Other Countries | |
|---|---|---|---|---|---|---|
| | | 1-2 yrs. | 2-4 yrs. | 4+ yrs. | Citizens | Non-Citizens |
| Mission ONE, Inc. | 1990 | - | - | - | 1 | - |
| Mission to the World (PCA), Inc. | 1978 | - | - | - | - | - |
| Partners International | 1997 | - | - | - | 79 | - |
| Samaritan's Purse | 2004 | - | 2 | - | - | 2 |
| United Pentecostal Ch. Intl., Foreign Missions Div. | 1955 | - | 2 | - | - | - |
| Venture International | 1998 | - | - | - | 2 | - |
| Walk Thru the Bible Ministries, Inc. | 2000 | - | - | - | - | - |
| World Bible Translation Center | | - | - | - | 2 | - |
| World Venture | 1956 | - | 2 | 4 | - | - |
| World-Wide Missions | 1987 | - | - | - | 1 | - |
| Totals: | | 12 | 12 | 93 | 89 | 3 |

## Kazakhstan

| | First Year | 1-2 yrs. | 2-4 yrs. | 4+ yrs. | Citizens | Non-Citizens |
|---|---|---|---|---|---|---|
| Advancing Renewal Ministries, Inc. | | - | - | 4 | 4 | - |
| All God's Children International | | - | - | - | 12 | - |
| Assemblies of God World Missions | 1991 | 1 | - | 2 | - | - |
| Awana Clubs International | 1992 | - | - | - | 2 | - |
| Christar | 1991 | - | - | 12 | 1 | 2 |
| Christian Aid Mission | | - | - | - | 20 | - |
| Christian Broadcasting Network Inc., the | 1995 | - | - | - | 2 | - |
| Church of God of Prophecy—Global Outreach | | - | - | - | 1 | - |
| Church of the Nazarene, World Mission Dept. | 1996 | - | - | - | - | - |
| Churches of Christ | 1990 | - | - | 2 | 2 | - |
| East-West Ministries International | 1995 | - | - | 6 | 50 | - |
| Evangelical Presbyterian Church—World Outreach | 1993 | - | - | - | 5 | - |
| Evangelism Explosion International | | - | - | - | - | 2 |
| Greater Grace World Outreach | 2001 | - | - | - | 2 | 7 |
| Mission to the World (PCA), Inc. | 1994 | - | 2 | - | - | - |
| Mission To Unreached Peoples | 2003 | - | - | - | - | - |
| OMS International, Inc. | 2003 | - | - | 1 | - | 1 |
| People International USA | 1992 | - | - | 5 | - | - |
| Presbyterian Evangelistic Fellowship | | - | - | 1 | - | - |
| RUN Ministries | 2002 | - | - | - | - | - |
| SEND International USA | 2005 | | | 5 | | |
| Seventh-day Adventists General Conference | 1886 | - | - | - | - | 2 |
| The Master's Mission, Inc. | 1993 | - | - | 2 | - | - |
| The Mission Society | 1993 | 3 | 6 | 6 | - | - |
| United Pentecostal Ch. Intl., Foreign Missions Div. | | - | 1 | - | - | - |
| Walk Thru the Bible Ministries, Inc. | | - | - | - | - | - |
| Totals: | | 4 | 9 | 46 | 101 | 14 |

## Kenya

| | First Year | 1-2 yrs. | 2-4 yrs. | 4+ yrs. | Citizens | Non-Citizens |
|---|---|---|---|---|---|---|
| ACM International | 1996 | - | - | 5 | - | - |
| Adventures in Missions | 1999 | 1 | - | 3 | - | - |
| Africa Inland Mission International | 1895 | 46 | 24 | 185 | - | 93 |
| African Enterprise | 1970 | - | - | - | 9 | - |
| African Leadership, Inc. | 1998 | - | - | - | 3 | - |
| Artists In Christian Testimony | 2003 | - | - | 2 | - | - |
| Assemblies of God World Missions | 1967 | 4 | - | 32 | - | - |
| Audio Scripture Ministries | 1985 | - | - | 1 | - | - |

| | | Personnel from U.S. | | | Other Countries | |
|---|---|---|---|---|---|---|
| | First Year | 1-2 yrs. | 2-4 yrs. | 4+ yrs. | Citizens | Non-Citizens |
| Awana Clubs International | 1992 | - | - | - | 4 | - |
| Baptist Bible Fellowship International | 1971 | - | - | 34 | - | - |
| Baptist International Missions, Inc. (BIMI) | | - | - | 4 | - | - |
| Baptist International Outreach | 1985 | - | - | 2 | - | 2 |
| Baptist Mid-Missions | 2006 | - | - | 2 | 2 | - |
| Bethany International Ministries | 1999 | - | - | 2 | - | - |
| Brethren Assemblies | | - | - | 1 | - | - |
| Bright Hope International | 1990 | - | - | - | 5 | - |
| Campus Crusade for Christ, Intl. | 1972 | 2 | - | 6 | 132 | - |
| Caring Partners International, Inc. | 1997 | - | - | - | - | - |
| Child Evangelism Fellowship, Inc. | 1966 | - | - | 5 | 27 | - |
| Childcare Worldwide | 1984 | - | - | - | 50 | - |
| Christ to the Nations | 2002 | - | - | - | 2 | - |
| Christian Aid Mission | | - | - | - | 71 | - |
| Christian Blind Mission International | 1971 | 1 | 1 | - | - | - |
| Christian Church of North America—Missions | 1996 | - | 2 | - | - | - |
| Christian Churches / Churches of Christ | | 2 | 3 | 35 | 8 | - |
| Christian Reformed World Relief Committee | 1983 | - | - | 1 | 2 | - |
| Ch. of God (Anderson, Ind.), Global Missions | 1922 | 4 | - | 5 | - | - |
| Church of God (Cleveland, TN) World Missions | 1977 | - | - | 9 | - | 4 |
| Church of God of Prophecy—Global Outreach | | - | - | - | 14 | - |
| Church of the Nazarene, World Mission Dept. | 1984 | - | - | 20 | - | - |
| Churches of Christ | 1965 | 8 | - | 22 | 6 | - |
| CMF International | 1977 | - | 26 | - | - | - |
| Compassion International, Inc. | 1980 | - | - | 1 | 48 | 1 |
| Daystar U.S. | 1989 | - | - | 4 | - | - |
| Eastern Mennonite Missions | | - | 4 | 2 | - | 2 |
| East-West Ministries International | 2002 | - | - | 2 | - | - |
| EFCA International Mission | 1996 | - | - | 8 | - | - |
| Elim Fellowship—International Department | 1940 | - | - | 5 | - | 9 |
| Empowering Lives International | 1995 | - | 3 | 2 | 67 | 1 |
| Episcopal Church USA—Domestic & Foreign | | - | - | 5 | - | - |
| Equip, Inc. | 1998 | - | - | - | 2 | - |
| Evangel Bible Translators | | - | - | - | 2 | - |
| Evangelical Covenant Ch.—Covenant Wld. Msn. | 1998 | 3 | - | - | - | - |
| Evangelical Luth. Ch. in Am., Div. for Global Msn. | 1969 | - | - | 4 | - | 1 |
| Fellowship International Mission | 2000 | - | - | 2 | - | - |
| Food for the Hungry, Inc. | 1976 | - | 4 | 1 | - | - |
| Free Methodist World Missions | 1944 | - | - | 2 | - | 2 |
| Friends United Meeting—Global Ministries | | - | - | 4 | 1 | - |
| Full Gospel Evangelistic Association | 2000 | - | - | 1 | 2 | - |
| Global Fellowship Inc. | 2006 | - | - | - | 2 | - |
| Global Outreach International | 2002 | - | - | 7 | - | - |
| Global Partners / Wesleyan World Missions | 1997 | - | 2 | - | - | - |
| Globe Missionary Evangelism | 1987 | - | - | 2 | - | - |
| Gospel Furthering Fellowship, The | | - | - | - | - | - |
| Greater Grace World Outreach | 2005 | - | - | - | 15 | - |
| Habitat for Humanity International | 1985 | - | 1 | - | - | 1 |
| Harvest | 2001 | - | - | - | 2 | - |
| Harvest International, Inc. | 2004 | - | 2 | - | 2 | - |

| | First Year | Personnel from U.S. 1-2 yrs. | 2-4 yrs. | 4+ yrs. | Other Countries Citizens | Non-Citizens |
|---|---|---|---|---|---|---|
| Have Christ Will Travel Ministries | 2000 | - | - | - | 5 | - |
| Hosanna | 2004 | - | - | - | 2 | - |
| Independent Faith Mission, Inc. | | - | - | 6 | - | - |
| International Christian Ministries | 1986 | - | - | 4 | 6 | - |
| International Gospel Outreach | 1986 | - | - | 4 | 6 | - |
| International Justice Mission | 2001 | - | - | - | 9 | - |
| International Outreach Ministries (IOM) | 1987 | - | - | 2 | - | - |
| Intl. Pentecostal Ch. of Christ—Global Msns. Dept. | 1936 | - | - | 8 | - | 8 |
| Intl. Pentecostal Holiness Ch. World Missions Mins. | 1972 | - | - | 6 | 2 | - |
| International Teams, U.S.A. | | - | - | 2 | - | 7 |
| InterVarsity Christian Fellowship/USA—Msns. Dept. | | 1 | - | 2 | - | - |
| Ireland Outreach International Inc. | 2004 | - | - | - | - | - |
| Kids Alive International | 2000 | - | 2 | 2 | 152 | 2 |
| Larry Jones Intl. Ministries (Feed the Children) | 1979 | - | - | - | 16 | 1 |
| Living Hope Ministries International | 2003 | - | - | 1 | - | - |
| Lott Carey Baptist Foreign Mission Convention | 1985 | - | - | - | 32 | - |
| Lutheran Church-Missouri Synod | 1999 | - | - | 2 | - | - |
| Macedonia World Baptist Missions, Inc. | 2006 | - | - | - | 2 | - |
| MAP International | 1987 | - | - | - | 21 | 1 |
| Medical Ambassadors International, Inc. | 1987 | - | - | 6 | 50 | - |
| Mission Ministries, Inc. | 1990 | - | - | 1 | 1 | - |
| Mission ONE, Inc. | 1990 | - | - | - | 38 | - |
| Mission to the Americas | 2001 | - | - | 1 | - | - |
| Mission to the World (PCA), Inc. | 1977 | 1 | 5 | - | - | - |
| Mission: Moving Mountains, Inc. | 1985 | - | - | 16 | 13 | 6 |
| Moravian Ch. in N. Am., Bd. of World Msn. | | - | - | - | - | - |
| Navigators, U.S. International Missions Group | | - | - | 2 | - | - |
| Network of International Christian Schools | 1996 | - | 4 | 2 | - | 1 |
| New Directions International, Inc. | 1984 | - | - | - | 21 | - |
| New Mission Systems International | 2003 | - | - | 9 | 3 | - |
| OC International, Inc. | 1985 | - | - | 6 | - | - |
| Pioneers USA | | - | - | 2 | - | - |
| Presbyterian Evangelistic Fellowship | | - | - | 2 | - | - |
| Reformed Baptist Mission Services | | - | - | - | - | 2 |
| Reformed Church in Am., Gen. Synod Council | 1985 | - | - | 6 | 2 | - |
| Salvation Army, U.S.A. | 1921 | - | - | 5 | - | - |
| Samaritan's Purse | 2005 | 2 | - | - | 44 | - |
| Seed International | 2000 | - | - | 1 | - | - |
| Seventh-day Adventists General Conference | 1906 | - | - | 17 | - | 29 |
| Share International | 1996 | - | - | - | 9 | - |
| SIM USA | 1977 | 4 | - | 21 | - | - |
| The God's Story Project | 2005 | - | - | - | 1 | - |
| The Master's Mission, Inc. | 1979 | - | - | 20 | 2 | 2 |
| Things To Come Mission, Inc. | 1986 | - | - | - | 15 | 4 |
| United Church of Christ—Wider Church Ministries | | - | 1 | - | - | - |
| United Pentecostal Ch. Intl., Foreign Missions Div. | 1972 | - | 4 | - | - | 1 |
| UWEZO International | 2005 | - | - | 1 | 1 | - |
| Walk Thru the Bible Ministries, Inc. | 1999 | - | - | - | 2 | - |
| Women to the World | 2006 | - | - | - | - | - |
| Word of Life Fellowship, Inc.—Intl. Ministries | 1970 | - | - | 2 | 31 | - |

| | First Year | Personnel from U.S. | | | Other Countries | |
|---|---|---|---|---|---|---|
| | | 1-2 yrs. | 2-4 yrs. | 4+ yrs. | Citizens | Non-Citizens |
| World Concern | 1984 | 3 | 1 | 3 | 66 | - |
| World Gospel Mission | 1932 | - | - | 46 | - | - |
| World Harvest Mission | 1990 | - | - | 6 | - | - |
| World Mission Prayer League | 1968 | - | - | 8 | - | 2 |
| World Missions & Evangelism, Inc. | | - | - | 10 | - | 4 |
| World Missions Far Corners, Inc. | 1992 | - | - | - | 6 | - |
| World Orphans | | - | - | - | 1 | - |
| World Reach, Inc. | 1983 | - | - | - | 11 | - |
| World Relief | 1998 | - | - | - | 11 | 1 |
| World Servants, Inc. | 1991 | - | - | - | - | - |
| World Venture | 1972 | - | 2 | 7 | - | - |
| World Vision Inc. | 1974 | - | - | - | - | - |
| World-Wide Missions | 1963 | - | - | - | 1 | - |
| Youth for Christ/USA—World Outreach | | - | - | 3 | - | - |
| Totals: | | 82 | 91 | 670 | 1060 | 187 |

**Kiribati**

| | First Year | 1-2 yrs. | 2-4 yrs. | 4+ yrs. | Citizens | Non-Citizens |
|---|---|---|---|---|---|---|
| Assemblies of God World Missions | 1989 | - | - | 1 | - | - |
| Medical Ambassadors International, Inc. | 2004 | - | - | - | - | - |
| Totals: | | - | - | 1 | - | - |

**Korea, North**

| | First Year | 1-2 yrs. | 2-4 yrs. | 4+ yrs. | Citizens | Non-Citizens |
|---|---|---|---|---|---|---|
| | | - | - | - | - | - |
| Seventh-day Adventists General Conference | | - | - | - | - | 1 |
| Totals: | | - | - | - | - | 1 |

**Korea, South**

| | First Year | 1-2 yrs. | 2-4 yrs. | 4+ yrs. | Citizens | Non-Citizens |
|---|---|---|---|---|---|---|
| | | - | - | - | - | - |
| Assemblies of God World Missions | 1928 | 2 | - | 4 | - | - |
| Awana Clubs International | 1983 | - | - | - | 2 | - |
| Baptist Bible Fellowship International | 1958 | - | - | 11 | - | - |
| Brethren Assemblies | | - | - | 2 | - | - |
| Cadence International | | - | 4 | - | - | 4 |
| Campus Crusade for Christ, Intl. | 1958 | - | - | - | 827 | 1 |
| Christian Churches / Churches of Christ | | - | - | 4 | 6 | - |
| Christians In Action Missions International | 1957 | - | - | - | 2 | - |
| Church of God of Prophecy—Global Outreach | | - | - | - | 2 | - |
| Church of the Nazarene, World Mission Dept. | 1948 | - | - | 6 | - | - |
| Churches of Christ | 1950 | 2 | - | 1 | 1 | - |
| David Livingstone KURE Foundation | | - | - | - | 24 | - |
| Evangelical Luth. Ch. in Am., Div. for Global Msn. | 1961 | - | 2 | - | - | - |
| Evangelistic Faith Missions | 1971 | - | - | - | - | - |
| Far East Broadcasting Company, Inc. | 1976 | - | - | 1 | 150 | - |
| Global Outreach Mission, Inc. | | - | - | - | 2 | - |
| Global Partners / Wesleyan World Missions | 1982 | - | - | - | - | - |
| Go Ye Fellowship | 1994 | - | - | 1 | - | - |
| Gospel Fellowship Association | 1967 | - | - | 4 | - | - |
| Greater Grace World Outreach | 2002 | - | 1 | 3 | - | - |
| Independent Faith Mission, Inc. | | - | - | 2 | - | - |
| International Gospel Outreach | 2000 | - | - | - | 2 | - |
| International Institute for Christian Studies | 2004 | - | - | - | - | - |
| Intl. Pentecostal Holiness Ch. World Missions Mins. | | - | - | - | - | - |

| | First Year | Personnel from U.S. | | | Other Countries | |
| --- | --- | --- | --- | --- | --- | --- |
| | | 1-2 yrs. | 2-4 yrs. | 4+ yrs. | Citizens | Non-Citizens |
| Macedonia World Baptist Missions, Inc. | 2002 | - | - | 2 | - | - |
| Mennonite Mission Network | | - | - | - | - | 2 |
| Mission to the World (PCA), Inc. | 1976 | - | - | - | - | - |
| Mission To Unreached Peoples | 2002 | - | - | - | - | - |
| Network of International Christian Schools | 1983 | 13 | 72 | 48 | - | 4 |
| New Tribes Mission | 1993 | - | - | 2 | 2 | - |
| OMS International, Inc. | 1907 | - | - | 2 | - | - |
| Orthodox Presbyterian Church | 1946 | - | - | 2 | - | - |
| Precept Ministries International | 1984 | - | - | - | 13 | - |
| Seventh-day Adventists General Conference | 1904 | - | - | 8 | - | 5 |
| Shield of Faith Mission International | 1954 | 1 | - | - | - | - |
| SIM USA | | - | - | 2 | - | - |
| Source of Light Ministries International, Inc. | 1985 | - | - | - | 2 | - |
| Tentmakers International | | - | - | - | - | - |
| U.S. Center for World Mission | | - | - | 1 | - | 1 |
| United Church of Christ—Wider Church Ministries | | - | 1 | - | - | - |
| United Pentecostal Ch. Intl., Foreign Missions Div. | 1985 | - | 1 | - | - | - |
| Walk Thru the Bible Ministries, Inc. | 2000 | - | - | - | 4 | - |
| Westminster Biblical Missions | 1973 | - | - | 1 | 15 | - |
| Word of Life Fellowship, Inc.—Intl. Ministries | 1989 | - | - | 4 | 8 | - |
| World Missions Far Corners, Inc. | 1976 | - | - | 2 | 7 | - |
| WorldHarvest | | - | - | - | - | - |
| Worldwide Tentmakers, Inc. | 2000 | - | - | - | - | - |
| | Totals: | 18 | 81 | 113 | 1069 | 17 |

**Kosovo**

| | First Year | 1-2 yrs. | 2-4 yrs. | 4+ yrs. | Citizens | Non-Citizens |
| --- | --- | --- | --- | --- | --- | --- |
| AMG International | | - | - | 2 | - | - |
| Assemblies of God World Missions | 1999 | 4 | - | 4 | - | - |
| Bethany International Ministries | 1999 | 2 | - | 1 | - | 1 |
| Christian Churches / Churches of Christ | | - | - | 2 | 1 | - |
| Church of the Nazarene, World Mission Dept. | 2005 | - | - | - | - | - |
| Eastern European Outreach, Inc. | 1999 | - | - | - | 2 | - |
| European Christian Mission International—USA | | - | - | 4 | - | - |
| Greater Europe Mission | 1974 | - | - | 3 | - | - |
| International Teams, U.S.A. | | - | - | 2 | - | - |
| Medical Ambassadors International, Inc. | 2003 | - | - | - | - | - |
| Paraclete, Inc. | 2004 | 2 | - | - | - | - |
| Samaritan's Purse | 1999 | 1 | - | - | 3 | - |
| World Relief | 2000 | - | 1 | - | 14 | - |
| | Totals: | 9 | 1 | 18 | 20 | 1 |

**Kuwait**

| | First Year | 1-2 yrs. | 2-4 yrs. | 4+ yrs. | Citizens | Non-Citizens |
| --- | --- | --- | --- | --- | --- | --- |
| Seventh-day Adventists General Conference | | - | - | - | - | 2 |
| Walk Thru the Bible Ministries, Inc. | 2002 | - | - | - | - | - |
| | Totals: | - | - | - | - | 2 |

**Kyrgyzstan**

| | First Year | 1-2 yrs. | 2-4 yrs. | 4+ yrs. | Citizens | Non-Citizens |
| --- | --- | --- | --- | --- | --- | --- |
| Assemblies of God World Missions | 1995 | 4 | - | 10 | - | - |
| Avant Ministries | | - | - | 2 | - | - |
| Christian Aid Mission | | - | - | - | 10 | - |

| | Personnel from U.S. | | | | Other Countries | |
|---|---|---|---|---|---|---|
| | First Year | 1-2 yrs. | 2-4 yrs. | 4+ yrs. | Citizens | Non-Citizens |
| Evangelism Explosion International | | - | - | - | - | 2 |
| Grace Brethren International Missions | 1998 | - | - | 2 | - | - |
| Greater Grace World Outreach | 1999 | - | - | 2 | 4 | 3 |
| People International USA | 1998 | - | 1 | 2 | - | - |
| Venture International | 1992 | - | - | - | 17 | - |
| Totals: | | 4 | 1 | 18 | 31 | 5 |

## Laos

| | First Year | 1-2 yrs. | 2-4 yrs. | 4+ yrs. | Citizens | Non-Citizens |
|---|---|---|---|---|---|---|
| Advancing Renewal Ministries, Inc. | | - | - | 2 | - | - |
| Assemblies of God World Missions | 1990 | 2 | - | 4 | - | - |
| Christian Aid Mission | | - | - | - | 62 | - |
| Christian Reformed World Relief Committee | 1997 | - | - | - | - | 3 |
| Church World Service | | - | - | 1 | 3 | - |
| Evangelical Covenant Ch.—Covenant Wld. Msn. | 1991 | 1 | - | 2 | - | - |
| Food for the Hungry, Inc. | 1998 | - | - | - | - | - |
| Global Fellowship Inc. | 1998 | - | - | - | 5 | - |
| Globe Missionary Evangelism | 2005 | - | - | 2 | - | - |
| Medical Ambassadors International, Inc. | 2003 | - | - | - | - | - |
| Mission ONE, Inc. | 1990 | - | - | - | 6 | - |
| Seventh-day Adventists General Conference | 1919 | - | - | - | - | 4 |
| United Pentecostal Ch. Intl., Foreign Missions Div. | | - | - | - | - | - |
| World Concern | 1990 | - | - | - | 29 | 1 |
| Totals: | | 3 | - | 11 | 105 | 8 |

## Latin America—General

| | First Year | 1-2 yrs. | 2-4 yrs. | 4+ yrs. | Citizens | Non-Citizens |
|---|---|---|---|---|---|---|
| Assemblies of God World Missions | 1910 | 3 | - | 81 | - | - |
| Baptist Medical & Dental Mission Intl., Inc. | 1974 | - | - | 4 | - | - |
| Campus Crusade for Christ, Intl. | | - | - | - | 4 | - |
| Christian and Missionary Alliance | | - | - | 171 | - | - |
| Church Ministries International | 1973 | - | - | - | - | 2 |
| Church World Service | 1946 | 175 | - | - | 3 | - |
| Cities for Christ Worldwide | 1975 | - | - | 2 | - | - |
| Cook Communications Ministries International | 1993 | - | - | - | - | - |
| Dawn Ministries, Inc. | | - | - | - | - | 1 |
| Final Frontiers Foundation, Inc. | 1989 | - | - | - | 180 | - |
| Free Methodist World Missions | | - | - | 3 | - | - |
| Global Action | 1998 | - | - | 2 | - | - |
| Global Youth Ministry Network | | - | - | - | - | 1 |
| Heifer International | 1944 | 25 | 31 | 14 | 64 | 6 |
| Help for Christian Nationals, Inc. | 1982 | - | - | 2 | - | - |
| International Cooperating Ministries | | - | - | - | - | - |
| InterVarsity Christian Fellowship/USA—Msns. Dept. | | - | - | 1 | - | - |
| Mailbox Club International Inc., The | 2000 | - | - | 1 | - | - |
| Mennonite Central Committee (MCC) | | - | - | 181 | - | - |
| Mission Aviation Fellowship | | - | 1 | 1 | - | - |
| Operation Mobilization | | - | - | 6 | - | - |
| Presbyterian Church (USA), Worldwide Ministries | | - | 90 | 88 | - | - |
| Presbyterian Evangelistic Fellowship | | - | - | 2 | - | - |
| Southern Baptist Convention Intl. Mission Board | | - | - | - | - | - |
| United World Mission | | - | - | 15 | - | - |

| | First Year | Personnel from U.S. 1-2 yrs. | Personnel from U.S. 2-4 yrs. | Personnel from U.S. 4+ yrs. | Other Countries Citizens | Other Countries Non-Citizens |
|---|---|---|---|---|---|---|
| VELA Ministries International | 1970 | - | - | - | - | 1 |
| Wycliffe Bible Translators, Inc. | 1934 | - | - | 678 | - | - |
| Young Life | | 7 | 4 | 10 | - | - |
| Totals: | | 210 | 126 | 1262 | 251 | 11 |

## Latvia

| | First Year | 1-2 yrs. | 2-4 yrs. | 4+ yrs. | Citizens | Non-Citizens |
|---|---|---|---|---|---|---|
| Assemblies of God World Missions | 1926 | - | - | 3 | - | - |
| Awana Clubs International | 2000 | - | - | - | 2 | - |
| Baptist International Missions, Inc. (BIMI) | | - | - | 4 | - | - |
| Bridge Builders International | 1994 | 2 | - | 1 | - | - |
| Calvary International | 1992 | - | - | 1 | 1 | - |
| Campus Crusade for Christ, Intl. | 1991 | - | - | 8 | 19 | - |
| Christian Associates International | 1992 | - | - | - | - | - |
| Churches of Christ | 1991 | - | - | 1 | 2 | - |
| Greater Europe Mission | 1992 | - | 2 | 4 | - | - |
| Peter Deyneka Russian Ministries | | - | - | - | - | - |
| Salvation Army, U.S.A. | | - | - | 1 | - | - |
| United Pentecostal Ch. Intl., Foreign Missions Div. | | - | - | - | - | 4 |
| Walk Thru the Bible Ministries, Inc. | 2000 | - | - | - | 1 | - |
| World Baptist Fellowship Mission Agency, Inc. | | - | - | 2 | - | - |
| Totals: | | 2 | 2 | 25 | 25 | 4 |

## Lebanon

| | First Year | 1-2 yrs. | 2-4 yrs. | 4+ yrs. | Citizens | Non-Citizens |
|---|---|---|---|---|---|---|
| Am. Baptist Chs. of the U.S.A., Intl. Ministries | 1998 | - | - | - | - | 2 |
| AMG International | | - | - | - | 2 | - |
| Arab World Ministries | | - | - | 2 | - | - |
| Armenian Missionary Association of America, Inc. | 1918 | 1 | - | 2 | - | - |
| Assemblies of God World Missions | 1925 | 1 | - | 8 | - | - |
| Campus Crusade for Christ, Intl. | 1968 | - | - | - | 18 | 2 |
| Ch. of God (Anderson, Ind.), Global Missions | 1914 | - | - | 1 | - | - |
| Church of the Nazarene, World Mission Dept. | 1950 | - | - | 2 | - | - |
| Evangelical Luth. Ch. in Am., Div. for Global Msn. | 1969 | 1 | - | - | - | - |
| International Partnership Ministries, Inc. | 1999 | - | - | - | 5 | - |
| Kids Alive International | 1948 | - | - | 1 | 20 | 2 |
| Mission ONE, Inc. | 1990 | - | - | - | 3 | - |
| Mutual Faith Ministries Intl. | | - | - | - | - | - |
| Seventh-day Adventists General Conference | 1970 | - | - | - | - | 4 |
| United Church of Christ—Wider Church Ministries | | - | 2 | - | - | - |
| United Pentecostal Ch. Intl., Foreign Missions Div. | 1992 | - | 2 | - | - | 2 |
| Venture International | 1987 | - | - | - | 2 | - |
| Walk Thru the Bible Ministries, Inc. | 2002 | - | - | - | - | - |
| World Venture | 1993 | - | - | 2 | - | - |
| Totals: | | 3 | 4 | 18 | 50 | 12 |

## Lesotho

| | First Year | 1-2 yrs. | 2-4 yrs. | 4+ yrs. | Citizens | Non-Citizens |
|---|---|---|---|---|---|---|
| Africa Inland Mission International | 1986 | - | 1 | 1 | - | 12 |
| Africa Inter-Mennonite Mission | 1972 | - | - | - | - | - |
| Assemblies of God World Missions | 1950 | - | - | 2 | - | - |
| Campus Crusade for Christ, Intl. | 1979 | - | - | - | 10 | - |
| Church of the Nazarene, World Mission Dept. | 1993 | - | - | 2 | - | - |

| | First Year | Personnel from U.S. | | | Other Countries | |
|---|---|---|---|---|---|---|
| | | 1-2 yrs. | 2-4 yrs. | 4+ yrs. | Citizens | Non-Citizens |
| Habitat for Humanity International | 1986 | - | 1 | - | - | 1 |
| Intl. Pentecostal Holiness Ch. World Missions Mins. | | - | - | - | - | - |
| Mennonite Mission Network | 1973 | - | - | - | - | 2 |
| Mission Aviation Fellowship | 1979 | 1 | 1 | 4 | - | - |
| Natl. Baptist Conv. USA, Inc.—Foreign Msn. Bd. | 1961 | - | - | - | - | - |
| Seventh-day Adventists General Conference | 1899 | - | - | 2 | - | 2 |
| United Church of Christ—Wider Church Ministries | | - | 12 | - | - | - |
| United Pentecostal Ch. Intl., Foreign Missions Div. | 1996 | - | 2 | - | - | - |
| Walk Thru the Bible Ministries, Inc. | 1999 | - | - | - | 1 | - |
| | Totals: | 1 | 17 | 11 | 11 | 17 |

## Liberia

| | First Year | 1-2 yrs. | 2-4 yrs. | 4+ yrs. | Citizens | Non-Citizens |
|---|---|---|---|---|---|---|
| Advent Christian Gen. Conf., Dept. of Wld. Msns. | 1988 | - | - | - | 10 | - |
| African Leadership, Inc. | 1998 | - | - | - | 1 | - |
| Agape Gospel Mission | | - | - | - | 6 | - |
| Assemblies of God World Missions | 1908 | - | - | - | - | - |
| Awana Clubs International | 1980 | - | - | - | 2 | - |
| Baptist Mid-Missions | 1938 | - | - | 2 | - | - |
| Campus Crusade for Christ, Intl. | 1979 | - | - | - | 26 | - |
| Carver International Missions, Inc. | 1955 | 1 | - | 5 | 3 | - |
| Child Evangelism Fellowship, Inc. | 1955 | - | - | - | 7 | - |
| Childcare Worldwide | 2003 | - | - | - | - | - |
| Christian Aid Ministries | | - | 15 | - | 23 | - |
| Christian Aid Mission | | - | - | - | 12 | - |
| Christian Churches / Churches of Christ | | - | - | 2 | - | - |
| Christian Literature International | | - | - | - | - | - |
| Church of God (Cleveland, TN) World Missions | 1974 | - | - | - | - | 4 |
| Ch. of God (Holiness), World Msn. Dept., Inc. | 1980 | - | - | - | 1 | - |
| Church of God of Prophecy—Global Outreach | | - | - | - | 6 | - |
| Church of the Nazarene, World Mission Dept. | 1990 | - | - | - | - | - |
| Episcopal Church USA—Domestic & Foreign | | - | - | 2 | - | - |
| Equip, Inc. | 1997 | 3 | - | - | 2 | 2 |
| Evangel Bible Translators | 1986 | - | - | 1 | 1 | - |
| Evangelical Luth. Ch. in Am., Div. for Global Msn. | 1862 | 1 | - | 1 | - | - |
| Global Partners / Wesleyan World Missions | 1978 | - | - | - | - | - |
| Greater Grace World Outreach | 1987 | - | - | - | 37 | - |
| Have Christ Will Travel Ministries | 1975 | - | - | - | 20 | - |
| International Gospel Outreach | 1988 | - | - | - | 2 | - |
| International Partnership Ministries, Inc. | 1998 | - | - | - | 11 | - |
| Intl. Pentecostal Holiness Ch. World Missions Mins. | | - | - | - | - | - |
| Lott Carey Baptist Foreign Mission Convention | 1908 | - | - | - | 150 | - |
| Lutheran Bible Translators, Inc. | 1969 | - | - | - | 27 | - |
| Mennonite Mission Network | 1988 | - | - | - | - | - |
| Northwest Medical Teams International, Inc. | 2003 | - | - | - | 25 | 1 |
| Partners International | 1964 | - | - | - | 507 | - |
| Presbyterian Evangelistic Fellowship | | - | - | - | 5 | - |
| Reformed Episcopal Board of Foreign Missions | | - | - | - | 8 | - |
| Salvation Army, U.S.A. | | - | - | 1 | - | - |
| Samaritan's Purse | 2003 | 7 | - | - | 77 | - |
| Seventh-day Adventists General Conference | 1927 | - | - | - | - | 2 |

| | First Year | Personnel from U.S. 1-2 yrs. | 2-4 yrs. | 4+ yrs. | Other Countries Citizens | Non-Citizens |
|---|---|---|---|---|---|---|
| SIM USA | 1952 | 1 | - | 3 | - | - |
| Source of Light Ministries International, Inc. | 1979 | - | - | - | 1 | - |
| United Pentecostal Ch. Intl., Foreign Missions Div. | 1924 | - | 2 | - | - | - |
| Walk Thru the Bible Ministries, Inc. | 2004 | - | - | - | 1 | - |
| World Relief | 2000 | - | - | - | - | 1 |
| World-Wide Missions | 1961 | - | - | - | 4 | - |
| Totals: | | 13 | 17 | 17 | 975 | 10 |

**Lithuania**

| | First Year | 1-2 yrs. | 2-4 yrs. | 4+ yrs. | Citizens | Non-Citizens |
|---|---|---|---|---|---|---|
| Assemblies of God World Missions | 1992 | - | - | 8 | - | - |
| Baptist Bible Fellowship International | 1991 | - | - | 2 | - | - |
| Campus Crusade for Christ, Intl. | 1991 | - | - | 5 | 9 | - |
| Christ to the Nations | 1989 | - | - | - | 5 | 2 |
| Churches of Christ | 1991 | - | - | 4 | 2 | - |
| Eastern Mennonite Missions | | - | 3 | 3 | - | - |
| Envoy International | | - | - | - | - | - |
| Episcopal Church USA—Domestic & Foreign | | - | - | 2 | - | - |
| Greater Grace World Outreach | 1996 | - | 2 | - | 2 | 1 |
| International Institute for Christian Studies | 2003 | - | 1 | - | - | - |
| Mennonite Mission Network | 1995 | - | - | - | - | - |
| Open Door Baptist Missions | 1992 | - | - | 4 | - | - |
| United Pentecostal Ch. Intl., Foreign Missions Div. | | - | - | - | - | 7 |
| Walk Thru the Bible Ministries, Inc. | 2001 | - | - | - | - | - |
| World Help | 1993 | - | - | - | - | - |
| World Venture | 1997 | - | - | 3 | 1 | - |
| Totals: | | - | 6 | 31 | 19 | 10 |

**Luxembourg**

| | First Year | 1-2 yrs. | 2-4 yrs. | 4+ yrs. | Citizens | Non-Citizens |
|---|---|---|---|---|---|---|
| Abundant Life Association, Inc. | 2006 | - | - | - | 4 | - |
| Assemblies of God World Missions | 1981 | - | - | 2 | - | - |
| Baptist Mid-Missions | 1986 | - | - | 2 | - | - |
| Biblical Ministries Worldwide | 1972 | - | - | 2 | - | 2 |
| Greater Europe Mission | 1989 | - | 2 | - | - | - |
| Totals: | | - | 2 | 6 | 4 | 2 |

**Macau**

| | First Year | 1-2 yrs. | 2-4 yrs. | 4+ yrs. | Citizens | Non-Citizens |
|---|---|---|---|---|---|---|
| Campus Crusade for Christ, Intl. | 1975 | - | - | - | 32 | 1 |
| Child Evangelism Fellowship, Inc. | 2000 | - | - | - | 1 | - |
| Christians In Action Missions International | 1976 | - | - | 1 | 1 | - |
| EFCA International Mission | 1993 | - | - | - | - | - |
| Global Mins., Ch. of the United Brethren in Christ | 1987 | - | - | 4 | - | - |
| Lutheran Church-Missouri Synod | 1988 | - | - | 3 | - | - |
| Mennonite Mission Network | 1996 | - | - | - | - | - |
| Seventh-day Adventists General Conference | 1888 | - | - | 2 | - | - |
| World Venture | 1986 | 1 | - | 11 | - | - |
| World-Wide Missions | | | | 1 | - | - |
| Totals: | | 1 | - | 22 | 34 | 1 |

**Macedonia**

| | First Year | 1-2 yrs. | 2-4 yrs. | 4+ yrs. | Citizens | Non-Citizens |
|---|---|---|---|---|---|---|
| Assemblies of God World Missions | 1991 | - | - | 2 | - | - |

| | | Personnel from U.S. | | | Other Countries | |
|---|---|---|---|---|---|---|
| | First Year | 1-2 yrs. | 2-4 yrs. | 4+ yrs. | Citizens | Non-Citizens |
| Campus Crusade for Christ, Intl. | 1996 | 8 | - | 4 | 7 | 2 |
| Church of the Nazarene, World Mission Dept. | 2000 | - | - | 1 | - | 1 |
| Envoy International | | - | - | - | - | - |
| Mission To Unreached Peoples | 2004 | - | - | 2 | - | - |
| Samaritan's Purse | 2001 | - | - | - | 1 | - |
| SEND International USA | 1993 | - | - | 11 | - | 3 |
| United Pentecostal Ch. Intl., Foreign Missions Div. | | - | 1 | - | - | - |
| WEC International | | - | - | 1 | - | - |
| Totals: | | 8 | 1 | 21 | 8 | 6 |

## Madagascar

| | | | | | | |
|---|---|---|---|---|---|---|
| Africa Inland Mission International | | 4 | - | - | - | 25 |
| Assemblies of God World Missions | 1990 | 2 | - | 8 | - | - |
| Campus Crusade for Christ, Intl. | 1979 | - | - | - | 33 | 4 |
| Child Evangelism Fellowship, Inc. | 1988 | - | - | - | 19 | - |
| Christian Blind Mission International | 1982 | - | 1 | - | - | - |
| Christians In Action Missions International | 1999 | - | - | - | - | 2 |
| Church of the Nazarene, World Mission Dept. | 1993 | - | - | 4 | - | - |
| Evangelical Lutheran Ch. in Am., Div. for Global Msn. | 1888 | - | 1 | 5 | - | - |
| Seventh-day Adventists General Conference | 1926 | - | - | 2 | - | 13 |
| Teen Missions International, Inc. | 1995 | - | - | - | 7 | - |
| United Pentecostal Ch. Intl., Foreign Missions Div. | 1970 | - | 2 | - | - | 1 |
| World Venture | 1966 | - | - | 2 | - | - |
| Totals: | | 6 | 4 | | | |

## Malawi

| | | | | | | |
|---|---|---|---|---|---|---|
| Action International Ministries | 2006 | - | - | 2 | - | - |
| African Bible Colleges, Inc. | 1988 | 8 | 4 | 14 | 25 | - |
| African Enterprise | 1982 | - | - | - | 6 | - |
| African Leadership, Inc. | 1998 | - | - | - | 2 | - |
| Assemblies of God World Missions | 1944 | 4 | - | 7 | - | - |
| Awana Clubs International | 1998 | - | - | - | 2 | - |
| Baptist International Missions, Inc. (BIMI) | | - | - | 1 | - | - |
| Brethren in Christ World Missions | 1983 | - | - | 4 | - | - |
| Bright Hope International | 2004 | - | - | - | 1 | - |
| Campus Crusade for Christ, Intl. | 1979 | - | - | - | 10 | - |
| Child Evangelism Fellowship, Inc. | 1988 | - | - | - | 2 | - |
| Christian Reformed World Relief Committee | 1989 | - | - | 3 | - | - |
| Church of God of Prophecy—Global Outreach | | - | - | - | 1 | - |
| Church of the Nazarene, World Mission Dept. | 1957 | - | - | 5 | - | 1 |
| Churches of Christ | 1907 | - | - | 5 | 4 | - |
| Emmanuel International Mission | 1987 | - | - | 1 | - | 4 |
| Episcopal Church USA—Domestic & Foreign | | - | - | 1 | - | - |
| Free Methodist World Missions | 1973 | - | - | 2 | - | - |
| Gospelink, Inc. | | - | - | - | 181 | - |
| Habitat for Humanity International | 1986 | - | 1 | - | - | 1 |
| Intl. Pentecostal Holiness Ch. World Missions Mins. | 1950 | - | - | 4 | - | - |
| Literacy & Evangelism International | | - | - | - | - | - |
| Natl. Baptist Conv. USA, Inc.—Foreign Msn. Bd. | 1900 | - | - | - | 1 | - |
| New Mission Systems International | 2003 | - | - | 3 | 2 | - |

| | First Year | Personnel from U.S. | | | Other Countries | |
|---|---|---|---|---|---|---|
| | | 1-2 yrs. | 2-4 yrs. | 4+ yrs. | Citizens | Non-Citizens |
| Reformed Church in Am., Gen. Synod Council | 1981 | - | - | 2 | 1 | - |
| Seventh-day Adventists General Conference | 1902 | - | - | 2 | - | 11 |
| SIM USA | 1900 | - | - | 15 | - | - |
| Teen Missions International, Inc. | 1988 | - | - | - | 21 | 2 |
| The Word for the World | 1994 | - | - | - | 4 | - |
| United Pentecostal Ch. Intl., Foreign Missions Div. | | - | 2 | - | - | 2 |
| Walk Thru the Bible Ministries, Inc. | 2001 | - | - | - | - | - |
| Wisc. Evangelical Luth. Synod, Bd. for Wld. Msns. | 1963 | - | - | 7 | - | - |
| World Relief | 1988 | - | - | 1 | 86 | - |
| World-Wide Missions | 1964 | - | - | - | 1 | - |
| Totals: | | 12 | 7 | 79 | 350 | 21 |

## Malaysia

| | First Year | 1-2 yrs. | 2-4 yrs. | 4+ yrs. | Citizens | Non-Citizens |
|---|---|---|---|---|---|---|
| Advent Christian Gen. Conf., Dept. of Wld. Msns. | 1960 | - | - | - | 6 | - |
| Asian Outreach U.S.A. | | - | - | - | - | - |
| Assemblies of God World Missions | 1928 | - | - | - | - | - |
| Campus Crusade for Christ, Intl. | 1968 | - | - | - | 96 | - |
| Christian Literature International | | - | - | - | - | - |
| Church of God (Cleveland, TN) World Missions | 1991 | - | - | 4 | - | - |
| Church of God of Prophecy—Global Outreach | | - | - | - | 1 | - |
| Churches of Christ | 1950 | 2 | - | 2 | 6 | - |
| EFCA International Mission | 1963 | - | - | - | - | - |
| Evangelical Congregational Church | | - | - | 1 | - | - |
| Food for the Hungry, Inc. | 2000 | - | - | 2 | - | - |
| Foursquare Missions International | 1984 | - | - | - | - | - |
| Globe Missionary Evangelism | 1983 | - | - | 2 | - | - |
| Gospel Revival Ministries | 1999 | - | - | - | 1 | - |
| Intl. Pentecostal Holiness Ch. World Missions Mins. | 1995 | - | - | - | - | - |
| Medical Ambassadors International, Inc. | 1999 | - | - | - | - | - |
| Mennonite Mission Network | | - | - | - | - | - |
| Mission To Unreached Peoples | 1995 | - | - | - | - | - |
| Missionary Ventures International | | - | - | - | - | 2 |
| New Tribes Mission | 1998 | - | - | 2 | - | - |
| Partners International | 1954 | - | - | - | 17 | - |
| Ripe for Harvest, Inc. | 1998 | - | - | 2 | - | - |
| RUN Ministries | 2004 | - | - | - | - | - |
| Salvation Army, U.S.A. | | - | - | 1 | - | - |
| The Brethren Church, Inc. | 1978 | - | - | - | 1 | - |
| United Pentecostal Ch. Intl., Foreign Missions Div. | 1975 | - | 1 | - | - | - |
| Walk Thru the Bible Ministries, Inc. | 2000 | - | - | - | - | - |
| Totals: | | 2 | 1 | 16 | 128 | 2 |

## Maldives

| | First Year | 1-2 yrs. | 2-4 yrs. | 4+ yrs. | Citizens | Non-Citizens |
|---|---|---|---|---|---|---|
| Assemblies of God World Missions | 1995 | - | - | - | - | - |
| Totals: | | - | - | - | - | - |

## Mali

| | First Year | 1-2 yrs. | 2-4 yrs. | 4+ yrs. | Citizens | Non-Citizens |
|---|---|---|---|---|---|---|
| Assemblies of God World Missions | 1989 | - | - | 6 | - | - |
| Avant Ministries | 1919 | - | - | 6 | - | 9 |
| Campus Crusade for Christ, Intl. | 1972 | - | - | - | 50 | - |

| | First Year | Personnel from U.S. | | | Other Countries | |
|---|---|---|---|---|---|---|
| | | 1-2 yrs. | 2-4 yrs. | 4+ yrs. | Citizens | Non-Citizens |
| Child Evangelism Fellowship, Inc. | 1993 | - | - | - | 1 | - |
| Christ for the City International | 2004 | - | - | - | - | 1 |
| Christian Churches / Churches of Christ | | - | - | 2 | - | - |
| Christian Reformed World Missions | 1984 | - | - | 6 | - | - |
| Christian Reformed World Relief Committee | 1984 | - | - | 1 | - | 1 |
| Evangelical Baptist Missions | | - | - | 10 | - | - |
| Macedonia World Baptist Missions, Inc. | 2005 | - | - | 2 | - | - |
| Mission Aviation Fellowship | 1985 | 2 | 3 | 5 | - | - |
| Partners International | 2001 | - | - | - | 22 | - |
| Seventh-day Adventists General Conference | 1982 | - | - | - | - | 2 |
| World Baptist Fellowship Mission Agency, Inc. | | 2 | - | - | - | - |
| World Venture | 1999 | - | - | 8 | - | - |
| Totals: | | 4 | 3 | 46 | 73 | 13 |

## Malta

| | First Year | 1-2 yrs. | 2-4 yrs. | 4+ yrs. | Citizens | Non-Citizens |
|---|---|---|---|---|---|---|
| Assemblies of God World Missions | 1985 | 1 | - | - | - | - |
| Baptist Mid-Missions | 2005 | - | - | 2 | - | - |
| Church of God of Prophecy—Global Outreach | | - | - | - | - | 1 |
| Intl. Pentecostal Holiness Ch. World Missions Mins. | 1988 | - | - | - | - | - |
| Ripe for Harvest, Inc. | 1999 | - | - | 1 | - | - |
| United Pentecostal Ch. Intl., Foreign Missions Div. | 2002 | - | 2 | - | - | - |
| Totals: | | 1 | 2 | 3 | - | 1 |

## Marshall Islands

| | First Year | 1-2 yrs. | 2-4 yrs. | 4+ yrs. | Citizens | Non-Citizens |
|---|---|---|---|---|---|---|
| Assemblies of God World Missions | 1961 | - | - | - | - | - |
| Gospel Fellowship Association | 1988 | - | - | 4 | - | - |
| Missionary Ventures International | 1999 | - | - | 2 | - | - |
| Seventh-day Adventists General Conference | 1930 | - | - | 2 | - | - |
| United Church of Christ—Wider Church Ministries | | - | 2 | - | - | - |
| Totals: | | - | 2 | 8 | - | - |

## Martinique

| | First Year | 1-2 yrs. | 2-4 yrs. | 4+ yrs. | Citizens | Non-Citizens |
|---|---|---|---|---|---|---|
| Church of the Nazarene, World Mission Dept. | 1976 | - | - | - | - | - |
| Totals: | | - | - | - | - | - |

## Mauritania

| | First Year | 1-2 yrs. | 2-4 yrs. | 4+ yrs. | Citizens | Non-Citizens |
|---|---|---|---|---|---|---|
| Seventh-day Adventists General Conference | | - | - | - | - | 2 |
| Totals: | | - | - | - | - | 2 |

## Mauritius

| | First Year | 1-2 yrs. | 2-4 yrs. | 4+ yrs. | Citizens | Non-Citizens |
|---|---|---|---|---|---|---|
| Assemblies of God World Missions | 1967 | - | - | 2 | - | - |
| Intl. Pentecostal Holiness Ch. Wld. Msns. Mins. | | - | - | - | - | - |
| United Pentecostal Ch. Intl., Foreign Missions Div. | | - | 2 | - | - | - |
| Totals: | | - | 2 | 2 | - | - |

## Mexico

| | First Year | 1-2 yrs. | 2-4 yrs. | 4+ yrs. | Citizens | Non-Citizens |
|---|---|---|---|---|---|---|
| Action International Ministries | 1990 | - | - | 1 | 2 | 2 |
| Advent Christian Gen. Conf., Dept. of Wld. Msns. | 1958 | - | - | 1 | 4 | - |
| Adventures in Missions | 1989 | - | - | 10 | - | - |
| Am. Baptist Chs. of the U.S.A., Intl. Ministries | 1870 | - | - | 6 | 1 | - |

| | First Year | Personnel from U.S. | | | Other Countries | |
|---|---|---|---|---|---|---|
| | | 1-2 yrs. | 2-4 yrs. | 4+ yrs. | Citizens | Non-Citizens |
| AmeriTribes | 1984 | - | - | 8 | - | - |
| AMG International | 1978 | - | 1 | 3 | - | - |
| AMOR Ministries | 1980 | 37 | - | - | 8 | 2 |
| Apostolic Christian Church Foundation, Inc. | 1972 | - | - | 1 | 1 | - |
| Arab World Ministries | | - | - | 4 | - | - |
| Assemblies of God World Missions | 1915 | 11 | - | 76 | - | - |
| Association of Free Lutheran Congregations | 1985 | - | - | 4 | 5 | - |
| Audio Scripture Ministries | 2004 | - | - | 1 | - | - |
| Avant Ministries | 1956 | - | - | 4 | - | 1 |
| Awana Clubs International | 1985 | - | - | 2 | 10 | - |
| Baptist Bible Fellowship International | 1946 | - | - | 8 | - | - |
| Baptist General Conference—Intl. Ministries | 1955 | - | - | 15 | - | - |
| Baptist International Missions, Inc. (BIMI) | | - | - | 55 | - | - |
| Baptist International Outreach | 1996 | - | - | 4 | 1 | - |
| Baptist Mid-Missions | 1960 | - | - | 11 | - | - |
| BCM International | | - | - | | 4 | - |
| Bethany International Ministries | 1972 | 2 | 3 | 10 | 72 | - |
| Biblical Ministries Worldwide | 1964 | - | - | 8 | 2 | 8 |
| Brethren Assemblies | | - | - | 44 | - | - |
| Brethren in Christ World Missions | 1993 | - | - | 2 | - | - |
| Calvary Commission, Inc. | 1980 | - | - | 10 | - | - |
| Calvary International | 1986 | - | - | 6 | - | - |
| CAM International | 1955 | - | - | 80 | - | - |
| Campus Crusade for Christ, Intl. | 1961 | 13 | - | 9 | 42 | - |
| Child Evangelism Fellowship, Inc. | 1939 | - | - | 1 | 1 | - |
| Childcare Worldwide | 1982 | - | - | | 3 | - |
| Children's Haven International | 1994 | - | - | 2 | - | - |
| Chosen People Ministries | | - | - | - | - | - |
| Christ for the City International | 1988 | - | - | - | 5 | 6 |
| Christian Aid Mission | | - | - | - | 3 | - |
| Christian Broadcasting Network Inc., the | 1998 | - | - | - | 4 | - |
| Christian Churches / Churches of Christ | | - | 4 | 50 | 20 | - |
| Christian Fellowship Union, Inc. | | - | - | 2 | - | - |
| Christian Literature International | | - | - | - | - | - |
| Christian Outreach International | 1997 | - | - | 3 | - | 3 |
| Christian Reformed World Missions | 1952 | 2 | 4 | 16 | - | - |
| Christian Reformed World Relief Committee | 1969 | - | - | - | - | - |
| Christians In Action Missions International | 1972 | - | - | - | - | - |
| Christ's Mandate for Missions | 2004 | - | - | 5 | 5 | - |
| Church of God (Cleveland, TN) World Missions | 1932 | 1 | - | - | - | - |
| Church of the Nazarene, World Mission Dept. | 1903 | - | - | 3 | - | 2 |
| Churches of Christ | 1929 | 2 | 6 | 38 | 16 | - |
| CMF International | 1980 | - | 18 | - | - | - |
| ComCare International | 1997 | - | - | 2 | 2 | - |
| Commission to Every Nation | 1997 | 6 | 4 | 5 | 3 | - |
| Compassion International, Inc. | 1976 | - | - | - | 20 | - |
| Congregational Methodist Ch., Div. of Msn. Mins. | 1965 | - | - | 5 | 2 | - |
| CrossWorld | 1971 | - | - | 8 | - | - |
| David Livingstone KURE Foundation | | - | - | - | 8 | - |
| DeNike Ministries | 1992 | - | - | 1 | - | - |

| | First Year | Personnel from U.S. | | | Other Countries | |
|---|---|---|---|---|---|---|
| | | 1-2 yrs. | 2-4 yrs. | 4+ yrs. | Citizens | Non-Citizens |
| EFCA International Mission | 1987 | - | - | 10 | - | - |
| Elim Fellowship—International Department | 1962 | - | - | 10 | - | - |
| Equip, Inc. | 1996 | - | - | 6 | - | - |
| Evangelical Baptist Missions | | 2 | - | 6 | - | - |
| Evangelical Congregational Church | | - | - | 1 | - | - |
| Evangelical Covenant Ch.—Covenant Wld. Msn. | 1946 | 3 | - | 14 | - | - |
| Evangelical Friends Mission | 1967 | - | - | 6 | - | - |
| Evangelical Luth. Ch. in Am., Div. for Global Msn. | 1956 | 1 | - | 2 | 1 | - |
| Evangelical Methodist Ch., Inc.—Bd. of Msns. | 1946 | - | - | 5 | - | - |
| Evangelism Explosion International | | - | - | - | - | 2 |
| Fellowship International Mission | 1988 | - | - | 13 | 3 | 2 |
| Floresta USA, Inc. | 1997 | - | - | - | 10 | - |
| Flying Doctors of Am. (Medical Mercy Msns., Inc.) | 1990 | - | - | - | - | - |
| Foundation For His Ministry | 1967 | - | - | - | 77 | 47 |
| Foursquare Missions International | 1943 | - | - | 4 | - | - |
| Free Methodist World Missions | 1917 | - | - | 10 | - | - |
| Full Gospel Evangelistic Association | 1950 | - | - | 5 | - | - |
| General Baptists International | 2003 | - | - | 4 | - | - |
| Global Fellowship Inc. | 1999 | - | - | - | 2 | - |
| Global Outreach International | 2000 | - | - | 9 | - | - |
| Global Outreach Mission, Inc. | | - | - | 17 | - | - |
| Global Partners / Wesleyan World Missions | 1920 | - | 3 | - | - | - |
| Global Recordings Network | 1958 | - | - | 2 | - | - |
| Globe Missionary Evangelism | 1985 | 1 | - | 11 | - | - |
| Go Ye Fellowship | | - | - | 4 | - | - |
| Good News Productions International | 1996 | - | 2 | 2 | 4 | - |
| Gospel Fellowship Association | 1967 | - | - | 10 | - | - |
| Grace Brethren International Missions | 1951 | - | - | 2 | - | 2 |
| Greater Grace World Outreach | 1987 | - | - | 3 | 4 | - |
| Hope for the Hungry | | - | - | 1 | - | 1 |
| Hosanna | 2003 | - | - | - | 2 | - |
| Impact International | 1970 | - | - | 2 | 2 | - |
| Independent Faith Mission, Inc. | | - | - | 2 | - | - |
| International Family Missions | 1988 | - | - | 8 | - | - |
| International Gospel Outreach | 1986 | - | - | 2 | 2 | - |
| International Institute for Christian Studies | 2004 | - | - | - | - | - |
| International Outreach Ministries (IOM) | 1986 | - | - | - | 5 | - |
| International Partnership Ministries, Inc. | 1991 | - | - | - | - | 2 |
| Intl. Pentecostal Ch. of Christ—Global Msns. Dept. | 1952 | - | - | 1 | - | 1 |
| Intl. Pentecostal Holiness Ch. Wld. Msn. Mins. | 1930 | - | - | 6 | - | - |
| International Teams, U.S.A. | | 3 | - | 13 | - | 6 |
| Josue Yrion World Evangelism and Missions, Inc. | 2002 | - | - | - | 1 | - |
| Latin America Mission | 1952 | 1 | - | 27 | 3 | 25 |
| Latin American Indian Ministries | 1976 | - | - | - | - | - |
| Latin American Lutheran Mission | 1942 | - | - | 3 | 1 | - |
| LOGOI Ministries | 1972 | - | - | - | 2 | - |
| Luke Society, Inc., The | 2002 | - | - | - | - | - |
| Macedonia World Baptist Missions, Inc. | 1988 | - | - | 17 | - | - |
| Medical Ambassadors International, Inc. | 1990 | - | - | 1 | 6 | - |
| Mennonite Mission Network | 1957 | - | - | 4 | - | - |

| | First Year | Personnel from U.S. | | | Other Countries | |
|---|---|---|---|---|---|---|
| | | 1-2 yrs. | 2-4 yrs. | 4+ yrs. | Citizens | Non-Citizens |
| Mexican Medical Ministries | 1963 | 9 | - | 22 | 6 | - |
| Ministries In Action | 2002 | - | - | - | - | - |
| Mission Aviation Fellowship | 1946 | 1 | - | - | - | - |
| Mission Ministries, Inc. | 1980 | - | - | 1 | 1 | - |
| Mission to the Americas | 1951 | - | 1 | 6 | 15 | - |
| Mission to the World (PCA), Inc. | 1977 | 13 | 35 | - | - | - |
| Missionary Gospel Fellowship | 1959 | - | - | 19 | - | - |
| Missionary Revival Crusade | 1949 | - | 1 | 19 | 6 | - |
| Missionary Ventures International | 1992 | - | - | 4 | - | - |
| Navigators, U.S. International Missions Group | | - | - | 8 | - | - |
| New Life Advance International | 1975 | - | - | 1 | - | - |
| New Tribes Mission | 1975 | - | - | 80 | - | - |
| New Way Missions | 1996 | - | - | - | - | - |
| N. Am. Baptist Conf.—Worldwide Outreach | 1992 | - | - | 2 | - | 4 |
| Northwest Medical Teams International, Inc. | 1985 | 2 | - | - | 15 | - |
| OC International, Inc. | 1967 | - | - | 4 | - | - |
| OMS International, Inc. | 1990 | - | - | 9 | - | 2 |
| Open Air Campaigners—Overseas Ministries | | 2 | - | - | 2 | - |
| Open Bible Churches, International Ministries | 1965 | - | - | 6 | - | - |
| Operation Mobilization | 1957 | 1 | - | 2 | - | - |
| Palm Missionary Ministries | 2004 | - | - | - | 2 | - |
| Pan American Missions | 1960 | - | - | 2 | - | - |
| Partners in Christ International | 1986 | - | - | 1 | 4 | - |
| Pentecostal Ch. of God—World Missions Dept. | | - | - | 6 | - | - |
| Pentecostal Free Will Baptist Church, Inc. | | - | - | - | 1 | - |
| Precept Ministries International | 1980 | - | - | - | 1 | - |
| Precious Seed Ministries | 1966 | - | - | 1 | 8 | - |
| Presbyterian Evangelistic Fellowship | | - | - | 8 | 2 | - |
| Reformed Church in Am., Gen. Synod Council | 1967 | - | - | 4 | 4 | - |
| Ripe for Harvest, Inc. | 1999 | - | - | - | 1 | - |
| Rosedale Mennonite Missions | 1999 | - | - | 2 | - | 2 |
| Salvation Army, U.S.A. | 1937 | - | - | 5 | - | - |
| Seed International | 1996 | - | 1 | 3 | - | - |
| Seventh-day Adventists General Conference | 1893 | - | - | 10 | - | 18 |
| Shield of Faith Mission International | 1970 | - | - | 6 | - | - |
| Source of Light Ministries International, Inc. | 1962 | - | - | - | - | - |
| Spanish World Ministries | | - | - | 5 | 5 | - |
| STEM (Short-Term Evangelical Missions) Intl. | 2002 | - | - | - | - | - |
| TEAM (The Evangelical Alliance Mission) | | - | - | 15 | - | - |
| The Brethren Church, Inc. | 1992 | - | - | 2 | - | - |
| The Church of God of the Apostolic Faith, Inc. | 1950 | - | - | 4 | - | - |
| The Mission Society | 1987 | 2 | 2 | 2 | - | - |
| TMA Ministries | 1980 | - | - | - | - | - |
| U.S. Center for World Mission | | - | - | - | - | 2 |
| United Church of Christ—Wider Church Ministries | | - | 2 | - | - | - |
| United Pentecostal Ch. Intl., Foreign Missions Div. | | - | 9 | - | - | 15 |
| Walk Thru the Bible Ministries, Inc. | 2000 | - | - | - | 4 | - |
| WEC International | | - | - | 18 | - | - |
| Westminster Biblical Missions | 1991 | - | - | - | 1 | 2 |
| Wisconsin Evangelical Lutheran Synod | 1964 | - | - | 2 | - | - |

| | First Year | Personnel from U.S. 1-2 yrs. | 2-4 yrs. | 4+ yrs. | Other Countries Citizens | Non-Citizens |
|---|---|---|---|---|---|---|
| Word of Life Fellowship, Inc.—Intl. Ministries | 1983 | - | - | - | 30 | 3 |
| World Baptist Fellowship Mission Agency, Inc. | | - | - | 23 | - | - |
| World Gospel Mission | 1945 | - | - | 12 | - | 2 |
| World Indigenous Missions | 1981 | - | - | 23 | 3 | - |
| World Mission Prayer League | 1945 | - | - | 2 | - | - |
| World Missions & Evangelism, Inc. | | - | - | 2 | - | - |
| World Missions Far Corners, Inc. | 1958 | - | - | 7 | 100 | - |
| World Servants, Inc. | 1997 | - | - | - | - | - |
| World Team | | - | - | 2 | - | - |
| World Vision Inc. | 1963 | - | - | - | - | - |
| World Witness, Assoc. Reformed Presbyterian Ch. | 1878 | - | 2 | 12 | - | - |
| World-Wide Missions | | - | - | 1 | 2 | - |
| YUGO Ministries | 1964 | 2 | 3 | 26 | - | - |
| | Totals: | 117 | 101 | 1156 | 582 | 162 |

## Micronesia, Federated States of

| | First Year | 1-2 yrs. | 2-4 yrs. | 4+ yrs. | Citizens | Non-Citizens |
|---|---|---|---|---|---|---|
| Baptist Mid-Missions | 1981 | - | - | 5 | 2 | - |
| Child Evangelism Fellowship, Inc. | 1957 | - | - | 2 | - | - |
| Church of the Nazarene, World Mission Dept. | 2000 | - | - | - | - | - |
| Conservative Cong. Christian Conf. | 1984 | - | - | 4 | - | - |
| Independent Faith Mission, Inc. | | 2 | - | 2 | - | - |
| Liebenzell USA | 1906 | - | - | 3 | 4 | - |
| United Pentecostal Ch. Intl., Foreign Missions Div. | | - | 2 | - | - | - |
| Worldwide Tentmakers, Inc. | 2000 | - | - | - | - | - |
| | Totals: | 2 | 2 | 16 | 6 | - |

## Middle East

| | First Year | 1-2 yrs. | 2-4 yrs. | 4+ yrs. | Citizens | Non-Citizens |
|---|---|---|---|---|---|---|
| Anglican Frontier Missions | 1999 | - | - | 4 | - | 4 |
| Assemblies of God World Missions | 1910 | 6 | - | 21 | - | - |
| Awana Clubs International | 1979 | - | - | 3 | 10 | 2 |
| Baptist Mid-Missions | 1999 | - | - | 2 | - | - |
| Christar | 1953 | - | - | 8 | - | - |
| Christian Aid Mission | | - | - | - | 39 | - |
| Ch. of God (Holiness), World Mission Dept., Inc. | 2002 | - | - | - | - | 2 |
| Elim Fellowship—International Department | | - | - | 2 | 4 | 1 |
| Entrust | 2002 | - | - | 6 | - | 2 |
| Final Frontiers Foundation, Inc. | 2004 | - | - | - | 10 | - |
| Go Ye Fellowship | | - | 2 | - | - | 4 |
| Great Commission Center International | 2001 | - | - | - | - | - |
| Greater Grace World Outreach | 1991 | - | - | 3 | - | 1 |
| Heart of God Ministries | | - | - | 3 | - | - |
| InterServe USA (International Service Fellowship) | 1951 | - | - | 11 | - | - |
| Macedonia World Baptist Missions, Inc. | 1996 | - | - | 4 | - | - |
| Mennonite Central Committee (MCC) | | - | - | 34 | - | - |
| Middle East Christian Outreach (MECO) | 1976 | - | - | - | - | - |
| Middle East Media—USA | 1976 | - | - | - | - | - |
| Mission Ministries, Inc. | 1995 | - | - | 2 | - | - |
| New Mission Systems International | | - | - | 2 | - | - |
| Operation Mobilization | | 10 | 3 | 23 | - | 9 |
| Partners International | 1959 | - | - | 2 | - | 2 |

| | Personnel from U.S. | | | | Other Countries | |
|---|---|---|---|---|---|---|
| | First Year | 1-2 yrs. | 2-4 yrs. | 4+ yrs. | Citizens | Non-Citizens |
| Pioneers USA | | 5 | - | 12 | - | - |
| Red Sea Team International | 1994 | - | - | 2 | - | 6 |
| Ripe for Harvest, Inc. | 1992 | - | - | 2 | - | - |
| Shelter for Life International, Inc. | 1993 | - | 1 | - | 200 | 1 |
| So. Baptist Convention Intl. Mission Board | | - | - | - | - | - |
| TEAM (The Evangelical Alliance Mission) | | - | - | 22 | - | - |
| United Pentecostal Ch. Intl., Foreign Missions Div. | 1992 | - | 2 | - | - | 2 |
| World Horizons | 1990 | - | - | 2 | - | 3 |
| Youth for Christ/USA—World Outreach | | - | - | 6 | - | - |
| | Totals: | 21 | 8 | 176 | 263 | 39 |

## Moldova

| | | | | | | |
|---|---|---|---|---|---|---|
| Assemblies of God World Missions | 1991 | - | - | 5 | - | - |
| Awana Clubs International | 1999 | - | - | - | 2 | - |
| Baptist International Evangelistic Ministries | | - | - | - | 8 | 2 |
| Campus Crusade for Christ, Intl. | 1995 | - | - | - | 51 | - |
| Child Evangelism Fellowship, Inc. | 1995 | - | - | 1 | - | - |
| Christian Aid Ministries | | - | - | - | 1 | - |
| Crossover Communications International | 1995 | - | - | 2 | - | - |
| Entrust | 1995 | - | - | 6 | - | - |
| Evangelism Explosion International | | - | - | - | - | 3 |
| Global Outreach International | 2004 | - | - | 2 | 1 | - |
| Greater Grace World Outreach | 2005 | - | - | - | - | 2 |
| Intl. Pentecostal Holiness Ch. World Missions Mins. | | - | - | - | - | - |
| InterVarsity Christian Fellowship/USA—Msns. Dept. | | - | - | 2 | - | - |
| Ministry to Educate and Equip Intl. (MTEE) | 2001 | - | 1 | - | - | - |
| New Hope International | 1992 | - | - | - | 3 | - |
| Northwest Medical Teams International, Inc. | 1993 | - | - | - | 7 | - |
| Precept Ministries International | 1994 | - | - | - | 5 | - |
| Salvation Army, U.S.A. | 1994 | - | - | 1 | - | - |
| TCM International Institute | | - | - | - | 1 | - |
| TITUS International | 1995 | - | - | 1 | 45 | - |
| Walk Thru the Bible Ministries, Inc. | 2000 | - | - | - | 1 | - |
| | Totals: | - | 1 | 20 | 125 | 7 |

## Monaco

| | | | | | | |
|---|---|---|---|---|---|---|
| Trans World Radio, International | 1960 | - | - | 2 | - | - |
| | Totals: | - | - | 2 | - | - |

## Mongolia

| | | | | | | |
|---|---|---|---|---|---|---|
| Asian Access | 1998 | - | - | - | - | - |
| Asian Outreach U.S.A. | | - | - | - | - | - |
| Assemblies of God World Missions | 1993 | 2 | - | 10 | - | - |
| Baptist Bible Fellowship International | 2005 | - | - | 2 | - | - |
| Christar | 1992 | - | - | 5 | - | - |
| Commission to Every Nation | 2000 | - | - | 1 | - | - |
| EFCA International Mission | 1993 | - | - | - | 2 | - |
| Far East Broadcasting Company, Inc. | 2001 | - | - | - | 6 | - |
| Food for the Hungry, Inc. | 1997 | - | 2 | - | - | - |
| Global Partners / Wesleyan World Missions | 1999 | - | - | - | - | - |

| | First Year | Personnel from U.S. | | | Other Countries | |
|---|---|---|---|---|---|---|
| | | 1-2 yrs. | 2-4 yrs. | 4+ yrs. | Citizens | Non-Citizens |
| Habitat for Humanity International | 2000 | - | 1 | - | - | 1 |
| Mennonite Mission Network | 1993 | - | - | 5 | - | 4 |
| Mission To Unreached Peoples | 2003 | - | - | 2 | - | - |
| New Tribes Mission | 1993 | - | - | 7 | - | - |
| Seventh-day Adventists General Conference | 1931 | - | - | 2 | - | 4 |
| Team Expansion, Inc. | | - | - | 2 | - | - |
| Walk Thru the Bible Ministries, Inc. | 2001 | - | - | - | - | - |
| WEC International | | - | - | 1 | - | - |
| World Relief | 2002 | - | 1 | - | - | - |
| World Venture | 1996 | - | - | 1 | - | - |
| | Totals: | 2 | 4 | 38 | 8 | 9 |

**Morocco**

| | First Year | 1-2 yrs. | 2-4 yrs. | 4+ yrs. | Citizens | Non-Citizens |
|---|---|---|---|---|---|---|
| Arab World Ministries | | 1 | - | 17 | - | - |
| Educational Services International (ESI) | 1999 | 33 | - | - | - | - |
| Fellowship International Mission | 1950 | - | - | 13 | 3 | - |
| Greater Grace World Outreach | 2003 | - | - | - | 1 | 2 |
| I. N. Network USA | 1983 | - | - | - | 6 | - |
| International Gospel Outreach | 2006 | - | - | 1 | - | - |
| International Outreach Ministries (IOM) | 1993 | - | - | 2 | - | - |
| United Pentecostal Ch. Intl., Foreign Msns. Div. | | - | 1 | - | - | 2 |
| Walk Thru the Bible Ministries, Inc. | 2002 | - | - | - | 1 | - |
| | Totals: | 34 | 1 | 33 | 11 | 4 |

**Mozambique**

| | First Year | 1-2 yrs. | 2-4 yrs. | 4+ yrs. | Citizens | Non-Citizens |
|---|---|---|---|---|---|---|
| Abundant Life Association, Inc. | 1990 | - | - | - | 50 | - |
| Africa Inland Mission International | 1985 | 2 | - | 21 | - | 19 |
| African Leadership, Inc. | 1998 | - | - | - | 1 | - |
| AMG International | | - | - | - | 2 | - |
| Armenian Missionary Association of America, Inc. | 1998 | - | - | - | - | - |
| Assemblies of God World Missions | 1973 | - | - | 2 | - | - |
| Awana Clubs International | 1993 | - | - | - | 2 | - |
| Baptist Mid-Missions | 2005 | - | - | 2 | - | - |
| BCM International | | - | - | - | 1 | - |
| Brethren Assemblies | | - | - | 2 | - | - |
| Bright Hope International | 2004 | - | - | - | - | 2 |
| Campus Crusade for Christ, Intl. | 1990 | - | - | - | 14 | 2 |
| Child Evangelism Fellowship, Inc. | 1994 | - | - | - | 4 | - |
| Christian Churches / Churches of Christ | | - | 2 | 6 | - | - |
| Christian Reformed World Relief Committee | 1993 | - | - | - | - | - |
| Church of God of Prophecy—Global Outreach | | - | - | - | 2 | - |
| Church of the Nazarene, World Mission Dept. | 1922 | - | - | 9 | - | 3 |
| Churches of Christ | 1960 | 4 | - | 2 | - | - |
| Episcopal Church USA—Domestic & Foreign | | - | - | 1 | - | - |
| Food for the Hungry, Inc. | 1987 | - | - | - | - | - |
| Global Outreach International | 2002 | - | - | 2 | - | - |
| Global Partners / Wesleyan World Missions | 1998 | - | 4 | - | - | - |
| Globe Missionary Evangelism | 2000 | - | - | 2 | - | - |
| Gospelink, Inc. | | - | - | - | 29 | - |
| Greater Grace World Outreach | 2003 | - | - | - | 3 | - |

| | First Year | Personnel from U.S. | | | Other Countries | |
|---|---|---|---|---|---|---|
| | | 1-2 yrs. | 2-4 yrs. | 4+ yrs. | Citizens | Non-Citizens |
| Habitat for Humanity International | 2000 | - | 1 | - | - | 1 |
| Hosanna | 2004 | - | - | - | 1 | - |
| Intl. Pentecostal Holiness Ch. World Missions Mins. | 1957 | - | - | - | - | - |
| Medical Ambassadors International, Inc. | 1999 | - | - | - | - | - |
| Mission Aviation Fellowship | 2000 | - | - | 1 | - | - |
| New Tribes Mission | 2002 | - | - | 4 | - | - |
| OC International, Inc. | | - | - | 2 | - | 4 |
| OMS International, Inc. | 1994 | - | - | 8 | - | 3 |
| Reformed Church in Am., Gen. Synod Council | 2004 | - | - | 2 | - | - |
| Samaritan's Purse | 2000 | 6 | - | - | 105 | - |
| SIM USA | 1936 | - | - | 8 | - | - |
| TEAM (The Evangelical Alliance Mission) | | - | - | 2 | - | - |
| Team Expansion, Inc. | 2005 | - | 3 | - | - | - |
| The God's Story Project | 2005 | - | - | - | - | 1 |
| United Pentecostal Ch. Intl., Foreign Missions Div. | | - | 2 | - | - | - |
| Walk Thru the Bible Ministries, Inc. | 1999 | - | - | - | 3 | - |
| World Relief | 1987 | - | 1 | - | 383 | 5 |
| World Venture | 2001 | - | - | 4 | - | - |
| World Vision Inc. | 1984 | - | - | - | - | - |
| Totals: | | 12 | 13 | 80 | 600 | 40 |

## Myanmar/Burma

| | First Year | 1-2 yrs. | 2-4 yrs. | 4+ yrs. | Citizens | Non-Citizens |
|---|---|---|---|---|---|---|
| American Leprosy Missions, Inc. | 1994 | - | - | - | 1 | - |
| AMG International | | - | - | - | 4 | - |
| Asian Access | 2003 | - | - | - | - | - |
| Asian Outreach U.S.A. | | - | - | - | - | - |
| Assemblies of God World Missions | 1930 | 2 | - | 2 | - | - |
| BCM International | | - | - | - | 6 | - |
| BILD International | | - | - | - | - | 1 |
| Campus Crusade for Christ, Intl. | 1972 | - | - | - | 120 | - |
| Christian Aid Mission | | - | - | - | 168 | - |
| Christian Churches / Churches of Christ | | - | - | - | 8 | - |
| Christian Literature International | | - | - | - | - | - |
| Ch. of God (Holiness), World Mission Dept., Inc. | 2004 | - | - | - | 16 | - |
| Church of the Nazarene, World Mission Dept. | 1984 | - | - | - | - | - |
| Church Planting International | 1996 | - | - | - | - | - |
| Cook Communications Ministries International | 2002 | - | - | - | - | - |
| Episcopal Church USA—Domestic & Foreign | | - | - | 1 | - | - |
| Evangel Bible Translators | 2003 | - | - | - | 2 | - |
| Global Fellowship Inc. | 2001 | - | - | - | 22 | - |
| Global Outreach International | 2003 | - | - | 2 | 1 | - |
| Global Outreach Mission, Inc. | | - | - | - | 2 | - |
| Global Partners / Wesleyan World Missions | 1997 | - | - | - | - | - |
| Good News Productions International | 1999 | - | - | - | 2 | - |
| Gospel for Asia, Inc. | 1992 | - | - | - | 752 | - |
| International Partnership Ministries, Inc. | 1997 | - | - | - | 2 | - |
| Intl. Pentecostal Holiness Ch. World Missions Mins. | | - | - | - | - | - |
| Medical Ambassadors International, Inc. | 2003 | - | - | - | - | - |
| New Mission Systems International | | - | - | - | 4 | - |
| Partners International | 1978 | - | - | - | 53 | - |

| | Personnel from U.S. | | | | Other Countries | |
|---|---|---|---|---|---|---|
| | First Year | 1-2 yrs. | 2-4 yrs. | 4+ yrs. | Citizens | Non-Citizens |
| Presbyterian Missionary Union | 2005 | - | - | - | 2 | - |
| Reformed Church in Am., Gen. Synod Council | 2004 | - | - | - | 1 | - |
| Seventh-day Adventists General Conference | 1919 | - | - | - | - | 2 |
| The God's Story Project | 2004 | - | - | - | 1 | - |
| United Pentecostal Ch. Intl., Foreign Missions Div. | | - | - | - | - | - |
| Village Ministries International | 2003 | - | - | - | 1 | - |
| Walk Thru the Bible Ministries, Inc. | 1999 | - | - | - | 2 | - |
| White Fields Inc. | | - | - | - | 12 | - |
| World Bible Translation Center | | - | - | - | 2 | - |
| World Concern | 1994 | - | - | - | 94 | - |
| World Help | 1997 | - | - | - | - | - |
| | Totals: | 2 | - | 5 | 1278 | 3 |

### N. Mariana Isls

| | | | | | | |
|---|---|---|---|---|---|---|
| Baptist International Missions, Inc. (BIMI) | | - | - | 4 | - | - |
| Church of the Nazarene, World Mission Dept. | 2000 | - | - | - | - | - |
| Far East Broadcasting Company, Inc. | 1974 | - | - | 4 | 3 | - |
| General Baptists International | 1947 | - | - | 2 | - | - |
| Pioneers USA | | - | - | 2 | - | - |
| World Baptist Fellowship Mission Agency, Inc. | | - | - | 2 | - | - |
| | Totals: | - | - | 14 | 3 | - |

### Namibia

| | | | | | | |
|---|---|---|---|---|---|---|
| Advent Christian Gen. Conf., Dept. of Wld. Msns. | 1999 | - | - | - | 2 | - |
| Africa Inland Mission International | 1981 | 2 | - | 5 | - | 7 |
| Assemblies of God World Missions | 1979 | - | - | 11 | - | - |
| Campus Crusade for Christ, Intl. | 1988 | - | - | - | 7 | 2 |
| Child Evangelism Fellowship, Inc. | 1994 | - | - | 3 | 1 | - |
| Church of God of Prophecy—Global Outreach | | - | - | - | - | 1 |
| Church of the Nazarene, World Mission Dept. | 1973 | - | - | 2 | - | - |
| Evangelical Luth. Ch. in Am., Div. for Global Msn. | 1983 | 6 | - | 1 | - | - |
| Lutheran Bible Translators, Inc. | 1996 | 3 | - | - | 11 | - |
| SIM USA | 1970 | - | - | 2 | - | - |
| United Church of Christ—Wider Church Ministries | | - | 2 | - | - | - |
| United Pentecostal Ch. Intl., Foreign Missions Div. | 1986 | - | 2 | - | - | - |
| Walk Thru the Bible Ministries, Inc. | 1999 | - | - | - | 2 | - |
| | Totals: | 11 | 4 | 24 | 23 | 10 |

### Nauru

| | | | | | | |
|---|---|---|---|---|---|---|
| Assemblies of God World Missions | 2000 | - | - | - | - | - |
| | Totals: | - | - | - | - | - |

### Nepal

| | | | | | | |
|---|---|---|---|---|---|---|
| Advancing Renewal Ministries, Inc. | | - | - | 2 | 6 | - |
| All God's Children International | | - | - | - | 3 | - |
| Am. Baptist Chs. of the U.S.A., Intl. Ministries | 1978 | - | - | 2 | - | - |
| Armenian Missionary Association of America, Inc. | 1986 | - | - | - | - | - |
| Asian Access | 2003 | - | - | - | - | - |
| Asian Outreach U.S.A. | | - | - | - | - | - |
| Awana Clubs International | 1996 | - | - | - | 6 | 2 |

| | First Year | Personnel from U.S. 1-2 yrs. | 2-4 yrs. | 4+ yrs. | Other Countries Citizens | Non-Citizens |
|---|---|---|---|---|---|---|
| Baptist Bible Fellowship International | 2004 | - | - | 2 | - | - |
| Baptist International Missions, Inc. (BIMI) | | - | - | 2 | - | - |
| BCM International | | - | - | - | 2 | - |
| Brethren in Christ World Missions | 1992 | - | - | - | 26 | - |
| Campus Crusade for Christ, Intl. | 1975 | - | - | - | 249 | - |
| Child Evangelism Fellowship, Inc. | 1988 | - | - | - | 1 | - |
| Christian Aid Mission | | - | - | - | 212 | - |
| Church of the Nazarene, World Mission Dept. | 1998 | - | - | - | - | - |
| Churches of Christ | | - | - | 2 | - | - |
| Evangel Bible Translators | | - | - | - | 2 | 1 |
| Evangelical Friends Mission | 1994 | - | - | 1 | 1 | 4 |
| Fellowship International Mission | 2003 | - | - | 2 | - | - |
| Foursquare Missions International | | - | - | 2 | - | - |
| Global Partners / Wesleyan World Missions | 1950 | - | - | - | - | 2 |
| Globe Missionary Evangelism | 2002 | - | - | 2 | - | - |
| Gospel for Asia, Inc. | 1988 | - | - | - | 556 | - |
| Greater Grace World Outreach | 1997 | - | - | - | 2 | - |
| Habitat for Humanity International | 1997 | - | 1 | - | - | 1 |
| HBI Global Partners | | - | - | - | 10 | - |
| I. N. Network USA | 1975 | - | - | - | 65 | - |
| International Partnership Ministries, Inc. | 1999 | - | - | - | - | 4 |
| International Teams, U.S.A. | | - | - | 2 | - | 3 |
| InterServe USA (International Service Fellowship) | 1956 | - | - | 4 | - | - |
| Medical Ambassadors International, Inc. | 1984 | - | - | - | 18 | - |
| Mennonite Mission Network | 1957 | - | - | 2 | - | - |
| Mission ONE, Inc. | 1990 | - | - | - | 6 | - |
| Mission To Unreached Peoples | 1985 | - | - | 3 | - | - |
| New Directions International, Inc. | 1989 | - | - | - | 23 | - |
| New Life Advance International | | - | - | - | 6 | - |
| Operation Mobilization | | 6 | 1 | 2 | - | 2 |
| Project Christ International | 1985 | - | - | - | 5 | - |
| Rock the World Youth Mission Alliance | | - | - | - | - | - |
| Seventh-day Adventists General Conference | 1957 | - | - | 4 | - | 11 |
| The God's Story Project | 2000 | - | - | - | 2 | - |
| United Church of Christ—Wider Church Ministries | | - | 10 | - | - | - |
| United Pentecostal Ch. Intl., Foreign Missions Div. | 1992 | - | 1 | - | 1 | - |
| Walk Thru the Bible Ministries, Inc. | 1999 | - | - | - | 2 | - |
| World Help | 1996 | - | - | - | - | - |
| World Mission Prayer League | 1956 | - | - | 5 | - | 1 |
| World Missions Far Corners, Inc. | 2001 | - | - | - | 6 | 1 |
| WorldHarvest | | - | - | - | - | - |
| World-Wide Missions | | - | - | 1 | 1 | - |
| Totals: | | 6 | 13 | 40 | 1211 | 32 |

## Netherlands

| | First Year | Personnel from U.S. 1-2 yrs. | 2-4 yrs. | 4+ yrs. | Other Countries Citizens | Non-Citizens |
|---|---|---|---|---|---|---|
| AMF International | 2005 | - | - | 1 | 1 | - |
| Assemblies of God World Missions | 1975 | 6 | - | 15 | - | - |
| Baptist Bible Fellowship International | 1979 | - | - | 2 | - | - |
| Baptist Mid-Missions | 1954 | - | - | 10 | - | - |
| BCM International | | - | - | 1 | 10 | - |

| | First Year | Personnel from U.S. | | | Other Countries | |
|---|---|---|---|---|---|---|
| | | 1-2 yrs. | 2-4 yrs. | 4+ yrs. | Citizens | Non-Citizens |
| Bethany International Ministries | 2003 | - | - | 1 | - | 1 |
| Biblical Ministries Worldwide | 1958 | - | - | 2 | 2 | - |
| Brethren Assemblies | | - | - | 2 | - | - |
| Campus Crusade for Christ, Intl. | 1969 | - | - | 2 | - | - |
| Christar | 1976 | - | - | 5 | - | - |
| Christian Associates International | 1987 | - | - | - | - | - |
| Church of the Nazarene, World Mission Dept. | 1967 | - | - | - | - | - |
| Churches of Christ | 1946 | - | - | 4 | 2 | - |
| EFCA International Mission | 1997 | 1 | - | 4 | - | - |
| Global Outreach Mission, Inc. | | - | - | - | 4 | - |
| Great Commission Ministries, Inc. | 2002 | 6 | - | 9 | - | - |
| Greater Europe Mission | 1952 | - | - | 12 | - | - |
| Intl. Pentecostal Holiness Ch. World Missions Mins. | 2003 | - | - | 2 | - | - |
| International Teams, U.S.A. | | - | - | - | - | 6 |
| Mennonite Mission Network | 2000 | - | - | - | - | - |
| New Tribes Mission | 2000 | - | - | - | 6 | - |
| Operation Mobilization | | - | 1 | - | - | 1 |
| Presbyterian Mission International (PMI) | 2001 | - | - | - | 1 | - |
| Tentmakers International | | - | - | - | - | - |
| Trans World Radio, International | | 2 | 1 | 8 | 2 | 4 |
| United Pentecostal Ch. Intl., Foreign Missions Div. | | - | 2 | - | - | 7 |
| World Harvest Mission | 1989 | - | - | 2 | - | - |
| World Venture | 1985 | - | - | - | - | - |
| | Totals: | 15 | 4 | 82 | 28 | 29 |

**Netherlands Antilles**

| | First Year | 1-2 yrs. | 2-4 yrs. | 4+ yrs. | Citizens | Non-Citizens |
|---|---|---|---|---|---|---|
| Assemblies of God World Missions | 1983 | 2 | - | 2 | - | - |
| Child Evangelism Fellowship, Inc. | | - | - | 2 | - | - |
| Church of God of Prophecy—Global Outreach | | - | - | - | 7 | - |
| Global Outreach Mission, Inc. | | - | - | 2 | 1 | - |
| Seventh-day Adventists General Conference | | - | - | 2 | - | - |
| Word of Life Fellowship, Inc.—Intl. Ministries | 1979 | - | - | - | 2 | - |
| | Totals: | 2 | - | 8 | 10 | - |

**New Caledonia**

| | First Year | 1-2 yrs. | 2-4 yrs. | 4+ yrs. | Citizens | Non-Citizens |
|---|---|---|---|---|---|---|
| Assemblies of God World Missions | 1967 | - | - | - | - | - |
| Baptist International Missions, Inc. (BIMI) | | - | - | 2 | - | - |
| Seventh-day Adventists General Conference | 1925 | - | - | - | - | 2 |
| United Pentecostal Ch. Intl., Foreign Missions Div. | 2002 | - | 2 | - | - | - |
| | Totals: | - | 2 | 2 | - | 2 |

**New Zealand**

| | First Year | 1-2 yrs. | 2-4 yrs. | 4+ yrs. | Citizens | Non-Citizens |
|---|---|---|---|---|---|---|
| Advent Christian Gen. Conf., Dept. of Wld. Msns. | 1995 | - | - | - | 2 | - |
| Adventures in Missions | 2004 | 1 | - | 2 | - | - |
| Asian Outreach U.S.A. | | - | - | - | - | - |
| Baptist Bible Fellowship International | 1971 | 2 | - | 16 | - | - |
| Baptist International Missions, Inc. (BIMI) | | - | - | 6 | - | - |
| Baptist Mid-Missions | 1973 | - | - | 6 | - | - |
| Biblical Ministries Worldwide | 1967 | - | - | 9 | - | 9 |
| Campus Crusade for Christ, Intl. | 1972 | 13 | - | 17 | 49 | - |

| | First Year | Personnel from U.S. | | | Other Countries | |
|---|---|---|---|---|---|---|
| | | 1-2 yrs. | 2-4 yrs. | 4+ yrs. | Citizens | Non-Citizens |
| Christian Churches / Churches of Christ | | - | - | 8 | - | - |
| Ch. of God (Anderson, Ind.), Global Missions | 1994 | - | - | 3 | - | 1 |
| Church of God of Prophecy—Global Outreach | | - | - | - | - | 2 |
| Church of the Nazarene, World Mission Dept. | 1952 | - | - | - | - | - |
| Churches of Christ | 1844 | - | - | 3 | 12 | - |
| Elim Fellowship— International Department | 1964 | - | - | 2 | - | - |
| Fellowship International Mission | 1995 | - | - | - | 2 | - |
| Global Partners / Wesleyan World Missions | 2000 | - | - | - | - | - |
| Gospel Fellowship Association | 1998 | - | - | 2 | - | - |
| International Teams, U.S.A. | | - | - | 2 | - | 4 |
| Mission to the World (PCA), Inc. | 2001 | 2 | - | - | - | - |
| Navigators, U.S. International Missions Group | | - | 1 | 4 | - | - |
| Presbyterian Mission International (PMI) | 2006 | - | - | - | 1 | - |
| Salvation Army, U.S.A. | | - | - | 1 | - | - |
| Teen Missions International, Inc. | 1996 | - | - | - | 1 | - |
| United Pentecostal Ch. Intl., Foreign Missions Div. | 1969 | - | 3 | - | - | 12 |
| WEC International | 1953 | - | - | 2 | - | - |
| Word of Life Fellowship, Inc.—Intl. Ministries | 1983 | - | - | - | 2 | - |
| World Baptist Fellowship Mission Agency, Inc. | | 2 | - | 8 | - | - |
| Youth for Christ/USA—World Outreach | | - | - | 3 | - | - |
| Totals: | | 20 | 4 | 94 | 69 | 28 |

## Nicaragua

| | First Year | 1-2 yrs. | 2-4 yrs. | 4+ yrs. | Citizens | Non-Citizens |
|---|---|---|---|---|---|---|
| Am. Baptist Chs. of the U.S.A., Intl. Ministries | 1917 | - | - | - | - | - |
| Assemblies of God World Missions | 1912 | 5 | - | 24 | - | - |
| Awana Clubs International | 2001 | - | - | 2 | - | 2 |
| Baptist Bible Fellowship International | 1969 | 2 | - | 15 | - | - |
| Baptist Medical & Dental Mission Intl., Inc. | 1974 | - | - | 4 | 26 | - |
| Brethren Assemblies | | - | - | 6 | - | - |
| Brethren in Christ World Missions | 1965 | - | - | 2 | - | - |
| CAM International | 1890 | - | - | 4 | - | - |
| Campus Crusade for Christ, Intl. | 1999 | - | - | 2 | 12 | - |
| Caring Partners International, Inc. | 1991 | - | - | - | - | - |
| Christ for the City International | 2002 | - | 4 | - | 1 | 2 |
| Christian Aid Ministries | | - | 8 | - | 10 | - |
| Christian Reformed World Missions | 1996 | - | 2 | 2 | - | - |
| Christian Reformed World Relief Committee | 1973 | - | 1 | - | - | 1 |
| Church of God (Cleveland, TN) World Missions | 1950 | 2 | - | - | - | - |
| Church of the Nazarene, World Mission Dept. | 1937 | - | - | - | - | - |
| Churches of Christ | | 2 | - | 3 | 6 | - |
| Commission to Every Nation | 2000 | - | - | 2 | - | - |
| Compassion International, Inc. | 2002 | - | - | - | 20 | - |
| Envoy International | | - | - | - | - | - |
| Equip, Inc. | 1998 | - | - | 2 | - | - |
| Food for the Hungry, Inc. | 1994 | - | 4 | - | - | 1 |
| Forward Edge International | 1985 | 1 | - | - | 1 | - |
| FRIENDS in Action, International | 2005 | 2 | - | - | - | - |
| Full Gospel Evangelistic Association | 1960 | - | - | 2 | - | - |
| Global Outreach International | 2001 | - | - | 2 | - | - |
| Global Partners / Wesleyan World Missions | 1997 | - | - | - | - | - |

| | First Year | Personnel from U.S. 1-2 yrs. | 2-4 yrs. | 4+ yrs. | Other Countries Citizens | Non-Citizens |
|---|---|---|---|---|---|---|
| Globe Missionary Evangelism | 1996 | 1 | - | 3 | - | - |
| Habitat for Humanity International | 1984 | - | 1 | - | - | 1 |
| Intl. Pentecostal Holiness Ch. World Missions Mins. | 1994 | - | - | 1 | - | - |
| International Teams, U.S.A. | | - | - | - | - | 1 |
| Larry Jones Intl. Ministries (Feed the Children) | 1989 | - | - | - | 6 | - |
| Living Water Teaching | 1986 | - | - | - | 2 | - |
| Luke Society, Inc., The | 2001 | - | - | - | - | - |
| Medical Ambassadors International, Inc. | 1999 | - | - | - | 3 | - |
| Mission to the Americas | 1997 | - | - | - | 2 | - |
| Mission to the World (PCA), Inc. | 2002 | - | - | - | | |
| Missionary Revival Crusade | | - | - | 3 | 1 | - |
| Missionary Ventures International | 1995 | - | - | 6 | - | - |
| Natl. Baptist Conv. USA, Inc.—Foreign Msn. Bd. | 1958 | - | - | - | 1 | - |
| Open Bible Churches, International Ministries | 2003 | - | - | 2 | - | - |
| Pentecostal Church of God—World Missions Dept. | | - | - | 2 | - | - |
| Pentecostal Free Will Baptist Church, Inc. | | - | - | - | 1 | - |
| Precious Seed Ministries | 1972 | - | - | - | 2 | - |
| Reformed Church in Am., Gen. Synod Council | 1991 | - | - | - | 2 | - |
| Rosedale Mennonite Missions | 1968 | - | - | 2 | 1 | 1 |
| Self-Help International | 1999 | - | - | - | 3 | - |
| Seventh-day Adventists General Conference | 1928 | - | - | - | - | 2 |
| TEAM (The Evangelical Alliance Mission) | | - | - | 2 | - | - |
| Trans World Missions | | - | - | - | 2 | 3 |
| United Church of Christ—Wider Church Ministries | | - | 1 | - | - | - |
| United Pentecostal Ch. Intl., Foreign Missions Div. | 1971 | - | 2 | - | - | 1 |
| Village Ministries International | 2003 | - | - | - | 3 | - |
| World Relief | 1991 | - | - | 1 | 23 | - |
| Totals: | | 15 | 23 | 94 | 129 | 15 |

## Niger

| | First Year | 1-2 yrs. | 2-4 yrs. | 4+ yrs. | Citizens | Non-Citizens |
|---|---|---|---|---|---|---|
| Assemblies of God World Missions | 1991 | 1 | - | 4 | - | - |
| Baptist International Missions, Inc. (BIMI) | | - | - | 2 | - | - |
| Calvary International | | - | - | 1 | - | - |
| Campus Crusade for Christ, Intl. | 1991 | - | - | - | 29 | 2 |
| Child Evangelism Fellowship, Inc. | 1994 | - | - | - | 1 | - |
| Christian Reformed World Relief Committee | 1991 | - | - | - | 1 | 2 |
| Elim Fellowship—International Department | 1991 | - | - | 4 | 4 | - |
| Evangelical Baptist Missions | | 1 | - | 8 | - | - |
| Fellowship International Mission | 1950 | - | - | 1 | - | 2 |
| Gospel Revival Ministries | 1997 | - | - | - | 2 | - |
| Medical Ambassadors International, Inc. | 1997 | - | - | - | - | - |
| Reformed Church in Am., Gen. Synod Council | 2001 | - | - | 2 | - | - |
| Samaritan's Purse | 2005 | 3 | - | - | 23 | 2 |
| Seventh-day Adventists General Conference | 1987 | - | - | - | - | 2 |
| SIM USA | 1924 | 5 | - | 61 | - | - |
| United Pentecostal Ch. Intl., Foreign Missions Div. | 1999 | - | 2 | - | - | - |
| World Missions & Evangelism, Inc. | | - | - | 2 | - | - |
| Totals: | | 10 | 2 | 85 | 60 | 10 |

## Nigeria

| | First Year | Personnel from U.S. | | | Other Countries | |
|---|---|---|---|---|---|---|
| | | 1-2 yrs. | 2-4 yrs. | 4+ yrs. | Citizens | Non-Citizens |
| ACM International | 1970 | - | - | 2 | - | - |
| Advent Christian Gen. Conf., Dept. of Wld. Msns. | 1960 | - | - | - | 25 | - |
| African Leadership, Inc. | 1998 | - | - | - | 1 | - |
| Agape Gospel Mission | | - | - | - | 12 | - |
| Assemblies of God World Missions | 1939 | - | - | 4 | - | - |
| Baptist Bible Fellowship International | 1987 | - | - | 2 | - | - |
| Baptist International Missions, Inc. (BIMI) | | - | - | 6 | - | - |
| Baptist International Outreach | 1988 | - | - | - | 3 | - |
| BILD International | | - | - | - | 6 | - |
| Brethren Assemblies | | - | - | 4 | - | - |
| Campus Crusade for Christ, Intl. | 1969 | 1 | - | 4 | 378 | 5 |
| Child Evangelism Fellowship, Inc. | 1982 | - | - | - | 7 | - |
| Christian Aid Mission | | - | - | - | 98 | - |
| Christian Blind Mission International | 1997 | - | 1 | - | - | - |
| Christian Broadcasting Network Inc., the | 1997 | - | - | - | 20 | - |
| Christian Churches / Churches of Christ | | - | - | 2 | - | - |
| Christian Literature International | | - | - | - | - | - |
| Christian Reformed World Missions | 1940 | 2 | 3 | 22 | - | - |
| Christian Reformed World Relief Committee | 1969 | - | - | - | 4 | - |
| Christ's Mandate for Missions | 2004 | - | - | - | 1 | - |
| Church of God (Cleveland, TN) World Missions | 1951 | 2 | - | - | - | - |
| Ch. of God (Holiness), World Msn. Dept., Inc. | 1995 | - | - | - | 1 | - |
| Church of the Nazarene, World Mission Dept. | 1977 | - | - | - | - | 4 |
| Churches of Christ | 1946 | 4 | - | 12 | 8 | - |
| Development Associates International (DAI) | 1996 | - | - | - | 2 | - |
| Elim Fellowship—International Department | 1975 | - | - | - | - | 2 |
| Equip, Inc. | 1995 | - | - | - | 4 | - |
| Evangelical Baptist Missions | | - | - | - | 2 | - |
| Evangelical Luth. Ch. in Am., Div. for Global Msn. | 1913 | - | - | 1 | - | - |
| Evangelical Presbyterian Church—World Outreach | 2003 | - | - | 2 | - | - |
| Evangelism Resources | 1995 | - | - | - | 2 | - |
| Fellowship International Mission | 1977 | - | - | 4 | - | - |
| Food for the Hungry, Inc. | 2000 | - | 2 | - | - | - |
| Foursquare Missions International | 1955 | - | - | 2 | - | - |
| Free Methodist World Missions | 1989 | - | - | 2 | - | - |
| Gospel Communications International, Inc. | 1970 | - | - | - | 6 | - |
| Gospel Revival Ministries | 1990 | - | - | - | 8 | - |
| Hosanna | 2004 | - | - | - | 2 | - |
| International Christian Ministries | 2000 | - | - | - | 4 | - |
| International Institute for Christian Studies | 1988 | - | - | 3 | 1 | 4 |
| Intl. Pentecostal Holiness Ch. World Missions Mins. | 1950 | - | - | - | - | - |
| Ireland Outreach International Inc. | 1994 | - | - | - | 9 | - |
| Liebenzell USA | 2005 | - | - | 1 | - | - |
| Lott Carey Baptist Foreign Mission Convention | 1965 | - | - | - | 140 | - |
| Lutheran Bible Translators, Inc. | 2003 | - | - | 2 | 3 | - |
| Lutheran Church-Missouri Synod | 1936 | - | - | 2 | - | - |
| Medical Ambassadors International, Inc. | 2003 | - | - | - | - | - |
| Mennonite Mission Network | 1959 | - | - | - | - | - |
| Mission Ministries, Inc. | 2000 | - | - | - | 2 | - |

| | First Year | Personnel from U.S. | | | Other Countries | |
|---|---|---|---|---|---|---|
| | | 1-2 yrs. | 2-4 yrs. | 4+ yrs. | Citizens | Non-Citizens |
| Mission to the World (PCA), Inc. | 1990 | - | - | - | - | - |
| Mission: Moving Mountains, Inc. | 2002 | | | | | |
| Missionary Ventures International | 1990 | - | - | - | 2 | - |
| Mutual Faith Ministries Intl. | | - | - | - | - | - |
| Navigators, U.S. International Missions Group | | - | - | 2 | - | - |
| N. Am. Baptist Conf.—Worldwide Outreach | 1939 | - | - | 2 | 1 | 7 |
| Pentecostal Free Will Baptist Church, Inc. | | - | - | - | 1 | - |
| Precept Ministries International | 1996 | - | - | - | 2 | - |
| Presbyterian Evangelistic Fellowship | | - | - | 1 | 2 | - |
| Ripe for Harvest, Inc. | 1998 | - | - | 1 | - | - |
| Salvation Army, U.S.A. | | - | - | 1 | - | - |
| Seventh-day Adventists General Conference | 1914 | - | - | 4 | - | 2 |
| SIM USA | 1893 | 6 | - | 56 | - | - |
| Source of Light Ministries International, Inc. | | - | - | - | 2 | - |
| The God's Story Project | 2000 | - | - | - | 1 | - |
| The Master's Mission, Inc. | 1987 | - | - | - | 5 | - |
| United Pentecostal Ch. Intl., Foreign Missions Div. | 1970 | - | 4 | - | - | 5 |
| Village Ministries International | 1991 | - | - | - | 39 | - |
| Walk Thru the Bible Ministries, Inc. | 2000 | - | - | - | 4 | - |
| Wisc. Evangelical Luth. Synod, Bd. for World Msns. | 1936 | - | - | - | - | - |
| Word of Life Fellowship, Inc.—Intl. Ministries | 2000 | - | - | 2 | 15 | - |
| World-Wide Missions | 1967 | - | - | | 1 | - |
| Totals: | | 15 | 10 | 146 | 824 | 29 |

**Norway**

| | First Year | 1-2 yrs. | 2-4 yrs. | 4+ yrs. | Citizens | Non-Citizens |
|---|---|---|---|---|---|---|
| Baptist International Missions, Inc. (BIMI) | | - | - | 2 | - | - |
| Churches of Christ | 1960 | - | - | - | 4 | - |
| Intl. Pentecostal Holiness Ch. World Missions Mins. | 1992 | - | - | 2 | - | - |
| International Teams, U.S.A. | | - | - | - | - | 2 |
| Navigators, U.S. International Missions Group | | - | - | 2 | - | - |
| New Tribes Mission | 2000 | - | - | - | 6 | - |
| Tentmakers International | | - | - | - | - | - |
| United Pentecostal Ch. Intl., Foreign Missions Div. | | - | 2 | - | - | 3 |
| Totals: | | - | 2 | 6 | 10 | 5 |

**Oceania—General**

| | First Year | 1-2 yrs. | 2-4 yrs. | 4+ yrs. | Citizens | Non-Citizens |
|---|---|---|---|---|---|---|
| Assemblies of God World Missions | 1972 | 2 | - | 9 | - | - |
| Final Frontiers Foundation, Inc. | 2001 | - | - | - | 2 | - |
| Great Commission Center International | 1999 | - | - | - | - | - |
| Southern Baptist Convention Intl. Mission Board | | - | - | - | - | - |
| United Pentecostal Ch. Intl., Foreign Missions Div. | 2004 | - | 2 | - | - | - |
| Wycliffe Bible Translators, Inc. | 1960 | - | - | 25 | - | - |
| Totals: | | 2 | 2 | 34 | 2 | - |

**Oman**

| | First Year | 1-2 yrs. | 2-4 yrs. | 4+ yrs. | Citizens | Non-Citizens |
|---|---|---|---|---|---|---|
| Arab World Ministries | | - | - | 4 | - | - |
| Reformed Church in Am., Gen. Synod Council | 2001 | - | - | 4 | - | - |
| Walk Thru the Bible Ministries, Inc. | 2002 | - | - | - | - | - |
| Totals: | | - | - | 8 | - | - |

| | First Year | Personnel from U.S. | | | Other Countries | |
| --- | --- | --- | --- | --- | --- | --- |
| | | 1-2 yrs. | 2-4 yrs. | 4+ yrs. | Citizens | Non-Citizens |
| **Pakistan** | | | | | | |
| Baptist Bible Fellowship International | 1959 | - | - | 4 | - | - |
| BILD International | | - | - | - | - | - |
| Campus Crusade for Christ, Intl. | 1960 | - | - | - | 83 | - |
| Child Evangelism Fellowship, Inc. | 1955 | - | - | - | 1 | - |
| Christ to the Nations | 2004 | - | - | - | 2 | - |
| Christar | 1953 | - | - | 10 | - | - |
| Christian Aid Mission | | - | - | - | 33 | - |
| Christian Blind Mission International | 1982 | - | 1 | - | - | - |
| Christian Churches / Churches of Christ | | - | - | - | 2 | - |
| Church of God (Cleveland, TN) World Missions | 1972 | 1 | - | - | - | - |
| Church of God of Prophecy—Global Outreach | | - | - | - | 2 | - |
| Church of the Nazarene, World Mission Dept. | 1996 | - | - | - | - | - |
| Church World Service | | - | - | - | 7 | - |
| Episcopal Church USA—Domestic & Foreign | | - | - | 3 | - | - |
| Full Gospel Evangelistic Association | 2003 | 3 | - | - | - | - |
| Global Partners / Wesleyan World Missions | 1992 | - | - | - | - | - |
| Gospel Revival Ministries | 2006 | - | - | - | 2 | - |
| Hosanna | 2006 | - | - | - | 2 | - |
| Key Communications | 1980 | - | - | - | 2 | - |
| Literacy & Evangelism International | | - | - | - | - | - |
| Mission ONE, Inc. | 1990 | - | - | - | 3 | - |
| Paraclete, Inc. | 2004 | - | - | - | - | - |
| People International USA | 2000 | - | - | - | 2 | - |
| Red Sea Team International | 1980 | - | - | - | 2 | 3 |
| Samaritan's Purse | 2005 | 4 | - | - | 18 | - |
| Seventh-day Adventists General Conference | 1914 | - | - | - | - | 4 |
| United Pentecostal Ch. Intl., Foreign Missions Div. | 1971 | - | 2 | - | - | - |
| Walk Thru the Bible Ministries, Inc. | 2002 | - | - | - | - | - |
| Westminster Biblical Missions | 1973 | - | - | 1 | 20 | - |
| World Mission Prayer League | 1946 | - | - | 2 | - | 2 |
| World Venture | 1954 | - | - | 4 | - | - |
| World Witness, Assoc. Reformed Presbyterian Ch. | 1906 | - | - | - | 400 | - |
| WorldHarvest | | - | - | - | - | - |
| | Totals: | 8 | 3 | - | - | - |
| **Palau** | | - | - | - | - | - |
| Assemblies of God World Missions | 1983 | - | - | 2 | - | - |
| Biblical Ministries Worldwide | | - | - | 2 | - | 2 |
| Church of the Nazarene, World Mission Dept. | 1995 | - | - | - | - | - |
| Liebenzell USA | 1929 | - | 1 | 1 | - | - |
| World Baptist Fellowship Mission Agency, Inc. | | - | - | 2 | - | - |
| | Totals: | - | 1 | 7 | - | 2 |
| **Palestine** | | | | | - | - |
| Anis Shorrosh Evangelistic Association | | - | - | 40 | - | - |
| Christ Community Church | 1928 | - | - | - | 7 | - |
| Evangelical Lutheran Ch. in Am., Div. for Global Msn. | 1967 | 2 | 2 | - | - | - |
| Friends United Meeting—Global Ministries | | - | 1 | 1 | - | - |
| United Pentecostal Ch. Intl., Foreign Missions Div. | | - | 2 | - | - | - |

| | First Year | Personnel from U.S. 1-2 yrs. | 2-4 yrs. | 4+ yrs. | Other Countries Citizens | Non-Citizens |
|---|---|---|---|---|---|---|
| Walk Thru the Bible Ministries, Inc. | 2002 | - | - | - | - | - |
| Totals: | | 2 | 5 | 41 | 7 | - |

## Panama

| | First Year | 1-2 yrs. | 2-4 yrs. | 4+ yrs. | Citizens | Non-Citizens |
|---|---|---|---|---|---|---|
| Am. Baptist Chs. of the U.S.A., Intl. Ministries | 2001 | - | - | - | - | - |
| Assemblies of God World Missions | 1967 | - | - | 8 | - | - |
| Avant Ministries | 1953 | - | - | 3 | 1 | - |
| Baptist Bible Fellowship International | 1976 | - | - | 8 | - | - |
| Baptist International Missions, Inc. (BIMI) | | - | - | 2 | - | - |
| CAM International | 1890 | - | - | 6 | - | - |
| Campus Crusade for Christ, Intl. | 1965 | - | - | 2 | 16 | - |
| Christian Churches / Churches of Christ | | 2 | - | 2 | - | - |
| Church of God (Cleveland, TN) World Missions | 1935 | - | - | 2 | - | - |
| Ch. of God (Holiness), World Mission Dept., Inc. | 2003 | - | - | - | 1 | - |
| Church of God of Prophecy—Global Outreach | | - | - | - | 2 | 2 |
| Church of the Nazarene, World Mission Dept. | 1953 | - | - | - | - | - |
| Churches of Christ | 1963 | - | - | 1 | 8 | - |
| Envoy International | | - | - | - | - | - |
| Episcopal Church USA—Domestic & Foreign | | - | - | 4 | - | - |
| Fellowship of Associates of Medical Evangelism | 1989 | - | - | - | 12 | - |
| Foursquare Missions International | | - | - | 2 | - | - |
| Free Will Baptist, Inc. Board of Intl. Missions | 1971 | - | - | 8 | - | - |
| Global Partners / Wesleyan World Missions | 1997 | - | - | - | - | - |
| Gospel Fellowship Association | 2002 | - | - | 2 | - | - |
| Intl. Pentecostal Holiness Ch. World Missions Mins. | 1988 | - | - | 2 | - | - |
| Latin America Mission | | - | 2 | - | 2 | - |
| Living Water Teaching | 2001 | - | - | - | - | 2 |
| Lutheran Church-Missouri Synod | 1941 | - | - | 6 | - | - |
| Medical Ambassadors International, Inc. | 2003 | - | - | - | - | - |
| Mission to the Americas | 1952 | - | - | - | 2 | 2 |
| Natl. Baptist Conv. of Am.—Foreign Msn. Bd. | 1969 | - | - | - | 4 | - |
| New Tribes Mission | 1953 | - | - | 50 | - | - |
| South American Missionary Society (USA) | 2004 | - | 1 | - | - | - |
| Trans World Missions | | - | - | - | - | 2 |
| United Pentecostal Ch. Intl., Foreign Missions Div. | 1980 | - | 2 | - | - | 1 |
| Word of Life Fellowship, Inc.—Intl. Ministries | 1988 | - | - | 1 | 10 | 1 |
| Totals: | | 2 | 5 | 109 | 58 | 10 |

## Papua New Guinea

| | First Year | 1-2 yrs. | 2-4 yrs. | 4+ yrs. | Citizens | Non-Citizens |
|---|---|---|---|---|---|---|
| Apostolic Christian Church Foundation, Inc. | 1961 | - | - | 2 | - | - |
| Assemblies of God World Missions | 2000 | - | - | - | - | - |
| Awana Clubs International | 1991 | - | - | 2 | 1 | - |
| Baptist Bible Fellowship International | 1961 | - | - | 10 | - | - |
| Baptist International Missions, Inc. (BIMI) | | - | - | 4 | - | - |
| Baptist Mid-Missions | 2006 | - | - | 2 | - | - |
| Brethren Assemblies | | - | - | 8 | - | - |
| Bright Hope International | 2000 | - | - | - | 1 | - |
| Campus Crusade for Christ, Intl. | 1978 | - | - | - | 5 | - |
| Christian Aid Mission | | - | - | - | 11 | - |
| Christian Blind Mission International | 1988 | - | 2 | - | - | - |

| | First Year | Personnel from U.S. | | | Other Countries | |
|---|---|---|---|---|---|---|
| | | 1-2 yrs. | 2-4 yrs. | 4+ yrs. | Citizens | Non-Citizens |
| Christian Churches / Churches of Christ | | - | 6 | 30 | - | - |
| Ch. of God (Holiness), World Mission Dept., Inc. | 2005 | 1 | - | - | - | - |
| Church of the Nazarene, World Mission Dept. | 1955 | - | - | 28 | - | 1 |
| Churches of Christ | 1971 | - | - | 5 | 3 | - |
| Evangel Bible Translators | | - | - | 2 | - | - |
| Evangelical Lutheran Ch. in Am., Div. for Global Msn. | 1886 | - | - | 2 | - | 1 |
| Evangelism Explosion International | | - | - | - | - | 10 |
| Foursquare Missions International | 1956 | - | - | 2 | - | - |
| FRIENDS in Action, International | 1995 | - | 2 | 2 | - | - |
| Global Partners / Wesleyan World Missions | 1961 | - | 4 | - | - | 2 |
| Gospel Fellowship Association | 1997 | 6 | - | 11 | - | - |
| Hosanna | 2006 | - | - | - | 2 | - |
| Kids Alive International | 1992 | - | - | 1 | 118 | - |
| Liebenzell USA | 1906 | - | - | - | - | 2 |
| Lutheran Bible Translators, Inc. | 1998 | - | - | 2 | - | - |
| Lutheran Church-Missouri Synod | 1948 | - | - | 1 | - | - |
| Medical Ambassadors International, Inc. | 2003 | - | - | - | 2 | 2 |
| Mission to the World (PCA), Inc. | 1987 | - | - | - | - | - |
| Mustard Seed International | 1974 | - | - | - | - | - |
| New Life Advance International | | - | - | - | - | - |
| New Tribes Mission | 1950 | 40 | - | 400 | - | - |
| Open Bible Churches, International Ministries | 1973 | - | - | 2 | - | - |
| Pioneer Bible Translators | 1977 | - | - | 33 | - | - |
| Pioneers USA | 1980 | - | - | 14 | - | - |
| Seventh-day Adventists General Conference | 1908 | - | - | - | - | 20 |
| United Pentecostal Ch. Intl., Foreign Missions Div. | 1973 | - | - | - | - | 3 |
| Word of Life Fellowship, Inc.—Intl. Ministries | 2000 | - | - | - | 3 | - |
| World Gospel Mission | 1996 | - | - | 5 | - | - |
| World-Wide Missions | 1975 | - | - | - | 1 | - |
| Wycliffe Bible Translators, Inc. | 1960 | - | - | 430 | - | - |
| | Totals: | 47 | 14 | 998 | 147 | 41 |

## Paraguay

| | First Year | Personnel from U.S. | | | Other Countries | |
|---|---|---|---|---|---|---|
| Apostolic Christian Church Foundation, Inc. | 1978 | - | - | 1 | 1 | - |
| Assemblies of God World Missions | 1944 | 2 | - | 14 | - | - |
| Baptist Bible Fellowship International | 1980 | - | - | 2 | - | - |
| Baptist International Missions, Inc. (BIMI) | | - | - | 2 | - | - |
| BCM International | | - | - | - | 2 | - |
| Bethany International Ministries | 2001 | 2 | - | - | - | - |
| Brethren Assemblies | | - | - | 14 | - | - |
| Campus Crusade for Christ, Intl. | 1966 | - | - | - | 11 | - |
| Christian Aid Mission | | - | - | - | 33 | - |
| Ch. of God (Anderson, Ind.), Global Missions | 2002 | - | - | - | - | 2 |
| Church of God (Cleveland, TN) World Missions | 1954 | - | - | 2 | - | - |
| Church of God of Prophecy—Global Outreach | | - | - | - | 4 | - |
| Church of the Nazarene, World Mission Dept. | 1980 | - | - | - | - | 4 |
| Churches of Christ | 1965 | - | - | 8 | - | - |
| Envoy International | | - | - | - | - | - |
| Foursquare Missions International | 1986 | - | - | 2 | - | - |
| Full Gospel Grace Fellowship | 1940 | - | - | - | 2 | - |

| | First Year | Personnel from U.S. | | | Other Countries | |
|---|---|---|---|---|---|---|
| | | 1-2 yrs. | 2-4 yrs. | 4+ yrs. | Citizens | Non-Citizens |
| Global Outreach Mission, Inc. | | - | - | 4 | - | - |
| Grace Brethren International Missions | 2002 | - | - | - | - | 2 |
| International Partnership Ministries, Inc. | 1995 | - | - | - | 3 | 1 |
| Intl. Pentecostal Holiness Ch. World Missions Mins. | | - | - | - | 2 | - |
| Latin America Mission | 2001 | - | 4 | 2 | - | 6 |
| Living Water Teaching | 1990 | - | - | 2 | - | - |
| Luke Society, Inc., The | 2001 | - | - | - | - | - |
| Medical Ambassadors International, Inc. | 2003 | - | - | - | - | - |
| Mennonite Mission Network | 1952 | - | - | - | - | - |
| Missionary Ventures International | 2002 | - | - | 2 | - | - |
| New Tribes Mission | 1946 | - | - | 60 | - | - |
| Open Air Campaigners—Overseas Ministries | 1991 | 4 | - | 4 | 8 | - |
| Salvation Army, U.S.A. | | - | - | 1 | - | - |
| Seventh-day Adventists General Conference | 1900 | - | - | - | - | 2 |
| SIM USA | 1987 | 1 | - | 16 | - | - |
| South America Mission, Inc. | 1991 | - | - | 5 | 5 | 1 |
| South American Missionary Society (USA) | 1998 | - | - | 1 | - | - |
| Spanish World Ministries | | - | - | 1 | 1 | - |
| STEM (Short-Term Evangelical Missions) Intl. | 1994 | - | - | - | - | - |
| The Brethren Church, Inc. | 1997 | - | - | - | - | 1 |
| The Mission Society | 1988 | 3 | 2 | 6 | - | - |
| United Church of Christ—Wider Church Ministries | | - | 2 | - | - | - |
| United Pentecostal Ch. Intl., Foreign Msn. Div. | 1973 | - | 2 | - | - | 6 |
| White Fields Inc. | | - | - | - | 2 | - |
| Word of Life Fellowship, Inc.—Intl. Ministries | 1979 | - | - | - | 13 | 2 |
| World Gospel Mission | 1986 | - | - | 4 | - | 1 |
| World-Wide Missions | 1963 | - | - | - | 1 | - |
| | Totals: | 12 | 10 | 153 | 88 | 28 |

## Peru

| | | | | | | - |
|---|---|---|---|---|---|---|
| Allegheny Wesleyan Methodist Connection | 1972 | - | - | 4 | - | - |
| Amazon Focus | 1995 | - | - | 4 | 25 | - |
| AMG International | | - | - | - | 5 | - |
| Assemblies of God World Missions | 1919 | 2 | - | 12 | - | - |
| Awana Clubs International | 1987 | - | - | - | 2 | - |
| Baptist Bible Fellowship International | 1958 | - | - | 17 | - | - |
| Baptist International Missions, Inc. (BIMI) | | - | - | 13 | - | - |
| Baptist International Outreach | 1995 | - | - | 4 | - | - |
| Baptist Mid-Missions | 1937 | - | - | 33 | 1 | - |
| BCM International | | - | - | - | 22 | - |
| BILD International | | - | - | - | 1 | - |
| Brethren Assemblies | | - | - | 22 | - | - |
| Calvary International | 2002 | - | - | 2 | - | - |
| Campus Crusade for Christ, Intl. | 1964 | - | - | - | 1 | 3 |
| Child Evangelism Fellowship, Inc. | 1946 | - | - | - | 1 | - |
| Childcare Worldwide | 1985 | - | - | - | 2 | - |
| Christ for the City International | 1989 | 1 | - | 1 | 1 | 1 |
| Christian Aid Mission | | - | - | - | 68 | - |
| Christians In Action Missions International | | - | - | - | - | - |
| Church of God (Cleveland, TN) World Missions | 1947 | - | - | 2 | - | - |

| | Personnel from U.S. | | | | Other Countries | |
| --- | --- | --- | --- | --- | --- | --- |
| | First Year | 1-2 yrs. | 2-4 yrs. | 4+ yrs. | Citizens | Non-Citizens |
| Church of God of Prophecy—Global Outreach | | - | - | - | 2 | - |
| Church of the Nazarene, World Mission Dept. | 1914 | - | - | 8 | - | - |
| Churches of Christ | 1958 | - | - | 4 | 2 | - |
| Commission to Every Nation | 2004 | 1 | - | - | - | - |
| Compassion International, Inc. | 1977 | - | - | - | 38 | - |
| Eastern Mennonite Missions | | - | 8 | - | - | 1 |
| EFCA International Mission | 1975 | 2 | - | 11 | 3 | - |
| Elim Fellowship—International Department | 1964 | - | - | 1 | - | - |
| Envoy International | | - | - | - | - | - |
| Flying Doctors of Am. (Medical Mercy Msns., Inc.) | 1990 | - | - | - | - | - |
| Food for the Hungry, Inc. | 1982 | 2 | 8 | - | 3 | - |
| Free Methodist World Missions | | - | - | 4 | - | - |
| Global Outreach International | 2005 | - | - | 2 | - | - |
| Global Outreach Mission, Inc. | | - | - | - | 4 | - |
| Global Partners / Wesleyan World Missions | 1903 | - | 2 | - | - | - |
| Greater Grace World Outreach | 2003 | - | - | 2 | - | - |
| Harvest | 1997 | - | - | - | 1 | - |
| Hosanna | 2005 | - | - | - | 2 | - |
| International Partnership Ministries, Inc. | 1996 | - | - | - | 13 | - |
| Intl. Pentecostal Holiness Ch. World Missions Mins. | 1996 | - | - | 2 | 2 | - |
| Josue Yrion World Evangelism and Missions, Inc. | 1997 | - | - | - | 1 | - |
| Kids Alive International | 1993 | - | - | 2 | - | 4 |
| Latin America Mission | 1975 | - | 2 | 6 | 3 | 5 |
| Latin American Indian Ministries | 1996 | - | - | - | - | - |
| Literacy & Evangelism International | 1995 | - | - | 2 | - | - |
| LOGOI Ministries | 1972 | - | - | - | 2 | - |
| Luke Society, Inc., The | 1988 | - | - | - | - | - |
| Macedonia World Baptist Missions, Inc. | 1987 | - | - | 15 | - | - |
| Medical Ambassadors International, Inc. | 1999 | - | - | - | 1 | - |
| Ministries In Action | 2005 | - | - | - | - | - |
| Mission to the World (PCA), Inc. | 1987 | 4 | 18 | - | - | - |
| Missionary Ventures International | 1999 | - | - | 8 | 1 | - |
| Network of International Christian Schools | 2001 | 1 | 12 | 2 | - | - |
| New Way Missions | 2006 | - | - | - | - | - |
| Pentecostal Free Will Baptist Church, Inc. | | - | - | - | 1 | - |
| Pioneers USA | 1997 | - | - | 17 | 1 | - |
| Precept Ministries International | 1992 | - | - | - | 1 | - |
| Presbyterian Evangelistic Fellowship | | - | - | 4 | 2 | - |
| Ripe for Harvest, Inc. | 1999 | - | 1 | 1 | - | - |
| Rock the World Youth Mission Alliance | | - | - | - | - | - |
| SIM USA | 1965 | 1 | - | 12 | - | - |
| Source of Light Ministries International, Inc. | 1975 | - | - | - | 2 | - |
| South America Mission, Inc. | 1926 | - | 1 | 28 | - | - |
| South American Missionary Society (USA) | 1979 | - | - | 6 | - | 2 |
| Spanish World Ministries | | - | - | 2 | 2 | - |
| TEAM (The Evangelical Alliance Mission) | | - | - | 6 | - | - |
| Team Expansion, Inc. | | - | 4 | - | - | - |
| The Brethren Church, Inc. | 1997 | - | - | - | 2 | - |
| The Mission Society | 1997 | 2 | 2 | 4 | - | - |
| United Pentecostal Ch. Intl., Foreign Missions Div. | 1962 | - | 4 | - | - | - |

| | First Year | Personnel from U.S. | | | Other Countries | |
|---|---|---|---|---|---|---|
| | | 1-2 yrs. | 2-4 yrs. | 4+ yrs. | Citizens | Non-Citizens |
| Walk Thru the Bible Ministries, Inc. | 2000 | - | - | - | - | - |
| White Fields Inc. | | - | - | - | 2 | - |
| Women to the World | 1988 | - | - | - | - | - |
| Word of Life Fellowship, Inc.—Intl. Ministries | 1986 | - | - | - | 20 | 2 |
| World Concern | 1987 | - | - | - | 6 | - |
| World Mission Prayer League | 1985 | 1 | - | 2 | - | - |
| World Missions Far Corners, Inc. | 1963 | - | - | 4 | 10 | - |
| World Reach, Inc. | 1998 | - | - | 2 | 3 | 1 |
| World Team | 1941 | - | - | - | - | 6 |
| World-Wide Missions | | - | - | 2 | - | - |
| Totals: | | 17 | 62 | 273 | 259 | 25 |

## Philippines

| | First Year | 1-2 yrs. | 2-4 yrs. | 4+ yrs. | Citizens | Non-Citizens |
|---|---|---|---|---|---|---|
| ACM International | 1998 | - | - | 2 | - | - |
| Action International Ministries | 1974 | - | - | 29 | 1 | 6 |
| Advent Christian Gen. Conf., Dept. of Wld. Msns. | 1953 | - | - | 2 | 30 | 1 |
| Adventist World Aviation | 2002 | - | - | 3 | 1 | - |
| Am. Baptist Chs. of the U.S.A., Intl. Ministries | 1900 | - | - | 2 | - | - |
| American Leprosy Missions, Inc. | 1953 | - | - | - | 2 | 1 |
| AMG International | 1979 | - | - | - | 312 | - |
| Asian Outreach U.S.A. | | - | - | - | - | - |
| Assemblies of God World Missions | 1926 | 19 | - | 53 | - | - |
| Association of Christian Schools Intl. (ACSI) | 1998 | - | - | 1 | - | - |
| Awana Clubs International | 1982 | - | - | - | 9 | - |
| Back to the Bible International | 1957 | - | - | - | 18 | - |
| Baptist Bible Fellowship International | 1948 | 6 | - | 46 | - | - |
| Baptist General Conference— Intl. Ministries | 1949 | - | - | 23 | - | - |
| Baptist International Missions, Inc. (BIMI) | | - | - | 35 | - | - |
| Baptist International Outreach | 1998 | - | - | 2 | 5 | - |
| BCM International | | - | - | - | 13 | - |
| Bethany International Ministries | 1982 | - | - | 6 | - | - |
| Brethren Assemblies | | - | - | 14 | - | - |
| Bright Hope International | 2004 | - | - | - | 3 | - |
| Cadence International | | - | 2 | - | 1 | 1 |
| Calvary International | 1990 | - | 1 | 13 | 8 | - |
| Campus Crusade for Christ, Intl. | 1965 | - | - | 21 | 148 | - |
| Child Evangelism Fellowship, Inc. | 1952 | - | - | - | 15 | - |
| Childcare Worldwide | 1996 | - | - | - | - | - |
| Christ Community Church | 1947 | - | - | - | 87 | - |
| Christ to the Nations | 1992 | - | - | - | 6 | - |
| Christar | 1951 | - | - | 17 | - | 4 |
| Christian Aid Mission | | - | - | - | 216 | - |
| Christian Aviation and Radio Mission | 1995 | - | - | - | 4 | - |
| Christian Blind Mission International | 1982 | 1 | - | - | - | - |
| Christian Broadcasting Network Inc., the | 1976 | - | - | - | 129 | - |
| Christian Churches / Churches of Christ | | - | - | 40 | 10 | - |
| Christian Cultural Development Foundation | 1985 | - | - | 2 | 4 | 2 |
| Christian Literature International | | - | - | - | - | - |
| Christian Reformed World Missions | 1961 | - | 2 | 10 | - | - |
| Christian Reformed World Relief Committee | 1970 | - | - | - | 1 | - |

| | Personnel from U.S. | | | | Other Countries | |
|---|---|---|---|---|---|---|
| | First Year | 1-2 yrs. | 2-4 yrs. | 4+ yrs. | Citizens | Non-Citizens |
| Christians In Action Missions International | 1979 | - | - | - | 7 | - |
| Christ's Mandate for Missions | 1995 | - | - | - | 75 | - |
| Church of God (Cleveland, TN) World Missions | 1947 | - | - | 16 | - | 8 |
| Church of God of Prophecy—Global Outreach | | - | - | - | 6 | - |
| Church of the Nazarene, World Mission Dept. | 1946 | - | - | 22 | - | 2 |
| Churches of Christ | 1928 | - | - | 20 | 16 | - |
| Commission to Every Nation | 1997 | - | - | 2 | - | - |
| Compassion International, Inc. | 1972 | - | - | - | 36 | - |
| CrossWorld | 1985 | - | - | 5 | - | - |
| David Livingstone KURE Foundation | | - | - | - | 42 | - |
| EFCA International Mission | 1951 | 2 | - | 14 | 3 | - |
| Elim Fellowship—International Department | 1997 | - | - | 1 | - | 1 |
| Emmanuel International Mission | 1985 | - | - | 1 | 4 | 1 |
| Evangelical Friends Mission | 1978 | - | - | - | 2 | - |
| Far East Broadcasting Company, Inc. | 1948 | - | - | 7 | 200 | - |
| Food for the Hungry, Inc. | 1982 | - | 3 | 1 | - | - |
| Free Gospel Church, Inc.—Missions Department | 1920 | - | 2 | - | 40 | - |
| Free Methodist World Missions | 1949 | - | - | 6 | - | - |
| General Baptists International | 1957 | - | - | 6 | - | - |
| Global Outreach International | 2000 | - | - | 2 | - | - |
| Global Partners / Wesleyan World Missions | 1932 | - | 4 | - | - | - |
| Globe Missionary Evangelism | 1986 | - | - | 2 | - | - |
| Good News Productions International | 1995 | - | - | 1 | 4 | - |
| Gospel Communications International, Inc. | 1980 | - | - | - | 5 | - |
| Gospel Fellowship Association | 1978 | 4 | - | 14 | - | - |
| Gospel Revival Ministries | | - | - | 1 | - | - |
| Grace Brethren International Missions | 1984 | - | - | 6 | - | 4 |
| Great Commission Ministries, Inc. | | - | - | - | 1 | - |
| Greater Grace World Outreach | 1997 | - | - | 1 | 2 | - |
| Habitat for Humanity International | 1986 | - | 4 | - | 3 | 1 |
| Harvest | 2001 | - | - | - | 2 | - |
| Help for Christian Nationals, Inc. | 2000 | - | - | - | - | 2 |
| I. N. Network USA | 1977 | - | - | - | 71 | - |
| Independent Faith Mission, Inc. | | - | - | 2 | - | - |
| International Gospel Outreach | 1999 | - | - | 2 | 4 | - |
| International Justice Mission | 2000 | - | - | - | 25 | - |
| International Partnership Ministries, Inc. | 2001 | - | - | - | 19 | - |
| Intl. Pentecostal Ch. of Christ—Global Msns. Dept. | 1992 | - | - | 1 | - | 1 |
| Intl. Pentecostal Holiness Ch. World Missions Mins. | 1975 | - | - | 6 | - | - |
| International Teams, U.S.A. | 1981 | - | 4 | 2 | 32 | 152 |
| Larry Jones Intl. Ministries (Feed the Children) | 1985 | - | - | - | 16 | - |
| Literacy & Evangelism International | 1999 | - | - | 2 | - | - |
| Medical Ambassadors International, Inc. | 1975 | - | - | - | 38 | - |
| Medical Missions Philippines, Inc. | | - | - | - | - | - |
| Mennonite Mission Network | 1998 | - | - | - | - | - |
| Mission Ministries, Inc. | 1980 | - | - | 1 | 41 | - |
| Mission to the World (PCA), Inc. | 1991 | 2 | 14 | - | - | - |
| Mission To Unreached Peoples | 1987 | - | - | 4 | 2 | - |
| Missionary Ventures International | 2000 | - | - | 2 | 4 | - |
| Mutual Faith Ministries Intl. | | - | - | - | - | - |

| | | Personnel from U.S. | | | Other Countries | |
|---|---|---|---|---|---|---|
| | First Year | 1-2 yrs. | 2-4 yrs. | 4+ yrs. | Citizens | Non-Citizens |
| Navigators, U.S. International Missions Group | | - | - | 10 | - | - |
| New Life Advance International | 2000 | 1 | - | - | - | - |
| New Tribes Mission | 1951 | - | - | 100 | - | - |
| OC International, Inc. | 1952 | - | - | 18 | - | - |
| OMF International | 1950 | - | - | 15 | 20 | 59 |
| OMS International, Inc. | 1982 | - | - | 6 | - | 1 |
| Partners International | 1968 | - | - | - | 26 | - |
| Pass the Torch Ministries | 2002 | - | - | 1 | 3 | - |
| Pentecostal Church of God—World Missions Dept. | | - | - | 6 | - | - |
| Pentecostal Free Will Baptist Church, Inc. | | - | - | 2 | - | - |
| Precept Ministries International | 1996 | - | - | - | 2 | - |
| Presbyterian Mission International (PMI) | 2000 | - | - | - | 1 | - |
| Reach Ministries International | 1968 | - | - | 6 | - | - |
| Ripe for Harvest, Inc. | 2000 | - | - | 1 | - | - |
| Seed International | 2003 | - | - | 1 | - | - |
| SEND International USA | 1947 | - | - | 29 | - | 10 |
| Seventh-day Adventists General Conference | 1906 | - | - | 26 | - | 27 |
| Source of Light Ministries International, Inc. | 1980 | - | - | - | 3 | - |
| Sowers International, The | 1993 | - | - | - | 8 | - |
| TEAM (The Evangelical Alliance Mission) | | - | - | 12 | - | - |
| Team Expansion, Inc. | | 1 | - | 4 | - | - |
| Teen Missions International, Inc. | 1982 | - | - | - | 6 | - |
| Tentmakers International | | - | - | - | - | - |
| The Brethren Church, Inc. | 2004 | - | - | - | 4 | - |
| The Mission Society | 1988 | - | - | 2 | - | - |
| The Waray-Waray Project | 1992 | - | - | - | 12 | - |
| Things To Come Mission, Inc. | 1958 | - | - | - | 300 | - |
| Training Evangelistic Leadership (T.E.L.), Inc. | 1977 | - | - | 7 | 9 | 1 |
| U.S. Center for World Mission | | 2 | - | 3 | - | 2 |
| United Church of Christ—Wider Church Ministries | | - | 4 | - | - | - |
| United Pentecostal Ch. Intl., Foreign Missions Div. | 1957 | - | 8 | - | - | 5 |
| Walk Thru the Bible Ministries, Inc. | 2000 | - | - | - | 68 | - |
| White Fields Inc. | | - | - | - | 22 | - |
| Word of Life Fellowship, Inc.—Intl. Ministries | 1973 | - | - | 9 | 61 | - |
| World Help | 1998 | - | - | - | - | - |
| World Indigenous Missions | 1987 | - | - | 4 | - | - |
| World Mission Prayer League | 1984 | - | - | 5 | - | - |
| World Missions Far Corners, Inc. | 1976 | - | - | 2 | 20 | - |
| World Team | 1981 | - | - | 13 | - | 6 |
| World Venture | 1948 | - | 6 | 28 | 3 | - |
| World-Wide Missions | 1971 | - | - | - | 1 | - |
| Wycliffe Bible Translators, Inc. | 1960 | - | - | 220 | - | - |
| Youth for Christ/USA—World Outreach | | - | - | 1 | - | - |
| **Totals:** | | 38 | 54 | 1001 | 2293 | 298 |

## Poland

| | | | | | | - |
|---|---|---|---|---|---|---|
| Assemblies of God World Missions | 1925 | - | - | 8 | - | - |
| Association of Free Lutheran Congregations | 1994 | - | - | 2 | - | - |
| Avant Ministries | 2004 | - | - | 8 | - | 1 |
| Back to the Bible International | 1993 | - | - | - | 5 | - |

| | First Year | Personnel from U.S. | | | Other Countries | |
| --- | --- | --- | --- | --- | --- | --- |
| | | 1-2 yrs. | 2-4 yrs. | 4+ yrs. | Citizens | Non-Citizens |
| Baptist Bible Fellowship International | 2001 | - | - | 2 | - | - |
| Baptist International Missions, Inc. (BIMI) | | - | - | 2 | - | - |
| BCM International | | - | - | 1 | 1 | - |
| Brethren Assemblies | | - | - | 6 | - | - |
| Campus Crusade for Christ, Intl. | 1977 | 2 | - | - | 97 | - |
| Child Evangelism Fellowship, Inc. | 1989 | - | - | - | 2 | - |
| Christian Associates International | | - | - | - | - | - |
| Christian Churches / Churches of Christ | | - | - | 2 | 60 | - |
| Church of the Nazarene, World Mission Dept. | 1999 | - | - | - | - | - |
| Church Resource Ministries (CRM) | 1995 | - | - | 2 | - | - |
| Churches of Christ | 1983 | - | - | 4 | 6 | - |
| Commission to Every Nation | 1999 | - | - | 2 | - | - |
| EFCA International Mission | 1993 | - | - | 4 | - | - |
| Elim Fellowship—International Department | 1997 | - | - | 1 | 1 | - |
| Envoy International | | - | - | - | - | - |
| European Christian Mission International—USA | | - | - | 4 | - | - |
| Fellowship International Mission | 1991 | - | - | 1 | - | - |
| Friends of Israel Gospel Ministry, Inc. | 1961 | - | - | - | 8 | - |
| Global Outreach International | 1997 | - | - | 2 | - | - |
| Great Commission Ministries, Inc. | 2002 | - | - | 2 | 1 | - |
| Greater Europe Mission | 1993 | - | - | 4 | - | - |
| Greater Grace World Outreach | 1985 | - | - | - | 6 | - |
| In Touch Mission International | 1984 | - | - | 7 | 28 | - |
| International Messengers | 1991 | - | - | 12 | 15 | 1 |
| Literacy & Evangelism International | | - | - | - | - | - |
| Lutheran Church-Missouri Synod, | 1943 | - | - | 3 | - | - |
| Mission To Unreached Peoples | 1989 | - | - | 4 | - | - |
| Pioneers USA | | - | - | 4 | - | - |
| Ripe for Harvest, Inc. | 2000 | - | 1 | 1 | - | - |
| SEND International USA | 1991 | - | - | 10 | - | 4 |
| TCM International Institute | | - | - | - | 1 | - |
| Team Expansion, Inc. | | - | 2 | - | - | - |
| United Pentecostal Ch. Intl., Foreign Missions Div. | | - | 2 | - | - | 3 |
| Word of Life Fellowship, Inc.—Intl. Ministries | 1987 | - | - | 1 | - | 1 |
| World Venture | 1988 | - | - | 9 | - | - |
| Worldwide Tentmakers, Inc. | 1990 | - | - | - | - | - |
| | Totals: | 2 | 5 | 108 | 231 | 10 |

## Portugal

| | First Year | | | | | |
| --- | --- | --- | --- | --- | --- | --- |
| Abundant Life Association, Inc. | 1989 | - | - | - | 60 | - |
| Assemblies of God World Missions | 1972 | - | - | 9 | - | - |
| Baptist Bible Fellowship International | 1987 | - | - | 10 | - | - |
| BCM International | | - | - | - | 2 | - |
| BILD International | | - | - | - | - | - |
| Brethren Assemblies | | - | - | 3 | - | - |
| Campus Crusade for Christ, Intl. | 1975 | - | - | - | - | 6 |
| Christian Associates International | 1997 | - | - | - | - | - |
| Christian Churches / Churches of Christ | | - | - | 4 | - | - |
| Church of God of Prophecy—Global Outreach | | - | - | - | 1 | - |
| Church of the Nazarene, World Mission Dept. | 1973 | - | - | 3 | - | 1 |

| | Personnel from U.S. | | | Other Countries | |
|---|---|---|---|---|---|
| First Year | 1-2 yrs. | 2-4 yrs. | 4+ yrs. | Citizens | Non-Citizens |
| Church Planting International | 1989 | - | - | - | 1 | - |
| Churches of Christ | 1969 | - | - | 2 | 4 | - |
| CLC Ministries International | | - | - | 2 | - | - |
| EFCA International Mission | 1994 | - | - | 4 | - | - |
| European Christian Mission International - USA | | - | - | 15 | - | - |
| Grace Brethren International Missions | 1990 | - | - | 5 | - | 2 |
| Greater Europe Mission | 1971 | - | - | 13 | - | - |
| Greater Grace World Outreach | 1999 | - | - | 1 | - | - |
| Intl. Pentecostal Holiness Ch. World Missions Mins. | 2001 | - | - | 2 | - | - |
| Missionary Revival Crusade | | - | - | - | - | - |
| Salvation Army, U.S.A. | 1971 | - | - | 1 | - | - |
| TEAM (The Evangelical Alliance Mission) | | - | - | 8 | - | - |
| United Pentecostal Ch. Intl., Foreign Missions Div. | 1972 | - | 4 | - | - | - |
| Word of Life Fellowship, Inc.—Intl.Ministries | 1976 | - | - | 3 | 7 | 1 |
| World Baptist Fellowship Mission Agency, Inc. | | 1 | - | 2 | - | - |
| World Partners USA | 1991 | - | - | 2 | - | - |
| World Venture | 1945 | - | - | 4 | - | - |
| Youth for Christ/USA—World Outreach | 1996 | - | - | 2 | - | - |
| Totals: | | 1 | 4 | 95 | 75 | 10 |

**Puerto Rico**                                                                                                                     -

| | First Year | 1-2 yrs. | 2-4 yrs. | 4+ yrs. | Citizens | Non-Citizens |
|---|---|---|---|---|---|---|
| Apostolic Christian Church Foundation, Inc. | 1996 | - | - | 2 | - | 4 |
| Baptist Bible Fellowship International | 1955 | - | - | 5 | - | - |
| Baptist International Missions, Inc. (BIMI) | | - | - | 13 | - | - |
| Baptist Mid-Missions | 1959 | - | - | 2 | - | - |
| Biblical Ministries Worldwide | 1986 | - | - | 2 | - | 2 |
| Brethren Assemblies | | - | - | 2 | - | - |
| Christian Churches / Churches of Christ | | - | - | 5 | 5 | - |
| Church of the Nazarene, World Mission Dept. | 1944 | - | - | 1 | - | 1 |
| Foursquare Missions International | | - | - | 2 | - | - |
| Global Partners / Wesleyan World Missions | 1952 | - | 2 | - | - | - |
| Gospel Fellowship Association | 1963 | - | - | 4 | - | - |
| Grace Ministries International | 1961 | - | 8 | - | - | - |
| International Partnership Ministries, Inc. | 2000 | - | - | - | 2 | - |
| Lutheran Church-Missouri Synod | 1993 | - | - | 8 | - | - |
| Macedonia World Baptist Missions, Inc. | 1991 | - | - | 6 | - | - |
| Ministries In Action | 2005 | - | - | 2 | - | - |
| Open Door Baptist Missions | 1995 | - | - | 2 | - | - |
| Pentecostal Free Will Baptist Church, Inc. | | - | - | - | 1 | - |
| Ripe for Harvest, Inc. | 1997 | - | - | 1 | - | - |
| Seventh-day Adventists General Conference | 1901 | - | - | 8 | - | - |
| United Pentecostal Ch. Intl., Foreign Missions Div. | 1964 | - | 2 | - | - | - |
| Wisc. Evangelical Luth. Synod, Bd. for World Msns. | 1963 | - | - | - | - | - |
| Totals: | | - | 12 | 65 | 8 | 7 |

**Qatar**                                                                                                                          -

| | First Year | 1-2 yrs. | 2-4 yrs. | 4+ yrs. | Citizens | Non-Citizens |
|---|---|---|---|---|---|---|
| Arab World Ministries | | - | - | 1 | - | - |
| Walk Thru the Bible Ministries, Inc. | 2003 | - | - | - | - | - |
| Totals: | | - | - | 1 | - | |

| | Personnel from U.S. | | | Other Countries | |
| --- | --- | --- | --- | --- | --- |
| First Year | 1-2 yrs. | 2-4 yrs. | 4+ yrs. | Citizens | Non-Citizens |

**Reunion**

| | | | | | - |
| --- | --- | --- | --- | --- | --- |
| Church of the Nazarene, World Mission Dept. | 2003 | - | - | 1 | - | 1 |
| United Pentecostal Ch. Intl., Foreign Missions Div. | 1999 | - | 2 | - | - | - |
| | Totals: | - | 2 | 1 | - | 1 |

**Romania**

| | First Year | 1-2 yrs. | 2-4 yrs. | 4+ yrs. | Citizens | Non-Citizens |
| --- | --- | --- | --- | --- | --- | --- |
| AMG International | 1992 | - | - | - | 48 | - |
| Assemblies of God World Missions | 1951 | 14 | - | 10 | - | - |
| Awana Clubs International | 1991 | - | - | - | 2 | - |
| Baptist Bible Fellowship International | 1990 | - | - | 9 | - | - |
| Baptist International Evangelistic Ministries | | - | - | - | 16 | - |
| Baptist International Missions, Inc. (BIMI) | | - | - | 12 | - | - |
| Baptist Mid-Missions | 1993 | - | - | 13 | - | - |
| Brethren Assemblies | | - | - | 4 | - | - |
| Calvary Commission, Inc. | 1990 | 3 | 4 | 2 | - | - |
| Campus Crusade for Christ, Intl. | 1980 | 1 | - | 8 | 153 | - |
| Christ to the Nations | 2005 | - | - | - | 1 | - |
| Christian Aid Ministries | | - | 32 | - | 100 | - |
| Christian Aid Mission | | - | - | - | 1 | - |
| Christian Associates International | | - | - | - | - | - |
| Christian Outreach International | 2002 | - | - | - | 1 | 1 |
| Christian Reformed World Relief Committee | 1998 | - | - | - | 3 | - |
| Church of God (Cleveland, TN) World Missions | 1922 | 2 | - | 2 | - | - |
| Church of God of Prophecy—Global Outreach | | - | - | - | 1 | - |
| Church of the Nazarene, World Mission Dept. | 1992 | - | - | 1 | - | - |
| Church Resource Ministries (CRM) | 1990 | - | - | 6 | - | - |
| Churches of Christ | 1964 | 2 | - | 12 | 2 | - |
| Commission to Every Nation | 2001 | - | - | 2 | - | - |
| CrossWorld | 1991 | - | - | 4 | - | - |
| EFCA International Mission | 1991 | - | 6 | 16 | - | - |
| Entrust | 1982 | - | - | 9 | 6 | - |
| Envoy International | | - | - | - | - | - |
| Episcopal Church USA—Domestic & Foreign | | - | - | 1 | - | - |
| European Christian Mission International—USA | | - | - | 5 | - | - |
| Evangelical Baptist Missions | | - | - | 3 | 1 | - |
| Food for the Hungry, Inc. | 1991 | - | 6 | 4 | - | - |
| Free Methodist World Missions | | - | - | 2 | - | - |
| Friendship International Ministries, Inc. | 1995 | 2 | - | 2 | 3 | 1 |
| Global Fellowship Inc. | 2001 | - | - | - | 8 | - |
| Global Outreach International | 1988 | - | - | 14 | 2 | 2 |
| Global Outreach Mission, Inc. | | - | - | - | 3 | - |
| Go Ye Fellowship | 1998 | 1 | - | - | - | - |
| Gospel Communications International, Inc. | 2002 | - | - | - | 2 | - |
| Greater Europe Mission | 1993 | 1 | - | 12 | - | - |
| Greater Grace World Outreach | 1991 | - | - | 1 | 2 | - |
| Harvest International, Inc. | 2000 | - | 4 | - | - | - |
| Heart to Heart Intl. Ministries | 1994 | 2 | 12 | - | 10 | - |
| I. N. Network USA | 1992 | - | - | - | 11 | - |
| In Touch Mission International | 1967 | - | - | - | 6 | - |
| International Gospel Outreach | 2006 | - | - | 2 | - | - |

| | Personnel from U.S. | | | Other Countries | |
| --- | --- | --- | --- | --- | --- |
| | First Year | 1-2 yrs. | 2-4 yrs. | 4+ yrs. | Citizens | Non-Citizens |
| International Institute for Christian Studies | 1991 | - | - | 1 | - | - |
| International Messengers | 1996 | - | - | 7 | 12 | - |
| Intl. Pentecostal Holiness Ch. World Missions Mins. | 1996 | - | - | 2 | - | - |
| International Teams, U.S.A. | | 3 | - | 6 | - | 13 |
| InterVarsity Christian Fellowship/USA—Msns. Dept. | | - | - | 3 | - | - |
| Kids Alive International | 1998 | - | - | - | 6 | - |
| Larry Jones Intl. Ministries (Feed the Children) | 1989 | - | - | - | 5 | - |
| Macedonia World Baptist Missions, Inc. | 2005 | - | - | 2 | - | - |
| Medical Ambassadors International, Inc. | 1992 | - | - | - | 3 | - |
| Ministry to Educate and Equip Intl. (MTEE) | | - | - | - | 1 | - |
| Mission Ministries, Inc. | 2000 | - | - | 1 | 1 | - |
| Mission to the World (PCA), Inc. | 2001 | - | 1 | - | - | - |
| New Hope International | 1971 | - | - | - | 9 | - |
| OC International, Inc. | 1996 | - | - | 11 | - | - |
| Operation Mobilization | | 2 | - | - | - | - |
| Ripe for Harvest, Inc. | 1999 | - | - | 1 | - | - |
| Romanian Missionary Society | 1968 | - | - | - | 70 | - |
| Salvation Army, U.S.A. | | - | - | 1 | - | - |
| Source of Light Ministries International, Inc. | 1992 | - | - | - | 2 | - |
| TCM International Institute | | - | - | - | 1 | - |
| The Master's Mission, Inc. | 1999 | - | - | 2 | 2 | - |
| TITUS International | 1999 | - | - | 5 | 20 | - |
| United Pentecostal Ch. Intl., Foreign Missions Div. | 1995 | - | 2 | - | - | 1 |
| Walk Thru the Bible Ministries, Inc. | 2000 | - | - | - | 2 | - |
| Word of Life Fellowship, Inc.— Intl. Ministries | 1993 | - | - | 1 | 16 | 1 |
| World Bible Translation Center | | - | - | - | 2 | - |
| World Harvest Mission | 2003 | - | - | 2 | - | - |
| World Help | 1991 | - | - | - | - | - |
| World Indigenous Missions | 1999 | - | - | 2 | - | - |
| World Link Ministries | 2003 | - | - | - | 30 | - |
| World Mission Prayer League | 1994 | - | - | 2 | - | - |
| World Missions & Evangelism, Inc. | | - | - | 2 | - | - |
| World Reach, Inc. | 1998 | - | - | - | - | 2 |
| World Venture | 1991 | - | - | 6 | - | - |
| Totals: | | 33 | 67 | 213 | 564 | 21 |

## Russia

| | First Year | 1-2 yrs. | 2-4 yrs. | 4+ yrs. | Citizens | Non-Citizens |
| --- | --- | --- | --- | --- | --- | --- |
| Artists In Christian Testimony | 2001 | - | - | 1 | - | - |
| Assemblies of God World Missions | 1990 | 7 | - | 41 | - | - |
| Avant Ministries | 1993 | - | - | 2 | 1 | - |
| Awana Clubs International | 1995 | - | - | - | 14 | - |
| Back to the Bible International | 1995 | - | - | - | 10 | - |
| Baptist Bible Fellowship International | 1993 | - | - | 22 | - | - |
| Baptist International Evangelistic Ministries | | - | - | 3 | 40 | 2 |
| Baptist International Missions, Inc. (BIMI) | | - | - | 16 | - | - |
| Baptist International Outreach | | - | - | - | - | - |
| Baptist Mid-Missions | 1992 | - | - | 4 | - | - |
| BCM International | | - | - | 1 | 2 | - |
| Cadence International | | - | 25 | - | 21 | 4 |
| Calvary International | 1992 | - | - | 2 | - | - |

| | First Year | Personnel from U.S. | | | Other Countries | |
|---|---|---|---|---|---|---|
| | | 1-2 yrs. | 2-4 yrs. | 4+ yrs. | Citizens | Non-Citizens |
| Campus Crusade for Christ, Intl. | 1991 | 36 | - | 65 | 160 | 34 |
| Centers for Apologetics Research (CFAR), the | 1993 | - | - | - | 6 | - |
| Child Evangelism Fellowship, Inc. | 1989 | - | - | - | 2 | 2 |
| Children's HopeChest | 1994 | - | - | 1 | 90 | - |
| Christ to the Nations | 1991 | - | - | - | 2 | - |
| Christar | 1994 | - | - | 1 | - | - |
| Christian Aid Mission | | - | - | - | 59 | - |
| Christian Associates International | 1993 | - | - | - | - | - |
| Christian Broadcasting Network Inc., the | 1992 | - | - | - | 8 | - |
| Christian Churches / Churches of Christ | | 2 | 4 | 16 | 6 | - |
| Christian Ministries International (CMI) | 1998 | - | - | - | 1 | - |
| Christian Reformed World Missions | 1994 | - | - | 1 | - | - |
| Ch. of God (Anderson, Ind.), Global Missions | 1994 | 1 | - | 2 | - | - |
| Church of God (Cleveland, TN) World Missions | 1992 | - | - | 6 | - | 2 |
| Church of God of Prophecy—Global Outreach | | - | - | - | 3 | 2 |
| Church of the Nazarene, World Mission Dept. | 1992 | - | - | 7 | - | - |
| Church Resource Ministries (CRM) | 1990 | - | - | 12 | - | - |
| Churches of Christ | 1952 | 2 | - | 12 | 20 | - |
| CLC Ministries International | | - | - | 2 | - | - |
| Development Associates International (DAI) | 2001 | - | - | - | 1 | - |
| Eastern European Outreach, Inc. | 1990 | - | - | - | 6 | 1 |
| East-West Ministries International | 1993 | - | - | 10 | 50 | - |
| EFCA International Mission | 1993 | 2 | 2 | 16 | 10 | - |
| Entrust | 1991 | - | - | 13 | 1 | - |
| Evangelical Baptist Missions | | - | - | 1 | - | - |
| Evangelical Covenant Ch.—Covenant Wld. Msn. | 1993 | - | - | 2 | - | - |
| Evangelical Lutheran Ch. in Am., Div. for Global Msn. | 1994 | 1 | - | 1 | - | - |
| Evangelism Explosion International | | - | - | - | - | 10 |
| Far East Broadcasting Company, Inc. | 1992 | - | - | - | 50 | - |
| Free Will Baptist, Inc. Board of Intl. Missions | 1999 | - | - | 2 | - | - |
| Friends of Israel Gospel Ministry, Inc. | 1994 | - | - | | 4 | - |
| Full Gospel Evangelistic Association | 2002 | - | 2 | | - | - |
| Global Outreach Mission, Inc. | | - | - | 3 | 4 | - |
| Global Partners / Wesleyan World Missions | 1993 | - | 8 | - | - | - |
| Globe Missionary Evangelism | 1995 | - | - | 2 | - | - |
| Gospelink, Inc. | | - | - | - | 21 | - |
| Grace Brethren International Missions | 2003 | - | 4 | - | - | - |
| Greater Europe Mission | 1995 | - | - | 1 | - | - |
| Greater Grace World Outreach | 1990 | - | - | 1 | 9 | 7 |
| HCJB Global | 1941 | - | - | 2 | - | - |
| Help for Christian Nationals, Inc. | 1996 | - | - | - | 2 | - |
| InterAct Ministries | 1989 | - | - | 9 | - | - |
| International Gospel Outreach | 1995 | - | - | 4 | - | - |
| International Teams, U.S.A. | | - | - | 4 | - | 5 |
| InterVarsity Christian Fellowship/USA—Msns. Dept. | | - | - | 6 | - | - |
| Jews for Jesus | 1993 | - | - | - | 4 | - |
| Larry Jones Intl. Ministries (Feed the Children) | 1992 | - | - | - | 17 | 1 |
| Luth. Ch.-Missouri Synod, Bd. for Msn. Svcs. | 1992 | - | - | 5 | - | - |
| Macedonia World Baptist Missions, Inc. | 2006 | - | - | 1 | - | - |
| Medical Ambassadors International, Inc. | 2004 | - | - | - | 2 | - |

| | First Year | Personnel from U.S. 1-2 yrs. | 2-4 yrs. | 4+ yrs. | Other Countries Citizens | Non-Citizens |
|---|---|---|---|---|---|---|
| Mennonite Mission Network | 1993 | - | - | 2 | - | - |
| Mission Aviation Fellowship | 1993 | - | - | 1 | - | - |
| Mission Possible Foundation, Inc. | 1990 | - | - | - | 28 | - |
| Mission To Unreached Peoples | 1993 | - | - | 2 | - | - |
| Missionary Revival Crusade | | - | - | - | - | - |
| Missionary Ventures International | 1994 | - | - | - | 2 | - |
| New Mission Systems International | 2002 | - | - | 2 | 3 | - |
| OMS International, Inc. | 1993 | - | 1 | 5 | - | 8 |
| Open Air Campaigners—Overseas Ministries | 2003 | - | 2 | - | 2 | - |
| Operation Mobilization | 1991 | - | 1 | - | - | - |
| Pentecostal Church of God—World Missions Dept. | | - | - | 2 | - | - |
| Perimeter Church, Global Outreach | 1985 | - | - | - | - | - |
| Peter Deyneka Russian Ministries | 1991 | - | - | - | - | - |
| Precept Ministries International | 1994 | - | - | - | 2 | - |
| Presbyterian Evangelistic Fellowship | | - | - | 2 | - | - |
| Ripe for Harvest, Inc. | 1996 | 1 | 1 | 3 | - | - |
| Salvation Army, U.S.A. | 1913 | - | - | 2 | - | - |
| Seed International | 2004 | - | - | 1 | - | - |
| SEND International USA | 1992 | - | - | 30 | - | 14 |
| Seventh-day Adventists General Conference | 1886 | - | - | 5 | - | 14 |
| TCM International Institute | | - | - | - | 1 | - |
| TEAM (The Evangelical Alliance Mission) | | - | - | 10 | - | - |
| The Mission Society | 1995 | 1 | - | 4 | - | - |
| United Pentecostal Ch. Intl., Foreign Missions Div. | 1990 | - | 7 | - | - | 5 |
| VELA Ministries International | 1993 | 1 | - | - | - | - |
| Walk Thru the Bible Ministries, Inc. | 2000 | - | - | - | 21 | - |
| WEC International | | - | - | 3 | - | - |
| White Fields Inc. | | - | - | - | 2 | - |
| Wisc. Evangelical Luth. Synod, Bd. for World Msns. | 1991 | - | - | 4 | - | - |
| Word To Russia | | - | - | 5 | 5 | - |
| World Bible Translation Center | | - | - | - | 2 | - |
| World Harvest Now, Inc. | | - | 4 | - | 3 | - |
| World Help | 1991 | - | - | - | - | - |
| World Indigenous Missions | 1995 | - | - | 2 | - | - |
| World Partners USA | 1994 | 1 | - | 8 | - | - |
| World Venture | 1992 | - | - | 12 | 2 | - |
| World Witness, Assoc. Reformed Presbyterian Ch. | 1991 | - | - | 10 | 8 | - |
| World-Wide Missions | | - | - | - | 1 | - |
| Young Life | | - | - | 1 | - | - |
| **Totals:** | | **55** | **61** | **416** | **708** | **111** |

## Rwanda

| | | | | | - | - |
|---|---|---|---|---|---|---|
| Africa Inland Mission International | | - | - | - | - | 4 |
| African Enterprise | 1988 | - | - | - | 10 | - |
| African Leadership, Inc. | 1998 | - | - | - | 1 | - |
| Assemblies of God World Missions | 1993 | - | - | 8 | - | - |
| Campus Crusade for Christ, Intl. | 1980 | - | - | - | 30 | - |
| Church of God of Prophecy—Global Outreach | | - | - | - | 6 | - |
| Church of the Nazarene, World Mission Dept. | 1990 | - | - | - | - | - |
| Compassion International, Inc. | 1980 | - | - | - | 30 | - |

| | | Personnel from U.S. | | | Other Countries | |
|---|---|---|---|---|---|---|
| | First Year | 1-2 yrs. | 2-4 yrs. | 4+ yrs. | Citizens | Non-Citizens |
| EFCA International Mission | 1994 | - | - | - | - | - |
| Episcopal Church USA—Domestic & Foreign | | - | - | 2 | - | - |
| Evangelical Friends Mission | 1986 | - | - | 2 | - | - |
| Food for the Hungry, Inc. | 1994 | - | - | - | - | - |
| Foursquare Missions International | 2005 | - | - | 2 | - | - |
| Free Methodist World Missions | 1942 | - | - | 1 | - | 1 |
| Global Outreach International | 1994 | - | - | 2 | - | - |
| Greater Grace World Outreach | 2004 | - | - | - | 15 | - |
| Harvest | 2000 | - | - | - | 2 | - |
| International Gospel Outreach | 1999 | - | - | 1 | - | - |
| Intl. Pentecostal Holiness Ch. World Missions Mins. | | - | - | - | - | - |
| International Teams, U.S.A. | | - | - | - | - | 2 |
| Seventh-day Adventists General Conference | 1920 | - | - | 4 | - | 10 |
| United Pentecostal Ch. Intl., Foreign Missions Div. | 1999 | - | 2 | - | - | - |
| World Concern | 1995 | - | - | - | 2 | - |
| World Relief | 1994 | 3 | 2 | 1 | 165 | 1 |
| World Venture | 1965 | - | 1 | 6 | - | - |
| Youth for Christ/USA—World Outreach | | - | - | 4 | - | - |
| Totals: | | 3 | 5 | 33 | 261 | 18 |

## Saint Kitts and Nevis

| | | | | | | |
|---|---|---|---|---|---|---|
| Baptist International Missions, Inc. (BIMI) | | - | - | 2 | - | - |
| Church of the Nazarene, World Mission Dept. | 1983 | - | - | - | - | - |
| Totals: | | - | - | 2 | - | - |

## Saint Lucia

| | | | | | | |
|---|---|---|---|---|---|---|
| Assemblies of God World Missions | 1996 | - | - | 2 | - | - |
| Church of the Nazarene, World Mission Dept. | 1972 | - | - | - | - | - |
| Macedonia World Baptist Missions, Inc. | 1994 | - | - | 6 | - | - |
| Ministries In Action | 2005 | - | - | - | - | - |
| Totals: | | - | - | 8 | - | - |

## Saint Martin

| | | | | | | |
|---|---|---|---|---|---|---|
| Ministries In Action | 2003 | - | - | - | - | - |
| Totals: | | - | - | - | - | - |

## Saint Vincent and the Grenadines

| | | | | | | |
|---|---|---|---|---|---|---|
| Baptist Mid-Missions | 1946 | - | - | 6 | - | - |
| BCM International | | - | - | - | 1 | - |
| Church of the Nazarene, World Mission Dept. | 1975 | - | - | - | - | - |
| Ministries In Action | 1974 | - | - | - | 2 | - |
| Seventh-day Adventists General Conference | | - | - | 2 | - | - |
| World Team | 1949 | - | - | 2 | - | - |
| Totals: | | - | - | 10 | 3 | - |

## Samoa

| | | | | | | |
|---|---|---|---|---|---|---|
| Church of God of Prophecy—Global Outreach | | - | - | 2 | - | - |
| Church of the Nazarene, World Mission Dept. | 1964 | - | - | - | - | - |
| United Pentecostal Ch. Intl., Foreign Msn. Div. | 1999 | - | 2 | - | - | - |
| Totals: | | - | 2 | 2 | - | - |

| | First Year | 1-2 yrs. | 2-4 yrs. | 4+ yrs. | Citizens | Non-Citizens |
|---|---|---|---|---|---|---|
| | | Personnel from U.S. | | | Other Countries | |

**Sao Tome and Principe**

| | First Year | 1-2 yrs. | 2-4 yrs. | 4+ yrs. | Citizens | Non-Citizens |
|---|---|---|---|---|---|---|
| Abundant Life Association, Inc. | 1990 | - | - | - | 1 | - |
| Church of the Nazarene, World Mission Dept. | 1997 | - | - | 2 | - | - |
| Seventh-day Adventists General Conference | | - | - | - | - | 2 |
| Totals: | | - | - | 2 | 1 | 2 |

**Saudi Arabia**

| | First Year | 1-2 yrs. | 2-4 yrs. | 4+ yrs. | Citizens | Non-Citizens |
|---|---|---|---|---|---|---|
| Walk Thru the Bible Ministries, Inc. | 2003 | - | - | - | - | - |
| Totals: | | - | - | - | - | - |

**Senegal**

| | First Year | 1-2 yrs. | 2-4 yrs. | 4+ yrs. | Citizens | Non-Citizens |
|---|---|---|---|---|---|---|
| Africa Inter-Mennonite Mission | 1996 | 5 | 2 | - | - | - |
| Assemblies of God World Missions | 1956 | - | - | 7 | - | - |
| Baptist General Conference—Intl. Ministries | | - | - | 6 | - | - |
| Baptist International Missions, Inc. (BIMI) | | - | - | 4 | - | - |
| Brethren Assemblies | | - | - | 5 | - | - |
| Campus Crusade for Christ, Intl. | 1985 | - | - | 1 | 20 | - |
| Christian Aid Mission | | - | - | - | 6 | - |
| Christian Broadcasting Network Inc., the | 2004 | - | - | 2 | 1 | - |
| Christian Reformed World Relief Committee | 1991 | - | - | 1 | - | - |
| Church of God of Prophecy—Global Outreach | | - | - | - | 1 | - |
| Church of the Nazarene, World Mission Dept. | 1988 | - | - | 2 | - | - |
| Evangelical Lutheran Ch. in Am., Div. for Global Msn. | 1976 | - | - | 7 | - | 3 |
| Fellowship International Mission | 2000 | - | - | 2 | - | - |
| Habitat for Humanity International | 2003 | - | 1 | - | - | 1 |
| International Gospel Outreach | 1988 | - | - | 1 | 2 | - |
| Mennonite Mission Network | 1996 | - | - | 7 | - | - |
| Mission to the World (PCA), Inc. | 1992 | - | 7 | - | - | - |
| Mission: Moving Mountains, Inc. | 1995 | - | - | 10 | - | 2 |
| New Tribes Mission | 1954 | - | - | 60 | - | - |
| Open Door Baptist Missions | 1998 | - | - | 2 | - | - |
| Partners International | 2001 | - | - | - | 8 | - |
| Pioneers USA | 1991 | - | - | 5 | - | - |
| Reformed Church in Am., Gen. Synod Council | 2002 | - | - | - | 2 | - |
| Seventh-day Adventists General Conference | 1952 | - | - | - | - | 2 |
| SIM USA | 1984 | - | - | 13 | - | - |
| WEC International | 1936 | - | - | 1 | - | - |
| World Venture | 1962 | - | 2 | 23 | 2 | - |
| Totals: | | 5 | 12 | 159 | 42 | 8 |

**Serbia and Montenegro**

| | First Year | 1-2 yrs. | 2-4 yrs. | 4+ yrs. | Citizens | Non-Citizens |
|---|---|---|---|---|---|---|
| Assemblies of God World Missions | 1993 | - | - | 4 | - | - |
| Brethren Assemblies | | - | - | 2 | - | - |
| Campus Crusade for Christ, Intl. | 1979 | - | - | - | 15 | 6 |
| Child Evangelism Fellowship, Inc. | 1989 | - | - | 2 | 4 | - |
| Churches of Christ | 1969 | - | 4 | 2 | 2 | - |
| CrossWorld | | - | - | 5 | - | - |
| Envoy International | | - | - | - | - | - |
| European Christian Mission International—USA | | - | - | 2 | - | - |

| | First Year | Personnel from U.S. | | | Other Countries | |
|---|---|---|---|---|---|---|
| | | 1-2 yrs. | 2-4 yrs. | 4+ yrs. | Citizens | Non-Citizens |
| Global Action | 1999 | - | - | - | - | 1 |
| Greater Europe Mission | | - | - | 2 | - | - |
| New Mission Systems International | | - | - | 2 | - | - |
| Precept Ministries International | 1994 | - | - | - | 2 | - |
| TMA Ministries | 1997 | 2 | - | - | - | - |
| United Pentecostal Ch. Intl., Foreign Missions Div. | | - | 1 | - | - | - |
| Walk Thru the Bible Ministries, Inc. | 2002 | - | - | - | - | - |
| World Bible Translation Center | | | | | 2 | - |
| | Totals: | 2 | 5 | 21 | 25 | 7 |

### Seychelles

| | First Year | 1-2 yrs. | 2-4 yrs. | 4+ yrs. | Citizens | Non-Citizens |
|---|---|---|---|---|---|---|
| Intl. Pentecostal Holiness Ch. World Missions Mins. | | - | - | - | - | - |
| United Pentecostal Ch. Intl., Foreign Missions Div. | 1988 | - | 2 | - | - | - |
| | Totals: | - | 2 | - | - | - |

### Sierra Leone

| | First Year | 1-2 yrs. | 2-4 yrs. | 4+ yrs. | Citizens | Non-Citizens |
|---|---|---|---|---|---|---|
| African Leadership, Inc. | 1998 | - | - | - | 1 | - |
| Assemblies of God World Missions | 1920 | - | - | 4 | - | - |
| Brethren Assemblies | | - | - | 2 | - | - |
| Campus Crusade for Christ, Intl. | 1981 | - | - | - | 27 | - |
| Christian Aid Mission | | - | - | - | 3 | - |
| Christian Reformed World Relief Committee | 1979 | - | - | - | - | - |
| Christians In Action Missions International | 1969 | - | - | - | 33 | - |
| Church of God of Prophecy—Global Outreach | | - | - | - | 8 | - |
| Church of the Nazarene, World Mission Dept. | 2004 | - | - | 2 | - | - |
| CityTeam Ministries | | - | - | - | 2 | - |
| Free Gospel Church, Inc.—Missions Department | 1928 | - | - | - | 15 | - |
| Global Fellowship Inc. | 1986 | - | - | - | 5 | - |
| Global Partners / Wesleyan World Missions | 1889 | - | - | - | - | - |
| International Christian Ministries | 2001 | - | - | - | 2 | 1 |
| International Gospel Outreach | 1988 | - | - | 1 | 2 | - |
| Intl. Pentecostal Holiness Ch. World Missions Mins. | | - | - | - | - | - |
| Lutheran Bible Translators, Inc. | 1974 | - | - | - | 24 | - |
| Medical Ambassadors International, Inc. | 2001 | - | - | - | 1 | - |
| Natl. Baptist Conv. USA, Inc.—Foreign Msn. Bd. | 1950 | - | - | - | 2 | - |
| Seventh-day Adventists General Conference | 1905 | - | - | - | - | 2 |
| United Pentecostal Ch. Intl., Foreign Missions Div. | 1975 | - | 2 | - | - | - |
| Walk Thru the Bible Ministries, Inc. | 2001 | - | - | - | - | - |
| World Partners USA | 1945 | - | - | 1 | - | - |
| World Relief | 1994 | 1 | 1 | - | 27 | 1 |
| World Venture | 2005 | - | - | 2 | 2 | - |
| World Vision Inc. | 1978 | - | - | - | - | - |
| | Totals: | 1 | 3 | 12 | 154 | 4 |

### Singapore

| | First Year | 1-2 yrs. | 2-4 yrs. | 4+ yrs. | Citizens | Non-Citizens |
|---|---|---|---|---|---|---|
| Asian Outreach U.S.A. | | - | - | - | - | - |
| Assemblies of God World Missions | 1926 | - | - | 10 | - | - |
| Awana Clubs International | 1984 | - | - | - | 1 | - |
| Baptist Bible Fellowship International | 1970 | - | - | 4 | - | - |
| Baptist General Conference—Intl. Ministries | | - | - | 2 | - | - |

| | | Personnel from U.S. | | | Other Countries | |
|---|---|---|---|---|---|---|
| | First Year | 1-2 yrs. | 2-4 yrs. | 4+ yrs. | Citizens | Non-Citizens |
| Baptist International Missions, Inc. (BIMI) | | - | - | 3 | - | - |
| Campus Crusade for Christ, Intl. | 1969 | - | - | 41 | - | - |
| Child Evangelism Fellowship, Inc. | 1970 | - | - | - | 2 | - |
| Christian Broadcasting Network Inc., the | 1996 | - | - | - | 3 | - |
| Christian Churches / Churches of Christ | | - | - | 4 | - | - |
| Church of God (Cleveland, TN) World Missions | 1989 | - | - | 2 | - | 2 |
| Church Resource Ministries (CRM) | 2000 | - | - | 4 | - | - |
| EFCA International Mission | 1957 | - | - | - | - | - |
| Elim Fellowship—International Department | | 1 | - | - | - | 2 |
| Evangelical Lutheran Ch. in Am., Div. for Global Msn. | 1966 | - | - | 1 | - | - |
| Evangelical Presbyterian Church—World Outreach | 2003 | - | - | 2 | - | - |
| Foursquare Missions International | | - | - | 2 | - | - |
| Good News Productions International | | - | - | 2 | 2 | - |
| Habitat for Humanity International | | - | 15 | 3 | 9 | 9 |
| HCJB Global | 2002 | - | - | 6 | - | 4 |
| International Pentecostal Holiness Church | 1987 | - | - | 6 | - | - |
| International Students, Inc (ISI) | | - | - | 1 | - | - |
| Missionary Ventures International | | - | - | 1 | - | - |
| Network of International Christian Schools | 1993 | - | 23 | 6 | - | 1 |
| New Tribes Mission | 1994 | - | - | 2 | 2 | - |
| OC International, Inc. | 1970 | - | - | 6 | - | - |
| OMF International | 1950 | - | - | 3 | 7 | 31 |
| Salvation Army, U.S.A. | | - | - | 1 | - | - |
| Seventh-day Adventists General Conference | 1904 | - | - | 2 | - | 6 |
| Source of Light Ministries International, Inc. | 2000 | - | - | - | 2 | - |
| Training Evangelistic Leadership (T.E.L.), Inc. | 1991 | - | - | - | 4 | - |
| Trans World Radio, International | | - | - | 11 | 21 | 16 |
| United Pentecostal Ch. Intl., Foreign Missions Div. | 1981 | - | 2 | - | - | - |
| Walk Thru the Bible Ministries, Inc. | 1998 | - | - | - | 7 | - |
| World Team | | - | - | - | - | 8 |
| World Venture | 1983 | - | - | 6 | - | - |
| WorldHarvest | | | | | | |
| Totals: | | 1 | 40 | 131 | 60 | 79 |

## Slovakia

| | | | | | | |
|---|---|---|---|---|---|---|
| Assemblies of God World Missions | 1960 | 1 | - | 3 | - | - |
| Awana Clubs International | 1997 | - | - | - | 2 | - |
| Baptist Bible Fellowship International | 1998 | 1 | - | 2 | - | - |
| Baptist International Missions, Inc. (BIMI) | | - | - | 4 | - | - |
| Baptist Mid-Missions | 1992 | - | - | 2 | - | - |
| Campus Crusade for Christ, Intl. | 1992 | 12 | - | 9 | 14 | - |
| Child Evangelism Fellowship, Inc. | 1989 | - | - | - | 2 | - |
| CrossWorld | 1991 | 1 | - | 4 | - | - |
| EFCA International Mission | 1993 | - | - | 4 | - | - |
| Entrust | 1983 | - | - | 3 | - | - |
| Envoy International | | - | - | - | - | - |
| Evangelical Lutheran Ch. in Am., Div. for Global Msn. | 1991 | - | 5 | 2 | - | - |
| Free Methodist World Missions | | - | - | 2 | - | - |
| Global Outreach International | 2000 | - | - | 1 | - | - |
| Go Ye Fellowship | | 1 | - | 1 | - | - |

| | First Year | Personnel from U.S. | | | Other Countries | |
|---|---|---|---|---|---|---|
| | | 1-2 yrs. | 2-4 yrs. | 4+ yrs. | Citizens | Non-Citizens |
| Greater Europe Mission | 1992 | - | - | 4 | - | - |
| I. N. Network USA | 1993 | - | - | - | 6 | - |
| International Messengers | 1994 | - | 1 | 3 | - | 1 |
| Mission to the World (PCA), Inc. | 1997 | - | 4 | - | - | - |
| New Hope International | 1971 | - | - | - | 3 | - |
| Precept Ministries International | 1991 | - | - | - | 1 | - |
| The Word for the World | 2003 | - | - | 2 | - | - |
| Trans World Radio, International | | 1 | 4 | 6 | 13 | 1 |
| United Pentecostal Ch. Intl., Foreign Missions Div. | 1930 | - | 2 | - | - | 2 |
| Youth for Christ/USA—World Outreach | | - | - | 1 | - | - |
| | Totals: | 17 | 16 | 53 | 41 | 4 |

## Slovenia

| | First Year | 1-2 yrs. | 2-4 yrs. | 4+ yrs. | Citizens | Non-Citizens |
|---|---|---|---|---|---|---|
| Assemblies of God World Missions | 1933 | - | - | 2 | - | - |
| Baptist Bible Fellowship International | 2005 | - | - | 2 | - | - |
| Bethany International Ministries | 1992 | - | - | 2 | - | 2 |
| Campus Crusade for Christ, Intl. | 1994 | - | - | 3 | 3 | - |
| Child Evangelism Fellowship, Inc. | 1997 | - | - | - | 2 | 2 |
| Church of the Nazarene, World Mission Dept. | | - | - | 1 | - | - |
| Global Fellowship Inc. | 2001 | - | - | - | 3 | - |
| Pioneers USA | | - | - | 1 | - | 1 |
| SEND International USA | 1997 | - | - | - | - | 1 |
| World Venture | 1991 | - | - | 2 | - | - |
| | Totals: | - | - | 13 | 8 | 6 |

## Solomon Islands

| | First Year | 1-2 yrs. | 2-4 yrs. | 4+ yrs. | Citizens | Non-Citizens |
|---|---|---|---|---|---|---|
| Assemblies of God World Missions | 1977 | - | - | 4 | - | - |
| Campus Crusade for Christ, Intl. | 1975 | - | - | - | 4 | - |
| Church of the Nazarene, World Mission Dept. | 1992 | - | - | 2 | - | - |
| Medical Ambassadors International, Inc. | 2004 | - | - | - | - | - |
| Seventh-day Adventists General Conference | 1914 | - | - | - | - | 4 |
| United Pentecostal Ch. Intl., Foreign Missions Div. | 1991 | - | 2 | - | - | - |
| | Totals: | - | 2 | 6 | 4 | 4 |

## South Africa

| | First Year | 1-2 yrs. | 2-4 yrs. | 4+ yrs. | Citizens | Non-Citizens |
|---|---|---|---|---|---|---|
| ACM International | 1996 | - | - | 2 | - | - |
| Advent Christian Gen. Conf., Dept. of Wld. Msns. | 1997 | - | - | - | 2 | - |
| Africa Inland Mission International | | - | - | 5 | 15 | 17 |
| Africa Inter-Mennonite Mission | 1982 | - | - | - | - | 2 |
| African Enterprise | 1962 | - | - | - | 16 | - |
| African Leadership, Inc. | 1998 | - | - | - | 4 | - |
| Am. Baptist Chs. of the U.S.A., Intl. Ministries | 1990 | - | - | 2 | - | - |
| Anis Shorrosh Evangelistic Association | | - | - | - | - | - |
| Asian Outreach U.S.A. | | - | - | - | - | - |
| Assemblies of God World Missions | 1917 | 13 | - | 44 | - | - |
| Awana Clubs International | 1982 | - | - | - | 4 | - |
| Baptist Bible Fellowship International | 1980 | 1 | - | 14 | - | - |
| Baptist International Missions, Inc. (BIMI) | | - | - | 19 | - | - |
| Baptist International Outreach | 1995 | - | - | 4 | 1 | - |
| BCM International | | - | - | - | 2 | - |

| | First Year | Personnel from U.S. | | | Other Countries | |
|---|---|---|---|---|---|---|
| | | 1-2 yrs. | 2-4 yrs. | 4+ yrs. | Citizens | Non-Citizens |
| Biblical Ministries Worldwide | 1976 | - | - | 12 | 6 | 6 |
| Brethren Assemblies | | - | - | 7 | - | - |
| Calvary International | 1995 | - | - | 2 | - | - |
| Campus Crusade for Christ, Intl. | 1971 | 3 | - | 6 | 112 | 10 |
| Child Evangelism Fellowship, Inc. | 1947 | - | - | 3 | 4 | - |
| Christ Community Church | 1903 | - | - | - | 9 | 7 |
| Christian Broadcasting Network Inc., the | 1997 | - | - | - | 3 | - |
| Christian Church of North America—Missions | 1980 | - | - | 4 | - | - |
| Christian Churches / Churches of Christ | | - | 3 | 32 | 4 | - |
| Christian Reformed World Relief Committee | 1999 | - | - | 1 | - | - |
| Church of God (Cleveland, TN) World Missions | 1951 | - | - | 1 | - | 1 |
| Church of God of Prophecy—Global Outreach | | - | - | - | 20 | - |
| Church of the Nazarene, World Mission Dept. | 1919 | - | - | 30 | - | 7 |
| Church Resource Ministries (CRM) | 2001 | - | - | 2 | - | - |
| Churches of Christ | 1900 | - | - | 14 | 26 | - |
| CityTeam Ministries | | - | - | - | 2 | - |
| CrossWorld | 1979 | - | - | 3 | - | - |
| Development Associates International (DAI) | 2001 | - | - | - | 2 | - |
| Emmanuel International Mission | 2004 | - | - | - | - | 2 |
| Episcopal Church USA—Domestic & Foreign | | - | - | 7 | - | - |
| Evangelical Baptist Missions | | 2 | - | 20 | - | - |
| Evangelical Lutheran Ch. in Am., Div. for Global Msn. | 1844 | 1 | - | 1 | 1 | - |
| Foursquare Missions International | 1928 | - | - | 4 | - | - |
| Global Outreach Mission, Inc. | | - | - | 1 | - | - |
| Global Partners / Wesleyan World Missions | 1901 | - | 10 | - | - | 2 |
| Globe Missionary Evangelism | 2000 | 1 | - | 2 | - | - |
| Gospel Fellowship Association | 1988 | - | - | 4 | - | - |
| Gospel Furthering Fellowship, The | | - | - | 2 | - | - |
| Greater Grace World Outreach | 2001 | - | - | 2 | - | - |
| Habitat for Humanity International | 1987 | - | 20 | 4 | 14 | 10 |
| HCJB Global | 1999 | - | - | 2 | - | - |
| Hope for the Hungry | | - | - | 1 | - | 1 |
| In Touch Mission International | 1977 | - | - | 6 | 6 | - |
| Independent Faith Mission, Inc. | | - | - | 6 | - | - |
| International Board of Jewish Missions, Inc. | 2001 | - | - | 2 | - | - |
| International Christian Ministries | 2002 | - | - | - | 4 | - |
| Intl. Pentecostal Holiness Ch. World Missions Mins. | 1911 | - | - | 19 | - | - |
| InterVarsity Christian Fellowship/USA—Msns. Dept. | | - | 2 | - | - | - |
| Jews for Jesus | 1989 | - | - | - | 2 | - |
| LeaderTreks | 2000 | - | 1 | - | - | - |
| Lott Carey Baptist Foreign Mission Convention | 1997 | - | - | - | 17 | - |
| Macedonia World Baptist Missions, Inc. | 2005 | - | - | 4 | - | - |
| Medical Ambassadors International, Inc. | 2003 | - | - | - | - | - |
| Mennonite Mission Network | 1982 | - | - | - | - | 2 |
| Mission to the World (PCA), Inc. | 1997 | - | 18 | - | - | - |
| Missionary Ventures International | | - | - | - | 1 | 2 |
| Natl. Baptist Conv. USA, Inc.—Foreign Msn. Bd. | 1894 | - | - | - | 1 | - |
| Navigators, U.S. International Missions Group | | - | - | 4 | - | - |
| New Tribes Mission | 2003 | - | - | 2 | 6 | - |
| OC International, Inc. | 1986 | - | - | 14 | - | 2 |

| | Personnel from U.S. | | | Other Countries | |
|---|---|---|---|---|---|
| First Year | 1-2 yrs. | 2-4 yrs. | 4+ yrs. | Citizens | Non-Citizens |
| OMS International, Inc. | - | - | - | - | 1 |
| Operation Mobilization | 7 | - | 6 | - | 2 |
| Precept Ministries International 1990 | - | - | - | 17 | - |
| Reformed Church in Am., Gen. Synod Council 2004 | - | - | - | - | 1 |
| Seventh-day Adventists General Conference 1887 | - | - | 2 | - | 13 |
| SIM USA 1889 | - | - | 8 | - | - |
| Source of Light Ministries International, Inc. | - | - | - | 1 | - |
| TEAM (The Evangelical Alliance Mission) | - | - | 21 | - | - |
| Teen Missions International, Inc. 1984 | - | - | 3 | 3 | - |
| The Word for the World 2004 | - | - | - | 1 | - |
| Things To Come Mission, Inc. 1989 | - | - | - | 1 | - |
| Trans World Radio, International 1994 | - | - | 17 | 23 | 6 |
| United Church of Christ—Wider Church Ministries | - | 7 | - | - | - |
| United Pentecostal Ch. Intl., Foreign Missions Div. 1948 | - | 8 | - | - | 2 |
| Walk Thru the Bible Ministries, Inc. 1999 | - | - | - | 44 | - |
| WEC International 1955 | - | - | 3 | - | - |
| White Fields Inc. | - | - | - | 11 | - |
| Word of Life Fellowship, Inc.—Intl. Ministries 1998 | - | - | 6 | 4 | - |
| World Missions & Evangelism, Inc. 2003 | 1 | - | 2 | 13 | - |
| World Missions Far Corners, Inc. 1958 | - | - | 2 | - | - |
| World Partners USA 1991 | - | - | 2 | - | - |
| World Thrust International, Inc. 1991 | - | - | - | 2 | - |
| World Venture 2004 | - | - | 4 | - | - |
| Youth for Christ/USA—World Outreach 1977 | - | - | 5 | - | - |
| Zion Evangelical Ministries of Africa 1903 | - | - | 5 | 21 | - |
| Totals: | 29 | 69 | 400 | 425 | 96 |

## South America—General

| | Personnel from U.S. | | | Other Countries | |
|---|---|---|---|---|---|
| First Year | 1-2 yrs. | 2-4 yrs. | 4+ yrs. | Citizens | Non-Citizens |
| ABWE (Assoc. of Baptists for World Evangelism) 1939 | - | 29 | 70 | - | - |
| Church of God (Cleveland, TN) World Missions | - | - | 2 | - | - |
| International Cooperating Ministries | - | - | - | - | - |
| Southern Baptist Convention Intl. Mission Board | - | - | - | - | - |
| Totals: | - | 29 | 72 | - | - |

## Spain

| | Personnel from U.S. | | | Other Countries | |
|---|---|---|---|---|---|
| First Year | 1-2 yrs. | 2-4 yrs. | 4+ yrs. | Citizens | Non-Citizens |
| Action International Ministries 2003 | - | - | 3 | - | - |
| AMG International 1989 | - | - | 1 | 2 | 4 |
| Arab World Ministries | - | - | 6 | - | - |
| Assemblies of God World Missions 1932 | 22 | - | 46 | - | - |
| Avant Ministries 1966 | 5 | - | 21 | - | 4 |
| Baptist Bible Fellowship International 1970 | - | - | 12 | - | - |
| Baptist International Missions, Inc. (BIMI) | - | - | 7 | - | - |
| Baptist Mid-Missions 1979 | - | - | 8 | - | - |
| BCM International | - | - | - | 6 | - |
| Bethany International Ministries 1992 | - | - | 2 | - | - |
| Biblical Ministries Worldwide 1958 | - | - | 6 | - | 6 |
| Brethren Assemblies | - | - | 11 | - | - |
| Brethren in Christ World Missions 1988 | - | - | 2 | - | - |
| Cadence International | - | 2 | - | - | 2 |
| CAM International 1971 | - | - | 16 | - | - |

| | First Year | Personnel from U.S. 1-2 yrs. | 2-4 yrs. | 4+ yrs. | Other Countries Citizens | Non-Citizens |
|---|---|---|---|---|---|---|
| Campus Crusade for Christ, Intl. | 1970 | 12 | - | 30 | - | 25 |
| Christ for the City International | 1994 | - | - | 2 | - | - |
| Christian Associates International | 1992 | - | - | - | - | - |
| Christian Churches / Churches of Christ | | - | - | 1 | - | - |
| Christian Fellowship Union, Inc. | | - | - | 2 | - | - |
| Christ's Mandate for Missions | 1980 | - | - | - | 1 | - |
| Church of God (Cleveland, TN) World Missions | 1937 | - | - | 4 | - | 9 |
| Church of God of Prophecy—Global Outreach | | - | - | - | 2 | - |
| Church of the Nazarene, World Mission Dept. | 1981 | - | - | - | - | - |
| Churches of Christ | 1964 | - | - | 2 | 6 | - |
| CMF International | | - | 7 | - | - | - |
| CrossWorld | 1985 | - | - | 4 | - | - |
| East-West Ministries International | 1998 | - | - | 4 | 10 | - |
| EFCA International Mission | 1994 | - | 4 | 8 | - | - |
| Equip, Inc. | 2004 | - | - | 2 | 2 | - |
| European Christian Mission International—USA | | - | - | 29 | 10 | - |
| Evangelical Covenant Ch.—Covenant Wld. Msn. | 1996 | 9 | - | 6 | - | - |
| Evangelical Methodist Church, Inc. | 2004 | - | - | - | - | 1 |
| Foursquare Missions International | 1975 | - | - | 2 | - | - |
| Free Methodist World Missions | | - | - | 2 | - | - |
| Free Will Baptist, Inc. Board of Intl. Missions | 1974 | 1 | 2 | 9 | - | - |
| Global Outreach Mission, Inc. | | - | - | - | 5 | - |
| Gospel Fellowship Association | 1978 | - | - | 6 | - | - |
| Gospel Furthering Fellowship, The | | - | - | - | 4 | - |
| Grace Brethren International Missions | 1984 | - | - | 4 | - | 2 |
| Greater Europe Mission | 1960 | - | - | 19 | - | - |
| HCJB Global | 1997 | - | - | - | - | 10 |
| Help for Christian Nationals, Inc. | 1990 | - | - | 2 | - | - |
| International Partnership Ministries, Inc. | 2000 | - | - | - | 2 | - |
| Intl. Pentecostal Holiness Ch. World Missions Mins. | 1988 | - | - | 4 | - | - |
| International Teams, U.S.A. | | 2 | 1 | 6 | - | 1 |
| Josue Yrion World Evangelism and Missions, Inc. | 2004 | - | - | - | 1 | - |
| Latin America Mission | 1990 | - | - | 4 | - | 4 |
| Liebenzell USA | 1995 | - | - | 2 | - | - |
| Macedonia World Baptist Missions, Inc. | 2003 | - | - | 2 | - | - |
| Mennonite Mission Network | 1976 | - | - | 2 | - | - |
| Mission to the World (PCA), Inc. | 1983 | - | 7 | - | - | - |
| Missionary Revival Crusade | 1969 | - | - | 11 | 2 | - |
| Navigators, U.S. International Missions Group | | - | - | 8 | - | - |
| OC International, Inc. | 1995 | - | - | 13 | - | - |
| OMS International, Inc. | 1972 | - | - | 11 | - | 3 |
| Open Door Baptist Missions | 1999 | - | - | 2 | - | - |
| Operation Mobilization | 1961 | - | - | 3 | - | 1 |
| Palm Missionary Ministries | 2002 | - | - | - | - | 2 |
| Precept Ministries International | 1992 | - | - | 1 | - | - |
| Salvation Army, U.S.A. | 1971 | - | - | 5 | - | - |
| SEND International USA | 1987 | - | - | 18 | - | 8 |
| South American Missionary Society (USA) | 1991 | - | - | 3 | - | - |
| Spanish World Ministries | | - | - | 2 | 2 | - |
| TEAM (The Evangelical Alliance Mission) | | - | - | 42 | - | - |

| | Personnel from U.S. | | | | Other Countries | |
|---|---|---|---|---|---|---|
| | First Year | 1-2 yrs. | 2-4 yrs. | 4+ yrs. | Citizens | Non-Citizens |
| United Pentecostal Ch. Intl., Foreign Missions Div. | | - | 6 | - | - | 8 |
| University of the Family | 1995 | - | - | - | - | 2 |
| WEC International | 1968 | - | - | 13 | - | - |
| Word of Life Fellowship, Inc.—Intl. Ministries | 1976 | - | - | 2 | 1 | - |
| World Baptist Fellowship Mission Agency, Inc. | | 2 | - | 4 | - | - |
| World Harvest Mission | 1998 | - | 5 | 6 | - | - |
| World Horizons | 1985 | - | - | 1 | - | 3 |
| World Indigenous Missions | 1996 | - | - | 5 | - | 1 |
| World Link Ministries | 1985 | - | - | 2 | 12 | 2 |
| World Missions & Evangelism, Inc. | | - | - | 2 | - | - |
| World Partners USA | 1985 | - | - | 9 | - | - |
| World Team | 1972 | - | - | 5 | - | 2 |
| World Venture | 1984 | - | - | 13 | - | - |
| Youth for Christ/USA—World Outreach | 1982 | - | - | 4 | - | - |
| Totals: | | 53 | 34 | 484 | 68 | 100 |

## Sri Lanka

| | First Year | 1-2 yrs. | 2-4 yrs. | 4+ yrs. | Citizens | Non-Citizens |
|---|---|---|---|---|---|---|
| Action International Ministries | 2005 | - | 1 | - | - | - |
| Asian Access | 2001 | - | - | - | - | - |
| Assemblies of God World Missions | 1923 | - | - | 6 | - | - |
| Awana Clubs International | 1992 | - | - | - | 2 | - |
| Back to the Bible International | 1955 | - | - | - | 40 | - |
| BCM International | | - | - | - | 1 | - |
| Campus Crusade for Christ, Intl. | 1967 | - | - | - | 34 | - |
| Childcare Worldwide | 1990 | - | - | - | - | - |
| Christian Aid Mission | | - | - | - | 19 | - |
| Church of God of Prophecy—Global Outreach | | - | - | - | 1 | - |
| Church of the Nazarene, World Mission Dept. | 2000 | - | - | - | - | - |
| Daystar U.S. | 1996 | - | - | 2 | - | - |
| Global Fellowship Inc. | 2000 | - | - | - | 28 | - |
| Global Partners / Wesleyan World Missions | 1993 | - | - | - | - | - |
| Globe Missionary Evangelism | 1984 | - | - | 2 | - | - |
| Gospel for Asia, Inc. | 1979 | - | - | - | 152 | - |
| Gospel Revival Ministries | 2006 | - | - | - | 2 | - |
| Habitat for Humanity International | 1994 | - | 1 | - | - | 1 |
| Hope for the Hungry | | - | - | 2 | 2 | - |
| I. N. Network USA | 1976 | - | - | - | 29 | - |
| Intl. Pentecostal Holiness Ch. World Missions Mins. | | - | - | - | - | - |
| Northwest Medical Teams International, Inc. | 2005 | 2 | - | - | 15 | - |
| Salvation Army, U.S.A. | | - | - | 2 | - | - |
| Samaritan's Purse | 2005 | 9 | - | - | 46 | 7 |
| Surfing the Nations | 1999 | - | - | - | 1 | - |
| TEAM (The Evangelical Alliance Mission) | | - | - | 2 | - | - |
| United Church of Christ—Wider Church Ministries | | - | 3 | - | - | - |
| United Pentecostal Ch. Intl., Foreign Missions Div. | 1949 | - | 2 | - | - | 3 |
| Village Ministries International | 1995 | - | - | - | 7 | - |
| Walk Thru the Bible Ministries, Inc. | 1999 | - | - | - | 2 | - |
| Totals: | | 11 | 7 | 16 | 381 | 11 |

| | First Year | Personnel from U.S. | | | Other Countries | |
|---|---|---|---|---|---|---|
| | | 1-2 yrs. | 2-4 yrs. | 4+ yrs. | Citizens | Non-Citizens |
| **Sudan** | | | | | | |
| Africa Inland Mission International | 1949 | 2 | 2 | - | - | 6 |
| African Leadership, Inc. | 1998 | - | - | - | 1 | - |
| Church of God of Prophecy—Global Outreach | | - | - | - | 2 | - |
| Church of the Nazarene, World Mission Dept. | 1999 | - | - | - | - | - |
| EFCA International Mission | 1997 | - | - | - | - | - |
| Emmanuel International Mission | 2003 | - | - | - | - | 1 |
| Empowering Lives International | 2005 | - | - | - | 12 | - |
| Episcopal Church USA—Domestic & Foreign | | - | - | 1 | - | - |
| Evangelical Covenant Ch.—Covenant Wld. Msn. | 1998 | 1 | - | - | - | - |
| Global Outreach International | 2004 | - | - | 1 | - | - |
| Gospel Revival Ministries | 1997 | - | - | - | 1 | - |
| Greater Grace World Outreach | 2003 | - | - | - | 2 | - |
| Hope for the Hungry | | - | 1 | - | - | 1 |
| In Touch Mission International | 1998 | - | - | - | 3 | - |
| International Gospel Outreach | 2006 | - | - | - | 2 | - |
| Intl. Pentecostal Holiness Ch. World Missions Mins. | 2003 | - | - | - | - | - |
| Medical Ambassadors International, Inc. | 2003 | - | - | - | - | - |
| Mission ONE, Inc. | 1990 | - | - | - | 36 | - |
| Mustard Seed International | | - | - | - | - | - |
| Northwest Medical Teams International, Inc. | 2003 | - | - | - | 20 | - |
| Partners International | 1995 | - | - | - | 60 | - |
| Reformed Church in Am., Gen. Synod Council | 2005 | - | - | 2 | 2 | - |
| Samaritan's Purse | 1997 | 32 | 6 | - | 444 | 15 |
| Seventh-day Adventists General Conference | 1978 | - | - | 2 | - | - |
| United Pentecostal Ch. Intl., Foreign Missions Div. | 2004 | - | 2 | - | - | - |
| Walk Thru the Bible Ministries, Inc. | 2001 | - | - | - | 1 | - |
| World Relief | 1999 | 3 | - | - | 90 | 3 |
| Totals: | | 38 | 11 | 6 | 676 | 26 |
| **Suriname** | | | | | | |
| Assemblies of God World Missions | 1959 | - | - | 2 | - | - |
| BCM International | | - | - | - | 5 | - |
| Campus Crusade for Christ, Intl. | 1979 | - | - | - | 7 | 2 |
| Child Evangelism Fellowship, Inc. | 1973 | - | - | - | - | 1 |
| Church of God of Prophecy—Global Outreach | | - | - | - | 1 | - |
| Church of the Nazarene, World Mission Dept. | 1984 | - | - | - | - | - |
| Global Partners / Wesleyan World Missions | 1945 | - | 3 | - | - | - |
| Hosanna | 2001 | - | - | - | 2 | - |
| Independent Faith Mission, Inc. | | - | - | 13 | - | - |
| Network of International Christian Schools | 1964 | - | 5 | 2 | - | 4 |
| Orthodox Presbyterian Church | 1987 | - | - | 2 | - | - |
| United Pentecostal Ch. Intl., Foreign Missions Div. | 2003 | - | 2 | - | - | 2 |
| World Team | 1957 | - | - | 2 | - | 2 |
| Totals: | | - | 10 | 21 | 15 | 11 |
| **Swaziland** | | | | | | |
| Adventures in Missions | 2004 | 1 | - | 6 | - | - |
| Assemblies of God World Missions | 1985 | - | - | 10 | - | - |
| BCM International | | - | - | - | 2 | - |

| | | Personnel from U.S. | | | Other Countries | |
|---|---|---|---|---|---|---|
| | First Year | 1-2 yrs. | 2-4 yrs. | 4+ yrs. | Citizens | Non-Citizens |
| Campus Crusade for Christ, Intl. | 1973 | - | - | - | 8 | - |
| Children's HopeChest | 2006 | - | - | - | - | - |
| Church of God of Prophecy—Global Outreach | | - | - | - | 4 | - |
| Church of the Nazarene, World Mission Dept. | 1910 | - | - | 1 | - | - |
| Churches of Christ | 1966 | - | - | 3 | 4 | - |
| Greater Grace World Outreach | 1999 | - | - | - | 3 | - |
| Intl. Pentecostal Holiness Ch. World Missions Mins. | | - | - | - | - | - |
| Natl. Baptist Conv. USA, Inc.—Foreign Mission Bd. | 1971 | 2 | - | - | - | - |
| Seventh-day Adventists General Conference | 1920 | - | - | - | - | 2 |
| TEAM (The Evangelical Alliance Mission) | | - | - | 2 | - | - |
| Trans World Radio, International | 1974 | - | - | 4 | 12 | 10 |
| United Church of Christ—Wider Church Ministries | | - | 2 | - | - | - |
| United Pentecostal Ch. Intl., Foreign Missions Div. | 1982 | - | 2 | - | - | - |
| Walk Thru the Bible Ministries, Inc. | 2000 | - | - | - | 2 | - |
| World-Wide Missions | | - | - | - | 1 | - |
| Totals: | | 3 | 4 | 26 | 36 | 12 |

## Sweden

| | | Personnel from U.S. | | | Other Countries | |
|---|---|---|---|---|---|---|
| Baptist Bible Fellowship International | 1985 | - | - | 4 | - | - |
| Biblical Ministries Worldwide | | - | - | 4 | - | 4 |
| Campus Crusade for Christ, Intl. | 1972 | 11 | - | - | - | 7 |
| Christian Associates International | | - | - | - | - | - |
| Churches of God, General Conference | 2005 | - | - | 2 | - | - |
| Elim Fellowship—International Department | 1990 | - | - | 2 | - | - |
| European Christian Mission International—USA | | - | - | 2 | - | - |
| Evangelical Baptist Missions | | - | - | 1 | 1 | - |
| Fellowship International Mission | 1977 | - | - | 3 | - | - |
| Global Outreach Mission, Inc. | | - | - | - | 1 | - |
| Greater Europe Mission | 1955 | - | - | 4 | - | - |
| Greater Grace World Outreach | 1976 | - | - | - | 4 | 2 |
| Mennonite Mission Network | | - | - | - | - | - |
| Mission Possible Foundation, Inc. | 2000 | - | - | - | - | - |
| Mission to the World (PCA), Inc. | 1999 | - | 2 | - | - | - |
| Operation Mobilization | | 2 | - | 1 | - | 1 |
| TEAM (The Evangelical Alliance Mission) | | - | - | 2 | - | - |
| United Pentecostal Ch. Intl., Foreign Missions Div. | | - | - | - | - | 2 |
| Wisc. Evangelical Luth. Synod, Bd. for World Msns. | 1971 | - | - | 1 | - | - |
| Totals: | | 13 | 2 | 26 | 6 | 16 |

## Switzerland

| | | Personnel from U.S. | | | Other Countries | |
|---|---|---|---|---|---|---|
| Assemblies of God World Missions | 1967 | - | - | - | - | - |
| Baptist International Missions, Inc. (BIMI) | | - | - | 2 | - | - |
| Campus Crusade for Christ, Intl. | | - | - | - | - | 2 |
| Child Evangelism Fellowship, Inc. | 1950 | - | - | 6 | - | 4 |
| Christian Associates International | | - | - | - | - | - |
| Church of the Nazarene, World Mission Dept. | 1978 | - | - | 19 | - | 9 |
| Churches of Christ | 1959 | - | - | 4 | 3 | - |
| Global Outreach Mission, Inc. | | - | - | 1 | - | - |
| Greater Grace World Outreach | 1994 | - | - | 2 | 2 | 1 |
| HCJB Global | 1983 | - | - | - | 4 | - |

| | First Year | Personnel from U.S. 1-2 yrs. | 2-4 yrs. | 4+ yrs. | Other Countries Citizens | Non-Citizens |
|---|---|---|---|---|---|---|
| Literacy & Evangelism International | 2005 | - | - | - | 1 | - |
| Reformed Baptist Mission Services | | - | - | - | 2 | - |
| Seventh-day Adventists General Conference | 1870 | - | - | - | - | 2 |
| SIM USA | | - | - | 2 | - | - |
| United Pentecostal Ch. Intl., Foreign Missions Div. | | - | 2 | - | - | 2 |
| Youth for Christ/USA—World Outreach | | - | - | 7 | - | - |
| Totals: | | - | 2 | 43 | 12 | 20 |

## Syria

| | | | | | | |
|---|---|---|---|---|---|---|
| Armenian Missionary Association of America, Inc. | 1918 | - | - | - | - | - |
| Assemblies of God World Missions | 1999 | - | - | - | - | - |
| Church of the Nazarene, World Mission Dept. | 1920 | - | - | - | - | - |
| Episcopal Church USA—Domestic & Foreign | | - | - | 1 | - | - |
| Walk Thru the Bible Ministries, Inc. | 2001 | - | - | - | - | - |
| World-Wide Missions | | - | - | - | 1 | - |
| Totals: | | - | - | 1 | 1 | - |

## Taiwan

| | | | | | | |
|---|---|---|---|---|---|---|
| Asian Outreach U.S.A. | | - | - | - | - | - |
| Assemblies of God World Missions | 1948 | - | - | 8 | - | - |
| Awana Clubs International | 2000 | - | - | 2 | 2 | - |
| Baptist Bible Fellowship International | 1946 | - | - | 13 | - | - |
| Baptist Mid-Missions | 1972 | - | - | 2 | - | - |
| Campus Crusade for Christ, Intl. | 1964 | - | - | - | 109 | 4 |
| Child Evangelism Fellowship, Inc. | 1951 | - | 2 | 2 | - | - |
| Christian Churches / Churches of Christ | | - | 2 | 21 | - | - |
| Church of the Nazarene, World Mission Dept. | 1956 | - | - | - | - | - |
| Churches of Christ | | 3 | - | 2 | - | - |
| EFCA International Mission | 1994 | - | - | 1 | - | - |
| Evangelical Covenant Ch.—Covenant Wld. Msn. | 1952 | - | - | 2 | - | - |
| Foursquare Missions International | 1988 | - | - | 2 | - | - |
| Free Methodist World Missions | 1952 | - | - | 6 | - | - |
| Globe Missionary Evangelism | 2000 | - | - | 2 | - | - |
| Great Commission Ministries, Inc. | | - | 2 | - | - | - |
| Heart of God Ministries | 1997 | - | - | 7 | - | - |
| International Gospel Outreach | 2003 | - | - | 2 | - | - |
| International Partnership Ministries, Inc. | 2003 | 1 | - | - | 1 | - |
| International Students, Inc (ISI) | | - | - | 1 | - | - |
| International Teams, U.S.A. | | - | - | - | - | 7 |
| Kids Alive International | 1971 | - | - | 2 | - | - |
| Liberty Corner Mission | | - | - | 2 | - | - |
| Liebenzell USA | 1955 | - | - | - | - | 2 |
| Lutheran Brethren World Missions | 1951 | - | - | 4 | - | - |
| Lutheran Church-Missouri Synod | 1951 | - | - | 9 | - | - |
| Macedonia World Baptist Missions, Inc. | 1985 | - | - | 2 | - | - |
| Mennonite Mission Network | 1954 | - | - | - | - | - |
| Mission to the World (PCA), Inc. | 1977 | 3 | 8 | - | - | - |
| Mission To Unreached Peoples | 1989 | - | - | 2 | - | - |
| Mustard Seed International | 1948 | - | - | - | - | - |
| Navigators, U.S. International Missions Group | | - | - | 4 | - | - |

| | First Year | Personnel from U.S. | | | Other Countries | |
|---|---|---|---|---|---|---|
| | | 1-2 yrs. | 2-4 yrs. | 4+ yrs. | Citizens | Non-Citizens |
| OC International, Inc. | 1951 | - | - | 5 | - | - |
| OMF International | 1950 | 1 | - | 8 | - | 38 |
| OMS International, Inc. | 1950 | - | - | 5 | - | 2 |
| Open Door Baptist Missions | 1999 | - | - | 1 | - | - |
| Overseas Radio & Television, Inc. (ORTV) | 1961 | - | - | - | 220 | 5 |
| Partners International | 1950 | - | - | - | 91 | - |
| Precept Ministries International | 1990 | - | - | - | 3 | 2 |
| Reformed Church in Am., Gen. Synod Council | 1970 | - | - | 3 | - | - |
| Ripe for Harvest, Inc. | 1999 | - | - | 1 | - | - |
| SEND International USA | 1966 | - | - | 19 | - | 8 |
| Seventh-day Adventists General Conference | 1902 | - | - | 9 | - | - |
| Sowers International, The | 1995 | - | - | - | 4 | - |
| TEAM (The Evangelical Alliance Mission) | | - | - | 16 | - | - |
| Team Expansion, Inc. | 1996 | - | - | 21 | - | - |
| United Church of Christ—Wider Church Ministries | | - | 5 | - | - | - |
| United Pentecostal Ch. Intl., Foreign Missions Div. | | - | 4 | - | - | - |
| Wisc. Evangelical Luth. Synod, Bd. for World Msns. | 1968 | - | - | 1 | - | - |
| World Gospel Mission | 1953 | - | - | 2 | - | - |
| World Team | 1999 | - | - | 6 | - | - |
| World Venture | 1952 | - | - | 11 | - | - |
| World-Wide Missions | 1966 | - | - | - | 1 | - |
| Totals: | | 8 | 23 | 206 | 431 | 68 |

## Tajikistan

| | First Year | 1-2 yrs. | 2-4 yrs. | 4+ yrs. | Citizens | Non-Citizens |
|---|---|---|---|---|---|---|
| Assemblies of God World Missions | 1997 | 1 | - | 7 | - | - |
| Christar | 1996 | - | - | 7 | - | - |
| Food for the Hungry, Inc. | 1996 | - | - | - | - | - |
| Foursquare Missions International | | - | - | 2 | - | - |
| Greater Grace World Outreach | 2005 | - | - | - | - | 6 |
| Health Emergent International Services | 1997 | - | - | 2 | - | - |
| Northwest Medical Teams International, Inc. | 2006 | 1 | - | - | 4 | - |
| People International USA | 1991 | - | 2 | - | - | - |
| Women to the World | | - | - | - | - | - |
| Totals: | | 2 | 2 | 18 | 4 | 6 |

## Tanzania

| | First Year | 1-2 yrs. | 2-4 yrs. | 4+ yrs. | Citizens | Non-Citizens |
|---|---|---|---|---|---|---|
| ACM International | 2004 | - | - | 4 | - | - |
| Africa Inland Mission International | 1909 | 8 | 4 | 29 | - | 26 |
| African Enterprise | 1970 | - | - | - | 8 | - |
| African Leadership, Inc. | 1998 | - | - | - | 2 | - |
| Assemblies of God World Missions | 1940 | 4 | - | 10 | - | - |
| Baptist Bible Fellowship International | 1988 | - | - | 13 | - | - |
| Baptist International Missions, Inc. (BIMI) | | - | - | 6 | - | - |
| Brethren Assemblies | | - | - | 2 | - | - |
| Calvary International | | - | 3 | - | - | - |
| Campus Crusade for Christ, Intl. | 1977 | - | - | - | 53 | 2 |
| Christian Aid Mission | | - | - | - | 18 | - |
| Christian Blind Mission International | 1971 | - | 1 | 1 | - | - |
| Christian Churches / Churches of Christ | | - | - | 21 | - | - |
| Christian Literature International | | - | - | - | - | - |

| | First Year | Personnel from U.S. 1-2 yrs. | 2-4 yrs. | 4+ yrs. | Other Countries Citizens | Non-Citizens |
|---|---|---|---|---|---|---|
| Christian Reformed World Relief Committee | 1990 | - | - | 1 | - | 1 |
| Ch. of God (And., Indiana), Global Missions | 1957 | 2 | - | 5 | - | - |
| Church of God of Prophecy—Global Outreach | | - | - | - | 7 | - |
| Church of the Nazarene, World Mission Dept. | 1990 | - | - | - | - | 2 |
| Churches of Christ | 1962 | 4 | - | 5 | 2 | - |
| CMF International | 1984 | - | 7 | - | - | - |
| Compassion International, Inc. | 1999 | - | - | - | 34 | - |
| Eastern Mennonite Missions | | - | - | 2 | - | 2 |
| EFCA International Mission | 1993 | 1 | 2 | 9 | - | - |
| Elim Fellowship—International Department | 1955 | - | - | 10 | - | 4 |
| Emmanuel International Mission | 1983 | - | 1 | - | - | 2 |
| Empowering Lives International | 2000 | - | - | - | 6 | - |
| Episcopal Church USA—Domestic & Foreign | | - | - | 4 | - | - |
| Equip, Inc. | 2004 | - | - | 2 | - | - |
| Evangelical Lutheran Ch. in Am., Div. for Global Msn. | 1924 | 1 | 2- | 19 | - | - |
| Floresta USA, Inc. | 2004 | - | - | - | 2 | - |
| Free Methodist World Missions | 1994 | - | - | 2 | - | 1 |
| Go Ye Fellowship | | - | - | 1 | 1 | - |
| Gospel Communications International, Inc. | 2002 | - | - | - | 2 | - |
| Gospel Furthering Fellowship, The | | - | - | 2 | - | - |
| Gospelink, Inc. | | - | - | - | 74 | - |
| Grace Ministries International | 1952 | 4 | 6 | - | - | - |
| Greater Grace World Outreach | 1999 | - | - | - | 9 | - |
| Habitat for Humanity International | 1986 | - | 3 | - | - | 3 |
| I. N. Network USA | 1997 | - | - | - | 21 | - |
| International Christian Ministries | 1999 | 2 | - | - | 2 | 4 |
| International Gospel Outreach | 2002 | - | - | 1 | 2 | - |
| Intl. Pentecostal Holiness Ch. World Missions Mins. | 1996 | - | - | 4 | - | - |
| MAP International | 1994 | - | - | - | - | - |
| Medical Ambassadors International, Inc. | 1987 | - | - | - | 3 | - |
| Mission ONE, Inc. | 1990 | - | - | - | 2 | - |
| Mission to the World (PCA), Inc. | 1990 | - | 2 | - | - | - |
| Moravian Ch. in N. Am., Bd. of World Msn. | 2003 | - | - | - | - | 2 |
| Perimeter Church, Global Outreach | | - | - | - | - | - |
| Pioneer Bible Translators | 1997 | - | - | 6 | - | 1 |
| Seed International | 2003 | - | - | 1 | - | - |
| Seventh-day Adventists General Conference | 1903 | - | - | 4 | - | 7 |
| SIM USA | 1990 | - | - | 2 | - | - |
| Team Expansion, Inc. | 1994 | - | - | 2 | - | 2 |
| The Mission Society | 2000 | - | 2 | 1 | - | - |
| The Word for the World | 2004 | - | - | - | - | 4 |
| United Pentecostal Ch. Intl., Foreign Missions Div. | 1980 | - | 4 | - | - | 1 |
| Walk Thru the Bible Ministries, Inc. | 2000 | - | - | - | 2 | - |
| World Gospel Mission | 1985 | - | - | - | - | - |
| World Outreach International—US | 1986 | - | - | 2 | - | - |
| Totals: | | 26 | 37 | 171 | 250 | 64 |

## Thailand

| | | | | | | |
|---|---|---|---|---|---|---|
| Am. Baptist Chs. of the U.S.A., Intl. Ministries | 1833 | - | - | - | - | - |
| AMG International | 1976 | - | - | - | 76 | 13 |

| | First Year | Personnel from U.S. 1-2 yrs. | 2-4 yrs. | 4+ yrs. | Other Countries Citizens | Non-Citizens |
|---|---|---|---|---|---|---|
| Asian Outreach U.S.A. | | - | - | - | - | - |
| Assemblies of God World Missions | 1968 | 13 | - | 19 | - | - |
| Baptist Bible Fellowship International | 1983 | 1 | - | 5 | - | - |
| Baptist General Conference—Intl. Ministries | 1990 | 2 | - | 8 | 1 | - |
| Baptist International Missions, Inc. (BIMI) | | - | - | 2 | - | - |
| Baptist Mid-Missions | 1998 | - | - | 9 | - | - |
| Bethany International Ministries | 1999 | - | 1 | 1 | - | 1 |
| Bright Hope International | 2000 | - | - | - | 4 | - |
| Calvary International | | - | - | 4 | - | 2 |
| Campus Crusade for Christ, Intl. | 1971 | 2 | - | 8 | 116 | 3 |
| Child Evangelism Fellowship, Inc. | 1957 | - | - | - | 1 | - |
| Childcare Worldwide | 1996 | - | - | - | - | - |
| Christian Aid Mission | | - | - | - | 30 | - |
| Christian Blind Mission International | 1982 | 1 | - | - | - | - |
| Christian Broadcasting Network Inc., the | 1999 | 1 | - | 1 | 47 | 3 |
| Christian Churches / Churches of Christ | | 2 | - | 41 | 12 | - |
| Christian Ministries International (CMI) | 1990 | - | - | 1 | 1 | 2 |
| Christ's Mandate for Missions | 2003 | - | - | - | 2 | - |
| Church of God of Prophecy—Global Outreach | | - | - | - | 2 | - |
| Church of the Nazarene, World Mission Dept. | 1989 | - | - | 6 | - | 3 |
| Church World Service | | - | 1 | - | 4 | - |
| Churches of Christ | 1903 | 4 | - | 16 | 4 | - |
| CMF International | 1994 | - | 6 | - | - | - |
| Compassion International, Inc. | 1970 | - | - | - | 31 | - |
| David Livingstone KURE Foundation | | - | - | - | 14 | - |
| Eastern Mennonite Missions | | - | 1 | 2 | - | - |
| EFCA International Mission | 1996 | 1 | - | 10 | 2 | - |
| Evangelical Covenant Ch.—Covenant Wld. Msn. | | - | - | 10 | - | - |
| Evangelical Lutheran Ch. in Am., Div. for Global Msn. | 1975 | - | - | - | - | 2 |
| Evangelical Presbyterian Church—World Outreach | 2003 | - | - | 4 | - | - |
| Food for the Hungry, Inc. | 2004 | - | 2 | 2 | - | - |
| Foursquare Missions International | 1987 | - | 2 | 2 | - | - |
| Free Methodist World Missions | | - | - | 2 | - | - |
| Global Fellowship Inc. | 1998 | - | - | - | 36 | - |
| Global Partners / Wesleyan World Missions | 2003 | - | 2 | - | - | - |
| Global Recordings Network | 1995 | - | - | 4 | 4 | - |
| Globe Missionary Evangelism | 1992 | - | - | 6 | - | - |
| Good News Productions International | 1998 | - | - | 4 | - | 2 |
| Gospel for Asia, Inc. | | - | - | - | - | - |
| Greater Grace World Outreach | 1989 | - | - | 2 | 1 | 3 |
| Habitat for Humanity International | 1998 | - | 21 | 5 | 14 | 12 |
| Harvest | 2005 | - | 2 | - | - | - |
| International Justice Mission | 2000 | 1 | 1 | 1 | 9 | 1 |
| Intl. Pentecostal Holiness Ch. World Missions Mins. | 1988 | - | - | 4 | - | - |
| International Teams, U.S.A. | | - | - | - | - | 9 |
| InterServe USA (International Service Fellowship) | 2002 | - | - | 2 | - | - |
| Larry Jones Intl. Ministries (Feed the Children) | 1986 | - | - | - | 8 | - |
| Medical Ambassadors International, Inc. | 1999 | - | - | - | 2 | - |
| Mennonite Mission Network | 2000 | - | - | - | - | - |
| Mission to the World (PCA), Inc. | 2000 | 1 | 6 | - | - | - |

| | First Year | Personnel from U.S. 1-2 yrs. | 2-4 yrs. | 4+ yrs. | Other Countries Citizens | Non-Citizens |
|---|---|---|---|---|---|---|
| Mission To Unreached Peoples | 1988 | - | - | 27 | - | - |
| Missionary Ventures International | | - | - | 2 | - | - |
| New Life Advance International | 1989 | - | - | 2 | - | - |
| New Tribes Mission | 1951 | - | - | 60 | - | - |
| OMF International | 1950 | 2 | - | 44 | - | 89 |
| Partners International | 1955 | - | - | - | 46 | - |
| Pass the Torch Ministries | 1988 | - | - | 1 | 1 | - |
| Perimeter Church, Global Outreach | | - | - | - | - | - |
| Pioneers USA | 1985 | 3 | - | 29 | 1 | - |
| Presbyterian Mission International (PMI) | 2000 | - | - | - | 1 | - |
| Ripe for Harvest, Inc. | 2001 | - | 1 | 3 | - | - |
| Rosedale Mennonite Missions | 1995 | - | - | 1 | - | 1 |
| Seed International | 2003 | - | - | 1 | - | - |
| Seventh-day Adventists General Conference | 1919 | - | - | 22 | - | 14 |
| SIM USA | 2005 | - | - | 5 | - | - |
| Sowers International, The | 1999 | - | - | - | - | 10 |
| Team Expansion, Inc. | | - | 4 | 5 | - | - |
| Tentmakers International | | - | - | - | - | - |
| United Church of Christ—Wider Church Ministries | | - | 6 | - | - | - |
| United Pentecostal Ch. Intl., Foreign Missions Div. | 1968 | - | 6 | - | - | - |
| Walk Thru the Bible Ministries, Inc. | 2001 | - | - | - | - | - |
| WEC International | 1947 | - | - | 6 | - | - |
| Wisc. Evangelical Lutheran Synod, Bd. for Wld. Msns. | 1993 | - | 2 | 1 | - | - |
| World Baptist Fellowship Mission Agency, Inc. | | - | - | 1 | 1 | - |
| World Concern | 1980 | - | 2 | 4 | 15 | - |
| World Help | 1998 | - | - | - | - | - |
| World Indigenous Missions | 2000 | - | - | 2 | - | - |
| World Missions Far Corners, Inc. | 1996 | - | - | 2 | 8 | 3 |
| World Partners USA | 1992 | - | - | 2 | - | - |
| World Venture | | - | - | 2 | - | - |
| World-Wide Missions | | - | 2 | - | - | - |
| Worldwide Tentmakers, Inc. | 2001 | - | - | - | - | - |
| Youth for Christ/USA—World Outreach | | - | - | 2 | - | - |
| Totals: | | 34 | 69 | 405 | 494 | 173 |

**Togo**

| | First Year | 1-2 yrs. | 2-4 yrs. | 4+ yrs. | Citizens | Non-Citizens |
|---|---|---|---|---|---|---|
| Assemblies of God World Missions | 1937 | 2 | - | 11 | - | - |
| Awana Clubs International | 1986 | - | - | - | 2 | - |
| Baptist International Missions, Inc. (BIMI) | | - | - | 8 | - | - |
| Campus Crusade for Christ, Intl. | 1979 | - | - | - | 33 | - |
| Child Evangelism Fellowship, Inc. | | - | - | - | 1 | - |
| Christian Blind Mission International | 1980 | - | 1 | - | - | - |
| Church of God of Prophecy—Global Outreach | | - | - | - | 2 | - |
| Church of the Nazarene, World Mission Dept. | 1998 | - | - | - | - | - |
| Churches of Christ | 1984 | 4 | - | 18 | - | - |
| Greater Grace World Outreach | 1990 | - | - | - | 47 | - |
| International Partnership Ministries, Inc. | 1991 | - | - | - | 22 | - |
| Intl. Pentecostal Holiness Ch. World Missions Mins. | 1993 | - | - | - | - | - |
| Ireland Outreach International Inc. | 2000 | - | - | - | - | - |
| Literacy & Evangelism International | | - | - | - | - | - |

| | First Year | Personnel from U.S. | | | Other Countries | |
|---|---|---|---|---|---|---|
| | | 1-2 yrs. | 2-4 yrs. | 4+ yrs. | Citizens | Non-Citizens |
| Lutheran Bible Translators, Inc. | 1996 | - | - | - | 3 | - |
| Lutheran Church-Missouri Synod | 1980 | - | - | 2 | - | - |
| Mennonite Mission Network | 1996 | - | - | - | - | 2 |
| Seventh-day Adventists General Conference | 1964 | - | - | 2 | - | 2 |
| SIM USA | 1997 | - | - | 2 | - | - |
| Source of Light Ministries International, Inc. | 1998 | - | - | - | 3 | - |
| United Pentecostal Ch. Intl., Foreign Missions Div. | 1972 | - | 2 | - | - | - |
| Walk Thru the Bible Ministries, Inc. | 2002 | - | - | - | - | - |
| | Totals: | 6 | 3 | 43 | 113 | 4 |
| **Tonga** | | | | | | |
| Assemblies of God World Missions | 1975 | 3 | - | 6 | - | - |
| Campus Crusade for Christ, Intl. | 1974 | - | - | - | 2 | - |
| Church of the Nazarene, World Mission Dept. | 2000 | - | - | - | - | - |
| United Pentecostal Ch. Intl., Foreign Missions Div. | | - | 2 | - | - | 1 |
| | Totals: | 3 | 2 | 6 | 2 | 1 |
| **Trinidad and Tobago** | | | | | | |
| Assemblies of God World Missions | 1945 | - | - | 2 | - | - |
| Baptist International Missions, Inc. (BIMI) | | - | - | 9 | - | - |
| Campus Crusade for Christ, Intl. | 1977 | - | - | - | 13 | - |
| Church of God of Prophecy—Global Outreach | | - | - | - | 7 | - |
| Church of the Nazarene, World Mission Dept. | 1926 | - | - | - | - | 4 |
| Churches of Christ | | - | - | 2 | 4 | - |
| Fundamental Baptist Mission of Trinidad & Tobago | | - | - | 5 | 6 | - |
| Intl. Pentecostal Holiness Ch. World Missions Mins. | 1983 | - | - | - | - | - |
| Pentecostal Ch. of God—World Missions Dept. | | - | - | 2 | - | - |
| Seventh-day Adventists General Conference | 1893 | - | - | 4 | - | 3 |
| STEM (Short-Term Evangelical Missions) Intl. | 1986 | - | - | - | - | - |
| TMA Ministries | 1994 | - | - | - | - | - |
| United Pentecostal Ch. Intl., Foreign Missions Div. | | - | 2 | - | - | - |
| Virginia Mennonite Board of Missions | 1976 | 2 | - | 1 | 1 | - |
| World Team | 1953 | - | - | - | - | 4 |
| | Totals: | 2 | 2 | 25 | 31 | 11 |
| **Tunisia** | | | | | | |
| Arab World Ministries | | - | 2 | 5 | - | - |
| Seventh-day Adventists General Conference | 1928 | - | - | - | - | 1 |
| Walk Thru the Bible Ministries, Inc. | 2002 | - | - | - | - | - |
| | Totals: | - | 2 | 5 | - | 1 |
| **Turkey** | | | | | | |
| AMG International | 1977 | - | - | - | 2 | - |
| Armenian Missionary Association of America, Inc. | 1951 | - | - | - | - | - |
| Christar | 1975 | - | - | 35 | - | - |
| EFCA International Mission | 1994 | - | - | - | - | - |
| Greater Grace World Outreach | 2005 | - | 2 | 2 | - | 5 |
| Intl. Pentecostal Holiness Ch. World Missions Mins. | 2001 | - | - | - | 6 | - |
| International Teams, U.S.A. | | - | - | 3 | - | 1 |
| InterServe USA (International Service Fellowship) | 1985 | - | - | 15 | - | - |

| | First Year | Personnel from U.S. | | | Other Countries | |
|---|---|---|---|---|---|---|
| | | 1-2 yrs. | 2-4 yrs. | 4+ yrs. | Citizens | Non-Citizens |
| Middle East Media—USA | 1976 | - | - | - | - | - |
| Mission To Unreached Peoples | 2002 | - | - | 8 | - | - |
| New Life Advance International | 1994 | - | - | 2 | - | - |
| Operation Mobilization | 1961 | 1 | 2 | 8 | - | 2 |
| Paraclete, Inc. | 2001 | 2 | - | - | - | - |
| Partners International | 1998 | - | - | - | 2 | - |
| People International USA | 1987 | - | 2 | 4 | - | 2 |
| Ripe for Harvest, Inc. | 2000 | - | - | 2 | - | - |
| Rosedale Mennonite Missions | 1987 | 1 | - | 6 | - | 7 |
| TEAM (The Evangelical Alliance Mission) | | - | - | 2 | - | - |
| Things To Come Mission, Inc. | 2001 | 2 | - | - | - | - |
| Turkish World Outreach | 1989 | - | - | 22 | 3 | 1 |
| United Church of Christ—Wider Church Ministries | | - | 6 | - | - | - |
| United Pentecostal Ch. Intl., Foreign Missions Div. | | - | 4 | - | - | 5 |
| Women to the World | 1985 | - | - | - | - | - |
| World Horizons | 1990 | - | - | 2 | - | 3 |
| World Witness, Assoc. Reformed Presbyterian Ch. | 1991 | - | - | 6 | 2 | - |
| World-Wide Missions | 1970 | - | - | - | 3 | - |
| Worldwide Tentmakers, Inc. | 1991 | - | - | - | - | - |
| | Totals: | 6 | 16 | 117 | 18 | 26 |
| **Turkmenistan** | | | | | - | - |
| Assemblies of God World Missions | 1996 | - | - | - | - | - |
| Back to the Bible International | 2001 | - | - | - | 4 | - |
| Evangelism Explosion International | | - | - | - | - | 2 |
| Greater Grace World Outreach | 1995 | - | - | - | 2 | - |
| People International USA | 1997 | - | - | - | 2 | - |
| | Totals: | - | - | - | 8 | 2 |
| **Turks and Caicos Islands** | | | | | | |
| Baptist International Missions, Inc. (BIMI) | | - | - | 1 | - | - |
| | Totals: | - | - | 1 | - | - |
| **Uganda** | | | | | | |
| Action International Ministries | 2002 | - | - | 4 | - | - |
| Africa Inland Mission International | 1918 | 2 | 4 | 16 | - | 27 |
| African Bible Colleges, Inc. | 1975 | - | - | - | - | - |
| African Enterprise | 1970 | - | - | - | 7 | - |
| African Leadership, Inc. | 1998 | - | - | - | 1 | - |
| AMG International | | - | - | - | 16 | - |
| Anglican Frontier Missions | 2004 | - | 2 | - | - | 2 |
| Assemblies of God World Missions | 1979 | - | - | - | - | - |
| Awana Clubs International | 1997 | - | - | - | 2 | - |
| Baptist Bible Fellowship International | 1986 | - | - | 2 | - | - |
| Baptist International Missions, Inc. (BIMI) | | - | - | 36 | - | - |
| Brethren Assemblies | | - | - | 3 | - | - |
| Bright Hope International | 2004 | - | - | - | 5 | - |
| Campus Crusade for Christ, Intl. | 1971 | - | - | 2 | 132 | - |
| Child Evangelism Fellowship, Inc. | 1965 | - | - | - | 2 | - |
| Childcare Worldwide | 1986 | - | - | - | 37 | - |

| | | Personnel from U.S. | | | Other Countries | |
|---|---|---|---|---|---|---|
| | First Year | 1-2 yrs. | 2-4 yrs. | 4+ yrs. | Citizens | Non-Citizens |
| Christ to the Nations | 1998 | - | - | - | 2 | - |
| Christian Blind Mission International | 1978 | - | 2 | - | - | - |
| Christian Literature International | | - | - | - | - | - |
| Christian Reformed World Relief Committee | 1982 | - | - | 2 | 1 | 3 |
| Ch. of God (Anderson, Ind.), Global Missions | 1983 | 2 | - | 1 | - | 4 |
| Church of God of Prophecy—Global Outreach | | - | - | - | 4 | - |
| Church of the Nazarene, World Mission Dept. | 1988 | - | - | 2 | - | - |
| Church Planting International | 1983 | - | - | - | - | - |
| Churches of Christ | 1969 | 4 | - | 24 | 4 | - |
| Compassion International, Inc. | 1980 | - | - | - | 44 | - |
| Development Associates International (DAI) | 2002 | - | - | - | 2 | - |
| Emmanuel International Mission | 1983 | - | - | - | - | 2 |
| Engineering Ministries International | 2003 | - | - | 5 | - | - |
| Evangelical Presbyterian Church—World Outreach | 2001 | - | - | 2 | - | - |
| Fellowship International Mission | 1989 | - | - | - | 2 | - |
| Foursquare Missions International | 1997 | - | - | 4 | - | - |
| Global Outreach International | 1984 | - | - | 22 | - | - |
| Good Shepherd Ministries International | 2004 | 2 | - | - | - | - |
| Gospel Communications International, Inc. | 1999 | - | - | - | 4 | - |
| Greater Grace World Outreach | 1996 | - | - | - | 47 | - |
| Habitat for Humanity International | 1984 | - | 1 | - | - | 1 |
| Harvest International, Inc. | 1997 | - | 2 | - | 2 | - |
| Hope for the Hungry | | 1 | - | - | - | 1 |
| HOPE International | | - | 1 | - | - | - |
| Hosanna | 2006 | - | - | - | 2 | - |
| I. N. Network USA | 1994 | - | - | - | 74 | - |
| In Touch Mission International | | - | - | 1 | 1 | - |
| International Christian Ministries | 1990 | - | - | - | 6 | - |
| International Gospel Outreach | 2005 | - | - | - | 4 | - |
| International Justice Mission | | 1 | - | - | 6 | - |
| Intl. Pentecostal Holiness Ch. World Missions Mins. | 2002 | - | - | 2 | - | - |
| International Teams, U.S.A. | | - | - | - | - | 5 |
| Larry Jones Intl. Ministries (Feed the Children) | 1990 | - | - | - | 7 | - |
| MAP International | 2006 | - | - | - | 4 | - |
| Medical Ambassadors International, Inc. | 1990 | - | - | 2 | 8 | - |
| Mission Aviation Fellowship | | - | - | 2 | - | - |
| Mission Ministries, Inc. | 1985 | - | - | 3 | - | - |
| Mission ONE, Inc. | 1990 | - | - | - | 6 | - |
| Mission to the World (PCA), Inc. | 1983 | 2 | - | - | - | - |
| Mission: Moving Mountains, Inc. | 1982 | - | - | - | 6 | - |
| Missionary Ventures International | 2002 | - | - | - | - | 2 |
| Northwest Medical Teams International, Inc. | 2004 | - | - | - | 40 | - |
| Orthodox Presbyterian Church | 1995 | 2 | 3 | 8 | - | - |
| Presbyterian Evangelistic Fellowship | | - | - | 2 | - | - |
| Salvation Army, U.S.A. | | - | - | 1 | - | - |
| Samaritan's Purse | 1999 | 5 | - | - | 117 | - |
| Seed International | 1999 | - | - | 1 | - | - |
| Servants in Faith & Technology (SIFAT) | 2005 | 1 | - | - | 1 | - |
| Seventh-day Adventists General Conference | 1926 | - | - | 6 | - | 10 |
| Source of Light Ministries International, Inc. | 1998 | - | - | - | 2 | - |

| | First Year | Personnel from U.S. 1-2 yrs. | 2-4 yrs. | 4+ yrs. | Other Countries Citizens | Non-Citizens |
|---|---|---|---|---|---|---|
| South American Missionary Society (USA) | 2004 | - | 1 | 2 | - | - |
| Teen Missions International, Inc. | 1992 | - | - | 1 | 6 | - |
| The Master's Mission, Inc. | 1998 | - | - | - | 2 | - |
| Things To Come Mission, Inc. | 2004 | - | - | - | - | 2 |
| Touch the World Youth Ministries | | - | - | 3 | - | - |
| United Pentecostal Ch. Intl., Foreign Missions Div. | 1970 | - | 2 | - | - | - |
| Walk Thru the Bible Ministries, Inc. | 1999 | - | - | - | 3 | - |
| Word of Life Fellowship, Inc.—Intl. Ministries | 2002 | - | - | - | - | 2 |
| World Concern | 1985 | - | - | - | - | 1 |
| World Gospel Mission | 1992 | - | 5 | 10 | - | - |
| World Harvest Mission | 1984 | - | 3 | 11 | - | - |
| World Orphans | | - | - | - | 1 | - |
| World Venture | 1961 | - | - | 18 | - | - |
| Youth for Christ/USA—World Outreach | | | | 1 | - | - |
| | Totals: | 22 | 26 | 199 | 610 | 62 |

## Ukraine

| | First Year | 1-2 yrs. | 2-4 yrs. | 4+ yrs. | Citizens | Non-Citizens |
|---|---|---|---|---|---|---|
| Action International Ministries | 1996 | - | - | 2 | - | 1 |
| Assemblies of God World Missions | 1993 | 7 | - | 23 | - | - |
| Association of Christian Schools Intl. (ACSI) | 1992 | - | - | 2 | - | - |
| Association of Free Lutheran Congregations | 2006 | - | 2 | - | - | - |
| Awana Clubs International | 1992 | - | - | - | 16 | 2 |
| Baptist Bible Fellowship International | 1993 | 1 | - | 4 | - | - |
| Baptist International Evangelistic Ministries | | - | - | - | 25 | - |
| Baptist International Missions, Inc. (BIMI) | | - | - | 13 | - | - |
| BCM International | | - | - | 2 | 10 | - |
| Calvary International | 1992 | - | - | 2 | - | - |
| Campus Crusade for Christ, Intl. | 1991 | 1 | - | 13 | 95 | 6 |
| Centers for Apologetics Research (CFAR), the | 1999 | - | 1 | - | 1 | - |
| Child Evangelism Fellowship, Inc. | 1989 | - | - | - | 6 | - |
| Children's HopeChest | 2006 | - | - | - | 2 | - |
| Chosen People Ministries | 1995 | - | - | - | - | - |
| Christ to the Nations | 1991 | - | - | 2 | 6 | - |
| Christian Aid Ministries | | - | 2 | - | - | - |
| Christian Aid Mission | | - | - | - | 162 | - |
| Christian Broadcasting Network Inc., the | 1991 | - | 2 | 1 | 180 | - |
| Christian Churches / Churches of Christ | | - | - | 30 | 8 | - |
| Christian Ministries International (CMI) | 1992 | - | - | - | 1 | - |
| Christian Outreach International | 1993 | - | - | 1 | 2 | 1 |
| Church Leadership Development International | 1994 | - | - | - | 2 | - |
| Church of God (Cleveland, TN) World Missions | 1992 | - | - | 3 | - | 2 |
| Ch. of God (Holiness), World Mission Dept., Inc. | 1996 | - | - | 2 | - | - |
| Church of God of Prophecy—Global Outreach | | - | - | 3 | 16 | - |
| Church of the Nazarene, World Mission Dept. | 1992 | - | - | - | - | - |
| Churches of Christ | 1952 | 3 | - | 18 | 8 | - |
| CMF International | 1994 | - | 7 | - | - | - |
| David Livingstone KURE Foundation | | - | - | - | 25 | - |
| Donetsk Christian University | 1991 | - | 2 | 5 | 45 | 5 |
| Eastern European Outreach, Inc. | 1994 | - | - | - | 30 | 1 |
| EFCA International Mission | 1993 | - | 2 | 8 | 8 | - |

| | | Personnel from U.S. | | | Other Countries | |
|---|---|---|---|---|---|---|
| | First Year | 1-2 yrs. | 2-4 yrs. | 4+ yrs. | Citizens | Non-Citizens |
| European Christian Mission International—USA | | - | - | 2 | - | - |
| Evangelism Explosion International | | - | - | - | - | 10 |
| Fellowship International Mission | 1994 | - | - | 2 | - | - |
| Fellowship of Evangelical Chs.—Intl. Ministries | 1987 | - | - | 2 | - | 2 |
| Free Methodist World Missions | 1999 | - | - | 5 | - | - |
| Global Action | 2001 | - | - | 1 | 8 | 1 |
| Global Outreach International | 2000 | - | - | 5 | - | - |
| Global Outreach Mission, Inc. | | - | - | - | 8 | - |
| Globe Missionary Evangelism | 2000 | - | - | 2 | - | - |
| Good News Productions International | 1997 | - | - | 2 | 2 | - |
| Gospelink, Inc. | | - | - | - | 41 | - |
| Great Commission Ministries, Inc. | | 7 | - | 10 | 3 | - |
| Greater Europe Mission | 1993 | - | - | 2 | - | - |
| Greater Grace World Outreach | 1991 | - | - | - | 14 | - |
| Harvest International, Inc. | 1996 | - | 1 | - | 2 | - |
| HCJB Global | 1998 | - | - | 2 | - | - |
| HOPE International | 1998 | - | - | 2 | - | - |
| Hosanna | 1999 | - | - | - | 3 | - |
| International Institute for Christian Studies | 1991 | - | - | - | - | - |
| International Messengers | 2000 | - | 1 | - | - | 4 |
| Intl. Pentecostal Holiness Ch. World Missions Mins. | 1990 | - | - | - | 9 | - |
| International Teams, U.S.A. | | - | - | 9 | - | 3 |
| InterVarsity Christian Fellowship/USA—Msns. Dept. | | - | 4 | 1 | - | - |
| Jews for Jesus | 1991 | - | - | - | 30 | - |
| Medical Ambassadors International, Inc. | 1992 | - | - | - | 4 | 2 |
| Mennonite Mission Network | 1996 | - | - | - | - | - |
| Ministry to Educate and Equip Intl. (MTEE) | 1996 | - | 2 | - | 12 | - |
| Mission Possible Foundation, Inc. | 1990 | - | - | - | 8 | - |
| Mission to the World (PCA), Inc. | 1993 | 13 | 18 | - | - | - |
| Mission To Unreached Peoples | 2004 | - | - | 2 | - | - |
| Missions to Military, Inc. | 1998 | - | - | 2 | - | - |
| New Hope International | 1971 | - | - | - | 15 | - |
| New Life Advance International | | - | - | - | - | - |
| OMS International, Inc. | 2003 | - | - | 4 | - | 4 |
| Open Air Campaigners—Overseas Ministries | 2002 | - | 3 | - | 3 | - |
| Operation Mobilization | | 3 | - | - | - | - |
| Peter Deyneka Russian Ministries | | - | - | - | - | - |
| Pioneer Bible Translators | 1999 | - | - | 4 | - | 1 |
| Precept Ministries International | 1994 | - | - | - | 9 | - |
| Presbyterian Mission International (PMI) | 2003 | - | - | - | - | 1 |
| Reformed Church in Am., Gen. Synod Council | 2003 | - | - | - | 1 | - |
| SEND International USA | 1991 | - | - | 48 | - | 9 |
| TCM International Institute | | - | - | - | 1 | - |
| TEAM (The Evangelical Alliance Mission) | | - | - | 7 | - | - |
| Team Expansion, Inc. | 1991 | - | - | 4 | - | - |
| TITUS International | 1993 | - | - | 6 | 15 | - |
| Ukrainian Childrens Fund | 1995 | - | - | - | 2 | - |
| United Pentecostal Ch. Intl., Foreign Missions Div. | | - | 1 | - | - | - |
| Walk Thru the Bible Ministries, Inc. | 1998 | - | - | - | 26 | - |
| Women to the World | 1991 | - | - | - | - | - |

| | | Personnel from U.S. | | | Other Countries | |
|---|---|---|---|---|---|---|
| | First Year | 1-2 yrs. | 2-4 yrs. | 4+ yrs. | Citizens | Non-Citizens |
| Word of Life Fellowship, Inc.—Intl. Ministries | 1992 | - | - | 2 | 22 | 6 |
| World Baptist Fellowship Mission Agency, Inc. | | - | - | 2 | - | - |
| World Gospel Mission | 1997 | - | - | 6 | - | - |
| World Harvest Mission | 1999 | - | - | 2 | - | - |
| World Help | 1992 | - | - | - | - | - |
| World Link Ministries | 2002 | - | - | - | 51 | - |
| World Reach, Inc. | 1991 | - | - | 2 | 4 | - |
| World Venture | 1992 | - | - | 11 | - | - |
| | Totals: | 35 | 48 | 283 | 941 | 61 |

**United Arab Emirates**

| | | | | | | |
|---|---|---|---|---|---|---|
| Arab World Ministries | | - | 1 | 2 | - | - |
| Evangelical Baptist Missions | | - | - | - | - | 2 |
| Seventh-day Adventists General Conference | | - | - | - | - | 2 |
| Walk Thru the Bible Ministries, Inc. | 2002 | - | - | - | - | - |
| Worldwide Tentmakers, Inc. | 1992 | - | - | - | - | - |
| | Totals: | - | 1 | 2 | - | 4 |

**United Kingdom**

| | | | | | | |
|---|---|---|---|---|---|---|
| ACM International | 1998 | - | - | 2 | - | - |
| Adventures in Missions | 2005 | 1 | 1 | 2 | - | - |
| Africa Inland Mission International | | - | 2 | 19 | 10 | 3 |
| Alongside Ministries International | 1980 | 2 | 2 | - | - | - |
| Am. Baptist Chs. of the U.S.A., Intl. Ministries | 2006 | - | - | - | - | 2 |
| Apostolic Team Ministries, Intl. | | - | - | 2 | - | - |
| Arab World Ministries | | - | - | 7 | - | - |
| Artists In Christian Testimony | 2005 | - | - | 2 | - | - |
| Asian Outreach U.S.A. | | - | - | - | - | - |
| Assemblies of God World Missions | 2001 | 4 | - | 15 | - | - |
| Avant Ministries | 1963 | - | - | 3 | - | - |
| Baptist Bible Fellowship International | 1971 | - | - | 55 | - | - |
| Baptist International Missions, Inc. (BIMI) | | - | - | 39 | - | - |
| Baptist Mid-Missions | 1972 | - | - | 11 | - | - |
| BCM International | | - | - | 10 | 16 | - |
| Biblical Ministries Worldwide | 1968 | - | - | 7 | - | 7 |
| Brethren in Christ World Missions | 1979 | 1 | 1 | 2 | - | 1 |
| Cadence International | | - | 2 | - | - | 2 |
| Campus Crusade for Christ, Intl. | 1967 | 13 | - | 17 | - | 2 |
| Chosen People Ministries | | - | - | - | - | - |
| Christar | 1966 | - | - | 12 | - | - |
| Christian Associates International | | - | - | - | - | - |
| Christian Broadcasting Network Inc., the | 1997 | - | - | - | 4 | 1 |
| Christian Churches / Churches of Christ | | - | 6 | 20 | - | - |
| Christian Literature International | | - | - | - | - | - |
| Christian Outreach International | 1985 | - | - | - | 1 | 1 |
| Christians In Action Missions International | 1965 | - | - | 4 | - | - |
| Church of God (Cleveland, TN) World Missions | 1955 | - | - | - | - | 2 |
| Church of the Nazarene, World Mission Dept. | 1909 | - | - | - | - | - |
| Churches of Christ | 1860 | 4 | - | 52 | 9 | - |
| CLC Ministries International | 1941 | - | - | 1 | - | - |

| | First Year | Personnel from U.S. | | | Other Countries | |
|---|---|---|---|---|---|---|
| | | 1-2 yrs. | 2-4 yrs. | 4+ yrs. | Citizens | Non-Citizens |
| CMF International | 1989 | - | 10 | - | - | - |
| Eastern Mennonite Missions | | - | 4 | - | - | - |
| EFCA International Mission | 1993 | - | 2 | 2 | - | - |
| Elim Fellowship—International Department | 1979 | - | - | 2 | - | - |
| Episcopal Church USA—Domestic & Foreign | | - | - | 1 | - | - |
| Evangelical Presbyterian Church—World Outreach | 1991 | - | - | 3 | - | - |
| Far East Broadcasting Company, Inc. | 1995 | - | - | 1 | - | 1 |
| Fellowship International Mission | 1993 | - | - | 2 | - | - |
| Fellowship of Evangelical Ch.—Intl. Ministries | 2001 | - | - | 3 | - | 3 |
| Friends of Israel Gospel Ministry, Inc. | 2000 | - | - | - | - | 2 |
| Global Outreach International | 2000 | - | - | 5 | - | - |
| Global Outreach Mission, Inc. | | - | - | 9 | 8 | - |
| Global Partners / Wesleyan World Missions | 1990 | - | 2 | - | - | - |
| Globe Missionary Evangelism | 1994 | - | - | 10 | - | - |
| Go Ye Fellowship | | 1 | - | - | - | - |
| Gospel Fellowship Association | 1972 | 1 | - | 19 | - | - |
| Grace Brethren International Missions | 1982 | - | - | 8 | - | - |
| Greater Europe Mission | 1970 | - | 2 | 2 | - | - |
| Greater Grace World Outreach | 1975 | - | - | 1 | 4 | 5 |
| Habitat for Humanity International | 1994 | - | 1 | - | 1 | - |
| HCJB Global | | - | - | - | 8 | - |
| Helps International Ministries | | - | - | 2 | - | - |
| International Board of Jewish Missions, Inc. | 1996 | - | - | 2 | - | - |
| Intl. Pentecostal Holiness Ch. World Missions Mins. | 1978 | - | - | 8 | - | - |
| International Teams, U.S.A. | | - | 1 | 13 | - | 15 |
| InterVarsity Christian Fellowship/USA—Msns. Dept. | | - | - | 5 | - | - |
| Jews for Jesus | 1992 | - | - | 2 | 4 | 1 |
| Josue Yrion World Evangelism and Missions, Inc. | 2000 | - | - | - | - | 1 |
| Luis Palau Evangelistic Assoc. | 1977 | - | - | - | 3 | - |
| Macedonia World Baptist Missions, Inc. | 1984 | - | - | 5 | - | - |
| Mennonite Mission Network | 1952 | - | - | 2 | - | - |
| Mission to the World (PCA), Inc. | 1990 | 6 | 23 | - | - | - |
| Missionary Revival Crusade | | - | 2 | - | - | - |
| Missionary Ventures International | 1990 | - | - | 2 | - | - |
| Navigators, U.S. International Missions Group | | 2 | - | 2 | - | - |
| New Tribes Mission | 1958 | - | - | 8 | 20 | - |
| OC International, Inc. | 2000 | - | - | 4 | - | - |
| OMS International, Inc. | | - | - | - | - | 7 |
| Operation Mobilization | 1961 | 13 | 5 | 21 | - | 14 |
| People International USA | 2002 | - | 2 | - | - | - |
| Precept Ministries International | 2002 | - | - | - | 1 | - |
| Presbyterian Evangelistic Fellowship | | - | - | 4 | - | - |
| Ravi Zacharias International Ministries | | - | - | 2 | - | - |
| Red Sea Team International | 1953 | - | - | - | - | 2 |
| Reformed Baptist Mission Services | | - | - | - | - | 2 |
| Ripe for Harvest, Inc. | 2001 | - | - | 4 | - | - |
| Salvation Army, U.S.A. | 1865 | - | - | 7 | - | - |
| Seventh-day Adventists General Conference | | - | - | 6 | - | 13 |
| Things To Come Mission, Inc. | 1972 | - | - | - | 2 | - |
| TMA Ministries | 1985 | 2 | - | - | - | - |

| | Personnel from U.S. | | | | Other Countries | |
|---|---|---|---|---|---|---|
| | First Year | 1-2 yrs. | 2-4 yrs. | 4+ yrs. | Citizens | Non-Citizens |
| U.S. Center for World Mission | | - | - | 2 | - | - |
| United Pentecostal Ch. Intl., Foreign Missions Div. | | - | 6 | - | - | 14 |
| Walk Thru the Bible Ministries, Inc. | 2003 | - | - | - | 4 | - |
| WEC International | 1913 | - | - | 9 | - | - |
| Word of Life Fellowship, Inc.—Intl. Ministries | 1980 | - | - | 2 | 2 | - |
| World Baptist Fellowship Mission Agency, Inc. | | 4 | 2 | 2 | - | - |
| World Harvest Mission | 1994 | 3 | 1 | 14 | - | - |
| World Missions Far Corners, Inc. | 1976 | - | - | 2 | - | - |
| World Team | 1986 | - | - | 2 | - | 4 |
| World Venture | 1998 | - | - | 6 | - | - |
| World Witness, Assoc. Reformed Presbyterian Ch. | 2002 | - | - | 3 | - | - |
| Worldwide Tentmakers, Inc. | 1995 | - | - | - | - | - |
| Young Life | | 2 | - | 6 | - | - |
| Youth for Christ/USA—World Outreach | 1983 | - | - | 8 | - | - |
| Totals: | | 59 | 73 | 509 | 97 | 105 |

## Uruguay

| | | | | | | |
|---|---|---|---|---|---|---|
| Armenian Missionary Association of America, Inc. | 1954 | - | - | - | - | - |
| Assemblies of God World Missions | 1946 | - | - | 10 | - | - |
| Baptist Bible Fellowship International | 1958 | - | - | 2 | - | - |
| Baptist General Conference—Intl. Ministries | 1991 | - | - | 2 | - | - |
| Biblical Ministries Worldwide | 1967 | - | - | 24 | 2 | 22 |
| Campus Crusade for Christ, Intl. | 1966 | - | - | - | 3 | - |
| Christian Aid Mission | | - | - | - | 6 | - |
| Church of God of Prophecy—Global Outreach | | - | - | - | 4 | - |
| Church of the Nazarene, World Mission Dept. | 1949 | - | - | - | - | - |
| Churches of Christ | 1952 | - | - | - | 1 | - |
| Free Will Baptist, Inc. Board of Intl. Missions | 1961 | 1 | - | 5 | - | - |
| Gospel Mission of South America | 1970 | - | - | 6 | - | - |
| International Board of Jewish Missions, Inc. | 1995 | - | - | 2 | - | - |
| International Partnership Ministries, Inc. | 2000 | - | - | - | 1 | 3 |
| Intl. Pentecostal Ch. of Christ—Global Msns. Dept. | 1996 | - | - | 3 | 3 | - |
| Intl. Pentecostal Holiness Ch. World Missions Mins. | 2004 | - | - | - | - | - |
| LOGOI Ministries | 1972 | - | - | - | 1 | - |
| Medical Ambassadors International, Inc. | 1999 | - | - | - | 1 | - |
| Mennonite Mission Network | 1954 | - | - | - | - | 4 |
| OMS International, Inc. | 2002 | - | - | 6 | - | 1 |
| SIM USA | 1995 | - | - | 6 | - | - |
| Spanish World Ministries | | - | - | 1 | 1 | - |
| United Pentecostal Ch. Intl., Foreign Missions Div. | 1932 | - | 2 | - | - | - |
| Word of Life Fellowship, Inc.—Intl. Ministries | 1976 | - | - | - | 2 | - |
| World Venture | 1995 | - | - | 4 | - | - |
| Totals: | | 1 | 2 | 71 | 25 | 30 |

## Uzbekistan

| | | | | | | |
|---|---|---|---|---|---|---|
| Assemblies of God World Missions | 1996 | - | - | 4 | - | - |
| Christian Aid Mission | | - | - | - | 27 | - |
| EFCA International Mission | 1995 | - | - | - | - | - |
| Evangelism Explosion International | | - | - | - | - | 2 |
| Food for the Hungry, Inc. | 2004 | - | 1 | - | - | - |

| | First Year | Personnel from U.S. | | | Other Countries | |
| --- | --- | --- | --- | --- | --- | --- |
| | | 1-2 yrs. | 2-4 yrs. | 4+ yrs. | Citizens | Non-Citizens |
| Greater Grace World Outreach | 1999 | - | - | - | 4 | - |
| International Outreach Ministries (IOM) | 1992 | - | - | 4 | - | - |
| InterVarsity Christian Fellowship/USA—Msns. Dept. | | - | - | 1 | - | - |
| Northwest Medical Teams International, Inc. | 1997 | 1 | - | - | 25 | - |
| Operation Mobilization | | 5 | 1 | 1 | - | - |
| People International USA | 1992 | 2 | - | 10 | 1 | 4 |
| Precept Ministries International | 1994 | - | - | - | 2 | - |
| Rosedale Mennonite Missions | 2000 | - | - | 2 | - | 2 |
| World Concern | 1993 | 2 | - | 1 | 136 | - |
| | Totals: | 10 | 2 | 23 | 195 | 8 |
| **Vanuatu** | | - | - | - | - | - |
| Assemblies of God World Missions | 1967 | 3 | - | 4 | - | - |
| Baptist Bible Fellowship International | 1999 | - | - | 2 | - | - |
| Church of the Nazarene, World Mission Dept. | 2001 | - | - | 2 | - | - |
| FRIENDS in Action, International | 2003 | - | 2 | - | - | - |
| United Pentecostal Ch. Intl., Foreign Missions Div. | 1970 | - | 5 | - | - | - |
| World Outreach International—US | 1995 | - | - | 2 | - | - |
| | Totals: | 3 | 7 | 10 | - | - |
| **Venezuela** | | | | | | |
| Assemblies of God World Missions | 1919 | 2 | - | 14 | - | - |
| Awana Clubs International | 1986 | - | - | - | 12 | - |
| Baptist Bible Fellowship International | 1966 | - | - | 4 | - | - |
| Baptist International Missions, Inc. (BIMI) | | - | - | 18 | - | - |
| Baptist Mid-Missions | 1924 | - | - | 7 | - | - |
| Brethren Assemblies | | - | - | 1 | - | - |
| Brethren in Christ World Missions | 1982 | - | - | 2 | - | - |
| Campus Crusade for Christ, Intl. | 1971 | 12 | - | 3 | 47 | - |
| Christian Churches / Churches of Christ | | - | - | 15 | - | - |
| Christian Outreach International | 1993 | - | - | 1 | 2 | - |
| Church of God (Cleveland, TN) World Missions | 1966 | - | - | 3 | - | 2 |
| Church of God of Prophecy—Global Outreach | | - | - | - | 3 | 1 |
| Church of the Nazarene, World Mission Dept. | 1982 | - | - | 6 | - | - |
| Church Resource Ministries (CRM) | 1992 | - | - | 14 | - | - |
| Churches of Christ | 1957 | 4 | - | 2 | 6 | - |
| EFCA International Mission | 1920 | 1 | 2 | 9 | - | - |
| Envoy International | | - | - | - | - | - |
| Fellowship International Mission | 1994 | - | - | - | - | 2 |
| Fellowship of Evangelical Chs.—Intl. Ministries | 1980 | - | - | 3 | - | 3 |
| Free Methodist World Missions | | - | - | - | - | - |
| Global Partners / Wesleyan Wld. Msns. | 2001 | - | - | - | - | - |
| Harvest | 1989 | - | - | - | 1 | - |
| International Board of Jewish Missions, Inc. | 1996 | - | - | 2 | - | - |
| Intl. Pentecostal Holiness Ch. World Missions Mins. | | - | - | - | - | - |
| Latin America Mission | 1987 | - | 2 | 1 | 1 | 2 |
| LOGOI Ministries | 1972 | - | - | - | 3 | - |
| Lutheran Church-Missouri Synod | 1951 | - | - | 3 | - | - |
| Macedonia World Baptist Missions, Inc. | 2002 | - | - | 4 | 2 | 2 |
| Medical Ambassadors International, Inc. | 1995 | - | - | - | 5 | - |

| | First Year | Personnel from U.S. | | | Other Countries | |
|---|---|---|---|---|---|---|
| | | 1-2 yrs. | 2-4 yrs. | 4+ yrs. | Citizens | Non-Citizens |
| Mission Aviation Fellowship | 1965 | 2 | 1 | 3 | - | - |
| Missionary Revival Crusade | | - | - | - | - | - |
| New Tribes Mission | 1946 | - | - | 50 | - | - |
| Pentecostal Free Will Baptist Church, Inc. | | - | - | - | 1 | - |
| Precept Ministries International | 1998 | - | - | - | 1 | - |
| Reformed Church in Am., Gen. Synod Council | 2003 | - | - | - | 2 | - |
| Seventh-day Adventists General Conference | 1910 | - | - | 2 | - | - |
| Spanish World Ministries | | - | - | 1 | 1 | - |
| STEM (Short-Term Evangelical Missions) Intl. | 2002 | - | - | - | - | - |
| TEAM (The Evangelical Alliance Mission) | | 1 | - | 16 | - | - |
| Team Expansion, Inc. | 1987 | - | - | 22 | 1 | - |
| Trans World Missions | | - | - | - | 2 | - |
| United Pentecostal Ch. Intl., Foreign Missions Div. | 1956 | - | 4 | - | - | - |
| WEC International | 1954 | - | - | 1 | - | - |
| Word of Life Fellowship, Inc.—Intl. Ministries | 1979 | - | - | - | 11 | 2 |
| World Indigenous Missions | 1997 | - | - | 5 | - | - |
| World Venture | 1986 | - | - | 4 | - | - |
| World-Wide Missions | | - | - | | 1 | - |
| Totals: | | 22 | 9 | 216 | 102 | 14 |

## Vietnam

| | First Year | 1-2 yrs. | 2-4 yrs. | 4+ yrs. | Citizens | Non-Citizens |
|---|---|---|---|---|---|---|
| All God's Children International | | - | - | - | 10 | - |
| Asian Outreach U.S.A. | | - | - | - | - | - |
| Assemblies of God World Missions | 1971 | 3 | - | 4 | - | - |
| Baptist International Outreach | | - | - | 2 | - | - |
| Calvary International | 1996 | - | - | 4 | - | - |
| Christian Aid Mission | | - | - | - | 64 | - |
| Church of God (Cleveland, TN) World Missions | 1995 | 1 | - | - | - | - |
| Church World Service | | - | - | - | - | 1 |
| Cook Communications Ministries International | 1999 | - | - | - | - | - |
| Educational Services International (ESI) | 2002 | 12 | - | - | - | - |
| Global Outreach International | 2003 | - | - | 2 | - | - |
| Globe Missionary Evangelism | 2002 | - | - | 2 | - | - |
| Habitat for Humanity International | | - | 1 | - | - | 1 |
| I. N. Network USA | 1991 | - | - | - | 57 | - |
| Intl. Pentecostal Holiness Ch. World Missions Mins. | | - | - | - | - | - |
| Medical Ambassadors International, Inc. | 1999 | - | - | - | 4 | - |
| Mission ONE, Inc. | 1990 | - | - | - | 1 | - |
| Mission To Unreached Peoples | 1997 | - | - | 2 | - | - |
| Northwest Medical Teams International, Inc. | 2005 | - | - | - | 1 | - |
| Partners International | 1991 | - | - | - | 451 | - |
| Samaritan's Purse | 2000 | 2 | - | - | 8 | - |
| Seventh-day Adventists General Conference | 1937 | - | - | 2 | - | - |
| Training Evangelistic Leadership (T.E.L.), Inc. | 1991 | - | - | 2 | 1 | 1 |
| United Church of Christ—Wider Church Ministries | | - | 1 | - | - | - |
| United Pentecostal Ch. Intl., Foreign Missions Div. | | - | - | - | - | - |
| Walk Thru the Bible Ministries, Inc. | 2000 | - | - | - | - | - |
| World Bible Translation Center | | - | - | - | 2 | - |
| World Concern | 1989 | 1 | - | - | 14 | - |
| World Indigenous Missions | 2004 | - | - | 2 | - | - |

| | First Year | Personnel from U.S. 1-2 yrs. | Personnel from U.S. 2-4 yrs. | Personnel from U.S. 4+ yrs. | Other Countries Citizens | Other Countries Non-Citizens |
|---|---|---|---|---|---|---|
| World Missions & Evangelism, Inc. | | - | - | 1 | - | - |
| World Missions Far Corners, Inc. | 1993 | - | - | 2 | - | - |
| Totals: | | 19 | 2 | 25 | 613 | 3 |
| **Virgin Islands** | | | | | | |
| Baptist International Missions, Inc. (BIMI) | | - | - | 2 | - | - |
| Church of God of Prophecy—Global Outreach | | - | - | - | 5 | - |
| Church of the Nazarene, World Mission Dept. | 1944 | - | - | - | - | - |
| Natl. Baptist Conv. of Am.—Foreign Msn. Bd. | 1978 | - | - | - | 6 | - |
| World Baptist Fellowship Mission Agency, Inc. | | - | - | 2 | - | - |
| Totals: | | - | - | 4 | 11 | - |
| **West Bank** | | | | | | |
| Helps International Ministries | | - | - | 2 | - | - |
| Totals: | | - | - | 2 | - | - |
| **Western Europe—General** | | | | | | |
| Awana Clubs International | 1991 | - | - | 2 | - | - |
| Dawn Ministries, Inc. | | - | - | - | - | 1 |
| TMA Ministries | 1982 | - | - | - | - | - |
| United World Mission | | - | 7 | 12 | - | - |
| Totals: | | - | 7 | 14 | - | 1 |
| **Yemen** | | | | | | |
| Arab World Ministries | | - | - | 6 | - | - |
| Assemblies of God World Missions | 2002 | - | - | 2 | - | - |
| Christar | 2006 | 1 | - | - | - | - |
| Seventh-day Adventists General Conference | | - | - | 2 | - | - |
| Walk Thru the Bible Ministries, Inc. | 2002 | - | - | - | - | - |
| Totals: | | 1 | - | 10 | - | - |
| **Yugoslavia** | | | | | | |
| Global Outreach Mission, Inc. | | - | - | - | 2 | - |
| Totals: | | - | - | - | 2 | - |
| **Zambia** | | | | | | |
| Action International Ministries | 2002 | 4 | - | 9 | - | 2 |
| Am. Baptist Chs. of the U.S.A., Intl. Ministries | 2006 | - | - | 2 | - | - |
| Assemblies of God World Missions | 1987 | 2 | - | 8 | - | - |
| Awana Clubs International | 1984 | - | - | - | 4 | - |
| Baptist Bible Fellowship International | 1989 | - | - | 16 | - | - |
| Baptist International Missions, Inc. (BIMI) | | - | - | 2 | - | - |
| Baptist International Outreach | 1987 | - | - | 5 | 2 | - |
| Baptist Mid-Missions | 1990 | - | - | 15 | - | - |
| Brethren Assemblies | | - | - | 25 | - | - |
| Brethren in Christ World Missions | 1906 | - | - | 3 | - | - |
| Campus Crusade for Christ, Intl. | 1975 | - | - | - | 61 | 1 |
| Child Evangelism Fellowship, Inc. | 1970 | - | - | - | 3 | - |
| Christian Literature International | | - | - | - | - | - |
| Christian Reformed World Relief Committee | 1990 | - | - | 1 | - | 2 |

| | First Year | Personnel from U.S. | | | Other Countries | |
|---|---|---|---|---|---|---|
| | | 1-2 yrs. | 2-4 yrs. | 4+ yrs. | Citizens | Non-Citizens |
| Ch. of God (Anderson, Ind.), Global Missions | 1986 | - | - | 3 | - | - |
| Church of God (Cleveland, TN) World Missions | 1965 | - | - | 3 | - | - |
| Church of God of Prophecy—Global Outreach | | - | - | - | 2 | - |
| Church of the Nazarene, World Mission Dept. | 1961 | - | - | 4 | - | - |
| Churches of Christ | 1919 | - | - | 2 | 3 | - |
| Global Partners / Wesleyan World Missions | 1930 | - | 4 | - | - | - |
| Gospel Fellowship Association | 2005 | - | - | 8 | - | - |
| Gospelink, Inc. | | - | - | - | 241 | - |
| Grace Ministries International | 1998 | - | 6 | - | 4 | 2 |
| Greater Grace World Outreach | 2004 | - | - | 3 | 2 | 2 |
| I. N. Network USA | 1985 | - | - | - | 12 | - |
| In Touch Mission International | 1995 | - | - | - | 5 | - |
| Independent Faith Mission, Inc. | | 4 | 1 | 9 | - | - |
| International Justice Mission | | - | 1 | - | 6 | - |
| International Partnership Ministries, Inc. | 2001 | - | - | - | 9 | - |
| Intl. Pentecostal Holiness Ch. World Missions Mins. | 1950 | - | 2 | - | - | - |
| International Teams, U.S.A. | | - | - | - | - | 2 |
| Ireland Outreach International Inc. | 2004 | - | - | - | 1 | - |
| Liebenzell USA | 1985 | - | - | 1 | - | 2 |
| Medical Ambassadors International, Inc. | 1999 | - | - | - | - | - |
| Mission to the World (PCA), Inc. | 2002 | - | 2 | - | - | - |
| Missionary Ventures International | 2000 | - | - | 2 | - | 2 |
| Natl. Baptist Conv. USA, Inc.—Foreign Msn. Bd. | 1993 | - | - | - | - | - |
| Navigators, U.S. International Missions Group | | - | - | 2 | - | - |
| Salvation Army, U.S.A. | 1922 | - | - | 1 | - | - |
| Seventh-day Adventists General Conference | 1905 | - | - | 2 | - | 8 |
| SIM USA | 1910 | 1 | - | 18 | - | - |
| Teen Missions International, Inc. | 1994 | - | - | 2 | 20 | - |
| The God's Story Project | 2000 | - | - | - | 1 | - |
| The Word for the World | 2004 | - | - | 2 | - | - |
| United Pentecostal Ch. Intl., Foreign Missions Div. | 1980 | - | 2 | - | - | - |
| Walk Thru the Bible Ministries, Inc. | 1999 | - | - | - | 8 | - |
| Wisconsin Evangelical Lutheran Synod | 1953 | - | - | 8 | - | - |
| Women to the World | 2005 | - | - | - | - | - |
| World Vision Inc. | 1981 | - | - | - | - | - |
| Totals: | | 11 | 18 | 156 | 384 | 23 |

## Zimbabwe

| | First Year | 1-2 yrs. | 2-4 yrs. | 4+ yrs. | Citizens | Non-Citizens |
|---|---|---|---|---|---|---|
| African Enterprise | 1980 | - | - | - | 5 | - |
| African Leadership, Inc. | 1998 | - | - | - | 1 | - |
| Assemblies of God World Missions | 1968 | - | - | 6 | - | - |
| Awana Clubs International | 1982 | - | - | - | 4 | - |
| BCM International | | - | - | 1 | - | - |
| Brethren in Christ World Missions | 1898 | - | - | 4 | - | - |
| Campus Crusade for Christ, Intl. | 1978 | - | - | 8 | 67 | 12 |
| Child Evangelism Fellowship, Inc. | 1951 | - | - | - | 2 | - |
| Christian Churches / Churches of Christ | | - | - | 34 | 14 | - |
| Church of God of Prophecy—Global Outreach | | - | - | - | 7 | - |
| Church of the Nazarene, World Mission Dept. | 1963 | - | - | - | - | 2 |
| Churches of Christ | 1902 | - | - | 2 | 1 | - |

| | | Personnel from U.S. | | | Other Countries | |
|---|---|---|---|---|---|---|
| | First Year | 1-2 yrs. | 2-4 yrs. | 4+ yrs. | Citizens | Non-Citizens |
| Fellowship of Associates of Medical Evangelism | 1961 | - | - | - | 10 | - |
| Gospelink, Inc. | | - | - | - | 75 | - |
| In Touch Mission International | | - | - | - | - | - |
| Independent Faith Mission, Inc. | | - | 2 | 2 | - | - |
| Intl. Pentecostal Holiness Ch. World Missions Mins. | 1950 | - | - | - | - | - |
| InterVarsity Christian Fellowship/USA—Msns. Dept. | | - | 2 | - | - | - |
| Lott Carey Baptist Foreign Mission Convention | 1998 | - | - | - | 18 | - |
| Mission Aviation Fellowship | 1964 | - | - | 1 | - | - |
| New Mission Systems International | | - | - | - | 2 | - |
| Seventh-day Adventists General Conference | 1894 | - | - | 4 | - | 13 |
| SIM USA | 1887 | - | - | 3 | - | - |
| TEAM (The Evangelical Alliance Mission) | | - | - | 15 | - | - |
| Teen Missions International, Inc. | 1985 | - | - | - | 6 | - |
| The Word for the World | 1984 | - | - | - | 2 | - |
| United Church of Christ—Wider Church Ministries | | - | 4 | - | - | - |
| United Pentecostal Ch. Intl., Foreign Missions Div. | 1968 | - | 2 | - | - | 1 |
| University of the Family | 1998 | - | - | - | 2 | - |
| Walk Thru the Bible Ministries, Inc. | 1999 | - | - | - | 6 | - |
| White Fields Inc. | | - | - | - | 3 | - |
| World Missions & Evangelism, Inc. | | - | - | - | - | - |
| World Relief | 2003 | - | - | - | 2 | - |
| Totals: | | - | 10 | 80 | 227 | 28 |

# Prices Now Reduced!

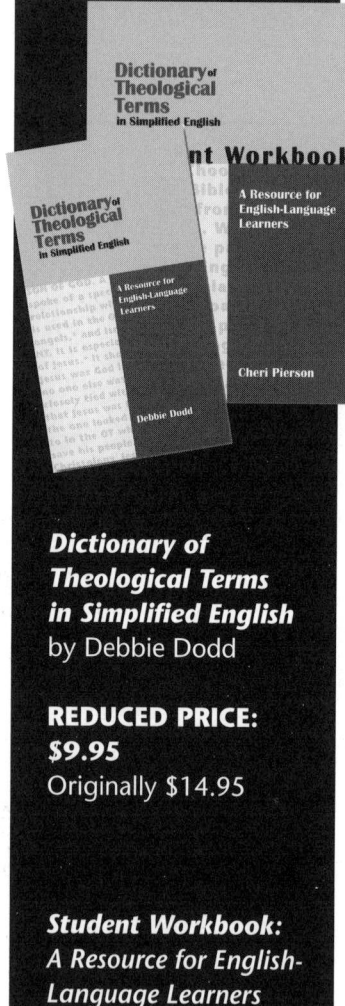

**Dictionary of
Theological Terms
in Simplified English**
by Debbie Dodd

**REDUCED PRICE:
$9.95**
Originally $14.95

**Student Workbook:
A Resource for English-
Language Learners**
by Cheri Pierson

**REDUCED PRICE:
$7.95**
Originally $9.95

*Dictionary of Theological Terms
in Simplified English* and
*Student Workbook*

**Clear, concise theological terms
for ESL/EFL students and professors.**

Most theological material today is written at a demanding readability level. This is a problem for international students and teachers with only a basic knowledge of the English language. The **Dictionary of Theological Terms in Simplified English** includes more than 650 common theological and biblical terms.

The companion piece to the **Dictionary** is the **Student Workbook**. Designed to strengthen one's understanding of theological terms, the workbook includes a dictionary quiz and references for: alphabetizing, guide words, word parts and families and short readings on theological topics.

**TO ORDER:**
Call 630.752.7158
Or go online to
**www.emisdirect.com**

Take **20% off** when you order
up to 10 copies.

Take **30% off** when you order
more than 10 copies!

# Evangelism Classics

*Be encouraged as you read.*
*Be strengthened as you work.*
*Be challenged as you share the gospel.*

For centuries, God has been raising up evangelist-leaders who exemplify what it means to live out the Great Commission. The twenty-two pocket-sized books in the Evangelism Classics series give you a glimpse at the lives and faith of some of these devoted men and women.

John R. Mott spurred global evangelism unlike any other Christian in the first half of the twentieth century. In *That the World May Believe*, believers are called to move beyond denominational, cultural and racial barriers to further the Kingdom of God.

Other books include original writings from godly saints such as George Muller, D.L. Moody, Brother Lawrence, Jonathan Edwards, Charles Finney, Phoebe Palmer, R.A. Torrey and others.

**22 Titles to choose from**

**Only $3.95 each**
+10% shipping and handling
$2.95 each when you order five or more
Get the entire set of twenty-two classics for just $50.00

Visit us at: **www.billygrahamcenter.org/emis**

To order, call 630.752.7960 or go online to: **www.emisdirect.com**

Published by the Evangelism and Missions Information Service (EMIS)
at the Billy Graham Center at Wheaton College, 500 College Ave., Wheaton, IL 60187

# EMQ
Evangelical Missions Quarterly

# A valuable resource for individuals and organizations involved in missions...

Since 1964 *Evangelical Missions Quarterly* (*EMQ*) has been providing practical information concerning missions. Today, *EMQ* has become the premier evangelical missions journal, read by thousands in North America and throughout the world.

## Available both in print and online, *EMQ* includes:
- articles by veteran missionaries and experts in fields pertinent to missions
- book reviews by experts in the missions field
- editorials on topics relevant to world missions today
- feedback from readers on past articles

## IN PRINT

The print edition allows you to build a valuable library with high-quality articles and editorials for future reference.

## ONLINE

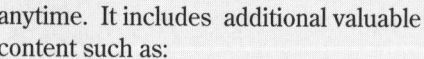

The online edition allows you to access *EMQ* and *EMQ* archives from any computer, anytime. It includes additional valuable content such as:

- more than forty years of archived *EMQ* articles
- current news and events not found elsewhere
- updated feedback from readers on posted articles

### Check it out at:
### www.emqonline.com

### New Subscriber Rates

One year (four issues) of *EMQ*
**$18.95**
One year of EMQonline
**$13.95**
One year of both *EMQ*
and EMQonline
**$28.95**

To order, call 630.752.7158
or go online to emisdirect.com

*EMQ* is published quarterly by the Evangelism and Missions Information Service (EMIS) at the Billy Graham Center at Wheaton College, 500 College Ave., Wheaton, IL 60189

# Chapter 5
# Canadian Protestant Agencies

This chapter contains the basic information for Canadian Protestant agencies engaged in Christian mission ministries outside Canada and the U.S. The comprehensive coverage includes agencies that directly support the work of such ministries or the work of overseas national churches/workers. The agencies supplied the information. The survey questionnaire used to gather the information is reproduced in the appendix.

The *Handbook* covers an agency's overseas ministry and support activities; it does not cover its mission work in Canada. Agencies with both overseas and Canadian mission ministries, however, were asked to include Canada-based ministry personnel in the total that appears in the "home ministry and office staff" line of the "Other Personnel" section.

Each agency will have at least seven of the basic categories of information listed below, with others included as applicable.

## Agency Name

Agencies are listed alphabetically. If the article "the" is in an agency's name, it will appear at the end of the name so the agency is in the most commonly referenced alphabetical order. Rare exceptions occur where the Christian public commonly uses the article "the" as the first word in the agency's name.

Agencies that have changed their name since the previous Handbook have their prior name listed also, with a cross-reference to the current or new name. A subdivision of a larger organization may be listed separately if it is organized to also serve the larger mission community rather than just its parent organization.

## Telephone and Fax Numbers

Area codes are in parentheses. Since area codes change rapidly, some may have changed since time of publication.

## Email Address

The Internet format and standards for capitalization are used. In some cases, agencies have a general email address (i.e.,Info@xxxx.org). Others have supplied an individual person's address within the organization. In cases where only a web address is given, it generally means a web page provides access to several email addresses so an inquiry can be immediately directed to the relevant department or person.

## Web Address

The Internet format and standards for capitalization are used. Most agencies have a web address; however, a few have chosen not to list it for security reasons.

## Postal Mailing Address

A post office box number usually appears whenever the agency has one. Exceptions occur when the agency prefers the street address.

## Chief Executive Officer

In a few cases where there are multiple primary contacts, or due to agency preference, two officers may be listed.

## Short Descriptive Paragraph

A brief description appears based on the denominational orientation and primary activities information supplied by the agency. Additional specific information, such as name changes, mergers or other unique aspects may also be included.

## Purpose Statement

Purpose statements are included when available. Some of the statements are concise and shown in their entirety, straight from the agency or its promotional material. For most, however, common or similar phrases such as "exists for the purpose of" are replaced by ellipses to present a more concise statement.

## Year Founded in Canada

This date is the year the agency or overseas mission component of a larger organization was founded or incorporated in Canada. In some cases the denomination or organization may have existed earlier in another country. For some organizations, the founding date of the missionary-sending component may be later than the founding of the larger organization. For organizations that have experienced mergers, the founding date is generally that of the oldest component involved in the merger.

## Income for Overseas Ministries

This is the part of an agency's overall income used or budgeted for ministry activities outside Canada and the U.S. or in activities that directly facilitate overseas ministries. "NA" indicates that income in this sense is not applicable, and usually applies to specialized service agencies or agencies whose income is reported under a sister or parent organization. "NR" indicates that the agency did not report income for overseas ministries, but may make this information available upon request.

## Gifts-in-Kind

If applicable, this is the portion of the income received in the form of donated gifts-in-kind commodities and/or services used for overseas ministries. Please note that some agencies do not include gifts-in-kind as part of their financial audit process, so the value of such gifts may not be included in their income for overseas ministries. Gifts-in-kind amounts that were an insignificant percentage (usually less than one percent) are not shown as a separate item.

## Fully Supported Canadian Personnel Overseas

Not all agencies have overseas personnel in the following categories, so the above heading will not always appear. If applicable, the following lines will appear with the appropriate numbers:

- "Expecting to serve more than four years" for persons from Canada who are fully supported by the agency
- "Expecting to serve one up to four years" for persons from Canada who are fully supported by the agency
- "Nonresidential mission personnel" for fully supported Canadian mission personnel not residing in the country or countries of their ministry, but assigned to work and travel overseas at least twelve weeks per year on operational aspects of the overseas ministry

## Other Personnel

If applicable for the agency, the following lines will appear:
- "Non-Canadian serving in own/other country" for persons with either citizenship in their country of service or another non-Canadian country, who are fully or partially supported from Canada. Such individuals are not included in the specific numbers for individual countries listed under the "Countries" heading at the bottom of many entries.
- "Bivocational/Tentmaker from Canada" for persons sponsored or supervised by the agency, but who support themselves partially or fully through non-church/non-mission vocations and live overseas for the purpose of Christian witness and/or encouraging believers
- "Short-Term less than one year from Canada" for persons who went on overseas projects or mission trips that lasted at least two weeks but less than one year through the agency, either fully or partially supported, or raising their own support
- "Home Ministry and office staff in Canada" for persons assigned to ministry and/or office duties in Canada either as full-time or part-time paid staff/associates

## Countries

These are the countries where the agency sends Canadian personnel or regularly supports national or other non-Canadian personnel. Following the name of the country is the number of Canadian personnel with terms of service of four years or more. In some cases, a continent or other general region is shown instead of a country. This may be due to several reasons, such as mission personnel whose ministry covers several countries.

Where an agency's work is maintained by nationals of countries other than Canada or the U.S., or by personnel serving less than four years, the country of activity may be listed without a number. Refer to the chapter entitled "Countries of Activity for Canadian Protestant Agencies" for more detailed country personnel totals.

"Unspecified Country" may also be listed for security reasons.

**Note:** Since the time we gathered the information, "Serbia/Montenegro" has been divided into two separate countries: Montenegro and the Republic of Serbia. Our statistical information uses the combined status.

# ABWE (Association of Baptists for World Evangelization)
980 Adelaide St. S., Ste. #34
London, ON N6E 1R3 CAN

**Phone:** (519) 690-1009
**Fax:** (519) 690-1618
**E-Mail:** office@abwecanada.org
**Web Site:** www.abwe.ca

*Rev. David W. Smith, Exec. Dir.*

A sending agency of Baptist tradition engaged in church planting, theological education, funds transmission, support of national churches and mobilization for mission.

**Purpose:** "...to serve local churches by assisting them to achieve their Canadian and international mission objectives."

**Year founded in CAN:** 1967
**Income for overseas min:** $1,500,000.00
**Fully supported CAN personnel overseas:**
  Expecting to serve more than 4 years: 25
  Expecting to serve 1 to 4 years: 3
  Non-residential mission personnel: 2
**Other personnel:**
  Short-term less than 1 year: 8
  Home ministry & office staff in CAN: 4
**Countries:** Bangladesh 1; Brazil 4; China; Croatia 2; Eastern Europe - General 1; Gambia, The 2; Liberia 1; Middle East 2; Portugal 2; Romania 2; Togo 4; Trinidad and Tobago 2; Ukraine 2

# Action International Ministries—Canada
3015 A 21st St. NE
Calgary, AB T2E 7T1 CAN

**Phone:** (403) 204-1421
**Fax:** (403) 204-1501
**E-Mail:** info@actioncanada.net
**Web Site:** www.actioncanada.net

*Dr. Wayne Whitbourne, Canadian Dir.*

An interdenominational sending agency of Evangelical tradition engaged in training, camping programs, childcare/orphanage programs, discipleship, leadership development, literature distribution and urban ministry to the poor.

**Purpose:** "...networks with local churches, national organizations and other mission agencies to reach people for Christ (evangelism), train them in Christian living (discipleship) and assist them in their physical and economic needs (development)."

**Year founded in CAN:** 1980
**Income for overseas min:** $1,383,914.00
**Fully supported CAN personnel overseas:**
  Expecting to serve more than 4 years: 17
  Expecting to serve 1 to 4 years: 2
  Non-residential mission personnel: 1
**Other personnel:**
  Short-term less than 1 year: 36
  Non-CAN serving in own/other country: 11
  Home ministry & office staff in CAN: 2
**Countries:** Brazil 2; Colombia 4; Ecuador 2; India 2; Philippines 5; Ukraine 1; Zambia 1

# Africa Inland Mission (Canada)
1641 Victoria Park Ave.
Toronto, ON M1R 1P8 CAN

**Phone:** (416) 751-6077
**Fax:** (416) 751-3467
**E-Mail:** general.can@aimint.net
**Web Site:** www.aimcanada.org
**Associations:** IFMA

*Dr. John P. Brown, Canadian Dir.*

A nondenominational sending agency of Baptist and Reformed tradition engaged in church planting, development, Christian education, missionary education, theological education and medical work.

**Purpose:** "...to plant maturing churches... through the evangelization of unreached people groups and the effective preparation of church leaders."

**Year founded in CAN:** 1953
**Income for overseas min:** $2,849,000.00
**Fully supported CAN personnel overseas:**
  Expecting to serve more than 4 years: 4
  Expecting to serve 1 to 4 years: 12
**Other personnel:**
  Short-term less than 1 year: 61
  Home ministry & office staff in CAN: 9
**Countries:** Kenya 2; Madagascar; Sudan 2; Tanzania

# African Enterprise Association of Canada
4509 W. 11th Ave.

Vancouver, BC V6R 2M5 CAN
**Phone:** (604) 228-0930
**Fax:** (604) 228-0936
**E-Mail:** aecanada@africanenterprise.com
**Web Site:** www.africanenterprise.com
*Mr. David Richardson, Exec. Dir./CEO*

A nondenominational support agency engaged in evangelism, development, justice & related issues, leadership development and short-term programs in more than 16 countries.

**Purpose:** "...to build strong partnerships for the mutual benefit of Africa and Canada...to enable African Enterprise to achieve its mission to: Evangelize the cities of Africa, through word and deed, in partnership with the church."

**Year founded in CAN:** 1964
**Personnel:**
  Short-term less than 1 year: 26
  Bi-vocational/tentmakers: 3
  Home ministry & office staff in CAN: 3

## Apostolic Church In Canada, The

27 Castlefield Ave.
Toronto, ON M4R 1G3 CAN
**Phone:** (416) 489-0453
**Fax:** (416) 489-6479
**E-Mail:** castlefield@sympatico.ca
**Web Site:** www.apostolic.ca
*Karl Thomas, President*

A network of apostolic churches of Pentecostal and evangelical tradition engaged in church planting, Bible distribution, evangelism, funds transmission and providing medical supplies. Countries of service and financial data from 1998.

**Purpose:** "...to establish a network of churches in apostolic relationship and reap a harvest through church planting."
**Year founded in CAN:** 1930
**Income for overseas min:** $250,000.00
**Gifts-in-kind:** $15,000.00
**Fully supported CAN personnel overseas:**
  Non-residential mission personnel: 2
**Other personnel:**
  Short-term less than 1 year: 60
  Bi-vocational/tentmakers: 3
  Non-CAN serving in own/other country: 22
  Home ministry & office staff in CAN: 11

## Apostolic Church of Pentecost of Canada

#119, 2340 Pegasus Way NE
Calgary, AB T2E 8M5 CAN
**Phone:** (403) 273-5777
**Fax:** (403) 273-8102
**E-Mail:** brian@acop.ca
**Web Site:** www.acop.ca
*Rev. Wes Mills, President*

A denominational sending agency of Baptist and Charismatic tradition engaged in church planting, discipleship, Christian education, leadership development, support of national workers, support of national churches and missionary training.

**Purpose:** "...an international network of ministers and churches providing fellowship, encouragement and accountability in the proclamation of the gospel of Jesus Christ by the power of the Holy Spirit."

**Year founded in CAN:** 1921
**Income for overseas min:** $1,800,000.00
**Gifts-in-kind:** $200,000.00
**Fully supported CAN personnel overseas:**
  Expecting to serve 1 to 4 years: 72
  Non-residential mission personnel: 50
**Other personnel:**
  Short-term less than 1 year: 150
  Bi-vocational/tentmakers: 5
  Home ministry & office staff in CAN: 2
**Countries:** Brazil; Burkina Faso; China; Congo, Democratic Republic of; Cote d'Ivoire; Estonia; Ghana; Guatemala; Honduras; Malawi; Mozambique; Russia; South Africa; Spain; Taiwan; Zimbabwe

## Arab World Ministries (Canada)

PO Box 3398
Cambridge, ON N3H 4T3 CAN
**Phone:** (519) 624-6170
**Fax:** (519) 624-6576
**E-Mail:** info@awmcanada.org
**Web Site:** www.awm.org
*Mr. Don Little, Exec. Director*

An interdenominational sending agency of Evangelical tradition engaged in church planting, discipleship, evangelism, support of national workers, short-term programs and tentmaking.

Year founded in CAN: 1967

Income for overseas min: $652,730.00

Fully supported CAN personnel overseas:
Expecting to serve more than 4 years: 18
Expecting to serve 1 to 4 years: 2

Other personnel:
Short-term less than 1 year: 17
Bi-vocational/tentmakers: 8
Home ministry & office staff in CAN: 6

Countries: Africa—General 8; Asia—General 3; France 2; Middle East 3; United Kingdom 2

## Avant Ministries Canada

2121 Henderson Hwy.
Winnipeg, MB R2G 1P8 CAN

Phone: (204) 338-7831
Fax: (204) 339-3321
E-Mail: amc@avmi.org
Web Site: www.avantministries.org
Associations: IFMA

*Mr. Grant Morrison, Canadian Director*

An interdenominational sending agency of Baptist tradition engaged in church planting, broadcasting, camping programs, discipleship, theological education and evangelism.

Purpose: "...to rapidly plant and develop churches where none exist."

Year founded in CAN: 1947

Income for overseas min: $1,915,000.00

Fully supported CAN personnel overseas:
Expecting to serve more than 4 years: 37
Expecting to serve 1 to 4 years: 4

Other personnel:
Short-term less than 1 year: 3
Home ministry & office staff in CAN: 8

Countries: Argentina 2; Austria 1; Bahamas, The 1; Belize; Bolivia 7; Brazil 2; Ecuador 4; France 1; Italy; Mali 9; Mexico 5; Poland 2; Spain 3

## Back to the Bible Canada

PO Box 10
Winnipeg, MB R3C 2G2 CAN
Phone: (204) 663-1782
Fax: (204) 663-1435
E-Mail: bttbible@backtothebible.ca
Web Site: www.backtothebible.ca

*Mr. Bob Beasley, CEO*

A nondenominational service agency of Baptist and Evangelical tradition engaged in broadcasting.

Purpose: "...a worldwide service ministry whose purpose is to lead believers into spiritual maturity and active service for Christ...and to reach unbelievers with the Gospel of Christ by teaching the Bible through media."

Year founded in CAN: 1954

Income for overseas min: $395,200.00

Personnel:
Home ministry & office staff in CAN: 5

## Baptist General Conference of Canada Global Ministries (BGCC Global Ministries)

#205 15824 131 Ave. NW
Edmonton, AB T5V 1J4 CAN

Phone: (780) 438-9127
Fax: (780) 435-2478
E-Mail: info@bgc.ca
Web Site: www.bgc.ca

*Jamey McDonald, Exec. Director*

A denominational sending agency of Baptist and Evangelical tradition engaged in church planting, theological education, partnership development and mobilization for mission. The mission agency of the Baptist General Conference of Canada.

Purpose: "...to involve every individual and every congregation in presenting the gospel and planting churches in their communities and around the world."

Year founded in CAN: 1981

Income for overseas min: $311,279.00

Fully supported CAN personnel overseas:
Expecting to serve more than 4 years: 6
Expecting to serve 1 to 4 years: 1

Other personnel:
Short-term less than 1 year: 2
Home ministry & office staff in CAN: 5

Countries: Asia—General 2; Ethiopia; Philippines 2; Portugal 1; Tanzania 1

## Barry Moore Ministries

PO Box 9100
London, ON N6E 3P3 CAN

Phone: (519) 661-0205
Fax: (519) 661-0206
E-Mail: bmoore@odyssey.on.ca

**Web Site:** www.bmoore.on.ca

*Rev. John Laari, Exec. Director*

An interdenominational service agency of Evangelical and Fundamental tradition engaged in evangelism, leadership development, support of national churches and training. More than 900 area-wide evangelistic crusades have been conducted throughout North America, Africa, Asia, and the islands of the seas.

**Purpose:** "...focused on communicating the gospel of Jesus Christ and bringing people to faith in Christ."

**Year founded in CAN:** 1960

**Personnel:**
   Home ministry & office staff in CAN: 3

## BCM International (Canada), Inc.

685 Main St. East
Hamilton, ON L8M 1K4 CAN

**Phone:** (905) 549-9810
**Fax:** (905) 549-7664
**E-Mail:** mission@bcmintl.ca
**Web Site:** www.bcmintl.ca

**Associations:** IFMA

*Mr. William Ricketts, Canadian Exec. Dir.*

A nondenominational support agency of Evangelical tradition engaged in childrens programs, bible memorization, camping programs, church planting, disability assistance programs, discipleship, Christian education, theological education, short-term programs, missionary training, training and translation work.

**Purpose:** "...to reach children...to develop churches worldwide."

**Year founded in CAN:** 1941

**Fully supported CAN personnel overseas:**
   Expecting to serve more than 4 years: 5

**Other personnel:**
   Non-CAN serving in own/other country: 5
   Home ministry & office staff in CAN: 1

**Countries:** Italy 2; Netherlands 1; Spain 2

## Bible Holiness Movement

PO Stn. A, Box 223
Vancouver, BC V6C 2M3 CAN

**Phone:** (250) 492-3376

*Wesley H. Wakefield, Bishop-General*

A denominational support agency of Holiness and Wesleyan tradition engaged in evangelism, audio recording/distribution, Bible distribution, literature distribution and support of national churches. Self-supporting, self-governed national workers in nine countries.

**Purpose:** "...to establish, conduct and maintain worldwide missionary work; to spread Scriptural holiness, vital Christianity and practical Godliness through a proper qualified ministry."

**Year founded in CAN:** 1949

**Income for overseas min:** $28,740.00

**Gifts-in-kind:** $3,700.00

**Personnel:**
   Short-term less than 1 year: 1

## Bible League of Canada, The

PO Box 5037
Burlington, ON L7R 3Y8 CAN

**Phone:** (905) 319-9500
**Fax:** (905) 319-0484
**E-Mail:** ministry@thebibleleague.ca
**Web Site:** www.thebibleleague.ca

*Rev. David J. Tigchelaar, Exec. Director*

An interdenominational specialized agency of Pentecostal and Reformed tradition engaged in Bible distribution, childrens programs, church planting, evangelism and Bible translation.

**Purpose:** "To provide Scriptures that bring people into the fellowship of Christ and His Church."

**Year founded in CAN:** 1948

**Income for overseas min:** $4,500,000.00

**Personnel:**
   Short-term less than 1 year: 18
   Home ministry & office staff in CAN: 17

## Bibles & Literature in French—Canada

Unicity PO 66066
Winnipeg, MB R3K 2E7 CAN

**Phone:** (204) 668-1273
**Fax:** (204) 668-1273
**E-Mail:** info@blfcanada.org
**Web Site:** www.blfcanada.org

*Mr. Harry Ens, Acting Canadian Director*

A nondenominational support agency of

Evangelical tradition engaged in literature production, Bible distribution, literature distribution and translation work.

**Purpose:** "...to provide Christian materials to meet the need of evangelism and discipleship in the French-speaking world."

**Year founded in CAN:** 2001

**Personnel:**
  Short-term less than 1 year: 2
  Home ministry & office staff in CAN: 1

# Biblical Literature Fellowship—Canada
# See: Bibles & Literature in French—Canada

# Brethren Assemblies (Canada)

(No central office)
connected to MSC Canada CAN

The Brethren Assemblies are also known as "Christian Brethren" or "Plymouth Brethren". Missionaries are sent from each local assembly (church) and not through a central agency. Personnel totals reported by MSC Canada.

**Fully supported CAN personnel overseas:**
  Expecting to serve more than 4 years: 236
  Expecting to serve 1 to 4 years: 1

**Other personnel:**
  Home ministry & office staff in CAN: 4

**Countries:** Angola 1; Argentina 2; Austria 8; Belgium 6; Bolivia 6; Botswana 2; Brazil 3; Chile 10; Colombia 1; Costa Rica 2; Cyprus 1; Czech Republic 2; Dominican Republic 3; Ecuador 5; Egypt 2; El Salvador 8; Finland 1; France 18; Ghana 3; Honduras 2; Hong Kong 2; India 4; Ireland 13; Italy 4; Japan 7; Kenya 2; Mexico 18; Netherlands 2; Nicaragua 2; Nigeria 4; Norway 2; Peru 5; Philippines 2; Poland 2; Puerto Rico 1; Russia 3; Saint Vincent and the Grenadines 1; Slovakia 2; South Africa 2; Spain 2; Unspecified Country 22; Uruguay 5; Venezuela 7; Zambia 36

# CAM International of Canada

PO Box 71034
Maple Hurst Postal Outlet
Burlington, ON L7T4J8 CAN
**Phone:** (905) 689-2473

**Fax:** (905) 689-2473
**E-Mail:** lljjhower@aol.com
**Web Site:** www.caminternational.org
**Associations:** IFMA
*Mr. Larry Hower, Director*

A nondenominational sending agency of Baptist and Evangelical tradition engaged in church planting, discipleship, theological education, evangelism and mobilization for mission.

**Purpose:** "...to contribute to fulfilling the Great Commission by partnering Canadians with the Spanish-speaking world..."

**Year founded in CAN:** 1965

**Income for overseas min:** $165,679.00

**Fully supported CAN personnel overseas:**
  Expecting to serve more than 4 years: 3

**Other personnel:**
  Short-term less than 1 year: 48
  Home ministry & office staff in CAN: 2

**Countries:** Guatemala 2; Mexico 1

# Campus Crusade for Christ of Canada, Inc.

20385 - 64 Ave.
Langley, BC V2Y 1N5 CAN
**Phone:** (604) 514-2000
**Fax:** (604) 514-2002
**E-Mail:** information@crusade.org
**Web Site:** www.crusade.org
*Mr. Leonard Buhler, President*

An interdenominational sending agency of Evangelical tradition engaged in evangelism, discipleship, leadership development and mobilization for mission.

**Purpose:** "...helping to fulfill the Great Commission in Canada and around the world, by developing movements of Evangelism and Discipleship."

**Year founded in CAN:** 1966

**Income for overseas min:** $6,884,009.00

**Gifts-in-kind:** $804,140.00

**Fully supported CAN personnel overseas:**
  Expecting to serve more than 4 years: 16
  Expecting to serve 1 to 4 years: 13
  Non-residential mission **Personnel:** 1

**Other personnel:**
  Home ministry & office staff in CAN: 70

**Countries:** Africa—General 2; Asia—General 5; India 2; Japan; Nigeria 2; Philippines 2; Russia 1; South Africa 2

## Canadian Assemblies of God

6724 Fabre St.
Montreal, PQ H2G 2Z6 CAN
**Phone:** (514) 279-1100
**Fax:** (514) 279-1131
**E-Mail:** info@caogonline.org
**Web Site:** www.caogonline.org

*Rev. David J. Mortelliti, General Superintendent*

A denominational support agency of Pentecostal tradition engaged in support of national churches, association of missions, broadcasting, leadership development, literature distribution and youth programs.

**Year founded in CAN:** 1912

**Income for overseas min:** $108,197.00

**Personnel:**
Home ministry & office staff in CAN: 3

## Canadian Baptist Ministries

7185 Millcreek Dr.
Mississauga, ON L5N 5R4 CAN
**Phone:** (905) 821-3533
**Fax:** (905) 826-3441
**E-Mail:** administration@cbmin.org
**Web Site:** www.cbmin.org

*Rev./Dr. Gary Nelson, Gen. Secretary*

A denominational sending agency of Baptist tradition engaged in leadership development, sustainable community development, joint pioneer outreach and global discipleship.

**Year founded in CAN:** 1912

**Income for overseas min:** $9,166,600.00

**Fully supported CAN personnel overseas:**
Expecting to serve more than 4 years: 40
Expecting to serve 1 to 4 years: 4

**Other personnel:**
Short-term less than 1 year: 500
Non-CAN serving in own/other country: 7
Home ministry & office staff in CAN: 33

**Countries:** Albania 1; Angola 3; Belgium 4; Bolivia 2; Brazil 3; Czech Republic 2; El Salvador; Hong Kong 2; Indonesia 5; Kenya 10; Middle East 6; Rwanda 2

## Canadian Bible Society / La Societe Biblique Canadienne

10 Carnforth Rd.
Toronto, ON M4A 1S4 CAN
**Phone:** (416) 757-4171
**Fax:** (416) 757-3376
**E-Mail:** donorenq@biblesociety.ca
**Web Site:** www.biblesociety.ca

*Rev. Phyllis M. Nesbitt, National Director*

An interconfessional support agency of Ecumenical tradition engaged in Bible distribution, linguistics, literature distribution, literature production, support of national churches and Bible translation.

**Purpose:** "...to promote and encourage, without doctrinal note or comment, the translation, publication, distribution and use of the Scriptures throughout Canada and Bermuda, and to cooperate with the United Bible Societies in its worldwide work."

**Year founded in CAN:** 1904

**Income for overseas min:** $2,694,000.00

**Personnel:**
Home ministry & office staff in CAN: 120

## Canadian Churches' Forum for Global Ministries

47 Queen's Park Crescent East
Toronto, ON M5S 2C3 CAN
**Phone:** (416) 924-9351
**Fax:** (416) 978-7821
**E-Mail:** admin@ccforum.ca
**Web Site:** www.ccforum.ca

*Patti Talbot, Chair*

An affiliated interdenominational service institution of the Canadian Council of Churches engaged in missionary training, children's programs, literature distribution and literature production.

**Purpose:** "...to provide a supportive, ecumenical environment where individuals interact with others involved in cross-cultural ministry for the purpose of discernment, orientation, renewal or re-entry."

**Year founded in CAN:** 1921

**Personnel:**
Home ministry & office staff in CAN: 2

## Canadian Convention of Southern Baptists (CCSB)

100 Convention Way
Cochrane, AB T3K 4S8 CAN
**Phone:** (403) 932-5688
**Fax:** (403) 932-4937
**E-Mail:** sjones@ccsb.ca
**Web Site:** www.ccsb.ca

*Rev. Gerald Taillon, Natl. Leader*

A denominational sending agency of Baptist tradition engaged in church planting, discipleship, extension education, theological education, evangelism and leadership development.

**Purpose:** "...churches in covenant giving ourselves away to advance the Kingdom of God."

**Year founded in CAN:** 1985

**Income for overseas min:** $127,336.00

**Fully supported CAN personnel overseas:**
Expecting to serve more than 4 years: 8

**Other personnel:**
Short-term less than 1 year: 20
Home ministry & office staff in CAN: 18

**Countries:** Africa—General 2; Chile 2; Eastern Europe—General 2; Western Europe—General 2

## Canadian Food for the Hungry International

201-2580 Cedar Park Pl.
Abbotsford, BC V2S 3S5 CAN
**Phone:** (604) 853-4262
**Fax:** (604) 853-4332
**E-Mail:** info@cfhi.ca
**Web Site:** www.cfhi.ca

*Mr. Ben Hoogendoorn, President/CEO*

A nondenominational service agency engaged in development, Christian education, leadership development, providing medical supplies, partnership development and relief and/or rehabilitation.

**Purpose:** "...to serve a suffering world by sending appropriate people, ideas and resources to needy communities influencing society to become advocates for the poor and empowering the Christian community with a Biblical view of poverty, social action and injustice."

**Year founded in CAN:** 1988

**Income for overseas min:** $40,874,000.00
**Gifts-in-kind:** $37,883,000.00
**Fully supported CAN personnel overseas:**
Expecting to serve more than 4 years: 5
Expecting to serve 1 to 4 years: 12
**Other personnel:**
Short-term less than 1 year: 24
Bi-vocational/tentmakers: 2
Non-CAN serving in own/other country: 1
Home ministry & office staff in CAN: 26

**Countries:** Bolivia 2; Brazil; Cambodia; Ethiopia; Indonesia; Peru; Romania; Thailand 2; Uganda 1

## Canadian South America Mission

PO Box 65057
St. Albert, AB T8N 5Y3 CAN
**Phone:** (780) 459-0941
**E-Mail:** cansam@samlink.org
**Web Site:** www.southamericamission.org
**Associations:** IFMA

*Mr. Bill Ogden, Exec. Director*

A nondenominational sending agency of Evangelical tradition engaged in leadership development, church planting, discipleship and support of national churches.

**Purpose:** "...to establish the church of Jesus Christ in South America by planting and nurturing churches, training church leaders, [and] developing church associations."

**Year founded in CAN:** 1982

**Income for overseas min:** $185,591.00

**Gifts-in-kind:** $185,591.00

**Fully supported CAN personnel overseas:**
Expecting to serve more than 4 years: 7

**Other personnel:**
Short-term less than 1 year: 10
Non-CAN serving in own/other country: 7
Home ministry & office staff in CAN: 1

**Countries:** Bolivia 2; Brazil 3; Peru 2

## Centre for World Mission— British Columbia

PO Box 1223 Metrotown RPO
Burnaby, BC V5H 4J8 CAN
**Phone:** (604) 856-3858
**Fax:** (604) 856-3858
**E-Mail:** cwmbc@telus.net
**Web Site:** www.cwmbc.org

*Ms. Sharon Walraven, Director*

An interdenominational support agency of Evangelical tradition engaged in mobilization for mission, Christian education, missions information service, partnership development, mission-related research and services for other agencies.

**Purpose:** "...to promote information on people groups of Canada and the world isolated by social and/or language barriers from mainstream society where a viable indigenous church is not yet existing."

**Year founded in CAN:** 1981

**Personnel:**
Home ministry & office staff in CAN: 1

## Child Evangelism Fellowship of Canada

PO Box 165 - Stn. Main
Winnipeg, MB R3C 2G9 CAN

**Phone:** (204) 943-2774
**Fax:** (204) 943-9967
**E-Mail:** info@cefcanada.org
**Web Site:** www.cefcanada.org

*Mr. Jerry Hanson, Nat'l. Director*

An interdenominational sending agency of Evangelical tradition engaged in evangelism, childrens programs, correspondence courses, discipleship, literature distribution and training.

**Purpose:** "...to assist and promote the evangelizing and discipling of children through leadership, coordination and administrative support to CEF ministries across Canada and overseas."

**Year founded in CAN:** 1970

**Income for overseas min:** $600,000.00

**Fully supported CAN personnel overseas:**
Expecting to serve more than 4 years: 8
Non-residential mission personnel: 2

**Other personnel:**
Non-CAN serving in own/other country: 6
Home ministry & office staff in CAN: 5

**Countries:** Albania 1; Asia—General 2; Australia 1; Bolivia 1; Brazil 1; Hungary 1; Japan 1

## Chosen People Ministries—Canada

PO Box 897, Station B
North York, ON M2K 2R1 CAN

**Phone:** (416) 250-0177
**Fax:** (416) 250-9235
**E-Mail:** info@chosenpeople.ca
**Web Site:** www.cpmcanada.ca
**Associations:** IFMA

*Rev. Joseph Gray, Director*

A nondenominational service agency of Evangelical tradition engaged in evangelism, church planting, discipleship and literature distribution.

**Purpose:** "...to serve as an arm of the local churches of the Lord Jesus Christ in fulfilling the Great Commission, with specific emphasis on the Jewish people."

**Year founded in CAN:** 1940

**Income for overseas min:** $102,513.00

**Personnel:**
Short-term less than 1 year: 2
Bi-vocational/tentmakers: 1
Non-CAN serving in own/other country: 3
Home ministry & office staff in CAN: 7

**Countries:** Israel; United Kingdom

## Christar Canada

PO Box 20164
St. Catharines, ON L2M 7W7 CAN

**Phone:** (800) 295-4158
**Fax:** (905) 646-8707
**E-Mail:** christar@on.aibn.com
**Web Site:** www.christar.org
**Associations:** IFMA

*Marty Frisk, Director*

An interdenominational sending agency of Baptist and Evangelical tradition engaged in discipleship, church planting, evangelism and tentmaking.

**Purpose:** "...proclaiming the gospel and establishing local indigenous churches, primarily among least-reached Asian communities worldwide."

**Year founded in CAN:** 1953

**Income for overseas min:** $300,000.00

**Fully supported CAN personnel overseas:**
Expecting to serve more than 4 years: 17

**Other personnel:**
Short-term less than 1 year: 8
Bi-vocational/tentmakers: 1
Home ministry & office staff in CAN: 4

**Countries:** Asia—General 14; Europe—General 3

# Christian Aid Mission

201 Stanton St.
Fort Erie, ON L2A 3N8 CAN

**Phone:** (800) 871-0882
**Fax:** (905) 871-5165
**E-Mail:** friends@christianaid.ca
**Web Site:** www.christianaid.ca

*Mr. James S. Eagles, President*

A nondenominational support agency of Evangelical tradition engaged in support of national workers, childcare/orphanage programs, Christian education, missions information service, support of national churches and relief and/or rehabilitation.

**Purpose:** "To aid, encourage and strengthen indigenous New Testament Christianity, particularly where Christians are impoverished, few or persecuted..."

**Year founded in CAN:** 1953

**Income for overseas min:** $1,300,000.00

**Gifts-in-kind:** $50,315.00

**Personnel:**
  Short-term less than 1 year: 2
  Home ministry & office staff in CAN: 11

# Christian and Missionary Alliance in Canada, The

30 Carrier Dr., Ste. 100
Toronto, ON M9W 5T7 CAN

**Phone:** (416) 674-7878
**Fax:** (416) 674-0808
**E-Mail:** info@cmacan.org
**Web Site:** www.cmacan.org

*Dr. Franklin A. Pyles, President*

A denominational sending agency of Evangelical tradition engaged in church planting, TEE and evangelism.

**Purpose:** "...a movement of churches transformed by Christ, transforming Canada and the world."

**Year founded in CAN:** 1981

**Income for overseas min:** $7,840,000.00

**Fully supported CAN personnel overseas:**
  Expecting to serve more than 4 years: 159
  Expecting to serve 1 to 4 years: 16

**Other personnel:**
  Bi-vocational/tentmakers: 15
  Home ministry & office staff in CAN: 28

**Countries:** Africa—General 10; Asia—General 4; Cambodia 7; China 12; Congo, Republic of the 3; Ecuador 3; France 3; Gabon 2; Germany 6; Guatemala 2; Guinea 4; Hungary 4; Indonesia 18; Japan 6; Laos 2; Malaysia 4; Mexico 20; Middle East 12; Netherlands 2; Niger 7; Philippines 2; Poland 4; Russia 4; Senegal 2; Serbia and Montenegro 2; Spain 1; Taiwan 2; Thailand 4; Venezuela 7

# Christian Blind Mission International—Canada

3844 Stouffville Rd., PO Box 800
Stouffville, ON L4A 7Z9 CAN

**Phone:** (905) 640-6464
**Fax:** (905) 640-4332
**E-Mail:** cbmi@cbmicanada.org
**Web Site:** www.cbmicanada.org

*Mr. David McComiskey, Exec. Director*

A nondenominational medical and rehabilitational agency engaged in the cure, prevention and care of disabling afflictions, including the training of nationals.

**Purpose:** "...to rescue and restore people trapped in poverty by disability."

**Year founded in CAN:** 1978

**Income for overseas min:** $8,540,527.00

**Gifts-in-kind:** $1,616,361.00

**Personnel:**
  Home ministry & office staff in CAN: 31

# Christian Reformed World Relief Committee of Canada

PO Box 5070 - Stn. LCD 1
Burlington, ON L7R 3Y8 CAN

**Phone:** (905) 336-2920
**Fax:** (905) 336-8344
**E-Mail:** crwrc@crcna.ca
**Web Site:** www.crwrc.org
**Associations:** AERDO, CWS, IFMA

*Ida Kaastra-Mutoigo, Dir. Canada*

A denominational service agency of Reformed tradition engaged in development, discipleship, justice, leadership development, partnership development and relief and/or rehabilitation.

**Year founded in CAN:** 1962

**Income for overseas min:** $8,275,036.00

**Fully supported CAN personnel overseas:**
  Expecting to serve more than 4 years: 14
  Expecting to serve 1 to 4 years: 7

Non-residential mission personnel: 3

**Other personnel:**
Short-term less than 1 year: 120
Non-CAN serving in own/other country: 20
Home ministry & office staff in CAN: 13

**Countries:** Bangladesh 1; Bolivia 1; Cambodia 2; Haiti 1; Kenya 1; Laos; Mali 1; Nicaragua 1; Niger 2; Romania 1; Uganda 1; Zambia 2

## Christian Studies International of Canada

13607-109 Ave.
Edmonton, AB T5M2G8 CAN
**Phone:** (780) 452-2715
**Fax:** (780) 465-3534
**E-Mail:** csidesk@telus.net
**Web Site:**
www.christianstudiesinternational.ca
*Dr. Henk W.H. Van Andel, Exec. Director*

A transdenominational service agency of Evangelical tradition engaged in Christian education, leadership development and tentmaking. An affiliate of International Institutes for Christian Studies.

**Purpose:** "...to recruit and support Christian professors to teach in public universities overseas, with the objective to provide students with an education rooted in a biblical worldview, preparing them to be godly servant leaders in their home country."

**Year founded in CAN:** 1995

**Income for overseas min:** $200,000.00

**Fully supported CAN personnel overseas:**
Expecting to serve more than 4 years: 3
Non-residential mission personnel: 4

**Other personnel:**
Bi-vocational/tentmakers: 4
Home ministry & office staff in CAN: 2

**Countries:** China 1; Nigeria 2

## Church of God (Anderson, IN) —Canadian Board of Missions

4717 - 56th St.
Camrose, AB T4V 2C4 CAN
**Phone:** (780) 672-0772
**Fax:** (780) 672-6888
**E-Mail:** wcdncog@cable-lynx.net
**Web Site:** www.chog.ca
*Rev. John D. Campbell, Exec. Dir. Min. Service*

A support agency of Holiness and Wesleyan tradition engaged in church planting, church construction, funds transmission, leadership development and providing congregational services to local congregations.

**Purpose:** "...focused on developing dynamic congregational life, effective leadership and church planting."

**Year founded in CAN:** 1905

**Income for overseas min:** $315,264.00

**Personnel:**
Short-term less than 1 year: 23
Home ministry & office staff in CAN: 3

## Compassion Canada

PO Box 5591
London, ON N6A 5G8 CAN
**Phone:** (519) 668-0224
**Fax:** (519) 685-1107
**E-Mail:** info@compassion.ca

**Web Site:** www.compassion.ca
**Associations:** AERDO
*Rev. Barry Slauenwhite, President/CEO*

An interdenominational service agency of Evangelical tradition engaged in child development, childrens programs, leadership development and support of national churches. Financial data from 2003.

**Purpose:** "...to advocate for children to release them from their spiritual, economic, social and physical poverty and enable them to become responsible and fulfilled Christian adults."

**Year founded in CAN:** 1963

**Income for overseas min:** $6,640,000.00

**Personnel:**
Home ministry & office staff in CAN: 43

## Crossroads Christian Communications Inc. (ERDF)

PO Box 5100
Burlington, ON L7R 4M2 CAN
**Phone:** (905) 332-6400
**Fax:** (905) 332-1880
**E-Mail:** dshelley@crossroads.ca
**Web Site:** www.crossroads.ca
*Mr. Byron Winsor, Exec. VP Admin.*

A nondenominational service agency of Pentecostal tradition engaged in broadcasting, agricultural programs, development, funds transmission, relief and/or rehabilita-

tion and supplying equipment.
**Year founded in CAN:** 1977
**Income for overseas min:** $2,680,897.00
**Gifts-in-kind:** $41,507.00
**Personnel:**
Home ministry & office staff in CAN: 160

## CrossWorld—Canada
1020 Matheson Blvd. E. #11
Mississauga, ON L4W 4J9 CAN
**Phone:** (905) 238-0904
**Fax:** (905) 629-8439
**E-Mail:** info.canada@crossworld.org
**Web Site:** www.crossworld.org
**Associations:** IFMA
*Rev. Dale Losch, Director*
A nondenominational sending agency of Baptist and Evangelical tradition engaged in church planting, discipleship, leadership development and support of national churches.
**Purpose:** "...to mobilize teams to make disciples and train leaders which will result in movements of reproducing churches among the unreached."
**Year founded in CAN:** 1931
**Income for overseas min:** $959,355.00
**Fully supported CAN personnel overseas:**
Expecting to serve more than 4 years: 14
Expecting to serve 1 to 4 years: 5
Non-residential mission personnel: 1
**Other personnel:**
Short-term less than 1 year: 21
Non-CAN serving in own/other country: 2
Home ministry & office staff in CAN: 9
**Countries:** Bosnia and Herzegovina; Brazil 7; Haiti 1; Ireland 2; Italy 1; Kosovo 1; Mexico; Senegal 2

## Czechoslovak Evangelical Mission
1601 Bramsey Dr.
Mississauga, ON L5J 2H8 CAN
**Phone:** (905) 822-8808
*Rev. Joseph R. Novak, President*
An interdenominational support agency of Baptist tradition engaged in literature production and literature distribution.
**Year founded in CAN:** 1984
**Income for overseas min:** $30,000.00

**Personnel:**
Short-term less than 1 year: 1
Home ministry & office staff in CAN: 1

## Emmanuel Relief and Rehabilitation International (also known as Emmanuel International)
See: Emmanuel International (ERRI)

## Emmanuel International (ERRI)
PO Box 4050
Stouffville, ON L4A 8B6 CAN
**Phone:** (905) 640-2111
**Fax:** (905) 640-2186
**E-Mail:** info@e-i.org
**Web Site:** www.e-i.org
**Associations:** AERDO
*Mr. Andrew Atkins, Exec. Dir. (Interim)*
An interdenominational sending agency of Evangelical tradition engaged in relief and/or rehabilitation, development, evangelism, partnership development and mobilization for mission.
**Purpose:** "...to encourage, strengthen and assist churches worldwide to meet the spiritual and physical needs of the poor in accordance with the Holy Scriptures..."
**Year founded in CAN:** 1975
**Income for overseas min:** $1,200,000.00
**Fully supported CAN personnel overseas:**
Expecting to serve more than 4 years: 14
Expecting to serve 1 to 4 years: 17
Non-residential mission personnel: 8
**Other personnel:**
Short-term less than 1 year: 18
Non-CAN serving in own/other country: 12
Home ministry & office staff in CAN: 9
**Countries:** Africa—General 12; Asia—General 2; Latin America—General

## Equip, Canada
PO Box 683
Duncan, BC V9L 3Y1 CAN
**Phone:** (250) 743-7171
**Fax:** (250) 743-7171
**Web Site:** www.equipinternational.com

*Rev. Barrie G. Flitcroft, Gen. Director*

An interdenominational sending agency of Baptist and Reformed tradition engaged in missionary training, agricultural programs, childcare/orphanage programs, development, disability assistance programs and medical work.

**Purpose:** "...to prepare, send and support evangelical missionaries to assist the church around the world to be responsive to the poor, sensitive to the Holy Spirit, focused on personal evangelism, and practically engaged in strengthening the Body of Christ."

**Year founded in CAN:** 1997

**Income for overseas min:** $108,000.00

**Personnel:**
Expecting to serve more than 4 years: 2
Expecting to serve 1 to 4 years: 2

**Countries:** Liberia 2

## Evangelical Covenant Church of Canada

PO Box 34025, RPO Fort Richmond
Winnipeg, MB R3T 5T5 CAN

**Phone:** (204) 269-3437
**Fax:** (204) 269-3584
**E-Mail:** messengr@escape.ca
**Web Site:** www.canadacovenantchurch.org

*Mr. Jeffrey Anderson, Superintendent*

A denominational conference of covenantal and evangelical tradition engaged in denominational funds transmission and mission mobilization for evangelism and church planting.

**Year founded in CAN:** 1904

**Income for overseas min:** $52,280.00

**Personnel:**
Home ministry & office staff in CAN: 3

## Evangelical Free Church of Canada Mission

PO Box 850, Langley Stn. LCD 1
Langley, BC V3A 8S6 CAN

**Phone:** (604) 513-2183
**Fax:** (604) 888-3108
**E-Mail:** info@efccm.org
**Web Site:** www.efccm.org

**Associations:** EFMA Candidate

*David McKinley, Exec. Director*

A denominational sending agency of Evangelical tradition engaged in church planting, theological education, evangelism, member care, mobilization for mission and short-term programs.

**Purpose:** "...exists to serve in the birth and growth of healthy churches internationally."

**Year founded in CAN:** 1976

**Income for overseas min:** $3,500,000.00

**Fully supported CAN personnel overseas:**
Expecting to serve more than 4 years: 55
Expecting to serve 1 to 4 years: 25
Non-residential mission personnel: 4

**Other personnel:**
Short-term less than 1 year: 70
Non-CAN serving in own/other country: 80
Home ministry & office staff in CAN: 7

**Countries:** Asia - General 4; Bolivia 10; Central Asia—General 2; Ecuador 2; Germany 2; Hungary 4; Japan 2; Lithuania 2; Mexico 4; Panama 2; Philippines 2; Russia; Thailand 2; Ukraine 15; Venezuela 2

## Evangelical Lutheran Church in Canada, ELCIC Mission in the World

302 - 393 Portage Ave.
Winnipeg, MB R3B 3H6 CAN

**Phone:** (204) 984-9164
**Fax:** (204) 984-9185
**E-Mail:** vim@elcic.ca
**Web Site:** www.elcic.ca/mission/world

*Mr. Kelvin Krieger, Program Coordinator*

The national mission office of a Lutheran denomination engaged in support of overseas partner churches, missions in Canada and campus ministry. Financial and personnel data from 2002.

**Purpose:** "...to share the Gospel of Jesus Christ with people in Canada and around the world through the proclamation of the Word, the celebration of the Sacraments and through service in Christ's name."

**Year founded in CAN:** 1985

**Income for overseas min:** $500,000.00

**Fully supported CAN personnel overseas:**
Expecting to serve more than 4 years: 5
Expecting to serve 1 to 4 years: 6

**Other personnel:**
Short-term less than 1 year: 3

Home ministry & office staff in CAN: 2

**Countries:** Cameroon 2; El Salvador 1; Hong Kong; Papua New Guinea 1; Peru 1; Slovakia; Thailand

# Evangelical Medical Aid Society

5155 Spectrum Way, Unit 30
Mississauga, ON L4W 5A1 CAN

**Phone:** (905) 625-4457
**Fax:** (905) 625-1812
**E-Mail:** main@cmds-emas.ca
**Web Site:** www.cmds-emas.ca

A nondenominational specialized agency of Evangelical tradition engaged in short-term programs, development, extension education, evangelism and medical work.

**Purpose:** "...to reveal Christ's love by working with national groups and to provide assistance in healing and teaching."
**Year founded in CAN:** 1948
**Income for overseas min:** $1,068,539.00
**Gifts-in-kind:** $73,295.00
**Personnel:**
    Short-term less than 1 year: 200
    Home ministry & office staff in CAN: 2

# Evangelical Mennonite Conference, Board of Missions

440 Main St.
Steinbach, MB R5G IZ5 CAN

**Phone:** (204) 326-6401
**Fax:** (204) 326-1613
**E-Mail:** emconf@mts.net
**Web Site:** www.emconf.ca
**Associations:** EFMA

*Mr. Len Barkman, Gen. Secretary*

A denominational sending agency of Mennonite and Evangelical tradition engaged in church planting, TEE, evangelism, leadership development, medical work, support of national churches and services for other agencies.

**Year founded in CAN:** 1953
**Income for overseas min:** $1,018,357.00
**Personnel:**
    Expecting to serve more than 4 years: 28
    Expecting to serve 1 to 4 years: 3

**Countries:** Burkina Faso 2; Mexico 11; Paraguay 15

# Evangelical Mennonite Mission Conf. Board of Missions & Service

Box 52059, Niakwa PO
Winnipeg, MB R2M 5P9 CAN

**Phone:** (204) 253-7929
**Fax:** (204) 256-7384
**E-Mail:** info@emmc.ca
**Web Site:** www.emmc.ca

*Mr. Len Sawatzky, Director of Missions*

A denominational sending agency of Mennonite tradition engaged in church planting, association of missions, missions information service, support of national churches and short-term programs.

**Purpose:** "...to inspire and facilitate local outreach and global mission."
**Year founded in CAN:** 1959
**Income for overseas min:** $650,000.00
**Fully supported CAN personnel overseas:**
    Expecting to serve more than 4 years: 6
    Expecting to serve 1 to 4 years: 6
**Other personnel:**
    Short-term less than 1 year: 6
    Non-CAN serving in own/other country: 10
    Home ministry & office staff in CAN: 5
**Countries:** Belize 2; Bolivia 4; Mexico

# Evangelical Missionary Church of Canada, World Partners

200-317 37th Ave. NE
Calgary, AB T2E 6P6 CAN

**Phone:** (403) 250-2759
**Fax:** (403) 291-4720
**E-Mail:** wpcinfo@emcc.ca
**Web Site:** www.emcc.ca

*Mr. Paul Brander, Assoc. Director*

A denominational sending agency of Evangelical tradition engaged in discipleship, church planting, correspondence courses, development, evangelism, medical work, relief and/or rehabilitation, short-term programs and Bible translation.

**Purpose:** "...to promote and provide opportunities for churches and individuals to participate in intentional, holistic ministry by sharing spiritual, human and material resources in cross-cultural and/or global contexts."

**Year founded in CAN:** 1998

**Income for overseas min:** $1,858,331.00

**Fully supported CAN personnel overseas:**
Expecting to serve more than 4 years: 8
Expecting to serve 1 to 4 years: 20
Non-residential mission personnel: 1

**Other personnel:**
Short-term less than 1 year: 10
Non-CAN serving in own/other country: 1
Home ministry & office staff in CAN: 4

**Countries:** Brazil; Cuba; El Salvador; Haiti; Hungary; Ireland; Mexico 6; Nigeria; Portugal 2; Romania; Spain; Tanzania

## Evangelical Tract Distributors

PO Box 146
Edmonton, AB T5J 2G9 CAN

**Phone:** (780) 477-1538
**Fax:** (780) 477-3795
**E-Mail:** etd-support@evangelicaltract.com
**Web Site:** www.evangelicaltract.com

*Mr. John Harder, President*

An interdenominational specialized agency of Evangelical tradition engaged in literature distribution, evangelism and literature production.

**Purpose:** "...to proclaim the Gospel of Jesus Christ and His message of forgiveness in as many languages as possible primarily by the printing of gospel tracts and any other appropriate media."

**Year founded in CAN:** 1935

**Income for overseas min:** $500,000.00

**Personnel:**
Home ministry & office staff in CAN: 7

## FAIR (Fellowship Agency for Internationafel Relief)

351 Elizabeth St.
Guelph, ON N1E 2X9 CAN

**Phone:** (519) 821-4830
**Fax:** (519) 821-9829
**E-Mail:** international@fellowship.ca
**Web Site:** www.febinternational.ca

*Mr. Norman E. Nielsen, Administrator*

A denominational support agency of Baptist tradition engaged in relief and/or rehabilitation, development and medical ministry. The relief arm of FEBInternational.

**Year founded in CAN:** 1974

**Income for overseas min:** $444,512.00

**Personnel:**
Home ministry & office staff in CAN: 1

## Far East Broadcasting Associates of Canada (FEB Canada)

3200-8888 Odlin Cresc.
Richmond, BC V6X 3Z8 CAN

**Phone:** (604) 717-8369
**Fax:** (604) 717-8383
**E-Mail:** dpatter@uniserve.com
**Web Site:** www.febcanada.org

*Mr. Don Patterson, Director*

An interdenominational specialized agency of Evangelical tradition engaged in broadcasting, audio recording/distribution, evangelism and literature distribution.

**Purpose:** "...to promote missions...to encourage evangelical Christians to participate in FEBCanada's ministries through prayer, financial support and personal involvement...to participate directly in FEB Radio International's broadcast ministry through the provision of staff, production of programs and the funding of missionaries and special projects."

**Year founded in CAN:** 1964

**Income for overseas min:** $1,142,719.00

**Fully supported CAN personnel overseas:**
Expecting to serve more than 4 years: 7
Expecting to serve 1 to 4 years: 2

**Other personnel:**
Home ministry & office staff in CAN: 25

**Countries:** Cambodia 1; Hong Kong 2; N. Mariana Isls 2; Philippines; Thailand 2

## FEBInternational

351 Elizabeth St.
Guelph, ON N1E 2X9 CAN

**Phone:** (519) 821-4830
**Fax:** (519) 821-9829
**E-Mail:** international@fellowship.ca
**Web Site:** www.febinternational.ca

*Rev. Richard Flemming, Director*

## Only one can be first.

He is first. That's why we created Prairie College of Applied Arts & Technology, the first - and only - school of its kind in Canada. So now you're able to pursue your ministry calling and a vocation - all in less than two years. Imagine that; make the Lord your priority and earn a great career all in one school. Now that has to be a first!

Learn more. Call us at **1.800.661.2425** or visit us online at **Prairie.edu**

## PRAIRIE
### Building a passionate Body of Christ

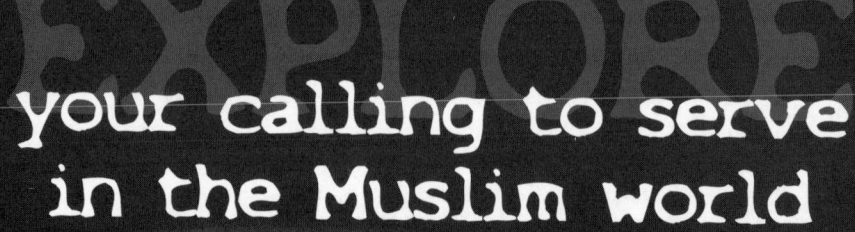

# EXPLORE
# your calling to serve in the Muslim world

## Short-term & Specialty Teams
2 weeks - 2 months to explore team life in the Muslim world or 6-12 months of relief and development work

## The Journey
Know God's tugging at your heart, but need more information? Whether you are considering an overseas career or a short-term trip, fill out "The Journey" online at www.frontiers.ca

## Frontiers | christian ministries inc

Find out how you can lead or join a peacemaking team in the Muslim world.

www.frontiers.ca   1.877.421.9090

A denominational overseas sending agency of the Fellowship of Evangelical Baptist Churches of Canada engaged in church planting and mobilization for mission.

**Year founded in CAN:** 1963

**Income for overseas min:** $3,187,236.00

**Fully supported CAN personnel overseas:**
Expecting to serve more than 4 years: 45
Expecting to serve 1 to 4 years: 3

**Other personnel:**
Short-term less than 1 year: 10
Non-CAN serving in own/other country: 5
Home ministry & office staff in CAN: 10

**Countries:** Belgium 6; Colombia 5; France; India; Italy; Japan 6; Kazakhstan 2; Kenya 2; Middle East 2; Netherlands 2; Pakistan 8; Philippines 2; Poland 3; Spain 2; Venezuela 5

## Frontiers Canada

**(See ad page 542)**
PO Box 9090
Edmonton, AB T5P 4K1 CAN
**Phone:** (780) 421-9090
**Fax:** (780) 421-9292
**E-Mail:** info@frontiers.ca
**Web Site:** www.frontiers.ca

*Rev. Nelson Wolf, Canadian Director*

An interdenominational sending agency of Evangelical tradition engaged in evangelism, development, discipleship, leadership development, support of national churches and relief and/or rehabilitation.

**Purpose:** "...working in close cooperation with local churches to see vital, worshipping witnessing churches established..."

**Year founded in CAN:** 1984

**Income for overseas min:** $998,546.00

**Fully supported CAN personnel overseas:**
Expecting to serve more than 4 years: 39

**Other personnel:**
Short-term less than 1 year: 6
Bi-vocational/tentmakers: 16
Home ministry & office staff in CAN: 19

**Countries:** Africa—General 7; Asia—General 14; Central Asia—General 9; Europe—General 2; Middle East 4; United Kingdom 3

## Fundamental Baptist Mission of Trinidad and Tobago (Canada)

Calvary Church, 746 Pape Ave.
Toronto ON M4K 3S7 CAN
**Phone:** (416) 466-3040 Ext.15
**Fax:** (416) 466-0945
**E-Mail:** pastoralcare@calvarychurch.ca

*Garry Francis, Secretary-Treasurer*

A support agency of Baptist and Fundamental tradition engaged in funds transmission and support of national workers. Financial data included in USA sister agency.

**Year founded in CAN:** 1990

**Personnel:**
Home ministry & office staff in CAN: 1

## Galcom International

115 Nebo Rd.
Hamilton, ON L8W 2E1 CAN
**Phone:** (905) 574-4626
**Fax:** (905) 574-4633
**E-Mail:** galcom@galcom.org
**Web Site:** www.galcom.org
**Associations:** IFMA

*Rev. Allan T. McGuirl, Intl. Director*

An interdenominational support agency of Evangelical and Baptist tradition engaged in designing, building and distributing high-tech communications equipment for other agencies used in evangelism and other ministries in 102 countries.

**Purpose:** "To provide durable technical equipment for communicating the Gospel worldwide."

**Year founded in CAN:** 1989

**Income for overseas min:** $1,695,219.00

**Personnel:**
Home ministry & office staff in CAN: 12

## Global Outreach Mission Inc.,Canada

261 Martindale Rd. #7, PO Box 1210
St. Catherines, ON L2W 1A1 CAN
**Phone:** (950) 684-1401
**Fax:** (905) 684-3069
**E-Mail:** glmiss@on.aibn.com
**Web Site:** www.missiongo.org
**Associations:** IFMA

*Dr. Brian M. Albrecht, President*

An interdenominational sending agency of Evangelical and Independent tradition engaged in church planting, broadcasting, evangelism, medical work, support of national workers and mobilization for mission.

**Purpose:** "...sharing the gospel planting and encouraging His church, helping the hurting physically and serving in every area of Christian development."

**Year founded in CAN:** 1943

**Income for overseas min:** $1,111,544.00

**Fully supported CAN personnel overseas:**
Expecting to serve more than 4 years: 26
Expecting to serve 1 to 4 years: 2

**Other personnel:**
Short-term less than 1 year: 64
Home ministry & office staff in CAN: 14

**Countries:** Belgium 1; Brazil 1; Congo, Republic of the 1; France 5; Guatemala 4; Haiti 1; India 6; Ireland 4; Romania 1; South Africa 2

## Global Recordings Network Canada

Unit 6, 120 Lancing Dr.
Hamilton, ON L8W 3A1 CAN

**Phone:** (905) 574-8220
**Fax:** (905) 574-6843
**E-Mail:** ca@globalrecordings.net
**Web Site:** www.globalrecordings.net/ca

**Associations:** IFMA

*Rev. Roy Grant, Natl. Director*

A nondenominational specialized agency of Baptist tradition engaged in audio recording/distribution, evangelism, support of national workers, mobilization for mission and translation work.

**Purpose:** "...to tell the story of Jesus in every language."

**Year founded in CAN:** 1969

**Income for overseas min:** $47,714.00

**Fully supported CAN personnel overseas:**
Expecting to serve more than 4 years: 4
Expecting to serve 1 to 4 years: 1

**Other personnel:**
Home ministry & office staff in CAN: 5

**Countries:** Kenya 4; South Africa

## Gospel for Asia

245 King St. E.
Stoney Creek, ON L8G 1L9 CAN

**Phone:** (905) 662-2101
**Fax:** (905) 662-8447
**E-Mail:** infocanada@gfa.org
**Web Site:** www.gfa.org

*Pastor Wendell Leytham, Director*

A nondenominational support agency of Evangelical tradition engaged in support of national workers totaling approximately 16,000 native missionaries, Bible distribution, broadcasting, church planting, evangelism and literature production.

**Year founded in CAN:** 1984

**Countries:** Bangladesh; Bhutan; Cambodia; China; India; Laos; Myanmar/Burma; Nepal; Sri Lanka; Thailand

## Gospel Mission of South America of Canada

PO Box 150
St. Charles, ON P0M 2W0 CAN

**Phone:** (705) 967-1262
**E-Mail:** canada@gmsa.org
**Web Site:** www.gmsa.org

*Rev. David Clarke, Chairman*

A nondenominational sending agency of Baptist and Fundamental tradition engaged in church planting, theological education and leadership development.

**Purpose:** "...to evangelize the people of Latin America by means of itinerant and localized work, with the object of establishing and developing indigenous churches."

**Fully supported CAN personnel overseas:**
Expecting to serve more than 4 years: 7
Expecting to serve 1 to 4 years: 4

**Other personnel:**
Non-CAN serving in own/other country: 11

**Countries:** Argentina 2; Chile 2; United Kingdom 1; Uruguay 2

## Gospel Missionary Union of Canada
## See: Avant Ministries Canada

## Greater Europe Mission (Canada)

100 Ontario St.
Oshawa, ON L1G 4Z1 CAN

**Phone:** (905) 728-8222
**Fax:** (905) 728-8958
**E-Mail:** gemcanada@gemission.com
**Web Site:** www.gemission.org
**Associations:** IFMA

*Rev. J. Howard Moore, Canadian Director*

A nondenominational sending agency of Evangelical tradition engaged in church planting, camping programs, theological education, evangelism, leadership development and youth programs.

**Purpose:** "...to assist the peoples of greater Europe in building up the Body of Christ so every person in greater Europe is within reach of a witnessing fellowship."

**Year founded in CAN:** 1959

**Income for overseas min:** $1,190,061.00

**Fully supported CAN personnel overseas:**
  Expecting to serve more than 4 years: 12
  Expecting to serve 1 to 4 years: 7

**Other personnel:**
  Short-term less than 1 year: 32
  Home ministry & office staff in CAN: 5

**Countries:** Croatia 2; Germany 4; Hungary 1; Latvia; Luxembourg 2; Portugal 2; Ukraine 1

## HCJB Global—Canada

6655 Kitimat Road, Unit #2
Mississauga, ON L5N 6J4 CAN

**Phone:** (905) 814-0176
**Fax:** (905) 814-6805
**E-Mail:** canada@hcjb.org
**Web Site:** www.hcjb.org

*Mr. Ian Leaver, Director*

An interdenominational support agency of Evangelical tradition engaged in broadcasting, discipleship, Christian education, medical work, partnership development and video/film production/distribution. Financial data from 2003.

**Year founded in CAN:** 1950

**Income for overseas min:** $1,300,000.00

**Fully supported CAN personnel overseas:**
  Expecting to serve more than 4 years: 10

Expecting to serve 1 to 4 years: 6

**Other personnel:**
  Home ministry & office staff in CAN: 7

**Countries:** Ecuador 10

## HCJB World Radio—Canada
## See: HCJB Global—Canada

## High Adventure Gospel Communication Ministries

PO Box 425, Station E
Toronto, ON M6H 4E3 CAN

**Phone:** (905) 898-5447
**Fax:** (905) 898-2500
**E-Mail:** mail@biblevoice.org
**Web Site:** www.biblevoice.org

*Mr. Don McLaughlin, Ministry Director*

A nondenominational agency of Evangelical tradition engaged in evangelism/Christian program placement on international radio.

**Year founded in CAN:** 1979

**Income for overseas min:** $750,000.00

**Personnel:**
  Short-term less than 1 year: 21
  Home ministry & office staff in CAN: 4

## HOPE International Development Agency

214 Sixth Street
New Westminster, BC V3L 3A2 CAN

**Phone:** (604) 525-5481
**Fax:** (604) 525-3471
**E-Mail:** hope@hope-international.com
**Web Site:** www.hope-international.com
**Associations:** AERDO

*Mr. David S. McKenzie, Exec. Director*

A nondenominational service agency engaged in development, agricultural programs, leadership development, relief and/or rehabilitation and training.

**Purpose:** "...supports water resource development, agriculture, health care, education and micro-enterprise projects in Africa, South Asia, Southeast Asia, Central and Latin America. We provide volunteer opportunities for people with skills in the above areas. We also offer short term serving and learning opportunities for students and young North Americans in various countries."

**Year founded in CAN:** 1975
**Income for overseas min:** $18,000,000.00
**Gifts-in-kind:** $15,000,000.00
**Fully supported CAN personnel overseas:**
  Expecting to serve 1 to 4 years: 1
  Non-residential mission personnel: 1
**Other personnel:**
  Short-term less than 1 year: 6
  Non-CAN serving in own/other country: 23
  Home ministry & office staff in CAN: 10
**Countries:** Afghanistan; Cambodia; Ethiopia; South Africa

## I. N. (International Needs) Network Canada

115 First St., Ste. 243
Collingwood, ON L9Y 4W3 CAN
**Phone:** (705) 446-3541
**E-Mail:** inca@innetwork.ca
**Web Site:** www.innetwork.ca
**Associations:** EFMA, IFMA
*Mr. John G. Denbok,Exec. Director*

A transdenominational service agency of Evangelical tradition engaged in church planting, association of missions, development, discipleship, Christian education and support of national workers. Country data from 2002.

**Purpose:** "...to link Canadian Christians and churches with overseas ministries of INC that seek to integrate evangelism, discipleship, and fulfillment of human needs through effective development."
**Year founded in CAN:** 1973
**Income for overseas min:** $1,600,000.00
**Personnel:**
  Short-term less than 1 year: 24
  Non-CAN serving in own/other country: 804
  Home ministry & office staff in CAN: 6
**Countries:** Bangladesh; Colombia; Czech Republic; Egypt; Eritrea; Ethiopia; Ghana; India; Morocco; Nepal; Philippines; Romania; Slovakia; Sri Lanka; Tanzania; Uganda; Vietnam; Zambia

## InterAct Ministries of Canada

PO Box 808
Carstairs, AB T0M 0N0 CAN
**Phone:** (403) 337-3312
**Fax:** (403) 337-3407
**E-Mail:** interact.canada@interactministries.org

**Web Site:** www.interactministries.org
**Associations:** IFMA
*Mr. Dan Mayerle, Canada Field Director*

A nondenominational service agency of Evangelical tradition engaged in church planting, discipleship, evangelism, support of national churches, short-term programs and training.
**Year founded in CAN:** 1967
**Income for overseas min:** $53,380.00
**Personnel:**
  Home ministry & office staff in CAN: 3

## International Child Care (Canada) Inc.

2476 Argentia Rd., #113
Mississauga, ON L9S 1N5 CAN
**Phone:** (905) 821-6318
**Fax:** (905) 821-1435
**E-Mail:** canada@intlchildcare.org
**Web Site:** www.intlchildcare.org
*Ms. Linda Pascoe, Operations Manager*

An interdenominational sending agency of Evangelical tradition engaged in childcare/orphanage programs and providing medical supplies. Statistics from 2003.
**Year founded in CAN:** 1978
**Income for overseas min:** $998,040.00
**Gifts-in-kind:** $144,756.00
**Fully supported CAN personnel overseas:**
  Expecting to serve more than 4 years: 2
  Expecting to serve 1 to 4 years: 4
**Other personnel:**
  Home ministry & office staff in CAN: 1
**Countries:** Haiti 2

## International Christian Aid Canada

PO Box 5090
Burlington, ON L7R 4G5 CAN
**Phone:** (905) 331-7799
**Fax:** (905) 331-7699
**E-Mail:** kenr@icac.ca
**Web Site:** www.icac.ca
**Associations:** AERDO
*Mr. Kenneth D. Roe, Exec. Director*

A nondenominational support agency of Evangelical tradition engaged in childcare/orphanage programs, development, providing medical supplies, medical work, support of national workers and relief and/or rehabilitation.

**Year founded in CAN:** 1973

**Income for overseas min:** $447,000.00

**Gifts-in-kind:** $80,000.00

**Fully supported CAN personnel overseas:**
  Non-residential mission personnel: 1

**Other personnel:**
  Non-CAN serving in own/other country: 95
  Home ministry & office staff in CAN: 4

**Countries:** Honduras; Kenya; Philippines

## International Christian Ministries Canada (ICM)

19978 - 72 Ave.
Langley, BC V2Y 1R7 CAN
**Phone:** (604) 771-5689
**E-Mail:** icmcanada@cs.com
**Web Site:** www.icmcanada.org

*Mr. Phil Jeske, President*

An interdenominational sending agency engaged in training, church planting, discipleship, TEE, theological education, leadership development and support of national workers.

**Purpose:** "...to serve the church by equipping and discipling its leaders."

**Year founded in CAN:** 1989

**Fully supported CAN personnel overseas:**
  Expecting to serve more than 4 years: 5

**Other personnel:**
  Non-CAN serving in own/other country: 6
  Home ministry & office staff in CAN: 2

**Countries:** Congo, Democratic Republic of 1; Eastern Europe—General 1; Kenya 1; Tanzania 1; Uganda 1

## International Teams, Canada (Evangelical International Crusades Canada, Inc.)

1 Union St.
Elmira, ON N3B 3J9 CAN
**Phone:** (519) 669-8844
**Fax:** (519)669-5644
**E-Mail:** ITCan@iteams.org
**Web Site:** www.iteams.ca

*Mr. Neil Ostrander, President*

A sending agency of Brethren tradition engaged in compassionate evangelism, childrens programs, church planting and youth programs.

**Purpose:** "...engages in authentic partnerships with local churches and other missions to mobilize teams of people around the world to compassionate evangelism and training next generation leaders."

**Year founded in CAN:** 1959

**Income for overseas min:** $1,094,000.00

**Gifts-in-kind:** $1,000.00

**Fully supported CAN personnel overseas:**
  Expecting to serve more than 4 years: 10
  Expecting to serve 1 to 4 years: 3
  Non-residential mission personnel: 2

**Other personnel:**
  Short-term less than 1 year: 98
  Home ministry & office staff in CAN: 16

**Countries:** Austria 2; Bolivia 1; Costa Rica 2; Ecuador; Greece; Rwanda 2; Unspecified Country 3

## InterServe Canada (International Service Fellowship)

10 HuntingdaleBlvd.
Scarborough, ON M1W 2S5 CAN
**Phone:** (416) 499-7511
**Fax:** (416) 499-4472
**E-Mail:** info@hardplaces.ca
**Web Site:** www.hardplaces.ca

*Mr. Craig Shugart, Natl. Director*

An interdenominational sending agency of Evangelical tradition engaged in tentmaking and recruiting/mobilizing for business as mission.

**Purpose:** "...to transform lives and communities through encounter with Jesus Christ in Asia and the Arab world."

**Year founded in CAN:** 1903

**Income for overseas min:** $2,180,009.00

**Fully supported CAN personnel overseas:**
  Expecting to serve more than 4 years: 37
  Expecting to serve 1 to 4 years: 2

**Other personnel:**
  Short-term less than 1 year: 19
  Bi-vocational/tentmakers: 5
  Home ministry & office staff in CAN: 9

**Countries:** Asia—General 22; Central Asia—General 8; Middle East 7

## InterVarsity Christian Fellowship of Canada

64 Prince Andrew Place
Toronto, ON M3C 2H4 CAN

**Phone:** (416) 443-1170
**Fax:** (416) 443-1499
**E-Mail:** National@ivcf.ca
**Web Site:** www.ivcf.ca

*Ms. Geri Rodman, President*

An interdenominational support agency of Evangelical tradition engaged in evangelism, camping programs, leadership development and short-term programs. Statistics from 2003.

**Purpose:** "...passionate about the transformation of youth, students and alumni into fully committed followers of Jesus."

**Year founded in CAN:** 1928

**Fully supported CAN personnel overseas:**
  Non-residential mission personnel: 7

**Other personnel:**
  Short-term less than 1 year: 6
  Home ministry & office staff in CAN: 155

## Into All The World

51 Bond Ct.
Guelph, ON N1H 8N6 CAN

**Phone:** (519) 763-6147
**E-Mail:** bill@iatw.ca
**Web Site:** www.iatw.ca

*Rev. Bill Lewis, Exec. Director*

A nondenominational sending agency of Charismatic and Ecumenical tradition engaged in church planting, evangelism, leadership development, support of national workers, short-term programs and discipleship.

**Purpose:** "A mission enabling agency that works with individuals and churches to fulfil the call of God on their life, with special concern about unreached and untargeted people in the 10-40 Window."

**Year founded in CAN:** 1981

**Income for overseas min:** $225,000.00

**Fully supported CAN personnel overseas:**
  Expecting to serve more than 4 years: 2
  Expecting to serve 1 to 4 years: 7

**Other personnel:**
  Short-term less than 1 year: 12
  Non-CAN serving in own/other country: 4

Home ministry & office staff in CAN: 3

**Countries:** Belize 2; Dominican Republic; Ethiopia; Kenya; Nigeria; South Africa; Uganda

## Italian Pentecostal Church of Canada See: Canadian Assemblies of God

## Janz Team Ministries Inc.

2121 Henderson Hwy.
Winnipeg, MB R2G 1P8 CAN

**Phone:** (204) 334-0055
**Fax:** (204) 339-3321
**E-Mail:** jtm@janzteam.org
**Web Site:** www.janzteam.org
**Associations:** IFMA

*Mr. Jack Stenekes, Director*

An interdenominational sending agency of Evangelical tradition engaged in evangelism, camping programs, Christian education, TESOL and music outreach.

**Purpose:** "...to be obedient to the Great Commission of Jesus Christ through evangelism and Christian education, contributing to the establishment and growth of vibrant churches."

**Year founded in CAN:** 1955

**Income for overseas min:** $1,520,955.00

**Fully supported CAN personnel overseas:**
  Expecting to serve more than 4 years: 61

**Other personnel:**
  Short-term less than 1 year: 32
  Non-CAN serving in own/other country: 3
  Home ministry & office staff in CAN: 3

**Countries:** Brazil; Germany 61

## Jusqu'aux Extremites de la Terre

29, ch. du Pied-de-Roi
Lac-Beauport, PQ G0A 2C0 CAN

**Phone:** (418) 849-3179
**E-Mail:** jeffeettonda@videotron.ca

*Jeff Street, Secretary-Treasurer*

An interdenominational service agency of Evangelical tradition engaged in support of national workers and leadership development in Francophone churches.

**Purpose:** "... a French language mission,

JET, exists to assist Francophone evangelical believers and churches to become directly involved in world missons and to raise up a generation of French speaking missionaries who will go out into the harvest."

**Year founded in CAN:** 2002

# Language Recordings International
# See: Gospel Recordings Network Canada

# Latin America Mission (Canada) Inc.

3075 Ridgeway Dr., Unit 14
Mississauga, ON L5L 5M6 CAN

**Phone:** (905) 569-0001
**Fax:** (905) 569-6990
**E-Mail:** info@lamcanada.ca

*Dr. Garth B. Wilson, Exec. Director*

An interdenominational sending agency of Evangelical tradition engaged in missionary placement, camping programs, childcare/orphanage programs, theological education, support of national workers and short-term programs. Financial data from 2003.

**Purpose:** "...an international community of men and women who, motivated by their love for the Lord Jesus Christ and in obedience to His commands, encourage, assist and participate with the Latin Church in the task of building the Church of Jesus Christ in the Latin world."

**Year founded in CAN:** 1961

**Fully supported CAN personnel overseas:**
Expecting to serve more than 4 years: 11
Expecting to serve 1 to 4 years: 4

**Other personnel:**
Short-term less than 1 year: 15
Non-CAN serving in own/other country: 5
Home ministry & office staff in CAN: 3

**Countries:** Colombia 2; Costa Rica 6; Honduras 2; Mexico 1

# Leprosy Mission Canada, The

75 The Donway W., Ste. 1410
North York, ON M3C 2E9 CAN

**Phone:** (416) 441-3618
**Fax:** (416) 441-0203
**E-Mail:** tlm@leprosy.ca

**Web Site:** www.leprosy.ca

*Rev. Peter A. Derrick, Exec. Director*

An interdenominational service agency of Congregational and Evangelical tradition engaged in hospitals and leprosy care, development, Christian education, funds transmission, support of national workers and relief and/or rehabilitation.

**Year founded in CAN:** 1892

**Income for overseas min:** $3,416,028.00

**Gifts-in-kind:** $181,921.00

**Fully supported CAN personnel overseas:**
Expecting to serve 1 to 4 years: 2
Non-residential mission personnel: 1

**Other personnel:**
Home ministry & office staff in CAN: 20

**Countries:** Nigeria

# Liebenzell Mission of Canada

RR #1
Moffat, ON L0P 1J0 CAN

**Phone:** (519) 822-9748
**E-Mail:** mission@liebenzell.ca
**Web Site:** www.liebenzell.ca
**Associations:** IFMA

*Rev. Jakob Koch, Exec. Director*

A nondenominational sending agency of Evangelical tradition engaged in church planting, Christian education, medical work, support of national churches, missionary training and discipleship.

**Purpose:** "...to glorify God by bringing the saving knowledge of Jesus Christ to people around the world, in the power of the Holy Spirit through fervent prayer."

**Year founded in CAN:** 1966

**Income for overseas min:** $91,250.00

**Fully supported CAN personnel overseas:**
Expecting to serve more than 4 years: 2

**Other personnel:**
Short-term less than 1 year: 11
Non-CAN serving in own/other country: 2
Home ministry & office staff in CAN: 3

**Countries:** Bangladesh; Ecuador; Germany; Guam; Papua New Guinea 2; Taiwan

# MBMS International

302-32025 George Ferguson Way
Abbotsford, BC V2T2K7 CAN

**Phone:** (604) 859-6267
**Fax:** (604) 859-6422
**E-Mail:** mbmsi@mbmsi.org
**Web Site:** www.mbmsinternational.org
**Associations:** EFMA

*Mr. Randy Friesen, Gen. Director*

A denominational sending agency of Mennonite tradition engaged in church planting, development, evangelism, recruiting/mobilizing, training and youth programs. MBMS is a bi-national organization and statistics cannot be separated into U.S. and Canadian. U.S. statistics are included in this Canadian listing.

**Purpose:** "...to participate in making disciples of all people groups, sharing the gospel of Jesus Christ cross-culturally and globally, in Spirit-empowered obedience to Christ's Commission and in partnership with local Mennonite Brethren churches."

**Year founded in CAN:** 1878
**Income for overseas min:** $3,069,321.00
**Fully supported CAN personnel overseas:**
Expecting to serve 1 to 4 years: 70
Non-residential mission personnel: 3
**Other personnel:**
Short-term less than 1 year: 495
Bi-vocational/tentmakers: 20
Non-CAN serving in own/other country: 14
Home ministry & office staff in CAN: 35
**Countries:** Africa—General; Angola; Austria; Brazil; Burkina Faso; Central Asia—General; Colombia; Congo, Democratic Republic of; Germany; India; Japan; Lithuania; Mexico; Middle East; Panama; Peru; Philippines; Portugal; Russia; South Africa; Thailand; Uruguay

# Mennonite Central Committee Canada

134 Plaza Dr.
Winnipeg, MB R3T 5K9 CAN
**Phone:** (204) 261-6381
**Fax:** (204) 269-9875
**E-Mail:** canada@mennonitecc.ca
**Web Site:** www.mcc.org/canada

*Mr. Don Peters, Exec. Director*

A transdenominational service agency of Mennonite tradition engaged in development, agricultural programs, justice, partnership development and relief and/or rehabilitation.

**Year founded in CAN:** 1963
**Income for overseas min:** $32,529,651.00
**Gifts-in-kind:** $12,519,107.00
**Fully supported CAN personnel overseas:**
Non-residential mission personnel: 5
**Other personnel:**
Short-term less than 1 year: 29
Non-CAN serving in own/other country: 606
Home ministry & office staff in CAN: 198
**Countries:** Africa—General; Bangladesh; Bolivia; Brazil; Cambodia; China; Colombia; Congo, Democratic Republic of; Egypt; El Salvador; Ethiopia; Europe—General; Guatemala; Haiti; Honduras; Hong Kong; India; Indonesia; Iran; Iraq; Jamaica; Jordan; Kenya; Korea, South; Laos; Lebanon; Mexico; Mozambique; Nepal; Nicaragua; Nigeria; Palestine; Philippines; Russia; Rwanda; Somalia; South Africa; Sri Lanka; Sudan; Syria; Tanzania; Thailand; Uganda; Vietnam; Zambia; Zimbabwe

# Mennonite Economic Development Associates (MEDA)

155 Frobisher Dr., Ste. I-106
Waterloo, ON N2V 2E1 CAN
**Phone:** (800) 665-7026
**Fax:** (519) 725-9083
**E-Mail:** meda@meda.org
**Web Site:** www.meda.org

*Mr. Allan Sauder, President*

An interdenominational service agency of Mennonite tradition engaged in development, agricultural programs, management consulting/training and technical assistance.

**Purpose:** "...that all people may experience Christ's love and utilize their abilities to earn a livelihood, provide for families and enrich their communities."

**Year founded in CAN:** 1953
**Income for overseas min:** $10,179,658.00
**Fully supported CAN personnel overseas:**
Expecting to serve 1 to 4 years: 1
Non-residential mission personnel: 16
**Other personnel:**
Short-term less than 1 year: 7
Non-CAN serving in own/other country: 156
Home ministry & office staff in CAN: 14
**Countries:** Mozambique; Nicaragua; Peru; Tajikistan; Tanzania

## Mission Aviation Fellowship of Canada (MAFC)
PO Box 368
Guelph, ON N1H 6K5 CAN
**Phone:** (519) 821-3914
**Fax:** (519) 823-1650
**E-Mail:** info@mafc.org
**Web Site:** www.mafc.org
**Associations:** IFMA
*Mr. Mark Outerbridge, CEO*

A nondenominational specialized agency of Evangelical tradition engaged in aviation services.
**Year founded in CAN:** 1973
**Income for overseas min:** $3,210,703.00
**Fully supported CAN personnel overseas:**
  Expecting to serve more than 4 years: 28
  Expecting to serve 1 to 4 years: 1
**Other personnel:**
  Short-term less than 1 year: 2
  Home ministry & office staff in CAN: 13
**Countries:** Angola 2; Australia 2; Botswana 2; Brazil 1; Central Asia - General; Chad 1; Indonesia 5; Kenya 2; Lesotho 1; Madagascar 2; Papua New Guinea 8; Uganda 1; Zambia 1

## Mission of Mercy Canada
4104-97 St.
Edmonton, AB T6E 5Y6 CAN
**Phone:** (780) 485-9995
**Fax:** (780) 485-9980
**E-Mail:** info@missionofmercy.ca
**Web Site:** www.missionofmercy.ca
*Mr. Gerry A. Johnson, Exec. Dir.*

A service agency of Pentecostal tradition engaged in extension education, church construction, funds transmission, medical work, support of national workers and relief and/or rehabilitation.
**Purpose:** "...to provide for the basic human needs of less fortunate people without regard to gender, religion, social or ethnic origin."
**Year founded in CAN:** 1978
**Income for overseas min:** $2,760,000.00
**Fully supported CAN personnel overseas:**
  Expecting to serve 1 to 4 years: 4
**Other personnel:**
  Home ministry & office staff in CAN: 5
**Countries:** India

## Mission Possible Canada
PO Box 40121
London, ON N5W 5Z5 CAN
**Phone:** (519) 285-2644
**Fax:** (519) 285-2411
**E-Mail:** missionpossible@odyssey.on.ca
**Web Site:** www.mpint.org
*Mr. James McKeegan, Board Chair*

An interdenominational support agency of Charismatic and Independent tradition engaged in Christian education, childcare/orphanage programs, evangelism, leadership development, short-term programs and discipleship. Operates via a joint ministry agreement with Mission Possible, USA.
**Purpose:** "...to equip Christ-Centered Leaders for the Kingdom through spiritual, character, educational and vocational development.
**Year founded in CAN:** 1994
**Income for overseas min:** $133,765.00
**Gifts-in-kind:** $16,549.00
**Countries:** Dominican Republic; Haiti

## Missionary Ventures Canada
336 Speedvale Ave. W.
Guelph, ON N1H 7M7 CAN
**Phone:** (519) 824-9380
**Fax:** (519) 824-9452
**E-Mail:** mvcanada@mvcanada.org
**Web Site:** www.mvcanada.org
*Mr. John Verdone, Executive Director*

An interdenominational service agency of Evangelical tradition engaged in short-term programs, evangelism, development, medical work, providing medical supplies and church construction.
**Purpose:** "To encourage and support indigenous missions...through personal involvement, financial sponsorship, and ministry development."
**Year founded in CAN:** 1991

## MSC Canada
509 - 3950 14th Ave.
Markham, ON L3R 0A9 CAN
**Phone:** (905) 947-0468
**Fax:** (905) 947-0352
**E-Mail:** msc@msc.on.ca
**Web Site:** www.msc.on.ca

*Mr. William Yuille, President*

A service agency for Brethren Assemblies missionaries sent by their local assemblies. Personnel totals are reported under Brethren Assemblies (Canada).

**Purpose:** "...to encourage and support service for the Lord by assembly-commended workers, in compliance with scriptural guidelines, government legislation and agreements with other organizations with which MSC is associated."

**Year founded in CAN:** 1940

**Income for overseas min:** $4,715,606.00

**Gifts-in-kind:** $33,172.00

**Personnel:**
Home ministry & office staff in CAN: 3

## Navigators of Canada, The
PO Box 27070
London, ON N5X 3X5 CAN
**Phone:** (519) 660-8300
**Fax:** (519) 660-4922
**E-Mail:** navscanada@navigators.ca
**Web Site:** www.navigators.ca
*Mr. Eric S. Stolte, President*

An interdenominational sending agency of Evangelical tradition engaged in discipleship, bible memorization, evangelism, leadership development and mobilization for mission.

**Purpose:** "...to advance the Gospel of Jesus and His Kingdom into the nations through spiritual generations of labourers living and discipling among the lost."

**Year founded in CAN:** 1960

**Income for overseas min:** $840,422.00

**Fully supported CAN personnel overseas:**
Expecting to serve more than 4 years: 13
Expecting to serve 1 to 4 years: 1

**Other personnel:**
Short-term less than 1 year: 7
Bi-vocational/tentmakers: 3
Home ministry & office staff in CAN: 16

**Countries:** Africa—General 3; Asia—General 2; Chile 2; Hungary 2; Slovakia 2; Turkey 2

## New Tribes Mission of Canada
PO Box 707
Durham, ON N0G 1R0 CAN
**Phone:** (519) 369-2622

**Fax:** (519) 369-5828
**E-Mail:** ntmc@ntmc.ca
**Web Site:** www.ntmc.ca
*Mr. Raymond Jones, Chairman*

A nondenominational sending agency of Evangelical tradition engaged in church planting, discipleship, literacy work, missionary training, Bible translation and translation work. Financial data from 1998.

**Purpose:** "...to assist the ministry of the local church through the mobilizing, equipping, and coordinating of missionaries to see indigenous New Testament churches established among unreached people groups..."

**Year founded in CAN:** 1969

**Income for overseas min:** $3,943,909.00

**Fully supported CAN personnel overseas:**
Expecting to serve more than 4 years: 300

**Other personnel:**
Home ministry & office staff in CAN: 44

**Countries:** Unspecified Country 300

## OMF International—Canada
Bldg. 21, 5155 Spectrum Way
Mississauga, ON L4W 5A1 CAN
**Phone:** (888) 657-8010
**E-Mail:** omfcanada@omf.ca
**Web Site:** www.omf.ca
**Associations:** IFMA

*Rev. Richard J. Konieczny, Nat'l. Director*

A nondenominational sending agency of Evangelical tradition engaged in church planting, theological education, evangelism, leadership development and support of national churches.

**Purpose:** "...to inspire and enable Canada's Christians to participate in the urgent evangelization of East Asia's peoples."

**Year founded in CAN:** 1888

**Income for overseas min:** $2,301,065.00

**Fully supported CAN personnel overseas:**
Expecting to serve more than 4 years: 63
Expecting to serve 1 to 4 years: 8

**Other personnel:**
Short-term less than 1 year: 35
Bi-vocational/tentmakers: 46
Non-CAN serving in own/other country: 66
Home ministry & office staff in CAN: 8

**Countries:** Asia—General 20; Australia; Cambodia 1; Hong Kong; Indonesia 3; Japan

7; Korea, South; Malaysia 2; Mongolia; Philippines 14; Singapore 2; Taiwan 3; Thailand 11; United Kingdom

## OMS International—Canada

293 Wellington St. N., Ste. 132
Hamilton, ON L8L 8E7 CAN
**Phone:** (905) 522-1605
**Fax:** (905) 522-2849
**E-Mail:** mail@omscanada.org
**Web Site:** www.omscanada.org
*Mr. Gordon Morley, Exec. Director*
An interdenominational sending agency of Methodist and Wesleyan tradition engaged in church planting, broadcasting, theological education, evangelism, support of national workers and support of national churches.
**Year founded in CAN:** 1948
**Income for overseas min:** $1,000,000.00
**Fully supported CAN personnel overseas:**
Expecting to serve more than 4 years: 13
Expecting to serve 1 to 4 years: 4
**Other personnel:**
Short-term less than 1 year: 16
Bi-vocational/tentmakers: 2
Home ministry & office staff in CAN: 6
**Countries:** Asia—General 4; Haiti 8; Hungary 1

## Open Doors with Brother Andrew Canada

30-5155 Spectrum Way
Mississauga, ON L4W 5A1 CAN
**Phone:** (905) 602-6404
**Fax:** (905) 602-6477
**E-Mail:** opendoorsca@od.org
**Web Site:** www.opendoorsca.org
*Rev. Paul W. Johnson, Director for Canada*
A nondenominational support agency of Evangelical tradition engaged in Bible distribution, correspondence courses, missions information service, leadership development, literature distribution and support of national workers.
**Year founded in CAN:** 1977

## Operation Mobilization Canada

212 West St.
Port Colborne, ON L3K 4E3 CAN

**Phone:** (905) 835-2546
**Fax:** (905) 835-2533
**E-Mail:** info@cdn.om.org
**Web Site:** www.omcanada.org
*Mr. Harvey Thiessen, Exec. Director*
A transdenominational sending agency of Evangelical tradition engaged in literature distribution, evangelism, literature production, mobilization for mission, short-term programs and discipleship.
**Purpose:** "...to motivate, develop and equip people for world evangelization, and to strengthen and help plant churches, especially among the unreached in the Middle East, South and Central Asia and Europe."
**Year founded in CAN:** 1965
**Income for overseas min:** $2,200,000.00
**Fully supported CAN personnel overseas:**
Expecting to serve more than 4 years: 31
Expecting to serve 1 to 4 years: 47
**Other personnel:**
Short-term less than 1 year: 54
Home ministry & office staff in CAN: 14
**Countries:** Afghanistan 3; Africa—General 5; Asia—General 3; Austria; Bosnia and Herzegovina; Central Asia—General 2; France 1; India 1; Middle East 6; Myanmar/Burma; Nepal; Pakistan 1; Sweden; Switzerland; Unspecified Country 3; Uruguay 2; Western Europe—General 4

## Outreach Canada

2 - 7201 72nd St.
Delta, BC V4G 1M5 CAN
**Phone:** (604) 952-0050
**E-Mail:** gkraft@outreach.ca
**Web Site:** www.outreach.ca
*Dr. Gerald Kraft, Exec. Director*
An interdenominational support agency of Evangelical tradition engaged in church planting, leadership development, management consulting/training, support of national churches, mobilization for mission, mission-related research and training.
**Purpose:** "...to assist the Body of Christ to make disciples of all peoples."
**Year founded in CAN:** 1977
**Income for overseas min:** $150,000.00
**Fully supported CAN personnel overseas:**
Expecting to serve 1 to 4 years: 4

Non-residential mission personnel: 4
**Other personnel:**
Home ministry & office staff in CAN: 13
**Countries:** Russia; South Africa

## Overseas Council for Theological Education & Missions, Inc.
See: reSource Leadership International

## Partners International Canada
56 - 8500 Torbram Rd.
Brampton, ON L6T 5C6 CAN
**Phone:** (905) 458-1202
**Fax:** (905) 458-4339
**E-Mail:** info@partnersinternational.ca
**Web Site:** www.partnersinternational.ca
*Mr. Robert B. Mitchell, Exec. Director*
An interdenominational support agency of Baptist and Evangelical tradition engaged in support of national workers, church planting, missionary education, partnership development, relief and/or rehabilitation and mission-related research.
**Year founded in CAN:** 1960
**Income for overseas min:** $2,205,081.00
**Personnel:**
Home ministry & office staff in CAN: 9

## Pentecostal Assemblies of Canada
2450 Milltower Ct.
Mississauga, ON L5N 5Z6 CAN
**Phone:** (905) 542-7400
**Fax:** (905) 542-0377
**E-Mail:** info@paoc.org
**Web Site:** www.paoc.org
*Mr. Murray Cornelius, Asst. Super. of Intl. Msns.*
A denominational sending agency of Pentecostal tradition engaged in association of missions, childcare/orphanage programs, church planting, support of national churches, relief and/or rehabilitation and missionary training. Financial data from 1998.
**Purpose:** "...to make disciples everywhere by the proclamation and practice of the gospel of Jesus Christ in the power of the

Holy Spirit; to establish local congregations and train spiritual leaders."
**Year founded in CAN:** 1919
**Income for overseas min:** $14,732,000.00
**Gifts-in-kind:** $600,000.00
**Fully supported CAN personnel overseas:**
Expecting to serve more than 4 years: 85
Non-residential mission personnel: 4
**Other personnel:**
Non-CAN serving in own/other country: 1
Home ministry & office staff in CAN: 46
**Countries:** Armenia 1; Asia—General 5; Brazil 2; Congo, Democratic Republic of 1; Cote d'Ivoire 1; Cuba 1; Dominica 1; Estonia 1; Ethiopia 4; Guatemala 4; Guinea 1; Haiti 2; Israel 3; Jamaica 1; Kenya 8; Malawi 5; Mozambique 6; Philippines 1; Rwanda 3; Senegal 6; South Africa 2; Tanzania 3; Thailand 8; Uganda 5; United Kingdom 2; Zambia 4; Zimbabwe 4

## Pioneers Canada
3528 Catherine St.
Dorchester, ON N0L 1G2 CAN
**Phone:** (519) 268-8778
**Fax:** (519) 268-2787
**Web Site:** www.pioneers.ca
**Associations:** IFMA
*Mr. Donnie Scearce, Exec. Director*
An interdenominational sending agency of Evangelical tradition engaged in church planting, evangelism, member care, partnership development, mobilization for mission and short-term programs.
**Purpose:** "...mobilizes teams to glorify God among unreached peoples by initiating church planting movements in partnership with local churches."
**Year founded in CAN:** 1982
**Income for overseas min:** $1,233,738.00
**Fully supported CAN personnel overseas:**
Expecting to serve more than 4 years: 29
Expecting to serve 1 to 4 years: 3
**Other personnel:**
Short-term less than 1 year: 27
Bi-vocational/tentmakers: 10
Non-CAN serving in own/other country: 2
Home ministry & office staff in CAN: 9
**Countries:** Africa—General 2; Asia—General 12; Belize 2; Bolivia 2; Brazil 2; Central

Asia—General 2; Eastern Europe—General 3; Indonesia 2; Peru 2

# Presbyterian Church in Canada—Life and Mission Agency

50 Wynford Dr.
Toronto, ON K0M 1G0 CAN
**Phone:** (416) 441-1111
**Fax:** (416) 441-2825
**E-Mail:** rfee@presbyterian.ca
**Web Site:** www.presbycan.ca
*Rev./Dr. Richard Fee, Gen. Secretary—L & MA*
A denominational sending agency of Presbyterian tradition engaged in support of national churches, development, theological education, leadership development, relief and/or rehabilitation and youth programs.
**Year founded in CAN:** 1875
**Fully supported CAN personnel overseas:**
  Expecting to serve more than 4 years: 16
  Expecting to serve 1 to 4 years: 4
  Non-residential mission personnel: 1
**Other personnel:**
  Bi-vocational/tentmakers: 9
  Non-CAN serving in own/other country: 1
**Countries:** Cyprus 1; Ghana 2; Guatemala 2; Guyana; Hungary 1; India 1; Kenya 1; Malawi; Nicaragua 1; Nigeria 1; Romania 1; Taiwan 3; Ukraine 2

# reSource Leadership International

#200 - 5726 Minoru Blvd.
Richmond, BC V6X 2A9 CAN
**Phone:** (604) 270-6045
**Fax:** (604) 270-6046
**E-Mail:** administrator@resourceleadership.com
**Web Site:** www.resourceleadership.com
*Rev. Gordon T. Smith, President*
An interdenominational support agency of Evangelical tradition engaged in theological education, leadership development, campus development and program development.
**Purpose:** "…generates funds for theological institutions that enable men and women to be equipped for effective Christian leadership for church and society in the developing world."

**Year founded in CAN:** 1979
**Income for overseas min:** $334,609.00
**Fully supported CAN personnel overseas:**
  Non-residential mission personnel: 1
**Other personnel:**
  Short-term less than 1 year: 3
  Home ministry & office staff in CAN: 4

# Salvation Army—Canada and Bermuda Territory, the

2 Overlea Blvd.
Toronto, ON M4H 1P4 CAN
**Phone:** (416) 425-2111
**Fax:** (416) 422-6201
**E-Mail:** donor_questions@can.salvationarmy.org
**Web Site:** www.salvationarmy.ca
*Commissioner M. Christine MacMillan, Territorial Commander*
A denominational sending agency of Evangelical and Wesleyan tradition engaged in relief and/or rehabilitation, camping programs, childcare/orphanage programs, childrens programs, church planting, development, Christian education, evangelism, leadership development and medical work.
**Year founded in CAN:** 1884
**Income for overseas min:** $10,000,000.00
**Fully supported CAN personnel overseas:**
  Expecting to serve more than 4 years: 22
  Expecting to serve 1 to 4 years: 16
  Non-residential mission personnel: 2
**Other personnel:**
  Short-term less than 1 year: 123
**Countries:** Africa—General 11; Argentina 1; Australia; Bangladesh 1; Caribbean—General; Chile 1; France; Germany 4; Pakistan; Papua New Guinea; Russia; Spain 2; United Kingdom 2

# Samaritan's Purse—Canada

20 Hopewell Way NE
Calgary, AB T3J 5H5 CAN
**Phone:** (403) 250-6565
**Fax:** (403) 250-6565
**E-Mail:** canada@samaritan.org
**Web Site:** www.samaritanspurse.org
*Mr. Fred Weiss, Exec. Director*
A nondenominational service agency of Evangelical tradition engaged in relief and/

or rehabilitation, development, medical work, partnership development, short-term programs and youth programs.

**Purpose:** "...providing spiritual and physical aid to hurting people around the world...meeting the needs of people who are victims of war, poverty, natural disasters, disease and famine...serving the church worldwide to promote the Gospel..."

**Year founded in CAN:** 1973

**Income for overseas min:** $31,000,000.00

**Fully supported CAN personnel overseas:**
Expecting to serve more than 4 years: 5
Expecting to serve 1 to 4 years: 31
Non-residential mission personnel: 6

**Other personnel:**
Short-term less than 1 year: 24
Home ministry & office staff in CAN: 49

**Countries:** Afghanistan; Cambodia; Cyprus; Eritrea; Hong Kong 2; Indonesia 1; Kenya; Kosovo; Liberia; Malaysia; Mexico; Niger; Pakistan; Sri Lanka; Sudan; Thailand 1; Vietnam 1

## Scripture Gift Mission (Canada)

106 - 17 Colbourne St. East
Orillia, ON L3V 1T4 CAN

**Phone:** (705) 325-1002
**E-Mail:** canada@sgm.org
**Web Site:** www.lifewords-global.com

*Rev. Lawson Murray, CEO*

A nondenominational support agency engaged in literature distribution.

**Purpose:** "...to give God's Word to the world's people."

**Year founded in CAN:** 1916

**Personnel:**
Home ministry & office staff in CAN: 1

## SEND International of Canada

1 - 22423 Jefferies Rd.
Komoka, ON N0L 1R0 CAN

**Phone:** (519) 657-6775
**Fax:** (519) 657-7027
**E-Mail:** info@sendcanada.org
**Web Site:** www.send.org/canada

**Associations:** IFMA

*Rev. Rob Magwood, Canadian Director*

An interdenominational sending agency of Baptist and Evangelical tradition engaged in church planting, evangelism, leadership development, support of national churches, short-term programs and discipleship.

**Purpose:** "...to start churches...evangelize the unreached...nurture disciples...develop leaders..."

**Year founded in CAN:** 1963

**Income for overseas min:** $1,900,000.00

**Fully supported CAN personnel overseas:**
Expecting to serve more than 4 years: 23
Expecting to serve 1 to 4 years: 10

**Other personnel:**
Bi-vocational/tentmakers: 1
Non-CAN serving in own/other country: 73
Home ministry & office staff in CAN: 11

**Countries:** Asia—General 3; Czech Republic 2; Japan; Kazakhstan; Macedonia 3; Philippines 5; Poland; Russia 6; Spain; Taiwan; Ukraine 4

## SIM Canada

10 Huntingdale Blvd.
Scarborough, ON M1W 2S5 CAN

**Phone:** (416) 497-2424
**Fax:** (416) 497-2444
**E-Mail:** info@sim.ca
**Web Site:** www.sim.ca

**Associations:** IFMA

*Mr. Gregg Bryce, Exec. Director*

An interdenominational sending agency of Evangelical tradition engaged in church planting, development, theological education, medical work, support of national churches and integrated/holistic ministries.

**Purpose:** "...to plant, strengthen and partner churches around the world."

**Year founded in CAN:** 1893

**Income for overseas min:** $11,511,259.00

**Fully supported CAN personnel overseas:**
Expecting to serve more than 4 years: 111
Expecting to serve 1 to 4 years: 9

**Other personnel:**
Short-term less than 1 year: 100
Non-CAN serving in own/other country: 3
Home ministry & office staff in CAN: 26

**Countries:** Angola 5; Asia—General 11; Benin 6; Bolivia 7; Botswana 1; Burkina Faso 9; Chile 2; Cote d'Ivoire 1; Ethiopia 15; Ghana

5; India; Kenya; Niger 19; Nigeria 8; Paraguay 2; Senegal 2; South Africa 7; Zambia 11

## Slavic Gospel Association— Canada

55 Fleming Dr., Ste. #26
Cambridge, ON N1T 2A9 CAN
**Phone:** (519) 621-3553
**Fax:** (519) 621-7571
**E-Mail:** canada@sga.org
**Web Site:** www.sga.org
**Associations:** IFMA

*Rev. Allan W. Vincent, Exec. Director*

An interdenominational support agency of Baptist and Evangelical tradition engaged in church planting, Bible distribution, childcare/orphanage programs, theological education, literature distribution and Bible translation.

**Year founded in CAN:** 1947

**Income for overseas min:** $817,786.00

**Fully supported CAN personnel overseas:**
Expecting to serve more than 4 years: 2

**Other personnel:**
Short-term less than 1 year: 21
Home ministry & office staff in CAN: 5

**Countries:** Ukraine 2

## South American Missionary Society in Canada

PO Box 21082
Barrie, ON L4M 6JI CAN
**Phone:** (705) 728-7151
**Fax:** (705) 728-6716
**E-Mail:** office@samscanada.ca
**Web Site:** www.samscanada.ca

*Dr. Trevor Smith, Chair*

A denominational sending agency of Anglican and Evangelical tradition engaged in mobilization for mission, evangelism, leadership development and support of national workers. Financial information from 1998.

**Purpose:** "...to find and send those whom God is calling to the mission field, and to widen and deepen the missionary vision of Canadian Anglicans."

**Year founded in CAN:** 1979

**Income for overseas min:** $293,925.00

**Personnel:**
Home ministry & office staff in CAN: 2

## TEAM (The Evangelical Alliance Mission of Canada)

2635 - 32nd St. SW
Calgary, AB T3E 2R8 CAN
**Phone:** (403) 248-2344
**Fax:** (403) 207-6025
**E-Mail:** team@teamcanada.org
**Web Site:** www.teamcanada.org
**Associations:** IFMA

*Mr. Lorne W. Strom, Canadian Director*

An interdenominational sending agency of Evangelical tradition engaged in church planting, development, evangelism, medical work, short-term programs and TESOL.

**Purpose:** "...to help [local] churches send missionaries to establish reproducing churches among the nations."

**Year founded in CAN:** 1890

**Income for overseas min:** $2,425,122.00

**Fully supported CAN personnel overseas:**
Expecting to serve more than 4 years: 44

**Other personnel:**
Short-term less than 1 year: 51
Home ministry & office staff in CAN: 10

**Countries:** Asia—General 10; Central Asia—General 3; Chad 2; Czech Republic 2; France 1; Germany 2; Italy 3; Japan 11; Middle East 1; Peru 2; South Africa 2; Spain 2; Venezuela 2; Zimbabwe 1

## Trans World Radio Canada

PO Box 25324
London, ON N6C 6B1 CAN
**Phone:** (888) 672-6510
**Fax:** (519) 672-6512
**E-Mail:** info@twrcanada.org
**Web Site:** www.twrcanada.org
**Associations:** IFMA

*Gerald Hayes, Exec. Director*

A nondenominational specialized agency of Evangelical tradition engaged in broadcasting, discipleship, evangelism, missions information service, member care and support of national workers.

**Year founded in CAN:** 1973

**Income for overseas min:** $1,352,469.00

**Fully supported CAN personnel overseas:**
Expecting to serve more than 4 years: 13

**Other personnel:**

Short-term less than 1 year: 2
Non-CAN serving in own/other country: 11
Home ministry & office staff in CAN: 9

**Countries:** Austria 5; Middle East; Netherlands 4; South Africa 4

# UFM International of Canada
See: CrossWorld—Canada

# Ukrainian Children's Christian Fund
10340 Freshwater Dr.
Richmond, BC V6V 1A6 CAN
**Phone:** (604) 278-0692
**Fax:** (604) 279-9080
**E-Mail:** pcf.lapka@shaw.ca
*Olga O. Lapka, President*

A nondenominational service agency of Baptist and Christian/Plymouth Brethren tradition engaged in evangelism, Bible distribution, camping programs, childrens programs, discipleship, Christian education, literature distribution, support of national workers and relief and/or rehabilitation.

**Year founded in CAN:** 1976

**Income for overseas min:** $72,000.00

# United Church of Canada, Justice, Global & Ecumenical Relations
3250 Bloor St. W., Ste. 300
Toronto, ON M8X 2Y4 CAN
**Phone:** (416) 231-5931
**Fax:** (416) 231-3103
**E-Mail:** info@united-church.ca
**Web Site:** www.united-church.ca
*Rev. James Sinclair, Gen. Secretary*

A denominational sending agency of Ecumenical tradition engaged in justice, development, theological education, leadership development, support of national churches and training. Supports ministry, training, development and relief projects in more than 37 countries.

**Year founded in CAN:** 1925

**Income for overseas min:** $13,700,000.00

**Fully supported CAN personnel overseas:**
Expecting to serve more than 4 years: 13
Expecting to serve 1 to 4 years: 14

Non-residential mission personnel: 8
**Other personnel:**
Short-term less than 1 year: 4

**Countries:** Angola; China; El Salvador; Fiji; Guatemala; Israel 1; Jamaica 2; Japan 3; Korea, South 3; Mozambique 2; Nicaragua; Palestine 1; Philippines; Switzerland 1

# Venture Teams International
#3A 3023 - 21 St. NE
Calgary, AB T2E 7T1 CAN
**Phone:** (403) 777-2970
**Fax:** (403) 777-2973
**E-Mail:** info@vti.ca
**Web Site:** www.vti.ca
*Mr. Mark Sorell, Exec. Director*

An interdenominational service agency of Baptist and Mennonite tradition engaged in evangelism, childrens programs, missionary training, youth programs and discipleship.

**Purpose:** "...to mentor, equip and inspire followers of Christ for purposeful global and community influence."

**Year founded in CAN:** 1979

**Income for overseas min:** $180,000.00

**Personnel:**
Short-term less than 1 year: 96
Home ministry & office staff in CAN: 5

# Voice of the Martyrs Inc., The
PO Box 117, Port Credit
Mississauga, ON L5G 4L5 CAN
**Phone:** (905) 670-9721
**Fax:** (905) 670-0246
**E-Mail:** thevoice@persecution.net
**Web Site:** www.persecution.net
*Mr. Klaas Brobbel, Exec. Director*

A nondenominational support agency of Evangelical tradition engaged in literature distribution, childcare/orphanage programs, missions information service, literature production, training and tentmaking.

**Purpose:** "...to be an effective source of information and support of persecuted Christians around the world."

**Year founded in CAN:** 1971

**Income for overseas min:** $811,000.00

**Personnel:**
Non-CAN serving in own/other country: 1
Home ministry & office staff in CAN: 8

# WEC International (Canada)

37 Aberdeen Ave.
Hamilton, ON L8P 2N6 CAN
**Phone:** (905) 529-0166
**Fax:** (905) 529-0630
**E-Mail:** wec-int@canada.com
**Web Site:** www.wec-int.org
*Mr. Henry Bell, Canadian Director*

An interdenominational sending agency of Evangelical tradition engaged in church planting, broadcasting, childcare/orphanage programs, evangelism, missionary training and tentmaking. 120 personnel serving in 26 countries.

**Purpose:** "...to evangelize the unreached peoples...to establish fully discipled, self-governing, self-supporting and reproducing churches able to fulfill their part in the Great Commission."

**Year founded in CAN:** 1936

**Income for overseas min:** $1,964,798.00

**Gifts-in-kind:** $7,093.00

**Fully supported CAN personnel overseas:**
  Non-residential mission personnel: 2

**Other personnel:**
  Short-term less than 1 year: 9
  Bi-vocational/tentmakers: 32
  Home ministry & office staff in CAN: 20

# Western Tract Mission, Inc.

401 33rd St. W.
Saskatoon, SK S7L 0V5 CAN
**Phone:** (306) 244-0446
**E-Mail:** wtm@sasktel.net
**Web Site:** www.westerntractmission.org
*Mr. Arnold Stobbe, Acting Director*

An interdenominational service agency of Evangelical tradition engaged in correspondence courses, discipleship, evangelism and literature distribution.

**Year founded in CAN:** 1941

**Personnel:**
  Home ministry & office staff in CAN: 6

# White Fields Missionary Society

PO Box 242
Edmonton, AB T5J 2J1 CAN
**Phone:** (780) 483-5750
**E-Mail:** canada@whitefields.org

**Web Site:** www.whitefields.org
*Mr. Stephen Lonetti, General Director*

A service agency of Evangelical tradition engaged in church planting and evangelism. Countries of service and personnel information included in White Fields, Inc. (USA).

**Purpose:** "...to provide collaborative start-up support to pastors and churches among their own people in other parts of the world."

**Year founded in CAN:** 1955

**Income for overseas min:** $227,252.00

# World Mission Prayer League

5408 49th Ave.
Camrose, AB T4V 0N7 CAN
**Phone:** (780) 672-0464
**Fax:** (780) 672-0464
**E-Mail:** wmplcdn@cable-lynx.net
**Web Site:** www.wmpl.org
*Rev. Rob Lewis, Exec. Director*

A denominational sending agency of Lutheran tradition engaged in evangelism, broadcasting, church planting, theological education, evangelism and medical work. Financial and personnel data from 1998.

**Year founded in CAN:** 1951

**Income for overseas min:** $83,433.00

**Fully supported CAN personnel overseas:**
  Expecting to serve more than 4 years: 4
  Expecting to serve 1 to 4 years: 2

**Other personnel:**
  Short-term less than 1 year: 3
  Home ministry & office staff in CAN: 2

**Countries:** Central Asia - General 4; Mexico

# World Relief Canada

600 Alden Rd., Ste. 310
Markham, ON L3R 0E7 CAN
**Phone:** (905) 415-8181
**Fax:** (905) 415-0287
**E-Mail:** worldrelief@wrcanada.org
**Web Site:** www.wrcanada.org
*Mr. Laurie Cook, CEO/President*

A interdenominational specialized agency of Evangelical tradition engaged in relief and/or rehabilitation, development and partnership development in 15 countries.

**Purpose:** "...partners with the evangelical

560 Mission Handbook 2007-2009

church in Canada and overseas to respond to the basic needs of the world's most oppressed, poor and suffering people, empowering them to meet their own needs in the name of Jesus Christ."

**Year founded in CAN:** 1982

**Income for overseas min:** $5,492,053.00

**Personnel:**
Home ministry & office staff in CAN: 12

## World Team Canada
7575 Danbro Cresc.
Mississauga, ON L5N 1N1 CAN
**Phone:** (905) 821-6300
**Fax:** (905) 821-6325
**E-Mail:** wt-canada@worldteam.org
**Web Site:** www.worldteam.org
**Associations:** IFMA

*Mr. Jonathan Wilson, Exec. Director*

An interdenominational sending agency of Evangelical tradition engaged in church planting, aviation services, support of national churches, partnership development, short-term programs and translation work.

**Purpose:** "...to glorify God by working together to establish reproducing churches focusing on unreached peoples of the world."

**Income for overseas min:** $2,033,600.00

**Gifts-in-kind:** $431,673.00

**Fully supported CAN personnel overseas:**
Expecting to serve more than 4 years: 34

**Other personnel:**
Non-CAN serving in own/other country: 159
Home ministry & office staff in CAN: 3

**Countries:** Australia; Brazil; Cambodia 2; Cameroon 2; Central African Republic; Chile; Dominican Republic 2; France; Guadeloupe; Haiti; Indonesia 4; Italy 2; Papua New Guinea; Peru 6; Philippines 4; Saint Vincent and the Grenadines; Singapore 8; Spain 2; Suriname; Taiwan; Trinidad and Tobago; Ukraine 2; United Kingdom

## World Vision Canada
1 World Dr.
Mississauga, ON L5T 2Y4 CAN
**Phone:** (905) 565-6100
**Fax:** (905) 696-2162
**E-Mail:** info@worldvision.ca
**Web Site:** www.worldvision.ca

*Mr. Dave Toycen, President/CEO*

A transdenominational service agency of Evangelical tradition engaged in development, childrens programs, relief and/or rehabilitation, training, youth programs and primary school education.

**Purpose:** "...an international partnership of Christians...working with the poor and oppressed to promote human transformation, seek justice and bear witness to the good news of the Kingdom of God."

**Year founded in CAN:** 1954

**Income for overseas min:**
$277,755,000.00

**Gifts-in-kind:** $62,000,000.00

**Fully supported CAN personnel overseas:**
Non-residential mission personnel: 10

**Other personnel:**
Short-term less than 1 year: 150
Home ministry & office staff in CAN: 550

## WorldServe Ministries Canada
1301 Johnson Rd.
White Rock, BC V4B 3Z3 CAN
**Phone:** (604) 531-3955
**Fax:** (604) 531-9168
**E-Mail:** office@worldserve.org
**Web Site:** www.worldserve.org

*Dr. David Hunt, President*

A transdenominational support agency of Evangelical tradition engaged in Bible distribution, church planting, evangelism, support of national workers, support of national churches and Bible translation.

**Purpose:** "...to serve and equip the Church worldwide."

**Year founded in CAN:** 1976

**Income for overseas min:** $3,960,000.00

**Personnel:**
Home ministry & office staff in CAN: 7

## Wycliffe Bible Translators of Canada, Inc.
4316 - 10 St. NE
Calgary, AB T2E 6K3 CAN
**Phone:** (403) 250-5411
**Fax:** (403) 250-2623
**E-Mail:** info@wycliffe.ca
**Web Site:** www.wycliffe.ca

*Mr. David H. Ohlson, Exec. Director*

A nondenominational sending agency of Baptist and Reformed tradition engaged in Bible translation, development, linguistics, literacy work, partnership development and translation work.

**Purpose:** "[To] challenge, train and assist Canadians to serve indigenous peoples through Bible translation and literacy-based development."

**Year founded in CAN:** 1968

**Income for overseas min:** $13,000,000.00

**Fully supported CAN personnel overseas:**
 Expecting to serve more than 4 years: 170
 Expecting to serve 1 to 4 years: 1
 Non-residential mission personnel: 3

**Other personnel:**
 Home ministry & office staff in CAN: 128

**Countries:** Africa—General 5; Asia—General 10; Australia 2; Austria 1; Brazil 5; Burkina Faso 4; Cameroon 20; Central Asia - General 10; Chad 2; Congo, Democratic Republic of 2; Ecuador 2; France 2; Ghana 3; Guatemala 4; Honduras 1; Kenya 4; Mali 2; Mexico 9; Mozambique 4; Netherlands 4; Niger 2; Nigeria 2; Papua New Guinea 19; Peru 6; Philippines 12; Senegal 3; South Africa 2; South Pacific 6; Switzerland 2; Thailand 12; Togo 2; Uganda 2; United Kingdom 4

## Young Life of Canada

#120 - 9440 202nd St.
Langley, BC V1M 4A6 CAN

**Phone:** (604) 881-6023
**Fax:** (604) 881-0204
**E-Mail:** national@younglife.ca
**Web Site:** www.younglife.ca

*Mr. Don Crompton, Natl. Director*

A nondenominational support agency of Evangelical tradition engaged in youth programs, camping programs and discipleship.

**Purpose:** "...loving teenagers in their world encouraging them to know Jesus Christ."

**Year founded in CAN:** 1954

## Youth for Christ, Canada

PO Box 93008
Langley, BC V3A 8H2 CAN

**Phone:** (604) 595-2498
**Fax:** (604) 595-2473

**E-Mail:** yfcnat@telus.net
**Web Site:** www.yfccanada.com

A transdenominational support agency of Evangelical tradition engaged in youth programs, camping programs, evangelism and mobilization for mission.

**Purpose:** "...to participate in the body of Christ in responsible evangelism of youth, presenting them with the person, work and teachings of Christ and discipling them into the Church."

**Year founded in CAN:** 1944

## Youth with a Mission Canada, Inc.

2718 Robinson Rd.
Winfield, BC V4V 1G6 CAN

**Phone:** (250) 766-5297
**Fax:** (250) 766-2387
**E-Mail:** revpaul@telus.net
**Web Site:** www.ywam.ca

*Mr. Paul Martinson, Team Leadership Member*

A nondenominational sending agency of Charismatic and Evangelical tradition engaged in discipleship, evangelism, leadership development, short-term programs, missionary training and youth programs.

**Purpose:** "...an international movement of Christians from many denominations dedicated to presenting Jesus personally to this generation, to mobilizing as many as possible to help in this task, and to the training and equipping of believers for their part in fulfilling the Great Commission."

**Year founded in CAN:** 1976

**Income for overseas min:** $8,500,000.00

**Personnel:**
 Short-term less than 1 year: 450
 Home ministry & office staff in CAN: 370

 QUINTEGRA RESOURCING

# Ethnic America Network
## Ministry Opportunities

*Connecting People to Opportunities*

**QUINTEGRA RESOURCING**

200 S. Meridian St.
Suite 420
Indianapolis
Indiana 46225

E-mail:
andersonfj@sbcglobal.net

www.quintegra.biz

The Billy Graham Center and Quintegra Resourcing have partnered with the Ethnic America Network to create a web-based tool to help facilitate the task of identifying, qualifying and enlisting seconded missionaries and ministry volunteers. The EAN now has access to the same recruitment processes and technology that Quintegra Resourcing provides to its business clients:

- Quick internet access to all posted opportunities
- On-line registration to facilitate candidate response
- Complete position descriptions for each opportunity
- Easy to communicate with and track candidates
- Built on flexible Microsoft platform

As we invite ministry-minded individuals to join with the EAN, this tool is growing as an enduring asset for the Kingdom of God. For more information, contact Fred Anderson at andersonfj@sbcglobal.net or register yourself at www.volunteerEAN.info.

# Chapter 6
# Indices to Canadian Protestant Agencies

M
any *Handbook* users find it valuable to locate agencies by particular categories of church tradition or ministry activity. This chapter provides the user with those indices. Agency responses on the Mission Handbook survey questionnaire helped define the listed categories. The organizations in each category appear in alphabetical order by organization name.

## Index by Church Tradition

If an agency needed more than one generic or denominational category to describe its traditional doctrinal and/or ecclesiastical stance, the agency may appear under as many as two of the given categories. We have arranged the list alphabetically by category and within each category by agency name. See question #8 of the survey questionnaire (in appendix) for the actual working of the question and the check-off list of choices.

## Index by Ministry Activity

Almost all agencies are involved in several types of ministry activities. Each agency may be listed under as many as six primary categories of activity. We asked those with more than six primary activities to indicate the six activities toward which they had committed the largest amount of resources.

We have divided the broad activities of education and evangelism into subcategories. For example, the evangelism category appears as "evangelism, mass" and "evangelism, student" and so on. See question #9 of the survey questionnaire (in appendix) for the actual wording of the question and the check-off list of activities.

Agencies sometimes have written in new categories under the "other" choice in previous surveys. Some of these, if used often enough, may be included in the check-off list for the next edition's survey questionnaire. Categories are occasionally dropped for lack of use. The most used categories have remained the same.

# Church Tradition

## Anglican
So. Am. Missionary Society in Canada

## Baptist
ABWE
Africa Inland Mission (Canada)
Apostolic Church of Pentecost of Canada
Avant Ministries Canada
Back to the Bible Canada
Baptist General Conference of Canada
CAM International of Canada
Canadian Baptist Ministries
Canadian Convention of Southern Baptists
Christar Canada
CrossWorld—Canada
Czechoslovak Evangelical Mission
Equip, Canada
FAIR
FEBInternational
Fundamental Baptist Msn. Trinidad/Tobago
Galcom International
Global Recordings Network Canada
Gospel Mission of South America of Canada
Partners International Canada
SEND International of Canada
Slavic Gospel Association—Canada
Ukrainian Children's Christian Fund
Venture Teams International
Wycliffe Bible Translators of Canada, Inc.

## Brethren
International Teams, Canada

## Charismatic
Into All The World
Mission Possible Canada
Youth with a Mission Canada, Inc.

## Christian/Plymouth Brethren
Brethren Assemblies (Canada)
MSC Canada

## Congregational
Leprosy Mission Canada, The

## Ecumenical
Canadian Bible Society/La Societe
    Biblique Canadienne
Canadian Churches' Forum for Global Mins.
United Church of Canada, Justice, Global

## Evangelical
Action International Ministries—Canada

Arab World Ministries (Canada)
Associated Gospel Churches
Barry Moore Ministries
BCM International (Canada), Inc.
Bibles & Literature in French—Canada
Campus Crusade for Christ of Canada, Inc.
Canadian South America Mission
Centre for World Mission—British Columbia
Child Evangelism Fellowship of Canada
Chosen People Ministries—Canada
Christian Aid Mission
Christian and Missionary Alliance in Canada
Christian Blind Mission Intl.—Canada
Christian Indigenous Development Overseas
Christian Studies International of Canada
Compassion Canada
Emmanuel International (ERRI)
Evangelical Covenant Church of Canada
Evangelical Free Church of Canada Mission
Evangelical Medical Aid Society
Evangelical Missionary Church of Canada
Evangelical Tract Distributors
Far East Broadcasting Associates of Canada
Frontiers Canada
Global Outreach Mission Inc.,  Canada
Gospel for Asia
Greater Europe Mission (Canada)
HCJB Global—Canada
High Adventure Gospel Communication Mins.
HOPE International Development Agency
I. N. (International Needs) Network Canada
InterAct Ministries of Canada
International Child Care (Canada) Inc.
International Christian Aid Canada
InterServe Canada (Intl. Service Fellowship)
InterVarsity Christian Fellowship of Canada
Janz Team Ministries Inc.
Jusqu'aux Extremites de la Terre
Latin America Mission (Canada) Inc.
Liebenzell Mission of Canada
Mission Aviation Fellowship of Canada
Missionary Ventures Canada
Navigators of Canada, The
New Tribes Mission of Canada
OMF International—Canada
Open Doors with Brother Andrew Canada
Operation Mobilization Canada
Outreach Canada
Pioneers Canada
reSource Leadership International
Salvation Army—Can. and Bermuda Territory
Samaritan's Purse—Canada
SIM Canada
TEAM (Canada)
Trans World Radio Canada
Voice of the Martyrs Inc., The

WEC International (Canada)
Western Tract Mission, Inc.
White Fields Missionary Society
World Relief Canada
World Team Canada
World Vision Canada
WorldServe Ministries Canada
Young Life of Canada
Youth for Christ, Canada

## Holiness
Bible Holiness Movement
Church of God (Anderson, Ind.)—Canadian

## Independent
Glad Tidings Missionary Society

Lutheran
Evangelical Lutheran Church in Canada, EL-CIC Mission in the World
World Mission Prayer League

## Mennonite
Evangelical Mennonite Conf., Bd. of Msns.
Evangelical Mennonite Mission Conf.
MBMS International
Mennonite Central Committee Canada
Mennonite Economic Dev. Associates

## Methodist
OMS International—Canada

## Pentecostal
Apostolic Church In Canada, The
Bible League of Canada, The
Canadian Assemblies of God
Crossroads Christian Communications Inc.
Mission of Mercy Canada
Pentecostal Assemblies of Canada

## Presbyterian
Presbyterian Church in Canada—Life/Msn.

## Reformed
Christian Reformed Wld. Relief Comm. Can.

# Ministry Activity

## Agricultural programs
Crossroads Christian Communications Inc.
Equip, Canada
HOPE International Development Agency
Mennonite Central Committee Canada
Mennonite Economic Dev. Assocs. (MEDA)

## Association of Missions
Canadian Assemblies of God
Evangelical Mennonite Mission Conf. Board
I. N. (International Needs) Network Canada

## Audio recording/distribution
Bible Holiness Movement
Far East Broadcasting Associates of Canada
Global Recordings Network Canada

## Aviation services
Mission Aviation Fellowship of Can. (MAFC)
World Team Canada

## Bible distribution
Apostolic Church In Canada, The
Bible Holiness Movement
Bible League of Canada, The
Bibles & Literature in French—Canada
Canadian Bible Society/La Societe Biblique
    Canadienne
Gospel for Asia
Open Doors with Brother Andrew Canada
Slavic Gospel Association—Canada
Ukrainian Children's Christian Fund
WorldServe Ministries Canada

## Bible memorization
BCM International (Canada), Inc.
Navigators of Canada, The

## Broadcasting, radio and/or TV
Avant Ministries Canada
Back to the Bible Canada
Canadian Assemblies of God
Crossroads Christian Communications Inc.
Far East Broadcasting Associates of Canada
Galcom International
Global Outreach Mission Inc., Canada
Gospel for Asia
HCJB Global—Canada
High Adventure Gospel Communication Mins.
OMS International—Canada
Trans World Radio Canada
WEC International (Canada)
World Mission Prayer League

## Camping programs
Action International Ministries—Canada
Avant Ministries Canada
BCM International (Canada), Inc.
Greater Europe Mission (Canada)
InterVarsity Christian Fellowship of Canada
Janz Team Ministries Inc.
Latin America Mission (Canada) Inc.
Salvation Army—Can. and Bermuda Territory

Ukrainian Children's Christian Fund
Young Life of Canada
Youth for Christ, Canada

## Childcare/orphanage

Action International Ministries—Canada
Christian Aid Mission
Equip, Canada
International Child Care (Canada) Inc.
International Christian Aid Canada
Latin America Mission (Canada) Inc.
Mission Possible Canada
Pentecostal Assemblies of Canada
Salvation Army—Can. and Bermuda Territory
Slavic Gospel Association—Canada
Voice of the Martyrs Inc., The
WEC International (Canada)

## Childrens programs

BCM International (Canada), Inc.
Bible League of Canada, The
Canadian Churches' Forum for Global Mins.
Child Evangelism Fellowship of Canada
Compassion Canada
International Child Care (Canada) Inc.
International Teams, Canada (Evangelical
International Crusades Canada, Inc.)
Salvation Army—Can. and Bermuda Territory
Ukrainian Children's Christian Fund
Venture Teams International
World Vision Canada

## Church construction

Ch. of God (Anderson, Ind.)—Canadian Bd.
Mission of Mercy Canada
Missionary Ventures Canada

## Church establishing/planting

ABWE
Africa Inland Mission (Canada)
Apostolic Church In Canada, The
Apostolic Church of Pentecost of Canada
Arab World Ministries (Canada)
Avant Ministries Canada
Baptist General Conference of Canada
BCM International (Canada), Inc.
Bible League of Canada, The
Brethren Assemblies (Canada)
CAM International of Canada
Canadian Conv. of So. Baptists (CCSB)
Canadian South America Mission
Chosen People Ministries—Canada
Christar Canada
Christian and Missionary Alliance in Canada
Church of God (Anderson, Ind.)
CrossWorld—Canada

Evangelical Covenant Church of Canada
Evangelical Free Church of Canada Mission
Evangelical Mennonite Conference
Evangelical Mennonite Mission Conf.
Evangelical Missionary Church of Canada
FEBInternational
Global Outreach Mission Inc.,  Canada
Gospel for Asia
Gospel Mission of South America of Canada
Greater Europe Mission (Canada)
I. N. (International Needs) Network Canada
InterAct Ministries of Canada
Intl. Christian Ministries Canada (ICM)
International Teams, Canada
Into All The World
Liebenzell Mission of Canada
MBMS International
MSC Canada
New Tribes Mission of Canada
OMF International—Canada
OMS International—Canada
Outreach Canada
Partners International Canada
Pentecostal Assemblies of Canada
Pioneers Canada
Salvation Army—Can. and Bermuda Territory
SEND International of Canada
SIM Canada
Slavic Gospel Association—Canada
TEAM (Canada)
WEC International (Canada)
White Fields Missionary Society
World Mission Prayer League
World Team Canada
WorldServe Ministries Canada

## Correspondence courses

Child Evangelism Fellowship of Canada
Evangelical Missionary Church of Canada
Open Doors with Brother Andrew Canada
Western Tract Mission, Inc.

## Development, community

Africa Inland Mission (Canada)
African Enterprise Association of Canada
Canadian Baptist Ministries
Canadian Food for the Hungry International
Christian Blind Mission Intl.—Canada
Christian Reformed World Relief Committee
Compassion Canada
Crossroads Christian Communications Inc.
Emmanuel International (ERRI)
Equip, Canada
Evangelical Medical Aid Society
Evangelical Missionary Church of Canada
FAIR (Fellowship Agency for Intl. Relief)

Frontiers Canada
HOPE International Development Agency
I. N. (International Needs) Network Canada
International Child Care (Canada) Inc.
International Christian Aid Canada
Leprosy Mission Canada, The
MBMS International
Mennonite Central Committee Canada
Mennonite Economic Dev. Assocs. (MEDA)
Missionary Ventures Canada
Presbyterian Church in Canada—Life and
Mission Agency
Salvation Army—Can. and Bermuda Territory
Samaritan's Purse—Canada
SIM Canada
TEAM (The Evangelical Alliance Msn. of Can.)
United Church of Canada, Justice, Global
World Relief Canada
World Vision Canada
Wycliffe Bible Translators of Canada, Inc.

**Disability assistance programs**
BCM International (Canada), Inc.
Christian Blind Mission Intl.—Canada
Equip, Canada
International Child Care (Canada) Inc.

**Discipleship**
Action International Ministries—Canada
Apostolic Church of Pentecost of Canada
Arab World Ministries (Canada)
Avant Ministries Canada
BCM International (Canada), Inc.
CAM International of Canada
Campus Crusade for Christ of Canada, Inc.
Canadian Baptist Ministries
Canadian Conv. of Southern Baptists (CCSB)
Canadian South America Mission
Child Evangelism Fellowship of Canada
Chosen People Ministries—Canada
Christar Canada
Christian Reformed World Relief Committee
CrossWorld—Canada
Evangelical Missionary Church of Canada
Frontiers Canada
HCJB Global—Canada
I. N. (International Needs) Network Canada
InterAct Ministries of Canada
International Christian Ministries Canada
Into All The World
Liebenzell Mission of Canada
Mission Possible Canada
Navigators of Canada, The
New Tribes Mission of Canada
Operation Mobilization Canada
SEND International of Canada

Trans World Radio Canada
Ukrainian Children's Christian Fund
Venture Teams International
Western Tract Mission, Inc.
Young Life of Canada
Youth with a Mission Canada, Inc.

**Education, church/sch. general**
Africa Inland Mission (Canada)
Apostolic Church of Pentecost of Canada
BCM International (Canada), Inc.
Canadian Food for the Hungry International
Centre for World Mission—British Columbia
Christian Aid Mission
Christian Studies International of Canada
Evangelical Covenant Church of Canada
HCJB Global—Canada
I. N. (International Needs) Network Canada
Janz Team Ministries Inc.
Leprosy Mission Canada, The
Liebenzell Mission of Canada
Mission Possible Canada
Salvation Army—Can. and Bermuda Territory
Ukrainian Children's Christian Fund

**Education, extension (other)**
Canadian Conv. of So. Baptists (CCSB)
Evangelical Medical Aid Society
Mission of Mercy Canada

**Education, missionary**
Africa Inland Mission (Canada)
Partners International Canada

**Education, theological**
ABWE
Africa Inland Mission (Canada)
Avant Ministries Canada
Baptist Gen. Conf. of Can. Global Mins.
BCM International (Canada), Inc.
CAM International of Canada
Canadian Conv. of So. Baptists (CCSB)
Evangelical Free Church of Canada Mission
Evangelical Lutheran Church in Canada
Gospel Mission of South America of Canada
Greater Europe Mission (Canada)
Intl. Christian Ministries Canada (ICM)
Latin America Mission (Canada) Inc.
OMF International—Canada
OMS International—Canada
Presbyterian Ch. in Can.—Life and Msn.
reSource Leadership International
SIM Canada
Slavic Gospel Association—Canada
United Church of Canada, Justice, Global
World Mission Prayer League

## Education, theological by extension (TEE)
Christian and Missionary Alliance in Canada
Evangelical Mennonite Conference
Intl. Christian Ministries Canada (ICM)

## Evangelism, mass
African Enterprise Association of Canada
Arab World Ministries (Canada)
Bible Holiness Movement
Campus Crusade for Christ of Canada, Inc.
Christian and Missionary Alliance in Canada
Emmanuel International (ERRI)
Evangelical Lutheran Church in Canada
Evangelical Missionary Church of Canada
Evangelical Tract Distributors
Far East Broadcasting Associates of Canada
Galcom International
Global Recordings Network Canada
Gospel for Asia
High Adventure Gospel Communication Mins.
International Teams, Canada
Janz Team Ministries Inc.
OMS International—Canada
Salvation Army—Can. and Bermuda Territory
Trans World Radio Canada
Venture Teams International
Western Tract Mission, Inc.
Youth for Christ, Canada

## Evangelism, personal and small group
African Enterprise Association of Canada
Apostolic Church In Canada, The
Arab World Ministries (Canada)
Avant Ministries Canada
Barry Moore Ministries
Bible Holiness Movement
Bible League of Canada, The
CAM International of Canada
Campus Crusade for Christ of Canada, Inc.
Canadian Conv. of So. Baptists (CCSB)
Chosen People Ministries—Canada
Christar Canada
Evangelical Covenant Church of Canada
Evangelical Free Church of Canada Mission
Evangelical Medical Aid Society
Evangelical Mennonite Conference
Evangelical Missionary Church of Canada
Frontiers Canada
Global Outreach Mission Inc., Canada
Greater Europe Mission (Canada)
InterAct Ministries of Canada
InterVarsity Christian Fellowship of Canada
Into All The World
MBMS International
Mission Possible Canada

Missionary Ventures Canada
MSC Canada
Navigators of Canada, The
OMF International—Canada
Operation Mobilization Canada
Pioneers Canada
Salvation Army—Can. and Bermuda Territory
SEND International of Canada
So. American Missionary Society in Can.
TEAM (The Evangelical Alliance Msn. of Can.)
Ukrainian Children's Christian Fund
Venture Teams International
WEC International (Canada)
White Fields Missionary Society
World Mission Prayer League
WorldServe Ministries Canada
Youth with a Mission Canada, Inc.

## Evangelism, student
Campus Crusade for Christ of Canada, Inc.
Canadian Conv. of So. Baptists (CCSB)
Child Evangelism Fellowship of Canada
InterVarsity Christian Fellowship of Canada
Navigators of Canada, The
World Mission Prayer League

## Funds transmission
ABWE
Apostolic Church In Canada, The
Ch. of God (Anderson, Ind.)—Can. Bd.
Crossroads Christian Communications Inc.
Evangelical Lutheran Church in Canada,
ELCIC Mission in the World
Fundamental Baptist Msn. Trinidad/Tobago
Leprosy Mission Canada, The
Mission of Mercy Canada

## Information services
Centre for World Mission—British Columbia
Christian Aid Mission
Evangelical Mennonite Mission Conf. Bd.
Open Doors with Brother Andrew Canada
Trans World Radio Canada
Voice of the Martyrs Inc., The

## Justice & Related
African Enterprise Association of Canada
Christian Reformed World Relief Committee
Mennonite Central Committee Canada
United Church of Canada, Justice, Global
Leadership development
Action International Ministries—Canada
African Enterprise Association of Canada
Apostolic Church of Pentecost of Canada
Barry Moore Ministries
Campus Crusade for Christ of Canada, Inc.

Canadian Assemblies of God
Canadian Baptist Ministries
Canadian Conv. of So. Baptists (CCSB)
Canadian Food for the Hungry International
Canadian South America Mission
Christian Reformed World Relief Committee
Christian Studies International of Canada
Ch. of God (Anderson, Ind.)—Canadian Bd.
Compassion Canada
CrossWorld—Canada
Evangelical Mennonite Conf., Bd. of Msns.
Frontiers Canada
Gospel Mission of South America of Canada
Greater Europe Mission (Canada)
HOPE International Development Agency
Intl. Christian Ministries Canada (ICM)
InterVarsity Christian Fellowship of Canada
Into All The World
Jusqu'aux Extremites de la Terre
Mission Possible Canada
Navigators of Canada, The
OMF International—Canada
Open Doors with Brother Andrew Canada
Outreach Canada
Presbyterian Ch. in Can.—Life and Mission
reSource Leadership International
Salvation Army—Can. and Bermuda Territory
SEND International of Canada
So. Am. Missionary Society in Canada
United Church of Canada, Justice, Global
Youth with a Mission Canada, Inc.

## Linguistics

Canadian Bible Society/La Societe Biblique
    Canadienne
Wycliffe Bible Translators of Canada, Inc.

## Literacy

New Tribes Mission of Canada
Wycliffe Bible Translators of Canada, Inc.

## Literature distribution

Action International Ministries—Canada
Bible Holiness Movement
Bibles & Literature in French—Canada
Canadian Assemblies of God
Canadian Bible Society/La Societe Biblique
    Canadienne
Canadian Churches' Forum for Global Mins.
Child Evangelism Fellowship of Canada
Chosen People Ministries—Canada
Czechoslovak Evangelical Mission
Evangelical Tract Distributors
Far East Broadcasting Associates of Canada
MSC Canada
Open Doors with Brother Andrew Canada

Operation Mobilization Canada
Scripture Gift Mission (Canada)
Slavic Gospel Association—Canada
Ukrainian Children's Christian Fund
Voice of the Martyrs Inc., The
Western Tract Mission, Inc.

## Literature production

Bibles & Literature in French—Canada
Canadian Bible Society / La Societe
    Biblique Canadienne
Canadian Churches' Forum for Global Mins.
Czechoslovak Evangelical Mission
Evangelical Tract Distributors
Gospel for Asia
Operation Mobilization Canada
Voice of the Martyrs Inc., The

## Management

Mennonite Economic Dev. Assocs. (MEDA)
Outreach Canada

## Medical supplies

Apostolic Church In Canada, The
Canadian Food for the Hungry International
International Christian Aid Canada
Missionary Ventures Canada

## Medicine, incl. dental and public health

Africa Inland Mission (Canada)
Christian Blind Mission Intl.—Canada
Equip, Canada
Evangelical Lutheran Church in Canada
Evangelical Medical Aid Society
Evangelical Mennonite Conference
Evangelical Missionary Church of Canada
FAIR (Fellowship Agency for Intl. Relief)
Global Outreach Mission Inc.,  Canada
HCJB Global—Canada
International Child Care (Canada) Inc.
International Christian Aid Canada
Leprosy Mission Canada, The
Liebenzell Mission of Canada
Mission of Mercy Canada
Missionary Ventures Canada
MSC Canada
Salvation Army—Can. and Bermuda Territory
Samaritan's Purse—Canada
SIM Canada
TEAM (Canada)
World Mission Prayer League

## Member Care

Evangelical Free Church of Canada Mission
Pioneers Canada
Trans World Radio Canada

## National church nurture/support
ABWE
Apostolic Church of Pentecost of Canada
Barry Moore Ministries
Bible Holiness Movement
Canadian Assemblies of God
Canadian Bible Society/La Societe Biblique
    Canadienne
Canadian South America Mission
Christian Aid Mission
Compassion Canada
CrossWorld—Canada
Evangelical Lutheran Church in Canada
Evangelical Mennonite Conference
Evangelical Mennonite Mission Conf.
Frontiers Canada
InterAct Ministries of Canada
Liebenzell Mission of Canada
MSC Canada
OMF International—Canada
OMS International—Canada
Outreach Canada
Pentecostal Assemblies of Canada
Presbyterian Ch. in Can.—Life and Mission
SEND International of Canada
SIM Canada
United Church of Canada, Justice, Global
World Team Canada
WorldServe Ministries Canada

## Partnership development
Baptist General Conf. of Can. Global Mins.
Canadian Food for the Hungry Intl.
Centre for World Msn.—British Columbia
Christian Blind Mission Intl.—Canada
Christian Reformed World Relief Committee
Emmanuel International (ERRI)
Galcom International
HCJB Global—Canada
High Adventure Gospel Communication Mins.
Mennonite Central Committee Canada
Partners International Canada
Pioneers Canada
Samaritan's Purse—Canada
World Relief Canada
World Team Canada
Wycliffe Bible Translators of Canada, Inc.

## Psychological counseling
Christian Blind Mission Intl.—Canada

## Recruiting/Mobilizing
ABWE
Baptist General Conf. of Can. Global Mins.
CAM International of Canada
Campus Crusade for Christ of Canada, Inc.

Centre for World Msn.—British Columbia
Emmanuel International (ERRI)
Evangelical Covenant Church of Canada
Evangelical Free Church of Canada Mission
FEBInternational
Global Outreach Mission Inc., Canada
Global Recordings Network Canada
InterServe Canada
Latin America Mission (Canada) Inc.
MBMS International
Navigators of Canada, The
Operation Mobilization Canada
Outreach Canada
Pioneers Canada
So. Am. Missionary Society in Canada
Youth for Christ, Canada

## Relief and/or rehabilitation
Canadian Food for the Hungry Intl.
Christian Aid Mission
Christian Blind Mission Intl.—Canada
Christian Reformed World Relief Committee
Crossroads Christian Communications Inc.
Emmanuel International (ERRI)
Evangelical Missionary Church of Canada
FAIR (Fellowship Agency for Intl. Relief)
Frontiers Canada
High Adventure Gospel Communication Mins.
HOPE International Development Agency
International Christian Aid Canada
Leprosy Mission Canada, The
Mennonite Central Committee Canada
Mission of Mercy Canada
Partners International Canada
Pentecostal Assemblies of Canada
Presbyterian Ch. in Can.—Life and Mission
Salvation Army—Can. and Bermuda Territory
Samaritan's Purse—Canada
Ukrainian Children's Christian Fund
World Relief Canada
World Vision Canada

## Research
Centre for World Mission—British Columbia
Outreach Canada
Partners International Canada

## Services for other agencies
Centre for World Mission—British Columbia
Evangelical Mennonite Conference
Galcom International

## Short-term programs
African Enterprise Association of Canada
Arab World Ministries (Canada)
BCM International (Canada), Inc.

Evangelical Free Church of Canada Mission
Evangelical Medical Aid Society
Evangelical Mennonite Mission Conf. Bd.
Evangelical Missionary Church of Canada
InterAct Ministries of Canada
International Child Care (Canada) Inc.
InterVarsity Christian Fellowship of Canada
Into All The World
Latin America Mission (Canada) Inc.
Mission Possible Canada
Missionary Ventures Canada
Operation Mobilization Canada
Pioneers Canada
Samaritan's Purse—Canada
SEND International of Canada
TEAM (Canada)
World Team Canada
Youth with a Mission Canada, Inc.
Crossroads Christian Communications Inc.
Galcom International
High Adventure Gospel Communication

## Support of national workers

Apostolic Church of Pentecost of Canada
Arab World Ministries (Canada)
Christian Aid Mission
Fundamental Baptist Msn., Trinidad/Tobago
Global Outreach Mission Inc., Canada
Global Recordings Network Canada
Gospel for Asia
I. N. (International Needs) Network Canada
International Christian Aid Canada
Intl. Christian Ministries Canada (ICM)
Into All The World
Jusqu'aux Extremites de la Terre
Latin America Mission (Canada) Inc.
Leprosy Mission Canada, The
Mission of Mercy Canada
OMS International—Canada
Open Doors with Brother Andrew Canada
Partners International Canada
So. Am. Missionary Society in Canada
Trans World Radio Canada
Ukrainian Children's Christian Fund
WorldServe Ministries Canada

## Technical assistance

Galcom International
Mennonite Economic Dev. Assocs. (MEDA)

## Tentmaking & Related

Arab World Ministries (Canada)
Christar Canada
Christian Studies International of Canada
InterServe Canada (Intl. Service Fellowship)
Voice of the Martyrs Inc., The

WEC International (Canada)

## TESOL

Janz Team Ministries Inc.
TEAM (Canada)

## Training, other

Action International Ministries—Canada
Barry Moore Ministries
BCM International (Canada), Inc.
Child Evangelism Fellowship of Canada
High Adventure Gospel Communication Mins.
HOPE International Development Agency
InterAct Ministries of Canada
Intl. Christian Ministries Canada (ICM)
Outreach Canada
United Church of Canada, Justice, Global
Voice of the Martyrs Inc., The
World Vision Canada

## Training/Orientation

Apostolic Church of Pentecost of Canada
BCM International (Canada), Inc.
Canadian Chs.' Forum for Global Mins.
Equip, Canada
Liebenzell Mission of Canada
MBMS International
New Tribes Mission of Canada
Pentecostal Assemblies of Canada
Venture Teams International
WEC International (Canada)
Youth with a Mission Canada, Inc.

## Translation, Bible

Bible League of Canada, The
Canadian Bible Society/La Societe Biblique
   Canadienne
Evangelical Missionary Church of Canada
New Tribes Mission of Canada
Slavic Gospel Association—Canada
WorldServe Ministries Canada
Wycliffe Bible Translators of Canada, Inc.

## Translation, other

BCM International (Canada), Inc.
Bibles & Literature in French—Canada
Global Recordings Network Canada
New Tribes Mission of Canada
World Team Canada
Wycliffe Bible Translators of Canada, Inc.

## Video/Film

HCJB Global—Canada

## Youth programs

Canadian Assemblies of God

Greater Europe Mission (Canada)
International Teams, Canada
MBMS International
Presbyterian Ch. in Can.—Life and Mission
Samaritan's Purse—Canada
Venture Teams International
World Vision Canada
Young Life of Canada
Youth for Christ, Canada
Youth with a Mission Canada, Inc.

## Chapter 7
# Countries of Activity for Canadian Protestant Agencies

I this chapter you will find the countries where agencies reported field personnel in answer to question #14 of the survey questionnaire (see appendix). The few exceptions to this are agencies whose whole program supports (with funds raised in Canada, but which may not be designated to specific personnel on a regular basis) churches or other initiatives in a country.

All countries are listed in alphabetical order according to the name most commonly recognized in North America. Countries that are part of the Commonwealth of Independent States (most of the former Soviet Union) have been listed separately. Examples of this include Armenia, Kyrgyzstan and Belarus. In a few cases we have listed a territory or other administrative district of a country because it is commonly viewed as a separate entity and mission agencies report it that way. The country of Serbia/Montenegro has separated into two separate countries as we go to print.

We have separated the personnel totals for all agencies into five categories. Under the "personnel from Canada" heading, the term of expected service has been divided into three categories: 4+ years, 2-4 years and 1-2 years for fully supported personnel. For non-Canadian personnel in the "Other Countries" heading, the categories are those who are citizens of that ministry country and those who are not citizens, and are fully or partially supported by funds raised in Canada by the associated agency. For example, a Korean with specific mission/ministry duties serving in Korea would be included in an agency's "citizens" column of the Korea section. A Korean serving in Russia would be listed in the "not citizen" column of the Russia section.

At the end of each country section, totals of each category for that country are given. Please note that the totals for the "other countries" heading do not necessarily reflect all non-Canadian mission personnel who draw support from Canadian agencies. Some agencies give grants for ongoing institutions and other programs without specifying individual recipients. This may be in addition to Canadian mission personnel based in that country or the agency may not have Canadian personnel living in that country.

Please note also that the totals will be minimum numbers only because of the bigger number of large agencies in this edition that reported their personnel only by general regions and not by specific countries. Their numbers are not included in this "countries of activity" section.

| | Personnel from CAN | | | Other Countries | |
|---|---|---|---|---|---|
| First Year | 1-2 yrs. | 2-4 yrs. | 4+ yrs. | Citizens | Non-Citizens |

### Afghanistan

| | First Year | 1-2 yrs. | 2-4 yrs. | 4+ yrs. | Citizens | Non-Citizens |
|---|---|---|---|---|---|---|
| HOPE International Development Agency | 2006 | - | - | - | 2 | - |
| Operation Mobilization Canada | | 1 | - | 3 | - | - |
| Samaritan's Purse—Canada | 2005 | 2 | - | - | - | - |
| Totals: | | 3 | - | 3 | 2 | - |

### Africa—General

| | First Year | 1-2 yrs. | 2-4 yrs. | 4+ yrs. | Citizens | Non-Citizens |
|---|---|---|---|---|---|---|
| Arab World Ministries (Canada) | 1881 | - | 1 | 8 | - | - |
| Campus Crusade for Christ of Canada, Inc. | 1998 | - | - | 2 | - | - |
| Canadian Conv. of So. Baptists (CCSB) | 2004 | - | - | 2 | - | - |
| Christian and Missionary Alliance in Canada | | - | - | 10 | - | - |
| Emmanuel International (ERRI) | 1975 | 8 | 8 | 12 | - | - |
| Frontiers Canada | | - | - | 7 | - | - |
| MBMS International | | - | 2 | - | - | - |
| Mennonite Central Committee Canada | 1975 | - | - | - | 7 | 5 |
| Navigators of Canada, The | | - | - | 3 | - | - |
| New Tribes Mission of Canada | | - | - | - | - | - |
| Operation Mobilization Canada | | 2 | - | 5 | - | - |
| Pioneers Canada | | - | - | 2 | 2 | - |
| Salvation Army—Canada and Bermuda Territory | | - | 1 | 11 | - | - |
| Voice of the Martyrs Inc., The | 1995 | - | - | - | 1 | - |
| Wycliffe Bible Translators of Canada, Inc. | 2000 | - | - | 5 | - | - |
| Totals: | | 10 | 12 | 67 | 10 | 5 |

### Albania

| | First Year | 1-2 yrs. | 2-4 yrs. | 4+ yrs. | Citizens | Non-Citizens |
|---|---|---|---|---|---|---|
| Canadian Baptist Ministries | 1993 | - | - | 1 | - | - |
| Child Evangelism Fellowship of Canada | 1996 | - | - | 1 | 1 | - |
| Totals: | | - | - | 2 | 1 | - |

### Angola

| | First Year | 1-2 yrs. | 2-4 yrs. | 4+ yrs. | Citizens | Non-Citizens |
|---|---|---|---|---|---|---|
| Brethren Assemblies (Canada) | 1958 | - | - | 1 | - | - |
| Canadian Baptist Ministries | 1956 | - | - | 3 | 1 | - |
| MBMS International | 1990 | - | - | - | - | 4 |
| Mission Aviation Fellowship of Canada (MAFC) | 1989 | - | - | 2 | - | - |
| SIM Canada | 1917 | - | 1 | 5 | - | - |
| United Ch. of Can., Justice, Global & Ecumenical | | 1 | - | - | - | - |
| Totals: | | 1 | 1 | 11 | 1 | 4 |

### Argentina

| | First Year | 1-2 yrs. | 2-4 yrs. | 4+ yrs. | Citizens | Non-Citizens |
|---|---|---|---|---|---|---|
| Avant Ministries Canada | 1911 | - | - | 2 | - | - |
| Brethren Assemblies (Canada) | 1987 | - | - | 2 | - | - |
| Evangelical Lutheran Church in Canada | | - | - | - | - | - |
| Gospel Mission of South America of Canada | | 3 | - | 2 | - | 5 |
| Salvation Army—Canada and Bermuda Territory | | - | - | 1 | - | - |
| Totals: | | 3 | - | 7 | - | 5 |

### Armenia

| | First Year | 1-2 yrs. | 2-4 yrs. | 4+ yrs. | Citizens | Non-Citizens |
|---|---|---|---|---|---|---|
| Pentecostal Assemblies of Canada | 2001 | - | - | 1 | - | - |
| Totals: | | - | - | 1 | - | - |

| | First Year | Personnel from CAN | | | Other Countries | |
|---|---|---|---|---|---|---|
| | | 1-2 yrs. | 2-4 yrs. | 4+ yrs. | Citizens | Non-Citizens |
| **Asia—General** | | | | | | |
| Arab World Ministries (Canada) | 1990 | - | - | 3 | - | - |
| Baptist Gen. Conf. of Can. Global Ministries | 1996 | - | - | 2 | - | - |
| Campus Crusade for Christ of Canada, Inc. | 1997 | 2 | 9 | 5 | - | - |
| Child Evangelism Fellowship of Canada | 2002 | - | - | 2 | - | - |
| Christar Canada | 1930 | - | - | 14 | - | - |
| Christian and Missionary Alliance in Canada | | - | - | 4 | - | - |
| Emmanuel International (ERRI) | 1977 | - | - | 2 | 4 | - |
| Evangelical Free Church of Canada Mission | 1999 | - | 2 | 4 | - | 6 |
| Frontiers Canada | | - | - | 14 | - | - |
| InterServe Canada (Intl. Service Fellowship) | 1975 | - | - | 22 | - | - |
| Navigators of Canada, The | | - | - | 2 | - | - |
| New Tribes Mission of Canada | | - | - | - | - | - |
| OMF International—Canada | 1865 | 5 | - | 20 | - | 21 |
| OMS International—Canada | | - | - | 4 | - | - |
| Operation Mobilization Canada | | - | - | 3 | - | - |
| Pentecostal Assemblies of Canada | | - | - | 5 | - | - |
| Pioneers Canada | | 2 | - | 12 | - | - |
| SEND International of Canada | 1988 | 1 | 1 | 3 | 4 | - |
| SIM Canada | | - | - | 11 | - | - |
| TEAM (The Evangelical Alliance Mission of Can.) | 1890 | - | - | 10 | - | - |
| Wycliffe Bible Translators of Canada, Inc. | 1979 | - | - | 10 | - | - |
| Totals: | | 10 | 12 | 152 | 8 | 27 |
| **Australia** | | | | | | |
| African Enterprise Association of Canada | | - | - | - | - | - |
| Child Evangelism Fellowship of Canada | 2000 | - | - | 1 | - | 1 |
| Mission Aviation Fellowship of Canada (MAFC) | | - | - | 2 | - | - |
| OMF International—Canada | | - | - | - | 2 | - |
| Salvation Army—Canada and Bermuda Territory | 1996 | - | 3 | - | - | - |
| World Team Canada | | - | - | - | 9 | - |
| Wycliffe Bible Translators of Canada, Inc. | 1956 | - | - | 2 | - | - |
| Totals: | | - | 3 | 5 | 11 | 1 |
| **Austria** | | | | | | |
| Avant Ministries Canada | 1966 | - | - | 1 | - | - |
| Brethren Assemblies (Canada) | 1983 | - | - | 8 | - | - |
| International Teams, Canada | | - | - | 2 | - | - |
| MBMS International | 1953 | - | 2 | - | - | - |
| Operation Mobilization Canada | 1960 | 2 | - | - | - | - |
| Trans World Radio Canada | | - | - | 5 | - | - |
| Wycliffe Bible Translators of Canada, Inc. | 1982 | - | - | 1 | - | - |
| Totals: | | 2 | 2 | 17 | - | - |
| **Bahamas, The** | | | | | | |
| Avant Ministries Canada | 1956 | - | - | 1 | - | - |
| Totals: | | - | - | 1 | - | - |
| **Bangladesh** | | | | | | |
| ABWE (Assoc. of Baptists for World Evangelization) | 1987 | - | - | 1 | - | - |

| | Personnel from CAN | | | Other Countries | |
|---|---|---|---|---|---|
| | First Year | 1-2 yrs. | 2-4 yrs. | 4+ yrs. | Citizens | Non-Citizens |

| | First Year | 1-2 yrs. | 2-4 yrs. | 4+ yrs. | Citizens | Non-Citizens |
|---|---|---|---|---|---|---|
| Christian Reformed Wld. Relief Committee of Can. | | - | - | 1 | 1 | - |
| Gospel for Asia | | - | - | - | - | - |
| I. N. (International Needs) Network Canada | 1974 | - | - | - | 93 | - |
| Liebenzell Mission of Canada | 2004 | - | - | - | - | 2 |
| Mennonite Central Committee Canada | 1970 | - | - | - | 63 | 7 |
| Salvation Army—Canada and Bermuda Territory | 1994 | - | 2 | 1 | - | - |
| Totals: | | - | 2 | 3 | 157 | 9 |

**Belgium**

| | First Year | 1-2 yrs. | 2-4 yrs. | 4+ yrs. | Citizens | Non-Citizens |
|---|---|---|---|---|---|---|
| African Enterprise Association of Canada | | - | - | - | - | - |
| Brethren Assemblies (Canada) | 1970 | - | - | 6 | - | - |
| Canadian Baptist Ministries | 1985 | - | - | 4 | - | - |
| FEBInternational | 1978 | - | - | 6 | - | - |
| Global Outreach Mission Inc., Canada | | - | - | 1 | - | - |
| Totals: | | - | - | 17 | - | - |

**Belize**

| | First Year | 1-2 yrs. | 2-4 yrs. | 4+ yrs. | Citizens | Non-Citizens |
|---|---|---|---|---|---|---|
| Avant Ministries Canada | 1955 | - | 2 | - | - | - |
| Evangelical Mennonite Mission Conf. | 1965 | - | - | 2 | - | - |
| Into All The World | 1993 | - | - | 2 | - | - |
| Pioneers Canada | | - | - | 2 | - | - |
| Totals: | | - | 2 | 6 | - | - |

**Benin**

| | First Year | 1-2 yrs. | 2-4 yrs. | 4+ yrs. | Citizens | Non-Citizens |
|---|---|---|---|---|---|---|
| SIM Canada | 1946 | - | - | 6 | - | - |
| Totals: | | - | - | 6 | - | - |

**Bhutan**

| | First Year | 1-2 yrs. | 2-4 yrs. | 4+ yrs. | Citizens | Non-Citizens |
|---|---|---|---|---|---|---|
| Gospel for Asia | 1995 | - | - | - | - | - |
| Totals: | | - | - | - | - | - |

**Bolivia**

| | First Year | 1-2 yrs. | 2-4 yrs. | 4+ yrs. | Citizens | Non-Citizens |
|---|---|---|---|---|---|---|
| Avant Ministries Canada | 1928 | - | 1 | 7 | - | - |
| Brethren Assemblies (Canada) | 1976 | - | - | 6 | - | - |
| Canadian Baptist Ministries | 1898 | - | - | 2 | 2 | - |
| Canadian Food for the Hungry International | 1998 | - | - | 2 | - | |
| Canadian South America Mission | 1922 | - | - | 2 | - | 2 |
| Child Evangelism Fellowship of Canada | 2004 | - | - | 1 | 1 | - |
| Christian Reformed Wld. Relief Committee of Can. | | - | - | 1 | - | 1 |
| Evangelical Free Church of Canada Mission | 2000 | - | 4 | 10 | - | 14 |
| Evangelical Mennonite Mission Conf. Board | 1969 | 2 | 2 | 4 | 6 | - |
| International Teams, Canada | | 1 | - | 1 | - | - |
| Mennonite Central Committee Canada | 1959 | - | - | - | 27 | 25 |
| Pioneers Canada | | - | - | 2 | - | - |
| SIM Canada | 1907 | - | - | 7 | - | - |
| Totals: | | 3 | 7 | 45 | 36 | 42 |

**Bosnia and Herzegovina**

| | First Year | 1-2 yrs. | 2-4 yrs. | 4+ yrs. | Citizens | Non-Citizens |
|---|---|---|---|---|---|---|
| CrossWorld—Canada | | 1 | - | - | - | - |
| Operation Mobilization Canada | | 1 | - | - | - | - |
| Totals: | | 2 | - | - | - | - |

| | Personnel from CAN | | | | Other Countries | |
|---|---|---|---|---|---|---|
| | First Year | 1-2 yrs. | 2-4 yrs. | 4+ yrs. | Citizens | Non-Citizens |
| **Botswana** | | | | | | |
| Brethren Assemblies (Canada) | 1991 | - | - | 2 | - | - |
| Ch. of God (Anderson, Ind.)—Can. Bd. of Msns. | | - | - | - | - | - |
| Mission Aviation Fellowship of Canada (MAFC) | | - | - | 2 | - | - |
| SIM Canada | 1973 | - | 1 | 1 | - | - |
| Totals: | | - | 1 | 5 | - | - |
| **Brazil** | | | | | | |
| ABWE (Assoc. of Baptists for World Evangelization) | | - | - | 4 | - | - |
| Action International Ministries—Canada | | - | - | 2 | 2 | - |
| Apostolic Church In Canada, The | 1980 | - | - | - | 6 | - |
| Apostolic Church of Pentecost of Canada | 1999 | - | 4 | - | - | - |
| Avant Ministries Canada | 1911 | - | - | 2 | - | - |
| Brethren Assemblies (Canada) | 1948 | - | - | 3 | - | - |
| Canadian Baptist Ministries | | - | - | 3 | - | - |
| Canadian Food for the Hungry International | 1998 | - | 1 | - | - | - |
| Canadian South America Mission | 1913 | - | - | 3 | - | 3 |
| Child Evangelism Fellowship of Canada | 1970 | - | - | 1 | - | 1 |
| CrossWorld—Canada | | - | - | 7 | - | - |
| Evangelical Missionary Ch. of Can., Wld. Partners | 1998 | 1 | 5 | - | - | - |
| Global Outreach Mission Inc.,  Canada | | - | - | 1 | - | - |
| Janz Team Ministries Inc. | 1968 | - | - | - | 1 | 2 |
| MBMS International | 1946 | - | 4 | - | - | - |
| Mennonite Central Committee Canada | 1947 | - | - | - | 12 | 15 |
| Mission Aviation Fellowship of Canada (MAFC) | | - | - | 1 | - | - |
| Pentecostal Assemblies of Canada | 1965 | - | - | 2 | - | - |
| Pioneers Canada | | - | - | 2 | - | - |
| World Team Canada | | - | - | - | - | 4 |
| Wycliffe Bible Translators of Canada, Inc. | 1964 | - | - | 5 | - | - |
| Totals: | | 1 | 14 | 36 | 21 | 25 |
| **Bulgaria** | | | | | | |
| SEND International of Canada | 1992 | - | - | - | - | - |
| Totals: | | - | - | - | - | - |
| **Burkina Faso** | | | | | | |
| Apostolic Church of Pentecost of Canada | 1950 | - | 8 | - | - | - |
| Evangelical Mennonite Conference, Bd. of Msns. | | 1 | - | 2 | - | - |
| MBMS International | 1994 | - | 2 | - | - | - |
| SIM Canada | 1930 | - | - | 9 | - | - |
| Wycliffe Bible Translators of Canada, Inc. | 1997 | - | - | 4 | - | - |
| Totals: | | 1 | 10 | 15 | - | - |
| **Cambodia** | | | | | | |
| Canadian Food for the Hungry International | 2001 | - | 1 | - | - | - |
| Christian and Missionary Alliance in Canada | | - | - | 7 | - | - |
| Christian Reformed Wld. Relief Comm. of Can. | | - | - | 2 | 2 | - |
| Far East Broadcasting Assocs. of Can. (FEB Can.) | 1993 | - | - | 1 | - | - |
| Gospel for Asia | 2005 | - | - | - | - | - |
| HOPE International Development Agency | 1992 | 1 | - | - | 5 | - |

| | Personnel from CAN | | | Other Countries | |
|---|---|---|---|---|---|
| | First Year | 1-2 yrs. | 2-4 yrs. | 4+ yrs. | Citizens | Non-Citizens |

| | First Year | 1-2 yrs. | 2-4 yrs. | 4+ yrs. | Citizens | Non-Citizens |
|---|---|---|---|---|---|---|
| Mennonite Central Committee Canada | 1979 | - | - | - | 9 | 10 |
| OMF International—Canada | 1994 | 2 | - | 1 | - | 4 |
| Samaritan's Purse—Canada | 2003 | - | 1 | - | - | - |
| World Team Canada | | - | - | 2 | - | 22 |
| World Vision Canada | 2006 | - | - | - | - | - |
| Totals: | | 3 | 2 | 13 | 16 | 36 |
| **Cameroon** | | | | | | |
| Evangelical Lutheran Church in Canada | 1999 | - | 2 | 2 | - | - |
| World Team Canada | | - | - | 2 | - | 18 |
| Wycliffe Bible Translators of Canada, Inc. | 1979 | 1 | - | 20 | - | - |
| Totals: | | 1 | 2 | 24 | - | 18 |
| **Caribbean—General** | | | | | | |
| Salvation Army—Canada and Bermuda Territory | | 1 | - | - | - | - |
| Totals: | | 1 | - | - | - | - |
| **Central African Republic** | | | | | | |
| World Team Canada | | - | - | - | - | 1 |
| Totals: | | - | - | - | - | 1 |
| **Central Asia—General** | | | | | | |
| Evangelical Free Church of Canada Mission | 1999 | - | - | 2 | - | 2 |
| Frontiers Canada | | - | - | 9 | - | - |
| InterServe Canada (Intl. Service Fellowship) | | - | - | 8 | - | - |
| MBMS International | | - | 2 | - | - | - |
| Mission Aviation Fellowship of Canada (MAFC) | | 1 | - | - | - | - |
| Operation Mobilization Canada | | - | 4 | 2 | - | - |
| Pioneers Canada | | - | - | 2 | - | - |
| TEAM (The Evangelical Alliance Msn. of Canada) | 1946 | - | - | 3 | - | - |
| World Mission Prayer League | 1945 | - | - | 4 | - | - |
| Wycliffe Bible Translators of Canada, Inc. | 1991 | - | - | 10 | - | - |
| Totals: | | 1 | 6 | 40 | - | 2 |
| **Chad** | | | | | | |
| Mission Aviation Fellowship of Canada (MAFC) | | - | - | 1 | - | - |
| TEAM (The Evangelical Alliance Msn. of Canada) | 1969 | - | - | 2 | - | - |
| Wycliffe Bible Translators of Canada, Inc. | 1993 | - | - | 2 | - | - |
| Totals: | | - | - | 5 | - | - |
| **Chile** | | | | | | |
| Brethren Assemblies (Canada) | 1952 | - | - | 10 | - | - |
| Canadian Convention of Southern Baptists (CCSB) | 1993 | - | - | 2 | - | - |
| Gospel Mission of South America of Canada | | 1 | - | 2 | - | 3 |
| Navigators of Canada, The | | - | - | 2 | - | - |
| Salvation Army—Canada and Bermuda Territory | | - | - | 1 | - | - |
| SIM Canada | 1986 | - | - | 2 | - | - |
| World Team Canada | | - | - | - | - | 4 |
| Totals: | | 1 | - | 19 | - | 7 |

| | Personnel from CAN | | | | Other Countries | |
| --- | --- | --- | --- | --- | --- | --- |
| | First Year | 1-2 yrs. | 2-4 yrs. | 4+ yrs. | Citizens | Non-Citizens |
| **China** | | | | | | |
| ABWE (Assoc. of Baptists for World Evangelization) | | - | 2 | - | - | - |
| Apostolic Church of Pentecost of Canada | 1950 | - | 3 | - | - | - |
| Christian and Missionary Alliance in Canada, The | | - | - | 12 | - | - |
| Christian Studies International of Canada | 2000 | - | - | 1 | - | - |
| Gospel for Asia | 1998 | - | - | - | - | - |
| Mennonite Central Committee Canada | | - | - | - | - | 18 |
| United Ch. of Can., Justice, Global & Ecumenical | | - | 4 | - | - | - |
| Totals: | | - | 9 | 13 | - | 18 |
| **Colombia** | | - | | | | |
| Action International Ministries—Canada | | - | - | 4 | - | 1 |
| Brethren Assemblies (Canada) | 1972 | - | - | 1 | - | - |
| Evangelical Lutheran Church in Canada | | - | - | - | - | - |
| FEBInternational | 1969 | - | - | 5 | 2 | - |
| I. N. (International Needs) Network Canada | 1994 | - | - | - | 8 | - |
| Latin America Mission (Canada) Inc. | 1989 | - | - | 2 | 3 | - |
| MBMS International | 1945 | - | 2 | - | - | - |
| Mennonite Central Committee Canada | 2001 | - | - | - | 2 | 5 |
| Totals: | | - | 2 | 12 | 15 | 6 |
| **Congo, Democratic Republic of** | | | | | | |
| African Enterprise Association of Canada | | - | - | - | - | - |
| Apostolic Church of Pentecost of Canada | 1965 | - | 1 | - | - | - |
| International Christian Ministries Canada (ICM) | 2002 | - | - | 1 | 1 | - |
| MBMS International | 1912 | - | 3 | - | - | - |
| Mennonite Central Committee Canada | 1960 | - | - | - | 10 | 6 |
| Pentecostal Assemblies of Canada | 2007 | - | - | 1 | - | - |
| World Vision Canada | 2006 | - | - | - | - | - |
| Wycliffe Bible Translators of Canada, Inc. | 1996 | - | - | 2 | - | - |
| Totals: | | - | 4 | 4 | 11 | 6 |
| **Congo, Republic of the** | | | | | | |
| Christian and Missionary Alliance in Canada, The | | - | - | 3 | - | - |
| Global Outreach Mission Inc., Canada | | - | 2 | 1 | - | - |
| Totals: | | - | 2 | 4 | - | - |
| **Costa Rica** | | | | | | |
| Brethren Assemblies (Canada) | 1956 | - | - | 2 | - | - |
| International Teams, Canada | | - | - | 2 | - | - |
| Latin America Mission (Canada) Inc. | 1973 | - | 2 | 6 | 2 | - |
| Totals: | | - | 2 | 10 | 2 | - |
| **Cote d'Ivoire** | | | | | | |
| Apostolic Church of Pentecost of Canada | 1969 | - | 1 | - | - | - |
| Pentecostal Assemblies of Canada | 1986 | - | - | 1 | - | - |
| SIM Canada | 1968 | 1 | - | 1 | - | - |
| Totals: | | 1 | 1 | 2 | - | - |
| **Croatia** | | | | | | |
| ABWE | 2001 | - | - | 2 | - | - |

| | Personnel from CAN | | | | Other Countries | |
|---|---|---|---|---|---|---|
| | First Year | 1-2 yrs. | 2-4 yrs. | 4+ yrs. | Citizens | Non-Citizens |
| Greater Europe Mission (Canada) | 1999 | - | - | 2 | - | - |
| SEND International of Canada | 1995 | - | - | - | - | - |
| Totals: | | - | - | 4 | - | - |
| **Cuba** | | | | | | |
| CAM International of Canada | | - | - | - | - | - |
| Evangelical Free Church of Canada Mission | 2000 | - | - | - | - | - |
| Evangelical Missionary Ch. of Can., Wld. Partners | 2005 | - | - | - | - | - |
| Pentecostal Assemblies of Canada | 2005 | - | - | 1 | - | - |
| Totals: | | - | - | 1 | - | - |
| **Cyprus** | | | | | | |
| Brethren Assemblies (Canada) | | - | - | 1 | - | - |
| Presbyterian Ch. in Can.—Life and Msn. Agency | 1990 | - | - | 1 | - | - |
| Samaritan's Purse—Canada | 2006 | 1 | - | - | - | - |
| Totals: | | 1 | - | 2 | - | - |
| **Czech Republic** | | | | | | |
| Brethren Assemblies (Canada) | | - | - | 2 | - | - |
| Canadian Baptist Ministries | | - | - | 2 | - | - |
| I. N. (International Needs) Network Canada | 1993 | - | - | - | 6 | - |
| SEND International of Canada | 1992 | - | - | 2 | - | - |
| TEAM (The Evangelical Alliance Msn. of Canada) | 1990 | - | - | 2 | - | - |
| Totals: | | - | - | 8 | 6 | - |
| **Dominica** | | | | | | |
| Pentecostal Assemblies of Canada | 1911 | - | - | 1 | - | - |
| Totals: | | - | - | 1 | - | - |
| **Dominican Republic** | | | | | | |
| Brethren Assemblies (Canada) | 1947 | - | - | 3 | - | - |
| International Child Care (Canada) Inc. | 1988 | - | - | - | - | - |
| Into All The World | 2004 | - | 1 | - | - | - |
| Mission Possible Canada | 1994 | - | - | - | - | - |
| World Team Canada | | - | - | 2 | - | 6 |
| Totals: | | - | 1 | 5 | - | 6 |
| **Eastern Europe—General** | | | | | | |
| ABWE (Assoc. of Baptists for World Evangelization) | 2002 | - | - | 1 | - | - |
| Canadian Convention of Southern Baptists (CCSB) | 2000 | - | - | 2 | - | - |
| International Christian Ministries Canada (ICM) | 1989 | - | - | 1 | 1 | 1 |
| Pioneers Canada | | - | - | 3 | - | - |
| Trans World Radio Canada | | - | - | - | 3 | - |
| World Team Canada | | - | - | - | - | 6 |
| Totals: | | - | - | 7 | 4 | 7 |
| **Ecuador** | | | | | | |
| Action International Ministries—Canada | | - | - | 2 | - | - |
| Avant Ministries Canada | 1896 | - | - | 4 | - | - |
| Brethren Assemblies (Canada) | 1983 | - | - | 5 | - | - |

| | First Year | 1-2 yrs. | 2-4 yrs. | 4+ yrs. | Other Countries Citizens | Non-Citizens |
|---|---|---|---|---|---|---|
| | | **Personnel from CAN** | | | **Other Countries** | |
| Christian and Missionary Alliance in Canada, The | | - | 2 | 3 | - | - |
| Evangelical Free Church of Canada Mission | 2000 | - | - | 2 | - | 2 |
| HCJB Global—Canada | | - | 6 | 10 | - | - |
| International Teams, Canada | | 1 | - | - | - | - |
| Liebenzell Mission of Canada | | - | - | - | - | - |
| Wycliffe Bible Translators of Canada, Inc. | 1965 | - | - | 2 | - | - |
| Totals: | | 1 | 8 | 28 | - | 2 |
| **Egypt** | | | | | | |
| Brethren Assemblies (Canada) | | - | - | 2 | - | - |
| I. N. (International Needs) Network Canada | 1997 | - | - | - | 2 | - |
| Mennonite Central Committee Canada | 1968 | - | - | - | 3 | 12 |
| Totals: | | - | - | 2 | 5 | 12 |
| **El Salvador** | | - | | | | |
| Brethren Assemblies (Canada) | 1991 | - | - | 8 | - | - |
| Canadian Baptist Ministries | | - | 2 | - | - | - |
| Evangelical Lutheran Church in Canada | 1988 | - | - | 1 | - | - |
| Evangelical Missionary Church of Canada | 2001 | - | - | - | 1 | - |
| Mennonite Central Committee Canada | 1982 | - | - | - | - | 7 |
| United Ch. of Can., Justice, Global & Ecumenical | | 1 | - | - | - | - |
| Totals: | | 1 | 2 | 9 | 1 | 7 |
| **Eritrea** | | | | | | |
| I. N. (International Needs) Network Canada | 1980 | - | - | - | - | - |
| Samaritan's Purse—Canada | 2003 | 1 | 1 | - | - | - |
| Totals: | | 1 | 1 | - | - | - |
| **Estonia** | | | | | | |
| Apostolic Church of Pentecost of Canada | 1991 | - | 10 | - | - | - |
| Pentecostal Assemblies of Canada | 1991 | - | - | 1 | - | - |
| Totals: | | - | 10 | 1 | - | - |
| **Ethiopia** | | | | | | |
| African Enterprise Association of Canada | | | - | - | - | - |
| Baptist Gen. Conf. of Can. Global Ministries | 1968 | - | 1 | - | - | - |
| Canadian Food for the Hungry International | 2005 | - | 1 | - | - | - |
| HOPE International Development Agency | 1985 | - | - | - | 14 | - |
| I. N. (International Needs) Network Canada | 1996 | - | - | - | 50 | - |
| Into All The World | 2002 | - | 2 | - | - | - |
| Mennonite Central Committee Canada | 1972 | - | - | - | 8 | 5 |
| Pentecostal Assemblies of Canada | 1992 | - | - | 4 | - | - |
| SIM Canada | 1927 | - | - | 15 | - | - |
| Totals: | | - | 4 | 19 | 72 | 5 |
| **Europe—General** | | | | | | |
| Christar Canada | 1980 | - | - | 3 | - | - |
| Frontiers Canada | | - | - | 2 | - | - |
| Mennonite Central Committee Canada | | - | - | - | 2 | 12 |
| Totals: | | - | - | 5 | 2 | 12 |

| | Personnel from CAN | | | | Other Countries | |
| --- | --- | --- | --- | --- | --- | --- |
| | First Year | 1-2 yrs. | 2-4 yrs. | 4+ yrs. | Citizens | Non-Citizens |
| **Fiji** | | | | | | |
| United Ch. of Can., Justice, Global & Ecumenical | - | - | 2 | - | - | - |
| Totals: | - | - | 2 | - | - | - |
| **Finland** | | | | | | |
| Brethren Assemblies (Canada) | 1982 | - | - | 1 | - | - |
| Totals: | - | - | - | 1 | - | - |
| **France** | | | | | | |
| Arab World Ministries (Canada) | 1976 | 1 | - | 2 | - | - |
| Avant Ministries Canada | | - | - | 1 | - | - |
| Bibles & Literature in French—Canada | 2006 | - | - | - | - | - |
| Brethren Assemblies (Canada) | 1949 | - | - | 18 | - | - |
| Christian and Missionary Alliance in Canada, The | | - | - | 3 | - | - |
| FEBInternational | 1982 | - | - | - | 2 | - |
| Global Outreach Mission Inc., Canada | | - | - | 5 | - | - |
| Operation Mobilization Canada | | - | - | 1 | - | - |
| Salvation Army—Canada and Bermuda Territory | 1994 | - | 2 | - | - | - |
| TEAM (The Evangelical Alliance Mn. of Canada) | 1952 | - | - | 1 | - | - |
| World Team Canada | | - | - | - | - | 17 |
| Wycliffe Bible Translators of Canada, Inc. | 1990 | - | - | 2 | - | - |
| Totals: | 1 | 2 | 33 | | 2 | 17 |
| **Gabon** | | | | | | |
| Christian and Missionary Alliance in Canada | | - | - | 2 | - | - |
| Totals: | - | - | 2 | - | - | - |
| **Gambia, The** | | | | | | |
| ABWE | | - | - | 2 | - | - |
| Totals: | - | - | 2 | - | - | - |
| **Germany** | | | | | | |
| African Enterprise Association of Canada | | - | - | - | - | - |
| Christian and Missionary Alliance in Canada, The | | - | 3 | 6 | - | - |
| Evangelical Free Church of Canada Mission | 2001 | 1 | - | 2 | - | 3 |
| Glad Tidings Missionary Society | | - | - | 1 | - | - |
| Greater Europe Mission (Canada) | 1990 | 3 | 2 | 4 | - | - |
| Janz Team Ministries Inc. | 1955 | - | - | 61 | - | - |
| Liebenzell Mission of Canada | | - | - | - | - | - |
| MBMS International | 1953 | - | 4 | - | - | - |
| Salvation Army—Canada and Bermuda Territory | 1991 | - | - | 4 | - | - |
| TEAM (The Evangelical Alliance Mn. of Canada) | 1994 | - | - | 2 | - | - |
| Totals: | 4 | 9 | 80 | | - | 3 |
| **Ghana** | | | | | | |
| African Enterprise Association of Canada | | - | - | - | - | - |
| Apostolic Church of Pentecost of Canada | 1950 | - | 2 | - | - | - |
| Bible Holiness Movement | 1987 | - | - | - | - | - |
| Brethren Assemblies (Canada) | | - | - | 3 | - | - |
| I. N. (International Needs) Network Canada | 1986 | - | - | - | 91 | - |

| | First Year | Personnel from CAN 1-2 yrs. | 2-4 yrs. | 4+ yrs. | Other Countries Citizens | Non-Citizens |
|---|---|---|---|---|---|---|
| Presbyterian Ch. in Can.—Life and Msn. Agency | | - | - | 2 | - | - |
| SIM Canada | 1956 | - | - | 5 | - | - |
| Wycliffe Bible Translators of Canada, Inc. | 1996 | - | - | 3 | - | - |
| Totals: | | - | 2 | 13 | 91 | - |
| **Greece** | | | | | | |
| International Teams, Canada | | 1 | - | - | - | - |
| Totals: | | 1 | - | - | - | - |
| **Greenland** | | | | | | |
| New Tribes Mission of Canada | | - | - | - | - | - |
| Totals: | | - | - | - | - | - |
| **Guadeloupe** | | | | | | |
| World Team Canada | | - | - | - | - | 2 |
| Totals: | | - | - | - | - | 2 |
| **Guam** | | | | | | |
| Church of God (Anderson, Ind.)—Canadian Bd. | | - | - | - | - | - |
| Liebenzell Mission of Canada | 2001 | - | - | - | - | - |
| Totals: | | - | - | - | - | - |
| **Guatemala** | | | | | | |
| Apostolic Church of Pentecost of Canada | | - | 9 | - | - | - |
| CAM International of Canada | | - | - | 2 | - | - |
| Christian and Missionary Alliance in Canada, The | | - | - | 2 | - | - |
| Global Outreach Mission Inc., Canada | | - | - | 4 | - | - |
| Mennonite Central Committee Canada | 1976 | - | - | - | 3 | 9 |
| Pentecostal Assemblies of Canada | 1991 | - | - | 4 | 1 | - |
| Presbyterian Ch. in Canada—Life and Msn. Agency | 1992 | - | - | 2 | - | - |
| United Ch. of Can., Justice, Global & Ecumenical | | - | 1 | - | - | - |
| Wycliffe Bible Translators of Canada, Inc. | 1955 | - | - | 4 | - | - |
| Totals: | | - | 10 | 18 | 4 | 9 |
| **Guinea** | | | | | | |
| Christian and Missionary Alliance in Canada, The | | - | - | 4 | - | - |
| Pentecostal Assemblies of Canada | 1988 | - | - | 1 | - | - |
| Totals: | | - | - | 5 | - | - |
| **Guyana** | | | | | | |
| Evangelical Lutheran Church in Canada | | - | - | - | - | - |
| Presbyterian Ch. in Can.—Life and Msn. Agency | 1997 | - | 2 | - | - | - |
| Totals: | | - | 2 | - | - | - |
| **Haiti** | | | | | | |
| Christian Reformed Wld. Relief Committee of Can. | | - | - | 1 | - | 1 |
| CrossWorld—Canada | | - | - | 1 | - | - |
| Evangelical Missionary Ch. of Can., Wld. Partners | 2002 | - | - | - | - | - |
| Global Outreach Mission Inc., Canada | | - | - | 1 | - | - |
| International Child Care (Canada) Inc. | 1967 | - | 4 | 2 | - | - |
| Mennonite Central Committee Canada | 1958 | - | - | - | 19 | 10 |

| | Personnel from CAN | | | | Other Countries | |
|---|---|---|---|---|---|---|
| | First Year | 1-2 yrs. | 2-4 yrs. | 4+ yrs. | Citizens | Non-Citizens |
| Mission Possible Canada | 1994 | - | - | - | - | - |
| OMS International—Canada | | 4 | - | 8 | - | - |
| Pentecostal Assemblies of Canada | 1983 | - | - | 2 | - | - |
| World Team Canada | | - | - | - | - | 9 |
| Totals: | | 4 | 4 | 15 | 19 | 20 |

## Honduras

| | | | | | | |
|---|---|---|---|---|---|---|
| Action International Ministries—Canada | | - | - | - | - | 1 |
| Apostolic Church of Pentecost of Canada | 2003 | - | 2 | - | - | - |
| Brethren Assemblies (Canada) | | - | - | 2 | - | - |
| International Christian Aid Canada | 1994 | - | - | - | 45 | - |
| Latin America Mission (Canada) Inc. | 2005 | 2 | - | 2 | - | - |
| Mennonite Central Committee Canada | 1981 | - | - | - | 2 | 9 |
| Wycliffe Bible Translators of Canada, Inc. | 1989 | - | - | 1 | - | - |
| Totals: | | 2 | 2 | 5 | 47 | 10 |

## Hong Kong

| | | | | | | |
|---|---|---|---|---|---|---|
| Brethren Assemblies (Canada) | 1994 | - | - | 2 | - | - |
| Canadian Baptist Ministries | 1992 | - | - | 2 | - | - |
| Evangelical Lutheran Church in Canada | 2000 | - | 2 | - | - | - |
| Far East Broadcasting Assocs. of Canada | 1986 | - | - | 2 | - | - |
| Mennonite Central Committee Canada | | - | - | - | - | 2 |
| OMF International—Canada | | - | - | - | 1 | - |
| Samaritan's Purse—Canada | 2000 | - | - | 2 | - | - |
| Totals: | | - | 2 | 8 | 1 | 2 |

## Hungary

| | | | | | | |
|---|---|---|---|---|---|---|
| Child Evangelism Fellowship of Canada | 1996 | - | - | 1 | - | 1 |
| Christian and Missionary Alliance in Canada, The | | - | - | 4 | - | |
| Evangelical Free Church of Canada Mission | 1990 | - | - | 4 | 1 | 3 |
| Evangelical Missionary Ch. of Can., Wld. Partners | 2006 | - | 3 | - | - | - |
| Greater Europe Mission (Canada) | 1994 | - | - | 1 | - | - |
| Navigators of Canada, The | | - | - | 2 | - | - |
| OMS International—Canada | | - | - | 1 | - | - |
| Presbyterian Ch. in Can.—Life and Msn. Agency | | - | - | 1 | - | - |
| SEND International of Canada | 1994 | - | - | - | - | - |
| Totals: | | - | 3 | 14 | 1 | 4 |

## India

| | | | | | | |
|---|---|---|---|---|---|---|
| Action International Ministries—Canada | | - | - | 2 | 5 | - |
| Apostolic Church In Canada, The | 1994 | - | - | - | 1 | 1 |
| Bible Holiness Movement | 1990 | - | - | - | - | - |
| Brethren Assemblies (Canada) | 1982 | - | - | 4 | - | - |
| Campus Crusade for Christ of Canada, Inc. | 1996 | - | - | 2 | - | - |
| Canadian Baptist Ministries | 1870 | - | - | - | 2 | - |
| FEBInternational | | - | - | - | 1 | - |
| Global Outreach Mission Inc., Canada | | - | - | 6 | - | - |
| Gospel for Asia | 1979 | - | - | - | - | - |
| I. N. (International Needs) Network Canada | 1979 | - | - | - | 202 | - |
| MBMS International | 1898 | - | 9 | - | - | - |

| | First Year | 1-2 yrs. | 2-4 yrs. | 4+ yrs. | Other Countries Citizens | Non-Citizens |
|---|---|---|---|---|---|---|
| | | Personnel from CAN | | | Other Countries | |
| Mennonite Central Committee Canada | 1942 | - | - | - | 20 | 5 |
| Mission of Mercy Canada | 1954 | 1 | 3 | - | - | - |
| Operation Mobilization Canada | | - | - | 1 | - | - |
| Presbyterian Ch. in Can.—Life and Msn. Agency | 1959 | - | - | 1 | - | - |
| SIM Canada | 1893 | - | - | - | 1 | - |
| Totals: | | 1 | 12 | 16 | 232 | 6 |

**Indonesia**

| | First Year | 1-2 yrs. | 2-4 yrs. | 4+ yrs. | Citizens | Non-Citizens |
|---|---|---|---|---|---|---|
| Canadian Baptist Ministries | 1973 | - | - | 5 | 1 | - |
| Canadian Food for the Hungry International | 2005 | 2 | - | - | - | 1 |
| Christian and Missionary Alliance in Canada, The | | - | 2 | 18 | - | - |
| Mennonite Central Committee Canada | 1948 | - | - | - | 13 | 12 |
| Mission Aviation Fellowship of Canada (MAFC) | | - | - | 5 | - | - |
| OMF International—Canada | 1952 | - | - | 3 | - | 2 |
| Pioneers Canada | | - | - | 2 | - | - |
| Samaritan's Purse—Canada | 1998 | 3 | - | 1 | - | - |
| World Team Canada | | - | - | 4 | - | 14 |
| Totals: | | 5 | 2 | 38 | 14 | 29 |

**Iran**

| | First Year | 1-2 yrs. | 2-4 yrs. | 4+ yrs. | Citizens | Non-Citizens |
|---|---|---|---|---|---|---|
| Mennonite Central Committee Canada | | - | - | - | - | 2 |
| Totals: | | - | - | - | - | 2 |

**Iraq**

| | First Year | 1-2 yrs. | 2-4 yrs. | 4+ yrs. | Citizens | Non-Citizens |
|---|---|---|---|---|---|---|
| Mennonite Central Committee Canada | 1998 | - | - | - | - | 1 |
| Totals: | | - | - | - | - | 1 |

**Ireland**

| | First Year | 1-2 yrs. | 2-4 yrs. | 4+ yrs. | Citizens | Non-Citizens |
|---|---|---|---|---|---|---|
| African Enterprise Association of Canada | | - | - | - | - | - |
| Brethren Assemblies (Canada) | 1968 | - | - | 13 | - | - |
| CrossWorld—Canada | | - | - | 2 | - | - |
| Evangelical Missionary Ch. of Can., Wld. Partners | 2005 | - | 1 | - | - | - |
| Global Outreach Mission Inc., Canada | | - | - | 4 | - | - |
| Totals: | | - | 1 | 19 | - | - |

**Israel**

| | First Year | 1-2 yrs. | 2-4 yrs. | 4+ yrs. | Citizens | Non-Citizens |
|---|---|---|---|---|---|---|
| Chosen People Ministries—Canada | | - | - | - | 1 | 1 |
| Pentecostal Assemblies of Canada | 1981 | - | - | 3 | - | - |
| United Ch. of Can., Justice, Global & Ecumenical | | - | - | 1 | - | - |
| Totals: | | - | - | 4 | 1 | 1 |

**Italy**

| | First Year | 1-2 yrs. | 2-4 yrs. | 4+ yrs. | Citizens | Non-Citizens |
|---|---|---|---|---|---|---|
| Avant Ministries Canada | | - | 1 | - | - | - |
| BCM International (Canada), Inc. | 1951 | - | - | 2 | 2 | - |
| Brethren Assemblies (Canada) | 1987 | - | - | 4 | - | - |
| CrossWorld—Canada | | - | - | 1 | - | - |
| FEBInternational | 1980 | - | - | - | - | - |
| TEAM (The Evangelical Alliance Mn. of Canada) | 1981 | - | - | 3 | - | - |
| World Team Canada | | - | - | 2 | - | 2 |
| Totals: | | - | 1 | 12 | 2 | 2 |

| | Personnel from CAN | | | | Other Countries | |
|---|---|---|---|---|---|---|
| | First Year | 1-2 yrs. | 2-4 yrs. | 4+ yrs. | Citizens | Non-Citizens |

**Jamaica**

| | | | | | | |
|---|---|---|---|---|---|---|
| Apostolic Church In Canada, The | 1949 | - | - | - | 14 | - |
| Mennonite Central Committee Canada | 1970 | - | - | - | 2 | 11 |
| Pentecostal Assemblies of Canada | 2006 | - | - | 1 | - | - |
| United Ch. of Can., Justice, Global & Ecumenical | | - | - | 2 | - | - |
| Totals: | | - | - | 3 | 16 | 11 |

**Japan**

| | | | | | | |
|---|---|---|---|---|---|---|
| Brethren Assemblies (Canada) | 1949 | - | - | 7 | - | - |
| Campus Crusade for Christ of Canada, Inc. | 2002 | - | 2 | - | - | |
| Child Evangelism Fellowship of Canada | | - | - | 1 | - | 1 |
| Christian and Missionary Alliance in Canada, The | | - | - | 6 | - | - |
| Evangelical Free Church of Canada Mission | | 2 | - | 2 | - | 4 |
| FEBInternational | 1963 | 3 | - | 6 | - | - |
| MBMS International | 1950 | - | 4 | - | - | - |
| OMF International—Canada | 1951 | - | - | 7 | - | 8 |
| SEND International of Canada | 1945 | - | 2 | - | - | 10 |
| TEAM (The Evangelical Alliance Msn. of Canada) | 1891 | - | - | 11 | - | - |
| United Ch. of Can., Justice, Global & Ecumenical | | - | - | 3 | - | - |
| Totals: | | 5 | 8 | 43 | - | 23 |

**Jordan**

| | | | | | | |
|---|---|---|---|---|---|---|
| Evangelical Lutheran Church in Canada | | - | - | - | - | - |
| Mennonite Central Committee Canada | 1985 | - | - | - | 2 | 4 |
| Totals: | | - | - | - | 2 | 4 |

**Kazakhstan**

| | | | | | | |
|---|---|---|---|---|---|---|
| FEBInternational | | - | - | 2 | - | - |
| SEND International of Canada | 2005 | - | - | - | - | 2 |
| Totals: | | - | - | 2 | - | 2 |

**Kenya**

| | | | | | | |
|---|---|---|---|---|---|---|
| Africa Inland Mission (Canada) | 2005 | - | 7 | 2 | - | - |
| African Enterprise Association of Canada | | - | - | - | - | - |
| Bible Holiness Movement | 2006 | - | - | - | - | - |
| Brethren Assemblies (Canada) | 1963 | - | - | 2 | - | - |
| Canadian Baptist Ministries | 1970 | - | - | 10 | 1 | - |
| Christian Reformed Wld. Relief Committee, Can. | | 1 | 1 | 1 | - | 3 |
| FEBInternational | 1998 | - | - | 2 | - | - |
| Global Recordings Network Canada | | - | - | 4 | - | - |
| International Christian Aid Canada | 1982 | - | - | - | 11 | - |
| International Christian Ministries Canada (ICM) | 1990 | - | - | 1 | 1 | - |
| Into All The World | 2002 | - | 1 | - | - | - |
| Mennonite Central Committee Canada | 1962 | - | - | - | 4 | 6 |
| Mission Aviation Fellowship of Canada (MAFC) | | - | - | 2 | - | - |
| Pentecostal Assemblies of Canada | 1918 | - | - | 8 | - | - |
| Presbyterian Ch. in Can.—Life and Msn. Agency | 1979 | - | - | 1 | - | - |
| Samaritan's Purse—Canada | 2005 | 1 | - | - | - | - |
| SIM Canada | | - | 1 | - | - | - |
| Wycliffe Bible Translators of Canada, Inc. | 1996 | - | - | 4 | - | - |
| Totals: | | 2 | 10 | 37 | 17 | 9 |

| | First Year | Personnel from CAN 1-2 yrs. | 2-4 yrs. | 4+ yrs. | Other Countries Citizens | Non-Citizens |
|---|---|---|---|---|---|---|
| **Korea, South** | | | | | | |
| Bible Holiness Movement | 1985 | - | - | - | - | - |
| Mennonite Central Committee Canada | | - | - | - | - | 3 |
| OMF International—Canada | 1969 | - | - | - | - | - |
| United Ch. of Can., Justice, Global & Ecumenical | | 1 | - | 3 | - | - |
| Totals: | | 1 | - | 3 | - | 3 |
| **Kosovo** | | | | | | |
| CrossWorld—Canada | | - | - | 1 | - | - |
| Samaritan's Purse—Canada | 2005 | 1 | - | - | - | - |
| Totals: | | 1 | - | 1 | - | - |
| **Laos** | | | | | | |
| Christian and Missionary Alliance in Canada | | - | - | 2 | - | - |
| Christian Reformed Wld. Relief Committee | | - | 2 | - | - | 2 |
| Gospel for Asia | 2005 | - | - | - | - | - |
| Mennonite Central Committee Canada | 1975 | - | - | - | 11 | 10 |
| Totals: | | - | 2 | 2 | 11 | 12 |
| **Latin America—General** | | | | | | |
| Emmanuel International (ERRI) | 1978 | - | 1 | - | 8 | - |
| New Tribes Mission of Canada | | - | - | - | - | - |
| Totals: | | - | 1 | - | 8 | - |
| **Latvia** | | | | | | |
| Greater Europe Mission (Canada) | 2003 | - | 2 | - | - | - |
| Totals: | | - | 2 | - | - | - |
| **Lebanon** | | | | | | |
| Mennonite Central Committee Canada | 1977 | - | - | - | 2 | 2 |
| Totals: | | - | - | - | 2 | 2 |
| **Lesotho** | | | | | | |
| Mission Aviation Fellowship of Canada (MAFC) | | - | - | 1 | - | - |
| Totals: | | - | - | 1 | - | - |
| **Liberia** | | | | | | |
| ABWE (Assoc. of Baptists for World Evangelization) | 2002 | - | - | 1 | - | - |
| Equip, Canada | 1997 | 2 | - | 2 | - | - |
| Samaritan's Purse—Canada | 2005 | 3 | - | - | - | - |
| Totals: | | 5 | - | 3 | - | - |
| **Lithuania** | | | | | | |
| Evangelical Free Church of Canada Mission | 2000 | - | 2 | 2 | 2 | 2 |
| MBMS International | 1994 | - | - | - | - | 2 |
| Totals: | | - | 2 | 2 | 2 | 4 |
| **Luxembourg** | | | | | | |
| Greater Europe Mission (Canada) | 1977 | - | - | 2 | - | - |
| Totals: | | - | - | 2 | - | - |

| | Personnel from CAN | | | | Other Countries | |
| | First Year | 1-2 yrs. | 2-4 yrs. | 4+ yrs. | Citizens | Non-Citizens |
|---|---|---|---|---|---|---|
| **Macedonia** | | | | | | |
| SEND International of Canada | 1993 | - | - | 3 | - | 2 |
| Totals: | | - | - | 3 | - | 2 |
| **Madagascar** | | | | | | |
| Africa Inland Mission (Canada) | 2005 | - | 2 | - | - | - |
| Mission Aviation Fellowship of Canada (MAFC) | | - | - | 2 | - | - |
| Totals: | | - | 2 | 2 | - | - |
| **Malawi** | | | | | | |
| African Enterprise Association of Canada | | - | - | - | - | - |
| Apostolic Church of Pentecost of Canada | 1955 | - | 4 | - | - | - |
| Bible Holiness Movement | 1990 | - | - | - | - | - |
| Pentecostal Assemblies of Canada | 1982 | - | - | 5 | - | - |
| Presbyterian Ch. in Can.—Life and Msn. Agency | 1995 | - | 2 | - | - | - |
| Totals: | | - | 6 | 5 | - | - |
| **Malaysia** | | | | | | |
| Christian and Missionary Alliance in Canada, The | | - | 2 | 4 | - | - |
| OMF International—Canada | 1952 | - | - | 2 | - | 2 |
| Samaritan's Purse—Canada | 2004 | 1 | - | - | - | - |
| Totals: | | 1 | 2 | 6 | - | 2 |
| **Mali** | | | | | | |
| Avant Ministries Canada | 1919 | - | - | 9 | - | - |
| Christian Reformed World Relief | | - | - | 1 | - | 1 |
| World Vision Canada | 2006 | - | - | - | - | - |
| Wycliffe Bible Translators of Canada, Inc. | 1988 | - | - | 2 | - | - |
| Totals: | | - | - | 12 | - | 1 |
| **Mexico** | | | | | | |
| Avant Ministries Canada | 1956 | - | - | 5 | - | - |
| Brethren Assemblies (Canada) | 1988 | - | - | 18 | - | - |
| CAM International of Canada | 2001 | - | - | 1 | - | - |
| Christian and Missionary Alliance in Canada, The | | - | - | 20 | - | - |
| CrossWorld—Canada | | 4 | - | - | - | - |
| Evangelical Free Church of Canada Mission | 1994 | 2 | 2 | 4 | 1 | 7 |
| Evangelical Mennonite Conf., Bd. of Msns. | | - | - | 11 | - | - |
| Evangelical Mennonite Mission Conf. Board | 1982 | - | 2 | - | 2 | 2 |
| Evangelical Missionary Ch. of Can., World Partners | 1998 | - | - | 6 | - | - |
| Glad Tidings Missionary Society | | - | - | 2 | - | 2 |
| Latin America Mission (Canada) Inc. | 1985 | - | - | 1 | - | - |
| MBMS International | 1905 | - | 9 | - | - | 2 |
| Mennonite Central Committee Canada | 1981 | - | - | - | 3 | 13 |
| Samaritan's Purse—Canada | 2003 | - | 1 | - | - | - |
| World Mission Prayer League | 1950 | - | 2 | - | - | - |
| Wycliffe Bible Translators of Canada, Inc. | 1942 | - | - | 9 | - | - |
| Totals: | | 6 | 16 | 77 | 6 | 26 |

| | Personnel from CAN | | | | Other Countries | |
|---|---|---|---|---|---|---|
| | First Year | 1-2 yrs. | 2-4 yrs. | 4+ yrs. | Citizens | Non-Citizens |
| **Middle East** | | | | | | |
| ABWE (Assoc. of Baptists for World Evangelization) | 1989 | - | - | 2 | - | - |
| Arab World Ministries (Canada) | 1983 | - | - | 3 | - | - |
| Canadian Baptist Ministries | | - | 2 | 6 | - | - |
| Christian and Missionary Alliance in Canada, The | | - | - | 12 | - | - |
| FEBInternational | 1990 | - | - | 2 | - | - |
| Frontiers Canada | | - | - | 4 | - | - |
| InterServe Canada (Intl. Service Fellowship) | | - | 2 | 7 | - | - |
| MBMS International | | - | 2 | - | - | - |
| Operation Mobilization Canada | | 2 | - | 6 | - | - |
| TEAM (The Evangelical Alliance Msn. of Canada) | 1960 | - | - | 1 | - | - |
| Trans World Radio Canada | | - | - | - | 8 | - |
| Totals: | | 2 | 6 | 43 | 8 | - |
| **Mongolia** | | | | | | |
| OMF International—Canada | 1993 | - | - | - | - | 1 |
| Totals: | | - | - | - | - | 1 |
| **Morocco** | | | | | | |
| I. N. (International Needs) Network Canada | 1983 | - | - | - | 6 | - |
| Totals: | | - | - | - | 6 | - |
| **Mozambique** | | | | | | |
| Apostolic Church of Pentecost of Canada | 1965 | - | 1 | - | - | - |
| Mennonite Central Committee Canada | 1982 | - | - | - | 2 | 5 |
| Mennonite Economic Dev. Associates (MEDA) | 1996 | - | - | - | 8 | 3 |
| Pentecostal Assemblies of Canada | 1927 | - | - | 6 | - | - |
| United Ch. of Can., Justice, Global & Ecumenical | | - | - | 2 | - | - |
| Wycliffe Bible Translators of Canada, Inc. | 1998 | - | - | 4 | - | - |
| Totals: | | - | 1 | 12 | 10 | 8 |
| **Myanmar/Burma** | | | | | | |
| Gospel for Asia | 1992 | - | - | - | - | - |
| Operation Mobilization Canada | | 1 | - | - | - | - |
| Totals: | | 1 | - | - | - | - |
| **N. Mariana Isls** | | | | | | |
| Far East Broadcasting Assocs. of Can. (FEB Can.) | 1995 | - | - | 2 | - | - |
| Totals: | | - | - | 2 | - | - |
| **Nepal** | | | | | | |
| Gospel for Asia | 1988 | - | - | - | - | - |
| I. N. (International Needs) Network Canada | 1975 | - | - | - | 65 | - |
| Mennonite Central Committee Canada | 1956 | - | - | - | 3 | 4 |
| Operation Mobilization Canada | | 1 | - | - | - | - |
| Totals: | | 1 | - | - | 68 | 4 |
| **Netherlands** | | | | | | |
| BCM International (Canada), Inc. | 1950 | - | - | 1 | 1 | - |
| Brethren Assemblies (Canada) | | - | - | 2 | - | - |

| | Personnel from CAN | | | Other Countries | |
|---|---|---|---|---|---|
| First Year | 1-2 yrs. | 2-4 yrs. | 4+ yrs. | Citizens | Non-Citizens |

| | | | | | | |
|---|---|---|---|---|---|---|
| Christian and Missionary Alliance in Canada, The | | - | - | 2 | - | - |
| FEBInternational | | - | - | 2 | - | - |
| OMF International—Canada | | - | - | - | - | - |
| Trans World Radio Canada | | - | - | 4 | - | - |
| Wycliffe Bible Translators of Canada, Inc. | 1983 | - | - | 4 | - | - |
| | Totals: | - | - | 15 | 1 | - |
| **New Zealand** | | | | | | |
| Action International Ministries—Canada | | - | - | - | 2 | - |
| African Enterprise Association of Canada | | - | - | - | - | - |
| | Totals: | - | - | - | 2 | - |
| **Nicaragua** | | | | | | |
| Brethren Assemblies (Canada) | | - | - | 2 | - | - |
| Christian Reformed Wld. Relief Committee Can. | | - | - | 1 | - | 1 |
| Mennonite Central Committee Canada | 1979 | - | - | - | 3 | 4 |
| Mennonite Economic Dev. Associates (MEDA) | 1995 | - | - | - | 37 | 2 |
| Presbyterian Ch. in Can.—Life and Msn. Agency | 1985 | - | - | 1 | - | 1 |
| United Ch. of Can., Justice, Global & Ecumenical | | - | 2 | - | - | - |
| | Totals: | - | 2 | 4 | 40 | 8 |
| **Niger** | | | | | | |
| Christian and Missionary Alliance in Canada, The | | - | - | 7 | - | - |
| Christian Reformed Wld. Relief Committee Can. | | - | - | 2 | - | 1 |
| Samaritan's Purse—Canada | 2005 | 1 | - | - | - | - |
| SIM Canada | 1924 | - | - | 19 | 2 | - |
| Wycliffe Bible Translators of Canada, Inc. | 1998 | - | - | 2 | - | - |
| | Totals: | 1 | - | 30 | 2 | 1 |
| **Nigeria** | | | | | | |
| Bible Holiness Movement | 1959 | - | - | - | - | - |
| Brethren Assemblies (Canada) | 1954 | - | - | 4 | - | - |
| Campus Crusade for Christ of Canada, Inc. | 1992 | - | - | 2 | - | - |
| Christian Studies International of Canada | 2001 | - | - | 2 | - | - |
| Evangelical Missionary Ch. of Can., Wd. Partners | 1998 | - | 2 | - | - | - |
| Into All The World | 2000 | - | - | - | 4 | - |
| Leprosy Mission Canada, The | 2006 | 2 | - | - | - | - |
| Mennonite Central Committee Canada | 1963 | - | - | - | 7 | 7 |
| Presbyterian Ch. in Can.—Life and Mn. Agency | 1980 | - | - | 1 | - | - |
| SIM Canada | 1893 | - | 2 | 8 | - | - |
| Wycliffe Bible Translators of Canada, Inc. | 1969 | - | - | 2 | - | - |
| | Totals: | 2 | 4 | 19 | 11 | 7 |
| **Norway** | | | | | | |
| Brethren Assemblies (Canada) | | - | - | 2 | - | - |
| | Totals: | - | - | 2 | - | - |
| **Oceania—General** | | | | | | |
| New Tribes Mission of Canada | | - | - | - | - | - |
| | Totals: | - | - | - | - | - |

| | First Year | Personnel from CAN | | | Other Countries | |
|---|---|---|---|---|---|---|
| | | 1-2 yrs. | 2-4 yrs. | 4+ yrs. | Citizens | Non-Citizens |
| **Pakistan** | | | | | | |
| FEBInternational | 1969 | - | - | 8 | - | - |
| Operation Mobilization Canada | | - | - | 1 | - | - |
| Salvation Army—Can. and Bermuda Territory | 1997 | - | 1 | - | - | - |
| Samaritan's Purse—Canada | 2003 | - | 1 | - | - | - |
| | Totals: | - | 2 | 9 | - | - |
| **Palestine** | | | | | | |
| Mennonite Central Committee Canada | 1949 | - | - | - | 1 | 5 |
| United Church of Canada, Justice, Global & Ecumenical Relations | | - | - | 1 | - | - |
| | Totals: | - | - | 1 | 1 | 5 |
| **Panama** | | | | | | |
| Evangelical Free Church of Canada Mission | 2000 | 1 | - | 2 | - | 3 |
| MBMS International | | - | - | - | - | 2 |
| | Totals: | 1 | - | 2 | - | 5 |
| **Papua New Guinea** | | | | | | |
| Evangelical Lutheran Church in Canada | 2000 | - | - | 1 | - | - |
| Liebenzell Mission of Canada | 2003 | - | - | 2 | - | - |
| Mission Aviation Fellowship of Canada (MAFC) | | - | - | 8 | - | - |
| Salvation Army—Can. and Bermuda Territory | 1998 | - | 1 | - | - | - |
| World Team Canada | | - | - | - | - | - |
| Wycliffe Bible Translators of Canada, Inc. | 1963 | - | - | 19 | - | - |
| | Totals: | - | 1 | 30 | - | - |
| **Paraguay** | | | | | | |
| Evangelical Mennonite Conf., Bd. of Msns. | | - | 2 | 15 | - | - |
| SIM Canada | 1987 | - | - | 2 | - | - |
| | Totals: | - | 2 | 17 | - | - |
| **Peru** | | | | | | |
| Brethren Assemblies (Canada) | 1977 | - | - | 5 | - | - |
| Canadian Food for the Hungry International | 2002 | - | 3 | - | - | - |
| Canadian South America Mission | 1926 | - | - | 2 | - | 2 |
| Evangelical Lutheran Church in Canada | 1994 | - | - | 1 | - | - |
| MBMS International | 1954 | - | 6 | - | - | 2 |
| Mennonite Economic Dev. Associates (MEDA) | 1996 | - | - | - | 6 | 1 |
| Pioneers Canada | | 1 | - | 2 | - | - |
| TEAM (The Evangelical Alliance Msn. of Canada) | 1961 | - | - | 2 | - | - |
| World Team Canada | | - | - | 6 | - | - |
| Wycliffe Bible Translators of Canada, Inc. | 1946 | - | - | 6 | - | - |
| | Totals: | 1 | 9 | 24 | 6 | 5 |
| **Philippines** | | | | | | |
| Action International Ministries—Canada | 1980 | - | - | 5 | - | - |
| Baptist Gen. Conf. of Can. Global Ministries | 1999 | - | - | 2 | - | - |
| Bible Holiness Movement | 1961 | - | - | - | - | - |
| Brethren Assemblies (Canada) | | 1 | - | 2 | - | - |

| | First Year | Personnel from CAN | | | Other Countries | |
| --- | --- | --- | --- | --- | --- | --- |
| | | 1-2 yrs. | 2-4 yrs. | 4+ yrs. | Citizens | Non-Citizens |
| Campus Crusade for Christ of Canada, Inc. | 1979 | - | - | 2 | - | - |
| Christian and Missionary Alliance in Canada, The | | - | 2 | 2 | - | - |
| Evangelical Free Church of Canada Mission | | - | - | 2 | - | 2 |
| Far East Broadcasting Assocs. of Can. (FEB Can.) | 1996 | - | 2 | - | - | - |
| FEBInternational | | - | - | 2 | - | - |
| Glad Tidings Missionary Society | | - | - | 1 | - | - |
| I. N. (International Needs) Network Canada | 1977 | - | - | - | 71 | - |
| International Christian Aid Canada | 1985 | - | - | - | 39 | - |
| MBMS International | | - | 1 | - | - | - |
| Mennonite Central Committee Canada | 1977 | - | - | - | - | 2 |
| OMF International—Canada | 1954 | 1 | - | 14 | 3 | 7 |
| Pentecostal Assemblies of Canada | 1987 | - | - | 1 | - | - |
| SEND International of Canada | 1945 | 2 | - | 5 | 8 | 10 |
| United Ch. of Can., Justice, Global & Ecumenical | | 2 | - | - | - | - |
| World Team Canada | | - | - | 4 | - | 9 |
| Wycliffe Bible Translators of Canada, Inc. | 1959 | - | - | 12 | - | - |
| Totals: | | 6 | 5 | 54 | 121 | 30 |

**Poland**

| | First Year | 1-2 yrs. | 2-4 yrs. | 4+ yrs. | Citizens | Non-Citizens |
| --- | --- | --- | --- | --- | --- | --- |
| Avant Ministries Canada | | - | - | 2 | - | - |
| Brethren Assemblies (Canada) | 1996 | - | - | 2 | - | - |
| Christian and Missionary Alliance in Canada, The | | - | 2 | 4 | - | - |
| FEBInternational | | - | - | 3 | - | - |
| SEND International of Canada | 1991 | - | - | - | - | 4 |
| Totals: | | - | 2 | 11 | - | 4 |

**Portugal**

| | First Year | 1-2 yrs. | 2-4 yrs. | 4+ yrs. | Citizens | Non-Citizens |
| --- | --- | --- | --- | --- | --- | --- |
| ABWE (Assoc. of Baptists for Wld. Evangelization) | | 1 | - | 2 | - | - |
| Baptist Gen. Conf. of Can. Global Ministries | 1998 | - | - | 1 | - | - |
| Evangelical Missionary Ch. of Can., Wld. Partners | 1998 | - | - | 2 | - | - |
| Greater Europe Mission (Canada) | 1996 | - | - | 2 | - | - |
| MBMS International | 1986 | - | 4 | - | - | - |
| Totals: | | 1 | 4 | 7 | - | - |

**Puerto Rico**

| | First Year | 1-2 yrs. | 2-4 yrs. | 4+ yrs. | Citizens | Non-Citizens |
| --- | --- | --- | --- | --- | --- | --- |
| Brethren Assemblies (Canada) | 1967 | - | - | 1 | - | - |
| Totals: | | - | - | 1 | - | - |

**Romania**

| | First Year | 1-2 yrs. | 2-4 yrs. | 4+ yrs. | Citizens | Non-Citizens |
| --- | --- | --- | --- | --- | --- | --- |
| ABWE (Assoc. of Baptists for World Evangelization) | 2000 | - | - | 2 | - | - |
| Canadian Food for the Hungry International | 2000 | - | 2 | - | - | - |
| Christian Reformed Wld. Relief Committee Can. | | - | - | 1 | - | 1 |
| Evangelical Missionary Ch. of Can., Wld. Partners | 2001 | 6 | - | - | - | - |
| Global Outreach Mission Inc., Canada | | - | - | 1 | - | - |
| I. N. (International Needs) Network Canada | 1992 | - | - | - | 11 | - |
| Presbyterian Ch. in Can.—Life and Msn. Agency | 1994 | - | - | 1 | - | - |
| Totals: | | 6 | 2 | 5 | 11 | 1 |

**Russia**

| | First Year | 1-2 yrs. | 2-4 yrs. | 4+ yrs. | Citizens | Non-Citizens |
| --- | --- | --- | --- | --- | --- | --- |
| Apostolic Church of Pentecost of Canada | 1992 | - | 2 | - | - | - |

| | First Year | 1-2 yrs. | 2-4 yrs. | 4+ yrs. | Personnel from CAN / Other Countries Citizens | Non-Citizens |
|---|---|---|---|---|---|---|
| Brethren Assemblies (Canada) | 1998 | - | - | 3 | - | - |
| Campus Crusade for Christ of Canada, Inc. | 1994 | - | - | 1 | - | - |
| Christian and Missionary Alliance in Canada | | - | - | 4 | - | - |
| Evangelical Free Church of Canada Mission | 1991 | - | 2 | - | 1 | 1 |
| MBMS International | | - | 2 | - | - | - |
| Mennonite Central Committee Canada | | - | - | - | 3 | 9 |
| Outreach Canada | | - | 2 | - | - | - |
| Salvation Army—Canada and Bermuda Territory | 1990 | - | 1 | - | - | - |
| SEND International of Canada | 1992 | 2 | 1 | 6 | 2 | 9 |
| Totals: | | 2 | 10 | 14 | 6 | 19 |

**Rwanda**

| | First Year | 1-2 yrs. | 2-4 yrs. | 4+ yrs. | Citizens | Non-Citizens |
|---|---|---|---|---|---|---|
| African Enterprise Association of Canada | | - | - | - | - | - |
| Canadian Baptist Ministries | | - | - | 2 | - | - |
| International Teams, Canada | | - | - | 2 | - | - |
| Mennonite Central Committee Canada | 1994 | - | - | - | 6 | 3 |
| Pentecostal Assemblies of Canada | 1998 | - | - | 3 | - | - |
| Totals: | | - | - | 7 | 6 | 3 |

**Saint Vincent and the Grenadines**

| | First Year | 1-2 yrs. | 2-4 yrs. | 4+ yrs. | Citizens | Non-Citizens |
|---|---|---|---|---|---|---|
| Brethren Assemblies (Canada) | 1990 | - | - | 1 | - | - |
| World Team Canada | | - | - | - | - | 2 |
| Totals: | | - | - | 1 | - | 2 |

**Senegal**

| | First Year | 1-2 yrs. | 2-4 yrs. | 4+ yrs. | Citizens | Non-Citizens |
|---|---|---|---|---|---|---|
| Christian and Missionary Alliance in Canada | | - | 1 | 2 | - | - |
| CrossWorld—Canada | | - | - | 2 | - | 2 |
| Glad Tidings Missionary Society | | - | - | 1 | - | - |
| Pentecostal Assemblies of Canada | 1989 | - | - | 6 | - | - |
| SIM Canada | 1984 | - | - | 2 | - | - |
| World Vision Canada | 2006 | - | - | - | - | - |
| Wycliffe Bible Translators of Canada, Inc. | 1987 | - | - | 3 | - | - |
| Totals: | | - | 1 | 16 | - | 2 |

**Serbia and Montenegro**

| | First Year | 1-2 yrs. | 2-4 yrs. | 4+ yrs. | Citizens | Non-Citizens |
|---|---|---|---|---|---|---|
| Christian and Missionary Alliance in Canada | | - | - | 2 | - | - |
| Totals: | | - | - | 2 | - | - |

**Singapore**

| | First Year | 1-2 yrs. | 2-4 yrs. | 4+ yrs. | Citizens | Non-Citizens |
|---|---|---|---|---|---|---|
| OMF International—Canada | 1950 | - | - | 2 | 3 | 1 |
| World Team Canada | | - | - | 8 | - | - |
| Totals: | | - | - | 10 | 3 | 1 |

**Slovakia**

| | First Year | 1-2 yrs. | 2-4 yrs. | 4+ yrs. | Citizens | Non-Citizens |
|---|---|---|---|---|---|---|
| Brethren Assemblies (Canada) | | - | - | 2 | - | - |
| Evangelical Lutheran Church in Canada | 2001 | 1 | - | - | - | - |
| I. N. (International Needs) Network Canada | 1993 | - | - | - | 6 | - |
| Navigators of Canada, The | | - | - | 2 | - | - |
| Totals: | | 1 | - | 4 | 6 | - |

| | First Year | Personnel from CAN 1-2 yrs. | 2-4 yrs. | 4+ yrs. | Other Countries Citizens | Non-Citizens |
|---|---|---|---|---|---|---|
| **Slovenia** | | | | | | |
| SEND International of Canada | 1997 | - | - | - | - | - |
| Totals: | | - | - | - | - | - |
| **Somalia** | | | | | | |
| Mennonite Central Committee Canada | 1971 | - | - | - | - | 3 |
| Totals: | | - | - | - | - | 3 |
| **South Africa** | | | | | | |
| African Enterprise Association of Canada | | - | - | - | - | - |
| Apostolic Church of Pentecost of Canada | 1965 | - | 8 | - | - | - |
| Brethren Assemblies (Canada) | | - | - | 2 | - | - |
| Campus Crusade for Christ of Canada, Inc. | 1988 | - | - | 2 | - | - |
| FEBInternational | 2002 | - | - | - | - | - |
| Global Outreach Mission Inc., Canada | | - | - | 2 | - | - |
| Global Recordings Network Canada | | 1 | - | - | - | - |
| HOPE International Development Agency | 1983 | - | - | - | 2 | - |
| Into All The World | 2004 | 2 | - | - | - | - |
| MBMS International | | - | - | - | - | 2 |
| Mennonite Central Committee Canada | 1971 | - | - | - | 13 | 8 |
| OMF International—Canada | | - | - | - | - | - |
| Outreach Canada | | - | 2 | - | - | - |
| Pentecostal Assemblies of Canada | 1917 | - | - | 2 | - | - |
| SIM Canada | 1989 | - | - | 7 | - | - |
| TEAM (The Evangelical Alliance Mn. of Canada) | 1892 | - | - | 2 | - | - |
| Trans World Radio Canada | | - | - | 4 | - | - |
| Wycliffe Bible Translators of Canada, Inc. | 1985 | - | - | 2 | - | - |
| Totals: | | 3 | 10 | 23 | 15 | 10 |
| **South Pacific** | | | | | | |
| Wycliffe Bible Translators of Canada, Inc. | 1986 | - | - | 6 | - | - |
| Totals: | | - | - | 6 | - | - |
| **Spain** | | | | | | |
| Apostolic Church of Pentecost of Canada | 1950 | - | 7 | - | - | - |
| Avant Ministries Canada | 1966 | - | - | 3 | - | - |
| BCM International (Canada), Inc. | 1949 | - | - | 2 | 2 | - |
| Brethren Assemblies (Canada) | 1975 | - | - | 2 | - | - |
| Christian and Missionary Alliance in Canada, The | | - | - | 1 | - | - |
| Evangelical Missionary Ch. of Can., Wld. Partners | 1998 | 1 | - | - | - | - |
| FEBInternational | 1980 | - | - | 2 | - | - |
| Salvation Army—Canada and Bermuda Territory | 1998 | - | - | 2 | - | - |
| SEND International of Canada | 1987 | - | - | - | - | 2 |
| TEAM (The Evangelical Alliance Msn. of Canada) | 1952 | - | - | 2 | - | - |
| World Team Canada | | - | - | 2 | - | 9 |
| Totals: | | 1 | 7 | 16 | 2 | 11 |
| **Sri Lanka** | | | | | | |
| Gospel for Asia | | - | - | - | - | - |
| I. N. (International Needs) Network Canada | 1976 | - | - | - | 29 | - |
| Mennonite Central Committee Canada | | - | - | - | - | 2 |

| | First Year | Personnel from CAN 1-2 yrs. | Personnel from CAN 2-4 yrs. | Personnel from CAN 4+ yrs. | Other Countries Citizens | Other Countries Non-Citizens |
|---|---|---|---|---|---|---|
| Samaritan's Purse—Canada | 2005 | 6 | - | - | - | - |
| Totals: | | 6 | - | - | 29 | 2 |
| **Sudan** | | | | | | |
| Africa Inland Mission (Canada) | 2005 | - | - | 2 | - | - |
| Mennonite Central Committee Canada | 1972 | - | - | - | - | 5 |
| Samaritan's Purse—Canada | 2004 | 5 | 1 | - | - | - |
| Totals: | | 5 | 1 | 2 | - | 5 |
| **Suriname** | | | | | | |
| World Team Canada | | - | - | - | - | 5 |
| Totals: | | - | - | - | - | 5 |
| **Sweden** | | | | | | |
| Operation Mobilization Canada | | - | 1 | - | - | - |
| Totals: | | - | 1 | - | - | - |
| **Switzerland** | | | | | | |
| Operation Mobilization Canada | | 2 | - | - | - | - |
| United Ch. of Can., Justice, Global & Ecumenical | | - | - | 1 | - | - |
| Wycliffe Bible Translators of Canada, Inc. | 1966 | - | - | 2 | - | - |
| Totals: | | 2 | - | 3 | - | - |
| **Syria** | | | | | | |
| Mennonite Central Committee Canada | 1991 | - | - | - | - | 2 |
| Totals: | | - | - | - | - | 2 |
| **Taiwan** | | | | | | |
| Apostolic Church of Pentecost of Canada | 1950 | - | 4 | - | - | - |
| Christian and Missionary Alliance in Canada, The | | - | - | 2 | - | - |
| Liebenzell Mission of Canada | | - | - | - | - | - |
| Navigators of Canada, The | | - | - | - | - | - |
| OMF International—Canada | 1951 | - | - | 3 | - | 2 |
| Presbyterian Ch. in Can.—Life and Mission Agency | 1958 | - | - | 3 | - | - |
| SEND International of Canada | 1966 | - | - | - | - | 10 |
| World Team Canada | | - | - | - | - | 6 |
| Totals: | | - | 4 | 8 | - | 18 |
| **Tajikistan** | | | | | | |
| Mennonite Economic Dev. Associates (MEDA) | 2004 | - | - | - | 31 | 1 |
| Totals: | | - | - | - | 31 | 1 |
| **Tanzania** | | | | | | |
| Africa Inland Mission (Canada) | 2005 | - | 3 | - | - | - |
| African Enterprise Association of Canada | | - | - | - | - | - |
| Baptist Gen. Conf. of Can. Global Ministries | 2004 | - | - | 1 | - | - |
| Bible Holiness Movement | 1998 | - | - | - | - | - |
| Evangelical Missionary Ch. of Can., World Partners | 2004 | - | 1 | - | - | - |
| I. N. (International Needs) Network Canada | 1997 | - | - | - | 21 | - |
| International Christian Ministries Canada (ICM) | 2000 | - | - | 1 | 1 | - |
| Mennonite Central Committee Canada | 1962 | - | - | - | 9 | 6 |

| | Personnel from CAN | | | | Other Countries | |
| --- | --- | --- | --- | --- | --- | --- |
| | First Year | 1-2 yrs. | 2-4 yrs. | 4+ yrs. | Citizens | Non-Citizens |
| Mennonite Economic Dev. Associates (MEDA) | 1991 | 1 | - | - | 64 | 3 |
| Pentecostal Assemblies of Canada | 1917 | - | - | 3 | - | - |
| Totals: | | 1 | 4 | 5 | 95 | 9 |

## Thailand

| | | | | | | |
| --- | --- | --- | --- | --- | --- | --- |
| Canadian Food for the Hungry International | 1998 | - | 2 | 2 | - | - |
| Christian and Missionary Alliance in Canada, The | | - | 2 | 4 | - | - |
| Evangelical Free Church of Canada Mission | | - | 1 | 2 | 1 | 2 |
| Evangelical Lutheran Church in Canada | 2000 | - | 1 | - | - | - |
| Far East Broadcasting Assocs. of Can. (FEB Can.) | 1994 | - | - | 2 | - | - |
| Gospel for Asia | | - | - | - | - | - |
| MBMS International | 1992 | - | 10 | - | - | - |
| Mennonite Central Committee Canada | 1960 | - | - | - | - | 2 |
| OMF International—Canada | 1951 | - | - | 11 | - | 7 |
| Pentecostal Assemblies of Canada | 1961 | - | - | 8 | - | - |
| Samaritan's Purse - Canada | 2002 | - | - | 1 | - | - |
| Wycliffe Bible Translators of Canada, Inc. | 1965 | - | - | 12 | - | |
| Totals: | | - | 16 | 42 | 1 | 11 |

## Togo

| | | | | | | |
| --- | --- | --- | --- | --- | --- | --- |
| ABWE (Assoc. of Baptists for World Evangelization) | | - | - | 4 | - | - |
| Wycliffe Bible Translators of Canada, Inc. | 1982 | - | - | 2 | - | - |
| Totals: | | - | - | 6 | - | - |

## Trinidad and Tobago

| | | | | | | |
| --- | --- | --- | --- | --- | --- | --- |
| ABWE (Assoc. of Baptists for World Evangelization) | 2002 | - | - | 2 | - | - |
| World Team Canada | | - | - | - | - | 4 |
| Totals: | | - | - | 2 | - | 4 |

## Turkey

| | | | | | | |
| --- | --- | --- | --- | --- | --- | --- |
| Navigators of Canada, The | | - | 1 | 2 | - | - |
| Totals: | | - | 1 | 2 | - | - |

## Uganda

| | | | | | | |
| --- | --- | --- | --- | --- | --- | --- |
| African Enterprise Association of Canada | | - | - | - | - | - |
| Canadian Food for the Hungry International | 2002 | - | - | 1 | - | - |
| Christian Reformed Wd. Relief Committee of Can. | | 2 | 1 | 1 | - | 4 |
| Ch. of God (Anderson, Ind.)—Canadian Bd. | | - | - | - | - | - |
| I. N. (International Needs) Network Canada | 1994 | - | - | - | 74 | - |
| International Christian Ministries Canada (ICM) | 1992 | - | - | 1 | 1 | - |
| Into All The World | 2002 | - | 1 | - | - | - |
| Mennonite Central Committee Canada | 1979 | - | - | - | 6 | 9 |
| Mission Aviation Fellowship of Canada (MAFC) | | - | - | 1 | - | - |
| Pentecostal Assemblies of Canada | 1969 | - | - | 5 | - | - |
| World Vision Canada | 2005 | - | - | - | - | - |
| Wycliffe Bible Translators of Canada, Inc. | 2000 | - | - | 2 | - | - |
| Totals: | | 2 | 2 | 11 | 81 | 13 |

## Ukraine

| | | | | | | |
| --- | --- | --- | --- | --- | --- | --- |
| ABWE (Assoc. of Baptists for World Evangelization) | 1993 | - | - | 2 | - | - |

| | First Year | Personnel from CAN | | | Other Countries | |
|---|---|---|---|---|---|---|
| | | 1-2 yrs. | 2-4 yrs. | 4+ yrs. | Citizens | Non-Citizens |
| Action International Ministries - Canada | 2004 | - | - | 1 | - | - |
| Evangelical Free Church of Canada Mission | 1992 | - | 5 | 15 | 3 | 17 |
| Greater Europe Mission (Canada) | 1968 | - | - | 1 | - | - |
| Presbyterian Ch. in Can.—Life and Mn. Agency | | - | - | 2 | - | - |
| SEND International of Canada | 1991 | - | 1 | 4 | 4 | 6 |
| Slavic Gospel Association—Canada | 1952 | - | - | 2 | - | - |
| Ukrainian Children's Christian Fund | | - | - | - | - | - |
| World Team Canada | | - | - | 2 | - | - |
| Totals: | | - | 6 | 29 | 7 | 23 |

**United Kingdom**

| | First Year | 1-2 yrs. | 2-4 yrs. | 4+ yrs. | Citizens | Non-Citizens |
|---|---|---|---|---|---|---|
| African Enterprise Association of Canada | | - | - | - | - | - |
| Arab World Ministries (Canada) | 1881 | - | - | 2 | - | - |
| Chosen People Ministries—Canada | | - | - | - | 1 | - |
| Frontiers Canada | | - | - | 3 | - | |
| Gospel Mission of South America of Canada | | - | - | 1 | - | 1 |
| OMF International—Canada | 1865 | - | - | - | 2 | - |
| Pentecostal Assemblies of Canada | 2004 | - | - | 2 | - | - |
| Salvation Army—Canada and Bermuda Territory | 1985 | - | 4 | 2 | - | - |
| World Team Canada | | - | - | - | - | 10 |
| Wycliffe Bible Translators of Canada, Inc. | 1960 | - | - | 4 | - | - |
| Totals: | | - | 4 | 14 | 3 | 11 |

**Uruguay**

| | First Year | 1-2 yrs. | 2-4 yrs. | 4+ yrs. | Citizens | Non-Citizens |
|---|---|---|---|---|---|---|
| Brethren Assemblies (Canada) | 1974 | - | - | 5 | - | - |
| Gospel Mission of South America of Canada | | - | - | 2 | - | 2 |
| MBMS International | 1950 | - | 2 | - | - | - |
| Operation Mobilization Canada | | - | - | 2 | - | - |
| Totals: | | - | 2 | 9 | - | 2 |

**Venezuela**

| | First Year | 1-2 yrs. | 2-4 yrs. | 4+ yrs. | Citizens | Non-Citizens |
|---|---|---|---|---|---|---|
| Brethren Assemblies (Canada) | 1947 | - | - | 7 | - | - |
| Christian and Missionary Alliance in Canada, The | | - | - | 7 | - | - |
| Evangelical Free Church of Canada Mission | 2000 | - | 1 | 2 | - | 3 |
| FEBInternational | 1990 | - | - | 5 | - | - |
| TEAM (The Evangelical Alliance Mn. of Can.) | 1906 | - | - | 2 | - | - |
| Totals: | | - | 1 | 23 | - | 3 |

**Vietnam**

| | First Year | 1-2 yrs. | 2-4 yrs. | 4+ yrs. | Citizens | Non-Citizens |
|---|---|---|---|---|---|---|
| I. N. (International Needs) Network Canada | 1991 | - | - | - | 57 | - |
| Mennonite Central Committee Canada | 1954 | - | - | - | 6 | 8 |
| Samaritan's Purse—Canada | 2006 | 1 | - | 1 | - | - |
| Totals: | | 1 | - | 1 | 63 | 8 |

**Western Europe—General**

| | First Year | 1-2 yrs. | 2-4 yrs. | 4+ yrs. | Citizens | Non-Citizens |
|---|---|---|---|---|---|---|
| Canadian Convention of Southern Baptists (CCSB) | 2006 | - | - | 2 | - | - |
| Operation Mobilization Canada | | - | 5 | 4 | - | - |
| Totals: | | - | 5 | 6 | - | - |

**Zambia**

| | First Year | 1-2 yrs. | 2-4 yrs. | 4+ yrs. | Citizens | Non-Citizens |
|---|---|---|---|---|---|---|
| Action International Ministries—Canada | 2000 | 2 | - | 1 | - | - |

|  | First Year | Personnel from CAN | | | Other Countries | |
|---|---|---|---|---|---|---|
|  |  | 1-2 yrs. | 2-4 yrs. | 4+ yrs. | Citizens | Non-Citizens |
| Bible Holiness Movement | 1990 | - | - | - | - | - |
| Brethren Assemblies (Canada) |  | - | - | 36 | - | - |
| Christian Reformed Wld. Relief Committee Can. |  | - | - | 2 | - | 2 |
| I. N. (International Needs) Network Canada | 1985 | - | - | - | 12 | - |
| Mennonite Central Committee Canada | 1962 | - | - | - | 3 | 7 |
| Mission Aviation Fellowship of Canada (MAFC) |  | - | - | 1 | - | - |
| Pentecostal Assemblies of Canada | 1967 | - | - | 4 | - | - |
| SIM Canada | 1910 | 3 | - | 11 | - | - |
|  | Totals: | 5 | - | 55 | 15 | 9 |

## Zimbabwe

|  | First Year | Personnel from CAN | | | Other Countries | |
|---|---|---|---|---|---|---|
| African Enterprise Association of Canada |  | - | - | - | - | - |
| Apostolic Church of Pentecost of Canada | 1955 | - | 6 | - | - | - |
| Mennonite Central Committee Canada | 1980 | - | - | - | 1 | 2 |
| Pentecostal Assemblies of Canada | 1948 | - | - | 4 | - | - |
| TEAM (The Evangelical Alliance Msn. of Can.) | 1939 | - | - | 1 | - | - |
|  | Totals: | - | 6 | 5 | 1 | 2 |

# Bibliography of Resources[1]

## Mission Directories on the Web

The websites listed in this section contain electronic directories of mission agencies. In most cases the directories contain full contact information for the organizations which are included.

### Worldwide

CrossSearch
www.crosssearch.com

Lausanne Committee for World Evangelization
www.lausanne.org

The Network for Strategic Missions
www.strategicnetwork.org

World Evangelical Alliance—Mission Commission
(Formerly World Evangelical Fellowship)
www.worldevangelicalalliance.com

### Regions

#### Asia

Asia-Pacific Missions & Evangelism Network, Inc.
www.amen21.net

#### Europe

European Evangelical Alliance
www.europeanea.org

European Missionary Association
www.missionnow.com

#### Latin America

**Ibero-America (Latin America, Spain, and Portugal)**
The Ibero-American Missions Handbook of COMIBAM Internacional
www.comibam.org

### Individual Countries

#### Australia

Australian Evangelical Alliance—Missions Interlink
www.evangelicalalliance.org.au

Evangelical Missionary Alliance, New South Wales
www.pastornet.net.au

## Brazil
InfoBrasil (site in Portuguese)
www.infobrasil.org

## Canada
Canadian Christian Relief and Development Association
www.ccrda.ca

Canadian Tentmaking Network
www.tentmaking.org

Evangelical Fellowship of Canada—Global Initiatives
www.evangelicalfellowship.ca

## Hong Kong
Hong Kong Association of Christian Missions
www.hkacm.org.hk (site in Chinese)

## India
India Missions Association
www.imaindia.org

## Japan
Japan Evangelical Missionary Association
www.keikyo.com

## Korea
Korean World Missions Association
www.kwma.org

## Malaysia
National Evangelical Christian Fellowship
www.necf.org.my

## Mexico
Cooperacion Misionera de Mexico
www.COMIMEX.org

## United Kingdom
Global Connections
www.globalconnections.co.uk

OSCAR
UK information service for world mission
www.oscar.org.uk

## United States of America

AERDO—Association of Evangelical Relief and Development Organizations
www.aerdo.org

AFMA: Alliance for Missions Advancement
www.theafma.org

AIMS: Accelerating International Mission Strategies
www.aims.org

ANAM: Association of North American Missions
www.anamissions.org

CWS: Church World Service
www.churchworldservice.org

EFMA: Evangelical Fellowship of Mission Agencies
www.efmamissions.org

FOM: The Fellowship of Missions
www.fellowshipofmissions.org

IFMA: Interdenominational Foreign Mission Association of North America
www.ifmamissions.org

## Non-Protestant

OCMC: Orthodox Christian Mission Center
www.ocmc.org

USCMA: US Catholic Mission Association
www.uscatholicmission.org

# Ministry Resource Links
## Finishers

*Finishers* challenges North American adults, especially at mid-life, to make an informed decision about opportunities in local and global ministries by providing information, coaching and pathways through partner agencies and churches.

**Canada: Email:** finishers@sim.ca  Website: www.finisherscanada.ca
**US: Email:** office@finishers.org  Website: www.finishers.org

## ICAP: International Christian Alliance on Prostitution

A global network led by an international team of practitioners and advocates which seeks to unite, equip and empower organizations seeking to of-

fer freedom and change to those involved in prostitution and those who have been trafficked for sexual exploitation. ICAP is an outgrowth of NCAP in the United Kingdom.
Email: contactICAP@gmail.com; Website: www.ncapuk.org

**MTI: Magazine Training Institute**
A multi-faceted program for Christians already publishing magazines or who are planning to start magazines by providing training resources through conferences, consulting, printed materials and audio tapes.
Email: info@magazinetraining.com; Website: www.magazinetraining.com

## Books on Mission in the Twenty-first Century

**Ahonen, Risto**. 2006. *Mission in the New Millennium: Theological Grounds for World Mission*. Helsinki: Finnish Evangelical Lutheran Mission. Note: Translated from Finnish by Michael Cox and John Mills.

**Barnett, Mike and Michael Pocock, eds**. 2006. *The Centrality of Christ in Contemporary Missions*. Pasadena, Calif.: William Carey Library, Evangelical Missiological Society Series Number 12.

**Bessenecker, Scott**. 2006. *The New Friars: The Emerging Movement Serving the World's Poor*. Downers Grove, Ill.: InterVarsity Press.

**Bonk, Jonathan**, ed. 2003. *Between Past and Future: Evangelical Mission Entering the Twenty-first Century*. Evangelical Missiological Society Series, no. 10. Pasadena, Calif.: William Carey Library.

**Clayson, David**, ed. 2005. *A New Vision: A New Heart, A Renewed Call*. Lausanne Occasional Papers from the 2004 Forum for World Evangelism, Pattaya, Thailand.

**Flemming, Dean**, E., 2005. *Contextualization in the New Testament: Patterns for Theology and Mission*. Downers Grove, Ill.: Intervarsity Press.

**Garner, Rod**. 2004. Facing the City: Urban Mission in the 21st Century. Werrington, England: Epworth Press.

**Gunter, W. Stephen and Elaine A. Robinson**. 2005. *Considering the Great Commission: Evangelism and Mission in the Wesleyan Spirit*. Nashville, Tenn.: Abingdon Press.

**Guthrie, Stan**. 2005. *Missions in the Third Millennium: 21 Key Trends for the 21st Century*. 2nd Edition. Carlisle, Cumbria; Waynesboro, Ga.: Paternoster Publishing.

**Jenkins, Philip**. 2002. *The Next Christendom: The Coming of Global Christianity*. New York: Oxford University Press.

**Kirk, J. Andrew**. 2006. *Mission Under Scrutiny: Confronting Contemporary Challenges*. Minneapolis, Minn.: Augsburg Fortress.

**Krabil, James R., Walter Sawatsky and Charles Edward van Engen, eds**. 2006. *Evangelical, Ecumenical, and Anabaptist Missiologies in Conversation: Essays in Honor of Wilbert R. Shenk*. Maryknoll, N.Y.: Orbis Books.

**Lewis, Donald M. and Mark A. Noll**. 2004. *Christianity Reborn: The Global Expansion of Evangelicalism in the Twentieth Century. Grand Rapids, Mich.: W.B. Eerdmans.

**Lord, Andrew**. 2005. *Spirit-Shaped Mission: A Holistic Charismatic Missiology*. Carlisle, United Kingdom: Paternoster Press.

**Sanneh, Lamin O. and Joel A. Carpenter**. 2005. *The Changing Face of Christianity: Africa, the West, and the World*. New York: Oxford University Press.

**Steffen, Tom and Mike Barnett**. 2006. *Business as Mission: From Impoverished to Empowered*. Pasadena, Calif.: William Carey Library, Evangelical Missiological Society Series Number 14.

**Unruh, Heidi Rolland and Ronald J. Sider**. 2005. *Saving Souls, Serving Society: Understanding the Faith Factor in Church-Based Social Ministry*; New York: Oxford University Press.

**Van Rheenan, Gailyn, ed**. 2006. *Contextualization and Syncretism: Navigating Cultural Currents*. Pasadena, Calif.: William Carey Library, Evangelical Missiological Society Series Number 13.

**Wan, Enoch, ed. 2006**. *Christian Witness in Pluralistic Contexts in the 21st Century*. Pasadena, Calif.: William Carey Library, Evangelical Missiological Society Series Number 11.

## Mission Journals and Newsletters

The following are important journals and news sources for mission research. Whenever known, subscription addresses are included. Section 1 contains a core list of English language titles of highest interest to readers of the Mission Handbook; annotations note specific reasons for inclusion. Section 2 offers additional titles, emphasizing the international research community.

### Section 1: Core English Language Periodicals

*Bibliographia Missionaria*. Vatican City: Pontifical Missionary Library, 1987-  . Annual. Pontifical Urbaniana University, 00120 Vatican City, Italy.

This annual bibliography covers a wide range of Catholic and Protestant literature from multiple language sources. The topical section, "Present State and Future of Mission," offers both articles and books of interest.

*Connections*. Hyderabad, India: World Evangelical Alliance Missions Commission, 2002-  . 3 issues per year. WEA Missions Commission. Web: www.worldevangelicalalliance.com

*Connections* aims to express the core values of the WEA Missions Commission and to communicate its perspective on contemporary mission issues. Each issue contains articles related to the issue's central theme along with book reviews and news and announcements concerning WEA activities in various areas of the world.

*Evangelical Missions Quarterly*. Wheaton, Ill.: Evangelism and Missions Information Service, 1964-  . 4 issues per year. *Evangelical Missions Quarterly*, Box 794, Wheaton, Ill. 60189, USA. Email: emq@wheaton.edu; Web: www.emqonline.com

Using both academic and missionary authors, *EMQ* tackles contemporary issues from a conservative perspective. Readers can also keep up to date in research by reading the book reviews and the internet resource guide, "Missions on the Web." The online edition also includes more than forty years of archived *EMQ* articles plus current information on missions around the world.

*International Bulletin of Missionary Research.* New Haven, Conn.: Overseas Ministries Study Center, 1981-   . Quarterly. *International Bulletin of Missionary Research*, P.O. Box 3000, Denville, NJ 07834 USA. Email: ibmr@omsc.org; Web: www.omsc.org.

*International Journal of Frontier Missions.* El Paso, Tex.: International Student Leaders Coalition for Frontier Missions, 1984-   . Quarterly. IJFM, 1539 East Howard Street, Pasadena, Calif. 91104, USA. Email: ijfm_subscriptions@wciu.edu; Web: www.ijfm.org. The editors seek to be "forerunners in missions to the frontiers."

*International Review of Mission.* Geneva, Switzerland: Commission on World Mission and Evangelism of the World Council of Churches, 1912-   . Quarterly. WCC Office, Rm. 1062, 475 Riverside Drive, New York, NY 10115, USA. Email: cm@wcc-coe.org; Web: www.wcc-coe.org
Covering a broad ecumenical spectrum, each issue contains ten to twelve scholarly articles on one topic. Of particular interest is the ongoing "Bibliography on Mission Studies."

*Missiology.* Scottdale, Pa.: American Society of Missiology, 1973-   . Quarterly. *Missiology*, American Society of Missiology, Web: www.asmweb.org.
As the official publication of the ASM, *Missiology* is a "forum for the exchange of ideas" among scholars in the field of missiology.

*Missionalia.* Menlo Park, South Africa: Southern African Missiological Society, 1973-   . 3 issues per year. The Editor, Missionalia, P. O. Box 35704, Menlo Park 0102, South Africa. Email: missionalia@bigfoot.com; Web: www.geocities.com/missionalia/missalia.htm
*Missionalia* is of particular interest to missionaries and scholars working in Africa. A significant portion of each issue is devoted to "Missiological Abstracts" with an annual index compiled in the last issue of each volume. The editors also provide a list of journals abstracted in each volume.
*Lausanne World Pulse.* Wheaton, Ill, USA: Evangelism and Missions Information Service, 1984-   . Free monthly online magazine. *Lausanne World Pulse.* Email: info@lausanneworldpulse.com.  Web: www.lausanneworldpulse.com
*Lausanne World Pulse* reports comprehensive news, analysis and information on evangelism and missions around the world.

**Section 2: International Mission Journals**

*Evangelikale Missiologie.* Korntal, Germany: Arbeitskreis für Evangelikale Missiologie, 1985- . 4 issues per year. AfeM - Geschäftsstelle, Kristina Weirich, Postfach 1360, D-51691 Bergneustadt, Germany. Email: afem.em@t-online.de; Web: www.afem-em.de.

*Exchange: Journal of Missiological and Ecumenical Research.* Leiden, The Netherlands: Brill Academic Publishers in cooperation with the Interuniversity Institute for Missiological and Ecumenical Research, 1972- . 4 issues per year. Brill Academic Publishers Inc., 112 Water Street, Suite 400, Boston, Mass. 02109. Email: cs@brillusa.com; Web: www.brill.nl.

*Mission: Journal of Mission Studies = Revue des Sciences de la Mission.* Ottawa, Ontario, Canada: Institut des Sciences de la Mission = Institute of Mission Studies, 1994- . 2 issues per year. *Mission,* Saint Paul University, 223 Hand Street, Ottawa, ON, Canada K1S 1C4. Email: scienceshumaines@ustpaul.ca; Web: www.ustpaul.ca.

*Mission Studies: Journal of the International Association for Mission Studies.* Leiden, Netherlands: IAMS, 1984- . 2 issues per year. IAMS Secretariat, Peter Bangs Vej 1 D, DK-2000 Frederiksberg, Copenhagen, Denmark. Email: iams@missionstudies.org; Web: www.missionstudies.org

*Missionsforum: en tidskrift från Svenska Missionsrådet.* (formerly known as Tidskriften Missionsforum) Stockholm, Sweden: Svenska Missionsradet, 1995- . 4 issues per year. Svenska Missionsradet, Starrbäcksgatan 11, se - 172 99 Sundbyberg, Sweden. Email: info@missioncouncil.se; Web: www.missioncouncil.se.

*Neue Zeitschrift für Missionswissenschaft. Nouvelle Revue de Science Missionnaire.* Immensee, [Switzerland]: Verein zur Förderung der Missionswissenschaft, etc., 1945- . 4 issues per year. Verlag NZM, Postfach 62, Calendariaweg 4, CH-6405 Immensee, Switzerland. Email: verlag@bag.ch; Web: wwwforummission.ch
*Norsk Tidsskrift for Misjon.* Oslo, Norway: Egede Institute in cooperation with Tapir Publishers, 1948- . 4 issues per year. NTM, Tapir Forlag, Nardovn. 14, 7005 Trondheim, Norway. Email: forlag@tapir.no; Web: http://tapirforlag.no/misjon

*Swedish Missiological Themes/Svensk Missionstidskrift.* Uppsala, Sweden: Swedish Institute of Missionary Research, 1913- . 4 issues per year. Swedish Institute of Missionary Research, P.O. Box 1526, SE-751 45 Uppsala, Sweden. Email: gustafbjorck@teol.uu.se; Web: www.teol.uu.se.

*Third Millennium: Indian Journal of Evangelization.* Gujarat, India: *Third Millennium,* 1998- . Quarterly. The Managing Editor, *Third Millennium,* Bishop's House, P.B. No. 1, Kalavad Road, Rajkot 360005, Gujarat, India. Email: navjeevanrjt@satyam.net.in.

*Transformation: An International Evangelical Dialogue on Mission and Ethics.* Oxford, England: Oxford Centre for Mission Studies, 1984- . 4 issues per year. *Transformation,* Vanguard University, 55 Fair Drive, Costa Mesa, Calif. 92626, USA. Email: transformation@vanguard.edu; Web: www.ocms.ac.uk.

*Wereld en Zending: Oecumenisch tijdschrift voor missiologie en missionaire Praktijk, voor Nederland en Belgie.* Kampen, The Netherlands: Uitgeverij Kok, [1972] - . 4 issues per year. Uitgeverij Kok, Postbus 130, 8260 GA, Kampen, The Netherlands. Email: abonnementen@kok.nl.

*Zeitschrift für Mission.* Stuttgart, Germany; Basel, Switzerland: Deutschen Gesellschaft für Missionswissenschaft und der Basler Mission, 1975- . 4 issues per year. Verlag Otto Lembeck, Gärtnerweg 16, D-60322 Frankfurt/Main, Germany. Email: verlag@lembeck.de; Web: www.lembeck.de.

*Zeitschrift für Missionswissenschaft und Religionswissenschaft.* Münster, Germany: Internationales Institut für missionswissenschaftliche Forschungen e. V., 1911- . 4 issues per year. ZMR, Institut für Missionswissenschaft, Hufferstr. 27, D-48149 Münster, Germany.

## General Reference Works

The majority of works in this section are recently published dictionaries, encyclopedias, atlases, handbooks, or other reference tools in the field of mission. A few historical works give context and perspective to statistics in the current *Mission Handbook.*

**Asian Christian Theologies: A Research Guide to Authors, Movements, Sources.** 2002-2004. Maryknoll, NY; Orbis Books; Delhi: ISPCK; Quezon City: Claretian Publishers. 3 vols.

**Evangelism and Missions Information Service.** 2007. *Mission Handbook: U.S. and Canadian Protestant Ministries Overseas, 2007-2009,* 20th ed. Wheaton, Ill.: EMIS.

____. 2004. *Mission Handbook: U.S. and Canadian Protestant Ministries Overseas, 2004-2006,* 19th ed. Wheaton, IL: EMIS.

____. 2000. *Mission Handbook: U.S. and Canadian Christian Ministries Overseas, 2001-2003,* 18th ed. Wheaton, IL: EMIS.

**Grimes, Barbara F., ed.** 2000. *Ethnologue: Languages of the World.* 14th ed. Dallas, Tex.: Summer Institute of Linguistics. CD-ROM and/or 2-volume print versions available at: www.ethnologue.com.

**Hillerbrand, Hans J., ed.** 2004. *Encyclopedia of Protestantism;* New York; Routledge.

**Johnstone, Patrick. 2001.** *Operation World.* 21st century edition. Carlisle, Cumbria, UK: Paternoster Lifestyle. CD-ROM and print editions available at www.authenticmedia.co.uk

**Linder, Eileen W., ed.** 2006. *Yearbook of American & Canadian Churches.* Nashville, Tenn.: Abingdon Press. Annual. Web: www.abingdonpress.com.

**Missionary Research Library. 1953-1966.** Various predecessor titles to the *Mission Handbook.* Editions     1-7. New York: Missionary Research Library.
· 1953: *Foreign Missionary Agencies in the United States*
· 1956: *Directory of Foreign Missionary Agencies in North America,* Revised ed.
· 1958: *Directory of North American Protestant Foreign Missionary Agencies,* 3rd ed.
· 1960: *Directory of North American Protestant Foreign Missionary Agencies,* 4th ed.
· 1962: *North American Protestant Foreign Mission Agencies,* 5th ed.
· 1964: *North American Protestant Foreign Mission Agencies,* 6th ed.
· 1966: *North American Protestant Foreign Mission Agencies,* 7th ed.

**Missionary Research Library and MARC.** 1968-1970. *Mission Handbook.* Editions 8-9. New York: Missionary Research Library; Pasadena, CA: MARC.
· 1968: *North American Protestant Foreign Mission Agencies,* 8th ed.
· 1970: *North American Protestant Ministries Overseas,* 9th ed.

**Mission Advanced Research and Communication Center (MARC). 1973-1997.** *Mission Handbook.* Editions 10-17. Pasadena, CA: MARC.
· 1973: *Mission Handbook: North American Protestant Ministries Overseas,* 10th ed.
· 1976: *Mission Handbook: North American Protestant Ministries Overseas,* 11th ed.
· 1979: *Mission Handbook: North American Protestant Ministries Overseas,* 12th ed.
· 1986: *Mission Handbook: North American Protestant Ministries Overseas,* 13th ed.
· 1989: *Mission Handbook: USA/Canada Protestant Ministries Overseas,* 14th ed.
· 1993: *Mission Handbook: USA/Canada Christian Ministries Overseas,* 15th ed.
· 1995: *Mission Handbook.* Directory Edition, 16th ed.
· 1997: *Mission Handbook, 1998-2000: U.S. and Canadian Christian Ministries Overseas,* 17th ed.
· See Evangelism and Missions Information Service for 18th, 19th and 20th editions.

**Moreau, A. Scott, ed.** 2000. *Evangelical Dictionary of World Missions.* Grand Rapids, Mich.: Baker Book House.

**Müller, Karl, Theo Sundermeier, Stephen B. Bevans and Richard H. Bliese, eds.** 1997. *Dictionary of Mission: Theology, History, Perspectives.* (American Society of Missiology Series, 24). Maryknoll, N.Y.: Orbis Books.

**United States Catholic Mission Association.** *Mission Statistics, 2004-2005.* Web: www.uscatholicmission.org

**Welliver, Dotsey and Minnette Smith, eds.** 2002. *Directory of Schools and Professors of Mission and Evangelism in the USA and Canada, 2002-2004.* Wheaton, Illinois: Evangelism and Missions Information Service. Web: www.billygrahamcenter.org/emis

### Endnote
1. A portion of this is based on the Selective Bibliography prepared by Ferne Lauraine Weimer, Billy Graham Center Library with Andrew Culbertson that was published in the previous edition.

# Appendix A
## Associations

**AERDO—Association of Evangelical Relief and Development Organizations**
AERDO is made up of evangelical Christian relief and development agencies from North America. For information on AERDO agencies, please check the website at www.aerdo.net

**AFMA—Alliance for Missions Advancement**
The AFMA membership is made up of mission agencies, churches that send missionaries, apostolic and prophetic networks, relief and development agencies, missions support organizations and businesses. For information on AFMA agencies, please check the website at www.theafma.org

**ANAM—Association of North American Missions**
The ANAM is made up of independent mission, ministry, or ministry agencies serving in North America. For information on ANAM agencies, please check the website at www.anamissions.org

**CCRDA—Canadian Christian Relief and Development Association**
The CCRDA membership is made up of Canadian Christian organizations and individuals involved in relief, development, and justice who are committed to integrated, transformational development. For information on CCRDA agencies, please check the website at www.ccrda.org

**CWS—Church World Service**
CWS is the relief, development, and refugee assistance ministry of 35 Protestant, Orthodox, and Anglican denominations in the United States. For information on CWS agencies, please check the website at www.churchworldservice.org

**EFMA—Evangelical Fellowship of Mission Agencies**
EFMA, the missions arm of National Association of Evangelicals, has a membership made up of support and sending mission agencies and churches that send missionaries. For information on EFMA agencies, please check the website at http://efma.gospelcom.net

**FOM—Fellowship of Missions**
The FOM membership is open to fundamental, premillennial agencies in North America. For information on FOM agencies, please check the website at www.fellowshipofmissions.org

**IFMA—Interdenominational Foreign Mission Association of North America**
The IFMA membership is made up primarily of nondenominational evangelical mission agencies in North America. For information on IFMA agencies, please check the website at www.ifmamissions.org

**OCMC—Orthodox Christian Mission Center**
The OCMC is the official mission agency of the Canonical Orthodox Bishops in the Americas (SCOBA). For information on OCMC agencies, please check the website at www.ocmc.org

**USCMA—US Catholic Mission Association**
For information on USCMA agencies, please check the website at www.uscatholicmission.org

# Appendix B

## Mission Handbook
### Canadian Protestant Ministries Overseas
### Questionnaire
Please return to: EMIS, P. O. Box 794, Wheaton, IL 60189-9908

1. What is your organization's name as you are known and would like to be listed in the Mission Handbook? [legal name]

_____

2. Mailing Address:

_____

(P. O. Box or Street)     (City)     (Province)                    (Postal code)

3. Telephone number: (_____) _____

   Fax number: (_____) _____

   E-mail _____

   Web Site _____

4. Chief Executive Officer in Canada:

_____

(Name)                                        (Title of Position)

5. Year organization founded in Canada: _____

6. Year Incorporated in Canada if different from year founded: _____

7. Which one of the following is most used in describing your organization's denominational orientation?

   ❏ Denominational          ❏ Transdenominational
   ❏ Nondenominational       ❏ Prefer that denominational orientation not be used
   ❏ Interdenominational     ❏ Other _____

8. Which one (or two if needed) of the following terms most clearly describes the general doctrinal and/or ecclesiastical stance of your organization (or that of your supporters if more appropriate)?

   ❏ Adventist                    ❏ Charismatic           ❏ Independent
   ❏ Anglican                     ❏ Congregational        ❏ Lutheran
   ❏ Baptist                      ❏ Ecumenical            ❏ Mennonite
   ❏ Brethren                     ❏ Episcopal             ❏ Methodist
   ❏ Christian ("Restoration      ❏ Evangelical           ❏ Pentecostal
     Movement")                   ❏ Friends               ❏ Presbyterian
   ❏ Christian/Plymouth           ❏ Fundamentalist        ❏ Reformed
     Brethren                     ❏ Holiness              ❏ Wesleyan
                                                          ❏ Other _____

9. Select up to six descriptors from the following list which are primary activities of your organization. If actively involved in more than six, please indicate only the six for which the most resources are currently committed.

❏ Adoption
❏ Agricultural assistance
❏ Apologetics
❏ Association of Missions
❏ Audio recording/distribution
❏ Aviation services
❏ Bible distribution
❏ Bible memorization
❏ Broadcasting, radio and/or TV
❏ Camping programs
❏ Childcare/orphanage
❏ Children's programs
❏ Church construction/financing
❏ Church planting/establishing
❏ Correspondence courses
❏ Development, community or other
❏ Disability assistance programs
❏ Discipleship
❏ Education, church/sch. general Christian
❏ Education, missionary (certificate)
❏ Education, theological education by extension (TEE)

❏ Education, extension (other)
❏ Education, theological
❏ Evangelism, mass
❏ Evangelism, personal & small group
❏ Evangelism, student
❏ Funds transmission
❏ Furloughed missionary support
❏ Information service (mission related)
❏ Justice related
❏ Leadership development
❏ Linguistics
❏ Literacy
❏ Literature distribution
❏ Literature production
❏ Management consulting/ training
❏ Medical supplies
❏ Medicine, incl. dental & public health
❏ Member care
❏ National worker support
❏ Nurture/support of national churches

❏ Partnership development
❏ Psychological counseling
❏ Purchasing services
❏ Recruiting/mobilizing
❏ Relief and/or rehabilitation
❏ Research (missions related)
❏ Services for other agencies
❏ Short-term programs coordination
❏ Supplying equipment
❏ Technical assistance
❏ Tentmaking and related
❏ TESOL
❏ Training/orientation, missionary
❏ Training, other
❏ Translation, Bible
❏ Translation, other
❏ Video/film production distribution
❏ Youth programs
❏ Other _____
_____
_____
_____

Which **one** of the activities above is most commonly associated with your organization?
_____

10. Is your organization a member of an association of missions?
❏ ANAM     ❏ AERDO     ❏ AFMA     ❏ EFMA     ❏ IFMA     ❏ CWS
❏ Other:_____

**FINANCIAL DATA**

11. What was your organization's **grand total income** for all ministries in Canada and overseas, raised in Canada in or fiscal 2005? (Denominations should report their board total.) $_____

12. Of the grand total for all ministries reported in Question 11, what was the amount of **income for overseas ministries**? $ _____

13. Of the amount reported in Question 12, what, if any, was the dollar amount of **gifts-in-kind commodities and/or services** that were donated for overseas activities to your organization? $ _____

## COUNTRIES OF SERVICE AND FIELD PERSONNEL

14. Personnel **FROM Canada and other countries:**

**NOTE: For <u>personnel from Canada</u>, include:**
- those engaged in cross-cultural ministry and fully supported under your organization as of Jan. 1, 2005
- those on furlough and those on loan to another organization if they are fully supported by your organization
- those on loan to your organization only if fully supported by you
- spouses, even if they don't have "official" ministry status but serve in a ministry or support role

**NOTE: For <u>personnel from countries other than Canada</u>, include:**
- personnel with specific mission/ministry duties who are fully or partially supported by/through your organization from funds raised in Canada

## PLEASE MAKE ADDITIONAL COPIES OF THIS PAGE IF NEEDED

| Country of Service  Note: Indicate a region only if a specific country is not suitable | Year Work Began | Number of personnel from Canada: Fully supported personnel with length of service expected to be: | | | Number of personnel from countries other than Canada: Fully or partially supported personnel. Show the number on the appropriate country of service line. | |
|---|---|---|---|---|---|---|
| | | From 1 up to 2 years | 2 to 4 years | More than 4 years | Citizens of their country of service | Not citizens of their country of service |
| | | | | | | |
| | | | | | | |
| | | | | | | |
| | | | | | | |
| | | | | | | |
| | | | | | | |
| | | | | | | |
| | | | | | | |
| | | | | | | |
| | | | | | | |
| | | | | | | |
| | | | | | | |
| | | | | | | |

**OTHER PERSONNEL** (Categories other than those reported in Question 14)

15. **Nonresidential mission personnel from Canada** (persons not residing in the country(s) of their ministry focus but assigned to overseas duties and traveling overseas at least 12 weeks per year on operational aspects of the ministry) who are supported by your organization.
_____ Fully supported by your organization _____ Partially supported

16. Number of **short-term personnel from Canada** who went on overseas service projects or mission trips less than 1 year, but at least 2 weeks, in 2005 through your organization, either fully or partially supported including those raising their own support:
_____

If you have a short-term program, where are initial contacts usually made with potential participants?
_____ Churches                    _____ Conferences (other than in churches)
_____ Schools                      _____ Other: _____
_____ Individually

How many of your **regular staff** in Canada and overseas have **duties related to short-term programs**?
_____ Full-time on S-T program
_____ Part-time on S-T program: 50%+ of total time _____ 10–49% _____

17. Number of **Canadian bi-vocational or "tentmaker" personnel sponsored or supervised by your organization** (persons who support themselves partially or fully through non-church/mission vocations and live overseas for the purpose of Christian witness, evangelism, and/or encouraging believers). _____

If you relate to "tentmakers," do you have staff assigned to maintain such contacts?
_____ Yes _____ No

**Note:** If countries of service for personnel in Items 14-16 are not already listed in the table in Item 14, please add the countries to the list. Also list countries with no personnel but with regular ongoing programs you support.

18. Number of **staff** and/or other employees **assigned to ministry and/or office duties in Canada**
_____ Full-time paid staff
_____ Part-time paid staff/associates
_____ Volunteer (ongoing) helpers

19. If your organization has a board-adopted short purpose or mission statement, please enclose a copy from a brochure, letterhead, newsletter or other copy that you share with others.

20. Please list any periodicals published by your organization: _____
_____    _____

21. Please give the name and title of the person in your organization in charge of one or all of the following departments: Recruiting, Training and Member Care.
Name: _____ Title: _____
Name: _____ Title: _____

If you have additional comments about your organization or this survey that you would like us to be aware of, please indicate here or enclose an additional sheet.

**THANK YOU** for responding to this survey! We appreciate it.
Submitted by: _____ Date: _____
Position: _____

# Appendix C

## Mission Handbook
## USA Protestant Ministries Overseas
## Questionnaire
Please return to: EMIS, P. O. Box 794, Wheaton, IL 60189-9908

1. What is your organization's name as you are known and would like to be listed in the Mission Handbook? [legal name]

_____

2. Mailing Address:

_____
(P. O. Box or Street)    (City)    (State)    (Zip)

3. Telephone number: (_____) _____

   Fax number: (_____) _____

   E-mail _____

   Web Site _____

4. Chief Executive Officer in the USA:

_____
(Name)    (Title of Position)

5. Year organization founded in USA: _____

6. Year Incorporated in USA if different from year founded: _____

7. Which one of the following is most used in describing your organization's denominational orientation?

   ❏ Denominational     ❏ Transdenominational
   ❏ Nondenominational     ❏ Prefer that denominational orientation not be used
   ❏ Interdenominational     ❏ Other _____

8. Which one (or two if needed) of the following terms most clearly describes the general doctrinal and/or ecclesiastical stance of your organization (or that of your supporters if more appropriate)?

   ❏ Adventist     ❏ Charismatic     ❏ Independent
   ❏ Anglican     ❏ Congregational     ❏ Lutheran
   ❏ Baptist     ❏ Ecumenical     ❏ Mennonite
   ❏ Brethren     ❏ Episcopal     ❏ Methodist
   ❏ Christian ("Restoration Movement")     ❏ Evangelical     ❏ Pentecostal
        ❏ Friends     ❏ Presbyterian
   ❏ Christian/Plymouth Brethren     ❏ Fundamentalist     ❏ Reformed
        ❏ Holiness     ❏ Wesleyan
            ❏ Other _____

9. Select up to six descriptors from the following list which are primary activities of your organization. If actively involved in more than six, please indicate only the six for which the most resources are currently committed.

❑ Adoption
❑ Agricultural assistance
❑ Apologetics
❑ Association of Missions
❑ Audio recording/distribution
❑ Aviation services
❑ Bible distribution
❑ Bible memorization
❑ Broadcasting, radio and/or TV
❑ Camping programs
❑ Childcare/orphanage
❑ Children's programs
❑ Church construction/financing
❑ Church planting/establishing
❑ Correspondence courses
❑ Development, community or other
❑ Disability assistance programs
❑ Discipleship
❑ Education, church/sch. general Christian
❑ Education, missionary (certificate)
❑ Education, theological education by extension (TEE)

❑ Education, extension (other)
❑ Education, theological
❑ Evangelism, mass
❑ Evangelism, personal & small group
❑ Evangelism, student
❑ Funds transmission
❑ Furloughed missionary support
❑ Information service (mission related)
❑ Justice related
❑ Leadership development
❑ Linguistics
❑ Literacy
❑ Literature distribution
❑ Literature production
❑ Management consulting/ training
❑ Medical supplies
❑ Medicine, incl. dental & public health
❑ Member care
❑ National worker support
❑ Nurture/support of national churches

❑ Partnership development
❑ Psychological counseling
❑ Purchasing services
❑ Recruiting/mobilizing
❑ Relief and/or rehabilitation
❑ Research (missions related)
❑ Services for other agencies
❑ Short-term programs coordination
❑ Supplying equipment
❑ Technical assistance
❑ Tentmaking and related
❑ TESOL
❑ Training/orientation, missionary
❑ Training, other
❑ Translation, Bible
❑ Translation, other
❑ Video/film production distribution
❑ Youth programs
❑ Other _____
_____
_____
_____

Which **one** of the activities above is most commonly associated with your organization?

_____

10. Is your organization a member of an association of missions?
❑ ANAM    ❑ AERDO    ❑ AFMA    ❑ EFMA    ❑ IFMA    ❑ CWS
❑ Other:_____

**FINANCIAL DATA**

11. What was your organization's **grand total income** for all ministries in the USA and overseas, raised in the USA in or fiscal 2005? (Denominations should report their board total.) $_____

12. Of the grand total for all ministries reported in Question 11, what was the amount of **income for overseas ministries?** $ _____

13. Of the amount reported in Question 12, what, if any, was the dollar amount of **gifts-in-kind commodities and/or services** that were donated for overseas activities to your organization? $ _____

## COUNTRIES OF SERVICE AND FIELD PERSONNEL

14. Personnel **FROM USA and other countries:**

**NOTE:** For <u>personnel from the US</u>, include:
- those engaged in cross-cultural ministry and fully supported under your organization as of Jan. 1, 2005
- those on furlough and those on loan to another organization if they are fully supported by your organization
- those on loan to your organization only if fully supported by you
- spouses, even if they don't have "official" ministry status but serve in a ministry or support role

**NOTE:** For <u>personnel from countries other than the US</u>, include:
- personnel with specific mission/ministry duties who are fully or partially supported by/through your organization from funds raised in the USA

**PLEASE MAKE ADDITIONAL COPIES OF THIS PAGE IF NEEDED**

| Country of Service | Year Work Began | Number of personnel from USA: Fully supported personnel with length of service expected to be: | | | Number of personnel from countries other than USA: Fully or partially supported personnel. Show the number on the appropriate country of service line. | |
| --- | --- | --- | --- | --- | --- | --- |
| Note: Indicate a region only if a specific country is not suitable | | From 1 up to 2 years | 2 to 4 years | More than 4 years | Citizens of their country of service | Not citizens of their country of service |
| | | | | | | |
| | | | | | | |
| | | | | | | |
| | | | | | | |
| | | | | | | |
| | | | | | | |
| | | | | | | |
| | | | | | | |
| | | | | | | |
| | | | | | | |
| | | | | | | |
| | | | | | | |
| | | | | | | |

266.0216
M67
2007-2009

117166

LINCOLN CHRISTIAN COLLEGE AND SEMINARY
616    Mission Handbook 2007-2009

**OTHER PERSONNEL** (Categories other than those reported in Question 14)

15. **Nonresidential mission personnel from the USA** (persons not residing in the country(s) of their ministry focus but assigned to overseas duties and traveling overseas at least 12 weeks per year on operational aspects of the ministry) who are supported by your organization.
_____ Fully supported by your organization _____ Partially supported

16. Number of **short-term personnel from the USA** who went on overseas service projects or mission trips less than 1 year, but at least 2 weeks, in 2005 through your organization, either fully or partially supported including those raising their own support:
_____

If you have a short-term program, where are initial contacts usually made with potential participants?
_____ Churches                    _____ Conferences (other than in churches)
_____ Schools                     _____ Other: _____
_____ Individually

How many of your **regular staff** in the USA and overseas have **duties related to short-term programs**?
____ Full-time on S-T program
Part-time on S-T program: 50%+ of total time _____ 10-49% _____

17. Number of **USA bi-vocational or "tentmaker" personnel sponsored or supervised by your organization** (persons who support themselves partially or fully through non-church/mission vocations and live overseas for the purpose of Christian witness, evangelism, and/or encouraging believers). _____

If you relate to "tentmakers," do you have staff assigned to maintain such contacts?
_____ Yes _____ No

**Note:** If countries of service for personnel in Items 14-16 are not already listed in the table in Item 14, please add the countries to the list. Also list countries with no personnel but with regular ongoing programs you support.

18. Number of **staff** and/or other employees **assigned to ministry and/or office duties in the USA** (e.g. administration).
_____ Full-time paid staff
_____ Part-time paid staff/associates
_____ Volunteer (ongoing) helpers

19. If your organization has a board-adopted short purpose or mission statement, please enclose a copy from a brochure, letterhead, newsletter or other copy that you share with others.

20. Please list any periodicals published by your organization: _____
_____    _____

21. Please give the name and title of the person in your organization in charge of one or all of the following departments: Recruiting, Training and Member Care.
Name: _____ Title: _____
Name: _____ Title: _____

If you have additional comments about your organization or this survey that you would like us to be aware of, please indicate here or enclose an additional sheet.

**THANK YOU** for responding to this survey! We appreciate it.
Submitted by: _____    3 4711 00179 4934    _____
Position: _____